MOON HANDBOOKS®

PATAGONIA

FIRST EDITION

WAYNE BERNHARDSON

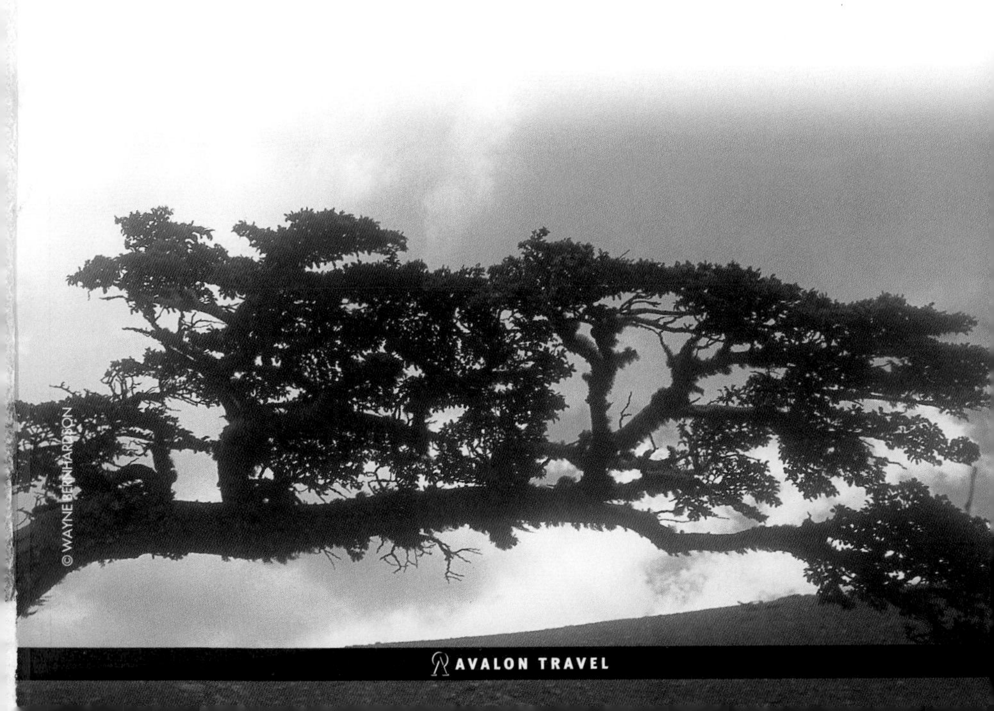

© WAYNE BERNHARDSON

AVALON TRAVEL

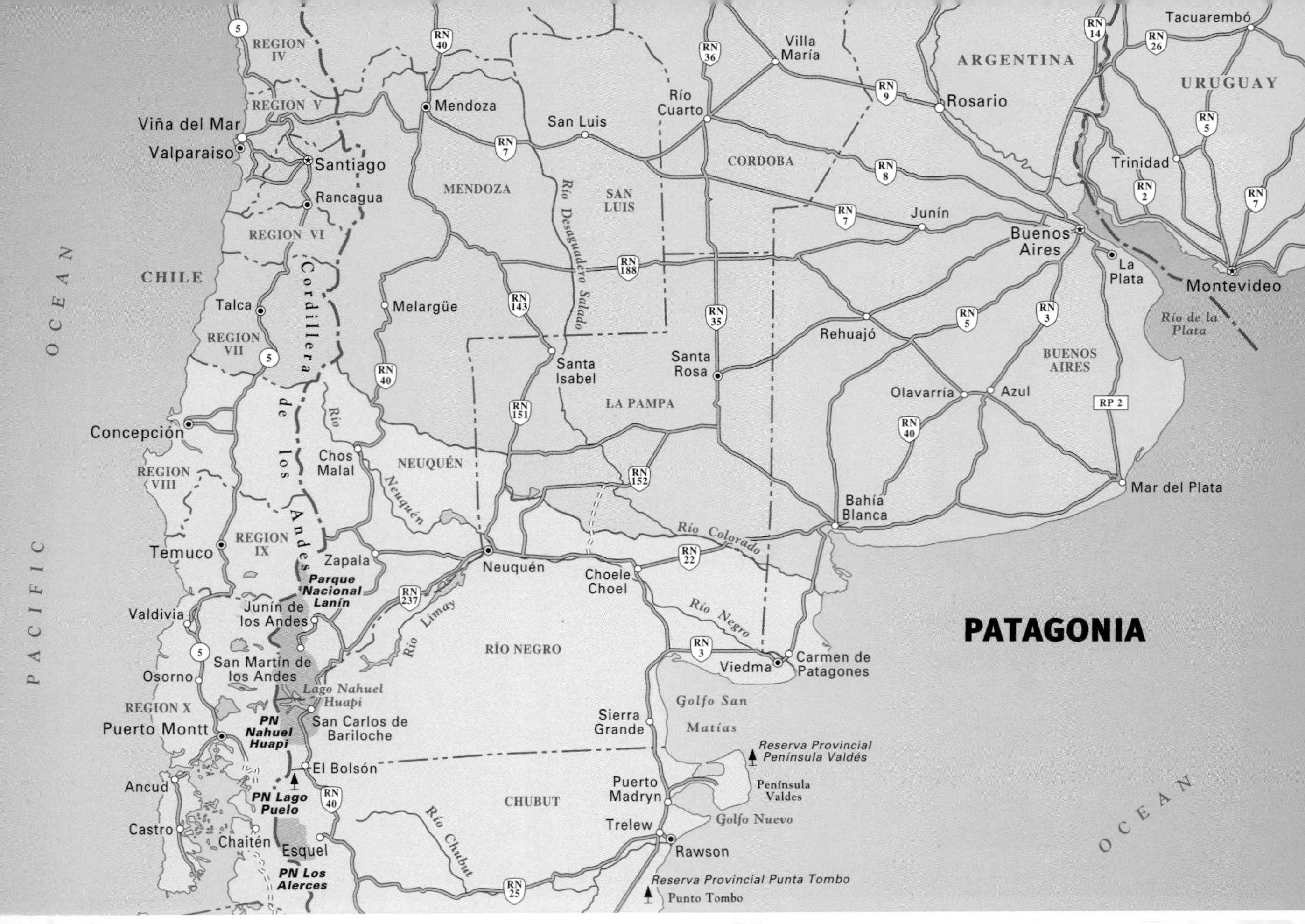
PATAGONIA
ARGENTINA
URUGUAY
CHILE
PACIFIC OCEAN
OCEAN
Tacuarembó
Villa María
Río Cuarto
Rosario
Trinidad
Montevideo
Buenos Aires
La Plata
Río de la Plata
Mendoza
San Luis
Santiago
Viña del Mar
Valparaiso
Rancagua
Junín
CORDOBA
MENDOZA
SAN LUIS
Río Desaguadero Salado
BUENOS AIRES
Talca
Melargüe
Santa Isabel
Santa Rosa
Rehuajó
Olavarría
Azul
LA PAMPA
Concepción
Chos Malal
NEUQUÉN
Río Neuquén
Mar del Plata
Bahía Blanca
Río Colorado
Temuco
Zapala
Neuquén
Choele Choel
Parque Nacional Lanín
Valdivia
Junín de los Andes
San Martín de los Andes
RÍO NEGRO
Río Limay
Río Negro
Viedma
Carmen de Patagones
Osorno
Lago Nahuel Huapi
San Carlos de Bariloche
Puerto Montt
PN Nahuel Huapi
Golfo San Matías
Sierra Grande
Reserva Provincial Península Valdés
El Bolsón
Ancud
PN Lago Puelo
CHUBUT
Río Chubut
Puerto Madryn
Península Valdes
Golfo Nuevo
Trelew
Castro
Chaitén
Esquel
Rawson
PN Los Alerces
Reserva Provincial Punta Tombo
Punto Tombo
Cordillera de los Andes
REGION IV
REGION V
REGION VI
REGION VII
REGION VIII
REGION IX
REGION X
RP 2
RN 14
RN 26
RN 5
RN 2
RN 7
RN 36
RN 9
RN 8
RN 40
RN 188
RN 143
RN 35
RN 3
RN 151
RN 152
RN 22
RN 237
RN 25

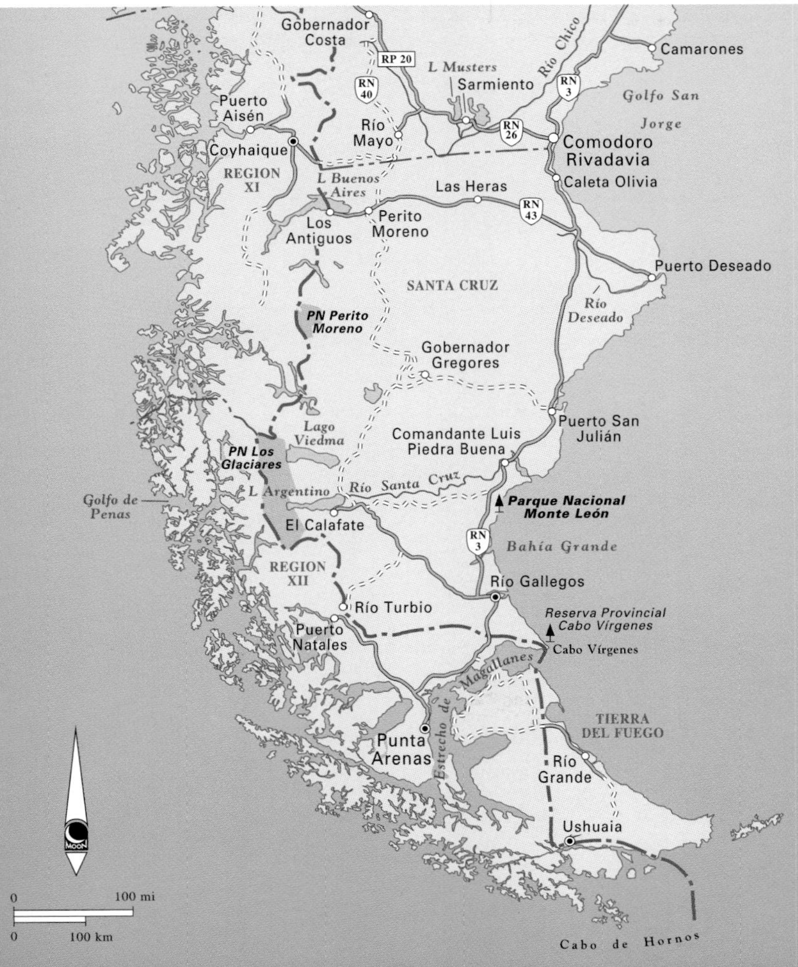

Gobernador Costa
RP 20
L Musters
Sarmiento
Río Chico
RN 3
Camarones
Golfo San Jorge
RN 40
Puerto Aisén
Río Mayo
RN 26
Coyhaique
Comodoro Rivadavia
REGION XI
L Buenos Aires
Las Heras
Caleta Olivia
RN 43
Los Antiguos
Perito Moreno
ATLANTIC
Puerto Deseado
SANTA CRUZ
Río Deseado
PN Perito Moreno
Gobernador Gregores
Puerto San Julián
Lago Viedma
Comandante Luis Piedra Buena
PN Los Glaciares
L Argentino
Río Santa Cruz
Golfo de Penas
Parque Nacional Monte León
El Calafate
RN 3
Bahía Grande
Falkland Islands (Islas Malvinas)
REGION XII
Río Gallegos
Río Turbio
Reserva Provincial Cabo Vírgenes
Stanley
Puerto Natales
Cabo Vírgenes
Estrecho de Magallanes
TIERRA DEL FUEGO
Punta Arenas
Río Grande
Ushuaia
0 100 mi
0 100 km
Cabo de Hornos

© WAYNE BERNHARDSON

CONTENTS

Discover Patagonia

Explore Patagonia

Know Patagonia

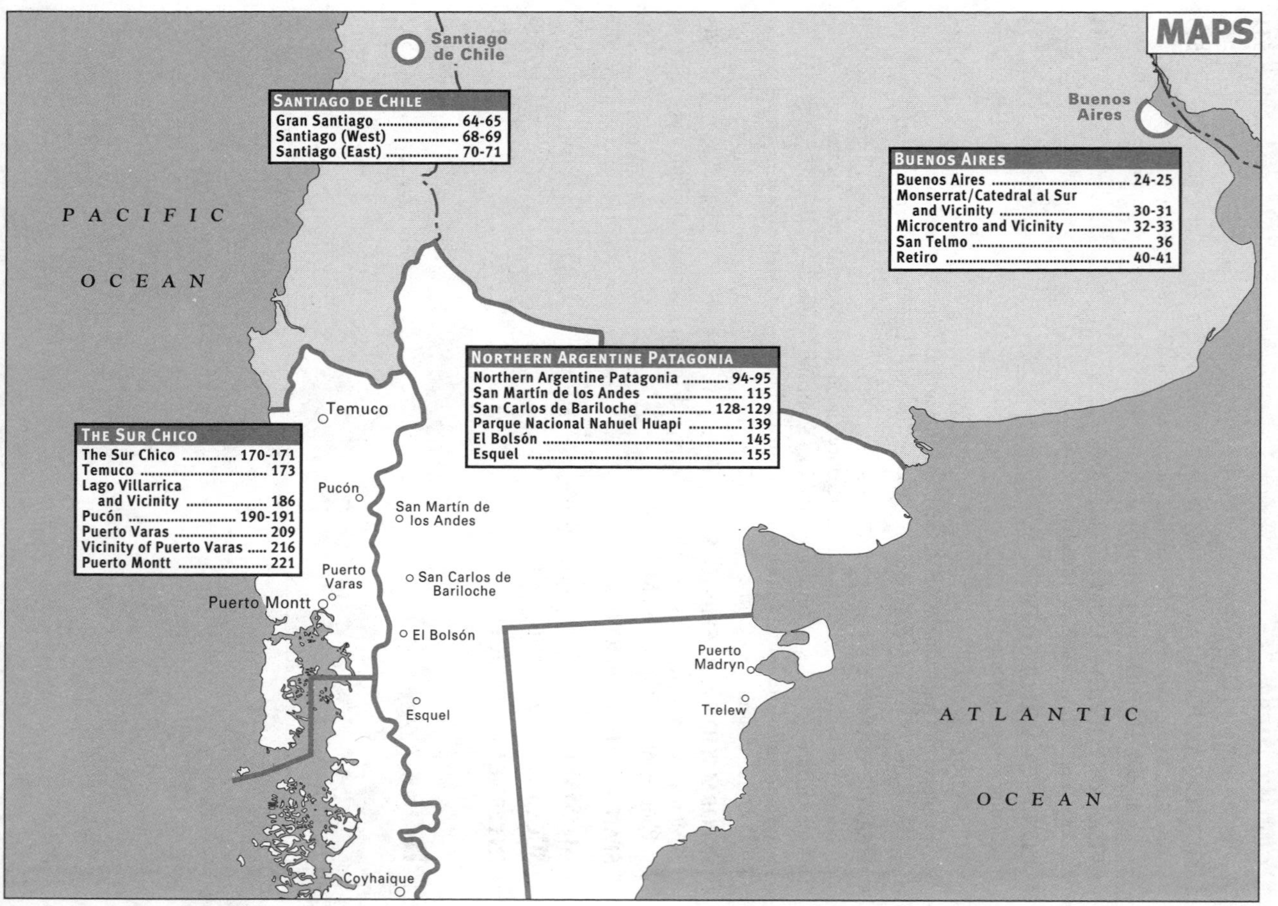
MAPS
Santiago de Chile
Santiago de Chile
Gran Santiago 64-65
Santiago (West) 68-69
Santiago (East) 70-71
Buenos Aires
Buenos Aires
Buenos Aires 24-25
Monserrat/Catedral al Sur
and Vicinity 30-31
Microcentro and Vicinity 32-33
San Telmo 36
Retiro 40-41
PACIFIC
OCEAN
Northern Argentine Patagonia
Northern Argentine Patagonia 94-95
San Martín de los Andes 115
San Carlos de Bariloche 128-129
Parque Nacional Nahuel Huapi 139
El Bolsón 145
Esquel 155
The Sur Chico
The Sur Chico 170-171
Temuco 173
Lago Villarrica
and Vicinity 186
Pucón 190-191
Puerto Varas 209
Vicinity of Puerto Varas 216
Puerto Montt 221
Temuco
Pucón
San Martín de los Andes
Puerto Varas
San Carlos de Bariloche
Puerto Montt
El Bolsón
Puerto Madryn
Trelew
Esquel
ATLANTIC
OCEAN
Coyhaique

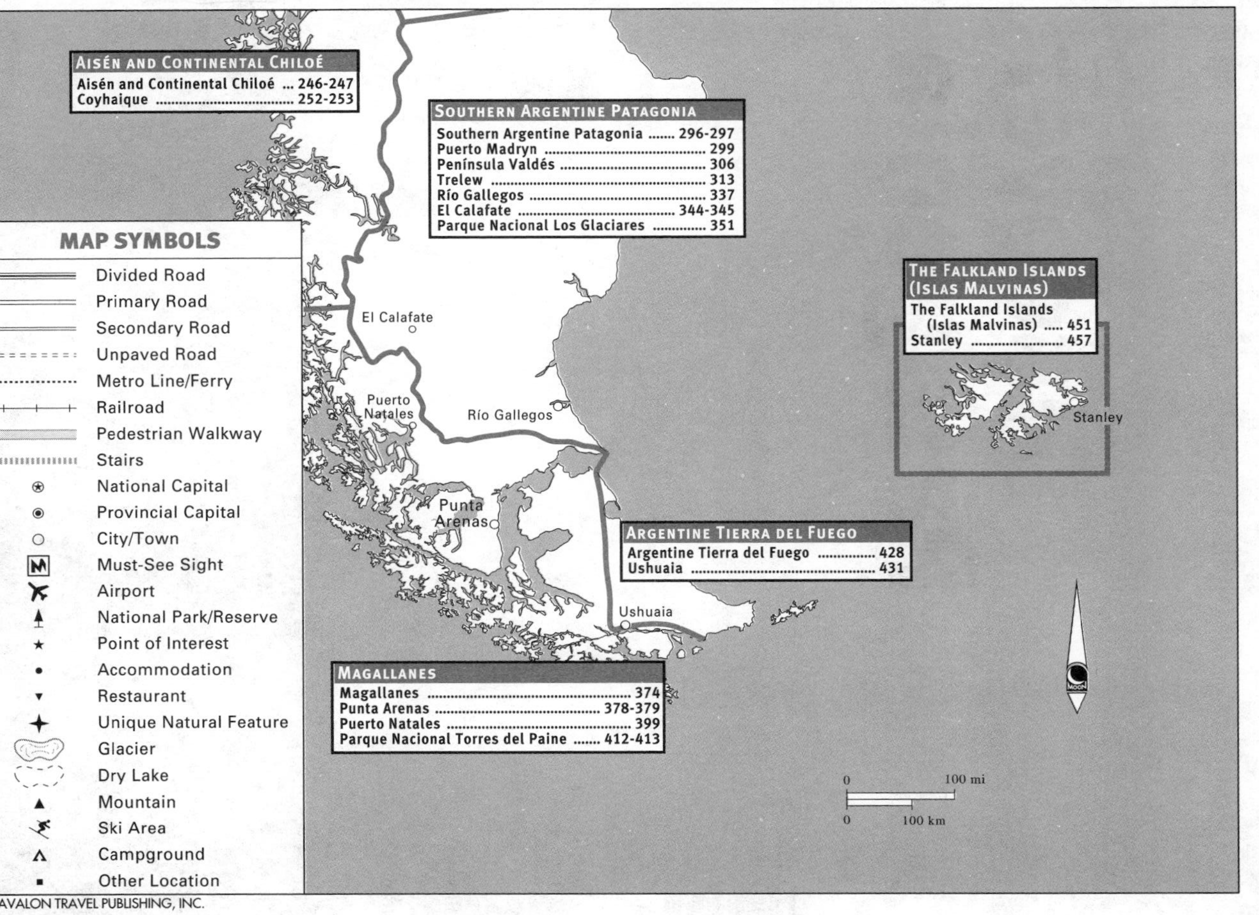

AISÉN AND CONTINENTAL CHILOÉ
Aisén and Continental Chiloé ... 246-247
Coyhaique ... 252-253
SOUTHERN ARGENTINE PATAGONIA
Southern Argentine Patagonia ... 296-297
Puerto Madryn ... 299
Península Valdés ... 306
Trelew ... 313
Río Gallegos ... 337
El Calafate ... 344-345
Parque Nacional Los Glaciares ... 351
THE FALKLAND ISLANDS (ISLAS MALVINAS)
The Falkland Islands (Islas Malvinas) ... 451
Stanley ... 457
ARGENTINE TIERRA DEL FUEGO
Argentine Tierra del Fuego ... 428
Ushuaia ... 431
MAGALLANES
Magallanes ... 374
Punta Arenas ... 378-379
Puerto Natales ... 399
Parque Nacional Torres del Paine ... 412-413
MAP SYMBOLS
Divided Road
Primary Road
Secondary Road
Unpaved Road
Metro Line/Ferry
Railroad
Pedestrian Walkway
Stairs
National Capital
Provincial Capital
City/Town
Must-See Sight
Airport
National Park/Reserve
Point of Interest
Accommodation
Restaurant
Unique Natural Feature
Glacier
Dry Lake
Mountain
Ski Area
Campground
Other Location
El Calafate
Puerto Natales
Río Gallegos
Punta Arenas
Ushuaia
Stanley
MOON
0
100 mi
0
100 km

Discover Patagonia

© WAYNE BERNHARDSON

Where the South American continent tapers to its tip, pointing toward Antarctica, Patagonia is a land of legend that's inspired the imagination ever since the first fantastic tales—of giants who dwarfed Europeans and hidden cities of gold—reached Madrid, Paris, Amsterdam, and London. In the region called the Southern Cone for its shape on the map, Patagonia became an enduring symbol of the unknown, a place where anything was possible.

Nearly five centuries after Magellan met his first Tehuelche on the South Atlantic shore, igniting rumors that persisted nearly 300 years about a race of aboriginal giants, Patagonia is still the land that drew Bruce Chatwin, in the 1970s, to look into a family anecdote about a giant ground sloth. Unlike the Patagonian giants, these megafauna indeed existed (though not within human memory), and Chatwin's resulting literary travelogue—not totally free of the fictions that have typified so much writing about Patagonia—helped revive the region's mystique.

Today, when the ease of air travel has made the exotic so familiar, Patagonia remains a destination whose staggering landscapes evoke exploration and mystery. Increasing numbers of overseas visitors are imagining their own Patagonia, and vigorously discovering the shores, steppes, rivers, lakes, forests, and mountains of southernmost Argentina and Chile—not to mention the remote Falkland Islands. For many visitors, one trip is not enough.

In the area covered by this book, shared between Argentina and Chile, Patagonia counts three UNESCO World Biosphere Reserves and four World Heritage Sites. On the Argentine side, these include the wildlife-packed Atlantic coastline of Península Valdés, the dramatic aboriginal rock art of Cueva de las Manos (Cave of Hands), and the Glaciar Moreno, a grinding river of ice that's a feast for the eyes *and* the ears. The Chilean side can boast the araucaria forests of its Andean lake district, the Jesuit-inspired chapels and churches of the Chiloé archipelago, the remote ice fields of Laguna San Rafael, and the soaring igneous summits of Torres del Paine.

Península Valdés, for that matter, is only one of many wildlife reserves on a seemingly endless South Atlantic shoreline. Northernmost Patagonia's forested lake district reminds visitors of North America's Pacific Northwest or the European Alps, while dinosaur-hunters have made major advances on the vast Patagonian steppes. Only New Zealand, Norway, and the Alaskan panhandle can equal Chile's Pacific fjords and archipelagic Tierra del Fuego's sub-Antarctic wildlands. The Falklands, arguably, boast the best assemblage of Antarctic wildlife this side of the frozen continent.

Patagonia is not all nature, though. Especially on the Chilean side, its Andean lake district is still home to the resilient Mapuche, who defended their territory against the Spaniards and their successors for more than three centuries. In southernmost Patagonia and Tierra del Fuego, sheep farmers created a distinctive cultural landscape, with dispersed settlements that have become vacation attractions in themselves, and a unique architectural heritage.

Two decades ago, relatively few braved travel to countries that suffered some of the most brutal, arbitrary military dictatorships on a continent that was infamous for them. Since the return to constitutional government, though, travel has steadily increased, and it's now an almost ideal place to travel. By North American or European standards, Patagonia remains affordable, and in some areas it's downright cheap.

By jet, the capitals of Argentina and Chile are about eight hours from Miami, 10 hours from New York, or 15 hours from Los Angeles—close enough for short-term visitors focused on special interests. Since Argentine standard time is only two hours ahead of New York and three hours behind Western Europe, and Chile is only an hour behind Argentina, even jet lag is only a minor issue.

Planning Your Trip

When planning any trip to Patagonia, don't overlook the fact that this is an enormous territory—far larger than most of the world's countries—and logistics can be complicated. Unless your trip is an open-ended overland excursion, this means choosing among numerous options both as to destinations and means of transportation. Capital cities like Buenos Aires and Santiago are compact and easy to travel around, but visiting other high-profile destinations like Argentina's Moreno glacier and Chile's Torres del Paine require either two- to three-hour flights or 15- to 30-hour bus trips. Driving is an option, but for most visitors this will mean a rental car from a provincial airport or city.

WHEN TO GO

The fact that the southern spring, summer, and fall months correspond to the northern hemisphere's coldest seasons adds to Patagonia's appeal. Still, seasonal wildlife migrations and Andean ski resorts make it a destination even during the austral winter.

The map of South America is deceptive, as its "Southern Cone" narrows and, beyond the archipelago of Tierra del Fuego, the next great landmass is Antarctica. Tierra del Fuego, though, ends at 56° S latitude—equivalent to the northern hemisphere city of Copenhagen, Denmark—and most of Patagonia lies in lower, more temperate latitudes.

On both sides of the border, the Andean lake district is a traditional summer destination, with locales like Bariloche and Pucón as busy as the ocean beaches; it's also a magnet for fly-fishing enthusiasts from October to April, and Bariloche's the focus of Argentina's ski industry from June to August.

Farther south, the season is lengthening, especially for foreign visitors. El Calafate, gateway to the Moreno Glacier, was once a January–February destination, but now many services stay open October to April, and even for July winter holidays. Península Valdés is a special case that depends on South Atlantic wildlife—the right whale's midwinter arrival in July brings the first tourists, who keep coming with the influx of elephant seals, orcas, and penguins until the end of March.

As an extension of Patagonia, Tierra del Fuego is still primarily a summer destination, though it also has a ski season. The city of Ushuaia is the South American gateway to Antarctica, where the spring breakup of pack ice determines the season.

Like Península Valdés, Falklands tourism depends much on the wildlife calendar, as migratory Magellanic and rockhopper penguins and elephant seals begin arriving in October and stay until March or even a little later. That said, there's some wildlife at all seasons, even though access becomes more difficult in winter.

Luggage: What sort of luggage you bring depends on what sort of trip you're planning, for how long, and where you're planning to go. For shoestring travelers planning months in southernmost South America, a spacious but lightweight backpack is the best choice; a small daypack for local excursions is also a good idea. Even for non-backpackers, light luggage is advisable, though traveling on airplanes, shuttles, and taxis can be logistically simpler than buses alone—door-to-door service is the rule. Even then, a small daypack for excursions is convenient. Small but sturdy lightweight locks are advisable for all sorts of luggage, if only to discourage temptation in the capital cities. In Patagonia itself, crime is almost negligible.

Clothing: A good rule of thumb is to bring appropriately seasonal clothing for comparable Northern Hemisphere latitudes. Buenos Aires's climate is mild in spring and autumn, hot and humid in summer, and cool but not cold in winter—humidity and winter winds, however, can make it feel colder than absolute temperatures might suggest (though frost is almost unheard of). For summer, then, light cottons are the rule, while a sweater and perhaps a light jacket suffice for the shoulder seasons. A warm but not polar-strength jacket and rain gear are advisable for winter. At a higher altitude than Buenos Aires, Santiago has a Mediterranean dry-summer, wet-winter climate; summer days can be hot, but nights invariably cool off. The Andean lake district gets the brunt of Pacific storms, and good rain gear and warm footwear are essential for hikers. In much of the region, an umbrella is less useful than a rain jacket or parka, as the winds can shred the sturdiest bumbershoot. Though summer temperatures can get hot in some parts of the region, warm clothing is imperative in high altitudes and latitudes; in southernmost Patagonia and Tierra del Fuego, state-of-the-art wet-weather gear is more than advisable.

Camping Gear: For many if not most visitors, Patagonia's appeal is its high, wild backcountry. In addition to wet-, cold-, and wind-resistant clothing, warm sleeping bags and a sturdy tent are imperative. Even car campers in Patagonia's more remote parts will appreciate good gear.

In much of the region, drinking water is potable straight from the stream, but it's not always obvious where otherwise limpid water has been polluted. Some sort of purification system is a good idea. In some but not all national parks, primarily in Argentina, wood fires are prohibited for either warmth or cooking. Gas canisters are available, but an adaptable multi-fuel camp stove is the best choice.

Rental gear is available in the gateways to some of the prime hiking areas, such as Bariloche, Puerto Natales, and El Chaltén.

Odds and Ends: Since public toilets sometimes lack toilet paper, travelers should always carry some, even though it's readily available in both countries. Some budget hotels have thin walls and squeaky floors, so earplugs can be useful. A compact pair of binoculars is a good idea for birders and others who enjoy wildlife and the landscape.

The Regions

Patagonia is notoriously hard to define, but for purposes of this book, it's a pragmatic matter that corresponds closely to political geography. On the Argentine side, it comprises the provinces of Neuquén, Río Negro, Chubut, Santa Cruz, and Tierra del Fuego, while in Chile it includes the lake-district jurisdictions of La Araucanía (Region IX) and Los Lagos (Region X), plus Patagonia proper, Aisén (Region XI) and Magallanes (Region XII).

The controversial Falkland Islands, while politically distinct and geographically isolated from the South American continent, share much of their natural environment and even traditional social institutions—their sprawling sheep farms were, arguably, the forerunners of the Patagonian sheep *estancias* in both Argentina and Chile. For purposes of this book, the Falklands ("Malvinas" to Argentines) are "insular Patagonia."

BUENOS AIRES

Since the 2002 devaluation, South America's highest-profile capital has become a bargain destination that's reason enough to visit the country—many visitors spend weeks or even months enjoying its first-rate accommodations, innovative cuisine, all-night entertainment, nonstop shopping, and matchless cultural resources. Despite its international sophistication, it's also a city of intimate neighborhoods where no one is truly anonymous.

SANTIAGO DE CHILE

Patagonia's other gateway capital is one of the continent's most underrated cities. While it lacks the high international profile of its Argentine neighbor, Santiago's setting at the base of the high Andes is far more impressive, and its accommodations, food, and entertainment scenes are catching up rapidly—not least because Chile is the continent's most politically stable and prosperous country.

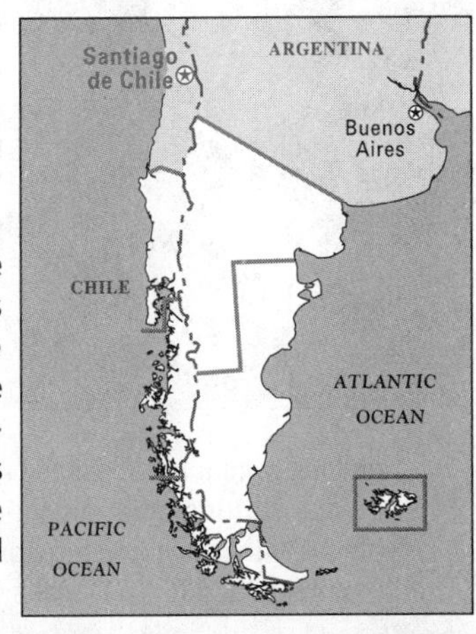

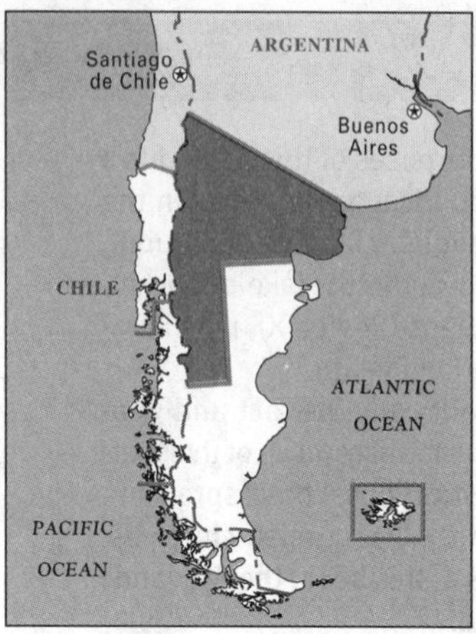

NORTHERN ARGENTINE PATAGONIA

Beyond the Río Colorado, which flows southeast from the Chilean border to the Atlantic Ocean, Argentine Patagonia consists of Neuquén, Río Negro, Chubut, and Santa Cruz provinces. For purposes of this book, northern Argentine Patagonia comprises Neuquén and Río Negro plus northwesterly parts of Chubut that correspond to the so-called lake district along the Chilean border.

While most of Argentine Patagonia is desert steppe, the densely wooded sector near the Chilean border boasts numerous national parks; centered around the city of San Carlos de Bariloche, this is the country's conventional holiday playground, but activities-oriented travel, including hiking, climbing, rafting and kayaking, and fly-fishing, has grown rapidly over the past decade. At select locations, ski resorts take advantage of its heavy winter snowpack.

For more than three centuries, northern Argentine Patagonia was a zone of conflict where Araucanian (Mapuche) Indians kept both Spanish and Argentine forces and settlers off guard, before finally bowing to Argentine sovereignty in the late 19th century. While marginalized economically, the Mapuche play an increasingly visible role in regional politics through their persistent land claims.

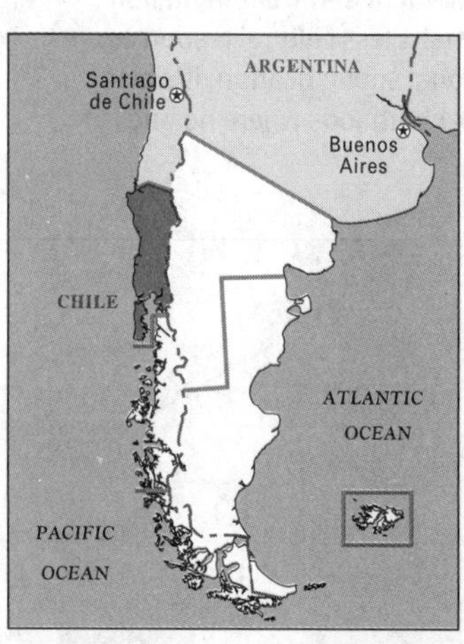

THE SUR CHICO

Often known imprecisely as Chile's "lake district," south of the Río Biobío, the "Little South" is a wonderland of rivers, lakes, forests, and volcanoes that comprises the Araucanía (Region IX)—the homeland of the Mapuche Indians—and Los Lagos (Region X). Within this vernacular region is also the Chiloé archipelago, a UNESCO World Heritage site rich in scenery, architecturally distinctive houses and churches, and extravagant folklore.

Though it's arguably not Patagonia at all—defining Patagonia is particularly complicated on the Chilean side—the Sur Chico is a popular destination for Chilean and foreign visitors alike, and it's common to cross the Andes into Argentine Patagonia here. It's also the official starting point for the Carretera Austral, the discontinuous southern highway that's linked previously inaccessible parts of southern Chile to the mainland, and for the ferries whose services help fill the gaps.

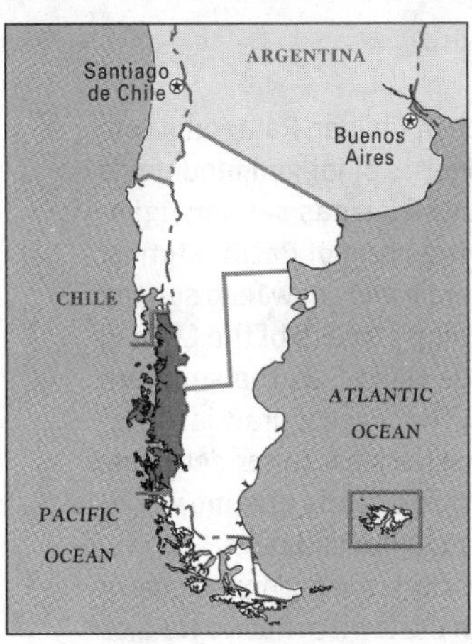

AISÉN AND CONTINENTAL CHILOÉ

Chile's most thinly populated region, Aisén (Region XI, formally speaking) is mostly wild islands-and-highlands country that bears strong resemblance to British Columbia and the Alaska panhandle. For purposes of this book, it also includes the southernmost part of Los Lagos (Region X), often known as "continental Chiloé," where the tiny ferry port of Caleta Gonzalo is the de facto (as opposed to the official) starting point of the Carretera Austral.

Along with Argentina's RN 3 and RN 40, the Carretera Austral is one of Patagonia's greatest road trips, but off-the-highway sights like Laguna San Rafael (accessible only by boat or air taxi) are highlights in their own right. There are numerous national parks and reserves along or near the highway, and Parque Natural Pumalín may be South America's most audacious private conservation initiative.

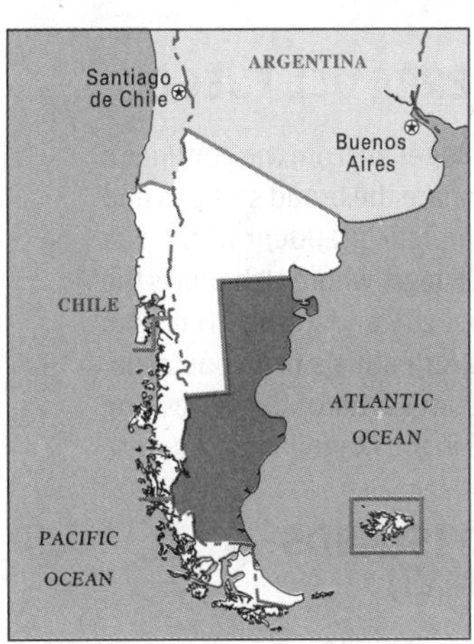

SOUTHERN ARGENTINE PATAGONIA

In this book, Southern Argentine Patagonia consists of Chubut province, excluding the northwesterly "lake district" area, and Santa Cruz province. All the way to the Chilean border, southern Patagonia's Atlantic coastline is a scenic cornucopia of whales, seals, penguins, and other wildlife. Along the Andean front range, the southern province of Santa Cruz is famous for the dramatic Moreno Glacier, a crackling outlier of the Campo de Hielo Sur, the southern Patagonian ice sheet.

Two legendary highways, the coastal RN 3 and the interior RN 40, connect the region with northerly provinces; RN 40 is an attraction in its own right, as Patagonia's "loneliest road," but its paving over the next few years may undercut some of its mystique. Most of the region's population is urban, but the rural economy supports everything from subsistence plots to extensive grazing of cattle and sheep.

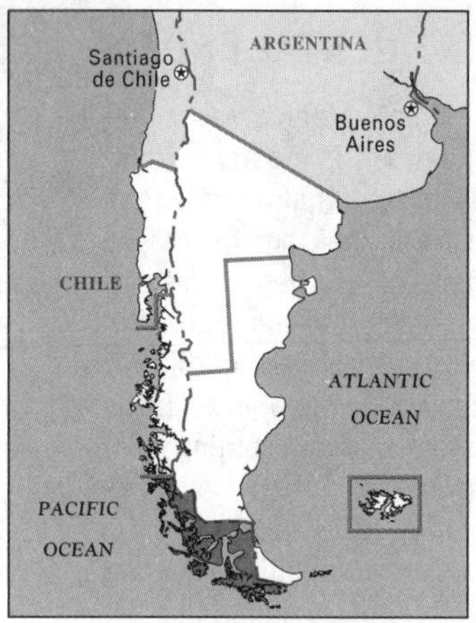

MAGALLANES

South of Aisén, much of Chilean Patagonia covered in this book consists of jagged mountains and almost uninhabited islands set among inland seas that bear the brunt of Pacific storms; copious quantities of rain and snow feed surging rivers and the sprawling glaciers of the Chilean side of the Campo de Hielo Sur, the southern continental ice field. The biggest draw is the igneous spires of Parque Nacional Torres del Paine, and in much of the region nearly pristine woodlands still cover the mountainsides.

The only significant city is the regional capital of Punta Arenas, though the town of Puerto Natales is a gateway to Torres del Paine. Most of the Chilean side of the Isla Grande Tierra del Fuego is thinly settled and its most scenic parts are almost inaccessible; but, across the Beagle Channel from Ushuaia, on Isla Navarino, Chile's Puerto Williams is the last major settlement north of Antarctica. Local cruise ships now visit Cape Horn, South America's southernmost point.

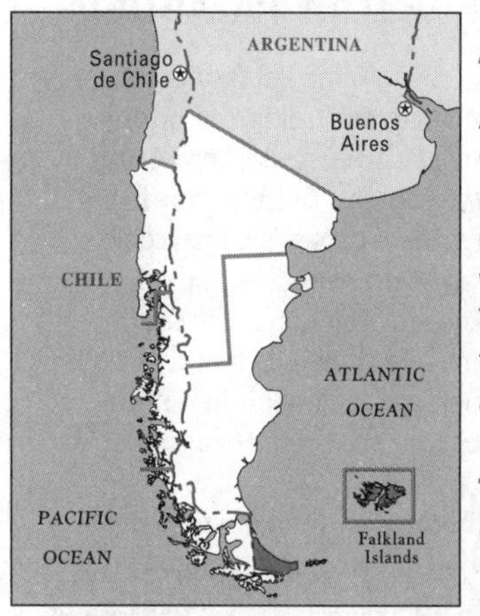

ARGENTINE TIERRA DEL FUEGO

Across the Strait of Magellan from the continent, Chile and Argentina share the broad steppes and mountainous sub-Antarctic grandeur of the Isla Grande de Tierra del Fuego, where Ushuaia is the world's southernmost city and Parque Nacional Tierra del Fuego was Argentina's first coastal national park. The Chilean sector of this sprawling archipelago appears in the Magallanes chapter.

THE FALKLAND ISLANDS (ISLAS MALVINAS)

In the open South Atlantic Ocean, more than 500 kilometers east of the South American mainland, the Falkland Islands acquired international notoriety in 1982, when a desperate Argentine dictatorship tried to deflect domestic discontent by militarily enforcing a longstanding territorial claim against the British-held Islands. Since the British regained them 10 weeks later, the Islands have prospered under a commercial fishing-license regime; they've also become a magnet for cruise ships and a smaller number of independent adventurers who all come to see their abundant sub-Antarctic wildlife while enjoying local hospitality.

Introducing Patagonia

For first-time visitors, the big sights are Argentina's Moreno Glacier and Chile's Torres del Paine. Since most passengers will arrive in Buenos Aires or Santiago, this simplifies logistics, but great distances mean that flying to Patagonia is unavoidable.

Fortunately, El Calafate's new airport has eliminated the tedious, time-consuming transfer from Río Gallegos to the Moreno Glacier; still, figure a night in Buenos Aires; two at El Calafate, gateway to the glacier; and an overnight at Punta Arenas, Chile. Two or three extra days would allow additional time in the capital, an excursion to the Fitz Roy sector of Parque Nacional Los Glaciares, or perhaps a stay at an *estancia.*

Adding only a few days means greater flexibility in itineraries, though distances can still mean airport time and returning to the hub airport at Buenos Aires is sometimes unavoidable. One possible extension takes you to the "uttermost part of the earth" at Ushuaia, the world's southernmost city in Argentine Tierra del Fuego.

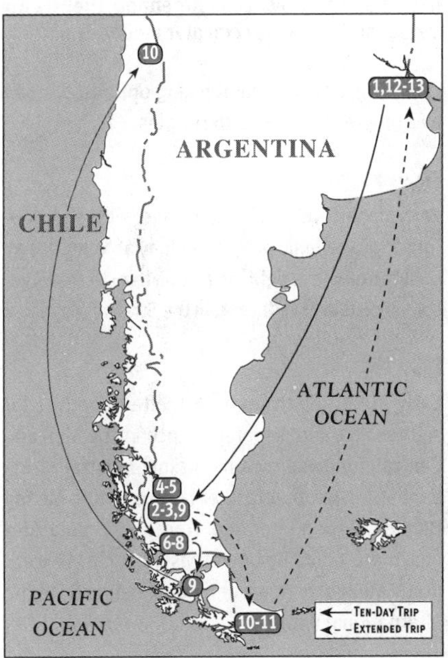

DAY 1

Morning arrival at Aeropuerto Internacional Ministro Pistarini (Ezeiza) and transfer to a **Buenos Aires** hotel, with afternoon free for sightseeing and evening for a tango floorshow.

DAYS 2–3

Morning flight to **El Calafate,** with afternoon excursion to nearby *estancia* for an *asado.* The following morning, a full-day excursion to **Moreno Glacier,** Parque Nacional Los Glaciares.

DAYS 4–5

Morning departure by bus or rental car for **El Chaltén,** in the Fitz Roy sector of **Parque Nacional Los Glaciares.** With an early arrival and good weather, a swift hike to view **Cerro Torre**'s glaciated needle. The next morning, a full-day hike to **Laguna de los Tres,** with stupendous views of **Cerro Fitz Roy,** followed by an evening return to El Calafate.

DAYS 6–8

Bus or air taxi to the Chilean town of **Puerto Natales,** gateway to **Parque Nacional Torres del Paine.** Overnight in Natales, with a scenic day hike in the vicinity, or in the park, with afternoon options for short hikes or a horseback ride. The next morning, a short but strenuous hike to the tarns beneath the Torres themselves; on the

© WAYNE BERNHARDSON

In Santa Cruz province in Argentina, the Fitz Roy range rivals Chile's Torres del Paine as Patagonia's most spectacular mountains.

following, any of several hiking options, with an evening return to Puerto Natales.

Day 9

Early departure for Punta Arenas, with short detour to Magellanic penguin colony at Seno Otway or, if the timing is right, afternoon ferry to the larger colony on Isla Magdalena, in the Strait of Magellan.

Day 10

Early flight to Santiago, with afternoon free for sightseeing and a seafood lunch at the Mercado Central, followed by a nighttime departure from Santiago's Aeropuerto Internacional Arturo Merino Benítez. With a later departure from Punta Arenas, there would be time to visit that city's exceptional Museo Regional and transfer directly to the international flight.

Ushuaia and Tierra del Fuego Extension

Day 9

Return to El Calafate by bus or air taxi, with possible afternoon excursion to bird-watching or rock-art sites.

Days 10–11

Morning flight to Ushuaia, capital of Tierra del Fuego province, followed by wildlife-viewing excursion on the legendary Beagle Channel. The next morning, a full-day excursion to Parque Nacional Tierra del Fuego, with multiple short hiking trails, but don't miss Ushuaia's prison museum.

Days 12–13

Return flight to Buenos Aires, with the afternoon and evening free for sightseeing and perhaps a tango floor show; the following day is open for exploring Buenos Aires before evening departure flight.

The Andean Lakes Loop

For touring both sides of the Andean lake district by rental car, it's easier to arrange a border-crossing vehicle on the Chilean side; it's important to clarify the insurance situation, as Chilean liability coverage is not normally valid in Argentina. Alternatively, it's simpler to rent a car separately on either side, especially if the bus-boat-bus crossing to Bariloche is on the docket.

Day 1

Morning arrival at **Santiago**'s Aeropuerto Internacional Arturo Merino Benítez, with quick connection to **Puerto Montt** and overnight in nearby **Puerto Varas;** alternatively, an afternoon's sightseeing in Santiago, with a seafood lunch at the Mercado Central, and a comfortable sleeper bus to Puerto Montt.

Day 2

For orientation, a leisurely drive around **Lago Llanquihue** via **Frutillar, Puerto Octay, Ensenada,** and Puerto Varas. With an early enough start, it's possible to continue south from Ensenada to **Cochamó** and **Puelo,** along the Estuario de Reloncaví, and back to Puerto Montt or Puerto Varas via the Caleta Puelche ferry shuttle.

Days 3–4

Morning departure for **Bariloche,** Argentina, on the bus-boat-bus crossing via **Lago Todos los Santos.** Accommodation in or near Bariloche.

The next day, a morning tour of Bariloche, followed by excursion on **Parque Nacional Nahuel Huapi**'s "Circuito Chico" loop, including a stiff trail hike to **Cerro López** or, more easily, driving within two kilometers of the López *refugio*.

Days 5–6

Morning departure for **Villa la Angostura,** on Lago Nahuel Huapi's north shore, with most of the day for hiking, mountain-biking, or kayaking in the vicinity. The next morning, a long but not taxing day hike to the myrtle forest of **Parque Nacional Los Arrayanes** and back; those with lesser stamina can take a comfortable boat either or both ways.

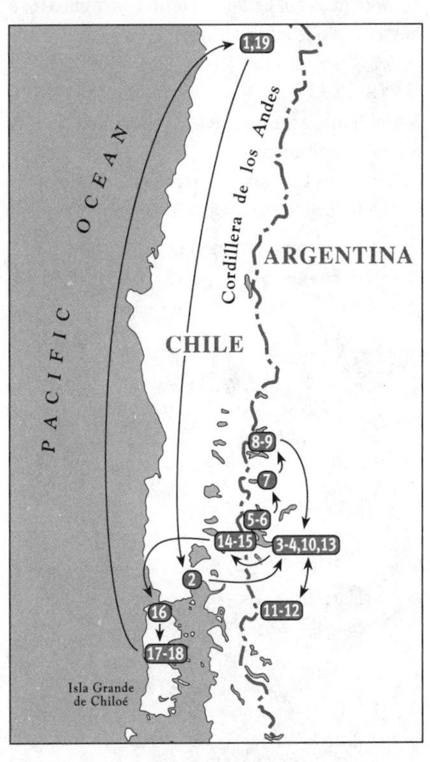

Day 7

Morning departure for **San Martín de los Andes** via the leisurely "Siete Lagos" (Seven Lakes) route. Afternoon boat excursion on **Lago Lácar,** or tour of city.

Days 8–9

Morning departure for north side of **Lago Huechulafquen, Parque Nacional Lanín,** via **Junín de los**

Andes. In-park accommodations or camping for hiking, horseback riding, or fishing.

The following morning, a full-day hike through *pewen* forest on the south side of **Lago Huechulafquen** and **Lago Paimún.**

Day 10

Return to Bariloche via Junín de los Andes and RN 40, with pause at **Estancia Fortín Chacabuco** for a horseback ride and an *asado.*

Days 11–12

Morning departure for Parque Nacional Nahuel Huapi's **Ventisquero Negro** ("Black Glacier"), south of Bariloche. Late afternoon arrival at **El Bolsón.**

The following morning, if it's market day, visit the lively Feria Artesanal El Bolsón and enjoy a short afternoon hike at **Parque Nacional Lago Puelo;** if it's not, hike to the summit of **Cerro Piltriquitrón** for a panoramic view of the Andes along the Chilean border, to the west.

© WAYNE BERNHARDSON

Feria Artesanal El Bolsón

Day 13

Early return to Bariloche, for bus connection to Puerto Montt or Puerto Varas.

Days 14–15

Morning departure for **Parque Nacional Puyehue,** with accommodations at the upmarket **Hotel Termas de Puyehue,** a hot-springs resort. Numerous short hikes in the vicinity.

The next morning, an arduous full-day hike to the shoulder of **Volcán Puyehue,** with spectacular views of the former rainforest area denuded by its 1960 eruption.

Day 16

Morning departure for **Ancud,** Chiloé, with an afternoon visit to the Humboldt penguin colony at **Puñihuil.**

Days 17–18

Morning departure for **Castro** and **Cucao,** Parque Nacional Chiloé, with short hikes near park headquarters. Simple B&B or *cabaña* accommodations near Cucao park entrance.

The next morning, a full-day hike along the Pacific shoreline of **Parque Nacional Chiloé,** returning to Puerto Montt or Puerto Varas for accommodations.

Day 19

Early flight to Santiago, with afternoon free for sightseeing and a seafood lunch at the Mercado Central, followed by a nighttime departure from Santiago's Aeropuerto Internacional Arturo Merino Benítez.

The Carretera Austral

For the most part, this is a Chilean itinerary through some of the continent's wildest scenery, but there's an optional detour into Argentine territory. Because public transportation is so limited along the southern highway, a rental car is virtually essential, unless time is no object. A high-clearance vehicle is a good idea, but four-wheel drive is not necessary.

Days 1–2

Morning arrival at **Santiago**'s Aeropuerto Internacional Arturo Merino Benítez, with onward connection to **Balmaceda** and transfer to **Coyhaique** hotel.

The next morning, a full-day excursion to **Parque Nacional Laguna San Rafael,** by air taxi from Coyhaique or high-speed catamaran from Puerto Chacabuco.

Day 3

Morning departure northbound to **Puerto Puyuhuapi,** breaking for hike to **Parque Nacional Queulat**'s hanging glacier. If space is available, overnight at **Termas de Puyuhuapi** hot-springs hotel; if not, overnight in Puerto Puyuhuapi at simpler but still acceptable accommodations.

Days 4–5

Morning visit to Puyuhuapi carpet factory, then northbound departure to **Chaitén** and **Caleta Gonzalo** (Parque Natural Pumalín), with possible hiking detour to hanging glacier west of Lago Yelcho. Accommodations in Chaitén or, depending on availability, camping or *cabañas* in Caleta Gonzalo.

The next morning, choose among any of several full-day hiking excursions within **Parque Natural Pumalín.**

Days 6–7

Morning departure to village of **Futaleufú.** Short afternoon excursions from town, after making preparations for rafting or other activities.

The next morning, an exhilarating full-day's rafting on the Class IV–V **Río Futaleufú,** one of the world's top whitewater experiences.

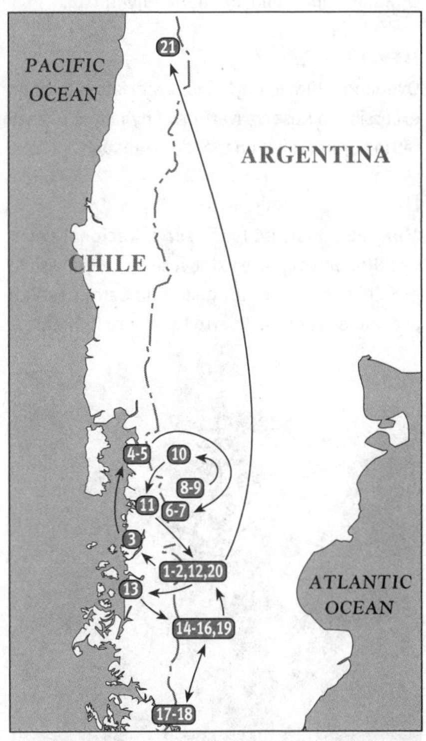

Days 8–9

Early departure for the historic Welsh mill town of **Trevelin,** Argentina, and **Parque Nacional Los Alerces,** with camping, *cabañas,* or hotel within the park. The next morning, a full-day lake excursion to the park's signature *alerce* woodlands.

Day 10

Morning departure for **Cholila,** site of Butch Cassidy's Patagonian home, and **Leleque,** site of

Benetton's impressive new museum, looping back to **Esquel** or Trevelin for accommodations. At Trevelin, late afternoon Welsh tea in lieu of dinner.

Day 11

Return loop to Chile via the village of **Palena,** with accommodations at La Junta's **Hostal Espacio y Tiempo, Cabañas El Pangue,** at Parque Nacional Queulat's north end, or Puerto Puyuhuapi.

Day 12

Overland return to Coyhaique, with late-afternoon excursion to **Reserva Nacional Coyhaique** or easy rafting or kayaking on the **Río Simpson.**

Day 13

Morning departure for **Reserva Nacional Cerro Castillo,** with day hike to the reserve and/or visit to pre-Columbian rock art near Villa Cerro Castillo; accommodations in **Puerto Ingeniero Ibáñez.**

© WAYNE BERNHARDSON

pedestrian bridge, Parque Nacional Queulat

Day 14

Car ferry on **Lago General Carrera** from Puerto Ingeniero Ibáñez to **Chile Chico.**

Day 15

Morning departure for **Puerto Guadal, Puerto Bertrand,** and **Cochrane** via Lago General Carrera's thrilling south shore road. Guadal and Bertrand both have excellent accommodations, but Cochrane has more complete services.

Day 16

Morning departure for **Caleta Tortel,** a uniquely scenic fishing village with boardwalks in lieu of streets. Simple bed-and-breakfast accommodations.

Days 17–18

Morning departure for **Villa O'Higgins,** via the Fiordo Mitchell ferry (delays possible if demand is heavy). The next morning, a full-day hiking excursion on the **Sendero de Chile,** or boat excursion to the **Ventisquero O'Higgins.**

Day 19

Early departure to Cochrane and **Puerto Río Tranquilo,** which has bed-and-breakfast accommodations. Wind permitting, half-day boat to lakeside limestone caverns at **Capilla de Mármol.**

Day 20

If the wind has let up, there's time to re-try the Capilla de Mármol. Either way, a leisurely return to Coyhaique via Cerro Castillo, with plenty of time for photography.

Day 21

Early northbound flight from Balmaceda, with afternoon free for sightseeing and a seafood lunch at Santiago's Mercado Central, followed by an evening departure from Aeropuerto Internacional Arturo Merino Benítez.

The Natural History Tour

In its more than 1.1 million square kilometers, divided between Chile and Argentina, Patagonia can offer an astonishing diversity of natural environments. While it's hard to define precisely what comprises Patagonia, the region is about the size of France, Germany, and the United Kingdom combined, or of California and Texas combined.

Nearly the entire Patagonian coastline abounds in wildlife like elephant seals, penguins, and sea lions, but the great distances require time and money to see them—public transportation is fine along the main highway but poor off it. The same is true of the Patagonian steppes, home to the llama-like guanaco and the ostrich-like rhea, and the southern Andean forests beyond the main tourist clusters. In terms of its natural assets, Tierra del Fuego is a southern extension of Patagonia.

Northern Argentine Patagonia boasts notable paleontological discoveries in and around the city of Neuquén, an accessible detour from the lake district, and in and around the city of Trelew, near Puerto Madryn and the wildlife Mecca of Península Valdés. Along much of the Andes, but particularly on the Chilean side, volcanism is an active presence.

Day 1

Morning arrival at **Santiago**'s Aeropuerto Internacional Arturo Merino Benítez, with transfer to hotel and sightseeing, including seafood lunch at the picturesque Mercado Central and a visit to the information offices of Conaf, the country's main national parks and conservation agency. Alternatively, in lieu of a hotel, a comfortable sleeper bus to **Temuco,** gateway to the upper Biobío's araucaria forests.

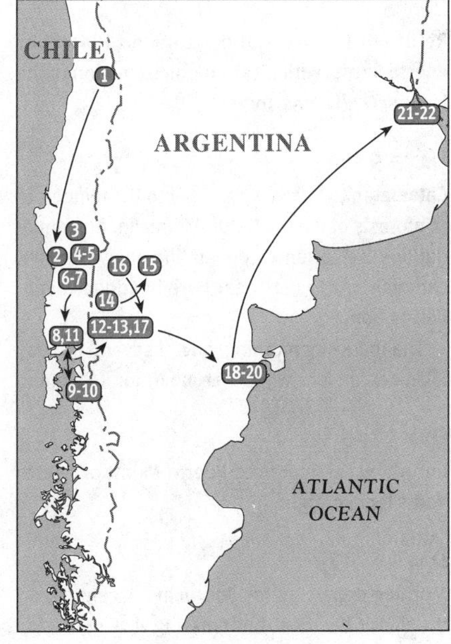

Day 2

Morning flight to Temuco and rental car to explore the streams, gallery forests, and araucaria woodlands of **Parque Nacional Tolhuaca** and the upper Biobío, with accommodations at **Malalcahuello.**

Day 3

Full-day hiking excursion to araucaria forests above Malalcahuello, on the slopes of **Volcán Lonquimay,** with a post-hike soak at the new hot-springs resort nearby.

Days 4–5

Leisurely drive of the upper Biobío circuit through **Lonquimay** and forested, thinly populated Pehuenche country, entering **Parque Nacional Conguillío** via the southern Melipeuco approach. After a visit to the park visitors center for orientation, camping or *cabaña* accommodations nearby.

On the following day, any of several hikes among Conguillío's lava fields and araucaria forests.

Days 6–7

Morning departure for **Lago Villarrica,** with accommodations in **Villarrica** or **Pucón.** Excursion to the **Cuevas Volcánicas** lava tubes, or an afternoon rafting on the **Río Trancura.**

The next morning—weather and seismic conditions permitting—a strenuous full-day climb to the crater of Volcán Villarrica, one of the continent's most active volcanoes. Alternatively, a full-day hiking in nearby Parque Nacional Huerquehue.

Day 8

Return to Temuco and bus to **Puerto Montt** or **Puerto Varas,** with an afternoon excursion to the **Lahuen Ñadi** *alerce* forest.

Days 9–10

Catamaran to **Chaitén,** gateway to the temperate rainforests of Parque Natural Pumalín. Accommodations in Chaitén or, depending on availability, camping or *cabañas* near park headquarters in **Caleta Gonzalo.**

The following morning, any of several full-day hiking excursions within **Parque Natural Pumalín.**

Day 11

Return by catamaran to Puerto Montt or Puerto Varas for overnight.

Days 12–13

Morning departure for **Bariloche,** Argentina, on the classic bus-boat-bus crossing via **Lago Todos los Santos.** Accommodation in or near Bariloche.

The next morning, tour of Bariloche and its

© WAYNE BERNHARDSON

arrayán forest at Parque Nacional Los Arrayanes, near Villa la Angostura

Museo de la Patagonia, emphasizing natural history and conservation in Argentina's national park system. In the afternoon, an excursion on **Parque Nacional Nahuel Huapi**'s "Circuito Chico" loop, including a stiff trail hike to **Cerro López** or, alternatively, a drive within two kilometers of López's *refugio* for panoramic views of the Andes and **Lago Nahuel Huapi.**

Day 14

Morning drive to **Villa la Angostura,** on Lago Nahuel Huapi's north shore, followed by a long but not taxing day hike to the myrtle forest of **Parque Nacional Los Arrayanes** and back; those with lesser stamina can take a comfortable boat either or both ways.

Day 15

Drive to **Estancia Fortín Chacabuco,** for a morning horseback ride offering spectacular panoramas of the Patagonian steppe, and a lunchtime *asado*. Continue to **Villa El Chocón**, a hydroelectric-company town that contains one of Neuquén province's several paleontological museums and dinosaur excavations. Accommodations at Villa El Chocón or the provincial capital city of **Neuquén.**

Day 16

Morning departure for dinosaur excavation site at **Los Barreales**, northwest of Neuquén city. If summer water levels are too high to visit the site, go directly west to Plaza Huincul's upgraded paleontological museum and then to **Parque Nacional Laguna Blanca**, a shallow steppe lake created by a lava-flow dam, that's home to black-necked swans and other wildlife. Decent accommodations in **Zapala** but, if it's early, continue to **Aluminé** on the dizzyingly scenic Rahue road, where the most easterly araucaria forests are.

© WAYNE BERNHARDSON

Elephant seals sun themselves on the beach at Caleta Valdés, Península Valdés.

Day 17

Return to Bariloche via **Junín de los Andes** and RN 40, followed by comfortable overnight sleeper bus to **Puerto Madryn.**

Days 18–20

Morning arrival at Puerto Madryn, followed by a visit to the city's new Ecocentro environmental museum. In the afternoon, time for in-town beach activities like diving or windsurfing.

The following morning, early departure by tour bus or rental car to **Península Valdés** where, depending on the season, there'll be elephant seals, penguins, orcas, or right whales. Many other species—rheas, guanacos, and sea lions, for instance—are present all year.

The morning after, full-day rental-car excursion to the gigantic Magellanic penguin colony at **Punta Tombo,** south of Trelew. On the way back, visit **Trelew**'s state-of-the-art paleontology museum and take Welsh tea at **Gaiman.**

Days 21–22

Morning flight to Buenos Aires, with the afternoon and evening free for sightseeing and perhaps a tango floorshow.

The following day, free for exploring Buenos Aires before evening departure flight.

The Southern Patagonian Road Trip

Because of Patagonia's vast expanses, overland travel tends to be for those with plenty of time. Most routes are well-served by reasonably priced public transportation, but those who can afford a vehicle can usually do them more efficiently and stop to see appealing second-tier sights. Four-wheel drive may not be necessary, but a high-clearance vehicle is worth the extra bucks.

Parallel to RN 3, the mother of all Argentine roads is RN 40, from the Bolivian border in Jujuy province to the Chilean border in Patagonia's Santa Cruz province. It's in Patagonia, though, that RN 40 has acquired an international reputation as *the* adventurous route between the northern lakes and southern glaciers. Only in the last few years has there been any semi-regular public transportation between Perito Moreno and El Calafate, and there's still not any between Perito Moreno and Río Mayo, though there are overland "expeditions" from Bariloche. While projects to pave the route are underway, in the near future any trip south of Río Mayo will still seem like an expedition, and travelers need to be prepared for several days' rugged travel—and weeks, if they want to explore off the main route.

As late as the 1980s, coastal RN 3 was nearly as rugged as RN 40 is now; today, it's almost entirely paved, with regular public transportation, but it still glows with the charisma of the world's southernmost highway, the Patagonian road that leads from Buenos Aires to the tip of Tierra del Fuego. To grasp the vastness that so impressed the first Europeans, and to view prodigious concentrations of wildlife, "Ruta Tres" is still a matchless itinerary.

Day 1

Arrival at Aeropuerto Internacional Ministro Pistarini (Ezeiza) and transfer to a **Buenos Aires** hotel, with afternoon free for sightseeing.

Day 2

Morning flight to **Trelew** and transfer to **Puerto Madryn,** with an afternoon visit to the city's Ecocentro environmental museum. There should still be time for the beach or more active pursuits like diving or windsurfing.

Day 3

Full-day rental-car excursion to **Península Valdés** where, depending on the season, there'll be elephant seals, penguins, orcas, or right whales. Many other species—such as rheas, guanacos, and sea lions—are present all year.

Day 4

Morning departure for **Trelew,** to visit its state-of-the-art paleontology museum, followed by a badlands hike through the *in situ* paleontological park at **Bryn Gwyn,** near Gaiman. Late afternoon Welsh tea and overnight at **Gaiman.**

Day 5

Morning departure for **Punta Tombo**'s massive Magellanic penguin colony. From Punta Tombo, a drive along the desolately scenic coastline past Cabo Raso to isolated **Camarones** for lunch, and on to the city of **Comodoro Rivadavia.** Time permitting, a visit to Comodoro's new downtown railroad museum.

Days 6–7

Morning visit to Comodoro's first-rate petroleum

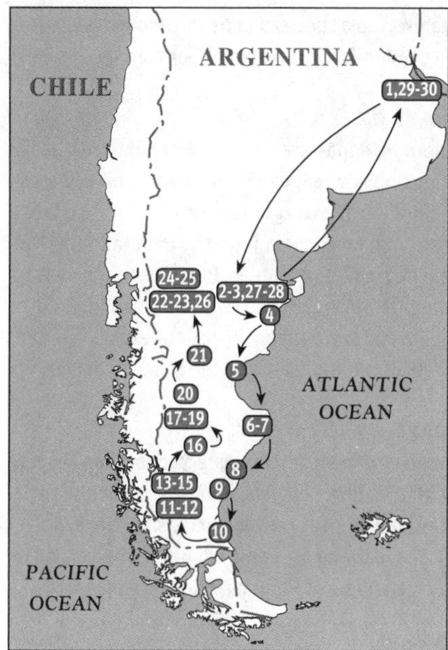

museum and an afternoon departure for picturesque Puerto Deseado and its unique estuary, the Ría Deseado.

The next morning, a full-day excursion on the Ría Deseado, home to penguins, cormorants, many other seabirds, and especially dolphins. Or, time and conditions permitting, sailing to the rockhopper penguin colony at offshore Isla Pingüinos.

Day 8

Long drive south to Puerto San Julián, where Magellan's crew wintered in 1520 and Sir Francis Drake later put down a mutiny. It's also home to large populations of dolphins and Magellanic penguins.

Day 9

Morning departure for the stunning headlands of Parque Nacional Monte León. Check the tide tables at the park visitors center at Estancia Monte León, in order to be able to walk the beach, enter the sea caves, and approach the cormorant-covered Isla Monte León. Exceptional accommodations at Estancia Monte León, Estancia Dor Aike, the nearby town on Comandante Luis Piedra Buena, or camping at the park itself.

Day 10

Morning or afternoon departure for Río Gallegos, capital of Santa Cruz province. Accommodations in town or at one of two historic *estancias:* Hill Station or the more remote Estancia Monte Dinero, near the large Magellanic penguin colony at Cabo Vírgenes.

Days 11–12

After a visit to Gallegos's regional museum, a post-lunch departure for El Calafate, gateway to Parque Nacional Los Glaciares. Time permitting, a visit to a working *estancia* for an *asado.*

The following morning, a full-day overland excursion to the Moreno Glacier, Parque Nacional Los Glaciares.

Days 13–15

Morning departure for El Chaltén, in the Fitz Roy sector of Parque Nacional Los Glaciares. With an early arrival and good weather, a swift hike to view Cerro Torre's namesake glaciated needle. Accommodations in or near town.

The following morning, a demanding full-day hike to Laguna de los Tres, with amazing views of Cerro Fitz Roy. On the next, a full-day boat excursion to Glaciar Viedma, including a short hike on the glacier itself. With a mid-afternoon return on a long summer day, there's time to drive north to Lago del Desierto, on the Chilean border.

Day 16

Morning departure for northbound RN 40, passing Tres Lagos en route to Lago Cardiel. Accommodations at Estancia Las Tunas, Estancia La Angostura, or Gobernador Gregores.

Days 17–18

Morning departure for Parque Nacional Perito Moreno, with accommodations at Estancia Menelik, Estancia La Oriental, or camping. Excursion to Lago Belgrano.

The next morning, hike to the summit of Cerro León, with panoramic views across the eastern steppe, west toward the Andes on the Chilean border, with numerous condors and guanacos en route.

Day 19

Morning departure for Bajo Caracoles and Cueva de las Manos, the world-famous rock-art site. Accommodations at any of several *estancias,* such as Estancia Lagos del Furioso, west of Bajo Caracoles, or Estancia Telken, south of the town of Perito Moreno.

Day 20

Morning departure for Perito Moreno and Los Antiguos, a lush "banana belt" town on the south shore of Lago Buenos Aires.

Day 21

Morning departure for Río Mayo and Sarmiento, gateway to a spectacular petrified-forest badlands. Accommodations in or near Sarmiento.

© WAYNE BERNHARDSON

Cerro Torre, Parque Nacional Los Glaciares

Days 22–23

Morning departure for Esquel, terminus of the famous narrow-gauge railway La Trochita (the so-called "Old Patagonian Express"). The next morning, an excursion on La Trochita to the Mapuche hamlet of Nahuel Pan. Afternoon visit to the historic Welsh mill town of Trevelin, its museum and surrounding historic sites; in late afternoon, a traditional Welsh tea in lieu of dinner.

Days 24–25

Morning departure for Parque Nacional Los Alerces, with camping, *cabañas,* or hotels within the park; day hike on any of several accessible trails.

The following morning, full-day lake excursion to *alerce* forests of Parque Nacional Los Alerces.

Day 26

Morning departure for Cholila, site of Butch Cassidy's Patagonian cabin, and the Benetton-sponsored historical museum at Leleque, looping back to Esquel for accommodations.

Day 27

Early departure for long drive across the Patagonian steppe to Trelew or Puerto Madryn. The main reward is the canyon scenery of the middle Río Chubut valley, at Paso de los Indios and Valle de los Mártires; carry food, as the few restaurants are dire.

Day 28

Rest and relaxation day at Puerto Madryn.

Days 29–30

Morning flight to Buenos Aires, with the afternoon and evening free for sightseeing and perhaps a tango floor show. Most of the following day free for exploring Buenos Aires before evening departure flight.

Explore Patagonia

Buenos Aires

South America's highest-profile capital, Buenos Aires has evolved dramatically since its shaky colonial origins. Massive post-independence immigration and prosperity turned a cozy "Gran Aldea" (Great Village) into a "Paris of the South" with broad avenues, colossal monuments, and mansard-capped mansions.

In the 20th century, Buenos Aires experienced spectacular spurts of growth and even more spectacular economic and political disasters. Yet somehow, like its melancholy signature music and dance of the tango, it's retained its identity and mystique.

Despite Argentina's problems, the River Plate's megalopolis still has much to offer urban explorers in a city that truly never sleeps. It's one of the most underrated destinations on an underrated continent—notwithstanding the 2002 economic and political crisis, *Travel + Leisure* called it Latin America's top tourist city.

Foreign visitors often conflate the city with Argentina—though provincial Argentines vociferously protest that "Buenos Aires is *not* Argentina." Despite a cosmopolitan outlook, many Porteños ("residents of the port") identify more strongly with their own Gran Aldea barrios or

Must-Sees

Look for M to find the sights and activities you can't miss and M for the best dining and lodging.

Plaza de Mayo: Buenos Aires's historic center is ground zero for Argentine public life (page 28).

Café Tortoni: For nearly a century and a half, the Avenida de Mayo's traditional gathering place has been an island of stability in a tumultuous ocean of political, social, and economic upheaval (page 28).

Teatro Colón: The continent's most important performing-arts venue retains its style and dignity (page 33).

Puerto Madero: Redevelopment of the capital's crumbling port opened the area to a generation of Porteños to whom the waterfront had been off-limits, and to tourists who lunch along the new yacht harbor (page 34).

Plaza Dorrego: Sunday is the day that antique vendors and spirited street performers clog San Telmo's principal plaza and surrounding streets (page 37).

Caminito: Professional and amateur photographers alike adore the vigorous street life and bright primary colors of the metal-clad houses that line the curving, cobbled pedestrian mall in the barrio of La Boca (page 38).

Cementerio de la Recoleta: For both the living and the dead, the barrio of Recoleta is the capital's prestige address (page 42).

© WAYNE BERNHARDSON

Plaza de Mayo and Casa Rosada

Museo de Arte Latinoamericano de Buenos Aires (MALBA): For decades, even during dictatorships, Argentina has had a thriving modern-art scene, but this new Palermo museum has given it a new focal point (page 43).

Museo Eva Perón: Promoted by Evita's partisans, Argentina's first museum dedicated to a woman is as notable for what it omits as for what it includes (page 43).

Museo Argentino de Ciencias Naturales: In the decidedly untouristed barrio of Caballito, this improving museum houses exhibits that shed light on the impressive Argentine dinosaur discoveries of recent decades (page 46).

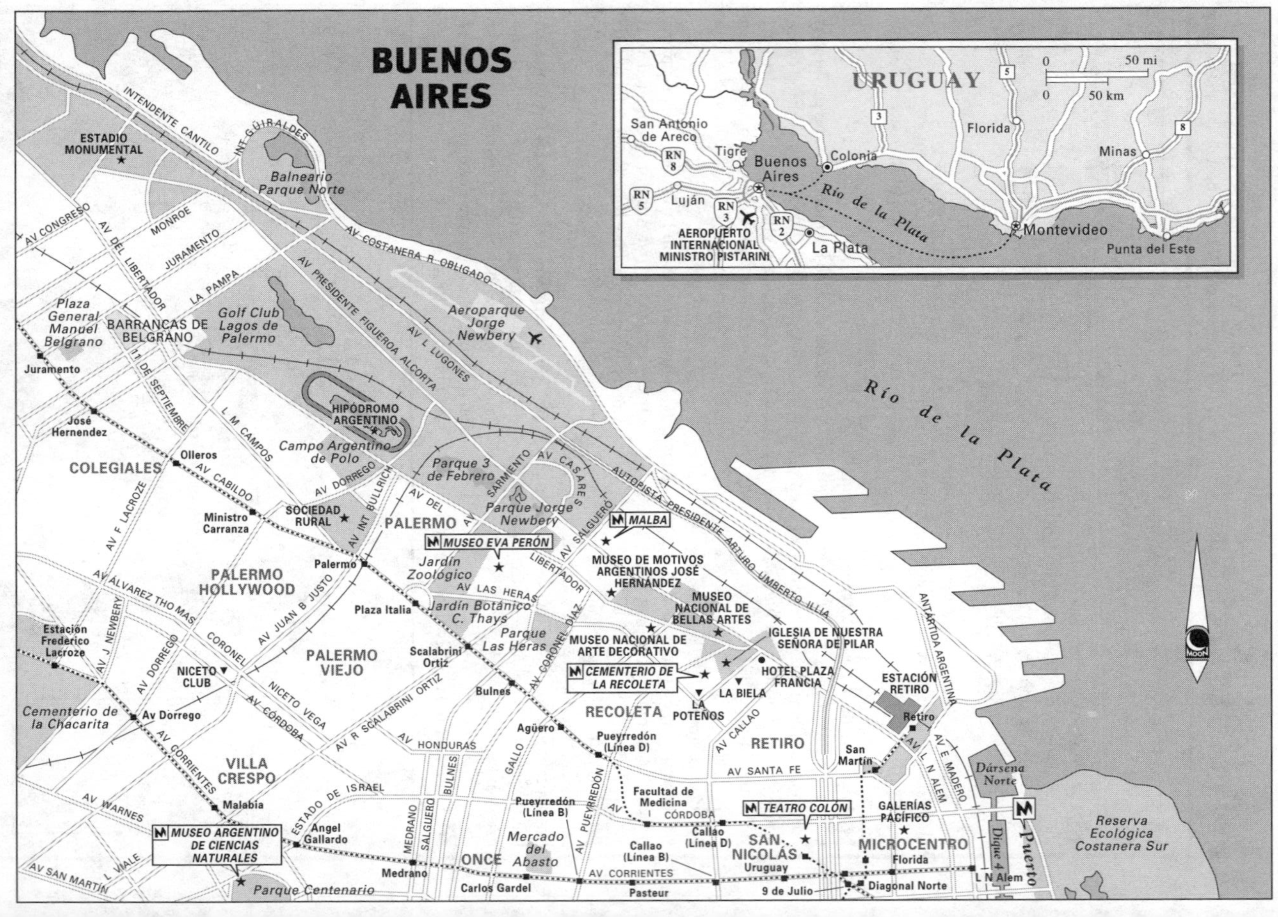
BUENOS AIRES
URUGUAY
0 50 mi
0 50 km
San Antonio de Areco
Tigre
Buenos Aires
Colonia
Florida
Minas
Luján
Río de la Plata
AEROPUERTO INTERNACIONAL MINISTRO PISTARINI
La Plata
Montevideo
Punta del Este
ESTADIO MONUMENTAL
INTENDENTE CANTILO
INT GÜIRALDES
Balneario Parque Norte
AV CONGRESO
AV DEL LIBERTADOR
MONROE
JURAMENTO
LA PAMPA
AV COSTANERA R. OBLIGADO
AV PRESIDENTE FIGUEROA ALCORTA
AV L LUGONES
Aeroparque Jorge Newbery
Plaza General Manuel Belgrano
BARRANCAS DE BELGRANO
Golf Club Lagos de Palermo
Juramento
11 DE SEPTIEMBRE
HIPÓDROMO ARGENTINO
José Hernendez
L M CAMPOS
Campo Argentino de Polo
Parque 3 de Febrero
SARMIENTO
AV CASARES
COLEGIALES
Olleros
AV CABILDO
AV DORREGO
AV INT BULLRICH
AV DEL
AUTOPISTA PRESIDENTE ARTURO UMBERTO ILLIA
SOCIEDAD RURAL
PALERMO
Parque Jorge Newbery
AV SALGUERO
MALBA
Ministro Carranza
AV F LACROZE
MUSEO EVA PERÓN
Jardín Zoológico
LIBERTADOR
MUSEO DE MOTIVOS ARGENTINOS JOSÉ HERNÁNDEZ
Palermo
PALERMO HOLLYWOOD
AV LAS HERAS
AV ÁLVAREZ THOMAS
AV JUAN B JUSTO
Plaza Italia
Jardín Botánico C. Thays
MUSEO NACIONAL DE BELLAS ARTES
IGLESIA DE NUESTRA SEÑORA DE PILAR
ANTÁRTIDA ARGENTINA
Estación Frederico Lacroze
AV J NEWBERY
CORONEL
PALERMO VIEJO
Scalabrini Ortiz
Parque Las Heras
AV CORONEL DÍAZ
MUSEO NACIONAL DE ARTE DECORATIVO
HOTEL PLAZA FRANCIA
ESTACIÓN RETIRO
NICETO CLUB
AV DORREGO
NICETO VEGA
AV R SCALABRINI ORTIZ
Bulnes
CEMENTERIO DE LA RECOLETA
LA BIELA
LA POTEÑOS
Cementerio de la Chacarita
Av Dorrego
AV CÓRDOBA
RECOLETA
Retiro
AV CALLAO
Agüero
AV HONDURAS
RETIRO
San Martín
AV L N ALEM
AV E MADERO
Dársena Norte
VILLA CRESPO
AV CORRIENTES
GALLO
Pueyrredón (Línea D)
AV SANTA FE
AV WARNES
ESTADO DE ISRAEL
BULNES
Facultad de Medicina
Malabia
MEDRANO
SALGUERO
Pueyrredón (Línea B)
AV PUEYRREDÓN
CÓRDOBA
TEATRO COLÓN
GALERÍAS PACÍFICO
Reserva Ecológica Costanera Sur
MUSEO ARGENTINO DE CIENCIAS NATURALES
Angel Gallardo
Mercado del Abasto
Callao (Línea D)
SAN NICOLÁS
MICROCENTRO
Dique 4
Puerto
Medrano
ONCE
Callao (Línea B)
Uruguay
Florida
AV SAN MARTÍN
L VIALE
Parque Centenario
Carlos Gardel
AV CORRIENTES
Pasteur
9 de Julio
Diagonal Norte
L N Alem
MOON

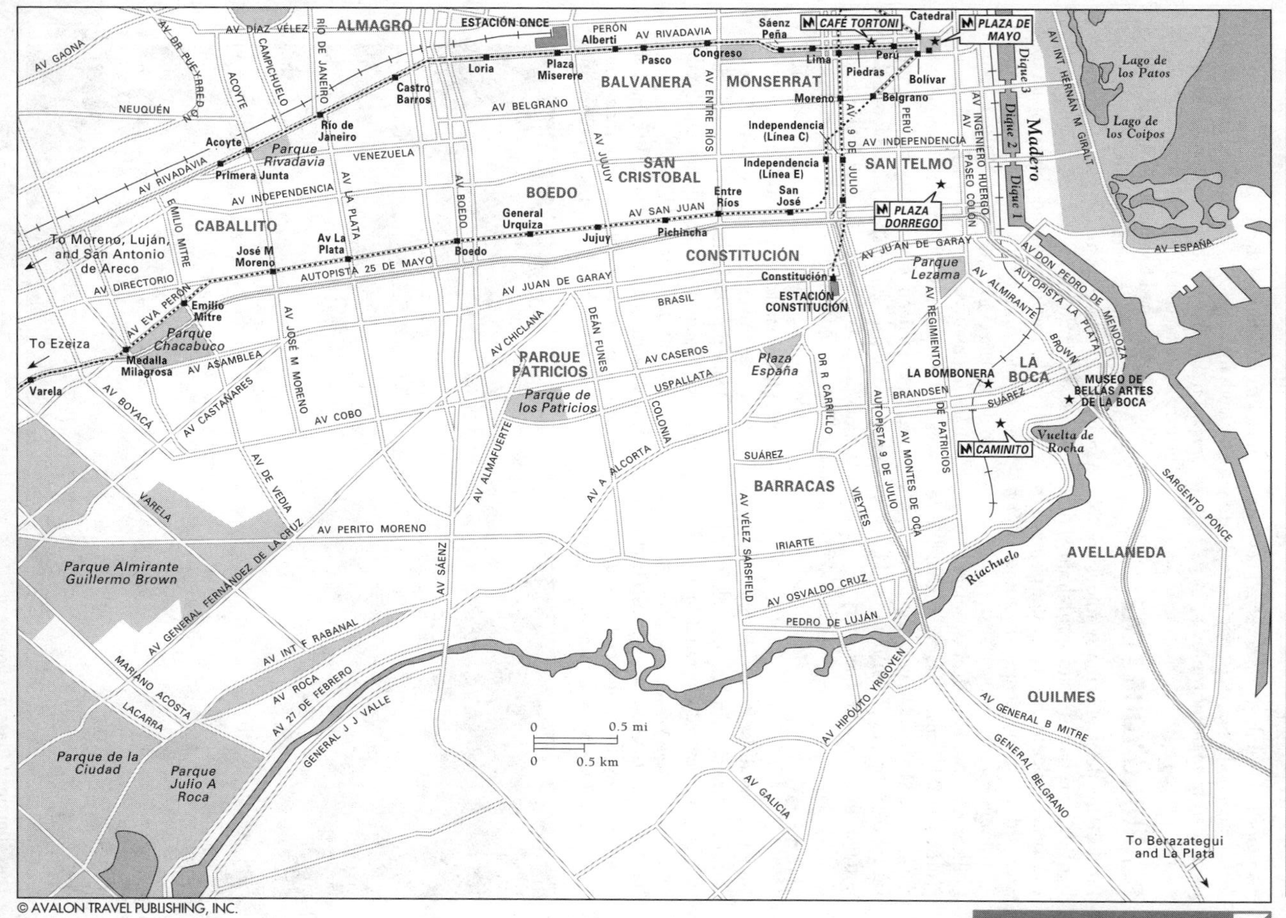

Buenos Aires

neighborhoods. Like New Yorkers, they often seem brash and assertive, their accent setting them apart from the provinces.

PLANNING YOUR TIME

Buenos Aires deserves as much time as possible, but Patagonia-bound visitors with limited time will have to pick and choose. Anyone planning an extended stay should consult the author's *Moon Handbooks Buenos Aires.*

Presuming no more than two days in town, visitors should focus on central highlights like the Plaza de Mayo and vicinity; the Teatro Colón; the southern barrios of San Telmo and La Boca; and the famous Recoleta cemetery.

HISTORY

Buenos Aires dates from the 1536 landing of Pedro de Mendoza, but his party failed to survive supply shortages and Querandí Indian opposition. Juan de Garay refounded the city in 1580, but for nearly two centuries it was a backwater, subordinate to Spain's viceregal capital of Lima.

Mendoza's lasting legacy was the escaped livestock that transformed the surrounding pampas grasslands into a fenceless ranch. Feral cattle and horses, nearly free for the taking, spawned Argentina's gaucho culture.

Buenos Aires had few markets, though, because low-value hides were too bulky to ship to Spain via Lima and Panama. This led to vigorous contraband trade with British and Portuguese vessels in the Paraná delta and obliged Spain to make Buenos Aires capital of the Virreinato del Río de la Plata (Viceroyalty of the River Plate).

Late colonial Porteños resisted British invasions in 1806 and 1807, but those invasions hastened the Revolution of May 1810, the beginning of the end of Spanish rule. In 1816, the Provincias Unidas del Río de la Plata (United Provinces of the River Plate) formally declared independence.

Following decades of disorder, isolationist caudillo Juan Manuel de Rosas took command of Buenos Aires province, ruling it from 1829 until 1852. By the time Rosas took power, the provincial capital's population was nearly 60,000; shortly after his departure, it reached 99,000.

Rosas' overthrow and exile brought explosive growth—the city's population more than doubled, to 230,000, by 1875. In 1880, it became

© WAYNE BERNHARDSON

the fountain at Plaza del Congreso

the federal capital and, by the early 20th century, Latin America's first city with more than a million inhabitants.

From Gran Aldea to Cosmopolitan Capital

Federalized Buenos Aires's first mayor, Torcuato de Alvear, immediately imposed his vision on the newly designated capital. Instead of the intimate *Gran Aldea* (Great Village), Buenos Aires would become a cosmopolitan showpiece. Where single-story houses once lined narrow colonial streets, broad boulevards like the Avenida de Mayo soon linked majestic public buildings.

Relandscaped spaces like the Plaza de Mayo, Plaza del Congreso, and Plaza San Martín reflected an ambitious country's aspirations—or pretensions. Some, though, castigated Alvear for favoring upper-class barrios like Recoleta and Palermo over immigrant neighborhoods like San Telmo and La Boca.

As European immigrants streamed into Buenos Aires, such differential treatment exacerbated social tensions. In 1913, it became the first South American city to open a subway system, but large families on subsistence wages squeezed into *conventillos* (tenements) in poorer neighborhoods. The gap between rich and poor frequently exploded into open conflict and instability.

In the 1930s, the military dictatorship that overthrew President Hipólito Yrigoyen further obliterated narrow colonial streets to create broad thoroughfares like Corrientes and Santa Fe, and the cross-town boulevard Avenida 9 de Julio. Despite lip service to working-class interests, the populist Perón regimes of the 1940s and 1950s splurged on pharaonic projects, heavy and heavily subsidized industry, and spending that squandered post–World War II surpluses.

The Dirty War and Its Aftermath

By 1970, as sprawling Gran Buenos Aires (Greater Buenos Aires) absorbed ever more distant suburbs, the capital and vicinity held eight million people, more than a third of the country's population. Continued instability became almost open warfare until 1976, when the military ousted the inept President Isabel Perón (Juan Perón's widow) in a bloodless coup that became a bloody reign of terror.

One rationale for taking power was civilian corruption, but the military and their civilian collaborators managed to attract international loans to demolish vibrant but neglected neighborhoods and create colossal public works. Much of the money found its way into offshore bank accounts.

Following the 1983 return to constitutional government, Argentina underwent several years' hyperinflation in which President Raúl Alfonsín's Radical government wasted enormous amounts of good will. President Carlos Menem's succeeding Peronist government, directed by Economy Minister Domingo Cavallo, brought a decade of stability during which foreign investment flowed into Argentina, and Buenos Aires in particular. The financial and service sectors flourished, and urban renewal projects like the Puerto Madero riverfront gave 1990s Porteños a sense of optimism. The boom had a dark side, though, a "crony capitalism" in which the president's associates enriched themselves through favorable privatization contracts.

Even before the late-2001 debt default, the economy contracted and Porteños began to suffer. After Menem's hapless successor Fernando de la Rúa resigned, in December, the country had a series of caretaker presidents until the May 2003 election of Peronist Néstor Kirchner.

As the economy stagnated and unemployment rose, homelessness also rose and scavengers became a common sight even in prosperous barrios. Strikes, strident pickets blocking bridges and highways, and frustration with politicians and the International Monetary Fund (IMF) contributed to the sense of *bronca* (aggravation). Yet somehow the city, with its blend of neighborhood integrity, cosmopolitan sophistication, and cultural life, continued to function.

ORIENTATION

The Ciudad Autónoma de Buenos Aires (Autonomous City of Buenos Aires), also known as the Capital Federal, lies within the boundaries formed by the Río de la Plata, its Riachuelo tributary, and the ring roads of Avenida General Paz and Avenida 27 de Febrero. Most visitors see only a key handful of its 47 barrios.

The historic center is **Monserrat** (also known as Catedral al Sur, "South of the Cathedral"), whose Plaza de Mayo has been the site of spectacle and debacle in Argentina's tumultuous politics. Immediately north, **San Nicolás** includes the compact, densely built **Microcentro** (also known as Catedral al Norte, "North of the Cathedral"), with major shopping and theater districts, and BA's Wall Street in "La City." Eastward, stretching north-south along the river, redeveloped **Puerto Madero** is the city's newest barrio.

Southern Monserrat gives way to the cobbled colonial streets of **San Telmo,** peopled with artists and musicians, tango bars, and the Plaza Dorrego flea market, with a scattering of old-money families and more than a scattering of *conventillos* (tenements) abandoned by old money. To the southeast, **La Boca** has never been prosperous, but it has a colorful history, an extravagantly colorful vernacular architecture and artists' colony, and an enviable community solidarity.

Across Avenida Córdoba, elegant **Retiro** marks a transition to the upper-middle-class residential barrios to the north and northwest. Immediately northwest, **Recoleta** retains that elegance in one of the world's most exclusive graveyards, the Cementerio de la Recoleta, where many affluent Argentines have elected to spend eternity. Barrio Norte, a mostly residential area overlapping Retiro and Recoleta, is more a real estate contrivancethan a barrio per se.

Beyond Recoleta, broad avenues lead to the open spaces of **Palermo,** a mostly middle- to upper-middle-class barrio with the city's finest dining and wildest night life. Woodsy **Belgrano** is a mostly residential barrio that hosts an assortment of museums and other cultural resources.

Sights

Buenos Aires's sights are mostly easily grouped by the barrios described above, though a few outlying barrios have scattered points of interest.

MONSERRAT/CATEDRAL AL SUR AND VICINITY

The barrio's axis is the **Avenida de Mayo,** which links the **Casa Rosada** presidential palace (1873–1898) with the **Congreso Nacional** (National Congress, 1906). The perpendicular **Avenida 9 de Julio** splits Monserrat in half.

Plaza de Mayo

The Plaza de Mayo derives its name from the date of the Revolution of 1810, but it owes its fame to the massive demonstrations that have taken place here in support and protest of the Peróns, the Falklands/Malvinas war, and other political causes.

At the plaza's northwest corner, the imposing **Catedral Metropolitana** (1827) holds the remains of national icon José de San Martín. At the southwest corner, only part of the colonial **Cabildo de Buenos Aires** (1725–1765) survived construction of the Avenida de Mayo. If the economy were as solid as the northeast corner's neoclassical **Banco de la Nación** (1939), Argentina would be a global powerhouse.

Café Tortoni

First among the Avenida de Mayo's surviving landmarks, the legendary Café Tortoni (Avenida de Mayo 825, tel. 011/4342-4328, www.cafetortoni.com.ar) dates from 1858. One of BA's most fiercely if quietly traditional places, the Tortoni has made no concessions to the 21st century and only a few to the 20th: upholstered chairs and marble tables stand among sturdy columns beneath a ceiling punctuated by stained-glass vitreaux, the wallpaper looks original between the dark-stained wooden trim, and the walls are decorated with pictures, portraits, and *filete,* the traditional calligraphy of Porteño sign-painters.

Among the patrons acknowledged on the walls are tango singer Carlos Gardel, La Boca painter Benito Quinquela Martín, dramatists Luigi Pirandello and Federico García Lorca, and pianist Arthur Rubinstein; more recently, the Tortoni

© WAYNE BERNHARDSON

Plaza de Mayo and Casa Rosada

has hosted King Juan Carlos I of Spain and Hillary Rodham Clinton.

Other Sights

At the west end of Avenida de Mayo, the **Plaza del Congreso** (officially, **Plaza de los Dos Congresos,** 1904), another frequent site for political demonstrations, faces the **Congreso Nacional** (1908), the notoriously dysfunctional Argentine legislature.

South of Plaza de Mayo, Monserrat's major colonial landmark is the **Manzana de las Luces,** comprising several ecclesiastical and educational institutions filling an entire block bounded by Alsina, Bolívar, Moreno, and Perú.

At Alsina and Defensa, the **Farmacia de la Estrella** (1900) is a classic apothecary distinguished by magnificent woodwork and health-oriented ceiling murals. Its exterior windows exhibit materials from the upstairs **Museo de la Ciudad** (Defensa 219, tel. 011/4343-2123 or 011/4331-9855), specializing in elements of everyday Porteño life. Hours are 11 A.M.–7 P.M. weekdays, 3–7 P.M. Sunday; admission costs US$.35 except Wednesday, when it's free.

A block south, the **Museo Etnográfico Juan B. Ambrosetti** (Moreno 350) has superb archaeological, ethnographic, and ethnohistorical displays on the northern Patagonian Mapuche and the Tierra del Fuego archipelago. Hours are 2:30–6:30 P.M. daily except Monday and Tuesday; admission costs US$.35. Guided tours take place on weekends.

From the roof of the **Casa de la Defensa** (Defensa 372), Porteños poured boiling oil on British invaders in 1806–1807. Half a block south, at Avenida Belgrano, the 18th-century **Iglesia y Convento de Santo Domingo** shares grounds with the Instituto Nacional Belgraniano, a patriotic institute that contains the tomb of Argentine flag designer General Manuel Belgrano.

MICROCENTRO AND VICINITY

Formally known as San Nicolás, the area bounded by Avenida Córdoba, Avenida Madero, Avenida Rivadavia, and Avenida Callao, encompasses the city's traditional financial, commercial, and entertainment centers. The area between Avenida 9 de Julio and the riverfront, immediately north of the Plaza de Mayo, is commonly called the Microcentro and, occasionally, "Catedral al Norte." North of Rivadavia, Calle San Martín is the axis of "La City," the financial district, with banks and exchange houses.

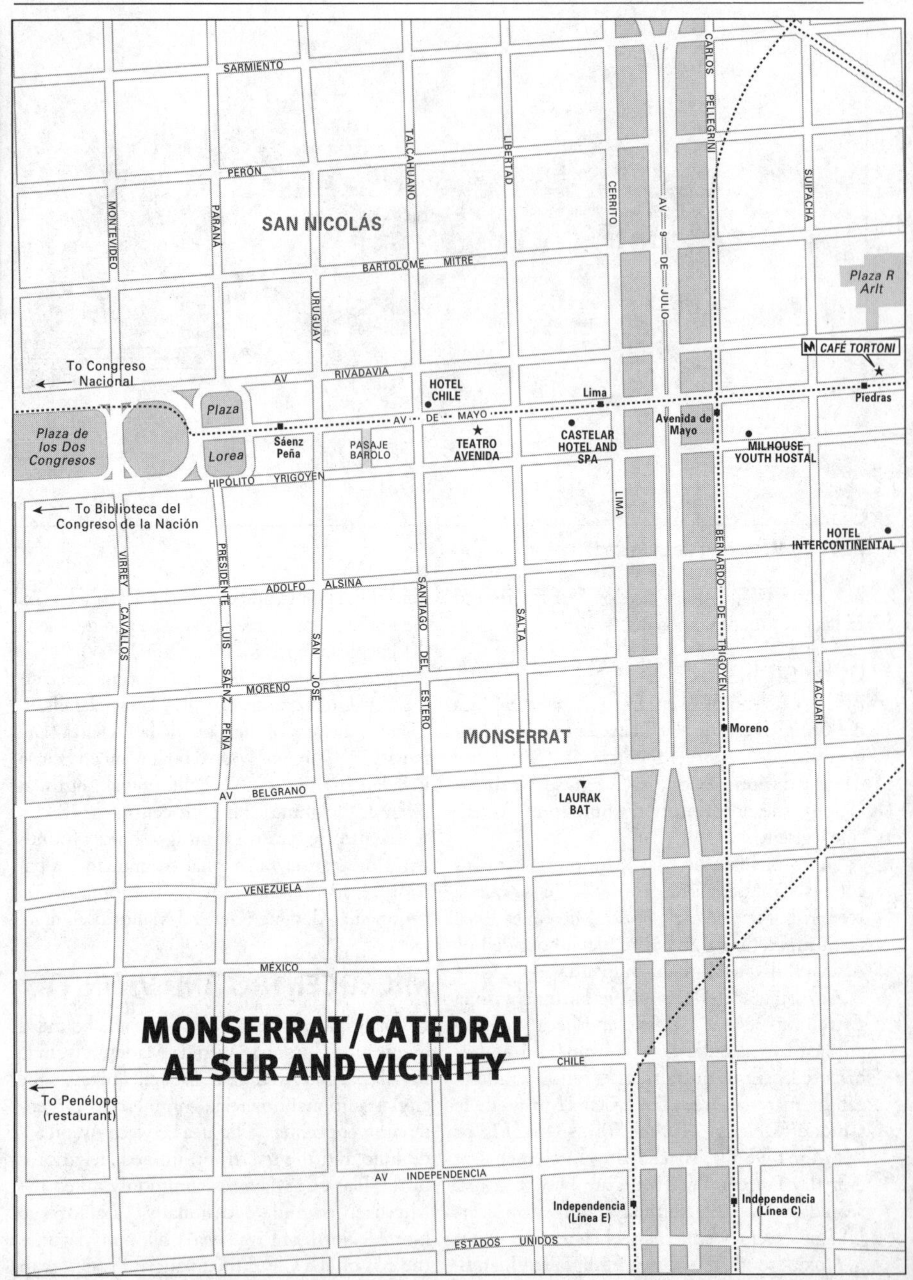
SARMIENTO
PERÓN
SAN NICOLÁS
BARTOLOMÉ MITRE
MONTEVIDEO
PARANÁ
URUGUAY
TALCAHUANO
LIBERTAD
CERRITO
AV 9 DE JULIO
CARLOS PELLEGRINI
SUIPACHA
Plaza R Arlt
CAFÉ TORTONI
To Congreso Nacional
AV RIVADAVIA
HOTEL CHILE
Lima
Piedras
Plaza de los Dos Congresos
Plaza Lorea
Sáenz Peña
PASAJE BAROLO
AV DE MAYO
TEATRO AVENIDA
CASTELAR HOTEL AND SPA
Avenida de Mayo
MILHOUSE YOUTH HOSTAL
HIPÓLITO YRIGOYEN
To Biblioteca del Congreso de la Nación
LIMA
HOTEL INTERCONTINENTAL
VIRREY CEVALLOS
PRESIDENTE LUIS SÁENZ PEÑA
ADOLFO ALSINA
SANTIAGO DEL ESTERO
SALTA
BERNARDO DE IRIGOYEN
SAN JOSÉ
MORENO
TACUARÍ
Moreno
MONSERRAT
AV BELGRANO
LAURAK BAT
VENEZUELA
MÉXICO
MONSERRAT/CATEDRAL AL SUR AND VICINITY
CHILE
To Penélope (restaurant)
AV INDEPENDENCIA
Independencia (Línea E)
Independencia (Línea C)
ESTADOS UNIDOS

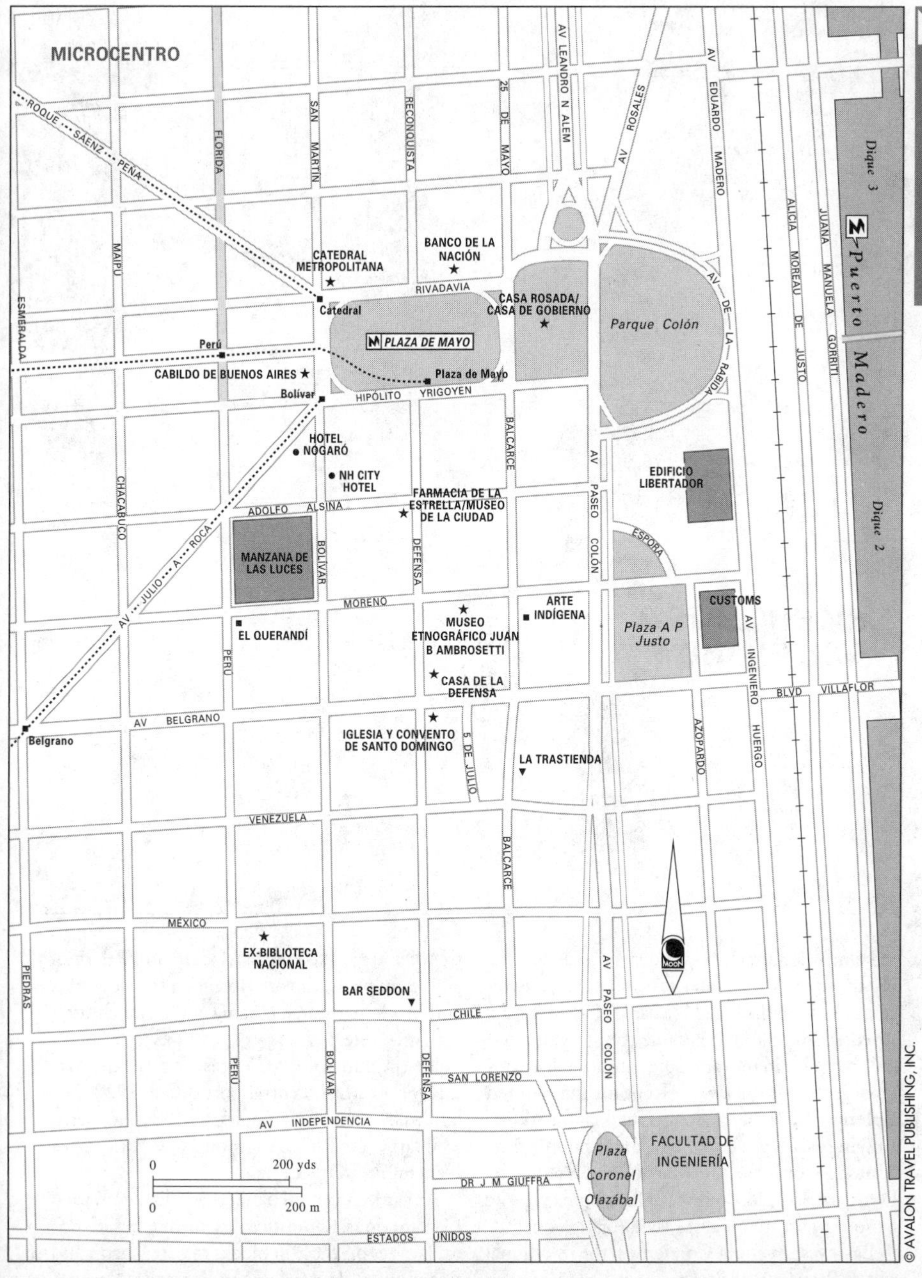
MICROCENTRO
ROQUE SAENZ PEÑA
FLORIDA
SAN MARTÍN
RECONQUISTA
25 DE MAYO
AV LEANDRO N ALEM
AV ROSALES
AV EDUARDO MADERO
Dique 3
Puerto Madero
Dique 2
ALICIA MOREAU DE JUSTO
JUANA MANUELA GORRITI
MAIPU
ESMERALDA
CATEDRAL METROPOLITANA
BANCO DE LA NACIÓN
RIVADAVIA
CASA ROSADA/ CASA DE GOBIERNO
Catedral
PLAZA DE MAYO
Parque Colón
AV DE LA RABIDA
Perú
CABILDO DE BUENOS AIRES
Plaza de Mayo
Bolívar
HIPÓLITO YRIGOYEN
BALCARCE
HOTEL NOGARÓ
NH CITY HOTEL
AV PASEO COLÓN
EDIFICIO LIBERTADOR
CHACABUCO
FARMACIA DE LA ESTRELLA/MUSEO DE LA CIUDAD
ADOLFO ALSINA
ESPORA
MANZANA DE LAS LUCES
BOLÍVAR
DEFENSA
AV JULIO A ROCA
MORENO
ARTE INDÍGENA
CUSTOMS
MUSEO ETNOGRÁFICO JUAN B AMBROSETTI
EL QUERANDÍ
Plaza A P Justo
PERÚ
CASA DE LA DEFENSA
AV INGENIERO HUERGO
BLVD VILLAFLOR
AV BELGRANO
Belgrano
IGLESIA Y CONVENTO DE SANTO DOMINGO
5 DE JULIO
AZOPARDO
LA TRASTIENDA
VENEZUELA
MÉXICO
EX-BIBLIOTECA NACIONAL
PIEDRAS
MOON
BAR SEDDON
CHILE
SAN LORENZO
AV INDEPENDENCIA
FACULTAD DE INGENIERÍA
Plaza Coronel Olazábal
0 200 yds
0 200 m
DR J M GIUFFRA
ESTADOS UNIDOS
Buenos Aires

Named for Argentina's independence day, the 16-lane **Avenida 9 de Julio** literally separates the Microcentro from the rest of the barrio. **Calle Florida,** a pedestrian mall that became the city's smartest shopping area in the early 20th century, is less fashionable than it once was except for the restored **Galerías Pacífico,** an architectural landmark occupying nearly an entire block also bounded by Avenida Córdoba, San Martín, and Viamonte. Don't overlook its dome murals, inspired by the famous Mexican muralist Davíd Alfaro Siqueiros.

East-west **Avenida Corrientes,** the traditional axis of Porteño nightlife, now takes a back seat to trendier areas like Puerto Madero and Palermo. There are plans, though, to widen the sidewalks and promote theater, cinema and other cultural activities here.

At the foot of Corrientes, the Beaux Arts **Correo Central** (central post office, 1928) is a landmark whose original architect, Norberto Maillart, based his design on New York City's General Post Office.

Argentina's central bank, the Italianate **Banco Central de la República Argentina,** has identical facades on the 200 blocks of San Martín and Reconquista. Its **Museo Numismático Dr. José**

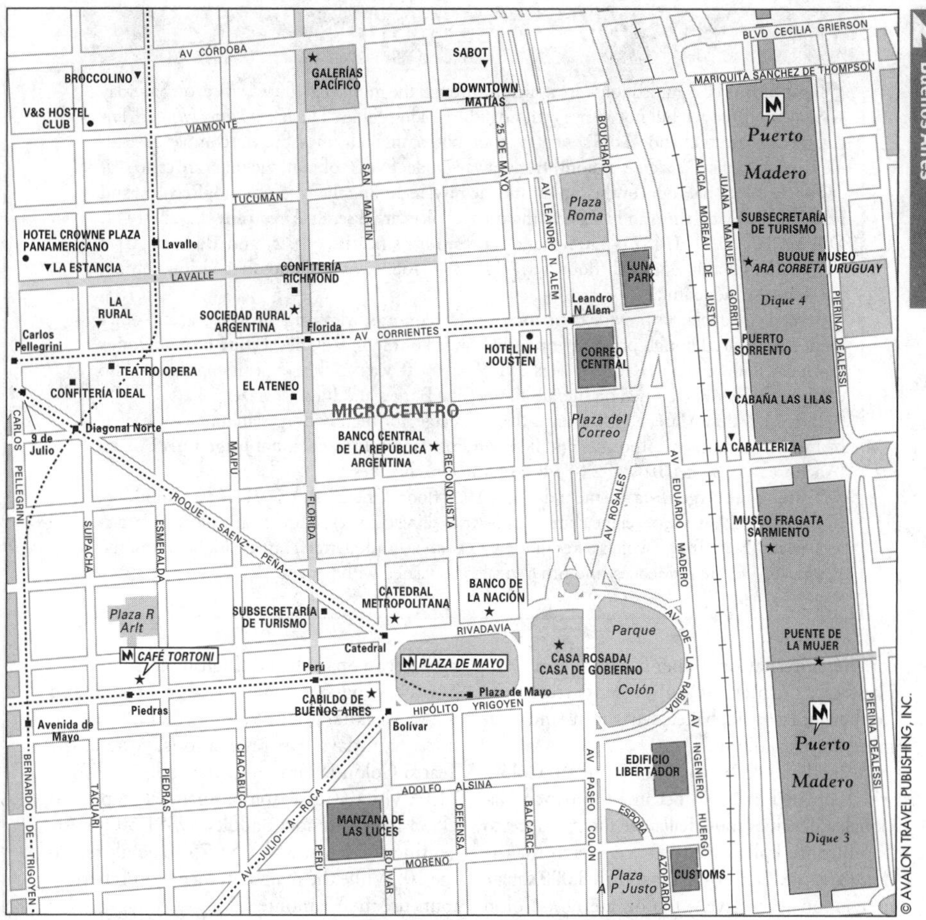

E. Uriburu (Reconquista 266, tel. 011/4393-0021), open 10 A.M.–3 P.M. weekdays, provides insights to Argentina's volatile economic history. Admission is free.

At Avenida 9 de Julio and Corrientes, the 67.5-meter **Obelisco** (Obelisk, 1936) is a city symbol erected for the 400th anniversary of Pedro de Mendoza's landing. From the Obelisco, the Diagonal Roque Sáenz Peña ends at **Plaza Lavalle,** where the **Palacio de Justicia** ("Tribunales" or Law Courts, 1904) has lent its colloquial name to the neighborhood.

Across the plaza is the stately **Teatro Colón** (1908) opera house (Libertad 621); for more information, see the separate entry below. To its north, fronting on Libertad and protected by bulky concrete planter boxes, the **Templo de la Congregación Israelita** (1932) is the capital's largest synagogue. Do not photograph this or any other Jewish community site without express permission.

Teatro Colón

Perhaps the continent's top performing-arts venue, the Teatro Colón (1908) is approaching its centenary down but not out. Unable to afford

ORGANIZED TOURS

Some of BA's best guided tours are available through the municipal tourist office, on Saturday and Sunday, often but not always with English-speaking guides. The *Buenos Aires Herald's* "Friday getOut!" section and *Clarín*'s events section both contain listings, but the complete schedule also appears in *Viva Bue,* a monthly giveaway guide. In case of rain, the tours are canceled.

For conventional tours of the capital and vicinity, including the Microcentro, Recoleta and Palermo, and San Telmo and La Boca, the usual choices are **Buenos Aires Tour** (Lavalle 1444, Oficina 10, tel. 011/4371-2304, buenosairestour@sinectis.com.ar) and **Buenos Aires Visión** (Esmeralda 356, 8th floor, tel. 011/4394-4682, www.buenosaires-vision.com.ar, bavision@ssdnet.com.ar).

Several city operators provide thematically oriented tours, with English-speaking and other guides available. Though primarily oriented toward outdoor activities, **Lihué Expediciones** (Paraguay 880, 7th floor, Retiro, tel./fax 011/5031-0070, viajes@lihue-expeditions.com.ar) also offers walking tours focused on literary figures like Borges and Julio Cortázar.

Borges's widow María Kodama leads free-of-charge, fortnightly Borgesian tours, sponsored by municipal tourism authorities and her own **Fundación Internacional Jorge Luis Borges** (Anchorena 1660, tel. 011/4822-8340); phone for schedules.

Travel Line Argentina (Esmeralda 770, 10th floor, Oficina B, tel. 011/4393-9000, fax 011/4394-3929, www.travelline.com.ar, info@ travelline.com.ar) conducts specialty excursions such as its "Evita Tour," which takes in the CGT labor headquarters, Luna Park Stadium, the Perón and Duarte residences, and other locales associated with her era.

top-tier international opera, ballet, and symphonic performers, it still presents front-line local talent in opera, ballet, symphony, and even more popular idioms.

As the Plaza de Mayo's original Teatro Colón, which opened in 1857, became the Banco Nacional, authorities chose Italian architect Francesco Tamburini's Italian Renaissance design for the new structure. Occupying more than 8,000 square meters, on seven levels, the ornate new Colón followed the lines of French and Italian classics. Seating 2,478 patrons, with standing room for another 700, it boasts world-class acoustics; a rotating stage simplifies rapid scene changes.

In the May–November season, the Teatro Colón (Libertad 621, tel. 011/4378-7344, www.teatrocolon.org.ar, boleteria@teatrocolon.org.ar) presents some 200 events; the ticket office is open 10 A.M.–8 P.M. Thursday–Saturday, 10 A.M.–5 P.M. Sunday, and 5 P.M. until the performance (if there is one) Monday. Presidential command performances take place May 25 and July 9, the winter patriotic holidays.

Fifty-minute, behind-the-scenes tours, always available in Spanish and English but sometimes in other languages, take place at 11 A.M. and 3 P.M. weekdays, and 9, 10, and 11 A.M. and noon Saturdays. For reservations, contact the Teatro Colón (Viamonte 1168, tel. 011/4378-7132, visitas@teatrocolon.org.ar). The price is US$3 for nonresident adults, US$1.50 for Argentine residents, and US$.75 for children to age 10. While the main entrance is on Libertad, tours use the Viamonte side.

PUERTO MADERO

Born amidst 19th-century corruption, modern Puerto Madero has reclaimed a riverfront that languished off-limits during the 1976–1983 military dictatorship. Comparable, in some ways, to Baltimore's Inner Harbor and London's Docklands, its focus is four rectangular *diques* (basins) bordered by brick warehouses recycled into stylish lofts, offices, restaurants, bars, and cinemas.

Sequentially numbered south to north, the *diques* stretch from La Boca to Retiro. Dique No. 3 holds a 450-berth yacht harbor; its **Museo**

Fragata Sarmiento (tel. 011/4334-9386), an early 20th-century naval training vessel, is a national historical monument, open 9 A.M.–10 P.M. Tuesday–Thursday, 9 A.M.–midnight Friday, Saturday, and Sunday. Admission costs US$.35; children under age 5 get in free.

The newest feature here is architect Santiago Calatrava's **Puente de la Mujer,** a modernistic pedestrian suspension bridge that rotates to allow vessels to pass between Dique No. 3 and Dique No. 2. Anchored at Dique No. 4, the **Buque Museo A.R.A. Corbeta Uruguay** (tel. 011/4314-1090) rescued Norwegian explorers Carl Skottsberg and Otto Nordenskjöld from Antarctica in 1903. Dating from 1874, the oldest Argentine vessel still afloat, it's open 9 A.M.–9 P.M. weekdays, 10 A.M.–9 P.M. weekends. Admission costs US$.35.

Toward the barrio's north end, the **Hotel de Inmigrantes** was Argentina's Ellis Island for European immigrants; it's now **Museo Nacional de la Inmigración** (Avenida Antártida 1355, tel. 011/4317-0285). Hours are 10 A.M.–5 P.M. weekdays, 11 A.M.–6 P.M. weekends. Admission is free.

© WAYNE BERNHARDSON

Redevelopment has turned the old warehouses along the Puerto Madero waterfront into upscale lofts and restaurants.

SAN TELMO AND VICINITY

San Telmo, with its narrow colonial streets, antique shops, and street fairs, appeals to Argentines and foreigners alike. Six blocks south of Plaza de Mayo, bounded by Chile on the north, Piedras to the west, Puerto Madero to the east, and Avenida Brasil, Parque Lezama, and Avenida Caseros to the south, it's a fine walkers' neighborhood—especially Sundays, when authorities close most of Calle Defensa to motor vehicles.

After elite families fled an 1870s yellow fever epidemic to northern barrios like Palermo and Belgrano, San Telmo became an area where impoverished immigrant families could find a foothold in *conventillos,* abandoned mansions where large families filled small spaces—often a single room. Today it's a mixed neighborhood where *conventillos* still exist, but young professionals have also recycled crumbling apartment buildings and even industrial sites into lofts. It's also closely identified with tango, or at least the high-priced spectacle with professional dancers.

While colonial Spanish law dictated rectangular city blocks of equal size, San Telmo breaks the rules. North-south **Calle Balcarce,** for instance, doglegs between Chile and Estados Unidos, crossing the cobblestone alleyways of **Pasaje San Lorenzo** and **Pasaje Giuffra.** The **Casa Mínima** (Pasaje San Lorenzo 380) takes the vernacular *casa chorizo* (sausage house) style to an extreme: This two-story adobe, given to a freed slave by his former owner, is barely wider than an average adult male's armspread.

To the east, on Paseo Colón's **Plaza Coronel Olazábal,** Rogelio Yrurtia's massive sculpture ***Canto al Trabajo*** (Ode to Labor), a tribute to hard-working pioneers, is a welcome antidote to pompous equestrian statues elsewhere.

San Telmo's heart, though, is **Plaza Dorrego** (Defensa and Humberto Primo), site of the hectic weekend flea market; see below for details.

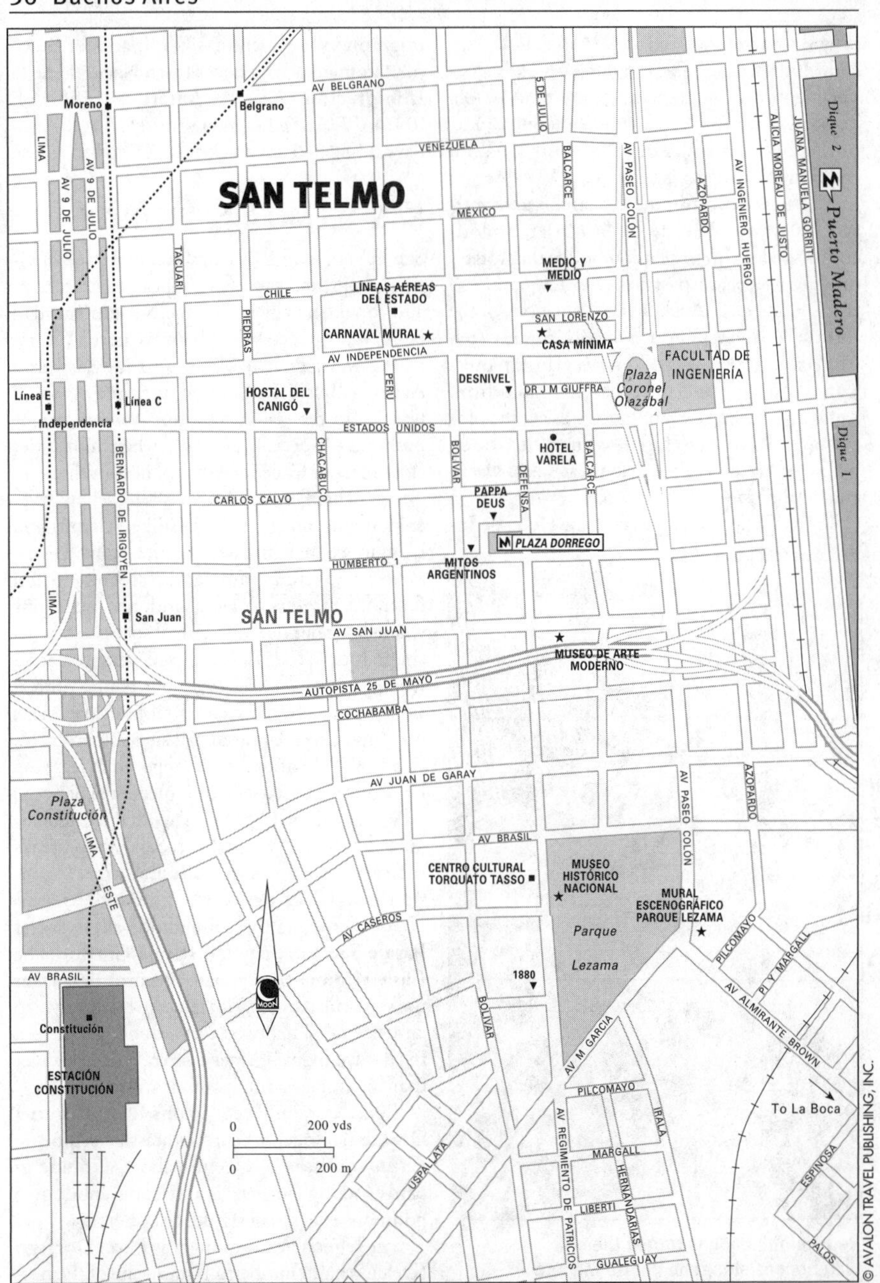
SAN TELMO
AV BELGRANO
Moreno
Belgrano
LIMA
AV 9 DE JULIO
AV 9 DE JULIO
VENEZUELA
5 DE JULIO
BALCARCE
AV PASEO COLÓN
AZOPARDO
AV INGENIERO HUERGO
ALICIA MOREAU DE JUSTO
JUANA MANUELA GORRITI
Dique 2
Puerto Madero
MÉXICO
TACUARÍ
MEDIO Y MEDIO
LÍNEAS AÉREAS DEL ESTADO
CHILE
PIEDRAS
SAN LORENZO
CARNAVAL MURAL
CASA MÍNIMA
AV INDEPENDENCIA
FACULTAD DE INGENIERÍA
Plaza Coronel Olazábal
DESNIVEL
DR J M GIUFFRA
Línea E
Línea C
Independencia
HOSTAL DEL CANIGÓ
PERU
ESTADOS UNIDOS
BERNARDO DE IRIGOYEN
CHACABUCO
BOLÍVAR
HOTEL VARELA
Dique 1
DEFENSA
BALCARCE
CARLOS CALVO
PAPPA DEUS
PLAZA DORREGO
HUMBERTO 1
MITOS ARGENTINOS
LIMA
San Juan
SAN TELMO
AV SAN JUAN
MUSEO DE ARTE MODERNO
AUTOPISTA 25 DE MAYO
COCHABAMBA
AV JUAN DE GARAY
AV PASEO COLÓN
AZOPARDO
Plaza Constitución
LIMA
AV BRASIL
CENTRO CULTURAL TORQUATO TASSO
MUSEO HISTÓRICO NACIONAL
MURAL ESCENOGRÁFICO PARQUE LEZAMA
ESTE
AV CASEROS
Parque Lezama
PILCOMAYO
PI Y MARGALL
AV BRASIL
1880
AV ALMIRANTE BROWN
Constitución
BOLÍVAR
AV M GARCIA
ESTACIÓN CONSTITUCIÓN
PILCOMAYO
To La Boca
0
200 yds
0
200 m
IRALA
USPALLATA
AV REGIMIENTO DE PATRICIOS
MARGALL
HERNANDARIAS
ESPINOSA
LIBERTI
GUALEGUAY
PALOS
MOON

Antique shops line both sides of Defensa, north and south of the plaza.

In a cavernous recycled warehouse, the **Museo de Arte Moderno** (Avenida San Juan 350, tel. 011/4361-1121) showcases contemporary abstracts by Argentine artists. Hours are 10 A.M.–8 P.M. Tuesday–Saturday, 11 A.M.–8 P.M. Sunday; it's closed in January. Admission costs US$.35 but is free Wednesdays; guided tours take place Tuesday, Wednesday, Friday, and Sunday at 5 P.M.

At Defensa and Avenida Brasil, a graffiti-covered statue of Pedro de Mendoza guards the entrance to **Parque Lezama,** where Mendoza ostensibly founded the city in 1536. It also contains the **Museo Histórico Nacional,** the national history museum; for more details, see below.

Plaza Dorrego

Six days a week, Plaza Dorrego is a nearly silent shady square where Porteños sip *cortados* and nibble lunches from nearby cafés. Sundays, though, it swarms with visitors who stroll among antiques stalls at the **Feria de San Pedro Telmo,** the most famous of the capital's street fairs. Items range from soda siphons to brightly painted *filete* plaques with *piropos* (aphorisms), oversized antique radios, and many other items. The plaza and side streets also fill with *tangueros* (tango dancers) puppet theaters, hurdy-gurdy men, and a glut of *estatuas vivas* ("living statues" or costumed mimes).

Starting around 9–10 A.M., the Feria lasts into late afternoon. The sidewalk and balcony cafés overlooking the plaza are ideal for enjoying the show.

Parque Lezama

The presumptive site of Pedro de Mendoza's encampment, Parque Lezama is an irregular quadrilateral on the banks above the old rivercourse, which has long since been covered by landfill. Shaded by mature palms and other exotics, and studded with monuments, it's the place where aging Porteños play chess, working-class families enjoy weekend picnics, and a Sunday crafts fair stretches south along Defensa.

Carlos Ridgley Horne built the Italianate mansion (1846) that now holds the surprisingly ahistorical **Museo Histórico Nacional** (Defensa 1600, tel. 011/4307-1182); its nadir is a chauvinistic account of General Julio Roca's so-called Conquista del Desierto (Conquest of the Desert) campaign against the Mapuche, which expanded the country's Patagonian frontier in the 1880s.

Despite the museum's shortcomings, the building is a well-kept landmark whose subterranean gallery hosts special exhibits and events. Hours are 11 A.M.–6 P.M. Tuesday–Friday, 2–7 P.M. Saturday, and 1–7 P.M. Sunday. Admission costs US$.35; guided tours take place at 3:30 P.M. weekends.

LA BOCA

On the twisting Riachuelo's west bank, La Boca owes its origins to French Basque and Genovese immigrants who manned packing plants and warehouses during the mid-19th-century beef export boom. Perhaps more than any other city neighborhood, it remains a community, symbolized by fervent identification—some would say fanatical obsession—with the Boca Juniors soccer team.

La Boca is, literally, the city's most colorful neighborhood, thanks to the brightly painted houses with corrugated zinc siding that line the curving **Caminito,** once a rail terminus. Now a tradition, these primary colors first came from marine paints salvaged from ships in the harbor.

One of the country's most polluted waterways, the **Riachuelo** is undergoing a visible cleanup of the corroded hulks that oozed contamination along the meander known as the **Vuelta de Rocha.** A new **Malecón** (levee) has made the riverside more presentable, but it's still not for sensitive noses.

Socially and politically, La Boca has a reputation for disorder and anarchy, but the late Benito Quinquela Martín, whose oils sympathetically portrayed its hard-working inhabitants, helped make it an artists' colony. Many Porteños consider the barrio dangerous, and some visitors prefer guided tours starting at the Caminito.

La Boca's real gateway, though, is Avenida Almirante Brown, at the southeast corner of Parque Lezama. There, the Catalinas del Sur theater group has erected the **Mural Escenográfico Parque**

Lezama, a three-dimensional mural depicting community life through colorful caricatures. From the foot of the avenue, where it intersects Avenida Pedro de Mendoza, the remaining massive girders of the former **Puente Nicolás Avellaneda** (1940), towering above the Riachuelo, are a civil engineering landmark.

Caminito

The starting point for most visitors remains the cobbled, curving Caminito. Once the terminus of a railroad line, the Caminito is now a pedestrian mall where painters display their watercolors (there are more artists on weekends than weekdays). Taking its name from a popular tango, the passageway veers northwest, between brightly colored houses with corrugated zinc siding, from Avenida Pedro de Mendoza.

Initially, these bright colors came from marine paints salvaged from ships in the harbor. The colors are inviting, but the poorly insulated buildings can be unbearably hot in summer and frigid in winter.

Museo de Bellas Artes de La Boca

To the east of the Caminito stands the Museo de Bellas Artes (Pedro de Mendoza 1835, tel. 011/4301-1080), in Quinquela Martín's former studio; it's open daily except Monday, 10 A.M.–5:45 P.M. Admission costs US$.35.

Estadio Doctor Camilo Cichero

For residents, the key landmark is the Estadio Doctor Camilo Cichero, the soccer stadium better known as **La Bombonera,** at Brandsen and Del Valle Iberlucea; murals of barrio life cover the walls along the Brandsen side. It's now home to the **Museo de la Pasión Boquense** (Museum of Boca's Passion, Brandsen 805, tel. 011/4362-1100, www.museoboquense.com), which integrates the soccer team's history with its role in the community. Hours are 10 A.M.–7 P.M. daily. Admission costs US$2.50 pp (US$4.50 pp with a guided tour).

RETIRO

Retiro popularly describes the area surrounding **Plaza San Martín,** but takes in much of the terrain north of Avenida Córdoba and overlaps the Barrio Norte sector.

Retiro (literally, a retreat) was once an isolated colonial monastery on the *barranca* (terrace) above the river. By 1862, General San Martín's equestrian statue marked its definitive urbanization and, on the centenary of the Liberator's birth in 1878, the original property was declared Plaza San Martín.

From the late 19th century, surrounding streets became BA's most elite residential area. The most extravagant residence, dating from 1909, was the **Palacio Paz** (Avenida Santa Fe 750), a 12,000-square-meter Francophile mansion built for newspaper magnate Jose C. Paz and now home to military offices.

On the plaza's north side, dating from 1905, the Art Nouveau **Palacio San Martín** (Arenales 761, tel. 011/4819-8092) was originally a three-house complex built for the Anchorena family. Purchased in 1936 for the Ministerio de Relaciones Exteriores y Culto (Foreign Ministry), it serves primarily ceremonial purposes. When there are no official functions, it's open for tours Thursday at 11 A.M. (Spanish only) and Friday at 3, 4, and 5 P.M. (Spanish and English). Admission is free.

At the plaza's southeastern edge, dating from 1935, the 33-story **Edificio Kavanagh** (Florida 1035) was BA's first skyscraper. At the northeast corner, the marble **Monumento a los Caidos de Malvinas** commemorates those who died in the 1982 Falkland Islands war with Britain.

Across Avenida del Libertador, the former Plaza Britania is now the **Plaza Fuerza Aérea Argentina** (the air force was the only branch of the Argentine military that performed credibly in the war). Its enduring centerpiece, though, is **Torre de los Ingleses** (1916), a Big Ben clone donated by the Anglo-Argentine community.

Immediately across Avenida Ramos Mejía, the **Estación Retiro** (1915) is a restored relic of the railroad era, when British-operated trains served Argentina's northern and northwestern provinces. Today, though, it receives mostly suburban commuter trains.

Retiro is a barrio where people purchase rather than make art, and the contemporary galleries around Plaza San Martín are almost all worth a look. Its one major museum is the **Museo Municipal de Arte Hispanoamericano Isaac Fernández Blanco** (Suipacha 1422, tel. 011/4327-0272 or 011/4327-0228, www.buenosaires.gov.ar/areas/cultura/museos/museoblanco.asp#museo), which stresses colonial and early independence–era art. Hours are 2–7 P.M. daily except Monday, when it's closed, and holidays, when hours are 3–7 P.M. only. Admission costs US$.35 except Thursday, when it's free. Guided tours take place at 4 P.M. Saturday and Sunday except January and/or February, when it closes.

RECOLETA AND BARRIO NORTE

Recoleta, where the line between vigorous excess and serene but opulent eternity is a thin one, is one of Buenos Aires's most touristed barrios, and one of its prime dining/nightlife zones. In everyday usage, "Recoleta" describes the area in and around its namesake cemetery, but it also encompasses much of Barrio Norte, a residential area of vague boundaries that extends westward from Retiro and north into Palermo.

Once a bucolic outlier, Recoleta urbanized rapidly when upper-class Porteños fled San Telmo after the 1870s yellow fever outbreaks. It is internationally known for the **Cementerio de la Recoleta** (Recoleta Cemetery, 1822), whose elaborate crypts and mausoleums cost more than many—if not most—Porteño houses. Flanking it is the Jesuit-built **Iglesia de Nuestra Señora de Pilar** (1732), a baroque church.

Bordering the church and cemetery are sizable green spaces including **Plaza Intendente Alvear** and **Plaza Francia,** frequented by street performers and a legion of *paseaperros* (professional dog walkers). On the southeastern corner, along Robert M. Ortiz, are some of Buenos Aires's most traditional cafés, most notably **La Biela** and **Café de la Paix.**

Alongside the church, the **Centro Cultural Ciudad de Buenos Aires** (Junín 1930, tel. 011/4803-1040, www.centroculturalrecoleta.org) is one of the capital's most important cultural centers; hours are 2–9 P.M. weekdays except Monday, and 10 A.M.–9 P.M. weekends and holidays.

Facing Plaza Francia, the **Museo Nacional de Bellas Artes** (1933) is the national fine-arts museum, described in detail below. Several other

© WAYNE BERNHARDSON

The Cementerio de la Recoleta is Buenos Aires's graveyard of the rich and famous.

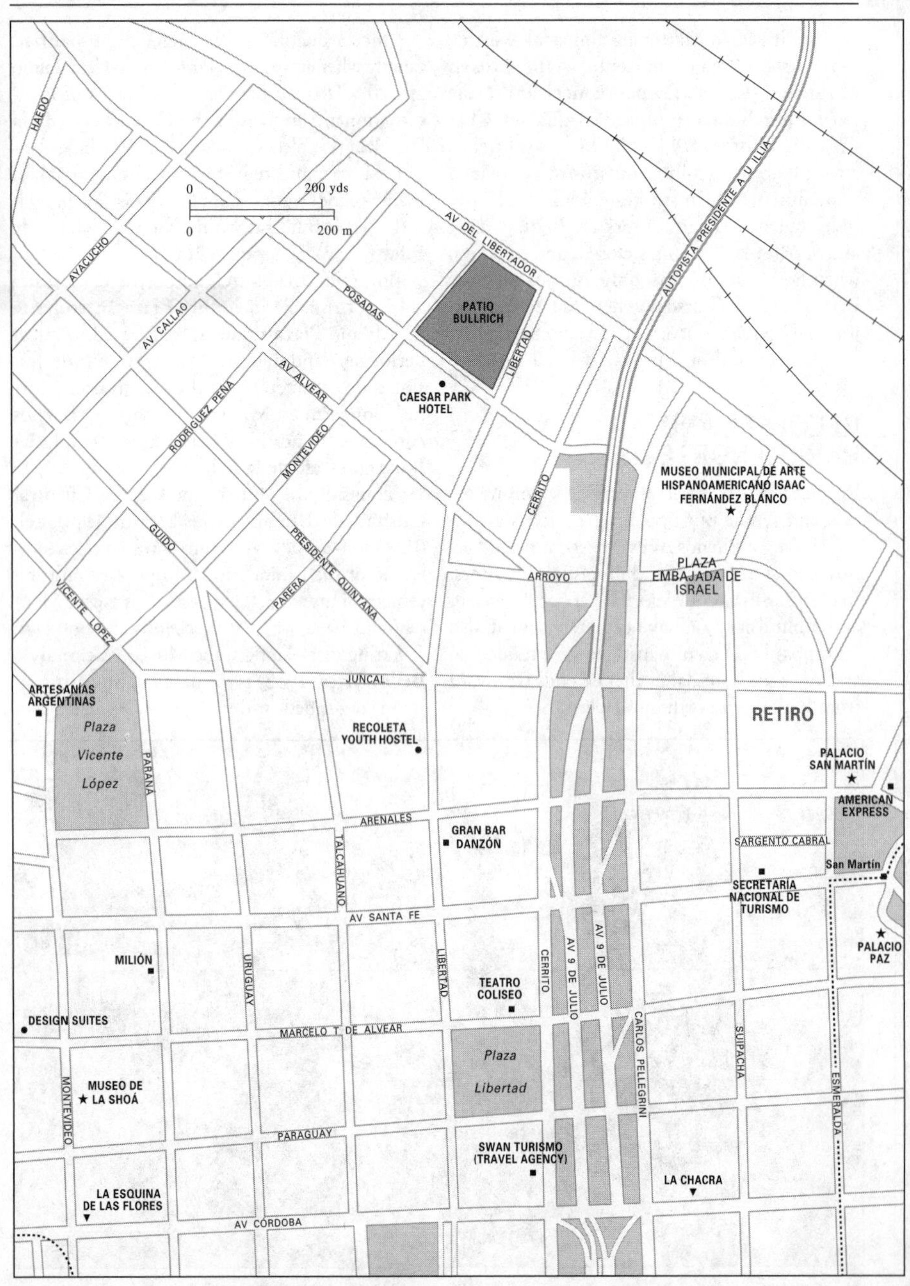
0
200 yds
0
200 m
HAEDO
AYACUCHO
AV CALLAO
POSADAS
AV DEL LIBERTADOR
AUTOPISTA PRESIDENTE A U ILLIA
PATIO BULLRICH
LIBERTAD
AV ALVEAR
CAESAR PARK HOTEL
RODRIGUEZ PEÑA
MONTEVIDEO
CERRITO
MUSEO MUNICIPAL DE ARTE HISPANOAMERICANO ISAAC FERNÁNDEZ BLANCO
GUIDO
PRESIDENTE QUINTANA
PARERA
ARROYO
PLAZA EMBAJADA DE ISRAEL
VICENTE LÓPEZ
JUNCAL
ARTESANÍAS ARGENTINAS
Plaza Vicente López
PARANÁ
RECOLETA YOUTH HOSTEL
RETIRO
PALACIO SAN MARTÍN
AMERICAN EXPRESS
ARENALES
GRAN BAR DANZÓN
TALCAHUANO
SARGENTO CABRAL
San Martín
SECRETARÍA NACIONAL DE TURISMO
AV SANTA FE
AV 9 DE JULIO
AV 9 DE JULIO
PALACIO PAZ
MILIÓN
URUGUAY
LIBERTAD
TEATRO COLISEO
CERRITO
DESIGN SUITES
MARCELO T. DE ALVEAR
CARLOS PELLEGRINI
SUIPACHA
Plaza Libertad
MONTEVIDEO
MUSEO DE LA SHOÁ
ESMERALDA
PARAGUAY
SWAN TURISMO (TRAVEL AGENCY)
LA CHACRA
LA ESQUINA DE LAS FLORES
AV CORDOBA

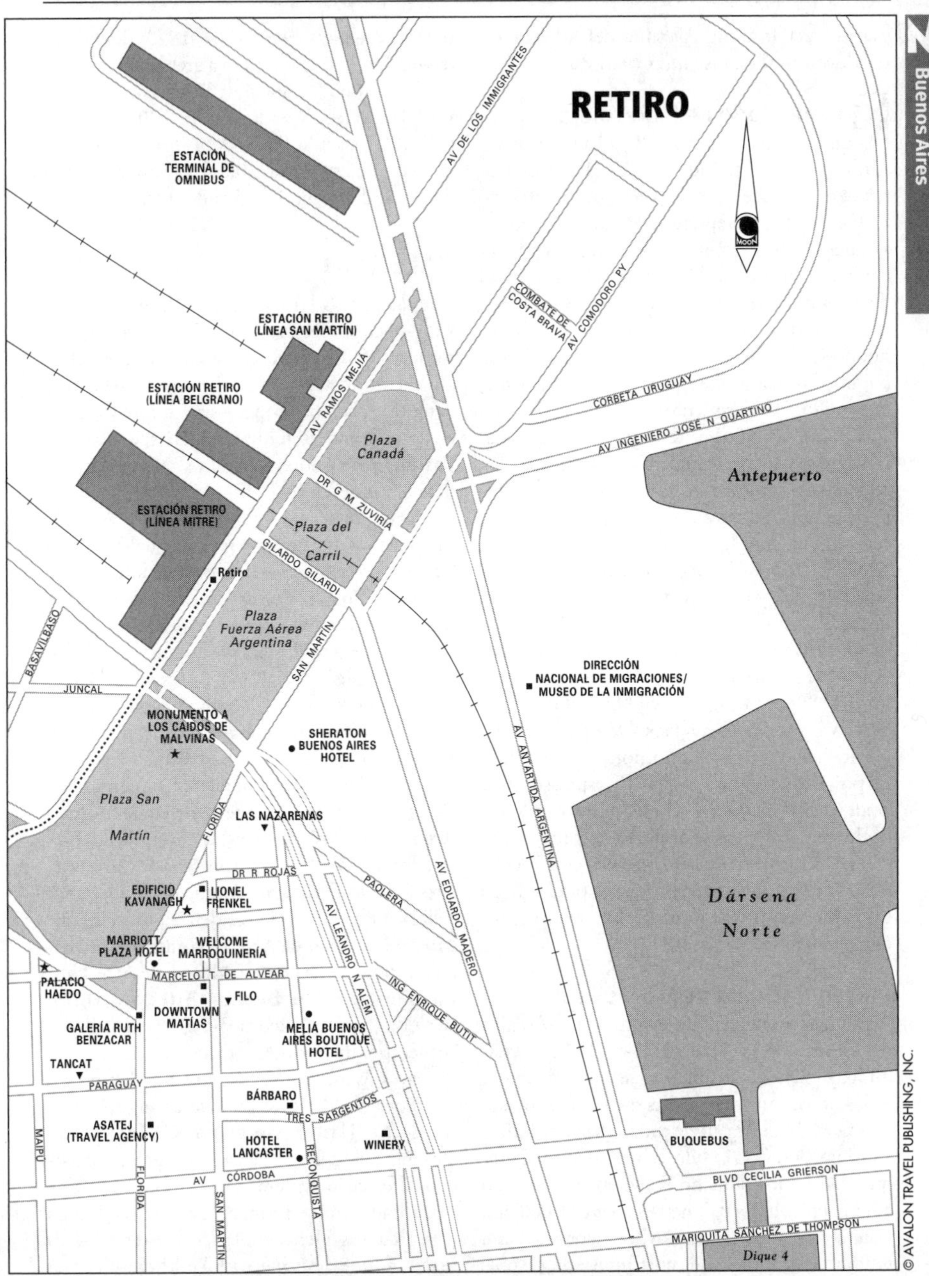

RETIRO
ESTACIÓN TERMINAL DE OMNIBUS
AV DE LOS IMMIGRANTES
ESTACIÓN RETIRO (LÍNEA SAN MARTÍN)
ESTACIÓN RETIRO (LÍNEA BELGRANO)
ESTACIÓN RETIRO (LÍNEA MITRE)
COMBATE DE COSTA BRAVA
AV COMODORO PY
CORBETA URUGUAY
AV INGENIERO JOSÉ N QUARTINO
AV RAMOS MEJÍA
Plaza Canadá
Antepuerto
DR G M ZUVIRÍA
Plaza del Carril
GILARDO GILARDI
Retiro
Plaza Fuerza Aérea Argentina
SAN MARTÍN
BASAVILBASO
JUNCAL
DIRECCIÓN NACIONAL DE MIGRACIONES/ MUSEO DE LA INMIGRACIÓN
MONUMENTO A LOS CAIDOS DE MALVINAS
SHERATON BUENOS AIRES HOTEL
AV ANTÁRTIDA ARGENTINA
Plaza San Martín
FLORIDA
LAS NAZARENAS
DR R ROJAS
PAOLERA
AV EDUARDO MADERO
EDIFICIO KAVANAGH
LIONEL FRENKEL
Dársena Norte
AV LEANDRO N ALEM
MARRIOTT PLAZA HOTEL
WELCOME MARROQUINERÍA
MARCELO T DE ALVEAR
PALACIO HAEDO
FILO
ING ENRIQUE BUTTY
DOWNTOWN MATÍAS
GALERÍA RUTH BENZACAR
MELIÁ BUENOS AIRES BOUTIQUE HOTEL
TANCAT
PARAGUAY
BÁRBARO
TRES SARGENTOS
ASATEJ (TRAVEL AGENCY)
MAIPÚ
HOTEL LANCASTER
WINERY
BUQUEBUS
AV CÓRDOBA
FLORIDA
SAN MARTÍN
RECONQUISTA
BLVD CECILIA GRIERSON
MARIQUITA SÁNCHEZ DE THOMPSON
Dique 4

plazas stretch along Avenida del Libertador, northwest of the museum toward Palermo.

Cementerio de la Recoleta

For quick and dead alike, Recoleta is Buenos Aires's most prestigious address. The roster of residents of the cemetery (Junín 1790, tel. 011/4803-1594) represents wealth and power as surely as the inhabitants of surrounding Francophile mansions and luxury apartments hoard their assets in overseas bank accounts. Socially, the cemetery is more exclusive than the neighborhood—cash can buy an impressive residence, but not a surname like Alvear, Anchorena, Mitre, Pueyrredón, or Sarmiento.

The top attraction, though, is the crypt of Eva Perón, who overcame humble origins with a relentless ambition that brought her to the pinnacle of political power with her husband, General and President Juan Perón, before her death in 1952. Even Juan Perón, who lived until 1974, failed to qualify for Recoleta; he lies across town in the Cementerio de la Chacarita.

There were other ways into Recoleta, however. One unlikely resident is boxer Luis Angel Firpo (1894–1960), the "wild bull of the Pampas," who nearly beat Jack Dempsey for the world heavyweight championship in 1923. Firpo, though, had pull—his sponsor was landowner Félix Bunge, whose family owns some of the cemetery's most ornate constructions.

The Cementerio de la Recoleta is open 7 A.M.–6 P.M. daily. Many travel agencies offer guided tours; the municipal tourist office sponsors occasional free weekend tours.

Museo Nacional de Bellas Artes

Argentina's traditional fine-arts museum (Avenida del Libertador 1473, tel. 011/4803-0802, www.mnba.org.ar, info@mnba.org.ar) mixes works of well-known European artists such as Picasso and Van Gogh with Argentine counterparts including Antonio Berni, Cándido López, Benito Quinquela Martín, Prilidiano Pueyrredón, and Lino Spilimbergo. In total, it houses about 11,000 oils, watercolors, sketches, engravings, tapestries, and sculptures. Among the most interesting works are López's, whose detailed oils recreate the history of the Paraguayan war (1864–1870) despite his having lost his right arm to a grenade.

The Museo Nacional de Bellas Artes is open weekdays except Monday 12:30–7:30 P.M.; weekend hours start at 9:30 A.M. Admission is free; guided tours take place Tuesday–Friday at 4 and 6 P.M., and weekends at 5 and 6 P.M.

PALERMO

Buenos Aires's largest barrio, Palermo boasts wide-open spaces thanks to 19th-century dictator Juan Manuel de Rosas, whose estate stretched almost from Recoleta all the way to Belgrano. After his exile, the property passed into the public domain and, ironically enough, the sprawling **Parque 3 de Febrero** takes its name from the date of his defeat in 1852.

Once part of the capital's unsavory *arrabales* (margins), its street corners populated by stylish but capricious *malevos* (bullies) immortalized in Jorge Luis Borges's stories, Palermo hasn't entirely superseded that reputation—in some areas, poorly lighted streets still make visitors uneasy. Yet it also has exclusive neighborhoods such as **Barrio Parque,** also known as **Palermo Chico,** with embassies, single-family mansions, and some of Buenos Aires's highest property values.

Barrio Parque has several key museums, including the gaucho-oriented **Museo de Motivos Argentinos José Hernández** (Avenida del Libertador 2373). Dating from 1918, the Beaux Arts **Palacio Errázuriz** (Avenida del Libertador 1902), once a private residence, contains the **Museo Nacional de Arte Decorativo.** The new kid is the state-of-the-art **Museo de Arte Latinoamericano de Buenos Aires** (MALBA; Avenida Figueroa Alcorta 3415), specializing in contemporary Latin American art.

Across Avenida del Libertador, the **Botánico** is an upper-middle-class enclave taking its name from the **Jardín Botánico Carlos Thays** (Avenida Santa Fe 3951), a lovely botanical garden infested with feral cats. Opposite nearby Plaza Italia, the rejuvenated **Jardín Zoológico** (Avenida Las Heras s/n, tel. 011/4806-7412) makes an ideal outing with children; it's open 10 A.M.–6 P.M. weekdays, 10 A.M.–6:30 P.M.

weekends. Admission costs US$1.50 per adult, but it's free for kids under age 13.

Once a neighborhood of imposing *palacetes,* the Botánico is still affluent but less exclusive than when, in 1948, Eva Perón enraged the neighbors by making one of those mansions the **Hogar de Tránsito No. 2,** a home for single mothers that now houses the **Museo Eva Perón** (Lafinur 2988).

The real center of action is slightly northwest at **Palermo Viejo,** where **Plaza Serrano** (also known as **Plaza Cortázar**) is a major axis of Porteño nightlife. Palermo Viejo further subdivides into **Palermo Soho** and the more northerly **Palermo Hollywood,** where many TV and radio producers have located facilities. Shaded by sycamores, many streets still contain low-rise *casas chorizos* (sausage houses) on deep, narrow lots.

At the northern end of the barrio, overlapping Belgrano, **Las Cañitas** is a gastronomic and nightlife area challenging Palermo Viejo among partygoers.

Museo de Motivos Argentinos José Hernández

It's tempting to call this the "museum of irony": Argentina's most gaucho-oriented institution (Avenida del Libertador 2373, tel. 011/4803-2384, www.naya.org.ar/mujose) occupies one of the country's most urbane, affluent, and cosmopolitan neighborhoods. Named for the author of the *gauchesco* epic *Martín Fierro,* it specializes in rural Argentiniana.

Even more ironically, oligarch Félix Bunge built the derivative French-Italianate residence with marble staircases and other extravagant features, and exhibits depict gentry like the Martínez de Hoz family—one of whom was the 1976–1983 military dictatorship's economy minister—as symbolic of a bucolic open-range lifestyle.

That said, the museum's worthwhile collections range from magnificent silverwork and vicuña textiles by contemporary Argentine artisans to pre-Columbian pottery, indigenous crafts, and even a typical *pulpería* or rural store.

The Museo José Hernández is open 1–7 P.M. Wednesday–Sunday. Admission costs US$.35 except Sunday, when it's free. It's normally closed in February.

Museo Nacional de Arte Decorativo

Matías Errázuriz Ortúzar and his widow Josefina de Alvear lived less than 20 years in the four-story Beaux Arts building (1918) that now houses the national decorative-arts museum (Avenida del Libertador 1902, tel. 011/4802-6606, www.mnad.org.ar). Its inventory consists of 4,000 items from family collections, ranging from Roman sculptures to contemporary silverwork, but mostly Asian and European pieces from the 17th to 19th centuries. Many items are anonymous; the best-known are by Europeans like Manet and Rodin.

The Museo de Arte Decorativo is open 2–7 P.M. daily; admission costs US$.70 except Tuesdays, when it's free. There are guided tours Wednesday, Thursday, and Friday at 4:30 P.M., by appointment only.

Museo de Arte Latinoamericano de Buenos Aires (MALBA)

Dedicated to Latin American art, Buenos Aires's most deluxe museum (Avenida Figueroa Alcorta 3415, tel. 011/4808 6500, www.malba.org) is a striking steel-and-glass structure designed by Córdoba architects Gastón Atelman, Martín Fourcade, and Alfredo Tapia. It devotes one entire floor to Argentine businessman and founder Eduardo F. Constantini's private collections, featuring prominent artists like the Mexicans Frida Kahlo and Diego Rivera, but there are also works by Antonio Berni, the Chilean Robert Matta, the Uruguayan Pedro Figari, and others. The second floor offers special exhibitions.

The Museo de Arte Latinoamericano de Buenos Aires is open Monday, Thursday, and Friday noon–8 P.M., Wednesday noon–9 P.M., and weekends 10 A.M.–8 P.M. Admission costs US$1.10 except Wednesdays, when it's free.

Museo Eva Perón

At her most combative, to the shock and dismay of neighbors, Eva Perón chose the upscale Botánico for the **Hogar de Tránsito No. 2,** a shelter for single mothers from the provinces. Even more galling, her Fundación de Ayuda

EVITA ON TOUR

Eva Perón became famous for her visit to Europe in 1947 when, as representative of an Argentina that emerged from World War II as an economic powerhouse, she helped legitimize a shaky Franco regime in Spain and, despite missteps, impressed other war-ravaged European countries with Argentina's potential. But even her death, five years later, did not stop her from touring.

Millions of Porteños said adios to Evita in a funeral cortege that took hours to make its way up Avenida de Mayo from the Casa Rosada to the Congreso Nacional, where her corpse lay in state. She then found a temporary resting place at the headquarters of the Confederación General del Trabajo (CGT), the Peronist trade union, where the shadowy Spanish physician Pedro Ara gave the body a mummification treatment worthy of Lenin, in preparation for a monument to honor her legacy.

Evita remained at the CGT until 1955, when the vociferously anti-Peronist General Pedro Aramburu took power and ordered her removal. Eventually, after a series of whistle stops that included the office of an officer who apparently became infatuated with the mummy, Aramburu shipped her into exile at an anonymous grave near Milan, Italy—even as a cadaver, Evita's presence was a symbolic reminder of Peronism's durability.

Despite banning the party, Aramburu had reason to worry. For many years, Argentines dared not even speak Perón's name, while the former strongman lived in luxury near Madrid. In 1970, though, as Argentine politics came undone in an era of revolutionary ferment, the left-wing Montoneros guerrillas kidnapped Aramburu and demanded to know her whereabouts.

When Aramburu refused to answer, they executed him and issued a public statement that they would hold the retired general's body hostage until Evita was returned to "the people." A common slogan of the time was "Si

© WAYNE BERNHARDSON

Palermo's Museo Eva Perón occupies the former Hogar de Tránsito No. 2, established by Evita to house homeless single mothers from the provinces.

Social María Eva Duarte de Perón took over an imposing three-story mansion to house the transients in their transition to the capital.

Since Evita's death in 1952, middle-class multistory apartment blocks have mostly replaced the elegant single family houses and distinctive apartments that once housed the Porteño elite (many have moved to exclusive northern suburbs). Fifty years later, on the July 26th anniversary of her death—supporting novelist Tomás Eloy Martínez's contention that Argentines are "cadaver cultists"—Evita's great-niece María Carolina Rodríguez officially opened the museum "to spread the life, work, and ideology of María Eva Duarte de Perón."

What it lacks is a critical perspective. Rather than a balanced account of her life, the museum's initial stage is a professionally presented chrono-

Evita viviera, sería Montonera" (If Evita were alive, she would be a Montonera); Perón himself, though, detested the leftists even as he cynically encouraged their activism to assist his return to power.

The police found Aramburu's body before the proposed post-mortem hostage swap could take place, but a notary to whom Aramburu had confided came forward with information as to Evita's whereabouts. In September 1971, Perón was stunned when a truck bearing Evita's casket and corpse arrived at his Madrid residence; remarried to dancer María Estela (Isabelita) Martínez, he neither expected nor wanted any such thing. His bizarre spiritualist adviser José López Rega, though, used the opportunity to try to transfer Evita's essence in Isabelita's body, as the mummy remained in the attic.

Perón returned to popular acclaim in 1973—leaving Evita in Madrid—and was soon elected president with Isabelita as his vice-president. Meanwhile, the Montoneros once again kidnapped Aramburu—from his crypt in Recoleta cemetery—until Evita's return.

Angry but increasingly ill and senile, Perón died the following year, but now president Isabelita brought Evita's corpse on a charter flight from Madrid to the presidential residence at Olivos, just north of the capital. It stayed there until March 1976, when General Jorge Rafael Videla's military junta overthrew Perón's living legacy.

Evita, for her part, finally achieved the respectability that she envied and resented during her rise to power. Though she was an illegitimate child who went by her mother's Basque surname Ibarguren, she landed in the family crypt of her father Juan Duarte, a provincial landowner—only a short walk from Aramburu's tomb.

Even that may not end Evita's wanderings. In mid-2002, there were rumors of yet another move—to San Telmo's Franciscan convent at Defensa and Alsina (ironically enough, set afire by Peronist mobs in 1955, but it's also the burial place of her confessor Pedro Errecart). Another possibility is Juan Perón's *quinta* (country house) in the northern suburb of San Vicente, where a new mausoleum would reunite the two (Perón presently rests at Chacarita cemetery).

Isabelita, for her part, has indicated her agreement in moving the caudillo's remains to San Vicente; maintaining her close relationship with Evita, she's even willing to see the Peronist icon lie alongside her late husband. The major objection, it seems, is that Isabelita, former caretaker president Eduardo Duhalde, and other Peronist politicians like the idea better than the Duarte heirs.

logical homage that sidesteps the demagoguery and personality cults that typified both Evita and her charismatic husband.

The Museo Eva Perón (Lafinur 2988, tel. 011/4807-9433, ievaperon@uol.com.ar) is open 10 A.M.–8 P.M. daily except Monday. The museum store has a selection of Evita souvenirs and a café-restaurant.

BELGRANO

Linked to central Buenos Aires by Subte and bus, Belgrano remains a barrio apart. In fact, it was once a separate city and then, in the 1880s, briefly the country's capital. The major thoroughfares are Avenida Cabildo, the northward extension of Avenida Santa Fe; Avenida Luis María Campos; and Avenida del Libertador.

Only a block off Cabildo, **Plaza General Manuel Belgrano** hosts a Sunday crafts market; immediately east, at Vuelta de Obligado 2042, the landmark **Iglesia de la Inmaculada Concepción** (1865), known as **La Redonda** for its circular floor plan, figures in Ernesto Sabato's psychological novel *On Heroes and Tombs.*

North of the plaza, the **Museo de Arte Español**

Enrique Larreta (Juramento 2291, tel. 011/4783-2640, museolarreta@infovia.com.ar) reflects the Hispanophile novelist who built it. Set among impressive Andalusian gardens, it's open 2–7:45 P.M. daily except Tuesday. Admission costs US$.35, but is free Thursdays. There are guided tours Sunday at 4 and 6 P.M. It usually closes in January.

When Belgrano was Argentina's capital, both executive and legislative branches met at what is now the **Museo Histórico Sarmiento** (Cuba 2079, tel. 011/4783-7555, museosarmiento@fibertel.com.ar), honoring President Domingo F. Sarmiento. Sarmiento never lived here, immediately east of the plaza, but the exhibits contain many personal possessions and a model of his provincial San Juan birthplace; it also chronicles the 1880s conflict that resulted in the capital's federalization. Hours are 2–7 P.M. Tuesday–Friday and 3–7 P.M. Sunday; admission costs US$.35, but is free Thursdays. Guided tours take place Sunday at 4 P.M.

A few blocks northwest, the **Museo Casa de Yrurtia** (O'Higgins 2390, tel. 011/4781-0385, www.casleo.secyt.gov.ar/index.htm) was the residence of sculptor Rogelio Yrurtia (1879–1950), creator of San Telmo's *Canto al Trabajo* and other works challenging the pomposity of Porteño public art. Hours Tuesday–Friday and Sunday from 3–7 P.M.; admission costs US$.35. Guided tours take place Tuesday–Friday at 3 P.M. and Sunday at 4 P.M.

OUTER BARRIOS

Beyond its most touristed barrios, Buenos Aires has a variety of worthwhile sights ranging from the mundane to the morbid. Some are less easily accessible by Subte, but have regular *colectivo* (city bus) service.

Museo Argentino de Ciencias Naturales

Once the city's outskirts, the barrio of Caballito gets few tourists, but its **Parque Centenario** is a good area for seeing an improving neighborhood popular with urban homesteaders. In impressive quarters dating from 1937, its natural history museum (Angel Gallardo 490, tel./fax 011/4982-1154, www.macn.secyt.gov.ar) houses one of the country's largest, best-kept collections, veering between a traditional stuff-in-glass-cases approach and more sophisticated exhibits that provide ecological, historical, and cultural context.

The main floor contains displays on geology and paleontology (including reconstructions of the massive Patagonian specimens *Giganotosaurus carolini,* the world's largest carnivorous dinosaur, and the herbaceous *Argentinosaurus huinculensis.* The upper floor stresses South American mammals (including marine mammals), comparative anatomy, amphibians and reptiles, birds, arthropods, and botany.

The Museo Argentino de Ciencias Naturales Bernardino Rivadavia is open 2–7 P.M. daily. Admission costs US$.60 for anyone older than six. It's roughly equidistant from Malabia and Angel Gallardo stations (Subte Línea B).

Cementerio de la Chacarita and Vicinity

For most cadavers, Buenos Aires's second cemetery is more affordable than Recoleta, but eternity at the Cementerio de la Chacarita (Guzmán 680, tel. 011/4553-9338) can still mean notoriety. Many high-profile Argentines, in fields ranging from entertainment to religion and politics, reside here, and the lines between these categories can be blurry.

The most universally beloved is tango singer Carlos Gardel, victim of a 1935 plane crash. Hundreds of admirers from around the globe have left dedicatory plaques, many thanking him for miracles, and every June 26 *Gardelianos* jam the cemetery's streets—platted like a small city—to pay homage.

In terms of devotion, only faith-healer-to-the-aristocracy Madre María Salomé can approach Gardel; on the second of every month—she died October 2, 1928—white carnations cover her crypt. Other famous figures include aviator Jorge Newbery; tango musicians Aníbal "Pichuco" Troilo and Osvaldo Pugliese; poet Alfonsina Storni; painter Benito Quinquela Martín; and theater and film comedian Luis Sandrini.

The most famous, though, is Juan Domingo Perón, whose vaulted corpse reposes across town from wife Evita's Recoleta tomb. His remains are incomplete, though—in 1987, vandals entered the crypt, amputating and stealing his hands in a still unresolved crime. Anti-Peronists speculated, despite slim evidence, that the thieves sought Perón's fingerprints for access to supposed Swiss bank accounts.

The Cementerio de la Chacarita covers 95 blocks with a total of 12,000 burial vaults, 100,000 gravesites, and 350,000 niches. Hours are 7 A.M.–6 P.M. daily. It's a short walk from Estación Federico Lacroze (Subte Línea B).

Besides Chacarita, there are two contiguous but formally separate cemeteries: the **Cementerio Alemán** (German Cemetery, Avenida Elcano 4530, tel. 011/4553-3206), and the **Cementerio Británico** (British Cemetery, Avenida Elcano 4568, tel. 011/4554-0092). Both keep identical hours to Chacarita.

The Británico is more diverse, with tombs belonging to Armenian, Greek, Irish, Jewish and other immigrant nationalities. Lucas Bridges, the son of pioneer Anglican missionaries in Tierra del Fuego and author of the classic Fuegian memoir *The Uttermost Part of the Earth,* lies here after dying at sea en route from Ushuaia to Buenos Aires.

Practicalities

ENTERTAINMENT

Porteños are night people—discos and dance clubs, for instance, may not even *open* until 1 A.M. or so, and don't close until dawn. Not everything takes place at those hours, though.

All Buenos Aires dailies have thorough event listings, especially in their Friday supplements. For major event tickets, contact **Ticketek** (tel. 011/4323-7200, www.ticketek.com.ar). Ticketek, which adds a US$1 service charge per ticket, has a Microcentro outlet at El Ateneo (Florida 340).

For discount tickets to certain events, including tango shows, cinemas, and live theater, check *carteleras,* agencies with last-minute specials. Among them are **Cartelera Espectáculos** (Lavalle 742, tel. 011/4322-1559); **Cartelera Baires** (Avenida Corrientes 1382, Local 24, tel. 011/4372-5058, www.entradascondescuento.com); and **Cartelera Vea Más** (Avenida Corrientes 1660, tel. 011/6320-5319, Local 2).

Cafés

No single place embodies tradition better than Monserrat's historic **Café Tortoni** (Avenida de Mayo 825, tel. 011/4342-4328, www.cafetortoni.com.ar); for its history, see the Sights entry. Most tourists come for coffee and croissants, but there's live tango and the bar serves inexpensive mixed drinks accompanied by a sizable *tabla* of sliced salami, paté, cheese, and olives that easily feeds two people.

Despite torn upholstery and cracked tiles, the past-its-prime **Confitería Ideal** (Suipacha 384, tel. 011/4326-0521) served as a set for Madonna's *Evita* debacle; there are proposals to rehab it. By contrast, the elegant but pricey **Confitería Richmond** (Florida 468, tel. 011/4322-1341), one of Borges's favorites, looks as good as the day it opened.

Recoleta's **La Biela** (Avenida Quintana 596/600, tel. 011/4804-0449) remains a classic Sunday breakfast spot. In good weather, try the patio, beneath the palm and palo borracho trees. It's slightly more expensive to eat outside, though, and the outdoor service can be absent-minded.

Bars and Clubs

The distinction between cafés and bars is more a continuum than a dichotomy. Some of the more stylish (or pretentious) bars go by the English word "pub," but may call themselves Irish.

Relocated to Monserrat after demolition of its classic Microcentro locale, **Bar Seddon** (Defensa 695) has made a successful transition to the capital's oldest neighborhood. **La Trastienda** (Balcarce 460, tel. 011/4342-7650) has recycled a Monserrat warehouse into an attractive theater with live music and drama.

Downtown Matías (Reconquista 701, tel. 011/4311-0327) is the Microcentro branch of

BA's oldest Irish-style pub; drinks are mostly in the US$2–3 range, with pub lunches around US$3. There's live music in various styles, including Celtic, depending on the night, and a 7–11 P.M. happy hour.

The artsy **Foro Gandhi** (Avenida Corrientes 1743, tel. 011/4374-7501) is a hybrid bookstore/coffeehouse/cultural center that offers films, poetry readings, tango and theater. Congreso's **Celta Bar** (Sarmiento 1702, tel. 011/4371-7338) makes great pizza, serves good drinks, and has hip live entertainment.

Retiro's **Bárbaro** (Tres Sargentos 415, tel. 011/4311-6856) takes its punning name from a slang term roughly translated as "cool." And it is, but unpretentiously so. Bordering Barrio Norte, **Milión** (Paraná 1048, tel. 011/4815-9925) is a tapas bar in a 1913 mansion; minimally altered for its current use, it offers garden, patio, and interior seating. It keeps late hours except Sunday night, when it closes at 1 A.M.

Nearby **Gran Bar Danzón** (Libertad 1161, tel. 011/4811-1108) is a sophisticated wine bar that doubles as a restaurant, with a fine sushi special at happy hour (7–9 P.M.). The sushi chef takes Mondays off.

Recoleta's **Los Porteños** (Avenida Las Heras 2100, tel. 011/4809-3548) is a corner bar holding only about 70 people for live blues with an exceptional house band on Friday and Saturday (Latin music) with a US$1 cover charge; drinks are reasonably priced, there's a decent bar-food menu, friendly staff, and an unpretentious crowd with a good age mix.

One of the city's most intimate entertainment venues, Palermo Viejo's **Club del Vino** (Cabrera 4737, tel. 011/4833-0048) offers a restaurant, wine bar, and small theater for live tango and folkloric music. Show prices vary but start around US$3, and the air quality's not bad by Porteño standards.

Palermo Hollywood's **Niceto Club** (Niceto Vega 5510, tel. 011/4779-6396) has become a top live-music venue, showcasing different musical styles, over the last several years; it's open Thursday, Friday, and Saturday nights.

Overhead trains shake **The Roxy** (Avenida Sarmiento and Avenida Casares, tel. 011/4899-0314, www.theroxybsas.com.ar), beneath a rickety railroad bridge in Parque Tres de Febrero, and the roof leaks in heavy rain, but it draws top performers like Charly García to a rowdy, sweaty ambiance—just what rock 'n' roll is supposed to be.

Jazz

Clásica y Moderna (Avenida Callao 892, tel. 011/4812-8707) is hybrid bookstore-café and live jazz venue in the same Barrio Norte location since 1938. Performers have included Susana Rinaldi, Mercedes Sosa, and Liza Minelli. It's open 8 A.M.–2 A.M. daily except Friday and Saturday, when it closes at 4 A.M.; regulars get better service than strangers.

Slightly different is nearby **Notorious** (Avenida Callao 966, tel. 011/4815-8473), a combination bar, CD-shop (listen to what interests you), and live-music venue. It's normally open 8 A.M.–midnight daily except Sundays and holidays, when it opens at 11 A.M.; live music goes later.

Tango and Milonga

Many tango venues are in the southerly barrios of Monserrat and San Telmo, with a few elsewhere and in outlying barrios. Professional shows range from simple, low-priced programs to extravagant productions at high, sometimes excessive prices. *Milongas* are bargains for those who want to participate.

Monserrat's **Café Tortoni** (Avenida de Mayo 825, tel. 011/4342-4328, www.cafetortoni.com.ar) hosts live song-and-dance shows at its separate Sala Alfonsina Storni for around US$4 per person plus drinks and food. Dating from 1920, the elegant **El Querandí** (Perú 302, tel. 011/5199-1770, www.querandi.com.ar, querandi@querandi.com.ar) is another classic; for US$35 per person, the nightly dinner (8:30 P.M.) and show (10:30 P.M.) occupy the upper end of the scale.

San Telmo's **Mitos Argentinos** (Humberto Primo 489, tel. 011/4362-7810) has a Sunday-afternoon show, 2–5 P.M., coinciding with nearby Plaza Dorrego's Feria de San Pedro Telmo. Both male and female singers are accompanied by live guitar and/or recorded music, and dancers per-

CELEBRATING THE TANGO

Despite its recency—the first event took place only in 1997—the Festival Buenos Aires Tango (tel. 0800/3378-4825, www.festivaldetango.com.ar,informacion@festivaldetango.com.ar) has become one of the city's signature special events. Lasting three weeks from mid-February to early March, this celebration of music, song, and dance ranges from the very traditional and conservative to the imaginative and even daring.

Shortly after its creation, the festival moved from December to February and March to follow Brazilian Carnaval, but it is not strictly a tourist-oriented affair; it is also widely accepted and anticipated by a demanding Porteño public. Unlike Brazilian Carnaval, it's not a mass spectacle, but rather a decentralized series of performances at relatively small, even intimate, venues around the capital. As such, it offers opportunities to see and hear not just established artists, but also developing performers.

Most of the funding for the city-sponsored festival goes to pay the artists, and admission is either free or inexpensive; however, tickets are usually available on a first-come, first-served basis on the day of the performance.

form to recorded music. There's no charge except for food and drink, which are reasonable.

Literally in the shadow of the redeveloped Mercado del Abasto, part of a municipal project to sustain the legacy of the "Morocho del Abasto" in his old neighborhood, the **Esquina Carlos Gardel** (Carlos Gardel 3200, tel./fax 011/4867-6363, www.esquinacarlosgardel.com.ar, info@esquinacarlosgardel.com.ar) has nightly shows from US$23 (show only) to US$32 (with dinner).

Those who prefer dancing to watching should try neighborhood *milongas.* Organized events charge in the US$2–3 range with live orchestra, less with recorded music. For classes, a good clearinghouse is Monserrat's **Academia Nacional del Tango** (Avenida de Mayo 833, tel. 011/4345-6968, www.sectur.gov.ar/cultura/ant/ant.htm), upstairs from Café Tortoni. The truly committed can take a three-year degree.

Upstairs at Confitería Ideal, **A Toda Milonga** (Suipacha 384, tel. 011/4729-6390, www.marrapoditango.unlugar.com, osvaldo_marrapodi@yahoo.com) takes place every Thursday 3–10 P.M. (admission US$1.50). San Telmo's **Centro Cultural Torquato Tasso** (Defensa 1575, tel. 011/4307-6506) offers live music events on Friday and Saturday and *milongas* with recorded music at 11 P.M. Sunday. Admission costs around US$4–5 for performing events and is nominal for the *milongas.* Instruction is also available.

In the barrio of San Cristóbal, **Club Gricel** (La Rioja 1180, tel. 011/4957-7157) offers live orchestra *milongas* Friday at 11 P.M. and Saturday at 10:30 P.M. (admission US$1.50). The 9:30 P.M. Sunday event, with recorded music, is cheaper.

Classical Music and Opera

The classical music and opera season lasts March through November but peaks in winter, June through August. The premier classical locale has long been the **Teatro Colón** (Libertad 621, tel./fax 011/4378-7344, www.teatrocolon.org.ar, boleteria@teatrocolon.org.ar).

Other venues include the Microcentro's **Teatro Opera** (Avenida Corrientes 860, tel. 011/4326-1225); Monserrat's **Teatro Avenida** (Avenida de Mayo 1212, tel. 011/4381-0662); and Retiro's **Teatro Coliseo** (M.T. de Alvear 1125, tel. 011/4807-1277, www.fundacioncoliseum.com.ar/teatro.htm).

Cultural Centers

Adjacent to Galerías Pacífico, the **Centro Cultural Borges** (Viamonte and San Martín, tel. 011/5555-5359, ccbor@tournet.com.ar) honors Argentina's most famous literary figure, and has rotating fine-arts exhibitions and performing-arts events. Hours are 10 A.M.–9 P.M. daily except Sunday, when it opens at noon (admission US$.70).

Recoleta's **Centro Cultural Ciudad de Buenos Aires** (Junín 1930, tel. 011/4803-1040, www.centroculturalrecoleta.org)has many free or inexpensive events. Hours are 2–9 P.M. Tuesday–Friday, 10 A.M.–9 P.M. weekends and holidays; guided visits (tel. 011/4803-4057) take place Wednesday at 6 P.M. and Saturday at 3 and 5 P.M.

Gay Venues

Buenos Aires has a vigorous gay scene, mostly around Recoleta, Barrio Norte, and Palermo Viejo, with a scattering of venues elsewhere. Lots of gay men hang out on Avenida Santa Fe between Callao and Pueyrredón, a good area to meet people and learn the latest. The monthly publication *La Otra Guía* lists gay-oriented and gay-friendly businesses.

EVENTS

Buenos Aires observes all the typical national holidays and quite a few special events as well. January and February, when most Porteños leave on vacation, are generally quiet; things pick up after school starts in March.

Dates for the pre-Lenten **Carnaval** (Carnival), February or March, vary year to year; though no equal for Brazilian festivities, Carnaval is enjoying a revival, with performances by barrio *murgas* (street musicians and dancers) rather than massive downtown events. Celebrations take place weekends rather than during the entire week.

Though it began in 1998 on Gardel's December 11 birthday, the increasingly important **Festival del Tango** (www.festivaldetango.com) now follows Brazilian Carnaval in March. Over several weeks, it includes dance competitions and free music/dance events.

April's book fair, the **Feria del Libro** (www.el-libro.com.ar), has been a literary fixture for nearly three decades. Most but not all exhibitors are from Latin America. It's recently moved from Recoleta to Palermo's Predio Ferial (Cerviño 4474, Avenida Sarmiento 2704, tel. 011/4777-5500). Admission costs about US$1.

For over a century, in July, the Sociedad Rural Argentina's **Exposición Internacional de Ganadería, Agricultura y Industria Internacional,** the annual agricultural exhibition at Palermo's Predio Ferial, has been one of the capital's biggest events.

SHOPPING

The main shopping areas are the Microcentro, along the Florida pedestrian mall toward Retiro; Retiro (around Plaza San Martín and along Avenida Santa Fe); Recoleta, near the cemetery;

© WAYNE BERNHARDSON

Galerías Pacífico—railroad offices recycled into an upscale shopping center

FERIAS OF BUENOS AIRES

For sightseers and spontaneous shoppers alike, Buenos Aires's diverse *ferias* (street fairs) are one of the city's greatest pleasures. Easily the most prominent is Sunday's standout **Feria de San Pedro Telmo,** which fills Plaza Dorrego and surrounding streets (authorities close Calle Defensa to vehicle traffic) with booths full of antiques, *filete* paintings, and other crafts. There are professional tango musicians and dancers, and dozens more street performers ranging from the embarrassingly mundane to the truly innovative. Lasting roughly 10 A.M.–5 P.M., it also offers sidewalk cafés and nearby upscale antique shops.

So successful is the Feria de San Pedro Telmo that, gradually, it's aided the now thriving **Feria Parque Lezama,** a Sunday crafts fair that's gradually spread north from its namesake park up Calle Defensa and under the freeway; only the broad Avenida San Juan has been able to stop it. Parque Lezama itself now gets Sunday street performers, though not so many as Plaza Dorrego.

In La Boca, the **Feria Artesanal Plazoleta Vuelta de Rocha** (Avenida Pedro de Mendoza and Puerto de Palos) takes place weekends and holidays 10 A.M.–6 P.M. Along the length of the nearby Caminito, painters, illustrators and sculptors sell their works in the **Feria del Caminito,** open 10 A.M.–6 P.M. daily.

After San Telmo, the most frequented tourist *feria* is probably Recoleta's crafts-oriented **Feria Plaza Intendente Alvear.** Immediately northeast of the Centro Cultural Recoleta, and also strong on street performers, it's begun to stretch south along Junín. Hours are 9 A.M.–7 P.M. weekends and holidays.

Gaucho souvenirs are on the docket at Sunday's Feria de San Pedro Telmo, on Plaza Dorrego.

On weekends and holidays, crafts stalls cover most of Belgrano's main square at the easy-going **Feria Artesanal Plaza General Manuel Belgrano** (Juramento and Cuba). Hours are 9 A.M.–7 P.M. or even later (when it's better). When it rains, the stalls are well sheltered with tarps.

and Palermo Viejo's tree-lined streets, where stylish shops sit between the newest restaurants and bars. Street markets take place in San Telmo, Recoleta, and Belgrano.

Shopping Centers

Developers have recycled many older buildings into upscale malls for one-stop shopping. The most notable is the Microcentro's magnificent **Galerías Pacífico** (Florida and Córdoba, tel. 011/5555-5100). Once a livestock auction house, Retiro's **Patio Bullrich** (Avenida del Libertador 750, tel. 011/4814-7400/7500) has become a palatial 24,000-square-meter commercial space with nearly 70 shops, plus restaurants and cinemas, on four levels.

Antiques

Sunday's outdoor **Feria de San Telmo,** one of the city's biggest tourist attractions (see the Sights entry), fills Plaza Dorrego with antiques and bric-a-brac. There are also many antique dealers in commercial galleries with small street-side frontage along Calle Defensa.

Art Galleries

Buenos Aires has a thriving modern-art scene, with the most innovative outlets in northern barrios. Retiro's **Galería Ruth Benzacar** (underground at Florida 1000, tel. 011/4313-8480, www.ruthbenzacar.com) showcases some of the country's most avant-garde artists. Recoleta's **Galería Rubbers** (Avenida Alvear 1595, tel. 011/4816-1864, www.rubbers.com.ar) is an excellent contemporary gallery.

Bookstores

Buenos Aires's signature bookstore is the Microcentro's **El Ateneo** (Florida 340, tel. 011/4325-6801, www.tematika.com.ar), with a huge selection on Argentine history, literature, and coffee-table souvenir books, plus domestic travel titles (it's also a publishing house).

The most elegant outlet, though, is Barrio Norte's affiliated **El Ateneo Grand Splendid** (Avenida Santa Fe 1880, tel. 011/4813-6052), occupying a recycled cinema that deserves a visit simply to see its seamless transformation: The stage is a café, the opera-style boxes hold chairs for readers, and floor-to-ceiling bookshelves line the curving walls of the upper levels.

The specialist **Librería Platero** (Talcahuano 485, Tribunales, tel. 011/4382-2215, fax 011/4382-3896, www.libreriaplatero.com.ar) has an enormous stock of new and out-of-print books (the latter in the basement stacks).

Librerías Turísticas (Paraguay 2457, tel. 011/4963-2866 or 4962-5547, turisticas@sinectis.com.ar) has an outstanding choice of maps and guidebooks, including its own guides to the capital's cafés.

Crafts

Monserrat's **Arte Indígena** (Balcarce 234, tel. 011/4343-1455) contains a representative assortment of indigenous crafts from around the country. In the Galerías Pacífico, items at **El Boyero** (Florida 760, tel. 011/5555-5307, www.elboyero.com) range from leather bags, boots, and belts to gaucho and Mapuche silverwork, *mate* gourds, and ceramics.

Artesanías Argentinas (Montevideo 1386, Barrio Norte, tel. 011/4812-2650, www.artesaniasargentinas.org) is a well-established artisans' outlet.

Leather Goods and Footwear

Retiro has several leather specialists, starting with **Lionel Frenkel** (San Martín 1088, tel. 011/4312-9806), also a crafts outlet. **Welcome Marroquinería** (Marcelo T. de Alvear 500, tel. 011/4312-8911) is another leather goods specialist.

Wine

San Telmo's wine-by-the-glass **Enoteka** (Defensa 891, tel. 011/4363-0011, www.laenoteka.com) is a good place to sample before purchase. Retiro's **Winery** (Avenida Leandro N. Alem 880, tel. 011/4311-6607) sells Argentine wines by the glass. The dean of wine outlets, though, is Palermo Viejo's **Club del Vino** (Cabrera 4737, tel. 011/4833-0048), one of the city's top restaurants, bars, and entertainment venues.

ACCOMMODATIONS

Buenos Aires has abundant accommodations in all categories. Since the economic implosion of early 2002, though, some upscale hotels have maintained differential rates for Argentines and foreigners—sometimes even continuing the former one-to-one exchange rate. If a hotel insists on this, there's not much you can do but go elsewhere or, if your language skills permit, argue the point. Note also that rates at upscale hotels often exclude the 21 percent IVA.

Under US$25

In recent years, good to excellent youth hostels have sprung up like tango halls in Gardel's time. Some but not all are Hostelling International affiliates.

Among non-hostel accommodations, San Telmo's **Hotel Varela** (Estados Unidos 342, tel. 011/4362-1231, hotelvarela@yahoo.com.ar, US$6–7 s or d) is a plain but spotless and reputable backpackers' choice. Some rooms have private bath.

On the edge of Palermo Viejo's nightlife, the HI affiliate **Tango Backpackers Hostel** (Thames 2212, tel. 011/4776-6871, www.tangobp.com, info@tangobp.com, US$5 pp for dorms, US$14 d) occupies a refurbished house with a rooftop terrace and *parrilla* for barbecues. Given their location in a party district (the hostel itself is on a fairly placid block), they're flexible on the 10 A.M. checkout time.

Northern barrios have few budget accommodations, but the HI affiliate **Recoleta Youth Hostel** (Libertad 1216, tel. 011/4812-4419, fax 011/4815-6622, www.trhostel.com.ar, reservas@trhostel.com.ar, US$8 pp, US$18 d) boasts the best location in its category (despite the name, it lies within Retiro).

The Microcentro's independent **V&S Hostel Club** (Viamonte 887, tel./fax 011/4322-0994, 011/4327-5131, www.hostelclub.com, hostelclub@hostelclub.com, US$9 pp, US$20/22 s/d) has both dorms and rooms with private bath. The century-old structure has central heating, a/c, and spacious and attractive common areas including kitchen, dining room, and a *parrilla.*

Near the Facultad de Medicina, **Hotel del Prado** (Paraguay 2385, tel. 011/4961-1192, www.hoteldelprado-ba.com.ar, reservas@hoteldelprado-ba.com.ar, US$12/15 s/d) is a remodeled older building with a quiet interior, good beds, and friendly owner-operators. Rooms have private bath, cable TV, telephone, and ceiling fans but no a/c.

Also an HI affiliate, Congreso's **St. Nicholas Youth Hostel** (Bartolomé Mitre 1691, tel. 011/4373-5920, US$6 pp with shared bath, US$16 d with private bath) is another rehab with ample common spaces; those common spaces, though, are so close to the dorms that it can be hard to get to sleep at an early hour.

Near Plaza de Mayo, the HI affiliate **Milhouse Youth Hostel** (Hipólito Yrigoyen 959, tel. 011/4345-9604, www.milhousehostel.com, info@milhousehostel.com, US$6 pp, US$20 d) is a well-managed, well-located, immaculate facility with large common areas.

Congreso's **Hotel Chile** (Avenida de Mayo 1297, tel./fax 011/4383-7877, US$14/19 s/d) is an Art Nouveau structure offering modernized rooms with private bath and breakfast. Corner balcony rooms on the upper floors enjoy panoramic views of the Plaza del Congreso and, craning the neck a bit eastward, the Plaza de Mayo and Casa Rosada.

US$25–50

Congreso's finest value is rejuvenated **Hotel de los dos Congresos** (Rivadavia 1777, tel. 011/4372-0466, fax 011/4372-0317, www.hoteldoscongresos.com, reservas@ hoteldoscongresos.com, US$27/31 s/d); its stately exterior belies the refurbished contemporary interior. Reservations are advisable for lofts, which have spiral staircases and Jacuzzi-equipped bathtubs.

Plainly but comfortably furnished, the 70-room **Ayacucho Palace Hotel** (Ayacucho 1408, tel./fax 011/4806-1815, www.ayacuchohotel.com.ar, reservas@ayacuchohotel.com.ar, US$29/36 s/d) offers some of the exterior style of more elegant Porteño hotels without extravagant prices.

On a deep but narrow lot, in a charming house dating from 1926, Palermo Viejo's **Como en Casa** (Gurruchaga 2155, tel. 011/4831-0517, fax 011/4831-2664, www.bandb.com.ar, info@bandb.com.ar, US$15 pp, US$35/45 s/d) has 11 cozy rooms with high ceilings, appealing common areas, and shady patios. Rates vary according to shared or private bath. It has Internet access and responsive English-speaking personnel, but lacks a/c.

US$50–100

Graham Greene, appropriately enough, stayed at the British-styled **Hotel Lancaster** (Avenida Córdoba 405, tel. 011/4312-4061, fax 011/4311-3021, www.lancasterhotel-page.com, lancast@infovia.com.ar, US$49/52 s/d with breakfast), which figures briefly in his novel *The Honorary Consul.*

One of the capital's most historic lodgings, dating from 1929, Monserrat's four-star **Castelar Hotel & Spa** (Avenida de Mayo 1152, tel. 011/4383-5000, fax 011/4383-8388, www.castelarhotel.com.ar, reservas@castelarhotel.com.ar, US$50–57 s or d) has hosted Spanish dramatist

Federico García Lorca (who lived six months in room 704), Chilean Nobel Prize poet Pablo Neruda, and Nobel Prize scientist Linus Pauling. Embellished with Carrara marble, it offers comfortable, well-equipped rooms with breakfast and spa access.

Devaluation has made Monserrat's four-star **Hotel Nogaró** (Diagonal Presidente Julio A. Roca 562, tel. 011/4331-0091, fax 011/4331-6791, www.nogarobue.com.ar, reservas@nogarobue.com.ar, US$107–133 d) a bargain with buffet breakfast. Dating from 1930 but recently renovated, this French-style, 150-room hotel features in-room safes and Internet connections.

Recoleta's **Hotel Plaza Francia** (Eduardo Schiaffino 2189, tel./fax 011/4804-9631, www.hotelplazafrancia.com, contact@hotelplazafrancia.com, US$65 s or d) is a boutique-style hotel near restaurants, entertainment, and open spaces. Rates include buffet breakfast, Internet connections, a/c, and other conveniences.

In a painstakingly remodeled *casa chorizo,* bed-and-breakfast **Malabia House** (Malabia 1555, tel./fax 011/4832-3345, 011/4833-2410, www.malabiahouse.com.ar, info@malabiahouse.com.ar, US$50–60 s, US$70–90 d) enjoys magnificent natural light, glistening wood floors, handsome furnishings, and small but attractive patios. Ground-floor rooms have external private baths; the slightly dearer upstairs rooms have a/c and interior baths. There's a 10 percent cash discount.

Just south of Plaza de Mayo, dating from 1931, the **NH City Hotel** Bolívar 160, tel. 011/4121-6464, fax 011/4121-6450, www.nh-hoteles.com, info@nh-city.com.ar, US$97 s or d) is a spectacularly modernized 300-room building that had the misfortune to reopen at the nadir of Argentina's economic meltdown of 2001–2002. Bad timing, though, has meant good rates for beautifully appointed rooms with contemporary conveniences, plus luxuries like a rooftop pool, gym and sauna, and a first-rate Spanish restaurant.

Barrio Norte's bright, modern **Design Suites** (Marcelo T. de Alvear 1683, tel./fax 011/4814-8700, www.designsuites.com, design@designsuites.com, US$96–144 s or d) is a boutique-style hotel with a heated pool, gym, and daily newspaper delivery (of the guest's choice). Each of its 40 suites has cable TV, telephone, Internet and fax connections, kitchenette, minibar, a/c, strongbox, and Jacuzzi.

US$100–150

Part of the Spanish luxury business chain, **Hotel NH Jousten** (Avenida Corrientes 240, tel. 011/4321-6750, fax 011/4321-6775, www.nh-hoteles.com, info@nh-jousten.com.ar, US$145 s or d) has 85 rooms in an elegant, tastefully recycled French-style castle. Quiet despite the busy avenue, thanks to double-paned windows, each room has cable TV, stereo, telephone, a/c, and modem connections. Rates include buffet breakfast; its highly regarded basement restaurant serves Spanish cuisine.

US$150–200

Retiro's **Meliá Buenos Aires Boutique Hotel** (Reconquista 945, tel. 011/4891-3800, fax 011/4891-3834, www.solmelia.com, buenosaires@meliaboutique.com.ar, US$190 d) has 125 rooms, including 18 suites, in a luminous facility with a gym and business center. Rates include a sumptuous buffet breakfast but not IVA; there are discounts from mid-December through February.

Near Puerto Madero, the massive high-rise **Sheraton Buenos Aires Hotel** (San Martín 1225, tel. 011/4318-9000, fax 011/4318-9346, www.starwood.com/redir/sheraton/buenosaires, sheraton@sheraton.com.ar, US$194–224 s or d) gets international business trade.

Now under international chain control, the landmark (1909) **Marriott Plaza Hotel** (Florida 1005, tel. 011/4318-3000, fax 011/4318-3008, www.marriott.com, marriott.plaza@ba.net, US$195–235 s or d) has undergone modernization without losing its German baroque charm.

Over US$200

Near the Obelisco, the **Hotel Crowne Plaza Panamericano** (Carlos Pellegrini 525, tel. 011/4348-5000, fax 011/4348-5251, www.crowneplaza.com.ar, hotel@crowneplaza.com.ar, US$260–315 d) comprises an older south tower and a newer north tower. Both are comfortable, but the more expensive north-tower rooms are technologically superior.

Monserrat's **Hotel InterContinental** (Moreno 809, tel. 011/4340-7100, fax 011/4340-7199, www.interconti.com.ar, buenosaires@interconti.com, US$303 s or d) consistently makes BA's best-hotels list. **Loi Suites Recoleta** (Vicente López 1955, tel. 011/5777-8950, fax 011/5777-8999, www.loisuites.com.ar, recoleta@loisuites.com.ar, US$200–345 s or d plus IVA) is the toniest link of a stylish new four-hotel chain. With some of BA's most innovative design, it takes fine advantage of natural light.

Popular with international entertainment figures, Retiro's **Caesar Park Hotel** (Posadas 1232, tel. 011/4819-1100, fax 011/4819-1165, www.caesar-park.com, hotel@caesar.com.ar, US$280 s or d plus IVA) now belongs to a Mexican luxury chain. Rates include an extravagant breakfast buffet.

Since 1928, the **Alvear Palace Hotel** (Avenida Alvear 1891, tel. 011/4805-2100, fax 011/4804-9246, www.alvearpalace.com, info@alvearpalace.com, US$410 and up s or d plus IVA) has symbolized elegance and luxury—not to mention wealth and privilege. Despite devaluation, it maintains both its standards and its prices—up to US$3,000 for the royal suite—for accommodations with Egyptian cotton sheets and Hermés toiletries, though discounts are possible. Francophobes may find the *ancien régime* decor cloying.

FOOD

Almost everything is affordable at present, at quality ranging from good to world-class, but some places are more affordable than others.

Monserrat/Catedral al Sur and Vicinity

In the barrio of San Cristóbal, west of Monserrat, **Miramar** (Avenida San Juan 1999, tel. 011/4304-4261) is both a *rotisería* takeaway and a no-frills restaurant unsuitable for a romantic night out, but great for unpretentious lunches or dinners. With fading posters from classic Argentine movies thumbtacked to the walls, this dingy corner bar serves surprisingly sophisticated entrées like oxtail soup and *gambas al ajillo* (garlic prawns) in the US$2.50–5.50 range.

Traditional Spanish/Basque seafood options include the author's choice, **Laurak Bat** (Avenida Belgrano 1144, tel. 011/4381-0682).

Microcentro and Vicinity

Pizzería Güerrín (Avenida Corrientes 1368, tel. 011/4371-8141) is a one-of-a-kind with exquisitely simple and simply exquisite by-the-slice *fugazza* (and *fugazzeta*). Seemingly unchanged since the days of Carlos Gardel, whose photographs line the walls, **Los Inmortales** (Avenida Corrientes 1369, tel. 011/4373-5303) is another classic pizzeria.

Open for lunch and dinner, **Broccolino** (Esmeralda 776, tel. 011/4322-9848) is an unfailingly reliable Italian choice, with impeccable service and a diverse menu. Entrées range from US$3.50–6, but most fall between US$4–5.

Several tourist-oriented *parrillas* make a fetish of staking their steaks over hot coals in circular barbecue pits, tended by bogus gauchos in full regalia, behind picture windows; while they play for the cliché and serve big crowds, their quality is outstanding and prices are reasonable. Try **La Estancia** (Lavalle 941, tel. 011/4326-0330). For a more typical Porteño experience, though, visit one of their barebones counterparts like Congreso's **Pippo** (Paraná 356, tel. 011/4374-0762) or **Chiquilín** (Montevideo 321, tel. 011/4373-5163).

The banker's favorite **Sabot** (25 de Mayo 756, tel. 011/4313-6587) serves top-quality Italo-Argentine dishes in a very masculine environment—women are few but welcome—with good-humored but professional service. Entrées like *matambre de cerdo* and *chivito,* plus some fish dishes, fall in the US$5–7 range. A pleasant surprise is the *mate de coca* from fresh coca leaves (for digestive purposes only!).

Puerto Madero

In recent years, redeveloped Puerto Madero has made its gastronomic mark, but more because of overall tourist appeal than quality—the food is mostly unimpressive. Most restaurants, though, have outdoor seating along the yacht harbor and, because the area's popular with foreigners from luxury hotels, restaurants are more accustomed to dealing with dinnertimes as early as, say, 7 P.M.

Opposite Dique No. 4, the best *parrilla* is

Cabaña Las Lilas (Alicia Moreau de Justo 516, tel. 011/4313-1336). Often packed for lunch despite high prices, it offers complimentary champagne and snacks while you wait; its *bife de chorizo* (US$7) may be BA's finest. Next door, **La Caballeriza** (Alicia Moreau de Justo 580, tel. 011/4314-2648) tries to keep pace. **Puerto Sorrento** (Alicia Moreau de Justo 410, tel. 011/4319-8730) is the best seafood option.

San Telmo and Vicinity

Despite the barrio's tourist allure, San Telmo's gastronomy lags behind other barrios, offering better lunchtime bargains than dinnertime indulgences.

Medio y Medio (Chile 316, tel. 011/4300-1396) bursts with lunchgoers seeking the Uruguayan caloric overload *chivito,* a steak sandwich piled high with lettuce, cheese, tomato, and bacon; a fried egg crowns the *chivito al plato,* a slab of beef that includes sides of potato salad, green salad, and fries.

Sunday visitors to Plaza Dorrego queue outside **DesNivel** (Defensa 855, tel. 011/4300-9081) for bargain-priced *parrillada* and pasta; it's open for lunch (except Monday) and dinner. Opposite Parque Lezama, **1880** (Defensa 1665, tel. 011/4307-2746) is a traditional *parrilla* with barrio atmosphere. Entrées, including pasta dishes like *ñoquis,* fall into the US$3–4 range.

Plaza Dorrego's **Pappa Deus** (Bethlem 423, tel. 011/4361-2110) is more imaginative than most nearby eateries, serving items like arugula and sun-dried tomatoes, plus a tremendous pumpkin-stuffed ravioli, but pricey desserts. Entrées cost around US$3–4.

Hostal del Canigó (Chacabuco 863, tel. 011/4304-5250) serves Catalonian seafood, other Spanish dishes, and standard Argentine items. Best at lunch, it occupies the classic dining room—dark mahogany woodwork and Spanish tiles—of the Casal de Catalunya cultural center.

La Boca

With sidewalk seating on the Vuelta de Rocha, **La Barbería** (Pedro de Mendoza 1959, tel. 011/4301-8770) serves lunchtime empanadas, tapas, pasta, pizza, sandwiches, seafood, and beer and cold hard cider from the tap. Prices fall into the US$3–7 range. Next-door **El Corsario** (Pedro de Mendoza 1981, tel. 011/4301-6579) is almost interchangeable.

In an area where taxis are obligatory at night and perhaps advisable in the daytime (though some cabbies have trouble finding it), **El Obrero** (Agustín Cafferena 64, tel. 011/4362-9912) is where celebrities go slumming for steaks. Its walls plastered with images of soccer icon Diego Maradona and little else, it draws international clientele like Bono, Robert Duvall, and others. There's no printed menu—check the chalkboards scattered around the dining room for entrées in the US$3–5 range.

Retiro

The hippest pizzería is the garishly decorated **Filo** (San Martín 975, tel. 011/4311-0312). Tourist-oriented *parrillas* include **Las Nazarenas** (Reconquista 1132, tel. 011/4312-5559) and **La Chacra** (Avenida Córdoba 941, tel. 011/4322-1409).

For a breather, try the vegetarian institution **La Esquina de las Flores** (Avenida Córdoba 1587, tel. 011/4813-3630), a health-food market and upstairs restaurant that helps diversify the Argentine diet through public workshops and radio and TV programs.

Tancat (Paraguay 645, tel. 011/4312-5442) is a first-rate and wildly popular Spanish *tasca,* with lunches around US$3–5 pp; don't miss the *jamón serrano* (ham) appetizer. Reservations are almost essential for tables, which are few, but there's usually space at the bar.

Recoleta and Barrio Norte

For spicy northwestern dishes like *locro* and empanadas, one of BA's best values is **El Sanjuanino** (Posadas 1515, tel. 011/4804-2909).

Open for lunch and dinner, **José Luis** (Avenida Quintana 456, tel. 011/4807-0606) is an Asturian seafood restaurant stressing fresher and lighter dishes than most of its counterparts. Entrées are mostly in the US$7 range.

Barrio Norte's **Los Pinos** (Azcuénaga 1500, tel. 011/4822-8704) occupies an old-style apothecary, its wooden cases still stocked with antique bottles and rising nearly to the ceiling. Fixed lunch and dinner specials fall into the US$3–5 range; a la carte beef, seafood, and pasta entrées are not much more expensive, as they include a side order.

Charging around US$6 per person, the Middle Eastern buffet at the **Restaurant del Club Sirio** (Pacheco de Melo 1902, tel. 011/4806-5764) is open nightly except Sunday.

Palermo

Palermo is, without question, Argentine gastronomy's center of innovation, mostly in southerly Palermo Soho but also in northerly Palermo Hollywood, the Botánico, and Las Cañitas.

The Botánico's **Bella Italia Café Bar** (República Árabe Siria 3330, tel. 011/4807-5120) is the midrange café version of the nearby namesake restaurant. For around US$3.50, it has outstanding squash gnocchi with a subtle cream sauce, along with fine cannelloni and salads.

For quality/price ratio, the hands-down choice for regional dishes is **La Cupertina** (Cabrera 5300, tel. 011/4777-3711). Tucumán-style chicken empanadas and *humitas en chala* (similar to tamales, wrapped in corn stalks) are exquisite and so cheap that price is no object, even with wine; there are also individual pizzas and exceptional desserts, especially the Spanish custard *natillas* and *arroz con leche.* Seating only about 20 diners, in simple surroundings, it keeps limited hours: 11:30 A.M.–3:30 P.M. daily except Monday and 7:30–11 P.M. daily except Sunday and Monday.

Near Plaza Serrano, **Spirit** (Serrano 1550, tel. 011/4833-4360) is an oyster bar serving an ample plate of seafood tapas, sufficient for two persons, for only US$10.

El Federal (Honduras 5254, tel. 011/4832-6500) draws an upscale clientele to high-priced versions of regional specialties from throughout the country, including Bariloche *jabalí* (wild boar) and Patagonian lamb. Open for lunch and dinner, its entrées range from US$6–7.

Known for live music in its intimate theater-club, the **Club del Vino** (Cabrera 4737, tel. 011/4833-8330, is also a fine restaurant with, as its name suggests, an exceptional wine selection. The menu includes the usual beef dishes (US$3–4), but also rabbit stew, conger eel with tomato and basil, chicken breast in orange sauce, and almond-stuffed trout, all in the US$4–7 range.

Las Cañitas has acquired a reputation for fashionability, but its classic is the venerable **El Portugués** (Báez 499, tel. 011/4771-8699). Some diners consider the half-portion *bife de chorizo* a double—consider sharing and then order more if you're still hungry.

Lotus Neo Thai (Ortega y Gasset 1782, tel. 011/4771-4449), Argentina's Thai pioneer, is one of few places with truly spicy dishes. Open for dinner only, a quiet upstairs locale with soothing music and lotus-themed decor, it's relatively expensive at US$5–9 for entrées.

Belgrano

Belgrano has decent restaurants—the city's Chinatown is here—but it's most notable for BA's best Peruvian dining. On a cul-de-sac near the railroad tracks, **Contigo Perú** (Echeverría 1627, tel. 011/4780-3960) has grown from humble beginnings to neighborhood success. Prices are moderate, even cheap. Hours are 10 A.M.–midnight daily except Monday.

INFORMATION

The **Secretaría Nacional de Turismo** (Avenida Santa Fe 883, Retiro, tel. 011/4312-2232 or 0800/555-0016, www.turismo.gov.ar) is open 9 A.M.–5 P.M. weekdays only; there's a branch at Aeropuerto Internacional Ezeiza (tel. 011/4480-0292) and another at Aeroparque Jorge Newbery (tel. 011/4771-0104). Airport branches are open 8 A.M.–8 P.M. daily.

The municipal **Subsecretaría de Turismo** maintains information kiosks in the Microcentro (Florida and Diagonal Roque Sáenz Peña), open 10 A.M.–6 P.M. daily except Sunday; at Puerto Madero's Dique 4 (tel. 011/4313-0187), open noon–6 P.M. weekdays, 10 A.M.–8 P.M. weekends; and at the Retiro bus terminal (tel. 011/4311-0528), open 7:30 A.M.–1 P.M. daily except Sunday. All distribute maps and brochures, and usually have English-speaking staff.

SERVICES

Buenos Aires has a capital city's selection of services, many of which keep long hours.

Money

Most visitors find the ubiquitous ATMs most convenient for changing money. The financial district's *casas de cambio,* along San Martín between Corrientes and Plaza de Mayo, usually offer the best rates for US cash, euros, and travelers' checks. For travelers' checks, they normally charge a commission or pay less than for cash; **American Express** (Arenales 707, Retiro, tel. 011/4310-3000) changes its own checks without commission.

Postal Services

The **Correo Central** (Sarmiento 151) is open 8 A.M.–8 P.M. weekdays, 10 A.M.–1 P.M. Saturday, but has many other branches. International parcels of more than one kilogram must use the **Correo Internacional** (Antártida Argentina near the Retiro train station, tel. 011/4316-7777). Hours are 11 A.M.–5 P.M. weekdays only.

Federal Express (Maipú 753, tel. 011/4393-6054) offers private courier service.

Communications

Locutorios for long-distance and fax services are so plentiful that it's pointless to mention specific locations. Many have Internet connections as well, but there are also Internet-exclusive locales.

Travel Agencies

Retiro's **American Express** (Arenales 707, tel. 011/4310-3535, fax 011/4315-1846, amex bueemp@aexp.com) offers the usual services.

Swan Turismo (Cerrito 822, 9th floor, Retiro, tel./fax 011/4129-7926, swanturismo@teletel.com.ar) is a full-service agency willing and able to deal with some of the Argentine travel system's eccentricities.

The nonprofit **Asatej** (Florida 835, 3rd floor, Retiro, tel. 011/4311-6953, fax 011/4311-6840, www.asatej.com.ar, asatej@asatej.com.ar) is focusing on incoming tourism as the economic crisis has reduced overseas travel by young Argentines. Also the Hostelling International headquarters, it's good at searching out the best airfares for anyone, not just students.

Libraries

The **Biblioteca Nacional** (National Library, Agüero 2502, Recoleta, tel. 011/4808-6000, www.bibnal.edu.ar) is open 9 A.M.–8 P.M. weekdays, noon–6 P.M. weekends.

Photography

Photo labs are abundant, but for slide film try a specialist like **Kinefot** (Talcahuano 250, tel. 011/4374-7445) or **Color Shot** (Corrientes 1550).

Immigration

The **Dirección Nacional de Migraciones** (Avenida Argentina 1355, Retiro, tel. 011/4317-0237) is open 8 A.M.–1 P.M. weekdays only.

Medical Services

Consider a private hospital or clinic, as budget and personnel constraints are causing problems for public facilities like Recoleta's **Hospital Rivadavia** (Avenida Las Heras 2670, tel. 011/4809-2002). The **Hospital Británico** (Perdriel 74, Barracas, tel. 011/4304-1082) and Belgrano's **Clínica Fleni** (Montañeses 2325, tel. 011/5777-3200, www.fleni.org.ar) are first-rate, though the latter does not serve every specialty.

GETTING THERE

Buenos Aires is the main port of entry for overseas visitors, and the hub for domestic travel.

Air

Most international carriers use the suburban airport at Ezeiza, though some short-haul flights use close-in Aeroparque; for airport details, see the Getting Around entry below. For international flight details, see the Getting Around entry in the Know Patagonia chapter.

Aerolíneas Argentinas has domestic and international flights. Their domestic arm, **Austral** (Perú 2, Monserrat, tel. 011/4320-2345), serves major Patagonian destinations.

American Falcon (Avenida Santa Fe 963, Retiro, tel. 011/4328-5541, www.americanfalcon.com.ar) flies from Aeroparque to Puerto Madryn, Comodoro Rivadavia, and Bariloche. **Southern Winds** (Avenida Santa Fe 784, Retiro, tel. 011/4515-8600, www.sw.com.ar) flies to Neuquén, Bariloche, and El Calafate.

Líneas Aéreas del Estado (LADE, Perú 714, San Telmo, tel. 011/4361-7071, www.lade.com.ar), the air force's commercial wing, flies to southern Buenos Aires province and Patagonian destinations.

Bus

Retiro's **Estación Terminal de Omnibus** (Avenida Ramos Mejía 1860, tel. 011/4310-0700, www.tebasa.com.ar) is a sprawling three-story structure serving some 140 separate carriers that cover the entire country and international destinations. It's walking distance from the northern terminus of Subte Línea C, at the Retiro train station.

Passengers leave from the 1st-floor *andenes* (platforms). Companies occupy more than 200 *ventanillas* (ticket windows) on the 2nd floor, roughly organized by geographical region; for readers of this book, the most important is Zona Sur (South, windows 1–21, 23, 25, 27–30, 32–34, and 101).

The departure level's Centro de Informes y Reclamos (tel. 011/4310-0700) provides general information and oversees taxis. The municipal tourist office is open 7:30 A.M.–1 P.M. only.

Reservations are a good idea during summer (January–February) and winter (late July) holidays, but also on long weekends like Semana Santa (Holy Week). Space precludes a complete list of domestic destinations, fares, and times here. For that information, check the Transportation entry under the destination itself.

GETTING AROUND

Airports

Buenos Aires has two airports under the concessionaire **Aeropuertos Argentinos 2000** (tel. 011/5480-6111, www.aa2000.com.ar). Popularly called "Ezeiza" after its Buenos Aires province location, **Aeropuerto Internacional Ministro Pistarini** is 35 kilometers southwest of downtown. Palermo's **Aeroparque Jorge Newbery** (Avenida Costanera Rafael Obligado s/n) is primarily domestic but handles a few flights from neighboring countries.

International passengers leaving from Ezeiza pay a US$30.50 departure tax, payable in local currency or US dollars; US$18 of this is normally collected on departure. On flights shorter than 300 kilometers to neighboring countries, such as Uruguay, the tax is US$6; on Aeroparque domestic flights, it's about US$3, normally included in the ticket price.

There's a variety of options to and from the airports, ranging from *colectivos* (city buses) to shuttles, taxis, and *remises* (meterless taxis that quote a fixed price for the trip).

To Aeroparque (about US$.35), the main ***colectivos*** are No. 33 from Plaza de Mayo, the Microcentro, and Retiro; No. 37-C ("Ciudad Universitaria") from Plaza del Congreso, Avenida Callao, Avenida las Heras, and Plaza Italia; northbound No. 45 from Plaza Constitución, Plaza San Martín, or Retiro; and No. 160-C or 160-D from Avenida Las Heras or Plaza Italia. Return buses leave from Avenida Costanera Rafael Obligado, just outside the terminal.

To Ezeiza (about US$.50), the backpackers' choice is the No. 86-A ("Aeropuerto"), from La Boca to Plaza de Mayo, Plaza del Congreso, and onward, but this takes up to two hours. Its *Servicio Diferencial* costs more (US$2) but has more comfortable reclining seats. At Ezeiza, both leave from just outside the Aerolíneas Argentinas terminal, a short walk from the main international terminal.

Retiro-based **shuttles** use the faster *autopista* (freeway). **Manuel Tienda León** (Avenida Madero and San Martín, tel. 011/4315-5115 or 0810/888-5366, www.tiendaleon.com.ar) runs 30 buses daily to and from Ezeiza (US$7) between 4 A.M. and 9:30 P.M. There are 25 daily to Aeroparque (US$3); buses from Ezeiza make Aeroparque connections for domestic flights.

Door-to-door **taxis** and ***remises*** are competitive with shuttles for three or more persons. Manuel Tienda León and other companies such as **Naon Remises** (tel. 011/4545-6500) go to Aeroparque (US$5) and Ezeiza (US$15–18). Ezeiza-bound *remises* and taxis usually add highways tolls (about US$1).

Colectivos (Buses)

Most visitors need to know relatively few of BA's

RIDING THE SUBTE

Operated by the private concessionaire Metrovías, the state-owned Subterráneos de Buenos Aires comprises five alphabetically designated lines, four of which (A, B, D, and E) begin in Monserrat or the Microcentro and serve outlying northern and western barrios, with numerous stations in between. Línea C is a north-south connector line between major railway stations at Retiro and Constitución. An additional north-south connector line, Línea H, is under construction between Retiro and outlying southern barrios, beneath Avenida Pueyrredón and Avenida Jujuy.

Subte hours are 5 A.M. to about 11 P.M. except Sundays and holidays, when the system opens later (around 8 A.M.) and closes earlier (about 10:30 P.M.) and services are less frequent. Fares are about US$.35; to save time, purchase magnetic tickets in quantities of two, five, 10, and 30 rides. Two or more people may use the same ticket (legally) by passing it back and forth across the turnstile; you do not need a ticket to exit the system.

Before going through the turnstiles, make sure of the direction; at some stations, trains in both directions use the same platform, but at others the platforms are on opposite sides. A few stations have one-way traffic only, but the next station down the line normally is one-way in the other direction.

For complaints or problems, contact Metrovías' Centro de Atención al Pasajero (tel. 0800/555-1616 toll-free).

Subte Routes

Línea A begins at Plaza de Mayo, Monserrat, and runs beneath Avenida Rivadavia to Primera Junta, in the barrio of Chacarita. A westward extension to the edge of Buenos Aires province is due to open by 2008.

Línea B begins at Avenida Leandro Alem, in the Microcentro, and runs beneath Avenida Corrientes and then northwesterly to Avenida los Incas, in Parque Chas, on an extension that is due to reach Villa Urquiza by 2007. At Federico Lacroze, the former terminus in the barrio of Chacarita, it connects with the suburban Ferrocarril Urquiza.

Línea C connects Retiro, which has commuter surface rail lines to northern suburbs, with Constitución, the transfer point for southern suburban commuter surface lines; Línea C also has transfer stations for all other Subte lines.

Línea D begins at Catedral, on Plaza de Mayo, and runs beneath Avenida Santa Fe and Avenida Cabildo through Palermo and Belgrano to Congreso de Tucumán, in the barrio of Núñez.

Línea E runs from Bolívar, on the Avenida de Mayo, to Plaza de los Virreyes, in the barrio of Flores. From Plaza de los Virreyes there's a light rail extension known as the Premetro.

Línea H is due to open in 2006; the economic crisis has slowed but not halted its construction. The first stretch will begin at Inclán, in the southern barrio of Parque Patricios, and connect with Plaza Miserere (Once), on Línea A; it should eventually extend north to Recoleta and Retiro and south to Nueva Pompeya.

bus routes. Detailed city atlases have abbreviated pocket versions available at kiosks and bookstores, but Porteño riders are also generous with information. Fares (around US$.35) depend on distance; on hearing your destination, the driver enters the fare in the automatic ticket machine, which takes only coins and gives small change.

Subway

Popularly known as the **Subte,** South America's first underground railway has modernized, but some antique cars, with varnished but worn woodwork, and elaborately tiled but chipped station murals help recall the early 20th century's prosperity and optimism.

Concessionaire Metrovías (www.metrovias.com.ar) has improved rolling stock, extended existing lines, remodeled older stations and built new ones, and replaced *fichas* (tokens) with electronic tickets.

Santiago de Chile

For most visitors, sprawling Santiago de Chile, its Mediterranean hillsides, and the snow-covered Andean crest are their first impressions of the country. Santiago may lack Buenos Aires's international profile, but its finest attractions can match or surpass those of Argentina's capital.

Since the 1990 return to constitutional government and subsequent economic expansion, the city has improved greatly. Both individuals and businesses, for instance, have restored or rehabbed houses and buildings in once rundown Barrio Brasil, and entrepreneurs have replaced unsalvageable structures with tasteful contemporary apartments. Barrio Bellavista has enjoyed a gastronomic and nightlife boom, and international commerce flourishes in Providencia and Las Condes.

The megacity of Santiago is really many cities, consisting of 32 different *comunas* (boroughs) with separate governments. Most sights are in the central city's colonial nucleus and adjacent boroughs like Recoleta, Independencia, and Quinta Normal, and eastern suburbs like Providencia, Las Condes, and Ñuñoa.

Must-Sees

Look for [M] to find the sights and activities you can't miss and [N] for the best dining and lodging.

Plaza de Armas: Numerous historic buildings and museums surround Santiago's 16th-century plaza, platted by Pedro de Valdivia (page 67).

Museo Chileno de Arte Precolombino: In an elegant colonial building, this museum houses an irreplaceable assortment of indigenous artifacts from throughout the Americas (page 72).

Mercado Central: North of the Plaza de Armas, this onetime colonial rubbish tip became a produce market and, more recently, a tourist draw for its *simpático* seafood eateries (page 72).

Palacio de la Moneda: Santiago's colonial presidential palace survived the 1973 headlines, and the public is once again welcome to stroll its passages (page 74).

Palacio de la Moneda, Centro Cívico

Cerro Santa Lucía: In the late 19th century, visionary mayor Benjamín Vicuña Mackenna started the transformation of a barren quarry, where Pedro de Valdivia founded Santiago, into a true garden spot (page 74).

La Chascona (Museo Neruda): On a cul-de-sac in bohemian Barrio Bellavista, Nobel poet Pablo Neruda's whimsical Santiago residence is a literary pilgrimage site that delights everyone (page 79).

Viña Cousiño Macul: Though surrounded by the sprawling capital, the surviving vineyards and subterranean bodegas of this classic Chilean winery are conveniently close for tours and tasting (page 80).

Viña Concha y Toro: In the southeastern suburb of Pirque, Concha y Toro is a bit more distant than Cousiño Macul, but it's still a prime visitor destination and one of Chile's best-known vineyards and wineries (page 80).

Five million people, more than a third of all Chileans, live in Gran Santiago (Greater Santiago). The locus of political and economic power, the capital has grown at the expense of the regions, but unevenly so—some *comunas* have become prosperous, others remain desperately poor.

Class-based residential segregation is striking, though less extreme than in cities like Lima and Mexico City. There are environmental costs, as well—more than a million automobiles sometimes clog narrow colonial streets. Idling behind sooty diesel buses, with smokestack industry adding a share, they aggravate one of the world's worst smog problems—especially in the almost windless autumn months of March and April.

Santiago's Mediterranean climate has a pronounced dry season (November–April) and wet winters (though droughts are not unusual). The daily maximum temperature averages 28°C in January, but it almost always cools off at night, thanks to the elevation. In July, the coolest month, the daily maximum averages 10°C.

PLANNING YOUR TIME

While Santiago has a lower profile than Buenos Aires, it still has much to offer. Presuming only two days, though, visitors should get to know the central Plaza de Armas and vicinity, including the Mercado Central and the Museo Precolombino; the Palacio de la Moneda; Cerro Santa Lucía; poet Pablo Neruda's "La Chascona" house; and a winery or two.

Anyone planning a longer stay should consult the author's *Moon Handbooks Chile.*

HISTORY

The conquistador Pedro de Valdivia founded "Santiago del Nuevo Extremo" on February 12, 1541, in a place where "The land is such that there is none better in the world for living in and settling down . . . because it is very flat, very healthy and very pleasant. . . ." Valdivia initially established good relations with Araucanian Indians, but during an absence in Peru, the Spaniards began to abuse the indigenes; their

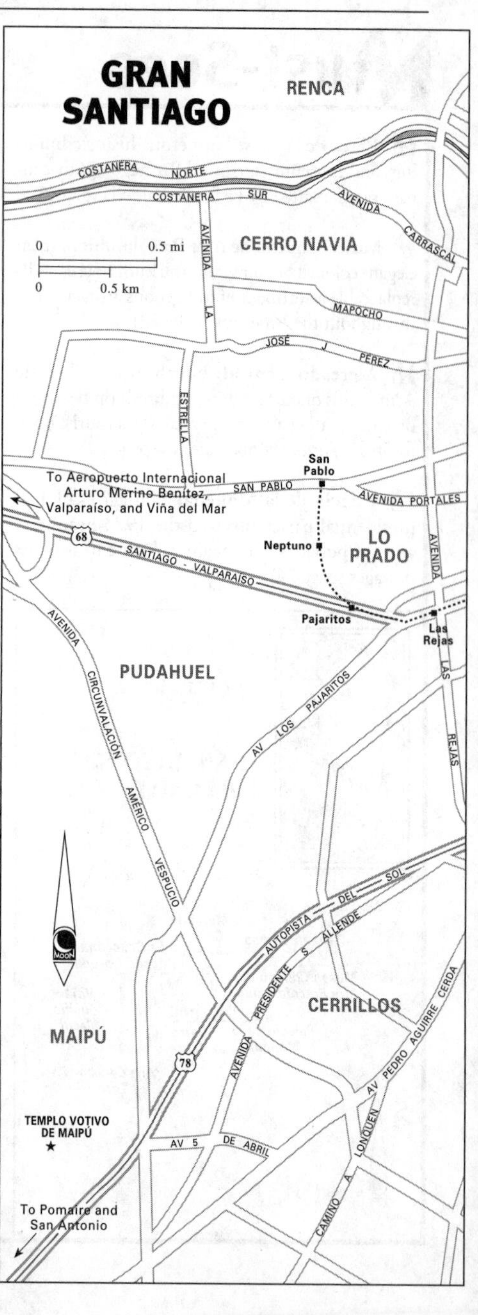

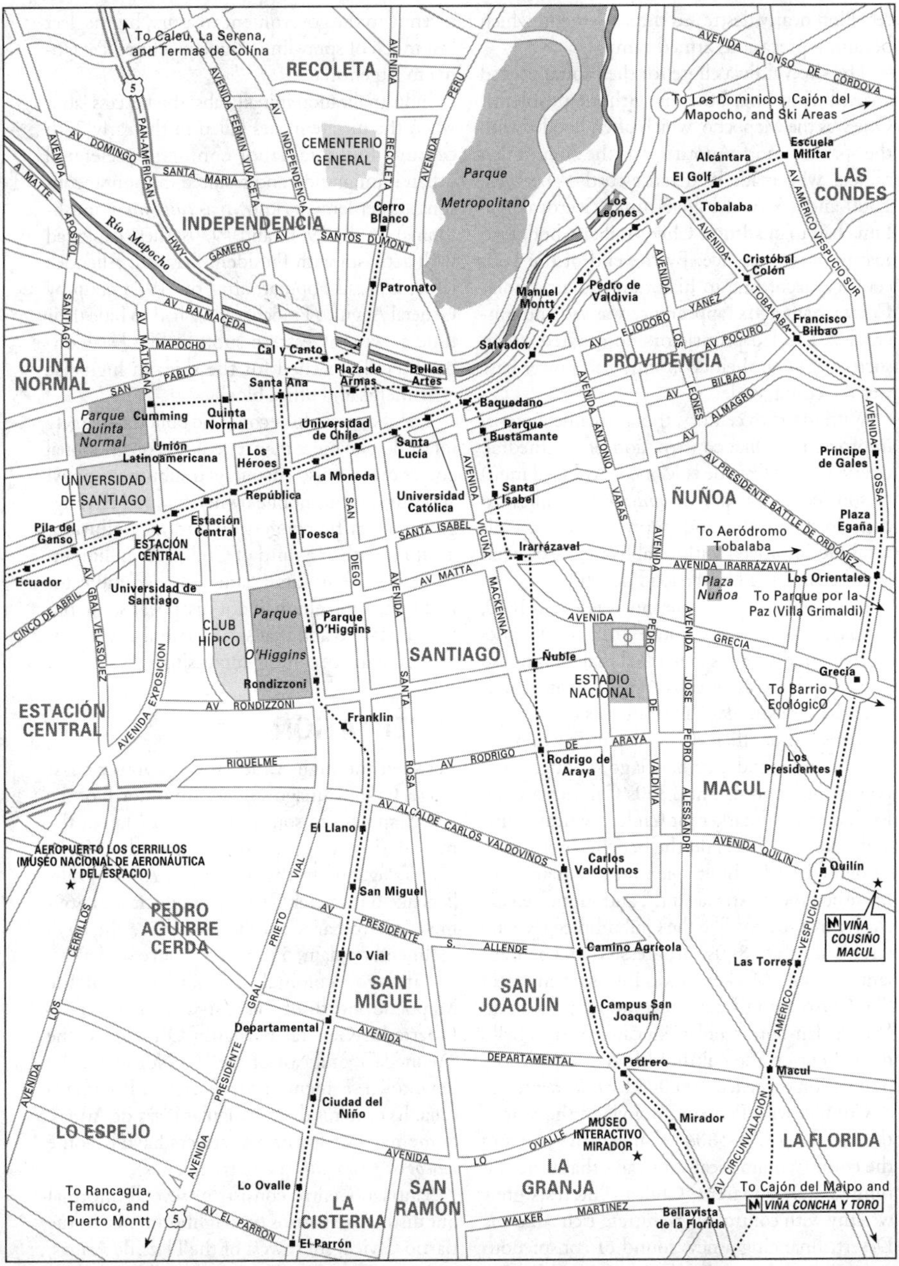

RECOLETA
INDEPENDENCIA
QUINTA NORMAL
PROVIDENCIA
LAS CONDES
ÑUÑOA
SANTIAGO
ESTACIÓN CENTRAL
MACUL
PEDRO AGUIRRE CERDA
SAN MIGUEL
SAN JOAQUÍN
LO ESPEJO
LA CISTERNA
SAN RAMÓN
LA GRANJA
LA FLORIDA

To Caleu, La Serena, and Termas de Colína
To Los Dominicos, Cajón del Mapocho, and Ski Areas
To Aeródromo Tobalaba
To Parque por la Paz (Villa Grimaldi)
To Barrio Ecológico
To Cajón del Maipo and VIÑA CONCHA Y TORO
To Rancagua, Temuco, and Puerto Montt

CEMENTERIO GENERAL
Parque Metropolitano
Río Mapocho
Parque Quinta Normal
UNIVERSIDAD DE SANTIAGO
ESTACIÓN CENTRAL
CLUB HÍPICO
Parque O'Higgins
ESTADIO NACIONAL
Plaza Ñuñoa
AEROPUERTO LOS CERRILLOS (MUSEO NACIONAL DE AERONÁUTICA Y DEL ESPACIO)
MUSEO INTERACTIVO MIRADOR
VIÑA COUSIÑO MACUL

Escuela Militar, Alcántara, El Golf, Tobalaba, Los Leones, Cristóbal Colón, Pedro de Valdivia, Manuel Montt, Francisco Bilbao, Salvador, Baquedano, Bellas Artes, Plaza de Armas, Cal y Canto, Santa Ana, Cerro Blanco, Patronato, Cumming, Quinta Normal, Universidad de Chile, Santa Lucía, Parque Bustamante, Unión Latinoamericana, Los Héroes, La Moneda, Universidad Católica, Santa Isabel, República, Estación Central, Pila del Ganso, Ecuador, Universidad de Santiago, Toesca, Irarrázaval, Príncipe de Gales, Plaza Egaña, Los Orientales, Parque O'Higgins, Ñuble, Grecia, Rondizzoni, Franklin, Rodrigo de Araya, Los Presidentes, El Llano, Carlos Valdovinos, Quilín, San Miguel, Camino Agrícola, Lo Vial, Las Torres, Campus San Joaquín, Departamental, Pedrero, Macul, Ciudad del Niño, Mirador, Lo Ovalle, Bellavista de la Florida, El Parrón rebellion nearly destroyed the settlement, which became a precarious armed camp.

The site Valdivia chose for the capital proved an enduring one, but not without problems. One was the Mapocho, which often flooded with the spring runoff. Another was the Araucanian raiders, who made its defense costly—between 1600 and 1606, the governing Viceroyalty of Lima had to quadruple Chile's military budget to maintain its presence. By the end of the 16th century, according to historian Eduardo Solar Correa, Santiago's "appearance was sad and miserable." Landed proprietors dominated urban society, though their economic and power base was the countryside.

With the 18th century, though, came material improvements like construction of a cathedral, creation of the Casa de la Moneda (colonial mint) to spur economic activity, *tajamares* (dikes) to contain the floods, and improved roads. Cultural life improved with establishment of what later become the Universidad de Chile.

By the time Chile became independent in 1810, Santiago was a modest, nondescript city. Charles Darwin, in the 1830s, remarked that "it is not so fine or so large as Buenos Ayres, but it is built after the same model." Earthquakes encouraged utilitarian rather than elaborate construction.

Post-independence Santiago, though, was poised for a boom. The 1850s California Gold Rush created a market for Chilean wheat, wine, and other produce, and the beneficiaries were a landed elite who built splendid city mansions, furnished them extravagantly, and supported exclusive institutions like the Club Hípico (Racing Club). By the 1870s, progressive mayor Benjamín Vicuña Mackenna was transforming areas like Cerro Santa Lucía into public parks, and Venezuelan-born scholar/educator Andrés Bello helped enrich the cultural life of a city whose population exceeded 100,000 by mid-century.

Conflict with Peru and Bolivia in the War of the Pacific (1879–1884) changed the city and the country dramatically, in ways that were not immediately apparent. Chilean interests grew wealthy with control of the nitrate-rich Atacama Desert, financing a new round of conspicuous consumption by mining magnates and bringing revenue to the government treasury, but neglect lost much of sprawling, vaguely defined Patagonia to Argentina.

Industrialization initially absorbed excess labor when the nitrate mines failed in the early 20th century, but rural labor conflicts accelerated urban immigration and resulted in spontaneous squatter settlements known as *callampas* (mushrooms). In the 1960s and 1970s, these exploded with activism with President Salvador Allende's leftist Unidad Popular; after the 1973 coup by General Augusto Pinochet, they had to bide their time as wealthy eastern suburbs like Las Condes literally reached for the skies in high-rise apartments and office blocks.

The dictatorship's economic policies—largely intact despite more than a decade's constitutional government—also encouraged suburban sprawl and private automobile ownership that have aggravated traffic congestion and air pollution. That more than a third of Chile's 15 million inhabitants live in Gran Santiago is an indicator that these problems will not disappear soon, but it's only fair to add that some central city neighborhoods are becoming increasingly livable.

ORIENTATION

Between the high Andes and the lower coast range, Gran Santiago sprawls from north of the Río Mapocho to south of the Río Maipo; the meandering Mapocho unites with the Maipo near Talagante, to the southwest. Andean outliers like 635-meter Cerro Santa Lucía and 869-meter Cerro San Cristóbal rise above the city's sedimentary plain, 550 meters above sea level.

Santiago's colonial core lies south of the Mapocho, north of the east-west Avenida del Libertador General Bernardo O'Higgins (the "Alameda"), and east of the Vía Norte Sur, the downtown segment of the Carretera Panamericana. Its center is the rectangular Plaza de Armas. Some narrow downtown streets have become *paseos* or *peatonales* (pedestrian malls).

Santiago Centro consists of several informal but distinctive barrios or neighborhoods. In the Barrio Cívico, southwest of the Plaza de Armas, major government offices surround the Plaza de la Constitución; farther west, across the Vía Norte Sur, once dilapidated Barrio Brasil is undergoing a residential renaissance. South of the Alameda, Barrio París Londres's winding streets break the grid pattern, as do those of Barrio Lastarria, east of Cerro Santa Lucía.

Beyond Santiago Centro, several other *comunas* have sights and services, most notably the easterly suburbs of Providencia and Las Condes. Some of these boast their own distinctive neighborhoods: north of the Mapocho, the restaurant and nightlife mecca of Barrio Bellavista lies half in Recoleta, half in Providencia. Providencia's traditional point of identification is Plaza Baquedano, universally known as Plaza Italia, where the eastbound Alameda becomes Avenida Providencia.

Las Condes and Vitacura are affluent eastward extensions of Providencia. Independencia, Quinta Normal and Estación Central have fewer sights, except for major museums and parks, and a few key services such as long-distance bus terminals.

Sights

Central Santiago has the highest density of sights in or around the Plaza de Armas, Plaza de la Constitución, Cerro Santa Lucía, and Barrio Bellavista, with a handful elsewhere. The municipal tourist authority, with separate offices near the Plaza de Armas and on Cerro Santa Lucía, offers free walking tours that include admission to some of the best museums; check for the most current itineraries.

PLAZA DE ARMAS AND VICINITY

On its west side, the Plaza's oldest surviving landmark is the **Catedral Metropolitana,** begun in 1748 but, because of setbacks including earthquakes and fires, not completed until 1830. Italian architect Joaquín Toesca designed its neoclassical façade, since modified with late-19th-century Tuscan touches.

On the north side, the next oldest structure is the **Municipalidad de Santiago** (1785). Immediately west, the **Palacio de la Real Audiencia** (1804) houses the Museo Histórico Nacional (see below); at the corner of Paseo Puente, the French-style **Correo Central** (Post Office, 1882) replaced the original government house. Half a block east of the plaza, dating from 1769, the **Casa Colorada** (Merced 860) houses the municipal tourist office and the city museum (see below).

One block west of the Plaza, occupying an entire block, the current **Ministerio de Relaciones Exteriores** (Foreign Ministry) was the Congreso de la República until the 1973 coup. One block from the southwest corner of the Plaza, the **Palacio de la Real Aduana** (Royal Customs House, Bandera 361) now accommodates the exceptional Museo Chileno de Arte Precolombino (Chilean Museum of Pre-Columbian Art; see separate entry below).

One block north of the Plaza, built of massive blocks, the **Templo de Santo Domingo** (begun in 1747, but not finished until 1808) stands at 21 de Mayo and Monjitas; two blocks north is the **Mercado Central,** the landmark central market that's also a major tourist draw for its seafood restaurants.

From 1913 until 1987, trains to Valparaíso, northern Chile and Mendoza (Argentina) used Eiffel-influenced architect Emilio Jecquier's monumental **Estación Mapocho;** closed in 1987 and reopened as a cultural center, it hosts events like Santiago's annual book fair. In the nearby Cal y Canto Metro station, parts of the foundations of the colonial **Puente Cal y Canto** bridge over the Mapocho have been exposed to view.

Museo Histórico Nacional (Palacio de la Real Audiencia)

After 1609, the Real Audiencia was Chile's colonial supreme court, but earthquakes twice destroyed its quarters. Architect Juan José de Goycolea y Zañartu designed the current neoclassical building, dating from 1808.

Three years later, during the independence struggle, the first Congreso Nacional met here,

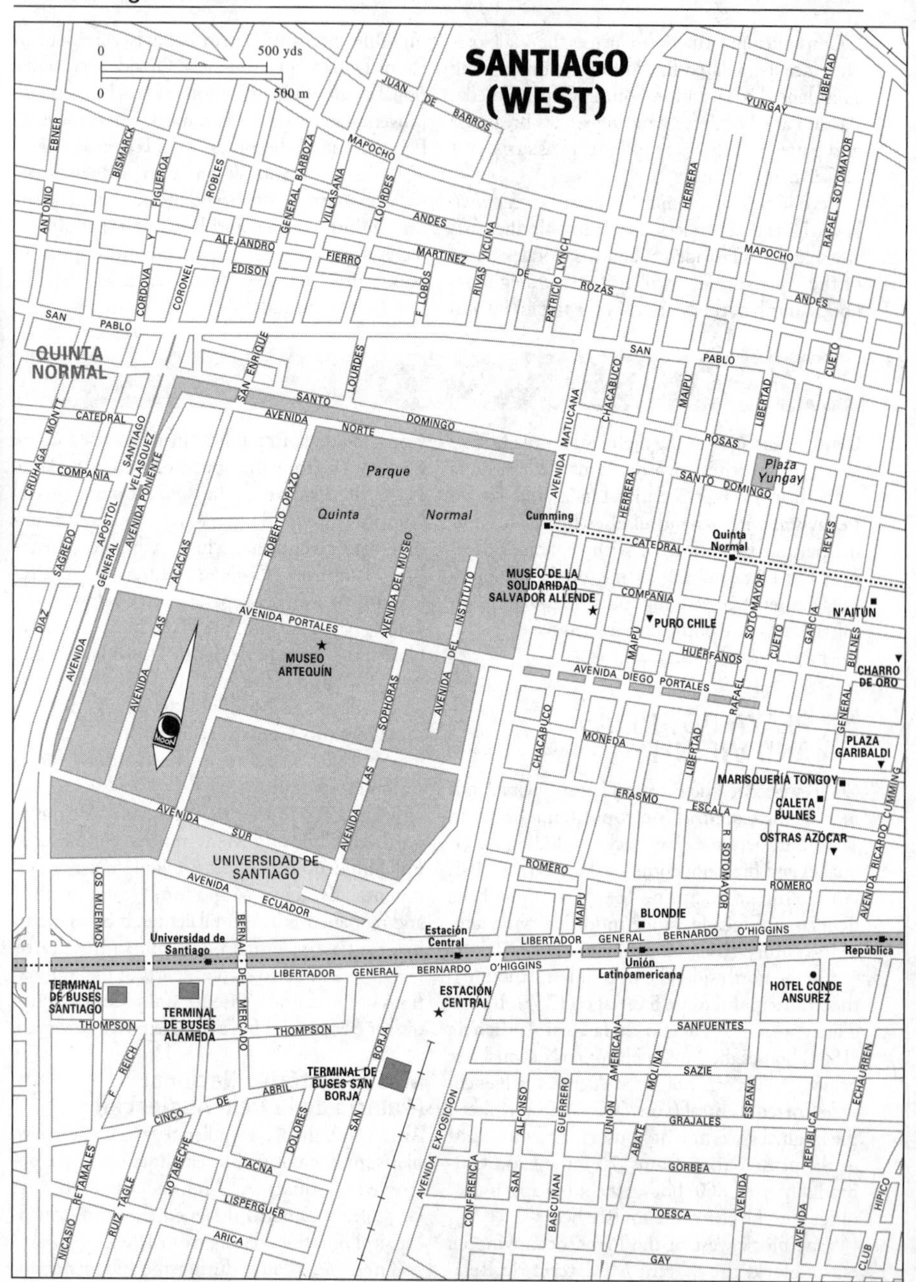
SANTIAGO
(WEST)
0
500 yds
0
500 m
QUINTA
NORMAL
Parque
Quinta
Normal
Plaza
Yungay
Cumming
Quinta
Normal
MUSEO DE LA
SOLIDARIDAD
SALVADOR ALLENDE
PURO CHILE
N'AITÚN
CHARRO
DE ORO
PLAZA
GARIBALDI
MARISQUERÍA TONGOY
CALETA
BULNES
OSTRAS AZÓCAR
MUSEO
ARTEQUÍN
UNIVERSIDAD DE
SANTIAGO
BLONDIE
Estación
Central
Universidad de
Santiago
Unión
Latinoamericana
República
HOTEL CONDE
ANSUREZ
ESTACIÓN
CENTRAL
TERMINAL
DE BUSES
SANTIAGO
TERMINAL
DE BUSES
ALAMEDA
TERMINAL DE
BUSES SAN
BORJA
JUAN DE BARROS
MAPOCHO
ANDES
MARTINEZ DE ROZAS
ALEJANDRO
FIERRO
EDISON
SAN PABLO
SANTO DOMINGO
AVENIDA NORTE
CATEDRAL
COMPAÑIA
ROSAS
HUÉRFANOS
AVENIDA PORTALES
AVENIDA DIEGO PORTALES
MONEDA
ERASMO ESCALA
ROMERO
AVENIDA SUR
AVENIDA ECUADOR
LIBERTADOR GENERAL BERNARDO O'HIGGINS
THOMPSON
SANFUENTES
SAZIE
GRAJALES
GORBEA
TOESCA
GAY
CINCO DE ABRIL
TACNA
LISPERGUER
ARICA
EBNER
BISMARCK
ANTONIO
FIGUEROA
ROBLES
GENERAL BARBOZA
VILLASANA
LOURDES
VICUÑA
RIVAS
F. LOBOS
PATRICIO LYNCH
CORDOVA Y
CORONEL
SAN ENRIQUE
HERRERA
LIBERTAD
YUNGAY
RAFAEL SOTOMAYOR
CUETO
MATUCANA
CHACABUCO
MAIPU
REYES
GARCIA
BULNES
GENERAL
AVENIDA RICARDO CUMMING
CRUHAGA
MONTT
SANTIAGO
VELASQUEZ
AVENIDA PONIENTE
GENERAL APOSTOL
SAGREDO
DIAZ
AVENIDA
ACACIAS
ROBERTO OPAZO
AVENIDA DEL MUSEO
AVENIDA DEL INSTITUTO
AVENIDA LAS
SOPHORAS
LAS
AVENIDA
R. SOTOMAYOR
LOS MUERMOS
BERNAL DEL MERCADO
F. REICH
SAN BORJA
DOLORES
JOTABECHE
RUIZ TAGLE
NICASIO RETAMALES
AVENIDA EXPOSICION
CONFERENCIA
SAN ALFONSO
BASCUÑAN GUERRERO
UNIÓN AMERICANA
MOLINA
ABATE
ESPAÑA
AVENIDA
REPÚBLICA
ECHAURREN
AVENIDA
CLUB HÍPICO
MOON

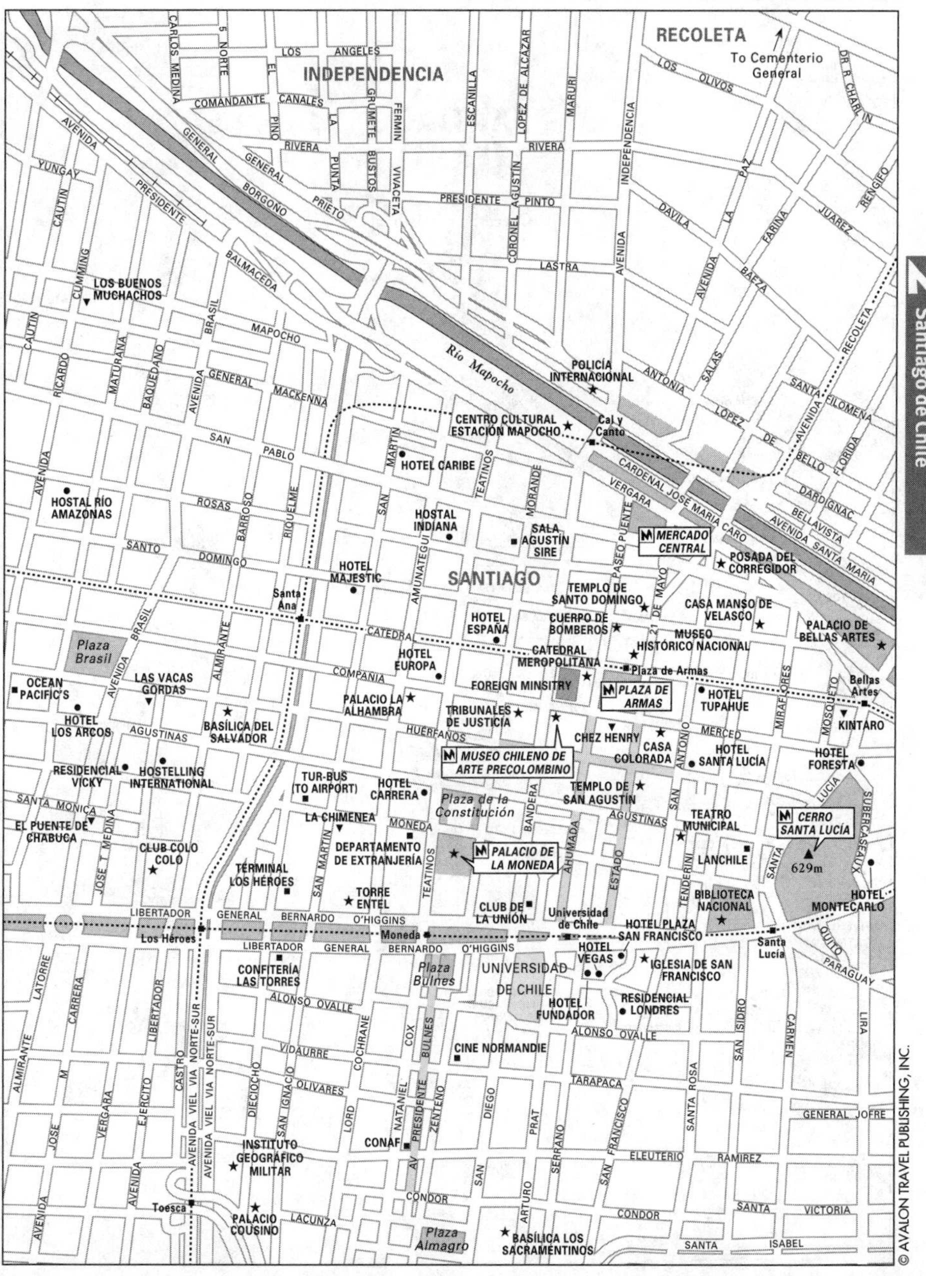

Santiago de Chile

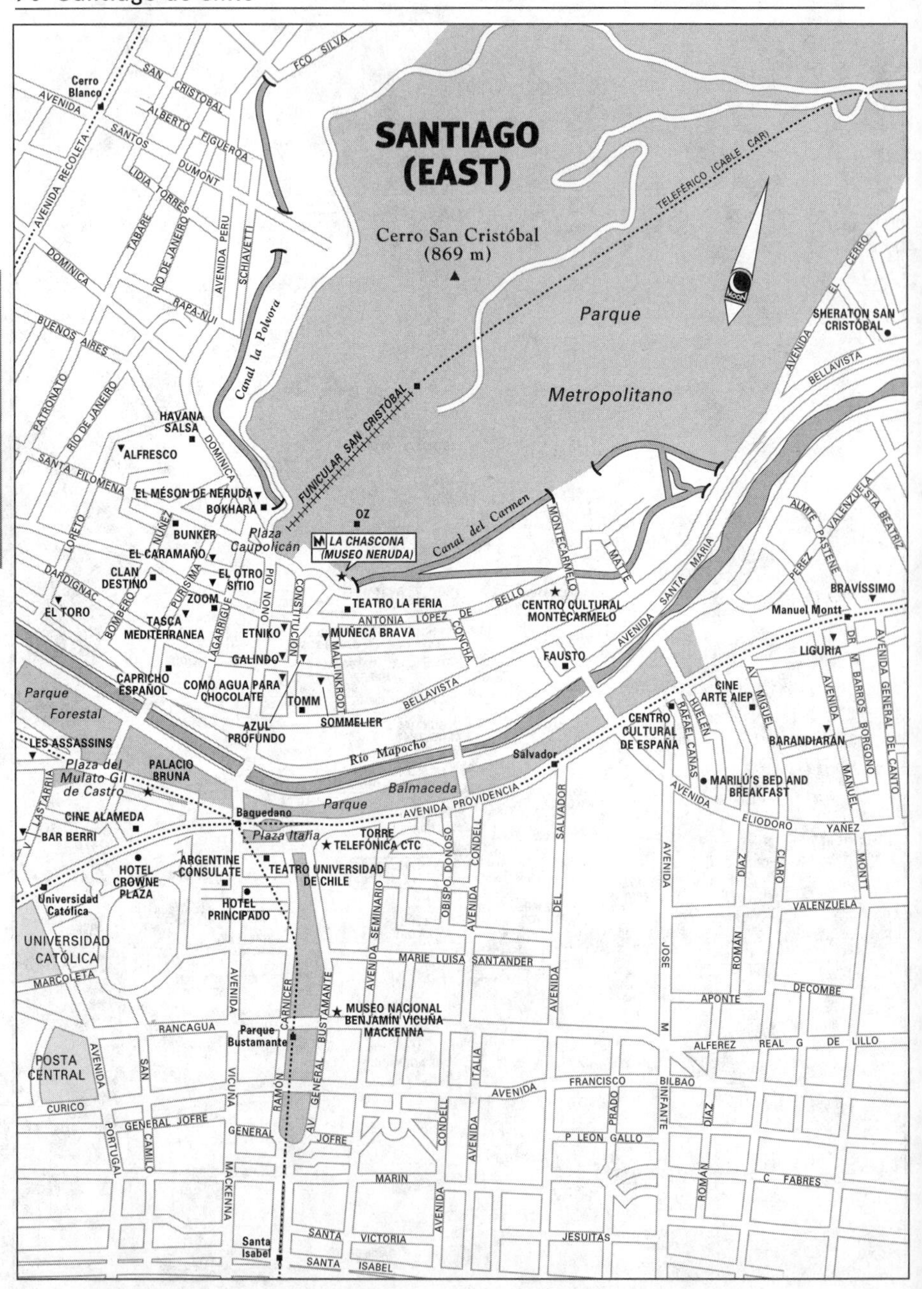
SANTIAGO (EAST)
Cerro San Cristóbal (869 m)
Parque Metropolitano
TELEFÉRICO (CABLE CAR)
FUNICULAR SAN CRISTÓBAL
Canal la Polvora
Canal del Carmen
Río Mapocho
Parque Forestal
Parque Balmaceda
Plaza Caupolicán
Plaza del Mulato Gil de Castro
Plaza Italia
LA CHASCONA (MUSEO NERUDA)
SHERATON SAN CRISTÓBAL
HAVANA SALSA
ALFRESCO
EL MÉSON DE NERUDA
BOKHARA
OZ
BUNKER
EL CARAMAÑO
CLAN DESTINO
EL OTRO SITIO
ZOOM
EL TORO
TASCA MEDITERRANEA
TEATRO LA FERIA
CENTRO CULTURAL MONTECARMELO
ETNIKO
MUÑECA BRAVA
GALINDO
FAUSTO
CAPRICHO ESPAÑOL
COMO AGUA PARA CHOCOLATE
TOMM
SOMMELIER
AZUL PROFUNDO
BRAVÍSSIMO
Manuel Montt
LIGURIA
CINE ARTE AIEP
CENTRO CULTURAL DE ESPAÑA
BARANDIARÁN
Salvador
MARILÚ'S BED AND BREAKFAST
LES ASSASSINS
PALACIO BRUNA
CINE ALAMEDA
Baquedano
BAR BERRI
TORRE TELEFÓNICA CTC
HOTEL CROWNE PLAZA
ARGENTINE CONSULATE
TEATRO UNIVERSIDAD DE CHILE
Universidad Católica
HOTEL PRINCIPADO
UNIVERSIDAD CATÓLICA
MUSEO NACIONAL BENJAMÍN VICUÑA MACKENNA
Parque Bustamante
POSTA CENTRAL
Santa Isabel
Cerro Blanco
FCO SILVA
SAN CRISTOBAL
AVENIDA
ALBERTO FIGUEROA
SANTOS DUMONT
LIDIA TORRES
AVENIDA RECOLETA
TABARE
RIO DE JANEIRO
AVENIDA PERU
SCHIAVETTI
DOMINICA
RAPA-NUI
BUENOS AIRES
PATRONATO
SANTA FILOMENA
LORETO
NUÑEZ
DARDIGNAC
BOMBERO
PURISIMA
LAGARRIGUE
PIO NONO
CONSTITUCION
MALLINKRODT
ANTONIA LOPEZ DE BELLO
CONCHA
BELLAVISTA
MONTECARMELO
MATTE
AVENIDA SANTA MARIA
AVENIDA EL CERRO
ALMTE PASTENE
VALENZUELA
STA BEATRIZ
PEREZ
DR M BARROS BORGOÑO
AVENIDA GENERAL DEL CANTO
AVENIDA MANUEL
AV MIGUEL CLARO
HUELEN
RAFAEL CAÑAS
AVENIDA ELIODORO YAÑEZ
MONT
LASTARRIA
AVENIDA PROVIDENCIA
AVENIDA SEMINARIO
OBISPO DONOSO
AVENIDA CONDELL
AVENIDA DEL SALVADOR
AVENIDA JOSE M INFANTE
DIAZ
ROMAN
VALENZUELA
MARIE LUISA SANTANDER
DECOMBE
APONTE
MARCOLETA
RANCAGUA
AVENIDA VICUÑA MACKENNA
RAMON CARNICER
AV GENERAL BUSTAMANTE
ALFEREZ REAL G DE LILLO
AVENIDA ITALIA
AVENIDA FRANCISCO BILBAO
PRADO
AVENIDA SAN CAMILO
CURICO
PORTUGAL
GENERAL JOFRE
P LEON GALLO
MARIN
C FABRES
SANTA VICTORIA
JESUITAS
SANTA ISABEL
Santiago de Chile

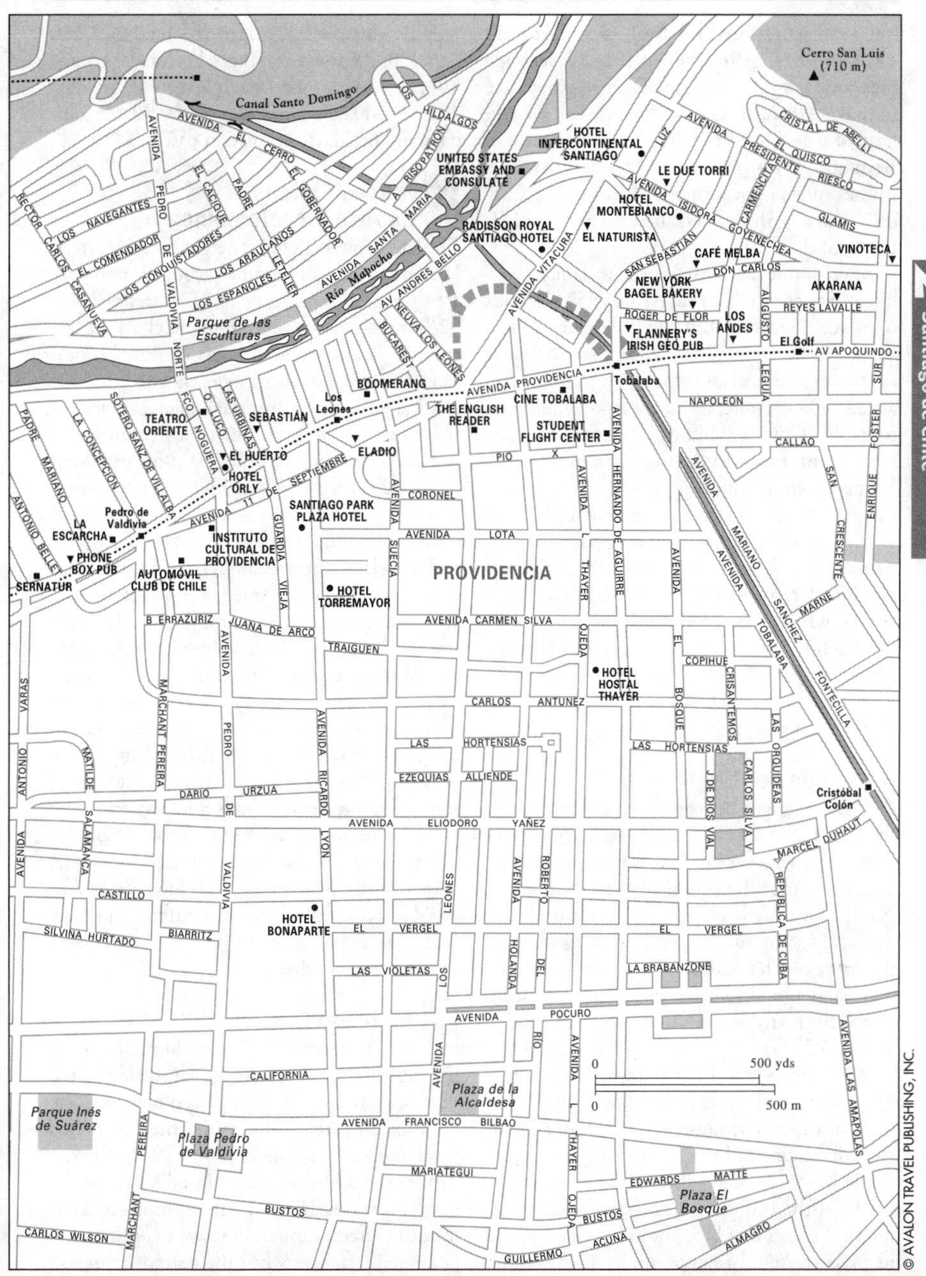

Santiago de Chile

but royalists restored the Real Audiencia from 1814 to 1817. After the battle of Chacabuco that same year, the Cabildo of Santiago met here to make Argentine General José de San Martín head of state, but San Martín declined in favor of Bernardo O'Higgins. After President Manuel Bulnes moved government offices to the Casa de la Moneda, the building became municipal offices and then a museum.

After a professional makeover, this once moribund museum (Plaza de Armas 951, tel. 02/6330462, bdevose@dibam.cl) deserves a visit. Thematically, its collections encompass Mapuche silverwork, colonial and republican furniture and art, material folklore, textiles, weapons, and photography. Chronologically, it traces Chile's development from indigenous times through Spanish colonial rule, the subsequent establishment of church and state, collapse of the Spanish empire, the early republic and its 19th century expansion, the oligarchy that ruled parliament, and the failed reforms that resulted in the 1973 coup—when the story abruptly ends.

Also hosting occasional special exhibits, the Museo is open 10 A.M.–6 P.M. daily except Monday; admission costs US$1 except Sunday, when it's free.

Museo de Santiago

Perhaps Santiago's best-preserved colonial house, the Casa Colorada was home to Mateo de Toro y Zambrano, who became Chile's interim governor, at age 83, after the colonial governor resigned. Named for its reddish paint, it hosted both José de San Martín and Bernardo O'Higgins after the battle of Chacabuco (1817), and the famous mercenary Lord Cochrane later lived here. Abandoned for many years, it underwent restoration after 1977.

While its style is colonial, only the two-story Merced façade is truly original, with its forged-iron balconies. The museum itself chronicles the city's development from its pre-Hispanic origins in the Mapocho valley through its founding by Valdivia, the evolution of colonial society, the political events that brought independence, and its modern transformation under 19th-century mayor Benjamín Vicuña Mackenna.

The Museo de Santiago (Merced 860, tel. 02/6330723, www.munistgo.cl/colorada) is open 10 A.M.–6 P.M. weekdays except Monday, 10 A.M.–5 P.M. Saturday, and 11 A.M.–2 P.M. Sundays and holidays. Admission costs US$1.

Museo Chileno de Arte Precolombino

The late Chilean architect Sergio Larraín García-Moreno donated a lifetime's acquisitions to create this exceptional museum (Bandera 361, tel. 02/6887348, www.precolombino.cl) in the late colonial Real Casa de Aduana (Royal Customs House, 1805). Following independence, the neoclassical building became the Biblioteca Nacional (National Library) and then the Tribunales de Justicia (Law Courts) until a 1968 fire destroyed most of its interior and archives. The two-story structure has twin patios separated by a broad staircase leading to the upstairs exhibits.

The permanent collections from Mesoamerica (Mexico and Central America), and the Central and Southern Andes are impressive; there are smaller displays on the Caribbean, the Amazon, and Andean textiles. Particularly notable are the carved wooden *chemamull*, larger-than-life-size Mapuche funerary statues. The museum also possesses Aguateca's Stele 6, from a Late Classic Maya site in Guatemala's Petén lowlands that's suffered severe depredations from looters.

The Museo Chileno de Arte Precolombino is open 10 A.M.–6 P.M. daily except Monday; it closes during Semana Santa (Holy Week) and on May 1, September 18, Christmas, and New Year's Eve. Admission costs US$3, but is free for students and children.

Mercado Central

In 1817, Bernardo O'Higgins himself shifted the disorderly market on the south side of the Plaza de Armas to an area once known as "the Dominican garbage dump" on the Mapocho's south bank, a few blocks north. When fire destroyed the informal market installations on the new "Plaza de Abasto" in 1864, municipal authorities hired Manuel Aldunate to create more permanent facilities, but the current structure (1872) is mainly the work of Fermín Vivaceta.

Shop additions fronting on the street have concealed the original façade except on the Ismael Valdés Vergara side, where it faces the river; there are entrances, however, on San Pablo, Paseo Puente, and 21 de Mayo. From the interior, the wrought-iron superstructure, embellished with the Chilean flag's recurring lone star, provides an airy setting for merchants to display their fresh fruit, vegetables, and seafood—according to food and travel writer Robb Walsh, "a display of fishes and shellfish so vast and unfamiliar that I felt I was observing the marine life of another planet."

Lunching and people-watching at tables set among the produce has become a popular tourist pastime, but Santiaguinos enjoy the market as much as foreigners. The smallish restaurants on the periphery are cheaper and almost as good as the two or three that monopolize the prime central sites.

BARRIO CÍVICO AND VICINITY

Straddling the Alameda, several blocks southwest of the Plaza de Armas, the Barrio Cívico is the country's political and administrative center. Facing the **Plaza de la Constitución,** the recently repainted, late-colonial **Palacio de La Moneda** (see below) is the locus of presidential authority. At 10 A.M. on even-numbered days, there's a presidential changing-of-the-guard ceremony here.

In a development that rankles Pinochet diehards, a dignified statue of former President Salvador Allende overlooks the Plaza's southeast corner, with a plaque inscribed with words from his last radio address: "I have faith in Chile and her destiny," September 11, 1973.

Across the street, at Moneda and Morandé, the **Intendencia de Santiago** (1914–1916) features an attractive corner entrance and a spectacular interior cupola. One block east of the Plaza, fronting on Moneda, the 19th-century **Iglesia de las Agustinas** (restored in 1994) replaced earlier temples destroyed by earthquakes. French architect Emilio Jecquier designed the flatiron-style **Bolsa de Comercio** (Stock Exchange, La Bolsa 84), begun in 1914 but delayed when World War I disrupted the arrival of materials from New York. Immediately south, reached by a cobbled passageway but fronting on the Alameda, the members-only **Club de la Unión** (1925) gave stockbrokers a place to schmooze on their lunch hours.

Palacio de la Moneda, Centro Cívico

Palacio de la Moneda

Never intended as the seat of government, the neoclassical Moneda became the presidential palace in 1846, when Manuel Bulnes moved his residence and offices to the former colonial mint. It made global headlines in 1973, when the Chilean air force strafed and bombed it in General Pinochet's coup against constitutional President Salvador Allende, who shot himself to death before he could be taken prisoner.

Around 1730, during an economic depression, local government requested the Spanish crown to establish a local mint. But Madrid, itself short of resources, designated businessman Francisco García Huidobro as treasurer of a mint at Huérfanos and Morandé—perhaps one of the earliest privatizations on record. When that mint proved inadequate, architect Joaquín Toesca began work on a new facility in 1784, but died six years before its completion in 1805.

Pinochet's regime restored the building to Toesca's original design by 1981, but it's no longer the presidential residence. Ricardo Lagos, the first Socialist elected President since Allende, has opened the main passageway for one-way public traffic from the Plaza de la Constitución entrance to the Plaza de la Libertad exit, 10 A.M.–6 P.M. weekdays only.

For a longer guided tour, contact the Dirección Administrativa del Palacio de La Moneda (tel. 02/6714103) at its office beneath Plaza de la Constitución, entered from Morandé. Theoretically, arranging a visit takes nearly three weeks, but an in-person request can accelerate the process. Intending visitors must show passports and complete a short application form.

CERRO SANTA LUCÍA AND VICINITY

East of Paseo Ahumada and north of the Alameda, the promontory called Welén by the Mapuche was the place where Pedro de Valdivia held out against the indigenous forces that threatened to expel the Spaniards from the Mapocho valley. Nearly three centuries later, in 1822, the Scotswoman María Graham marveled at the view of:

> *. . . the city, its gardens, churches and its magnificent bridge all lit up by the rays of the setting sun . . . what pen or pencil can impart a thousandth part of the sublime beauty of sunset on the Andes?*

It took visionary mayor Benjamín Vicuña Mackenna to realize Santa Lucía's potential, as his efforts—along with convict labor and donations from wealthy citizens—transformed a barren quarry into an urban Eden with more than 60 hectares of gardens, fountains and statuary, including his own tomb.

From the summit, approached by meandering footpaths and reached by a steep climb to a tiny parapet, there are stupendous views of the Andes—at least on a rare clear day—and panoramas of the city and Cerro San Cristóbal. A lower but broader terrace offers less panoramic but almost equally impressive views toward Providencia and the Andes.

Royalists built **Fuerte Hidalgo** (1816) toward the park's north end to defend against Chilean revolutionaries. On its lower northeastern slope, the recent **Jardín Japonés** (Japanese Garden) is a notable addition; along the Alameda, look for the tile mural of Nobel Prize poetess Gabriela Mistral.

Fenced except around its lowest periphery and steepest slope, Cerro Santa Lucía has two main entrances: from the Alameda just east of Plaza Vicuña Mackenna, where twin staircases climb around the fountains of **Plaza Neptuno,** and by a cobbled road from the east end of Agustinas. There's also a modern glass elevator, at the east end of Huérfanos, that's often out of service. In an exaggerated effort to improve security, authorities require all visitors to sign in (as if muggers would do so), but the park's not really a dangerous place.

Hours are 9 A.M.–8 P.M. daily, but the best introduction is a guided tour (English and Spanish) starting from its municipal tourist-office branch at 11 A.M. Thursday. Tours include Vicuña Mackenna's tomb and the still-functioning gun emplacement (several years ago, authorities halted the customary midday cannon shot because of neighbors' complaints, but broader public pressure restored the tradition at a lower decibel level).

© WAYNE BERNHARDSON

view of the Andean front range from Cerro Santa Lucía

Between Cerro Santa Lucía and Paseo Ahumada, the most imposing landmark is the classicist **Biblioteca Nacional** (National Library, 1914–1927) facing the Alameda between MacIver and Miraflores. Two blocks north, the neoclassical **Teatro Municipal** (Municipal Theater, 1857) has seen performances by Sarah Bernhardt, Igor Stravinsky, Plácido Domingo, Anna Pavlova, and the Chilean classical pianist Claudio Arrau.

BARRIO PARÍS LONDRES AND VICINITY

South of the Alameda, dating from 1618, the major landmark is the **Iglesia y Convento de San Francisco** (Alameda 834), Chile's oldest colonial building and a survivor of repeated fires and earthquakes; the former convent is also home to the **Museo de Arte Colonial,** an ecclesiastical colonial art collection (see below).

Until the early 1920s, the Franciscans controlled much of this area, but a financial crisis forced them to sell 30,000 square meters to developer Walter Lihn. Lihn demolished several buildings and patios, and their gardens, but architects Roberto Araya and Ernesto Holzmann created an intimately livable neighborhood of meandering cobbled streets in their place.

Betraying the neighborhood's legacy, the house at **Londres 38** was a torture center during Pinochet's dictatorship. Two blocks west of Iglesia San Francisco, the **Casa Central de la Universidad de Chile** (1863–1872), the state university's main campus, stretches along the Alameda.

Iglesia y Convento de San Francisco

Pedro de Valdivia himself established the Ermita del Socorro to house an image of the Virgen del Socorro—to which he credited Santiago's survival from Mapuche attacks—that he had brought to Chile. In 1554, in exchange for 12 city lots, the Franciscan order built a church to house the image, but an earthquake destroyed the original structure in 1583. After finishing the present church in 1618, they built a pair of cloisters and gradually added patios, gardens, a refectory, and other structures. Earthquakes toppled the original towers in 1643 and 1751, but Fermín Vivaceta's 19th-century clock tower has withstood every shock since. The church's interior is notable for its Mudéjar details and carved cypress doors.

Over four and a half centuries, the Franciscans have kept faith with Valdivia by continuing to host the Virgen del Socorro. In addition, their **Museo de Arte Colonial** boasts 42 separate canvases, representing the life of St. Francis of Assisi, from the late 17th-century Cuzco school. A later wall-size painting chronicles the Franciscan lineage and their patrons.

The Museo de Arte Colonial (Londres 4, tel. 02/6398737) is open 10 A.M.–1:30 P.M. and 3–6 P.M. Tuesday– Saturday, 10 A.M.–2 P.M. Sundays and holidays. Admission costs US$1 for adults, US$.50 for children.

BARRIO LASTARRIA AND VICINITY

East of Cerro Santa Lucía, between Parque Forestal and the Alameda, Barrio Lastarria is a neighborhood of narrow streets and cul-de-sacs that's home to several intimate restaurants and bars.

The barrio's main axis is its namesake street José Victorino Lastarria, whose **Plaza del Mulato Gil de Castro** is an adaptive reuse uniting several early-20th-century buildings into a commercial/cultural cluster with two notable museums: the **Museo Arqueológico de Santiago** and the eye-catching **Museo de Artes Visuales.** Between Rosal and Merced, Lastarria has become an attractive pedestrian mall.

To the north, the Mapocho's banks and floodplain were home to slums and rubbish dumps until the early 20th century, when mayor Enrique Cousiño redeveloped it as the **Parque Forestal,** stretching from Estación Mapocho on the west to the Pío Nono bridge on the east. Shaded with mature trees and dotted with statues and fountains, it's a verdant refuge from summer's midday heat.

Toward the west, directly north of Cerro Santa Lucía, stands the **Museo Nacional de Bellas Artes,** the city's traditional fine-arts museum. South across the Alameda, toward downtown, is the central campus of the **Universidad Católica** (Catholic University, 1913).

Museo Arqueológico de Santiago

With its excellent but almost unchanging exhibits on Chile's indigenous peoples from colonial times to the present, Santiago's deceptively named archaeological museum—"ethnohistorical" would be more accurate—is worthwhile for first-time visitors only.

Within the Plaza del Mulato Gil de Castro complex, the Museo Arqueológico (Lastarria 321, tel. 02/6383502) is open 10:30 A.M.–2 P.M. daily except Sunday, 3:30–7 P.M. weekdays only. Admission is free.

Museo de Artes Visuales

With a permanent collection of 650 pieces by 250 contemporary Chilean artists, among them Roberto Matta and Alfredo Jaar, Santiago's visual-arts museum (Lastarria 307, tel. 02/6649397, www.mavi.cl), also in the Plaza del Mulato Gil complex, opened in early 2001. About 140 of these pieces, ranging from engravings to paintings, photographs, and sculptures, are on display at any one time. Flawless lighting accentuates each piece's individual qualities in its half-dozen spacious rooms, which feature high ceilings and polished wooden floors.

Privately owned and financed, the Museo de Artes Visuales is open 10:30 A.M.–6:30 P.M. daily except Monday. Admission costs US$1.50 for adults except Sunday, when it's free; it's US$.50 for children 8–12.

Museo de Bellas Artes

Built for the centennial of Chile's independence and fashioned after Paris's Petit Palais, Santiago's neoclassical fine-arts museum is the pride of Parque Forestal. Collections range from colonial and religious art to nearly contemporary figurative and abstract works by artists like the recently deceased Roberto Matta. It also has a sample of French, Italian, and Dutch painting, and prestigious special exhibits. While Bellas Artes is a traditional museum, its ambitious website is making the works of 2,000 Chilean artists accessible to world in a "museum without walls."

The Museo de Bellas Artes (José Miguel de La Barra s/n, tel. 02/6330655, www.mnba.cl) is open 10 A.M.–6 P.M. weekdays except Monday, noon–4:30 P.M. weekends and holidays. Admission costs US$1; children pay half.

BARRIO BRASIL AND VICINITY

West of the Vía Norte Sur, Barrio Brasil was a prestigious early-20th-century residential area that fell upon hard times, but has recently rebounded without losing its character. The best way to approach the barrio is the Huérfanos pedestrian suspension bridge that crosses the Vía Norte Sur to an area where recently constituted private universities have rehabbed buildings, salvaged libraries and built collections, and introduced a youthful vigor. It's also good for moderately priced accommodations and food.

The barrio's focus is its lovingly landscaped namesake **Plaza Brazil.** Dating from 1892, its most impressive landmark may be the neo-Gothic **Basílica del Salvador** (Huérfanos 1781), if only because it's still standing after the 1985 earthquake. Dating from 1926, the most idiosyncratic building is the former **Club Colo Colo** (Cienfuegos 41), an erstwhile private residence whose grinning gargoyles and smiling skulls, jutting out from its façade, always attract attention.

On Santiago Centro's western edge, beyond Barrio Brasil proper, wooded **Parque Quinta Normal** offers relief from a densely built area and is home to several museums. The other main attraction is the **Museo de la Solidaridad Salvador Allende,** a modern-art collection and cultural center that occupies the former **Escuela Normal No. 1 de Niñas** (Girls' Normal School, Herrera 360).

Parque Quinta Normal

At the western edge of Santiago Centro, Parque Quinta Normal is a traditional open space whose 40 hectares constituted the city's first de facto botanical garden. It also provides playgrounds, soccer fields, tennis courts, skating rinks, and pools, and a cluster of museums.

The most notable museum is the **Museo Nacional de Historia Natural** (Natural History Museum), a research facility that also has public exhibits on archaeology, ethnography, physical anthropology, mineralogy, paleontology, botany, and zoology. Dating from 1830, when the government contracted French naturalist Claude Gay to inventory Chile's natural resources, the Museo de Historia Natural (tel. 02/6804615) is open 10 A.M.–6 P.M. daily except Monday. Admission costs US$1 for adults, US$.50 for kids, but is free Sundays and holidays except January 1, Easter Sunday, May 1, September 18–19, November 1, and December 25, when it's closed.

Parque Quinta Normal's main entrance is on Matucana at the west end of Compañía, with other gateways on Avenida Portales, Santo Domingo, and Apostól Santiago; it now has its own Metro station. Grounds are open 8 A.M.–8:30 P.M. daily except Monday.

Museo de la Solidaridad Salvador Allende

Many of the works in this contemporary-art museum, created in 1971 with donations by artists who identified with Chile's Marxist experiment, spent 17 years of military dictatorship in anonymous storage. Among those represented are Roberto Matta, Joan Miró, David Alfaro Siqueiros, and Alexander Calder; despite the artists' leftist sympathies, few of those works are explicitly political.

Since the return to democracy, the Museo (Herrera 360, tel. 02/6817542, www.mssa.cl) has settled into permanent quarters in the former Escuela Normal No. 1 de Niñas (Girls' Normal School) near Parque Quinta Normal. Hours are 10 A.M.–7 P.M. daily except Monday; admission is free.

Palacio Cousiño

South of the Alameda, 19th-century Calle Dieciocho was an aristocratic area of Parisian-style mansions long before the oligarchy moved to the eastern suburbs. One of its keystone families was the Cousiños, Portuguese immigrants who made fortunes in wine and mining.

Funds for the Palacio Cousiño (1878) came from the estate of Luis Cousiño, an art collector who inherited his father's mining fortune (Luis Cousiño died young, but his widow Isidora Goyenechea continued construction). The three-story house has marble staircases, a music hall, winter garden, and even a one-person elevator, the country's first.

The Palacio remained in family hands until

1941, when the city purchased it for a museum and as a guesthouse for high-profile visitors like Charles DeGaulle, Marshal Tito, and Golda Meir. A 1968 fire, which destroyed the 3rd-floor interior, prevented England's Queen Elizabeth II from spending the night on her state visit.

The Palacio Cousiño (Dieciocho 438, tel. 02/6985063, www.palaciocousino.co.cl) is open 9:30 A.M.–1:30 P.M. daily and 2:30–5 P.M. weekdays only. Admission, including guided tours in Spanish or English, costs US$3 for adults, US$.80 for children.

PROVIDENCIA AND VICINITY

At the east end of the Alameda, lively **Plaza Italia** (formally known as Plaza Baquedano) marks the boundary of the *comuna* of Providencia, the westernmost of the affluent eastern suburbs that also include Las Condes, Vitacura, and Ñuñoa. While this mostly staid, middle-class to upper-middle-class area has shopping malls that look like something straight out of the San Fernando Valley, it also has Bohemian enclaves like Barrio Bellavista (Santiago's main restaurant and nightlife area) and bar-hopper zones like Avenida Suecia. Except in compact Bellavista, points of interest are more spread out than in Santiago Centro, but public transportation is good.

From Plaza Italia, the northbound Puente Pío Nono (Pío Nono bridge) crosses the Mapocho to **Barrio Bellavista** (see below for more detail). The area's most conspicuous landmark is the 31-story **Torre Telefónica CTC** (Avenida Providencia 111), the company headquarters in the form of a 140-meter cell phone!

South of Plaza Italia, Avenida Vicuña Mackenna separates the *comunas* of Santiago Centro, on the one hand, and Providencia and Ñuñoa, on the other. On the Providencia side, the **Museo Nacional Benjamín Vicuña Mackenna** (Avenida Vicuña Mackenna 94, tel. 02/2229642) honors the mayor, historian, journalist, and diplomat responsible for the capital's 1870s modernization. Hours are 10 A.M.–6:10 P.M. weekdays and 10 A.M.–1 P.M. Saturday; admission costs US$1 for adults, half that for children and seniors.

On the Mapocho's north bank between the Padre Letelier and Pedro de Valdivia bridges, the open-air **Parque de las Esculturas** (Avenida Santa María 2201, tel. 02/3407303) showcases abstract works by contemporary Chilean sculptors. Open 10 A.M.–7 P.M. daily, it also has an enclosed gallery with rotating exhibitions.

BARRIO BELLAVISTA AND VICINITY

At the foot of massive Cerro San Cristóbal, compact Bellavista is a walker's delight. In the daytime, Santiaguinos cross the Pío Nono bridge to stroll its leafy streets, parks, and plazas and enjoy modest lunch specials at some of the city's most innovative restaurants. At night, they crowd the same places for elaborate dinners before a night at nearby bars, discos, salsa clubs, theaters, and other diversions. Daytime visitors, by the way, may not even realize that this is a nightlife center—most dance clubs, for instance, do not *open* until 1 A.M. or so, and few have prominent signs.

While most visitors see Bellavista as a single neighborhood, **Avenida Pío Nono** is a dividing line between the two *comunas* that comprise the barrio—rough-edged Recoleta to the west and modish Providencia to the east. There's more style than substance to this, as security-obsessed Providencia makes more conspicuous efforts to prevent auto burglaries and other petty crime in what is, for the most part, a safe area.

On weekends, Pío Nono itself is a frenetic blend of crafts market, cheap sidewalk restaurants, and beer joints. While not so bad as that might sound, it's less appealing than the barrio's perpendicular and parallel side streets.

For a notion of Bellavista's best, relax on a bench at **Plazuela Camilo Mori,** a small triangular plaza at Antonia López de Bello and Constitución. Walking north, turn into the cul-de-sac at Márquez de la Plata 0192, where poet Pablo Neruda lived at the house he called **La Chascona,** now a museum (see below for more detail). A short walk to the northwest, **Plaza Caupolicán** is the main entry point to the 722-hectare **Parque Metropolitano,** a hillside and hilltop public park. A funicular railway carries visitors past the city zoo to the summit, whose terrace offers exceptional views on clear days; from there, a *teleférico* (cable gondola) connects the park to eastern Providencia.

On the Recoleta side, at the north end of Avenida La Paz, famous figures from Chile's past are among the two million who repose in the **Cementerio General** (General Cemetery, 1897).

La Chascona (Museo Neruda)

Inconspicuous from the street side of its cul-de-sac, Pablo Neruda's hillside house is by no means extravagant—in fact, it may be the most conventional of his three houses (the others, also open for visits, are in Valparaíso and the beach community of Isla Negra). Opposite the house, a small amphitheater tucked into the slope is an ideal complement to the residence, restored since its military sacking in 1973 (Neruda, a committed Salvador Allende supporter, died only about a month after the coup).

The Fundación Neruda (Márquez de La Plata 0192, tel. 02/7378712, www.fundacionneruda.org) offers hour-long guided tours on a drop-in basis, from 10 A.M.–6 P.M. daily except Monday. Tours cost US$3 for adults, US$1.50 for children.

Cementerio General

Among the cemetery's Gothic, Greek, Moorish, and Egyptian-style sepulchers, all but two of Chile's presidents are interred—Bernardo O'Higgins's remains rest in the Alameda's Altar de la Patria and Gabriel González Videla lies in his native La Serena. Other notable figures include diplomat Orlando Letelier (killed by a car bomb in Washington, D.C. under orders from a Pinochet subordinate), Venezuelan-born educator Andrés Bello, and cultural icon, folksinger, and songwriter Violeta Parra. Nobel Prize poets Gabriela Mistral and Pablo Neruda originally rested here as well, but Mistral's body was moved to her Elqui valley birthplace and Neruda's to his Isla Negra beach residence.

Salvador Allende moved in the other direction—with the end of the Pinochet dictatorship, after 17 years in Viña del Mar, he regained his freedom to travel to a monumental memorial here. Another indicator of change is sculptor Francisco Gazitúa's *Rostros* (Faces), memorializing the regime's victims.

OUTLYING SIGHTS

Several points of interest are scattered elsewhere around town.

Los Dominicos

One of few survivals from colonial Las Condes, when it was bucolic farmland, the **Iglesia y Convento San Vicente Ferrer de los Dominicos** sits on lands that Pedro de Valdivia himself seized from Mapuche cacique Apoquindo for Valdivia's mistress Inés de Suárez. Willed to the Dominican order by a subsequent owner, the property deteriorated during more than a century of litigation, but the Dominicans managed to add its twin Byzantine domes in 1847.

Alongside the church, where Avenida Apoquindo dead-ends at Padre Hurtado, **Los Graneros del Alba** (Avenida Apoquindo 9085) is Santiago's biggest crafts market, also popular for its country cuisine and impromptu entertainment. Popularly known as "Los Dominicos," it's open 10 A.M.–7:30 P.M. daily all year. Several buses out the Alameda, Avenida Providencia, and Avenida Apoquindo go directly to the church and market; the quickest alternative is Línea 1 to Metro Escuela Militar and then either the bus or a taxi (about US$3.50) out Avenida Apoquindo.

Estadio Nacional

South of Providencia and east of Santiago Centro, middle-class Ñuñoa has few landmarks but enjoys a vigorous cultural life on and around **Plaza Ñuñoa,** thanks partly to nearby campuses of the Universidad Católica and the Universidad de Chile.

With the Andean front range in the distance, Ñuñoa's one unforgettable landmark is the **Estadio Nacional** (National Stadium, Avenida Grecia and Campo de Deportes). First famous for the 1962 World Cup, it became infamous as an impromptu prison camp after the 1973 coup, when some 7,000 Allende sympathizers (and suspected sympathizers) were incarcerated. Many were tortured and more than a few were executed (including folksinger Victor Jara and U.S. citizens Charles Horman and Frank Teruggi). Today, the stadium is once again the site of the country's most important soccer matches.

Frequent buses to Plaza Ñuñoa leave from Plaza Italia (Plaza Baquedano), while Metrobús make a direct connection from Estación Salvador on Línea 1 of the Metro. The Estadio Nacional is within reasonable walking distance of Línea 5's Ñuble station.

Viña Cousiño Macul

In the southeastern *comuna* of Peñalolén, Cousiño Macul is one of Chile's oldest wineries, in the same family since 1856 since Matías Cousiño purchased the vineyards. Its *bodegas* (cellars) and Museo del Vino (Wine Museum) are open for English-language tours weekdays at 11 A.M., with Spanish-language tours weekdays at 4 P.M. and Saturday at 11 A.M. Tours are free, but tastings of estate wines, held in an attractive bar cum sales room, cost US$2 per glass (reserve wines US$3 per glass). The house produces cabernet, merlot, chardonnay, sauvignon blanc, and Riesling.

Bus No. 210 from the Alameda goes within walking distance of Viña Cousiño Macul (Avenida Quilín 7100, tel. 02/3514135, fax 02/3514181, www.cousinomacul.cl, sschotte@cousinomacul.cl).

Parque por la Paz

The most subtly eloquent memorial to the Pinochet dictatorship's victims, Peñalolén's Parque por la Paz (Park for Peace) occupies the grounds of Villa Grimaldi, an isolated mansion that was the principal torture center for the Directorio de Inteligencia Nacional (DINA), General Manuel Contreras's ruthless intelligence service. Before it closed, more than 200 political prisoners died here, and many more were interrogated and tortured.

In the regime's final days, the military bulldozed nearly every building to destroy evidence, but the nonprofit Fundación Parque por la Paz has transformed the property into a pilgrimage site that honors and remembers the victims without any overt political posturing. It has permanently locked the original street-side gates, by which prisoners entered the grounds, with a declaration that it is "never to be opened again."

Parque por la Paz, in the 8300 block of José Arrieta, is open 11 A.M.–8:30 P.M. daily except Monday; admission is free. Several bus lines pass nearby: No. 242 from Avenida Providencia, No. 337 from Estación Central and the Alameda, and No. 433 from Plaza Italia.

Chip Travel (Avenida Santa María 227, Oficina 12, tel. 02/7775376, www.chip.cl, vchip@rdc.cl) is the only operator offering alternative "Human Rights Legacy" tours that take in Parque por la Paz, the Cementerio General, the Fundación Pinochet, and the Escuela Militar.

Viña Concha y Toro

In suburban Pirque, Viña Concha y Toro (Victoria Subercaseaux 210, tel. 02/4765269, www.conchaytoro.com) offers guided English-language tours with tasting (US$6 pp) of its vineyards, grounds, cellars and museum at 11:30 A.M. and 3 P.M. weekdays, 10 A.M. and noon Saturday. Spanish-language tours take place at 10:30 A.M. and 4 P.M. weekdays, 11 A.M. Saturday, but there's a good chance a bilingual guide can handle English-speakers on these tours. While reservations are advisable, it's often possible to join an existing group that might include—who knows?—Mick Jagger, Bono, Helmut Kohl, Nicaraguan poet Ernesto Cardenal, and others who have toured the facilities.

Practicalities

ENTERTAINMENT AND EVENTS

Just as it's the center of Santiago's restaurant scene, Barrio Bellavista is the city's night life focus—in a neighborhood where most clubs don't *open* until after midnight and hardly anybody goes before 2 A.M., it's hard to believe that, during Pinochet's dictatorship, Santiaguinos endured an 11 P.M. *curfew.*

There are also nightspots in and around Santiago Centro, around Providencia's Avenida Suecia, and near Plaza Ñuñoa, in the largely middle-class borough of the same name. Many bars and dance clubs, especially gay venues, have no obvious public signs except during opening hours.

Bars

Barrio Lastarria's **Bar Berri** (Rosal 321, tel. 02/6384734) is a quiet neighborhood bar with fixed-price lunches.

A throwback to the Allende years, Barrio Brasil's **N'aitún** (Avenida Ricardo Cumming 453, tel. 02/6718410) is an activist bookstore that has an upstairs bar with basic food—sandwiches and snacks—along with folk-oriented music and political theater.

Bellavista's **La Casa en el Aire** (Antonia López de Bello 0125, tel. 02/7356680) is a direct descendent of 1960s and 1970s *peñas,* with folkloric music, storytelling, films, and the like in an alternative milieu. The consistently best rock-music locale is Plaza Ñuñoa's **La Batuta** (Jorge Washington 52, tel. 02/2747096).

North of Avenida Providencia, Avenida Suecia and cross streets are home to a swarm of theme-oriented bars that tend toward kitsch, but the drinks are good, often imaginative, and a bargain during happy hours that can last until midnight. Among them are Australian-run **Boomerang** (General Holley 2285, tel. 02/3345081) and **Brannigan's** (Avenida Suecia 035, tel. 02/2325172). Many of these places are also popular for light meals, though the food is only ordinary.

Discos and Dance Clubs

Bellavista's **Oz** (Chucre Manzur 6, tel. 02/7377066) is a techno disco and events center in a cavernous ex-warehouse on Cerro San Cristóbal's southern slope; open Thursday, Friday, and Saturday 11:30 P.M.–4:30 A.M., it collects US$12 pp cover.

Salsa is booming on Bellavista's Recoleta side, thanks to the Habana Vieja ambience at **Havana Salsa** (Dominica 142, tel. 02/7371737), but canned music is the rule.

Nightclubs

Several venerable venues hold stage and floor shows, often but not always featuring clichéd versions of Chilean culture like the *cueca,* along with typical cuisine. The most interesting is **Confitería Las Torres** (Alameda 1570, tel. 02/6986220), a magnificent 19th-century building that hosts live tango on weekends. If you can't visit Buenos Aires's Café Tortoni, this is Santiago's best option.

South of the Alameda, the garish **Los Adobes de Argomedo** (Argomedo 411, tel. 02/2222104) is a popular stop for foreign tour groups' farewell dinners, but it gets plenty of Chilean business as well. The floorshow is participatory—get ready to *cueca.*

In the same Barrio Brasil location since 1939, **Los Buenos Muchachos** (Avenida Ricardo Cumming 1031, tel. 02/6980112) seats up to a thousand people for lunch or dinner and a show. It has its own orchestra and floorshows.

Gay and Lesbian Venues

Barrio Bellavista's Recoleta side is home to most of Santiago's gay clubs. The most discreet is **Capricho Español** (Purísima 65, tel. 02/7777674), whose patrons often meet for a quiet drink and/or dinner before a night on the town.

Holding up to a thousand partygoers on Thursday, Friday, and Saturday nights is the gigantic **Bunker** (Bombero Núñez 159, tel. 02/7773760), which appeals to those who can afford the US$10-plus cover charge. A bit less central, **Fausto** (Avenida Santa María 0832, tel. 02/7771041) draws a mixed-age crowd on separate levels linked by broad staircases that encourage interaction.

Cultural Centers

The **Instituto Chileno-Norteamericano de Cultura** (Moneda 1467, tel. 02/6963215) sponsors art exhibits and other events, and has an English-language library. The most elaborate and active foreign cultural center, though, is Providencia's **Centro Cultural de España** (Avenida Providencia 927, tel. 02/2351105).

Cinema

Several multiscreen cinemas, both in Santiago Centro and outlying *comunas,* show current films, often in English with Spanish subtitles. Children's films and animated features, though, normally appear in Spanish. For locations and phone numbers, see any Santiago newspaper.

Performing Arts

Santiago has many live theater and music venues, with offerings ranging from serious classical and contemporary drama to vulgar burlesque, and from traditional folk to rock and classical; the best source of information is the daily *El Mercurio*'s entertainment section.

The landmark **Teatro Municipal** (Agustinas 794, tel. 02/3690282) is Santiago's most prestigious performing-arts venue, hosting classical music, opera, and occasional popular musicals. Only opening performances are truly formal, and Santiaguinos sometimes show up in surprisingly casual clothes.

Musicians rave about the acoustics at the **Teatro Universidad de Chile** (Avenida Providencia 043, tel. 02/6345295), best known for ballet and classical music, though it hosts the occasional rock event.

Repertory groups play Bellavista venues like **Teatro Bellavista** (Dardignac 0110, tel. 02/7356264), **Teatro El Conventillo** (Bellavista 173, tel. 02/7774164), and **Teatro La Feria** (Crucero Exeter 0250, tel. 02/7377371).

Festivals

September's patriotic holidays are an excuse for parties and parades, but the month can be contentious—September 11, the date of Pinochet's coup, usually sees disturbances around Providencia's Avenida 11 de Septiembre. September 18, **Día de la Independencia** (Independence Day), sees cheerful barbecues in the parks, but September 19's **Día del Ejército** (Armed Forces Day) is more divisive.

At the Estación Mapocho, November's 10-day **Feria de Libro** (Book Festival) draws both Chilean writers and internationally recognized authors.

SHOPPING

Santiago may not be one of the great shopping meccas, but quality handicrafts and antiques from around the country are widely available. Many visitors, of course, take home Chilean wines.

Books

The **Feria Chilena del Libro** (Huérfanos 623, tel. 02/6396758) is a chain with several branches elsewhere. For academic and antiquarian tastes, try downtown's **Librería Luis Rivano** (San Diego 119, Local 7) or Providencia's **Librería Chile Ilustrado** (Avenida Providencia 1652, tel. 02/2358145), in the same complex as the Phone Box Pub.

The English Reader (Avenida Los Leones 116, tel. 02/3347388) carries a large inventory of English-language books. Vitacura's **Librería Eduardo Albers** (Avenida Vitacura 5648, tel. 02/2185371) has a selection of guidebooks (including this one) and other general-interest books in English and German.

Music

For CDs or tapes of present and past Chilean music, try the **Feria del Disco** (Ahumada 286, tel. 02/6715290).

Handicrafts

Downtown's best souvenir shops are **Chile Típico** (Moneda 1025, Local 149, tel. 02/6965504) and **Huimpalay** (Huérfanos 1162, tel. 02/6721395), with premium prices. Cerro Santa Lucía's **Centro de Exposición de Arte Indígena** (Alameda 499, tel. 02/6641352), in the semi-subterranean Grutas del Cerro Welén, has the best Mapuche, Aymara, and Rapanui crafts; it's open 10 A.M.–6 P.M. daily except Sunday.

Bellavista is the destination for lapis lazuli jewelry, at locales like **Lapiz Lazuli House** (Bellavista 014, tel. 02/7321419). **Chile Vivo** (Dardignac 15, tel. 02/7353959) displays a large crafts selection ranging from basketry to lapis lazuli, leather, silverwork, and woodcarvings.

Antiques

For the best antique shops, visit the vicinity of Cerro Santa Lucía for locales like **Antigüedades Haddad** (José Miguel de la Barra 496, tel. 02/6392157), or Bellavista for **Arte del Mundo** (Dardignac 67, tel. 02/7352507).

Wine

If visiting wineries isn't on your agenda but buying wine is, there are several representative outlets in Las Condes, including **Vinoteca** (Isidora Goyenechea 3520, tel. 02/3341987) and **The Wine House** (Avenida Vitacura 3446, tel. 02/2073533).

ACCOMMODATIONS

Nearly all of Santiago's budget to midrange accommodations are in and around Santiago Centro, while most luxury hotels are in Providencia and Las Condes. At the lower end, taxes are not an issue, but midrange and top-end hotels discount IVA for foreign visitors. Many upper-range hotels belong to international chains.

Unless otherwise indicated, hotels below are in Santiago Centro, with some of them more closely defined by their barrio. Many hotels in other *comunas* are primarily business-oriented, but are still open to ordinary travelers or tourists.

US$10–25

Youthful Israelis seek their traveling companions in a rundown but relatively safe area at **Hostal Indiana** (Rosas 1343, tel. 02/6714251, US$6 pp). Near Metro Los Héroes, Barrio Brasil's simple **Residencial Vicky** (Moneda 2055, tel. 02/6960787, US$6) enjoys a better neighborhood.

A short walk from Metro Cal y Canto, **Hotel Caribe** (San Martín 851, tel. 02/6966681, US$7 pp) provides cheap breakfasts and other meals, free luggage storage, obliging management, and Internet access, but other equally good, more conveniently located places cost only a little more.

Used mostly by groups and a steady influx of independent foreigners, the well-managed **Hostelling International** (Cienfuegos 151, tel. 02/6718532, fax 02/6728880, histgoch@entelchile.net, US$10 pp) has spacious common areas, dorm-style accommodations (four to six beds per room), free Internet on a handful of computers, and cheap laundry service. Its cafeteria has lunches and dinners in the US$2–3 range, and the Saturday night *asado* (US$5 pp, wine and salad included) is a bargain.

In the winding cobbled streets south of the Alameda, such good value that reservations are almost imperative, **Residencial Londres** (Londres 54, tel. 02/6339192, fax 02/6382215, unico54@ctcinternet.cl, US$11 pp with shared bath) is the Hilton or Hyatt of Santiago's backpacker hotels, but with more charm than the international chains. Breakfast costs extra.

US$25–50

In a quirky 19th-century adobe, **Hostal Río Amazonas** (Rosas 2234, tel./fax 02/6719013, tel. 02/6984092, www.hostalrioamazonas.cl, amazona@entelchile.net, US$22/30 s/d) offers large rooms with breakfast and private bath, some with sleeping lofts. A couple slightly cheaper rooms share baths.

At the north end of Cerro Santa Lucía, underrated **Hotel Foresta** (Subercaseaux 353, tel. 02/6396262, fax 02/6322996, hforesta@terra.cl, US$30/40 s/d) has suffered from traffic noise, but the recent undergrounding of a nearby avenue should help. Rates include breakfast.

Nearby **Hotel Montecarlo** (Subercaseaux 209, tel. 02/6392945, fax 02/6335577, info@hotelmontecarlo.cl, US$32/38 s/d) offers what might charitably be called compact rooms, with breakfast and private bath. While decent enough, it's a lesser value than the Foresta. Barrio Brasil's **Hotel Los Arcos** (Agustinas 2173, tel. 02/6990998, US$22 pp) is a cozy place on a quiet block that deserves consideration (breakfast is extra).

In Providencia, close to Metro Salvador, **Marilú's Bed & Breakfast** (Rafael Cañas 246, tel. 02/2355302, fax 02/2643318, banbchile@yahoo.com, www.bedandbreakfast.cl, US$27–30 s, US$32–44 d) occupies the 1st and 3rd floors of an apartment building. Some of the variably sized rooms have shared baths, while others have private baths; there is no smoking indoors. Common areas have TV, with tea and coffee available all day, and the management handles both English and French.

One of downtown's best midrange values, **Hotel Santa Lucía** (Huérfanos 779, 4th floor, tel. 02/6398201, fax 02/6331844, santalucia@terra.cl, US$26–35 s, US$36–45 d) provides rooms with breakfast and amenities like cable TV, refrigerator/bar, and telephone.

US$50–100

At recommended **Hotel Conde Ansurez** (Avenida República 25, tel./fax 02/6960807, hotel@ansurez.cl, US$50/60 s/d), one side of the 44-room building fronts the noisy Alameda—ask for a room, with private bath and buffet breakfast, in the back.

In Barrio París Londres, easy walking distance from Metro Universidad de Chile, comfy **Hotel Vegas** (Londres 49, tel. 02/6322498, fax 02/6325084, www.hotelvegas.net, info@hotelvegas.net, US$48 s, US$55 d) manages to stay cool in summer despite the lack of a/c.

Magnificently restored and modernized, **Hotel España** (Morandé 510, tel. 02/6966066, www.hotelespania.com, hotelespania@entelchile.net, US$50–60 s, US$55–65 d) has spacious cheerful rooms with contemporary baths, exceptional natural light on the 4th floor in particular, plus cable TV, Internet connections, and electronic strong boxes. A couple smaller bargain rooms go for US$30/35 s/d.

In contrast to Providencia's otherwise corporate accommodations, **Hotel Hostal Thayer** (Luis Thayer Ojeda 746, tel. 02/2339703, fax 02/2337022, hotelhostalthayer@terra.cl, US$40/50 s/d) is an intimate boutique-style hotel with contemporary conveniences.

In recent decades, many high rises have replaced handsome French-style buildings that once graced Providencia's streets, but one survivor is the 23-room **Hotel Orly** (Avenida Pedro de Valdivia 027, tel. 02/2318947, fax 02/2520051, h.orly@ctcinternet.cl, US$85/95 s/d), whose ornate facade and mansard roof denote midsize rooms with breakfast and assiduous service.

Nestled into a highrise neighborhood, the 33-room **Hotel Montebianco** (Isidora Goyenechea 2911, tel. 02/2330427, fax 02/2330420, contacto@hotelmontebianco.cl, US$69/88 s/d) is a bargain by Las Condes standards, with buffet breakfast, a/c, and other amenities. Convenient to the Metro and the Bosque Norte restaurant cluster, this minor gem offers more personalized atmosphere than nearby megahotels.

Overlooking the Mapocho from the base of Cerro San Cristóbal, with garden space that other luxury hotels lack, Providencia's **Sheraton San Cristóbal** (Avenida Santa María 1742, tel. 02/2335000, fax 02/2341729, isabel.guzman@sheraton.com, US$90 s or d) has stylishly decorated view rooms with a substantial buffet breakfast included. At this price, it's an exceptional value, but fluctuations are possible.

US$100–150

Business-oriented **Hotel Plaza San Francisco** (Alameda 816, tel. 02/6393832, fax 02/6397826, www.plazasanfrancisco.cl, hotel@plazasanfrancisco.cl, US$119–130 s or d) offers bargain rates for "standard" rooms during the summer off-season; most of the year, it's a bit dearer, with substantially more expensive luxury suites.

Melding modernity with traditional style in Barrio París-Londres, business-oriented **Hotel Fundador** (Paseo Serrano 34, tel./fax 02/6322566, www.hotelfundador.cl, hotelfundador@hotelfundador.cl, US$130 s or d) is one of downtown's best values.

Boasting nearly 300 rooms, half of them nonsmoking, **Hotel InterContinental Santiago** (Luz 2920, tel. 02/3942000, fax 02/3942075, www.interconti.cl, hotel@interconti.cl, US$116–125 s, US$126–135 d) has spacious rooms and admirable service. It's easy walking distance to the Bosque Norte restaurant zone and Metro.

US$150–200

Las Condes' skyscraping **Marriott Hotel** (Avenida Kennedy 5741, tel. 02/4262000, fax 02/4262001, US$189 s or d) is one of Santiago's newest hotels and also one of the city's tallest buildings. The early reports are highly positive.

Also in Las Condes, the 310-room high-rise **Hotel Hyatt Regency Santiago** (Avenida Kennedy 4601, tel. 02/2181234, fax 02/2182279, hyattscl@chilepac.net, US$195 s or d) has made *Condé Nast Traveler*'s top 10 list of Latin American hotels; its lofty atrium, topped by a glass dome, lets natural light stream inside. Midsize to capacious rooms, some with stupendous Andean views, also include access to a gymnasium, a swimming pool, and tennis courts.

Over US$200

At Providencia's **Hotel Santiago Park Plaza** (Ricardo Lyon 207, tel. 02/3724000, fax 02/2336668, bookings@parkplaza.cl, US$210/220 s/d), the antique-studded foyer belies the modernity of its wired rooms and recreational facilities, including a glassed-in rooftop pool.

Virtually self-contained, downtown's business-oriented **Hotel Crowne Plaza** (Alameda 136, tel. 02/6381042, fax 02/6336015, reservations@crownesantiago.cl, US$239 s or d) features recreational facilities including a gymnasium, swimming pool, shops, and even its own post office.

FOOD

On a global level, Santiago's diverse and innovative gastronomy is an underappreciated secret. The distribution of restaurants generally mirrors that of hotels, with cheaper eateries downtown and most upscale restaurants in Providencia and Las Condes—though Barrio Bellavista, across the Rio Mapocho, offers the city's most original dining and congenial ambiance.

Santiago Centro

For morning espresso, try standup bars like **Café Caribe** (Ahumada 120) and **Café Haití** (Ahumada 140). While these places have the best and cheapest coffee, their clientele are *overwhelmingly* male because of provocatively clad waitresses.

For whimsical decor, traditional Chilean food, and reasonable prices (about US$3–4 for lunch), there's the classic **La Chimenea** (Príncipe de Gales 90, tel. 02/6970131). On the south side of the Plaza de Armas, **Chez Henry** (Portal Fernández Concha 962, tel. 02/6966612) was once among Santiago's best; with the gastronomic boom, it's lost luster, but still merits consideration for seafood and Chilean specialties like *pastel de choclo,* at midrange prices (US$6–10).

In Barrio Lastarria, near Cerro Santa Lucía, **Les Assassins** (Merced 297-B, tel. 02/6384280) is a tiny venue that gets crowded around lunchtime, but it's an excellent value for French food.

Kintaro (Monjitas 450, tel. 02/6382448) is one of Santiago's cheapest sushi options, with large fresh fish and shrimp plates—more than most diners can consume in a sitting—in the US$9 range. Sashimi and rice-based plates like *donburi* are also on the menu.

Barrio Brasil

Several years after opening, **Las Vacas Gordas** (Cienfuegos 280, tel. 02/6971066) still combines high standards with high volume and low prices, but it's almost always crowded (except Sunday night, when it's closed). It's primarily *parrillada,* but pasta and fish are also on the menu. The high decibel level is a drawback, but service is exceptional for such a busy place.

Open for lunch and dinner, **El Puente de Chabuca** (Brasil 75, tel. 02/6967962) serves moderately priced Peruvian food in a classic Barrio Brasil building.

For bargain-priced Mexican tacos complemented by enchiladas, quesadillas, and similar *antojitos,* try **Charro de Oro** (Avenida Ricardo Cumming 342-A, tel. 02/6972695). Some fillings seem spicy for the Chilean palate, but will probably not bother those accustomed to Mexican food. It sometimes keeps erratic hours, though it's ostensibly open for lunch and dinner daily except Sunday, and to 3 A.M. Friday and Saturday.

The barrio's best Mexican option, though, is **Plaza Garibaldi** (Moneda 2319, tel. 02/6994278), drawing diners who once wouldn't be seen dead in this part of town. Brightly decorated, operated by a former Mexico City exile, its creative menu merits a visit even for those who live in areas where Mexican food is common. Entrées (US$6–10) and the margaritas and Mexican beers are first-rate.

There are several seafood restaurants on Calle Bulnes (not to be confused with Avenida Bulnes). **Caleta Bulnes** (Bulnes 86, tel. 02/6988151) has good seafood—US$5 for a tasty *chupe de locos*—and is open Sunday night when most other barrio restaurants are closed. Across the street, comparably priced **Marisquería Tongoy** (Bulnes 91, tel. 02/6971144) is a popular seafood choice whose main floor is nonsmoking.

Ocean Pacific's (Avenida Ricardo Cumming 221, tel. 02/6972413) is another traditional seafood restaurant with midrange prices. The equally traditional **Ostras Azócar** (Bulnes 37, tel. 02/6816109, 02/6822293) serves a more affluent clientele.

Barrio Bellavista

North of the Mapocho, Barrio Bellavista is Santiago's gourmet ghetto, with dozens of first-rate restaurants virtually side-by-side—but not on Pío Nono itself, where most are little better than greasy spoons. Most of the best are east of Pío Nono, on the Providencia side, but there are still many outstanding possibilities on the westerly Recoleta side.

Surviving amidst rampant gentrification by serving exceptional sandwiches and simple but well-prepared Chilean dishes, Bohemian **Galindo** (Dardignac 098, tel. 02/7770116) is one of the Providencia side's oldest eateries. Even more casual is **El Caramaño** (Purísima 257, tel. 02/7377043), so absent of decor—not even a street sign—that you need to bang the door to get in, lending it a sort of speakeasy atmosphere. For Spanish food, **La Tasca Mediterránea** (Purísima 161, tel. 02/7353901) is a bookstore/café-type venue.

One of Santiago's best in any category, the Peruvian **El Otro Sitio** (Antonia López de Bello 53, tel. 02/7773059) is expensive (US$8–12 for entrées) but worth the splurge. Under the same management, nearby **Todo Fresco** (Antonia López de Bello 61, tel. 02/7350988) has fresh seafood, fine service, and airy decor, but can be distractingly noisy. Entrées are comparably priced except for *centolla* (king crab), which, when available, costs at least double that.

Dining at **Azul Profundo** (Constitución 111, tel. 02/7380288) must be the closest possible experience to eating at Pablo Neruda's—its whimsical decor, including its signature deep-blue exterior,

Avenida Pío Nono, Barrio Bellavista

a doorway bowsprit, and maritime memorabilia within, seem to have come straight from the poet's beloved Isla Negra residence. Seafood, of course, is the specialty, and they've put as much effort into its kitchen as its character; though not cheap, with entrées at US$10 and up, it's worth the price.

Serving unconventional—at least for Santiago—Japanese and Vietnamese specialties, popular **Etniko** (Constitución 172, tel. 02/7320119) is more of a scene than a restaurant, but the food is better than palatable. One block east, **Muñeca Brava** (Mallinkrodt 170, tel. 02/7321338) looks like a scene—or scenes from the films evoked by its elaborate cinematic decor—but the menu, especially the seafood, is consistently excellent. Entrées start in the US$8–10 range.

Unlike most barrio restaurants, the Franco-Chilean **Sommelier** (Dardignac 0163, tel. 02/7320034) is a subdued, self-consciously sophisticated locale with rich but not overpowering continental dishes (US$12 and up). The service sometimes lags behind the food.

Looking like a set from the movie based on its Mexican namesake novel, **Como Agua Para Chocolate** (Constitución 88, tel. 02/7778740) is one of Bellavista's smartest restaurants. Mexican-Caribbean style entrées start around US$8–10; try the *reineta a la plancha* (grilled fish) with coconut sauce, the elaborate dessert menu, and large wine list.

It's stretching things to call it Bellavista—it's really in Recoleta's Patronato garment district—but Argentine-run **El Toro** (Loreto 33, tel. 09/4196307) has earned a loyal following for its crepes, moderately priced lunches, and nonconformist sidewalk atmosphere.

One of Bellavista's best is politically conscious **Off the Record** (Antonia López de Bello 0155, tel. 02/7777710, www.offtherecord.cl), a bar/restaurant whose wood-paneled walls sport photos of the Chilean arts community. Excellent meat, seafood, and pasta entrées, and combinations, fall into the US$6–10 range, with wines by the glass (about US$2.50). It's open Monday–Saturday 9 A.M.–1 A.M., Sunday 6–9 P.M. only.

Amongst Bellavista's exclusive and inventive eateries, Italian *cucina* might seem the odd man out, but **Il Siciliano** (Dardignac 0102, tel. 02/7372265) has surmounted the stodginess of its upscale competitors elsewhere in town. Three-course lunches (around US$9–10 pp) are the best bet; dinners are more expensive.

Providencia

Liguria (Avenida Providencia 1373, tel. 02/2357914) is a hangout with plain but reliable Chilean meals at moderate prices (around US$5). **Eladio** (Avenida 11 de Septiembre 2250, 5th floor, tel. 02/2314224) specializes in beef but its varied menu will satisfy almost anyone, with moderately priced entrées (US$3.50–7.50) and good, cheap pisco sours (about US$1).

Within a surprisingly secluded cluster of bookstores and other specialty shops on an otherwise hectic avenue, the **Phone Box Pub** (Avenida Providencia 1670, tel. 02/2359972) is a pub-grub kind of place with a shady grape arbor and lunches in the US$6–8 range, plus imported beers on tap and in the bottle.

El Huerto (Orrego Luco 054, tel. 02/2332690) is a landmark vegetarian restaurant, with dishes so appetizing that even dedicated carnivores don't seem to notice the lack of meat. Its adjoining café **La Huerta** has a limited menu but lower prices—try the fresh fruit bowl with yogurt, granola, and honey (about US$4.50).

In an old but spacious Providencia house, painted in exuberant primary colors, **Barandiarán** (Manuel Montt 315, tel. 02/2366854) prepares tangy appetizers and *ceviches,* spicy Peruvian entrées (US$8–10), and a diverse dessert menu. The *corvina* with mango sauce rates special mention, but the lamb dishes are a bit heavy on the cilantro.

It's no longer a secret—go early for dinner or ring for reservations at **Puerto Perú** (Avenida Condell 1298, tel. 02/3639886), a once modest Peruvian place south of Avenida Providencia, near the Ñuñoa border. Prices are still lower than at Bellavista's best, but the difference in quality is negligible.

Providencia has Santiago's best ice creameries: **Bravíssimo** (Avenida Providencia 1406, tel. 02/2352511), **Sebastián** (Andrés de Fuenzalida 26, tel. 02/2319968, and **La Escarcha** (Avenida Providencia 1762).

Las Condes and Vitacura

For Sunday brunch and fine lunches, the hands-down choice is **Café Melba** (Don Carlos 2898, tel. 02/2324546), just around the corner from the British Embassy on Avenida Bosque Norte. There's sidewalk seating, and the omelettes, fresh juices, and similar breakfast fare are unmatchable in their category.

Though its limited menu is obvious from its name, a good and cheaper option is the nearby **New York Bagel Bakery** (Roger de Flor 2894, tel. 02/2463060).

The best pub-style food is at **Flannery's Irish Geo Pub** (Encomenderos 83, tel. 02/2336675), which offers a variety of lunchtime specials (US$4–7), along with Guinness and other imported beers on tap. **Da Dino** (Avenida Apoquindo 4228, tel. 02/2081344) has one of the city's finest, most diverse pizza menus.

The Hyatt Regency Santiago's highly regarded **Anakena** (Avenida Kennedy 4601, tel. 02/3633177) has one of a handful of Thai menus in town. Popular with the diplomatic corps, **Shoogun** (Enrique Foster Norte 172, tel. 02/2311604) is an upscale Japanese venue.

Near Las Condes' new Ritz-Carlton Hotel, Kiwi-run **Akarana** (Reyes Lavalle 3310, tel. 02/2319667) is Café Melba's more elegant, full-service restaurant. Occupying one of the area's few surviving WWII vintage houses, with both interior and patio seating, it serves entrées ranging from pumpkin ravioli (US$9) to New Zealand fish and chips (US$10) and Moroccan-style lamb filets (US$15). The Vietnamese chicken salad (US$6) and the mixed appetizer of salmon, tuna, and rhea (US$7) deserve consideration, and there are also gourmet pizzas.

INFORMATION

Santiago is home to Chile's central tourism agency but also to municipal authorities and some private information sources.

Tourist Offices

Sernatur (Avenida Providencia 1550, tel. 02/7318300, info@sernatur.cl), the national tourist service, is open 9:30 A.M.–8 P.M. weekdays, 9:30 A.M.–6 P.M. weekends. It has competent English-speaking personnel who distribute maps and information on city attractions and services, and brochures on the rest of the country. Its international airport office (tel. 02/6019320) is open 8:15 A.M.–9:30 P.M. daily.

Half a block east of the Plaza de Armas, the municipal **Oficina de Turismo** (Merced 860, tel. 02/6327785, tur-ims@entelchile.net) also has a satellite office on Cerro Santa Lucía (tel. 02/6644206). Both are open 10 A.M.–6 P.M. Monday–Thursday, 10 A.M.–5 P.M. Friday. There is also a municipal tourist kiosk at the intersection of the Huérfanos and Ahumada pedestrian malls.

National Parks

South of the Alameda, the **Corporación Nacional Forestal** (Conaf, Avenida Bulnes 291, tel. 02/3900282 or 02/3900125, www.conaf.cl) provides information on national parks and other protected areas; it also has inexpensive maps, as well as books and pamphlets. Hours are 9 A.M.–1 P.M. and 2–4:30 P.M. weekdays only.

Libraries

The **Biblioteca Nacional** (Alameda 651, tel. 02/3605200) is the national library.

Newspapers

The notoriously conservative daily *El Mercurio* partially compensates for its editorial bias with broad international, business, cultural, and entertainment coverage. The tabloid *La Nación* is the official government daily, but its editorial line seems more diverse and independent. The tabloid *Santiago News* is an English-language weekly.

SERVICES

Like accommodations and restaurants, most services are in Santiago Centro, Providencia, and Las Condes, with a few addresses elsewhere.

Money

ATMs are so abundant that exchange houses have become virtual dinosaurs except for changing traveler's checks or leftover cash. Most are downtown on Agustinas, between Bandera and Ahumada, with others in Providencia and at the airport (where rates are poorer).

For replacing lost or stolen traveler's checks, contact AmEx or Thomas Cook representatives (see the Travel Agencies entry below).

Postal Services

The **Correo Central** (Plaza de Armas 983) is open 8 A.M.–10 P.M. weekdays, 8 A.M.–6 P.M. Saturday. In addition to poste restante (general delivery), it has a philatelic office here and branch offices around town.

For courier service, try **Federal Express** (Avenida Providencia 1951, tel. 02/2315250).

Communications

There are many long-distance *centros de llamados,* such as downtown's **Entelchile** (Paseo Huérfanos 1133) and **Telefónica CTC** at Metro stations and elsewhere. Santiago's area code is 02.

The number of Internet outlets has grown so rapidly that none needs individual mention. Prices have fallen to around US$1 per hour or less.

Immigration

For visa extensions, visit the **Departamento de Extranjería** (Moneda 1342, Santiago Centro, tel. 02/6725320), open 8:30 A.M.–3:30 P.M. daily. Replacing a lost tourist card requires a trip to the **Policía Internacional** (General Borgoño 1052, Independencia, tel. 02/7371292), across the Mapocho from the old railroad station. Hours are 8:30 A.M.–12:30 P.M. and 3–7 P.M. weekdays.

Laundry

Laundries include Santiago Centro's **Lavandería Autoservicio** (Monjitas 507, tel. 02/6321772), Barrio Brasil's **Lavandería Lolos** (Moneda 2296, tel. 02/6995376), and Providencia's **Laverap** (Avenida Providencia 1645).

Travel Agencies

Las Condes' **Turismo Cocha** (Avenida El Bosque Norte 0430, tel. 02/2301000, fax 02/2035110) is the AmEx representative. **Turismo Tajamar** (Orrego Luco 023, tel. 02/2329595, Providencia) is the Thomas Cook affiliate.

The **Student Flight Center** (Hernando de Aguirre 201, Oficina 401, Providencia, tel. 02/3350395, fax 02/3350394, sfc@sertur.cl) provides discounts for both students and the general public.

Photography

For simple camera repairs and service, try **Von Stowasser** (Santa Magdalena 16, Providencia, tel. 02/2315559). For more complex needs, visit **Photo Service** (Avenida Suecia 84, 8th floor, Providencia, tel. 02/3354460).

Medical Services

The **Posta Central** (Avenida Portugal 125, Santiago Centro, tel. 02/6341650) is a public clinic; the private **Clínica Universidad Católica** (Lira 40, tel. 02/6334122) is nearby. The private **Clínica Alemana** (Avenida Vitacura 5951, Vitacura, tel. 02/2129700) is highly regarded.

GETTING THERE

Santiago has international air links to most South American capitals and some provincial cities, to Europe, North America, and the Caribbean, and across the Pacific. Domestic destinations include Puerto Montt, the gateway to Chilean Patagonia, and the Patagonian cities of Coyhaique and Punta Arenas.

International overland passengers arrive by road from Perú and Argentina, and domestic passengers arrive from many destinations throughout the country.

Air

LAN's domestic service **LanExpress** (Agustinas 640, tel. 02/6323442) flies southbound to Puerto Montt, Balmaceda, and Punta Arenas, as does **Sky Airlines** (Andrés de Fuenzalida 55, Providencia, tel. 02/3533169). **Aerolíneas del Sur** (Roger de Flor 2915, Las Condes, tel. 02/2109000), an Aerolíneas Argentinas affiliate, has recently begun service on the same routes; it flies six times weekly to Punta Arenas, more often in summer.

Bus

Santiago's four bus terminals are on or near the Alameda; some companies have offices at more than one.

Tur-Bus, its discount subsidiary **Cóndor Bus,** and **Pullman Bus** use the **Terminal de Buses Alameda** (Alameda 3750, tel. 02/2707500; Metro: Universidad de Santiago) for a wide variety of destinations. Most southbound carriers use the nearby **Terminal Santiago** (also known as Terminal de Buses Sur, Alameda 3848, tel. 02/3761755).

Northbound long-distance carriers use **Terminal San Borja** (San Borja 184, tel. 02/7760645, www.paseoestacion.cl; Metro: Estación Central). Some northbound carriers also use **Terrapuerto Los Héroes** (Tucapel Jiménez 21, tel. 02/4200099, heroebus@entelchile.net), where some Terminal Santiago buses pick up additional passengers.

Fares can fluctuate both seasonally and among companies, so comparison pricing is advisable. For Patagonia-bound travelers, the main domestic destination is Puerto Montt (US$14, 12–13 hours). Most international carriers use Terminal Santiago, but several use Terminal Los Héroes: **Tas Choapa** (tel. 02/6969326) and **Cruz del Sur** (tel. 02/7790607) to San Carlos de Bariloche (21 hours, US$36) via Osorno; and **Nar-Bus** (tel. 02/7781235) to Junín de los Andes, San Martín de Los Andes, and Neuquén via Temuco.

GETTING AROUND

Santiago has abundant public transport at reasonable cost, particularly by Metro. Sernatur's free-of-charge *Plano de Santiago* map is a big help in finding your way around.

Airport

Serving all international and virtually all domestic flights, the state-of-the-art **Aeropuerto Internacional Arturo Merino Benítez** (tel. 02/6019001, 02/6019709) is 26 kilometers west of Santiago Centro, in the *comuna* of Pudahuel.

For airport transport, the cheapest option (US$1.50 pp) is **Centropuerto** (tel. 02/6019883), which has some 40 buses daily from Plazoleta Los Héroes, just off the eastbound lanes of the Alameda outside Los Héroes Metro station. The slightly more expensive Tur-Bus has similar services.

For shuttle services, it's better to call a day in advance. **Transvip** (tel. 02/6773000) provides door-to-door service for the entire city, starting around US$5 to Santiago Centro; Providencia, Las Condes and other eastern *comunas* are slightly more expensive. This is the best option for travelers with heavy luggage, or those who arrive late at night.

Hotels can help arrange taxi or radio-taxi service, which can be cost-effective if shared by several people.

Metro and Metrobús

Santiago's quiet, clean, and efficient **Metro** (www.metrosantiago.cl) would be the pride of many European cities. Three interconnected lines cover most points of interest; others, and extensions of existing lines, are under construction.

For most visitors Línea 1, running beneath the Alameda, Avenida Providencia, and Avenida Apoquindo, is the most useful. Línea 2 connects the northern Cal y Canto station, near the former Estación Mapocho, with the southern *comuna* of Lo Ovalle. Línea 5 (there is no Línea 3 or 4 as yet) connects Quinta Normal with the southeastern *comuna* of La Florida. There are three transfer stations: Los Héroes (Línea 1 and Línea 2), Baquedano (Línea 1 and Línea 5), and Santa Ana (Línea 2 and Línea 5).

Hours are 6:30 A.M.–10:30 P.M. daily except Sundays and holidays, when it's open 8 A.M.–10:30 P.M. Fares depend on the hour of the day. An *unitario* ticket, from 7:15–9 A.M. and 6–7:30 P.M. weekdays, costs US$.60; the rest of the day and on weekends, the *unitario rebajado* fare is about US$.50. The turnstile swallows the ticket, which is not needed to exit the system.

Multivía (multi-trip ticket) purchasers get small discounts, but the electronic ticket itself requires a US$2.50 investment that's less useful for short-term users. More than one person, though, may use a *multivía* ticket by passing it back across the turnstile (this is not illegal).

Metrobús is a system of feeder lines from the outer suburbs into the Metro system and back. Fares are slightly cheaper than ordinary city buses—about US$.45.

CAR RENTALS IN SANTIAGO

Santiago's numerous car-rental agencies, both international franchises and local companies (the latter generally cheaper), are scattered throughout the city. Most airport rentals are franchises. Note that demand is high for economy cars, so reserve well in advance for the best rates. To cross into Argentina, additional paperwork and fees are necessary.

Alameda: Avenida Libertador Bernardo O'Higgins 4332, Estación Central, tel. 02/7790609 or 02/7798545, alamed@alamedarentacar.cl, www.alamedarentacar.cl

Alamo: Avenida 11 de Septiembre 2155, Oficina 1204, Providencia, tel. 02/2334343, fax 02/2334766

Ansa: Eliodoro Yáñez 1198, Providencia, tel. 02/2510256

Atal: Avenida Costanera Andrés Bello 1051, Providencia, tel. 02/2359222, fax 02/2360636

Automóvil Club de Chile (Acchi): Avenida Vitacura 8620, Vitacura, tel. 02/2125702 or 02/2746261, fax 02/2295295

Avis: Av Santa María 1742, Providencia, tel. 02/2747621, fax 02/6019757

Econorent: Avenida Manquehue Sur 600, Las Condes, tel. 02/2208292, fax 02/2241175

Chilean: Bellavista 0185, Providencia, tel./fax 02/7379650

First: Rancagua 0514, Providencia, tel. 02/2256328

Hertz: Avenida Costanera Andrés Bello 1469, Providencia, tel. 02/2359666, fax 02/2360252

Lacroce: Seminario 298, Providencia, tel. 02/6651325, fax 02/6651321, lacroce.car.rental@entelchile.net, www.lacroce.cl

Lys: Miraflores 541, tel. 02/6337600, fax 02/6399332, rent@lys.cl

United: Padre Mariano 420, Providencia, tel. 02/2361483

Santiago de Chile

Bus

City buses are numerous, cheap (about US$.50) and run all day and all of the night to virtually every part of town, but many are rundown and spew clouds of diesel into Santiago's already smoggy skies. Along the Alameda there are dedicated bus lanes and fixed stops, intended to speed up traffic, but in much of the city the buses contribute to congestion. After the Metro closes, this is the main means of getting around town.

Destinations are marked on window signs and at fixed stops, but frequent changes can make this more complex than it sounds. Regional authorities are trying to impose automatic fare machines on private bus drivers, but most still make change. Inspectors may ask for your ticket, so don't lose it.

Taxi

Black with yellow roofs, regular taxis charge about US$.50 to start the meter and US$.15 more for every subsequent 200 meters. There is also a system of radio taxis with fixed fares within certain zones; among the choices are **Radio Taxi Arauco** (tel. 02/2461114) and **Radio Taxi Alameda** (tel. 02/7764730).

Taxi Colectivos

Resembling normal cabs but designated by illuminated roof signs, *taxi colectivos* carry up to four or five passengers on fixed itineraries. Slightly more expensive than regular buses, they cover many of the same routes but are usually quicker.

Car Rental

All the major international agencies and several locals offer rental cars, both at the airport and in town. For suggestions, see the accompanying sidebar.

Northern Argentine Patagonia

On a bridge over the Río Colorado in southern Buenos Aires province, midway between Bahía Blanca and the Río Negro, a roadside sign reading "Patagonia Starts Here" marks the boundary of southernmost South America's vast, legendary region. No other part on the continent—not even Amazonia—excites the imagination like it. Ever since Magellan's chronicler Antonio Pigafetta reported encounters with a giant "so tall that the tallest among us reached only to his waist," the unknown southern latitudes have projected a mystique that's been a mixture of anticipation and apprehension. In our contemporary language, Patagonia became a brand—literally so today, as an internationally known clothing company has assumed its name.

Argentine Patagonia comprises the area south of the Río Colorado, primarily the provinces of Neuquén, Río Negro, Chubut, and Santa Cruz. While the four provinces' 1.6 million residents are barely 4.5 percent of the country's 36.2 million, they cover more than 27 percent of Argentine territory, an area roughly equivalent to Texas or the United Kingdom.

Geographically, Argentine Patagonia is more diverse than simple statistics suggest, with its

Must-Sees

Look for M to find the sights and activities you can't miss and M for the best dining and lodging.

M Volcán Lanín: In the northernmost sector of Argentina's fabled lake district, one of the region's most recognizable summits is the snow-capped centerpiece of **Parque Nacional Lanín,** whose forests include stands of distinctive monkey-puzzle trees; the lakes and the streams that drain its slopes are recreational wonderlands (page 121).

M Parque Nacional Los Arrayanes: Easily accessible from the upmarket resort of **Villa la Angostura,** the cinnamon-barked myrtles of Lago Nahuel Huapi's north shore form a fairyland forest that's ideal for hikers of almost any ability (page 124).

M Centro Cívico: Surrounding the main plaza of **San Carlos de Bariloche,** the Euro-Andean architectural legacy of the "capital of Patagonia," with native woods and stone, has become a standard for the entire lake district (page 129).

Volcán Lanín, Parque Nacional Lanín

M Lago Nahuel Huapi: In 1903, Francisco P. Moreno's donation of 7,500 hectares along the Chilean border helped preserve this alluring finger lake as part of **Parque Nacional Nahuel Huapi,** Argentina's first national park, taking in the forests, pinnacles, and ice fields of some of the Andes' most accessible scenery (page 141).

M Feria Artesanal El Bolsón: Barely an hour south of Nahuel Huapi, in a lush valley renowned for its soft fruits and hops, El Bolsón is the anti-Bariloche in its disregard for commercial fashion; its thrice-weekly market is the perfect place to seek out local crafts and sample regional snacks and brews (page 146).

M Cerro Piltriquitrón: Rising to 2,284 meters, immediately east of El Bolsón, this granite summit offers panoramic views of the snow-covered Andean summits along the Chilean border. At the parking area, 1,200 meters above sea level, local artists have converted a forest burn area into an imaginative sculpture ground (page 151).

M Circuito Lacustre: In **Parque Nacional Los Alerces,** this boat-and-foot excursion from Puerto Limonao leads to old-growth forests of "false larch" trees, which survive abundantly along the Chilean border west of the city of Esquel (page 164).

NORTHERN ARGENTINE PATAGONIA
MENDOZA
NEUQUÉN
LA PAMPA
BUENOS AIRES
RÍO NEGRO
CHILE
ARGENTINA
To Santiago
To Buenos Aires
To Buenos Aires
Santa Rosa
General Acha
Bahía Blanca
Carmen de Patagones
Viedma
San Antonio Oeste
Sierra Grande
Choele Choel
General Roca
Cipolletti
Neuquén
Añelo
25 de Mayo
Villa el Chocón
Plaza Huincul
Picún Leufú
Zapala
Chos Malal
Piedra del Aguila
Ingeniero Jacobacci
Aluminé
Junín de Los Andes
San Martín de los Andes
Villa la Angostura
San Carlos de Bariloche
Chillán
Los Angeles
Temuco
Pucón
Valdivia
Osorno
Río Colorado
Río Negro
Río Neuquén
Río Limay
Embalse Los Barreales
Golfo San Matías
Meseta de Somuncurá
P.N. Lihue Calel
P.N. Laguna Blanca
P.N. Lanín
P.N. Nahuel Huapi
ESTANCIA HUECHAHUE
ESTANCIA FORTÍN CHACABUCO
VOLCÁN LANÍN
PARQUE NACIONAL LOS ARRAYANES
LAGO NAHUEL HUAPI
CENTRO CÍVICO
RN 143
RN 40
RN 5
RN 33
RP 10
RN 151
RP 20
RN 35
RN 152
RP 7
RN 22
RP 13
RP 46
RN 22
RN 3
RN 251
RN 250
RN 237
RN 23
RN 3
RP 6
RN 231

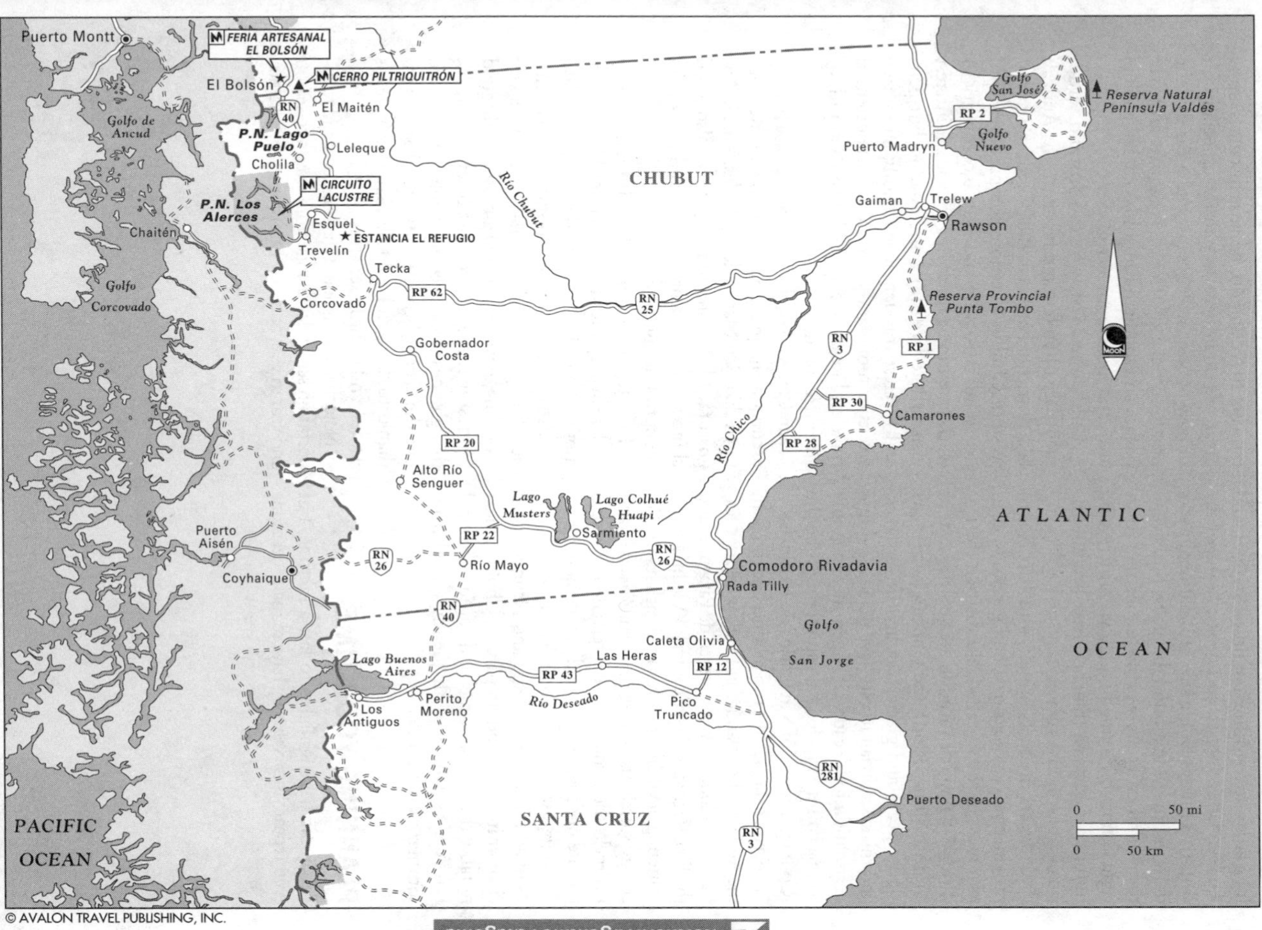
Puerto Montt
FERIA ARTESANAL EL BOLSÓN
El Bolsón
CERRO PILTRIQUITRÓN
RN 40
El Maitén
Golfo de Ancud
P.N. Lago Puelo
Leleque
Cholila
CIRCUITO LACUSTRE
P.N. Los Alerces
Chaitén
Esquel
ESTANCIA EL REFUGIO
Trevelín
Tecka
Golfo Corcovado
RP 62
Corcovado
RN 25
CHUBUT
Río Chubut
Golfo San José
Reserva Natural Península Valdés
RP 2
Puerto Madryn
Golfo Nuevo
Gaiman
Trelew
Rawson
Reserva Provincial Punta Tombo
RN 3
RP 1
Gobernador Costa
RP 30
Camarones
Río Chico
RP 20
RP 28
Alto Río Senguer
Lago Musters
Lago Colhué Huapi
Sarmiento
ATLANTIC
Puerto Aisén
RP 22
RN 26
Río Mayo
RN 26
Comodoro Rivadavia
Coyhaique
Rada Tilly
RN 40
Golfo
San Jorge
Caleta Olivia
OCEAN
Lago Buenos Aires
Las Heras
RP 12
RP 43
Perito Moreno
Los Antiguos
Río Deseado
Pico Truncado
RN 281
Puerto Deseado
0 50 mi
0 50 km
SANTA CRUZ
RN 3
PACIFIC
OCEAN

long Atlantic coastline, boundless steppes, and Andean lakes, forests, and peaks. Many of the country's finest wildlife sites and national parks draw visitors from around the globe, but several towns and cities are worthwhile in their own right. Though varying in quality, an increasing number of *estancias* (ranches) have become enticing guest-house getaways.

Between them, Neuquén and Río Negro provinces, Patagonia's overland gateways, contain most of the so-called lake district, the traditionally popular vacation area on the eastern Andean slope. Along the Chilean border, its alpine peaks and glaciers, indigo finger lakes, and thick Valdivian forests have made it a prime destination for decades; if Argentine Patagonia were a country, its logical capital might be the Río Negro resort of San Carlos de Bariloche.

Together, though, the two provinces extend from the Andes to the Atlantic, and the coastal zone features the colonial city of Carmen de Patagones and the Río Negro provincial capital of Viedma, and a scattering of wildlife reserves and beach resorts. An energy storehouse for its petroleum reserves and hydroelectric resources, the intervening steppe is the site of some of the world's most momentous dinosaur discoveries of recent decades.

In addition to Río Negro and Neuquén, this chapter includes Andean parts of Chubut, most notably the city of Esquel and Parque Nacional Los Alerces, which are frequently visited from southern Río Negro.

PLANNING YOUR TIME

Patagonia has highlights to last a lifetime, but even repeat visitors usually have to make decisions on what to see and do. Because distances are so great, it's often necessary to fly, especially for those who visit widely separated areas like the northerly lake district of Neuquén and Río Negro, and southern Patagonia's coastal wildlife areas and massive Andean glaciers.

Unlike the coast, where sights and settlements are often few and far apart, the Andean lake district of Neuquén, Río Negro, and northwestern Chubut is a more compact area with dense infrastructure and easy accessibility. A week here can be rewarding for special-interest visitors like fly-fishing aficionados, but general-interest travelers would easily enjoy two weeks or more, and dedicated sports-oriented travelers like climbers could spend a month or an entire summer.

San Carlos de Bariloche makes an ideal hub for excursions in and around the lake district, but towns like San Martín de los Andes, Villa la Angostura, El Bolsón, and Esquel are also good choices—not to mention lodges and *estancias* in the surrounding countryside.

In Patagonia's southerly latitudes, January and February are the most popular vacation months, but they are also the most expensive months. The shoulder months of November–December and March–April have lesser crowding, lower prices, and almost equally good (and sometimes better) weather. By April, though, the days are getting significantly shorter, but the region becomes a winter destination, thanks to skiing in Bariloche, San Martín de los Andes, and a few lesser areas.

Note that, throughout Patagonia, overland transportation schedules change from season to season and year to year, and may be disrupted by weather.

Coastal Río Negro Province and Vicinity

CARMEN DE PATAGONES

On the north bank of what was then the Río Curru Leuvú, Carmen de Patagones (founded 1779) was once the Spanish empire's farthest outpost in what is now Argentina, and it's the only Patagonian city that can claim a genuine colonial heritage. Modern "Patagones" is actually Buenos Aires province's most southerly city, but the Río Negro capital of Viedma on the south bank has a greater variety of hotels, restaurants, and other services.

Befitting its dual heritage, the city's name is a blend of the indigenous (Patagones, after the region's aborigines) and the European (after its patron, the Virgen del Carmen). The original colonists came from Maragatería, in Spain's León province; in 1827, in the conflict over the buffer state of Uruguay, their descendents fended off Brazilian invaders. Locals still go by the nickname of *maragatos.*

Orientation

Carmen de Patagones (population 18,095) is 279 kilometers south of Bahía Blanca and 915 kilometers south of Buenos Aires via RN 3, the coastal highway that continues west and then south to Chubut, Santa Cruz, and Tierra del Fuego. Two bridges connect it to Viedma, but most locals commute via launches that shuttle across the river. Most points of interest lie between the river and the Centro Cívico on Plaza 7 de Marzo, two blocks inland.

Sights

Patagones's most conspicuous landmark, the twin towers of the Salesian-built **Iglesia Parroquial Nuestra Señora del Carmen** (1883) rise above the west side of **Plaza 7 de Marzo,** which commemorates the victory over Brazil in 1827. Immediately west, engineer José Pérez Brito's **Torre del Fuerte** (1780) is the sole remnant of Patagones's frontier fortifications.

South of the tower, between a set of antique cannons, the broad staircase of **Pasaje San José de Mayo** descends to the adobe **Rancho de Rial** (1820), home of the town's first elected mayor.

From the city of Viedma, the colonial town of Carmen de Patagones is just a short boat ride across the Río Negro.

One block east, dating from 1823, the restored **Casa de la Cultura** (Mitre 27) was once a flourmill. Immediately across the street, fitted with period furniture, the 19th-century **Casona La Carlota** (Bynon and Mitre) is open for guided tours; the museum (see below) has details.

To the south, on the flood-prone waterfront, the restored **Mazzini & Giraudini** was a thriving merchant house a century ago. The adjacent open space of **Parque Piedra Buena** was once the home of naval hero and Patagonian/South Atlantic explorer Luis Piedra Buena; a block west, the **Casa Histórica del Banco de la Provincia de Buenos Aires** (J.J. Biedma 64), the former provincial bank, is now the regional history museum (see separate entry below).

At Patagones's historical museum, **Museo Histórico Regional Emma Nozzi** (J.J. Biedma 64, tel. 02920/462729), a stereotypically chauvinistic attitude—the unspoken but unmistakable notion that General Roca's 19th-century "Conquest of the Desert" was a greater good that justified a genocidal war against Patagonia's native peoples—undercuts the quality of its pre-Columbian artifacts. In context, its most interesting exhibit is the so-called **Cueva Maragata,** one of several riverbank excavations that sheltered the first Spanish colonists.

© WAYNE BERNHARDSON

Iglesia Parroquial Nuestra Señora del Carmen, Carmen de Patagones

The building itself has served a variety of uses, ranging from a naval stores depot to a girls' school to branches of Banco de la Provincia and Banco de la Nación to retail. Banco de la Provincia restored the structure, which suffered serious flood damage in 1899, for use as a museum in 1984; historical photographs display the flood's devastation, which caused lower-lying Viedma's evacuation.

Immediately opposite the riverside launch dock, the Museo Histórico is open 10 A.M.–noon weekdays and 7–9 P.M. daily December–mid-March; admission is free. The rest of the year, hours are 10 A.M.–noon and 2:30–4:30 P.M. weekdays, 7–9 P.M. Saturday and holidays.

Entertainment and Events

Carmen's annual **Fiesta del 7 de Marzo,** commemorating the date of the victory over Brazilian forces, fills the first week of March. Most activities take place on Plaza Villarino, four blocks north of Plaza 7 de Marzo.

The **Cine Garibaldi** (España 206) shows recent films.

Accommodations and Food

Viedma has more and better hotels and restaurants, but there's adequate shoestring accommodations, with private bath, at **Residencial Reggiani** (Bynon 422, tel. 02920/15-608619, US$6/10 s/d), opposite Plaza Villarino. The Francophile-style **Hotel Percaz** (Comodoro Rivadavia 384, tel. 02920/464104, US$8/12 s/d) is drab but tidy.

Confitería Sabbatella (Rivadavia 218) is ideal for breakfast, coffee, or sandwiches. **Pizzería Neptuno** (Rivadavia 310) sells the obvious, while the riverfront **Rigoletto** (J.J. Biedma 10) serves seafood.

Information and Services

The **Dirección Municipal de Turismo** (Bynon 186, tel. 02920/461777, Int. 253, subcom@patagones.mun.gba.gov.ar) is helpful and well-stocked with maps and brochures. Summer hours are 7 A.M.–9 P.M. weekdays, 10 A.M.–1 P.M. and 6–9 P.M. weekends; the rest of the year, hours are 7 A.M.–7 P.M. weekdays only.

Banco de la Nación (Paraguay 2) has an ATM at the southeast corner of Plaza 7 de Marzo. **Correo Argentino** (Paraguay 38) is immediately to the east; the postal code is 8504. **Locutorio Patagones** (Olivera 9) is on the south side of Plaza 7 de Mayo.

Getting There and Around

Services to and from Patagones's **Terminal de Omnibus** (Barbieri and Méjico, tel. 02920/462666), two blocks north and three blocks east of Plaza 7 de Marzo, are less frequent than Viedma's; many long-distance buses stop at both, however.

Balsas (passenger launches) cross the river to Viedma every few minutes.

VIEDMA

It lacks Patagones's colonial character, but fast-growing Viedma long ago surpassed the older city in services and significance, as it's the capital of Río Negro despite its distance from other cities in this Atlantic-to-the-Andes province. Locals swim and kayak along its willow-shaded riverfront, with its new riverside *parrilla* restaurants and sailing school.

Founded simultaneously with Patagones, in 1779, Viedma became the de facto capital of Patagonia exactly a century later and then, following the "Conquest of the Desert," capital of Río Negro territory. Later, the capital was briefly relocated to Choele Choel after an 1899 flood. In 1955 Viedma became capital of the new Río Negro province; 1980s President Raúl Alfonsín tried to transfer the federal capital here from Buenos Aires—a foolishly visionary boondoggle that, fortunately, never came to be.

Orientation

Viedma (population 46,767) is 280 kilometers south of Bahía Blanca and 439 kilometers north of Puerto Madryn via coastal RN 3. It's 982 kilometers east of Bariloche, Río Negro's largest city, via Neuquén and the Río Negro valley.

Like most Argentine cities, Viedma has a regular grid, and at least three separate activity zones: the waterfront Costanera Avenida Villarino and its Centro Cívico; the provincial government center around Plaza San Martín, four blocks southwest; and the traditional Plaza Alsina, several blocks south of the Centro Cívico. Street names change on either side of Colón, which runs roughly northeast-southwest, except for the diagonal Buenos Aires, which is continuous between 25 de Mayo and Yrigoyen.

Sights

On the southwest side of **Plaza Alsina,** the entire block bounded by Yrigoyen, Colón, Rivadavia, and Alvaro Barros is a national historical monument dating from the 1880s, when the Salesian order first installed itself here. Among its works were the Italian-built **Vicariato Apostólico de la Patagonia Septentrional** (Vicarage of Southern Patagonia, 1883–1897); Padre Juan Aceto envisioned its neo-Renaissance brick façade and tower.

For many years, the structure served as the **Colegio San Francisco de Sales,** a boys' school, and an orphanage. Since 1975, it has been the **Centro Histórico Cultural Salesiano,** comprising two museums: the **Museo Salesiano Cardenal Cagliero** (Rivadavia 34), offering the Salesian viewpoint on evangelizing the Patagonian frontier, and the **Museo Tecnológico del Agua y del Suelo** (Colón 498, 1st floor, tel. 02920/431569), focusing on irrigation's role in the province. The former is open 9 A.M.–noon and 3:30–6:30 P.M. weekdays, the latter 9–11 A.M. and 5–9 P.M. daily.

Part of the same complex, facing Plaza Alsina, the **Catedral de la Merced** (1912) replaced an earlier church that came down after the 1899 flood; the adjacent neoclassical **Obispado de Viedma** (Bishopric of Viedma, 1945) replaced the **Hospital de San José.**

Provincial public buildings cluster around Plaza San Martín: the **Casa de Gobierno** (Government House), the dignified **Residencia del**

Gobernador (Governor's Residence), and the hideous deco high-rise **Legislatura Provincial.** On the plaza's north side, the **Museo Gobernador Eugenio Tello** (San Martín 263, tel. 0290/425900) is an archaeological and secular historical museum, open 9 A.M.–4:30 P.M. weekdays only.

Daily except Monday at 5 P.M., the catamaran *Curru Leuvu II* offers 1.5-hour river excursions from the **Muelle de Lanchas,** at the foot of 25 de Mayo. Tickets costs US$2 per adult, US$1 for children to age 12.

Entertainment and Events

Viedma's biggest event is January's **Regata del Río Negro** (www.regatadelrionegro.com.ar). Its highlight is "the longest regatta in the world," a 500-kilometer kayak race from Neuquén.

Shopping

Craftspeople populate an informal **Mercado Artesanal** on Plaza Alsina. For wines, try the large selection at **La Bodega de Marzio** (San Martín 319, tel. 02920/422087).

Accommodations

Across RN 3 on the west side of town, the well-kept waterside **Camping Municipal** (tel. 02920/421341, US$1.50 pp and per tent) offers some shade, hot showers, clean toilets, and mosquitoes.

Residencial Luis Eduardo (Sarmiento 366, tel. 02920/420669, US$7/11 s/d) offers good shoestring value with breakfast included.

Viedma's biggest surprise is the former Hotel Nuevo Roma, a dreary place literally rejuvenated as the **Hotel Spa Inside Patagónico** (25 de Mayo 174, tel. 02920/430459, US$13 pp), which includes a pool, sauna, and gym; it also offers personal trainers, dance classes, massage, and even cellulitis treatment.

Overlooking Plaza Alsina, the utilitarian **Hotel Peumayén** (Buenos Aires 334, tel. 02920/425222, fax 02920/425243, hotelpeumayen@speedy.com.ar, US$11/16 s/d) is a decent choice with carpeted rooms, a/c, parking, and TV, with discounts for cash.

Friendly **Hotel Nijar** (Mitre 490, tel. 02920/422833, nijarh@arnet.com.ar, US$15s, US$21 d) is an immaculate modern hotel with good service, parking, breakfast, and other amenities, and a 10 percent cash discount. Overlooking the river, there's four-star **Hotel Austral** (Avenida Villarino 292, tel. 02920/422615, viedma@hoteles-austral.com.ar, US$27/30 s/d).

Food

El Nuevo Munich (Buenos Aires 161, tel. 02920/421108) has pizza, substantial sandwiches, and draft beer. **Camila's Café** (Buenos Aires and Saavedra) is good for coffee and desserts.

Sahara Pizza & Pasta (Saavedra 326, tel. 02920/15-607790) is Viedma's most popular pizzeria, but **Los Tíos** (Belgrano 265, tel. 02920/422790) runs a close second. For *parrillada,* try **El Tío** (Avenida Zatti and Colón, tel. 02920/420757).

Ideal for lunch beneath the riverside willows, **La Balsa** (Avenida Villarino 55, tel. 02920/431974) specializes in fish and seafood at moderate prices. **El Náutico** (Avenida Villarino 205, tel. 02920/430086) is a waterside pizzeria.

Viedma's most promising culinary development is the ambitious **Capriasca** (Alvaro Barros 685, tel. 02920/426754), with diverse entrées (US$4–5) including pastas, Patagonian lamb, beef, and seafood; the bittersweet chocolate mousse is a good dessert choice. The kitchen is prompt and the rehabbed period house, its walls partly opened to reveal its structure and the rest painted in pastels, is a plus, but it suffers from an out-of-the-way location.

Fiore Helados (Buenos Aires and Aguiar, tel. 02920/421600) serves fine ice cream.

Information

The riverfront **Oficina de Informes Turísticos** (Villarino s/n between Colón and Alvaro Barros, viprotur@impsat1.com.ar), though it's open 8 A.M.–8 P.M. daily in summer, seems to operate on automatic pilot. Winter hours are 9 A.M.–1 P.M. and 4–8 P.M. daily. There's also an office at the bus terminal.

The provincial **Secretaría de Turismo** (Avenida Caseros 1425, tel. 02920/422150, www.rionegrotur.com.ar) provides information and printed matter for the entire province.

For motorists, **ACA** (tel. 02920/422441) is at RN 3 Km 692.

Services

Banco Patagonia (Buenos Aires 184) and several others have ATMs. **Tritón Turismo** (Namuncurá 78, tritontur@speedy.com.ar, tel. 02920/430129) changes money, rents cars, and arranges excursions.

Correo Argentino is at Rivadavia 151; the postal code is 8500. **Telefónica** has a *locutorio* at Mitre 531. **Inter.com Servicios** (Saavedra 213) provides Internet access.

Lavandería Automática Siglo XXI (Mitre 343) does the laundry.

For medical emergencies, try **Hospital Artémides Zatti** (Avenida Rivadavia 351, tel. 02920/422333).

Getting There

Aerolíneas Argentinas/Austral (Colón 212, tel. 02920/423033) flies two or three weekly nonstops to Aeroparque, and sometimes flies there via Bahía Blanca. **LADE** (Buenos Aires 320, tel. 02920/424420) flies Tuesdays to Puerto Madryn and Trelew, and Wednesdays to Bahía Blanca, Mar del Plata, and Aeroparque.

Sefepa (Cagliero s/n, tel. 02920/422130, www.trenpatagonico.com.ar, comercial@sefepa.com.ar) connects Estación Viedma, on the southeast edge of town, with Bariloche via **train** two or three times weekly, with evening departures. The 15-hour trip costs US$9–12 in hardbacked *turista,* US$19–22 in reclining Pullman, or US$32–37 in *camarote* sleepers; children 5–12 pay half.

Viedma's **Terminal de Omnibus** (Guido 1580, tel. 02920/426850) is 13 blocks south of downtown, at the corner of Avenida General Perón.

Sample destinations, fares, and times include Las Grutas (US$4, 2.5 hours), Puerto Madryn (US$9, five hours), Trelew (US$9.50, 5.5 hours), Neuquén (US$14, eight hours), Esquel (US$16, 10 hours), Comodoro Rivadavia (US$18, 11 hours), Buenos Aires (US$21–25, 12 hours), Bariloche (US$19, 14 hours), and Río Gallegos (US$29, 20 hours).

Getting Around

There's no scheduled transfers to **Aeropuerto Gobernador Castello** (tel. 02920/425311), five kilometers south of town on RP 51, but a cab or *remise* costs only about US$3.

On-demand ***balsas*** cross the river Carmen de Patagones from the Muelle de Lanchas at the foot of 25 de Mayo, from 7 A.M.–8 P.M. weekdays.

Tritón Turismo (Namuncurá 78, tel. 02920/430129) is the only car-rental option.

GOLFO SAN MATÍAS AND VICINITY

From Viedma, RN 3 turns west and slightly inland toward the port of San Antonio Oeste, paralleling the shoreline of the Golfo San Matías, but day-trippers and visitors with their own vehicles should consider a detour along coastal RP 1.

Here, about 30 kilometers east of Viedma at Río Negro's mouth, **Balneario El Cóndor** draws beachgoers from the provincial capital; there are decent accommodations at **Hospedaje Río de los Sauces** (tel. 02920/497193, US$11/14 s/d) and several seafood restaurants. From Viedma's Plaza Alsina, Empresa Ceferino (tel. 02920/424542) has five buses daily (US$.65).

Buses and RP 1 continue another 30 kilometers to **La Lobería,** where the **Reserva Faunística Provincial Punta Bermeja** protects a 4,000-strong colony of southern sea lions *(Otaria flavescens),* present all year; the scenic coastline is also a prime birding area. There is a visitors center, a *confitería* for light meals, and exposed tent sites at **Camping La Lobería** (tel. 02920/428883, US$1 pp and per tent).

West of La Lobería, the pavement ends but RP 1's scenery improves to include massive dunes at **Bahía Creek** (for secluded camping) and another sea lion colony at **Reserva Provincial Caleta de los Loros;** fishing is also popular. Here, at Punta Mejillón, the highway swerves inland, where it's possible to return to RN 3 via unpaved RP 52, or else continue west toward San Antonio Este, where paved RN 251 also turns north to RN 3.

Some 187 kilometers west of Viedma, but east of RN 3, hordes of summer and weekend visitors converge on **Las Grutas** (permanent population 2,708), a beach resort named for the wave-eroded grottoes that have penetrated the sedimentary headlands. Because of a phenomenal tidal range, the available beachfront can recede to just tens of meters, making it suitable for only the most gregarious beachgoers. There are nearly a hundred hotels, *hospedajes,* and campgrounds; for suggestions, visit the Secretaría Municipal de Turismo in the Galería Antares (Primera Bajada s/n, tel. 02934/497470). Las Grutas has frequent buses to San Antonio Oeste, 12 kilometers northeast.

About 125 kilometers south of San Antonio Oeste and 140 kilometers north of Puerto Madryn, RN 3 passes through **Sierra Grande** (population 6,768), a onetime iron-mining town that's the northernmost point with gasoline at Patagonian discount prices—at least a third cheaper than in Las Grutas or San Antonio Oeste. Southbound drivers should nurse their fuel to get here, while the northbound should top off the tank.

While the mine has closed, the highway helps keep Sierra Grande alive, filling its modest hotels and simple roadside restaurants. Trying to encourage stopovers, the municipality has promoted descents into the inoperative iron mine once run by **Hierro Patagónico Rionegrino** (Hiparsa). These cost around US$5 pp, with discounts for children; for details, contact Hotel Jarillal (RN 3 Km 1270, tel. 02934/481095, hoteljarillal@infovia.com.ar). The Subsecretaría de Turismo (Calle 2 No 300, tel. 02934/15-447776) can also provide information.

Interior Neuquén Province

NEUQUÉN

Capital of its namesake province, Neuquén is primarily a gateway to the northern Patagonian lake district, but it's also an ideal base for visiting a triangle of dinosaur sites to the northwest, west, and southwest. At the confluence of two major rivers, once a major railroad junction, it's a clean contemporary city that benefits from abundant energy resources, a productive financial sector, and proximity to the upper Río Negro valley's agricultural plenty.

Orientation

At the confluence of the Río Neuquén and the Río Limay, Neuquén (population 201,729) is 537 kilometers east of Bahía Blanca via RN 22, 559 kilometers southwest of Santa Rosa via a series of paved highways, and 429 kilometers northeast of San Carlos de Bariloche via RN 237. It is also the main access point to destinations like Aluminé, in the lake district's little-visited northernmost part. Note that RN 22 through the upper Río Negro valley and west toward Zapala is a narrow highway with heavy truck traffic and many dangerously impatient drivers.

Most points of interest and services lie north of Félix San Martín, the main east-west thoroughfare (also known as RN 22); the main north-south street is Avenida Argentina/Avenida Olascoaga; street names change on either side of Avenida Argentina and either side of the old railroad station, which is now the Parque Central. North of the Parque Central, several diagonals complicate the otherwise regular grid.

Sights

Nearly all Neuquén's sights are in the **Parque Central,** the recycled railyard bounded by Avenida San Martín/Avenida Independencia on the north, Salta/Manuel Láinez to the west, Tucumán/Tierra del Fuego on the east, and Sarmiento/Mitre on the south.

Occupying the 1902 repair shed for the Ferrocarril del Sud, the **Museo Nacional de Bellas Artes** (Avenida San Martín and Brown) has become a branch of the national fine-arts museum, with rotating exhibits of painting, sculpture, and other plastic arts. Hours are 8 A.M.–8 P.M. weekdays, 4–8 P.M. weekends; admission is free. It is due, however, to be replaced by a nearby and more contemporary facility.

Just north of the bus terminal, the **Sala de Arte Emilio Saraco** (Avenida Olascoaga s/n, tel.

0299/449-1200, Int. 4490) occupies the railroad station's former cargo terminal, with contemporary art exhibits. Hours are 8 A.M.–8 P.M. weekdays, 4–8 P.M. weekends; admission is free. Across the tracks to the north, **Juntarte en el Andén** is an outdoor art space at the former passenger terminal.

Two blocks east, the **Museo de la Ciudad Paraje Confluencia** (Avenida Independencia and Córdoba) traces Neuquén's cultural evolution and history from early archaeological sites through European contact, the Mapuche nation's development, and their resistance to General Roca's euphemistically named "Conquest of the Desert." Hours are 8 A.M.–8 P.M. weekdays, 4–8 P.M. weekends and holidays. Admission is free.

Entertainment and Events

La Casona (Alvear 59) is a bar with live music some nights. For current films, there's the **Cine Teatro Español** (Avenida Argentina 271, tel. 0299/442-2048).

January's annual **Regata del Río Negro** is a 500-kilometer kayak marathon that starts here and ends a week later in Viedma; for more detail, see the Viedma entry above.

Shopping

Near Avenida Independencia and Avenida Argentina, the Parque Central's **Paseo de los Artesanos** (Vuelta de Obligado s/n) is open 10 A.M.–9 P.M. daily except Monday and Tuesday.

The province of Neuquén sponsors **Artesanías Neuquinas** (San Martín 57, tel. 0299/442-3806, www.artesaniasneuquen.com.ar), which has an excellent, diverse crafts selection at reasonable prices. **Cardón** (Avenida Argentina 392, tel. 0299/448-0155) sells leather goods, *mates,* and silverwork. **Artesanías Mapuches** (Roca 76, tel. 0299/443-6750) focuses on indigenous crafts, primarily silverwork.

Accommodations

Oddly enough, nearly all Neuquén's accommodations lie in the slightly scruffy, but not unsafe, retail area between RN 22 and the bus terminal.

Easily reached by *colectivo* No. 103, Neuquén's **Camping Municipal** (Obreros Argentinos and Copahue, tel. 0299/448-5228, US$1 pp plus US$1.50 per tent) lies on the banks of the Río Limay, on the south side of town. It's closed in winter.

Rooms at friendly, centrally located **Hostería Belgrano** (Rivadavia 283, tel. 0299/4480612, US$6.50/11 s/d, hostal2@infovia.com.ar) are small—some claustrophobically so—but also immaculate. **Residencial Inglés** (Félix San Martín 534, tel. 0299/442-2252, US$7/11 s/d) is quiet, clean and family-run, but rates do not include breakfast.

Under the same management as Hostería Belgrano, modernized **Hotel Alcorta** (Ministro Alcorta 84, tel. 0299/442-2652, hostal2@infovia.com.ar, US$13/19 s/d) has most contemporary conveniences, but lacks the intangibles. **Hotel Ideal** (Avenida Olascoaga 243, tel. 0299/442-2431, hotelidealneuquen@yahoo.com.ar, US$11–14 s, US$18–22 d) has clean, comfortable rooms with breakfast, parking, and modern amenities.

Rooms at family-run **Residencial del Neuquén** (Roca 109, tel. 0299/442-2403, US$12/16 s/d) are also small, but it's spotless with breakfast, cable TV, and private bath. Rooms at **Hotel Charbel** (San Luis 268, tel. 0299/442-4143, hotelcharbel@hotmail.com, US$13/20 s/d) are clean and substantially larger, with most conveniences and a bar/restaurant.

The classic **Hotel Iberia** (Avenida Olascoaga 294, tel. 0299/442-2372, luislo@neunet.com.ar, US$20/26 s/d) has tidy, ample rooms with basic conveniences.

Remodeled three-star **Hotel Royal** (Avenida Argentina 145, tel. 0299/442-2408, reservas@royalhotel.com.ar, US$25/34 s/d) has large rooms and baths, with cable TV and breakfast included; there's also a 10 percent cash discount.

Neuquén's best value may be the nearly new **Hotel El Prado** (Perito Moreno 484, tel. 0299/448-6000, hotelelprado@hotmail.com, US$20–28 s, US$30–37 d), which has large, well-furnished rooms with private bath, a/c, cable TV, telephone, key cards, and Internet access jacks. In addition, there's an abundant buffet breakfast and superb service.

Downtown, four-star **Hotel del Comahue** (Avenida Argentina 387, tel. 0299/442-2439,

NEUQUÉN'S DINOSAUR TRIANGLE

Where there's oil, there's dinosaurs, and Neuquén's sedimentary steppe is a late Cretaceous hot spot. By rental car, a triangle of sites northwest, west, and southwest of the provincial capital makes an ideal (if long) full-day excursion though one of these, Lago Barreales, is more difficult to reach and open only in the fall and winter months. The other two, Plaza Huincul and Villa El Chocón, are easily accessible by public transportation.

Centro Paleontológico Lago Barreales

The best place to see an onsite excavation is this reservoir northwest of Neuquén, where paleontologists demonstrate the separation and rescue of fossil deposits, as well as the cleaning and extraction of the fossils themselves. Beasts in the sediments here include the sauropod *Futalognkosaurus* (a long-tailed quadruped with a long neck and small head), teropods (bipedal carnivores with huge claws such as *Megaraptor*), and ornithopods (small bipedal herbivores), as well as bivalves, crocodiles, turtles, and pterosaurs.

Only when the water level falls in autumn, usually early April, can the Museo de Geología y Paleontología de la Universidad Nacional del Comahue, under the direction of Jorge Calvo, resume its work, so this is the ideal time to go. The long-term plan is to create an open-air dinosaur park in the vicinity.

On the north shore of Barreales, the Centro Paleontológico Lago Barreales (RP 51 Km 65, tel. 0299/15-404-8614, www.proyectodino.com.ar) is open 9 A.M.–12:30 P.M. and 3–7 P.M. daily. Admission costs US$.65 for adults, US$.35 for kids under 12. Foreign university students can hire on to participate in the digs for US$420 for a week, US$700 for two weeks, with tent accommodations, full board, and transportation from Neuquén included.

Actually reaching the site can be complicated, but the simplest route is to take RP 7 from Cipoletti almost to Añelo, about 100 kilometers northwest of Neuquén, and then turn south on a gravel road to the north shore of Barreales. It's signed, but still requires close attention.

***Pianitzkysaurus floresi*, Museo Paleontológico Municipal Ernesto Bachmann, Villa El Chocón**

Museo Municipal Carmen Funes (Plaza Huincul)

At the oil town of Plaza Huincul, about midway between Neuquén and Zapala, the municipal museum's prize exhibit is a replica skeleton of *Argentinosaurus huinculensis,* the world's largest dinosaur at 45 meters long and 18 meters high. So large is the herbivore *A. huinculensis* that an adult male human barely reaches its knee, and one of the dorsal vertebrae measures 1.6 meters.

Former oil worker Guillermo Heredia found the fossil only three kilometers away, along the highway, in 1987. In addition to the imposing skeleton, there's a clutch of dinosaur eggs some 80 million years old, and remains of crocodiles found in Picún Leufú, about 75 kilometers to the south.

Directly on the highway, the expanding Museo Municipal Carmen Funes (Avenida Córdoba 55, tel. 0299/496-5486) is open 9 A.M.–8 P.M. daily except Sundays and holidays, when it closes at 9 P.M. Admission costs US$.65, but is free for children under age 12.

In consultation with museum director Rodolfo Coria, metallurgist Omar Vejar (tel. 0299/496-0522, cel. 0299/15-5884076) produces scale models of Patagonian dinosaur skeletons; prices start around US$70 for the smallest items, around 30 centimeters in length.

Plaza Huincul (population 12,047), 110 kilometers west of Neuquén via RN 237 and RN 22, has an **Oficina de Información Turística** (RN 22 s/n, tel. 0299/496-7637) right on the highway. Bus services from Neuquén are frequent and comfortable.

Museo Paleontológico Municipal Ernesto Bachmann (Villa El Chocón)

If Plaza Huincul boasts the world's largest herbivore, Villa El Chocón can claim its carnivorous counterpart in *Giganotosaurus carolinii.* On the shores of the Embalse Exequiel Ramos Mexía, an enormous hydroelectric reservoir southwest of Neuquén, the municipal museum also features models of *Carnotaurus* and the smaller *Pianitzkysaurus.* There are dinosaur tracks in the vicinity.

G. carolinii takes its name from amateur paleontologist Rubén Carolini, who discovered the fossil, while Rodolfo Coria, Leonardo Salgado, and Jorge Calvo first identified it. Measuring 14 meters in length and 4.65 meters high at the hip, it weighed up to 10,000 kilograms.

Unfortunately, because the hydroelectric dam (generating 3.35 million kwh per annum) drowned the Río Limay's sedimentary canyon here, many probable paleontological sites have disappeared beneath the water. The Museo Paleontológico Municipal Ernesto Bachmann, open 8 A.M.–9 P.M. daily, also offers exhibits on the area's archaeology and a whitewashed history of the dam and former *estancia* owner Manuel Bustigorry. Admission costs US$.35.

Villa El Chocón, 136 kilometers southwest of Neuquén via RN 237, originated as a company town during the dam's construction. The **Dirección Municipal de Turismo** (tel. 0299/490-1230), at the northern approach to town off RN 22, is open 8 A.M.–7 P.M. daily; there's a paleontological excavation site within easy walking distance.

On the shoreline, **La Posada del Dinosaurio** (tel. 0299/490-1200, fax 0299/490-1201, http://posadadinosaurio.com.ar, US$40 d) offers excellent accommodations, with a good, reasonably priced restaurant and outstanding service. Camping also exists nearby.

www.hoteldelcomahue.com.ar, US$54/61 s/d) is the pick of the litter, also offering 10 percent cash discounts.

Food

Neuquén is strong on pizza and pasta, at places like the traditional **La Mamma** (9 de Julio 56, tel. 0299/442-5291), **El Sótano** (Brown 162, tel. 0299/443-1122), and **La Tartaruga** (Roca 193, tel. 0299/443-6880). **Franz y Peppone** (9 de Julio and Belgrano, tel. 0299/448-2299) blends the Teutonic and the Mediterranean.

La Tejuela (Alberdi 59, tel. 0299/443-7114) has a beef and seafood menu. **Pasty** (Félix San Martín 246, tel. 0299/443-5860) serves fine, fairly priced pasta and chicken dishes, with well-intentioned but inconsistent service; the sidewalk seating is a mixed blessing, as the highway runs almost alongside it.

Decorated in soothing pastels, **Mediterráneo** (Avenida Argentina 584, tel. 0299/442-9325) lives up to its name in both food and decor, with an exceptional Middle Eastern and Mediterranean buffet of appetizers; the seafood and succulent meat entrées run about US$6–9. This is Neuquén's one real can't-miss dining choice.

Neuquén may not have Argentina's finest ice cream, but **Helados Las Malvinas** (Avenida Argentina 16, tel. 0299/443-9207) and **Heladería Pire** (Diagonal Alvear 29, 0299/442-2206) are worthy enough.

Information

Directly on RN 22, the **Subsecretaría de Turismo** (Félix San Martín 182, (tel. 0299/442-4089, www.neuquentur.gov.ar, turismo@neuquen.gov.ar) is open 7 A.M.–8 P.M. weekdays, 8 A.M.–8 P.M. weekends. In terms of content, accuracy, and usefulness, their brochures and maps are among the country's best. Sometimes a bus-terminal office also operates here.

For motorists, **ACA** is at Rivadavia and the diagonal 25 de Mayo, tel. 0299/442-4860.

Services

As a provincial capital, Neuquén has a full complement of services.

There are ATMs at **Banco de la Provincia de Neuquén** (Avenida Argentina 13) and several others nearby. Neuquén has two exchange houses, **Cambio Olano** (J.B. Justo 97, tel. 0299/442-6192) and **Cambio Pullman** (Ministro Alcorta 144, tel. 0299/442-2438).

Correo Argentino is at Rivadavia and Santa Fe; the postal code is 8300.

Arlequín I (Avenida Olascoaga 222) has both telephone and Internet access, but there are many other *locutorios*.

Neighboring Chile has a **consulate** (tel. 0299/442-2727) at La Rioja 241. **Migraciones** (tel. 0299/442-2061) is at Santiago del Estero 466.

The travel agency **Zanellato** (Avenida Independencia 366, tel. 0299/443-0105) is the AmEx representative, but there are many others downtown.

Lava Ya (Avenida Independencia 326, tel. 0299/443-4318) does the washing.

Try the **Hospital Regional** (Buenos Aires 421, tel. 0299/449-0800) for emergencies or routine care.

Getting There

Aerolíneas Argentinas and **Austral** (Santa Fe 52, tel. 0299/442-2409) have at least seven flights weekly to Aeroparque.

Southern Winds (San Martín 107, tel. 0299/442-0124) flies most mornings and some afternoons to Aeroparque.

LADE (Brown 163, tel. 0299/443-1153) flies changing schedules to Bariloche, San Martín de los Andes, Aeroparque, Comodoro Rivadavia, and Puerto Madryn.

On the Parque Central's southern edge, Neuquén's **Terminal de Omnibus** (Mitre 147, tel. 0299/442-4903) is a hub for provincial, national, and some international services (to the Chilean cities of Temuco and Osorno/Puerto Montt). Reservations are advisable for international buses.

Sample provincial and long-distance destinations, fares, and times include Zapala (US$4.50, 2.5 hours), Aluminé (US$10, 5.5 hours), Bariloche (US$11–14, 5.5 hours), San Martín de los Andes (US$13, 6.5 hours), Villa La Angostura (US$12, 6.5 hours), Puerto Madryn (US$16, 9.5 hours), Trelew (US$20, 10.5 hours), El Bolsón (US$14–16, 7.5 hours), Esquel (US$18–21, nine hours), Buenos Aires (US$23–32, 13 hours), Comodoro Rivadavia (US$27, 16.5 hours), and Río Gallegos (US$47, 28 hours).

Chile-bound buses normally leave around 11 P.M. or midnight. Carriers include **Narbus/Igi Llaima** (tel. 0299/442-3661) to Temuco (US$20, 11–12 hours) via Zapala and the Pino Hachado pass; **Igi Llaima** (tel. 0299/442-3661) to Temuco over Paso Tromen via Junín de los Andes; and **Andesmar** (tel. 0299/442-2216) to Osorno and Puerto Montt via Paso Cardenal Samoré (US$24, 12 hours). Services vary seasonally, but there's usually daily service except to Puerto Montt (Tuesday, Thursday and Saturday).

Getting Around

Aeropuerto Internacional Juan Domingo Perón (tel. 0299/444-0244) is seven kilometers west of town on the north side of RN 22 (despite its name, it has no international services at present). A taxi or *remise* costs US$3–4.

Neuquén has several car-rental agencies, including **AI** (Perticone 735, tel. 0299/443-8714); **Avis** (San Martín 5901, tel. 0299/444-1297), at the airport; and **Dollar** (Carlos Rodríguez 518, tel. 0299/442-0875).

ZAPALA

Argentine backpackers once used forlorn Zapala, the erstwhile end of the line for the Ferrocarril Roca's northern spur, as a jumping-off point to some of the lake district's least-visited parts. With the railroad shut down, and little immediate prospect of connecting the dots over the Andes in a bi-national transit corridor, this bleak steppe town draws fewer visitors than it once did. It's a convenient stopover en route to San Martín de los Andes, though, and offers good access to bird-rich Parque Nacional Laguna Blanca and an outrageously scenic route to the trout-fishing Mecca of Aluminé.

Orientation

Zapala (population 31,265) is 189 kilometers west of Neuquén via RP 22, which continues northwest toward Las Lajas and the Chilean border at Pino Hachado, and 244 kilometers northeast of San Martín de los Andes via RN 40 and RN 234. RP 13 leads west to the ski resort of Primeros Pinos, while paved RP 46 leads southwest to Parque Nacional Laguna Blanca and down the spectacular Bajada de Rahué into the Río Aluminé valley.

Zapala's main drag is Avenida San Martín, which leads south from the traffic circle intersection of RN 22 and RN 40.

Museo Olsacher

Zapala's most worthwhile sight is its mineralogical museum, a recycled warehouse with minerals from around the world and paleontological exhibits from Neuquén. Its prize is the remains of the herbivorous dinosaur *Zapalasaurus antipani*, but there are also displays on marine reptiles, paleobotany, systematic mineralogy (2,035 minerals from 84 countries), Argentine economic minerals, and invertebrate and vertebrate paleontology. A specialized library holds more than 11,500 items.

Alongside the bus terminal, the Museo Olsacher (Etcheluz and Ejército Argentino, tel. 02942/431959) is open 8 A.M.–2 P.M. and 6–9 P.M. weekdays except Monday, and 5–9 P.M. weekends and holidays; admission is free.

Shopping

Zapala's **Escuela de Cerámica** (Luis Monti 240) has a long tradition in artisanal pottery.

Accommodations and Food

While accommodations and food options are limited, their quality is acceptable or better.

South of the old railroad line, the free **Camping Municipal** (Sapag s/n) has poplar windbreaks, hot showers, and marginal toilets. Otherwise, Zapala's cheapest is **Residencial Coliqueo** (Etcheluz 165, tel. 02942/421308, US$6.50/10 s/d). **Hotel Huincul** (Avenida Roca 311, tel. 02942/431442, US$7.50/11 s/d) also has a restaurant.

Near the bus terminal, the immaculate **Pehuén Hotel** (Etcheluz and Elena de la Vega, tel. 02942/423135, US$7.50/12.50 s/d) stays cool even in summer. **Hotel Hue Melén** (Almirante

Brown 929, tel. 02942/422407, hotelhuemelen@hotmail.com, US$16/23 s/d) has a restaurant as well; there's a 10 percent cash discount.

For breakfast, coffee, and snacks, there's **El Chancho Rengo** (Avenida San Martín and Etcheluz, tel. 02942/422795). Directly on RN 22 near the roundabout, **La Zingarella** (Houssay 654, tel. 02924/422234) is the choice for pasta and *parrillada.*

Capriccio (Etcheluz 151, tel. 02942/423156) prepares very good homemade pasta, such as fresh ravioli and pizza, in utilitarian surroundings. It's only so-so compared with ice creameries elsewhere, but **Helados Don Héctor** (Etcheluz 527) is not a desperation choice.

Information

The **Dirección Municipal de Turismo** (Avenida San Martín and Almirante Brown, tel. 02942/421132, turismozapala@argentina.com) occupies an A-frame on the median strip of the main avenue. Summer hours are 7 A.M.–8 P.M. weekdays, 8 A.M.–noon and 4–7 P.M. weekends; the rest of the year, it's open 8 A.M.–8 P.M. weekdays only.

Zapala's **APN** office (Ejército Argentino 260, tel. 02942/431982, lagunablanca@apn.gov.ar) provides information on Parque Nacional Laguna Blanca.

Services

Banco de la Provincia del Neuquén (Cháneton 460) has an ATM.

Correo Argentino is at Avenida San Martín 324; the postal code is 8340. **Telefónica** (Etcheluz 527) has long-distance telephone service and slow Internet connections.

For medical needs, try the **Hospital Regional** (Luis Monti 155, tel. 02924/431555).

Getting There and Around

LADE (Uriburu 397, tel. 02942/430134) flies Wednesdays to San Martín de los Andes and Bariloche.

Zapala's **Terminal de Omnibus** (Etcheluz and Uriburu, tel. 02924/423191) has provincial and long-distance services; some Chile-bound carriers will pick up passengers here. Ruta Sur goes to Temuco (US$15) at 3 A.M. Monday, Thursday, and Sunday.

Sample destinations, fares, and times include Neuquén (US$4, 2.5 hours), San Martín de los Andes (US$6, 3.5 hours), Bariloche (US$9, five hours), and Buenos Aires (US$29, 18 hours). Most often, for Buenos Aires, it's easiest to transfer in Neuquén.

Aluminé Viajes goes to Laguna Blanca (US$2, one hour) and Aluminé (US$5, 2.5 hours) Monday, Wednesday, and Friday at 7 P.M., and at 6 P.M. Tuesday, Thursday, Saturday, and Sunday.

Taxis or *remises* to **Aeropuerto Zapala** (tel. 02924/431496), at the junction of RN 40 and RP 46 southwest of town, cost about US$3.50.

PARQUE NACIONAL LAGUNA BLANCA

In the stark volcanic steppe southwest of Zapala, alkaline Laguna Blanca is a shallow but plankton-rich interior drainage lake that supports large breeding populations of the black-necked swan *(Cygnus melancoryphus).* Designated an internationally significant wetland under the Ramsar convention, it's also the spot to spot coots, ducks, grebes, gulls, upland geese, and occasional flamingos; even the flightless *choike* (rhea) sometimes scurries along the barren shoreline for a drink.

Orientation

From a junction 10 kilometers south of Zapala via RN 40, paved RP 46 leads 20 kilometers southwest to the park, comprising 11,250 hectares of undulating terrain 1,276 meters above sea level; the lake itself covers 1,700 hectares to a depth of 10 meters. RP 46 continues southwest to Rahué and Aluminé, a recommended scenic detour to San Martín de los Andes.

Sights

From the visitors center on RP 46, a short signed nature trail winds through the steppe to the shoreline, the best place to see the abundant bird life. A roofed shelter, open on the leeward side, holds a classic 1915 Zeiss telescope that awaits repair; even if the money comes through, it's still worth carrying a pair of lightweight binoculars. Swans are present all year, but the bird life is best November–March.

Practicalities

On the north side of RP 46, about one kilometer east of the visitors center, a free APN campground offers shade and shelter from the strong, steady westerlies that gust across the steppe. There's no food available here, though—bring everything from Zapala or elsewhere. In reality, Laguna Blanca makes a better day trip than an overnight.

Directly on RP 46, Laguna Blanca's steadily improving Centro de Visitantes has helpful rangers, informative exhibits, clean toilets, and a crafts outlet. It's open 9 A.M.–6 P.M. daily mid-December–March; the rest of the year it's open weekends and holidays only.

Public transportation is limited; for details, see the Zapala entry. If schedules are inconvenient, considering hiring a *remise.*

The Lake District

ALUMINÉ AND VICINITY

West of Laguna Blanca, paved RP 46 passes 2,839-meter Cerro Chachil, with more distant views of Volcán Lanín, on the border with Chile, and of fuming Volcán Villarrica, across the line. From the Cuesta del Rahué, where the first araucaria (monkey puzzle) trees make their appearance, the zigzag road descends into the valley of the Río Aluminé, a prime trout and whitewater river whose singularly appropriate name derives from a Mapuche compound meaning "glittering jewel."

Aluminé proper is nothing special but, for visitors with their own vehicles, it offers the best services in an area with almost unlimited recreational opportunities in Parque Nacional Lanín's northernmost parts. The southbound route through the Aluminé valley, to Junín de los Andes and San Martín de los Andes, is far more scenic than RN 40.

Cuesta del Rahué, easternmost habitat of the araucaria (monkey puzzle) tree

Orientation

Aluminé (population 3,384; 900 meters above sea level) is 138 kilometers southwest of Zapala via RP 46, which is gradually being paved, and a paved stretch of RP 23; it is also 102 kilometers north of Junín de los Andes via RP 23, a good but mostly gravel road.

Whitewater Rafting

November and December's heavy runoff makes the Class II–IV Río Aluminé a superb whitewater opportunity, but low water the rest of the year makes the rock-strewn riverbed hazardous. For river excursions (about US$10–15 pp), contact **Aluminé Rafting** (Villegas 610, tel. 02942/496322), **Malí Viajes** (Joubert and Julio Ayoso, tel. 02942/496310, malialumine@alumine.com.ar), or **Amuyén Servicios Turísticos** (Villegas 348, tel. 02942/496368).

Events

Mid-March's **Fiesta del Pehuén** pays homage to the distinctive monkey puzzle tree that provided sustenance to the region's aboriginal inhabitants. Mapuche communities still harvest the fallen nuts.

Accommodations and Food

Hostería Nid-Car (Cristián Joubert 559, tel. 02942/496131, cagonzalez@hotmail.com, nidcaralumine@yahoo.com.ar, US$9/15 s/d) is the shoestring choice with breakfast included. Across from Plaza San Martín, looking better without than within, **Hostería Aluminé** (Cristián Joubert 336, tel. 02942/496347, hosteriaalumine@hotmail.com, US$11/16 s/d) has spacious if spartan rooms, but breakfast is extra. Rooms with shared bath are about 20 percent cheaper.

Aluminé's best hotel, **Pehuenia Hotel & Resort** (Capitán Crouzelles and RN 23, tel. 02942/496340, hotelpehuenia@uol.com.ar, US$18/25 s/d) is a multistory European-style chalet with comfortable rooms, some with river views, though the beds are little soft; some of the common areas are worn, their walls scuffed, and their carpets frayed. Rates include an abundant but mediocre breakfast; the dinner is notably better.

At Rahué, 16 kilometers south of Aluminé, **Hostería Rahué-Quillén** (RP 46, tel./fax 02942/496129, panchoyaliciaquillen@alumine.com.ar, US$32/40 s/d) is a comfortable lodge catering primarily to hunters and fishermen. Rates include an abundant, diverse breakfast; lunch and dinner cost an additional US$9. It's open January–mid-April only.

The area's top accommodations, though, is the all-inclusive **Piedra Pintada Resort** (tel. 02942/496396, www.piedrapintada.com.ar, info@piedrapintada.com.ar, US$195 pp), 35 kilometers northwest of town on the south shore of Lago Pulmari. Alongside the aboriginal rock-art site that gives the resort its name, it's a 2,000-hectare property with a dozen luxury doubles and an appealing restaurant that uses produce from its own organic garden. It also provides fine access to the northernmost sector of Parque Nacional Lanín and the scenic loop road to Villa Pehuenia.

Information and Services

For information, consult the diligent **Subsecretaría de Turismo** (Cristián Joubert 321, tel. 02942/496001, www.alumine.net, subsecretariadeturismo@alumine.com.ar), directly on the central Plaza San Martín. In summer, it also operates a Centro de Informes in the hamlet of Rahué, at the junction of RP 46 and RP 23.

Banco de la Provincia del Neuquén (Villegas 392) has an ATM.

Correo Argentino is at Villegas 560; the postal code is 8345. There's a ***locutorio*** at Juan Benigar 334.

The **Centro Tecnológico Quintu Che** (Avenida RIM 26 No. 430) has Internet access.

Getting There

Aluminé's **Terminal de Ómnibus** (4 de Caballería 139, tel. 02942/496048) occupies a triangular block immediately south of Plaza San Martín. **Albús** leaves daily at 3:30 A.M. to Zapala and Neuquén (US$10, 5.5 hours) while **Aluminé Viajes** leaves daily at 7 A.M. to Zapala (US$5, three hours) except Sunday, when it leaves at 3:45 P.M.

Transporte Tillería goes to Junín de los Andes (US$5) and San Martín de los Andes (US$6, three hours) Tuesday and Friday at 7 A.M.

Northern Argentine Patagonia

JUNÍN DE LOS ANDES AND VICINITY

Where the steppe meets the sierra, the Río Chimehuín gushes from the foot of 3,776-meter Volcán Lanín to become one of Argentina's top trout streams near Junín de los Andes. Styling itself Neuquén province's "trout capital," economical Junín also provides the best access to the central sector of Parque Nacional Lanín, which takes its name from the symmetrical cone straddling the Chilean border.

In addition to its natural attractions, Junín is promoting itself as a pilgrimage site for links to the recently beatified Chilean Laura Vicuña, a young girl who willed her own death to protest her widowed mother's affair with an Argentine landowner, and for the ostensible blend of Catholic and Mapuche traditions here. Founded in 1883 as a military camp, during General Roca's euphemistically named "Conquista del Desierto," it's Neuquén's oldest city.

Orientation

At the confluence of the Río Chimehuín and its tributary Río Curruhué, Junín (population 10,243) is 402 kilometers southwest of Neuquén via RN 22, RN 40, and RN 234, and 41 kilometers northeast of San Martín de los Andes via RN 234. It is 218 kilometers north of San Carlos de Bariloche, the lake district hub, via RN 234, RN 40, and RN 237. RP 23 leads north to Aluminé, while nearby RP 60 and RP 62 are unpaved roads leading west to the Chilean border.

Junín's main thoroughfare is north-south RN 234, known as Blvd. Juan Manuel de Rosas within the city limits. Centered on Plaza San Martín, its compact grid lies mostly east of the highway and west of the Chimehuín. Avoid confusing the Avenida San Martín, which runs north-south along its namesake plaza, and the parallel Félix San Martín, two blocks west.

Sights

The focus of the Salesian-organized **Museo Mapuche** (Ginés Ponte 540) is its indigenous artifacts and historical exhibits, but it also displays a sample of fossils. Hours are 9 A.M.–noon daily except Sunday, and 2–7 P.M. weekdays only.

In what was once a Lebanese-run general store, the private **Museo Moisés Roca Jalil** (Coronel

Río Chimehuín, one of Argentina's prime trout streams, near Junín de los Andes

Suárez 311) houses an ample selection of Mapuche artifacts, including elaborate weavings. Though closed recently, it's normally open 10 A.M.–noon Monday, Wednesday, and Friday.

Recent developments reflect Junín's ambition to become a religious tourism destination. The recently modernized **Santuario Nuestra Señora de las Nieves y Beata Laura Vicuña** (Ginés Ponte and Don Bosco) has become an airy, luminous structure that incorporates Mapuche elements into its design; it also shelters an urn that contains one of Laura Vicuña's vertebrae. It's open for guided tours 9 A.M.–7 P.M. daily.

In the western foothills, the **Vía Crucis** is an ambitious stations-of-the-cross project that stretches two kilometers to the cross-topped summit of **Cerro de la Cruz.**

Events

January's **Feria y Exposición Ganadera** is the landowner's extravaganza of blue-ribbon cattle, horses, and sheep, as well as rabbits and poultry. Gauchos get to show off their skills here as well, but they take center stage at mid-February's **Festival del Puestero.**

Junín's pre-Lenten **Carnaval del Pehuén** fills the streets with parades, costumed celebrants, and water balloons and confetti. Late August's **Semana de Artesanía Aborígen** gives the Mapuche a chance to showcase their finest crafts.

Shopping

Junín's **Paseo Artesanal,** on Padre Milanesio immediately north of the tourist office, accommodates a cluster of artisans working in ceramics, leather, wood, and wool.

Sports and Recreation

Both Argentines and foreigners flock here for fishing on the Chimehuín, the Aluminé, their tributaries, and Parque Nacional Lanín's glacial lakes. Catch-and-release is the norm; for licenses and suggested guides, visit the tourist office on Plaza San Martín. For nonresidents of the province, licenses cost US$11 per day, US$50 per week, or US$70 for the season; the national parks have their own separate licenses.

The **Club Andino Junín de los Andes** in the Paseo Artesanal (Padre Milanesio 568) provides information on hiking and climbing Volcán Lanín and other excursions in the park, as does the Parques Nacionales office (see below).

Estancia Huechahue

On the banks of the Río Aluminé, about 30 kilometers east of Junín via RN 234, the 15,000-hectare Anglo-Argentine Estancia Huechahue is a forested cattle ranch that doubles as a recreational getaway for serious gaucho-style riders, or those who want to become serious riders. From November–April, owner Jane Williams's 70 well-trained horses take a maximum of 12 guests at a time over the mountainous *estancia* and into Parque Nacional Lanín.

For accompanying non-riders, or for a change of pace, there's hiking, birding, fishing, swimming, and even tennis. Among its attractions, Huechahue also features volcanic caves, Tehuelche rock-art sites, and wildlife sites including An-

on the trail at Estancia Huechahue

dean nesting sites (not to mention deer and feral wild boar).

Most visitors arrange packages from overseas; drop-ins are not possible, but with at least a few days' notice it may be possible to arrange a stay. The basic rate of US$212 per person, in twin-bedded rooms in two separate guesthouses, includes full board (traditional Patagonian fare rather than the European-style cuisine of some contemporary *estancias*), drinks (beer, wine, and spirits), and activities (though fishing guides are extra). It also includes transportation between Huechahue and San Martín de los Andes' Aeropuerto Chapelco; transportation to or from Bariloche is possible for an additional charge. For more information contact Jane Williams at Estancia Huechahue (huechahue@fronteradigital.net.ar).

Accommodations and Food

The riverside municipal **Camping La Isla** (Ginés Ponte s/n, tel. 02972/491461, US$1 pp) has good facilities but collects a small additional charge for showers, which have limited hours: 8–10 A.M. and 8–10 P.M. Across the way, **Camping y Albergue Beata Laura Vicuña** (Ginés Ponte 861, tel. 02972/491149, campinglv@fronteradigital.net.ar, US$1.70 pp) is comparable but also has four-person hostel accommodations (US$4 pp).

Directly on the highway, **Residencial Marisa** (Blvd. Juan Manuel de Rosas 360, tel. 02972/491175, residencialmarisa@jdeandes.com.ar, US$7–9 s, US$10–13 d) has both doubles and bunks; breakfast is an inexpensive extra.

Other budget choices include Plaza San Martín's basic **Hostería del Montañés** (San Martín 555, tel. 02972/491155, US$9/14 s/d), **Residencial El Cedro** (Lamadrid 409, tel. 02972/492044, US$9/14 s/d), and **Hostería Posada Pehuén** (Coronel Suárez 560, tel. 02972/491569, posadapehuen@hotmail.com, US$10/15 s/d).

On Junín's northern outskirts, **Hotel Alejandro Primero** (Blvd. Juan Manuel de Rosas and Chubut, tel. 02972/491182, alejandro1@jandes.com.ar, US$15/23 s/d) also has a restaurant.

Aging but agreeable, the riverside **Hostería Chimehuín** (Coronel Suárez and 25 de Mayo, tel. 02972/491132, fax 02972/492503, hosteriachimehuin@fronteradigital.net.ar, US$8 pp with shared bath, US$14/23 s/d with private bath) has 23 comfortable rooms and a restaurant. Breakfast includes homemade scones and other specialties.

For pizza and pasta, plus sandwiches and empanadas, try the traditional favorite **Roble Bar** (Ginés Ponte 331, tel. 02972/491111). Though it's primarily a *parrilla,* **Ruca Hueney** (Padre Milanesio 641, tel. 02972/491113) has a more diverse menu (try the *pollo al ajillo,* garlic chicken, for US$4) and good service even with large numbers of diners. Most entrées do not exceed US$6.

In an attractive new building styled after Bariloche's landmark civic center, the awkwardly named **Casa de Turismo** (Padre Milanesio 586, tel. 02972/492555) has a good but mostly standard Argentine menu; the standout item is the butter-grilled trout (US$5.50).

Down the block, **Heladería San Martín** (Padre Milanesio 520, tel. 02972/492577) has Junín's best ice cream in a tobacco-free atmosphere.

Information

Facing Plaza San Martín, the **Subsecretaría de Turismo y Cultura** (Padre Milanesio 596, tel. 02972/491160, turismo@jdeandes.co.ar) is open 8 A.M.–11 P.M. daily in summer, 8 A.M.–9 P.M. the rest of the year. It also sells fishing permits.

For information on Parque Nacional Lanín, the **APN** occupies an office on the Paseo Artesanal, immediately to the north, where it sells park entry permits (US$4). Hours are 9 A.M.–8:30 P.M. weekdays, 2:30–8:30 P.M. weekends.

Services

Banco de la Provincia del Neuquén (Avenida San Martín and Lamadrid) has an ATM.

Correo Argentino is at Suárez and Don Bosco; the postal code is 8371. For telephone services, use the ***locutorio*** at Padre Milanesio 540, half a block north of the tourist office.

Laverap Pehuén (Ginés Ponte 340) cleans dirty clothes.

A new hospital is under construction, but meanwhile use the **Hospital de Area** (Ginés Ponte and Padre Milanesio, tel. 02972/491162).

Getting There

Aeropuerto Aviador Carlos Campos–Chapelco (RN 234 Km 24, tel. 02972/428388) lies midway between Junín and San Martín de los Andes. For flight details, see the Getting There entry for San Martín de los Andes, below.

Services to and from Junín's **Terminal de Omnibus** (Olavarría and Félix San Martín, tel. 02972/492038) resemble those to and from San Martín, including services across the Andes to Pucón and Temuco, Chile. For details, see the Getting There entry for San Martín, below.

SAN MARTÍN DE LOS ANDES

In little more than a century since its founding as a frontier military outpost, San Martín de los Andes has become one of the Patagonian lake district's most fashionable—and expensive—resorts. Nestled in the hills near Lago Lácar, it owes its tourist appeal to its surrounding scenery, the trout that thrash in the lakes and streams of Parque Nacional Lanín, and the ski boom that began in the 1940s at nearby Chapelco.

San Martín is picturesque in its own right, thanks to the legacy of architect Alejandro Bustillo, whose rustically stylish Centro Cívico builds on his designs at Bariloche. Unlike Bariloche, though, San Martín has shunned the high-rise horrors that have degraded Bustillo's legacy there; its biggest blight is the growing number of timeshares and the increasingly aggressive marketing of them. The height limit has its own downside, though, in promoting its perceived exclusivity—in that sense, San Martín de los Andes is Argentina's Jackson Hole, where fashion often trumps nature.

Orientation

At the east end of Lago Lácar, 642 meters above sea level, San Martín de los Andes (population 22,269) is 189 kilometers north of San Carlos de Bariloche via RN 237, RN 231, and RN 234; it is 109 kilometers north of Villa la Angostura via RN 234, part of which is a narrow and unpleasantly dusty but scenic road in Parque Nacional Lanín's southern sector. It's 259 kilometers from Bariloche via the roundabout but faster alternative of RN 237, RN 40, and RN 234 via Junín.

THE SLOPES OF CHAPELCO

Overlooking San Martín de los Andes, at a maximum elevation of 1,920 meters, Cerro Chapelco draws enthusiastic winter crowds to 29 different runs, the longest combination of which is about 5.3 kilometers. The diversity of conditions means it's suitable for both experienced skiers and novices. The **Fiesta Nacional del Montañes,** the annual ski festival, takes place in August, when there are also provincial skiing championships.

Chapelco Aventura (Avenida San Martín and Elordi, tel. 02972/427460, www.chapelco.com.ar) is the resort office in San Martín. Rental equipment is available onsite, but also in town at **Bumps** (Villegas 465, tel. 02972/428491) and **La Colina** (San Martín 532, tel. 02972/427414).

Lift-ticket prices depend on timing; the season runs mid-June–mid-October, but is subdivided into low, mid-, or peak season. One-day rates range from US$16–29 for adults, US$13–23 for children ages 5–11 and seniors age 60 and above. The corresponding prices for three-day passes are US$48–85 for adults, US$40–68 for children and seniors. Week-long passes cost US$93–161 for adults, US$74–131 for children and seniors, while the rates for 15-day passes are US$181–316 and US$146–254 respectively. Season passes cost US$770 for adults, US$616 for children and seniors. Skiers over age 70 pay nothing.

San Martín's main thoroughfare is RN 234, which divides into the one-way avenues of Avenida Roca and Avenida San Martín (the main commercial drag) as it runs northeast-southwest through town. Most points of interest and services lie within a few blocks of the Centro Cívico surrounding Plaza San Martín, bounded by the two avenues and the block-long streets of Rosas and Frey.

Centro Cívico

The masterpiece of lavishly landscaped **Plaza San Martín** is Alejandro Bustillo's **Intendencia Parque Nacional Lanín** (Emilio Frey 749), which matches the style of its Bariloche counterpart for

SAN MARTÍN DE LOS ANDES

Plaza San Martín
FREY
SECRETARÍA MUNICIPAL DE TURISMO
MUSEO PRIMEROS POBLADORES
ARTESANÍAS NEUQUINAS
CERRO TORRE, TIEMPO PATAGÓNICO
CHAPELCO TURISMO
ABOLENGO
PATALIBRO
PUCARÁ VIAJES
CAFÉ DE LA PLAZA
MENDIETA
ABUELA GOYE
HOTEL ROSA DE LOS VIAJES
KOSEM
HOSTERÍA ANAY
EL ALMACÉN
PIZZERÍA LA NONNA
HOTEL CHAPELCO SKI
ANDINA INTERNACIONAL AEROLÍNEAS ARGENTINAS/AUSTRAL
AHUMADERO EL CIERVO
LAVERAP
HOTEL INTERMONTI
TRATTORIA MI VIEJO PEPE
SAN MARTÍN ORVIS SHOP
PURA VIDA
EL CLARO TURISMO
LA RESERVA
CAMPING DEL ACA
To Junín de los Andes, Parque Nacional Lanín
AV DR KOESSLER
LOS CIPRESES
RAMAYON
MASCARDI
SARMIENTO
E ELORDI
BELGRANO
CAP DRURY
CNEL PEREZ
M MOENO
M MONENO
RIVADAVIA
CORONEL DIAZ
CORONEL ROHDE
JUEZ DEL VALLE
GRAEFF
AV COSTANERA
GRAL ROCA
R ROCA
P MORENO
CALDERON
A FOSBERY
3 DE CABALLERA
C WEBER
AV SAN MARTIN
GRAL VILLEGAS
G OBEID
BROWN
RESIDENCIAL LAURA
COOPERATIVA DE ARTESANOS
CENTRO CULTURAL AMANCAY
EL ESTABLO
JORGE CARDILLO FLY SHOP
LA OVEJA NEGRA
HG RODADOS
Plaza Sarmiento
HOTEL CRISMALÚ
AVIS
CHARLOT
HOTEL CAUPOLICÁN
LOCALIZA
HOSTERÍA CUMELÉN
SEE DETAIL
SALSABIL
HOSTERÍA LA MASÍA
HOSTERÍA LAS LUCARNAS
POST OFFICE
BANCO DE LA NACIÓN
RESIDENCIAL ITALIA
RESIDENCIAL CASA ALTA
HOSTERÍA LAS LENGAS
HOSTERÍA LA CHEMINEE
INTENDENCIA PN LANÍN
AUSTRIA SKI-BAR
FENOGLIO
PUMA HOSTEL
HOTEL COLONOS DEL SUR
ALIHUEN
HOTEL PATAGONIA PLAZA
LA CHACHA
HOSTAL DEL LAGO
PATAGONIA PISCIS
ICI VIAJES
HOSTAL DEL ESQUIADOR
HOSPITAL ZONAL RAMÓN CARRILLO
HOSTERÍA DEL CHAPELCO
DOWNTOWN MATÍAS
ALBERGUE RUKALHUE
HOSTERÍA LA POSTA DEL CAZADOR
TERMINAL DE ÓMNIBUS
Lago Lácar
To Playa Catritre, Villa la Angostura, Bariloche
0 200 yds
0 200 m

Northern Argentine Patagonia

Parque Nacional Nahuel Huapi and has influenced architects and designers throughout the region. The exterior consists of roughly hewn stone blocks, rustically carved wooden beams, attic windows that jut out from the main structure, and wooden roof shingles. Other buildings in the vicinity resemble, but cannot quite match, Bustillo's prototype.

On the opposite side of the plaza, the **Museo Primeros Pobladores** (Rosas 758, 02792/428676, Int. 2, museoprimerospobladores@yahoo.com.ar) is a modest but worthy effort at acknowledging all the area's cultural influences, from pre-Columbian hunter-gatherers to settled Mapuche farmers and their struggles with the Spanish and Argentine invaders, and the European colonists who helped create the contemporary city. The material exhibits include items such as arrowheads, spear points, and ceramics, but there's also an account of Parque Nacional Lanín's creation and its significance to the area. Hours are 10 A.M.–3 P.M. and 6–9 P.M. weekdays, 3–10 P.M. weekends; admission costs US$.35.

Entertainment and Events

At February 4's **Día de la Fundación,** the anniversary of San Martín's creation as a frontier fortress in 1898, the military still march down the avenues, followed by firemen and an offbeat equestrian array of foxhunters, gauchos, and riders on polo ponies.

San Martín's main performing-arts outlet is the **Centro Cultural Amancay** (Roca 1154, tel. 02972/428399), which offers recent movies at its **Cine Amankay** (tel. 02972/427274).

This is also a bar-goer's town, at places like the theme-oriented **Austria Ski-Bar** (San Martín and Moreno, tel. 02972/427071) and **Downtown Matías** (Coronel Díaz and Calderón, tel. 02972/421699).

El Almacén (Capitán Drury 857, tel. 02972/425663) is an exceptional by-the-glass or by-the-bottle wine bar, with a food menu limited to sandwiches and tapas, plus one nightly special.

Shopping

San Martín has a significant concentration of souvenir outlets, starting with the Mapuche weavings, silverwork, and carvings at **Artesanías Neuquinas** (Rosas 790, tel. 02972/428396), the provincially sponsored crafts cooperative. There's also a good selection at Plaza Sarmiento's **Cooperativa de Artesanos** (Avenida San Martín 1050, tel. 02972/429097).

El Establo (San Martín 1141, tel. 02972/429257) specializes in rural clothing like boots, leather, and ponchos, plus *mate* gourds and paraphernalia. For textiles, try **La Oveja Negra** (Avenida San Martín 1025, tel. 02972/428039) or **Kosem** (Capitán Drury 838, tel. 02972/427269).

Fenoglio (Avenida San Martín 536, tel. 02972/427515) is a popular choice for homemade-style chocolates.

Patalibro (Avenida San Martín 866, Local 11, tel. 02972/421532) has a selection of books on Patagonia, including some in English.

Sports and Recreation

Like Jackson Hole, and thanks to the proximity of Parque Nacional Lanín, San Martín de los Andes is a Mecca for outdoor recreationists for everything from hiking and climbing to mountain biking, whitewater rafting, trout fishing, and skiing (for details on Cerro Chapelco, see the sidebar "The Slopes of Chapelco").

Climbing snow-topped Volcán Lanín requires some technical skill, but it's possible for enthusiastic amateurs with a qualified guide such as **Horacio Peloso,** at Cerro Torre (San Martín 950, tel. 02972/429162), which also rents equipment.

Secondary roads around Lago Lácar and the park are ideal for mountain biking. Rental bikes are available from **HG Rodados** (Avenida San Martín 1061, tel. 02972/427345).

Rivers on the Argentine side generally have lower flows and fewer challenging rapids than their Chilean counterparts, but the Class III-plus Río Aluminé flows through spectacular scenery a couple hours north of San Martín. It's best with the spring runoff in November and December; contact **Pucará Viajes** (Avenida San Martín 941, tel. 02972/427862, pucara@smandes.com.ar).

Closer to San Martín, the Class II Río Hua Hum provides a gentler experience. Contact **ICI Viajes** (Villegas 459, tel. 02972/427800, www.interpatagonia.com/iciviajes, iciviajes@smandes.com.ar); **El Claro Turismo** (Villegas 977, tel. 02972/428876, www.elclaroturismo.com.ar, elclaro@smandes.com.ar); or **Tiempo Patagónico** (San Martín 950, tel. 02972/427113, www.tiempopatagonico.com, info@tiempopatagonico.com.ar).

For fishing gear and advice, visit the **San Martín Orvis Shop** (Villegas 835, tel. 02972/425892) or **Jorge Cardillo Fly Shop** (Villegas 1061, tel. 02972/428372).

Accommodations

San Martín has abundant accommodations, but prices are higher than almost anywhere else in the region. Reservations are advisable in the summer months, at Semana Santa, and throughout ski season. At these peak times, single occupants may have to pay double rates, but the 2002 devaluation has made and kept things fairly affordable.

Under US$10

On the highway to Junín, the wooded **Camping ACA** (Avenida Koessler 2176, tel. 02972/429430, US$2.50 pp off season, US$9 per site in summer) is spacious enough even in peak season, but the best sites go early. There are other campgrounds north and south of town, in Parque Nacional Lanín.

US$10–25

Albergue Rukalhue (Juez del Valle 682, tel. 02972/427431, info@rukalhue.com.ar, US$6 pp) offers hostel accommodations in respectable facilities. Peak-season reservations are essential at the HI-affiliated **Puma Hostel** (Fosbery 535, tel. 02972/422443, fax 02972/428545, www.pumahostel.com.ar, puma@smandes.com.ar, US$6 pp in dorms, US$20 d), an attractive and well-run 50-bed facility on the north side of the arroyo.

Hostería Las Lucarnas (Coronel Pérez 632, tel. 02972/427085, US$18 d) is also a decent budget choice. Slightly larger, with greater privacy, is **Hostería Cumelén** (Elordi 931, tel. 02972/427304, cumelen@smandes.com.ar, US$19 d). **Hotel Crismalú** (Rudecindo Roca 975, tel. 02972/427283, crismalu@smandes.com.ar, US$19 d) is one of the better choices in its range.

Run by relocated Porteño shrinks, cozy **Hostal del Lago** (Rohde 854, tel. 02972/427598, hostalago@hotmail.com, US$17/20 s/d) has six reasonably spacious rooms with good beds, desks, cable TV, and decent breakfast, but it could use a color scheme consultant.

There are several simple, economical *residenciales:* **Residencial Laura** (Mascardi 632, tel. 02972/427271, US$20 d); **Residencial Casa Alta** (Obeid 659, tel. 02972/427456, casaalta@smandes.com.ar, US$21 d), open in summer only; and **Residencial Italia** (Coronel Pérez 977, tel. 02972/427590, US$21 d).

At the north end of town, preserving its original style, the worn but well-kept **Hostería Parque Los Andes** (RN 234, Km 2, tel. 02972/428211, hosteriaparquelosandes@smandes.com.ar, US$24 s or d) is still a good value, though some rooms are smallish and others have too-soft beds. After Chilean poet Pablo Neruda fled on horseback over the Andes to avoid political persecution in the 1940s, he may have shared drinks with Juan Perón in the hotel's gallery bar.

Try also **Hostal del Esquiador** (Coronel Rohde 975, tel. 02972/427674, hostaldelesquiador@smandes.com.ar, UD$24 d), a block from the bus terminal.

US$25–50

Hotel Rosa de los Viajes (Avenida San Martín 821, tel. 02972/427484, rosahotel@smandes.com.ar, US$17/30 s/d) is a small (only 20 rooms) and homey place, but both foot and auto traffic are heavy in this part of town.

Set among attractive gardens, **Hostería Anay** (Capitán Drury 841, tel. 02972/427514, anay@smandes.com.ar, US$25/37 s/d) has 10 cozy rooms and enjoys a welcome setback from the street in a bustling area.

Sedate **Hotel Intermonti** (Villegas 717, tel./fax 02972/427454, www.hotelintermonti.com.ar, info@hotelintermonti.com.ar, US$32/40 s/d) has 24 well-furnished midsize rooms, plus attractive common areas.

Central **Hotel Chapelco Ski** (Belgrano 869, tel. 02972/427480, hotelchapelcoski@smandes.com.ar, US$28/35 s/d) is a little worn and has limited parking, but is otherwise OK.

Near the lake, **Hostería del Chapelco** (Brown

297, tel. 02972/427610, hcchapelco@smandes.com.ar, US$32/38 s/d) has the best location of any hotel in its range; some second-story rooms have balconies with lake or mountain views.

Upstairs rooms are better than downstairs at **Hostería La Posta del Cazador** (Avenida San Martín 175, tel. 02972/427501, laposta@satlink.com, US$37 s or d), a Middle European–style place on a quiet block near the lake. The credit-card surcharge is high—pay cash.

Just far enough off the main drag to ensure some quiet, **Hotel Colonos del Sur** (Rivadavia 686, tel. 02972/427224, info@colonosdelsur.com.ar, US$30/40 s/d) has smallish rooms with bathtubs in a category where showers are the rule.

US$50–100

The alpine-styled **Hotel Caupolicán** (Avenida San Martín 969, tel. 02972/427900, hotelcaupolican@smandes.com.ar, US$47/62 s/d) offers ample rooms with contemporary furnishings on the avenue's busiest section.

Hostería Las Lengas (Coronel Pérez 1175, tel. 02972/427659, navarroclaudia@speedy.com.ar, US$47/63 s/d) is an intimate B&B with a French-Swiss style and ample natural light.

On sprawling wooded grounds, with rustic style and contemporary comforts, **Hostería La Masía** (Obeid 811, tel. 02972/427688, www.hosterialamasia.com.ar, info@hosterialamasia.com.ar, US$47/63 s/d) is exceptional for the price.

Hostería La Cheminee (Avenida Roca and Mariano Moreno, tel. 02972/427617, lacheminee@smandes.com.ar, US$81 d) is one of San Martín's best.

Over US$100

Four-star **Hotel Patagonia Plaza** (San Martín and Rivadavia, tel./fax 02972/422280, patagoniaplaza@smandes.com.ar, US$110–270 d) has become downtown's premier accommodations, with 90 rooms ranging from relatively simple doubles to sprawling suites. Cash-paying customers get a 10 percent discount.

Food

Try **Café de la Plaza** (Avenida San Martín and Coronel Pérez, tel. 02972/428488) for coffee, croissants, sandwiches, and desserts. **Abolengo** (Avenida San Martín 806, tel. 02972/427732) is a cozy, comfortable place for rich hot chocolate on a cool night. **Alihuen** (Rivadavia 759, tel. 02972/423643) is a teahouse with outstanding desserts.

Pizzería La Nonna (Capitán Drury 857, tel. 02972/422223) serves about 30 varieties of pizzas, including wild boar, trout, and venison, in the US$4–8 range; there are also calzones and empanadas. While the food is good enough, it gets intolerably noisy when crowded—either take earplugs or, alternatively, go early or late, or consider takeout.

Trattoria Mi Viejo Pepe (Villegas 725, tel. 02972/427415) is a more elaborate Italian option. Tasty *ñoquis* and other pastas make tobacco-free **Pura Vida** (Villegas 745, tel. 02972/429302) one of San Martín's best values; while it's not strictly vegetarian, it has a diverse selection of excellent vegetarian entrées.

Reflecting San Martín's Lebanese roots, **Salsabil** (Obeid 832, tel. 02972/427556) prepares Middle Eastern dishes like hummus, tabbouleh, falafel, and kebabs. For smoked meats, as well as cheeses and mushrooms, go to **Ahumadero El Ciervo** (Villegas 724, tel. 02972/427361).

La Chacha (San Martín and Rivadavia, tel. 02972/429376) is primarily a *parrilla* that serves out-of-the-routine items like kid goat and roast pig, a flavorful chicken in plum sauce, and fresh raspberries in season. Dinner lines form early outside popular *parrilla* **Patagonia Piscis** (Villegas 598, tel. 02972/423247) and the more fashionable **Mendieta** (San Martín 713, tel. 02972/429301).

For a romantic dinner, try the sophisticated but understated **La Reserva** (Belgrano 940, tel. 02972/428734), serving moderately priced Patagonian tapas, salads, and entrées like squash *panzotti* in the US$7-and-up range.

For ice cream, try either of **Charlot**'s two locations (Avenida San Martín 467, Avenida San Martín 1017, tel. 02972/428561), with dozens of imaginative flavors. **Abuela Goye** (Capitán Drury 812, tel. 02972/429409) is another outstanding choice, with superb chocolate confections as well.

Information

At the east end of Plaza San Martín, the **Secretaría Municipal de Turismo** (Avenida San Martín and Rosas, tel. 02972/427347, www.smandes.gov.ar, munitur@smandes.com.ar) does an outstanding job of providing advice, maps, and brochures, plus an up-to-the-minute data base of accommodations and rates; in peak season, though, heavy demand can stretch its resources nearly to the breaking point. Summer hours are 8 A.M.–10 P.M. daily; the rest of the year, it closes at 9 P.M.

Across the plaza, the APN's **Intendencia de Parque Nacional Lanín** (Emilio Frey 749, tel. 02972/427233, 429004) provides information on the park from 8 A.M.–1 P.M. weekdays only, with a selection of maps and brochures.

Services

Banco de la Nación (Avenida San Martín 687) and several others have ATMs. **Andina Internacional** (Capitán Drury 876) is the only exchange house.

Correo Argentino (General Roca and Coronel Pérez) is the post office. **Codesma** (Capitán Drury 761) has telephone, fax, and Internet services.

Chapelco Turismo (Avenida San Martín 876, tel. 02972/427550) offers conventional overland excursions to Parque Nacional Lanín (including Lago Huechulafquen), Villa Traful, Villa la Angostura, and even San Martín's Chilean counterpart of Pucón.

For laundry, **Laverap** (tel. 02972/428820) has two locations: Capitán Drury 880 and Villegas 972.

Hospital Zonal Ramón Carrillo (Avenida San Martín and Coronel Rohde, tel. 02972/427211) is very central.

Getting There

Note that air schedules, in particular, change frequently, especially in the winter ski season.

Aerolíneas Argentinas (Capitán Drury 876, tel. 02972/427004) flies occasionally to Buenos Aires, sometimes to Aeroparque and others to Ezeiza; its partner Austral flies more frequently to Aeroparque.

LADE (Villegas 231, tel. 02972/427672) occupies a booth in the bus terminal; it flies occasionally to Aeroparque (Buenos Aires), Bariloche, El Bolsón, El Maitén, Esquel, and Comodoro Rivadavia, and to Zapala and Neuquén.

San Martín's **Terminal de Ómnibus** (Villegas 231, tel. 02972/427044) has regional, long-distance, and international connections (to Chile).

Transportes Ko Ko (tel. 02972/427422) goes to Villa la Angostura (US$6, three hours) via the scenic Siete Lagos route, sometimes continuing to Bariloche, but most of their services to Bariloche (US$8, 4.5 hours) use the longer but smoother and faster Rinconada route. **Albús** (tel. 02972/428100) also goes to Villa la Angostura, three times daily by the Siete Lagos route, twice to Bariloche. Transporte Tillería goes to Aluminé (US$6, three hours) Tuesday and Friday at 4 P.M.

Internationally, **Igi-Llaima** (tel. 02972/428100) and **Empresa San Martín** (tel. 02972/427294) alternate service to Pucón and Temuco, Chile (US$15, eight hours), daily except Sunday; San Martín continues to Valdivia. In summer, **Buses Lafit** (tel. 02972/427422) goes once or twice daily to the Chilean border post of Pirehueico (US$4.50, two hours) and on to Panguipulli (US$9, 4.5 hours).

Other typical destinations, fares, and times include Junín de los Andes (US$2, 45 minutes), Neuquén (US$10, 5.5 hours), and Buenos Aires (US$40–45, 21 hours).

Getting Around

Aeropuerto Aviador Carlos Campos-Chapelco (RN 234 Km 24, tel. 02972/428388) lies midway between San Martín and Junín de los Andes. For airport transfers, contact Transportes Caleuche (tel. 02944/422115).

In summer only, **Transportes Ko Ko** (tel. 02972/427422) runs several buses daily (US$1) to Lago Lolog.

From the pier at the foot of Obeid, **Naviera Lácar y Nonthue** (Avenida Costanera s/n, tel. 02972/427380) goes seven times daily to Quila Quina (US$5.50 round-trip), on Lago Lácar's south shore, and daily to Hua Hum (US$18). It also does nighttime excursions.

For rental cars, try **Avis** (Avenida San Martín 998, tel. 02972/427704) and **Localiza** (Villegas 977, tel. 02972/428876).

PARQUE NACIONAL LANÍN

In westernmost Neuquén, stretching from Lago Ñorquinco in the north to a southeasterly diagonal that runs between Lago Nonthué on the Chilean border and Confluencia on RN 237, Parque Nacional Lanín comprises 412,000 hectares of arid steppe, verdant mid-altitude forests ringing glacial finger lakes, alpine highlands, and volcanic summits. From Aluminé in the north to Junín de los Andes and San Martín de los Andes in the south, several longitudinal highways intersect westbound access roads, all of them graveled.

Where the park's eastward-flowing Pleistocene glaciers receded, they have left a series of deep finger lakes that drain into the upper and lower tributaries of the Río Limay. Unlike Parque Nacional Nahuel Huapi, to the south, these lakes and the dense Valdivian forests that surround them have suffered less commercial development, but they are recovering from the early-20th-century timber exploitation and livestock grazing that, in some areas, still persist.

From north to south, Aluminé, Junín de los Andes, and San Martín de los Andes are the park's main access points. This section begins at Aluminé and works southward, though most park visitors use either Junín or San Martín as their base.

THE SIETE LAGOS ROUTE

Between Villa la Angostura and San Martín de los Andes, northbound RN 234 traverses the forests and skirts the lakes of two national parks, Nahuel Huapi and Lanín, on the popular **Ruta de los Siete Lagos.** The route takes its name from the seven scenic lakes that it passes along or near, but only its northern half, through Lanín, is paved. This is notable because the southern Nahuel Huapi section may well be Argentina's dustiest road or, when it rains heavily, perhaps the muddiest.

Because of billowing dust clouds, tours that take this otherwise enjoyable route don't necessarily see the landscape; the ideal time is immediately after a light rain. The narrow Nahuel Huapi segment requires defensive driving to avoid head-on collisions; vehicles are also a serious hazard for cyclists, but many international adventure travel companies include the route as part of their mountain-bike itineraries. There are plans to pave the remainder.

In addition to tours, the Siete Lagos route offers scheduled bus service; for details, see the Getting There entries for Villa la Angostura and San Martín de los Andes.

Flora and Fauna

Precipitation that reaches up to 3,000 millimeters per annum encourages the growth of dense humid Valdivian woodlands. Lanín's signature species is the coniferous *pehuén* or monkey puzzle tree *(Araucaria araucana),* for centuries a subsistence resource for the Mapuches and Pehuenches (a sub-group whose own name stresses their dependence on the tree's edible nuts). Along with the broadleaf deciduous southern beech *raulí (Nothofagus nervosa),* the *pehuén* forms part of a transitional forest that overlaps southern beech species that dominate the more southerly Patagonian forests, such as the *coihue, lenga,* and *ñire.* In places, the solid bamboo *colihue* forms almost impenetrable thickets.

At higher elevations, above 1,600 meters, extreme cold and wind reduce the vegetative cover to shrubs and grasses. At lower elevations, to the east, the drier climate supports shrubs and Patagonian steppe grasses.

Except for its trout, Lanín is less celebrated for its wildlife than for its landscapes. Fortunate visitors, though, may see the secretive spaniel-size deer known as the *pudú (Pudu pudu)* or the larger Andean *huemul (Hippocamelus bisulcus).* The major predator is the puma, present on the steppes and in the forest, while the torrent duck frequents the faster streams and the Andean condor glides on the heights. The lakes and rivers attract many other birds.

Sector Aluminé

Immediately east of Aluminé, RP 18 follows the south bank of the Río Rucachoroi for 23 kilo-

© WAYNE BERNHARDSON

araucaria trees, Parque Nacional Lanín

meters to Lago Rucachoroi, site of a Mapuche reserve. From Rahué, 17 kilometers south of Aluminé, RP 46 leads west to **Lago Quillén,** an area of dense monkey puzzle forests that's also home to Mapuche families.

Nineteen kilometers north of Aluminé via RP 23, scenic RP 11 climbs eastward through araucaria forests along the Río Pulmari and **Lago Ñorquinco,** the park's northernmost access point. On what would be an excellent mountain-bike route, the road loops north-northeast toward the Chilean border at Icalma and the small Argentine resort of Villa Pehuenia.

Sector Lago Tromen

From a junction 11 kilometers north of Junín, northwesterly RP 60 leads to the Chilean border at Paso Mamuil Malal, where Lago Tromen marks the most convenient approach to the summit of **Volcán Lanín.** Because of the northeasterly exposure, both hiking and climbing routes open earlier here than on the southern side of the peak, which lies partly in Chile.

Before climbing Lanín, obtain permission from the APN in San Martín, who will ask to inspect your gear, which should contain crampons, ice axe, plastic tools, and appropriate clothing and peripherals (gloves, hats, insulated jackets, sunglasses, and sunscreen).

From the trailhead at the Argentine border, the **Camino de Mulas** route takes five to seven hours to the **Refugio Club Andino Junín de los Andes** (altitude 2,600 meters; capacity 10 persons); beyond here, snow gear is essential. The shorter but steeper **Espina del Pescado** route starts at the Argentine army's **Refugio Regimiento Infantería de Montaña** (elevation 2,350 meters; capacity 15 persons); it's possible to approach either route from the Lago Huechulafquen side (see below) as well. A new *refugio,* with a capacity of 60 persons at an elevation of 2,600 meters, is under consideration.

Volcán Lanín

Looming above the landscape, straddling the Chilean border at 3,776 meters above sea level, lop-sided Volcán Lanín is the literal and metaphorical center of its namesake national park. Covered by permanent snow, rising 1,500 meters above any other peak in the vicinity, its irregular cone is an elevated beacon visible for hundreds of kilometers to the east and, where the rugged terrain permits, to the north and south.

Sector Lago Huechulafquen

About four kilometers north of Junín, RP 61 leads northwest along the Río Chimehuín and the north shore of Lago Huechulafquen for 52 kilometers to Puerto Canoas and **Lago Paimún** (the end of the road). En route, several trailheads lead north; the most interesting is the **Cara Sur** (Southern Face) approach to Volcán Lanín along the wooded Arroyo Rucu Leufú, which meets the trail coming south from Lago Tromen (see above). Hikers not wishing to continue to the base of Lanín, about a four-hour walk, or the seven hours to the RIM *refugio,* can still enjoy the stroll through the araucaria woodland; climbers should obtain permission from the APN ranger here.

© WAYNE BERNHARDSON

Volcán Lanín, Parque Nacional Lanín

From the Piedra Mala campground at Lago Paimún, a 30-minute hike goes to **Cascada El Saltillo,** a 20-meter waterfall. It's no longer possible to walk around Lago Paimún, most of whose north shore is closed for environmental reasons, but summer hikers can cross the narrows, known as La Unión, that separates Huechulafquen and Paimún on a *balsa* (cable platform) for about US$1. The rest of the year, it's possible to hire a rowboat to get across; on the north shore, a Mapuche family runs the basic **Camping Ecufén.**

From La Unión, the trail continues through *coihue* and *pehuén* forest for about five hours to **Aila,** where there's a Mapuche-run campground, and another eight hours to the rustic **Termas de Epulafquen.** From Epulafquen, RP 62 returns to Junín de los Andes.

Lago Lolog

Only about 15 kilometers north of San Martín, little developed Lago Lolog has several campgrounds and regular summer transportation; see the accommodations entry below and the San Martín Getting Around entry for details.

Lago Lácar

San Martín's own lake, Lago Lácar, is wilder toward the Chilean border, where there is camping, hiking, and whitewater rafting at the outlet of the Río Hua Hum. For transportation details, both overland and by water, see the San Martín entry.

Accommodations and Food

Except in nearby towns, accommodations and food are in short supply, as the park is less developed than Nahuel Huapi to the south.

Sector Lago Tromen: Alongside the Gendarmería post, **Camping Lanín** (tel. 02972/491355, US$1 pp) has facilities that include picnic tables, fire pits and bathrooms with showers. It's open in January, February, and March only.

Appealing chiefly to fly-fishing fanatics, **Hostería San Huberto** (RP 60 Km 28, tel. 02972/491238, www.sanhubertolodge.com.ar) charges from US$150/200 s/d with full board. Reservations are essential as it has only six twin rooms.

Sector Lago Huechulafquen: Free campgrounds along on the shores of Lago Huechulafquen and Lago Paimún are very rustic, while the paying sites are better maintained, with better services, and are community-oriented.

Camping Bahía Cañicul (RP 61 Km 48) has sites for US$1.70 pp over age 13; those 13 and under cost US$1 pp. It also has a small store, but supplies are cheaper and more diverse in Junín. **Camping Raquithué** (RP 61 Km 54) costs US$1.30 pp for anyone over age six; those six and under stay free. The attractive **Camping Piedra Mala** (RP 61 Km 60) charges US$1.70 pp for those older than 10; those 10 and under stay free, but pay a small charge for using the showers.

A few kilometers before Lago Paimún, **Hostería Huechulafquen** (RP 61 Km 55, tel. 02972/426075, hosteriahuechulafquen@yahoo.com.ar, US$40 pp with half board, US$48 pp full board) is less elaborate but still pleasant. The three-star **Hostería Paimún** (RP 61 Km 58, tel. 02972/491211, fax 02972/491201, adelvalle@jandes.com.ar, US$43 pp with half board, US$50 pp full board) is primarily a fishing lodge.

Lago Lolog: The basic **Camping Puerto Arturo** is free of charge.

Hua Hum: Westbound from San Martín, gravel RP 48 follows the north shore of Lago Lácar to the Chilean border at Hua Hum. En route, **Estancia Quechuquina** (RP 48 Km 30) is a rustic teahouse with exceptional cakes and cookies, open noon–7:30 P.M. daily for lunch and tea. Though it has no accommodations, it does have lake access and makes an ideal day trip. It opens in mid-December and stays open until Semana Santa.

Other Practicalities

In addition to the APN Intendencia at San Martín, there are ranger stations at all the major lakes and some other points of interest. While the rangers are helpful, they do not, in general, have maps or other printed matter. The park has recently instituted an admission fee of US$4 per person, valid for one week, which must be purchased at APN and local tourist offices outside the park rather than at the park entrance itself.

San Martín de los Andes, Junín de los Andes, and Aluminé are the main gateways to the park. Public transportation is limited, but consult those entries for further information. While international buses to Chile, via the southerly Hua Hum and the northerly Tromen passes, may carry passengers, they are often full.

VILLA LA ANGOSTURA AND VICINITY

On the north shore of Lago Nahuel Huapi, Villa la Angostura traditionally lies within Bariloche's economic orbit. Thanks to its proximity to less developed parts of the lake, to Parque Nacional Los Arrayanes, and the Cerro Bayo winter-sports center, though, it's quickly establishing its own destination identity for both Argentines and foreign visitors. It has excellent accommodations and restaurants, but there's an air of exclusivity and prices are on the high side.

Orientation

Villa la Angostura (population 7,311) is 80 kilometers northwest of Bariloche via RN 237 and RN 231 (the international highway to Osorno, Chile) and 109 kilometers south of San Martín de los Andes via RN 234, the scenic but narrow and dusty Siete Lagos (Seven Lakes) route. It is 870 meters

Snow falls on a *Nothofagus* forest, Villa la Angostura.

above sea level, but the surrounding mountains rise sharply from the Nahuel Huapi shoreline.

RN 231 passes directly through the part of town known as El Cruce, where many services line both sides of the highway (which is known as Avenida Los Arrayanes and its westward extension Avenida Los Lagos). Three kilometers south, the largely residential La Villa also has a cluster of hotels and restaurants; Parque Nacional Los Arrayanes occupies the entirety of Península Quetrihué, the southward-jutting peninsula linked to La Villa by the 91-meter isthmus that gives Villa la Angostura its name (The Narrows). There are other sectors of interest as well, including Las Balsas and Puerto Manzano to the southeast, and Barrio Norte and Río Correntoso to the northwest.

Sights

Foot, bicycle, and kayak are the best means of seeing Villa la Angostura's attractions. For hiking in the nearby mountains, where the trails are too steep and narrow for bicycles, consider hiring a taxi or *remise* to the trailhead.

Recently relocated to El Cruce, Villa la Angostura's **Museo Histórico Regional** (Blvd. Nahuel Huapi and El Calafate, 02944/494476, ext. 21) deals primarily with the pioneering timber industry, the agriculture that followed it, and the families who established themselves here. It does, however, acknowledge the enduring presence of the Mapuche who constituted a separate nation overlapping the Argentine and Chilean borders, and their displacement by the Argentine state.

Four blocks south of the bus terminal, the Museo Histórico Regional is open 11 A.M.–5 P.M. Tuesday–Saturday. Admission is free.

June–September at nearby Cerro Bayo, **Centro de Ski Cerro Bayo** operates 26 kilometers of runs ranging from 1,050 to 1,782 meters above sea level, with five chairlifts and five tow bars. Lift passes depend on the time of the season, but range from US$12–19 for a half-day, US$14–23 for a full day, US$35–61 for three days, and US$80–138 for a week. Season passes costs US$480; children get discounts of about one-third in all categories, while adults 65 or older ski free.

Only nine kilometers southeast of El Cruce, Cerro Bayo (tel. 02944/494189, www.cerrobayoweb.com, informes@cerrobayoweb.com) also has accommodations, restaurants, and rental equipment on site. Empresa 15 de Mayo operates four buses daily (US$1) from town, starting at 11 A.M.; the last one returns at 7 P.M.

From El Cruce, a narrow four-kilometer road zigzags to **Mirador Belvedere,** a wide parking area and overlook with views along Lago Correntoso to the north, the almost absurdly short Río Correntoso that connects it to Lago Nahuel Huapi, and the hoary peaks that mark the Chilean border to the west.

About midway up the route, an eastbound forest trail leads to **Cascada Inayacal,** a 50-meter waterfall. From the parking area, a three-kilometer trail to 1,992-meter **Cerro Belvedere** climbs through *coihue* forest before dipping into a saddle and then ascending steeply over Cerro Falso Belvedere before continuing to the summit. The road, which has several blind curves, can be difficult in wet weather.

Parque Nacional Los Arrayanes

According to local folklore, Walt Disney's cartoon feature *Bambi* took the idea for its forest from the *arrayán* woodland at the tip of Península Quetrihué, a former estancia that became a national park in 1971. The eye-catching red-barked forests of *Myrceugenella apiculata,* with their bright white flowers, do indeed bear a resemblance, but a Disney archivist has pointed out that Walt never visited the area. In fact, *Bambi* was in production prior to his 1941 trip to Argentina.

So close to La Villa that it feels more like a sprawling city park—in fact, it's larger than the city itself—Los Arrayanes occupies the entire 1,753 hectares of Península Quetrihué, which stretches south into Lago Nahuel Huapi. Its namesake forest comprises only about 20 hectares, but the rest of the peninsula bristles with trees like the *maitén* and the southern beeches *coihue, lenga* and *ñire,* colorful shrubs like the *notro* and *chilco,* and dense bamboo thickets of *colihue.*

The park's environmental standout may be the *arrayán,* whose individual specimens reach 25 meters and 650 years of age, but it's also an ideal place for hiking and mountain biking—the undulating 12-kilometer trail to or from the tip of the peninsula makes an ideal half-day excursion (on a bicycle or doing one-way by boat) or a full-day by hiking in both directions. Argentine rangers often exaggerate the time needed on certain trails, but the three hours they suggest is about right for this highly pleasurable walk-in-the-woods, which passes a pair of lakes. Only at the park entrance, near La Villa, are there any truly steep segments.

At the entrance, rangers collect a US$4.50 admission charge (US$2.25 for Argentine residents). Unfortunately, even those who only intend to make the 20-minute stroll to the panoramic **Mirador Arrayán** must also pay the fee. Near the dock at the peninsula's southern tip, a *confitería* with a cozy fireplace serves sandwiches, coffee, and hot chocolate.

Non-hikers can reach the *arrayán* forest in about half an hour on the *Catamarán Futaleufú,* run by El Cruce's **Angostura Turismo** (Avenida Arrayanes 208, Local 1, tel. 02944/494405); the cost is US$7 one way, plus a US$1 boarding tax. Cyclists can rent bikes in El Cruce, but both hikers and bikers must leave the park by 4 P.M. Horses are prohibited, as is camping.

Shopping and Events

On weekends only, locals and parachutists peddle their own wares at **Feria de Artesanos,** El Cruce's artisan's fair, on Belvedere between Avenida Los Arrayanes and Las Fucsias.

For four days in early February, the provincial **Fiesta de los Jardines** (Garden Festival) occupies center stage.

Sports and Recreation

English-speaking Anthony Hawes operates **Alma Sur Eco Trips** (tel. 02944/15-564724, www.almasur.com, info@almasur.com), which arranges activities ranging from hiking and horseback riding to mountain biking, fishing, and whitewater rafting and kayaking.

Accommodations

In the recent past, Villa la Angostura was almost exclusively upscale, but recent developments include some fine budget options.

Some 500 meters west of the tourist office, the improved **Camping Unquehue** (Avenida Los Lagos s/n, tel. 02944/494922, unquehue@ciudad.com.ar, US$3 pp) offers wooded sites, with hot showers available in the communal baths.

The next cheapest choices are the classy HI-affiliate **Bajo Cero Hostel** (Río Caleufú 88, tel. 02944/495454, www.bajocerohostel.com, US$6.50 pp in dorms, US$23 d) and the **Hostel la Angostura** (Barbagelata 157, tel. 02944/494834, www.hostellaangostura.com.ar, hostellaangostura.com.ar, US$7 pp in dorms, US$20 d), an attractive place on spacious grounds.

Two blocks north of the bus terminal, at **Residencial Río Bonito** (Topa Topa 260, tel. 02944/494110, riobonito@ciudad.com.ar, US$18 d), the private rooms enjoy a quiet garden setting; breakfast is included. El Cruce's **Residencial Don Pedro** (Belvedere and Los Maquis, tel. 02944/494269, US$20 d) is comparable.

About one kilometer west of El Cruce, **Hostería Las Cumbres** (Avenida Siete Lagos s/n, tel. 02944/494945, www.hosterialascumbres.com, info@hosterialascumbres.com, US$26 d) is an eight-room, owner-operated hotel that's a fine budget choice. Home-cooked dinners are also available.

In a secluded location near Lago Correntoso, skier-friendly **Hostel lo del Francés** (Lolog 2057, tel. 02944/15-564063, www.lodelfrances.com.ar, hosteldelfrances@hotmail.com, US$10 pp for hostel bunks, US$27 d) has only three rooms but offers home-cooked dinners, great gardens, a bar, and other common areas, including a walk-in fireplace for recharging the batteries in ski season. It is an HI affiliate; because capacity is so limited, reservations are essential.

Just off Avenida Arrayanes, El Cruce's **Hostería Posta de los Colonos** (Los Notros 19, tel. 02944/494386, postadeloscolonos@infovia.com.ar, US$30/47 s/d) has nearly pristine, well-heated rooms with comfy beds, cable TV, and breakfast, but also thin walls and creaky floors. While it's not a noisy locale per se, small noises carry well and the planned addition of sound insulation will be welcome.

Dating from 1938, originally built for the APN, La Villa's lakeside classic **Hotel Angostura** (Nahuel Huapi 1911, tel. 02944/494224, www.hotelangostura.com, info@hotelangostura.com, US$47 d) has 20 rooms, some with lake views, and three separate bungalows sleeping up to six people. While its aged floors are also creaky and the hot water is slow to reach the shower early in the morning, this once-romantic hotel still has style, personality, good beds, no TVs or phones in the rooms, and friendly service.

In Puerto Manzano, about six kilometers southeast of El Cruce, **Hosteria Naranjo en Flor** (Chucao 62, tel. 02944/494863, naranjoenflor@infovia.com.ar, US$60 d) is an eight-room hotel on a forested lot with views of Lago Nahuel Huapi and the Andes. It also has a pool, and a restaurant that pulls in nonguests as well.

Across the Río Correntoso, three kilometers northwest of El Cruce, the historic **Hotel Correntoso** (tel. 02944/15-619727, www.correntoso.com, info@correntoso.com, US$145–190 s or d) started as a fishing lodge in 1917 and became a major attraction before burning nearly to the ground. Almost abandoned, it's undergone a recent rehab that's restored its former glory plus—there's a lakeside fishing bar, a wine bar, and an outstanding restaurant as well. It also has a Buenos Aires contact (Avenida Figueroa Alcorta 3351, tel. 011/4803-0030).

The area's standout is the sophisticated Relais & Chateaux affiliate **Hostería Las Balsas** (tel. 02944/494308, www.lasbalsas.com, balsas@satlink.com, US$200 d, US$300 suite), a 12-room, three-suite Bustillo classic on Bahía las Balsas south of El Cruce. All rooms have lake views; rates include unlimited spa access and breakfast, and there's a highly regarded hybrid restaurant with French and traditional Argentine dishes.

Food

In addition to its hotel restaurants (see the accommodations entry above), Villa la Angostura offers a diversity of dining options at moderate to upscale prices. There's a cluster on and around El Cruce's Avenida Arrayanes, but several other worthwhile options are in the vicinity.

For breakfast, sandwiches, coffee, and desserts, try **Rincón Suizo** (Avenida Arrayanes 44, tel. 02944/494248). **Las Varas** (Avenida Arrayanes 235, tel. 02944/494740) is a standard *parrilla.* **Tante Frida** (Avenida Arrayanes 209) is a teahouse with exceptional ice cream, but the extraordinary ice creamery *Jauja* (Avenida Arrayanes 141, tel. 02944/495671) has also established a branch here (though with fewer flavors than in Bariloche or El Bolsón).

The spacious but still crowded **Nativa Café** (Avenida Arrayanes 198, tel. 02944/495093) is a fine pizzeria whose toppings include *jabalí* (wild boar) and *ciervo* (venison, which is farmed in the region). **La Buena Vida** (Avenida Arrayanes 167, Local 4, tel. 02944/495200) is a smaller, homier place, with excellent service, that serves a fine risotto.

North of Puente Correntoso, **El Mirador de los Cerros** (Avenida Siete Lagos 5018) enjoys a spectacular panorama from its hillside deck, though the kitchen and the service can be slow and the menu is limited to pizza, sandwiches, and regional appetizers. Also enjoying fine views, especially at sunset, **Raíces** (Avenida Siete Lagos 3314, tel. 02944/15-556903) is another good choice for appetizers and drinks.

A recent addition to the restaurant scene, **La Camorra** (Avenida Cerro Bayo 65, tel. 02944/495554) offers a blend of Italian, Spanish, and criollo cuisine in dishes such as stews, pot roast, polenta, focaccia, and especially risotto.

Not necessarily the area's best restaurant, but conceivably its best value, moderately priced **La Encantada** (Cerro Belvedere 69, tel. 02944/495515) serves exceptional *ahumados* (smoked appetizers), exquisite trout empanadas, and fine pizzas and pastas and provides attentive service (including savvy wine suggestions).

Reservations are imperative at the current star of the cuisine scene, the **Tinto Bistro** (Blvd. Nahuel Huapi 34, tel. 02944/494924). Run by brother-to-royalty Martín Zorreguieta (his sister Máxima married the Dutch Crown Prince William in 2002), it offers an

Asian/Patagonian fusion food, with entrées in the US$6–9 range. Typical dishes include appetizers like Patagonian roll with lamb dipped in honey/soy sauce and Thai-flavored pastas with shrimp and crayfish (spicy by Argentine standards). Open for dinner only, from 8:30 P.M.–midnight, it offers what may be the area's finest wine selection (including some very expensive vintages).

Set on wooded grounds, Puerto Manzano's comfy **Waldhaus** (Avenida Arrayanes 6431, tel. 02944/495123) serves continental-style dishes like carpaccio, fondue, goulash, and raclette, with a Patagonian touch. At least the equal of Tinto, with entrées in the US$8 range, it's open for lunch and for dinner (when reservations are obligatory), and has a fine wine list.

Information and Services

At El Cruce, the **Secretaría Municipal de Turismo** (Avenida Siete Lagos 93, tel. 02944/494124, www.villalaangostura.gov.ar) is open 8 A.M.–9 P.M. daily except in winter, when it closes at 8 P.M.

The APN's **Seccional Villa la Angostura** (Nahuel Huapi s/n, tel. 02944/494152) is in La Villa.

Virtually all services are in El Cruce, where **Banco Patagonia** (Avenida Arrayanes 275) has an ATM.

Correo Argentino is at Avenida Arrayanes 282, Local 4; the postal code is 8407. **VLA Comunicaciones** (Avenida Arrayanes 90, Local 2) has phone and Internet connections, but those connections are still slower than in Bariloche.

Getting There

El Cruce's convenient **Terminal de Omnibus** (Avenida Siete Lagos and Avenida Arrayanes, tel. 02944/494961) has frequent connections to Bariloche, several buses daily to San Martín de los Andes via the dustily scenic Siete Lagos route, and long-distance services to Neuquén. Chile-bound buses from Bariloche stop here, but reservations are advisable because these often run full.

Typical destinations, times, and fares include Bariloche (US$2.50, 1.5 hours), San Martín de los Andes (US$5.50, three hours), and Neuquén (US$11, six hours).

SAN CARLOS DE BARILOCHE AND VICINITY

If Patagonia ever became independent, its logical capital might be San Carlos de Bariloche—"Bariloche" to most visitors—the highest profile destination in an area explorer Francisco P. Moreno once called "this beautiful piece of Argentine Switzerland." It's not just that Bariloche, with its incomparable setting on the shores of Lago Nahuel Huapi, is the lake district's largest city, transportation hub, and gateway to Argentina's first national park; in the 1930s, the carved granite blocks and rough-hewn polished timbers of its landmark Centro Cívico made a promising precedent for harmonizing urban expansion with the wild surroundings.

Dating from 1902, Bariloche was slow to grow—when former U.S. President Theodore Roosevelt visited in 1913, he observed that

> *Bariloche is a real frontier village. . . . It was like one of our frontier towns in the old-time West as regards the diversity in ethnic type and nationality among the citizens. The little houses stood well away from one another on the broad, rough, faintly marked streets.*

When Roosevelt crossed the Andes from Chile, Bariloche was more than 700 kilometers from the nearest railroad, but it began to boom after completion of the Ferrocarril Roca's southern branch in 1934. Its rustically sophisticated style has spread throughout the region—even to structures as commonplace as phone booths—but unrelenting growth, promoted by unscrupulous politicians and developers, has cost the city much of its hybrid Euro-Andean charm. For much of the day, for instance, the Bariloche Center, a multi-story monstrosity authorized by the brief and irregular repeal of height-limit legislation, literally overshadows the Centro Cívico.

As Bariloche's population has grown from about 60,000 in 1980 to almost 90,000 today, its congested downtown *microcentro* has become a clutter of chocolate shops, hotels, and time-shares,

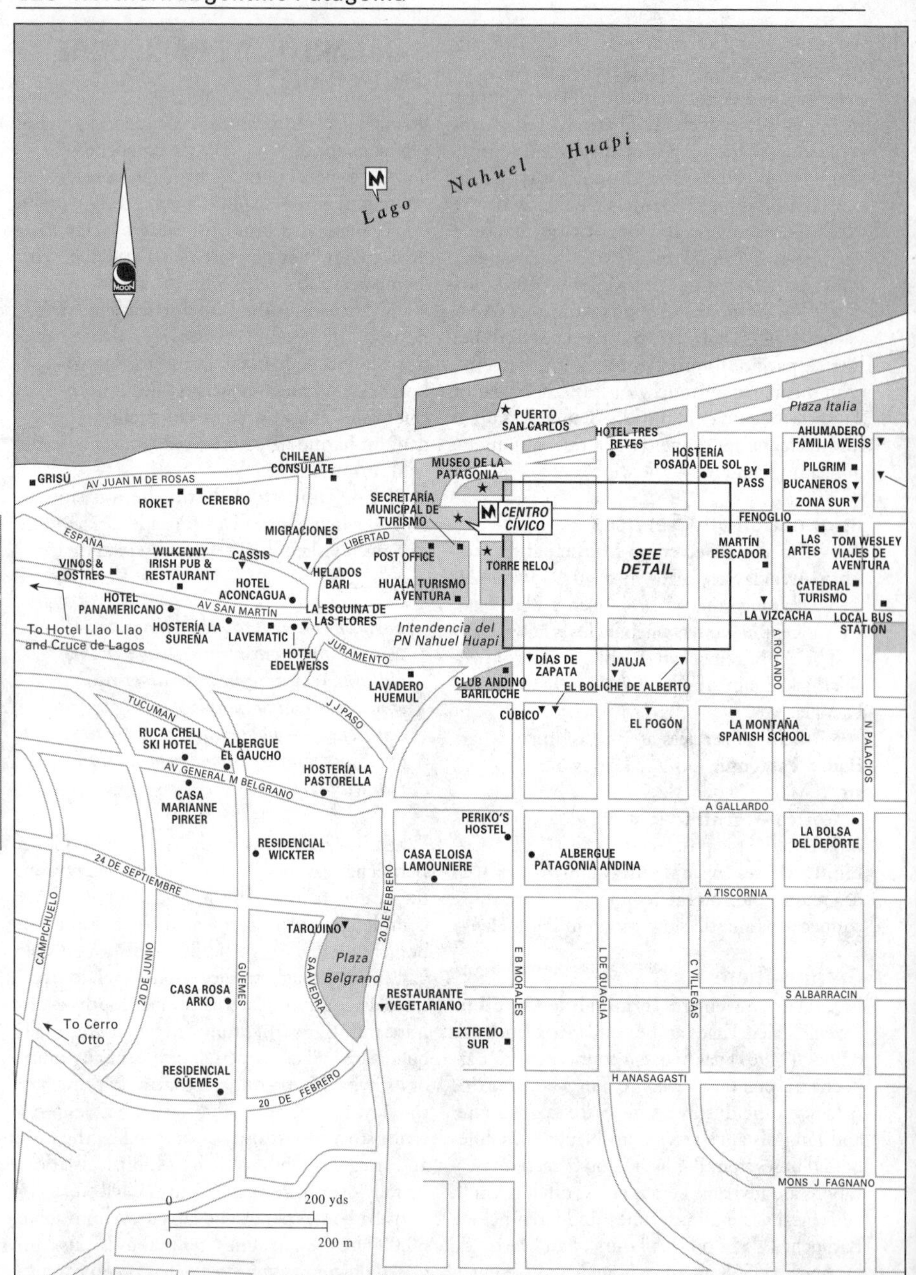

Lago Nahuel Huapi
PUERTO SAN CARLOS
HOTEL TRES REYES
Plaza Italia
AHUMADERO FAMILIA WEISS
HOSTERÍA POSADA DEL SOL
BY PASS
PILGRIM
BUCANEROS
ZONA SUR
CHILEAN CONSULATE
MUSEO DE LA PATAGONIA
GRISÚ
AV JUAN M DE ROSAS
ROKET
CEREBRO
SECRETARÍA MUNICIPAL DE TURISMO
CENTRO CÍVICO
MIGRACIONES
FENOGLIO
ESPAÑA
LIBERTAD
MARTÍN PESCADOR
LAS ARTES
TOM WESLEY VIAJES DE AVENTURA
SEE DETAIL
WILKENNY IRISH PUB & RESTAURANT
CASSIS
VINOS & POSTRES
POST OFFICE
TORRE RELOJ
HELADOS BARI
HOTEL ACONCAGUA
HUALA TURISMO AVENTURA
CATEDRAL TURISMO
HOTEL PANAMERICANO
AV SAN MARTÍN
LA ESQUINA DE LAS FLORES
LA VIZCACHA
LOCAL BUS STATION
To Hotel Llao Llao and Cruce de Lagos
HOSTERÍA LA SUREÑA
LAVEMATIC
Intendencia del PN Nahuel Huapi
HOTEL EDELWEISS
JURAMENTO
A ROLANDO
DÍAS DE ZAPATA
JAUJA
LAVADERO HUEMUL
CLUB ANDINO BARILOCHE
EL BOLICHE DE ALBERTO
TUCUMAN
J J PASO
CÚBICO
EL FOGÓN
LA MONTAÑA SPANISH SCHOOL
N PALACIOS
RUCA CHELI SKI HOTEL
ALBERGUE EL GAUCHO
AV GENERAL M BELGRANO
HOSTERÍA LA PASTORELLA
CASA MARIANNE PIRKER
A GALLARDO
PERIKO'S HOSTEL
LA BOLSA DEL DEPORTE
RESIDENCIAL WICKTER
CASA ELOISA LAMOUNIERE
ALBERGUE PATAGONIA ANDINA
24 DE SEPTIEMBRE
A TISCORNIA
20 DE FEBRERO
TARQUINO
CAMPICHUELO
20 DE JUNIO
GUEMES
SAAVEDRA
Plaza Belgrano
E B MORALES
L DE QUAGLIA
C VILLEGAS
S ALBARRACIN
CASA ROSA ARKO
RESTAURANTE VEGETARIANO
To Cerro Otto
EXTREMO SUR
RESIDENCIAL GÜEMES
H ANASAGASTI
20 DE FEBRERO
MONS J FAGNANO
0
200 yds
0
200 m

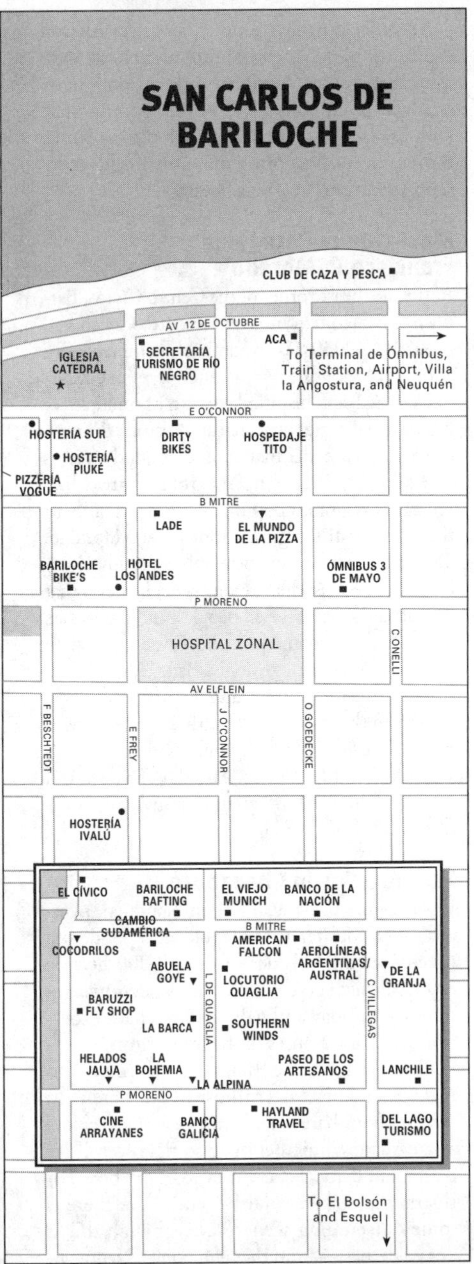

and notorious for high-school graduation bashes that leave some hotel rooms in ruins. Student tourism may be declining, in relative terms at least, but Bariloche still lags behind aspirations that were once higher than nearby Cerro Catedral's ski areas. Like other Patagonian destinations, it's booming in the summer months of December, January, and February.

Bariloche holds a unique place in Argentine cinema as the location for director Emilio Vieyra's *Sangre de Vírgenes* (Blood of the Virgins), a Hammer-style vampire flick that was well ahead of its time when shot in 1967 (it's now available on DVD). Perhaps Vieyra envisaged the unsavory side of things to come, but Bariloche's bloodsuckers are only part of the story—the city and its surroundings still have much to offer, at reasonable cost. Many of the best accommodations, restaurants, and other services lie between along Avenida Bustillo between Bariloche proper and Llao Llao, about 25 kilometers to the west.

Orientation

On Lago Nahuel Huapi's southeastern shore, 764 meters above sea level, Bariloche (population 89,475) is 1,596 kilometers from Buenos Aires and 429 kilometers southwest of Neuquén via RN 237, but 982 kilometers west of the Río Negro provincial capital of Viedma, on the Atlantic coast. It is 123 kilometers north of El Bolsón via RN 258.

As RN 237 enters Bariloche from the east, it becomes Costanera Avenida 12 de Octubre, Avenida Juan Manuel de Rosas, and then Avenida Bustillo, as it continues west to the resort of Llao Llao. En route, it skirts the landmark Centro Cívico; one block south, the parallel Avenida Bartolomé Mitre is the main commercial street, but the entire area within a few blocks of the lake is densely built. North-south streets—some of them staircases—climb steeply from the lakeshore.

Centro Cívico and Vicinity

Despite the kitsch merchants who pervade the plaza with Siberian huskies and St. Bernards for photographic poses, and the graffiti that often deface sculptor Emilio Sarneguet's equestrian statue of the controversial General Roca, the handsome array of buildings that border it would be the pride of many cities around the world. The view north to Lago Nahuel Huapi is a bonus, even when the boxy Bariloche Center blocks the afternoon sun.

The Centro Cívico was a team effort, originally envisioned by architect Ernesto de Estrada in 1936, and executed under the stewardship of APN director Exequiel Bustillo until its inauguration in 1940. On its south side, when the Municipalidad's **Torre Reloj** (Clock Tower) sounds at noon, figures from Patagonian history appear to mark the hour. Other buildings of interest, with steep-pitched roofs and gracefully arched *recovas* that offer shelter from inclement winter weather, include the **Correo** (post office) and the **Museo de la Patagonia** (see separate entry below).

© WAYNE BERNHARDSON

Bariloche's Centro Cívico set the style for architecture in northern Argentine Patagonia's lake district.

Exequiel Bustillo's brother, architect Alejandro Bustillo, designed the **Intendencia de Parques Nacionales** (National Park Headquarters, San Martín 24), one block north, to harmonize with the Centro Cívico. Together, the structures form a national historical monument and represent Argentine Patagonia's best.

Museo de la Patagonia Francisco P. Moreno

At the northeast corner of the Centro Cívico, Bariloche's Patagonian museum (Centro Cívico s/n, tel. 02944/422309) is an admirably comprehensive effort at placing the region (and more) in ecological, cultural, and historical context. Its multiple exhibition halls touch on natural history through taxidermy (far better than most of its kind); insects (inexplicably including subtropical areas like Iguazú); Patagonia's population from antiquity to the present; the region's aboriginal Mapuche, Tehuelche, and Fuegian peoples; caudillo Juan Manuel de Rosas; the Conquista del Desierto that displaced the region's first peoples; and Bariloche's own urban development. There is even material on Stanford University geologist Bailey Willis, a visionary consultant who did the first systematic surveys in the region in the early 20th century.

The Museo de la Patagonia is open 10 A.M.–12:30 P.M. and 2–7 P.M. Tuesday–Friday, and 10 A.M.–1 P.M. Monday and Saturday. Admission costs about US$1.

Estancia Fortín Chacabuco

Just over the provincial line in Neuquén, plantations of Monterey, lodgepole, and ponderosa pine cover the hillsides of this 10,000-hectare estancia, which grazes 2,500 sheep, offers miles of trails for full-day and half-day horseback excursions, and also houses fly-fishing visitors.

On the edge of the Patagonian steppe at Lago Nahuel Huapi's easternmost point, barely 20 minutes from Bariloche, Fortín Chacabuco enjoys a rain-shadow microclimate so that even if it's pouring in Bariloche, it's likely to be dry here. For riders, the terrain is fairly gentle, but there is some outstanding scenery even though this is not wilderness—from the high points, Neuquén-bound buses from Bariloche are readily visible.

Fortín Chacabuco's full-day excursions (US$35 pp) include transportation from Bariloche and back, a morning trail ride followed by a traditional gut-busting *asado* for lunch, and a shorter afternoon ride. Anglo-Argentine operator Alastair Whewell sometimes leads upwards of 20 riders per day, but the average is around 15.

Rides take place all year except for May and June. For more details, contact Estancia Fortín Chacabuco (tel. 02944/15-567449) or Estancias Patagónicas (www.estanciaspatagonicas.com). Accommodations rates are in the US$150 per-person range with full board.

Entertainment

The densely built *microcentro* has an active nightlife, with pubs, theaters, cinema, and discos open until all hours.

Cine Arrayanes (Perito Moreno 39, tel. 02944/422860) shows recent movies.

Bariloche's cluster of downtown bars also offers menus of palatable pub grub. Choices include the **Wilkenny Irish Pub & Restaurant** (San Martín 435, tel. 02944/424444), which has a 6–9 P.M. happy hour; **Pilgrim** (Palacios 167, tel. 02944/421686), also an Irish-style venue; and the traditional German-style **El Viejo Munich** (Mitre 102, tel. 02944/422336), a customary stop for sandwiches, snacks, and cold draft beer. **Cúbico** (Elflein 47, tel. 02944/522260) is a modernist downtown wine bar.

Like their Buenos Aires counterparts, Bariloche nightspots open late—around 1 A.M.—and close around daybreak. The most central of the bunch is **By Pass** (Rolando 157, tel. 02944/420549), while several others lie a few blocks west of the Centro Cívico: **Cerebro** (Juan Manuel de Rosas 406, tel. 02944/424948); **Roket** (Juan Manuel de Rosas 424, tel. 02944/431940); and **Grisú** (Rosas 574, tel. 02944/422269).

Events

More than just a pretty landscape, the Nahuel Huapi area also has an active cultural life. Llao Llao's Camping Musical Bariloche (cmbariloche@infovia.com.ar) sponsors the summertime **Festival de Música de Verano,** which includes chamber music and brass concerts in January and February.

March's **Muestra Floral de Otoño** is an end-of-the-summer flower show, while May 3 marks the **Fiesta Nacional de la Rosa Mosqueta,** in which local bakers and confectioners make the most of the wild rosehips, a European introduction that's become a plague in the lake district. July's **Fiesta Nacional de la Nieve** (National Snow Festival) marks the beginning of the ski season.

In the spring, gardeners again get their turn at October's **Fiesta del Tulipán** (Tulip Festival) and the **Muestra Floral de Primavera** (Spring Flower Show). Late December is the time for **Navidad Coral** (Christmas Chorus).

Shopping

Bariloche artisans lives off souvenir shoppers, who frequent the outdoor **Paseo de los Artesanos** (Villegas and Perito Moreno), open 10 A.M.–9 P.M. daily.

Vinos & Postres (Avenida San Martín 597, tel. 02944/436300) is the Bariloche outpost of Buenos Aires's Club del Vino, with a wide selection of Argentine wines.

Traditionally, chocoholics flock to locales like **Fenoglio** (Mitre 301, tel. 02944/423119), **Las Artes** (Mitre 369, tel. 02944/424434), and **Abuela Goye** (Quaglia 221, tel. 02944/423311), which is also a standout ice creamery.

La Barca (Quaglia 247, tel. 02944/423170) is an excellent bookstore.

Sports and Recreation

Thanks to nearby Parque Nacional Nahuel Huapi, Bariloche is the base for organizing outdoor activities ranging from fishing, hiking, and climbing to mountain biking, horseback riding, whitewater rafting and kayaking, and skiing. For details on skiing, see the sidebar "The Slopes of Bariloche."

Mid-November–mid-April, the entire lake district is a **fishing** enthusiast's paradise for its lakes (where trolling is the rule) and streams (for fly-fishing). Bariloche's **Club de Caza y Pesca** (Costanera 12 de Octubre and Onelli, tel. 02944/422785) is a good source of information. For rental equipment, try **Baruzzi Fly Shop** (Urquiza 250, tel. 02944/424922) or **Martín**

Pescador (Rolando 257, tel. 02944/422275, martinpescador@bariloche.com.ar).

Non-Argentines can purchase licenses at the APN's Intendencia on the Centro Cívico at a cost of cost US$11 per day, US$50 per week, or US$70 per month; note that national park fishing regulations may differ from those of the province.

The APN can provide some information on **hiking and climbing,** but the best source is the **Club Andino Bariloche** (20 de Febrero 30, tel. 02944/422266, www.clubandino.com.ar, cab@bariloche.com.ar), which also organizes park excursions and sells trail maps.

Bariloche's general high-quality roads, both paved and gravel, and the area's many wide trails make **cycling** an attractive option. Mountain-bike rental, with gloves and helmet, costs about US$15 per day.

Dirty Bikes (Eduardo O'Connor 681, tel. 02944/425616, www.dirtybikes.com.ar, dirtybikes@speedy.com.ar) rents bikes and also offers half-day to multiday excursions that include other activities as well. **Bariloche Bike's** (Moreno 520, tel. 02944/424657) also rents bikes.

Local **horseback-riding** trips can last anywhere from two hours (about US$10) to a full day, with multiday excursions also possible. The main operators are **Cabalgatas Carol Jones** (Modesta Victoria 5600, tel. 02944/426508, www.caroljones.com.ar, caroljones@infovia.com.ar) and **Tom Wesley Viajes de Aventura** (Mitre 385, tel. 02944/435040, www.tomwesley.com, info@tomwesley.com).

See also the separate entry for Estancia Fortín Chacabuco.

For **rafters and kayakers,** the Río Limay, at the outlet of Lago Nahuel Huapi, is a half-day, Class II float through agreeable scenery east of Bariloche. The more challenging Río Manso, midway between Bariloche and El Bolsón to the south, is a full-day, mostly Class III descent (around US$40 pp) with some taxing Class IV rapids on multiday trips.

Operators offering river trips include **Aguas Blancas** (Morales 564, tel. 02944/432799, aguasblancas@infovia.com.ar); **Bariloche Rafting** (Mitre 86, Local 5, tel./fax 02944/422997, rafting@bariloche.com.ar); **Extremo Sur** (Morales 765, tel. 02944/427301, www.extremosur.com, info@extremosur.com); and **Huala Turismo Aventura** (San Martín 66, tel. 02944/522438, www.patagoniarafting.com, info@patagoniarafting.com).

Accommodations

Bariloche has plentiful accommodations options in all categories, from camping to hostels, B&Bs, hotels, and luxury lodges. Quality hostel accommodations, in particular, have proliferated, and there are now more than a dozen; for B&Bs, the best area is Barrio Belgrano, southwest of the Centro Cívico. The finest hotels are west of the city proper, on and along the Llao Llao road.

Bariloche's municipal tourist office keeps a thorough database of accommodations and, when summer demand is high, they're an excellent resource. Remember that many low- to midrange hotels cater to high school graduation trips, so it may be better to avoid them toward the end of the calendar academic year.

Under US$10

There are numerous campgrounds west of town on and around Avenida Bustillo, such as the lakefront **Camping Petunia** (Avenida Bustillo 13500, tel. 02944/461969, www.campingpetunia.com, campingpetunia@bariloche.com), where rates are US$2 per person for adults, US$1 per person for kids.

Bariloche's cheapest hostel—still very decent—is the tobacco-free **La Bolsa del Deporte** (Palacios 405, tel. 02944/423529, www.labolsadeldeporte.com.ar, viaene@bariloche.com.ar, US$4 per-person for dorms, US$10 d). For a shoestring hotel, try **Hotel Los Andes** (Perito Moreno 594, tel. 02944/422222, US$6.50/8 s/d).

US$10–25

Only 500 meters west of the bus terminal, the promising **Tango Inn Hostel** (12 de Octubre 1915, tel. 02944/430707, www.tangoinn.com, US$5–6 pp for dorms, 14–24 d, with breakfast) is one of Bariloche's newest hostels, with a restaurant, cafeteria, and bar.

The nonsmoking **Periko's Hostel** (Morales 555, tel. 02944/522326, US$5.50 pp, www.perikos.com) has mostly dorm rooms, but also

© WAYNE BERNHARDSON

West of Bariloche, Hotel Llao Llao is one of South America's most famous hotels.

some new stylish doubles (US$17 d) on the upper floors and a secluded garden (uncommon in this part of town). On wooded grounds in a quieter barrio west of town, its more cramped sister (and HI affiliate) **Alaska Hostel** (Lilinquén 326, tel. 02944/461564, info@alaska-hostel.com, US$5.50 pp) is walking distance from Avenida Bustillo Km 7.5. Several buses, including Nos. 10, 20, and 21 will drop passengers here.

Across the street from Periko's, **Albergue Patagonia Andina** (Morales 564, tel. 02944/422783, info@elpatagoniaandina.com.ar, US$5–6 pp) is less spacious but equally welcoming, with ample common areas. Also good is the newly popular **Albergue El Gaucho** (Belgrano 209, tel. 02944/522464, www.hostelelgaucho.com.ar, albergueelgaucho@hotmail.com, US$4–5.50 pp), which has mostly dorms but also a handful of doubles (US$13); all rooms have private bath. It also rents bicycles, and the staff can manage English, German, and Italian.

Barrio Belgrano is home to several family-run B&Bs that, in the US$6–7 per-person range, are good alternatives to the city's otherwise impersonal budget hotels, but phone ahead. Choices include **Casa Rosa Arko** (Güemes 691, tel. 02944/423109), **Casa Eloisa Lamouniere** (24 de Septiembre 55, tel. 02944/422514), and **Casa Marianne Pirker** (24 de Septiembre 230, tel. 02944/429689, franzpirker@bariloche.com.ar).

Other shoestring choices include **Hospedaje Tito** (Eduardo O'Connor 745, tel. 02944/523563, US$11 d), and Barrio Belgrano's **Residencial Wickter** (Güemes 566, tel. 02944/423248, wikter@hotmail.com, US$14 d) and **Residencial Güemes** (Güemes 715, tel. 02944/424785, US$9/15 s/d).

The hillside **Hostería Ivalú** (Frey 535, tel. 02944/423237, US$18 d) is a decent out-of-the-center choice to the south. Downtown's **Hostería Posada del Sol** (Villegas 148, tel. 02944/423011, posadadelsolbariloche@hotmail.com, US$22 s or d) is comparable.

Near the cathedral, try **Hostería Piuké** (Beschtedt 136, tel. 02944/423044, US$14/20 s/d), or the rather cluttered **Hostería Sur** (Beschtedt 101, tel. 02944/422677, hosteriasur@ciudad.com.ar, US$13/23 s/d).

US$25–50

Barrio Belgrano's obliging **Ruca Cheli Village Ski Hotel** (24 de Setiembre 275, tel./fax

02944/424528, www.rucacheli.com.ar, rucacheli@ciudad.com.ar, US$17/28 s/d) has reasonably large rooms that are good enough if you can tolerate the lurid wallpaper; rates include a buffet breakfast.

West of Barrio Belgrano, **Hostería Quime Quipán** (Avenida de los Pioneros Km 1, tel. 02944/425423, www.hosteriaquimequipan.com.ar, quimequipan@bariloche.com.ar, US$28 d) is adequate but a steep walking distance away from downtown.

Hostería La Sureña (San Martín 432, tel. 02944/422013, hosteria@infovia.com.ar, US$22/30 s/d) is an attractive chalet-style place whose main drawback is its busy avenue setting.

Though it's not kept pace with the times—the aging plumbing can delay the morning's first shower and the breakfast is utterly forgettable—**La Posada del Angel** (Avenida Bustillo Km 12.5, tel. 02944/461263, posadadelangel@infovia.com.ar, US$27/32 s/d) does enjoy friendly family service, a large pool, and five wooded hectares screened by pines from the busy avenue. The rooms themselves are ample and comfortable, but their small windows limit alpine views.

Also on the Llao Llao road, the woodsy **Hostería Pájaro Azul** (Avenida Bustillo 10800, tel. 02944/461025, www.hosteriapajaroazul.com.ar, hostpajaroazul@bariloche.com.ar, US$32/35 s/d) has cozy pine-paneled rooms with mountain views through, again, relatively small windows.

Some of the 13 rooms at attractive **Hostería La Pastorella** (Avenida Belgrano 127, tel. 02944/424656, www.lodgebariloche.com/pastorella, lapastorella@bariloche.com.ar, US$33/41 s/d) are a little too cozy for comfort, but it does offer a diverse breakfast and amenities including a sauna.

Past its prime, the **Hotel Aconcagua** (San Martín 289, tel. 02944/424718, www.aconcaguahotel.com.ar, aconcagua@invofia.com.ar, US$45 s or d) was once one of the city's best, but it's now only average in its price range.

US$50–100

Recently rehabbed, the lakefront **Hotel Tres Reyes** (Avenida 12 de Octubre 135, tel. 02944/426121, fax 02944/424230, www.hoteltresreyes.com, reservas@hoteltresreyes.com, US$42–51 s, US$51–58 d) is a stylish classic dating from 1951. Though some rooms are smallish, this is a solid downtown hotel whose more expensive rates correspond to lake views.

Hotel Edelweiss (San Martín 202, tel. 02944/426165, www.edelweiss.com.ar, reservas@edelweiss.com.ar, US$90–105 s or d) has 100 spacious standard to superior rooms, plus more elaborate suites.

Over US$100

Llao Llao's **Hotel Tunquelén** (Avenida Bustillo Km 24, tel. 02944/448600, www.tunquelen.com, US$113–133 s or d) might be the area's top choice were it not for the nearby Hotel Llao Llao.

Not just a hotel but an attraction in its own right, **Hotel Llao Llao** (Avenida Bustillo Km 25, tel. 02944/448530, fax 02944/445781, www.llaollao.com, US$221 up s or d) is an Alejandro Bustillo classic dating from 1940, its interior completely renovated in the 1990s. Rates depend on the size, view, and amenities of the room, and the season; there are also more elaborate suites.

Downtown's top hotel is the five-star **Hotel Panamericano** (San Martín 536, tel. 02944/425846, www.panamericanobariloche.com, hotel@panameri.com.ar, US$350 s or d), a sprawling complex on both sides of the avenue, linked by a glassed-in, elevated walkway. It also holds a casino and a spa, but it's just not up to the standards—not to mention the style or location—of the Llao Llao.

Food

For breakfast, coffee, sandwiches, and sweets, try *confiterías* like **La Alpina** (Perito Moreno 98, tel. 02944/425693) or **Zona Sur** (Mitre 396, tel. 02944/434258).

Primarily a takeaway place, **La Esquina de las Flores** (20 de Febrero 313) is the Bariloche outpost of Buenos Aires's famous natural foods market and restaurant. For smoked *ciervo* (venison), *jabalí* (wild boar), and *trucha* (trout), pay a visit to expanded **Ahumadero Familia Weiss** (Palacios and V.A. O'Connor, tel. 02944/435789), a tourist-oriented *parrilla* and beer garden that packages these items for takeaway as well.

Downtown's **De la Granja** (Villegas 216, tel. 02944/435939) isn't Bariloche's best, but its crepes (especially the smoked trout) and fried empanadas are above average at moderate prices; the desserts, though, are not up to par.

Unrelated to its namesake ice creamery, **Jauja** (Quaglia 366, tel. 02944/422952) is a Bariloche fixture for its derivative European-style menu at above-average prices.

Downtown's **La Bohemia** (Moreno 48, tel. 02944/522327) prepares quality versions of Argentine standards like pasta and *parrillada,* not to mention smoked meats, and has live music, sometimes including tango, after 9:30 P.M. Try the *lomo a la pimienta* (pepper steak, US$5) and the prosciutto appetizer.

Primarily a *parrilla* but also serving excellent trout, **Tarquino** (24 de Septiembre and Saavedra, tel. 02944/421601) is a Hansel-and-Gretel construction with high ceilings, erected around living trees. Most entrées, including venison ravioli and *ñoquis,* fall under US$6, but a handful are dearer.

Bariloche abounds in pizzerias, starting with the inexpensive, unpretentious, and excellent **Cocodrilos** (Mitre 5, tel. 02944/426640), though **El Mundo de la Pizza** (Mitre 759, tel. 02944/423461) has greater variety. **Pizzería Vogue** (Palacios 156, tel. 02944/431343) is arguably hipper—or smugger—than either. Across the street, **Bucaneros** (Palacios 187, tel. 02944/423674) is more engaging if less inventive.

The full-portion *bife de chorizo* at **El Boliche de Alberto,** Avenida Bustillo Km 8.8, tel. 02944/462285) is too big for all but the most ravenous adolescents, even the fatty half-portion (US$3.50) and the side dishes are too large for a single diner and even for some couples. Given its popularity, it's best to go a little early, around 8–8:30 P.M.; it also has downtown branches specializing in *parrillada* (Villegas 347, tel. 02944/431433) and pasta (Elflein 49, tel. 02944/431084).

Other worthwhile downtown *parrillas* include the reliable **La Vizcacha** (Rolando 279, tel. 02944/422109), which offers exceptional value, and **El Fogón** (Elflein 163, tel. 02944/524603).

Across from the Club Andino, the so-so Mexican food at **Días de Zapata** (Morales 362, tel. 02944/423128) is at least a break from the routine. More of a break is the recommended **Días de Zapata** (20 de Febrero 730, tel. 02944/421820).

Fresh-made chocolates are one of Bariloche's most popular items.

Recently relocated from Esquel, downtown's **Cassis** (España 268, tel. 02944/431382, www.cassis-patagonia.com.ar) is another gourmet-style Patagonian restaurant specializing in game dishes like hare and rabbit, along with versions of traditional items like lamb and trout.

Serving game specialties like *choike* (rhea) and rabbit, **Hasta Que Llegue El Tren** (12 de Octubre 2400, tel. 02944/457200) is an upscale new wine bar/restaurant in the old train station.

With its blend of sea-and-sierra cuisine, the Spanish **Tasca Brava** (Avenida Bustillo 7000, tel. 02944/462599) offers lakeside views in a cozy Bustillo clone with glossy varnished logs, windows, and staircases on a stone foundation, around a circular fireplace. Standouts include the *rabas* (calamari) appetizer and *gambas* (jumbo shrimp), and there's wine by the glass.

For *picadas* pizzas, and draft beer, don't miss **Cervecería Blest** (Avenida Bustillo 11600, tel. 02944/461026); it closes relatively early, at midnight. The kitchen at **Paraje Bairoleto** (Avenida Bustillo 7966, tel. 02944/525251) prepares a brilliant *lomo a la pimienta* (pepper steak) in its airy but rather impersonal dining room; the service, though, is exemplary, and it also has an onsite pub.

Despite its almost intimidating size, the service at cavernous **El Patacón** (Avenida Bustillo Km 7, tel. 02944/442800, www.elpatacon.com.ar) is very personal and the food meticulously prepared. Former U.S. President Bill Clinton has been among the diners for dishes like an outstanding provoletta appetizer(US$3.50) and venison ravioli (US$6).

Possibly Bariloche's best—perhaps even one of the country's top 10—**Chachao** (Avenida Bustillo 3800, tel. 02944/520574, chachaobistro@terra.com) offers what might be called nouvelle Patagonian cuisine. Options include an assortment of cheeses and smoked game, crepes, guanaco with grilled vegetables, *lomo a la frambuesa* (steak with raspberry sauce), Patagonian lamb with elaborate vegetable garnishes, teriyaki trout, and beer from El Bolsón. It's on the high side, with entrées for about US$10 and up, but worth every centavo. Bring your own bilingual dictionary, though, if you're concerned about dishes like "prawns muffled in flour of piñones on mattress of espinaca with caulker's sauce."

Approaching Llao Llao, **Atalaya** (Avenida Bustillo 23500, tel. 02944/448436) is an outstanding teahouse, with panoramic views of Lago Nahuel Huapi, that doubles as a classy nighttime restaurant. It's open noon–midnight daily.

Bariloche has several exceptional ice creameries, starting with **Helados Bari** (España 7, tel. 02944/422305), near the Centro Cívico, and **Abuela Goye** (Quaglia 221, tel. 02944/422311). The real standout, though, is **Helados Jauja** (Perito Moreno 18, tel. 02944/437888), whose dizzying diversity includes unconventional wild fruit flavors, half a dozen or more chocolates, and sometimes the remarkable *mate cocido* (there's even greater variety at their home base in El Bolsón).

Information

Bariloche's **Secretaría Municipal de Turismo** (Centro Cívico s/n, tel. 02944/429850, 429896, www.barilochepatagonia.com, secturismo@bariloche.com.ar) is open 8 A.M.–9 P.M. daily, but in peak season it's overwhelmed with visitors in search of accommodations and other information. There's a satellite office in a kiosk at the Paseo de los Artesanos (Perito Moreno and Villegas), open 9:30 A.M.–1 P.M. and 5–8:30 P.M. daily.

The APN's **Intendencia del Parque Nacional Nahuel Huapi** (San Martín 24, tel. 02944/423111) is one block south of the Centro Cívico. One block farther south, the **Club Andino Bariloche** (20 de Febrero 30, tel. 02944/424531) provides details and permits for hiking in the park; it's open 9:30 A.M.–1 P.M. and 4:30–8:30 P.M. daily except Sunday.

The **Secretaría de Turismo de Río Negro** (Avenida 12 de Octubre and Emilio Frey, tel. 02944/425973, secturrn@rnonline.com.ar) distributes information on the entire province.

For motorists, **ACA** is at 12 de Octubre 785, tel. 02944/422611.

Services

Bariloche has the most complete traveler services of any lake-district locality.

Cambio Sudamérica (Mitre 63) changes foreign cash and traveler's checks. **Banco de la Nación** (Mitre 180) and **Banco Galicia** (Moreno and Quaglia) are two of many downtown banks with ATMs.

Correo Argentino (Centro Cívico s/n) is alongside the municipal tourist office; the postal code is 8400.

Locutorio Quaglia (Quaglia 220) is one of many phone and fax options; **El Cívico** (Urquiza 187), just off the Centro Cívico, has Internet service until 1 A.M., but there are many others.

Hayland Travel (Moreno 126, 6th floor, tel. 02944/420377) is the AmEx representative. **Del Lago Turismo** (Villegas 222, tel. 02944/430056, cordille@bariloche.com.ar) is a full-service agency that will arrange a variety of excursions around the area.

For trips throughout the region and beyond, including Patagonian excursions via the still rugged RN 40 to El Calafate, contact **Overland Patagonia** through either of Bariloche's Hostelling International affiliates: Periko's **Youth Hostel** (Morales 555, tel. 02944/522326, www.perikos.com, info@perikos.com) or **Alaska Youth Hostel** (Lilinquén 326, tel. 02944/461564, www.alaskahostel.com). They also offer four-day tours on the Siete Lagos route, four days to Parque Nacionales Los Alerces, an 11-day combination of the two that adds three days' hiking, and an 18-day adventure to Ushuaia, Tierra del Fuego.

Another recent option is **Corredor Patagónico** (12 de Octubre 1915, tel. 02944/525488, www.corredorpatagonico.com), which offers transportation and tours along both RN 40 (to El Chaltén and El Calafate) and Chile's Carretera Austral (re-entering Argentina at Los Antiguos). Like Overland Patagonia, they also offer trips in the vicinity of Bariloche and as far afield as Ushuaia.

La Montaña Spanish School (Elflein 251, tel. 02944/524212, www.lamontana.com, info@lamontana.com) charges around US$120 per week for 20 hours' instruction.

Neighboring Chile has a **consulate** (tel. 02944/422842) at Avenida Juan Manuel de Rosas 180.

For visa matters, visit **Migraciones** (Libertad 191, tel. 02944/423043).

Lavadero Huemul (Juramento 37, tel. 02944/522067) is one of many downtown laundries.

The **Hospital Zonal** (tel. 02944/426119) is at Perito Moreno 601.

Getting There

Bariloche is northern Argentine Patagonia's transportation hub, with regional and international connections.

LanChile (Moreno 234, 2nd floor, tel. 02944/431043) now flies between Santiago and Bariloche Fridays and Sundays, sometimes via the southern Chilean city of Puerto Montt.

Domestically, **Aerolíneas Argentinas/Austral** (Mitre 185, tel. 02944/422425) normally flies to Aeroparque but a handful of flights make international connections at Ezeiza; a few flights go to El Calafate, and there's the occasional connection to Esquel and Trelew.

Bariloche is something of a hub for **LADE** (Mitre 531, 1st floor, tel. 02944/423562), with low-priced flights to Buenos Aires and to Patagonian destinations including Comodoro Rivadavia, Trelew, Neuquén, El Bolsón, El Maitén, and Esquel, but most of these are only weekly and schedules change frequently.

American Falcon (Mitre 159, tel. 02944/425200) flies to and from Aeroparque several times weekly. **Southern Winds** (Quaglia 262, Local 13, tel. 02944/423704) flies to Neuquén and Aeroparque, and to El Calafate.

On the eastern outskirts of town, across the Río Ñireco, Bariloche's new but relatively small **Terminal de Ómnibus** (Avenida 12 de Octubre s/n, tel. 02944/432860) is immediately east of the train station, with which it shares taxis and parking facilities. There are international services (to Osorno and Puerto Montt, Chile), long-distance services throughout the republic, and provincial and regional routes.

For Patagonian travelers one of the most encouraging developments is **Corredor Patagónico** (12 de Octubre 1915, tel. 02944/525488, www.corredorpatagonico.com), which is providing the first regularly scheduled service from Bariloche to the towns of Perito Moreno, El Chaltén, and El Calafate via RN 40, with overnights in Perito Moreno and El Chaltén. In peak summer season, southbound departures are at 7 A.M. on odd-numbered days; samples fare and times include Perito Moreno (US$50, 12 hours), El Chaltén (US$43 and 16 hours more), and El Calafate (US$15 and four hours more). Hotel accommodations and meals are extra.

Four companies cross the Andes to the Chilean cities of Osorno (5.5 hours) and Puerto Montt (US$14, 6.5 hours): **Andesmar** (tel. 02944/430211), **Bus Norte** (tel. 02944/430303), **Tas Choapa** (tel. 02944/422288), and **Vía Bariloche** (tel. 02944/432444). Most leave by 10 A.M.

Sample domestic destinations, fares, and times include Villa La Angostura (US$4, 1.5 hours), El Bolsón (US$4.50, two hours), San Martín de los Andes (US$8, 4.5 hours), Esquel (US$7.50, four hours), Neuquén (US$11–14, 5.5 hours), Viedma (US$20, 14 hours), Trelew (US$23, 13 hours), Puerto Madryn (US$26, 14 hours), Comodoro Rivadavia (US$23, 12 hours), Buenos Aires (US$32–50, 22–23 hours), and Río Gallegos (US$47, 24 hours).

Well east of downtown, **Sefepa** (Avenida 12 de Octubre s/n, tel. 02944/431777, www.trenpatagonico.com.ar, trenpatagonico@bariloche.com.ar) connects Bariloche with Viedma via **train** Thursday and Sunday at 5 P.M. The 15-hour trip costs US$9–12 in hard-backed *turista,* US$19–22 in reclining Pullman, or US$32–37 in *camarote* sleepers; children 5–12 pay half.

Cruce de Lagos (www.crucedelagos.com) operates the long-running bus-boat shuttle over the Andes to Puerto Montt, Chile (US$178 pp with lunch) via Puerto Pañuelo, Puerto Blest, Puerto Frías, Peulla (Chile), Petrohué, and Puerto Varas. With an overnight at Peulla, the trip costs US$220 pp. For bookings, contact the local representative **Catedral Turismo** (Palacios 263, tel. 02944/425444). Foreigners pay an additional US$4.50 in national park entry fees; it is possible to do this trip in segments or as a round-trip, say from Puerto Pañuelo to Puerto Blest and back.

Getting Around

Aeropuerto Teniente Candelaria (tel. 02944/422767) is 15 kilometers east of Bariloche via RN 237 and RP 80. Micro Ómnibus 3 de Mayo's No. 72 bus goes directly to the airport (US$.50), while cabs and *remises* cost about US$3.

Omnibus 3 de Mayo (Perito Moreno 840, tel. 02944/425648) goes to Cerro Catedral (US$1) every 30 minutes, sometimes via Avenida de los Pioneros and others via Avenida Bustillo. In summer, 3 de Mayo goes four times daily to Lago Mascardi.

3 de Mayo's No. 20 bus goes every 20 minutes to Llao Llao and Puerto Pañuelo, which is also the final destination of some of its seven Nos. 10 and 11 buses via Colonia Suiza, on the Circuito Chico route through Parque Nacional Nahuel Huapi, at 8:05 A.M., noon, and 5:20 P.M. Return times from Puerto Pañuelo via Colonia Suiza are 9:40 A.M. and 1:40 and 6:40 P.M.

3 de Mayo's Nos. 50 and 51 buses go to Lago Gutiérrez (US$1.10) every 30 minutes, while in summer the company's Línea Mascardi goes to Villa Mascardi (US$2) and Puente Los Rápidos (US$3) three times daily. Their Línea El Manso goes twice Friday and once Sunday to Río Villegas and El Manso (US$2), on the southwestern edge of Parque Nacional Nahuel Huapi.

Bariloche has several rental agencies, including **Baricoche** (Moreno 115, 1st floor, tel. 02944/427638), **Budget** (Mitre 106, 1st floor, tel. 02944/422482), **Correcaminos** (Libertad 114, tel. 02944/426076), **Dollar** (Villegas 282, tel. 02944/430333), **Europcar** (Rolando 258, tel. 02944/426420), and **Localiza** (Avenida San Martín 531, tel. 02944/424767).

PARQUE NACIONAL NAHUEL HUAPI

In 1903, Patagonian explorer Francisco Pascasio Moreno donated three square leagues of "the most beautiful scenery my eyes had ever seen," at the west end of Lago Nahuel Huapi near the Chilean border, to "be conserved as a natural public park." Explicitly mentioning the United States' example in creating large public reserves, Moreno's burst of idealism actually returned part of a personal land grant to the Argentine state. First known as Parque Nacional del Sur, this property became today's Parque Nacional Nahuel Huapi.

Since then, countless Argentine and foreign visitors have enjoyed the benefits of Moreno's charity and foresight in a reserve that now encompasses a far larger area of glacial lakes and limpid rivers, densely forested moraines and mountains, and snow-topped Andean peaks that mark the international border. So many, in fact, have experienced the park that it's debatable whether authorities have fulfilled Moreno's wish that "the current features of their perimeter not be altered, and that there be no additional constructions other than those that facilitate the comforts of the cultured visitor."

Prior to the "Conquest of the Desert," Araucanian peoples freely crossed the Andes between Chile and Argentina, via the Paso de los Vuriloches south of ice-covered, 3,554-meter Cerro Tronador, the park's highest peak. The pass lent its name to Bariloche which, a century after its founding in 1903, has morphed from lakeside hamlet to a sprawling city whose wastes threaten the pure air, water, and woodlands that surround it.

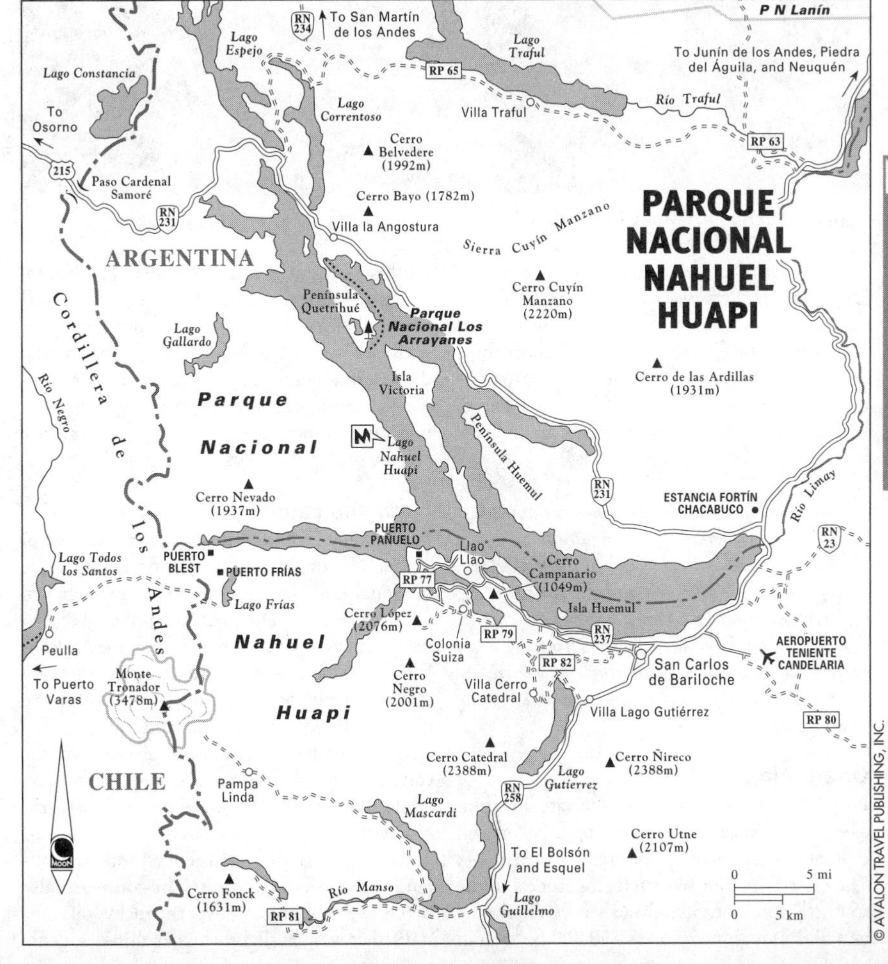

© WAYNE BERNHARDSON

Lago Nahuel Huapi, Parque Nacional Nahuel Huapi

For all that, Nahuel Huapi remains a beautiful spot that connects two countries via a series of scenic roads and waterways. In 1979, regrettably, Argentine and Chilean military dictatorships fortified the borders and mined the approaches because of a territorial dispute in Tierra del Fuego, but a papal intervention cleared the air and perhaps reflected Moreno's aspirations:

> ***This land of beauty in the Andes is home to a colossal peak shared by two nations: Monte Tronador unites both of them. . . . Together, they could rest and share ideas there; they could find solutions to problems unsolved by diplomacy. Visitors from around the world would mingle and share with one another at this international crossroads.***

Orientation

From Moreno's original 8,100-hectare donation along the Chilean border, the park has grown dramatically. Stretching from the northerly Lago Queñi, west of San Martín de los Andes, to the southerly Río Manso, midway between Bariloche and El Bolsón, it now covers 750,000 hectares in southwestern Neuquén and western Río Negro. Together with the contiguous Parque Nacional Lanín to the north, it forms an uninterrupted stretch of well over a million hectares, but part of the area is a *reserva nacional* that permits commercial development. At the park's western edge, imposing Tronador is the highest of a phalanx of snow-covered peaks signifying the border.

Flora and Fauna

Nahuel Huapi's flora and fauna resemble those of Parque Nacional Lanín to the north and Parque Nacional Los Alerces to the south, but differ in some key respects. There are three principal ecosystems: the easterly Patagonian steppe, the Andean-Patagonian forest, and the high Andes above 1,600 meters, which consists of low shrubs and sparse grasses adapted to cold, wind, and snow.

Guanacos graze the semi-arid grasslands of the eastern steppe, stalked by foxes and even pumas, while raptors like the cinereous harrier *(Circus cinereus)* and American kestrel *(Falco sparverius)* patrol the skies. Toward the west, open woodlands of coniferous cypress, the southern false beech *ñire,* and *maitén* cover the rocky soils.

Farther west, at slightly higher altitudes, dense

HONORING THE EXPERT: THE LEGACY OF PERITO MORENO

The career of Francisco Pascasio Moreno (1852–1919) began improbably at his father's Buenos Aires insurance agency, but by age 20 the young, inquisitive Moreno had founded the Sociedad Científica Argentina (Argentine Scientific Society). From 1875, a time when much of Patagonia was hostile and unknown territory, he explored the Río Negro and Limay valleys up to Lago Nahuel Huapi (twice), and the Río Santa Cruz to its source at Lago San Martín. On his 1879–1880 Nahuel Huapi expedition, he fell prisoner to previously friendly Manzanero Indians—for whom he evinced a sympathy that was unfashionable during General Roca's Conquista del Desierto—fleeing down the Limay on a precarious log raft.

Dedicated to the public good, in 1884 Moreno donated his natural-history collections to the Museo Antropológico y Etnológico de Buenos Aires, an institution that became the Museo de Historia Natural de La Plata—compared by U.S. Patagonian surveyor Bailey Willis to the Smithsonian Institution. In 1897, recognizing Moreno's intimate knowledge of the region, the government named the *perito* (expert) its delegate to a commission settling border differences with Chile; five years later, he oversaw the placement of permanent boundary markers.

The following year, honoring his services, the government granted him a substantial Nahuel Huapi property near the Chilean border, which the altruistic Moreno gave back on the stipulation that it become the cornerstone of a national-park system. Five years later, in 1908, he founded the Argentine Boy Scouts; in 1913, he hosted former U.S. President Theodore Roosevelt at Bariloche.

Only a few years later, dismayed by changes in a country that ignored his ideas, betrayed and bitter like Argentine liberator José de San Martín a century earlier, Moreno died in near poverty in Buenos Aires. In Patagonia, his public legacy is a few frequently confused place names—a street in Bariloche, his namesake lake to the west, a dusty town in Santa Cruz province, Parque Nacional Perito Moreno, and the famous Glaciar Perito Moreno.

Yet according to Willis (whose own name graces a peak near Bariloche), Moreno was the first to grasp Patagonia's potential as a "national asset" that needed impartial research to be properly unlocked: "Among men of Moreno's nationality personal ambition is more often than not the ruling motive. But he was selfless where knowledge of the truth was his objective."

false beech forests of *coihue, lenga,* and *ñire* cover the slopes, while the lakeshores and stream banks burst with a flowering understory of *notro* shrubs and climbing vines like *mutisia,* with scattered clusters of the cinnamon-barked *arrayán (Myrceugenella apiculata).*

Near Puerto Blest, rainfall up to 4,000 millimeters per annum supports a humid Valdivian forest of Guaiteca cypress *(Pilgerodendron uviferum), mañío macho (Podocarpus nubigena), mañío hembra* (Prince Albert's yew, *Saxegothaea conspicua*), and the tree fern *fuinque (Lomatia ferruginea).* Nahuel Huapi, though, lacks Lanín's araucaria forests and the more southerly *alerce* tree is less abundant here than in Chubut province.

The *huemul* (Andean deer, *Hippocamelus bisulcus*) and the miniature deer *pudú (Pudu pudu)* both exist here, but sightings are rare. Other mammals include the carnivorous *huillín* (otter, *Lontra provocax*) and the gopher-like *tuco-tuco (Ctenomys sociabilis),* an endemic rodent.

Normally ocean-going, the king cormorant has a colony along Lago Nahuel Huapi, where the kelp gull *(Larinus dominicanus)* often trails the boats that sail the lake. Nahuel Huapi, its tributary streams, and other lakes teem with trout and other fish as well.

Lago Nahuel Huapi

Nahuel Huapi's focal point is its namesake lake, whose finger-like channels converge near the

Llao Llao peninsula to form the main part of its 560-square-kilometer surface. With a maximum depth of 454 meters, it drains into the Río Limay, a major tributary of the Río Negro, east of Bariloche.

In the middle of Nahuel Huapi's northern arm, **Isla Victoria** is the former site of the APN's park ranger's school (since relocated to Tucumán) that trained rangers from throughout the Americas. From Puerto Pañuelo, the *Modesta Victoria* (tel. 02944/426109) sails to the island (US$13 plus US$4 national park entry fee) at 10:30 A.M. while the *Espacio* (tel. 02944/431372, US$14 plus the national park fee) goes at 1:30 P.M.; both continue to Parque Nacional Los Arrayanes, on Península Quetrihué. To Isla Victoria only (US$9), Bioceánica has departures at 10:30 A.M. and 2:30 P.M. Note that Los Arrayanes is more accessible from Villa la Angostura, on the north shore of the lake.

hikers on the trail to Refugio López, Parque Nacional Nahuel Huapi

Circuito Chico

Bariloche's single most popular excursion leads west out Avenida Bustillo to Península Llao Llao and returns via the hamlet of Colonia Suiza, at the foot of Cerro López. En route, it passes or touches several points of interest worthwhile in their own right; public buses will pick up and drop off passengers almost anywhere.

For a panoramic view of Nahuel Huapi and its surroundings, take the **Aerosilla Campanario** (Avenida Bustillo Km 17.5, tel. 02944/427274) to the 1,050-meter summit of **Cerro Campanario,** where there's an expensive *confitería.* Open 9 A.M.–6 P.M. daily, the chairlift charges US$5 per person.

The bus-boat "Cruce de Lagos" to Chile starts at **Puerto Pañuelo,** but excursions to Isla Victoria and Parque Nacional Los Arrayanes (across the lake) also leave from here. The area's outstanding cultural landmark is the **Hotel Llao Llao,** a Bustillo creation opened to nonguests for guided tours (free of charge, except for parking); for details on accommodations, see the Bariloche entry above.

Almost immediately west of Puerto Pañuelo, a level footpath from the parking area leads southwest to an arrayán forest in **Parque Municipal Llao Llao;** the trail rejoins with the paved road at **Lago Escondido.** The road itself passes a trailhead for **Cerro Llao Llao,** a short but stiff climb that offers fine panoramas of Nahuel Huapi and the Andean crest. On the descent, the trail joins a gravel road that rejoins the paved road from Puerto Pañuelo, which leads south before looping northeast toward Bariloche; a gravel alternative heads east to **Colonia Suiza,** known for its Sunday crafts fair (Wednesday also in summer). There is also a regular Sunday *curanto* (a mixture of beef, lamb, pork, chicken, sausage, potatoes, sweet potatoes, and other vegetables, baked on heated earth-covered stones) and a spectacular assortment of sweets and desserts.

From Colonia Suiza, a zigzag dirt road suitable for mountain bikes climbs toward the Club Andino's **Refugio López,** 1,620 meters above sea level; near the junction of the paved and gravel roads (see above), a steep footpath climbs 2.5 hours to the *refugio,* which is open mid-December–mid-April.

For most of the way, the route is obvious, but

THE SLOPES OF BARILOCHE

After decades of decline and eclipse by resorts like Las Leñas (Mendoza), Bariloche is reestablishing itself as a ski destination with new investment and technological improvements at **Catedral Alta Patagonia** (Base Cerro Catedral, Casilla de Correo 1630, tel. 02944/423776, www.catedralaltapatagonia.com), only a short hop west of town. It's still more popular with Argentines and Brazilians than long-distance travelers, but new snow-making and grooming equipment have complemented the blend of 15 beginner-to-advanced runs, and lift capacities have also improved. From a base of 950 meters, the skiable slopes rise up another thousand.

As elsewhere, ticket prices depend on timing; the season runs mid-June–mid-October, but is subdivided into low, mid-, or peak season. One-day rates range from US$16–28 for adults, US$13–23 for children ages 5–11 and seniors age 65–74. The corresponding prices for three-day passes are US$43–75 for adults, US$34–61 for children and seniors. Week-long passes cost US$90–157 for adults, US$72–127 for children and seniors, while the rates for 15-day passes are US$164–285 and US$132–232 respectively. Season passes cost US$714 for adults, US$580 for children and seniors. Those over age 75 ski free.

Basic rental equipment is cheap, but quality gear is more expensive. In addition to the onsite facilities, try downtown's **Baruzzi Fly Shop** (Urquiza 250, tel. 02944/424922) or **Martín Pescador** (Rolando 257, tel. 02944/422275).

In addition to downhill skiing, there are also cross-country routes at close-in Cerro Otto.

where it seems to disappear into a grove of *lengas,* it actually climbs steeply to the left, brushing the dirt road, before continuing toward the *refugio.* In fact, it's much simpler if a little longer to walk the upper sections along the road (in any event, the last kilometer or so is on the road itself, which deteriorates into something not even suitable for 4WD).

From Refugio López, a good place to take a break and a beer, the route climbs to **Cerro Turista,** a strenuous scramble over rugged volcanic terrain. With an early start, it's possible to reach the 2,076-meter summit of **Cerro López.**

Many Bariloche agencies offer the Circuito Chico as a half-day tour (about US$6–7 pp), but it's also possible on cheaper public transportation; for details, see the Bariloche Getting Around entry.

Cerro Otto

From Bariloche's Barrio Belgrano, westbound Avenida de los Pioneros intersects a gravel road that climbs first gently and then steeply to the 1,405-meter summit of Cerro Otto. While it's a feasible eight-kilometer hike or mountain-bike ride, it's also possible to reach the peak via the gondolas of **Teleférico Cerro Otto** (Avenida de los Pioneros Km 5, tel. 02944/441035) for US$8 per person; city buses Nos. 50 and 51 go directly to the base station.

On the summit road, at 1,240 meters, the Club Andino's **Refugio Berghof** has 40 bunks, serves meals and drinks, and also houses the **Museo de Montaña Otto Meiling** (guided tours US$0.50), honoring an influential early mountaineer who built his residence here. There is a nearby area suitable for cross-country skiing and rock climbing.

Cerro Catedral

About 20 kilometers southwest of Bariloche, the 2,388-meter summit of Cerro Catedral overlooks **Villa Catedral,** the base of the area's major winter-sports complex (see the sidebar "The Slopes of Bariloche" for ski details). From Villa Catedral, the **Cablecarril y Silla Lynch** (US$8 pp, open 10 A.M.–5:30 P.M. daily) carries visitors to **Confitería Punta Nevada** at 1,900 meters and the **Refugio Lynch,** which also has a *confitería.* Hikers can continue along the ridgetop route to the Club Andino's 40-bed **Refugio Emilio Frey,** 1,700-meters above sea level; it's open all year in an area whose spire-like summits are a magnet for rock climbers.

Monte Tronador

Though its inner fire died long ago, the ice-clad volcanic summit of Tronador still merits its name (the "Thunderer") when frozen blocks plunge and crash off its face into the valley below. The peak that surveyor Bailey Willis called "majestic in savage ruggedness" has impressed everyone from early Jesuit explorer Miguel de Olivares to Perito Moreno, Theodore Roosevelt, and the hordes of tourists that view it every summer. Its ascent, though, is for skilled snow-and-ice climbers only.

Source of the Río Manso, Tronador's icy eastern face gives birth to the **Ventisquero Negro** (Black Glacier), a jumble of ice, sand, and rocky detritus, and countless waterfalls. Passing Pampa Linda, at the end of the road from Lago Mascardi, whistle-blowing rangers prevent novice (and other) hikers from approaching the **Garganta del Diablo,** the area's largest accessible waterfall, too closely.

From Pampa Linda, hikers can visit the Club Andino's basic **Refugio Viejo Tronador,** a kiln-shaped structure that can sleep a maximum of 10 climbers in bivouac conditions, via a trail on the south side of the road. On the north side, another trail leads to its more comfortable 60-bed **Refugio Meiling,** 2,000 meters above sea level. Well-equipped backpackers can continue north to Laguna Frías via the 1,335-meter Paso de las Nubes and return to Bariloche on the bus-boat shuttle via Puerto Blest and Puerto Pañuelo; it's also possible to do this route from Bariloche or Puerto Pañuelo.

Reaching the Tronador area requires a roundabout drive via southbound RN 258 to the south end of Lago Mascardi, where westbound RP 81 follows the south bank of the Río Manso; at Km 9, a northbound lateral crosses the river and becomes a single-lane dirt road to Pampa Linda and the base of Tronador. Because of its narrowness, traffic is one-way inbound in the morning (until 2 P.M.) and outbound in the afternoon (after 4 P.M.). At other hours, it's open to cautious two-way traffic. From mid-November, the Club Andino provides transportation from its Bariloche headquarters to Pampa Linda at 9 A.M. daily, returning at 5 P.M., for US$4.50 per person (two hours).

Hostería Pampa Linda (see the accommodations entry below) organizes horseback rides in the vicinity.

Accommodations and Food

Park campgrounds are numerous, especially in those areas accessible by road. Club Andino's *refugios* charges around US$3 per person for overnight stays, US$.50 for day use, US$.75 for breakfast, and US$1 for kitchen use. Since bunks are limited, it's a good idea to make reservations through the Club Andino, but day hikers can buy simple meals and cold drinks at them.

Hotels and other accommodations are scattered around various sectors of the park. At the Villa Catedral ski area, the cheapest option is Club Andino's **Hostería Knapp** (tel./fax 02944/460021, www.hosteria-knapp.com.ar, hosteria@hosteria-knapp.com.ar), where rates are US$25 pp with breakfast for accommodations with a restaurant, bar, and ski-equipment rentals (though it's open all year). Half-board is also available, and triples and quadruples are available for slightly less per person; rates fall considerably in spring and summer.

At the northwest end of Lago Mascardi, on the Pampa Linda road, **Hotel Tronador** (tel. 02944/441062, www.hotel-tronador.com, hoteltronador@bariloche.com.ar) is a lake-district classic in the Bustillo tradition; rates of US$51/61 s/d with full board are more than reasonable. Near the end of the road, the rustically contemporary **Hostería Pampa Linda** (tel. 02944/490517, pampalinda@bariloche.com.ar) charges a reasonable US$30/45 s/d with breakfast, US$38/58 s/d with half-board, and US$45/73 s/d with full board.

Information

For detailed information on the park, contact the APN office or the Club Andino in Bariloche; see the Bariloche entry for contact details. The *refugios* in the highlands are good sources of information within the park.

The Club Andino's improved trail map, *Refugios, Sendas y Picadas,* at a scale of 1:100,000 with more detailed versions covering smaller areas at a scale of 1:50,000, is a worthwhile acquisition. The fifth edition of Tim Burford's *Chile and Argentina: The Bradt Trekking Guide* (Bradt Travel Guides, 2001) covers several park trails in considerable detail, but its maps are for orientation only. The third edition of Clem Lindenmayer's *Trekking in the Patagonian Andes* (Lonely Planet, 2003) has more useful maps, but doesn't seem to have been updated as thoroughly.

EL BOLSÓN

El Bolsón, Argentine Patagonia's counterculture capital, may be the place to replace your faded tie-dyes, but it's also a beautiful spot in a fertile valley between stunning longitudinal mountain ranges that provide some of the region's finest hiking. So far, despite completion of the paved highway from Bariloche, this self-styled "ecological municipality" and declared nonnuclear zone has managed to stymie the incursion of five-star hotels and stylish ski areas in favor of simpler—earthier, even—services and activities.

El Bolsón's alternative lifestyle dates from the 1960s, and grew in the 1970s as an island of tolerance and tranquility even during the country's nastiest military dictatorship ever. More affordable than Bariloche, it embraces visitors and turns the valley's agricultural bounty—apples, cherries, pears, raspberries, strawberries—into delectable edibles, and makes local hops into a distinctive beer. Motorists will appreciate that this is the northernmost place to buy gasoline at Patagonian discount prices.

Orientation

Río Negro's southernmost city, on the Chubut border, El Bolsón (population 13,845, elevation 300 meters) is 123 kilometers south of Bariloche via RN 258 and 167 kilometers north of Esquel via RN 258 and RN 40. West of the Río Quemquemtreu, which flows south through the valley, the Cordón Nevado's snowy ridge marks the Chilean border, while the Cerro Piltriquitrón's knife-edge crest rises steeply to the east.

Most services are on or around north-south Avenida San Martín, the main thoroughfare, which leads south to Lago Puelo; the diagonal Avenida Belgrano becomes the main southbound highway to Chubut. The real civic center is the elliptical Plaza Pagano, which surrounds an artificial lake and is the site of the popular street fair.

© WAYNE BERNHARDSON

Plaza Pagano, El Bolsón

Feria Artesanal El Bolsón

Nearly encircling Plaza Pagano, the buskers, bakers, candle-makers, flower arrangers, and countless other crafts workers have transformed Bolsón's street fair from a once-a-week gathering to a Tuesday, Thursday, and Saturday event. Instead of a restaurant lunch, snack to the max on the Belgian waffles, homemade empanadas, sandwiches, sausages, and sweets, and wash them all down with fresh-brewed draft beer. It all starts around 10 A.M. and winds down around 3 P.M.

Other Shopping

In addition to the crafts at the Feria Artesanal, the Mapuche-oriented **Centro Artesanal Cumey Antú** (Avenida San Martín 2020), toward the south end of town, sells indigenous textiles. On the east side, **Cabaña Micó** (Isla Malvinas 2753, tel. 02944/492691) is the place to find fresh fruit from its own vines in season, and homemade preserves the rest of the year.

Entertainment and Events

Founded in 1926, the city celebrates its **Aniversario** every January 28. Bolsón's brewers take center stage in mid-February's four-day **Festival Nacional del Lúpulo** (National Hops Festival).

In summer, the **Morena Café** (San Martín and Pablo Hube, tel. 02944/492725) offers live music. **La Bandurria** (Perito Moreno and Dorrego, tel. 02944/491929) and **La Posada del Alquimista** (Avenida Belgrano and Beruti, tel. 02944/492908) also have live music.

Sports and Recreation

Several El Bolsón travel agencies arrange excursions such as boating on Lago Puelo, hiking and climbing, horseback riding, mountain biking, rafting on the nearby Río Azul and the more distant Río Manso, parasailing, and the like. Where logistics are complex, as in reaching some trailheads, they can be a good option.

Among the operators are **Grado 42** (Avenida Belgrano 406, Local 2, tel. 02944/493124, grado42@elbolson.org), **Patagonia Adventure** (Pablo Hube 418, tel. 02944/492513, patago@red42.com.ar), and **Viva Más Patagonia** (Avenida San Martín 2526, tel. 02944/455555, vivamaspatagonia@elbolson.com).

© WAYNE BERNHARDSON

Feria Artesanal El Bolsón

Accommodations

El Bolsón has quality accommodations for every budget except the four- and five-star luxury category (but what lacks in luxury often compensates with character). Some of the best values are not in town itself, but scattered around the northern and southern outskirts.

At the north end of town, directly on the highway to Bariloche, a truly unique option is **Camping El Bolsón** (RN 258 s/n, tel. 02944/492595, cervezaselbolson@elbolson.com, US$2.50 pp)—perhaps the only campground in the country with its own brewery and beer garden. At the southeast edge of town, grassy **Camping La Chacra** (Avenida Belgrano s/n, tel. 02944/492111, lachacra@elbolson.com, US$2.50 pp) is a good alternative.

Albergue Sol del Valle (25 de Mayo 2367, tel. 02944/492087, US$3.50 pp) is a good downtown hostel. About four kilometers north of town, the HI affiliate **El Pueblito Hostel** (Barrio Luján s/n, tel. 02944/493560, reservas@hostels.org.ar, US$3 pp in dorms, US$9 d) is a comfortable, sociable place on a large property, with bunks for 40 people. From downtown Bolsón, there are hourly buses between 7:45 A.M. and 8:45 P.M., except at 7:45 P.M.

Residencial Edelweiss (Angel del Agua 360, tel. 02944/492594, US$4 pp) is basic, with shared bath and kitchen privileges. **Hospedaje Salinas** (Roca 641, tel. 02944/492396, US$5 pp) may be cozy in summer but cold in winter; rates also include kitchen privileges. Rather better choices include **Residencial Valle Nuevo** (25 de Mayo 2329, tel. 02944/492087, US$14 d), and **Hospedaje Unelén** (Azcuénaga 134, tel. 02944/492729, US$15 d), which stays open all year.

About three kilometers southeast of Plaza Pagano, Alejandro Canale raises brilliantly colorful flowers for dried arrangements on the lower slopes of Piltriquitrón at **Hostería Sukal** (Subida los Maitenes s/n, tel. 02944/492438, www.sukalelbolson.com, sukal@elbolson.com, US$10 pp). A miracle for the price, it also enjoys spectacular views of the Andean crest across the valley; the farm-fresh breakfast (US$2) more than justifies its price.

More central, the four-room B&B **La Posada de Hamelin** (Granollers 2179, tel. 02944/492030, gcapece@elbolson.com, US$14/21 s/d) is comparably priced, but breakfast also costs an additional US$2.

Casablanca Hostería (José Hernández and Onelli, tel. 02944/493784, US$20 s or d) offers smallish but well-furnished rooms with private bath and breakfast, which varies daily (a strong point, as Argentine hotel breakfasts are often uniformly mediocre). It's open from January to Semana Santa, and again in July winter holidays.

On the west side of the highway on the northern outskirts of town, the **Hostería del Campo** (RN 258 s/n, tel. 02944/492297, delcampo@elbolson.com, US$20 s or d) has quiet motel-style rooms with covered parking, set among spacious gardens, but breakfast is extra and there's a credit-card surcharge.

The **Amancay Hotel** (Avenida San Martín

3217, tel. 02944/492222, hotelamancay@elbolson.com, US$22/28 s/d) is an aging but still-serviceable hotel showing wear but not tear; rates include breakfast.

Six kilometers north of town, by a well-signed dirt road that diverges from the Bariloche highway, the French-run riverside **La Casona de Odile** (Barrio Luján s/n, tel. 02944/492753, www.interpatagonia.com/odile, odile@red42.com.ar, US$15 pp) is a bargain with homemade breakfast; a home-cooked French dinner with wine doubles the price, though, and Odile herself is a heavy smoker (nonguests may partake of dinner with reservations; for more details see under Food, below). It's open October or November to late April, and also can accommodate disabled individuals.

Across from the Amancay, the **Cordillera Hotel** (Avenida San Martín 3210, tel. 02944/492235, cordillerahotel@elbolson.com, US$25/35 s/d) has large rooms whose east-facing balconies provide fine views of Cerro Piltriquitrón; by category, it's Bolsón's best, and its standards are good, but there are more distinctive (and cheaper) options surrounding town. Rates include buffet breakfast.

Food

Given the ready accessibility of fresh fruit and vegetables, El Bolsón's food exceeds expectations, even though it may lack Buenos Aires's (or even Bariloche's) sophistication. Forgo at least one restaurant lunch to snack at Plaza Pagano's **Feria Artesanal** (see separate entry above). **Verde Menta** (San Martín 2137, tel. 02944/493576) is a natural-foods grocery at the south end of town.

There are several good breakfast-and-coffee spots, including **La Calabaza** (San Martín 2518, tel. 02944/492910), and **La Tosca** (San Martín and Roca, tel. 02944/493669), immediately behind the tourist office; the latter has occasional live music. Relocated **La Salteñita** (Avenida Belgrano 515, tel. 02944/493749) still serves the best spicy northern empanadas for takeaway.

Economical **Arcimboldo** (Avenida San Martín 2790, tel. 02944/492137) specializes in pastas. **Las Brasas** (Sarmiento and Hube, tel. 02944/492923) is one of Bolsón's better *parrillas.*

Martín Sheffield (Avenida San Martín 2740, tel. 02944/491920) is a welcome new presence, with cooked-to-order chicken, Patagonian trout, and lamb, plus local beer on tap. Service is excellent and attentive. **Il Rizzo** (Avenida San Martín 2599, tel. 02944/491380) is for pizza and pasta.

Though the food's not quite up to its aspirations yet, promising **Tente en Pié** (Avenida San Martín 3410, tel. 02944/455654) deserves a visit for trout and other game entrées, and vegetarian dishes like chop suey, in the US$3–5 range. The decor is appealing, and the service good.

Cerro Lindo (Avenida San Martín 2524, tel. 02944/492899) has evolved from a good but simple pizzeria (try the smoked boar) to a full-fledged restaurant with regional specialties that include half a dozen versions of trout, plus venison, stuffed leg of lamb, and the like, in the US$5–7 range. It badly needs a tobacco-free section, though—the air is fresher on the sidewalk. Service is good, and it has a decent wine list.

Still, Bolsón's best is **Jauja** (San Martín 2867, tel. 02944/492448), where Alejandro Canale's vivid flower arrangements set the stage for succulent pastas such as gnocchi with a garlic cream sauce, vegetarian dishes such as *milanesa de soja* (breaded soybean steak), a wide selection of fish and pizza, outstanding homemade bread, and local brews.

Ignore the in-house restaurant desserts, though, and step out the door to their **Helados Jauja,** one of the country's top two or three ice creameries, with an almost paralyzing choice of inventive flavors. The author's longstanding favorite is *mate cocido con tres de azúcar* (boiled and slightly sweetened *mate*), though even some Argentines blanch at the idea of consuming their favorite bitter infusion in frozen form.

Information

At the north end of Plaza Pagano, El Bolsón's improved **Dirección Municipal de Turismo** (Avenida San Martín and Roca, tel./fax 02944/492604, www.bolsonturistico.com.ar, sec_turismo@elbolson.com) provides decent maps of accommodations and other services, and even employs a helpful accommodations specialist who will make suggestions and book hotels. Summer hours are 9 A.M.–11 P.M. weekdays, 9 A.M.–11 P.M. Saturday, and 10 A.M.–10 P.M. Sunday; the rest of the year, hours are 9 A.M.–9 P.M., sometimes a little later, daily.

For details on hiking and climbing in the vicinity, visit the **Club Andino Piltriquitrón,** on Sarmiento between Roca and Feliciano (tel. 02944/492600).

For motorists, **ACA** is at Avenida Belgrano and San Martín (tel. 02944/492260).

Services

Banco de la Nación (Avenida San Martín 2598) and **Banco Patagonia** (Avenida San Martín 2831) have ATMs.

Correo Argentino is at Avenida San Martín 2806; the postal code is 8430. At the south end of Plaza Pagano, **La Barra** (Juez Fernández 429) has long-distance phone service. **Rancho Internet** (Avenida San Martín and Pablo Hube) has the best Internet connections.

Laverap (José Hernández 223, tel. 02944/493243) does the washing.

The **Hospital de Area** (Perito Moreno s/n, tel. 02944/492240) is behind Plaza Pagano.

Radio Alas (FM 89.1 Mhz) provides an eclectic blend of music and community-service programs, from 8 A.M.–2 P.M. weekdays and 8 A.M.–midnight weekends.

Getting There

El Bolsón has regional air and bus connections, but Bariloche has more complete services.

LADE (Roca 446, tel. 02944/492206) flies northbound weekly to Bariloche, Neuquén, and Buenos Aires, and southbound to El Maitén, Esquel, and Comodoro Rivadavia. Flights leave from the **Aero Club El Bolsón** (tel. 02944/491125) at the north end of Avenida San Martín.

El Bolsón lacks a central **bus** terminal, though one may be built in the future in the vicinity of the airfield. Most companies, though, are within a few blocks of each other.

Andesmar (Belgrano and Perito Moreno, tel. 02944/492178) goes to Bariloche and Buenos Aires (usually with a change in Neuquén), and south to Esquel. **Vía Bariloche** (Sarmiento and Roca, tel. 02972/455554) goes to Esquel, Bariloche, and Buenos Aires; **Transportes Esquel** (Belgrano 406, tel. 02944/493124) also goes to Esquel via Parque Nacional Los Alerces.

Grado 42 (Belgrano 406, tel. 02944/493124) represents TAC, which goes to Esquel and to Bariloche, and makes connections in Neuquén for Mendoza, Córdoba, and other northern destinations. **Don Otto** (Belgrano and Berutti, Local 3, tel. 02944/493910) goes to Bariloche and Comodoro Rivadavia, with connections in Esquel for Trelew and Puerto Madryn. **Maputur/Mar y Valle** (Perito Moreno 2331, tel. 02944/491440) goes directly to Puerto Madryn.

The usual destinations from El Bolsón are Bariloche (US$4.50, two hours) and Esquel (US$5, 2.5 hours). Fares to other northbound destinations are slightly more expensive than those from Bariloche; fares to southbound destinations are slightly cheaper than those from Bariloche.

Getting Around

For a small town, El Bolsón has excellent public transportation for excursions like Cerro Piltriquitrón, Mallín Ahogado, and Lago Puelo. For details, see the appropriate entry. There are also abundant radio taxis and *remises.*

For rental bikes, try **La Rueda** (Avenida Sarmiento 2972, tel. 02944/492465).

VICINITY OF EL BOLSÓN

One of El Bolsón's greatest virtues is its convenience to trailheads for hiking and secondary roads for mountain biking. Most are just far enough away, though, to require an early start for those without their own vehicle; consider hiring a *remise* to the trailheads. Spanish-speaking hikers should look for Gabriel Bevacqua's inexpensive local hiking guide *Montañas de la Comarca,* for sale in the local tourist office. Its simple orientation map is adequate for initial planning.

Both east and west of town, there are backcountry *refugios* where hikers can either camp or hire a bunk or floor space, and cook or purchase meals. While these are fairly basic, they are inexpensive and comfortable enough, and the *refugieros* who run them are building a series of connector trails to supplement the access points and create a hikers' circuit. Some of these are already operative.

Two blocks north of Plaza Pagano, westbound Azcuénaga crosses the Quemquemtreu and continues six kilometers to a footpath overlooking its southerly confluence with the Río Azul and, in the distance, Lago Puelo; the short but precipitous northbound trail leads to the natural metamorphic silhouette colloquially known as the **Cabeza del Indio** ("Indian's Head"). Local Mapuche themselves sometimes hold ceremonies here.

About six kilometers north of town via the Bariloche road, a northwesterly gravel road leads to a signed southeasterly turnoff to the municipal **Reserva Forestal Loma de Medio–Río Azul** (admission US$.35). Its main attraction is an 800-meter loop trail to the **Cascada Escondida,** where the river follows a fault before tumbling down the titled face in a classic bridal veil. It's best during the heavy spring runoff, when the volume of water turns the single falls into two or three larger ones.

About 10 kilometers north of town by the same main road, but via a northeasterly lateral, the **Cascada Mallín Ahogado** is a 20-meter waterfall on the Quemquemtreu tributary of the Arroyo del Medio. Diverted for agriculture, it's best in early spring runoff. The caretaker has carved scale models of traditional oxcarts, wheelbarrows, and the like.

A parallel main road continues 15 kilometers northwest to Club Andino's 70-bunk **Refugio Perito Moreno** (tel. 02944/493912, US$3.50 pp); a small ski area, at a base elevation of 1,000 meters, has a T-bar lift to 1,450 meters. From the *refugio,* the 2,206-meter summit of **Cerro Perito Moreno** is about a three-hour hike. The *refugio* is busiest in summer, when it gets a lot of schoolkids, and meals are also available here.

Cajón del Azul

Immediately west of Mallín Ahogado, 15 kilometers northwest of El Bolsón, a signed gravel road suitable only for 4WD vehicles drops steeply into the canyon of the Río Azul, which flows eastward out of the Andes before turning sharply south at the confluence with the Río Blanco. Beyond the Arco Iris campground, where the road

© WAYNE BERNHARDSON

An increasingly integrated trail network links Refugio Cajón del Azul to other Andean huts west of El Bolsón.

© WAYNE BERNHARDSON

view of Lago Puelo and the Chilean border from Cerro Piltriquitrón, near El Bolsón

ends, two precarious *pasarelas* (pedestrian bridges) cross the rivers before the trail becomes an up-and-down hike that leads to a sheer-sided gorge. Here, beneath a sturdy log bridge, the spring runoff explodes like a cannon shot.

Just across the bridge, about 2.5 hours from the confluence, **Refugio Cajón del Azul** is open all year. Run by an English-speaking semi-hermit named Atilio who offers a free cup of coffee, tea, or *mate* to every arrival, it also has mattresses for overnighters in a communal dormitory. Though dark, the spacious and rustically comfortable *refugio* even has a water-driven turbine to provide electricity. Most supplies arrive on horseback, though in summer and fall Atilio's irrigated *chacra* provides fresh apples, cherries, peaches, plums, raspberries, and the like. The westbound trail continues another hour or more to **Refugio El Retamal.**

An alternative northwesterly trail from the Arco Iris trailhead dead-ends at **Refugio Dedo Gordo,** providing access to the summit of its namesake 2,065-meter summit. Before the final climb to Refugio Cajón del Azul, a new but poorly signed trail climbs steeply southward and then drops into the drainage of the Arroyo Teno and to **Refugio Hielo Azul.** This route allows overnight hikers to loop back to El Bolsón.

Cerro Piltriquitrón

East of Bolsón, the piedmont rises steadily and then sharply to the granite summit of 2,284-meter Piltriquitrón, where a clear day reveals the snow-covered phalanx of peaks along the Chilean border, from Tronador and beyond in the north to Lago Puelo and beyond the Cordón Esperanza in the south. Over the border, the Fuji-perfect cone of Volcán Osorno lies almost immediately west of Tronador.

From Bolsón, a winding dirt road climbs 13 kilometers to an overlook and parking area at the 1,200-meter level, where a steep footpath leads to the **Bosque Tallado** (www.elbosquetallado.com). Here, chainsaw sculptors from around the country have transformed trunks from a scorched *lenga* forest into 25 memorable sculptures. Admission to the forest is US$1 per person.

Beyond the Bosque Tallado, the trail climbs to Club Andino's **Refugio Piltriquitrón** (tel. 02944/492024) at 1,400 meters. Bunks cost

US$2.50 per person, but you need your own sleeping bag; meals are also available. This was once a ski area, and the path climbs even more steeply along the rusty T-bar cable before leveling off and rounding Piltriquitrón; marked by paint blazes, it then climbs steeply again, over loose talus, to the summit. From the *refugio,* it takes about two hours; carry water and high-energy snacks.

In summer, Bolsón's **Grado 42** (Avenida Belgrano 406, Local 2, tel. 02944/493124) goes to the parking area at 9:30 A.M. daily, returning at 4:30 P.M. The fare is US$3.50 one way, US$5 round-trip.

Interior Chubut Province

PARQUE NACIONAL LAGO PUELO

Fed by four rivers and numerous arroyos, nearly surrounded by forested peaks, the turquoise body of Lago Puelo is the showpiece of its namesake national park. In addition to its scenery, it's popular for camping, swimming, boating, and hiking, and offers a little-used option for crossing into Chile (unlike most Argentine lakes and streams, Lago Puelo drains toward the Pacific).

Orientation

Just 15 kilometers south of El Bolsón, Lago Puelo lies across the Chubut provincial line. The park itself encompasses 27,675 hectares of mostly mountainous forested land, except for the lakeshore deltas of the Río Azul in the north, and the Río Turbio, across the lake to the south. Though the lake is only 200 meters above sea level, the summits rise above 1,500 meters.

Flora and Fauna

Lago Puelo's flora and fauna closely resemble those of Nahuel Huapi to the north and Los Alerces to the south. Its relatively low elevations and exposure to Pacific storms, though, create a milder microclimate around the lakeshore that permits the growth of tree species like the *ulmo (Eucryphia cordifolia),* with its showy white flowers, and the *lingue (Persea lingue).* The *huemul* (Andean deer) and *pudú* (miniature deer) are both present but rarely seen.

Sports and Recreation

There are several trailheads near the park's scantily outfitted Centro de Informes, where a couple bilingual guides hang out to offer inexpensive guided hikes. The most popular is the **Sendero al Mirador del Lago,** to the east, which climbs 130 meters to an overlook.

To the west, the **Senda Los Hitos** fords the Río Azul and leads five kilometers east to Arroyo Las Lágrimas, where through-hikers to Chile can complete Argentine border formalities with the Gendarmería. Five kilometers farther west, just beyond Los Hitos, the Chilean Carabineros handle their part of the paperwork; from there, it's possible to continue to the Chilean town of Puelo, with onward connections to Puerto Montt.

For most visitors, though, the chance to sail the lake is the main attraction. The *Juana de Arco* (tel. 02944/493415) and *Popeye 2000* carry passengers on half-hour excursions (US$3.50 pp) after 2:30 P.M.; they also offer 11 A.M. departures to the Chilean border (US$10 pp).

The *Catamarán Lago Puelo* (tel. 02944/492663, lagopuelo@elbolson.com) sails Friday and Sunday to Río Turbio (US$10), on the lake's south shore.

Practicalities

Immediately east of the visitors center, **Camping Lago Puelo** (tel. 02944/499186) charges US$2 per person. There's a small *confitería* here, and limited supplies are available.

In addition, there's a free site at Arroyo Las Lágrimas, about five kilometers west of the visitors center, on the footpath to the Chilean border, and other free sites at Río Turbio, at the south end of the lake.

Near the park entrance, the APN's understaffed **Oficina de Informes** (tel. 02944/499232, lagopuelo@apn.gov.ar) lags behind the area's other parks, with scanty exhibits on its natural attractions. At the entrance, they collect fees of US$1 per person for Argentine residents, US$2 per person for foreigners; that admission is valid for 48 hours at other nearby parks, including Nahuel Huapi and Los Alerces.

From El Bolsón, Vía Bariloche **buses** shuttle down Avenida San Martín to the park entrance and back 10 times every weekday between 6:45 A.M. and 9 P.M., but only eight Saturday between 9 A.M. and 9 P.M. The first of seven Sunday buses leaves at 10:30 A.M., the last at 9 P.M. Return times are 30–45 minutes later.

EL MAITÉN

In 1979, Paul Theroux's overrated opus *The Old Patagonian Express* made the dying narrow-gauge railway that ran south from Ingeniero Jacobacci to Esquel a global household word. Its antique steam locomotives no longer traverse the entire 402-kilometer route from Río Negro to Chubut, but the dusty township of El Maitén, with its rusting rails, weathered workshops, and twirling turntables, is the best place to savor this picturesque economic folly. Like Esquel, it also retains enough rolling stock to let committed trainspotters board this living anachronism and fill their photo albums in the process.

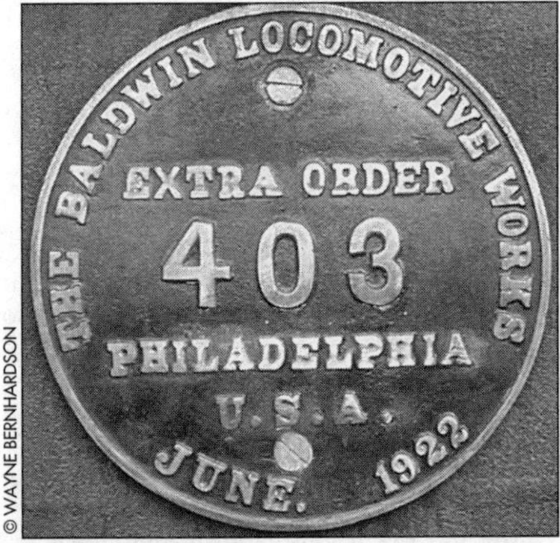

© WAYNE BERNHARDSON

locomotive plaque at El Maitén

Orientation

El Maitén (population 3,399) is 70 kilometers southeast of El Bolsón via gravel RP 6 or via paved RN 258 and gravel RP 70. It's 130 kilometers north of Esquel via RP 40, with the last 32 kilometers unpaved.

La Trochita

Gringos may cite the Gospel according to Theroux, but most Argentines prefer to call it La Trochita (a diminutive for "gauge") or El Trencito ("Little Train"). The yards are still open, though only a couple locomotives (an American Baldwin and a 1922 German Henschel) are in running order; the mostly Belgian cars date from 1922 to about 1960.

February's combined **Fiesta Provincial del Trencito** and **Fiesta Nacional del Tren a Vapor** (National Steam Train Festival) fill El Maitén's handful of hotels and campgrounds. Celebrating the railroad, it also features live music, horseback races, and bronco-busting, and regional delicacies.

In summer, the train does a 2.5-hour excursion to Bruno Thomae and back (US$5.50 pp) Tuesday, Thursday, Friday, and Saturday at 3 P.M.; the rest of the year, frequencies fall to weekly. For current schedules, contact El Maitén's **Secretaría de Turismo** (tel. 02945/495150, turismai@ar.inter.net) or **Estación El Maitén** (Carlos Pellegrini 841, tel. 02945/495190, latrochita@epuyen.net.ar).

Practicalities

On the Río Chubut on the east side of town, the **Camping Municipal** (tel. 02945/495189) charges about US$1 per person. **Hostería Refugio Andino** (Avenida San Martín 1317, tel. 02945/15-681121, US$4.50 pp) has both accommodations and a restaurant.

LADE (Avenida San Martín s/n, tel. 02945/495159) flies once or twice per week to destinations like El Bolsón, Bariloche, Esquel, Comodoro Rivadavia, and Neuquén.

Transportes El Maitén (tel. 02944/493124) goes from El Bolsón to El Maitén Wednesday and Saturday at 1 P.M., returning at 3 P.M. **Vía Bariloche** (Avenida San Martín 1317, tel.

02945/15-681121) goes to Esquel (US$4.50, two hours) Tuesday, Thursday, and Saturday at 1 P.M.

ESQUEL

Across the Chubut border, the gateway to Parque Nacional Los Alerces and the end of the line for the famous narrow-gauge train internationally known as "The Old Patagonian Express," Esquel is a deceptively tranquil town of wide avenues divided by densely planted medians. At the same time, it's a city divided by a dispute and a plebiscite that rejected a nearby mine, promoted by Canada's Meridian Gold and local politicians, which would have used toxic cyanide to leach the valuable mineral; there's always a cop or two posted outside Meridian's downtown offices. What's more, it's a place where Mapuche militancy is palpable, in graffiti that says "neither Argentine nor Chilean, but Mapuche."

Orientation

Esquel (population 28,117) is 167 kilometers south of El Bolsón via RN 258, RN 40, and RN 259, all of which are smoothly paved. Alternatively, many visitors take the gravel highway RP 71, south of the town of Epuyén, to go directly to Parque Nacional Los Alerces. Esquel is also 608 kilometers west of Trelew via a series of paved highways across the Patagonian steppe, and 581 kilometers northwest of Comodoro Rivadavia via equally good roads.

The city itself is a compact grid on the north bank of the Arroyo Esquel. Southbound RN 259 leads to a junction to Parque Nacional Los Alerces, the Welsh-settled town of Trevelin, and the Chilean border at Futaleufú.

Sights

Esquel's most notable sight, not to mention one of its most popular excursions, is the narrow-gauge steam train **La Trochita,** which arrives and departs from the **Estación Ferrocarril Roca** (Roggero and Urquiza); see the separate entry below and the El Maitén entry above for more detail.

Esquel has a pair of modest museums. The **Museo de Culturas Originarias Patagónicas** (Belgrano 330, tel. 02945/451929) is an archaeological and ethnographic institution focusing on Patagonia's first peoples; it's open 7 A.M.–12:30 P.M. and 4–9 P.M. weekdays, 9 A.M.–1 P.M. weekends, with an admission charge of US$.35.

The **Museo de Arte Naif** (Avenida Alvear and Avenida Fontana) occupies new quarters on the 1st floor of the old bus terminal; it's open 9:30 A.M.–12:30 P.M. and 5–9 P.M. weekdays, 5–8 P.M. Saturdays. Admission costs US$.35.

La Trochita

From the old Roca railway station, now a museum, La Trochita still makes entertaining excursions to the Mapuche hamlet of Nahuel Pan. Its wooden passenger wagons, equipped with salamander stoves and hard-backed benches, are classics of their era, and the entire line is a national historical monument.

© WAYNE BERNHARDSON

La Trochita, the famous narrow-gauge steam train, arrives at Esquel.

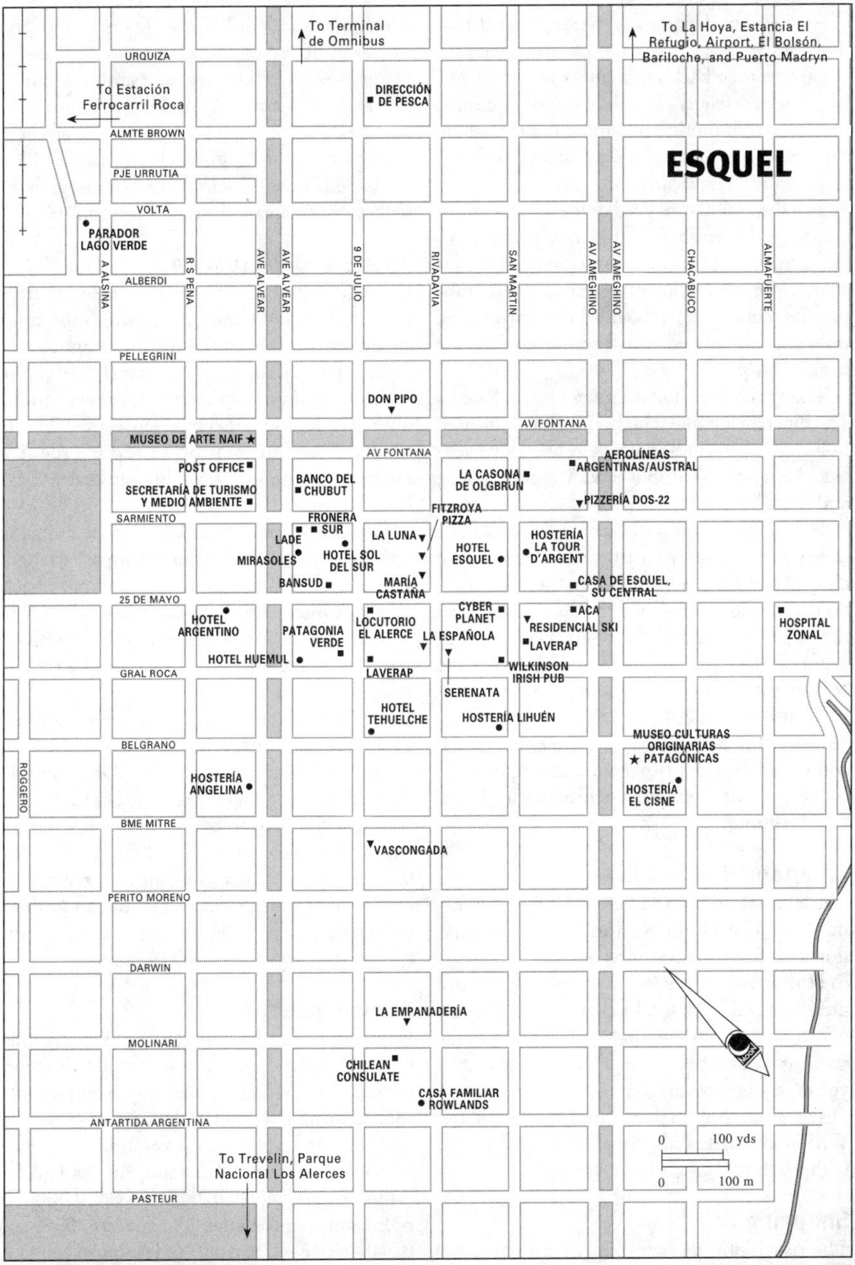

ESQUEL

To Terminal de Omnibus
To La Hoya, Estancia El Refugio, Airport, El Bolsón, Bariloche, and Puerto Madryn
To Estación Ferrocarril Roca
To Trevelin, Parque Nacional Los Alerces

URQUIZA
ALMTE BROWN
PJE URRUTIA
VOLTA
ALBERDI
PELLEGRINI
AV FONTANA
SARMIENTO
25 DE MAYO
GRAL ROCA
BELGRANO
BME MITRE
PERITO MORENO
DARWIN
MOLINARI
ANTARTIDA ARGENTINA
PASTEUR

A ALSINA
R S PENA
AVE ALVEAR
9 DE JULIO
RIVADAVIA
SAN MARTIN
AV AMEGHINO
CHACABUCO
ALMAFUERTE
ROGGERO

DIRECCIÓN DE PESCA
PARADOR LAGO VERDE
DON PIPO
MUSEO DE ARTE NAIF
POST OFFICE
SECRETARÍA DE TURISMO Y MEDIO AMBIENTE
BANCO DEL CHUBUT
LA CASONA DE OLGBRUN
AEROLÍNEAS ARGENTINAS/AUSTRAL
PIZZERÍA DOS-22
FITZROYA PIZZA
FRONERA SUR
LADE
MIRASOLES
HOTEL SOL DEL SUR
LA LUNA
HOTEL ESQUEL
HOSTERÍA LA TOUR D'ARGENT
BANSUD
MARÍA CASTAÑA
CASA DE ESQUEL, SU CENTRAL
HOTEL ARGENTINO
PATAGONIA VERDE
HOTEL HUEMUL
LOCUTORIO EL ALERCE
LAVERAP
LA ESPAÑOLA
CYBER PLANET
SERENATA
ACA
RESIDENCIAL SKI
LAVERAP
WILKINSON IRISH PUB
HOSPITAL ZONAL
HOTEL TEHUELCHE
HOSTERÍA LIHUÉN
MUSEO CULTURAS ORIGINARIAS PATAGÓNICAS
HOSTERÍA EL CISNE
HOSTERÍA ANGELINA
VASCONGADA
LA EMPANADERÍA
CHILEAN CONSULATE
CASA FAMILIAR ROWLANDS

0 100 yds
0 100 m

Northern Argentine Patagonia

As the train departs the station, Esquel residents leave their houses and cars to wave as it chugs past their back yards and crosses the highway. Each passenger coach has a guide and some very good folk-music performers, but the rolling stock generates so much noise that it's difficult to understand them clearly.

The theoretical top speed of the antique steam engines is 60 km/h, but they rarely exceed 45 km/h and average only about 30 km/h. In one instance, the concessionaire even staged a "robbery" as mounted riders boarded the slow-moving train and "demanded" small amounts of money for the show.

Taking about an hour to reach Nahuel Pan, La Trochita remains about an hour before returning to Esquel. In the meantime, there are good oven-baked empanadas, drinks, and Mapuche crafts, and short horseback rides.

Normally, the train to Nahuel Pan and back leaves at 9 A.M. and return to Esquel at noon daily in summer, but sometimes there are afternoon departures as well and the occasional trip all the way to El Maitén (nine hours, US$33), with a stop at the Leleque museum. The rest of the year, excursions are less frequent. The local fare is US$9 per person, cash only; you can usually buy a ticket without a reservation. For more detail, contact La Trochita (Roggero and Urquiza, tel. 02945/451403, www.latrochita.org.ar, latrochita@chubutur.gov.ar).

Entertainment and Events

The **Semana de Esquel** marks the city's founding in 1906. The **Fiesta Nacional de Esqui** (national ski festival) takes place in September.

Hotel Argentino (25 de Mayo 862) has a great bar with a classic kitchen-sink collection of memorabilia and junk, a long bar, and friendly staff, but don't expect to get to get to sleep early if you're staying upstairs.

For something a little slicker, there's the **Wilkinson Irish Pub** (San Martín and Roca), with a 6–8 P.M. happy hour.

Shopping

The Asociación de Artesanos de Esquel sponsors Plaza San Martín's **Feria Artesanal Permanente;** hours are 7–10:30 P.M. Thursday and Friday, 6–11:30 P.M. weekends.

For wood carvings, try **Artesanías Manolo** (Alsina 483). **Casa de Esquel** (25 de Mayo 415, tel. 02945/452544) is a bookstore and crafts outlet. **La Casona de Olgbrun** (San Martín 1137, tel. 02945/453841) sells crafts but also edibles such as chocolates and smoked salmon.

Sports and Recreation

Hiking, climbing, horseback riding, whitewater rafting and kayaking, fishing, and skiing are all on the docket; for information on skiing, in particular, see the separate entry for La Hoya below. Rafters and kayakers should note that the Río Futaleufú, across the Chilean border, is one of the world's top whitewater rivers; Argentina's Corcovado is an easier Class II–III outing.

Patagonia Verde (9 de Julio 926, tel. 02945/454396, www.patagonia-verde.com.ar) arranges activities like hiking, climbing, and horseback riding. **Frontera Sur** (Sarmiento 784, tel. 02945/450505, www.fronterasur.net, fronterasur@fronterasur.net) organizes water sports like rafting (US$30 for a full day) and kayaking on the Class II–III Río Corcovado, as well as hiking, riding, and mountain biking.

For fishing licenses, contact the **Dirección de Pesca** (9 de Julio 1643, tel. 0297/451226); the season runs November–mid-April. **Andrés Müller** (Sarmiento 120, tel. 02945/454572, fax 02945/453901, framumi@ar.inter.net) is a reliable independent fishing guide, while **Rincón Andino** (Miguens 40, tel. 02945/451891, www.rinconandino.com.ar) is a specialist operator.

Accommodations

Esquel has abundant budget accommodations but little in the upper categories, and things can get tight in the summer high season and ski season. Standards in general, though, are good.

There are several campgrounds around and just outside of town: **Autocamping La Colina** (Humphreys 554, tel. 02945/454962, US$1.50 pp); **Camping Millalén** (Ameghino 2063, tel. 02945/456164, US$2 pp); and **Autocamping La Rural** (RN 259 Km 1, tel. 02945/452580, US$2 pp, plus a one-time charge of US$2 per car, tent, and family group).

Shoestring backpackers can try basic **Hotel Argentino** (25 de Mayo 862, tel. 02945/452237, US$5–6 pp), which has rooms with shared or private bath, plus a great street-level bar. There are also, however, simple B&Bs like the **Casa Familiar Rowlands** (Rivadavia 330, tel. 02945/452578, US$3.50 pp) with shared bath; breakfast costs US$1 more.

Other inexpensive options include **Hotel Huemul** (Alvear 1015, tel. 02945/450817, US$5/9 s/d) and **Hostería El Cisne** (Chacabuco 778, tel. 02945/452256, US$7/10 s/d). No longer a Hostelling International affiliate, **Parador Lago Verde** (Volta 1081, tel. 02945/452251, fax 02945/453901, info@patagonia-verde.com.ar, US$10/14 d) still offers good value.

Hostería Lihuén (San Martín 822, tel. 02945/452589, ejarque@esquel-net.com.ar, US$13/15 s/d) is a friendly, decent place. **Residencial Ski** (San Martín 961, tel. 02945/451646, elcalafate@ciudad.com.ar, US$13/18 s/d) is showing its age.

Comfortable **Hostería los Tulipanes** (Avenida Fontana 365, tel. 02945/452748, US$13/20 s/d) is a real find—the decor may be tacky, but the beds are firm, the baths spacious, and the breakfast abundant and diverse. There's also genuine warmth in the details, like chocolates by the bedside, in this family-run hostelry.

Improved **Hotel Esquel** (San Martín 1044, tel. 02945/452534, hotelesquel@hotmail.com, US$14/24 s/d) and the alpine-styled **Hostería La Tour D'Argent** (San Martín 1063, tel. 02945/454612, latourdargent@ciudad.com.ar, 22/33 s/d) are also good choices.

An unremarkable façade makes a misleading approach to the spacious, well-furnished rooms at **Hostería Angelina** (Avenida Alvear 758, tel./fax 02945/452763, hosteriangelina@argentina.com, US$27/33 s/d), whose gregarious owner goes out of his way to make guests feel welcome. Rates include telephone, cable TV, parking, and central heating; the buffet breakfast (US$2 pp) includes croissants, ham, cheese, bread, cereal, fruit and fruit salad, coffee, and tea.

Esquel has a pair of solid three-star hotels: **Hotel Sol del Sur** (9 de Julio 1086, tel. 02945/452189, soldelsur@commlab.com.ar, US$30/40 s/d) and spacious **Hotel Tehuelche** (9 de Julio 825, tel. 02945/452420, tehuelche@ar.inter.net, US$43/58 s/d).

Food

Esquel is no place for haute cuisine, but its restaurants do what they do well. **María Castaña** (25 de Mayo 605, tel. 02945/451752) serves breakfast, coffee, and good sandwiches. **La Luna** (Rivadavia 1080, tel. 02945/453800) offers palatable lunches for about US$5, with limited sidewalk seating. **La Empanadería** (Molinari 633) bakes a variety of empanadas.

Fitzroya Pizza (Rivadavia 1048, tel. 02945/450512) is a first-rate pizzeria, with an enormous variety of toppings, in the US$3.50–7 range; solo diners can order half portions. Other good pizzerias include **Don Pipo** (Fontana 649, tel. 02945/453458), though it seems to have slipped a notch, and **Pizzería Dos-22** (Ameghino and Sarmiento, tel. 02945/454995).

Esquel's best new restaurant is the bistro-style **Mirasoles** (Avenida Alvear 1069, tel. 02945/15-686196), with red-brick walls, wooden floors, plenty of space between diners, and excellent service even when busy. Italo-Argentine entrées like *ñoquis* and appetizers like *mozzarrela caprese* are the best choices.

La Española (Rivadavia 940, tel. 02945/451509) is a *parrilla* that also serves Middle Eastern dishes. **Vascongada** (9 de Julio and Mitre, tel. 02945/452229) serves large portions of regional specialties.

Serenata (Rivadavia 939, tel. 02945/455999) has Esquel's finest ice cream.

Information

Open 7 A.M.–11 P.M. daily, the **Secretaría de Turismo y Medio Ambiente** (Avenida Alvear 1120, tel. 02945/451927, www.esquel.gov.ar, turismo@esquel.gov.ar) maintains a thorough database on accommodations and other services here and in Parque Nacional Los Alerces. A satellite office at the bus terminal is open 6–9 A.M., 11:30 A.M.–2 P.M., and 5:30–8:30 P.M. daily.

The private **Ente Mixto de Turismo** (tel.

02945/451566) has a desk at the bus terminal, but its information is skeletal.

For motorists, **ACA** is at 25 de Mayo and Ameghino, tel. 02965/452382.

Services

Banco del Chubut (Alvear 1131) and **BanSud** (25 de Mayo 737) have ATMs.

Correo Argentino is at Alvear 1192; the postal code is 9200. **Su Central** (25 de Mayo 415) has both phone and Internet access, but the best Internet connections are at **Locutorio El Alerce** (25 de Mayo and 9 de Julio). **Cyber Planet** (San Martín 996) has fast connections but also a plague of video gamers.

Chile's honorary **consulate** (Molinari 754, tel. 02945/451189) is open 8:30 A.M.–1:30 P.M. weekdays only.

For laundry (about US$3 per load), **Laverap** (tel. 02945/455959) has two locations: Avenida San Martín 941 and 9 de Julio and Roca.

For medical services, contact the **Hospital Zonal** (25 de Mayo 150, tel. 02945/450222).

Getting There

Esquel has limited air services, better bus connections, and rail fantasies.

Aerolíneas Argentinas/Austral (Avenida Fontana 406, tel. 0297/453614) flies twice or three times weekly to Buenos Aires via Bariloche, and occasionally to Trelew.

LADE (Alvear 1085, tel. 02945/452124) usually flies twice weekly to Bariloche, Neuquén and Buenos Aires, and weekly or so to El Bolsón, El Maitén, Río Mayo, and Comodoro Rivadavia.

Esquel's **Terminal de Omnibus** (Avenida Alvear 1871, tel. 02945/451566, terminalesq@ciudad.com.ar) is a contemporary facility four blocks northeast of downtown. It has good local and regional services, but long-distance connections are better in Bariloche.

Transportes Jacobsen/Vía Bariloche (tel. 02945/453528) connects Esquel with El Maitén at 12:30 P.M. Tuesday, Thursday, and Saturday, returning at 3 P.M.

Jacobsen also serves the nearby provincial destinations of Trevelin (frequently); La Balsa/Futaleufú (Monday and Friday at 8 A.M. and 5:30 P.M., with Wednesday service in summer); and Corcovado/Carrenleufú (Sunday and Monday at 4 P.M., Wednesday and Friday at 10 A.M.).

In summer, **Transportes Esquel** (tel. 02945/453529) goes to Parque Nacional Los Alerces and Lago Puelo at 8 A.M. (connecting with lake excursions) and 2 P.M. daily. Fares are US$2.50 to La Villa, US$3.50 to Bahía Rosales, US$4 to Lago Verde, US$5 to Lago Rivadavia, US$6 to Cholila, and US$7 to Puelo, where there are easy connections to El Bolsón. Winter schedules may differ.

Typical destinations, fares, and times include Trevelin (US$1.50, 30 minutes), La Balsa/Futaleufú (US$4, 1.5 hours), El Maitén (US$4.50, two hours), El Bolsón (US$5, 2.5 hours), Corcovado/Carrenleufú (US$4.50, three hours), Bariloche (US$7–9, 4.5 hours), Neuquén (US$18–21, 10.5 hours), Trelew (US$15, eight hours), Puerto Madryn (US$17, nine hours), Comodoro Rivadavia (US$16, nine hours), and Buenos Aires (US$40–45, 29 hours).

For the moment, **La Trochita** (tel. 02945/541403) is a **tourist train** only, but there's talk of reopening the line to Ingeniero Jacobacci.

Getting Around

Aeropuerto Esquel is 20 kilometers east of town on RN 40; a taxi or *remise* is the only option.

Opposite the bus terminal, **Los Alerces Rent a Car** (Avenida Alvear 1830, tel. 02945/456008, losalercesrentacar@ciudad.com.ar) is the only car-rental option.

VICINITY OF ESQUEL

In addition to Parque Nacional Los Alerces, the area's biggest attraction (see separate entry below), Esquel has many other points of interest within an hour or two.

La Hoya

Only 13 kilometers north of Esquel, run by the provincial government, La Hoya is a modest ski area with improving infrastructure. Thanks to its location on the Andes' drier eastern side, it gets a fine powder that compensates for its relatively small size, and it's also substantially cheaper than Bariloche.

Ranging from 1,200 to 2,500 meters above sea level, La Hoya has 25 runs totaling about 22 kilometers on 60 hectares. Its modern lifts include the 1,100-meter Telesilla del Bosque, which also carries hikers to high-country trailheads in summer (US$2), and the 1,018-meter Telesilla del Cañadón. In the June–October season, it also has a ski school; the **Fiesta Nacional del Esquí** (National Ski Festival) takes place the second week of September.

Full-day lift passes run from US$7 (low season) to US$11 (high season), with small children's discounts. Six-day passes cost US$36–56 for adults, US$26–38 for children, while season passes cost US$83 for adults, US$60 for children.

Equipment can be rented on site or in Esquel at **Bolsa de Ski** (Rivadavia and 25 de Mayo, tel. 02945/452379). In town, contact the **Centro de Montaña La Hoya** (25 de Mayo 646, tel. 02945/453018, www.camlahoya.com.ar). Note that, with low capacity, the lift lines can be long.

Estancia El Refugio

East of Esquel, the arid steppe stretches toward the coast, but the classic *casco* of Estancia El Refugio (tel./fax 02945/452653, www.estancia elrefugio.com, elrefugio@esquelonline.com.ar) occupies a sheltered hideaway with sprawling gardens and lawns, in the midst of a 16,000-hectare cattle and sheep ranch. Only half an hour from town, it's close enough to serve as a base for fishing, riding, and other excursions (which the *estancia* organizes), but offers the most genteel accommodations in the vicinity, with five rooms and suites in the main chalet, and another two in a separate guest house.

Estancia El Refugio charges US$48 per person with half-board, plus US$9 per person for additional meals. It's 24 kilometers from Esquel via a dirt road off southbound RN 40, only a short distance east of its junction with RN 258.

Museo Leleque

Midway between Esquel and El Bolsón, on what was one of Argentina's largest *estancias,* the Museo Leleque (RN 40 Km 1440, www.latrochita.com .ar/museo.htm, museoleleque@ciudad.com.ar) covers Patagonia from prehistory to the present. Funded by Italian fashion icon Carlo Benetton, who purchased the Argentine Southern Land Company and several other Patagonian properties, it houses and organizes the collections of Ukrainian immigrant Pablo S. Korschenewski, who left Buenos Aires half a century ago to live in Patagonia, exploring the countryside on foot and by horseback.

In the process, Korschenewski collected over 14,000 artifacts including arrowheads, thin stone blades, bone drills, ceremonial stone axes, grinding stones, and pottery shards. Making contact with Benetton, he struck a chord and persuaded him to turn the historic buildings at Leleque, once a general store, hotel, and school, into a contemporary museum that now gets 8,500 visitors, mostly Argentines, per annum. Not just archaeological, the exhibits stress contact and post-contact history of the region's first peoples, regional and oral histories, photographs, and documents. One prize is a receipt signed by Butch Cassidy, who lived in nearby Cholila from 1901 to 1905, under the alias Santiago Ryan.

Administered by the Fundación Ameghino, the Museo Leleque is 90 kilometers north of Esquel. It's open 11 A.M.–7 P.M. daily except Wednesday in January and February; the rest of the year, hours are 11 A.M.–5 P.M. except Wednesday and in May and June, when it shuts down entirely. Admission costs US$1; the museum also has a souvenir shop and a *confitería* for snacks and coffee.

Cholila

Though it's barely a wide spot in the road, the community of Cholila has become an offbeat pilgrimage site ever since U.S. author Anne Meadows pinpointed the house of *yanqui* outlaws Robert Leroy Parker and Harry Longabaugh in her historical travelogue *Digging Up Butch and Sundance* (3rd edition, University of Nebraska Press, 2003). Bruce Chatwin also told the tale of the Cholila cabin—perhaps taking literary license—in his classic *In Patagonia.*

Butch and Sundance presumably tried to go straight here, but fled to Chile in 1905 when accused of a robbery in Río Gallegos and the Pinkertons got on their scent. Since the death of its elderly

© WAYNE BERNHARDSON

Butch Cassidy and the Sundance Kid built this cabin near Cholila.

occupant Aladín Sepúlveda in 1999, the unoccupied and now crumbling cabin has become a target for souvenir hunters. It is also in legal limbo, unsaleable as one of the Daher family owners died intestate; the Sepúlveda family also claims a right of occupancy. The provincial government hopes to lease the cabin from the Daher survivors, restore it, and hire the Sepúlvedas as caretakers.

Near the northeastern entrance of Parque Nacional Los Alerces, just north of Cholila at Km 21 of RP 71 near the signed junction to the Casa de Piedra teahouse, the house is visible on the west side of the highway; in fact, there are informal directional signs. Transportes Esquel buses between El Bolsón and Esquel via Los Alerces pass within sight of the cabin.

Beyond the cabin entrance, a westbound lateral leads to the **Casa de Piedra** (tel. 02945/498056, US$25 d), a hybrid B&B/teahouse that's open from December through Semana Santa. It makes an ideal detour even for day-trippers.

TREVELIN AND VICINITY

Unlike coastal Chubut, the Andean interior has few settlements where the Welsh imprint remains, but tranquil Trevelin, with historic houses and teahouses to rival Gaiman, is the exception. Only half an hour south of Esquel, it owes its very name to a Welsh compound meaning "mill town" after its first flourmill, since preserved as a history museum.

Trevelin (population 4,849), 24 kilometers south of Esquel via RN 259, is also unique for its disorientingly octagonal Plaza Coronel Fontana, from which RN 259 continues southward as Avenida San Martín; it is the main commercial street and thoroughfare to Corcovado and the Chilean border post of Futaleufú. Other streets fan out from the plaza.

Chile-bound motorists should fill the tank here, as Futaleufú has no permanent service station and, in any event, Chilean gasoline prices are double those in Argentine Patagonia.

Sights

In 1922, Welsh immigrants founded the Molino Harinero de la Compañía Andes, the flour mill that is now the **Museo Molino Viejo** (Molino Viejo 488, tel. 02945/480189). Commercially closed in 1953, it was then used for wool storage; a fire gutted its interior in 1972, but the solid brick walls survived to become the city's historical museum. Its contents include everyday items of early Trevelin, such as period clothing, furniture, carriages, and agricultural machinery, but also photographs, maps, and documents. It also devotes substantial space to the Mapuche and Tehuelche, and notes an early-20th-century banditry crackdown, by the army, that was tough on honest settlers.

November–March, museum hours are 11 A.M.–8 P.M. daily; the rest of the year it's open 9 A.M.–noon and 2–8 P.M. daily. Admission costs US$1 for adults, half that for children under age 12.

Two blocks northeast of the plaza, the offbeat **Museo Cartref Taid** (Malacara s/n, tel. 02945/480108) holds the **Tumba de Malacara,** a tomb with the remains of the horse that helped its rider, Trevelin founder John D. Evans, flee an Araucanian raid during the Argentine army's 1880s war against the indigenes. Hours are 9 A.M.–12:30 P.M. and 2 P.M.–dusk; admission costs US$.65.

At the south end of town, built of brick, the **Capilla Bethel** (ApIwan and Laprida) is a Welsh chapel dating from 1897; it has also served as a school.

About 19 kilometers south of Trevelin via RN 259 and a short southbound lateral, **Reserva Provincial Nant-y-Fall** is a provincial park with a 400-meter footpath to a string of waterfalls, the highest of which is 67 meters. The source for Nant-y-Fall is **Lago Rosario,** a sub-alpine lake on a Mapuche reservation, 24 kilometers southwest of Trevelin via RP 17 and a short eastbound lateral.

Six kilometers west of Nant-y-Fall, the provincial **Estación de Salmonicultura** (salmon hatchery) offers guided tours 8 A.M.–1 P.M. weekdays. There are several campgrounds and *cabañas* along RN 259, which leads to the Chilean border.

In the Valle 16 de Octubre, about five kilometers east of Trevelin via gravel road, the historic **Escuela No. 18** stands near the site of a 1902 plebiscite that determined that Trevelin would stay on the Argentine side of the border (the original adobe building no longer exists). The onetime school now holds the **Museo del Plebiscito 1902,** an outlier of Trevelin's regional museum, that commemorates the 1902 events; it's open 11 A.M.–8:30 P.M. Thursday–Sunday in summer, 11 A.M.–6:30 P.M. the same days the rest of the year.

For information on the Chilean village of **Futaleufú,** which offers some of the world's most thrilling whitewater rafting and kayaking, see the Aisén chapter.

In summer, Plaza Coronel Fontana hosts a Sunday **crafts market;** the rest of the year, it takes place alternate Sundays.

Accommodations

Except for *cabañas,* which are primarily for large family groups, accommodations are scarce. On the high ground east of the plaza, the HI affiliate **Casaverde Hostel** (Los Alerces s/n, tel. 02945/480091, www.casaverdehostel.com.ar, casaverdehostel@ciudad.com.ar, US$5–6 pp in dorms, US$16–18 d) is a true prize: comfortable rooms, a bar, and extensive hilltop grounds, with views of the Andes to the west. It's small, though, so reservations—or good timing—are essential. It also rents bicycles and helps arrange language courses. Breakfast is about US$1.40 extra.

Other good options include **Residencial Pezzi** (Sarmiento 353, tel. 02945/480146, US$7 pp, open summer only) and **Residencial Estefanía** (Perito Moreno and Sarmiento, tel. 02945/480148, santidoc@ciudad.com.ar, US$12/18 s/d).

Food

Like Gaiman, Trevelin is the place to go for Welsh tea; though teahouses are not so numerous here, the quality is still outstanding. The traditional favorite, though its quarters are contemporary, is **Nain Maggie** (Perito Moreno 179, tel. 02945/480232), but there's nothing wrong with **Las Mutisias** (Avenida San Martín 170, tel. 02945/480165). Late-afternoon teas, which are very filling, cost about US$6 per person.

For takeaway food, try the inexpensive **Los Troncos** (Avenida San Martín and Perito Moreno), a *parrilla* and *rotisería* with fine baked empanadas. Four blocks south of the plaza, **Ruca Laufquén** (Avenida San Martín 419, tel. 02945/480400) is a reliable *parrilla.* **Küimey Ruca** (Avenida Fortín Refugio s/n, tel. 02945/480088), a block northwest of the plaza, is a popular pizzeria.

Reservations are advisable at **Patagonia Celta** (25 de Mayo s/n, tel. 02945/480722), which has a more diverse menu of Argentine regional specialties in agreeable surroundings, with excellent service. Despite the name, it has no direct Welsh connections.

Opposite the plaza, the recently opened **Cosas de Antaño** (28 de Julio 200, tel. 02945/480689) occupies a Bustillo-inspired building with rough-hewn stone and rough-cut timbers. With entrées like trout with almond or hazelnut sauce, as well as fondues, the food may not yet be up to its aspirations, but it's worth a gamble in the US$3–5 price range. The service is more well-meaning than professional, and it has a good wine list.

Information

December–March, the improved **Secretaría de Turismo y Medio Ambiente** (Plaza Coronel Fontana s/n, tel. 02945/480120, www.trevelin.org, turismotrevelin@ciudad.com.ar) is open 8 A.M.–10 P.M. weekdays, 9 A.M.–10 P.M. weekends; the rest of the year, hours are 9 A.M.–6 or 7 P.M. daily.

Services

Banco del Chubut (Avenida San Martín and Brown) has an ATM.

Correo Argentino (Avenida San Martín and Brown) is across the street from the bank; the postal code is 9203. For phone calls, the **Locutorio Central San Martín** (San Martín 559) is five blocks south of Plaza Coronel Fontana.

Gales al Sur (Avenida Patagonia 185, tel. 02965/480427) organizes excursions and activities in Trevelin and vicinity.

Lavitrev (Avenida San Martín 559, tel. 02945/480393) does the washing.

Hospital Trevelin (Avenida San Martín and John Evans, tel. 02945/480132) is three blocks south of Plaza Coronel Fontana.

Getting There and Around

Transportes Jacobsen/Vía Bariloche shuttles between Esquel and Trevelin frequently during the daylight hours; some of its buses continue to the main Chilean border crossing at La Balsa/Futaleufú (Monday, Wednesday, and Friday at 8:30 A.M. and 5:30 P.M.), while others use the alternate Chilean border post at Carrenleufú (Monday and Sunday at 4 P.M., Tuesday and Friday at 10 A.M. from Esquel). Long-distance travelers have to return to Esquel.

CORCOVADO

Some 65 kilometers south of Trevelin via gravel RP 17, the riverside hamlet of Corcovado is popular for rafting, kayaking, and fly-fishing, and provides an alternative international route to the Argentine border post of Carrenleufú and the Chilean town of Palena. It has basic services, including camping, *cabañas,* and a couple of *parrillas,* and a tourist office in summer only.

Motorists continuing to the border, 11 kilometers away via westbound gravel RP 44, should fill their tanks at inexpensive Argentine Patagonian prices here.

PARQUE NACIONAL LOS ALERCES

Parque Nacional Los Alerces owes its existence and its name to the coniferous *Fitzroya cupressoides,* the monarch of the humid Valdivian forests, also known as false larch or Patagonian cypress. Easily western Chubut's most popular attraction, the park draws campers and fishing aficionados to its lush forests and deep blue finger lakes. Despite the magnificent setting, with the snowy summits of the Andean range to the west, hikers may find it frustrating because it has relatively few trails, forcing them to walk the shoulders of dusty roads with heavy automobile traffic.

Geography and Climate

About 45 kilometers west of Esquel via RN 259 and RP 71, Los Alerces is a 263,000-hectare unit on the eastern Andean slope. The highest summit is 2,253-meter Cerro Torrecillas, but most of the cordillera is low enough to permit the penetration of Pacific storms while areas to the north or south might lie completely in the rain shadow.

Lago Verde, Parque Nacional Los Alerces

Past glaciations have left a series of navigable finger lakes that provide access to some of the park's finest sights. Summers are mild, with temperatures reaching 24°C with cool nights, but winters average barely 2°C, with considerable snowfall.

Most destinations within the park are described with reference to "La Villa," the village-like cluster of services at Lago Futalaufquen's south end.

Flora and Fauna

In addition to its signature *alerce,* the park's other conifers include the Chilean incense cedar *(Austrocedrus chilensis)* and the Guaiteca cypress *(Pilgerodendron uviferum),* both of which have limited geographical distribution. Most of the rest of the forest consists of the broadleaf southern beeches *coihue (Nothofagus dombeyi), lenga (Nothofagus pumilio),* and *ñire (Nothofagus antarctica).* The *arrayán* is near the southern limit of its range here.

For hikers, one of the worst plagues is the *colihue (Chusquea coleou),* a solid bamboo that forms impassable thickets. The exotic *Rosa mosqueta,* a European introduction, is an aggressive species that is displacing native plants in many areas.

In this dense forest, Los Alerces' fauna are less conspicuous, but the Andean deer or *huemul* is present, along with its distant miniature relative the *pudú.* Birds include the *chucao* (a common songbird), the austral parakeet, and the Patagonian woodpecker.

Sights and Activities

Travel agencies in Esquel sell tickets for the **Circuito Lacustre,** the park's most popular excursion to the old-growth *alerce* forests; for more details, see the separate entry below.

On the Río Desaguadero, east of RP 71 at the south end of Lago Futalaufquen, the **Sendero del Poblamiento Prehistórico** is an easy 500-meter nature trail that passes a natural overhang with fading pre-Columbian rock art, some of it clearly geometrical; it then climbs through forest to an overlook with expansive panoramas to the north.

Hikers need to register with rangers to hike the steep route to the 1,916-meter summit of **Cerro Alto El Dedal,** reached by a trailhead from Puerto Bustillo, two kilometers north of La Villa; figure about five hours round-trip. From the same trailhead, **Cinco Saltos** is a shorter and easier hike to a series of waterfalls.

From Puerto Limonao, four kilometers north of La Villa, the 25-kilometer **Sendero Lago Krüger** follows Lago Futalaufquén's south shore to the smaller Lago Krüger, where there is a campground and a *refugio,* which is due to reopen after repairs; register with rangers before beginning the hike. Daily boat service to Lago Krüger costs about US$17 per person.

In the park's southernmost sector, reached via Trevelin, the 448-megawatt **Central Hidroeléctrico Futaleufú** is a massive dam project that drowned several natural lakes to create a 9,200-hectare reservoir that powers Puerto Madryn's Aluar aluminum plant, 550 kilometers east. Guided tours (US$1 pp) take place 8 A.M.–8 P.M. daily.

Circuito Lacustre

Los Alerces' traditional excursion is the "lake circuit" starting at Puerto Limonao, at the south end of Lago Futalaufquen, to the Río Arrayanes outlet of Lago Verde; at **Puerto Mermoud,** a catwalk crosses to **Puerto Chucao,** on Lago Menéndez, where another boat continues to **Puerto Sagrario.**

From Puerto Sagrario, passing blue-green **Lago Cisne,** a looping nature trail goes to the *alerce* grove of **El Alerzal** and the landmark **El Abuelo,** the oldest and most impressive single specimen. While there are guides on the hike to and from El Abuelo, it's possible to separate from the group; it is not possible, however, to hike elsewhere in an area that's mostly limited-access *zona intangible.*

It's possible to start the excursion at either Puerto Limonao (US$25 pp) or Puerto Chucao (US$17 pp). Scheduled departures are at 10 A.M. from Limonao, returning by 6:30 P.M., and noon from Chucao, returning by 4:45 P.M. Any Esquel travel agency can make reservations, which are highly advisable, but it's possible to purchase tickets here on a space-available basis.

Accommodations and Food

Los Alerces has numerous campgrounds and a handful of other accommodations, mostly in the vicinity of Lago Futalaufquen. In addition to the reasonably priced organized campgrounds, there are other free but often poorly maintained sites.

Accessible by road, organized campgrounds all have picnic tables, fire pits, toilets with hot showers, and easy access to groceries and restaurants; some have electrical outlets. Among them are **Camping Los Maitenes** (tel. 02945/451003, US$2 pp), only 200 meters from the Intendencia at the south end of Lago Futalaufquen; **Camping Bahía Rosales** (tel. 02945/471004, US$2.50 pp), 14 kilometers from La Villa on the eastern lakeshore; **Camping Lago Verde** (tel. 02945/454421, US$2 pp), 36 kilometers north of La Villa, on its eponymous lake; and **Camping Lago Rivadavia** (tel. 02945/454381, US$2.50 pp), 42 kilometers north of La Villa at the south end of its namesake lake.

Reached only by a 25-kilometer footpath or launch from Puerto Limonao, **Camping & Hostería Lago Krüger** (tel. 02945/452997, www.lagokruger.com) is the park's sole backcountry campsite and hotel. Having undergone a major renovation, it charges about US$5 per person for camping, US$70 per person with full board in the *hostería.*

About 25 kilometers north of La Villa, on Futalaufquén's north arm, **Hostería Cume Hue** (RP 71 s/n, tel. 02945/453639, www.cumehue.com.ar, US$33–43 pp with full board) has clean, comfortable rooms in an attractive setting, but seems to make little effort to promote itself. The restaurant is mediocre.

For groups of any size, the cheapest non-camping options are places like **Cabañas Los Tepues** (RP 71 s/n, tel. 02945/452129, lostepues@hotmail.com, US$27 d), eight kilometers north of La Villa; and **Cabañas Tejas Negras** (RP 71, tel. 02945/471046, tejasnegras@ciudad.com.ar, US$40 d), about 12 kilometers north of La Villa.

About six kilometers north of La Villa, **Hostería Quimé-Quipán** (RP 71 s/n, tel./fax 02945/454134, US$60 d with half-board) has simple but comfortable rooms, some with lake views; its restaurant is adequate, but hardly haute cuisine.

Four kilometers north of La Villa, the park's prestige accommodations is the Bustillo-built **Hostería Futalaufquen** (tel. 02945/471008, fax 02945/471009, www.brazosur.com, www.newage-hotels.com, hosteria@ar.inter.net, US$93–

125 to US$120–161 s or d, depending on view). With only nine rooms, it enjoys a privileged end-of-the-road location on Lago Futalaufquén's western shore; distinctive features include beamed Tudor-style ceilings, a walk-in granite fireplace, copper chandeliers, and a polished wooden bar. Rates, which include half-board, vary from low season (mid-October–mid-December and March to the end of April; high season is mid-December–late February and Semana Santa. The restaurant is open to nonguests (reservations only for dinner).

Other Practicalities

Colloquially known as "La Villa," Villa Futalaufquen, at the south end of Lago Futalaufquen on the eastern approach from Esquel, is the park headquarters. The APN's **Museo y Centro de Informes** (tel. 02945/471015, Int. 23, losalerces@apn.gov.ar, infoalerces@apn.gov.ar) is both a museum, with exhibits on the park's history and natural history, and a notably helpful ranger information center. Hours are 7 A.M.–9 P.M. daily from mid-December–April, and 9 A.M.–5 P.M. daily the rest of the year.

At both the northern Lago Rivadavia and eastern La Portada entrances, rangers collect a US$4-per-person admission charge, which is valid for a week and includes other area parks, such as Lago Puelo. After 9 P.M., when the tollbooths close, there's no one to collect the charge.

In addition to the APN headquarters, La Villa also has a gas station, grocery, post office, public telephones, and a first-aid station.

Transportes Esquel **buses** between Esquel and El Bolsón pick up and drop off passengers along RP 71 within the park; some northbound buses go only as far as Lago Rivadavia before returning to Esquel.

GOBERNADOR COSTA

Some 153 kilometers south of Esquel, Gobernador Costa is a cow town with little to see, but offers the best motorist services on the long haul between Esquel and Río Mayo on RN 40 (south of here, the paved route becomes RP 20, while graveled RN 40 veers west through Alto Río Senguer). **Lago General Vintter,** on the Chilean border via graveled westbound RP 19, is popular with fishermen.

Accommodations and Food

On the north side of the highway, the **Camping Municipal** (US$2 pp) has hot water and electricity. **Residencial Jair** (San Martín and Sarmiento, tel. 02945/15-680414, US$5.50) has decent rooms with private bath.

Hostería y Parrilla Mi Refugio (Avenida Roca s/n, tel. 02945/491097, US$9 pp) provides newish rooms with firm, comfortable beds, but the cheap bathroom fixtures could use an upgrade. Breakfast is included, and its restaurant serves pretty good versions of Argentine standards like beef, pasta, and *milanesa.*

Other Practicalities

Banco del Chubut (Sarmiento and San Martín) has an ATM.

Gobernador Costa's **bus** terminal has northbound services to Esquel, eastbound services to Trelew, and southbound services to Río Mayo, Sarmiento, and Comodoro Rivadavia.

RÍO MAYO

For southbound travelers on RN 40, the crossroads town of Río Mayo is the end of the line for public transportation; in fact, few vehicles of any kind use the spine-jarring gravel section that intersects RP 43, the paved route between Comodoro Rivadavia and the Chilean border, 124 kilometers to the south. Though it has little to see in its own right, it's a common stopover for cyclists, bikers, and others with their own mobility, as well as the odd southbound safari from Bariloche.

Depending primarily on wool for its livelihood, though petroleum is also making a comeback, Río Mayo (population 2,940) is 224 kilometers south of Gobernador Costa, and 274 kilometers west of Comodoro Rivadavia via paved RN 26 and RP 20. There is public transportation on the 189 kilometers of westbound RN 26 to Coyhaique, Chile; some buses take the slightly longer route via RP 55. For information on RN 40's southern reaches, between

Perito Moreno and the Chilean border, see the Southern Argentine Patagonia chapter.

Sights and Events

Río Mayo's modest **Museo Regional Federico Escalada** (Avenida Ejército Argentino s/n, tel. 02903/420400) shares quarters with the tourist office and keeps the same hours, 8 A.M.–1 P.M. and 4–7 P.M. weekdays only.

Featuring sheep-shearing contests and horseback races, early January's **Festival Nacional de la Esquila** in the Predio Olegario Paillaguala (fairgrounds) is the principal festival.

Accommodations and Food

Camping El Labrador (Belgrano and Sarmiento) charges US$3 per vehicle. Modernized **Hotel Akatá** (San Martín 640, tel. 02903/420054, US$7 pp) has rooms with private bath and a so-so restaurant.

Reservations are a good idea for **Hotel El Viejo Covadonga** (San Martín 573, tel. 02903/420020, elviejocovadonga@hotmail.com, US$7 pp), which is popular with tour operators who do the RN 40 circuit between Bariloche and El Calafate. Though it no longer sports its classic Old West–style bar, which the previous owners absconded with, this spruced-up hotel has gracious management and it's also the best place to eat.

Information and Services

For tourist information, visit the **Casa de la Cultura** (Avenida Ejército Argentino s/n, tel. 02903/420400, turismoriomayo@yahoo.com.ar, riomayoturistico@yahoo.com.ar); hours are 9 A.M.–noon and 4–6 P.M. weekdays only.

Banco del Chubut (Yrigoyen and Antártida Argentina) has an ATM. Río Mayo's postal code is 9030. The **Cooperativa Eléctrica** (9 de Julio 409) has Internet access.

Hospital Río Mayo (Sarmiento and Belgrano, tel. 02903/420022) provides medical services.

Getting There

LADE (San Martín 520, tel. 02903/420060) flies semi-regularly to Comodoro Rivadavia and to Esquel and Aeroparque.

Schedules are subject to change from Río Mayo's **Terminal de Ómnibus** (Fontana and Irigoyen). **Etap** (tel. 02903/420167) has northbound services to Esquel (US$9, seven hours) twice weekly, usually Monday and Thursday, and eastbound daily to Comodoro Rivadavia (US$6, four hours). The Esquel buses change passengers at the La Laurita junction of RP 22 and RP 20.

Westbound international buses to Coyhaique, Chile (US$8, four hours) leave Monday and Friday at 5:30 P.M., but often fill up in Comodoro, so reservations are essential.

The Sur Chico

South of the Río Biobío, popularly known as Chile's "lake district" for the scenic finger lakes left by receding Pleistocene glaciers, the Sur Chico has long enticed Chilean and Argentine tourists to its matchless scenery of ice-capped volcanic cones soaring above dense native forests. Only in the past decade-plus have significant numbers of them, plus adventurous foreigners, begun to venture beyond conventional lakeside resorts into the Andean backcountry for activities like hiking, horseback riding, and whitewater rafting. National parks and reserves cover large swathes of the cordillera.

Politically, the Sur Chico comprises Region IX (La Araucanía, the Mapuche homeland) and Region X (Los Lagos), which includes the Chiloé archipelago and, on the mainland across the Golfo de Ancud and the Golfo de Corcovado, what is colloquially known as continental Chiloé. Economically diverse cities like Temuco, Osorno, and Puerto Montt, which rely on forestry, agricultural services, and manufacturing in addition to tourism, are the gateways, but smaller lakeside towns like Villarrica, Pucón, and Puerto Varas make better bases for excursions. There are several routes across the Andes to Argentina, which has its own lake district centered on the city of Bariloche; Puerto Montt, the de facto terminus of the continental Panamericana, is the hub for air, land, and sea access to Chilean Patagonia and also a gateway to the Argentine side.

Southeast of Temuco, Lago Villarrica is a

Must-Sees

Look for **M** to find the sights and activities you can't miss and **M** for the best dining and lodging.

Parque Nacional Conguillío: The fame of the monkey-puzzle tree was such that, nearly a century ago, the famous conservationist John Muir went far out of his way to visit the area that now protects much of southern South America's endemic araucaria forests (page 182).

Parque Nacional Villarrica: Every summer, hundreds of hikers slog up the snow-covered slopes of Chile's most active volcano, immediately south of Pucón, for the views and the thrills (page 195).

Parque Nacional Huerquehue: Just northwest of Pucón, Huerquehue is the place for shaded woodland hikes alongside rushing streams in ruggedly scenic terrain (page 197).

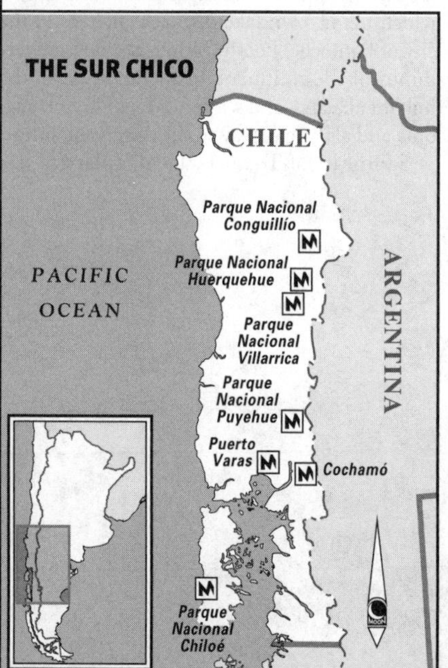

fumaroles on Volcán Puyehue, Parque Nacional Puyehue

Parque Nacional Puyehue: Its remaining forests resemble the rainforest woodlands north and south of it, but the most impressive sight is the barren high country wrought by the lava flows and ash from the 1960 eruption of its namesake volcano (page 202).

Puerto Varas: On Lago Llanquihue's western shore, studded with shingled houses that recall the Middle European origins of its first settlers, Puerto Varas has the Sur Chico's finest services and restaurants, making it the ideal gateway to the bus-boat crossing to the Argentine "lake district" city of Bariloche (page 208).

Cochamó: Southwest of Puerto Varas, the backcountry of Cochamó boasts Yosemite-like granite monoliths surrounded by lush mid-latitude rainforests. Hiking it can be a slog, so many visitors prefer horseback excursions (page 219).

Parque Nacional Chiloé: Only on Chiloé's wild west coast can hikers traipse through dense dwarf woodlands where, according to legend, the troll-like Trauco awaits the unwary (page 241).

beehive of activity for its access to national parks like Villarrica and Huerquehue, but the lake district's heart is farther south, where Lago Todos los Santos is widely considered the country's single most beautiful body of water. Near picturesque Puerto Varas, Volcán Osorno, an almost perfectly symmetrical cone rising above Lago Llanquihue, offers some of the most breathtaking views anywhere, but there are dozens of other high volcanic summits, scenic lakes and rivers, and shores and estuaries to fill weeks or months of sightseeing and activities.

Like the Araucanía, Los Lagos has a vigorous tourist industry and infrastructure, but there's a tension between the natural landscape and resource-based industries like forestry and fisheries. In 2001, vigorous opposition by Chilean conservationists derailed a plan to turn thousands of hectares of native forest into chips for export; still, water pollution from large-scale salmon farming in both freshwater lakes and saltwater estuaries continues to cause concern. Over-exploitation of valuable native finfish, as well as shellfish like abalone and giant mussels, is also a problem.

This chapter also includes insular Chiloé, easily reached by shuttle ferries and soon to be reached by bridge, and parts of continental Chiloé, south to the town of Hornopirén (also known as Río Negro), where a summer-only ferry sails to the tiny cove of Caleta Gonzalo, the de facto start of the Carretera Austral. Because of continental Chiloé's physical isolation from the rest of Region X—only air taxis, catamarans, slow-moving ferries and roundabout buses through Argentina connect it to Puerto Montt and Castro—the bulk of its coverage appears in the Aisén chapter.

PLANNING YOUR TIME

Because the Chilean lakes district is relatively compact, with excellent highways and secondary roads, and with frequent and comfortable public transportation, this is the least problematical part of "Patagonia" for travelers. Still, in the summer peak season, hotel and rental-car reservations are advisable, though accommodations are abundant enough that something's usually available.

For visitors, the best bases are the Lago Villarrica resorts of Villarrica and Pucón to the north, and the Lago Llanquihue town of Puerto Varas or the mainland city of Puerto Montt to the south. For visitors with vehicles, staying at any of these locales keeps the driving to a minimum, but public transportation is good enough that a car is rarely necessary. For those staying outside town, though, it's helpful to have one.

Seeing the main sights in either of these two clusters requires around a week. This would permit a day trip to Parque Nacional Conguillío and perhaps an overnight near the thermal-baths complex at Malalcahuello, or looping around the park from Temuco via the upper Biobío. In Villarrica or Pucón, there would be ample time for activities like hiking in Parque Nacional Huerquehue, climbing Volcán Villarrica, rafting the Río Trancura, and simply relaxing on Lago Villarrica's black-sand beaches.

From either Puerto Varas or Puerto Montt, attractions like Parque Nacional Vicente Pérez Rosales, the wild backcountry of Cochamó, the seafood port of Angelmó, and the island of Chiloé are almost equally accessible. Many visitors prefer to stay in Puerto Varas, which is quieter, more picturesque, and has better services in a more compact area (though Puerto Montt also has respectable hotels and restaurants, and other positive aspects).

HISTORY

Human presence in the Sur Chico dates from at least 13,000 years ago, when hunter-gatherer bands roamed the area around Monte Verde, 35 kilometers west of Puerto Montt. One of the continent's oldest and most significant archaeological sites, Monte Verde benefited from ideal conditions for preservation despite the humid climate, as more than a meter of volcanic ash and peat covered the remains of mastodons, shellfish, seeds, fruits, and roots consumed by the dozen or so families who lived there. From the remaining refuse, researchers have learned that these bands hunted

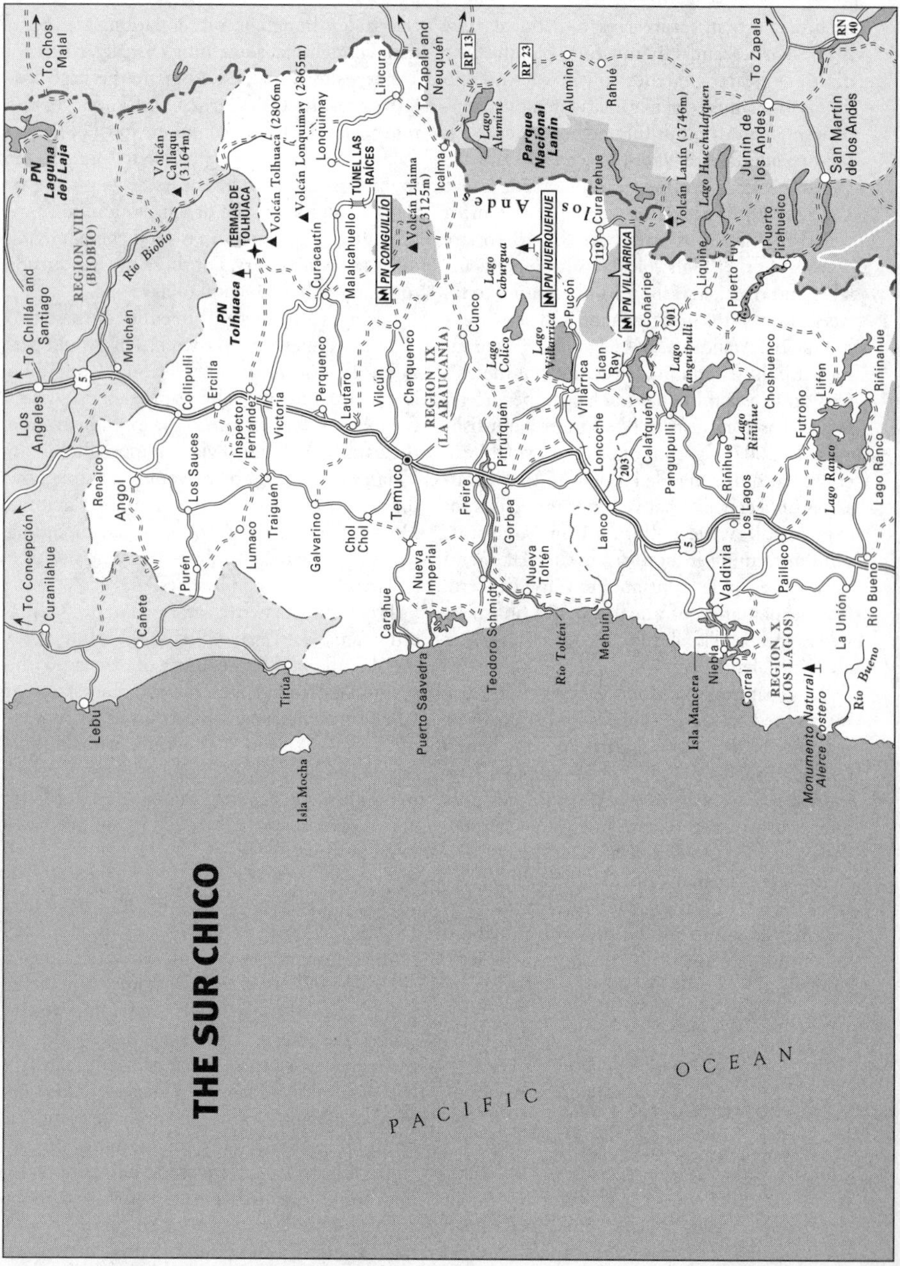

THE SUR CHICO

PACIFIC OCEAN

To Chos Malal
PN Laguna del Laja
Volcán Callaquí (3164m)
REGION VIII (BIOBÍO)
Río Biobío
To Chillán and Santiago
Los Angeles
Mulchén
Collipulli
Ercilla
PN Tolhuaca
TERMAS DE TOLHUACA
Volcán Tolhuaca (2806m)
Volcán Lonquimay (2865m)
Lonquimay
Liucura
To Zapala and Neuquén
TÚNEL LAS RAÍCES
Curacautín
Malalcahuello
PN CONGUILLÍO
Volcán Llaima (3125m)
Icalma
Lago Aluminé
Aluminé
Rahué
RP 13
RP 23
Parque Nacional Lanín
Los Andes
PN HUERQUEHUE
Lago Caburgua
Curarrehue
Volcán Lanín (3746m)
Lago Huechulafquen
Junín de los Andes
To Zapala
RN 40
San Martín de los Andes
Puerto Pirehueico
Puerto Fuy
PN VILLARRICA
Pucón
Lago Villarrica
Cunco
Lago Colico
Cherquenco
Vilcún
Lautaro
Perquenco
Victoria
Inspector Fernández
REGION IX (LA ARAUCANÍA)
Temuco
Freire
Pitrufquén
Villarrica
Lican Ray
Coñaripe
Liquiñe
Loncoche
Calafquén
Lago Panguipulli
Panguipulli
Choshuenco
Lago Riñihue
Riñihue
Futrono
Llifén
Lago Ranco
Riñinahue
Lago Ranco
To Concepción
Curanilahue
Renaico
Angol
Los Sauces
Traiguén
Lumaco
Purén
Galvarino
Chol Chol
Nueva Imperial
Carahue
Gorbea
Nueva Toltén
Lanco
Los Lagos
Valdivia
Paillaco
La Unión
Río Bueno
Cañete
Tirua
Lebu
Isla Mocha
Puerto Saavedra
Teodoro Schmidt
Río Toltén
Mehuín
Isla Mancera
Niebla
Corral
REGION X (LOS LAGOS)
Monumento Natural Alerce Costero
Río Bueno

ARGENTINA
To Neuquén
San Carlos de Bariloche
Parque Nacional Nahuel Huapi
Lago Nahuel Huapi
Lago Mascardi
Puerto Blest
El Bolsón
Parque Nacional Lago Puelo
Esquel
Trevelin
To Río Mayo
Parque Nacional Los Alerces
Lago Amutui Quimei
Futaleufú
Lago Yelcho
Cordillera de
PARQUE NACIONAL PUYEHUE
Lago Puyehue
Lago Rupanco
Peulla
PN Vicente Pérez Rosales
COCHAMÓ
Petrohué
Ralún
Las Cascadas
Ensenada
PUERTO VARAS
Entre Lagos
Lago Llanquihue
Puerto Octay
Puerto Montt
Lenca
Seno de Reloncaví
PN Hornopirén
Hornopirén
Parque
Natural
Pumalín
Ayacara
Caleta Gonzalo
Volcán Michinmahuida (2404m)
Chaitén
Puerto Cárdenas
Volcán Corcovado (2300m)
To Coyhaique
Osorno
Río Negro
Purranque
Frutillar
Fresia
Los Muermos
Río Maullín
Calbuco
Golfo de Ancud
Islas Chauques
Isla Talcan
Isla Tranqui
Golfo de Corcovado
Bahía Mansa
Maullín
Carelmapu
Pargua
Chacao
Ancud
Linao
Quemchi
Tenaún
Achao
Rilán
Quellén
Chepu
Mocopulli
Dalcahue
Castro
Puqueldón
Chonchi
Huillinco
Cucao
Quellón
Isla Grande de Chiloé
Lago Chaiguata
Río de la Zorra
PARQUE NACIONAL CHILOÉ
To Puerto Chacabuco and Puerto Natales
RN 234
RN 237
RN 231
RN 258
RN 40
215
225
5
7
0
30 mi
30 km
MOON
© AVALON TRAVEL PUBLISHING, INC.

and foraged in an area within a radius of about 100 kilometers.

Unlike the central Andean highlands of Peru and Bolivia, the pre-Columbian Sur Chico never developed great cities or monuments—while its people developed agricultural skills, they were shifting cultivators who occupied dispersed settlements and lacked any centralized political authority. In practice, this benefited their resistance to the Inca empire and, later, Spanish invaders; the Mapuche used guerrilla tactics to harass their opponents. More egalitarian than hierarchical, their top leadership was interchangeable rather than irreplaceable.

Thus, by the early 1600s, Mapuche resistance had reduced most Spanish settlements south of the Biobío to ashes and ruin. Except for the river port of Valdivia, reestablished in the mid-17th century, this remained a precarious area for Spanish settlers until a series of treaties between the Chilean government and indigenous forces in the 1880s. Many of the cities and towns in the north in this area—Victoria, Curacautín, Lonquimay, Temuco, Cunco, Villarrica, and Pucón—originally constituted a string of fortresses along the Mapuche frontier.

Chile counts more than a million Mapuche among its 15 million citizens. While many have left for the cities, large numbers still remain in the countryside where, in the more liberal political climate following the Pinochet dictatorship, they have become more outspoken in asserting rights to their ancestral lands.

Part of the controversy dates from the officially encouraged immigration which took place after the mid-19th century, when the government recruited German émigrés to settle in the area around present-day Puerto Montt and Lago Llanquihue. In fact, in the ensuing years, Llanquihue and other lakes to the north became the region's highways, linking towns like Puerto Varas and Puerto Octay via sail and steamer until the railroad's advent in the early 20th century.

German immigrants have left a palpable imprint on the region's economy (through commerce and manufacturing), landscape (through dairy farming and other agricultural pursuits), architecture (some of the country's finest European-style houses), and food (Germanic goodies known collectively as *kuchen* are almost universal). Many other nationalities flowed into the region, however, mostly Spaniards and Italians.

Araucanía Region

TEMUCO

Fast-growing Temuco (population 232,528) is the gateway to Chile's Andean lake district, numerous national parks, and many other attractions, though its own tourist appeal is limited—while it's a Mapuche market town, the city's architecture is largely utilitarian and economically it relies on agricultural and forest products. Unfortunately, like Santiago, it's begun to suffer air-pollution problems, especially in winter, as the widespread use of low-quality wood-burning stoves has contributed to a growing incidence of respiratory infections.

History

As a city, Temuco dates from February 24, 1881, when President Aníbal Pinto sent Interior Minister Manuel Recabarren, veteran General Gregorio Urrutia, engineer Teodoro Schmidt, and the Chilean army under to found Fuerte de Temuco (originally Fuerte Recabarren). Later that year, averting an attack on the fortress, the Chileans reached a treaty agreement and, within 15 years, the railroad had arrived. Before the turn of the century, colonists had flooded into the region, their farmers displacing the aboriginal inhabitants, and the population exceeded 7,000. The early push from the railroad sustained that growth well into the 20th century, providing easy access to metropolitan markets and technology.

Orientation

On the north margin of the braided Río Cautín, Temuco is 677 kilometers south of Santiago and

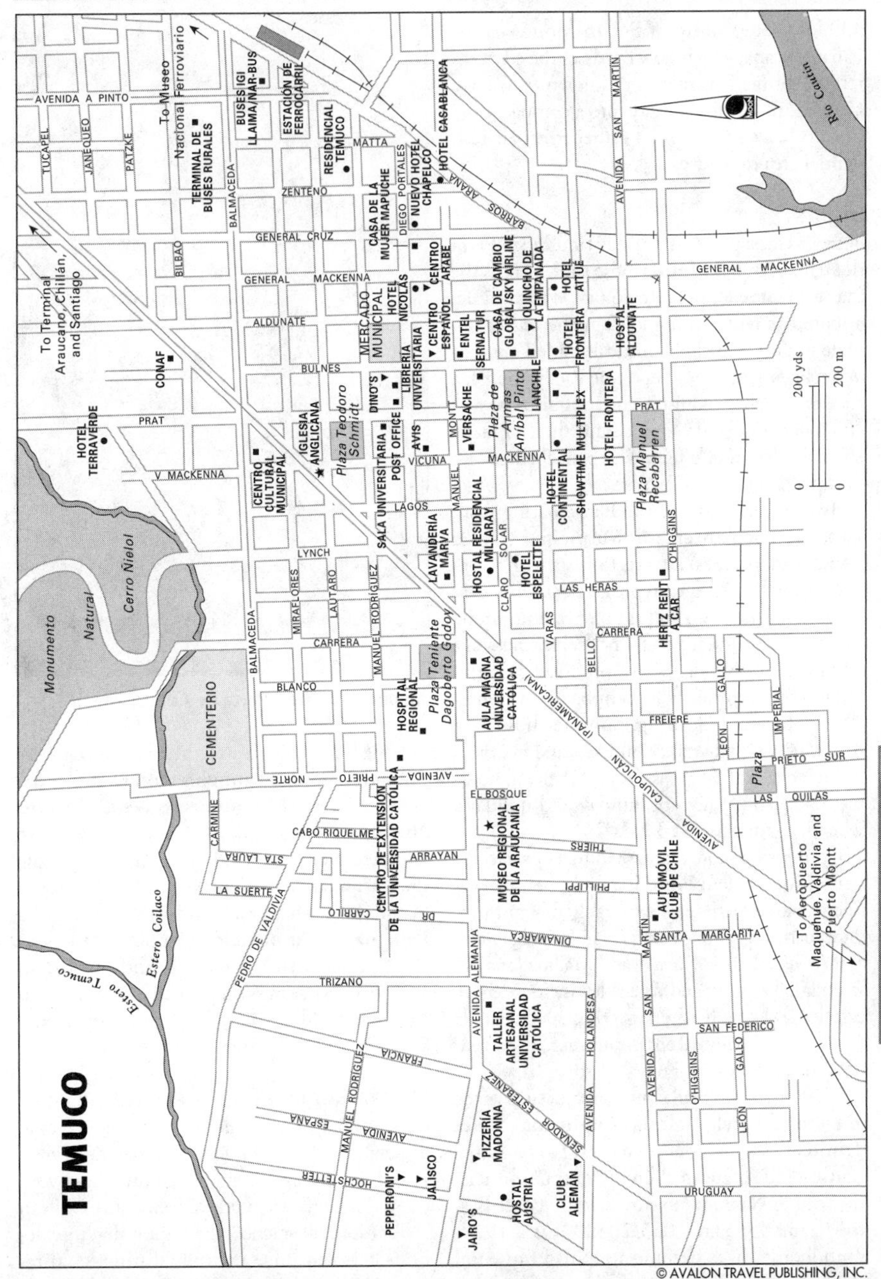
TEMUCO
To Museo Nacional Ferroviario
To Terminal Araucano, Chillán, and Santiago
To Aeropuerto Maquehue, Valdivia, and Puerto Montt
Río Cautín
Monumento Natural Cerro Ñielol
CEMENTERIO
Estero Coilaco
Estero Temuco
TERMINAL DE BUSES RURALES
BUSES IGI LLAIMA/NAR-BUS
ESTACIÓN DE FERROCARRIL
RESIDENCIAL TEMUCO
CASA DE LA MUJER MAPUCHE
NUEVO HOTEL CHAPELCO
HOTEL CASABLANCA
MERCADO MUNICIPAL
HOTEL NICOLÁS
CENTRO ÁRABE
CENTRO ESPAÑOL
LIBRERÍA UNIVERSITARIA
ENTEL
SERNATUR
CASA DE CAMBIO GLOBAL/SKY AIRLINE
QUINCHO DE LA EMPANADA
HOTEL AITUÉ
HOTEL FRONTERA
HOSTAL ALDUNATE
LANCHILE
SHOWTIME MULTIPLEX
HOTEL CONTINENTAL
Plaza de Armas Aníbal Pinto
Plaza Manuel Recabarren
CONAF
HOTEL TERRAVERDE
IGLESIA ANGLICANA
Plaza Teodoro Schmidt
DINO'S
POST OFFICE
AVIS
VERSACHE
SALA UNIVERSITARIA
CENTRO CULTURAL MUNICIPAL
LAVANDERÍA MARVA
HOSTAL RESIDENCIAL MILLARAY
HOTEL ESPELETTE
HERTZ RENT A CAR
Plaza Teniente Dagoberto Godoy
HOSPITAL REGIONAL
AULA MAGNA UNIVERSIDAD CATÓLICA
CENTRO DE EXTENSIÓN DE LA UNIVERSIDAD CATÓLICA
MUSEO REGIONAL DE LA ARAUCANÍA
AUTOMÓVIL CLUB DE CHILE
TALLER ARTESANAL UNIVERSIDAD CATÓLICA
PIZZERÍA MADONNA
CLUB ALEMÁN
HOSTAL AUSTRIA
JAIRO'S
JALISCO
PEPPERONI'S
Plaza
AVENIDA A PINTO
TUCAPEL
JANEQUEO
PATZKE
BALMACEDA
MATTA
ZENTENO
GENERAL CRUZ
GENERAL MACKENNA
ALDUNATE
BULNES
PRAT
V MACKENNA
VICUÑA
MACKENNA
LAGOS
LYNCH
LAUTARO
MIRAFLORES
BILBAO
MONT
MANUEL
MANUEL RODRÍGUEZ
SOLAR
CLARO
LAS HERAS
VARAS
CARRERA
BELLO
BLANCO
FREIERE
GALLO
LEÓN
IMPERIAL
O'HIGGINS
AVENIDA PRIETO NORTE
PRIETO SUR
LAS QUILAS
EL BOSQUE
CARMINE
CABO RIQUELME
ARRAYAN
STA LAURA
LA SUERTE
DR CARRILLO
THIERS
PHILIPPI
DINAMARCA
SANTA MARGARITA
TRIZANO
PEDRO DE VALDIVIA
AVENIDA ALEMANIA
AVENIDA HOLANDESA
AVENIDA SAN MARTÍN
SAN FEDERICO
FRANCIA
ESPAÑA
AVENIDA
HOCHSTETTER
SENADOR ESTEBANEZ
URUGUAY
AVENIDA CAUPOLICAN (PANAMERICANA)
BARROS ARANA
DIEGO PORTALES
200 yds
200 m
0

339 kilometers north of Puerto Montt via the Panamericana, which now bypasses the city center; the former Panamericana, known as Avenida Caupolicán, divides the city into a compact original grid to the east and a rather irregular residential area to the west.

Sights

Temuco's focal point is the lushly landscaped **Plaza de Armas Aníbal Pinto,** whose showpiece is the massive **Homenaje a la Región de la Araucanía,** a sculpture representing a Mapuche *machi* (female healer), the euphemistically titled *Soldado de la Pacificación* ("Soldier of the Pacification"), a *Colono* ("Early Colonist"), the conquistador and epic poet Alonso de Ercilla, and the Mapuche *toqui* (leader) Kallfulifán. The bandshell gallery hosts rotating cultural exhibits.

Two blocks north of the Plaza, dating from 1928, Temuco's **Mercado Municipal** (Diego Portales and Bulnes) attracts tourists with its accomplished crafts and typical restaurants that range from the plain and simple to, if not quite sublime, at least very good. Locals, however, take advantage of abundant fresh produce and utilitarian commodities like manufactured household goods and clothing. Summer hours are 8 A.M.–8 P.M. daily except Sundays and holidays, when it closes at 3 P.M.; the rest of the year, hours are 8 A.M.–6 P.M. except Sunday and holidays, when it again closes at 3 P.M.

Comprising more than 700 different stalls, the **Feria Libre Aníbal Pinto** is a lively, mainly Mapuche and sometimes disagreeably fragrant produce market sprawling along Avenida Aníbal Pinto and Avenida Barros Arana near the railroad station. In addition to fruits and vegetables, there are cheap eateries and Mapuche crafts. Hours are roughly 8 A.M.–5 P.M. daily except in summer, when vendors stick around until 6 P.M. or so.

Most other landmarks are scattered, such as the gingerbread-style **Iglesia Anglicana Santa Trinidad** (Vicuña Mackenna and Lautaro), the century-old Anglican church. For trainspotters, the **Museo Nacional Ferroviario** (Avenida Barros Arana 0565, tel. 045/203203) is a 1920s roundhouse that's become a railroad museum, about one kilometer north of the main station.

© WAYNE BERNHARDSON

Mapuche weaver, Plaza de Armas, Temuco

Chile's national flower the *copihue (Lapageria rosea)* flaunts its autumn blooms in the deciduous forest of **Monumento Natural Cerro Ñielol,** a 90-hectare hilltop reserve about one kilometer north of the Plaza de Armas via Calle Prat. Popular with picnickers, Ñielol is also a historical site—in 1881, under the shade of **La Patagua del Armisticio,** Mapuche leaders finally acceded to the city's founding. Conaf charges US$1 admission per pedestrian, US$.30 for each child, and US$1 per car; hours are 8:30 A.M.–11 P.M. daily.

Museo Regional de la Araucanía

Created in 1940, Temuco's improving regional museum tackles what might, in a rhetorical sense, sound euphemistic—the "encounter" between the indigenous Mapuche and Spanish-Chilean civilization. In practice, the notion that interactions between these radically distinct cultures were a give-and-take rather than simple domination and submission is a good starting point for reassessing regional history, even if the execution is imperfect.

Housed in the former Carlos Thiers residence, a German immigrant–style national monument dating from 1924, the Museo stresses the historical centrality of the Mapuche and their ancestors, and acknowledges the diversity of various subgroups—the sedentary and shifting agriculturalists of the floodplains and forests, the fisher-gatherer Lafkenche of the Pacific littoral, and the hunter-gatherer Pehuenche of the Andean cordillera.

On the other hand, lapses in rethinking the past persist—the openly expressed perspective on "pacification" in the 300-year war between the two civilizations recalls the U.S. military's Vietnam war approach. Exhibits implicitly credit the Mapuche resistance with fashioning deadly weapons from available materials, but overlook their horsemanship and tactical skills.

Coverage of post-war developments are better. Arrival of the "Ferrocarril de La Frontera" (Frontier Railroad) brought Catholic missionaries and immigrants from northwestern and Mediterranean Europe. Maps and photographs help chronicle Temuco's urban development, which the 1960 earthquake disrupted. One glaring omission is the marginalization of the contemporary Mapuche.

Unearthed by researchers or donated by local residents, the collections comprise more than 3,000 archaeological, ethnographic, pictorial, photographic and historical items. The Mapuche materials, dating mostly from about A.D. 1400–1800, also include 19th-century jewelry and textiles. In addition, there's a specialized library on the Mapuche, anthropology and regional history, and cartography. All coverage is in Spanish only, however.

The Museo de la Araucanía (Avenida Alemania 084, tel. 045/211108, museoaraucania@terra.cl) is about 10 blocks west of the Plaza de Armas. Summer hours are 9 A.M.–7 P.M. weekdays, 10 A.M.–7 P.M. Saturday, 10 A.M.–5 P.M. Sundays and holidays; the rest of the year, hours are 9 A.M.–5:45 P.M. weekdays, 11 A.M.–2 P.M. Sunday only. Admission is US$1 for adults, US$.50 for children, but is free Sundays and holidays.

Entertainment and Events

Temuco isn't exactly a 24-hour city, but there's usually something going on at local cultural facilities or its two universities. The biggest single celebration is February's **Aniversario de la Ciudad,** commemorating the city's founding—at that time, it was really a fortress—on February 24, 1881. During the festivities, a high-quality crafts fair nearly fills the Plaza de Armas.

The **Centro Cultural Municipal** (Avenida Caupolicán and Avenida Balmaceda) includes the **Teatro Municipal Pablo Neruda** (tel. 045/265868) for performing arts, plus an exhibition hall and the city library. The **Aula Magna Universidad Católica** (Manuel Montt 256, tel. 045/205421) has an annual event schedule including live theater and films.

The **Showtime Multiplex** (Antonio Varas 840, tel. 045/644779) is the main commercial cinema. The **Sala Universitaria** (Prat 332, tel. 045/325877) shows films during the university year, as does the Universidad Católica's Centro de Extension (Avenida Prieto Norte 371, tel. 045/232760).

Shopping

Indigenous women sell their crafts, mainly pottery and textiles, directly to the public at the cooperative **Casa de la Mujer Mapuche** (Portales 1190, tel. 045/233886); profits go directly to members in both cash and educational opportunities. There's a bigger selection at the **Mercado Municipal** (Diego Portales and Aldunate), which keeps longer hours but has far more kitsch.

Other crafts alternatives are the **Sala de Exposiciones** (tel. 045/236785), beneath the Plaza de Armas bandshell, and the **Taller Artesanal Universidad Católica** (Avenida Alemania 0422, tel. 045/212081). The latter is open 9 A.M.–1 P.M. and 3–6 P.M. weekdays.

Accommodations

Temuco's budget accommodations are only so-so, but by spending just a little more travelers can get better value. Upper-range choices are generally good.

US$10–25

The Hostelling International affiliate is 20-bed

Residencial Temuco (Manuel Rodríguez 1341, 2nd floor, tel./fax 045 233721, hostemuco@hotmail.com, US$10 pp), where rates include breakfast and kitchen facilities; there is also laundry service. Since it's small and also serves the wider public, reservations are a good idea; note also that it lacks a street sign.

Hostal Aldunate (Aldunate 864, tel./fax 045/642438, US$10 pp shared bath, US$13/23 s/d private bath, breakfast included) occupies a quiet but still central neighborhood.

At gracefully aging **Hostal Casa Blanca** (Manuel Montt 1306, tel./fax 045/272677, www.hostalcasablanca.cl, US$8.50 pp shared bath, US$13/24 s/d private bath), all rates include breakfast, but only rooms with private bath have cable TV.

US$25–50

Hotel Chapelco (General Cruz 401, tel. 045/749393, fax 045/952734, www.hotelchapelco.cl, US$22/29 s/d with private bath and breakfast) is a respectable option near the train tracks at the east end of downtown.

In residential west Temuco, **Hostal Austria** (Hochstetter 599, tel./fax 045/247169, www.hostalaustria.cl, US$25/45 s/d) offers quiet, comfortable, spotless, and tobacco-free accommodations with private bath, cable TV, and *Gemütlichkeit* (warmth).

Near the Mercado Municipal, **Hotel Nicolás** (General Mackenna 420, tel. 045/210020, fax 045/213468, www.hotelnicolas.cl, US$29/40 s/d with private bath and TV) is more central.

Once Temuco's most prestigious quarters, the timeless **Hotel Continental** (Varas 708, tel. 045/238973, fax 045/233830, hcontine@ctcinternet.cl, US$13–25 s, US$24–41 d) is a living monument boasting a spectacularly anachronistic dining room and an equally classic wooden bar; plaques indicate rooms where illustrious tourists like Presidents Pedro Aguirre Cerda and Salvador Allende, and Nobel Prize poets Gabriela Mistral and Pablo Neruda, have spent the night. Breakfast is included, but rates vary according to whether the room has just a washbasin (with shared exterior toilet and shower), shares the bath with an adjacent room, or has its own private bath.

Hotel Aitué (Antonio Varas 1048, tel. 045/212512, fax 045/212608, www.hotelitue.cl, US$37/43 s/d) is a business-oriented facility with responsive service, an excellent value with IVA discounted.

US$50–100

Hotel Frontera (Bulnes 733, tel. 045/200400, fax 045/200401, www.hotelfrontera.cl, US$60–80 s, US$70–90 d) is a complex of two facing buildings that comprise one business-oriented hotel and conventional center. The one across the street has greater amenities—swimming pool, gym, and the like—but its only advantage is easier access, as guests at either building are entitled to use all facilities.

At the foot of Cerro Ñielol, **Hotel Terraverde** (Prat 0220, tel. 045/239999, fax 045/239455, www.panamericanahoteles.cl, US$74/85 s/d) is a five-star choice by local standards.

Food

The truly basic *puestos* (food stalls) in and around the chaotic **Mercado Pinto,** between the Terminal de Buses Rurales and the EFE train station on both sides of its namesake street, are Temuco's cheapest choices, but the hygiene is questionable at some of them.

Known best as a crafts market and a sight in itself, the downtown **Mercado Municipal** (Portales and Aldunate) is an even better choice for straightforward seafood—try **La Caleta,** Puesto 45, tel. 045/213002). Figure about US$5–6.50 for a good, filling meal; the market, though, is primarily a lunch venue, and most eateries close by 7 P.M.

The chain restaurant **Dino's** (Bulnes 360, tel. 045/213660) has reliable sandwiches and standard Chilean fare. **El Quincho de la Empanada** (Aldunate 698, tel. 045/216307) is a one-of-a-kind specializing in empanadas.

Among the better downtown choices are the **Centro Español** (Bulnes 483, tel. 045/238664) and the **Centro Arabe** (General Mackenna 462, tel. 045/215080) for Middle Eastern food.

More stylish, contemporary dining is available west of the Panamericana, at places like **Pepperoni's** (Hochstetter 425, tel. 045/405656), a good pizza-and-pasta place where entrées start around US$4.50 but range upwards of US$10 depending on ingredients; shrimp dishes, for instance, are considerably more expensive. The service is exemplary, and there's an adequate tobacco-free section.

Other good options in the area are the Tex-Mex **Jalisco** (Hochstetter 435, tel. 045/243254), which has more of a pub feel; **Jairo's** (Avenida Alemania 0830, tel. 045/248849) for seafood; **Pizzería Madonna** (Avenida Alemania 0660, tel. 045/249191); and the more traditional **Club Alemán** (Senador Estébanez 772, tel. 045/240034).

Information

On the north side of the Plaza de Armas, **Sernatur** (Claro Solar 899, tel. 045/211969, fax 045/215509, infoaraucania@sernatur.cl) distributes free city maps and regional leaflets; it often but not always has an English speaker on hand. Summer hours are 8:30 A.M.–8 P.M. daily; March–December hours are 9 A.M.–2 P.M. and 3–5 P.M. weekdays only.

The **Automóvil Club de Chile** (Acchi, San Martín 0278, tel. 045/910522) can help motorists. For national parks information, visit **Conaf** (Avenida Bilbao 931, 2nd floor, tel. 045/298114).

Librería Universitaria (Diego Portales 861, tel. 045/215330) is strong on Mapuche ethnography and regional history.

Services

Though it's primarily an administrative and commercial center, Temuco has a full complement of traveler's services as well.

Banco de Crédito (Bulnes 615) has an ATM, but there are many other ATMs and also exchange houses, such as **Casa de Cambio Global** (Bulnes 655, Local 1).

Correos de Chile is at Diego Portales and Prat.

Entel (Prat 505) offers long-distance telephone and Internet access, but there are many others.

Lavandería Marva (Manuel Montt 415, tel. 045/945201; Manuel Montt 1099, tel. 045/952200) does the washing.

The **Hospital Regional** is at Manuel Montt 115 (tel. 045/296100).

Getting There

Temuco is Araucanía's major transportation hub, with air connections north and south, and even more abundant bus connections north and south along the Panamericana, and east into the Andes. It's presently the terminus of the railroad from Santiago, a service that may be extended southward.

LanChile (Bulnes 687, tel. 045/211339) flies several times daily to Santiago; southbound, there are one or two flights daily to Puerto Montt. **Sky Airline** (Bulnes 655, tel. 045/747300) flies four times weekly to Santiago and to Puerto Montt.

The chaos of long-distance **bus** carriers that once congested downtown streets has been relieved by construction of the new **Rodoviario Araucario** (Avenida Rudecindo Ortega 01580, tel. 045/255005), at the eastern foot of Cerro Ñielol. This has not completely concentrated services—the **Terminal de Buses Rurales** (Avenida Aníbal Pinto 032, tel. 045/210494) hosts regional carriers, and several long-distance companies have ticket offices and even terminals around the axis formed with the perpendicular Avenida Balmaceda. In addition, some buses for Curacautín, Lonquimay, and the upper Biobío leave from **Rodoviario Curacautín** (Avenida Barros Arana 191).

Among the regional carriers at the Terminal de Buses Rurales are **Flota Erbuc** (tel. 045/272204), which goes several times daily to Curacautín via Lautaro or Victoria, continuing to Malalcahuello and Lonquimay; **Nar-Bus** (tel. 045/407740), to Capitán Pastene (for Parque Nacional Tolhuaca), Cherquenco (for the Llaima sector of Parque Nacional Conguillío), Icalma, Cunco, and Melipeuco; and **Buses Jac** to Villarrica and Pucón, though departures are more frequent from its other office.

From the Rodoviario Araucario, many carriers connect Temuco with Panamericana destinations from Santiago to Puerto Montt; some have, as indicated, downtown ticket offices. These include **Pullman Sur** and **Cruz del Sur** (tel. 045/730310), which also serves Ancud and Castro,

Chiloé; **Tas Choapa** (tel. 045/212422, Antonio Varas 609); **Tur-Bus** (Claro Solar 598, tel. 045/230979), which shares offices with its budget line Cóndor Bus; and Igi Llaima, which shares attractive new facilities with **Nar-Bus** (Miraflores 1535, tel. 045/407777). **Buses Jac** (Avenida Balmaceda 1005, tel. 045/210313) shuttles frequently to Villarrica and Pucón.

Sample domestic destinations, with approximate fares and times, include Villarrica (US$3, one hour), Pucón (US$4, 1.5 hours), Curacautín (US$2.50, 1.5 hours), Ancud (US$11, eight hours), Osorno (US$5, three hours), Puerto Montt (US$7, five hours), Castro (US$12, nine hours), Santiago (US$13–16, eight hours). *Salón cama* buses to Santiago cost around US$22–26.

Most Argentina-bound buses use the Paso Mamuil Malal crossing southeast of Pucón (to Junín de los Andes and San Martín de los Andes), but some take the Paso Pino Hachado route, directly east of Temuco via Curacautín and the upper Biobío town of Lonquimay (to Zapala and Neuquén). In addition, there are connections to Bariloche via the Panamericana to Osorno and Ruta 215 east over Paso Cardenal Samoré.

Since the distances are long, the terrain mountainous, and the roads partly gravel, some buses across the Andes leave early—some well before daylight. Carriers serving Junín de los Andes and San Martín de los Andes (US$15, eight hours) include **Buses San Martín** (tel. 045/234017) and **Buses Ruta Sur** (Miraflores 1151, tel. 045/210079). **Igi Llaima** and **Nar-Bus** (both at Miraflores 1535, tel. 045/407707) alternate daily 5 A.M. services to Zapala and Neuquén (US$23, 10 hours), and also go to San Martín.

To Bariloche (US$20, nine hours), the main carriers are Tas Choapa and Cruz del Sur; it's necessary to change in Osorno.

The **Estación de Ferrocarriles del Estado** (Avenida Barros Arana s/n, tel. 045/233416) is eight blocks northeast of the Plaza de Armas. Nightly EFE **trains** go north to Santiago (12.5 hours) and intermediate stops at 8:30 and 9:30 P.M. Fares range from US$16–32. Tickets are also available from EFE's downtown ticket office (Bulnes 582, tel. 045/233522), alongside Sernatur.

Getting Around

City transport is frequent and cheap, with both buses and *taxi colectivos.*

Just six kilometers south of town, Temuco's **Aeropuerto Maquehue** (tel. 045/554801) occupies part of an air-force base but is due to move in the near future. Call ahead. **Araucanía Transfer** (tel. 045/339900) arranges airport transfers (around US$4 pp), as do taxis from the northeast corner of the Plaza de Armas.

From downtown to the Rodoviario, catch Micro No. 2 or No. 7 from Portales and Bulnes, or *taxi colectivo* 11-P or 25-A from the corner of Prat and Claro Solar.

For backcountry excursions around Temuco, especially the circuit through Parque Nacional Conguillío or the upper Biobío, car rental is the most convenient option. Rental agencies include the **Automóvil Club de Chile** (Acchi, San Martín 0278, tel. 045/248903); **Avis** (Vicuña Mackenna 448, tel. 045/238013); **Hertz** (Las Heras 999, tel. 045/318585); and **Verschae** (Lagos 521, tel. 045/231575).

VICINITY OF TEMUCO

There are worthwhile excursions in all directions from Temuco, but most visitors focus on the Andean cordillera.

Parque Nacional Tolhuaca

Native woodlands of araucarias and other species adorn the foothill slopes of Parque Nacional Tolhuaca, where the Río Malleco drains south-southwest into marshy Laguna Malleco before plunging into its lower course toward the coast. Improved access roads have increased visitation, especially in summer and on weekends, but most people stay in the immediate vicinity of Laguna Malleco—the rest of the park is still ideal for camping, hiking, and fishing.

In the Andean foothills, ranging from 1,000 meters above sea level around Laguna Malleco to 1,821 meters on the ridgelines of Reserva Nacional Malleco to the north, Tolhuaca is a compact 6,374-hectare unit on the Río Malleco's north bank. It has a cool, humid climate, with an average annual temperature of 9°C and

2,500–3,000 millimeters of rainfall, but enjoys mild, fairly dry summers. The park's namesake peak, 2,806-meter Volcán Tolhuaca, lies beyond park boundaries to the southeast.

At higher elevations, Tolhuaca has nearly pure araucaria forests in well-drained soils, but the dense gallery forests along the Malleco consist of *coigue, olivillo,* and other evergreen species, along with deciduous *raulí* and *roble.* Bamboo-like *quila (Chusquea quila)* forms an impenetrable undergrowth in some areas. *Junquillos* (reeds) grow in the lakeside sediments, while massive *nalcas (Gunnera chilensis), chilco* (*Fuchsia magellanica,* firecracker fuchsia), ferns, mosses, and other water-loving plants blanket the riverbanks.

Except for waterfowl and coypu in Laguna Malleco, Tolhuaca's fauna are inconspicuous, but there are puma, *pudú* (miniature deer), foxes, and skunks.

As ash and other sediments from the surrounding ridges and peaks sluice into the river and downstream, water-loving reeds are colonizing the shoreline of 76-hectare **Laguna Malleco,** a glacial remnant where Conaf has a loaner rowboat for fishermen and birders. It's an easy walk from the campground, and swimming is possible is several pools en route.

From Laguna Malleco's north shore, the 1,800-meter **Sendero El Salto** winds through thick native forest to **Salto Malleco,** a thunderous 50-meter cascade that plumbs over the rugged basalt into the river's lower drainage. Even more copious foliage surrounds the continuing trail.

Also from Laguna Malleco, **Sendero Prados de Mesacura** switchbacks north to intersect the **Sendero Lagunillas,** which follows the contour east through nearly waterless araucaria woodlands—the volcanic soil absorbs nearly all the precipitation. From a spot about five kilometers east of Laguna Malleco, toward Termas de Tolhuaca, the eight-kilometer **Sendero Laguna Verde** skirts the southwestern slope of 1,606-meter Cerro Laguna Verde to arrive at its namesake lake, covering some 3.6 hectares.

At Laguna Malleco, Conaf's shady 25-site **Camping Inalaufquén** (US$13 per site) has barbecue pits, picnic tables, running water, and clean bathrooms with flush toilets and cold showers. Single travelers can try for a discount if it's not crowded. For travelers with their own vehicle and more money, Hotel Termas de Tolhuaca is an option; see the separate entry below.

No supplies whatsoever are available at Laguna Malleco—bring everything you need.

Tolhuaca lacks a formal visitors center, but Conaf rangers at Laguna Malleco offer daily chats at the outdoor amphitheater. Park admission costs US$3 per person for adults, US$1 for children.

No public transportation goes directly to the park, but one bus daily (4 P.M.) goes from Victoria's Terminal de Buses Rurales, 58 kilometers north of Temuco on the Panamericana, to the hamlet of San Gregorio, on a decent gravel road that leads east from the village of Inspector Fernández. This, unfortunately, stops 20 kilometers short of Laguna Malleco, but the road is still a good alternative for hitchhikers, motorists, or mountain bikers.

From Curacautín, 87 kilometers northeast of Temuco via Lautaro or 119 kilometers via Victoria, an improved gravel road reaches the hot-springs resort of Termas de Tolhuaca (see separate entry below), 33 kilometers to the north. From Termas de Tolhuaca, what was once a hazardous four-wheel-drive road to Laguna Malleco is now passable for ordinary vehicles, at least in summer. *Taxi colectivos* from Curacautín go as far as Termas de Tolhuaca, but it's another nine kilometers to Malleco.

The Upper Cautín and Biobío

From Victoria, 58 km north of Temuco on the Panamericana, a smooth and scenic two-lane highway parallels the branch railroad that once ran from Púa to Curacautín, Lonquimay, and the upper Biobío, a little-visited and underappreciated area north of Parque Nacional Conguillío. Blessed with its own native forests, rushing rivers, and volcanic grandeur, the upper Biobío is, along with Conguillío, part of a UNESCO World Biosphere Reserve declared to protect its remaining araucaria stands.

In addition to the main road, this area is also accessible via a shorter paved alternative that heads northeast from Lautaro (30 km north of Temuco). From the upper Biobío, it's also possible to loop back around on good gravel roads to Melipeuco, Conguillío's southern gateway, or back to Temuco.

Curacautín

The mid-sized town of Curacautín (population 12,812) dates from 1882, when the Chilean military established Fuerte Ultra Cautín on Pehuenche territory on the banks of the Río Cautín. Today, it's the northern access to Parque Nacional Conguillío and the gateway to the upper Cautín and upper Biobío. It's 87 kilometers northeast of Temuco via Lautaro or 119 kilometers via Victoria.

Facing the highway at the west end of town, homey **Hostal Rayén** (Manuel Rodríguez 104, US$9 pp) has rooms with breakfast and shared bath. **Hostal Las Espigas** (Miraflores 315, tel.045/881138, rivaseugenia@hotmail.com, US$10 pp) has rooms with private bath.

Curacautín has few places to eat, the best of which is probably **La Cabaña** (Yungay 157), opposite the plaza. **Café Vizzio's** (Serrano 248) has good sandwiches, desserts, and coffee.

Banco Estado's ATM now works with foreign ATM cards. **CTC Telefónica** (O'Higgins 610-B) has both long-distance service and Internet access, but there are several new Internet outlets.

In summer only, Curacautín's **Oficina de Informaciones Turísticas,** on the north side of the Plaza de Armas, is open 10 A.M.–6 P.M. weekdays and 9 A.M.–1:30 P.M. Saturday.

Curacautín's **Terminal Rodoviario** (Manuel Rodríguez s/n) is just north of the Plaza de Armas and directly on the Lonquimay highway. Erbuc has five buses daily to and from Temuco (US$3) via Victoria and four via Lautaro; there are five to Lonquimay. Erbuc goes to Captrén, the entrance to Parque Nacional Conguillío (US$1) Monday and Friday at 5:45 A.M. and 5:30 P.M.; it's also possible to hire a cab to Conguillío.

Igi Llaima and Nar-Bus pass through town daily en route to Zapala and Neuquén, Argentina, but make reservations in Temuco to be sure of a seat.

Termas de Tolhuaca

Reached by an improved gravel road that heads north out of Curacautín for 35 kilometers, the once humble hot springs of Termas de Tolhuaca has morphed into a spa, but is still a pretty good value by international standards, and a good alternative for those who want to visit Parque Nacional Tolhuaca but don't want to camp in the park, which is nine kilometers farther on by road. The resort began in 1898, but today's facility is a dramatic improvement over the rustic Russian-built original.

Accommodations at the 100-bed **Hotel Termas de Tolhuaca** (Calama 240, Curacautín, tel. 045/881164, fax 045/881211, www.termasdetolhuaca.co.cl, US$60 pp with full board) includes unlimited access to pools and baths; it has its own restaurant. Camping is also possible for US$10 per site for up to six people; public-pool access costs US$8 per person (US$4 for children), and there are limited supplies on site.

Manzanar

Barely a wide spot in the road, 18 kilometers east of Curacautín and 680 meters above sea level, Manzanar is home to **Hotel Termas de Manzanar** (tel./fax 045/881200, www.termasdemanzanar.cl), a riverside spa resort set back from the south side of the highway. It offers a variety of accommodations options ranging from simple rooms with shared bath (US$28/48 s/d for B&B to US$44/80 with full board) to *cabañas* with private bath and Jacuzzi (US$43/70 s/d for B&B to US$60/103 with full board).

Malalcahuello

Ten kilometers east of Manzanar, the hamlet of Malalcahuello occupies a cool high valley in the shadow of the 2,865-meter Volcán Lonquimay (known also as Volcán Mocho). At altitudes upwards of 980 meters, Malalcahuello is substantially cooler than areas to the west, and nights can get chilly even in summer.

Thanks to its accessibility to the **Reserva Nacional Malalcahuello**—trailheads start near the highway itself—it's an ideal destination for hikers and horseback riders. Its newest asset is the hot-springs resort **Centro Termal Malalcahuello.**

Its summit crater filled by a glacier that spills onto the adjoining flanks, symmetrical **Volcán Lonquimay** is the reserve's focal point. Slightly northeast of town, it dates from the late Pleistocene times but has erupted as recently as 1933, almost simultaneously with nearby Volcán Llaima, and lava flows spilled down its northeastern flanks in 1990. Trails to nearby Cerro Cautín (2.5 hours) and Lonquimay's summit start here.

Malalcahuello also has a sparkling new ski area, the **Corralco Centro de Montaña** (Avenida 11 de Septiembre 2250, Local 107, Providencia, Santiago, tel. 02/2090030, www.corralco.com, US$100 d for accommodations), on the site of an older place that was nearly in ruins. Lift tickets cost US$11–14 per day, depending on the date, or about US$260 for the entire mid-June–October season.

The **Centro Termal Malalcahuello** (Recabarren 03160, Temuco, tel. 045/1963541, www.malalcahuello.cl) is a hot-springs megaproject that fits well into its natural setting about two kilometers south of the highway through town via a dirt road. With state-of-the-art indoor and outdoor pools, spa treatments, and therapists, it has a handful of *cabañas* (US$200 for up to four people, access to baths included) for accommodations and a restaurant that's still finding its way. Admission to the pools costs US$13 per adult, US$8.50 per child between 2 and 12 years of age. Additional services include massages, mud baths, steam baths, and the like. A hotel is under construction.

Swiss-run **La Suizandina** (tel. 045/1973725 or 09/8849541, fax 045/1973724, www.suizandina.com) is a combination of campground, hostel, *cabaña,* and sparkling new guesthouse just west of town on the north side of the highway. Rates are US$4 per person for camping; US$12–17 per person in the centrally heated *cabaña,* which has four four-bedded rooms; and US$22–46 per person in the comfortable, centrally heated guesthouse.

Multilingual Tom and Eva Buschor include a Swiss-style breakfast (Tom is a professional baker) and also serve Swiss specialties like fondue and raclette for reasonably priced lunches or dinners accompanied by fresh desserts and Chilean wines.

Conaf's ranger station at Malalcahuello is a good source for advice; speakers of English, German, French, and Italian can contact the Buschors at La Suizandina, which arranges excursions to Conguillío, Lonquimay, and other local attractions, organizes transportation, and offers information and advice to individuals who wish to undertake them independently.

Erbuc buses between Temuco and Lonquimay go directly through Malalcahuello.

Lonquimay

From Malalcahuello, the highway heads southeast to enter the 1930s **Túnel Las Raíces,** where the Púa-Lonquimay railway ran a tourist train as recently as the 1990s. Now open to vehicle traffic, the one-lane, 4.5-kilometer tunnel has sprung leaks that produce meter-long icicles in winter, and it's overdue for an upgrade that would include new pavement, roof reinforcement, and a second parallel tunnel that would permit two-way rather than alternating traffic as at present. This would simplify access to the Pino Hachado border crossing.

Beyond the tunnel, the highway turns northeast to the village of Lonquimay, in the placid upper Biobío drainage—the traditional starting point for descending what was Chile's wildest whitewater river until a series of downstream dams submerged the rapids.

Instead of a standard grid, Lonquimay has a peculiar ovoid city plan still centered, though, on the usual Plaza de Armas. It also has an obliging **tourist office** (O'Higgins and Carrera Pinto, tel. 045/891911), and restaurants and hotels that traditionally close at the end of February. From Malalcahuello, a steep eastbound dirt road over Cuesta las Raíces is a shorter alternate route to Lonquimay, which is 900 meters above sea level, but it's open in summer and autumn only.

Along this route, eight kilometers west of Lonquimay, **Los Arenales de Lonquimay** (Casilla 5, Lonquimay, tel. 045/891911 for lodging, tel. 09/3132208 for service, www.turismolonquimay.cl) is a promising new ski area where the Fondo por Solidaridad e Inversión Social (Fund for Solidarity and Social Investment, FOSIS) has created a joint venture between the Hungarian owner and the local Pehuenche population. If all works well, the Pehuenche will build and operate ten *cabañas,* but for the moment the only accommodations are in town. Los Arenales presently has two beginner, two intermediate, and four expert runs for skiing and snowboarding, but anticipates expansion; there is also childcare, a ski school, and a café-restaurant. Lift tickets are cheap at US$13 per person, with ski or snowboard rentals around US$13–15.

Hospedaje Navidad (Caupolicán 915, tel. 045/891111, US$8.50 pp) has rooms with shared bath and breakfast. Five Erbuc buses daily connect Lonquimay with Temuco.

Alto Biobío

South of Lonquimay, a gravel road tracks south past Lago Galletué, the official source of the Biobío and part of Conaf's **Reserva Nacional Galletué,** and continues southeast past the border post of Icalma (for the Argentine town of Aluminé). There is no regular public transport across this route. There are numerous simple campgrounds along this main road, which then turns west toward Melipeuco and Parque Nacional Conguillío. From Lonquimay, a newly paved road crosses Conaf's **Reserva Nacional Alto Biobío** via the 1,884-meter Paso Pino Hachado, the route used by buses to the Argentine cities of Zapala and Neuquén.

Melipeuco

In the Río Allipén valley, built precariously on an ancient mudflow 92 kilometers east of Temuco via Cunco and 45 kilometers west of Icalma, the Mapuche town of Melipeuco is Parque Nacional Conguillío's southern access point and an alternative route into the upper Biobío loop around Lonquimay. In the 1970s, this was a conflictive area in the agrarian reform movement, and the issue is still alive today.

Melipeuco (population 2,333) operates a summer-only tourist office on Pedro Aguirre Cerda, across from the YPF gas station. There's a crafts market here as well.

Melipeuco's cheapest accommodations are found at cozy **Hospedaje Icalma** (Pedro Aguirre Cerda 729, tel. 045/581108, US$5–7 pp), which also arranges Conguillío excursions. **Hostería Huetelén** (Pedro Aguirre Cerda 1, tel. 045/581005, lospionerosmelipeuco@chile.com, US$33 s or d with private bath) is a more formal option, but its restaurant is mediocre; for food, try **Ruminot** (Pedro Aguirre Cerda 496).

Nar-Bus has seven buses daily to and from Temuco's Terminal de Buses Rurales (US$2, 1.5 hours). There's no scheduled public transport to Conguillío, but taxis or pickup trucks take passengers to the visitors center for about US$12–15.

Cunco and Vicinity

About 32 kilometers west of Melipeuco, Cunco is the gateway for rafting on the Río Allipén, a roughly three-hour excursion (US$17 pp) with German-run **Esmeralda Raft** (tel. 09/8467617, www.esmeraldaraft.de). You'll find them on the Allipén bridge about five kilometers south of town to the road to Lago Colico.

About five kilometers west of Cunco via a paved lateral, **Hostería Adela y Helmut** (Faja 16000, Km 5 Norte, Cunco, tel. 09/7244479, www.adelayhelmut.com, US$8.50 pp in dorms, US$30–37 d, breakfast US$4 extra) is a small German-Mapuche guesthouse that grows its own produce and makes snacks and desserts.

PARQUE NACIONAL CONGUILLÍO

Directly east of Temuco, 3,125-meter Volcán Llaima's smoldering crater is the Parque Nacional Conguillío's most eye-catching feature—since colonial times, Chile's second-most-active volcano has recorded dozens of violent eruptions and other events, some as recently as 1999. Within its 60,833 hectares, though, this UNESCO biosphere reserve also abounds with dozens of lava flows, secondary cones, alpine lakes, river canyons, and the araucaria forest that it was created to protect—the name Conguillío derives from the Mapudungun *kongüjim,* "to enter the *pewen* forest."

In fact, the *pewen's* fame was such that, in late 1911, pioneer U.S. conservationist John Muir traveled to the region simply to see, sketch, and photograph the tree in its native habitat—"A glorious and novel sight, beyond all I had hoped for." As he so often did in California's Sierra Nevada, Muir slept in the open air, beneath the trees he had come to visit.

For foreigners and Chileans alike, Conguillío is one of the most popular excursions from Temuco. It justifies a day trip but deserves more.

Geography and Climate

From Temuco, Conguillío's western limit is only about 80 kilometers away via Cherquenco, but by either Curacautín or Melipeuco it's about 120 kilometers. Altitudes range from around 900 meters in the Río Truful Truful valley, to 3,125 meters on Llaima's summit. In the park's northeastern corner, the ruggedly glaciated Sierra Nevada averages above 2,500 meters.

Since most of Conguillío's 2,500 millimeters of precipitation falls as snow between May and September, the mild summer temperatures, averaging around 15°C, make its numerous lakes and streams popular recreational destinations. Even in summer, though, occasional heavy rains can make the road from Curacautín impassable.

Flora and Fauna

Conguillío originally was two separate parks, the other named Los Paraguas after the umbrella shape of the mature araucaria that, above 1,400 meters, mixes with southern beeches like *coigue (Nothofagus dombeyi), ñirre (Nothofagus antarctica)* and *lenga (Nothofagus pumilio). Coigue* is also common at lower elevations, around 900 meters, but mixed with *roble (Nothofagus obliqua);* above 1,200 meters, *raulí (Nothofagus alpina)* succeeds *roble.*

Traditionally, the Pewenche branch of the Mapuche collected the coniferous araucaria's nuts, much as indigenous groups gathered piñon nuts in western North America. The name Pewenche literally means "people of the pewen," the local species of an endemic southern hemisphere genus that once enjoyed a greater distribution throughout the Americas.

Given that much of Conguillío's terrain consists of barren volcanic slopes, lava fields and open woodlands, prime wildlife habitat is scarce and so is wildlife. Birds are most common and resemble those at Tolhuaca or Malalcahuello, but the small reptile *lagartija (Liolaemus tenuis)* flourishes in the drier environments.

Volcán Llaima, Parque Nacional Conguillío

Sights and Activities

Towering just west of the park's geographic center, glacier-covered **Volcán Llaima** is a Holocene structure of accumulated lava flows within an eight-kilometer-wide caldera that exploded about 7,200 years ago. It has two active craters, one on the summit and another on its southeastern shoulder.

East of Llaima, the sprawling lava flows of **El Escorial** dammed the Río Truful Truful to form **Laguna Arco Iris** and **Laguna Verde;** to the north, beneath the Sierra Nevada, **Laguna Conguillío** has a similar origin.

Near Conaf's Centro de Información at the southwest corner of Laguna Conguillío, the **Sendero Araucarias** is a short woodland nature trail suitable for any hiker. For a longer and more challenging excursion that's still a day hike, take the trail from **Playa Linda** at the east end of Laguna Conguillío to the foot of the **Sierra Nevada,** which rewards the hiker with overwhelming views through nearly pure araucaria. This route

THE CHILEAN PATH TO CONSERVATION

One of Latin America's most far-sighted conservation projects ever is the Lagos administration's **Sendero de Chile** (Chilean Trail), a 7,500-kilometer foot-, bicycle, and horse path linking the altiplano of the Norte Grande, near the Peruvian border, with southern Patagonia's sub-Antarctic tundra. Intended for both environmental and recreational purposes, its initial segments opened in 2001, but the ambitious goal is to finish the project by 2010, the bicentennial of Chilean independence.

Comparable to the United States' Pacific Crest Trail in the terrain it covers, but more like the older Appalachian Trail in that authorities hope to encourage community maintenance, the trail will pass through a representative sample of precordillera and upper Andean ecosystems. There is even the unprecedented possibility of cooperation with Argentina where the route passes through the vicinity of the Campo de Hielo Sur, the southern Patagonian ice sheet that once occasioned a bitter border dispute between the two countries.

Conama, the state environmental agency entrusted with the project, will permit no motorized transport whatsoever on the two-meter-wide dirt and gravel trail. Mostly following the Andean foothills, the route will have detours to important natural, cultural, or even commercial features such as archaeological sites, wineries, and crafts markets.

Conama hopes the trail will attract both urban day-trippers and Chilean and international outdoor enthusiasts who want to hike some or all of its length. Along the route there will be rustic cabins and campsites, built in locally appropriate styles, as well as mileage markers and informational panels on flora and fauna. Since one project goal is to encourage local development, there will be special emphasis on local place names and cultural monuments.

In early 2001, President Ricardo Lagos himself inaugurated the first kilometer at Parque Nacional Conguillío; as of 2005, upwards of 800 kilometers were open, including 36 kilometers at Conguillío, 25 kilometers in Parque Nacional Puyehue, 15 kilometers in Parque Nacional Chiloé, 60 kilometers in Reserva Nacional Cerro Castillo, eight kilometers near Villa O'Higgins, and 30 kilometers in Reserva Nacional Magallanes.

This progress may not be so great as it implies, as parts of it link preexisting trails in national parks, reserves, and monuments. Some segments, though, will pass through private land, and private companies and individuals will become involved. To follow its progress, visit the Sendero de Chile website, www.senderodechile.cl.

continues across the mountains to Termas Río Blanco, but it's a hazardous one on which hikers have died.

At **Laguna Captrén,** at the park's northern entrance, the **Sendero de Chile** was the initial section of the nonmotorized trail intended to unite the country from the Peruvian border to Tierra del Fuego. At Laguna Arco Iris, to the south, an early settler built the wooden **Casa del Colono** as a homestead cabin. From Laguna Verde, also known as Laguna Quililo, a short wooded footpath reaches the beach at **La Ensenada.**

Conaf's **Sendero Cañadon Truful-Truful,** a 900-meter nature trail, follows the river's course where erosion has uncovered the rainbow chronology of Llaima's eruptions and ash falls. Along the 800-meter **Sendero Los Vertientes,** subterranean springs emerge from the volcanic terrain.

From **Sector Los Paraguas,** on the park's west side, well-equipped climbers can scale Llaima; camping is possible in summer, and there is also a *refugio.* There is an alternative route from Captrén, which has better public transport, on the north side. Before climbing, ask Conaf permission in Temuco.

Skiing takes place at Los Paraguas' upgraded **Centro de Ski Las Araucarias** (tel. 045/562313, www.skiaraucarias.cl); it has Temuco offices at Bulnes 351, Oficina 47 (tel. 045/274141). Lift tickets cost about US$24 per day. Temuco's **Club de Esquí Llaima** (Las Heras 299, tel. 045/237923, cecmano@hotmail.com) provides classes and rental equipment.

Accommodations and Food

Along the south shore of Laguna Conguillío, Conaf has five campgrounds under private concession: The campground administration is at **Los Ñirres** (44 sites), while there are smaller clusters at **Los Carpinteros** (12 sites), **La Caseta** (12 sites), **El Estero** (10 sites) and **El Hoyón** (10 sites). Rates are US$23 per site for up to five persons in summer and during Semana Santa, but Conaf sets aside a handful of sites at El Estero for bicyclists and backpackers (US$5 pp). Ten kilometers northwest of Laguna Conguillío, there are another 12 sites at **Laguna Captrén.** For camping reservations, contact René Peña at Fundación Raíces (tel. 045/736200, rpena@telsur.cl).

Between the park administration and Los Ñirres campground, built around pewen trunks, the older units at **Cabañas Conguillío** (US$56 for up to four persons) are more quaint than practical; newer units (US$85 for up to eight persons) are a better choice (the older units' days are supposed to be numbered). In the peak summer season, a restaurant and store operates on the lakeshore.

At Laguna Verde, 18 kilometers north of Melipeuco, the new **Cabañas La Baita Conguillío** (tel. 09/7332442, icorrea@labaitaconguillio.cl, US$75) can accommodate up to eight persons.

At Sector Los Paraguas, the **Refugio Escuela Ski** (tel. 045/237923 in Temuco, US$50 pp) features bunks for 70 and a restaurant; rates include lift tickets (the infrastructure is basic) and full board. In summer, operator Oscar Gutiérrez offers climbing and hiking excursions in the vicinity.

The modern **Centro de Ski las Araucarias** (tel. 045/562313, www.skiaraucarias.cl) has a variety of accommodations. Its **Refugio Las Paraguas** has dorm beds (US$11 pp with your own sleeping bag) and one six-bed apartment (US$80), while the **Refugio Pehuén** also has dorms (US$13 pp) and doubles with shared bath (US$33) and private bath (US$42). Facilities at the **Apartment Hotel Llaima** (US$100) can sleep up to four persons.

Information

At Laguna Conguillío, Conaf's Centro de Información Ambiental has good natural-history exhibits and a cozy fireplace; it's open 10 A.M.–1 P.M. and 3–7:30 P.M. daily in January and February, when it organizes children's programs and hiking excursions, and provides evening naturalist talks.

Conaf also has ranger stations at the Laguna Captrén and Truful-Truful park entrances.

Getting There

Because public transportation is inconvenient to almost every sector of the park, it's worth considering a car rental, but it's not absolutely essential. Even with a car, the steep, narrow, and sometimes muddy road between Laguna Captrén and Curacautín can be difficult to negotiate.

Reaching Curacautín and Melipeuco, the northern and southern gateways to the main park loop, is easy enough by public bus; see the appropriate entries above for details. From Curacautín, Erbuc (tel. 045/881670) goes to Laguna Captrén (US$1) Monday and Friday at 5:45 A.M. and 5:30 P.M., but that is the only scheduled transport. From either Curacautín or Melipeuco, it's possible to hire a taxi or pickup truck to Conguillío.

Sector Los Paraguas is the most difficult sector to reach by public transportation. Nar-Bus goes to the village of Cherquenco (US$1.50), but then it's another 17 kilometers to the ski lodge at Los Paraguas. An alternative route, requiring a high-clearance vehicle and preferably four-wheel drive, goes from Captrén to Los Paraguas.

VILLARRICA

Southeast of Temuco, lakeside Villarrica marks the beginning of Chile's most traditional resort region, where generations of families have spent their summers on the shores of lakes left by receding Pleistocene glaciers. It also shares its name with Volcán Villarrica, a fuming 2,840-meter cone that's Chile's most active volcano, to the southeast. Much of this area was once wide-open country, but a construction boom of hotels and country houses between Villarrica and the neighboring resort of Pucón, to the east, is rapidly filling the gaps.

History

Fiery eruptions from Volcán Villarrica may have deterred some settlers, but the Mapuche resistance

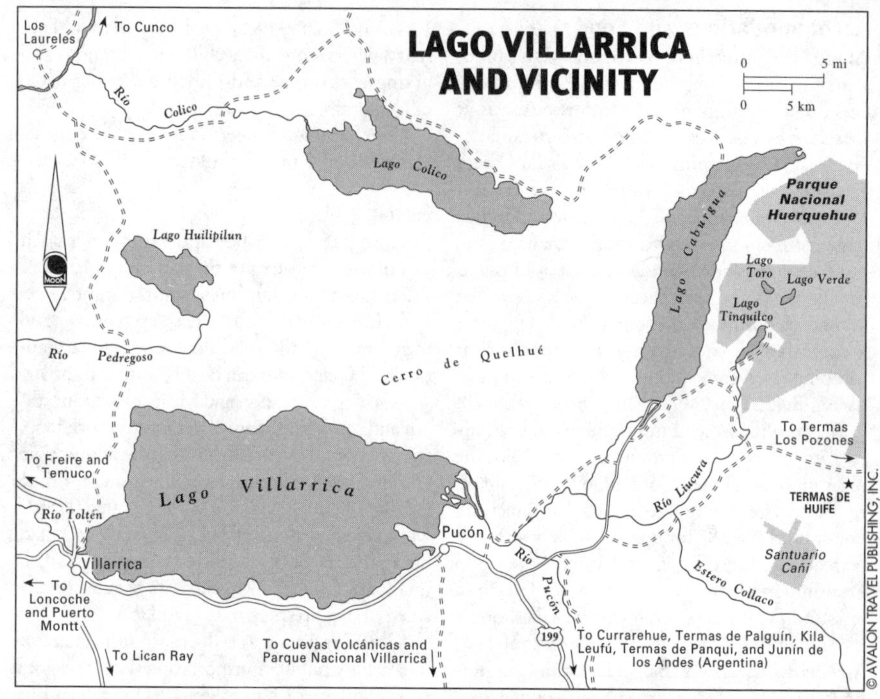

to the Spaniards and Chileans was more effective. In 1552, 50 colonists under Gerónimo de Alderete's command established Santa María Magdalena de Villarrica, but Mapuche assaults forced its abandonment several times despite speculation about precious metals in the area (the overly optimistic founding name "Villarrica" means "rich town"). After driving out the Spaniards in 1602, the Mapuche enjoyed nearly three centuries of uninterrupted possession until, in 1883, Chilean colonel Gregorio Urrutia reached an agreement with the Mapuche chief Epuléf to regularize the Chilean presence.

Villarrica's 1897 declaration of city status brought an influx of immigrants, many of them German, who gradually transformed the area into a dairy zone and, eventually, a durable resort area with an international reputation.

Orientation

Some 87 kilometers southeast of Temuco via the Panamericana and Ruta 199, an international highway to Argentina, Villarrica (population 30,859) occupies a favored site at Lago Villarrica's southwestern edge, at its Río Toltén outlet. While the town has a regular grid pattern, the focus of local activity is not the Plaza de Armas but rather the lakeshore, along with the main commercial thoroughfare Avenida Pedro de Valdivia and its perpendicular Camilo Henríquez.

Sights and Activities

Stone tools, early Mapuche ceramics, and contemporary indigenous jewelry, silver, and leatherwork constitute the collections of the **Museo Histórico y Arqueológico de Villarrica** (Pedro de Valdivia 1050, tel. 045/413445). Hours are 9 A.M.–1 P.M. and 3–7:30 P.M. weekdays; admission costs US$.50.

Directly in front of the Museo stands the landmark **Ruca,** a traditional Mapuche dwelling thickly thatched with *junquillo* and *totora* reeds.

The lakefront **Embarcadero,** featuring a cluster of small jetties toward the foot of General Körner, is the starting point for water-based excursions.

Entertainment

Peña La Tranquera (Acevedo 761) is a bar offering live folk music. **Pub del Sur** (Camilo Henríquez 382), a recent addition to the nightlife scene with agreeable ambiance, opens early (around 7 P.M.) and also has live music.

Shopping

Immediately behind the tourist office, Villarrica's **Feria Artesanal** showcases Mapuche crafts and food in summer, but the rest of the year it's fairly moribund. Strong all year is the **Mercado Fritz** (Aviador Acevedo 600).

Permanent crafts outlets include the **Tornería Suiza** (Prat 675, tel. 045/411610) and **Tejidos Ray-Ray** (Anfión Muñoz 386, tel. 045/412006); the latter is strong on woolens.

Accommodations

Like other Andean lake-district resorts, Villarrica's accommodations prices peak in January and February, but Semana Santa, September's Fiestas Patrias, and the ski season can all see higher prices.

In addition to the permanent places listed here, many economical *hospedajes* open in summer only—look for signs or ask at the tourist office.

For shoestring backpackers only, rates at the barebones **Hotel Fuentes** (Vicente Reyes 665, tel. 045/411595, US$6–8 pp) vary depending on whether the room has shared or private bath. Some rooms even lack windows, but its bar/restaurant has long been a gathering place.

Cyclists in particular flock to the Swiss-run hostel **La Torre Suiza** (Bilbao 969, tel./fax 045/411213, www.torresuiza.com, US$8 pp for dorms, US$20–24 d), an immaculately modernized house with firm, comfortable beds, easily regulated hot showers, Internet access, and a tobacco-free interior. Rates, which depend on whether the room has shared or private bath, include a substantial European-style breakfast. Owners Béat and Claudia Zbinden also help with self-guided cycling trips.

Traditionally popular **Hostería Rayhuén** (Pedro Montt 668, tel./fax 045/411571, US$17/25 s/d) has cozy rooms with private bath and breakfast, and also serves other meals at its family-style restaurant, which has garden as well as indoor seating. The owner, though, can be overbearingly friendly.

Rates at **Hotel Villa Linda** (Avenida Pedro de Valdivia 678, tel. 045/411392, hotelvillalinda@hotmail.com, US$20/37 s/d) include private bath and breakfast. **Hotel Villarrica** (Körner 255, tel./fax 045/411641, US$35/44 s/d) offers good value for its tranquil lakeside location in a residential area.

Comfy, rustically styled **Hostería Bilbao** (Camilo Henríquez 43, tel. 045/411186, www.7lagos.com/bilbao, US$25/46 s/d) also enjoys a lakeshore site.

Rates at renovated **Hostería Kiel** (Körner 153, tel. 045/411631, fax 045/410925, reservas@bungalowlandia.cl, US$27/42 s/d) include breakfast and private bath. Set among lush gardens, **Hotel El Ciervo** (Körner 241, tel. 045/411215, fax 045/411426, www.hotelelciervo.cl, US$46–53 s, US$61–72 d) is a traditional favorite; some rooms have fireplaces.

Modern **Hotel Montebianco** (Pedro de Valdivia 1011, tel. 045/411798, www.marpack.cl, US$46/58 s/d) has made good first impressions and has an outstanding restaurant, but it's also on Villarrica's busiest street.

Overlooking the lake from the high ground, the Oregonian owners at **Hostería de la Colina** (Las Colinas 115, tel./fax 045/411503, www.hosteriadelacolina.com, US$40–85 s, US$60–100 d) provide a full American-style breakfast, attractive gardens, and other amenities, including a large English-language library. The highest rates correspond to garden *cabañas*.

Food

For sandwiches and desserts, try **Café Bar 2001** (Camilo Henríquez 379, tel. 045/411470). At the Mercado Fritz crafts market, inexpensive **La Cocina de María** (Aviador Acevedo) offers typical Chilean dishes like chicken with rice, fried chicken, and empanadas.

Over the past few years, **The Travellers** (Valentín Letelier 753, tel. 045/412830) has earned a comfortable niche with its diverse choice of Chilean, Asian, and Mexican fusion dishes at moderate prices. In a traditional lakeside setting, **El Rey del Marisco** (Valentín Letelier 1030, tel. 045/412093) serves fine but traditional fish and shellfish dishes in the US$6.50–8 range. **El Tabor** (Epulef 1187, tel. 045/411901) gets high marks for seafood, with a popular *tenedor libre* buffet (US$10–15) on weekends.

Hotel Montebianco's **La Vecchia Cucina** (Pedro de Valdivia 1011, tel. 045/411798) offers fine pasta entrées for US$6.50–8, with slightly cheaper pizzas and fabulous homemade ice cream, all with professional service. Another good alternative, serving continental and Chilean cuisine, is the **Club Social Treffpunkt** (Valentín Letelier 690). **Bahía Perú** (Valentín Letelier 893, tel. 045/413841) is a promising new Peruvian restaurant.

The best choice for meat is **La Cava de Roble** (Valentín Letelier 658, tel. 045/416446), whose specialties include game dishes like venison and wild boar. For moderately priced Chinese food, the option is **Cheng Chong** (Valentín Letelier 795).

Information

Well-stocked with maps, brochures, and lists of accommodations and prices, Villarrica's municipal **Oficina de Turismo** (Pedro de Valdivia 1070, tel. 045/206619, turis@entelchile.net) keeps long summer hours: 8:30 A.M.–11 P.M. daily January–March; the rest of the year hours are 9 A.M.–1 P.M. and 2:30–6 P.M. weekdays only except in December, when they're 8:30 A.M.–8:30 P.M. daily.

Services

Turismo Christopher (Pedro de Valdivia 1033) and **Turcamb** (Camilo Henríquez 576, Local 6) are the only exchange houses. There are several ATMs along Avenida Pedro de Valdivia.

For postal services, **Correos de Chile** is at Anfión Muñoz 315.

The **Centro de Llamados** (Camilo Henríquez 544) and **Entel** (Camilo Henríquez 446) both have long-distance and Internet service.

For laundry service, try **Todo Lavado** (General Urrutia 699, Local 7, tel. 045/414452).

For medical assistance, there's the **Hospital Villarrica** (San Martín 460, tel. 045/411169).

Getting There

Villarrica's **Terminal de Buses** is at Avenida Pedro de Valdivia 621, though some carriers have individual offices nearby.

Buses Regionales Villarrica (Vicente Reyes 619, tel. 045/411871, has frequent buses to Pucón (US$1, 45 minutes), where there are connections to other **regional** destinations like Curarrehue and Puesco.

Buses Jac (Bilbao 610, tel. 045/411447) shuttles at least every 15–30 minutes between Temuco (US$1.50, one hour) and Pucón (US$1, 45 minutes). It also goes nine times daily to Caburgua (US$1.50) via Pucón in summer, less frequently the rest of the year.

Northbound **long-distance** services to Santiago and intermediates on the Panamericana are frequent, but some southbound services require backtracking to Temuco; alternatively, transfer at Freire from any Temuco-bound bus, or at Loncoche from any Valdivia-bound bus.

Many companies go to Santiago, including **Buses Jac** and **Tur-Bus** (Anfión Muñoz 657, tel. 045/411534), which have the only direct services to Osorno, Puerto Varas, and Puerto Montt.

Depending on the carrier and seasonal demand, Santiago fares can range from US$10–20, while rates for *salón cama* sleepers can double that. Other sample destinations, fares, and times include Osorno (US$7, 3.5 hours) and Puerto Montt (US$9, five hours).

International buses serve the Argentine cities of Junín de los Andes, with connections to Neuquén, and San Martín de los Andes; these buses leave from Temuco and board additional passengers in Villarrica and Pucón. **Buses San Martín** (Anfión Muñoz 604, tel. 045/411584) and **Igi Llaima** (tel. 045/412733), at the main terminal, alternate daily services.

For services to Bariloche, it's necessary to return to Temuco or make connections in Osorno.

Getting Around

Automotriz Castillo (Anfión Muñoz 415, tel.

045/411618, hugo77@ctcreuna.cl) is the only car-rental agency.

PUCÓN

At the foot of ominously smoldering Volcán Villarrica, Pucón has gained fame as *the* destination for Chile-bound hikers, climbers, mountain bikers, windsurfers, and whitewater rafters and kayakers. Still popular with conventional Chilean holidaymakers in the summer peak, it enjoys a longer season than most Andean lake-district resorts because hordes of youthful international travelers frequent the area from November to April. It has few sights of its own because almost everything worth seeing or doing is outside town, but when the sun sets everyone swarms to party at local hotels, restaurants, and bars.

That doesn't mean Pucón lacks its serious side. Over the past several years, the landmark cooperative Hostería ¡Ecole!, along with the affiliated Fundación Lahuén, has actively promoted forest conservation in the surrounding countryside.

© WAYNE BERNHARDSON

Pucón, on Lago Villarrica, is the Chilean lake district's adventure travel capital.

Orientation

Where the Río Pucón enters the lake, 25 kilometers east of the town of Villarrica via Ruta 119, Pucón (population 13,837) occupies a compact grid bounded by the lakeshore to the north and west, Avenida Colo Colo to the east, and Volcán Villarrica's lower slopes to the south. Its main commercial axis is Avenida Bernardo O'Higgins, which continues as Ruta 119 toward Curarrehue and the Argentine border at Paso Mamuil Malal.

Language Classes

Hostería ¡Ecole! (General Urrutia 592, tel. 045/441675, fax 045/441660, www.ecole.cl, ecole-spanishschool@entelchile.net) organizes a variety of activity-based Spanish-language courses.

Entertainment and Events

There's not much in the way of formal entertainment venues, but somehow Pucón has plenty to do.

Filling an entire city block east of the Plaza de Armas, built primarily for those with money to burn or who fantasize beating the house, the colossal **Casino de Pucón** (Ansorena 23, tel. 045/441873) used part of its profits to build a performing-arts venue and a cinema.

There's a lot of turnover in bars, but several have managed to last more than a few seasons: **Bar del Pelao** (O'Higgins 624); **La Taverna de Barbazul** (Lincoyán 361); **Krater** (O'Higgins 447, tel. 045/441339); and **Mama's & Tapas** (O'Higgins 587, tel. 045/449002). All these places serve food as well, but that's not their forte.

Early February's **Triatlón Internacional de Pucón** (Pucón International Triathlon) grows in popularity every year. The **Aniversario de Pucón** celebrates the city's founding on February 27.

Shopping

There's a permanent **Mercado Artesanal** (artisans' market) on Ansorena between O'Higgins and Brasil. **Artesanos de Pucón** is on Alderete between Fresia and Ansorena.

Accommodations

Pucón has good and abundant budget accommodations, but the best values are just a little

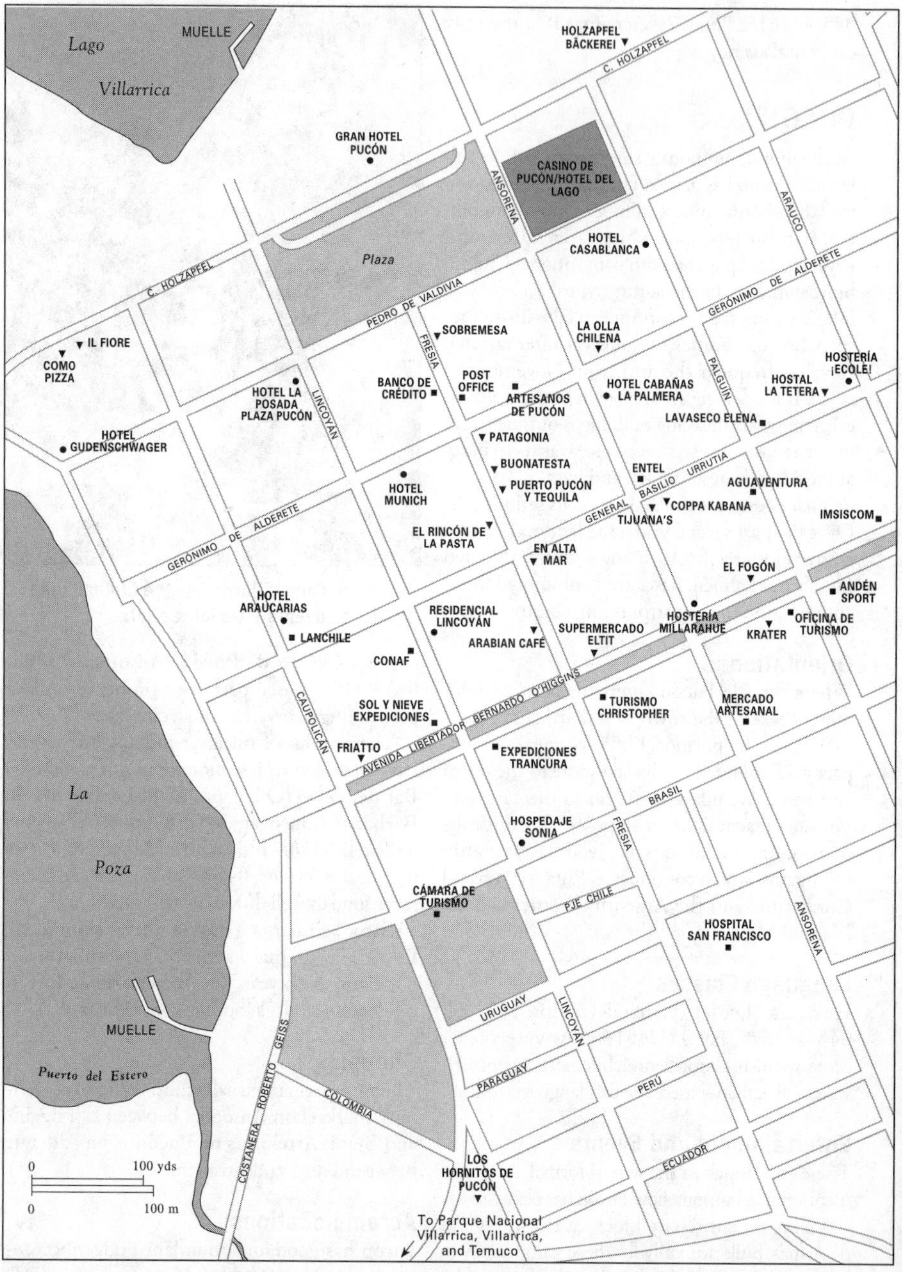

Lago Villarrica
MUELLE
HOLZAPFEL BÄCKEREI
C. HOLZAPFEL
GRAN HOTEL PUCÓN
CASINO DE PUCÓN/HOTEL DEL LAGO
ANSORENA
ARAUCO
Plaza
HOTEL CASABLANCA
C. HOLZAPFEL
PEDRO DE VALDIVIA
GERÓNIMO DE ALDERETE
SOBREMESA
LA OLLA CHILENA
FRESIA
IL FIORE
COMO PIZZA
HOTEL LA POSADA PLAZA PUCÓN
LINCOYÁN
BANCO DE CRÉDITO
POST OFFICE
ARTESANOS DE PUCÓN
HOTEL CABAÑAS LA PALMERA
PALGUÍN
HOSTERÍA ¡ECOLE!
HOSTAL LA TETERA
LAVASECO ELENA
HOTEL GUDENSCHWAGER
PATAGONIA
BUONATESTA
PUERTO PUCÓN Y TEQUILA
ENTEL
GENERAL BASILIO URRUTIA
AGUAVENTURA
HOTEL MUNICH
COPPA KABANA
TIJUANA'S
IMSISCOM
GERÓNIMO DE ALDERETE
EL RINCÓN DE LA PASTA
EN ALTA MAR
EL FOGÓN
ANDÉN SPORT
HOTEL ARAUCARIAS
LANCHILE
RESIDENCIAL LINCOYÁN
ARABIAN CAFÉ
SUPERMERCADO ELTIT
HOSTERÍA MILLARAHUE
KRATER
OFICINA DE TURISMO
CONAF
AVENIDA LIBERTADOR BERNARDO O'HIGGINS
TURISMO CHRISTOPHER
MERCADO ARTESANAL
SOL Y NIEVE EXPEDICIONES
CAUPOLICÁN
FRIATTO
EXPEDICIONES TRANCURA
BRASIL
La Poza
HOSPEDAJE SONIA
FRESIA
CÁMARA DE TURISMO
PJE CHILE
HOSPITAL SAN FRANCISCO
ANSORENA
URUGUAY
LINCOYÁN
MUELLE
PARAGUAY
PERU
Puerto del Estero
COSTANERA ROBERTO GEISS
COLOMBIA
ECUADOR
LOS HORNITOS DE PUCÓN
0 100 yds
0 100 m
To Parque Nacional Villarrica, Villarrica, and Temuco

The Sur Chico

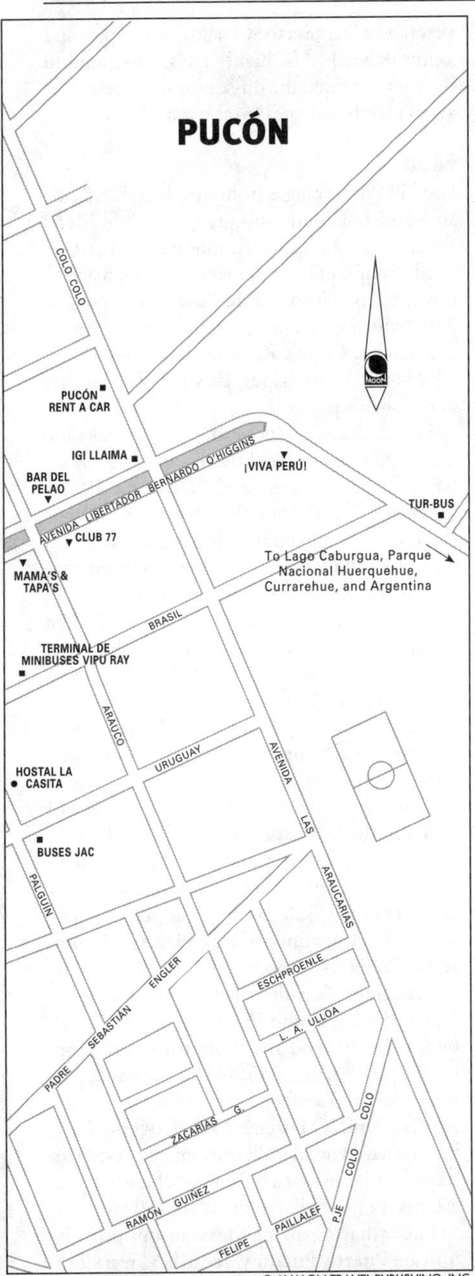

more expensive. There are some truly opulent upscale options.

US$10–25

Over the past decade-plus, comfortable **Hospedaje Sonia** (Lincoyán 485, tel. 045/441269, hospedajesonia@hotmail.com, US$10 pp, US$23–25 d without breakfast) has become a gathering place for international travelers, offering good-value accommodations with kitchen privileges and also arranging its own tours of local highlights.

In a quiet site only about 100 meters north of the Tur-Bus terminal, Swiss-run **Hospedaje Travel Pucón** (Blanco Encalada 190, tel. 045/444093, pucontravel@terra.cl, US$10 pp) has spacious rooms with both breakfast (US$3 extra) and kitchen privileges. For additional bucks, it also offers a variety of massage options ranging from reiki to Thai, for US$20–35.

US$25–50

Residencial Lincoyán (Lincoyán 323, tel. 045/441144, www.lincoyan.cl, US$15 pp with breakfast) is a friendly family-style place.

More than just a comfy bed, **Hostería ¡Ecole!** (General Urrutia 592, tel. 045/441675, fax 045/441660, www.ecole.cl, US$12–17 pp) has become a destination in itself. Owned and operated by a committed cooperative of Chilean and international environmental activists, it provides informally stylish B&B-style accommodations with shared bath, with discounts for Hostelling International members (breakfast costs extra, but is well worth it). In addition, it has an exceptional but moderately priced, mostly vegetarian restaurant and a book exchange, operates its own excursions in the vicinity, and provides information and advice to independent travelers. On the downside, it's become so popular that reservations are essential in summer, and not a bad idea the rest of the year. There are a few even cheaper backpacker bunks.

Alongside ¡Ecole!, the more subdued Swiss-Chilean **Hostal La Tetera** (General Urrutia 580, tel./fax 045/441462, www.tetera.cl, US$21/30 s/d) offers stylishly comfortable rooms with good beds, individual reading lights, and shared bath; the walls may be a little thin, but it attracts a quiet clientele and has Pucón's best breakfasts.

US$50–100

One of Pucón's best midrange values is **Hotel La Palmera** (Ansorena 221, tel. 045/441083, fax 045/443127, www.cepri.cl/lapalmera, US$37–41 s, US$49–57 d), which also has garden *cabañas.*

With its spa and other upgrades, **Hotel Araucarias** (Caupolicán 243, tel. 045/441286, fax 045/441693, hotel@araucarias.cl, US$45/70 s/d) is an exceptional value with IVA discounts.

Set on ample grounds, with a large pool, **Hotel La Posada Plaza Pucón** (Pedro de Valdivia 191, tel. 045/441088, fax 045/441762, www.hotelplazapucon.cl, US$41–61 s, US$57–70 d) is comparable.

The classically aging **Hotel Gudenschwager** (Pedro de Valdivia 12, tel./fax 045/441156, www.puconturismo.cl/gudens, US$59/76 s/d) fronts directly on the lake.

Over US$100

Enjoying its own black-sand beach, the mammoth lakefront **Gran Hotel Pucón** (Holzapfel 190, tel./fax 045/441001, www.granhotelpucon.cl, US$124/165 and up s/d) dates from the 1930s, when the state railroad agency Ferrocarriles del Estado decided on Pucón as the next great tourist destination. It now focuses on packages from two or three days to a week.

Part of the pharaonic new casino a block to the northwest of Gran Hotel Pucón, the 82-room **Hotel del Lago** (Ansorena 23, tel. 045/291000, fax 045/291200, www.hoteldellago.cl, US$180–240 s or d with breakfast) is a self-contained eyesore whose main redeeming feature is a cinema that shows first-run movies.

Two kilometers west of Pucón on the Villarrica road, poised among hillside gardens with immaculate flower beds, pools, and cascades, the Bauhaus-style **Hotel Antumalal** (tel. 045/441011/2, fax 045/441013, www.antumalal.com, US$100–140 s, US$140–185 d) prides itself on personal service—on arrival, the staff place a fresh fruit basket in every room and each guest's name on the door (rooms are unnumbered) and even wash your car. Each of its 20 rooms boasts lake views and a fireplace; there is also a heated pool and a private beach. The higher rates correspond to the summer peak; the off-season rates are a giveaway. Half-board rates are also available.

Food

Food in Pucón ranges from simple regional cuisine and fast food—no greasy chain outlets, though—to sophisticated international fare. A good example of both, at the western approach to town, is **Los Hornitos de Pucón** (Caupolicán 710), which specializes in oven-baked takeaway empanadas. **Coppa Kabana** (Urrutia 407, tel. 045/444371) serves sandwiches and plain lunches at reasonable prices.

Even if there's no room to stay, don't miss the most vegetarian lunches or dinners and the lively tobacco-free atmosphere at **Hostería ¡Ecole!** (Urrutia 592, tel. 045/441675). For about US$5–6, this is some of the country's best-value food.

La Olla Chilena (Jerónimo de Alderete 402-B) features freshly prepared, attractively presented versions of Chilean standards like *pastel de choclo* in the US$5 range, plus a superb and inexpensive (US$1.50) *consomé reina* (chicken soup). The service is warm and friendly. **Club 77** (O'Higgins 635) has similar fare, while **El Fogón** (O'Higgins 480, tel. 045/444904) is a *parrilla.*

One of Pucón's many Italian venues, **El Rincón de la Pasta** (Fresia 284, tel. 045/444258) offers superb and varied pasta dishes, with an equally great variety of sauces, with most entrées in the US$6–8 range. Service is impeccable. The Argentine-style **Pizzería Buonatesta** (Fresia 243, tel. 045/441434) is equally outstanding. Near the lakefront are two other Italian venues: **Como Pizza** (Holzapfel 71, tel. 045/441109), and the more formal **Il Fiore** (Holzapfel 83, tel. 045/441565), which also serves beef and seafood.

¡Viva Perú! (O'Higgins 761, tel. 045/444285) has injected an overdue diversity into the restaurant scene, but it can't match Santiago's best Peruvian eateries. Entrées fall into the US$6–10 range.

Pucón has a pair of Mexican options: the upscale **Puerto Pucón y Tequila** (Fresia 245, tel. 045/441592) and the more modest **Ti-**

juana's (Ansorena 303). The **Arabian Café** (Fresia 354, tel. 045/443469) serves Middle Eastern specialties.

At **En Alta Mar** (General Urrutia 315, tel. 045/442294), the seafood is good and fresh, and the pisco sours are excellent, but the quality doesn't quite match the prices—US$8–10 for most entrées. The service can be surprisingly distracted at what presumes to be one of Pucón's better restaurants. For meat and seafood, some locals prefer **Sobremesa** (Fresia 123, tel. 045/444627).

Patagonia (Fresia 223, tel. 045/443165) serves sandwiches, coffee, juices, and particularly exquisite desserts, including homemade ice cream and crepes, as well as artisanal chocolates. The **Holzapfel Bäckerei** (Holzapfel 524, tel. 045/441334) serves *kuchen* and similar regional specialties, as well as ice cream. **Friatto** (O'Higgins 136-B) also serves very fine ice cream.

Information

The municipal **Oficina de Turismo** (O'Higgins 483, tel. 045/293002) opens 8:30 A.M.–10 P.M. daily in summer; the rest of the year, hours are 8:30 A.M.–7 P.M. weekdays, 10 A.M.–6 P.M. weekends.

Pucón's private **Cámara de Turismo** (Brasil 115, tel. 045/441671, www.puconturismo.cl) is open 8 A.M.–midnight in January and February, 10 A.M.–1 P.M. and 4–9 P.M. the rest of the year.

For national parks, **Conaf** (Lincoyán 336, 1st floor, tel. 045/443781) now has centrally convenient offices.

Services

Turismo Christopher (O'Higgins 335) and **Supermercado Eltit** (O'Higgins 336) change US and Argentine cash. The supermarket now has an ATM, as does **Banco de Crédito** (Fresia 174).

Correos de Chile (Fresia 183) handles the mail.

Entel (Ansorena 299) has long-distance and Internet services. **Imsiscom** (O'Higgins 575) is one of few Internet providers that offers an iMac option, though most of its machines are PCs.

Lavaseco Elena (General Urrutia 520-B) charges about US$5 per load, washed, dried, and folded.

For medical services, contact **Hospital San Francisco** (Uruguay 325, tel. 045/441177).

Getting There

Bus is the main means of transport to and from Pucón, but there are occasional summer flights from Santiago.

LAN (General Urrutia 102, tel. 045/443514) normally flies out of Temuco.

Long-distance **bus** service is an extension of that from Villarrica, so schedules and fares do not appear in detail here. The two main carriers have their own terminals: **Tur-Bus** (O'Higgins 910, tel. 045/443328) and **Buses Jac** (Palguín 605, tel. 045/443693). **Intersur** and **Buses San Martín** share the Tur-Bus terminal, while other companies have separate terminals around the east end of town.

Buses Jac and Tur-Bus have frequent service to Santiago, while Tur-Bus also goes to Puerto Montt. Other Santiago carriers include **Igi Llaima** (O'Higgins and Colo Colo, tel. 045/442061) and **Cóndor Bus** (Colo Colo 430, tel. 045/443023).

San Martín buses to Argentina use the Tur-Bus terminal, while Igi Llaima uses its own terminal.

Buses Regionales Villarrica services to Villarrica start at the **Terminal de Minibuses Vipu Ray** (Brasil between Palguín and Arauco). Buses Jac also goes frequently to Villarrica (45 minutes, US$.60), and has nine buses daily to Caburgua (US$1), 18 daily to Curarrehue (US$1) and one to the Argentine border at Puesco at 7:30 A.M., returning at 6 P.M. In summer, they also go to Parque Nacional Huerquehue (US$1.50) at 7:30 A.M., 11:15 A.M., and 5:30 P.M.; the rest of the year, there are departures Monday, Wednesday, and Friday at 8:30 A.M. and 4 P.M., returning at 10 A.M. and 5 P.M.

Taxibuses Rinconada (Ansorena 299, tel. 045/441905) goes to Huepil, on the Termas de Huife road, at 12:30 P.M. weekdays, and at 4:15 P.M. to Huife Alto via Termas de Huife and Los Pozones, returning the following morning.

Getting Around

Several adventure travel agencies on Avenida O'Higgins also rent mountain bikes; for addresses, see the Vicinity of Pucón entry below.

For rental cars, try **Pucón Rent A Car** (Colo Colo 340, tel./fax 045/443052).

VICINITY OF PUCÓN

As the locus of adventure travel in the Andean lake district, Pucón offers activities ranging from climbing Volcán Villarrica to rafting the Río Trancura, hiking at Huerquehue, horseback riding, fly-fishing, skiing, and visits to nearby thermal baths. Competition—often cutthroat competition—can keep prices low and temperatures high among numerous local operators. Occasionally, though, they manage to cooperate in putting groups together, especially outside the summer peak.

Commercial operators (in alphabetical order) include French-run **Aguaventura** (Palguín 336, tel. 045/444246, www.aguaventura.com); **Andén Sport** (O'Higgins 535, tel. 045/441048, fax 045/441236); **Expediciones Trancura** (O'Higgins 211-C, tel. 045/443436, fax 045/441189, www.trancura.com); **Politur** (O'Higgins 635, tel./fax 045/441373, www.politur.com); and **Sol y Nieve Expediciones** (O'Higgins 192, tel./fax 045/441070, www.chile-travel.com/solnieve.htm).

Best known as a place to stay, noncommercial **Hostería ¡Ecole!** (General Urrutia 592, tel. 045/441675, fax 045/441660) organizes groups to visit the Fundación Lahuén's nearby Santuario Cañi forest reserve, and other alternative excursions, and offers suggestions for independent excursions.

Cuevas Volcánicas

On Volcán Villarrica's southern slopes, but outside the national park, the misleadingly named "volcanic caves" are in fact lava tubes, but this privately run attraction provides a professional introduction to volcanism. Starting with a (Spanish-only) video on volcanic hazards, it ranges through displays on volcanic geology and seismic technology (ranging from a classic seismograph as well as modern computer monitors). The highlight is a 340-meter descent into the tubes themselves (unless you're a bat, the darkness at the bottom is absolute).

Reached by a fork off the road to Parque Nacional Villarrica, the Cuevas Volcánicas (tel. 045/442002, cuevasvolcanicas@hotmail.com) are 14.5 kilometers south of the main Villarrica-Pucón highway. Some of the well-trained guides can manage English if necessary; admission and the one-hour tour cost US$10 per person for adults, US$7 per person for children.

Río Trancura

Barely half an hour east of Pucón, the Trancura is not one of Chile's premier whitewater rivers—there's plenty of still water between rapids—but the Class IV waterfalls make parts of its upper sector a wild ride indeed. Heavy competition has kept prices down to about US$20 per person for the Alto Trancura, half that for the calmer Bajo Trancura. Both are morning or afternoon excursions, but the Alto Trancura means a little longer on the water as well. For booking information, see the list of travel agencies above.

One alternative to rafting or kayaking is hydrospeeding, a sort of whitewater-body-board experience that's gained popularity the past couple years. A trip down the Trancura Alto costs about US$20.

Kila Leufú

At Palguín Bajo, east of Pucón, Kila Leufú is a working Mapuche farm that offers a variety of horseback-riding trips, the chance to participate (or not) in farm activities, a *ruca* for socializing, and accommodations, all at reasonable prices. Camping costs US$5 per person with breakfast. Comfortable accommodations with shared bath cost US$9 per person with breakfast, with additional meals for US$4 (lunch) and US$5 (dinner), including vegetarian options.

Kila Leufú (tel. 09/7118064, www.kilaleufu.cl) is 23 kilometers east of Pucón on the Curarrehue road, just beyond the Cabedañe bridge and the Termas de Palguín turnoff. For more details, contact Kila Leufú's Margo Martínez, who speaks English, German, and French in addition to Spanish.

From Pucón, Curarrehue-bound Buses Jac services pass by Kila Leufú's front door.

Hot Springs

The entire volcanic cordon of the Andean lake district is dotted with *termas,* but there's a particularly dense concentration near Pucón. Several have become retreats or resorts ranging from basic day-use facilities to upscale but not-quite-lavish hotels.

On the Río Liucura northeast of Pucón, **Termas de Huife** is the area's most upmarket option, a modern chalet-style resort with spa facilities in 40°C waters and offering massage therapy. For US$10 in summer, US$8.50 the rest of the year, day-trippers can use the outdoor pools. The resort provides its own transportation from Pucón for $18 return, but infrequent buses also pass near the entrance. Both restaurant and cafeteria meals are available.

Termas Huife is 30 kilometers northeast of Pucón via Paillaco, on the road to Parque Nacional Huerquehue. For more details, contact **Hotel y Termas Huife** (Gerónimo de Alderete 324, Pucón, tel./fax 045/445970, www.termashuife.cl, US$88–101 s, US$132–151 d). The higher rates are in effect mid-December–mid-March only.

Just two kilometers beyond Huife, the minimalist **Termas Los Pozones** is a popular budget option; admission to a series of riverside pools ranging from 30–40°C costs US$6 per person in the day time, US$8 per person at night, when some Pucón travel agencies run tours. Bring food and other supplies, as there's almost nothing on site. Pucón's Taxibuses Rinconada (Ansorena 299, tel. 045/441905) has one or two buses daily; see the Pucón transportation entry for details.

In 1998 **Termas de Palguín,** the area's oldest hot-springs resort, 30 kilometers southeast of Pucón on its namesake river, suffered a major fire that destroyed its landmark hotel. Rebuilt in a less distinctive style on a more modest scale, the current **Hotel Termas de Palguín** (Casilla 1-D, Pucón, tel. 045/441968, US$60/100 s/d with full board) is once again open year-round. For nonguests, admission to the pools or private tubs costs US$6 per person; there is also a restaurant.

The area's most unconventional thermal baths, 58 kilometers from Pucón via the paved road to Curarrehue and an improved gravel road that heads north, **Termas de Panqui** exudes distinctly New Age vibes with its material and spiritual hodgepodge of Mapuche *rucas,* Lakota tipis, yoga, tai chi, meditation, and full-moon retreats in a rustic setting that, admittedly, has a great deal to offer. There are also hot pools, mud baths, and a vegetarian restaurant.

Day-use admission costs US$13 per person, while tipi accommodations cost US$18 per person and rather dark hotel rooms US$27 per person; they also arrange transportation from Pucón for US$9 per person. For more information, contact Termas de Panqui (Avenida O'Higgins 555, Oficina 2, Pucón, tel. 045/442039, fax 045/442040, ingeluz@yahoo.com).

Santuario Cañi

In a high roadless area about 21 kilometers east of Pucón, the Fundación Lahuen administers 400 hectares of mixed araucaria forest in the Santuario Cañi, Chile's first private nature reserve. A project is underway to create a "Sendero Pehuén" to connect the reserve with Parque Nacional Huerquehue, as part of the ambitious Sendero de Chile project; it will have campgrounds, *refugios,* trail markers, and hygienic facilities.

For the moment, access is limited to guided hikes under the auspices of the Fundación Lahuen, arranged through the Fundación, at Hostería ¡Ecole! (Urrutia 592, Pucón, tel. 045/441675, fax 045/441660), and other local operators. For information in the United States, contact Ancient Forests International (Box 1850, Redway, CA 95560, tel. 800/447-1483, tel./fax 707/923-3001).

PARQUE NACIONAL VILLARRICA

Dominating the skyline south of Pucón, 2,847-meter Volcán Villarrica's glowing crater is a constant reminder that what Spanish conquistador poet Alonso de Ercilla called its "great neighbor volcano" could, at any moment, obliterate the town in a cataclysm of volcanic bombs, a cloud of ash, or beneath a mudflow triggered by lava and melting snow. Closely monitored and occasionally closed to climbers, its summit remains one of the area's most popular excursions.

More than just the volcano, Parque Nacional Villarrica comprises 63,000 hectares of mostly forested Andean cordillera that stretches from Pucón to the 3,746-meter summit of Volcán Lanín, most of which lies within Argentina's Parque Nacional Lanín (intending climbers must cross the border to the Argentine side).

Geography and Climate

Immediately south of Pucón, the park ranges from 600 meters above sea level on the lower slopes to 3,746 meters at Volcán Lanín. Barren lava flows and volcanic ash cover much of its surface, but unaffected areas are lushly forested. The other major summit is 2,360-meter Volcán Quetrupillán, halfway to the Argentine border; from Quetrupillán to the east, several alpine lakes are accessible by foot.

Summertime temperatures generally range from a minimum of about 9°C to a maximum of around 23°C, while wintertime lows average about 4°C. Most precipitation falls between March and August, when Pacific storms can drop up to two meters of snow, but it can rain at any time of year. The park receives about 2,500–3,500 millimeters rainfall per annum.

entrance to Parque Nacional Villarrica

Flora and Fauna

At lower elevations, up to about 1,500 meters, mixed araucaria and *nothofagus* woodlands cover the slopes—the araucaria reaches the southern limit of its distribution at Volcán Quetrupillán. The *mañío (Podocarpus nubigena),* an ornamental in the Northern Hemisphere, also makes an appearance here. Native bunch grasses have colonized some volcanic areas.

Among the mammals are puma, *pudú,* foxes, and skunks, as well as the aquatic coypu. Waterfowl like coots and ducks inhabit the lakes and other watercourses, while large raptors like the black-shouldered kite and peregrine falcon are occasionally sighted in the skies.

Sights and Activities

Villarrica's accessibility from Pucón makes it a favorite destination in both summer and winter.

Chile's most active volcano, **Volcán Villarrica** is a cauldron of bubbling lava and venting steam that's erupted dozens of times, including a major 1971 event that expelled 30 million cubic meters of lava in a flow that stretched for 14 kilometers.

A strenuous but nontechnical climb, Villarrica requires crampons, an ice ax, rain and wind gear, high-energy snacks, and a guide—except for those who manage to wrangle one of the few individual private permits from Conaf. For those who contract a tour with one of Pucón's adventure travel agencies, it involves a crash course in mountaineering; in good weather, the summit's about six hours from the ski area, but bad weather sometimes forces groups to turn back. When the sulfurous crater is especially active, Conaf closes the route.

While the ascent can be a slog through wet snow, the descent involves body-sledding down the volcano's flanks with only an ice axe for braking. Rates for the trip are around US$30–40 per person, but can be more in peak season.

When winter snows cover the lower slopes, the **Centro de Ski Volcán Villarrica** operates four lifts with nine runs ranging from 500 to 1,500 meters in length. Lift tickets cost around US$26 per day in

© WAYNE BERNHARDSON

Volcán Villarrica from Parque Nacional Huerquehue

peak season, US$20 per day in the shoulder season; there are also three-day, one-week, and season passes. For more information, contact Pucón Ski (Holzapfel 190, tel. 045/441176, 045/441901, www.skipucon.cl) in the Gran Hotel Pucón.

About midway between Volcán Villarrica and **Volcán Quetrupillán,** a rough summer-only road crosses the park from Termas de Palguín to the hot-springs town of Coñaripe. Best suited to four-wheel-drive or at least high-clearance vehicles, though some daring (or foolhardy) Chileans attempt it with ordinary passenger cars, it passes through a scenic araucaria forest that includes the park's only campground.

From Volcán Villarrica's southern slopes, a series of hiking trails crosses the park to Termas de Palguín and continues to Puesco, where Buses Jac has a daily bus back to Pucón. For more detail on this hike, which has some hard-to-follow sections, see Tim Burford's *Chile and Argentina: The Bradt Trekking Guide* (Bradt, 2001) or Clem Lindenmayer's *Trekking in the Patagonian Andes* (Lonely Planet, 2003).

Accommodations and Food

In Sector Quetrupillán on the park's southern boundary, on the steep, narrow road between Termas de Palguín and Coñaripe, Conaf's **Camping Chinay** (US$8 for up to five persons) lies in the midst of an araucaria forest.

At the ski area, rebuilt after a fire in early 2001, the **Refugio Villarrica** serves cafeteria meals, but skiers stay in Pucón.

Information

On the road to the ski area, eight kilometers from Pucón, Conaf's **Guardería Rucapillán** is the best information source; rangers collect a US$2-per-person admission charge (US$.50 for children) here. There are also ranger stations at Sector Quetrupillán and Sector Puesco.

Getting There and Around

Transportation is limited except for organized tours. To Sector Rucapillán, only a few kilometers south of Pucón, taxis are the only non-tour option. Buses Jac has one bus daily from Pucón to Sector Puesco.

PARQUE NACIONAL HUERQUEHUE

Fast becoming one of the region's most popular parks, Huerquehue comprises 12,500 hectares of scenic Andean precordillera with alpine lakes, rushing rivers, and waterfalls set among dense native forest.

Geography and Climate

Huerquehue is 35 kilometers northeast of Pucón via the hamlet of Paillaco. Elevations range from about 720 meters above sea level near Lago Tinquilco to the 2,000-meter summit of Cerro Araucano, but glaciers and rivers have eroded deep canyons. It receives just over 2,000 millimeters of rainfall per annum, mostly between May and September, some falling as snow at higher elevations. While temperatures are generally mild, rain can fall at any time of year.

Flora and Fauna

On the park's lower slopes, the dominant forest species is the *coigue (Nothofagus dombeyi),* while *lenga (Nothofagus pumilio)* gives way gradually to araucaria at higher elevations. Birds, ranging from woodpeckers to thrushes, flit within the forest, while Andean condors sometimes soar among the ridgetops and summits.

Sights and Activities

Huerquehue is a hiker's park, with a good network of trails beginning at the north end of Lago Tinquilco. From here, the well-watered **Sendero Lago Verde** (Lago Verde Trail) zigzags from 700 meters altitude at the trailhead to 1,300 meters at its namesake lake. Light gaps in the *coigue* woodlands yield glimpses of Volcán Villarrica across the Liucura and Pucón valleys to the south, while the surrounding ridges sport araucaria forests.

From Lago Tinquilco, it's about two hours-plus of steady hiking to **Lago Chico,** where the terrain levels off; at a trail junction beyond Lago Chico, the left fork goes to **Lago Verde,** while the right fork goes to **Lago El Toro** and continues to Conaf's simple **Refugio Renahue,** where camping is also possible. From here an eastbound trail continues to **Termas de Río Blanco,** a thermal springs linked by gravel road to Cunco, Lago Colico, and Lago Caburgua's north end.

Accommodations and Food

On Lago Tinquilco's eastern shore, near the park gate, Conaf's wooded **Camping Tinquilco** (US$13 per site except in January and February, when it's US$16) can accommodate up to five persons on each of its 18 sites.

Just beyond the park entrance, near the Lago Verde trailhead, the rustically chic Canadian-Chilean **Refugio Tinquilco** (tel. 09/5392728; tel. 02/7777673, fax 02/7323079 in Santiago) charges US$9 for hostel-type bunks (with a US$2 surcharge for sheets, if necessary); it also has rooms with king-size beds for US$32 d with shared bath, US$40 d with private bath. Set on densely wooded grounds, it also has its own private beach, and offers meals to guests or nonguests: US$2–4 for breakfast, US$6 for lunch or dinner. More elaborate multicourse dinners with aperitifs and wine cost around US$14.

Information

At the Lago Tinquilco gate, Conaf's **Centro de Educación e Intepretación Ambiental** is open 10 A.M.–8 P.M. daily in summer. Rangers here collect a US$3.50-per-person admission fee (US$1 for children). Refugio Tinquilco is also a good source of information for hiking alternatives beyond the main Lago Verde route.

Getting There and Around

Thanks to increasing demand, **Buses Jac** now offers summer service from Pucón to Huerquehue (US$1.50) at 7:30 A.M. and 11:15 A.M., and 5:30 P.M. daily; the rest of the year, buses leave Pucón Monday, Wednesday, and Friday at 8:30 A.M. and 4 P.M., returning at 10 A.M. and 5 P.M.

Most Pucón adventure travel agencies also offer excursions to Huerquehue.

Los Lagos Region

OSORNO

More a crossroads than a destination in its own right, Osorno relies more on dairying, forestry, and manufacturing than tourism for its livelihood, but it's the gateway to destinations like Lago Puyehue, Parque Nacional Puyehue, and Argentina's Andean lake district. The city dates from 1558, but the Mapuche uprising of 1599 destroyed it and six other cities within five years, even resulting in the death of Spanish governor Oñez de Loyola.

Spanish authorities needed nearly two centuries to refound the city in 1793 with the construction of Fuerte Reina Luisa, a riverside fortification that helped keep out the Mapuche. It failed to flourish until the mid-19th century, as overland communications were too arduous and even hazardous to permit rapid growth of internal markets. This began to change with the arrival of German immigrants in the mid-19th century, and accelerated after the definitive "pacification" of the area south of the Biobío in the 1880s, followed by the arrival of the railroad in 1895 and its extension to Puerto Montt by 1911. Through most of the 20th century, it achieved steady growth.

Orientation

Osorno (population 132,245) is 913 kilometers south of Santiago and 109 kilometers north of Puerto Montt via the Panamericana. Also an east-west crossroads, it's 126 kilometers from the Argentine border at Paso Cardenal Samoré via paved Ruta 215.

Central Osorno, about two kilometers west of the Panamericana, has a slightly irregular grid bordered by the Río Damas to the north, Calles Angulo and Eduvijes to the east, Manuel Rodríguez to the south, and the Río Rahue to the west.

Sights

Despite its colonial origins, Osorno has few really venerable sights—the so-called **Distrito Histórico** west of the Plaza de Armas includes mostly early-20th-century landmarks like the crumbling **Estación de Ferrocarril** (railroad station, 1912), the restored **Sociedad Molinera de Osorno,** a flour mill now occupied by a pasta factory, and many weathered private residences. A modest standout is the ramparts and towers of **Fuerte Reina Luisa** (1793)—all that remains of the erstwhile colonial fortress at the foot of Eleuterio Ramírez.

The de facto historic district, though, is on Juan Mackenna between Avenida Matta and Freire, where half a dozen pioneer houses are national monuments: the **Casa Mohr Pérez** (Mackenna 939), the **Casa Enrique Schüller** (Mackenna 1011), the **Casa Sürber** (Mackenna 1027), the **Casa Germán Stückrath** (Mackenna 1047), the **Casa Federico Stückrath** (Mackenna 1069), and the **Casa Conrado Stückrath** (Mackenna 1095).

The **Museo Histórico Municipal** (Avenida Matta 809, tel. 064/238615) exhibits diverse materials ranging from Paleo-Indian archaeology and Mapuche culture to Osorno's colonial founding, its destruction at the hands of the Mapuche and subsequent refounding, the 19th century city and immigration, and naval hero Eleuterio Ramírez. There are also a natural-history room and a new child-oriented interactive basement display.

Occupying the former Schilling Buschmann residence (1929), a handsome neocolonial building, the municipal historical museum is open 9 A.M.–5 P.M. weekdays all year and 3–6 P.M. Saturday except in summer, when weekend hours are 11 A.M.–7 P.M. Admission is free.

Shopping

Detalles Hecho a Mano (Mackenna 1100, tel. 064/238462) sells regional crafts. **Plazuela Yungay** (Prat and Ramírez) has an outdoor artisans' market. There are also crafts outlets at the **Mercado Municipal** (Errázuriz 1300).

Entertainment

Osorno ain't Santiago or even Pucón, but it doesn't completely lack cultural activities or things to do at night.

Show Time (Ramírez 650, tel. 064/233890) is a two-screen movie theater.

Osorno has an improving bar scene at spots like **La Pinte** (Freire 677, tel. 064/235944). **Mario's Discotheque** (Mackenna 555, tel. 064/234978) is for dancing.

The municipal **Centro Cultural** (Avenida Matta 556, tel. 064/238898) hosts theater and music events, along with rotating art exhibits. Hours are 8:30 A.M.–1:45 P.M. and 4–5:15 P.M. daily.

Accommodations

Osorno has good alternatives in all categories, though the cheapest places are only so-so.

Under US$10

Open January–mid-March only, the improved municipal **Camping Olegario Mohr** (tel. 064/204860, US$10 per tent) occupies wooded grounds on the banks of the Río Damas just across the Panamericana. In addition to grassy sites with picnic tables, fire pits, clean toilets, and hot showers, it now has swimming pools for adults and children, and tennis courts. Eastbound buses and taxi *colectivos* on Avenida Buschmann pass within a couple hundred meters of the site.

US$10–25

East of the bus terminal, **Hospedaje Sánchez** (Los Carrera 1595, tel./fax 064/232560, crisxi@telsur.cl, US$8.50 pp) is modest but acceptable.

Two blocks east of the Plaza, you'll find shingled **Residencial Schulz** (Freire 530, tel. 045/237211, fax 045/246266, US$16/25 s/d), where standard rates include private bath. It also has some slightly cheaper rooms with shared bath.

US$25–50

Under the same ownership, **Hostal Bilbao Express** (Bilbao 1019, tel./fax 064/262200, US$17/26 s/d) and the **Hostal Bilbao** (Juan Mackenna 1205, tel./fax 064/264444, US$24/34 s/d) are outstanding in their range.

Four blocks south of the terminal, **Hotel Villa Eduviges** (Eduviges 856, tel./fax 064/235023, www.hoteleduviges.cl, US$23/35 s/d) has rooms with private bath and breakfast in a charming older building. Rates at **Hostal Rucaitué** (Freire 546, tel. 064/239922, fax 064/236344, hrucaitue@surnet.cl, US$25/43 s/d) include breakfast, TV, and private bath.

Hotel Pumalal (Bulnes 630, tel./fax 064/242477, pumalal@entelchile.net, US$29/43 s/d) is a recent addition to the hotel scene.

Since its original 1930 incarnation as the Hotel Burnier, the 65-room **Gran Hotel Osorno** (O'Higgins 615, tel. 045/232171, fax 045/239311, granhotelosorno@entelchile.net, US$33/49 s/d) has traditionally been among the town's best. Though well past its peak, the Deco landmark is still good value, with standard amenities like private bath, telephone, and cable TV.

US$50–100

Hotel Waeger (Cochrane 816, tel. 064/233721, fax 064/237080, hotelwaeger@telsur.cl, US$45/65) is a classic German-style regional hotel. **Hotel Lagos del Sur** (O'Higgins 564, tel. 064/245222, fax 064/243696, www.hotelagosdelsur.cl, US$54/68 s/d) is a nearly new hotel with handsomely decorated rooms.

The contemporary, immaculate **Hotel García Hurtado de Mendoza** (Mackenna 1040, tel. 064/237111, fax 064/237115, www.hotelgarciahurtado.cl, US$66/86) is one of the city's best.

Food

For real budget meals, nothing's better than the choice seafood at the numerous *comedores* in the **Mercado Municipal** (Prat and Errázuriz)—avoid the *fried* fish, though. It's also a good place to purchase fresh produce and groceries, as is the **Supermercado Las Brisas** (Mackenna 1150), whose **Kaffeestube** (tel. 064/230262) serves inexpensive sandwiches and lunches.

Upstairs from its namesake bakery, **Pastelería Rhenania** (Ramírez 977, tel. 064/235457) serves sandwiches and pastries, with separate tobacco-free seating. **Dino's** (Ramírez 898, tel. 064/233880) also specializes in sandwiches and light meals, along with its franchise rival **Bavaria** (O'Higgins 743, tel. 064/231302). **Bocatto** (Ramírez 938, tel. 064/238000) has similar offerings but also pizza and Osorno's best ice cream.

The **Club Alemán,** also known as the **Deutscher Verein** (O'Higgins 563, tel. 064/232784), reflects the German community's significance more in name than in menu, which is fairly standard Chilean. The **Club de Artesanos** (Juan Mackenna 634, tel. 064/230307) is a labor-union restaurant with a good Chilean menu.

Chung Hwa (Matta 517, tel. 064/233445) serves Cantonese food, while **Del Piero** (Manuel Rodríguez 1081, tel. 064/256767) works at pizza and pasta.

Information

Sernatur (O'Higgins 667, tel. 064/237575, fax 064/234104, infosorno@sernatur.cl) occupies an office on the ground floor of the Edificio Gobernación Provincial, on the west side of the Plaza de Armas. Hours are 8:30 A.M.–7 P.M. weekdays in summer, when it normally has English-speaking staff; the rest of the year hours are 8:30 A.M.–1 P.M. and 2:30–5:30 P.M. daily except for Friday, when afternoon hours are 2–4:30 P.M. Sernatur supports a private information office at the long-distance **Terminal de Buses** (Errázuriz 1400, tel. 064/234149).

At the northwest corner of the Plaza de Armas, the municipal **Departamento de Turismo**'s information kiosk is open mid-December–mid-March 10 A.M.–1:30 P.M. and 2:30–8 P.M. daily except Sunday, when hours are 10 A.M.–2 P.M. only.

For motorists, the **Automóvil Club de Chile (Acchi)** (tel. 064/540080) is at Manuel Bulnes 463.

For national-parks information, contact **Conaf** (Martínez de Rozas 430, tel. 064/234393).

Services

Exchange houses include **Turismo Frontera** (Ramírez 959, Local 11) and **Cambiotur** (Juan Mackenna 1004). **Banco de Chile** has an ATM at Juan Mackenna and Avenida Matta.

On the west side of the Plaza de Armas, **Correos de Chile** (O'Higgins 645) is the postal service.

Entel (Ramírez 1107) has long-distance and Internet service, but there are many others.

Lavandería Limpec (Arturo Prat 678, tel. 064/238966) offers prompt laundry service.

For medical services, contact Osorno's **Hospital Base** (Avenida Bühler 1765, tel. 064/230977); Avenida Bühler is the southward extension of Arturo Prat.

Getting There

Osorno has limited air connections, but it's a major ground-transportation hub for bus services along the Panamericana, throughout the region, and across the Andes to Argentina.

LAN (Ramírez 802, tel. 064/314900) flies at least daily to Santiago, usually via Temuco or Concepción.

The long-distance **Terminal de Buses** is at Avenida Errázuriz 1400, tel. 064/234149. Some but not all regional buses use the Mercado Municipal's **Terminal de Buses Rurales** (Errázuriz 1300, tel. 064/232073).

From the Terminal de Buses Rurales, two companies go to Puyehue and Aguas Calientes: **Buses Expreso Lago Puyehue** (tel. 064/243919) and **Buses Barría** (tel. 064/230628). From 7 A.M. to 9 P.M., there are departures about every half hour on a route that's also served by *taxi colectivos* across the street.

At the main terminal, **Transur** (tel. 064/234371) goes to the eastern Lago Llanquihue destination of Las Cascadas (US$2). **Buses Via Octay** (tel. 064/237043) goes frequently to the northern Lago Llanquihue town of Puerto Octay (US$1) and to the western lakeside village of Frutillar.

Many carriers connect Osorno with Panamericana destinations between Santiago in the north and Puerto Montt to the south. Sample destinations, fares, and times include Puerto Montt (US$2.50, 1.5 hours), Temuco (US$4.50, three hours), Ancud (US$5.50, 3.5 hours), and Santiago (US$15–18, 14 hours).

Services to Punta Arenas (US$60, 26–34 hours) and to Coyhaique (US$30) start in Puerto Montt and pick up passengers here. Note that buses to Chilean Patagonian destinations like Coyhaique and Punta Arenas use Paso Cardenal Samoré, east of Osorno, but carry through passengers only—Chilean domestic bus lines are not allowed to drop passengers within Argentina.

Most buses across the Andes to Bariloche (US$15, six hours) and other Argentine destinations also begin in Puerto Montt and use Paso Cardenal Samoré; see the Puerto Montt Transportation entry for more details.

Getting Around

Aeropuerto Carlos Hott Siebert (tel. 064/232529), alternatively known as Cañal Bajo, is seven kilometers east of Osorno via Avenida Buschmann. It's off the city bus routes, but cabs cost only about US$3.

Both the **Automóvil Club de Chile** (Bulnes 463, tel. 064/232269) and **Econorent** (Freire 848, tel. 064/235303) have rental cars.

TERMAS DE PUYEHUE

From modest beginnings in 1908, on sprawling wooded grounds near the border of Parque Nacional Puyehue, Termas de Puyehue has become one of Chile's most elegant hot-springs resorts. Housing up to 300 guests in 130 spacious rooms, its stately hotel features a thermal spa with huge swimming pool, offering massage, mud baths, algal treatments, and many other amenities, along with a sophisticated restaurant and bar, a small museum, a library, game rooms, and even an events hall that hosts classical music concerts. Since 1939, electricity has come from its own small hydroelectric plant.

Hotel Termas de Puyehue (Ruta 215 Km 76, tel. 02/2936000, fax 02/2831010, www.puyehue.cl, US$98–126 s, US$104–142 d) sits at the junction where the main highway continues toward Anticura and the Argentine border; a paved lateral heads to Aguas Calientes, a more modest hot springs, and the Antillanca sector of Parque Nacional Puyehue. Rates vary according to view and amenities; half-board is available for US$18 more per person, full board for US$34 more per person. Outside the peak summer season (January–mid-March), rates drop about 20–25 percent.

Termas de Puyehue also has offices in Osorno (Manuel Matta 1216, tel. 064/232881) and Santiago (Avenida Vitacura 2898, 2nd level, Las Condes, tel. 02/2342440, fax 02/3332370).

PARQUE NACIONAL PUYEHUE

Barely an hour from Osorno, accessible Puyehue still has plenty of untamed wilderness among its 106,772 hectares of Valdivian rain forest—at least where lava flows and ash from its volcanic vents and summits have not left it as barren as the Atacama desert. Statistically, it's one of Chile's most visited national parks, but statistics can deceive—the highly developed hot-springs resort at Aguas Calientes and its Antillanca ski area draw its mostly Chilean crowds.

Geography and Climate

Ranging from the lower Río Golgol valley, only about 250 meters above sea level, to the 2,240-meter summit of Volcán Puyehue, the park is about 80 kilometers east of Osorno and extends

© WAYNE BERNHARDSON

fumaroles on Volcán Puyehue, Parque Nacional Puyehue

all the way to the Argentine border. Volcán Casablanca (1,980 meters) is another major landmark, and the park has abundant creeks, rivers, and lakes that are ideal for fishing.

The annual rainfall, about 5,000 millimeters (much of it falling as snow at higher elevations), supports verdant *valdivian* forest. Temperatures are relatively mild at lower elevations, averaging about 14°C in summer and 5°C in winter, with highs near 25°C and lows around freezing.

Flora and Fauna

Puyehue's lush lower *valdivian* forest is a mixed woodland of species like *ulmo (Eucryphia cordifolia),* some specimens of which reach 40 meters or more in height, along with *olivillo (Aextoxicon punctatum), tineo (Weinmannia trichosperma), mañío (Podocarpus nubigena),* and *coigue (Nothofagus dombeyii).*

Beneath the dense canopy grow smaller trees like the myrtle relative *arrayán (Myrceugenella apiculata),* while the solid bamboo *quila (Chusquea quila)* forms impassable thickets in some areas; the endemic *chilco* (*Fuchsia magellanica,* firecracker fuchsia), along with intensely green ferns and mosses, provides spots of color. The striking *nalca (Gunnera chilensis)* sports umbrella-sized leaves at the end of edible stalks up to two meters in height.

At some higher elevations, though, lava flows and volcanic ash from Volcán Puyehue's 1960 eruption have left the landscape so barren that grasses and shrubs have only recently begun to colonize the area, despite substantial rainfall.

Pudú may inhabit the dense forest, but it's difficult to see them or other woodland and riverine species like foxes, otters, and coypu. Some 100 or so bird species flit from tree to tree, along with waterfowl like the *pato cortacorriente* (torrent duck, *Merganetta armata*) that fishes in the river rapids, and the condors that soar on the thermals overhead.

Sights and Activities

Puyehue consists of three distinct sectors: Aguas Calientes at its southwestern border, Antillanca at its southeastern border, and Anticura, mostly north of Ruta 215.

Aguas Calientes

From the Termas de Puyehue junction, a paved road leads four kilometers south to **Termas Aguas Calientes** (www.termasaguascalientes.com) where, for most visitors, the highlight is its namesake thermal baths, open to hotel guests, campers, and day-trippers alike. Rates are more affordable than Termas de Puyehue.

Several short nature trails and one longer hike start here. The 1,800-meter **Sendero El Pionero** switchbacks through dense Valdivian forest to a ridgetop with panoramic northern vistas of Lago Puyehue, the wooded Río Golgol valley, and the Volcán Puyehue's barren cone. Along its namesake river, the **Sendero Rápidos del Chanleufú** passes through 1,200 meters of gallery forest. The 11-kilometer **Sendero Lago Bertín** climbs steadily to a rustic lakeside *refugio* that may be closed, however, because of hantavirus concerns.

Antillanca

From Aguas Calientes, the road becomes a gravel surface that leads another 18 kilometers to the base of Volcán Casablanca, where Antillanca is a popular hotel and ski resort between early June and late October; in summer it's open for hikers, mountain bikers, fishermen, and general recreationists even though there's no campground in the area. Pool access for nonguests costs US$4 per person, while mountain-bike rental costs US$9–15 per day.

Ranging from 1,050 meters at its base to 1,514 meters above sea level on Cerro Haique, the ski area itself has beginner, intermediate, and expert slopes. For more details, contact the Centro Turístico Deportivo Antillanca at the Club Andino Osorno (Casilla 765, O'Higgins 1073, Osorno, tel. 064/232297, fax 064/238877, www.skiantillanca.com); see also the listing for Accommodations and Food, below.

Anticura

From Termas de Puyehue, Ruta 215 heads northeast up the Río Golgol valley for 17 kilometers to Anticura, before continuing to Chilean customs at Pajaritos and on to the international border. At Anticura, there is camping and access to several short trails and some longer ones.

The 950-meter **Sendero Educativo Salto del Indio** is a signed nature trail leading to a waterfall on the Río Golgol; it takes its name from a local legend that a fugitive Mapuche hid to avoid forced labor in a colonial gold mine. An overnight excursion up the Río Anticura valley leads to **Pampa Frutilla.** Areas east of Pajaritos, the Chilean border post, require Conaf permission to hike or otherwise explore.

From El Caulle, two kilometers west of Anticura, a 16-kilometer trail climbs steeply to the flanks of **Volcán Puyehue,** where Conaf has a well-kept *refugio.* You can camp here, or continue through a barren volcanic landscape of fumaroles and lava flows to rustic thermal pools where it's also possible to camp. Note that a private inholder at El Caulle may demand a "toll" for the right to pass through his property en route. It is possible to continue hiking to Riñinahue, at the south end of Lago Ranco, rather than return to El Caulle.

Volcán Puyehue itself is a flat-topped Holocene caldera, measuring 2.4 kilometers in diameter; it sits within a larger caldera measuring five kilometers across. The most recent eruptions have come not from the summit caldera, but from vents on its western, southern, and eastern flanks, and a small cone on the southern flank.

Accommodations and Food

Some visitors to the area stay at Termas de Puyehue (see separate entry above), but accommodations within the park range from campgrounds to *cabañas* to hotels.

Aguas Calientes: Termas Aguas Calientes (tel. 064/236988 in Osorno) operates two campgrounds: the 36-site **Camping Chanleufú** (US$23 for up to four persons) and the 20-site **Camping Los Derrumbes** (US$13 for up to four persons). At the former, fees include access to the baths, but at the latter they do not.

Accommodations at **Cabañas Aguas Calientes** (tel. 064/374533, fax 064/374529, US$112–123 for up to four persons) include access to the baths. It also has a restaurant.

Antillanca: At the ski area, the 73-room **Hotel Antillanca** (Ruta 215, Km 98, tel. 064/235114, fax 064/235672, www.skiantillanca.com) has a contemporary sector and an older but more-than-acceptable *refugio.* In the peak ski season, July–mid-August hotel rates reach US$85/120 s/d, while *refugio* rooms cost about US$60/80. In the shoulder ski season, prices drop by about 25 percent and, in summer, another 20 percent.

In Osorno, contact the Centro Turístico Deportivo Antillanca through the Club Andino Osorno (Casilla 765, O'Higgins 1073, tel. 064/232297, fax 064/238877).

Anticura: The **Fundación Raíces** (tel. 045/298255 in Temuco) operates the eight-site **Camping Catrué** (US$6.50 for two persons, US$10 for up to four), whose basic facilities include running water, picnic tables, fire pits, and pit toilets. It's also in charge of *cabañas* (US$40–83, depending on number of guests).

Information

At Antillanca, Conaf's **Centro de Información Ambiental** is open 9 A.M.–6 P.M. daily except in summer, when it's open until 8 P.M. In summer, there are daily slide talks in late afternoon; permanent exhibits focus on natural history (flora and fauna), and on geomorphological topics like volcanism. Conaf maintains a smaller information center at Anticura.

Because the park straddles an international highway, there is no admission charge.

Getting There and Around

Paved all the way to the Argentine border, Ruta 215 passes directly through the park. From Osorno's Mercado Municipal (Errázuriz 1300), both **buses** and ***taxi colectivos*** serve Termas de Puyehue and Aguas Calientes, with additional service to Anticura and the Chilean border post at Pajaritos; for details, see the Osorno Getting There entry.

In winter, the **Club Andino Osorno** (O'Higgins 1073, tel. 064/232297) shuttles between Osorno and the Antillanca ski area.

PUERTO OCTAY

From prosaic 19th-century beginnings as a port at Lago Llanquihue's north end, the idyllic Puerto Octay has become one of the region's most picturesque locales, enjoying magnificent views across the lake to Volcán Osorno. Local pleasure boats, though, have supplanted the steaming freighters that once connected Octay with Puerto Varas, and it's become a low-key destination for summer holidaymakers who arrive by paved road from Osorno, 50 kilometers to the northwest. The German immigrant presence is palpable in its architecture, food and the checkerboard landscape of dairy farms and woodlands, and in its apparent middle-class contentment.

Puerto Octay (population 3,403) also includes Península Centinela, a wooded spit protruding into the lake that's home to several hotels and campgrounds. From town, it's possible to travel Llanquihue's western shore to the resort village of Frutillar, or its eastern shore to Ensenada and Parque Nacional Vicente Pérez Rosales, via a road whose northern half is now paved.

Sights

Puerto Octay dates from 1852, but its architectural legacy of European-style neoclassical and chalet houses dates from the early 20th century. None of these is a recognized national monument, but at least a dozen private residences and other buildings contribute to its captivating ambiance.

One of those buildings is the **Casa de la Cultura Emilio Winkler** (Independencia 591), housing part of the **Museo El Colono,** a well-organized collection of maps, photographs, and other materials on early German colonization. The building is too small, though, to contain an assortment of antique farm equipment that spills out of a barn and onto the grounds of a separate facility at the point where the gravel road to Península Centinela splits off the paved road to Frutillar. It's open 9:30 A.M.–1 P.M. and 3–7 P.M. daily except Sunday, when hours are 11 A.M.–1 P.M. and 3–7 P.M. Mid-December–mid-March it's closed Monday. Admission costs US$1.

Puerto Octay Backpacker Zapato Amarillo

About two kilometers north of town on the Osorno road, the Swiss/Chilean-run Puerto Octay Backpacker Zapato Amarillo (tel./fax 064/391575, www.zapatoamarillo.8k.com, US$10–14 pp) has become a destination in its own right as much as a place to stay. Comfortably stylish hostel-type accommodations, on ample grounds, include kitchen facilities and breakfast. Prices fall slightly April–October.

In addition to accommodations, though, it offers initial shuttles from Puerto Octay, laundry service, information, Internet access, dinner (summer only, US$7 pp), rental bikes (US$8 per day), canoes (US$12 per day), a small sailboat (US$20 per day), and transfers to La Picada for a hike to Petrohué (US$8 pp). Spanish, German, and English are all spoken.

Accommodations

Downtown has camping and basic *hospedajes,* but Avenida Andrés Schmoelz leads south out of Puerto Octay proper for about two kilometers todead-end on Península Centinela, which has luxury lodgings but also some affordable alternatives. See also the entry for the outstanding Zapato Amarillo hostel, a short distance north of town, above.

Five hundred meters south of the Plaza de Armas, **Camping El Molino** (Costanera Pichi Juan 124, tel. 064/391375) has lakefront campsites for US$12 for up to five persons. At Península Centinela, the woodsier **Camping Centinela** (tel. 064/391276, US$10 per site) is more isolated.

In downtown Octay, try **Hospedaje Teuber** (German Wulf 712, tel. 064/391260, US$9 pp), **Hospedaje Barrientos** (Independencia 488, tel. 064/391381, US$9 pp), and **Hospedaje Costanera** (Pedro Montt 306, tel. 064/391329, US$10 pp). The peninsula's most affordable choice is **Hostería La Baja** (tel. 064/391269, US$10 pp, breakfast included).

At the end of the road, the peninsula's showpiece is the renovated and expanded **Hotel y Cabañas Centinela,** tel./fax 064/391326, www.hotelcentinela.cl, US$83–92 s or d with breakfast), a chalet-type structure which, in its 1930s heyday, hosted guests like the Prince of Wales. Separate *cabañas* start around US$82–106 pp, depending on the *cabaña* and number of guests. Off-season rates March–mid-December are about 15–20 percent lower; nonguests may also use the restaurant here.

Food

Puerto Octay has nothing really out of the ordinary—it's mostly Chilean standbys like **Restaurant Cabañas** (Pedro Montt 713, 064/391450) and **Baviera** (Germán Wulf 582, tel. 064/391460). The well-regarded *parrilla* **El Fogón de Anita** (tel. 064/391455) has moved to a location about one kilometer north of town on the Osorno highway. New on the scene is the **Puerto Muñoz Gamero** (Muñoz Gamero 107, tel. 064/391485).

The restaurant at **Hotel Centinela,** on the peninsula, is also open to the public.

Information

On the east side of the Plaza de Armas, the **Oficina Municipal de Turismo** (Esperanza 555, tel. 064/391491) is a small freestanding office alongside the Municipalidad. Hours are 9 A.M.–9 P.M. daily, December–February only.

Getting There

Puerto Octay has no proper bus terminal—buses and minibuses stop on German Wulf just south of the Plaza de Armas. **Via Octay** (tel. 064/230118) goes to Osorno's main bus terminal several times daily, while **Thaebus** goes half a dozen times daily to Puerto Montt via Frutillar and Puerto Varas. Four times daily, **Arriagada** goes south to Las Cascadas, roughly halfway to Ensenada.

FRUTILLAR

Perhaps the most self-consciously immaculate example of German colonization in the entire region, the western Lago Llanquihue village of Frutillar is almost a caricature of Teutonic orderliness—where a sign on the beach says "Deporte, Picnic y Camping Prohibido" (Sports, Picnicking and Camping Prohibited), it nearly feels as if it *should* say "Sport, Picknick und Camping Verboten."

Still, with its almost perfectly preserved European-style houses, Frutillar exudes both style and charm; for a *Dorf* of its size, it also has impressive cultural resources, including a fine museum and one of Chile's most important music festivals. Mirrored in the waters beyond Frutillar's sandy beaches, Volcán Osorno rises symmetrically to the east.

© WAYNE BERNHARDSON

water-driven mill, Museo Colonial Alemán de Frutillar

Orientation

Frutillar (population 9,118) is 63 kilometers south of Osorno and 50 kilometers north of Puerto Montt via the Panamericana. It comprises two separate sectors: The busy commercial zone of Frutillar Alto adjoins the Panamericana, while Avenida Carlos Richter leads to the waterside resort of Frutillar Bajo, pinched between the sandy lakeshore and a steeply rising hill, about two kilometers east. Avenida Philippi runs north-south along the lakeshore, linked to the parallel Vicente Pérez Rosales by a series of block-long streets; most services and other points of interest face the lake from the west side of Philippi.

Sights

Middle European–style architecture is Frutillar Bajo's trademark, in structures like the 1911 **Iglesia Luterana** (Lutheran church) at Philippi 1000, but handsome houses and other distinctive buildings face the entire lakefront.

The highlight, though, is the Universidad Austral's **Museo Colonial Alemán de Frutillar,** an indoor-outdoor facility set among immaculate gardens at the base of the hill. Antique farm machinery in mint condition adorns the grounds, while buildings like the **Molino** (a water-powered mill), the **Casa del Herrero** (a working smithery), the **Campanario** (a storage structure with a conical roof supported by a central pillar), and the **Casa del Colono** (a large residence that houses collections of period furniture and household implements) are precise historical reconstructions.

Built partly with aid from the German Federal Republic, the Museo Colonial (Vicente Pérez Rosales s/n, tel. 065/421142) is at the west end of Arturo Prat, one short block from the lakeshore. It's open 10 A.M.–1 P.M. and 2–8 P.M. daily mid-December–mid-March; the rest of the year, hours are 10 A.M.–1 P.M. and 2–6 P.M. Admission costs about US$2.50 for adults, US$1 for children.

The museum shop sells souvenirs like horseshoes forged in the Casa del Herrero and woodcarvings of museum buildings.

Events

Frutillar's major annual event is the **Semanas Musicales de Frutillar** (www.semanasmusicales.cl), a 10-day extravaganza that has showcased classical, jazz, and ethnic music since 1968. In late January and early February, events take place both during the daytime and at night, when performances are both more formal and more expensive. Many events take place at the **Teatro del Lago,** built on the site of the former Hotel Casona del Lago (destroyed by fire), on lakeshore landfill between Antonio Varas and Manuel Rodríguez; the series also includes concerts in other regional cities like Osorno and Puerto Montt.

The next most important event is November's **Semana Frutillarina,** celebrating its founding as a lakeport in 1856.

Accommodations

Frutillar's accommodations scene is strong at the mid- to upscale range, but real budget alternatives are relatively few; during the annual music festival, prices can spike even higher than regular summer rates. All the listings below are in Frutillar Bajo, though there are a handful of cheaper *residenciales* in Frutillar Alto.

The otherwise upscale **Hostería Winkler** (Philippi 1155, tel. 065/421388, US$10 pp) is also the Hostelling International affiliate, so good budget accommodations are available. Open in summer only, the simple **Residencial Bruni** (Las Piedras 60, tel. 065/421309, US$12 pp) is two blocks inland from the lake.

Also notable for its restaurant, **Hospedaje Trayén** (Philippi 963, tel. 065/421346, US$20 pp) has rooms with private bath and cable TV. In addition to hostelling accommodations, **Hostería Winkler** (Philippi 1155, tel. 065/421388, US$25 pp) has rooms with private bath and breakfast.

With only eight rooms, occupying a historic house dating from 1911, **Hotel Klein Salzburg** (Philippi 663, tel. 065/421201, fax 065/421750, www.salzburg.cl, US$35/55 s/d) is more a B&B than a hotel, but it's a very fine one.

On a hillock with lovely flower gardens, **Hotel Frau Holle** (Antonio Varas 54, tel. 065/421345, frauholle@surnet.cl, US$33/57 s/d) embodies the best of Frutillar. Frutillar in general is pretty quiet, but it's even quieter at **Hotel Casona del 32** (Caupolicán 28, tel./fax 065/421369, US$52/61 s/d), at the north end of town.

Hotel Residenz am See (Philippi 539, tel. 065/421539, fax 065/421858, US$33 pp) offers rooms with private bath and a European-style breakfast. Accommodations at the nearly new **Apart Hotel Badenhoff** (Vicente Pérez Rosales 673, tel. 065/421649, US$70 d) include kitchen facilities.

Renovated **Hotel Ayacara** (Philippi 1215, tel./fax 065/421550, www.hotelayacara.com, US$49–81 s, US$62–97 d) occupies a gabled century-old lakefront mansion; each of its eight rooms—the more expensive enjoy lake views—is distinctive.

Food

Along the lakefront, Frutillar has several ideal breakfast and *onces,* starting with the **Salón de Te Trayen** (Philippi 963, tel. 065/421346), but also including the **Andes Café** (Philippi 1057, tel. 09/2087691) and the **Bauernhaus** (Philippi 779, tel. 09/8222489), which serves consistently spectacular kuchen and other desserts.

For fixed-price meals around US$5, the best bet is the **Casino de Bomberos** (Philippi 1065, tel. 065/421588). The traditional **Club Alemán** (San Martín 22, tel. 065/421249) is more formal and more expensive, but not unreasonable. **Parrilla Don Carlos** (Balmaceda and Philippi, tel. 065/421709) serves Argentine-style beef.

Decorated in a whimsical Hansel/Gretel motif, with dolls on broomsticks hanging from the ceilings, **Selva Negra** (Antonio Varas 24, tel. 065/42116) offers fine food and exceptionally attentive service, with entrées in the US$6–8 range. Occasionally the owner even circulates among the diners.

In summer, look along the lakeshore for stands with fresh raspberries, raspberry jam, and raspberry kuchen, all area specialties.

Information

The municipal **Oficina de Información Turística** (Avenida Philippi s/n, between San Martín and O'Higgins, tel. 065/421198) occupies a small kiosk. December–March, it's open 10 A.M.–9 P.M. daily; hours are erratic the rest of the year.

Services

Frutillar has no exchange houses, but **Banco Santander** (Philippi 555) has an ATM.

Correos de Chile (Pérez Rosales and San Martín) delivers the mail.

For long-distance phone calls, there's a **Centro de Llamados** (Avenida Philippi and Manuel Rodríguez) in Frutillar Bajo. **Cyber Café Tacitas** (Arturo Prat and Philippi) provides Internet access and also rents bicycles.

Lavandería Frutillar (Carlos Richter 335, tel. 065/421555) in Frutillar Alto washes clothes.

For medical services, contact the **Hospital de Frutillar** (Las Piedras s/n, tel. 065/421386).

Getting There and Around

Bus services arrive and leave from Frutillar Alto; *taxi colectivos* shuttle back and forth to Frutillar Bajo. The two major long-distance carriers are **Tur-Bus** (Diego Portales 150, tel. 065/421390) and **Cruz del Sur** (Alessandri 360, tel. 065/421552); both run north (Santiago and intermediates) and south (to Puerto Montt) along the Panamericana. **Thaebus,** at the Alessandri terminal, runs half a dozen buses daily to Puerto Octay.

PUERTO VARAS

North of Puerto Montt, picturesque Puerto Varas appeals to conventional tourists who loll on Lago Llanquihue's beaches, admire its century-old mansions, sup in some of Chile's best restaurants, and follow the bus-boat crossing to the famous Argentine resort of Bariloche via Lago Todos los Santos. Increasing numbers of more adventurous visitors, though, also appreciate its access to the Río Petrohué's whitewater rafting, Volcán Osorno's snow-clad slopes, Cochamó's wild backcountry, and other outdoor attractions. To the southeast, beyond Cochamó, a new bridge over the Río Puelo also provides an alternate route to Hornopirén and the Carretera Austral.

Varas's architectural heritage, stemming from its German colonization as a 19th-century lake port, lends it its character. While a recent building boom has resulted in nondescript housing developments on the outskirts, it's also brought more stylish infill downtown; many visitors prefer Varas to nearby Puerto Montt, and not just as a base for excursions.

Orientation

At the southwestern shore of Lago Llanquihue, Puerto Varas (population 24,309) is 996 kilometers south of Santiago, 20 kilometers north of Puerto Montt, and a short distance east of Ruta 5, the Panamericana. The boundaries of its compact central grid are the lakeshore to the east, Diego Portales to the north, San Bernardo to the west, and Del Salvador to the south. On all sides except the shoreline, hills rise steeply toward quiet residential neighborhoods that include many places to stay.

From the corner of Del Salvador, the Costanera becomes paved Ruta 225 to the village of Ensenada, the lakeport of Petrohué on Lago Todos los Santos in Parque Nacional Vicente Pérez Rosales, and toward the Cochamó backcountry.

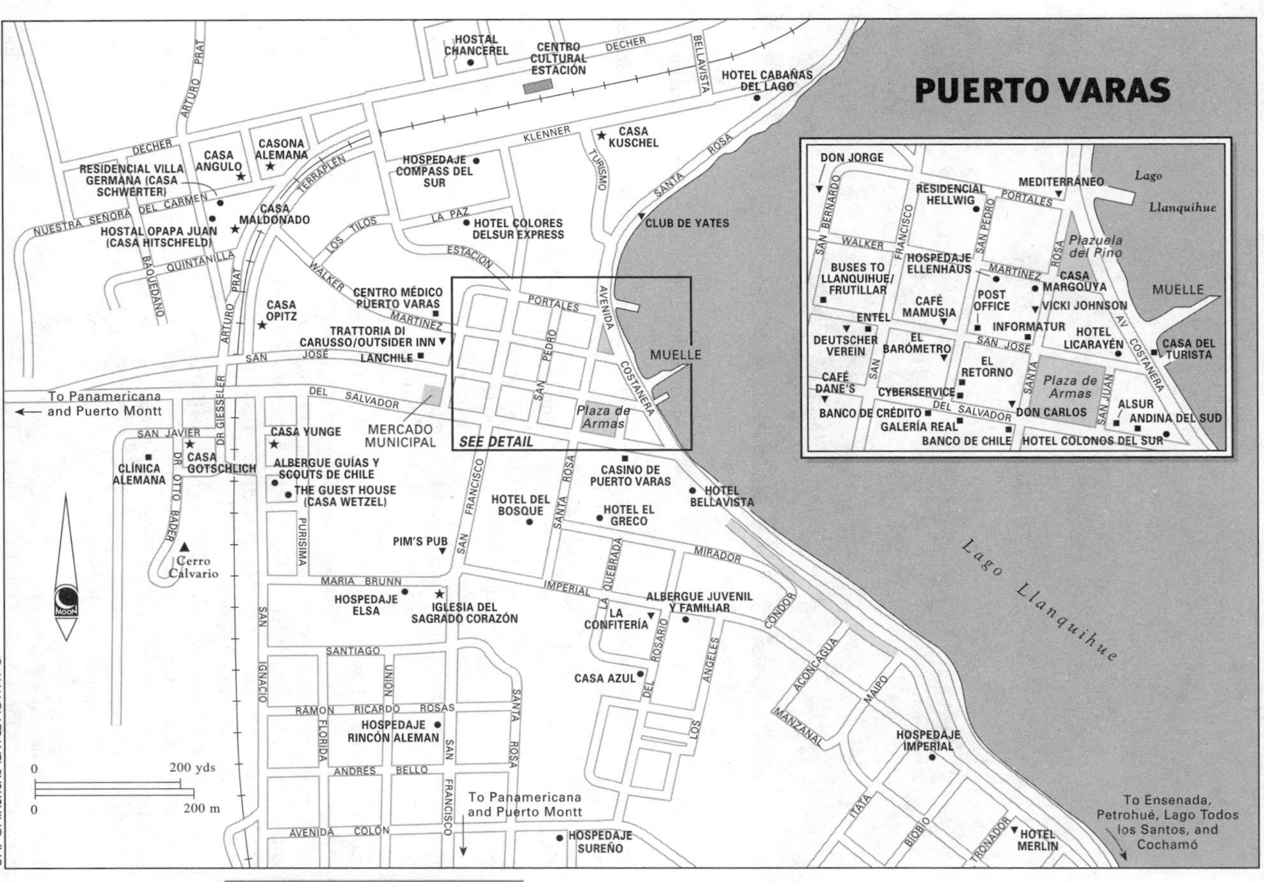

The Sur Chico

Lago Llanquihue and Volcán Osorno, from Puerto Varas

Sights

Other than the lake and its inspiring views toward Volcán Osorno, Varas's main attraction is its Germanic colonial architecture. The most imposing single structure is the **Iglesia del Sagrado Corazón** (1915), a national monument whose steeple soars above the town from the corner of San Francisco and María Brunn.

Numerous private residences are national monuments; they and many others appear in a map brochure entitled *Paseo Patrimonial;* despite repeated assurances, there have been no reprints, but it's still worth asking about. The monuments, mostly in residential neighborhoods northwest and west of downtown, include the **Casa Kuschel** (1910) at Klenner 299, the **Casona Alemana** (1914) at Nuestra Señora del Carmen 788, **Casa Maldonado** (1915) at Quintanilla 852, **Casa Angulo** (1910) at Miraflores 96, **Casa Opitz** (1913) at Terraplén 861, **Casa Gotschlich** (1932) at Dr. Otto Bader 701-05, and **Casa Yunge** (1932) at San Ignacio 711. A couple impressive non-monuments are *hospedajes:* the **Casa Schwerter** (1941–1942) at Nuestra Señora del Carmen 873, and the **Casa Hitschfeld** (1930) at Arturo Prat 107.

For some years after the Santiago-Puerto Montt railroad closed, the former **Estación del Ferrocarril** (Klenner s/n) sat empty, but it's been recently revamped into the Centro Cultural Estación, a gallery and events center.

Entertainment and Events

Puerto Varas has less nightlife than might be expected in a town that gets so much tourist traffic. It has filled what was, until recently, an unsightly vacant lot with the pharaonically ugly **Casino de Puerto Varas** (Del Salvador 21, tel. 065/346600).

Commemorating the city's founding in 1854, the **Aniversario de Puerto Varas** lasts two weeks in late January and early February. Soon thereafter, painters from around the country display their work at the **Concurso de Pintura El Color del Sur.**

Shopping

On the **Plazuela del Pino,** a triangular plaza bounded by the lakefront, Santa Rosa, and Walker Martínez, various *carretas* (carts) offer local crafts and food items.

Accommodations

Puerto Varas has abundant accommodations, some of them very distinctive, in all categories.

© WAYNE BERNHARDSON

Iglesia del Sagrado Corazón, Puerto Varas

Some of the cheapest ones are seasonal, but there are always good options.

Under US$10

In January and February, two makeshift hostels accommodate student backpackers: the **Albergue Juvenil y Familiar** (Rosario and Imperial, US$5), in the Liceo Pedro Aguirre Cerda secondary school, and the **Albergue Guías y Scouts de Chile** (San Ignacio 879, tel. 065/232774, US$5 pp). Both offer hot showers and kitchen privileges.

US$10–25

Puerto Varas has several decent places in the U$10-per-person range with shared bath and breakfast, such as cozy **Residencial Hellwig** (San Pedro 210, tel. 065/232472, US$8 pp), **Hospedaje Sureño** (Colón 179, tel. 065/232648, US$8 pp with shared bath, US$25 d with private bath), and **Hospedaje Elsa** (María Brun 427, tel. 065/232803, US$8 pp with shared bath, US$25 d with private bath). All the rooms at **Hospedaje Imperial** (Mirador 0653, tel. 065/232451, fax 065/232749, US$8 pp, US$23 d) have private baths.

Replacing the backpacker standby Colores del Sur, **Casa Margouya** (Santa Rosa 318, tel. 065/511648, www.margouya.com, US$11–13 pp, US$22 d) can lodge up to 17 guests in a variety of singles, doubles, and dorms, which share two bathrooms. Rates include breakfast, free tea and coffee, and free Internet access, with Spanish, English, and French spoken.

US$25–50

Open in January and February only, all rooms at **Hospedaje Rincón Alemán** (San Francisco 1004, tel. 065/232087, lquilaqueo@surnet.cl, US$27 d) come with private bath and breakfast.

Easy walking distance from downtown, but in a quiet barrio opposite the old railway station, **Hospedaje Compass del Sur** (Klenner 467, tel. 065/232044, 09/7186197, www.compassdelsur.cl, US$17/28 s/d) occupies a German colonial–style house with large rooms and kitchen privileges; breakfast, with muesli and real coffee (not Nescafé), costs US$2 extra. Moderately priced laundry service is also available.

Downtown's highly regarded **Hospedaje Ellenhaus** (Walker Martínez 239, tel. 065/233577, ellenhaus@yahoo.com, US$11/20 s/d with shared bath, US$30 d with private bath) is a step above the other budget places.

In a quiet hilltop neighborhood about 15 minutes from the Plaza de Armas, German-run **Casa Azul** (Manzanal 66, tel. 065/232904, www.casaazul.net, US$15/22 s/d with shared bath, US$31 d with private bath) has become a travelers' favorite for its rustically stylish and comfortable rooms. Kitchen access is included, but the huge breakfast of fresh fruit and homemade bread costs US$4 extra. Dog people will enjoy the enormous, almost intimidatingly friendly brindle Brazilian fila named Butch.

Residencial Villa Germania (Nuestra Señora del Carmen 873, tel. 065/233162, US$35 d with private bath and breakfast) occupies the landmark Casa Schwerter, a national monument. Perched on a hilltop overlooking downtown, **Hotel del Bosque** (Santa Rosa 710, tel.

065/232897, fax 065/233085, www.travelsur.com, US$30/40 s/d with private bath and breakfast) enjoys exceptional views of Lago Llanquihue and the surrounding mountains.

Though it's recently changed hands, the **Outsider Inn** (San Bernardo 318, tel./fax 065/232910, outsider@telsur.cl, US$31/47 s/d) has provided some of Varas's best value for money over the past several years. There's no reason to think this nearly pristine place won't continue to do so.

The brown shingle Casa Hitschfeld, another national monument, is home to **Hostal Opapa Juan** (Arturo Prat 107, tel. 065/232234, www.opapajuan.cl, US$20 pp with private bath and breakfast). Nearby, though it may look remote on the map, **Hostal Chancerel** (Decher 400, tel./fax 065/234221, www.turismochancerel.cl, US$31/49 s/d) is still less than a 15-minute walk from the Plaza de Armas. Rates include spacious rooms with private bath, breakfast, cable TV, and central heating. Other meals and German-style *onces* are also available.

One of Varas's most distinctive accommodations, its natural wood walls enhanced with work by regional artists, the boutique-style **Hotel El Greco** (Mirador 134, tel. 065/233880, fax 065/233388, www.hotelelgreco.com, US$46/50 s/d) is a recycled German-style building with a dozen impeccable, moderately sized rooms.

US$50–100

Restored to its pioneer style, **The Guest House** (O'Higgins 608, tel. 065/231521, www.vicki-johnson.com, US$40/60 s/d) occupies the German-colonial Casa Wetzel, a national monument. With stylishly furnished rooms and ample, well-lighted common spaces, it's Varas's most intimate accommodations.

Directly on the Costanera, **Hotel Licarayén** (San José 114, tel. 065/232305, fax 065/232955, info@hotelicarayen.cl, US$45/65 s/d) hasn't quite kept up with competitors in its price range, but does offer amenities like a sauna and gym.

Under the same management as the more central Hotel Colonos del Sur but in quieter surroundings, **Hotel Colonos del Sur Express** (tel./fax 065/233394, www.colonosdelsur.com, US$70/75 s/d) has more personality than its downtown sibling, with truly grand views from some rooms; rates include breakfast and access to the sauna at Colonos del Sur.

On the lakeshore just south of the casino, the 38-room **Hotel Bellavista** (Vicente Pérez Rosales 60, tel. 065/232011, fax 065/232013, www.hotelbellavista.cl, US$60/70 s/d) has outstanding lake views but fewer amenities than some other places in its category. It's substantially cheaper off-season.

US$100–150

On the lakeshore, the contemporary **Hotel Colonos del Sur** (Del Salvador 24, tel. 065/233309, fax 065/233394, www.colonosdelsur.com, US100/110 s/d with breakfast) is a luxury lodging with a restaurant and bar, café, heated pool, and sauna.

Stretching impressively above the lakeshore, the hillside **Hotel Cabañas del Lago** (Klenner 195, tel. 065/232291, fax 065/232707, calago@entelchile.net, US$107/114 s/d with breakfast) has equally impressive views and a heated pool.

Food

Puerto Varas has some of Chile's best restaurants, and even the run-of-the-mill places are pretty good. **Café Dane's** (Del Salvador 441, tel. 065/232371) wins no style prizes, but its breakfasts, *onces,* and Chilean specialties like *pastel de choclo* are more than a step above most places offering similar fare. **El Barómetro** (San Pedro 418, tel. 065/346100) is a popular meeting place with good sandwiches, desserts, and coffee. Though a bit out of the way, **La Confitería** (Del Rosario 1010, tel. 065/338188) merits a detour for its pastries and kuchen.

Café Mamusia (San José 316, tel. 065/233343) serves fine Chilean specialties, especially *pastel de choclo,* in the US$6–10 range, with a fixed-price *menu de casa* for US$6; the pisco sours are strong, but service is erratic. The very traditional **Deutscher Verein** (German Club, San José 415, tel. 065/232246) offers fixed-price midday meals.

In the Mercado Municipal, **Donde El Gordito** (San Bernardo 560, Local 7, tel. 065/233425) is a modest seafood venue that's good value for the price. **Don Jorge** (San Bernardo 240, tel. 09/6559759) is a no-frills locale specializing in beef and Chilean dishes. **Don Carlos** (Santa Rosa and Del Salvador) is a *parrilla* that's made good first impressions.

The lakeside **Mediterráneo** (Santa Rosa 68, tel. 065/237268) does a fine stir-fry with a variety of meats and has good fish dishes, mostly in the US$7 range. For fine summer afternoons and evenings, it has outdoor seating. Farther north along the lakefront, the **Club de Yates** (Santa Rosa 0161, tel. 065/232000) is Varas's newest upscale seafood option.

Trattoria Di Carusso (San Bernardo 318, tel. 065/233478) makes tremendous pizza (the crust is especially notable) and seafood. The best pizza choice, though, is moderately priced **El Retorno** (San Pedro 465, tel. 065/346441). **Pim's Pub** (San Francisco 712, tel. 065/233998) is a popular meeting place and restaurant, serving Tex-Mex food like fajitas, and margaritas for aperitifs.

On the lakefront southeast of downtown, **Color Café** (Los Colonos 1005, tel. 065/234311) is a friendly wine bar, with an appealing natural wood interior; though a little pricey, pasta dishes like ravioli are excellent.

Widely acknowledged as one of Chile's finest restaurants, relocated **Hotel Merlín** (Imperial 0605, tel. 065/233105, www.merlinrestaurant.com) counts the country's rich and famous among its clientele, but even shoestring travelers should consider a splurge here—prices are not *that* outrageous, though almost everyone spends upwards of US$20 per person. German celebrity chef Richard Knobloch has adapted fresh local and regional ingredients, particularly seafood and fresh fruit, into a hybrid international cuisine. Its new quarters, including an attractive bar with a separate menu, are a charmer, and imaginative items like the salad of strawberries on fresh lettuce and the double mousse (white and dark chocolate, garnished with garden-fresh berries) are worth every peso. There's also an exceptional wine list. Despite the name, this surprisingly unpretentious place has no accommodations.

Along with Merlín, **Ibis** (Vicente Pérez Rosales 1117, tel. 065/232017, www.ibisrestaurant.com) is one of southern Chile's finest dining experiences, with prices to match. Appetizers cost around US$6, most entrées are in the US$10-and-up range, and desserts are from US$3–4. With drinks and side orders, it's easy to spend more than US$30 per person. Still, again along with Merlín, it's one of the best splurges outside of Santiago for mid-sized portions of items like *corvina al cheff,* with shrimp, scallop, and crab sauce; they're also one of few Chilean restaurants to offer *criadillas*—often known as Rocky Mountain oysters in North America. On the down side, they really don't *need* Elton John and the Doobie Brothers.

© WAYNE BERNHARDSON

tourist pier on Lago Llanquihue, Puerto Varas

For chocoholics, **Vicki Johnson** (Santa Rosa 318, tel. 065/232240) prepares an awesome variety of takeaway truffles.

Information

At the foot of the pier on the Avenida Costanera, Puerto Varas's **Casa del Turista** (Piedraplén s/n, tel. 065/237956, corporacion@puertovaras.org) is open 9 A.M.–9 P.M. daily in summer; the rest of the year, hours are 9 A.M.–2 P.M. and 3–6 P.M. In addition to its regular staff, it has a computerized "Turismático" station to peruse the area's attractions and services. There is an incomplete private website, www.puertovarasvirtual.com.

Informatur (San José and Santa Rosa, tel. 065/338542, www.informatur.com), sponsored by an alliance of various service operators, keeps a selective database of accommodations.

Services

TravelSur (San Pedro 451, tel./fax 065/236000) is a general travel agency that also changes money. **Banco de Chile** has an ATM at Del Salvador 201, **Banco de Crédito** at Del Salvador 305.

Correos de Chile (San José 242) is the post office.

Entel (San José 413) provides long-distance telephone service. **Cyberservice** (Del Salvador 264, Local 6, tel. 065/237911) offers quick Internet access.

Lavandería Alba (Walker Martínez 511, tel. 065/232908) washes the clothes.

The **Clínica Alemana** (Dr. Otto Bader 810, tel. 065/232336) sits atop Cerro Calvario in southwestern Puerto Varas. The **Centro Médico Puerto Varas** (tel. 065/232792) is at Walker Martínez 576.

Getting There

Puerto Varas is close enough to the area's principal airport (at Puerto Montt), has good regional and long-distance bus connections, and is also on the popular bus-boat route to Argentina.

LAN/LanExpress (Avenida Gramado 560, tel. 065/234799) flies out of Puerto Montt; see the Puerto Montt entry for details.

Rather than a central terminal, both regional and long-distance **bus** companies use their own (sometimes shared) offices within a couple blocks of the Plaza de Armas. Some long-distance carriers from Puerto Montt pick up northbound passengers here; some regional carriers have no fixed offices but pick up and drop off passengers en route through the city.

Santiago carriers **Pullman Bus** (Walker Martínez 317, tel. 065/341140), **Pullman Sur,** and **Cruz del Sur** (Walker Martinez 239-B, tel. 065/231925; terminal at San Francisco 1317, tel. 065/236969) share offices with **Buses Norte Internacional,** which goes daily to San Carlos de Bariloche, Argentina (US$15). **Buses JAC** and **Cóndor Bus** (both at Walker Martínez 227, tel. 065/237255) also go to Santiago.

Other northbound carriers to Santiago (US$15–20, 12 hours) and intermediates include **Intersur** and **Tur-Bus** (both at San Pedro 210, tel. 065/233787) and **Tas Choapa** (Walker Martínez 230, tel. 065/233831). Santiago fares can even be a little higher, depending on the service level; the most expensive are nighttime buses with reclining seats.

Puerto Montt–based **Thaebus** shuttles frequently to Puerto Varas, stopping at the corner of San Bernardo and Walker Martínez. It also goes at 9 A.M. and 2:30 P.M. daily to Petrohué, on Lago Todos los Santos (US$2.50), returning at 11 A.M. and 5 P.M. **Expresos Puerto Varas** (tel. 065/232253) also goes frequently to Puerto Montt; it is commonly known as "Mitsubishi" for its minibus fleet.

From a stop outside the Galería Real (Del Salvador 257), **Buses J.M.** (tel. 09/6471716) goes to Ensenada and Petrohué up to five times daily in summer, but only twice the rest of the year. November–February, **Buses Interlagos** (tel. 065/257015) goes to Ensenada and Petrohué every 20 minutes or so; otherwise, services range from one or two per day in winter to hourly or so as the summer approaches.

Buses Fierro (tel. 065/253022) goes from Puerto Montt (US$3) to Cochamó at 8:15 A.M., 12:30 P.M., and 5 P.M. weekdays, 8:15 A.M., 12:30 P.M., and 4 P.M. Saturday, and 8:15 A.M. and 5 P.M. Sunday and holidays; Puerto Varas departures are about half an hour later. Occasionally, in summer, there are competing services; Fierro also has daily service to Ralún and Canutillar.

Puerto Varas is one of the intermediate points on the **bus-boat shuttle** from Puerto Montt to Bariloche (Argentina) via Lago Todos los Santos, so it's possible to purchase tickets and board the bus to Petrohué here. Most of the year, buses leave Puerto Montt at 8 A.M. daily for Petrohué, returning at 6 P.M.; from April–mid-

September, though, they run Wednesday–Sunday only, leaving Puerto Montt at 9 A.M. and returning at 5 P.M. The Puerto Montt operator **Andina del Sud** has an office here at Del Salvador 72, tel./fax 065/232811.

Getting Around

There are no regularly scheduled airport departures, but **ETM** (tel. 065/294294) will drop off or pick up passengers to and from Varas for US$12 for one person and only US$15 for up to four persons. Otherwise it's necessary to make the connection indirectly via Puerto Montt.

TravelSur (San Pedro 451, tel./fax 065/236000) arranges rental cars. **Campo Aventura** (San Bernardo 318, tel./fax 065/232910, www.campo-aventura.com) is the Avis representative.

VICINITY OF PUERTO VARAS

Puerto Varas is the gateway for sights like Volcán Osorno and Lago Todos los Santos, in Parque Nacional Vicente Pérez Rosales, and the backcountry of Cochamó. Varas is also the staging point for adventure activities like whitewater rafting, hiking, climbing, mountain biking, horseback riding, and fishing. Paved Ruta 225 follows the lakeshore east to Ensenada; at a fork two kilometers farther east, the main road goes northwest to Petrohué, while another paved route heads southeast to Ralún, Cochamó, and Puelo.

Among Varas's standard travel agencies are **Andina del Sud** (Del Salvador 72, tel./fax 065/232811, www.andinadelsud.com) and **TravelSur** (San Pedro 451, tel./fax 065/236000). Adventure travel operators include **Alsur** (Del Salvador 100, tel./fax 065/232300, www.alsurexpeditions.com), **Aqua Motion** (San Francisco 328, tel./fax 065/232747, www.aqua-motion.com); and **Tranco Expediciones** (San Pedro 422, tel. 065/311311, www.trancoexpediciones.cl).

Most of adventure-travel agencies rent mountain bikes and other outdoor-sports equipment. Just north of the pier, **Canoas Tour** (Avenida Costanera s/n, tel. 065/233587) rents kayaks for lake use, but **KoKayak** (San José 308, tel. 065/346433, www.paddlechile.com) organizes more ambitious kayak trips.

Ensenada

At Lago Llanquihue's east end, 45 kilometers from Puerto Varas, the shoreline village of Ensenada lies midway between the perfect cone of 2,660-meter Volcán Osorno, to the northeast, and the serrated caldera of 2,015-meter Volcán Chacabuco, to the southwest. Most services are on or near the junction with the northbound road to Las Cascadas and Puerto Octay.

Just north of the Las Cascadas junction, **Hotel Ensenada** (tel. 065/212017 or 065/212028, www.hotelensenada.cl, US$50 d with shared bath, US$80–90 d with private bath) is a century-old classic that oozes character out of the woodwork—all the rooms are spacious, even the 3rd-floor rooms with shared baths, and museum pieces fill the common areas. It's closed April–September.

In a class of its own, built by Seattle tech entrepreneur Michael Darland, the punning **Yan Kee Way Lodge** is an over-the-top luxury resort with whimsical (even kitschy) decor targeting big-bucks travelers willing and able to cough up US$300 per person double occupancy for expedition holidays and US$600 per person for fly-fishing—per day. Accommodations include regular hotel rooms and two-unit bungalows (which share a wall). The dining room and elaborate kitchen at its **Latitude 42** pull in travelers from around the country. For more information, contact Southern Chile Expeditions (Casilla 149, Puerto Varas, tel. 065/212030, fax 065/212031, www.southernchilexp.com).

Several buses use Ruta 225 between Puerto Varas, Ensenada, and Petrohué; others continue to Ralún, Cochamó, and Puelo. For more details, see the Puerto Varas Getting There entry.

Parque Nacional Vicente Pérez Rosales

Established in 1926, Chile's very first national park is a geographical extravaganza whose dominant features are Volcán Osorno, a symmetrical snowcapped cone that's often called the "Fujiyama of South America," and fjordlike Lagos Todos los Santos, which forms an elongated lacustrine highway toward the Argentine border. It

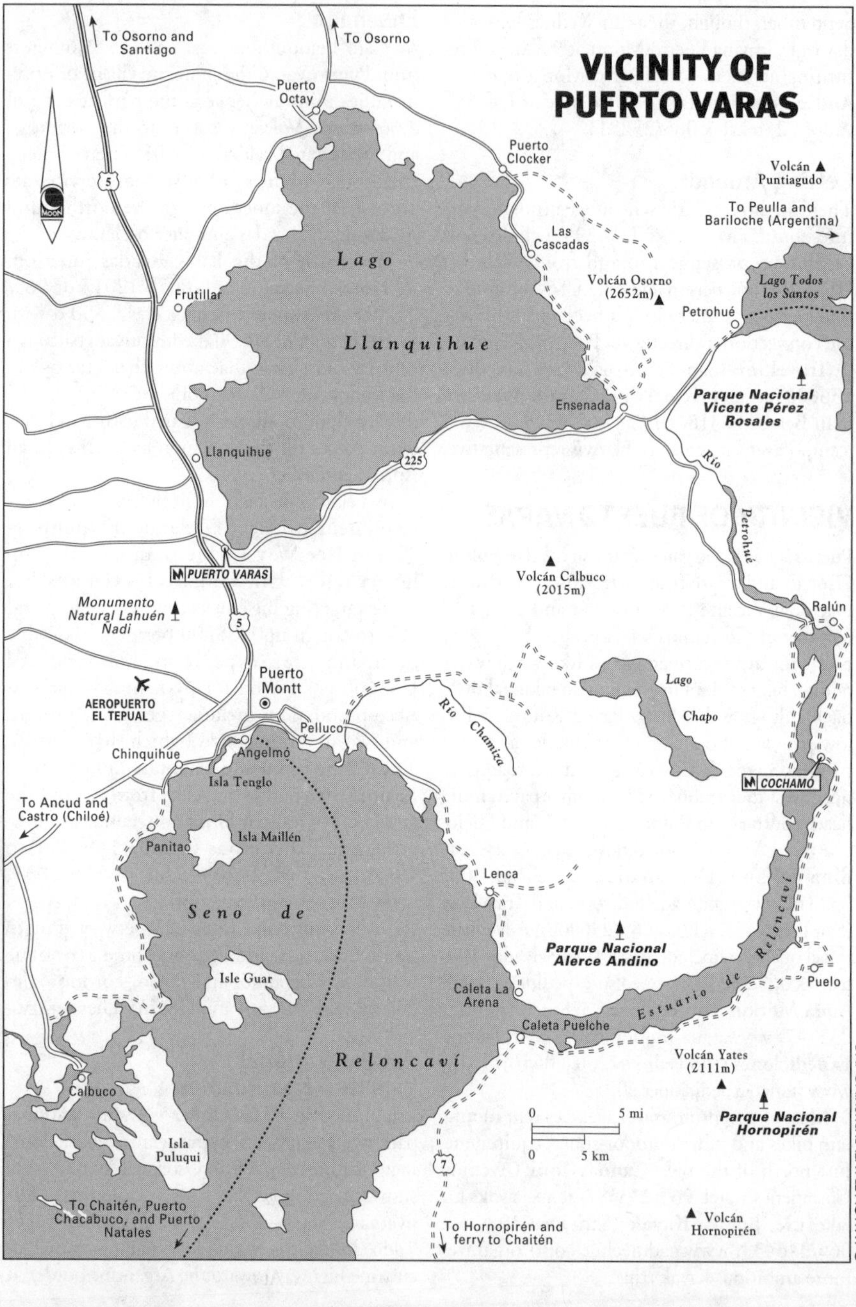

VICINITY OF PUERTO VARAS

To Osorno and Santiago
To Osorno
Puerto Octay
Puerto Clocker
Volcán Puntiagudo
To Peulla and Bariloche (Argentina)
Las Cascadas
Lago Llanquihue
Volcán Osorno (2652m)
Lago Todos los Santos
Frutillar
Petrohué
Parque Nacional Vicente Pérez Rosales
Ensenada
Llanquihue
225
5
Río Petrohué
PUERTO VARAS
Volcán Calbuco (2015m)
Monumento Natural Lahuén Ñadi
Ralún
Puerto Montt
AEROPUERTO EL TEPUAL
Lago Chapo
Río Chamiza
Pelluco
Angelmó
Chinquihue
COCHAMÓ
Isla Tenglo
To Ancud and Castro (Chiloé)
Panitao
Isla Maillén
Lenca
Seno de Reloncaví
Parque Nacional Alerce Andino
Isle Guar
Caleta La Arena
Puelo
Estuario de Reloncaví
Caleta Puelche
Volcán Yates (2111m)
Calbuco
Parque Nacional Hornopirén
0 5 mi
0 5 km
Isla Puluqui
7
To Chaitén, Puerto Chacabuco, and Puerto Natales
To Hornopirén and ferry to Chaitén
Volcán Hornopirén

© WAYNE BERNHARDSON

Hotel Peulla, Parque Nacional Vicente Pérez Rosales

also, though, contains rushing rivers, steep forested canyons, and a scattering of alpine lakes.

The 251,000-hectare park takes its name from Vicente Pérez Rosales, an adventurer and explorer whose mid-19th-century travels literally cleared the way for European settlement, as he hired the indigenous Huilliche to set fire to the forests near Lago Llanquihue. Pérez Rosales later made a name for himself during the California Gold Rush.

Boat traffic began to cross Lago Todos los Santos as early as 1890, with the first tourists arriving in 1903. Long before Europeans saw the area, though, indigenous peoples had used the southerly Paso de Vuriloche to traverse the Andes, and Jesuit missionaries used a slightly different route south of Volcán Tronador, the area's highest peak.

Geography and Climate

Some 50 kilometers northeast of Puerto Varas via Ruta 225, Parque Nacional Vicente Pérez Rosales ranges in altitude from 50 meters above sea level near Ensenada to about 3,460 meters on the summit of Cerro Tronador, a glaciated volcano on the Argentine border that has no recorded historic eruptions. The 2,652-meter summit of Volcán Osorno is its most conspicuous accessible feature; other high peaks include 2,493-meter Volcán Puntiagudo on the park's northern border and 1,710-meter Cerro La Picada, northeast of Volcán Osorno.

Several rivers drain from the cordillera into Lago Todos los Santos, most notably the Río Negro; at 191 meters above sea level, the lake is the source of the Río Petrohué, diverted southward into the Golfo de Reloncaví by lava flows that reached the shores of Lago Llanquihue just north of Ensenada.

The park receives about 2,500 millimeters rainfall per annum at lower elevations but up to 4,000 millimeters, much of it falling as snow, near the Argentine border. The lake moderates the ambient temperature, which averages about 16°C in summer and 6.5°C in winter, though it gets much colder at altitude. Summertime highs reach about 25°C.

Flora and Fauna

Ecologically, up to 1,000 meters above sea level, the park's dense *valdivian* rainforest consists of the southern beech *coigue* mixed with glossy-leaved *ulmos* and shrubs like *quila,* as well as ferns and climbing vines. At higher elevations *coigue* mixes with the related *lenga;* the rare coniferous *alerce (Fitzroya cuppresoides)* grows in a few steep areas.

Within the park are 33 mammal species, among them puma, *pudú,* foxes, and skunks, and 117 bird species, including Chilean torrent ducks, kingfishers, coots, woodpeckers, and hummingbirds. Rainbow and brown trout have been introduced into its lakes and streams, though there are also native trout.

Sights and Activities

While it hasn't erupted since the mid-19th century, the youthful Holocene crater of 2,652-meter **Volcán Osorno** has active fumaroles and is potentially very dangerous. From the deck of the *Beagle,* Darwin observed its eruption of January 19–20, 1835:

> *At midnight the sentry observed something like a large star, which gradually increased in size until about three o'clock, when it presented a very magnificent spectacle. By the aid of a glass, dark objects, in constant succession, were seen, in the midst of a great glare of red light, to be thrown up and to fall down. The light was sufficient to cast on the water a long bright reflection.*

Adventure travel operators in Puerto Octay and Puerto Varas offer one-day guided climbs of Osorno, ranging from US$100 for up to four persons to US$200 per person. It is a difficult ascent, requiring either technical skills on snow and ice or guides with technical skills. Conaf, which regulates climbing here, requires one guide for every three climbers on commercial trips; for independent climbers, it requires proof of experience and presentation of gear before issuing permits.

At the east end of Lago Todos los Santos, the source of its namesake river, **Sector Petrohué** is most popular as the port for the passenger ferry to Peulla, which leaves in mid-morning and returns in early afternoon. Andina del Sud, which operates the Peulla ferry, also runs a daily excursion to **Isla Margarita,** an island which rears its head above the middle of the lake, in January and February only.

Since most of Sector Petrohué lacks an integrated trail network, visiting remote areas requires either hiring a private launch or contracting an activities-oriented tour, but there are a few easily accessible options. From **Playa Larga,** the black-sand beach north of Hotel Petrohué, the five-kilometer **Sendero Rincón del Osorno** follows the western shore of the lake. Six kilometers southwest of Petrohué, on the south side of the highway, Conaf charges US$2 admission for the **Sendero Saltos del Petrohué,** a short riverbank trail that follows a series of basalt bedrock rapids and falls too rough for rafting or kayaking. Below the falls, Puerto Varas operators start their Class III–IV descents of the **Río Petrohué,** which is suitable for novice rafters but interesting enough for those with more experience. Sites suitable for rock climbing are nearby.

Where the Río Negro and the Río Peulla empty into Lago Todos los Santos, 20 nautical miles from Petrohué, the hamlet of **Peulla** earns its livelihood from tourist traffic that patronizes Hotel Peulla and its restaurant, whether overnight, on day excursions from Petrohué, or en route to Bariloche. Chilean customs and immigration is only a short distance east of here.

Day-trippers and through travelers have time enough to walk to **Cascada de Los Novios,** a waterfall just a few minutes from Hotel Peulla. Only overnighters will have time for the eight-kilometer climb of the **Sendero Laguna Margarita.**

Accommodations and Food

Within the park, accommodations and food are both limited; hotel reservations are advisable.

Just below Volcán Osorno's permanent snow line, 1,200 meters above sea level, the 50-bunk **Refugio Teski Ski Club** (tel. 09/2623323, US$10 pp) also serves breakfast (US$4) and lunch and dinner (US$7 each). From a turnoff three kilometers north of the Ensenada junction, the *refugio* is a nine-kilometer climb along a gravel road.

On the south side of the Río Petrohué, reached by rowboat shuttle from the visitors center, the no-frills **Hospedaje Küschel** charges US$10 per person for beds, half that for camping. North of the visitors center, Conaf's 24-site **Camping Playa Petrohué** charges US$10 for up to four persons.

Recently rebuilt after burning to the ground in 2002, the Middle European–style **Hotel Petrohué** (tel./fax 065/212025, www.petrohue.com, US$97/139 s/d with breakfast) is, by all accounts, at least the equal of what had always been a very fine hotel. Rates with half-board cost US$108/161 s/d, while packages with excursions included are US$163/271 s/d. Its restaurant and bar are open to the public; otherwise, only limited supplies at high prices are available at Petrohué's only shop.

At the east end of the lake, the venerable **Hotel Peulla** (tel. 065/258041, hpeulla@ctcinternet.cl, US$101/148 s/d) is only so-so. Rates include half-board at its restaurant **Tejuela,** which has drawn some criticism for both price and quality. There's also an unofficial campsite, plus summer-only accommodations at **Hospedaje Hernández** (US$10 pp).

Other Practicalities

At Petrohué, Conaf's Centro de Visitantes contains exhibits on the park's geography, geology, fauna, flora, and history.

Regular bus service connects Petrohué with Puerto Varas and Puerto Montt; for details, see the Puerto Varas Getting There entry, above.

Mid-September–mid-April, daily except Sunday, Puerto Montt's **Andina del Sud** (Antonio Varas 437, tel./fax 065/257797, www.andinadelsud.com) operates 8 A.M. buses to Ensenada and Petrohué via Puerto Varas, connecting with its own bus-boat crossing to Bariloche (Argentina); return buses leave at 6 P.M. The rest of the year, the Bariloche crossing takes two days, with an obligatory overnight at Hotel Peulla; buses run weekdays only, leaving Puerto Montt at 8:30 A.M. but returning at 10:45 P.M.

At Petrohué, a dockside kiosk sells tickets for the three-hour trip to Peulla, where it connects with the bus to the Argentine border at Puerto Frías and a relay of bus-boat links to Bariloche. Hikers and cyclists can also take this route; round-trip tickets to Peulla cost US$30 for adults, slightly less for children; lunch at Hotel Peulla costs an additional US$10 per person. From Puerto Varas, the fare is US$38; for more details, contact **Turismo Peulla** (San Juan 430, 2nd floor, Puerto Varas, tel. 065/236150, info@turismopeulla.cl).

Cochamó and Vicinity

Two kilometers east of Ensenada, where international Ruta 225 continues to Petrohué, another paved road follows the Río Petrohué southeast for 30 kilometers, where it forks as the river enters the Estuario de Reloncaví. While the right fork heads south to Canutillar, the graveled left fork crosses the bridge over the Petrohué and continues to **Ralún,** where another gravel road forks north to **Cayutué,** on the south arm of Lago Todos los Santos.

The main road, though, continues another 15 kilometers to Cochamó, where the 2,111-meter Volcán Yates, at the south end of the Estuario, provides a backdrop for the shingled **Iglesia Parroquial María Inmaculada** and its soaring steeple. The area's big attraction, though, is the yet untamed grandeur of the upper Río Cochamó, where ribbon-like waterfalls tumble over exfoliated granite domes that rise above the luxuriant rainforest. Still, only small numbers of hikers, dedicated technical climbers, and horseback riders challenge the muddy trail, part of which follows a 19th-century log road that crossed the Andes to Argentina, to the scenic valley of **La Junta** and beyond.

Cochamó is the base for **Campo Aventura,** an eco-lodge and horse-trekking company that offers one- to 10-day horseback trips to its backcountry camp at La Junta, 17 kilometers east and 300 meters above sea level. Unfortunately for wilderness enthusiasts, new road construction is slowly but inexorably proceeding up the valley to La Junta, though much of the area is likely to remain roadless for some time and there may be an attempt to declare the log road a national monument, which would be an obstacle to construction of an improved road.

The present road and trail follow the north bank of the river as far as La Junta, where it's necessary to ford the river to Campo Aventura's south-bank camp, which has comfortable lodging, camping (US$4 pp), and its own small network of hiking trails. If the river is high, the crossing can be dangerous for hikers and, on rare occasions, even riders, but Campo Aventura has installed its own cable car to simplify the process. A three-day, two-night horseback package costs US$165 per person; for more details, contact Campo Aventura's Puerto Varas office (San Bernardo 318, tel./fax 065/232910, www.campo-aventura.com). In addition, the company also offers boat trips to nearby thermal baths and a sea lion colony, sea kayaking, and fishing and trekking excursions.

From Campo Aventura, the gravel road continues south over a new bridge across the Río Puelo and then joins Ruta 7, the Carretera Austral, to **Caleta Puelche.** Here it's possible to return north toward Puerto Montt via the ferry shuttle to Caleta La Arena, or continue south to Hornopirén, the vehicle ferry port for southbound travelers; for more detail, see the separate entry for Hornopirén.

Cochamó proper has **Hotel Cochamó** (Catedral 19, tel. 065/216212, US$8–10 pp) and well-heated **Residencial Edicar** (tel. 065/216526, US$10 pp), which has good views over the estuary. Both places include breakfast.

Both horseback-tour clients and non-riders overnight (US$14 pp) at the three stylish *cabañas* at **Campo Aventura Eco-Lodge,** five kilometers south of Cochamó proper and 500 meters east of the Puelo road, on the south side of the bridge over the Río Cochamó. Breakfast costs an additional US$5; seafood and vegetarian lunches and dinners are also available at their restaurant.

Open mid-September–mid-May, Campo Aventura has equally stylish if simpler dormitory-style accommodations at La Junta, with wood-fired hot showers and a campground as well. Meals, wine, and fresh bread are also available here, but it's best to make advance arrangements for meals at the Eco-Lodge.

Buses Fierro (tel. 065/253022) goes from Puerto Montt (US$3) to Cochamó at 8:15 A.M., 12:30 P.M., and 5 P.M. weekdays, 8:15 A.M., 12:30 P.M., and 4 P.M. Saturday, and 8:15 A.M. and 5 P.M. Sunday and holidays, via Puerto Varas. Confirm bus times at Campo Aventura's Varas offices, which is near the bus stop and can also arrange transfers by private vehicle or even kayak (even for non-kayakers).

PUERTO MONTT AND VICINITY

No Chilean city enjoys a more impressive setting than Puerto Montt, where a cordon of forested mountains and snowcapped volcanoes stretches south along the waters of Chile's island-studded "Inside Passage." While the mid-sized port can't match the prosperity and cultural diversity of cities in comparable surroundings, like Seattle and Vancouver, improvements are underway. Municipal authorities are turning part of the waterfront, with its dramatic views, into a park, anchor businesses like the Ripley department store are helping make downtown a retail mecca, pedestrian malls are sprouting chic sidewalk cafés, and pubs and bars are proliferating.

As a city whose potential, to this point, exceeds its achievements, the capital of Region X (Los Lagos) remains primarily a gateway to the Andean lake district, the Chiloé archipelago, Chilean Patagonia, and parts of Argentina. As a transport hub where mainland Chile ends and archipelagic Chile begins, it enjoys air, land, or sea connections in all directions but west. Increasing numbers of cruise ships are even calling at its port of Angelmó, though there's barely room for them to maneuver in and out of the congested harbor.

History

Puerto Montt dates from 1853, when German colonists landed at the north end of the Seno de Reloncaví in what was then called "Melipulli," a Huilliche word whose definition—"four hills"—aptly described the new settlement's site. It grew slowly until 1912, when completion of the railroad cut travel time to Santiago to only 26 hours and it became the jumping-off point for southbound colonists headed for continental Chiloé, Aisén, and Magallanes.

In 1960, a catastrophic earthquake destroyed the port and most of what Jan Morris called "structures in the Alpine manner, all high-pitched roofs and quaint balconies." Rebuilt in a mostly utilitarian style, Puerto Montt is only now beginning to sport newer buildings of distinction; the earlier style survived to a greater degree in nearby Puerto Varas.

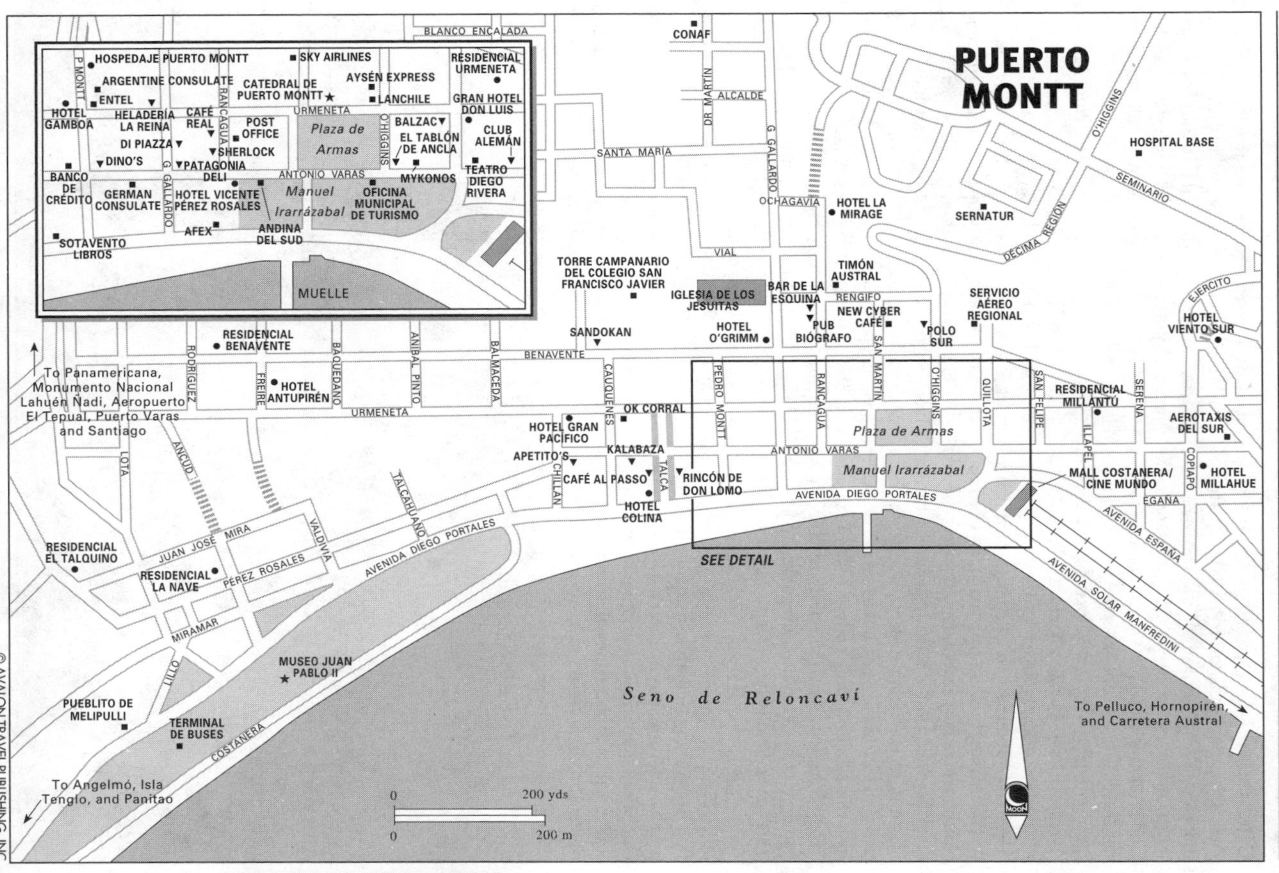

The Sur Chico

Orientation

Puerto Montt (population 155,895) is 1,016 kilometers south of Santiago via the Panamericana, which bypasses the city center en route to the Chiloé archipelago. Like Valparaíso, it occupies a narrow shelf at the foot of a series of hills, but not quite so high as those at Valparaíso. Westbound Avenida Diego Portales becomes Avenida Angelmó, the main approach to the ferry, fishing, and forest-products port of Angelmó, which attracts tourists to its permanent crafts fair and seafood restaurants; eastbound, it becomes Avenida Soler Manfredini, the starting point for the discontinuous Carretera Austral, a series of both paved and gravel highways linked, where necessary, by ferries. This highway ends at Villa O'Higgins, 1,240 kilometers to the south in Region XI (Aisén), but most travelers cover at least part of the route via air or ferry from Puerto Montt or Chiloé.

Sights

Puerto Montt's strength is its magnificent geographical setting, but it also has a handful of architectural monuments and other sights. On the south side of **Plaza Manuel Irarrázaval,** built of *alerce* in the style of the Parthenon, the **Catedral de Puerto Montt** (1856) is city's oldest building. Surrounded by woods, the hillside **Torre Campanario del Colegio San Francisco Javier** (1894) rises behind the **Iglesia de los Jesuitas** (1872), at the corner of Guillermo Gallardo and Rengifo.

Recently upgraded, the waterfront **Museo Juan Pablo II** holds collections on natural history, archaeology (including dioramas of the-Monte Verde early-man site 35 km west of town), and anthropology, early Spanish and 19th-century German colonization, and the city's history from its origins as the indigenous hamlet of Melipulli to the massive 1960 earthquake and up to the present. For many locals, the high point was the 1987 visit of Pope John Paul II, also documented here, which resulted in its renaming. Directly east of the bus terminal, the Museo (Avenida Diego Portales 991, tel. 065/261822, museojp@yahoo.com) is open 9 A.M.–7 P.M. weekdays, 10 A.M.–6 P.M. weekends. Admission costs US$.40 for adults, US$.15 for children.

Puerto Montt and **Angelmó,** two kilometers west, have gradually grown together along the waterfront, but the port retains its own identity and attracts more visitors than other parts of

© WAYNE BERNHARDSON

formal starting point of the Carretera Austral, Puerto Montt

© WAYNE BERNHARDSON

windows of Puerto Montt

town, thanks to its sprawling crafts market and gaggle of *marisquerías,* always jammed with lunch and dinner patrons. Taxi *colectivos* out Avenida Diego Portales go directly to the port area, which is also the departure point for southbound ferries.

Monumento Nacional Lahuén Ñadi

Little native forest remains near Puerto Montt, but substantial stands of *alerce, ulmo, mañío, coigue,* and other species survive in this 200-hectare woodland between the city and Aeropuerto El Tepual, despite the steady encroachment of trophy houses surrounded by high fences and guarded by Rottweilers.

Located on the private Fundo El Rincón, the Conaf-administered park features a small visitors center, a cafeteria, a short nature trail, and one slightly longer hiking trail. Midway between the Panamericana and the airport, a bumpy gravel road leads to the park, about three kilometers to the north; water can cover parts of the road when rains are heavy, but the surface is firm gravel and vehicles without four-wheel drive pass easily.

Any airport-bound bus will drop you at the junction, which is about 30 minutes' walk from the park. Admission costs about US$2.30.

Entertainment

Built with Mexican aid after the 1960 earthquake, named for the famous muralist, the **Teatro Diego Rivera** (Quillota 116, tel. 065/261817) is Puerto Montt's main performing-arts venue for theater, dance, and the occasional film. Upstairs in the same building, named for a prominent Chilean painter of the mid-20th century, the **Sala Hardy Wistuba** is a gallery with rotating exhibits of painting, sculpture, and photography; it's open 10 A.M.–1 P.M. and 3–7 P.M. weekdays, 10 A.M.–6 P.M. weekends. Admission to exhibitions is free.

Puerto Montt has a smattering of pubs and bars, including the superficially Western-themed **OK Corral** (Cauquenes 128, tel. 065/266287) and the popular new **Sherlock** (Antonio Varas and Rancagua, tel. 065/288888). **El Biógrafo** (Rancagua 235, tel. 065/344166) features live music, while nearby **Bar de la Esquina** (Rancagua 245) sometimes showcases live blues.

In the former train station, miraculously transformed into the Mall Costanera, the **Cine Mundo** (Illapel 10, Local 303, tel. 065/348055) shows current movies.

Shopping

Directly opposite the bus terminal, the **Pueblito**

CHILE'S INSIDE PASSAGE

Even in the darkest days of the 1970s, as Chile chafed under dictatorship and foreign travelers were few, the occasional adventurer found his way south in search of a sailing passage through the archipelagic labyrinth of Chile's southern canals. Nearly uninhabited, the myriad islands south of Chiloé exerted an inexorable magnetism on map-mongers, but only a few fast talkers made their way aboard the rust-bucket *Río Baker,* the funky freighter that plied the route from Puerto Montt to Puerto Natales, or the ferry *Evangelistas* that replaced it in the last years of the Pinochet regime.

Today, fortunately, it's easier than ever to sail what might be called "the poor man's cruise," a three-day voyage through the western fjords of Aisén and Magallanes. The *Magallanes,* which shuttles the 900 nautical miles between Puerto Montt and Puerto Natales, is not a cruise ship. Rather, it's a cargo ferry that also carries passengers in reasonable comfort through some of South America's finest scenery—at least when the weather clears in one of the earth's stormiest regions.

Sailing south from Puerto Montt, on a sunny departure day, there are seemingly infinite views of the volcanic continental cordon of Osorno, Calbuco, Yates, Michinmahuida, and Corcovado. As the ship proceeds south through the Golfo de Ancud, Golfo de Corcovado, and Canal Moraleda, Michinmahuida's snowfields seem to rotate slowly in the distance until they finally fade from view. To the west, the lighthouse at **Melinka,** a tiny outpost in the Guaitecas archipelago, is the only conspicuous sign of settlement beyond Chiloé.

On entering the Canal Moraleda, the vessel normally heads south to the Canal Errázuriz and west toward the open Pacific via the Canal Chacabuco; here passengers will spot Puerto Chacabuco's small-scale fishing fleet, pursued by seabirds.

The usual route west to the Pacific is through the Canal Chacabuco, the most southerly option between Isla Humos and Isla FitzRoy, but there are more northerly alternatives like Canal Darwin between Isla Quemada and Isla Luz; occasionally, the captain chooses an even more northerly route via Canal Ninualac, between Isla James and Isla Melchor.

As the ship rounds Cabo Tres Montes, there are no alternatives to crossing the **Golfo de Penas** (Gulf of Sorrows), as the nautically challenged seek relief through medication before cafeteria trays start flying like Frisbees in the open ocean swells. Most passengers feel literal relief at entering the protected Canal Messier, passing through **Angostura Inglesa,** a constricted narrows where, it seems, the queasier passengers might leap off the deck to dry land. Just to the north, the route passes the rusting hulk of the shipwrecked *Capitán Leonidas,* run aground on the Cotopaxi rocks.

The *Magallanes* usually pauses at the fishing hamlet of **Puerto Edén,** where Kawasqar (Alacaluf) Indians still board to sell souvenirs or travel to Puerto Natales themselves. Beyond

de Melipulli (Diego Portales s/n, tel. 065/263524) is a permanent artisans' market, but crafts stalls also line both sides and cover the sidewalks of Avenida Angelmó west of Independencia. Typical items include woolens, copperware, and standard souvenirs.

Timón Austral (Rengifo 430-A) is an antiques and antiquarian book dealer. **Sotavento Libros** (Diego Portales 580, tel. 065/256650) specializes in local and regional history and literature.

Accommodations

Puerto Montt has plenty of accommodations, but many of those at the bottom end tend to the unremarkable if not quite dire.

US$10–25

Uphill from the bus terminal, **Residencial El Talquino** (Pérez Rosales 114, tel. 065/253331, US$6 pp with breakfast) also offers kitchen privileges for a small additional charge.

Puerto Edén, the scenery is enthralling, with emerald forests, countless waterfalls, and glaciers that don't quite reach the sea but still glisten when the sun burns through the clouds. Approaching Puerto Natales, passengers grab their backpacks and prepare to head for the *hospedajes,* to make their plans for Torres del Paine and Patagonia.

Practicalities

Because the *Magallanes* is faster than the *Puerto Edén,* which used to run this route, the frustration that many passengers felt when weather or mechanical difficulties caused delays should diminish. For contact information, details on booking, and rates, see the information in the Puerto Montt entry. The boat sails Mondays all year, returning from Puerto Natales Thursdays, but longer summer days usually mean good visibility even with changeable weather.

New on the route, a Japanese ferry remodeled in Chile, the *Magallanes* can carry 337 passengers versus the *Puerto Edén*'s maximum of 175 or so. The former needs only 58 hours between Puerto Montt and Puerto Natales, with a pause at Puerto Edén, while the slower *Puerto Edén* needs about 72 hours.

The *Magallanes* is 123 meters long and 21 meters wide and has a pub, dining room, self-service cafeteria, and spacious upper decks and terraces. Its eight AAA cabins have two bunks each with individual reading lights, private bath, writing desk, chair, locking closet, regulated heat, and an exterior window. Sixteen AA cabins have two upper and two lower bunks and the same amenities. Fourteen A cabins have the same amenities but lack exterior windows. The 132 Literas C lack locking closets and have exterior baths. If you're susceptible to seasickness, bring medication and take it well before crossing the Golfo de Penas.

The food is cafeteria food, but it's improved in quality and increased in quantity—though truly big eaters might consider carrying some snacks. Both bridge and cabin staff are friendly, even the food servers, and prices at the bar are surprisingly moderate. The no-smoking policy, though, is inconsistently enforced.

Navimag carries twice as many foreigners as Chileans on the Puerto Montt–Puerto Natales route, which takes three full days but can still be delayed by bad weather. At the outset of the voyage, there is an orientation and safety talk. Videos and other entertainment do occur on board, including a closing-night party.

In the course of the voyage, many people make acquaintances and enduring friendships, and even some marriages have resulted. There's easy access to the bridge, the crew are personable and informative, and it's possible to follow the route on their charts. Some passengers, though, bring their own GPSs and charts, the most comprehensive of which is the British Admiralty's Hydrographer of the Navy Chart No. 561, Cabo Pilar to Golfo Coronado, at a scale of 1:750,000.

To the west, **Casa Perla** (Trigal 312, tel. 065/262104, www.casaperla.com, US$8 pp with breakfast) offers rooms with shared bath, hot showers, kitchen privileges, and laundry facilities; while it's not the most appealing neighborhood, the sociable owners speak English, and the cozy common areas include a small library.

Newish but already a bit worn, **Hostal Aysén** (Avenida Angelmó 1866, tel. 065/272051, US$8.50 pp) has sizeable rooms with shared bath, good beds, and breakfast included.

Nearer the port, responsive **Hospedaje Rocco** (Pudeto 233, tel./fax 065/272897, www.hospedajerocco.cl, US$10 pp with shared bath and breakfast) also offers Internet access and kitchen privileges.

Convenient to the Angelmó ferry dock, **Residencial Costanera** (Avenida Angelmó 1528, tel./fax 065/255244, US$10 pp) is an older house partitioned into smallish but adequate bedrooms with shared bath and breakfast. The common spaces are good and, uncommonly for Puerto Montt budget accommodations, there is plenty of parking.

Hospedaje Puerto Montt (Pedro Montt 180, tel. 065/252276, US$10 pp with shared bath) is friendly and central, but downstairs rooms are darkish with a maximum number of beds packed into each room. The breakfast is abundant.

Residencial La Nave (Ancud 103, tel. 065/253740, US$20 s or d with private bath) is well-located and well-regarded in its range. Near the waterfront, **Hotel Colina** (Talca 81, tel./fax 065/273501, US$24 s or d) is good value even if its location, and the quality of construction, aren't the quietest.

Deco-style **Residencial Millantú** (Illapel 146, tel./fax 065/263550, sperezs@telsur.cl, US$15/25 s/d) offers rooms with private bath and breakfast, but is slowly declining.

US$25–50

Decorated with the works of Swiss-Chilean owner/artist Rossy Oelckers, rooms at **Hospedaje Suizo** (Independencia 231, tel. 065/252640, 257565, US$7–13 pp) vary in size and style, but all have shared bath; breakfast costs US$2.50 more. It's straight uphill from the port entrance on Avenida Angelmó.

Once one of Puerto Montt's better budget choices, well-located **Residencial Urmeneta** (Urmeneta 290, 2nd floor, tel. 065/253262, US$13/22 s/d with shared bath, US$19/30 with private bath) is showing its age.

Hotel Gamboa (Pedro Montt 157, tel. 065/252741, US$13 pp with shared bath, US$17/30 s/d with private bath) is a classic hotel with sizable rooms that retain most of their original style, though some of the modern furniture is tacky.

In the summer peak season, **Hotel Millahue** (Copiapó 64, tel. 065/253829, fax 065/256317, hmillahue@surnet.cl, US$27/34 s/d) is often full.

Rooms at friendly but aging **Hospedaje Benavente** (Benavente 948, tel./fax 065/256369, charges US$9 pp with shared bath, US$18 pp with private bath) are adequate, but the Gamboa, among others, is a better option.

US$50–100

The contemporary **Hotel Le Mirage** (Rancagua 350, tel. 065/255125, fax 065/256302, hlemirage@telsur.cl, US$45/54 s/d) often fills with groups; rates include private bath, cable TV and most other conveniences, but it's worn for its age.

Hotel O'Grimm (Gallardo 211, tel. 065/252845, fax 258600, www.ogrimm.com, US$65/75 s/d) has attentive service and large rooms with all modern conveniences. Its attractive bar also has a basement pub with occasional live music, but it's acoustically insulated.

Puerto Montt's best new hotel, the business-oriented **Hotel Gran Pacífico** (Urmeneta 719, tel. 065/482100, fax 065/482110, www.hotelgranpacifico.cl, US$76/88 s/d) has spacious, comfortable, and immaculate rooms that are also soundproofed; those facing southeast have the best views. External amenities include a gym and sauna.

Overlooking the town from a hillside perch, frequented by foreign tour groups, remodeled **Hotel Viento Sur** (Ejército 200, tel. 065/258701, fax 065/258700, www.hotelvientosur.cl, US$80–90 s, US$90–98 d) boasts great views, stylistic integrity, finely finished woodwork, and a restaurant. Rates include a buffet breakfast.

US$100–150

A block east of the Plaza de Armas, **Gran Hotel Don Luis** (Quillota 146, tel. 065/259001, fax 065/259005, www.hotedonluis.cl, US$96–105 s or d) is a quality choice.

Hotel Antupirén (Freire 186, tel. 065/313637, fax 065/313638, hotelant@telsur.cl, US$80/110 s/d) is a business-oriented facility with attentive, efficient service and a good buffet breakfast. Some smaller, slightly cheaper rooms are lesser values.

Gran Hotel Don Vicente Pérez Rosales (Antonio Varas 447, tel. 065/432900, fax 065/437699, www.granhoteldonvicente.cl, US$93/130 s/d) is a traditional downtown favorite.

Food

With only a couple exceptions, downtown Puerto Montt restaurants include reasonably priced but run-of-the-mill places like **Apetito's** (Chillán 96, tel. 065/252470; **Café al Passo** (Talca 81, tel. 065/253501); **Dino's** (Antonio Varas 550, tel. 065/252785), with its chain predictability; **Mykonos** (Antonio Varas 326, tel. 065/262627); and **Rincón de Don Lomo** (Talca 84, tel. 065/254597). Figure about US$3–5 for lunch, somewhat more for dinner.

DiPiazza (Gallardo 118, tel. 065/254174) is only a so-so pizzería, but with moderate prices—individual-sized pizzas start around US$3, and inexpensive pasta plates are also on the menu. The rejuvenated **Club Alemán** or **Deutscher Verein** (German Club, Antonio Varas 264, tel. 065/252551) is a step up in both price and quality. So is the seafood at the Centro Español's **Polo Sur** (O'Higgins 233, 2nd floor, tel. 065/343753). **El Tablón del Ancla** (Antonio Varas 350) is a cheerful new bar/restaurant that's worth a look.

Any of numerous *palafito marisquerías* clustered at the port of Angelmó are worth trying for fish, shellfish, and *curanto,* but streetside restaurants like the flashy **Marfino** (Avenida Angelmó 1856, tel. 065/259044) deserve consideration. One of the best new options is **El Cuento del Mar** (Avenida Angelmó 2476, tel. 061/271500), with fine fish and shellfish entrées in the US$7–10-and-up range. Though some of the waiters seem to be novices, the management is congenial and accommodating.

For sandwiches, *onces,* coffee, and desserts like German-style kuchen, try **Café Real** (Rancagua 137, tel. 065/253750), **Patagonia Deli** (Antonio Varas 486, tel. 065/482898), and **Kalabaza** (Antonio Varas 629, tel. 065/266010). **Heladería La Reina** (Urmeneta 508, tel. 065/253979) continues to produce Puerto Montt's finest ice cream.

Information

Puerto Montt has a variety of information sources.

Mid-January–mid-March, Puerto Montt's **Oficina Municipal de Turismo** (Varas and O'Higgins, tel. 065/261701), a kiosk just south of the Plaza de Armas, is open 9 A.M.–9 P.M. daily; the rest of the year hours are 9 A.M.–1 P.M. and 3–7 P.M. daily except Sunday.

Within the hilltop Intendencia Regional, **Sernatur** (tel. 065/254580) is open 8:30 A.M.–5:30 P.M. weekdays except Friday, when it closes an hour earlier.

Neighboring **Argentina's consulate** (Pedro Montt 160, 6th floor, tel. 065/253996) is open 8 A.M.–1 P.M. weekdays only. **Germany's consulate** is at Antonio Varas 525, Oficina 306 (tel. 065/252828).

Conaf's **Patrimonio Silvestre** unit at Dr. Martín 566 (tel. 065/486711) can provide national-park information.

Services

Puerto Montt has a full complement of travelers' services.

Exchange houses include **Afex** (Diego Portales 516, tel. 065/256604) and the bus terminal's **La Moneda de Oro** (Diego Portales s/n, tel. 065/255108). **Banco de Crédito** has an ATM at Antonio Varas 560, but there are many others downtown.

Correos de Chile is at Rancagua 126.

For long-distance services, **Entel** has new quarters at the corner of Pedro Montt and Urmeneta, as well as a small office just outside the Angelmó ferry port.

Latin Star Communication Center (Avenida Angelmó 1684) stays open late for Internet access. Downtown, try the **New-Cyber Café** (San Martín 230, tel. 065/350339).

Most travel agencies catering to overseas visitors are in Puerto Varas, but British-run **Travellers** (Avenida Angelmó 2456, tel./fax 065/258555, info@travellers.cl) is an experienced resource for the entire region and beyond. In addition to arranging flights, ferry tickets, and rental cars, changing money, and setting up adventure travel excursions with the most reliable local operators, they sell guidebooks and IGM topographic maps and have a large book exchange.

Puerto Montt's **Hospital Regional** (Seminario s/n, tel. 065/261134) is northeast of the hilltop Intendencia Regional, reached via O'Higgins and the zigzag Avenida Décima Región.

Getting There

Other than Santiago, Puerto Montt is the main gateway for air, land, and sea connections to Chilean Patagonia and across the Andes to Argentina. Only in summer can overland travelers begin the entire Carretera Austral by heading southeast from here, as Transmarchilay's Hornopirén-Caleta Gonzalo ferry link operates in January and February only; otherwise, it's necessary to take the ferry or catamaran from Puerto Montt to Chaitén.

LanChile/LanExpress (O'Higgins 167, Local 1-B, tel. 065/253315) flies several times daily to Santiago, usually nonstop but sometimes via Valdivia, Temuco, or Concepción, or a combination of these. It also flies at least twice daily to Balmaceda/Coyhaique and three or four times daily to Punta Arenas. One Saturday-morning Punta Arenas flight continues to the Falkland Islands (sometimes via Río Gallegos, Argentina), while another stops in Balmaceda/Coyhaique. Once a week, usually Sunday, it flies from Santiago to Puerto Montt and on to San Carlos de Bariloche, Argentina.

Sky Airlines (San Martín 189, Local 3, tel. 065/437555) flies three times daily to Santiago and once to Balmaceda/Coyhaique.

No carrier has lasted long on the air-taxi route from Puerto Montt to Chaitén, a common starting point for overland trips on the Carretera Austral, but some continue to try. The current entrants are **Servicio Aéreo Regional** (Quillota 254, Local 1, tel. 065/266666, cschuwirth@hotmail.com) and **Aerotaxis del Sur** (Antonio Varas 70-A, tel. 065/252523, aerotaxisdelsur@entelchile.net).

Puerto Montt's **Terminal de Buses** (Avenida Portales and Lota, tel. 065/294533) is about one kilometer southwest of the Plaza de Armas. Services are frequent to rural, regional, and most long-distance destinations, as well as Bariloche, Argentina. Buses to Chilean Patagonia destinations like Coyhaique and Punta Arenas, which pass through Argentina, are less frequent but reliable.

Several companies go to Puerto Varas (US$1, 30 min), including **Expreso Puerto Varas, Thaebus** (tel. 065/420120, less frequently), and **Buses Fierro** (tel. 065/253022), whose route continues

CROSSING THE LAKES

In Walter Salles's 2004 film *The Motorcycle Diaries,* a youthful Ernesto (Che) Guevara and his friend Alberto Granados push their dying motorcycle through a freak summer snowstorm around Lago Frías en route to Chile. In the early 1950s, the two Argentines were following the **Cruce de Lagos,** a route that's become one of the South American continent's classics since it opened in the early 20th century. Former U.S. President Theodore Roosevelt crossed the Andes from Lago Llanquihue to San Carlos de Bariloche in 1913, and countless thousands of tourists have followed suit.

Connecting the Chilean and Argentine "lake districts," passing through Chile's Parque Nacional Vicente Pérez Rosales and Argentina's Parque Nacional Nahuel Huapi, the Cruce de Lagos is a boat-bus-boat shuttle between Puerto Montt and Bariloche. While many people do it in a day, passively enjoying the mountain scenery, there are hotels and campgrounds at each end of Lago Todos los Santos, on the Chilean side of the border, which provide opportunities for exploratory hikes, though the trail system is not extensive.

The more active can go white-water rafting on the Río Petrohué, canyon up Vicente Pérez Rosales's steep ravines, or even scale snowcapped Volcán Osorno, a 2,652-meter peak that's a technical challenge. There are fewer places to stay on the Argentine side, except between Bariloche and Puerto Pañuelo, but there is a good network of footpaths that would make it possible to hike part of the route. Quite a few cyclists pedal the roads between the water segments of the trip.

The Cruce de Lagos (www.crucedelagos.com) is open all year, but best from October to April. From the Chilean side, it's not necessary to continue beyond Lago Todos los Santos to the Argentine side—some people go only as far as Peulla and return to Petrohué, Puerto Varas, or Puerto Montt.

to Ensenada, Cochamó (US$4.50), and Río Puelo (US$6), daily at 8:15, 12:30, and 5 P.M.

Fierro also goes to Lago Chapo (US$1.25), the northerly access point to Parque Nacional Alerce Andino, several times daily; and to Lenca (US$1.10), the southerly access point to Alerce Andino, five times daily except on weekends, when it goes only twice.

Daily except Sunday at 8 A.M. and at 1:30, 3, and 5 P.M., **Buses Jordán** (tel. 065/254938) goes to Hornopirén, also known as Río Negro (US$5, 3.5 hours), the summer ferry port to Caleta Gonzalo. Caleto Gonzalo is the gateway to Parque Natural Pumalín and most of the Carretera Austral.

Numerous carriers serve the capital city of Santiago (US$14–20, 12–13 hours) and intermediates. **Transportes Turismo Futaleufú** goes to Futaleufú (US$28, 11 hours) via Argentina Thursday at 7 A.M. **Turibús/Trans Austral** (tel. 065/231233) goes to Coyhaique (US$30) Monday and Thursday via Argentina. Several companies operate between Puerto Montt and Punta Arenas (US$44–60, 32 hours), including **Buses Pacheco** (tel. 065/252926), **Queilén Bus** (tel. 065/253468), and **Turibús** (tel. 065/253245), all of which normally begin in Castro (Chiloé) and pick up passengers here and in Osorno. These are through buses, not permitted to drop passengers in Argentina.

Four companies cross the Andes to San Carlos de Bariloche, Argentina (US$16–18, seven hours), via Osorno and the Cardenal Samoré pass: **Andesmar** (tel. 065/252926), **Buses Norte Internacional** (tel. 065/254731), **Tas Choapa** (tel. 065/254828), and **Vía Bariloche** (tel. 065/253841).

Andina del Sud (Antonio Varas 437, tel. 065/257797) operates the bus-boat relay to Bariloche (US$150) via Puerto Varas, Ensenada, Petrohué, and Peulla. These leave Puerto Montt in the morning, arriving early evening in Bariloche; summer departures are daily, but the rest of the year they're weekdays only and require an overnight stay in Peulla.

From Puerto Montt there are passenger and passenger/vehicle **ferries** or **bus-ferry combinations** to Chiloé and Chaitén in Region X, Puerto Chacabuco (the port of Coyhaique) in Region XI (Aisén), and Puerto Natales in Region XII (Magallanes). Since these routes follow the relatively sheltered inland sea, seasickness is generally a minor problem except on the open-sea crossing of the Golfo de Penas (literally, Gulf of Sorrows), en route to Puerto Natales. For sea routes within these regions, such as excursions to Laguna San Rafael from Puerto Chacabuco, see the appropriate chapter for details.

Puerto Montt's **Terminal de Transbordadores** (Avenida Angelmó 2187) is the ferry port. To Puerto Chacabuco, **Navimag** (tel. 065/432300, fax 065/276611) sails the passenger/vehicle ferry *Puerto Edén* Wednesday and Saturday at 2 P.M., with extensions to Laguna San Rafael; to Puerto Natales, the newer, larger *Magallanes* sails Monday evenings. Note that weather can play havoc with the Puerto Natales schedule, which must cross the exposed Golfo de Penas.

Navimag cabins to Puerto Chacabuco range from US$59–90 per person with breakfast included; other meals are available in the cafeteria. Bicycles cost an additional US$17, motorcycles US$26, and private vehicles (automobiles or light trucks) US$120; other vehicles pay US$50 per linear meter.

Substitution of the larger *Magallanes* for the smaller *Puerto Edén* has reduced some of the passenger pressure on the popular Puerto Montt–Puerto Natales route, but reservations are still advisable in the peak summer season; if in Santiago, visit the Navimag/Terra Australis office there, or else try the Travellers agency in Angelmó. Still, it's worth trying for a last-minute berth or cabin. Fares depend on the season and the quality of the accommodations, but usually range from US$275–820 per person with full board. Bicycles cost an additional US$28, motorcycles US$40, and private vehicles (automobiles or light trucks) US$280; other vehicles pay US$63 per linear meter.

Also at the Terminal de Transbordadores, **Transmarchilay** (tel. 065/270430, fax 270415, transporte@tmc.cl) runs shorter ferry routes between Puerto Montt and Chaitén (nine hours) on the ferry *La Pincoya,* four times weekly, and sometimes has service to Puerto Chacabuco and

THE REDWOOD OF THE SOUTH

Like the California redwoods, the coniferous *alerce (Fitzroya cupressoides)* is long-lived (up to 4,000 years), tall (up to 70 meters, though most mature specimens top out around 40), and an attractive, easily worked, and water- and insect-resistant timber. Native to Chile and Argentina, it is much more abundant on the Chilean side, where its native habitat ranges from coastal Valdivia south to archipelagic and continental Chiloé. In Argentina, it's found from Lago Nahuel Huapi south to Parque Nacional Los Alerces.

Although it grows mostly between 400 and 700 meters above sea level, the *alerce* also occurs in poorly drained marshlands at lower altitudes. The branches of younger specimens touch the ground, but the reddish-barked lower trunks of mature trees are barren. The Mapuche know it as the *lawen,* but Darwin gave the tree its botanical name, after the famous commander of his equally famous vessel. Still, the great scientist offers only a few descriptive remarks in *The Voyage of the Beagle.*

© WAYNE BERNHARDSON

alerce trees

Laguna San Rafael. Fares to Chaitén range from US$16 per person for fixed seats to US$19 for reclining seats. Vehicle fares are US$100 for automobiles and small trucks, US$24 per linear meter for larger vehicles; bicycles cost US$11, motorcycles US$22.

In high-speed **catamarans, Aysén Express** (O'Higgins 167, Oficina 307, tel. 065/435735, www.aysenexpress.cl) island-hops from Puerto Montt to Chaitén (US$36), Puerto Chacabuco (US$65), and intermediates. From the smaller port of Chinquehue, 13 kilometers west of town, **Catamaranes del Sur** (tel. 065/482308, www.catamaranesdelsur.cl) has provided similar services, but its future is up in the air.

September–May, **Cruceros Marítimos Skorpios** (Avenida Angelmó 1660, tel. 065/252996, fax 065/275660, www.skorpios.cl) operates **luxury cruises** to Laguna San Rafael that begin in Puerto Montt; rates on the 140-passenger *Skorpios II* start at US$823 per person and range up to US$1,400 per person.

Getting Around

From the bus terminal, **Buses ETM** (tel. 065/256253) connects to inbound and outbound flights at **Aeropuerto El Tepual** (tel. 065/252019), which is 16 kilometers west via the Panamericana and a paved lateral. The fare is US$1.50.

For car rentals, try the **Automóvil Club** (Esmeralda 70, tel. 065/254776); **Avis** (Urmeneta 783, tel. 065/255155); **Budget** (Antonio Varas 162, tel. 065/286277); **Full Fama's** (Diego Portales 506, tel. 065/258060, fax 065/259840); **Hertz** (Antonio Varas 126, tel. 065/259585); and **Travi** (Cardonal 2010, tel. 065/257137). Note that taking a vehicle into Argentina requires notarial permission, which local agencies are best at arranging.

PARQUE NACIONAL ALERCE ANDINO

Occupying most of the peninsula only a short distance east of Puerto Montt and south of Lago Chapo, adjoining the Carretera Austral, Alerce Andino takes its name from the Andean false larch, which survives both in and around the 39,255-hectare unit. Hiking its woodland trails and camping on the shores of several alpine lakes are its main attractions.

Geography and Climate

Altitudes at Alerce Andino range from sea level just east of La Arena, on the Estuario de Reloncaví, to 1,558 meters above on Cerro Cuadrado, in the park's most easterly sector. While the altitudes are not extreme, the precipitous terrain and dense forest cover make off-trail travel difficult. At higher elevations, there are more than 50 lakes and tarns of glacial origins.

There are several approaches to the park. From the village of Chamiza, 10 kilometers east of Puerto Montt, a gravel road leads 19 kilometers east to Sector Correntoso and Laguna Sargazo and, a few kilometers beyond, the west end of Sector Lago Chapo. The east end of Lago Chapo is also accessible from the village of Canutillar, reached via a roundabout route through Puerto Varas and Ensenada, while the Carretera Austral passes near the westerly entrance to Sector Chaica, about 32 kilometers southeast of Puerto Montt.

With its maritime west coast climate, Alerce Andino gets up to 4,500 millimeters rainfall per annum at lower elevations and substantial snowfall above 700–800 meters. Temperatures are mild, though, averaging about 7°C in winter and 15°C in summer.

Flora and Fauna

Officially designated a national monument, the long-lived *alerce (Fitzroya cupressoides)* spurred the park's creation in 1982. Ranging about 400–700 meters above sea level, it mixes with other species like *coigue, tineo, mañío (Podocarpus nubigena),* and *canelo (Canelo winteri).* Evergreen rain forest of *coigue, tepa (Laurelia philippiana),* and *ulmo* reaches from sea level up to 900 meters or more, while nearly prostrate *lenga* covers much of the highest areas.

In such dense forest, wildlife is rarely seen, but there are puma, *pudú,* gray fox, skunks, and vizcachas. Bird life includes the Andean condor, the kingfisher, and waterfowl like the *pato real* or Chiloé wigeon *(Anas sibilatrix).* The park's lakes and river sport native trout and introduced species like rainbow and brown trout.

The most abundant wildlife, though, is the large but slow-moving biting fly known as the *tábano,* abundant in early summer. Insect repellent, long trousers, and long sleeves are all good precautions, but they're no guarantee of invulnerability.

Sights and Activities

Footpaths connect the northern and southern sectors of the park, but heavy winters can cause damage to them. From Sector Correntoso, the **Sendero Laguna Fría** climbs 4.5 kilometers up the valley of the Río Sargazo to **Laguna Fría,** where a trail over the drainage divide leads south to **Laguna Chaiquenes,** reached by trail from the southerly **Sector Chaica.**

For the most up-to-date information on park trails, contact Conaf's Patrimonio Silvestre office in Puerto Montt or the Travellers agency in Angelmó, which arranges trips there but is also helpful to independent hikers and campers.

Accommodations and Food

At the northern approach to the park, try Conaf's **Camping Correntoso** (US$5 for up to five persons); its **Camping Chaica** (US$1.50 pp) is at the head of the Río Chaica valley. Backcountry camping remains an option and **Refugio Laguna Sargazo** (US$3) is once again open, though *refugios* at Río Pangal and Laguna Fría remain closed.

Just outside the park boundaries, the secluded **Alerce Mountain Lodge** (Carretera Austral Km 36, tel. 065/286969, www.mountainlodge.cl) offers package tours of the area, including hiking and horseback riding. Two-day, one-night packages with full board cost US$265/460 s/d, while three-day, two-night packages cost US$530/920 s/d, four-day, three-night packages US$785/1360, and five-day, four-night packages US$1015/1760. Off-season rates (May–October) are about 15–20 percent lower.

Other Practicalities

Conaf has **ranger posts** at both Sector Correntoso and Sector Chaica; park admission costs US$1.50.

Buses Fierro goes to Lago Chapo (US$1.25), the northerly access point to Parque Nacional Alerce Andino, several times daily. There are also rural buses, from in front of the Puerto Montt terminal, at 7:30 A.M., returning at 6 P.M., daily except Sunday.

Fierro also operates five buses each weekday, two daily on weekends, to the Carretera Austral junction at Lenca (US$1.10), where a seven-kilometer gravel road ascends the Río Chaica valley to the park, but there is no public transport along this route.

HORNOPIRÉN (RÍO NEGRO) AND VICINITY

At La Arena, 45 kilometers southeast of Puerto Montt, the mouth of the Estuario de Reloncaví interrupts the graveled Carretera Austral, but frequent ferries cross the water to Puelche and continue to Hornopirén (also known as Río Negro), 48 kilometers farther south. Hornopirén (population 6,583) is the access point for its little-visited namesake national park, only a few kilometers to the east; it is also the northern port for the summer vehicle/passenger ferry to Caleta Gonzalo and Parque Natural Pumalín (for more details on these destinations, see the separate entries below).

Parque Nacional Hornopirén

Only a short distance west of town, Parque Nacional Hornopirén is an almost totally undeveloped 48,232-hectare unit surrounded by several volcanoes, including 1,210-meter Apagado, 1,572-meter Hornopirén, and 2,187-meter Yates.

Accommodations and Food

The new **Camping Río Negro Hornopirén** (O'Higgins s/n, tel. 065/217436, US$13) has eight sites with hot water, fire pits, and electricity. Rates at aging but charming **Hotel Hornopirén** (Ignacio Carrera Pinto 388, tel. 065/217256, US$14 pp with shared bath) include breakfast; lunch and dinner are optional. In addition, there's a cluster of new *hospedajes* near the ferry ramp, such as **Hostería Catalina** (Ingenieros Militares s/n, tel. 065/217359, mmontiel@entelchile.net, US$14 pp with shared bath, US$38 d with private bath).

While you're waiting for the ferry, family-run **El Fogón del Navegante** (Ignacio Carrera Pinto s/n) can offer fresh homemade bread, tangy pisco sours, appetizers including a tasty salmon ceviche (US$2.50), and Chilean shellfish dishes like *locos* (abalone) and *picoroco* (giant barnacle). Behind a steeply pitched ceiling supported by foot-thick beams, its windows provide expansive harbor views.

Other Practicalities

Hours at Hornopirén's new **Oficina de Información Turística,** near the ferry ramp, are 10:30 A.M.–4:30 P.M. daily except Thursday, when it closes at 2:30 P.M. It's open January and February only.

From Puerto Montt, **Buses Fierro** (tel. 065/253022) goes to Hornopirén (US$4, three hours) daily except Sunday at 8 A.M. and 1:30 and 3 P.M., and Sunday at 3 and 6:30 P.M. Both buses and private vehicles must cross the Estuario de Reloncaví from La Arena to Puelche, where **Transmarchilay**'s *BZ Quellonina* makes 10 crossings daily between 7:15 A.M. and 9:30 P.M. The half-hour voyage costs US$11 for cars, US$12.50 for light trucks, US$7 for motorcycles, US$3.50 for bicycles; passengers pay US$1 per person.

In January and February only, Transmarchilay's ferry *Mailén* sails daily to Caleta Gonzalo (six hours) at 9 A.M. Passengers pay US$14 per person, while cyclists pay an extra US$9 and motorcyclists US$17. Automobiles and light trucks pay US$88, while larger vehicles pay US$24 per lineal meter.

Insular Chiloé

The heartland of Chilean folklore, greener than Washington and Oregon, Chiloé is a rain-drenched archipelago whose wild western woodlands are darker than the Black Forest and traversed by trails that lead to secluded ocean beaches with rolling dunes. Its cultural landscape is a mosaic of field and forest, and it is home to some of Chile's most diverse seafood.

Some 180 kilometers long and 50 kilometers wide, one of about 40 islands in the group, the Isla Grande is not only Chile's largest island, but South America's second largest—only Tierra del Fuego (shared between Chile and Argentina) is larger. The sheltered inlets on its more densely populated east coast are ideal for sea kayaking, linking peasant villages with a unique vernacular architecture of elaborately shingled houses—a handful of them *palafitos* on stilts—and churches.

Though it can rain at any time of year, summer is the best time to visit, as the days are long enough at least to hope for a break in the drizzle. On the Pacific side penguins—the ranges of the Humboldt and Magellanic species overlap here—also breed in summer.

HISTORY

Pre-Columbian Chiloé was the province of the Huilliche, the most southerly branch of the Mapuche, who netted and trapped fish, gathered shellfish like sea urchins, and cultivated maize and especially potatoes in its cool, damp climate. Their insularity bred a self-reliance that persists to the present, as its residents have adapted native materials into technologically simple but useful artifacts.

Spain founded the city of Castro in 1567, but Jesuit missionaries soon established a circuit around what was often called the "last outpost of Christianity." Before their 1767 expulsion from the Americas, the Jesuits encouraged the construction of churches and chapels that were predecessors of the 50-plus scattered around the archipelago today, which have resulted in its designation as a UNESCO World Heritage Site.

Refugees fleeing the mainland Mapuche insurrection of the early 17th century found a haven here, creating the first permanent European presence. Their geographical isolation took political form in a conservatism that made them the Spanish Empire's last holdouts in Chile, which failed to conquer the fortress of Ancud in 1826.

Economically, isolation meant poverty, though not starvation. Darwin remarked, only a few years after Spain's expulsion, that "there is no demand for labour, and consequently the lower orders cannot scrape together money sufficient to purchase even the smallest luxuries," and that barter was a way of life. Emigration for employment became a way of life—buses still leave the Isla Grande for southern Patagonia every day—but developments of the past two decades have improved the economy and reduced isolation. Ferries frequently cross the Canal Chacao to the mainland, a suspension bridge is in the works, and salmon farming, whatever its environmental drawbacks, has brought a measure of prosperity. In summer, the tourist economy also makes a substantial contribution.

ANCUD

On a sheltered harbor that enjoys good ocean access, the late colonial outpost of Ancud defended Spain's Pacific coastline from foreign powers and privateers so well that it held out for nearly a decade after Chile's 1818 declaration of independence. Only the Peruvian port of Callao held out longer.

Now Chiloé's largest town, the former fortress was once a major port of entry but the 1912 arrival of the railroad to Puerto Montt undercut Ancud's economic base, and it now relies on fishing for its livelihood. Its high headlands provide exceptional coastal views.

Orientation

On the northern coast of the Isla Grande, facing the Canal de Chacao that divides the archipelago from the mainland, San Carlos de Ancud (population 27,292) is 90 kilometers southwest of

Puerto Montt, 27 kilometers west of the Pargua-Chacao ferry crossing, and 87 kilometers north of Castro via the Panamericana, which skirts the eastern approach to the city. It occupies a hilly peninsular site whose irregular terrain has generated an equally irregular but compact city plan around the roughly trapezoidal Plaza de Armas.

Sights

At the southwest corner of the Plaza de Armas, the recently remodeled **Museo Azul de las Islas de Chiloé,** alternatively known as the **Museo Aurelio Bórquez Canobra,** is Ancud's regional museum. Informally known as the Museo Chilote, it focuses on the archipelago's natural environment and wildlife, regional archaeology, European settlement, ecclesiastical art and architecture, the 1960 earthquake (which literally shook the island into the present), the Castro-Ancud railway (destroyed by the quake), and a vivid relief map of the archipelago. The patios also include sculptures of folkloric figures like the sinister, forest-dwelling Trauco and the siren mermaid La Pincoya.

The Museo Chilote (Libertad 370, tel. 065/622413) is open 10:30 A.M.–7:30 P.M. daily in January and February, 9 A.M.–5:45 P.M. weekdays, 10 A.M.–12:45 P.M. weekends and 3–5:45 P.M. Saturdays only the rest of the year. Admission costs US$1 for adults, US$.50 for children.

Guarding the harbor from a promontory just west of the intersection of Cochrane and San Antonio, the colonial **Fuerte San Antonio** (1770) was Spain's last Chilean redoubt during the independence struggles—Chilean forces finally lowered the Spanish flag and raised their own in 1826. Its cannon emplacements are still intact.

Entertainment and Events

Performing-arts events take place at the **Teatro Municipal de Ancud** (Blanco Encalada 660), on the east side of the Plaza de Armas, and the **Casa del la Cultura** (Libertad 663), alongside the museum.

For drinks, try the **Retro Pub** (Maipú 615; see also Food, below).

Late January's **Semana Ancuditana** (Ancud Week) celebrates the city's founding and the island's folkloric music and dance, and traditional food. Throughout December and January, though, there are similar events in nearby communities.

© WAYNE BERNHARDSON

fishing fleet in Ancud

The Sur Chico

Shopping

Chiloé's crafts offerings include ceramics, wood carvings, and woolens. Local outlets include the **Museo Chilote** (see above), the **Mercado Municipal** (Dieciocho between Libertad and Blanco Encalada), and **Artesanía Francisquita** (Libertad 530).

In January and February only, a small **Feria de Artesanos** fills the north end of the Plaza de Armas. A permanent **Feria Artesanal** (Arturo Prat and Pedro Montt) occupies the site of the old rural bus terminal, but it focuses on fruits, vegetables, and seafood.

Accommodations

Ancud has plenty of accommodations ranging from camping to mostly midrange choices, with a handful of not-quite-upscale alternatives.

Surveying the shoreline from its location above Playa Gruesa, about 600 meters north of downtown, **Camping Arena Gruesa** (Costanera Norte 290, tel. 065/623428, arenagruesa@yahoo.com, US$4 pp) has 60 lighted sites with scant privacy but hot showers, firewood, and other conveniences; in a residential neighborhood, its major drawbacks are barking dogs and crowing roosters.

The Hostelling International representative is **Hospedaje Vista al Mar** (Avenida Salvador Allende 918, tel./fax 065/622617, www.vistaalmar.cl, US$9 pp). Crammed with kitschy decor, friendly **Hospedaje Alto Bellavista** (Bellavista 449, tel. 065/622384, US$10 pp with shared bath, US$25 d with private bath) has reasonably spacious, comfy rooms and serves an abundant breakfast; parking is limited.

Thanks to its gracious, responsive management, **Hospedaje Germania** (Pudeto 357, tel./fax 065/622214, roseminiortloff@hotmail.com, US$17 d with shared bath, US$25 d with private bath) is worth consideration.

Ancud's best new option is the nearly pristine, Swiss-run **Hostal Nuevo Mundo** (Avenida Costanera Salvador Allende 748, tel. 065/628383, www.newworld.cl, US$10 pp in dorms, US$24/29 s/d), which also offers panoramic sunsets.

On a busy one-way street, **Hotel Lacuy** (Pudeto 219, tel./fax 065/623019, hotellacuy@yahoo.es, US$24/32 s/d) is only a so-so choice, with breakfast and private bath. On the north side of the Plaza de Armas, **Hotel Balai** (Pudeto 169, tel./fax 065/622541, www.hotelbalai.cl, US$28/37 s/d) is a modern facility.

The bayfront **Hotel Polo Sur** (Avenida Salvador Allende 630, tel. 065/622200, www.turismopolosur.cl, US$25/40 s/d) offers well-located, utilitarian accommodations with breakfast and private bath.

Upscale accommodations are relatively scarce but pretty good, starting with cheerful **Hotel Galeón Azul** (Libertad 751, tel. 065/622567, fax 065/622543, galeonazul@surnet.cl, US$72/86 s/d). Easily Ancud's finest, with the best views as well, is **Hotel Ancud** (San Antonio 30, tel. 065/622340, fax 065/622350, tel. 02/2349610 in Santiago, www.hosteriancud.com, US$75/85 s/d).

Food

Most restaurant menus are similar in content—fish and shellfish—and in price. The Mercado Municipal's **Sacho** (Arturo Prat s/n, Local 7 tel. 065/622260) has a longstanding reputation for enormous standard seafood portions at moderate prices—in the US$5–6 range for most items. Salads are easily large enough for two. As the market is rebuilt, Sacho and its counterparts will have to relocate, as least temporarily.

Similar fare is available at **El Cangrejo** (Dieciocho 155, tel. 065/623091); **Capri** (Mocopulli 710); and the local favorite **Chiloé** (Pudeto 35). Slightly elaborate seafood venues include **La Pincoya** (Prat 61, tel. 065/622613); **Polo Sur** (Avenida Salvador Allende 630, tel. 065/622200); and **Kurantón** (Prat 94, tel. 065/622216), which also serves beef and pizza.

Until recently, the out-of-the-ordinary choice has been the **Retro Pub** (Maipú 615, tel. 065/626410), a pub-restaurant that dared to serve pizza and even some Mexican dishes. New on the scene, though, **La Candela** (Libertad 499) has a diverse international menu with items like crab cakes, Peruvian *ají de gallina,* and sushi, plus Ancud's best coffee.

Casa Mar (Costanera Salvador Allende and Errázuriz, tel. 065/624481) is both a restaurant and an events center, pricier than La Candela, but it has moderately priced lunches.

Information

Sernatur (Libertad 665, tel. 065/622800, infochiloe@sernatur.cl) is the island's best-equipped office in terms of maps, brochures, and up-to-date accommodations data. In summer, it's open 8:30 A.M.–8 P.M. weekdays, 10 A.M.–1:30 P.M. and 3–7:30 P.M. weekends; the rest of the year, hours are 7:30 A.M.–5:30 P.M. weekdays only.

The private **Asociación De Turismo De Ancud (ATA)** maintains a fairly thorough website (www.ancudmagico.cl) with details of some services.

Services

Ancud has no exchange houses, but **Banco de Crédito** has an ATM at Ramírez 257.

For postal services, **Correos de Chile** is at Pudeto and Blanco Encalada.

Entel (Pudeto 219) has long-distance and Internet services.

Centro Internet (Avenida Salvador Allende 740, tel. 065/622607) also provides Internet access, but there are many others.

Clean Center (Pudeto 45, tel. 065/623838) does the washing.

Hospital de Ancud (Almirante Latorre 405, tel. 065/622356) can handle medical problems.

Getting There

Ancud's long-distance **Terminal de Buses** (Aníbal Pinto and Marcos Vera) is about 1.2 kilometers east of downtown. There are many northbound buses to Puerto Montt and on to Santiago and intermediates, southbound buses to Castro, and services to Punta Arenas via Argentina with **Queilén Bus** (tel. 065/622140) and **Turibús** (tel. 065/622289).

Typical destinations, times, and fares include Castro (US$2, one hour), Chonchi (US$3.50, 1.5 hours), Puerto Montt (US$3.50, two hours), Temuco (US$10, seven hours), Santiago (US$15–20, 15 hours), and Punta Arenas (US$60, 32 hours).

For buses to destinations other than those on or along the Panamericana, the **Terminal de Buses Rurales** is at Pedro Montt and Arturo Prat.

VICINITY OF ANCUD

Ancud's U.S.-run **Austral Adventures** (Cochrane 432, tel./fax 065/625977, www.austral-adventures.com) conducts day tours and sea-kayak excursions; it specializes, though, in extended explorations of the archipelago's inner waters and points south on the 15-meter *Cahuella,* whose exterior resembles a traditional Chilote fishing boat but whose interior has contemporary comforts. For more information, see the Organized Tours entry in the Know chapter.

Isla Puñihuil

About 27 kilometers southwest of Ancud, offshore Isla Puñihuil is home to breeding colonies of both Magellanic and Humboldt penguins. The Fundación Otway (tel. 09/5647866, otwafund@ctcinternet.cl), which administers the site, conducts half-hour Zodiac tours of the colony for US$5 per person once you get there, but there is no public transport.

CASTRO

The Isla Grande's first urban settlement, picturesque Castro dates from 1567, when Martín Ruiz de Gamboa made it the base for evangelizing the archipelago's southern Huilliche and Chonos populations. Despite the activities of Franciscan, Mercedarian, and Jesuit missionaries, it remained a poor and isolated backwater, subject to earthquakes, tsunamis, fires, and sacking by privateers.

On seeing the city in 1834, barely two decades after Chilean independence, Darwin found it "a most forlorn and deserted place." Even in the early 20th century, Castro had barely a thousand inhabitants, and its isolation had fostered a distinctive townscape still characterized by its surviving *palafitos,* the stilted waterfront houses with their elaborately carved shingles. By 1912, a narrow-gauge railroad linked Castro with Ancud and the rest of the country, as farm exports increased port activity.

The 1960 earthquake devastated the city, but salmon farming in the late 1970s began a recovery that has continued to this day. Improved ferry connections have brought regular tourist

© WAYNE BERNHARDSON

palafitos (houses on stilts), Castro

traffic of Chileans and foreigners, the latter mostly Argentines.

Orientation

Castro (population 29,148), 88 kilometers south of Ancud via the paved Panamericana, is a central location for excursions throughout the Isla Grande. Its compact central grid occupies a broad plain above the Estero de Castro, a sheltered ocean inlet, but the Avenida Pedro Montt curves around the shoreline at sea level.

Sights

Castro has a greater number of tourist-oriented sights than any other city on the island, but it's also a fine base for excursions.

On the north side of the Plaza de Armas, Castro's landmark **Iglesia San Francisco** represents both change and continuity in Chiloé's architectural tradition. After fire destroyed its Franciscan-built predecessor in 1902, ecclesiastical authorities broke with tradition in hiring an Italian architect, Eduardo Provasoli, who incorporated both neo-Gothic and classical elements into the twin-tower structure. At the same time, employing local master builders and artisans ensured that Chilote elements would survive in the iron-clad wooden structure.

Now a national monument, begun in 1906 but not completed until 1912, the church has changed its colors without surrendering its flamboyance—instead of salmon and violet, its galvanized-iron exterior is now banana yellow with violet towers and dashes of reddish trim. The natural-wood interior is more somber, embellished with traditional Catholic statuary—some of it grisly renderings of the crucifixion.

Half a block south of the Plaza de Armas, the **Museo Regional de Castro** (Esmeralda s/n, tel. 065/635967) displays Huilliche artifacts and ethnographic materials, "appropriate technology" from the surrounding countryside, accounts on the island's urban development, and greatly improved photographic exhibits. Summer hours are 9:30 A.M.–8 P.M. daily except Sunday, when it's open 10:30 A.M.–1 P.M. The rest of the year, hours are 9:30 A.M.–1 P.M. and 3–6:30 P.M. daily except Sunday, when it's open 10:30 A.M.–1 P.M. Admission is free, but donations are welcome.

Now sitting in the newly developed **Plazuela El Tren,** a waterfront park on Avenida Pedro

© WAYNE BERNHARDSON

Iglesia San Francisco, Castro

Montt, the **Locomotora Ancud-Castro** hauled passengers and freight on the narrow-gauge railroad between 1912 and 1960, when an earthquake and tsunami ended train service on the island. The route either followed or paralleled the present-day Panamericana.

Occupying airy, well-lighted quarters that once were warehouses, Castro's **Museo de Arte Moderno de Chiloé** (MAM, Galvarino Riveros s/n, tel. 065/635454) stresses up-and-coming Chilean, mostly Chilote, painters, sculptors, and multimedia specialists. On the grounds of the Parque Municipal at the west Riveros, the MAM is open 10 A.M.–7 P.M. daily in summer, when it invites selected artists to show their latest work. In November, December, and March, hours are 11 A.M.– 2 P.M. daily, but it's closed the rest of the year except by appointment. Admission is free.

Until the 1960 earthquake and tsunami of 1960, shingled, stilted ***palafitos*** lined nearly all the Isla Grande's eastern shore estuaries, but only a handful survive today, most notably in Castro and vicinity. Traditionally, Chilote fishermen would tie their vessels to the pilings out their back door, but the houses themselves front on city streets.

Castro has the largest remaining assortment of this unique vernacular architecture, along the Costanera Avenida Pedro Montt at the northern approach to town, only two blocks from the Plaza de Armas at the Costanera's south end, and on both sides of the bridge over the Río Gamboa, southwest of the city center via the Panamericana.

At the south end of the Costanera, Castro's waterfront **Feria Artesanal** integrates tourist appeal—typical woolens, souvenir basketry, and *palafito marisquerías*—with practical items like food (including edible algae) and fuel (blocks of peat). While Dalcahue's Sunday crafts market gets more hype, this daily market rates nearly as highly.

Entertainment and Events

For exhibitions, the **Centro Cultural de Castro** (Serrano 320) is open 11 A.M.–1 P.M. and 4–9 P.M. daily, but it also serves as a performing-arts venues.

The **Casa Salvador Allende** (Gabriela Mistral 357) is a leftish cultural center that holds Saturday-night *peñas,* spontaneous musical gatherings.

Late January's **Festival de Huaso Chilote** is an excuse for high-speed horse races at the Parque Municipal. Mid-February's **Festival Costumbrista** is a weekend event with island crafts, folkloric music and dance, traditional foods like *curanto* and *yoco* (a pork dish), and liquors like *chicha* (cider, usually made from apples).

Accommodations

Accommodations of all sorts are abundant, but there's a notably better selection of top-end places than in Ancud.

Of several budget accommodations, the best value is **Hospedaje Mirador** (Barros Arana 127, tel. 065/633795, maboly@yahoo.com, US$8.50 pp, US$10 pp with breakfast). The waterfront **Hostal Costa Azul** (Lillo 67, tel./fax 065/632440, costazul@chiloeweb.com, US$14 pp with private bath) has cable TV in all rooms and breakfast is included.

Hostal Quelcún (San Martín 581, tel. 065/632396, fax 065/638717, quelcun@telsur.cl, US$8 pp with shared bath, US$17/30 s/d with private bath) has carpeted, centrally heated rooms with breakfast included.

At **Hostal Casablanca** (Los Carrera 308, tel./fax 065/632726, nelysald@surnet.cl, US$10 pp, US$40 d with breakfast) the shared-bath singles are tiny but spotless and comfy, while doubles with private bath are substantially larger.

Half a block off the Plaza de Armas, rates for the smallish but tidy rooms at **Hotel Chilhué** (Blanco 278, tel./fax 065/632596, hotelchilhue@yahoo.com, US$15/21 s/d with shared bath, US$30/36 s/d with private bath) include breakfast.

One of Castro's best-kept secrets is **Hostal Casa Kolping** (Chacabuco 217, tel. 065/633273, US$25/40 s/d), an architecturally noteworthy and immaculately maintained hotel in a quiet location south of the Plaza. Off-season rates, about 25 percent lower, are a steal.

Decorated in attractive native woods, **Hostal Don Camilo** (Ramírez 566, tel. 065/632180, audiex@telsur.cl, US$37/40 s/d) is a good value. Under the same management as the more elite Hostería de Castro, also embellished with native wood and carpeted floors, **Hostal Casita Española** (Los Carrera 359, tel. 065/635186, hosteriadecastro@telsur.cl, US$33/42 s/d) is comparable.

Behind its hideous façade, **Hotel Esmeralda** (Esmeralda 266, tel. 065/637900, fax 065/637910, hesmeralda@telsur.cl, US$22 pp with shared bath, US$49/65 s/d with private bath) has large modern rooms. Other amenities include breakfast, parking, a restaurant, and a pool hall.

Rates at **Gran Hotel Alerce Nativo** (O'Higgins 808, tel. 065/632267, fax 065/632309, hotelalerc@telsur.cl, US$54/66) include private bath, cable TV, and breakfast.

Dating from 1910, the highly regarded, architecturally distinctive **Hotel Unicornio Azul** (Pedro Montt 228, tel. 065/622359, hotelunicornioazul@surnet.cl, US$54/67 s/d) was a budget hotel as recently as the 1980s, but steady improvements have driven prices upward. Traditionally, the **Hostería de Castro** (Chacabuco 202, tel. 065/632301, fax 065/635688, www.hosteriadecastro.cl, US$65/74 s/d) rivals it for the honor of being Castro's best hotel. With IVA or cash discounts around 20 percent, this can be a much better value.

Food

For breakfasts, sandwiches, coffee, and desserts, try **Café del Mirador** (Blanco Encalada 388, tel. 065/633958) or **Café La Brújula del Cuerpo** (O'Higgins 308, tel. 065/633229). **La Tavolata** (Balmaceda 245, tel. 065/633882) serves quality pizza and pasta at moderate prices.

Most of the best are seafood venues, such as **Sacho** (Thompson 213, tel. 065/632079); **Chilos** (Sotomayor and San Martín, tel. 065/635782); **Dónde Eladio** (Lillo 97, tel. 065/635285); and **El Bucanero** (Lillo s/n, tel. 065/637260).

Widely acknowledged as one of the city's best, **Octavio** (Avenida Pedro Montt 261, tel. 065/632855) offers waterfront dining with style and fine service at moderate cost with a diverse menu—entrées range from US$4 (chicken) to US$12 (king crab). On the minus side, the pisco sours are a little small, and switching off—or removing—the TV would enhance the experience.

Information

In summer, Castro's private **Asociación Gremial Hotelera Gastronómica** operates a small information booth on the north side of the Plaza de Armas, open 9 A.M.–9 P.M. daily; the rest of the year, hours are 10 A.M.–5 P.M. daily except Sunday, when it's open 10 A.M.–2 P.M. only. It has adequate city maps, an accommodations price list of member hotels only, and limited information on the vicinity of Castro.

Conaf (Gamboa 424, tel. 065/622289) can provide information on Parque Nacional Chiloé.

Services

Castro has two exchange houses, **Cambio de Monedas Juan Suárez** (Gamboa 411) and **Julio Barrientos** (Chacabuco 286). **Banco de Crédito** (Gamboa 393) has an ATM.

Correos de Chile (O'Higgins 388) handles the mail.

Entel (O'Higgins 480) has long-distance and Internet access, but there are many others such as **Cadesof** (Gamboa 447, 2nd floor, tel. 065/632629).

The **Clean Center** (Serrano 490) does the washing.

Hospital de Castro is at Freire 852, tel. 065/632445.

Getting There

Most transport in and out of Castro is by land; maritime service to Chaitén is, metaphorically speaking, up in the air. Until recently, Catamaranes del Sur has connected Castro to Puerto Montt by sea; Aysén Express may or may not take the service over.

Most bus companies work out of the deceptively named **Terminal de Buses Rurales** (San Martín 667), which is also used by many long-distance carriers. **Cruz del Sur** (San Martín 486, tel. 065/632389) has its own terminal, also used by **Turibús** (tel. 065/632389) and **Transchiloé** (tel. 065/635152). Some companies have ticket agents at both locales.

Cruz del Sur goes south to Chonchi and north to Ancud and Puerto Montt, and offers continuing service to Santiago and intermediates. Transchiloé has similar routes. Several carriers go to Punta Arenas, including **Queilén Bus** (tel. 065/632173), **Buses Pacheco** (tel. 065/631188), and Turibús.

At the Terminal de Buses Rurales, **Buses Arroyo** (tel. 065/635604) goes two or three times daily to Cucao, the gateway to Parque Nacional Chiloé; Ojeda has additional services on the same route. **Dalcahue Expreso** (tel. 065/635164) goes at least half hourly to Dalcahue weekdays, but less frequently on weekends. **Buses Lemuy** and **Buses Gallardo** (tel. 065/634521) serve Chonchi (US$1.25). *Taxi colectivos* to Chonchi leave from the corner of Chacabuco and Esmeralda.

Sample destinations, fares, and times include Ancud (US$2, one hour), Puerto Montt (US$5, three hours), Temuco (US$12, eight hours), Santiago (US$18–22, 19 hours), and Punta Arenas (US$60, 34 hours).

VICINITY OF CASTRO

Several companies conduct day trips and longer tours of the area, including destinations like Dalcahue, Chonchi, Parque Nacional Chiloé, and offshore islands. Among them are **Turismo Quelcún** (San Martín 581, tel. 065/632396), **Turismo Queilén Bus** (San Martín 667, tel. 065/632173), at the Terminal de Buses Rurales, and **Pehuén Turismo** (Blanco Encalada 299, tel. 065/632361, fax 065/635254, www.turismopehuen.cl).

Dalcahue

Artisans from around Chiloé customarily present their best at Dalcahue's Sunday market, still its biggest attraction, but this modest fishing village, about 20 kilometers northeast of Castro, is gaining importance as a base for sea-kayak excursions among the islands off the archipelago's sheltered eastern shore.

Nothing remains of Dalcahue's *palafitos,* obliterated by the 1960 tsunami, but its 19th-century **Iglesia Parroquial** is one of the architectural monuments that helped the island's wooden churches gain UNESCO World Heritage Site status. Most visitors come to Dalcahue (population 4,933) for Sunday's **Feria Artesanal,** though a flood of imported kitsch has nearly inundated the quality basketry, woodcarvings, and woolens that once typified this lively market.

Most visitors choose to stay at Castro, which has much better accommodations than Dalcahue, but the waterfront **Brisas Marinas** (Pedro Montt s/n) makes an ideal lunch break, with outstanding seafood at moderate prices.

Frequent **Dalcahue Expreso** buses to and from Castro stop at both the main bus terminal (Freire and O'Higgins) and the waterfront Feria Artesanal. There are also *taxi colectivos* to and from Castro.

Chonchi

Nicknamed the Ciudad de los Tres Pisos (City of Three Levels) for its sheer hillsides and steep streets, San Carlos de Chonchi (population 4,588) was one of Chiloé's first Jesuit missions, thanks to its strategically central location. Not founded officially until 1767, the year of the Jesuits' expulsion, it managed to keep its own spontaneous street plan and avoid the imposition of the regulation Spanish colonial grid, which would have played havoc with its hilly topography. It is 23 kilometers south of Castro.

Even if the 1960 tsunami split Chonchi's *palafitos* into toothpicks, the earthquake spared its historic **Iglesia San Carlos de Chonchi** (1900) and many houses along **Calle Centenario,** an area designated a *zona típica* national monument. The new **Museo de las Tradiciones Chonchinas** (Centenario 116) replicates a typical Chilote kitchen and displays impressive photographs of the 1960 tsunami.

Set on spacious grounds with fruit trees and a gazebo, the seaside **Hospedaje La Esmeralda** (Irarrázabal s/n, tel. 065/671328, grady@telsur.cl, US$7.50–8.50 pp with shared bath, US$11 pp for more spacious rooms with private bath and in-room heating) is a backpackers' favorite; the room known as "The Bridge" has the best views of the harbor. Other meals—salmon dinners are a tradition—are also available, along with rental bikes, a rowboat and fishing gear, and boat tours of the vicinity. Owner Carl Grady, who is English, also speaks German and Spanish.

The municipal **Oficina de Información Turística** (Sargento Candelaria and Centenario) is open 9 A.M.–7 P.M. daily in summer only.

Cruz del Sur and **Transchiloé,** which share offices at Pedro Montt 233, tel. 065/671218, have frequent services between Castro and Chonchi; *taxi colectivos* to Castro (US$1) are also frequent. Buses from Castro that are bound for Cucao (Parque Nacional Chiloé) stop here en route; in addition, there are one or more Pepe Vera minibuses to Cucao (US$1.50) from the Terminal Municipal.

PARQUE NACIONAL CHILOÉ

South of Ancud and west of the Panamericana, Chiloé's Pacific coast is an almost roadless area of abrupt headlands, broad sandy beaches, and sprawling dunes at the foot of forested mountains dissected by numerous transverse rivers. Much of this landscape, in fact, differs little from Darwin's description in *The Voyage of the Beagle* as he rode west toward Cucao, now the gateway to Parque Nacional Chiloé:

> *At Chonchi we struck across the island, following intricate winding paths, sometimes passing through magnificent forests, and sometimes through pretty cleared spots, abounding with corn and potato crops. This undulating woody country, partially cultivated, reminded me of the wilder parts of England, and therefore had to my eye a most fascinating aspect. At Vilinco [Huillinco], which is situated on the borders of the lake of Cucao, only a few fields were cleared . . .*

Since its creation in 1982, Parque Nacional Chiloé has protected a representative sample of the Isla Grande's natural habitat and wildlife, while providing recreational access to growing numbers of outdoors enthusiasts, both Chileans and foreigners. At the same time, Conaf administration has been less successful in integrating the area's indigenous Huilliche residents into its future, and matters have changed little from the 19th century when Darwin observed that "they are very much secluded from the rest of Chiloé, and have scarcely any sort of commerce . . ."

Geography and Climate

On the Isla Grande's thinly settled, densely forested Pacific coast, Parque Nacional Chiloé comprises 43,057 hectares in three distinct sectors: 35,207-hectare **Sector Anay,** west of Chonchi near the village of Cucao; 7,800-hectare **Sector Chepu,** southwest of Ancud; and the 50-hectare **Sector Islote Metalqui,** a rugged offshore island.

Altitudes range from sea level to 850 meters in the Cordillera de Piuchén. Annual rainfall in the marine west coast climate varies from about 2,000 millimeters on the coast to 3,000 millimeters at the highest elevations. Temperatures are mild, averaging about 10°C over the course of the year, with few extremes of either heat or cold.

Flora and Fauna

At some lower elevations, mixed evergreen forest of the endemic *coigue* or *roble de Chiloé (Nothofagus nitida)* covers the valleys and slopes, along with the coniferous *mañío (Podocarpus nubigena)* and climbing vines; in others, enormous

© WAYNE BERNHARDSON

chapel at Cucao

ferns cover the soil beneath the *ulmo, arrayán,* and the twisted *tepu (Tepualia stimulais).* Near its northern limit here, the world's most southerly conifer, the *ciprés de los Guaitecas (Pilgiroden-dron uviferum),* also grows in swampy soils with the *tepu;* the *alerce* reaches the southern limit of its geographical range at altitudes above 600 meters.

In such dense forest, it's rare to see mammals, though the *pudú* and the Chiloé fox (*Dusicyon fulvipes,* first identified by Darwin) survive here. Both sea otters and sea lions inhabit coastal areas, while the 110 bird species include Magellanic and Humboldt penguins, oystercatchers, and cormorants on the coast. The dense forest is home to the elusive *chucao.*

Sights and Activities

Cucao is the base for visiting Sector Anay, the park's most accessible and popular area, which has several hiking trails of varying length. Because of the damp climate, wool socks and water-resistant boots are advisable for hikers.

From Conaf's Centro de Visitantes at Chanquín, just across the river from the village, the **Sendero Dunas de Cucao** winds through vestigial forest and traverses a broad dunefield to arrive at a long white sandy beach, one kilometer to the west. Violent surf, treacherous currents, and frigid Pacific waters make the beach unsuitable for swimming, so the scenery is the main attraction.

Near Conaf's Chanquín campground, winding through boggy, slippery terrain, the 700-meter **Sendero Interpretivo El Tepual** makes as many twists and turns as the trunks of the *tepu* trees over which it passes.

North of Cucao, a longer coastal trail goes three kilometers to the Huilliche settlement at **Lago Huelde** and continues to the **Río Cole Cole,** nine kilometers farther, where there is a simple Conaf *refugio* with a fire pit for cooking. Eight kilometers beyond Cole Cole, there's a similar *refugio* at **Río Anay.** Inquire about conditions at these *refugios* before planning to spend the night, and consider a tent as an alternative.

For non-hikers, inexpensive rental horses are available at Cucao, but they're not suitable for forest trails like El Tepual and, because many of them are untrained for amateur riders, there have been accidents.

For organized excursions to more remote parks of the park, on foot, horseback or via canoe or kayak, contact the Fundación Raíces (tel. 09/9913733, pnchiloe@conaf.cl).

Accommodations and Food

In and around Cucao, several family-run campgrounds charge around US$2–3 per person, but the only formal campground within park boundaries is **Camping Chanquín** (US$4.50 pp), about 200 meters beyond Conaf's visitors center. Designed for privacy, its 20 sites offer running water, firewood, hot showers, and toilets. At *refugios* or along trails, camping is free of charge.

Non-campers can try any of several Cucao *hospedajes,* among them **Hospedaje El Paraíso** (tel. 09/2965465, US$8.50 pp) and the slightly more upscale **Posada Cucao** (tel. 09/8969855, US$10 pp). All of them offer meals as well.

Fundación Raíces (contact Lidia López Tresinger, tel. 09/9913733, pnchiloe@conaf.cl) rents *cabañas* for US$43; camping costs US$3.50 per person.

At Cucao, in the bus station, **Doña Rosa** offers local fare, while the German-run **Parador Darwin,** just across the bridge, offers a more imaginative menu. Unfortunately, the latter is up for sale, so its survival is open to question.

Cucao has a minimarket, and its possible to buy fresh fish, potatoes, and the like from local fishermen and farmers, but supplies are more diverse and cheaper in Castro and Chonchi.

Information

About one kilometer west of the concrete bridge over the Río Cucao, rangers collect a US$1.60-per-person admission charge at Chanquín, where Conaf's **Centro de Visitantes** is open 9 A.M.–7:30 P.M. daily. It contains exhibits on the park's flora and fauna, the aboriginal Huilliche, mining history, and regional legends and traditions. The surrounding grounds contain samples of Chilote technology, including a cider press and wooden sleighs used to drag heavy loads over boggy ground.

Getting There

Cucao, the park's main access point, is 52 kilometers southwest of Castro via the Panamericana and a rugged gravel road (almost always passable but which never seems to improve) and 32 kilometers west of Chonchi. From Castro, there are two to five buses daily, depending on the season, to Cucao, with **Buses Arroyo** (tel. 065/635604) and Ojeda. In summer, from Chonchi, there are also buses to and from Cucao.

Ancud's **Buses Chepu** (Arturo Prat s/n) goes to Sector Chepu, at the northern end of the park (US$1), daily in summer but Monday, Wednesday, and Friday only the rest of the year.

Aisén and Continental Chiloé

With the smallest population of any Chilean region, Aisén is a natural wonderland of islands, mountains, fjords, lakes, rivers, and forests that's drawing growing numbers of visitors since completion of the Carretera Austral from Caleta Gonzalo in the north to Villa O'Higgins in the south. Its only sizeable city is the regional capital of Coyhaique, which has a small but state-of-the-art airport and is a good base for exploring the area. Some visitors, though, begin at Region X ferry port of Chaitén and work their way south along the Carretera Austral. Others arrive at Coyhaique's port of Puerto Chacabuco, via ferry or catamaran from Puerto Montt.

In addition to the Carretera Austral and its several national parks, Aisén's major attraction is Parque Nacional Laguna San Rafael, where the ice meets the sea, but it's accessible only by sea or by air taxi. In general, the climate resembles that of coastal British Columbia, with the seasons reversed (December, January, and February are summer). Consequently, weather can be wet, windy, and cool any time of year, especially at

Must-Sees

Look for [M] to find the sights and activities you can't miss and [N] for the best dining and lodging.

Parque Nacional Laguna San Rafael: Southwest of Coyhaique, the ice still reaches the sea at Laguna San Rafael—though it's receding alarmingly fast (page 260).

Parque Nacional Queulat: The hanging glacier at this park once reached what is now the northern Carretera Austral and, while it's receded dramatically over the past two centuries, it still provides a clue as to what Yosemite valley might have looked like before its glaciers melted (page 264).

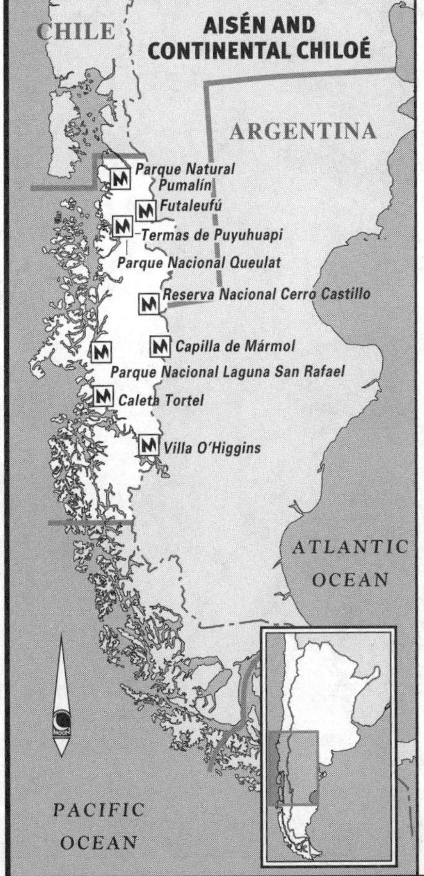

Termas de Puyuhuapi: It's not really an island, but this surprisingly affordable hot-springs resort might as well be, for its splendid isolation opposite the northern Carretera Austral (page 267).

Futaleufú: Almost every rafter and kayaker places the Río Futaleufú among the world's top 10 whitewater rivers, and many put it at the top of the list (page 269).

Parque Natural Pumalín: It's been politically controversial, but South America's largest private conservation project is gradually winning acceptance for its commitment to preserving huge extents of midlatitude rain forest and simultaneously making them accessible to the public (page 275).

Reserva Nacional Cerro Castillo: Growing in popularity, the trekking beneath the spires of this readily accessible reserve on the southern Carretera Austral makes it second only to Torres del Paine, probably, in its popularity with multiday hikers. It's a distant second, though, so there's no Paine gridlock (page 280).

Capilla de Mármol: Accessible by water only, the sinuous walls of these blue/white grottos are on the shores of Lago General Carrera (page 283).

Caleta Tortel: A road reaches its outskirts now, but the only way to get around this quaint seaside fishing village is still the boardwalks and staircases that connect its waterfront and scattered houses and businesses (page 290).

Villa O'Higgins: In scenic mountain surroundings, this orderly outpost of Chilean bureaucracy is almost the end of the road—the Carretera Austral stops just south of here—but it's also the jumping-off point for the new "Cruce de Lagos" to the Argentine trekking capital of El Chaltén (page 291).

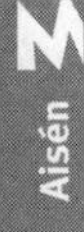

AISÉN AND CONTINENTAL CHILOÉ

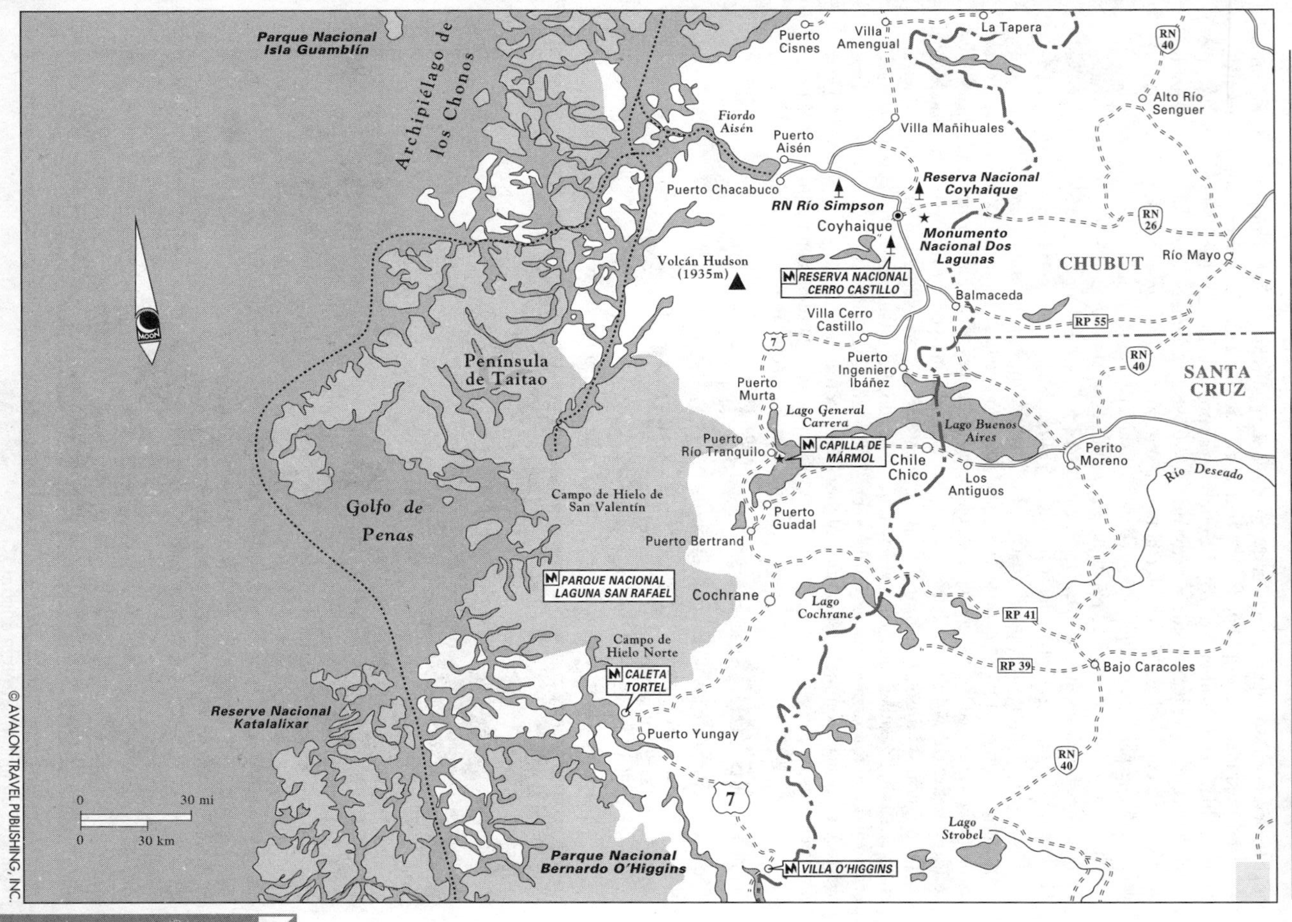
Parque Nacional Isla Guamblín
Archipiélago de los Chonos
Puerto Cisnes
Villa Amengual
La Tapera
RN 40
Alto Río Senguer
Fiordo Aisén
Puerto Aisén
Villa Mañihuales
Puerto Chacabuco
RN Río Simpson
Reserva Nacional Coyhaique
Coyhaique
Monumento Nacional Dos Lagunas
RN 26
Río Mayo
CHUBUT
Volcán Hudson (1935m)
RESERVA NACIONAL CERRO CASTILLO
Balmaceda
RP 55
Villa Cerro Castillo
7
Península de Taitao
Puerto Ingeniero Ibáñez
SANTA CRUZ
Puerto Murta
Lago General Carrera
Lago Buenos Aires
Puerto Río Tranquilo
CAPILLA DE MÁRMOL
Chile Chico
Los Antiguos
Perito Moreno
Río Deseado
Golfo de Penas
Campo de Hielo de San Valentín
Puerto Guadal
Puerto Bertrand
PARQUE NACIONAL LAGUNA SAN RAFAEL
Cochrane
Lago Cochrane
RP 41
Campo de Hielo Norte
CALETA TORTEL
RP 39
Bajo Caracoles
Reserve Nacional Katalalixar
Puerto Yungay
0
30 mi
30 km
Lago Strobel
Parque Nacional Bernardo O'Higgins
VILLA O'HIGGINS
MOON

Aisén

higher elevations, so hikers should carry good rain and trekking gear and hope for the best. Summer highs can climb above 25°C around Coyhaique, but cooler temperatures are the rule. Mid-summer days are long, with sunsets around 10 P.M., thanks partly to daylight savings time.

Thanks to tourism, Aisén is increasingly prosperous, but agriculture and extractive industries like forestry and mining are also important. More recently, the salmon-farming industry has brought both prosperity and controversy, as its environmental cost has proved greater than some residents believe it's worth.

Throughout Chilean Patagonia, overland transportation schedules change from season to season and year to year, and may be disrupted by weather, particularly on the Aisén portion of the Carretera Austral.

PLANNING YOUR TIME

Because distances are great, public transportation is limited, and the roads are few and often slow, Aisén more than any other Chilean region can justify a rental car, preferably with high clearance. Vehicles are also few, though, and rental reservations are advisable for visitors flying into Balmaceda/Coyhaique, which is roughly the midway point on the Carretera Austral.

Coyhaique is the best base for excursions north and south, and to Laguna San Rafael by catamaran or air taxi. Northbound on the Carretera Austral, it takes at least a week or 10 days to see even adequately the roadside or near-roadside highlights like Parque Nacional Queulat, the hot springs at Termas de Puyuhuapi, Parque Natural Pumalín, and the Río Futaleufú's world-class whitewater—not counting a possible side trip into Argentina.

Southbound on the highway, it needs at least a week and preferably longer to enjoy Cerro Castillo, Lago General Carrera, the one-of-a-kind fishing settlement of Caleta Tortel, and the wild end-of-the-road scenery at Villa O'Higgins.

For visitors heading south from Puerto Montt, with rental cars, ferry reservations are advisable, especially for the summer service between Hornopirén and Caleta Gonzalo.

HISTORY

Europeans first viewed Aisén's channels in 1553, when Pedro de Valdivia ordered Francisco de

The catamaran *Patagonian Express* arrives at Termas de Puyuhuapi hot springs, one of many highlights along the Carretera Austral.

Ulloa to explore the Strait of Magellan from the Pacific side. When Ulloa landed on Península Taitao, though, the forerunners of today's Kawasqar (Alacaluf) had been navigating the same waterways for millennia; on the nearby continent, the Tehuelche (Aónikenk) and their predecessors had long stalked the steppes for guanaco and the forest for *huemul.*

Aisén's thinly populated, rugged recesses held little appeal for the Spaniards. At first, tales of "Trapananda" drew a few fortune hunters in search of the fabulous wealthy but literally fantastic "City of the Caesars" (tales of hidden riches persist to the present, and a small Conaf reserve northeast of Coyhaique even bears the name Trapananda). After gold fever subsided, the Spaniards settled in more temperate areas where they could extract tribute and labor from the indigenous population, a more dependable source of wealth until introduced diseases reduced their numbers dramatically.

In the 1670s, both Bartolomé Díaz Gallardo and Antonio de Vea came upon Laguna San Rafael and the Campo de Hielo Norte, the northern continental ice sheet. The most dedicated explorers, though, were Jesuit missionaries in search of souls, working their way south from Chiloé, by both land and sea until their expulsion from the Americas in 1767. The list of non-Spaniards reads like a who's who: John Byron, grandfather of the famous poet George Gordon (Lord Byron), suffered a shipwreck in the late 18th century, and FitzRoy and Darwin saw Laguna San Rafael on board the *Beagle* a few decades later. Under Admiral Sir Thomas Baker, commander of the British Navy's South American Squadron, the latter charted much of the area's waters, their work later supplemented by Chilean naval officer Enrique Simpson in the 1870s.

In 1798, Spain made the region's first land grant, an enormous tract between the Río Yelcho in the north and the Río Bravo in the south, but Argentine overland explorers were the first non-indigenous travelers to see much of the area. Despite concern about the Argentine presence, which led to territorial disagreements that have only been resolved within the last decade, Chile had trouble enough controlling areas south of the Biobío, let alone remote Aisén. Consequently, it did little to promote settlement until the early 20th century, when it granted the Valparaíso-based Sociedad Industrial Aisén a huge, long-term concession for sheep ranching and forest exploitation near what is now Coyhaique.

News of the concession set off a land rush, from the Chilean heartland and Argentina's Chubut province, by settlers who challenged the Sociedad's state-sanctioned dominance. While these smallholders held their own against the Sociedad, both of them, along with the Chilean state, bear responsibility for large-scale deforestation that followed under a misguided law that encouraged cutting and burning to establish land titles. Today, when hillsides of deciduous *ñirres* turn red in the fall, it's a pale reminder of what the entire region must have looked like seven decades ago, before deliberate fires and unintentional wildfires denuded countless slopes and left only pale trunks scattered among pasture grasses, from Mañihuales in the north to Puerto Ibáñez in the south. One unanticipated consequence was that silt carried by the Río Simpson, from erosion triggered by deforestation and grazing, clogged the harbor of the region's main port, Puerto Aisén, necessitating its shift to Puerto Chacabuco.

Since the 1970s, the major development in Aisén and continental Chiloé has been construction of the Carretera Austral, parts of which are now being paved, to Villa O'Higgins. With improved relations between Argentina and Chile, cross-border contacts have also improved, and pressure has increased to open up the area to hydroelectric projects on the Río Futaleufú and the Río Baker, both of them also prime recreational resources. While Aisén seems likely to grow, it seems unlikely to attract the large-scale growth, through massive immigration, advocated by some regional politicians.

Coyhaique and Vicinity

Originally known as Baquedano, today's regional capital was at first so remote and obscure that letters addressed here often ended up in an Atacama desert mining town of the same name. After a decade of confusion following its founding in 1929, its name became Coyhaique, but it did not become the provincial capital until 1973, when it succeeded Puerto Aisén.

Founded as a service center for the Sociedad Industrial Aisén, its growth spurred by the colonists who flooded the region in its wake, Coyhaique is a mostly modern city whose infrastructure hasn't quite kept up with its growth—in heavy rain, downtown streets drain so poorly and the flow of water in the gutters is so broad that the city sets out impromptu pedestrian bridges at some intersections. Recent improvements, though, include a rehabilitated Plaza de Armas and conversion of congested Calle Horn into Paseo Horn, a pedestrian mall that's become a popular gathering place.

Still the region's only substantial city, Coyhaique has a complete array of services, including several new restaurants, pubs, and travel agencies. One of the gateways to the Carretera Austral both north and south, it also offers an alternate route into Argentina.

ORIENTATION

Beneath the basaltic barricade of Cerro Macay, at the confluence of the Río Simpson and the Río Coyhaique, 455 kilometers south of Caleta Gonzalo and 566 kilometers north of Villa O'Higgins, Coyhaique (population 44,850) sits roughly at the midpoint of Carretera Austral's continental segment. It is 634 kilometers from Puerto Montt via the Carretera Austral.

To the west, a paved highway leads to Puerto Aisén and Puerto Chacabuco, while another paved highway leads southeast to Balmaceda and the Argentine border at Paso Huemules. On the Argentine side, the mostly paved road continues to the Atlantic port of Comodoro Rivadavia, 600 kilometers to the east on what is optimistically called the *Corredor Bioceánico* (Bi-Oceanic Corridor) with Puerto Chacabuco.

Coyhaique's street plan is not for the geometrically challenged, based as it is on a pair of concentric pentagons, the inner of which surrounds the Plaza de Armas. Beyond this, it's more regular and less disorienting, but still presents problems for anyone unaccustomed to the irregular angles of many intersections.

Avenida Baquedano, on the northeast edge of town, connects the paved Puerto Chacabuco road with the gravel road that leads east to the Argentine border at Coyhaique Alto. Avenida Ogana is the main route to Balmaceda and to the southbound Carretera Austral.

SIGHTS

Nearly all visitors to Coyhaique's disorienting pentagonal **Plaza de Armas,** where 10 streets radiate like spokes from a wheel, get lost returning to their hotels. Bewildered travelers can thank the city's founder, Luis Marchant González, a policeman who decided in 1929 that the Carabineros' five-sided badge made an ideal city-planning template. Recently re-landscaped, it still boasts many mature trees, and the forest cover itself makes landmarks more difficult to spot for orientation.

Coyhaique's **Museo Regional de la Patagonia,** recently relocated to new quarters in the Casa de la Cultura (Eusebio Lillo 23, tel. 065/213174), documents regional history through a large and well-presented series of historical photographs and early settlers' household implements. Hours are 9 A.M.–9 P.M. daily in summer, 8:30 A.M.–1 P.M. Monday–Saturday and 3–7 P.M. weekdays the rest of the year. Admission is US$.60.

Nearby, on the Baquedano median strip, the **Monumento al Ovejero** commemorates the pioneer sheep farmers who settled the region. The series of statues consists of a mounted shepherd, his flock, and his sheep dogs.

THE DICTATOR'S HIGHWAY?

The highway where Santiaguinos come to test their SUVs, rather than on the streets of Las Condes and Vitacura, the Carretera Austral is so crucial to Aisén that Coyhaique's modest museum used to devote its largest exhibit to it, and many residents still give General Pinochet the credit—one conspicuous photo showed a grandfatherly Pinochet, in civilian dress, beaming at a local schoolboy. A frequent comment is that the military regime was "the last one to pay attention to the region," and one Pinochet partisan claimed that "the politicians would never have built this highway. There are no votes here."

But Pinochet may get more credit than he deserves. The original highway studies date from 1968, during the Christian Democrat administration of President Eduardo Frei Montalva, and the project advanced during the early 1970s administration of Socialist Allende. Though work accelerated during the dictatorship, civilian contractors actually did more than the military.

The Carretera's final irony is that the man who finished it, President Ricardo Lagos, is the man who stared down Pinochet in 1988, boldly addressing the dictator through a TV camera: "You promise the country another eight years of torture, disappearances, and human rights violations." Lagos's bravery probably turned the tide in a plebiscite that began the end of the military regime. Maps once labeled "Carretera Longitudinal Austral Presidente Pinochet" now simply say "Carretera Longitudinal Austral."

Villa O'Higgins, the end-of-the-road hamlet, is governed by the far-right UDI. Still, the entire town showed up in April 2000, when the newly elected Socialist President Ricardo Lagos, Pinochet's political nemesis, formally dedicated the Río Bravo-Villa O'Higgins segment, the final piece in the puzzle.

The notoriously timid *huemul*, the emblematic, endangered Andean deer that graces Chile's coat-of-arms that along with the Andean condor and the motto "by reason or force," is surprisingly common and even docile along this last segment. In a sense, it's a tangible symbol of change and openness that the highway increasingly represents—not force alone, but reason as well. The highway that began as a military exercise now belongs to everyone, and even the occasional skid off the straight-and-narrow won't change the direction.

While some pioneer settlements along the Carretera Austral are acquiring an air of permanence, this is still wild country, where camping is mostly free and easy, with just enough creature comforts for those on bigger budgets. Most Chileans take their vacations in January and February, when prices are at their highest and public transport most frequent. The spring months of October and November and the autumn months of March and April can be good times to travel here, though public transport is less frequent.

At the same time the Carretera Austral is one of the loveliest highways in the Americas—there's no bad scenery anywhere—it's also one of the most hazardous. Blind curves in dense forests and sheer mountains, narrow segments with steeply sloping shoulders, and frequent loose gravel all require drivers to pay the closest attention to avoid head-on collisions, rollovers, and other possible accidents.

COYHAIQUE

Río Simpson

EJÉRCITO
TAPERA
EXPEDICIONES COYHAIQUE
PORTALES
HOSPITAL BASE
DR JORGE IBAR
BALMACEDA
PRESIDENTE IBAÑEZ
RODRÍGUEZ
21 DE MAYO
MORALEDA
CARRERA
PATAGONIA HOTEL
OBISPO MICHELATO
GENERAL PARRA
NAVIMAG
CASINO DE BOMBEROS
RIQUELME
PATAGONIA ADVENTURE EXPEDITIONS
TRAVELL
PARRA
LANEXPRESS
OBISPO G. VIELMO
LA CASONA
HOSTAL ARAUCARIAS
HOSTERÍA COIHAIQUE
DUSSEN
BUSES NORTE
BALMACEDA
MANOS AZULES
TURISMO PRADO
PIEL ROJA
CAFETERÍA ALEMANA
LA OLLA
SERNATUR
AYSÉN EXPRESS
GABRIELA MISTRAL
TRANSPORTES AÉREOS SAN RAFAEL
BAR WEST
LAVANDERÍA QL
SKY AIRLINE
RINCÓN DEL POETA/CÓNDOR
CAFÉ ORIENTE
CONDELL
BANCO SANTANDER
BILBAO
EL MASTIQUE
BUSES SURAY
FERIA ARTESANAL DE COYHAIQUE
LA FIORENTINA
CIBER PATAGONIA
18 DE SEPTIEMBRE
HOSTAL ARRIERO PATAGÓN
HORN
Plaza de Armas
MONTT
E. LILLO
MAGALLANES
CAMBIOS EMPERADOR
CAFÉ RICER
ENTELCHILE
CINE COIHAIQUE
POST OFFICE
12 DE OCTUBRE
LOBERÍAS DE CHACABUCO
TRANSPORTE AÉREO DON CARLOS/TAXI BUS DON CARLOS
HOTEL LUIS LOYOLA
TERMINAL DE BUSES
PATAGONIA EXPLORER AVIACIÓN
CYBERNAUTA
RESIDENCIAL PUERTO VARAS
LITO'S
GEOTURISMO PATAGONIA
AUTOMUNDO
ERRAZURIZ
COCHRANE
LAUTARO
PRAT
HOSPEDAJE LAUTARO
HOSTAL BELISARIO JARA
FRANCISCO
SIMPSON
FREIRE
LILLO
CAFÉ SAMOA
BUSES TO PUERTO INGENIERO IBAÑEZ
BUDGET RENT A CAR
BILBAO
EUSEBIO
BOLIVAR
SERRANO
SIMÓN
IGNACIO
To Local Airport
HOSPEDAJE NATTI
RESIDENCIAL MÓNICA
HOSPEDAJE LOS 4 HERMANOS
PATRIMONIO SILVESTRE
AVENIDA OGANA
LOS COIGÜES
SIMPSON
COLÓN
SARGENTO ALDEA
MOON
Recinto Ogarra
IGNACIO SERRANO
LOS MAÑIOS
LOS ARRAYANES
To Aeropuerto Balmaceda and Carretera Austral Sur

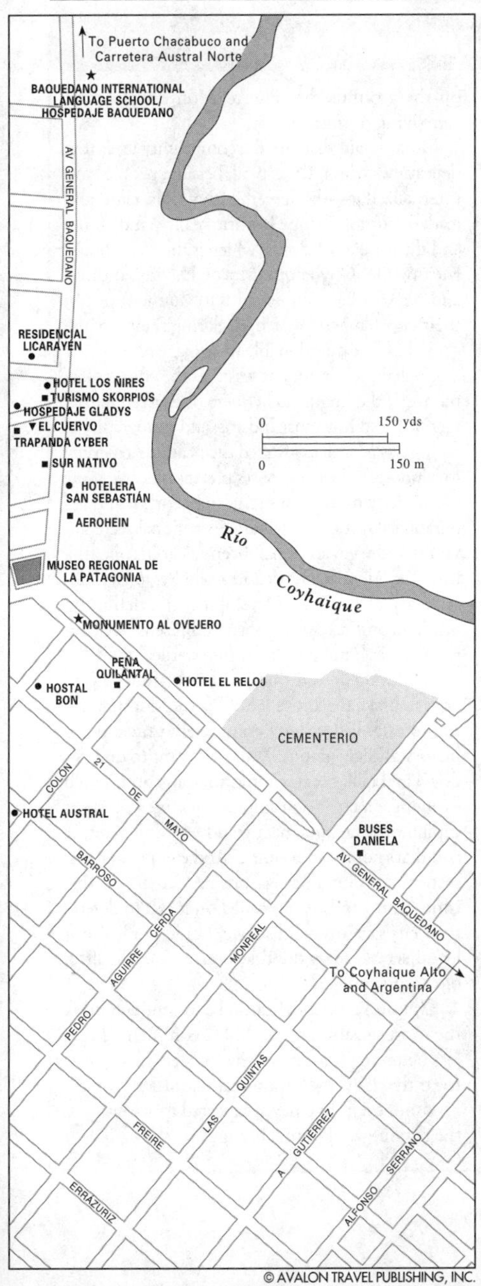

ENTERTAINMENT

Coyhaique has a growing number of bars, but so far their aspirations surpass their appeal. **Piel Roja** (Moraleda 495, tel. 067/236635), for instance, has pizza and pub grub, psychedelic decor that probably infringes Fillmore copyrights, and a 7–9 P.M. happy hour, but something's lacking. Despite its pioneer-style house, swinging doors, pistols on the wall, and cold beer on tap, **Bar West** (Bilbao 110, tel. 065/210007) serves mediocre pisco sours and plays too much insipid pop music. The liveliest place may be **El Cuervo** (General Parra 72, tel. 067/215015), which has a karaoke bar.

Peña Quilantal (Baquedano 791, tel. 065/234394) sometimes showcases live folkloric music, but is just as likely to offer run-of-the-mill pop.

Cine Coihaique (Cochrane 321) shows occasional recent films.

LANGUAGE CLASSES

Intensive Spanish classes with room and full board cost US$300 per person weekly at **Baquedano International Language School** (Baquedano 20, tel. 067/232520, fax 067/231511, www.patagoniachile.cl/bils, pguzmanm@entelchile.net); rates include four hours instruction daily except Sunday, primarily in summer when the main instructor does not have local teaching obligations.

SHOPPING

At the **Feria Artesanal de Coyhaique,** on the west side of the Plaza de Armas, local horse gear is the main attraction, though there are also wood carvings and woolens. **Manos Azules** (Riquelme 435, tel. 065/230719) is another crafts outlet.

Rincón del Poeta (Dussen 357-B, tel. 061/241868) is a small but promising bookstore that carries a handful of English-language titles as well as good Chilean literature.

ACCOMMODATIONS

Coyhaique's accommodations scene is a little unusual, with plenty of budget and midrange choices and relatively little at the upper end.

THE PHANTOM CAPITAL

For better or worse, wrote the 19th-century Argentine-American naturalist William Henry Hudson in his classic *Idle Days in Patagonia,* Argentine Patagonia's destiny was to remain a desert: "During the last twenty years the country has been crossed in various directions, from Atlantic to the Andes, and from the Río Negro to the Straits of Magellan, and has been found all barren." Hudson disparaged the delusions of early explorers who fantasized a "City of the Caesars," an austral El Dorado, adding that "The mysterious illusive city, peopled by whites, which was long believed to exist in the unknown interior, in a valley called Trapananda, is to moderns a myth, a mirage of the mind, as little to the traveler's imagination as the glittering capital of great Manoa, which Alonzo Pizarro and his false friend Orellana failed to discover."

What, then, would Hudson say of the three Chilean cities that, in 2001, were aiming to (dare we say?) "capitalize" on the Patagonian mystique by claiming to be the political and cultural center of a region that transcends borders and exists at least partly in the imagination? In Chile, at least, "Patagonia" has no juridical reality (even if the concept exerts a powerful hold on the mind), but that didn't stop Puerto Montt, Punta Arenas, and Coyhaique from conducting public press campaigns to champion their claims to a title that, each one thought, would help promote its tourist industry.

The furor started in early 2001, when the Consejo Comunal de Punta Arenas, the city council, sent a note to Chile's Interior Ministry protesting Puerto Montt mayor Rabindranath Quinteros's claim that Puerto Montt was "capital of Patagonia." Punta Arenas mayor Juan Morano argued that "By tradition and history the title is ours, and nobody's adventurous phrases will change that, no matter how much authority they may have." The Consejo even considered a complaint to the Servicio Nacional de Consumidores (National Consumer Protection Service, Sernac) on the grounds that Puerto Montt authorities were lying to tourists.

Morano said that "it's the community itself that determines who is the capital, because people have internalized it—the agreements of politicians and leaders cannot change historic reality, and in the end the people will decide which is the real capital." Meanwhile, Coyhaique Mayor David Sandoval and his Consejo Municipal (city council) put in their two centavos' worth, declaring their city the capital of this questionable imaginary region.

Coyhaique's argument was that the efforts of its pioneers, the linguistic heritage of the Tehuelche, Chonos, and Kawasqar Indians, and cartography as far back as Magellan justified their cause. According to Sandoval, "Puerto Montt's pretensions owe more to publicity motivations than to historical and geographical factors." Coyhaique's regional secretary said that the governor had been "clear in soliciting from the Subsecretaria de Desarollo Regional (Subsecretary of Regional Development) a definition of what constitutes Patagonia; in this sense we consider any argument over the title sterile."

Sandoval stressed that "what we are trying to do is to brake the arrogance of Puerto Montt in trying to establish criteria completely unrelated to history and geography. What we want to do is sit down and talk, because tomorrow Argentina could easily pick a city according to the same criteria as capital of Patagonia, or it could be Punta Arenas, and that's not the idea either." At the same time, the secretary of Punta Arenas' private Cámara de Turismo (Tourism Bureau) called on locals to defend their city's claims because "we should not lose nor let others take away this title, because it could affect our tourist image."

Chilean President Ricardo Lagos, though, took the most sensible approach. He commented that "it's better to project yourselves as a city than to arrogantly claim the idea of capital of Patagonia." Hudson, even if he never expected to see cities in the region, would probably agree.

With a few exceptions budget accommodations are not all that great.

US$10–25

Reached by a narrow staircase so narrow your elbows can touch the sides, some rooms at **Hospedaje Los 4 Hermanos** (Colón 495, tel. 067/232647, US$8 pp) can be claustrophobic, but it's often full and singles are at a premium—phoning ahead is a good idea. The comparable **Hospedaje Natti** (Almirante Simpson 417, tel. 067/231047, US$8 pp) is a good alternative.

In a quiet location at the north edge of town, **Hospedaje Baquedano** (Baquedano 20, tel. 067/232520, pguzmanm@entelchile.net, US$9 pp) has English-speaking ownership—with traces of Maine and Tennessee in the accent—but has only one cozy *cabaña* with private bath and a separate kitchen.

Hostal Arriero Patagón (Bilbao 262, 2nd floor, tel. 067/231596, arriero@patagoniachile.cl, US$19 d) is a promising new B&B, but the management seems a little absent-minded. So-so **Residencial Puerto Varas** (Serrano 168, tel. 067/235931, US$24 d with shared bath) hasn't kept pace with some of Coyhaique's better budget places, but will still do in a pinch; breakfast costs extra.

The backpackers' choice is the Spanish-run, HI affiliate **Albergue Las Salamandras** (Sector los Pinos s/n, tel. 067/211865, www.salamandras.cl, US$10 pp with kitchen privileges) on secluded piney grounds about two kilometers southwest of town on the old airport road. Most rooms in this attractive building, with large communal spaces, are dormitories, but there are also a couple doubles (US$13 pp) and camping is also possible.

US$25–50

Cozier and simply better than most other places in its range, cheerful **Residencial Mónica** (Eusebio Lillo 666, tel. 067/234302, US$9 pp with shared bath, US$13 pp with private bath) includes breakfast, but in a few rooms too many beds crowd the available space. Motel-style **Residencial Licarayén** (J.M. Carrera 33-A, tel. 067/233337, eduardo_lepe@yahoo.es, US$15 pp) is OK for a night.

Coyhaique's best new choice is quiet, well-located **Hospedaje Gladys** (General Parra 65, tel. 067/251076, US$13 pp with shared bath, US$20 pp with private bath), whose spotless rooms, with cable TV, are spacious enough, though the lurid red bedspreads are distracting. Breakfast (US$3 extra) is worth the price.

Friendly, popular **Hotel Austral** (Colón 203, tel. 067/232522, US$25/42) is a good mid-range choice. **Hotelera San Sebastián** (Avenida Baquedano 496, tel. 067/233427, US$33/44) is comparable.

Hostal Bon (Serrano 91, tel. 067/231189, US$23 pp) has plain but comfortable accommodations with breakfast. Though it's spacious and well-kept, **Hostal Araucarias** (Obispo Vielmo 71, tel. 067/232707, US$23 pp) seems pricey for a place whose open floor plan lets sounds carry upstairs.

US$50–100

Relocated to a site overlooking the Río Coyhaique, genial **Hotel El Reloj** (Baquedano 828, tel./fax 067/231108, htlelreloj@patagonia chile.cl, US$42/52 with breakfast) is one of Coyhaique's best values, with an outstanding restaurant as well.

Hotel Los Ñires (Avenida Baquedano 315, tel./fax 067/232261, www.doncarlos.cl, US$39/54 s/d)has inviting rooms with central heating, cable TV, and private bath. Large if comfortable beds nearly monopolize the floor space in a few rooms, but the baths are spacious, the hot water abundant, and the water pressure steady.

Hotel Luis Loyola (Prat 455, tel./fax 067/234200, hotel-loyola-coyhaique@chile.net, US$41/55 s/d) is a modern, central, and comfortable hotel.

One of Coyhaique's best values, despite a nondescript exterior, the **Patagonia Hotel** (General Parra 551, tel. 067/254960, fax 067/254962, www.patagoniahotel.cl, US$69 s or d) offers comfortable carpeted rooms in a quiet location, with telephone, cable TV, and Internet access.

Hostal Belisario Jara (Bilbao 662, tel./fax 067/234150, belisariojara@entelchile.net, US$68/83 s/d) has more personality than most Coyhaique hotels.

On sprawling grounds on the west side of town, Coyhaique's priciest is the motel-style **Hostería Coihaique** (Magallanes 131, tel. 067/231137, fax 067/233274, www.hotelsa.cl, hotelsa@ctcinternet.cl, US$84/98 s/d), which is quiet and comfortable enough, but the twins are surprisingly small.

FOOD

Cafetería Alemana (Condell 119, tel. 065/231731) has a well-deserved reputation for outstanding sandwiches, *onces,* and desserts; down the block is its sister **Café Oriente** (Condell 201, tel. 065/231622). For inexpensive light meals, try **Café Samoa** (Prat 653, tel. 065/232864).

For home cooking with class, try the lunches (US$3) at **El Mastique** (Bilbao 141, tel. 067/235594); its dinner menu is more limited. Despite an uninviting—almost foreboding—exterior and its obscure location, **Lito's** (Lautaro 147, tel. 067/254528) has a spacious dining area with an attractive bar and above-average versions of Chilean specialties like beef (US$6), fish, and seafood.

With a standard Chilean menu enhanced by top-quality ingredients, the **Casino de Bomberos** (General Parra 365, tel. 065/231437) is a traditional favorite, but it's become one of the country's more expensive fire-station restaurants. **La Fiorentina** (Prat 230, tel. 065/238899) has good pizza, *pastel de choclo,* and crisp service at moderate prices.

Loberías de Chacabuco (Prat 386, tel. 067/239786) is a seafood venue that seems to be slumming these days, though they've maintained their quality and kept prices reasonable. **La Olla** (Prat 176, tel. 065/234700) is one of Coyhaique's better (and more expensive) restaurants, but the budget-conscious can enjoy moderately priced (around US$5) lunches. The *pollo al ajillo* (garlic chicken) is excellent, but the service can be slow and the pisco sours a little sugary for some palates.

For light cooking to international standards, Hotel El Reloj's **El Ovejero** (Baquedano 828, tel./fax 065/231108) comes highly recommended for entrées like *congrio al ajillo* (conger eel with garlic, US$8) and Patagonian desserts like rhubarb mousse; on long summer nights, grab a window seat for fine views over the Río Coyhaique.

On the west side of the Plaza de Armas, a longtime favorite with locals and travelers alike, **Café Ricer** (Paseo Horn 48, tel. 067/232920) has some of Coyhaique's best food and drink, including Patagonian specialties like barbecued lamb (about US$10) and even Middle Eastern items like stuffed grape leaves; humongous sandwiches and snacks are considerably cheaper. Most people eat in the downstairs café, but the more formal upstairs restaurant has better atmosphere, its walls lined with historic photographs of the city and the region. There is live music downstairs on weekends.

Another good option, popular with foreign tour operators, is **La Casona** (Obispo Vielmo 77, tel. 067/238894) for lamb, *pastel de jaiva* (crab soufflé) and other regional entrées in the US$7–10 range. The service equals or even surpasses the food.

INFORMATION

In comfortable new quarters, **Sernatur** (Bulnes 35, tel. 067/240290, infoaisen@sernatur.cl) is open 8:30 A.M.–8 P.M. weekdays, 10 A.M.–6 P.M. weekends December–February; the rest of the year, hours are 8:30 A.M.–5 P.M. weekdays only. It has English-speaking staff and a useful message board.

Conaf's **Patrimonio Silvestre** (Los Coihues s/n, tel. 067/212125, fax 067/212130) provides information on national parks and reserves. **Codeff** (12 de Octubre 288, Oficina 205, tel. 067/234451) is an environmental NGO.

SERVICES

Coyhaique has the region's most complete services, by far. Changing money, in particular, is far easier than elsewhere on the Carretera Austral.

Turismo Prado (21 de Mayo 417) and **Cambios Emperador** (Freire 171) both exchange cash and traveler's checks. **Banco Santander** has an ATM at Condell 184.

For postal services, **Correos de Chile** (Cochrane 202) is near the Plaza de Armas.

Entelchile (Arturo Prat 340) has telephone and Internet connections, but other Internet outlets keep longer hours and will let you hook up your own laptop for around US$1 per hour: **Ciber Patagonia** (21 de Mayo 525, tel. 067/254700), **Cybernauta** (Bilbao 484, tel. 067/670323), and **Trapananda Cyber** (General Parra 86).

For laundry, try **Lavandería QL** (Bilbao 160, tel. 067/232266) or **Lavandería All Clean** (General Parra 55, Local 2, tel. 067/219635), next door to Residencial Gladys.

For medical attention, contact the **Hospital Base** (J.M. Carrera s/n, tel. 067/231286).

GETTING THERE

Coyhaique is the region's transportation hub, with flights north and south, and bus service along the Carretera Austral, to Region X (Los Lagos) and Region XII (Magallanes) via Argentina, and to Argentina itself. Note that buses to Chilean destinations in other regions may not drop passengers in Argentina.

Air

Commercial jets leave from **Aeropuerto Balmaceda,** a modern facility 50 kilometers southeast of Coyhaique that would be the pride of many large Chilean cities. Small planes still use convenient **Aeropuerto Teniente Vidal,** only five kilometers southwest of town.

LanExpress (Moraleda 402, tel. 065/231188, flies several times daily to Puerto Montt and Santiago, and Saturday only to Punta Arenas. **Sky Airline** (Prat 203, tel. 067/240827) flies daily to Puerto Montt and the Chilean capital.

Transporte Aéreo Don Carlos (Subteniente Cruz 63, tel./fax 067/231981, www.doncarlos.cl) flies air taxis once or twice weekly to destinations including Caleta Tortel (US$31), Chile Chico (US$40), Cochrane (US$67), and Villa O'Higgins (US$100). **Transportes Aéreos San Rafael** (18 de Septiembre 469, tel. 065/232048, fax 065/233408) flies to the remote island settlement of Melinka (US$22) and on to Quellón, Chiloé (US$43) Thursday. In addition to Don Carlos and San Rafael, two other air taxi companies offer charter service to Parque Nacional Laguna San Rafael and elsewhere in the region: **Aerohein** (Baquedano 500, tel. 067/252177, tel./fax 067/232772, www.aerohein.cl) and **Patagonia Explorer Aviación** (Freire 365, tel. 09/8172172). For details on park charters, see the separate Parque Nacional Laguna San Rafael entry.

Bus

More carriers have begun to use Coyhaique's upgraded **Terminal de Buses** (Lautaro and Magallanes), but several still use their own offices elsewhere in town. Note that services both north and south along the Carretera Austral are most frequent in summer, and may be considerably reduced in winter.

To Puerto Aisén (US$1.50) and Puerto Chacabuco (US$2, one hour), there are frequent departures with **Buses Suray** (Prat 265, tel. 067/238387), **Buses Don Carlos** (Subteniente Cruz 63, tel. 067/231981), and **Interlagos** (tel. 067/240840), at the main terminal.

At the main terminal, **Buses São Paulo** (tel. 067/254369) goes north to Mañihuales daily at 1 P.M. via the paved Viviana junction, and to off-highway destinations like Villa Ortega and La Tapera. **Buses Daniela** (Baquedano 1122, tel. 067/231701) goes to Puerto Puyuhuapi, with connections to Chaitén, Wednesday and Sunday at 8 A.M.

Buses Norte (General Parra 337, tel. 067/232167) goes north to Chaitén and intermediates up to four times weekly at 8 A.M. At the main terminal, **Terra Austral** (tel. 067/254335) goes to Puerto Cisnes daily except Sunday at 3:30 P.M.

Sample northbound destinations and fares along the Carretera Austral include Mañihuales (US$4), Villa Amengual (US$6.50), Puerto Cisnes (US$9, six hours), Puerto Puyuhuapi (US$11, six hours), La Junta (US$12.50), Santa Lucía (US$19), and Chaitén (US$23.50, 12 hours).

Southbound minibuses to Puerto Ibáñez (US$6), the north-shore ferry port for Chile Chico on Lago General Carrera, leave from the corner of Prat and Errázuriz. Among the carriers are **Transportes Yamil Alí** (tel. 067/250346), **Darío Figueroa Castro** (tel. 067/233286), and **Minibus Don Tito** (tel. 067/250280).

Other minibus services go as far as Villa Cerro

Castillo, where the pavement presently ends on the southbound Carretera Austral: **Minibuses Javier Alí** (tel. 09/3131402) and **Minibuses Tomás Urreta** (tel. 09/9500276); these leave from the corner of Prat and Lautaro, near the restaurant Moneda de Oro, but with a day's notice they'll pick you at your hotel.

Leaving from 12 de Octubre and Errázuriz, **Transportes El Cóndor** (tel. 09/5686125, tel. 067/411904 in Chile Chico) goes Wednesday and Sunday to Puerto Guadal, at the east end of Lago General Carrera, and intermediates.

At the main terminal, **Interlagos** (tel. 067/240840) goes beyond Cerro Castillo to Cochrane and intermediates at 10 A.M. daily, as does **Acuario 13** (tel. 067/240990) daily except Monday. **Don Carlos** (Subteniente Cruz 63, tel. 067/231981) goes Tuesday, Wednesday, Thursday, and Saturday.

Fares for southbound destinations include Villa Cerro Castillo (US$5, two hours), Bahía Murta (US$8.50, five hours), Puerto Río Tranquilo (US$9, 5.5 hours), Puerto Guadal (US$12, seven hours), Puerto Bertrand (US$12, eight hours), and Cochrane (US$17, 10 hours).

From the main terminal, **Queilén Bus** (tel. 067/240760) goes twice weekly to Puerto Montt (US$30) via Argentina. Also at the main terminal, **Bus Sur** (tel. 067/211460) goes to Punta Arenas, also via Argentina, twice weekly (US$47, 20 hours).

Sharing offices at the main terminal, **Buses Giobbi** and **Turibús** (tel. 067/232067 for both) offer international service to Comodoro Rivadavia (US$30, nine hours), Argentina, via Río Mayo and Sarmiento, with northbound connections to Esquel and Bariloche.

Sea

Coyhaique is not a seaport, but several maritime transporters keep offices here. **Navimag** (Presidente Ibáñez 347, Oficina 1, tel. 067/223306, fax 067/233386) sells tickets for its ferries from Puerto Chacabuco to Puerto Montt, and to Parque Nacional Laguna San Rafael.

Aysén Express (Condell 149, Local 5, tel. 067/670331, www.aysenexpress.cl) island-hops from Puerto Chacabuco to Puerto Montt. **Geoturismo Patagonia** (Eusebio Lillo 315, tel. 067/256100) is the representative of Catamaranes del Sur, which has catamaran service to Parque Nacional Laguna San Rafael but has suspended passenger services from Chaitén to Puerto Montt.

Turismo Skorpios (General Parra 21, tel. 067/213755) operates multiday luxury cruises from Puerto Chacabuco to Parque Nacional Laguna San Rafael.

GETTING AROUND

To the Airport

Taxis to Aeropuerto Teniente Vidal are cheap enough (about US$4), but air-taxi companies usually provide transfers. To the commercial Aeropuerto Balmaceda about 45 minutes away via a smooth paved highway, there are several door-to-door minivan services (US$4 pp), including **Transfer Coyhaique** (tel. 067/210495) and **Transfer AM** (tel. 067/250119).

Car Rental

Even shoestring travelers indulge themselves on car rentals in Aisén, since public transport is less frequent than in other parts of Chile and some sights are off the main north-south route. Because vehicles are limited and demand can be high, summer reservations are advisable—even essential.

Among Coyhaique's several rental agencies are **Hertz** rep Sur Nativo (Baquedano 457, tel. 067/231648), **Automundo** (Bilbao 510, tel. 067/231621, fax 067/231794), **Andes Patagónicos** (Paseo Horn 48, tel. 067/216711), and **Budget** (Errázuriz 454, tel. 067/255171).

VICINITY OF COYHAIQUE

Coyhaique makes a great base for outdoors activities like hiking, fly-fishing, rafting and even winter skiing. Fishing probably tops the list, as the season runs from November–May in the region's abundant lakes and rivers.

Among the reliable operators are fly-fishing specialist **Aisén Bridges Travel** (tel./fax 067/233302, www.aisen.cl), which is located on the outskirts of town and is easiest to contact by phone (English spoken); **Andes Patagónicos** (Paseo Horn 48, Local 11, tel. 067/216711, www.andespatagonicos.cl); **Expediciones Coyhaique** (Portales 195, tel./fax 067/232300, www.expecoy.es.vg), also fly-fishing-oriented; **Cóndor Excursions** (Dussen 357, tel. 067/670349, info@condorexcursions.com); U.S.-run, Puerto Bertrand-based **Patagonia Adventure Expeditions** (Riquelme 372, tel./fax 067/219894, www.adventurepatagonia.com), a trekking, fishing, and whitewater operator that also offers rafting and kayaking on the nearby Río Simpson; and Cochrane-based U.S.-Chilean **Salvaje Corazón** (tel. 067/211488, fax 067/237490, www.salvajecorazon.com), also best contacted by phone (English, Hebrew, Portuguese, and some French also spoken).

Reserva Nacional Coyhaique

Few cities anywhere in the world have so much wild country so near as this mountainous 2,676-hectare reserve, with its top-of-the-world views of Coyhaique, Cerro Macay, and Cerro Castillo to the south, the Río Simpson valley to the west, and the Patagonian plains sprawling away to the east. Local residents enjoy their weekend picnics and barbecues here, only five kilometers north of town, but there's always space away from the crowds and on weekdays it's almost empty.

Altitudes in the reserve range from 400 meters to 1,361 meters on the summit of Cerro Cinchao. More than a meter of rain and snow falls throughout the year, but summers are mild and fairly dry, with an average temperature of 12°C.

While the reserve is wild and almost undeveloped, it's not exactly pristine. Forests of *coigue (Nothofagus betuloides)* and *lenga (Nothofagus pumilio)* blanket the hillsides, but plantations of exotic pines and larches have replaced some of the native forest devastated in the 1940s. So close to the city, birds are the most conspicuous wildlife.

The reserve's main sights are literally that—the seemingly infinite panoramas in nearly every direction. It's possible to get different perspectives on those panoramas on nature trails like the 800-meter **Sendero Laguna Verde,** the four-kilometer **Sendero Laguna Venus,** and the **Sendero Las Piedras,** which leads to the 1,361-meter summit of Cerro Cinchao.

Most visitors stay in town, but Conaf (tel. 067/212125 in Coyhaique) has a rustic six-site campground at **Laguna Verde** and a 10-site campground at **Casa Bruja.** Each charges US$5.50 for up to six persons; two of the Laguna Verde sites have roofed shelters. All sites have picnic tables, fresh water, and fire pits; the Casa Bruja site has toilets and hot showers. Bring as much food as necessary for the duration. At the park entrance, Conaf rangers collect an admission fee of US$1 for adults, US$.35 for children.

Three kilometers north of Coyhaique via the paved highway to Puerto Chacabuco, a dirt lateral climbs steeply east to Reserva Nacional Coyhaique. The road itself is passable for most vehicles in summer, but difficult or impossible with rain. It's close enough to the city, though, that anyone in decent physical condition should be able to walk from the highway to the park entrance in about half an hour.

Monumento Natural Dos Lagunas

East of Coyhaique, international Ruta 240 is no longer the main road to the Argentine border at Coyhaique Alto, but it still passes **Laguna El Toro** and **Laguna Escondida,** which shelter grebes, black-necked swans, and other wild waterfowl in this 181-hectare unit on the edge of the Patagonian steppe. Conaf rangers charge US$1 admission for adults, US$.30 for children, and rent six campsites for US$5 each for up to six persons.

Centro de Ski El Fraile

One of Chile's most obscure ski resorts, the Centro de Ski El Fraile (tel. 067/215878, is 29 kilometers south of Coihaique via the Carretera Austral and an eastbound gravel road. It's a small area, with only two lifts and five runs up to two kilometers long, but the snow quality is good, with options for skiers of all abilities.

Lift passes cost around US$13 per person, per day; it's normally open Thursday–Sunday, but daily except Monday during school holidays. Facilities include a café and rental shop. Transportation is available by reservation through

Coyhaique's Buses Norte (General Parra 337, tel. 067/232788).

Reserva Nacional Río Simpson

Northwest of Coyhaique, midway to Puerto Chacabuco, paved Ruta 240 passes through the Río Simpson valley, flanked by the steep walls and canyons that form this accessible 41,634-hectare forest reserve.

Altitudes are only about 100 meters along the river itself, but rise to 1,878 meters in the cordillera. Because most elevations are lower than Reserva Nacional Coyhaique, the weather is milder (averaging around 15–17°C in summer), but it's also wetter, as Pacific storms drop up to 2,500 millimeters of precipitation on their way inland.

Like Reserva Nacional Coyhaique, Río Simpson's forests consist largely of native southern beeches *(Nothofagus spp.),* but the heavy rainfall fosters verdant undergrowth of ferns, fuchsias, and similar species. *Huemuls* are found in the more remote areas, as are puma and *pudú,* along with many birds, including the Andean condor. Bird species, though, diminish in the autumn and winter, returning in the spring.

Opposite the old visitors center, at Km 37, look for the **Cascada La Virgen,** a waterfall that plunges vertically through intense greenery on the north side of the highway. At the visitors center itself, a trail descends to the beach, where both swimming and fishing are possible.

Five kilometers east of park headquarters, Conaf's eight-site **Camping San Sebastián** (Ruta 240 Km 32, US$11 for up to eight persons) has bathrooms with hot showers.

Conaf's **Centro de Información Ambiental** (Ruta 240 Km 37) boasts a small natural-history museum (admission US$.60) and botanical garden. For some time, it's been due to move to a new location at Las Chimeneas (Km 30), but progress has been slow.

From Coyhaique, any Don Carlos bus will drop passengers at the campground, museum, or anywhere along the route.

Puerto Chacabuco

The forests destroyed by fire in the 1940s were more than just embellishments on Aisén's landscape; their dense foliage softened the impact of heavy storms on the hillsides and impeded soil erosion. One side effect of this fire-fed devastation was to increase the sediment load of the Río Simpson and silt up the harbor at Puerto Aisén, forcing authorities to build new port facilities at Puerto Chacabuco, 14 kilometers west.

Now the main maritime gateway to the region, Puerto Chacabuco is also the departure point for trips and cruises to Parque Nacional Laguna San Rafael, and a stop on some voyages between Puerto Montt and Puerto Natales.

Just beyond the port, the so-so **Hotel Moraleda** (O'Higgins 82, tel. 067/351155, US$9.50 pp) is cheap. With 60 rooms in three separate modules, the significantly superior **Hotel Loberías del Sur** (J.M. Carrera 50, tel. 067/351115, www.catamaranesdelsur.cl, US$62/85 s/d) is also the best place to eat, and not excessively expensive.

Buses shuttle frequently between Puerto Chacabuco and Coyhaique, 82 kilometers east via Ruta 240.

Puerto Chacabuco's **Terminal de Transbordadores** (ferry terminal) is part of the port complex. Both long-distance ferries and excursions to Parque Nacional Laguna San Rafael leave from here; for details of services to and from Laguna San Rafael, see the separate entry below. Frequencies may vary between summer and the rest of the year.

Navimag (tel. 067/351111, fax 067/351192) operates passenger/vehicle ferries from Puerto Montt to Puerto Chacabuco, with extensions to Parque Nacional Laguna San Rafael. For fares on these routes, see the Puerto Montt entry in the Sur Chico chapter and the Parque Nacional Laguna San Rafael entry, below.

PARQUE NACIONAL LAGUNA SAN RAFAEL

Flowing ice meets frigid sea at Parque Nacional Laguna San Rafael, where icy pinnacles tumble from the crackling western face of Ventisquero San Rafael, a 60-meter-high glacier that descends from the Campo de Hielo Norte, the sprawling northern continental ice field, to become bobbing icebergs. Misleadingly named, Laguna San Rafael itself is really an ocean inlet, though its salinity is relatively low as the icebergs slowly thaw and the receding glacier discharges quantities of fresh water into it.

One of Chile's largest national parks, encompassing 1,742,000 hectares of rugged terrain, Laguna San Rafael is also a UNESCO World Biosphere Reserve for its extraordinary scenery and environments. While remote from any settlement, it's a popular summer excursion for both Chileans and foreigners, and accessible throughout the year.

History

For an area so thinly populated and so rarely visited, Laguna San Rafael has an impressive history. The first European here was the Spaniard Bartolomé Díaz Gallardo, who crossed the low-lying Istmo de Ofqui (Isthmus of Ofqui) from the Golfo de Penas. Jesuit missionaries visited the area in 1766 and 1767, bestowing its present name, but the Spanish king expelled them from the continent soon afterward.

During the voyage of the *Beagle,* Darwin made extensive observations here, while naval officer Enrique Simpson delivered the first comprehensive report to the Chilean government in 1871. Nearly seven decades later, in 1940, the government started work on a canal across the isthmus to improve communications with the far south, but soon gave up the project. In 1959 it declared the area a national park, but as late as the 1980s it entertained proposals to build a road to facilitate cargo transshipments.

Geography and Climate

Laguna San Rafael is about 225 kilometers southwest of Puerto Chacabuco by sea via a series of narrow longitudinal channels, but only about 190 kilometers from Coyhaique as the crow flies. To the east rises the rugged Patagonian mainland; to the west lie the Archipiélago de Chonos, with its myriad islands, and the Península de Taitao.

Altitudes range from sea level to 4,058-meter Monte San Valentín, the southern Andes' highest peak. Sea-level temperatures are relatively mild, averaging about 8°C, with upwards of 2,500 millimeters rainfall per annum; at higher elevations, though, precipitation doubles, temperatures are colder, and the resulting snowfall feeds 19 major glaciers that form the 300,000-hectare Campo de Hielo Norte. Seemingly endless Pacific storms can darken the skies for weeks on end, but when the overcast lifts the views are spectacular.

Flora and Fauna

In areas not covered by ice, up to about 700 meters, grows mixed Valdivian forest so dense that, in Darwin's words, "our faces, hands and shin-bones all bore witness to the maltreatment we received, in attempting to penetrate their forbidding recesses." The main tree species are two species of *coigue, Nothofagus dombeyii* and *Nothofagus nitida, mañío macho (Podocarpus nubigena), tepu (Tepualia stimulais),* and other species, with a dense understory of shrubs, ferns, mosses, and vines. Above 700 meters, there is almost equally dense forest of *lenga (Nothofagus pumilio)* and *ñirre (Nothofagus antarctica),* with occasional specimens of the coniferous Guaiteca cypress *Pilgerodendron uviferum.*

Most of the easily visible wildlife congregates around the shoreline, beginning with eye-catching seabirds like the flightless steamer duck *(Tachyeres pteneres),* Magellanic penguin *(Spheniscus magellanicus),* the soaring black-browed and sooty albatrosses *(Diomedea melanophris* and *Phoebetria palpebrata),* and various gull species. Marine mammals include the southern elephant seal *(Mirounga leonina),* southern sea lion *(Otaria flavescens),* and the southern sea otter *(Lutra felina).*

Forest-dwelling animals are harder to see, but mammals like *pudú* and *huemul* graze the uplands, while foxes and pumas prowl for their prey.

Sights and Activities

Calving off the face of **Ventisquero San Rafael,** deep indigo icebergs bob and drift in the waters of **Laguna San Rafael,** an oval body of water measuring nine kilometers at its widest and six kilometers at its narrowest, connected to the southern canals by the narrow Río Témpanos.

The world's lowest-latitude tidewater glacier, Ventisquero San Rafael may not be so for much longer, as its retreating face may be a casualty of global warming. Since 1960, it has been in continuous retreat.

Few visitors actually set foot in the park, as most visitors arrive by ferry or catamaran, transferring to smaller craft to approach the glacier's face and navigate among the icebergs. Those who do manage to land and stay a while can hike the **Sendero al Ventisquero,** which leads through seven kilometers of evergreen forest to a glacial overlook.

Accommodations and Food

Conaf's three-site **Camping Laguna Caiquenes,** at park headquarters, charges US$4 per site; no campfires are permitted, however. Its **Casa de Huéspedes Laguna Caiquenes,** with kitchen facilities, can accommodate up to six persons for US$94, park admission included. For reservations, contact Conaf's Coyhaique Patrimonio Silvestre office (Los Coihues s/n, tel. 067/212125, fax 067/212130).

No supplies except fresh water are available, so bring everything from Coyhaique or Puerto Chacabuco. Both ferries and catamarans feed their passengers; the catamarans usually have an open bar and chill the whisky with ice chipped off passing bergs.

Information

Conaf's administration and ranger station is on the northeastern shore of Laguna San Rafael. Anyone who literally sets foot in the park pays a US$4 admission fee, but boat people do not, as the offshore waters fall under naval rather than Conaf jurisdiction (according to Conaf statistics, which exclude maritime passengers, the park hosted only 564 visitors in 2003).

Getting There

Still the only practical means of reaching the park, air and sea transportation both have their drawbacks—air travel is expensive and fleeting, while sea travel can be moderately priced but slow, or relatively fast and expensive. From the town of Puerto Río Tranquilo, on the north arm of Lago General Carrera, a new gravel road is advancing slowly toward Bahía Exploradores, only about 65 kilometers north of the glacier, but its completion will not eliminate the need for boat travel, only shorten it.

Light airplanes only can land at Laguna San Rafael's 775-meter gravel airstrip; several Coyhaique-based companies can carry up to five passengers for US$600–700, remaining only about an hour at the park. Among them are **Transporte Aéreo Don Carlos** (Subteniente Cruz 63, tel./fax 067/231981, www.doncarlos.cl), **Transportes Aéreos San Rafael** (18 de Septiembre 469, tel. 067/232048, fax 067/233408), **Aerohein** (Baquedano 500, tel. 067/252177, tel./fax 067/232772, www.aerohein.cl), and **Patagonia Explorer Aviación** (Freire 365, tel. 09/8172172).

Long-established **Navimag** offers slow-sailing ferries to Laguna San Rafael, while other operators offer options ranging from comfortable cruise ships to high-speed catamarans. For ferries and cruise ships, the overnight voyage can take 12–16 hours from Puerto Chacabuco, while the catamarans can return the same day. Ferries and cruise ships, on the other hand, spend five or six hours at the glacier, while catamarans have two or three hours at most. While these excursions are most frequent in summer, they may take place all year.

Navimag cruises begin in Puerto Montt and call in Puerto Chacabuco before continuing to Laguna San Rafael. From Puerto Montt, fares for the five-day, four-night voyage on Navimag's *Puerto Edén* range from US$400 per person for bunks in shared cabins with exterior baths to US$800/1400 s/d in private cabins with external views; from Puerto Chacabuco, the comparable round-trip fares are US$200 per person to US$750/1300 s/d. For more detail, contact Navimag offices in Santiago, Puerto Montt, Coyhaique, or Puerto Chacabuco, or see its website (www.navimag.com).

September–May, **Cruceros Marítimos Skorpios** (Augusto Leguía 118, Las Condes, Santiago, tel. 02/2311030, fax 02/2322269, www.skorpios.cl) offers four-day, three-night cruises from Puerto Chacabuco on the 74-passsenger *Skor-*

pios I. Rates range from US$480 per person in low season to US$900 per person in high season (mid-December–mid-March), depending on the cabin; some cruises include a side trip to hot springs in the Quitralco fjord. Skorpios also has a Coyhaique office.

Aysén Express's catamaran *Sognekongen* (US$165 pp in summer) offers off-season specials for as little as US$70 per person; for details, contact their Coyhaique office (Condell 149, Local 5, tel. 067/670331, yessicah@aysenexpress.cl). Rates on **Catamaranes del Sur**'s 70-passenger *Iceberg Expedition* (US$299 pp) include full meals and an open bar; for more details or reservations, contact Coyhaique's **Geo Turismo** (Eusebio Lillo 315, tel. 067/234098, lpuchi@geoturismopatagonia.cl).

The Northern Carretera Austral

From Coyhaique, the paved Carretera Austral is briefly contiguous with Ruta 240 to Puerto Aisén and Puerto Chacabuco, but after nine kilometers it becomes a gravel road that veers northeast toward Villa Ortega. Ruta 240 continues west and, passing through the **Túnel Farellón** above the Río Simpson en route, it reaches the Viviana junction after 39 kilometers. Here, a smooth paved highway turns northeast up the Río Mañihuales valley and joins the Carretera Austral about 13 kilometers southeast of Villa Mañihuales.

Heavy rains can and do cut the highway north to Chaitén, as happened in March of 2001, when several communities were isolated for days.

VILLA MAÑIHUALES

Villa Mañihuales, a pioneer village 76 kilometers north of Coyhaique via the roundabout Viviana junction, is the headquarters for Conaf's **Reserva Nacional Mañihuales,** a 3,596-hectare forest reserve that takes its name from the native *mañío* (Podocarpus) forest (despite Conaf's presence, the reserve does not yet exist officially, as it still awaits formal recognition from other government agencies).

Facilities at Conaf's five-site **Camping Las Lavanderas** (US$6.50 for up to six persons) include picnic tables and toilets, but cold showers only. **Residencial Mañiguales** (Ibar 280, tel. 067/431403, US$8 pp) has rooms with shared bath; there are a couple simple eateries.

All buses from Coyhaique pass through Villa Mañihuales en route to northbound Carretera Austral destinations.

VILLA AMENGUAL

About 58 kilometers north of Villa Mañihuales, overlooking the Río Cisnes canyon in the shadow of 2,095-meter Cerro Alto Nevado, the pioneer village of Villa Amengual dates only from 1983 and owes its existence to the Carretera Austral. A few kilometers south, an eastbound gravel road climbs the river valley to the settlement of La Tapera and a rarely used border crossing to Argentina.

Distinguished by its shingled chapel, built in the Chilote immigrant style, Villa Amengual is a popular stop for cyclists, if only because it's one of few places with food and accommodations between Villa Mañihuales and Puerto Puyuhuapi, another 60 kilometers north over rugged terrain. **Residencial El Encanto** (Castro 33-A, US$6 pp) and **Residencial El Paso** (Arias 12, US$6 pp) both have simple rooms with shared bath.

Again, all northbound buses from Coyhaique pass through here, but some turn west toward Puerto Cisnes from a highway junction only a few kilometers north of Amengual.

PUERTO CISNES

At the mouth of its namesake river, the town of Puerto Cisnes (population 2,507) owes its origins to a 1920s lumber mill, but still serves as a key port for scattered fishing hamlets in and around the Canal Puyuhuapi; rarely visited Parque Nacional Isla Magdalena is just across the water to the west.

Construction of a link to the Carretera Austral has partially reoriented the town inland and, in

© WAYNE BERNHARDSON

chapel at Villa Amengual

recent years, the economy has diversified with salmon farming and tourism, the latter primarily oriented toward fly-fishing.

One of Aisén's architectural oddities is Cisnes's **Biblioteca Pública Genaro Godoy,** a wooden structure with hexagonal neoclassical columns and a pediment decorated with bas reliefs of figures from Greek mythology.

Visitors can hire a launch to the 157,616-hectare **Parque Nacional Isla Magdalena,** occupying most of its namesake island and several smaller islands, but it can cost around US$200 or a bit less with skilful negotiations. Contact Alberto Miranda (tel. 067/345538) or Raúl Rogel Vargas (Gabriela Mistral 165, tel. 067/346600).

Accommodations and Food

Puerto Cisnes has several passable accommodations, starting with the reasonably priced **Hospedaje Bellavista** (Séptimo de Línea 112, tel. 067/346408, US$8 pp with shared bath). **Hostería El Gaucho** (Holmberg 140, tel. 067/346514), US$11 pp) is slightly dearer, as is comfy **Hostal Michay** (Gabriela Mistral 112, tel. 067/346462, US$13–15 pp).

Well-kept **El Guairao** (Piloto Pardo 58, tel. 067/346473, US$33 d) has motel-style rooms with satellite TV; it also has the best restaurant, but there are other options along the waterfront.

Information

For information, visit the **Biblioteca Pública** (Sotomayor s/n), on the south side of the Plaza de Armas, which is open 10 A.M.–8 P.M. weekdays, 2–7 P.M. weekends, in summer only.

Getting There

Transportes Terra Austral (Piloto Pardo 368, tel. 067/346757) and **Buses Alegría** (Piloto Pardo 354, tel. 067/346434) alternate 6 A.M. departures daily except Sunday to Coyhaique (US$10). **Transportes Entre Verde** (Séptimo de Línea 112, tel. 067/346408) goes to La Junta (US$6.50) at 4 P.M. Monday and Friday; otherwise, for northbound connections, it's necessary to wait at the highway junction or backtrack toward Coyhaique.

PARQUE NACIONAL QUEULAT

From the Río Cisnes junction, the steep, narrow Carretera Austral zigzags over the 500-meter Portezuelo Queulat as it enters the 154,093-hectare Parque Nacional Queulat, which rises from the ocean fjords of Canal Puyuhuapi through nearly impenetrable evergreen forests that, except on a handful of well-kept trails, deter all but the most resolute hikers. Beneath snowcapped summits, meltwater cascades off bluish hanging glaciers into frigidly limpid rivers that have cut deep canyons en route to the sea, and many visitors come to enjoy the fishing.

Queulat's accessibility has made it a popular destination for those exploring the Carretera, but most see only a sample of its attractions. In 2003, it recorded 5,930 visitors, the great majority in summer; 43 percent of these were foreigners.

At the same time, Queulat could be a poster child for climate change—according to Conaf, as late as 1837 its spectacular hanging glacier came within 100 meters of the sea, but that distance is now 7.8 kilometers. Much of this change, though, dates from a major 1960 flood.

Geography and Climate

Roughly midway between Chaitén and Coihaique, Queulat ranges from sea level on Canal Puyuhuapi to the 2,225-meter summit of Cerro Alto Nevado. Up to 4,000 millimeters of precipitation, fairly evenly distributed throughout the year, feeds its upper snowfields and glaciers, rushing rivers, and peaceful finger lakes; the more westerly areas are the wettest. The mean annual temperature is around 8°C.

Flora and Fauna

At lower elevations, Queulat's humid climate fosters dense evergreen forests of southern *coigue (Nothofagus betuloides)* and *tepa (Laurelia philippiana),* which reaches heights of 30 meters or more, with a dense understory of bamboo-like *quila (Chusquea quila),* fuchsia, and ferns. On some slopes, the coniferous Guaiteca cypress *(Pilgerodendron uviferum)* shades massive specimens of the broad-leaved shrub *nalca (Gunnera chilensis),* while at higher altitudes the *coigue* mixes with *lenga (Nothofagus pumilio).*

hanging glacier, Parque Nacional Queulat

Even along the highway, look for the timid *pudú,* no bigger than a border collie, as it emerges from the forest. Foxes, pumas, and Patagonian skunks are also present. The seldom-seen *chucao* is a solitary songbird that, legend says, brings good luck if it sings on your right, but bad luck if it sings on your left. The elegant black-necked swan paddles on the fjords and even some lakes.

Sights and Activities

Many points of interest are on or near the Carretera Austral, but the best base of operations is the **Sector Ventisquero,** where Conaf's Centro de Información, 22 kilometers from Puerto Puyuhuapi via the highway and a short eastbound lateral, is the starting point for several dead-end trails. Even the most sedentary can walk the 200-meter **Sendero El Mirador** to a vista point that looks east up the valley to the **Ventisquero Colgante,** a hanging glacier that conjures images of what California's Yosemite valley must have looked like before the ice melted. The trail itself winds through rain forest so dark that you nearly need a flashlight at midday, even when the sun shines bright above.

Crossing its eponymous river on a suspension bridge, the 600-meter **Sendero Río Guillermo** arrives at **Laguna Témpanos** which, despite its name, is iceberg-free. On the turbulent river's north bank, the 3.5-kilometer **Sendero Ventisquero Colgante** climbs unrelentingly to even more breathtaking views of Queulat's hanging glacier. As the afternoon sun warms the atmosphere, chunks of ice tumble onto the rocks below.

West of the bridge crossing, on the south bank, the 350-meter **Sendero Interpretativo El Aluvión** loops through a part of the valley where the 1960 flood carried huge boulders and flattened tall trees. It's signed in Spanish and pretty good English (despite a couple misspellings).

Just beyond Guardería Pudú, the park's southern entrance, the 1.7-kilometer **Sendero Río de**

las Cascadas winds through dripping rainforest until it arrives at a granite amphitheater where ribbons of glacial meltwater mark the river's source. Farther on, where the highway begins to switchbacks into the famous of the Río Queulat, a short staircase trail approaches the **Salto Río Padre García,** a waterfall named for the Chiloé-based Jesuit missionary who, in 1766–1767, may have been the first European to see the area.

Queulat's numerous rivers and lakes, particularly the northern **Lago Risopatrón** and **Lago Rosselot** (part of which comprises a separate reserve near the town of La Junta), are prime destinations for fly-fishing devotees.

Accommodations and Food

Accommodations are decentralized, to say the least, but there are plenty of options from La Junta in the north to the Río Ventisquero and vicinity in the south. For accommodations in nearby towns, see the separate entries for Puerto Puyuhuapi and La Junta.

Near the main trailheads, Conaf's scenic **Camping Ventisquero** (US$6.50 for up to 10 persons) has 10 relatively barren sites with sheltered cooking areas and immaculate toilets, but if the shower water were any colder the pipes would freeze.

On the western shore of Lago Risopatrón, 12 kilometers north of Puerto Puyuhuapi, Conaf's 10-site **Camping Angostura** (US$7 for up to six persons) has similar facilities in a dramatically different setting of humid temperate rainforest with soggy soils.

About 17 kilometers south of Puerto Puyuhuapi and five kilometers north of the turnoff to Sector Ventisquero, a garden of technicolor lupines marks **Hospedaje Las Toninas** (US$10 pp with breakfast and shared bath), a shingled roadside inn where cyclists, campers, and backpackers can sleep cheaply and ingest enormous plates of fresh crab salad at giveaway prices. Inexpensive campsites are also available.

About half an hour north of Puerto Puyuhuapi on Lago Risopatrón, **Cabañas El Pangue** (Km 240, tel. 067/325128, www.elpangue.cl, US$45–77 s, US$55–89 d) offers spacious cabins with natural wood, large double beds, and sunken tubs in a woodsy setting; the higher rates correspond to the summer peak season. There are larger units, accommodating up to seven persons, that cost less on a per-person basis; meals are also available for US$5 for breakfast, US$6.60 for special breakfast, US$8.30 for *onces,* US$9–12 for lunch or dinner, US$17 per person for a lamb barbecue outdoors. The management also rents canoes, rowboats and motorboats, and horses, and has a sauna and Jacuzzi.

Other Practicalities

Conaf has built a new, instructive Centro de Información Ambiental at Sector Ventisquero, where rangers can provide guidance on hiking and other activities. Visitors can also consult with rangers at Guardería Pudú (the park's southern entrance) and Guardería El Pangue (its northern entrance).

Conaf collects a US$2.40 admission charge at Sector Ventisquero only.

Buses from Coyhaique to Puerto Puyuhuapi and Chaitén pass directly through the park on the Carretera Austral, though they drop passengers at least half an hour's walk west of Sector Ventisquero.

PUERTO PUYUHUAPI

Thanks to its history as a pioneer port established by German immigrants in 1940, Puerto Puyuhuapi has a greater air of permanence than any other settlement on the Carretera Austral between Coyhaique, 225 kilometers to the south, and Chaitén, 195 kilometers to the north. Many of its streets, residents, and businesses still bear names like Hopperdietzel, Grosse, Ludwig, Rossbach and Übel.

At the north end of the Seno Ventisquero, a sheltered extension of the larger Canal Puyuhuapi, Puerto Puyuhuapi is now also a gateway to Parque Nacional Queulat and the elite hot-springs resort of Termas de Puyuhuapi.

Alfombras de Puyuhuapi

Since its founding by textile engineer Walter Hopperdietzel in 1940, Alfombras Puyuhuapi has produced handmade woolen carpets, tinted with Swiss dyes, for both internal and export markets. Most of its 20 employees are women weavers from the archipelago of Chiloé. They produce items that sell for upwards of $1,000, but smaller, more affordable pieces are also on display in the showroom. The benchmark price is US$150 per square meter.

Factory tours take place weekdays at 10:30, 11, and 11:30 A.M., and 4, 4:30 and 5 P.M., weekends and holidays at 11:30 A.M. only; admission costs US$1.50 for adults, US$.70 for children. The sales office is open 8:30 A.M.–1 P.M. and 3–7 P.M. daily. For more information, contact Alfombras de Puyuhuapi (Ernesto Ludwig s/n, tel. 067/325131, www.puyuhuapi.com, alfombras@puyuhuapi.com).

Accommodations and Food

Residencial Elizabeth (Circunvalación s/n, tel. 067/325106, US$7 pp for B&B) also serves lunch and dinner. The best budget option is **Hostería Marily** (Avenida Otto Übel s/n, tel. 067/325102, US$8 pp with shared bath, US$11 pp with private bath); though it has no frills, everything works, the beds are comfortable, and rates include breakfast.

Open December–March only, with exceptional management, the nonsmoking **Casa Ludwig** (Avenida Übel 850, tel./fax 067/325220, l.ludwig@entelchile.net, US$11–16 pp with shared bath, US$47 d with private bath) is an eight-room B&B occupying a cavernous four-story landmark house. Attic rooms with shared bath are cheaper than the downstairs rooms (some of which have sea views), but still comfy and cozy, and the breakfast is excellent. English and German are spoken; the sitting room has a large German-language library with a few English titles. There are lower rates in December and March.

Set among delightful gardens, **Hostería Alemana** (Avenida Übel 450, tel. 067/325118, hosteria_alemana@entelchile.net, US$28/42 s/d) is good enough but lacks the charm of the Ludwig.

In addition to hotel dining rooms, there are also salmon dinners and *kuchen* at inconsistent **Café Rossbach** (Ernesto Ludwig s/n), alongside the carpet factory. Open in summer only, the rustically stylish **Lluvia Marina** (Avenida Übel 720, tel. 067/325214) is the best choice—the only choice, really—for a splurge; entrées like an excellent *chupe de locos* fall in the US$6–7.50 range.

Other Practicalities

Near the Copec gas station and Café Rossbach, Puyuhuapi's **Oficina de Información Turística** (Ernesto Ludwig s/n) is theoretically open 10 A.M.–2 P.M. and 3–9 P.M. daily in summer, but sometimes nobody shows up. Transportation schedules are posted outside, other information inside.

Buses Norte (O'Higgins 39, tel. 067/325130) passes through Puerto Puyuhuapi en route between Coyhaique and Chaitén, as do buses between Puerto Cisnes and La Junta.

TERMAS DE PUYUHUAPI

South of Puerto Puyuhuapi, sumptuous in style but more affordable than it looks, Termas de Puyuhuapi (Bahía Dorita s/n, tel. 067/325129) is a secluded spa resort that's not literally an island but, since there's no road and the only access is by launch across the Seno Ventisquero (Ventisquero Sound), it might as well be. Both hotel guests and day visitors can enjoy naturally heated outdoor pools and hiking trails that veer through the forest understory of dense *quila* (solid bamboo) thickets, *chilco* (firecracker fuchsia), colossal tree ferns and rhubarb-like *nalcas* with leaves the size of umbrellas.

Hotel guests only, though, have access to the modern spa facilities including a gym, heated indoor pool, and massage room, which, perched in a tower, enjoys 360-degree views of its scenic surroundings. When the weather lifts, the panorama is the Andean front range of Parque Nacional Queulat, where traces of snow linger even at summer's end. More than just traces remain on the enormous hanging glacier that's just out of sight.

Spacious waterfront rooms, stocked with genteel touches like terrycloth robes and individual umbrellas, look out onto the dock where the catamaran *Patagonia Express* starts its weekly run to Parque Nacional Laguna San Rafael, on the final day of package holidays that range from four days

© WAYNE BERNHARDSON

Termas de Puyuhuapi is an upscale but unpretentious hot springs hotel.

and three nights to six days and five nights. Activities like hiking, fly-fishing, and excursions along the Carretera Austral are additional.

While the hotel primarily works with multiday packages, overnight accommodations are possible on a space-available basis, normally Thursday and Friday only. In peak season (Christmas–mid-March), rates start at US$100 s or d with a buffet breakfast; the rest of the year, rates begin at US$90. Spa access costs US$12 per person more. Fixed-price lunches and dinners from the recently remodeled kitchen and dining room, which include salmon from the resort's own hatchery, cost US$22, while deluxe buffet dinners cost US$26.

It sounds exclusive (and it ain't proletarian), but Puyuhuapi also lets the riffraff in for day-use of the outdoor pools and baths (US$20 pp for adults, US$10 pp for children) and of the spa (US$35 pp). The cafeteria at the pools, open only in daytime, has a cheaper but more limited menu than the hotel restaurant.

Termas de Puyuhuapi has its main office in Santiago through **Patagonia Connection** (Fidel Oteíza 1951, Oficina 1006, Providencia, tel. 02/2256489, fax 02748111, www.patagonia-connection.com).

Puyuhuapi provides free transport for its package guests; otherwise, launches leave from its mainland information center on the Carretera Austral, 14 kilometers south of Puerto Puyuhuapi, charging US$5 per adult, US$4 per child, each way. Scheduled departures from the hotel are at 9:30 A.M., noon, and 3 and 6:30 P.M., returning at 10 A.M. and 12:30, 3, and 7 P.M., but there are occasional unscheduled crossings as well.

LA JUNTA

At the crossroads town of La Junta, new penetration roads proceed west along the Río Palena to the port of Raúl Marín Balmaceda and east toward the Río Figueroa valley and the Argentine border. La Junta gained a measure of notoriety when, in 2001, municipal authorities erected an unauthorized monolith to General Pinochet—still popular here for building the north-south Carretera Austral.

On a broad plain at the confluence of the two rivers, just south of the regional border between Aisén and Los Lagos, La Junta is the main access point to **Reserva Nacional Lago Rosselot,** a 12,725-hectare forest reserve whose longitudinal finger lake is known for its fishing.

Rates at **Residencial Valderas** (Antonio Varas s/n, tel. 067/314105, US$9 pp with shared bath) include breakfast. The best choice, though, is the roadside **Hostal Espacio y Tiempo** (Carretera Austral s/n, tel. 067/314141, www.espacioytiempo.cl, US$50/73 with breakfast and private bath), which also offers fishing and other excursions in the area.

Like other destinations along the Carretera Austral, La Junta is a regular stop for buses en route between Coyhaique and Chaitén. **Buses Lago Verde** (Antonio Varas s/n) goes north to Chaitén (US$9.50) at 8 A.M. Monday, Wednesday, and Friday. **Entre Verde** (tel. 067/314725) goes to Puerto Cisnes at 7 A.M. Monday and Friday.

LAGO YELCHO

About 30 kilometers north of La Junta, where the Carretera Austral bridges the Río Palena, lies the boundary between Region XI (Aisén) and Region X (Los Lagos). Los Lagos' first major attraction is elongated Lago Yelcho, which stretches from Puerto Cárdenas in the north to Puerto Ramírez in the southeast, and formed the lacustrine part of the highway between Chaitén and Futaleufú until completion of the Carretera Austral eliminated the need for ferries. Kayakers, though, can still paddle from Puerto Ramírez to Puerto Cárdenas and even to the Pacific.

At **Villa Santa Lucía,** 70 kilometers north of La Junta and 78 kilometers south of Chaitén, the Carretera Austral continues north but the eastbound lateral Ruta 235 drops steeply to the lakeshore and **Puerto Ramírez,** where **Hostería Verónica** (tel. 065/264431, tel. 09/9170088, US$10 pp with breakfast and shared bath, US$20 pp with full board) is the main accommodations option. Nearby **Puerto Piedra Lodge** (tel. 065/731505 in Chaitén, pto_piedralodge@hotmail.com) focuses on relatively cheap all-inclusive fishing holidays (US$100 pp per day including transfers from Chaitén), but will take individual guests if there's space available.

At Puerto Ramírez, Ruta 235 continues southeast toward Palena and a minor border crossing to Argentina, while the alternative Ruta 231 proceeds northeast toward the whitewater-rafting and kayaking capital of Futaleufú and a far more efficient border crossing. For details, see the separate entries for Futaleufú and Palena below.

Midway between Villa Santa Lucía and Puerto Cárdenas, on the west side of the Carretera Austral, the north side of the **Puente Ventisquero** (Glacier Bridge) is the starting point for a two-hour hike through soggy evergreen forest to the **Ventisquero Cavi,** a hanging glacier. **Camping Ventisquero** (US$1.50 pp) is a no-frills facility that also operates a summer café-bus, with sandwiches and kuchen.

Across the highway from the Ventisquero Cavi, the lakeside **Hotel Yelcho en la Patagonia** (tel. 065/731337, US$70/80 s/d) is a fashionable fishing lodge whose comfortable upstairs rooms offer lake views through groves of *arrayanes;* the ground-level bar/restaurant has high-beamed ceilings and decent-enough food for a place that specializes in fly-fishing holidays through its Santiago office (Alonso Ovalle 612, Oficina 4, tel. 02/6330501, www.yelcho.cl). On the same grounds, it also has 15 campsites (US$32 for up to four persons) with electricity, roofed shelters, and hot showers.

At the north end of the lake, where Lago Yelcho becomes the Río Yelcho, **Puerto Cárdenas** has three simple places to stay, all reachable by the same message number, tel. 065/264429: **Hospedaje Lulú, Residencial Los Pinos,** and **Residencial Yelcho.** All are open in summer only. The 250-meter suspension bridge that crosses the river here was the first of its kind in Chile.

FUTALEUFÚ

With its reputation for world-class whitewater—some say it's *the* best—Futaleufú draws outdoor recreationists like a magnet. But what works for this tidy village, its forested mountains, and its namesake river—spectacular natural beauty, cleanliness, and isolation—also works against it. The 1,153 people who live here may be on borrowed time, possibly powerless to fend off Endesa, the powerful Spanish electric utility that wants to build three massive dams where at least three international rafting and kayaking enterprises have elaborate summer camps, and several Chilean operators spend at least part of the season.

For the time being, though, the "Fu" remains one of the world's most challenging rivers. Both foreign and Chilean operators hope to kindle local and national enthusiasm for preserving the river and its surroundings, and the March 2000 Whitewater Challenge World Championships brought rafters and kayakers from 14 different countries. Fly-fishing has also had a substantial impact on the local economy.

Orientation

Only eight kilometers west of the Argentine border, at the confluence of the Río Espolón and the Río Futaleufú, the village is 155 kilometers southeast of Chaitén via the Carretera Austral, Ruta 235 from Villa Santa Lucia, and Ruta 231 from Puerto Ramírez, at the east end of Lago Yelcho.

Futaleufú's plan is a rectangular grid whose focus, if not precisely its center, is the manicured Plaza de Armas. On the south side of the Plaza, Bernardo O'Higgins leads east toward the Argentine border, while Arturo Prat, on the west side, leads south toward westbound Ruta 231.

Activities

Whitewater is clearly the major attraction, but hiking, climbing, mountain biking, and horseback riding are also attracting attention. Several U.S. rafting/kayaking operators maintain summer camps in the vicinity October–April; for details, see the Organized Tours entry in the Know Patagonia chapter. Santiago-based operators are also listed there.

The Class III Espolón is a good starter river, and even parts of the Fu are suitable for those with limited experience, but rapids like the Class V Terminator can be a challenge even for professionals. According to former U.S. Olympic kayaker Chris Spelius, who runs a camp here, "Big water can be forgiving to a certain extent, but this river's so big that it can take a normal human being with a life jacket and hold him under water longer than a normal human being can hold his breath." Even on commercially rafted Class IV stretches there are what Chris calls "Death Spots" that need a capable guide to be avoided. According to Lawrence Alvarez, another U.S. operator, about 10 percent of those who raft on the Fu become "swimmers" at some point.

A leisurely float on the Espolón costs about US$30, while a Class III raft descent goes for US$50. For a half-day Class IV descent on the Fu, figure about US$60; a full-day Class IV–V experience costs about US$80. The former involves descent of the river "between the bridges," a nonstop succession of Class III–IV rapids. Novices get out before tackling the Class V Casa de Piedra rapid.

For hikers, one of the area's best trails follows the Fu's south bank, beginning with an undulating oxcart road opposite the Expediciones Chile camp about 10 kilometers west of town; ask for directions at Expediciones Chile (Gabriela Mistral 296, tel. 065/721386). The trail continues past peasant homesteads above rapids like the Terminator before continuing through southern beech forest so dense that, in mid-afternoon on a sunny day, it's as dark as dusk. It eventually emerges onto a terrace with a couple new trophy houses; a nearby bridge recrosses the river to the Ruta 231.

For river rafting and other activities, drop-in visitors can try local operators and offices including **Austral Excursiones** (Hermanos Carrera 500, tel. 065/721239), **Futaleufú Explore** (O'Higgins 772, tel. 065/721265), **Expediciones Chile** (Gabriela Mistral 296, tel. 065/721386, www.exchile.com), and the Hostería Río Grande's **Patagonia Adventure Center** (O'Higgins 397, tel. 065/721320, www.pacchile.cl).

For horseback riding, contact **Rancho las Ruedas** (Piloto Carmona 337, tel. 065/721294), in the woods at the north end of Arturo Prat.

Accommodations

Futaleufú has more and better accommodations than any other place of its size on or along the Carretera Austral; many are utilitarian, but a growing number have both character and style.

Just south of town on Ruta 231, prior to crossing the bridge over the river, **Camping Puerto Espolón** (US$4 pp) has shady sites with grass, clean toilets, and hot showers.

Affordable accommodations with shared bath and breakfast include **Hospedaje El Campesino** (Prat 107, tel. 065/721275, US$8 pp), **Residencial Carahue** (O'Higgins 332, tel. 065/721221, US$8 pp), and **Hotel Continental** (Balmaceda 595, tel. 065/721222, US$8 pp). **Hospedaje Adolfo** (O'Higgins 302,tel. 065/721256, US$8 pp) is a step above the others in comfort. **Posada Ely** (Balmaceda 409, tel. 065/721205, US$12 pp with breakfast) has rooms with private bath.

Under new ownership, on the east side of the Plaza de Armas, promising **La Antigua Casona** (Manuel Rodríguez 215, tel. 065/721311, US$42/50 s/d) is a work in progress, but the rejuvenated rooms are spacious, the beds are comfortable, and the breakfast diverse. The restaurant is worth consideration for lunch or dinner (US$13) as well. The more upmarket **Posada Campesina La Gringa** (Sargento Aldea 456, tel.

065/721260, tel. 02/2359187 in Santiago, US$48/70 s/d with breakfast) enjoys a spacious garden setting.

Easily the area's most stylish place, in a sylvan setting west of town on the road to Chaitén, **Hostal La Confluencia** (tel. 065/232300 in Puerto Montt, reservasalsur@surnet.cl, US$39 pp) is a Doug Tompkins property that offers B&B for no more than four persons in a pair of double rooms.

Hostería Río Grande (O'Higgins 397, tel. 065/721320, US$50/80 s/d, www.pacchile.cl) has rustically styled common areas, a bar/restaurant that's become a mecca for rafters and kayakers, and a dozen simple, tastefully decorated twin-bedded rooms. The small TV lounge is full of kayak videos.

Rooms at rustically styled, family-run **Hotel El Barranco** (O'Higgins 172, tel. 065/721314, elbarranco@chile.com, US$78/97 with breakfast) look into lush woods. While it's attractive enough, it's arguably overpriced for this market.

Food

Just like the accommodations, the food is a bit better in Futaleufú than in most other towns its size, though Chilean standards like beef, chicken, and sandwiches are the rule. In addition to the dining room at Hostería Río Grande, choices include **El Encuentro** (O'Higgins 633, tel. 065/721247), **Escorpio** (Gabriela Mistral 255, tel. 065/721228), and **Futaleufú** (Pedro Aguirre Cerda 407, tel. 065/721295).

Sur Andes (Aguirre Cerda 308, tel. 065/721405) has espresso and desserts. Though possibly overbuilt for a burg of Futa's size, **Martín Pescador** (Balmaceda 603, tel. 065/721279) offers cozy living-room style for an aperitif, good salmon (around US$6), and a small English-language library (not a book exchange).

Information and Services

Futaleufú's **Oficina de Turismo Municipal** (O'Higgins 536, tel. 065/721370) is on the south side of the Plaza de Armas. December–March, it's open 9 A.M.–9 P.M. daily.

Visitors arriving from or departing for Argentina should know that Chilean customs and immigration here is far better organized than at Palena, where Carabineros handle the formalities. The border is open 8 A.M.–8 P.M. daily.

Banco del Estado (O'Higgins and Manuel Rodríguez) is the only place to change money. Bring cash to Futa, as there's no ATM, it's complicated to cash traveler's checks for services, and only a few places accept credit cards.

Telefónica del Sur (Balmaceda 419) has long-distance telephone service, but public Internet access has yet to arrive here.

Señora Vicky (Sargento Aldea 273, tel. 067/721276) does the washing.

Getting There

Transporte Cordillera (O'Higgins 234, tel. 067/721248) shuttles passengers to the international border, eight kilometers east, for connections to the Argentine towns of Trevelin and Esquel. Departures are at 8:30 A.M. Monday, Wednesday, and Friday, but may be more frequent in summer.

Several companies go to Chaitén (US$10, four hours) at 7:30 A.M. daily, including Transportes Cordillera and **Turismo Futaleufú** (Pedro Aguirre Cerda 505, tel. 065/721280; the latter also goes to Osorno and Puerto Montt (US$31, 11 hours) Tuesday and Friday at 7:45 A.M. via Argentina.

PALENA

From the Puerto Ramírez junction, where Ruta 231 leads northwest toward Futaleufú, Ruta 235 continues southeast to the hamlet of Palena, which is far less frequented but no less scenic. While lacking Futaleufú's critical mass of tourist services, it compensates with a pastoral integrity that manifests itself in events like late January's rodeo, and it also provides an alternative road into Argentina.

In the valley of its namesake river, Palena is 43 kilometers southeast of Puerto Ramírez and only five kilometers east of the Argentine border post at Carrenleufú. The Carabineros, who manage the crossing on the Chilean side, can be agonizingly slow.

Palena has a pair of simple, affordable accommodations almost side-by-side: **Hospedaje**

THE HUASO AND THE RODEO

Less celebrated than the Argentine gaucho, the Chilean *huaso* resembles his trans-Andean counterpart in many ways, but differs dramatically in others. Both, of course, are horsemen, but the gaucho arose from a background of fierce independence on the Pampas, while the subservient *huaso* originated on the landed estates that dominated economic and social life in colonial and republican Chile.

Though the *huaso* was a hired hand or even a peon attached to the property, on Sundays he and his colleagues could blow off steam in racing their horses, betting, and drinking. As the spontaneous rodeo grew too raucous, though, it drew the disapproval of landowners, who responded by organizing competitions that, over time, became more genteel versions of the *huaso* tradition.

Today, though Chilean rodeo remains popular, it is, according to historian Richard Slatta, a nostalgic exercise that's "a middle- and upper-class pastime, not a profession" as it has become in North America. Riders wear colorful ponchos, flat-brimmed hats, oversized spurs, and elaborately carved wooden stirrups.

Chilean rodeo's signature event is the *atajada,* in which a pair of *jinetes* (riders) guide and pin a calf or steer to the padded wall of the *medialuna,* the semicircular rodeo ring. Since it's harder to control the steer by the body than the head—the chest is best—the horsemen get more points for this. They lose points if the steer strikes any unpadded part of the wall, or escapes between the horses.

There are no cash prizes, though the event ends by acknowledging the champions and other riders with wine and empanadas. Compared to Canada, the United States, and even Mexico, Chilean rodeo is truly *machista*—women prepare and serve food, dress in costume, and dance the traditional *cueca* with the men, but they do not ride. In small settlements along the Carretera Austral, the Chilean rodeo probably comes closest to its historic origins.

© WAYNE BERNHARDSON

rodeo at Palena

La Chilenita (Pudeto 681, tel. 065/741212, US$5.50 pp) and **Hospedaje El Passo** (Pudeto 661, tel. 065/741226, US$5.50 pp). Both also serve meals, as does **Los Pioneros** (Pérez Rosales 663, tel. 065/741262).

Palena's **Oficina de Información Turística** (O'Higgins 740, tel. 065/741217, tur-muni@entelchile.net) keeps long hours in summer only.

Buses Río Palena (Pedro Montt 853,tel. 065/741319) connects the town with Chaitén (US$6, four hours) Monday, Wednesday, and Friday at 6:45 A.M., returning at 3:30 P.M.

CHAITÉN

Between the snowy volcanic cones of Michinmahuida and Corcovado, the modest port of Chaitén is the main gateway to continental

Chiloé. Receiving regular ferry and catamaran traffic from Puerto Montt, it's the starting point for many trips down the Carretera Austral and the year-round access point for Parque Natural Pumalín, the controversial conservation initiative of U.S. entrepreneur Douglas Tompkins.

Chaitén's services and infrastructure are rapidly improving. Town streets are being paved, and the highway itself is being paved and widened south of town.

Orientation

Chaitén (population 4,065) is 46 kilometers north of Puerto Cárdenas by a segment of the Carretera Austral that is presently being widened and paved, and 56 kilometers south of Caleta Gonzalo, a summer-only ferry port that's also the headquarters of Parque Natural Pumalín. Most services and other points of interest are within a block or two of the Costanera Avenida Corcovado, which runs north-south along the Bahía de Chaitén waterfront. The Plaza de Armas is two blocks east, between O'Higgins and Pedro Aguirre Cerda.

The Costanera leads north to Caleta Gonzalo, while Avenida Ignacio Carrera Pinto heads east and then south toward Puerto Cárdenas.

Accommodations and Food

Chaitén has abundant budget accommodations, some of which is pretty good, but relatively little in either midrange or above. Israeli travelers favor **Hospedaje Casa de Rita** (Almirante Riveros and Prat, tel. 065/721502, US$4 pp for floor space, US$6 pp with shared bath). Family-run **Hospedaje Ancud** (Libertad 105, tel. 067/731535, US$6 pp with shared bath and breakfast) prepares additional meals as well.

Other affordable choices include **Hospedaje Anita** (Pedro de Valdivia 129, tel. 065/731413), which also offers camping (US$4 pp); family-operated **Hospedaje Don Carlos** (Almirante Riveros 53, tel./fax 065/731287, mali178@hotmail.com, US$8 pp with shared bath, US$23 d with private bath); **Residencial Astoria** (Corcovado 442, tel. 065/731263, US$8 pp); **Hostería Sebastián** (Almirante Riveros 163, tel./fax 065/731225, US$8 pp); and the waterfront **Hostería Llanos** (Corcovado 378, tel. 067/731332, US$10 pp with shared bath and breakfast, US$12 pp with private bath).

The midrange **Hostería Corcovado** (Corcovado 408, tel. 065/731221, corcovado@chile.com, US$11–13 pp with an ample breakfast) is also a restaurant that serves homemade meals, including seafood, in the US$4–6.50 range. Comparable or slightly better places include attractive **Hotel Schilling** (Corcovado 230, tel. 065/731295, constsch@telsur.cl, US$16–24 pp with private bath); **Cabañas Brisas del Mar** (Corcovado 278, tel. 067/731266, fax 067/731284, cababrisas@telsur.cl, US$50 s or d with breakfast and cable TV); and **Hostería los Coihues** (Pedro Aguirre Cerda 398, tel. 067/731461, juancac@surnet.cl, US$40/60 s/d).

Owned by Pumalín visionary Doug Tompkins, recycled **Hostería Puma Verde** (O'Higgins 54, tel./fax 065/731184, pumaverde@telsur.cl, US$39/55 s/d but no IVA discounts) is an intimate, tobacco-free B&B whose dining room also serves meals to nonguests. A spacious lawn, planted with cherry and apple trees, separates the main house from a separate outbuilding that's quieter. Rooms themselves are an upscale adaptation of the Chilean south's traditional shingle-covered houses, with steep-pitched roofs; the antiqueish beds and other furniture are solid, and mattresses firm, but the showers are a bit small. Befitting a Tompkins property, framed conservation posters and photographs decorate the walls; in fact, Tompkins has upgraded the entire block of O'Higgins with trees and flower planters.

Hotel Mi Casa (Avenida Norte 206, tel. 065/731285, hotelmicasa@123.cl, US$48/67 s/d) exudes old-fashioned charm: wallpapered rooms with wood paneling, armoires, twin beds, central heating, and small bathrooms. Rates include a substantial breakfast (bread and cheese, strudel, tea or coffee); its restaurant is worth consideration for lunch or dinner as well. Note that some beds are soft because they have two mattresses rather than a mattress and box spring—check before taking the room.

Other than hotel restaurants, Chaitén has relatively few places to eat. Several locales along the waterfront serve seafood, including the homey

Cocinería Marita (Corcovado 455). In recent years, **Flamengo** (Corcovado 218, tel. 067/731314) has evolved from a budget restaurant to a more upscale venue also specializing in seafood, and it's often packed.

Information and Services

Chaitén has built a new **Oficina de Información Turística** (Costanera Corcovado s/n), at the foot of O'Higgins, but more effort has gone into construction than into training the staff, who are young and well-meaning, but not particularly knowledgeable. Hours are 8 A.M.–10 P.M. daily in summer.

At the bus terminal, **Chaitur** (O'Higgins 67, tel./fax 065/731429, nchaitur@hotmail.com) is a good source of information all year, with Spanish-, English-, and French-speaking staff. It also sells maps and has a small book exchange.

Across from the bus terminal, Parque Pumalín has its own **Centro de Información** (O'Higgins 62, tel./fax 065/731341).

Banco Estado (Libertad 298) changes U.S. cash and traveler's checks; its ATM now works with MasterCard and Cirrus, but it's the last chance north of Coyhaique.

On the north side of the Plaza de Armas, **Correos de Chile** (O'Higgins 230) is the post office. On the east side of the plaza, the new **Entelchile** office (Libertad 402) has long-distance telephones and the fastest Internet access.

Lavandería Masol (Todesco 272, Local B, tel. 065/731566) does the laundry.

Hospital de Chaitén (Avenida Ignacio Carrera Pinto 153, tel. 067/731244) provides medical services.

Getting There

Chaitén has air connections with Puerto Montt, sea links with Puerto Montt and Chiloé, and roads south to Futaleufú and Coyhaique and north to Caleta Gonzalo.

Reservations are essential for air taxis to Puerto Montt (about US$53), which leave from the airstrip a short distance south of town. Services change frequently, but the current carriers are **Servicio Aéreo Regional** (Pedro Aguirre Cerda s/n, tel. 065/731384) and **Aerotaxis del Sur** (Riveros and Ignacio Carrera Pinto, tel. 065/731315).

Chaitén's ferry dock is a short distance northwest of town via the Costanera. **Transmarchilay** (Corcovado 266, tel. 065/731272, fax 065/731282) sails three times weekly to Castro and four times weekly to Puerto Montt (nine hours) on the vehicle ferry *La Pincoya.* Fares to both destinations range from US$16 per person for fixed seats to US$19 per person for reclining seats. Vehicle rates are US$102 for passenger vehicles and small trucks, plus US$3 for the driver, and US$24 per lineal meter for other vehicles; bicycles cost US$11 and motorcycles US$22. In summer only, Transmarchilay also sails from Caleta Gonzalo, 56 kilometers north of Chaitén, to the town of Hornopirén.

In addition to the ferries, **Aysén Express** catamarans occasionally go to Puerto Montt (US$36), but these services change frequently; for details, contact **Chaitur** (O'Higgins 67, tel. 065/731429).

Nearly all buses stop at the main **Terminal de Buses** (O'Higgins 67, tel. 067/731429) before continuing down the Carretera Austral, but some companies are scattered around town. The main destinations are Futaleufú and Coyhaique and intermediates, but there are also services north to Caleta Gonzalo (Parque Pumalín).

Services to Coyhaique (US$25, 12 hours) are daily in summer, three or four times weekly the rest of the year, with **Buses Norte** from the main terminal. Departure time is around 9 A.M. **B y V Tour** (Libertad 432, tel. 065/731390) goes to Coyhaique four times weekly at 10 A.M.

B y V also goes to Caleta Gonzalo (US$5) Monday, Wednesday, and Friday at 9 A.M. in summer, less frequently the rest of the year. In summer, **Chaitur** and other companies go to Caleta Gonzalo (US$6, two hours) daily at 5 P.M. and will make special trips if demand is sufficient.

Buses Lago Verde, on Todesco between Corcovado and Portales, goes south to La Junta (US$9.50) Monday, Wednesday, and Friday afternoons.

From the main terminal, **Turismo Futaleufú** goes to Futaleufú (US$10, four hours) at 3:30 P.M. daily in summer, daily except Sunday in winter. **Transportes Cordillera** goes daily at 3:15 P.M. to Futaleufú.

Buses Río Palena goes to Palena (US$10, four hours) at 3:30 P.M. Monday, Wednesday, and Friday from the corner of Corcovado and Todesco. In winter, Buses Norte sometimes goes to La Junta, Puerto Cisnes, Lago Verde, and Palena.

VICINITY OF CHAITÉN

English-speaking Nicholas LaPenna at **Chaitur** (O'Higgins 67, tel. 065/731429, fax 065/731266, nchaitur@hotmail.com) organizes excursions as far north as Caleta Gonzalo and south to Termas de Amarillo, the Yelcho glacier, and other Carretera Austral sights, and guides fly-fishing trips. Chaitur also serves as a general travel agency for Chilean airlines, catamarans, ferries, and accommodations, including the *cabañas* at Parque Pumalín.

Casa Avión

About 20 kilometers southeast of Chaitén, on the south side of the Carretera Austral, stands one of the region's most offbeat landmarks. In 1974, well before the highway's completion, the Chilean Air Force crashed a DC-3 in the vicinity; unable to fly it out, they salvaged the engine and left the fuselage. Using two oxcarts, farmer Carlos Anabalón hauled it to his roadside property, divided it into three rooms, and lived in the Casa Avión (Airplane House) until the year 2000, when he traded it to a Chaitén policeman for a four-wheel-drive Jeep.

Termas El Amarillo

At a highway junction about 25 kilometers southeast of Chaitén, a gravel road turns north for five kilometers to the forested, no-frills hot-springs site of Termas El Amarillo. Admission to the outdoor pools costs US$3 per person; it also has walk-in campsites (US$6) and a restaurant.

At the highway junction itself, **Residencial Marcela** (tel. 065/264442, US$9/17 s/d with shared bath and breakfast) also has *cabañas* with private bath and kitchen for US$33 for up to six persons.

PARQUE NATURAL PUMALÍN

In 1991, U.S. businessman Douglas Tompkins and his wife Kristine McDivitt cashed out their

Casa Avión, near Chaitén

THE SAGA OF PUMALÍN

In the decade-plus since he purchased 17,000 hectares of temperate rainforest on Fiordo Reñihué, north of Chaitén, Californian Douglas Tompkins has become the gringo Chile knows best—or at least the gringo many Chileans think they know best. Since then, as Tompkins acquired a total of some 360,000 hectares in southernmost Region X (Los Lagos) and Aisén, probably not even President Ricardo Lagos has appeared more often in the Chilean press.

Reported to be Chile's largest landholder, in a country where the *latifundio* has often been anathema, Tompkins is a polarizing figure, but not in the usual sense. Traditionally, objections to large landholdings come from the political left, which fought vociferously against the wealthy *fundos* before the coup of 1973, and advocated redistribution of their properties to landless peasants. The right, by contrast, upheld the status quo and sanctity of private property, and their position seemingly triumphed after 1973.

Tompkins, founder of the Esprit clothing empire, turned conventional Chilean politics head over heels. Taking advantage of Chile's openness toward foreign investors, he used the proceeds from Esprit's sale to consolidate several large undeveloped properties not for profit but for preservation. While other entrepreneurs were clear-cutting native forest and replanting with fast-growing exotics for the quickest possible profit, Tompkins formed a trust to turn his lands into a de facto national park under a Chilean law that allows private *santuarios de la naturaleza* (nature sanctuaries).

Tompkins anticipated that his Proyecto Pumalín, in a thinly populated and once inaccessible area along the Argentine border south of Hornopirén and north of Chaitén, would make him a hero in Chile and it did—among the small but growing Chilean environmental movement for whom forest preservation was a hot-button issue, and who distrusted the growing power of multinational corporations. For them, the multimillionaire capitalist who believed in philanthropy and biodiversity was a real if improbable hero.

On the other hand, Tompkins' actions aroused distrust and hostility from conservative sectors that, economically at least, might seem to have much in common with him. He ran afoul, though, of conservative business, military, and religious interests, all with slightly different but overlapping rationales for adamant opposition to the project.

One reason was overt nationalism. Traditionally, Latin American armies place high value on controlling their borders, even those of such remote access and difficult terrain as Pumalín, and many civilians shared their opinions. In some cases, nationalist arguments bordered on hysteria; the army argued that any dispute with Tompkins might result in U.S. intervention, while Christian Democratic Senator Sergio Páez called Pumalín a "geopolitical catastrophe" and, preposterously, claimed that if Tompkins' property became a nature sanctuary, the land might eventually be ceded to the state of California.

The conservative daily press, ironically and disingenuously, argued what pro-Allende radicals could have said in the 1970s: the occupation of so much land by a wealthy foreigner would squeeze economic opportunities for Chilean workers. Owned by the Copec group, which has substantial investments in Chile's forestry sector, *La Tercera* has given the Tompkins story consistently critical front-page coverage. One of Tompkins' fiercest local critics, former Chaitén mayor José Miguel Fritis, apparently turned against him when Tompkins declined to purchase what he considered an overpriced property of the mayor's.

The Catholic Church, to which most of Tompkins' critics belong, has its own disagreements with the philanthropist's ideology. In their opinion, Tompkins's "deep ecology" beliefs contradict the church's teaching that humans are superior to other living things, and they disagree vehemently with what they consider his pro-choice approach to birth control and abortion.

This opposition has been effective at times, blocking Tompkins' purchase of 30,000 hectares from Valparaíso's Universidad Católica in favor of the electric utility Endesa, and consistently delaying the park's formal establishment. After drawing fire from the Asociación de Productores de Salmón y Truchas (Salmon and Trout Producers' Association) when he complained about water pollution from fish farming, in mid-2001 Tompkins threatened to abandon the Pumalín project because of "harassment" from local and national politicians, but soon reversed his position in what some critics derided as a publicity stunt.

Tompkins has many local and national supporters, though. Some legislators and government officials favor the park and its tourism potential, but are reluctant to speak because of consequences from business interests and the political right. PPD Deputy Guido Girardi, one of the country's most outspoken environmentalists, said that opposition to Pumalín was a combination of "extreme nationalism" and lobbying by forestry companies. The Lagos administration has been supportive, and visiting Sernatur chief Oscar Santelices said: "The park is just in the beginnings of what could be a world-class reserve, thanks to the considerable funds invested. In all honesty, this could be the gateway to success for Chilean eco-tourism."

At the same time, even some Tompkins supporters agree his actions have not been so transparent as they might have been—his earliest purchases, in particular, seemed almost surreptitious, and might have benefited from traditional political lobbying. As the project has developed, though, public access has steadily improved through hiking trails, campgrounds, *cabañas,* a very good restaurant, and a visitors center, not to mention small-scale sustainable-agriculture experiments and other features to benefit the small local population.

One of the latest issues in the Pumalín saga is construction of a road from Hornopirén, in the north, to Caleta Gonzalo in the south, thus eliminating a discontinuous stretch of the Carretera Austral that now requires a ferry. The nationalist opposition prefers a route through the heart of Pumalín, with expensive bridges and tunnels, while Tompkins and his supporters argue that a coastal road would be cheaper and serve the local population better.

To the chagrin of Tompkins' opponents, right-of-center politician Sebastián Piñera, after spending four days at Pumalín, proclaimed his support for Tompkins' position. One outraged member of Piñera's Renovación Nacional (RN) party, Senator Antonio Horvath, went so far as to resign his party leadership post, though he probably would have given it up soon anyway. Cristián Salazar N., of the Corporación Defensa de la Soberanía (Corporation for the Defense of Sovereignty), grumbled in *La Tercera* that "It's time that Tompkins and his entourage of ecologists take off their masks and expose the motives for their sick obsession with isolating the park from the rest of the country."

In late 2004, Tompkins finally received government approval to convert Pumalín into a national sanctuary administered by a seven-member, all-Chilean board of directors.

For more details on the park, contact **Parque Pumalín** (Buin 356, Puerto Montt, tel. 065/250079, 065/251911, fax 065/255145, www.parquepumalin.cl, pumalin@telsur.cl) or the **Foundation for Deep Ecology** (Building 1062, Fort Cronkhite, Sausalito, CA 94965, tel. 415/229-9339, fax 415/229-9340, www.deepecology.org, info@deepecology.org).

© WAYNE BERNHARDSON

The ferry from Hornopirén arrives at Caleta Gonzalo, gateway to Parque Pumalín.

fortunes from the Esprit and Patagonia clothing empires and began purchasing large blocks of temperate rainforest to create the region's largest destination—literally so—in Parque Pumalín, a 317,000-hectare private nature reserve straddling the highway north of Chaitén. Since then, says the *New York Times,* only Pinochet has had his name in the Chilean press more than Tompkins, who's even received death threats from ultranationalists who accuse him of trying to split the country in half. Tompkins also has many Chilean supporters, though, and most criticisms of the park are far less extreme.

Tompkins has allayed many of those concerns by building trails, cabins, campgrounds, and a restaurant and visitors center that have lured visitors from Chaitén to Caleta Gonzalo, a summer ferry port on the Reñihué fjord, and other points along the highway and the park's extensive shoreline. In late 2004 in a ceremony in Santiago, the park finally received formal legal recognition from the government of President Ricardo Lagos.

Geography and Climate

Pumalín stretches from 42° S in the north, where it's contiguous with Parque Nacional Hornopirén, to nearly 43° S just east of Chaitén in the south. Most visitors, though, see the areas along both sides of the Carretera Austral just north of Chaitén en route to Caleta Gonzalo.

Elevations range from sea level to the snowy summit of 2,404-meter Volcán Michinmahuida, in the most southerly sector of the park, but even these statistics are misleading—the topography rises so steeply in some areas that trails require ladders rather than switchbacks.

Pumalín wouldn't look like it does without rain—lots of rain. While there are no reliable rainfall statistics, probably more than 4,000 millimeters falls every year. At higher elevations, of course, it accumulates as snow.

Flora and Fauna

Pumalín takes its name from the puma *(Felis concolor),* but the principal reason for its creation was to protect the temperate southern rainforest, whose single most significant species is the *alerce (Fitzroya cupressoides).* There are also several species of southern beech *(Nothofagus),* not to mention the numerous other rain-forests species common to southern Chilean environments.

In addition to the puma, the *pudú* inhabits the sopping rainforests, while foxes prowl along the shoreline and other open areas. Southern sea lions inhabit headlands and rookeries, stealing salmon from the fish farms that float offshore beyond the park boundaries—and placing themselves at risk from the powerful companies that bring in much of the region's income.

Hikers here and in other parts of the southern Chilean rainforests should watch for miniature *sanguijuelas* (leeches), which can work their way into boots and trousers (some leeches are used for medical purposes in Chile).

Sights and Activities

From a trailhead near the café at Caleta Gonzalo, the **Sendero Cascadas** climbs and winds through thick rainforest to a high falls; figure about 1.5 hours each way. At the Centro de Información, it's possible to arrange a tour of the apiaries at **Fundo Pillán,** across the Fiordo de Reñihué, and to obtain fishing licenses (hunting is strictly prohibited).

From a trailhead about 12 kilometers south of Caleta Gonzalo, west of the highway, the **Sendero Laguna Tronador** crosses a *pasarela* (hanging bridge) before ascending a string of slippery stepladders up nearly vertical slopes to the **Mirador Michinmahuida,** a platform where, on clear days, there are astounding views of the volcano's icy summit. The trail continues through nearly pristine forest, dropping gradually to the shores of an amphitheater lake where Tompkins's employees have built a stylish two-site campground with picnic tables, a deck, and an outhouse. It's about 1.5 hours to or from the trailhead.

Only a short distance farther south, on the east side of the highway, **Sendero los Alerces** crosses the Río Blanco to a large *alerce* grove. Just a little farther south on the west side, the **Sendero Cascadas Escondidas** is one of those rare trails that is longer and more strenuous than the signposted three hours would suggest. It is mostly boardwalk—through the swampy, soggy forest—and catwalk along precipitous rock walls, with some steep stepladders as well. The hardest part, though, is boulder-hopping the river on slippery granite or, better and perhaps safer, wading across. On the other side, the trail climbs steeply for another 15–20 minutes, then drops into a narrow canyon and a dangerous-looking stepladder anchored by a rope (the bravest hikers can continue around the rock on the rope to get the best view of the "hidden" falls).

Accommodations and Food

At Caleta Gonzalo, the walk-in **Camping Río Gonzalo** (US$2.50 pp) has forested sites with fire pits (firewood is for sale), clean toilets, and cold showers. There is a separate large shelter for cooking. Those without tents can rent one of the roofed *fogones* normally reserved for picnickers during the daytime.

Fourteen kilometers south of Caleta Gonzalo, **Auto-Camping Cascadas Escondidas** has four drive-in sites (US$10) with clean toilets, cold showers, and roofed decks for pitching tents and eating without having to sit on the soggy ground.

Seventeen kilometers south of Caleta Gonzalo, **Camping Lago Negro** (US$3 pp, US$9 per roofed site) resembles Cascadas Escondidas, with four roofed sites and an open tent-camping area. Accessible by an 800-meter footpath, **Camping Punta del Lago** has two lakeside sites. Three kilometers farther south, **Camping Lago Blanco** (US$10) resembles Camping Lago Negro, with half a dozen roofed sites.

Tompkins's stylish **Cabañas Caleta Gonzalo** (tel. 065/250079, fax 065/255145 in Puerto Montt, pumalinreservas@telsur.cl; tel. 1712/1964150 locally, US$80) can accommodate up to six people. All nine have private bath and hot water, but lack kitchen facilities.

Dignified by a stone fireplace with a copper vent, the airy **Café Caleta Gonzalo,** open 7:30 A.M.–11:30 P.M. daily, maintains high standards for local cuisine with organic fruit, vegetables, dairy products and meat, and seafood. Four-course lunches or dinners, with fresh bread, fall in the US$10 range. The breakfast really shines with fresh homemade bread, local honey, butter, and cheese; there's also a sandwich menu and juices. Unusually for Chile, it's a totally nonsmoking environment, and the only place in Chile with a culinary exhortation from celebrity foodie Alice Waters.

Information

At Caleta Gonzalo, Pumalín's **Centro de Visitantes** (tel. 1712/1964151) distributes brochures, provides information, and displays informational panels with large-scale black-and-white photographs of the park; it also sells books, maps, film, park products like organic honey and jam, and local crafts items. If it's not open, café personnel can unlock it for you.

Pumalín maintains additional information offices in Chaitén (O'Higgins 62, tel./fax 065/731341); in Puerto Montt (Buin 356, tel. 065/250079, fax 065/255145, pumalin@telsur.cl); and in the United States (The Conservation Land Trust, Building 1062, Fort Cronkhite, Sausalito, CA 94965, tel. 415/229-9339, fax 415/229-9340, www.theconservationlandtrust.org).

Pumalín also has a detailed website (www.parquepumalin.cl) in Spanish and English. In addition, the park publishes a monthly magazine, *Puma Verde.*

Getting There

In January and February only, **Transmarchilay**'s ferry *Mailén* sails daily to Hornopirén (six hours) at 4 A.M.; reservations are advisable for vehicles. Passengers pay US$14 per person, while cyclists pay an extra US$9 and motorcyclists US$17. Automobiles and light trucks pay US$88, while larger vehicles pay US$24 per lineal meter.

For land transportation, see the separate entry for Chaitén, above.

Organized Tours

Because most of Pumalín is inaccessible by public transportation, it's worth considering organized tours by a variety of operators. **Alsur** (Del Salvador 100, Puerto Varas, tel./fax 065/232300, www.alsurexpeditions.com) arranges activity-oriented excursions—hiking, sea kayaking, and sailing—throughout the park.

Puerto Montt's **Marina del Sur** (Camino a Chinquehue Km 4.5, tel. 065/251958, www.marinadelsur.cl) organizes luxury yacht tours in the vicinity. Chiloé-based **Austral Adventures** (Cochrane 432, Ancud, tel./fax 065/625977, www.austral-adventures.com) offers customized cruises on the 15-meter motor vessel *Cahuella*.

The Southern Carretera Austral

Even more thinly settled than the area north of Coyhaique, southern Aisén is wild country, with few and scattered services; barely 10,000 people live in nearly 46,000 square kilometers. The only towns with more than a thousand inhabitants are Chile Chico, near the Argentine border on the south shore of Lago General Carrera, and Cochrane, directly on the Carretera Austral.

The highway is now paved all the way to Villa Cerro Castillo, 98 kilometers south of Coyhaique, as is the lateral to Puerto Ibáñez. In late 1999, it finally reached its terminus at Villa O'Higgins, though the last 100 kilometers still requires a ferry shuttle from Puerto Yungay to Río Bravo.

RESERVA NACIONAL CERRO CASTILLO

Straddling the Carretera Austral beyond the airport turnoff to Balmaceda, marking the divide between the drainages of the Río Simpson to the north and he Río Ibáñez to the south, Cerro Castillo is a 179,550-hectare unit whose map boundaries look like pieces of a jigsaw puzzle. Its signature landmark is Cerro Castillo itself, whose soaring basaltic battlements, above the tree line, truly resemble a medieval castle.

Elevations range from about 500 meters to the 2,320-meter summit of Cerro Castillo, embellished by three south-facing glaciers. Like most of the rest of the region, it gets substantial rainfall and snow at higher altitudes, but some east-facing areas enjoy a rain-shadow effect.

Nearly pure stands of *lenga (Nothofagus pumilio)* dominate the forest landscape up to about 1,200 meters, but there are also *coigue (Nothofagus betuloides), ñirre (Nothofagus antartica),* and many shrubs. Steppe-like grasslands typify the rain-shadow areas.

Among the mammals are puma, *huemul (Hippocamelus bisulcus),* two fox species, and skunks. Birds are common, including the soaring Andean condor, various owl species, the austral blackbird or *tordo (Curaeus curaeus),* and the austral parakeet or *cachaña (Enicognathus ferrugineus).*

Sights and Activities

About eight kilometers south of Laguna Chiguay, a faint westbound road from a nearly abandoned highway construction camp is the starting point for **Sendero Las Horquetas,** a four-day backpack that climbs the valley of Estero la Lima to pass beneath the spires of Cerro Castillo before descending to Villa Cerro Castillo, a small village on the Carretera Austral. This is much easier from the north than from the south, where the approach is far more rugged. For hiking details, see the third edition of Clem Lindenmayer's *Trekking in the Patagonian Andes* (Lonely Planet, 2003) or the fifth

© WAYNE BERNHARDSON

Oxcarts still ply parts of the Carretera Austral in Aisén.

edition of Tim Burford's *Chile and Argentina: The Bradt Trekking Guide* (2001).

Practicalities

At the reserve's northeastern edge, Conaf's woodsy **Camping Laguna Chiguay** (Km 67, US$4 per site) is just west of the highway. At the southern approach, there are simple accommodations at Villa Cerro Castillo, just outside the reserve boundary.

Conaf maintains a ranger station on the highway opposite the Laguna Chiguay campground.

All public transportation between Coyhaique, on the one hand, and Puerto Ibáñez and Villa Cerro Castillo on the other, pass through the reserve's northern sector.

PUERTO INGENIERO IBÁÑEZ

Prior to completion of the Carretera Austral, Puerto Ingeniero Ibáñez was a major lacustrine port on Lago General Carrera's north shore, connecting Coyhaique with Chile Chico, on the south shore, and other lake ports. Its current livelihood derives from agriculture, both livestock and tree fruit like apples and pears.

Since completion of the highway bypass, it's lost some of its economic clout, but the ferry from here to Chile Chico, for an easy border crossing to Argentina, is still quicker than the roundabout road system. It's about 110 kilometers south of Coyhaique via the Carretera Austral and a paved lateral that bears south about 10 kilometers east of Villa Cerro Castillo. There's also a rugged road but scenic crossing to Argentina along the lake's north shore (across the line, it is called Lago Buenos Aires).

Lodging can be found at simple **Residencial Ibáñez** (Dickson 31, tel. 067/423227, US$6 pp), which also serves meals. Two blocks north, **Residencial Vientos del Sur** (Dickson 282, tel. 067/423208, US$5.50 pp) is similar. The top choice, though, is the Swiss-Chilean **Shehen Aike** (Risopatrón 055, tel. 067/423284, tel. 02/3567064 in Santiago, www.shehenaike.cl, US$39 s or d). In addition to comfortable *cabañas,* it organizes local activities and may soon add a restaurant.

Several companies operate minibuses to Coyhaique (US$6, two hours)—**Transportes Yamil Alí** (tel. 067/250346), **Darío Figueroa Castro** (tel. 067/233286), and **Minibus Don Tito** (tel. 067/250280).

Mar del Sur (Baquedano 146, Coyhaique,

tel. 067/231255) sails the ferry *Pilchero* to Chile Chico (two hours) at 6 P.M. Monday, 10 A.M. Wednesday, 4:30 P.M. Thursday, 11 A.M. Saturday, and 5 P.M. Sunday, but schedules are subject to change. Fares are US$3.50 peradult passenger, half that for children. Bicycles pay an additional US$6.50, motorcycles US$12. Passenger vehicles and light trucks pay US$32, while large vehicles pay US$12 per linear meter.

VILLA CERRO CASTILLO

Founded in 1966, under the Frei Montalva administration, the former frontier outpost of Villa Cerro Castillo is finally acquiring an air of permanency, though its exposed site makes it one of the Carretera Austral's bleaker settlements. Just south of here, 89 kilometers from Coyhaique, the paved section of the highway ends and the gravel begins. Hikers who begin the trek through Reserva Nacional Cerro Castillo at Las Horquetas will exit the reserve here.

Alero de las Manos

Only five kilometers south of town, via a lateral off the highway, the positive and negative hands of the pre-Columbian rock art at Alero de las Manos resembles that of the landmark Argentine site at Cueva de las Manos. Beneath a volcanic overhang, the paintings differ in that they are many fewer, much younger (only about 3,000 years old), and do not include representations of animals. In some cases, rocks have split from the overhang and fallen to the ground, probably concealing even more images.

Alero de las Manos (admission US$1 pp including a guided tour) is open 10 A.M.–6 P.M. daily. There's a small visitors center with clean toilets.

Practicalities

Though improving, accommodations are limited here and can fill up fast. All of them use the same community telephone (tel. 067/419200) for messages.

Hospedaje El Castillo (O'Higgins 522, US$4 pp) is only adequate, while **Pensión Andreita** (Carlos Ibáñez del Campo 297, US$6 pp) is cheap enough and has lots of blankets but also lumpy beds and pretty awful food. Other choices include **Hospedaje El Rodeo** (Pedro Aguirre Cerda 281, US$5.50 pp) and **Hospedaje Villarrica** (US$7 pp).

Improved and slightly more expensive, **Hospedaje La Querencia** (O'Higgins 522, US$8 pp) has firm beds and better food, but only one full bathroom for a maximum 15 guests (there are additional toilets). Its restaurant unavoidably gets lots of single men quaffing beers until closing.

Open long hours in summer only, the helpful **Oficina de Información Turística** (O'Higgins s/n) provides a good town map and list of services.

Several **minibus** services connect Cerro Castillo with Coyhaique; all regularly scheduled services between Coyhaique, to the north, and Puerto Río Tranquilo and Cochrane, to the south, pass by the entrance to town.

BAHÍA MURTA

West of Villa Cerro Castillo, the Carretera Austral climbs above the valley of the Río Ibáñez before veering south to Lago General Carrera and the tiny lakeside town of Bahía Murta, one of the best areas to see fall colors. There are a couple simple accommodations: **Hostería Lago General Carrera** (Avenida 5 de Abril 647, US$5.50 pp) and **Residencial Patagonia** (Pasaje España 64, US$6.50 pp). Both use the same community telephone (tel. 067/419600), and both have food.

PUERTO RÍO TRANQUILO

Until completion of the Carretera Austral, Puerto Río Tranquilo was a lake port with a weekly supply boat from Puerto Ibáñez; today it's a slowly but steadily growing settlement at Lago General Carrera's west end, 25 kilometers south of Puerto Murta. At the north end of town, a new road toward Bahía Exploradores, an inlet of the larger Estero Capquelán, has reached the midway point at Lago Bayo; with a boat connection and an hour's hike, you get to Laguna San Rafael.

Capilla de Mármol

The area's best excursion goes to Capilla de Mármol, a string of swirling marble grottos on the shoreline, reached by launch from town. The 1.5-hour trip costs around US$25–30 for up to five persons, but may not be possible if winds are high. Ask at Residencial Los Pinos (see Practicalities, below) or elsewhere to hire a launch. It's best late in the season, when water levels permit launches to approach more closely and explore the grottos more thoroughly.

Practicalities

Río Tranquilo has better than average accommodations for a town its size; unless otherwise indicated, all of them use the same community telephone (tel. 067/419500) for messages.

Two blocks west of the highway, local favorite **Residencial Darka** (Los Arrayanes 330, US$8 pp) has smallish rooms with twin beds and shared bath.

Right on the highway, **Hostería Costanera** (Carretera Austral s/n, tel. 067/411121, US$10 pp) is friendly enough but suffers the shortcomings of many cheap Chilean hotels—too many beds in too many rooms. Some rooms are claustrophobically tiny, others spacious; some beds are firm, others sag like hammocks.

Also on the highway, **Residencial Carretera Austral** (1 Sur 223, US$11 pp) also has *cabaña* accommodations that can work out cheaper for a group. In addition, it has a modest restaurant.

With 10 rooms arranged along each side of a corridor, friendly, family-run **Hostal Los Pinos** (Godoy 51, tel. 067/411576, US$11 pp, US$31 d) has spotless accommodations with breakfast and either shared or private bath. Low-season prices are about 10–15 percent cheaper. Its restaurant is also above average for a town its size, serving fixed-price lunches or dinners for about US$5–6 in a tobacco-free dining room.

Scheduled buses on the Carretera Austral between Coyhaique and Cochrane drop and pick up passengers here. **Transporte El Cóndor** (Los Arrayanes 380, tel. 067/411904) goes to Puerto Guadal and Chile Chico (US$11) Tuesday and Friday at 6:30 A.M.

CRUCE EL MAITÉN AND VICINITY

Cruce El Maitén, about 50 kilometers south of Puerto Río Tranquilo at the westward outlet of Lago General Carrera, is not a settlement but rather a crossroads with the eastbound highway to

Capilla de Mármol, Lago General Carrera

Puerto Guadal and Chile Chico. Nevertheless, there are several important services in the vicinity.

Almost right at the junction, **Hacienda Tres Lagos** (Km 274, tel./fax 067/411323, US$116/129 s/d and up) is one of the highway's best accommodations options. Oriented toward packages of three days or more, its spacious, well-lighted *cabañas* are appealing enough, but it also provides a sauna, horseback riding, fishing, and excursions to sights on and off the highway. Its restaurant **El Parador Austral,** open to the public, has a superb kitchen. In Santiago, contact Hacienda Tres Lagos (Roberto del Río 1111, Providencia, tel. 02/2322680, fax 02/2320869, www.patagoniadreamhotel.com).

One kilometer north of Hacienda Tres Lagos, **Mallín Colorado** (Km 273, US$114 s or d) has several log-style *cabañas* with similar amenities. For more information, in Santiago, contact Patagonia Pacífica (Marcel Duhaut 2979, Providencia, tel. 02/2741807, fax 2042785, www.patagonia-pacific.cl).

About 14 kilometers north of the junction, near the handsome suspension bridge at the outlet of Lago General Carrera, the **Pasarela Sur Lodge** (Km 260, tel. 067/411425, www.pasarelasurlodge.cl, US$70 s or d) primarily attracts fishing-oriented visitors, but can also arrange other activities like rafting, hiking, and horseback riding. It also has a decent restaurant.

© WAYNE BERNHARDSON

bridge over the outlet of Lago General Carrera, near Cruce El Maitén

PUERTO GUADAL

Another of the former lake ports now linked by highway, at the west end of Lago General Carrera, Puerto Guadal is more picturesque than most towns in the area. It lies 13 kilometers east of the El Maitén junction; from here, a rugged and narrow road leads northeast to Chile Chico and the Argentine border at Los Antiguos.

Puerto Guadal has upgraded its free campground along the lakeshore. Otherwise, the cheapest accommodations are **Hostería Huemules** (Las Magnolias 382, tel. 067/411202, US$9 pp), which also has a restaurant.

Cabañas Antué (Los Pinos 456, tel. 067/431215, US$40 for up to five persons) has hot showers, full kitchens, and wood stoves; check in at Supermercado Plaza, Las Camelias 147.

On the eastern outskirts of town, the elegantly simple **Terra Luna** (tel. 067/431263, fax 067/431264, www.terra-luna.cl) enjoys an exceptional woodsy setting overlooking the lakeshore. While the French-run resort specializes in weeklong activities-oriented packages, they also rent "ministudio" accommodations for US$25 s or d in the off-season, US$35 s or d in summer; rooms in the main lodge go for US$70 s or d off season, US$120 s or d in summer. Breakfast is included, other meals are extra; the kitchen can do a lot with a little, even on short notice. English and French are spoken; their Santiago contact is Azimut 360 (General Salvo 159, Providencia, tel. 02/2363880, fax 2/2353085, www.azimut360.com).

Other than the Terra Luna, **Café de la Frontera** (Los Lirios 399) is the best place to eat.

Transportes Austral (Los Notros 430, tel. 067/431275) goes to Coyhaique (US$12) Monday and Thursday, while **Transporte El Cón-**

dor goes Wednesday and Sunday. To Chile Chico (US$8), try **Turismo Seguel** (Los Notros 560, tel. 067/431214) Monday and Thursday.

CHILE CHICO AND VICINITY

Settled from Argentina in the early 20th century, on the southern shore of Lago General Carrera, Chile Chico developed in virtually autonomous isolation from the rest of Chile, and connections are still better with Argentina than with most of mainland Chile. One of the region's easiest border crossings, it also enjoys access to remote protected areas like Reserva Nacional Jeinimeni, and is the starting (or finishing) point for the wild rugged highway to or from Puerto Guadal and the Carretera Austral. From Los Antiguos, just across the border, travelers can make connections to the Atlantic-coast city of Caleta Olivia, nearby Perito Moreno, and southern Argentine Patagonian destinations like El Chaltén and El Calafate, which now have reliable bus transportation.

Despite brief mining booms, most recently with the Fachinal gold and silver mine to the west, Chile Chico's enduring economic base has been the production of temperate fruits, thanks to its mild lakeshore microclimate. This has not exactly brought prosperity, though, as even after the completion of the first motor road from Coyhaique to Puerto Ibáñez, in 1952, the town remained remote from any sizable market. Ash deposits from the 1991 eruption of Volcán Hudson depressed agricultural production, which has only recovered in the past few years.

Motorists crossing from Argentina should fill the tank in Los Antiguos, where gasoline costs about half what it does in Chile Chico.

THE ASHES OF VOLCÁN HUDSON

In the vicinity of Lago General Carrera, which continues east across the Argentine border as Lago Buenos Aires, travelers will see the lingering effects of the August 1991 eruption of 1,935-meter Volcán Hudson, northwest of Villa Cerro Castillo. Chile's second largest 20th-century eruption deposited more than a cubic kilometer of ash in Chile, about two cubic kilometers in Argentine Patagonia, and another two cubic kilometers over the South Atlantic Ocean; in some areas, the ash fall reached a depth of more than 1.5 meters. Northwesterly winds carried the plume southeast to the Falkland Islands and South Georgia, in the South Atlantic, and eventually as far as Australia. Heavy winds, in excess of 100 kilometers per hour, also remobilized already fallen ash to cover pasture and watercourses, killing tens of thousands of cattle and sheep. The region's agriculture has gradually recovered, but the possibility of another eruption always exists.

Orientation

Only five kilometers west of the Argentine border, Chile Chico (population 3,042) is 122 kilometers northeast of Cruce El Maitén via the narrow, precipitous road along the south shore of Lago General Carrera. Avenida O'Higgins, one block south of the lakeshore, is the main thoroughfare in both directions; the central grid extends about 10 blocks from east to west, and four blocks from north to south. The Plaza de Armas is in the northwest corner of town.

Museo de la Casa de la Cultura

Much improved in recent years, but still lacking interpretive panels, Chile Chico's museum displays regional painting and sculpture along with paleontological materials, historical artifacts from early colonists, and, connected by the second story by a walkway leading straight to its deck, the restored *Los Andes,* which once ferried passengers and cargo around the lake. The Museo (O'Higgins and Lautaro, tel. 067/411268, fax 067/411355) is open 10 A.M.–7 P.M. daily except Sunday, December–March only. Admission is free.

Reserva Nacional Lago Jeinemeni

From Chile Chico, a four-wheel-drive-only road parallels the border (not to mention another similar road on the Argentine side) to Reserva Nacional Lago Jeinemeni, a rarely visited protected area of 161,000 hectares. There is little infrastructure except for a campground (US$4.50); Conaf rangers collect US$1 admission.

Accommodations

On quiet grounds about one kilometer east of town, **Hospedaje No Me Olvides** (Camino Internacional s/n, US$7 pp) is rustic but friendly. The more central **Hospedaje Eben Ezer** (Manuel Rodríguez 302, tel. 067/411535, US$8 pp) is unexceptional but acceptable. **Hospedaje Brisas del Lago** (Manuel Rodríguez 443, tel. 067/411204, US$8 pp) is a decent alternative.

Other central options include **Hotel Plaza** (Balmaceda and O'Higgins, tel. 067/411215, US$10 pp); **Hostal Turismo** (Avenida O'Higgins 750, tel. 067/411030, US$10 pp); and **Hotel Ventura** (Carrera 290, tel. 067/411311, US$13 pp). **Hospedaje Don Luis** (Balmaceda 175, tel. 067/411384, US$15 pp with breakfast) is the best of the central places.

On the eastern outskirts of town, the Belgian-Chilean **Hostal de la Patagonia** (Camino Internacional s/n, tel./fax 067/411337, US$15 pp) is an ivy-covered country-inn with large, rustically decorated but cozy rooms with private bath and breakfast (excellent homemade bread); there's also one tiny single with shared bath for US$12. Camping and additional meals are also available.

Food

There's nothing really outstanding, though the dining room at **Hostal de la Patagonia** (see above) is pretty good. On the east side of the plaza, **Café Elizabeth y Loly** (González 25, tel. 067/411288) serves reliable breakfasts, sandwiches, and *onces.*

Café Wild West (González 115, tel. 067/411382) serves standard Chilean meals of decent quality. **Pub El Minero** (Carrera 205, tel. 067/411521) serves moderately priced lunches and drinks.

Information and Services

Chile Chico's **Oficina de Información Turística** is within the Casa de la Cultura (O'Higgins 333, tel. 067/411359, www.chilechico.cl) occupies an office alongside the Municipalidad. In summer only, it's open Tuesday–Saturday 10 A.M.–1:30 P.M. and 2:30–7:30 P.M., Sunday 10 A.M.–1 P.M. only.

For national-parks information, contact **Conaf** (Blest Gana 121, tel. 067/411325). Open 10 A.M.–1 P.M. weekdays only, **Banco del Estado** (González 112) is slow to change both U.S. cash and traveler's checks (the latter only with high commissions and even worse bureaucracy). Unfortunately, it's the only option.

For postal services, **Correos de Chile** (Manuel Rodríguez 121) is on the north side of the Plaza de Armas.

There are several long-distance telephone offices: **Entel** (O'Higgins between Pedro Montt and Lautaro), **Fonosol** (O'Higgins at Marchant Pereira), and at **Café Elizabeth y Loly** (González 25).

Hospital Chile Chico (Lautaro 275, tel. 067/411334) provides medical services.

Getting There

Transporte Aéreo Don Carlos (González just south of Avenida O'Higgins, tel. 067/411490) flies daily except Sunday to Coyhaique (US$40) from **Aeródromo Chile Chico** (Camino Internacional s/n, tel. 067/411284), just east of town on the road to the Argentine border.

Transporte Jaime Acuña (Augusto Grosse 150, tel. 067/411590) shuttles passengers to the Argentine border at Los Antiguos (US$3, 30 minutes) four times daily except Sunday, when there is no service. **Transportes La Unión** (O'Higgins s/n, tel. 067/411904) goes to Comodoro Rivadavia (Argentina, US$13) daily except Sunday at 1 P.M.

Transportes Seguel (O'Higgins 394, tel. 067/411443) goes to Puerto Guadal (US$7, three hours) Monday and Friday at 2 P.M. **Transportes Ale** (Rosa Amelia 880, tel. 067/411739) goes Wednesday and Saturday to Puerto Guadal and Cochrane (US$16, six hours). **Transportes El Cóndor** (tel. 067/411904) goes to Puerto Río Tranquilo (US$11) Tuesday and Friday at 4 P.M., with connections to Coyhaique.

In a kiosk on the jetty, **Mar del Sur** (Manuel Rodríguez s/n, tel. 067/411864) sells tickets for the vehicle-passenger ferry *El Pilchero,* which sails to Puerto Ingeniero Ibáñez, on the lake's north shore, at 8 A.M. Tuesday, 4 P.M. Wednesday, 4:30 P.M. Friday, and 1:30 P.M. Sunday. Schedules are subject to change; for fares, see the entry for Puerto Ingeniero Ibáñez, above.

December–March, the Mar del Sur kiosk also sells tickets for the bus from Los Antiguos (Argentina) to El Chaltén, Argentina's trekking mecca.

PUERTO BERTRAND AND VICINITY

Separated from Lago General Carrera by a short and narrow channel, Lago Bertrand, is the source of the Río Baker, Chile's largest river in terms of its flow. Beautifully sited on the lake's southeastern shore, the village of Puerto Bertrand is a convenient base for exploring the area, though there are also several handsome lodges in the immediate vicinity. It is 11 kilometers south of Cruce El Maitén.

Sights and Activities

For water sports—rafting, kayaking, and fly-fishing—the **Río Baker** itself is the big draw. Because it has relatively few rocks and play spots, the Baker's Class II and III rapids draw fewer rafters and kayakers than the rugged Futaleufú, but its fast current, huge flow, large waves and occasional deep holes make it exciting enough for beginners (a bit farther south of Puerto Bertrand, only a handful of world-class kayakers could survive the **Cascada Nef Baker,** a thunderous eight-meter waterfall at the Baker's confluence with the Río Nef). A string of fly-fishing lodges line the highway south of Puerto Bertrand, beneath the glistening backdrop of the northern Patagonian ice field.

October–April, Bertrand-based, U.S.-run **Patagonia Adventure Expeditions** (tel./fax 067/219894, contact@adventurepatagonia.com) arranges rafting, kayaking, hiking, climbing, and horseback riding in the vicinity; there is also a specialist fly-fishing guide. Half-day trips down the Baker cost US$25 per person; a more ambitious 212-kilometer, eight- to 12-day descent to the ocean costs US$1,800–2,400 per person. Kayak instruction costs US$100 per day, while fly-fishing on the Baker costs US$130 for half a day, US$210 for a full day (alternatively, US$180 ppfor two people). Their Chilean postal address is Casilla 519, Coyhaique, where they also have a permanent office.

Practicalities

There are primarily budget accommodations in Puerto Bertrand itself and fishing lodges that cater mostly to week-long holidays in the vicinity, but if space is available the lodges will take drop-in guests.

Easily the cheapest option, in town, is the riverside **Camping Municipal** (US$3 pp). **Hospedaje Vargas** (US$10) and **Hospedaje Casa Ester** (US$10) are both rustic options.

The upstairs front room at **Hostería Bertrand** (tel./fax 067/419900, US$13 pp) has central heating of a sort—the chimney pipe from the 1st-floor woodstove passes directly through the middle of the room. Its restaurant is also a good place to eat.

Also in town, Argentine-run **Hostería Río Baker** (tel./fax 067/411447, US$67/117 s/d) enjoys a stunning riverside location with great fly-fishing possibilities. It has contact numbers in Buenos Aires (tel. 54/11/4863-9373) and Mendoza (tel. 54/261/420-2196).

Along the highway three kilometers south of town, the **Cabañas Rápidos Río Baker** (tel. 067/411199, tel. 067/236867 in Coyhaique, tel. 09/8215900, aligduran@hotmail.com, US$120 for up to six persons) is one of several places of its type.

Also south of town, on the west side of the highway, the six-room **Patagonia Baker Lodge** (tel. 067/411903, www.pbl.cl, US$90/110 s/d with breakfast) is a new riverside facility that stresses fly-fishing. One larger suite goes for US$120/150 s/d.

Four kilometers south of town, **Lodge Patagonia Australis** (tel. 067/239696 in Coyhaique, US$39/70 s/d with breakfast) needs to pay attention to details—after more than three years in operation, parts of it still seem unfinished.

Buses between Coyhaique and Cochrane, and between Chile Chico and Cochrane, pass near the entrance to town.

CRUCE PASO ROBALLOS AND VICINITY

At the confluence of the Río Baker and Río Nef, roughly 15 kilometers south of Puerto Bertrand,

© WAYNE BERNHARDSON

highway sign on the Carretera Austral

the **Cascada Nef Baker** is a thunderous waterfall on the property of Dimanc Cárcamo, who charges US$2.50 for cars to enter. The Carretera Austral continues south to Cochrane and Villa O'Higgins, while an eastbound lateral ascends the Río Chacabuco valley to 647-meter Paso Roballos, the region's most southerly border crossing passable to motor vehicles (others farther south are for nonmotorized transport only). Across the border, at the bleak crossroads of Bajo Caracoles (gasoline available), Argentina's dusty RN 40 leads south to El Calafate, an alternative approach to Chile's Parque Nacional Torres del Paine.

Between the highway junction and the border, **Estancia Chacabuco** is a large sheep farm recently sold by its Belgian owners to conservationist Doug Tompkins, who outbid Chilean interests concerned—or obsessed—with his property acquisitions in Patagonia. Tompkins, however, has vowed to donate the land to Conaf, the state conservation agency, for a national park.

COCHRANE

Once literally the end of the road, the tidy town of Cochrane may still have more horses than automobiles but, says one immigrant, "If you park your horse in front of the bar now, you'll get a ticket for shitting on the sidewalk." While attractive enough for a frontier settlement, thanks to its neatly landscaped Plaza de Armas and broad paved streets, its main appeal lies in the surrounding countryside of **Reserva Nacional Lago Cochrane,** sometimes known as **Reserva Nacional Tamango,** north and northeast of town.

Cochrane is still an obligatory stop for southbound wanderers, partly because it's the last accommodations and food for nearly 300 kilometers and partly because it's home to **Casa Melero,** Patagonia's greatest general store. It's *the* place to buy camping gear, canoes, chainsaws, chocolate, fine wines, fishing gear, and almost anything else you can't find between here and Antarctica. Cochrane is also, apparently, the end of the line for the traveling salesman responsible for the lurid red bedspreads seen in many cheap hotels along the Carretera Austral.

Orientation

Cochrane (population 2,217) is 345 kilometers south of Coyhaique and 225 kilometers north of Villa O'Higgins via the Carretera Austral. Its core is a rectangular grid that's only about three blocks from north to south, but about nine blocks from west to east, where the Río Cochrane marks its limit.

Note that recent changes have meant inconsistencies in street numbering, but the town is small enough that orientation remains fairly simple.

Accommodations

Even budget accommodations are a little more expensive in Cochrane, though the simple **Residencial Cochrane** (Dr. Steffens 451, tel. 067/522377, US$8 pp) is an exception. **Residencial El Fogón** (San Valentín 651, tel. 067/522240, US$8 pp) also has one of Cochrane's better restaurants.

Residencial Lago Esmeralda (San Valentín 141, tel. 067/522621, US$9) has some legitimate, comfortable singles, rather than the closet-sized partitions that often pass for singles in this part of the country. It also has a passable restaurant, but the shower fixtures in the shared baths can be awkward.

The other current budget favorite is family-run **Hostal Latitude 47° Sur** (Lago Brown 564, tel.

067/522280, turislat47sur@hotmail.com, US$11 pp), though remodeled **Residencial Paola** (Lago Brown 150, tel. 067/522215, US$13 pp) offers good value. **Residencial Cero a Cero** (Lago Brown 464, tel. 067/522158, US$14 pp with private bath) is similar. Rooms vary at **Residencial Sur Austral** (Arturo Prat 334, tel. 067/522150, US$14 pp), but the best of them are comfortable and spacious.

Popular with cycling groups, the comfortably furnished **Residencial Rubio** (Teniente Merino 871, tel. 067/522173, US$16 pp) has spacious, spotless rooms with twin beds, private bath, and breakfast (some cheaper rooms have shared bath).

On spacious, well-landscaped grounds, **Hotel Wellmann** (Las Golondrinas 36, tel. 067/522171, US$39 d with breakfast) is both central and comfortable.

Directly across the street from Cero a Cero, on barren grounds urgently needing landscaping, Spanish-run **Hotel Ultimo Paraíso** (Lago Brown 455, tel./fax 067/522361, US$47/58 s/d) is otherwise exceptional, with eight well-heated, spacious, and attractive rooms with private bath. The guests-only restaurant charges US$12 for lunch or dinner.

Food

Part of its namesake *hospedaje,* **El Fogón** (San Valentín 651) had long been probably Cochrane's best restaurant; today, while that's no longer true, it's still not bad. While the name implies a *parrilla,* the menu is more diverse than that, with fish, including conger eel, hake, and salmon, and fowl, in the US$7–10 range. Their specialty, though, is the *doble infarto* ("double heart attack") of steak, eggs, onions, and French fries smothered in a pepper cream sauce.

The outstanding homemade meals at family-run **Ñirrantal** (O'Higgins 650-C, tel. 067/522604) has taken over the top spot among local restaurants, with diverse entrées ranging from pizza to beef and everything in between. While the service can be erratic, it's so well-intentioned and the food is so good that that's only a minor drawback.

If neither of those meets your needs, the dining rooms at **Residencial Sur Austral** (Prat 281) and **Residencial Lago Esmeralda** (San Valentín 141) also deserve consideration.

Information and Services

December–March only, the municipal **Oficina de Información Turística** operates from a kiosk at the southeast corner of the Plaza de Armas; it's open daily except Sunday 10 A.M.–8 P.M.

For specific information on nearby parks and reserves, visit Conaf (Río Nef 417, tel. 067/522164).

On the east side of the Plaza de Armas, **Banco del Estado** (Esmeralda 460) will change cash or travelers' checks, but change elsewhere if possible.

For postal needs, **Correos de Chile** is at Esmeralda 199. There are several long-distance phone offices, including the **Centro de Llamados Latitude 47° Sur** (Dr. Steffen 576), on the south side of the Plaza de Armas, which has erratic Internet access. There's free public Internet access (but high demand) at the public library in the **Centro Cultural** (San Valentín 555).

In addition to its phone and Internet service, **Latitude 47° Sur** (Dr. Steffen 576, tel. 067/522280) arranges fly-fishing and other excursions in the vicinity.

Hospital Cochrane (O'Higgins 755, tel. 067/522131) provides medical assistance.

Getting There

Alongside Residencial Sur Austral, **Transporte Aéreo Don Carlos** (Prat 281, tel. 067/522150) flies Monday and Thursday to Villa O'Higgins and back to Coyhaique.

Buses Don Carlos (Prat 281, tel. 067/522150) goes overland to Coyhaique (US$14, ten hours) Wednesday–Friday and Sunday at 8:30 A.M. **Interlagos** (San Valentín 466, tel. 067/522606) goes to Coyhaique daily at 9 A.M. (US$16, 10–11 hours).

Buses Los Ñadis (Los Helechos 420, tel. 067/522196) goes to Villa O'Higgins (US$10), a subsidized route on which local residents have priority, Monday at 8:30 A.M.

Transportes Ale (Las Golondrinas 399, tel. 067/522448) goes to Puerto Guadal and Chile Chico (US$16) Thursday and Sunday at 10 A.M.

Buses Acuario 13 (Río Baker 349, tel.

067/522143) goes to Caleta Tortel (US$8, three hours) at 8:15 A.M. Monday–Thursday and Sunday.

Transporte López (Dr. Steffens 147, tel. 067/522276) goes to San Lorenzo Monday and Thursday at 11 A.M.

RESERVA NACIONAL LAGO COCHRANE

Informally but inaccurately known as Reserva Nacional Tamango, Reserva Nacional Lago Cochrane is most notable as home to the endangered *huemul (Hippocamelus bisulcus),* which appears on Chile's coat of arms. On the north shore of its namesake lake, the 6,925-hectare reserve is only six kilometers northwest of the town of Cochrane. Admission at the Guardería Húngaro entrance to the reserve costs US$2.40 per person.

Launch excursions to see the *huemuls,* to the east end of the lake, cost US$47–62 for up to seven persons. While there is no regular public transportation to the reserve, it's close enough that hitching is possible and even hiring a taxi is not prohibitively expensive.

On the north bank of the Río Cochrane, Conaf's **Camping Las Correntadas** (US$10) has four sites with picnic tables, wash basins, and fire pits. There is also a four-person *cabaña* (US$33), which has a bathroom and hot shower.

Accessible only by a 45-minute boat ride or an eight-kilometer hike, Conaf's lakeside **Camping Playa Paleta** also has four campsites and three *cabañas* with bath but without shower. Prices are the same as at Las Correntadas.

CALETA TORTEL

Where the Río Baker meets the sea, Caleta Tortel is a distinctively picturesque fishing village that has no streets in the traditional sense—boardwalks and staircases link its houses and handful of businesses. For nearly half a century the only access to this isolated hamlet (founded in 1955) was either slow or expensive—or both—by air, river, or sea. Since completion of the road link from the Carretera Austral along the river's south bank, though, it's accessible overland, and the wait was worth it.

In addition to the town itself—a real charmer—there is hiking to destinations such as **Cerro La**

© WAYNE BERNHARDSON

Inhabitants of Caleta Tortel get around on boats and boardwalks.

Bandera or, more ambitiously, to **Cascada Pisagua,** which requires hiring a launch to reach the trailhead.

Caleta Tortel (population 507) is about 130 kilometers southeast of Cochrane via the Carretera Austral and a westbound lateral along the Río Baker's south bank. Motor vehicles arrive at a parking lot at the Rincón Alto sector, from which it's necessary to wheel or haul your luggage down Tortel's steep staircases (and back up when you leave).

For accommodations, try Sergio Barria's **Hostal Costanera** (Antonio Ronchi 141, tel. 067/234815, US$12.50 pp with shared bath); one exceptional room has high ceilings and exceptional sea views, but the others are also more than acceptable. There are several other *hospedajes* and simple but decent seafood restaurants along the waterfront.

At the parking lot, the Municipalidad maintains a small tourist office that has maps and suggestions for hikes and excursions.

Transporte Aéreo Don Carlos flies Wednesdays to Coyhaique (US$32) from the airstrip immediately east of town.

From the parking lot above the town, **Buses Acuario 13** links Tortel with Cochrane (US$8, three hours) at 2:30 P.M. Tuesday–Thursday and Sunday.

PUERTO YUNGAY

Until 1999 Puerto Yungay, on the north shore of the Fiordo Mitchell, was the end of the Carretera Austral, but now it's the port for a flat-bottomed, four-car ferry to a ramp at Río Bravo, the last link to Villa O'Higgins, the highway's most southerly outpost. When the road opened in December of that year, according to Sergeant Eduardo Martínez of the Cuerpo Militar de Trabajo (CMT, Chile's Army Corps of Engineers), it was the site of the highway's biggest traffic jam waiting for the ferry: "There were so many cars backed up that we were working from 7 A.M. until midnight. Some days we couldn't handle all of them, so they had to camp and wait until the next day."

The CMT may someday carve a road along the sheer rock wall of the north side of the fjord, but it won't be as fast as the ferry to Río Bravo, where the road to Villa O'Higgins resumes. There, some visionary (or hallucinatory) politicians envision a further southern link to the famous Parque Nacional Torres del Paine, a project that could take 20–25 years and still require eight or nine ferry crossings (already, though, a segment of this road is under construction).

Four *cabañas* formerly belonging to the CMT were to be donated to the communities of Tortel and Villa O'Higgins, for use as information centers, accommodations, and cafes, but nothing has happened yet. The ferry from Puerto Yungay now runs on demand during daylight hours; for more information or reservations, try contacting the Departamento de Vialidad in Cochrane, at the corner of Avenida O'Higgins and Esmeralda (tel. 067/521242).

VILLA O'HIGGINS

For decades, the frontier outpost of Villa O'Higgins was accessible only by air taxi from Coyhaique, or by water from Argentina. It depended on Argentine supplies, and highway construction materials entered via Argentine roads and ferries on Lago O'Higgins (Lago San Martín to Argentines). Now, though, the ferry from Puerto Yungay drops passengers and vehicles at Río Bravo, a boat ramp 100 kilometers northwest of Villa O'Higgins, for the last leg of the trip down the Carretera Austral.

When the new road finally opened, said ex-policeman Arturo Gómez, curious tourists overran the town's 12 square blocks. "We were at full capacity, and most of the people here have scarce resources and couldn't arrange things so soon." People camped, slept in spare rooms, and rented a handful of *cabañas.* "We didn't evolve step-by-step," said then-Mayor Alfredo Ronín. "We went from horseback to jet."

Villa O'Higgins (population 463) is now booming with new construction, and the town has big plans. The idea, added Ronín, "is to promote the ice, because that's what we've got the most of." Thanks to work on the new Sendero de Chile, and the motor launch that helps link the town with remote parts of the

THE NEW CRUCE DE LAGOS

The traditional lake-land-lake crossing from Chile to Argentina goes from Puerto Montt to Bariloche, but if Aisén and Santa Cruz authorities have their druthers, the next big thing will be the route from Villa O'Higgins to El Chaltén.

Increasing numbers of hardy travelers are making the journey from Villa O'Higgins to the Lago O'Higgins port of Bahía Bahamóndez for the twice-weekly, 50-kilometer, 3.5-hour journey (US$20) by the 62-passenger motor launch *Quetru* to the Chilean border post of Candelario Mansilla. From Candelario Mansilla, the *Quetru* makes an optional excursion to **Glaciar O'Higgins** and **Glaciar Chico** before returning to Mansilla (to pick up arrivals from Argentina) and return to Bahamóndez.

From Candelario Mansilla, where there are simple accommodations (US$11 pp), camping (US$2 per tent), and meals, the Chilean Carabineros handle immigration and customs procedures. By foot, bicycle, horseback, or vehicle, it's another 15 kilometers to the international border and 7.5 kilometers more to the Argentine Gendarmería, who handle customs and immigration here. In some cases, hikers may need to ford the Río Obstáculo; beyond the borderline, the existing road becomes a footpath unsuitable for cyclists, who will have to push. At Candelario Mansilla, it's possible to hire a guide (US$17) and horses (US$17 pp plus US$17 for each pack animal).

From the Gendarmería post, at the north end of Laguna del Desierto, there are 20-passenger launches (US$15, 30–45 minutes) to the south end of the lake at 1:30 and 4:45 P.M. Alternatively, hikers can walk the 15 kilometers in about five hours. At the south end, where the launches leave for the border at 10:45 A.M. and 2 P.M., there is also **Camping Laguna del Desierto** (US$2 pp).

From Laguna del Desierto, there are buses to El Chaltén (US$9, one hour) at 1:30 and 4:45 P.M. Buses from El Chaltén to Laguna del Desierto leave at 9:30 A.M. and 12:45 P.M.; schedules are subject to change.

There are environmental issues here—deforestation, erosion, etc.—and some romantics will deplore the loss of frontier feeling as buses replace bicycles. Whatever the ultimate result, though, crossing the borders here is a huge improvement over the days when Chilean and Argentine forces exchanged gunfire over what was one of the last outstanding border disputes between the two countries.

lake and with Argentina, the backcountry is increasingly accessible to hikers.

Sights and Activities

Directly east of town, a footpath leads to a scenic overlook that's part of the **Parque Cerro Santiago,** Chile's first municipal nature reserve. Hoping to attract adventurous hikers and climbers, local authorities have forged a trail from patching together and signing existing forest paths to a backwoods shelter near the **Ventisquero Mosco** (Mosco glacier).

Villa O'Higgins lies in the broad valley of the **Río Mayer,** a prime trout stream. Just outside town, a secondary road leads south and crosses the river on the **Puente Colgante August Grosse,** a 123-meter suspension bridge; from the south side of the bridge, an exposed zigzag trail leads west above the south bank of **Lago Ciervo,** a scenic route that eventually drops onto the shore of **Lago Negro,** where camping is possible. With an early start, this can also be a long day hike, but the new trail is tiring because it climbs and drops more than is necessary, and is difficult to follow in a few places.

To the west, the steeply rising peaks of the **Campo de Hielo Sur,** the southern Patagonian icecap, may be the next big thing for hikers for whom Torres del Paine has become too tame. Beyond the bridge, the road continues south to

Bahía Bahamóndez, where there's a new launch destined to carry tourists up Lago O'Higgins to the **Ventisquero O'Higgins,** the O'Higgins glacier. The town also owns a ferry capable of carrying passengers and vehicles to the Argentine side, but at present it has no authority to do so.

It is possible, however, to make a very difficult border crossing by chartering a boat or taking the scheduled weekly motor launch *Pirincho* to the south end of **Lago O'Higgins** and making a long and sometimes difficult hike through rugged country to **Laguna del Desierto,** on the Argentine side. From this point there's a road to the village of **El Chaltén,** in Argentina's Parque Nacional Los Glaciares. Some people have even done this by mountain bike, but that involves carrying the bike and supplies for a good part of the way, though it's well enough trod that a guide is no longer necessary. Consult with Carabineros on border formalities.

Accommodations and Food

There are many places to camp inexpensively in and around town, and the number of permanent accommodations is growing though still limited (several of them use the same community telephone for messages). It's been hard to get a meal anywhere out of season, though this is likely to change as the influx of tourists grows.

Until recently, Villa O'Higgins had only one permanent lodge, the simple but well-kept **Hospedaje Patagonia** (Río Pascua s/n, tel. 067/234813, US$8 pp), opposite the Plaza de Armas, with comfortable beds and a decent breakfast. In summer, they serve lunch and dinner as well.

Run by the former mayor, **Hostal Runín** (tel. 067/216711, US$11 pp with private bath and breakfast) has comfortable rooms with hot showers and good meals for about US$5–6. When it's crowded in town, he permits camping in the garden.

About two kilometers south of town, **Cabañas Península la Florida** (tel. 067/234813 for reservations, US$50) has comfortable accommodations for up to four persons.

Recently opened **José Adolfo** (Lago O'Higgins s/n, tel. 067/234814) makes an effort to offer appealing food within the limits of what's available locally.

Other Practicalities

Villa O'Higgins has no formal tourist office, but local resident and guide **Hans Silva** (tel. 067/670313) maintains an informative website about the area, www.villaohiggins.cl, in Spanish only.

From the airstrip directly opposite the main drag, **Transportes Aéreos Don Carlos** flies to Coyhaique (US$100) Monday and Thursday.

Bus services to Cochrane remain infrequent and subject to change, with preference for local residents. For the moment, the only service is **Los Ñadis,** which leaves from Hospedaje Cordillera (Lago Salto 302) at 9:30 A.M. Tuesday.

For the latest on the lake-land-lake crossing to El Chaltén, Argentina, see the sidebar "The New Cruce de Lagos."

Southern Argentine Patagonia

Argentina's second- and third-largest provinces, extending from the ocean to the Andes, Santa Cruz and Chubut might be considered Argentina's "Deep South," whose vast open spaces and small population lend themselves to Patagonia's "wild and remote" stereotype. That said, there are several substantial cities and towns with hotels and other services, many good roads (and others not so good), and a decent public-transportation infrastructure.

Note that details on the northern stretches of RN 40, from the Río Negro provincial border to the southern Chubut town of Río Mayo, appear in the Northern Argentine Patagonia chapter. Those sections of RN 40 southbound to the Chilean border and northbound to the town of Perito Moreno appear in this chapter.

PLANNING YOUR TIME

Southern Argentine Patagonia has virtually limitless highlights, but distances are great and flying is almost essential for short-term visitors—overland transportation is too time-consuming to

Must-Sees

Look for [M] to find the sights and activities you can't miss and [M] for the best dining and lodging.

Ecocentro Puerto Madryn: Home to living tidepools, native gardens, a research center, and more, this environmental center is a testament to the ecological commitment of Puerto Madryn, coastal Patagonia's largest beach resort (page 300).

Reserva Provincial Península Valdés: It's hard to choose among coastal Patagonia's countless wildlife reserves, but Península Valdés has everything: guanacos, rheas, penguins, elephant seals, sea lions, orcas, and the great right whales. It doesn't have everything at the same time, though, so every season's a different experience (page 305).

Reserva Provincial Punta Tombo: Every austral spring, nearly 250,000 pairs of Magellanic penguins waddle ashore to breed in this remote spot, where there are plenty of other seabirds and shorebirds as well (page 320).

Parque Nacional Monte León: Where the tides strike the headlands, the South Atlantic has gouged deep kelp-filled caverns in this recently created coastal park. In addition, there's plenty of wildlife, including penguins and guanacos (page 334).

Estancia Monte Dinero: On the coastal steppe southeast of Río Gallegos, Monte Dinero is a model working ranch that also offers homey accommodations and easy access to the giant penguin colony and other sites at **Cabo Vírgenes** (page 340).

Hostería Alta Vista: Southwest of El Calafate, this country lodge on historic Estancia Anita is the place to vacation like the Braun-Menéndez dynasty (page 350).

Parque Nacional Los Glaciares: The constantly calving 60-meter face of groaning **Glaciar Moreno,** east of El Calafate, is one of the continent's most awesome sights (and sounds). Its **Sector Fitz Roy,** near the hamlet of El Chaltén, offers some of the Andes' most exhilarating scenery, hiking, and climbing (page 350).

Parque Nacional Perito Moreno: West of RN 40, Argentine Patagonia's loneliest highway, this remote park offers endless vistas and varied terrain—ranging from sub-Antarctic forests to high Andean grasslands (page 366).

Cueva de las Manos: East of RN 40, where the Río Pinturas has carved a canyon into the steppe, this UNESCO World Heritage Site's rock art includes hundreds of human hands and other more abstract designs nearly 10,000 years old (page 368).

SOUTHERN ARGENTINE PATAGONIA
RÍO NEGRO
CHUBUT
ARGENTINA
Meseta del Canquel
Cordillera de los Andes
To Viedma and Buenos Aires
To Barlioche
RESERVA PROVINCIAL PENÍNSULA VALDÉS
Puerto Pirámides
Reserva Provincial Punta Loma
Golfo Nuevo
RP 2
PLAYA EL DORADILLO
Puerto Madryn
ECOCENTRO PUERTO MADRYN
Trelew
Rawson
Playa Unión
RESERVA PROVINCIAL PUNTA TOMBO
Cabo Raso
RP 1
Gaiman
Dolavon
RN 3
Camarones
Reserva Provincial Cabo dos Bahías
RP 30
RP 28
Comodoro Rivadavia
Rada Tilly
Golfo San Jorge
RN 281
Río Chico
RN 25
Los Altares
Paso de Indios
Río Chubut
Caleta Olivia
RP 12
Pico Truncado
RN 26
Lago Colhué Huapi
Sarmiento
Lago Musters
Reserva Provincial Bosque Petrificado José Ormachea
Las Heras
Río Deseado
RP 20
RP 22
Río Mayo
RN 40
RP 43
Perito Moreno
ESTANCIA TELKEN
ESTANCIA LOS TOLDOS
CUEVA DE LAS MANOS
ESTANCIA CASA DE PIEDRA
RP 57
RP 41
Los Antiguos
Lago Buenos Aires
Gobernador Costa
Alto Río Senguer
RN 26
RP 55
BALMACEDA
Tecka
RP 62
El Maitén
Leleque
RN 40
Cholila
Esquel
Trevelín
El Bolsón
RN 258
PN Nahuel Huapi
PN Lago Puelo
PN Los Alerces
Chaitén
Coyhaique
Puerto Aisén
Puerto Puyuhuapi
7
Puerto Montt
Golfo de Ancud
Golfo Corcovado

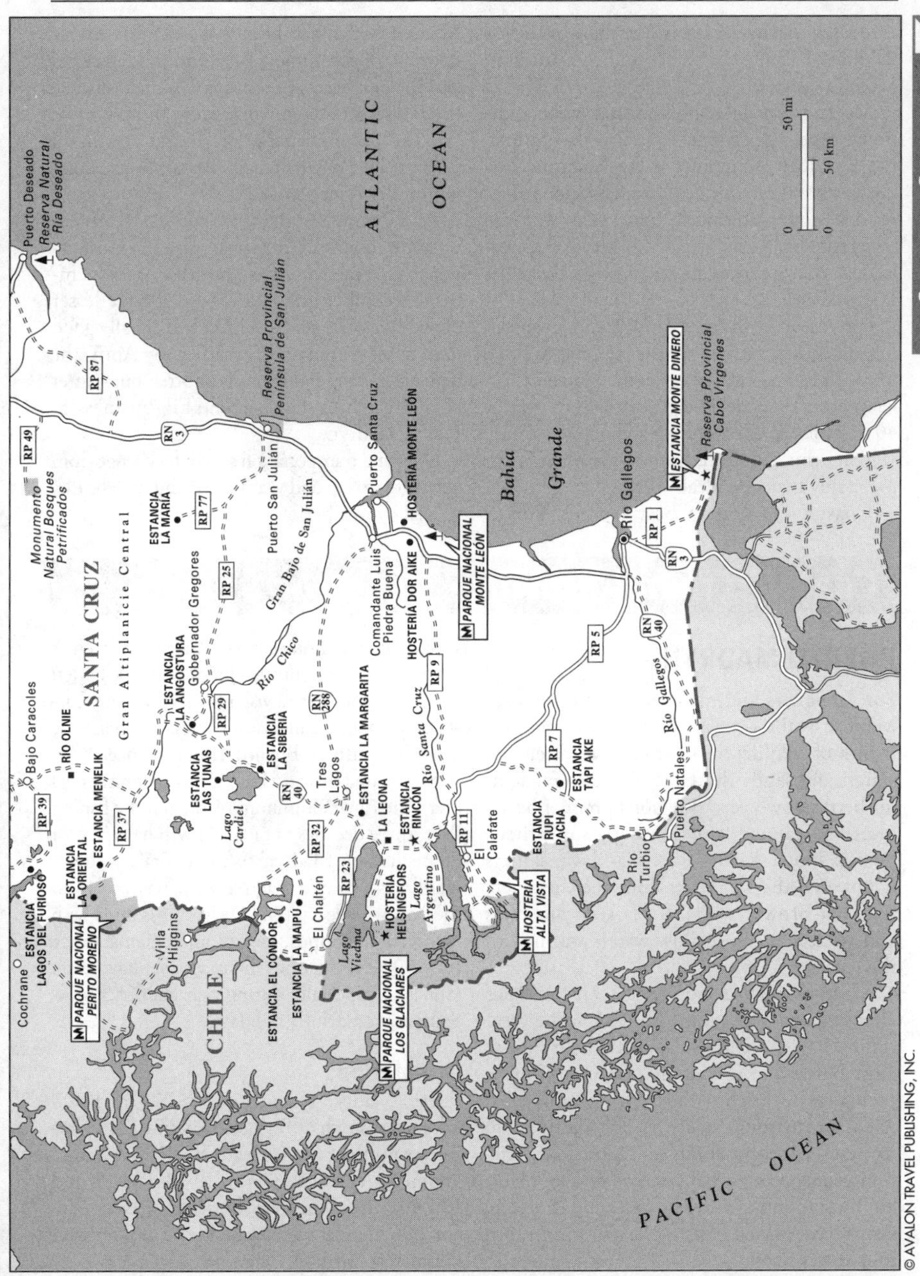

Southern Argentine Patagonia

see widely separated sights like the world-class wildlife of Península Valdés and the stunning Moreno Glacier.

Moreno Glacier visitors should make additional time—perhaps at least a week—to hike the Fitz Roy sector of Parque Nacional Los Glaciares and even Chile's Parque Nacional Torres del Paine (dedicated climbers can wait the entire summer for the weather to clear at these latitudes). Many choose an extension to Tierra del Fuego as well.

For visitors with time, money, and a vehicle, one of the best ways to see the region is to drive south on RN 3—all the way to the Moreno Glacier or even Tierra del Fuego—and return via RN 40 to Bariloche or beyond. In addition to a sturdy vehicle, this would require at least a month, preferably two, and ideally three.

Coastal Patagonia's best base is Puerto Madryn, which has the largest and most diverse selection of accommodations and other services and the best access to secondary attractions like the Welsh settlements of Trelew and Gaiman. For the national parks of the far south, El Calafate and El Chaltén are best options, along with full-service *estancias.*

January and February are the most popular vacation months, but they are also the most expensive. The shoulder months of November–December and March–April have lesser crowding, lower prices, and almost equally good (and sometimes better) weather. By April, the days are getting significantly shorter, but winter whale-watching has become big business at Puerto Madryn.

Overland transportation schedules change from season to season and year to year and may be disrupted by weather.

Coastal Chubut Province

PUERTO MADRYN

For foreigners and many Argentines, Puerto Madryn is the gateway to coastal Patagonia's wealth of wildlife; the Golfo Nuevo's sheltered waters and sandy shoreline have also made it, for better or worse, the region's premier beach resort. In January and February, sunbathers, cyclists, inline skaters, joggers, and windsurfers irrupt onto the *balnearios* along the Costanera Avenida Brown, while divers seek out reefs and wrecks as the shallow waters warm with the season.

Madryn's tourist season, in fact, only weakens after Semana Santa until July, when the great right whales of Península Valdés help fill the city's hotels and restaurants. Conscious of its ecological birthright, Madryn has promoted itself as an environmentally friendly destination; its new Ecocentro complex, focused on maritime conservation, is a positive development, but mushrooming souvenir stores and chocolate shops have turned parts of the waterfront into tourist traps.

At the same time, the bright green lawns of suburban-style homes have worsened the city's water deficit. The burning dunes along the barren Costanera could use a visionary like the late Carlos Gesell, who planted shade trees to stabilize the dunes of southern Buenos Aires province.

Stimulated by the Muelle Storni (commercial pier), the Aluar aluminum plant, and the fishing fleet, three decades of rapid growth have almost obliterated the Madryn's Welsh heritage (though it still has a sister city in Nefyn, Gwynedd). On the positive side, cultural life has blossomed with a university campus, theater, and cinema. Since the 2002 devaluation, many visitors have been Chileans, especially during that country's mid-September patriotic holidays.

Orientation

Puerto Madryn (population 57,571) is 1,308 kilometers south of Buenos Aires and 1219 kilometers north of Río Gallegos via RN 3. It is 673 kilometers east of Esquel via RN 3, RN 25, and RN 40, 719 kilometers southeast of Neuquén, and 896 kilometers from Bariloche. It is only 65 kilometers north of Trelew.

Most services are within a few blocks of the

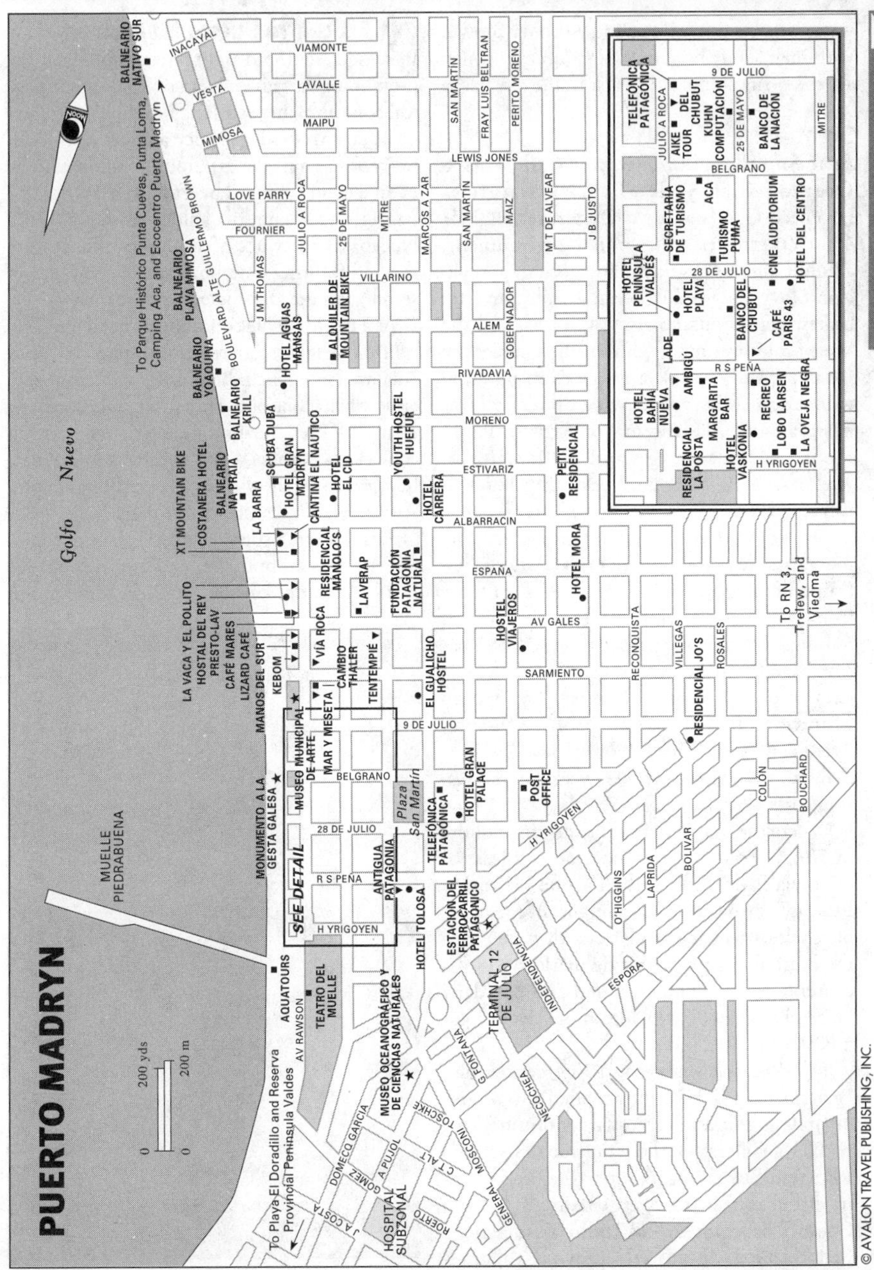

Southern Argentine Patagonia

waterfront Avenida Roca and Avenida Brown, with their sandy beaches and *balnearios,* which are the main points of interest in the city itself.

Sights

At the north end of downtown, the **Museo Oceanográfico y de Ciencias Naturales** (Domecq García and Menéndez, tel. 02965/451139) stresses the regional environment, wildlife, and history, including geology and paleontology, botany and oceanography, invertebrates, marine mammals, fish, birds, and the Welsh colonization of Chubut. It occupies the **Chalet Pujol** (1915), a neoclassical building with a domed hexagonal tower, built by businessman and Madryn mayor Agustín Pujol. Hours are 9 A.M.–noon and 2:30–8:30 P.M. weekdays, 4:30–8:30 P.M. weekends; admission is free, but donations are appropriate.

One of Madryn's oldest structures, the former **Estación del Ferrocarril Patagónico** (Hipólito Yrigoyen and Marcos A. Zar) dates from 1889; after serving briefly as the city bus terminal, the onetime train station is due to become the Centro de Estudios Históricos de la Ciudad (City Historical Center). The **Museo Municipal de Arte** (Municipal Art Museum, Avenida Roca 444, tel. 02965/453204) is open 2–8 P.M. weekdays, 4–10 P.M. weekends; admission costs US$.35.

Where the first Welsh colonists came ashore in 1865, about three kilometers southeast of town via Blvd. Brown, the **Parque Histórico Punta Cuevas** preserves remnants of the humble shelters whose foundations they dug into the bluff above the high-tide mark. A visitors center, open 3–7 P.M. daily and 5–9 P.M. daily December–March, provides more details; admission costs US$.35.

For Puerto Madryn's 1965 centennial, Porteño artist Luis Perlotti created two monumental sculptures: downtown's **Monumento a La Gesta Galesa** (on the waterfront at Avenida Roca and Belgrano), to honor the Welsh contribution to the area's settlement, and Punta Cuevas's **Monumento al Indio Tehuelche,** a well-deserved tribute to the province's aboriginal inhabitants.

Ecocentro Puerto Madryn

In season, southern right whales approach the promontory of this emblem of Madryn's ecological commitment, a striking building that draws on Patagonia's "Magellanic" architectural tradition and permits the maximum illumination by natural light. Crowned by a tower that yields distant views of Península Valdes across the Golfo Nuevo, it's the work of a nonprofit institution striving to bring environmental education, research, and the arts under the same roof.

As a maritime-life educational center, the Ecocentro has superb interpretive displays of South Atlantic fauna, including birds, seals, and especially whales; one of the finest, though, is a living tidal pool. Even the surrounding gardens serve an educational purpose—rather than planting water-hungry lawns, the directors have chosen to preserve the native coastal desert flora.

Reached by a spiral staircase, the three-level tower holds a library, an exhibition room for local artists and authors, and a reading room.

Ecocentro Puerto Madryn

Painting, photography, and sculpture are all on display; the spacious ground-floor atrium accommodates the largest works. There are also a 150-seat theater for concerts and lectures, a crafts and souvenir shop, and a café.

Reached by Blvd. Almirante Brown, about five minutes from downtown by taxi, 15 minutes by bicycle, and 40 minutes on foot, the Ecocentro (Julio Verne 3784, tel. 02965/457470, www.ecocentro.org.ar, mar@ecocentro.org.ar) is open 10 A.M.–7 P.M. daily except Tuesday. Admission costs US$3 for adults, US$2 for retired individuals, and US$1 for kids. English-speaking personnel can answer specific questions.

Entertainment and Events

The **Teatro del Muelle** (Rawson 60, tel. 02965/457966) offers theater programs, usually on weekends. The **Cine Auditorium** (28 de Julio 129, tel. 02965/455653) shows current movies and hosts theater productions as well.

For occasional live music, try the **Margarita Bar** (Roque Sáenz Peña 15), which has good pub food and drinks, but the drinks are considerably costlier than the food (which is rock-bottom cheap, but recently upgraded). **La Oveja Negra** Hipólito Yrigoyen 144) is another popular bar.

July 28's **Fundación de la Ciudad** celebrates the anniversary of the initial Welsh landing at Punta Cuevas. Festivities continue for several days.

Shopping

The waterfront avenues are full of souvenir shops now, but the best choice for souvenirs and crafts remains **Manos del Sur** (Avenida Roca 546, tel. 02965/472539).

Recreo (25 de Mayo and Roque Sáenz Peña, tel. 02965/472971) carries an outstanding selection of books on Patagonia, including some English-language titles.

Sports and Recreation

Water sports are the primary attraction on the crescent of sandy beaches that stretches from Aluar's Muelle Storni in the north almost to Punta Cuevas in the south. In these sheltered waters, hazards like rip currents are nonexistent, but at low tide the water retreats hundreds of meters on the gradually sloping beach.

At the beaches along Blvd. Almirante Brown, several *balnearios* rent water-sports equipment and have snack bars and restaurants. From north to south, they are **Balneario Na Praia** (Blvd. Brown between Lugones and Perlotti), **Balneario Krill** (Blvd. Brown and Luis Perlotti), **Balneario Yoaquina** (Blvd. Brown and José Hernández), **Balneario Playa Mimosa** (Blvd. Brown and Fragata Sarmiento), and **Balneario Nativo Sur** (Blvd. Brown and Inacayal).

Several *balnearios* also rent items like inline skates and mountain bikes, and some operators who arrange diving excursions and other activities have space at them; other operators are scattered around town.

Divers favor Madryn because of its clear waters, natural and artificial reefs, and shipwrecks; most operators do initial dives for novices, PADI certification courses, and underwater photography. Operators working out of the *balnearios* include **Ocean Divers** (Balneario Yoaquina, tel. 02965/472569, www.oceandivers.com.ar, oceandivers@oceandivers.com.ar), **Tito Botazzi** (Balneario Krill, tel. 02965/474110, www.titobottazzi.com.ar, teresa@titobottazzi.com.ar), **Patagonia Buceo** (Balneario Rayentray, Blvd. Brown and Castelli, tel. 02965/452278, patagoniabuceo@yahoo.com.ar), and **Madryn Buceo** (Balneario Nativo Sur, 3ra Rotonda, tel. 02965/15-513997, www.madrynbuceo.com, madrynbuceo@mixmail.com). Operators elsewhere include **Aquatours** (Avenida Roca 550, tel. 02965/451954, www.aquatours.com.ar, patagonia9@hotmail.com), **Lobo Larsen** (Avenida Hipólito Yrigoyen 144, tel. 02965/15-516314, www.lobolarsen.com, lobolarsenbuceo@infovia.com.ar), and **Scuba Duba** (Blvd. Brown 893, tel. 02965/452699, www.scubaduba.com.ar, info@scubaduba.com.ar).

Accommodations

In addition to up-to-date hotel prices, the Secretaría de Turismo keeps a register of rental apartments on a daily, weekly, or monthly basis. Note that in peak season, hotels may double rates even for a single person. Hotel occupancy is high, but the trend in summer is toward apartment complexes, as people come here to spend two weeks on the beach.

Under US$10

On the Punta Cuevas road, the wooded 800-site **Camping ACA** (tel. 02965/452952, US$7 for up to four persons) offers discounts to members and affiliates. A short distance beyond, sites at the Club Náutico Atlántico Sud's more spacious **Camping El Golfito** (tel. 02965/454544, US$2 pp) are more exposed.

US$10–25

Freshly modernized, the amiable, motel-style **Hostel Viajeros** (Gobernador Maíz 545, tel. 02965/456457, info@hostelviajeros.com, US$5.50 pp) has doubles and triples with pleasing garden spaces. A step down is the **Youth Hostel Huefur** (Estivariz 245, tel. 02965/453926, huefur245@hotmail.com, US$5–6 pp).

Madryn's HI affiliate is the exceptional **El Gualicho Hostel** (Marcos A. Zar 480, tel. 02965/454163, www.elgualichohostel.com.ar, US$6–7 pp in dorms, US$18 d). Comfortably furnished and attractively decorated, it also has a shady patio that encourages socializing.

Affordable non-hostel options include **Hotel del Centro** (28 de Julio 149, tel. 02965/473742, US$6/10 s/d), **Hotel Vaskonia** (25 de Mayo 43, tel. 02965/472581, buce23@infovia.com.ar, US$9/12 s/d), and **Residencial Jo's** (Bolívar 75, tel. 02965/471433, residencialjos@infovia.com.ar, US$12/15 s/d).

The spartan **Petit Residencial** (Marcelo T. de Alvear 845, tel. 02965/451460, fax 02965/456428, hotelpetit@arnet.com.ar, US$7 pp) is a friendly place with small motel-style rooms and ample parking; breakfast is US$1.50 extra.

Other good choices include **Hotel Mora** (Juan B. Justo 654, tel. 02965/471424, nelyomarmora@hotmail.com, US$15/18 s/d), where breakfast costs US$1 more; the simple but tidy, 40-room **Hotel Gran Palace** (28 de Julio 390, tel. 02965/471009, US$15/19 s/d); and **Hotel Gran Madryn** (Lugones 40, tel. 02965/472205, granmadryn1@hotmail.com, US$15/20 s/d).

Attractive **Residencial La Posta** (Avenida Roca 33, tel. 02965/472422, fax 02965/454573, residenciallaposta@infovia.com.ar, US$15/20 s/d) fills up fast. Though its smallish rooms don't get many style points, the homey, well-kept **Hotel Carrera** (Marcos A. Zar 844, tel. 02965/450759, www.hotelcarrera.com.ar, US$17/23 s/d) offers personalized service in a quiet neighborhood, with a very decent breakfast to boot.

On a quiet residential block, one of the best values in its range, tranquil **Hotel Aguas Mansas** (José Hernández 51, tel. 02965/473103, www.aguasmansas.com, aguasmansas@aguasmansas.com, US$18/23) is a contemporary place that doesn't raise rates in summer. Set back from the busy avenue, centrally located **Residencial Manolo's** (Avenida Roca 763, tel. 02965/472390, ibaloren@hotmail.com, US$23 d) has firm beds but slightly cramped rooms.

US$25–50

Adequate, but showing its age, the **Costanera Hotel** (Almirante Brown 759, tel. 02965/453000, hotelcostanera@infovia.com.ar, US$20/32 s/d) lives mostly off its convenient beachfront location. Nicely furnished, in a quiet area, **Hotel El Cid** (25 de Mayo 850, tel./fax 02965/471416, hotelcid@infovia.com.ar, US$25/33 s/d) is a good choice.

Recreating the style of Madryn's early Welsh houses, but with contemporary comforts, **Hotel Bahía Nueva** (Avenida Roca 67, tel./fax 02965/451677, www.bahianueva.com.ar, US$26/33 s/d) also has spacious gardens and ample parking, in a central beachfront location. **Hotel Playa** (Avenida Roca 181, tel. 02965/451446, www.playahotel.com.ar, US$32–43 s or d) draws its character from its age.

Down the block, **Hostal del Rey** (Blvd. Brown 681, tel. 02965/471093, rcvcentral@ar.inter.net, US$35/43 s/d) benefits from its proximity to the beach.

Over US$50

Hotel Tolosa (Roque Sáenz Peña 253, tel. 02965/471850, www.hoteltolosa.com.ar, US$37–50 s, US$43–62 d) lacks the retro touch, but is still a fine downtown choice. Top-of-the line **Hotel Península Valdés** (Avenida Roca 155, tel. 02965/

471292, fax 02965/452584, www.hotel-peninsula-valdes.com, US$53 d) has fine standard rooms, but spectacular ocean views make the larger panoramic rooms worth consideration for only a little more.

Food

Good choices for breakfast, snacks, and coffee include **Café París 43** (Roque Sáenz Peña 112) and the **Lizard Café** (Avenida Roca and Gales, tel. 02965/455306).

Madryn's only Welsh teahouse, **Del Chubut** (Avenida Roca 369, tel. 02965/451311) also sells takeaway *alfajores* (cookies sandwiched around sweet fillings like *dulce de leche*) and *torta galesa* (a dense black cake).

La Barra (Blvd. Brown and Lugones, tel. 02965/455550) is one of Madryn's better pizzerias, with moderate prices, but **Tentempié** (Avenida Gales 191, tel. 02965/455384) has lighter versions. Reinvented as a sports bar, **Ambigú** (Avenida Roca 97, tel. 02965/472541) has eight TVs, but pizza is still the best bet here (though the scallops aren't bad).

Though the service can seem surly, **La Vaca y El Pollito** (Avenida Roca and Alfonsina Storni, tel. 02965/458486) serves a thick, juicy *bife de chorizo* (US$5) that's arguably the best-value steak in town; truly fresh bread accompanies every meal.

Made in the metal-clad Magellanic style, with Georgian flourishes and a brick interior adorned with artifacts from the early days of settlement, **Antigua Patagonia** (Mitre and Roque Sáenz Peña, tel. 02965/458738) has a varied menu of meat, excellent fish (try the *abadejo*), seafood, and pasta, with most entrées in the US$4–5 range. For warm nights, there's outdoor seating and a play area for kids.

The large menu at **Mar y Meseta** (Avenida Roca 485, tel. 02965/458740) boasts intriguing dishes like gnocchi with lamb, prawn ravioli, and rabbit in chocolate sauce, but not everything is available every night. Consider the king crab salad (US$5) or the seafood *parrillada* (US$6.50), which includes fresh fish, king crab, and scallops. Service is attentive and cheerful, but the kitchen sometimes seems a little *too* quick for a leisurely meal.

Cantina El Náutico (Avenida Roca 790, tel. 02965/471404) and **Puerto Marisko** (Avenida Rawson 7, tel. 02965/450752) are traditional seafood favorites.

For Madryn's most ambitious menu, try **Nativo Sur** (Blvd. Brown 1900 at Humphreys, tel. 02965/457403), with delicious appetizers like bruschetta (US$2.50) and gazpacho with chicken chunks, and entrées like grilled pork (US$5.50) and an abundant mixed-seafood plate (US$6) of fish, king crab, octopus, scallops, and shrimp. Be prepared to wait, though—the service can be haphazard, and the kitchen so slow you may think they've left to hunt the Patagonian hare (US$5.50). Fortunately, there's a good wine list; in summer, the shady interior *quincho* stays cooler than the exposed beachside tables.

Under the same ownership, the less expensive **Yoaquina** (Blvd. Brown 1050, tel. 02965/456058) has very good lasagna (US$4) and excellent raspberries with cream for dessert, but the *ahumados* (smoked meats) are disappointing.

Madryn has several superb ice creameries, including the 40-plus flavors at **Vía Roca** (Avenida Roca 517, tel. 02965/450704), **Kebom** (Avenida Roca 540), and **Café Mares** (Avenida Roca 600).

Information

The **Secretaría de Turismo** (Avenida Roca 223, tel. 02965/453504, 02965/456067, www.madryn.gov.ar, informes@madryn.gov.ar) does an exemplary job of providing information (in, Spanish, English, French, and German), and will help find accommodations when beds are scarce. Hours are 7 A.M.–9 P.M. January–March; the rest of the year, weekday hours are 7 A.M.–1 P.M. and 3–9 P.M. weekdays, 8:30 A.M.–1:30 P.M. and 3:30–8:30 P.M. weekends and holidays.

For motorists, **ACA** (tel. 02965/456684) is at Belgrano 19.

The **Fundación Patagonia Natural** (Marcos A. Zar 760, tel. 02965/474363, www.patagonianatural.org, patagonianatural@speedy.com.ar) is an NGO working to preserve Patagonia's natural wealth.

Services

There are numerous ATMs, including **Banco**

de la Nación (9 de Julio 117) and **Banco del Chubut** (25 de Mayo 154). The only exchange house is **Cambio Thaler** (Avenida Roca 497).

Correo Argentino is at Belgrano and Gobernador Maíz; the postal code is 9120.

Telefónica Patagónica (Marcos A. Zar 289; Avenida Roca and 9 de Julio) has phone, fax, and Internet services, but there are several others. **Kuhn Computación** (25 de Mayo 362, tel. 02945/472961) lets you hook up your own laptop.

Nievemar (Avenida Roca 493, tel. 02965/455544) is the AmEx affiliate. For suggestions on tour operators, see the Vicinity of Puerto Madryn entry below.

Laverap (Avenida Gales 112) or **Presto-Lav** (Avenida Brown 605, tel. 02965/451526) can do the washing.

Puerto Madryn's **Hospital Subzonal** (tel. 02965/451240) is at Pujol 247.

Getting There

Nearly all commercial flights land at Trelew, 65 kilometers to the south; for details, see the Trelew entry.

LADE (Avenida Roca 119, tel. 02965/451256) uses nearby **Aeródromo El Tehuelche** (tel. 02965/451909) for sporadic southbound flights to Trelew and Comodoro Rivadavia, and northbound flights to Neuquén and to Aeroparque.

In peak summer and winter vacation months, **American Falcon** flies to and from Buenos Aires; its local representative is **Turismo Cuyun-Co** (Avenida Roca 165, tel. 02965/451845).

Madryn's new **Terminal 12 de Julio** (Italia s/n, tel. 02965/451789) stands directly behind the old terminal (and former railroad station). It has frequent connections to nearby Trelew with **Línea 28 de Julio** (tel. 02965/472056), plus extensive regional and long-distance connections. **Mar y Valle** (tel. 02965/472056) goes to Puerto Pirámides at 9:55 A.M. daily; in summer and during the whale-watching season it adds a 5 P.M. departure.

Sample destinations, fares, and times include Trelew (US$2, one hour), Puerto Pirámides (US$3, 1.5 hours), Comodoro Rivadavia (US$10, 6.5 hours), Esquel (US$14, nine hours), Neuquén (US$17, 10 hours), Bariloche (US$20, 12 hours), Río Gallegos (US$28, 18 hours), and Buenos Aires (US$29–35, 20 hours).

Getting Around

For LADE flights from Madryn's Aeródromo El Tehuelche, use a taxi or *remise.* For commercial flights to and from Trelew, **Transportes Eben-Ezer** (tel. 02965/472474, 02965/15-660463) charges US$4.50 per person for door-to-door service.

Bicycle-rental outlets include **XT Mountain Bike** (Avenida Roca 742, tel. 02965/472232), which also leads guided tours, and **Alquiler de Mountain Bike** (25 de Mayo 1136, tel. 02965/474426).

Because the area's attractions are so spread out, but roads are fairly good, renting a car is a good option here. Agencies include **Avis** (Avenida Roca 27, tel. 02965/451491); **Localiza** (Avenida Roca 536, tel. 02965/456300); **Puerto Madryn Turismo** (Avenida Roca 624, tel. 02965/452355); and **Rent A Car Patagonia** (Avenida Roca 293, tel. 02965/452095).

VICINITY OF PUERTO MADRYN

Tour agencies in Madryn go farther afield as well, to Trelew, Gaiman, Punta Tombo, and, of course, Península Valdés. Operators include **Aike Tour** (Avenida Roca 353, tel. 02965/450720); **Cuyun-Co** (Avenida Roca 165, tel. 02965/451845); **Huinca Travel** (25 de Mayo 309, tel. 02965/454411, www.huincatravel.com); **Puerto Madryn Turismo** (Avenida Roca 41, tel. 02965/456453; Avenida Roca 624, tel. 02965/452355); and **Turismo Puma** (28 de Julio 46, tel. 02965/451063). Full-day excursions run in the US$25–35 range, not including meals; whale-watching is additional, even on full-day tours to Península Valdés.

Reserva Provincial Punta Loma

Close enough to Madryn to make it an ideal mountain-bike excursion, Punta Loma lacks the large numbers and diversity of wildlife at the more famous Península Valdés, but its ample sea lion colonies, along with cormorants, giant petrels, gulls, terns, and snowy sheathbills are reason enough to visit. Though only 15 kilometers southwest of Madryn via an undulating gravel road, it still gets far fewer visitors than Valdés.

Near the sea lion colony, there's a visitors center and an overlook that permits good views of the animals. Hours are 8 A.M.–8 P.M. daily; admission costs US$3.50 for foreigners, US$1.50 for Argentine residents, and US$.75 for Chubut residents. There's no scheduled public transportation, but Madryn operators will arrange excursions or a small group can go cheaply by hiring a *remise.*

Playa El Doradillo

From the headlands at Playa El Doradillo, 17 kilometers northeast of Madryn via RP 42, deep water lets whales approach the shore—the next best choice to an in-the-water view at Península Valdés. Like Punta Loma, this is close enough for a bicycle trip or a shared taxi.

RESERVA PROVINCIAL PENÍNSULA VALDÉS

Coastal Patagonia's top destination, the UNESCO World Biosphere Reserve of Península Valdés is the place where the great southern right whale arrives to breed and birth in the winter months. Protected since 1935, the *ballena franca* occupies an almost unique position as a "natural monument"—a designation normally reserved for territorial ecosystems—within the Argentine national-park system.

Península Valdés itself, a provincial reserve rather than a national park, has more to offer than just the whales. Some marine mammal species—ranging from sea lions to elephant seals and orcas—cover the beaches or gather in the waters of the Golfo San José, Golfo Nuevo, or the open South Atlantic all year. There are also masses of burrowing Magellanic penguins and flocks of other seabirds, plus herds of grazing guanacos and groups of sprinting rheas in the arid interior grasslands.

The peninsula's main activity center is the hamlet of Puerto Pirámides, which like Puerto Madryn enjoys a long tourist season because of the whale- and orca-watching periods. Once the export point for salt from the Salina Grande depression, it has grown haphazardly, and water continues to be a problem in this desert environment.

Sometimes called Puerto Pirámide, the village

cliffs near Puerto Pirámides, Península Valdés

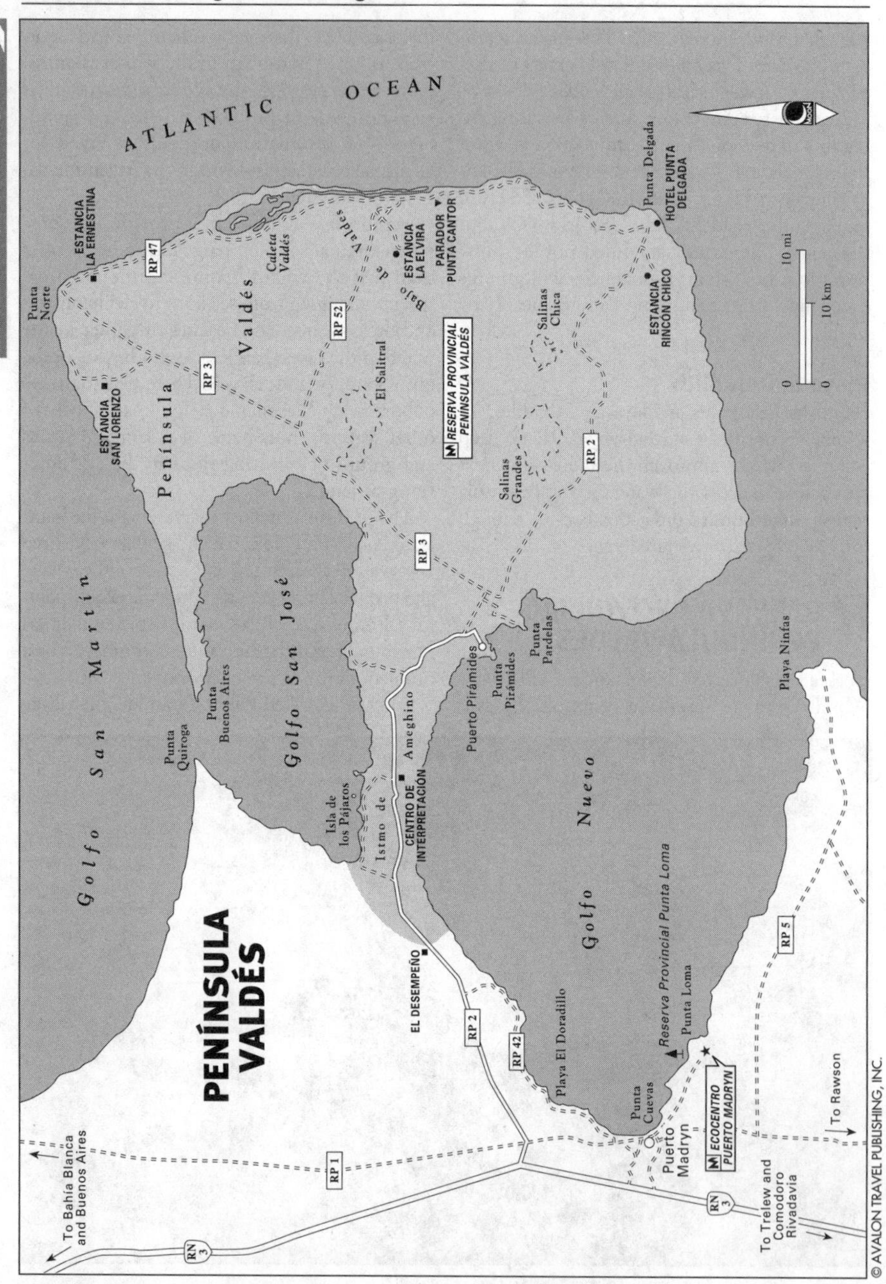
PENÍNSULA VALDÉS
ATLANTIC OCEAN
Península Valdés
Golfo San Martín
Golfo San José
Golfo Nuevo
Punta Norte
ESTANCIA LA ERNESTINA
RP 47
Caleta Valdés
Bajo de Valdés
ESTANCIA LA ELVIRA
PARADOR PUNTA CANTOR
RP 52
El Salitral
RESERVA PROVINCIAL PENÍNSULA VALDÉS
Salinas Chica
Salinas Grandes
RP 2
RP 3
ESTANCIA SAN LORENZO
Punta Delgada
HOTEL PUNTA DELGADA
ESTANCIA RINCÓN CHICO
0
10 mi
10 km
Punta Pardelas
Punta Pirámides
Puerto Pirámides
Istmo de Ameghino
CENTRO DE INTERPRETACIÓN
Isla de los Pájaros
Punta Quiroga
Punta Buenos Aires
Playa Ninfas
EL DESEMPEÑO
RP 42
Playa El Doradillo
Reserva Provincial Punta Loma
Punta Loma
Punta Cuevas
Puerto Madryn
ECOCENTRO PUERTO MADRYN
RP 5
To Rawson
To Trelew and Comodoro Rivadavia
RN 3
RP 1
To Bahía Blanca and Buenos Aires
MOON
© AVALON TRAVEL PUBLISHING, INC.

has recently reasserted its plurality. According to local accounts, when the Argentine navy used the area as a firing range, they destroyed two of the three pyramidal promontories that gave the settlement its original moniker.

In addition, Pirámides has nominated a right whale named Bona Fide as an itinerant ambassador and illustrious citizen of Chubut province. According to mayor Alejandro Albaini, "With all these honors, we are sending a message to those, like the Japanese fishing boats, that hunt our whales. They'd better not hurt our ambassador now."

Geography and Climate

Connected to the mainland by the narrow Istmo de Ameghino, Península Valdés is 56 kilometers northeast of Puerto Madryn via RP 2, but a visit to the major wildlife sites involve a circuit of roughly 400 kilometers to Puerto Pirámides and Punta Delgada via RP 2, Caleta Valdés and Punta Norte via RP 47, and RP 3 back to Puerto Pirámides. Beyond Puerto Pirámides, all these are gravel and dirt roads that can be hazardous to inexperienced drivers, especially with low-clearance vehicles.

Broad sandy beaches line much of the coast, but the many steep headlands that rise above them are dangerous to descend because of unconsolidated sediments. Sheep *estancias* take up most of the interior, whose Salina Grande depression lies 42 meters below sea level, one of the world's lowest points. The climate is extremely dry, with high evaporation due to long hours of sunlight and almost perpetual winds.

Flora and Fauna

Most of Peninsula Valdés consists of rolling *monte* (scrubland) with patches of pasture that can expand considerably in wet years. The stocking rate for the sheep *estancias* is relatively low, permitting the guanacos and rheas to thrive alongside domestic stock.

Marine mammals—whales, orcas, elephant seals and sea lions—are the big draw, but there are also Magellanic penguin colonies. In addition to penguins, there are breeding populations of the Dominican gull *(Larus domincanus)*, white heron *(Casmerodius albus)*, black-crowned night heron *(Nycticorax nycticorax)*, olivaceous cormorant *(Phalacrocorax olivaceus)*, black cormorant *(Phalocrocorax magellanicus)*, steamer duck

© WAYNE BERNHARDSON

A right whale swims along the surface near Puerto Pirámides, Península Valdés.

(Tachyeres leucocephalus), Patagonian crested duck *(Lophonetta specularoides),* Magellanic oystercatcher *(Haematopus ostralegus),* and black oystercatcher *(Haematopus ater).* Several species of gulls, terns, and plovers are visitors, along with the Chilean flamingo and the snowy sheathbill.

Whales: June–December, the breeding, breaching, blowing, and birthing of *Eubalaena australis* brings whale-watchers from around the world to the warm, shallow waters of the Golfo Nuevo and Golfo San José. Since 1971, when the first census was taken, the Península Valdés population has grown from 580 to about 3,000.

Inhabiting the South Atlantic from about 20° S to 55° S, the southern right whale is a giant that reaches 17 meters in length and weighs up to 100 tons, though most individuals are smaller; females are larger than males. They are baleen whales, filtering krill and plankton as seawater passes through sieves in their jaws.

Right whales acquired their English name from whalers who sought them ought because dead specimens, instead of sinking, floated to the surface; hence, they were the "right whales" for hunting. Identifiable by keratin calluses on their heads, about 1,300 of Valdés's population have names; this has given researchers the ability to follow their movements and even trace their kinship.

After the cows give birth, whale calves get closest to the catamarans and rafts that do commercial whale-watching at Puerto Pirámides. Over the course of the season, though, it is possible to see all stages of the species' mating and breeding cycle.

Orcas: For much of the year, *Orcinus orca* swims the South Atlantic waters in search of squid, fish, penguins, and dolphins, but October–April, pods of "killer whales" patrol the Punta Norte shoreline in search of sea lion pups—a nine-meter specimen can kill and consume up to eight pups per day. The largest of the dolphin family, the 950-kilogram animal is a conspicuous sight thanks to its sleek black body, white underbelly, and menacing dorsal fin, which can rise two meters above the water's surface.

Elephant Seals: The peninsula's sandy beaches are the only continental breeding site for *Mirounga leonina,* though there are also breeding colonies on sub-Antarctic islands in Chile and the Falklands (Malvinas), as well as South Georgia and other circumpolar islands. Largest of the pinnipeds, it's a true seal with no external ear (as opposed to the southern sea lion, for example), but its distinguishing characteristic is the male's inflatable proboscis, which truly resembles an elephant's trunk.

Ungainly on land, the 2,500–4,000-kilogram "beachmaster" males come ashore in the spring to take charge of harems that number up to 100 females; the much smaller females weigh only about 500 kilograms. Reaching seven meters in length, the beachmasters engage in bloody fights with younger bachelors that leave all parties scarred and even disfigured.

Females spend most of their pregnancy at sea, giving birth when they return to land in the spring. Pups spend only a few weeks nursing, gaining weight quickly, before the mother abandons them (some die crushed beneath battling males). At sea, the elephant seal is an extraordinary diver, plunging up to 600 vertical meters in search of squid before surfacing for air half an hour later.

Sea Lions: Present all year on the beaches and reefs beneath the peninsula's headlands, *Otaria flavescens* is common from southern Brazil and Uruguay all the way around the tip of South America and north to Peru. With its thick mane, the 300-kilogram, 2.3-meter male reminds many observers of the African lion, though Spanish-speakers know it as the *lobo marino* (sea wolf). The female is only about 1.8 meters long and weighs only about 100 kilograms.

Unlike the larger elephant seal, the sea lion has external ears. Also unlike the elephant seal, it propels itself on land with both front and rear flippers, and the male is quick enough to attack and drag away elephant seal pups. More often, though, it feeds on krill and the odd penguin.

For Spanish speakers, by the way, this is the *lobo marino de un pelo;* the *lobo marino de dos pelos,* or southern fur seal *(Arctocephalos australis),* whose pelt was far more valuable to commercial sealers, is found farther south.

Penguins: *Spheniscus magellanicus,* the braying and burrowing jackass penguin, is the only species present on the peninsula. From September to

March or April, it breeds and raises its young in remote areas like Caleta Valdés and Punta Norte, but summer swimmers in the shallow waters at Puerto Pirámides have had close encounters.

Sights and Activities

Many visitors book excursions in Puerto Madryn, but these day trips are often too brief for more than a glimpse of what the peninsula offers, especially if the operators spend too much time at lunch. Staying in Puerto Pirámides and contracting tours there can be a good alternative, especially for whale-watching, as you have the flexibility to pick the best time to go out.

Five operators, some of whom also have offices in Puerto Madryn, offer whale-watching in semirigid rafts (which get closer to the animals) and in larger catamarans: **Tito Botazzi** (Primera Bajada, tel. 02965/495050, www.titobottazzi.com), **Hydrosport** (Primera Bajada, tel. 02965/495065, www.hydrosport.com.ar), **Pinino Aquatours** (Primera Bajada, tel. 02965/495015, www.whales argentina.com.ar, capitanpinino@infovia.com.ar), **Jorge Schmid** (Segunda Bajada, tel./fax 02965/495012, www.puntaballena.com.ar, puntaballena@puntaballena.com.ar), and **Peke Sosa** (Segunda Bajada, tel. 02965/471291, www.pekesosa.com.ar). Prices range from around US$17–35, depending on the vessel and the length of the tour.

© WAYNE BERNHARDSON

lighthouse at Punta Delgada, Península Valdés

In the waters of Golfo San José, 800 meters north of the isthmus, penguins, gulls, cormorants, and herons all nest on the offshore bird sanctuary of **Isla de los Pájaros.** The island itself is off limits to humans, but a stationary shoreline telescope permits views of the breeding birds. Near the telescope is a replica chapel from Fuerte San José, the area's first Spanish settlement (1779, but destroyed by the Tehuelche in 1810).

Argentina's primary whale-watching center, **Puerto Pirámides,** has the peninsula's major concentration of tourist services, including its most affordable accommodations and food. June–December, whales are the main attraction, but traditional beachgoers take over in January and February. Visitors without their own vehicle can hike or bike to the southern sea lion colony at Punto Pirámide, four kilometers west, which offers outstanding panoramas and sunsets over the Golfo Nuevo.

Beneath the headlands at the peninsula's southeastern tip, **Punta Delgada** is home to substantial elephant seal and sea lion colonies, reached by a trail from the lighthouse at the former naval station (now a hotel). The hotel concessionaires provide well-prepared English-speaking guides, free of charge, to lead tour groups and individuals; they have also turned the lighthouse into a small but well-presented museum. Their restaurant is open to the public, and they also offer horseback tours of the area.

Another large colony of elephant seals and sea lions is visible from the steep cliffs a short distance north of Punta Delgada, but there is no safe access.

On the peninsula's eastern shore, about midway between Punta Delgada and Punta Norte, **Caleta Valdés** is a sheltered bay that's fast becoming a lagoon as its ocean outlet fills with sediments. In the meantime, though, Magellanic penguins swim north to a breeding colony and elephant seals haul up onto the shore in the mating season. Even guanacos may be seen along the beach.

Where RP 47 and RP 3 meet at the peninsula's northern tip, **Punta Norte** features as its big attraction a mixed colony of southern elephant seals and sea lions, but October–April this is also the best place to see the orcas that lunge onto the beach to grab unwary pups. Punta Norte also has a small but outstanding museum that puts marine mammals in both natural and cultural perspective—thanks to exhibits on the aboriginal Tehuelche and a historical account of the sealing industry.

Near Punta Norte, reached by a northwesterly road off RP 3, **Estancia San Lorenzo** conducts tours of its own Magellanic penguin colony, but is not open as accommodations.

Accommodations and Food

Puerto Pirámides has sprouted many more places to stay, eat, and recreate than ever before. Demand is high, though; in summer and in the whale-watching season reservations are advisable. There are *estancia* accommodations scattered around Punta Delgada, Caleta Valdés, and Punta Norte, but no camping is permitted beyond Puerto Pirámides.

Immediately behind the dunes, Puerto Pirámides' shoreline **Camping Municipal** (tel. 02965/495084) charges US$1.50 per person plus US$.35 per shower (water is limited and the showers timed). The bathrooms are clean, and there's a store with basic supplies, but only a few sites have shade.

The next cheapest option is **Hospedaje El Español** (Avenida de las Ballenas s/n, tel. 02965/495025, US$3.50 pp), which can accommodate up to 36 people in spartan accommodations with shared baths and hot showers. At the entrance to town, the **Hostería ACA** (tel. 02965/495004, www.piramides.net, US$14/19 s/d for members, US$18/23 s/d for nonmembers) was once Piramides' top choice, but several others have overtaken it.

Hostería La Estancia del Sol (Avenida de las Ballenas s/n, tel. 02965/495007, hosteriestancia delsol@hotmail.com, US$26 d) is a step up, but is by no means extravagant.

Right on the beach, the **Posada Austral Patagonia Franca** (Primera Bajada, tel. 02965/495006, www.patagoniafranca.com, info@patagoniafranca.com) is a sparkling new construction with views across the Golfo Nuevo. Rates are US$35/42 s/d Monday–Thursday, US$42/48 s/d weekends.

Its handsome brick superstructure reproducing the region's Welsh heritage, **Hostería Paradise** (Avenida de las Ballenas s/n, tel./fax 02965/495003 or 02965/495030, www.hosteriaparadise.com.ar, paradise@satlink.com) is a substantial improvement on the traditional choices. Rates are US$110 s or d with breakfast, while there's a spacious suite for US$170. Fixed-price lunches or dinners cost US$15 for foreigners, US$9 for Argentines; there's a sandwich and pizza menu as well.

In a casual ambiance that blends traditional artifacts and artwork with pop music, **La Estación** (Avenida de la Ballenas s/n, tel. 02965/495047) serves excellent fresh fish and salads, but the kitchen is slow and the service amateurish.

On the bluffs overlooking Punta Delgada, alongside the lighthouse at the east end of RP 2, **Hotel Punta Delgada** (tel. 02965/15-406304; Avenida Roca 536, Puerto Madryn, tel. 02965/458444, www.puntadelgada.com, faro@puntadelgada.com) is an upgraded property on lease from the navy, with 30 comfortable double rooms with private baths. High-season rates, September 1–January 1, are US$110/134 s/d with breakfast, US$134/184 with half-board, and US$150/215 with full board; low-season rates, January 1–April 15, are about 10 percent cheaper. Tour buses often stop at its restaurant, which is open to nonguests.

Near Punta Delgada and run by a young Madryn couple, the best of the new tourist-oriented *estancias* is **Estancia Rincón Chico** (tel. 02965/15-688302, Blvd. Almirante Brown 1783, Puerto Madryn, tel. 02965/471733, www.rinconchico.com.ar, rinconchico@infovia.com.ar). Five kilometers south of RP 2, its purpose-built hotel has eight comfortable, well-furnished doubles, with a sheltered *quincho* for barbecues. For three months a year, they host elephant-seal researchers from the University of California at Santa Cruz, as the seals frequent their long coastal frontage. High-season rates, September 1–January 31, are US$120/138 s/d with breakfast, US$144/180 with half-board, and US$156/222 with full board; low-season rates, February 1–April 15 and June 15–August 30, are about 10–15 percent less. Prices do not include taxes.

Set in a sheltered depression west of Caleta Valdés, along RP 47, **Estancia La Elvira** (tel. 02965/15-698709, 02965/15-406183, www.laelvira.com.ar, laelvira@laelvira.com.ar) lacks the mature landscaping of Rincón Chico, but the rooms and common areas are attractive enough. Rates are US$90/110 s/d with breakfast, US$114/144 s/d with half-board, and US$142/203 s/d with full board. For nonguests, they operate the roadside **Parador Punta Cantor,** which gets tour buses at lunchtime, near the elephant-seal colony.

Toward Punta Norte, along the west side of RP 47, the seven-room **Estancia la Ernestina** (tel. 02965/15-661079; Avenida Gales 54, Puerto Madryn, tel. 02965/471143, www.laernestina.com.ar, info@laernestina.com.ar) is an amiable place with access to the large Magellanic penguin colony at Estancia San Lorenzo. Three of the rooms have only two baths among them. Rates are US$140/220 s/d with full board, drinks, and excursions.

Information

At El Desempeño, at the west end of the Istmo de Ameghino, provincial authorities have erected a toll booth to collect an admission fee of US$12 for most foreigners, US$9 for Mercosur residents, US$5 for Argentine residents, and US$2 for Chubut residents. Immediately east, the reserve's **Centro de Interpretación** (open 8 A.M.–8 P.M. daily) includes a complete right whale skeleton and other natural-history items, but also historical material ranging from the Tehuelche presence to Spanish colonization and Argentine settlement for salt mining and sheep ranching. An adjacent observation tower offers panoramas across the northerly Golfo San José to the southerly Golfo Nuevo, and east across the peninsula's interior.

Sarah Mansfield Taber's *Dusk on the Campo: A Journey in Patagonia* (New York: Henry Holt and Company, 1991) tells the tale of peninsula pioneers, in both historical and ethnographic perspective.

Getting There and Around

In summer, from Puerto Madryn, **Mar y Valle** (tel. 02965/472056) has daily bus departures for Puerto Pirámides (US$6.50, 1.5 hours) at 8:55 A.M. and 5 P.M.; return buses leave at 11 A.M. and 7 P.M. In the winter months, there are morning departures only, Thursday and Saturday only.

Tour buses may permit passengers to disembark at Puerto Pirámides and return another day, on a space available basis, but make arrangements in advance.

Distances from Puerto Pirámides to other destinations on the peninsula are too great for any transport except motor vehicles, so it's worth considering a **rental car** in Puerto Madryn. Many consider day trips from Madryn too rushed.

TRELEW

Though less conspicuously tourist-oriented than Puerto Madryn, the Río Chubut city of Trelew retains more visible remnants of its Welsh birthright than its oceanside sister city. It also offers excellent access to the lower Chubut Welsh communities of Gaiman and Dolavon, to the dolphin-watching beach resort of Playa Unión, and the massive Punta Tombo penguin colony. Its own main attraction is the state-of-the-art paleontological museum that documents the great Argentine dinosaur discoveries of recent decades.

Dating from 1886, when the railroad united Puerto Madryn with the farms of the lower Río Chubut, Trelew takes its name from Welsh colonist and railroad promoter Lewis Jones (in Welsh, *tre* means "town" while *lew* simply abbreviated "Lewis"). It has since experienced immigration cycles—Italians and Spaniards, as well as Argentines from elsewhere in the country—and boom-and-bust periods thanks to the wool industry, customs preferences, and industrial promotion.

© WAYNE BERNHARDSON

The annex of the former Distrito Militar (army headquarters) now holds Trelew's tourist office.

Through all this, Trelew has retained its immigrant identity through events like the Eisteddfod (a Welsh poetry and music festival) and other cultural activities.

Orientation

On the Río Chubut's north bank, Trelew (population 88,397) is 65 kilometers south of Puerto Madryn and 377 kilometers northeast of Comodoro Rivadavia via RN 3. It is 608 kilometers west of Esquel via paved RN 25, RP 62 and RN 40.

Most points of interest and services lie on or within a few blocks northeast of the central Plaza Independencia.

Sights

From its office opposite **Plaza Independencia,** Entretur distributes an informative brochure (Spanish only) describing most city landmarks. On the pleasingly landscaped plaza itself, the Victorian-style **Kiosco del Centenario** (1910) marked the centennial of Argentine independence.

Once separated by walls and gates from the rest of the plaza, the former **Distrito Militar** (army headquarters, Mitre 350) also served as police headquarters and then municipal offices; it now houses the **Museo de Artes Visuales,** with exhibits of historical photography, as well as contemporary photography, painting, and sculpture. Dating from 1900, it's overdue for maintenance. Entretur's own offices occupy the adjacent **Anexo** (Annex, Mitre 387). Museum hours are presumably 9 A.M.–noon and 6–9 P.M. weekdays only, but can be variable.

In 1920, Trelew's Spanish community built the **Teatro Español** (25 de Mayo 237), on the plaza's north side, to replace an earlier construction destroyed by fire. Half a block east of the plaza, on San Martín between Belgrano and Rivadavia, the **Teatro Verdi** (1914) served the Italian community; at San Martín and Belgrano, the Welsh community's **Salón San David** (1913) hosts the musical festivities of the Eisteddfod. Half a block north, the Welsh **Capilla Tabernacl** (1889) is Trelew's oldest surviving building.

Two blocks northeast of the plaza, early Patagonian tourists stayed at the **Hotel Touring Club** (1906), the former Hotel Martino, which underwent a major upgrade in the 1920s with imported European materials (the Touring Club

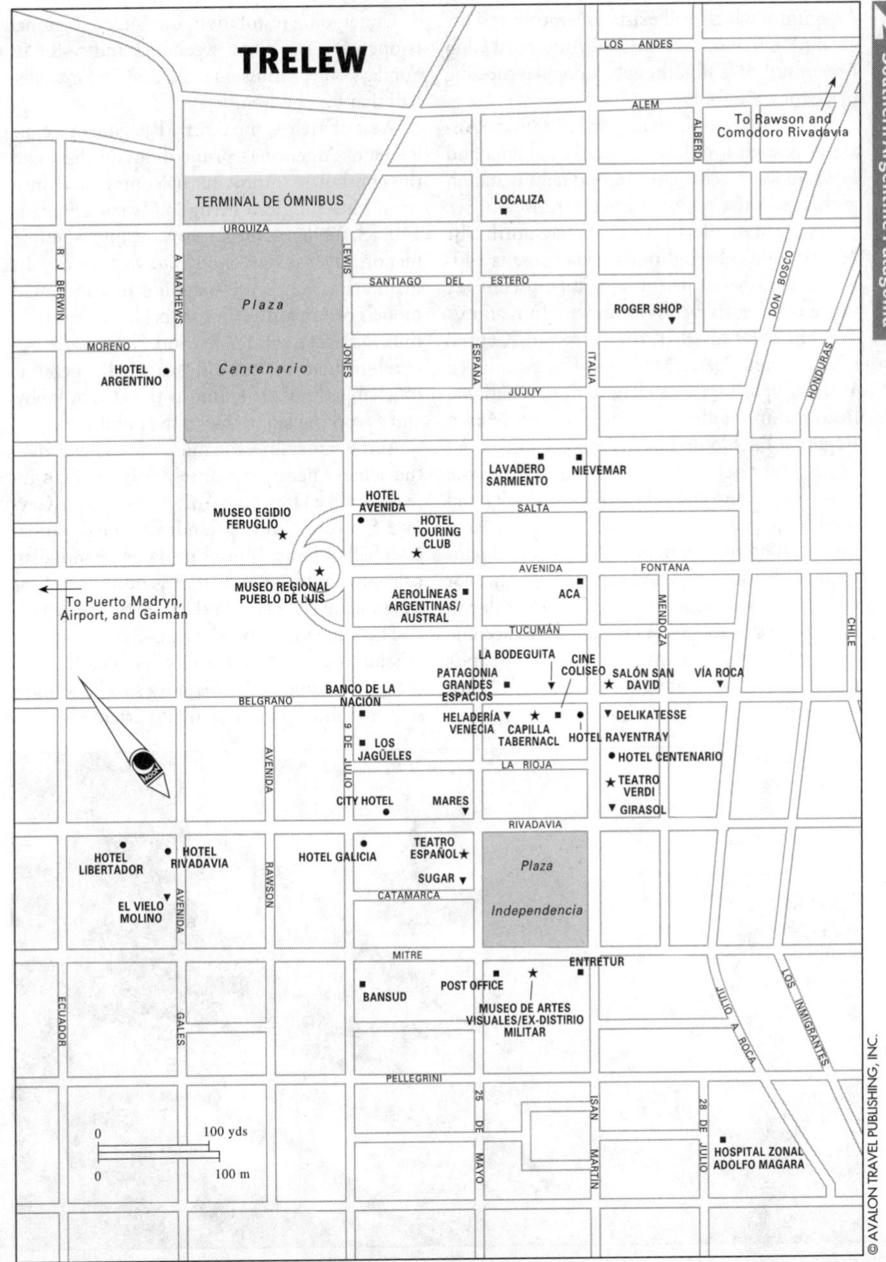
TRELEW
LOS ANDES
ALEM
ALBERDI
To Rawson and Comodoro Rivadavia
TERMINAL DE ÓMNIBUS
LOCALIZA
URQUIZA
R. J. BERWIN
A. MATHEWS
LEWIS
SANTIAGO DEL ESTERO
Plaza
Centenario
ROGER SHOP
DON BOSCO
MORENO
HOTEL ARGENTINO
JONES
ESPAÑA
ITALIA
HONDURAS
JUJUY
LAVADERO SARMIENTO
NIEVEMAR
HOTEL AVENIDA
MUSEO EGIDIO FERUGLIO
HOTEL TOURING CLUB
SALTA
AVENIDA
FONTANA
MUSEO REGIONAL PUEBLO DE LUIS
AEROLÍNEAS ARGENTINAS/ AUSTRAL
ACA
To Puerto Madryn, Airport, and Gaiman
MENDOZA
CHILE
TUCUMÁN
LA BODEGUITA
CINE COLISEO
PATAGONIA GRANDES ESPACIOS
SALÓN SAN DAVID
VÍA ROCA
BANCO DE LA NACIÓN
BELGRANO
HELADERÍA VENECIA
CAPILLA TABERNACL
HOTEL RAYENTRAY
DELIKATESSE
9 DE JULIO
LOS JAGÜELES
LA RIOJA
HOTEL CENTENARIO
AVENIDA
TEATRO VERDI
CITY HOTEL
MARES
GIRASOL
RIVADAVIA
HOTEL LIBERTADOR
HOTEL RIVADAVIA
HOTEL GALICIA
TEATRO ESPAÑOL
RAWSON
Plaza
Independencia
SUGAR
CATAMARCA
EL VIELO MOLINO
AVENIDA
MITRE
ENTRETUR
POST OFFICE
BANSUD
MUSEO DE ARTES VISUALES/EX-DISTIRIO MILITAR
JULIO A. ROCA
LOS INMIGRANTES
ECUADOR
GALES
PELLEGRINI
25 DE MAYO
SAN MARTÍN
28 DE JULIO
0
100 yds
0
100 m
HOSPITAL ZONAL ADOLFO MAGARA

Argentino, which still exists, is a moribund organization that once rivaled the Automóvil Club Argentino). It is still, though, a popular meeting place for *trelewenses.*

Half a block north, dating from 1889, the **Antigua Estación del Ferrocarril** (Fontana and Lewis Jones) was the city's second railway station and is now the regional history museum; see below for more detail. Immediately north, the **Museo Egidio Feruglio** (Avenida Fontana 140) is a state-of-the-art paleontological museum; see the separate entry below for more information.

From 1889 to 1961, the Ferrocarril Central Chubut from Puerto Madryn to Trelew stopped at this English-style railway station, a national historical monument, that now houses **Museo Regional Pueblo de Luis** (Avenida Fontana and Lewis Jones, tel. 02965/424062). An antique steam locomotive and other equipment still stand outside the building. Packed with memorabilia of the Welsh immigration, including historical photographs, furnishings, and clothing, the interior is short on interpretation; this, however, is due to be remedied as the museum expands to become an "Ecomuseo" documenting the landscape's transformation by aboriginal peoples and European settlers.

Undergoing restoration, the Museo Regional is open 8 A.M.–8 P.M. weekdays and 5–8 P.M. Sundays only; admission costs US$.75 for adults, half that for children.

West of Trelew, the central Patagonian steppe is one of Argentina's prime dinosaur digs, and the constantly improving paleontological museum **Museo Egidio Feruglio** (Avenida Fontana 140, tel. 02965/420012, www.mef.org.ar, info@mef.org.ar) is reason enough to visit the city. Its main attraction is the magnificently mounted models of Argentine dinosaurs like the carnivorous *Pianitzkysaurus floresi* and *Carnotaurus sastrei,* but there are also dinosaur eggs, a genuine touchable dinosaur femur in the atrium lobby, and a working lab visible to the public.

At the same time, the museum acknowledges the achievements of pioneering Patagonian researchers like Florentino Ameghino, George Gaylord Simpson, and Alejandro Pianitzky in its own hall of fame. It owes its name to an Italian paleontologist who came to Argentina in 1925 as a petroleum geologist for the state company YPF.

The museum is open 10 A.M.–8 P.M. daily. Admission costs US$3 for adults, half that for children 12 and under; there is also a small café and a souvenir shop. The Museo also arranges excur-

Pianitzkysaurus, Museo Egidio Feruglio, Trelew

sions to Parque Paleontológico Bryn Gwyn, near Gaiman; for details, see the separate entry below.

Entertainment and Events

The **Cine Coliseo** (Belgrano 371, tel. 02965/425300) shows recent films.

Mid-September's **Certámen Internacional de Coros,** which takes place in odd-numbered years, draws on the Welsh tradition of choral music. Later that same month, the **Fiesta Provincial del Pingüino** coincides with the spring arrival of penguins at Punta Tombo.

October 20's **Aniversario de la Ciudad** celebrates Trelew's 1886 founding. Late October's **Eisteddfod de Chubut** focuses on the Welsh traditions, particularly folk music and poetry, of the lower Chubut valley.

Shopping

For souvenirs and clothing, including horse gear, leather, and woolens, visit **Los Jagüeles** (25 de Mayo 144, tel. 02965/422949).

Accommodations

The best shoestring choices are **Hotel Avenida** (Lewis Jones 49, tel. 02965/434172, US$4/7 s/d), which has rooms with shared bath and a cheap breakfast; and **Hotel Argentino** (Mathews 186, tel. 02965/436134, US$7/10 s/d), immediately north of Plaza Centenario.

Upstairs rooms at **Hotel Rivadavia** (Rivadavia 55, tel. 02965/434472, fax 02965/423491, www.cpatagonia.com/rivadavia, hotelriv@infovia.com.ar, US$5 pp, US$8/15 s/d) have better beds and bathrooms, in addition to cable TV, than the more economical downstairs rooms. Breakfast costs about US$1.25 extra.

The fast-aging, 1970s-era **City Hotel** (Rivadavia 254, tel./fax 02965/433951, cityhotelsrl@infovia.com.ar, US$10/13 s/d) is central and remains tidy; the rooms are smallish but bright and cheerful.

For a taste of old Patagonia—perhaps because it's well past its prime—try the landmark **Hotel Touring Club** (Avenida Fontana 240, tel. 02965/433998, htouring@internet.siscotel.com, US$13/17 s/d).

Recently rehabbed **Hotel Galicia** (9 de Julio 214, tel. 02965/433802, www.sipatagonia.com/hotelgalicia,hotelgalicia@arnet.com.ar, US$13/17 s/d) has impressive public areas—note the elegant marble staircase—along with slightly less impressive rooms; still, with cable TV and breakfast, this is one of Trelew's best values.

Hotel Centenario (San Martín 150, tel. 02965/420542, www.hotelcentenario.com.ar, hotelcentenario@infovia.com.ar, US$20/23 s/d) is not quite the value of the Galicia. Four-star in designation, the 90-room **Hotel Libertador** (Rivadavia 31, tel./fax 02965/420220, www.hotellibertadortw.com, hlibertador@infovia.com.ar, US$24–32 s, US$30–38 d) is a decent but far-from-exceptional hostelry with friendly personnel and a buffet breakfast, but rather dull rooms.

Closer to four-star in reality, **Hotel Rayentray** (San Martín 101, tel. 02965/434702, www.cadenarayentray.com.ar, rcvcentral@ar.inter.net, US$30/37 s/d) has amenities including a restaurant, gym, sauna, and swimming pool.

Food

Even those who don't stay at the hotel should consider breakfast or coffee at the **Confitería Touring Club** (Avenida Fontana 240, tel. 02965/433998), to partake of its timeless ambiance. **Sugar** (25 de Mayo 247, tel. 02965/435978) is a sandwich and short-order option.

Girasol (San Martín 188, tel. 02965/437280) is primarily a *parrilla* rather than the Chinese *tenedor libre* it once was.

La Bodeguita (Belgrano 374, tel. 02965/436276) serves good pasta (particularly canneloni) and pizza, with decent service. **Lo de Juan** (Moreno 360, tel. 02965/421534) is a pizzería with a diversity of other dishes as well. **Delikatesse** (Belgrano 409, tel. 02965/430716) serves mainly pasta and pizza, but also wild-game dishes.

About three blocks north of Plaza Independencia, in an elegantly recycled flour mill dating from 1910, **El Viejo Molino** (Avenida Gales 250, tel. 02965/428019) is Trelew's most ambitious new restaurant; its best dishes are variations on the traditional *parrillada,* as well as pastas.

For ice cream, try **Heladería Venecia** (Belgrano 321), **Mares** (25 de Mayo 195), and **Vía Roca** (Belgrano and Roca).

Roger Shop (Moreno 463, tel. 02965/430690), Trelew's only Welsh teahouse, is the place to purchase traditional black cake.

Information

Occupying recycled quarters at the southeast corner of Plaza Independencia, the municipal **Entretur** (Mitre 387, tel. 02965/420139, www.trelewpatagonia.gov.ar, turismo@trelew.gov.ar) is open 8 A.M.–9 P.M. weekdays and 9 A.M.–1 P.M. and 3–8 P.M. weekends. There are also offices at the bus terminal (open daily except Sunday, 10 A.M.–noon and 6–9 P.M.) and airport (for arriving flights only).

For motorists, **ACA** is at Avenida Fontana and San Martín, tel. 02965/435197.

Services

Many visitors stay in Puerto Madryn, but Trelew agencies also operate excursions to destinations like Rawson and Playa Unión, the lower Río Chubut valley's Welsh villages, Punta Tombo, and even Península Valdés.

Several banks have ATMs, including **Banco de la Nación** (Avenida Fontana and 25 de Mayo) and **BanSud** (9 de Julio 320). **Patagonia Grandes Espacios** (Belgrano 330, tel. 02965/435161) changes cash and traveler's checks.

Correo Argentino is at Calle 25 de Mayo and Mitre; the postal code is 9100. **Locutorio del Centro** (25 de Mayo 219), on the north side of Plaza Independencia, has telephone, fax, and Internet services.

Nievemar (Italia 98, tel. 02965/434114), the AmEx representative, also arranges excursions to the Welsh settlements and Punta Tombo.

Lavadero Sarmiento (Sarmiento 363, tel. 02965/434233) washes clothes.

For medical needs, contact the **Hospital Zonal Adolfo Margara** (28 de Julio 160, tel. 02965/427542).

Getting There

Aerolíneas Argentinas/Austral (25 de Mayo 33, tel. 02965/420210) flies once or twice daily to Aeroparque, and occasionally to destinations such as El Calafate, Río Gallegos, and Ushuaia.

LADE (Urquiza 150, tel. 02965/435740) occupies offices in the bus terminal; it flies sporadically to Puerto Madryn, Viedma, and Aeroparque northbound; Esquel, Bariloche, and Neuquén westbound; and Comodoro Rivadavia, Río Gallegos, El Calafate, Río Grande, and Ushuaia southbound.

The **Terminal de Ómnibus** (Urquiza 150, tel. 02965/420121) is six blocks northeast of Plaza Independencia.

Empresa Mar y Valle (tel. 02965/432429) has regular service to Puerto Pirámides, leaving Trelew at 7:45 A.M., with additional summer service; for more detail, see the Puerto Madryn entry. **El Ñandú** (tel. 02965/427499) goes to the coastal town of Camarones Monday and Friday at 8 A.M., and Wednesday at 6 P.M., but departures may be daily in summer.

Typical destinations, fares, and times include Camarones (US$8, three hours), Puerto Pirámides (US$4.50, three hours), Comodoro Rivadavia (US$7–10, five hours), Viedma/Carmen de Patagones (US$11–14, seven hours), Esquel (US$13, nine hours), Neuquén (US$17, 10 hours), Río Gallegos (US$20–23, 17 hours), Bariloche (US$17–27, 13 hours), and Buenos Aires (US$23–33, 21 hours).

Getting Around

Aeropuerto Internacional Marcos A. Zar (RN 3 s/n, tel. 02965/433443) is five kilometers north of town on the east side of the Puerto Madryn highway. Cabs or *remises* cost about US$3.

Línea 28 de Julio (tel. 02965/432429) has hourly buses to Puerto Madryn (US$1.50), and 18 daily to Gaiman (US$.65) and Dolavon (US$1.10) between 7:10 A.M. and 11 P.M. weekdays; on Saturday there are 14 between 7:20 A.M. and 9:40 P.M., and 11 on Sundays and holidays between 7:30 A.M. and 9:30 P.M.

Empresa Rawson goes to Rawson (US$.50) and Playa Unión every 15 minutes, starting at 5:30 A.M.

Car-rental agencies include **Avis** (San Martín 146, tel. 02965/434634) and **Localiza** (Urquiza 310, tel. 02965/435344), both of which also have airport desks. For camper and motor-home rentals, contact the local agent for **Gaibu Motorhome Time** (Salvador Allende 1064, tel.

02965/15-407412, claudiofrasch@hotmail.com, infovaldes@gaibu.com); for more details, see the car-rental entry in the Know Patagonia chapter.

RAWSON AND PLAYA UNIÓN

Rawson (population 22,355) is Chubut's low-profile capital and, in truth, there's not a lot to see in this nondescript bureaucratic outpost. Its suburb of Playa Unión, though, is a minor ecotourism destination for the glossy black-and-white Commerson's dolphins that dart around and under the launches that motor through the waters fronting its long sandy beach.

To see the dolphins (which are also common in other coastal destinations like Puerto Deseado), contact **Toninas Adventure** (tel. 02965/15-666542, toninas_adventure@yahoo.com), which charges about US$8 per person. While waiting, or afterward, consider a seafood lunch at dockside cantinas like **El Marinero** or **Cantina Marcelino** (tel. 02965/496960) at the south end of town.

Playa Unión also has decent accommodations at **Hotel Atlansur** (Costanera Avenida Rawson 339, tel. 02965/15-698735, US$10/13 s/d, breakfast extra) and **Hostería Le Bon** (Rifleros 68, tel. 02965/496638, US$13/17 s/d).

In Rawson, the **Secretaría de Turismo y Areas Protegidas de la Provincia del Chubut** (Avenida 9 de Julio 280, tel. 02965/481113, www.chubutur.gov.ar, chubutur@arnet.com.ar, info@chubutur.gov.ar) has information on the entire province. Playa Unión has its own **Centro de Atención al Turista** (Avenida Rawson and Centenario, tel. 02965/4496887), open 7:30 A.M.–7:30 P.M. daily except Sunday, when hours are 9 A.M.–noon and 4–9 P.M.

Buses from Trelew to Rawson run every 15 minutes; from the Rawson terminal, it's necessary to catch another local bus or taxi to Playa Unión.

GAIMAN AND VICINITY

More than any other lower Chubut valley settlement, Gaiman has sustained, and capitalized on, its Welsh heritage. Traditionally famous for its tourist teahouses, sturdy stone buildings, and community events like the Eisteddfod, it's recently become more of a destination, thanks to the addition of several B&B accommodations, rather than a simple excursion.

Gaiman (population 4,300), 17 kilometers east of Trelew via RN 25, dates from 1874, when Welsh immigrants first harnessed the river to irrigate their fields and orchards. The aboriginal Tehuelche gave it the name Gaiman, meaning "Stony Point."

Sights

The best starting point for a visit is the **Amgueddfa Hanesyddol** (Sarmiento and 28 de Julio, tel. 02965/491007), the regional historical museum in the former train station. Staffed by Welsh and English-speaking volunteers, it holds documents, photographs, and possessions of early immigrants. Hours are 10 A.M.–11:30 P.M. and 3–7 P.M. weekdays except Monday, when it's closed, and 3–7 P.M. weekends; admission costs US$.35.

© WAYNE BERNHARDSON

Welsh teahouses line the streets of Gaiman.

Two blocks to the northwest, Dolavon-bound trains no longer pass through the **Twnnel yr Hen Reilfford,** a 300-meter brick tunnel that's now open to pedestrians and slow-moving vehicles (westbound only). One block west of the tunnel exit, dating from 1899, the **Coleg Camwy** (Bouchard and M.D. Jones) may have been Patagonia's first secondary school. At the east end of 28 de Julio, the **Mynwent** (cemetery) is full of historic headstones, many of them in Welsh.

Parque El Desafío

Though it has nothing to do with Gaiman's Welsh heritage, founder Joaquín Alonso's magnum opus (Avenida Almirante Brown s/n, tel. 02965/491340) is a whimsical labor of love by a man who seems incapable of throwing anything away, turning everyone else's trash into lighthearted *objets d'arts.* In the process, he's created credible mural replicas of works by Florencio Molina Campos, Benito Quinquela Martín, and even Pablo Picasso *(Guernica).* Perhaps the most amusing single item is the *palo borracho* (a pun on the spiny northern Argentine tree *Chorisia speciosa,* colloquially known as "drunken stick" because of its water-swollen trunk); the leaves of this drunken stick, though, are beer and wine bottles.

According to the *Guinness Book of Records,* Alonso's one-hectare property contains 50,000 wine and beer bottles, 30,000 aluminum cans, 25,000 spools of thread, 12,000 bottle caps, and 5,000 plastic bottles, along with automobiles, TVs, refrigerators, washing machines, and 200-liter water tanks. It's easy to amuse yourself for an hour or so just looking at the odds and ends, and even easier if your Spanish is good enough to appreciate the aphorisms on small plaques scattered around the park.

Parque El Desafío is open from dawn to 6 P.M. Admission costs US$2 per adult, US$.80 for children. With every admission, Alonso hands out a small souvenir.

Geoparque Paleontológico Bryn Gwyn

Exposed by early meanderings of the Río Chubut after an earlier subtropical sea evaporated, Bryn Gwyn's sedimentary badlands are an open book of ancient fossils. While the oldest Tertiary beds are too recent for dinosaur bones, there is evidence of giant anteaters and ungu-

Parque El Desafío, Gaiman

lates from the time when this was savanna, as well as marine mammals like seals, dolphins, and whales, plus penguins.

Visitors to the park, eight kilometers south of Gaiman via RP 5, can hike the well-organized trail, which climbs gradually and then steeply up the cliffs, from the *confitería* at the south end. There are at least a dozen excavation sites, with some fossils in the open and others preserved in glass cases.

Affiliated with Trelew's Museo Feruglio, the park charges US$1.40 admission for adults, US$1 for children; groups of more than 20 can arrange guided visits. Hours are 10 A.M.–5 P.M. daily. There's no scheduled transportation, but *remises* from Gaiman are not unreasonable.

Shopping

For crafts, visit the **Paseo Artesanal Crefft Werin** (Avenida Eugenio Tello and Miguel Jones, tel. 02965/491134), opposite Plaza Roca. Try **El Arbol** (Belgrano 259, tel. 02965/15-685582) for chocolates, cheeses, and the like.

Accommodations

Gaiman's quality of accommodations is pretty high, especially as some of the top teahouses have begun to offer B&B-style lodging. Options are still limited, though, so reservations are a good idea.

Alongside the fire station, the flood-prone **Camping Bomberos Voluntarios** (Hipólito Yrigoyen between Libertad and Independencia, US$1 pp) has picnic tables, clean toilets, and hot showers.

Hostería Dyffryn Gwyrdd (Avenida Eugenio Tello 103, tel. 02965/491777, www.dwhosteria.com.ar, infodw@dwhosteria.com.ar, US$10 pp) is not one of those teahouses, but it's a respectable place with private bath and breakfast, though definitely a work in progress. Run by Italo-Argentines, its Welsh name is misleading.

Plas y Coed (M.D. Jones 123, tel. 02965/491133, US$12/20 s/d) is a B&B annex of Gaiman's landmark teahouse. At **Hostería Gwesty Tywi** (Michael D. Jones 342, tel. 02965/491292, www.advance.com.ar/usuarios/gwestywi, gwestywi@infovia.com.ar, US$13/20 s/d with breakfast), the rooms vary and some have shared rather than private baths. There are discounts for stays longer than a few days.

Gaiman's only proper hotel, **Hotel Unelem** (Avenida Eugenio Tello and 9 de Julio, tel. 02965/491663, unelem@argentina.com, US$12–13 d with breakfast) has large rooms with private bath, some with fireplaces.

Te Gwyn (9 de Julio 147, tel. 02965/491009, 02965/491653, tygwyn@cpsarg.com, US$14 pp) is a quality teahouse that's added several stylishly furnished rooms—the beds are handsome, and they've turned antique sewing machines into desks. Some rooms have balconies facing the river—a mixed blessing, as they also face a playground where families with children play until midnight or even later, and the mosquitoes are ferocious. Still, it's a remarkable bargain with breakfast (a reprise of the previous afternoon's tea), and would still be a good value at the old 1:1 exchange rate.

Food

Gaiman may be picturesque, but it's pointless to come here without indulging yourself on cakes, jams, scones, pies, and a bottomless teapot. Since tea starts around 3 P.M., either skip lunch or go later and then skip dinner; for about US$5.50–6 per person, it's a de facto all-you-can-eat. Watch out for tour buses—when one is parked outside, slow service is almost certain.

Gaiman's oldest teahouse is **Plas y Coed** (M.D. Jones 123, tel. 02965/491133), which wins points for exceptional sweets and personalized service. Ivy-covered **Ty Nain** (Hipólito Yrigoyen 283, tel. 02965/491126) is the most stylish of the bunch, but **Ty Gwyn** (9 de Julio 147, tel. 02965/491009) is also appealing. The newest teahouse, **Ty Cymraeg** (Mathews 74, tel. 02965/491010) blends a traditional style with all modern conveniences; its scones, grape jam, and lemon pie are all outstanding.

Across the river, reached by a roundabout route over the bridge at the south end of J.C. Evans, **Ty Caerdydd** (tel. 02965/491053) is an enormous teahouse set among its own irrigated fields, which produce fresh fruits and berries used in its own products, and elaborate flower gardens. Lady Di, as Princess of Wales, was once a celebrity guest.

Overnighters can't gorge themselves on Welsh teas every day. New restaurants include **Pizzería Gustos** (Avenida Eugenio Tello 156, tel. 02965/491453) and **La Vieja Cuadra** (M.D. Jones 418). Gaiman's most ambitious and atmospheric restaurant, **El Angel** (M.D. Jones 257, tel. 02965/491460) is open for dinner Saturdays only; reservations are imperative.

Other Practicalities

In the Casa de Cultura (Belgrano 235, tel. 02965/491571), Gaiman's **Oficina de Informes Turísticos** is open 8 A.M.–3 P.M. weekdays only.

Correo Argentino is at Juan Evans and Hipólito Yrigoyen, just north of the bridge over the river; the postal code is 9105. There's a ***locutorio*** on Avenida Tello between 25 de Mayo and 9 de Julio.

Empresa 28 de Julio's frequent **buses** between Trelew and Dolavon stop on the south side of Plaza Roca.

DOLAVON

Unlike Gaiman, sleepy Dolavon (population 2,481) has never become a tourist town, but the brick buildings along its silent streets display a greater architectural harmony than its larger neighbor—even though, founded in 1919, it's much newer. Its major landmark, dating from 1930, is the **Molino Harinero** (Maipú 61, tel. 02965/492290), a grain mill that's now a hybrid museum and restaurant. *Norias* (waterwheels) in nearby canals still distribute Río Chubut water to the fields and orchards.

From the Trelew terminal, Empresa 28 de Julio runs 10 buses daily to and from Dolavon via Gaiman.

LOS ALTARES

From Trelew, passing Gaiman and Dolavon, paved westbound RN 25 stays atop the steppe for more than 100 kilometers before dropping into the Río Chubut valley at Valle de los Mártires, where the landscape resembles Utah's Bryce Canyon, with striking sandstone hoodoos resisting the ravages of erosion. The road continues through the Valle de las Ruinas, slightly less impressively, from the floodplain hamlet of Los Altares through the Valle Paso de los Indios, where it rejoins the steppe.

At Los Altares, a wide spot on the road with a population of only about 120, there's a municipal campground with decent facilities. The only other accommodations is the **ACA Hostería** (RN 25 Km 321, US$7 pp), a tidy but worn and crumbling facility whose pool table is the town's main source of amusement. Everything works, and there's hot water, but it's on such a shoestring budget that, when a lightbulb fails, they have to go out and buy one. The rooms themselves are spartan and dark.

While the accommodations are no prize, **Parrilla El Vasco** across the highway offers better-than-expected food at reasonable prices.

RESERVA PROVINCIAL PUNTA TOMBO

On the barren shores of the South Atlantic, 110 kilometers southeast of Trelew, nearly a quarter million pairs of Magellanic penguins come ashore every austral spring to nest on only 210 hectares at remote Punta Tombo. Despite its isolation, 50,000 visitors a year find their way down graveled RP 1 and a dusty southeasterly lateral to the continent's largest single penguin colony. In addition to penguins, though, there are impressive numbers of other seabirds, including giant petrels, kelp and dolphin gulls, and king and rock cormorants, and shorebirds including oystercatchers and flightless steamer ducks.

Half-day tours from Trelew (around US$27 pp) arrive at the site around 11 A.M., but the birds are dispersed enough that it rarely seems crowded. Provincial authorities have fenced off most of the nesting grounds and human visitors must stay on marked trails and boardwalks; still, since the penguins themselves do not respect the fences, it's possible to get up-close-and-personal photographs while respecting the birds' distance. Note, though, that penguin beaks can inflict a nasty gash.

© WAYNE BERNHARDSON

Magellanic penguin, Cabo Dos Bahías

Punta Tombo's infrastructure is limited—a visitors center is in the works, but local *estancieros* are disinclined to part with any more property than they already have. The simple *confitería,* while nothing special, has fresh-baked lamb empanadas and clean, modernized toilets.

At the entrance, provincial authorities collect US$5 per person for adult foreigners, US$2 for Argentine residents, and US$1 for Chubut residents. No camping is permitted; if you're driving, penguins have the right-of-way.

While it's also possible for a group to hire a taxi for a day trip to the reserve, renting a car in Trelew or Puerto Madryn would make it possible to follow the scenic desert coastline south past the ghost town of Cabo Raso to the picturesque fishing port of Camarones (see below) and the wildlife reserve of Cabo Dos Bahías, which has both penguins and sea lions. From Camarones it's possible to return to Trelew or Puerto Madryn via paved RN 3.

CAMARONES AND VICINITY

Toward the south end of its namesake bay, the sleepy fishing port of Camarones has only two paved streets, but so many wide gravel ones that it seems as if the town is waiting for something big to happen. Its citizens may wait quite a while, but Camarones is just picturesque enough and close enough to the wildlife reserve at Cabo Dos Bahías, and getting here from Punta Tombo via the desolate Cabo Raso route is interesting enough, that it makes a worthwhile off-the-beaten-road loop for anyone with a vehicle.

Alternatively, there's public transportation via southbound RN 3 from Trelew and eastbound RP 30, a distance of about 250 kilometers. The town holds a **Fiesta Nacional del Salmón** (National Salmon Festival) the second weekend of February.

Reserva Provincial Cabo Dos Bahías

Only 30 kilometers southeast of Camarones, Dos Bahías is one of several similar but not identical reserves in coastal Chubut. Its 12,000-strong colony of Magellanic penguins is smaller than Punta Tombo's, but Dos Bahías' open terrain makes it easier to appreciate the colony's extent.

In addition to penguins, Dos Bahías has a substantial southern sea lion colony on offshore **Isla Moreno,** though they're hard to see from the mainland without binoculars. It also has terrestrial wildlife, including armadillos, foxes, guanacos, and rheas, not to mention many of the same seabirds that characterize Punta Tombo.

Unlike Punta Tombo, it's possible to camp at the beaches en route to Dos Bahías and at the reserve itself, though there are no other services. There is also no scheduled transportation, though it's possible to hire a car with driver in Camarones (try Hotel Viejo Torino). At the reserve's entrance, provincial authorities collect a US$3 admission fee from adult foreigners.

Practicalities

Open all year, the sheltered sites at the waterfront **Camping Camarones** (US$2 per site) have electricity, and the clean bathrooms have hot showers.

Residencial Bahía del Ensueño (Belgrano and 9 de Julio, tel. 0297/496-3007, US$4 pp) is the shoestring choice. Better but still basic, **Hotel Kau-i-keukenk** (Sarmiento and Roca, tel. 0297/496-3004, US$8 pp with breakfast) has a reliable if unexceptional restaurant.

Though it's work in progress, the cheerful **Hotel Viejo Torino** (Brown 100, tel. 0297/496-3003, US$12 pp) represents an effort to create a decent hotel with an attractive seafood and pasta restaurant, which is doing good business—though the food falls short of its aspirations and the well-intentioned service is inexperienced. Rooms are simply but comfortably furnished, with firm beds and up-to-date baths with plentiful hot water.

There are still only three or four **El Ñandú buses** weekly to Trelew (US$8, 3.5 hours), which arrive and leave the same afternoon.

THE WILDLIFE ROUTES OF COASTAL CHUBUT

For Patagonia travelers, arrow-straight RN 3 is the quickest ticket south, but visitors with their own wheels—whether two or four—should explore coastal Chubut's dusty backroads. It's common enough to rent a car for Península Valdés, where a bicycle is less useful because camping is prohibited, but the loop from Rawson south to Punta Tombo and Camarones, returning via RN 3, is an intriguing alternative for automobiles, motorbikes, and bicycles.

Along southbound RP 1, the big attraction is Punta Tombo's penguins, but most visitors see them on a tour. Rather than returning to Puerto Madryn or Trelew, the self-propelled can get an *estanciero*'s view of the thinly settled area by following the dusty, narrow, but smooth gravel road south past desolate Cabo Raso, with its steep gravel beach, and on to picturesque Camarones.

From Camarones, the provincial wildlife reserve at Cabo Dos Bahías makes an ideal excursion before returning to RN 3 via a paved lateral and heading back north—perhaps for tea in Gaiman—or continuing south toward Comodoro Rivadavia. With an early start, this could be a day trip, but an overnight in Camarones is a better option.

COMODORO RIVADAVIA AND VICINITY

Comodoro Rivadavia's motto is "a city with energy," and in that sense Chubut's most southerly city is Houston-by-the-Sea. For nearly a century, ever since drillers seeking water hit a crude gusher instead, it's been the locus of Argentina's petroleum industry; thanks to the former state oil company Yacimientos Petrolíferos Fiscales (YPF), since privatized, it has an outstanding petroleum museum.

On the hills north and south of town, the landscape is a jumble of drilling rigs, petroleum pipelines, storage tanks, and seismic survey lines. Ironically enough, though, Comodoro appears to be leading the way in alternative energy—Cerro Chenque's high-tech windmills, overlooking downtown from the north, are a conspicuous symbol of change.

As the only large coastal city between Trelew and Río Gallegos, Comodoro Rivadavia's services make it a frequent stopover for southbound motorists. Other destinations, though, have more to see and do.

Orientation

Comodoro Rivadavia (population 135,813) is 377 kilometers south of Trelew and 780 kilometers north of Río Gallegos via RN 3. It is 581 kilometers southeast of Esquel via paved RN 26, RP 20, and RN 40.

Hilly Comodoro lacks a central plaza, and most activity takes place within a triangular area formed by the Atlantic shoreline, east-west Avenida San Martín (the main commercial street), and north-south Avenida Alsina and Avenida Chiclana.

Sights

For a panoramic view of the city and Golfo San Jorge's curving coastline, climb the footpath to the summit of **Cerro Chenque,** immediately north of downtown. Nearly barren, prone to landslides that have covered RN 3, it's now the site of **Parque Eólico Antonio Morán,** South America's largest assemblage of windmills.

On the Avenida Rivadavia median strip, a stiff climb from downtown, the **Museo Patagónico Antonio Garcés** (Rivadavia and Chacabuco, tel. 0297/447-7101) is an orderly but uninspiring facility that offers vignettes of Comodoro's development through fossils, aboriginal artifacts, and photographs. Hours are 8 A.M.–7 P.M. weekdays, 3–7 P.M. weekends; admission is free.

Railroads were never the factor in Patagonia, especially southern Patagonia, that they were in the Argentine Pampas. In Comodoro's old railway station, though, the developing **Museo Ferroportuario** (Avenida Rivadavia and 9 de Julio, tel. 0297/447-3330, Interno 345) chronicles the train that hauled wool and produce from the city of Sarmiento, 149 kilometers to the west; intended to reach Lago Buenos Aires, the line never penetrated any farther west, though it also carried crude from nearby oilfields to the port. Museum hours are 8 A.M.–7 P.M. weekdays, 3–7 P.M. weekends; admission is free.

About three kilometers north of downtown, the Universidad Nacional de Patagonia's first-rate **Museo Nacional del Petróleo** (San Lorenzo 250, tel. 0297/455-9558, museodelpetroleo@arnet.com.ar) is a YPF legacy. Occupying the grounds of Comodoro's initial gusher, it presents a professional account of Argentina's oil industry, from the natural and cultural environment to the evolution of petroleum technology and its social and historical consequences. Summer hours are 9 A.M.–1 P.M. and 3–8 P.M. weekdays except Monday, and 3–8 P.M. weekends only; the rest of the year, hours are 8 A.M.–6 P.M. weekdays except Monday and 3–8 P.M. weekends and holidays. Admission costs US$1.50 per person, with senior discounts available. From the Comodoro bus terminal, take the No. 7 Laprida or No. 8 Palazzo bus.

Nearby, on sprawling shoreline grounds, the **Chalet Huergo** (1923) was the residence of YPF administrators and, during the oil-boom years, host to guests like the Shah of Iran. Today, though, it's the centerpiece of a public park and home to special events and exhibitions.

About 15 kilometers north of town, on the west side of RN 3, the **Museo Paleontológico Astra** has two elements: a roadside display of antique drilling gear, and an elaborate exhibit of Patagonian fossils and minerals that is well worth a visit but is rarely open.

Rada Tilly

About 17 kilometers south of Comodoro via RN 3, Rada Tilly is Comodoro's main beach resort and the access point for a sea lion colony at **Punta del Marqués,** where the animals are visible from an overlook. The **Museo Regional** (Combate de Martín García 175, tel. 0297/445-1598) has exhibits on natural history but also ethnography and rock art; it's open 9:30 A.M.–8 P.M. Tuesday–Friday, 4–8 P.M. Saturday, Sunday, and holidays. Admission costs US$.35.

For further information, Rada Tilly's **Dirección de Turismo** (Avenida Brown 117, tel. 0297/445-2423, www.radatilly.gov.ar, turismoradatilly@infovia.com.ar) is open 7:30 A.M.–2:30 P.M. weekdays and 1–7 P.M. weekends and holidays. There are frequent buses from Comodoro's downtown terminal.

Entertainment and Events

A classic of its era, the **Cine Teatro Español** (Avenida San Martín 664, tel. 0297/447-7700) offers recent movies and theater productions. A recent entry is the **Cine Coliseo** (San Martín 570, tel. 0297/444-5500).

Accommodations

Because Comodoro is the largest city in almost a thousand kilometers of highway, hotels can fill up fast and reservations are a good idea in summer.

Comodoro proper has no campgrounds, but Rada Tilly's **Camping Municipal** (Avenida Capitán Moyano s/n, tel. 0297/445-2918, US$1 pp, plus US$1 per tent) has sheltered sites with fire pits and electricity, plus clean toilets and hot showers.

Downtown Comodoro has several run-of-the-mill shoestring choices: **Hospedaje Belgrano** (Belgrano 546, tel. 0297/447-8349, US$5–7 s, US$7–10 d); the drab but well-located **Hotel Español** (9 de Julio 850, tel. 0297/446-0116, US$7–9 pp); and **Hospedaje Cari-Hue** (Belgrano 563, tel. 0297/447-2946, US$10/17 s/d). Breakfast is about US$1 at all of them.

Hostería Rua Marina (Belgrano 738, tel.

0297/446-8777, US$9 pp, US$13/22 s/d) is suitable in a pinch; the higher-end rooms come from its newer sector. **Residencial Comodoro** (España 919, tel. 0297/446-2582, fax 0297/444-0718, US$13/22 s/d) is deservedly the city's most popular budget choice. The aging public areas at **Hotel Azul** (Sarmiento 724, tel./fax 0297/447-4628, US$18/23 s/d) are a misleading introduction to what are, in fact, pretty decent rooms.

The traditionally upscale **Hotel Comodoro** (9 de Julio 770, tel. 0297/447-2300, info@comodorohotel.com.ar, US$25–32 s, US$32–50 d) has fallen behind some newer options.

Really two hotels in one, the **Austral Hotel** (Rivadavia 190, US$33/38 s/d) and the recent addition **Hotel Austral Plaza** (Moreno 725, tel. 0297/447-2200, fax 0297/447-2444, www.australhotel.com.ar, info@australhotel.com.ar, US$55/68 s/d) share a reception, telephones, bar, *confitería,* and restaurant. While the Austral's rooms are comfy enough, if a little small, they are less extravagant than the Plaza's, which cost almost twice as much. Guests at both eat the same buffet breakfast.

Hotel Lucania Palazzo (Moreno 676, tel. 0297/449-9300, www.lucania-palazzo.com, reserva@lucania-palazzo.com, US$57/64 s/d) is a new four-star high-rise with all the amenities.

Food

For breakfast and sandwiches, try the **Café del Sol** (Avenida San Martín and 25 de Mayo).

Comodoro has several quality *parrillas,* including **Bom Bife** (España 789, tel. 0297/446-8412) and **La Rastra** (Rivadavia 348, tel. 0297/446-2140).

Pizzería Giulietta (Belgrano 851, tel. 02965/446-1201) serves fine pasta as well; in the same vein, there's **Cayo Coco** (Rivadavia 102, tel. 0297/447-3033) and **La Cantina** (Belgrano 845).

Peperoni (Rivadavia 481, tel. 0297/446-9683) serves fish and seafood, pastas, and short orders like *milanesa.* **La Barca** (Belgrano 935, tel. 0297/447-3710) is a downtown fish-and-seafood locale, while waterfront **Puerto Cangrejo** (Avenida Costanera s/n, tel. 0297/444-4590) serves large portions of good seafood in the US$6–7 range; the service is good, but the nonsmoking section is small.

Under the direction of a disciple of Porteño celebrity chef Joan Coll, the Hotel Austral Plaza's **Tunet** (Rivadavia 190, tel. 0297/447-2200) has become Comodoro's top restaurant, and even if they bring you the wrong dish—the service isn't quite up to snuff—it's likely to be so good you won't care. Good choices are the seafood risotto and the Ensalada Williams, a mixed salad of smoked salmon, mozzarella, carrots, and mushrooms; most entrées, especially seafood, are in the US$7–10 range.

Chocolate's (San Martín 231) serves Comodoro's best ice cream.

Information and Services

Comodoro's **Dirección de Turismo** (Rivadavia 430, tel. 0297/446-2376, www.comodoro.gov.ar, turismocomodoro@comodoro.gov.ar), is open 8 A.M.–7 P.M. weekdays, 2–7 P.M. weekends in summer; the rest of the year, hours are 8 A.M.–3 P.M. weekdays only. It also has quarters at the bus terminal, open 8 A.M.–10 P.M. daily except weekends, when hours are 9 A.M.–9 P.M.

For motorists, **ACA** is at Dorrego and Alvear, tel. 0297/446-4036.

Banco de la Nación (San Martín 102) is one of several ATMs along the main commercial drag. **Cambio Thaler** (San Martín 272) is the only formal exchange house.

Correo Argentino is at Avenida San Martín and Moreno; the postal code is 9000. **Locutorio Pellegrini** (Pellegrini 930) has phone, fax, and Internet services, but there are several others.

Turismo Ceferino (9 de Julio 880, 1st floor, tel. 0297/447-3805) is the AmEx representative.

The **Chilean consulate** (tel. 0297/446-2414) is at Almirante Brown 456, Oficina 3.

Laverap (Rivadavia 287) does the laundry.

For medical assistance, try the **Hospital Regional** (Hipólito Yrigoyen 950, tel. 0297/444-2287).

Getting There

Comodoro is a minor hub for air and overland transportation in the province.

Aerolíneas Argentinas/Austral (9 de Julio 870, tel. 0297/444-0050) flies two or three times daily to Aeroparque.

Comodoro is the best place to catch a flight on **LADE** (Rivadavia 360, tel. 0297/447-0585), which flies irregularly northbound to Puerto Madryn and Aeroparque; westbound to Río Mayo, Esquel, El Maitén, El Bolsón, Bariloche, and Neuquén; and southbound to Puerto Deseado, Gobernador Gregores, San Julián, El Calafate, Río Gallegos, Río Grande, and Ushuaia.

Comodoro's **Terminal de Omnibus Teniente General Angel Solari** (Pellegrini 730, tel. 0297/446-7305) has regional, long-distance, and limited international service (to Coyhaique, Chile).

Buses to Coyhaique (US$30, nine hours) often run full, so reservations are essential. **Giobbi** (tel. 0297/447-4841) departs at 1 A.M. Mondays and Fridays for Coyhaique, while **Turibús** (tel. 0297/446-0058) goes Tuesday and Saturday at 8 A.M. Schedules can vary, however.

Other sample destinations, fares, and times include Caleta Olivia (US$2.50, one hour), San Julián (US$8, 5.5 hours), Trelew (US$7–10, five hours), Puerto Deseado (US$7, four hours), Puerto Madryn (US$8–11, six hours), Los Antiguos (US$11, six hours), Esquel (US$13, eight hours), Río Gallegos (US$15, 10 hours), Bariloche (US$22, 14 hours), and Buenos Aires (US$32, 25 hours).

Getting Around

From the downtown bus terminal, the No. 8 Patagonia Argentina (Directo Palazzo) bus goes directly to **Aeropuerto General Mosconi** (RN 3, tel. 0297/454-8093), which is nine kilometers north of town.

Car-rental agencies include **Localiza** (Rivadavia 535, tel. 0297/446- 3526) and **Dubrovnik** (Moreno 941, tel./fax 0297/444-1844).

VICINITY OF COMODORO RIVADAVIA

In the distances of sprawling southern Patagonia, "vicinity" is a relative term, but westbound RN 26 and RP 20 can merit a detour.

Sarmiento

In what was once Tehuelche territory, 149 kilometers west of Comodoro Rivadavia, Sarmiento (population 8,022) is an oil town and farming service center. It sits between two large lakes, Lago Musters and Lago Colhué Huapi, part of whose waters flow eastward via a pipeline to relieve the thirst of arid Comodoro Rivadavia.

While uninteresting in its own right, Sarmiento is the gateway to impressive petrified forests a short distance south, while westbound RP 20 to Río Mayo runs through colorful badlands.

Sarmiento is an oil town, and the best accommodations fill up fast. In town, the best is **Hotel Ismar** (Patagonia 248, tel. 0297/489-3293, US$9 d with shared bath, US$9/13 s/d with private bath), though the management's a little brusque and they'd do well to oil the hinges.

Ten kilometers west of town via RP 20, just over the Río Senguer bridge, **Hostería Labrador** (tel. 0297/489-3329, agna@coopsar.com.ar, US$22 pp) is a working farm that also offers accommodations and breakfast that include their own fresh fruit, chocolates, and other regional products. The owners speak English and Dutch as well as Spanish.

There's no elaborate food in Sarmiento, but **Heidy's** (Perito Moreno 600, tel. 0297/489-8308) serves large portions of pretty good ravioli at low prices, and an excellent flan for dessert.

Sarmiento's hard-working **Dirección Municipal de Turismo** (Avenida Regimiento de Infantería 25 and Pietrobelli, tel. 0297/489-8220, turismo@coopsar.com.ar) keeps long hours.

There are three **ETAP buses** to and from Comodoro, and others to Río Mayo and Esquel as well.

Reserva Provincial Bosque Petrificado José Ormachea

Thirty kilometers south of Sarmiento, fossil stumps, trunks, and chips of wood and bark litter the polychrome shale-and-sandstone landscape of the José Ormachea petrified forest. Here, 75 million years ago, a two-tier tropical to subtropical forest covered what is now a brilliantly colored desert. Probably uprooted by hurricanes, then buried by ash blown westward as volcanism and tectonic uplift built the Andes, the fallen trees petrified as ensuing climatic change turned

© WAYNE BERNHARDSON

Fossil logs lie scattered across the badlands of the Bosque Petrificado José Ormachea.

the densely vegetated fluvial landscape into a desert. The petrified trees, often exceeding a meter in diameter, may have reached 100 meters in height.

From the park visitors center, there's a stunningly scenic two-kilometer nature trail that passes through the contemporary moonscape that was once the forest. It's best when the slanting afternoon sun brings out the hues of Cerro Colorado, to the southeast, but worthwhile at any time. The provincial park system is considering opening supervised road tours (with their vehicles only) to visit presently inaccessible parts of the park. Souvenir taking is absolutely prohibited.

At the park entrance, reached by a gravel road from Sarmiento, rangers collect a US$5-per-person admission charge and provide a guided tour of the small museum; there's also a covered shelter for picnics. This is a common day tour from Comodoro, but it's also possible to hire a *remise* from Sarmiento. Hours are 8 A.M.–8 P.M. daily October–March, 9 A.M.–6:30 P.M. the rest of the year.

Coastal Santa Cruz Province

CALETA OLIVIA

South of Comodoro Rivadavia, entering Santa Cruz province, there's heavy truck traffic and plenty of reckless driving on winding RN 3, before arriving at the forlorn oil port of Caleta Olivia. Caleta (population 36,323), 79 kilometers south of Comodoro, is a hub for westbound traffic to Lago Buenos Aires, Los Antiguos, and the Chilean border. It is 346 kilometers north of Puerto San Julián, the next major stop on RN 3, but only 216 kilometers northwest of Puerto Deseado, an underrated wildlife destination.

The city's only conspicuous attraction, dominating a downtown traffic circle that marks the center of town, is the **Monumento al Obrero Petrolero** (1969), popularly known as "El Gorosito." Facing north, Pablo Daniel Sánchez's 10-meter sculpture of a shirtless oil worker turning an oil valve symbolizes thinly peopled Patagonia's contribution to (or exploitation by) Argentina's populous heartland.

Accommodations and Food

Open all year, the seaside **Balneario Municipal** (Brown and Guttero, tel. 0297/485-0976, US$1 pp, US$2 for a family) has clean toilets and hot showers.

Hotel Capri (José Hernández 1145, tel. 0297/485-1132, US$3.50–5 pp) has rooms with shared bath or private bath; breakfast is US$1 extra. **Posada Don David** (Hipólito Yrigoyen 2385, tel. 0297/485-7661, US$6–7 s, US$9–12 d) has similar offerings.

Hospedaje Rodas (Matheu 12, tel. 0297/485-1880, US$5 pp) offers good value with private bath. **Hotel Robert** (Avenida San Martín 2151, tel. 0297/485-1452, hrobert@mcolivia.com.ar, US$13–17 s, US$23–26 d) passes for a top hotel here, and its restaurant, **La Rosa,** comes recommended.

Pizzería Variedades (Independencia 52, tel. 0297/485-2653) also has a wide variety of takeaway empanadas. Down the block, **El Puerto** (Avenida Independencia 1060, tel. 0297/485-1313) is a good option, especially for seafood.

Heladería Centro (Independencia 1175) has fine ice cream.

Information and Services

The municipal **Centro de Informes** (Avenida San Martín and Güemes, tel. 0297/485-0988) is open 8 A.M.–9 P.M. in summer, 8 A.M.–5 P.M. the rest of the year.

There are several **ATMs** along Avenida San Martín.

Correo Argentino is at Hipólito Yrigoyen 2194. **Telefonía Caleta** (Avenida Independencia 1147) has long-distance services.

Getting There

Caleta's **Terminal de Ómnibus** (Avenida Tierra del Fuego and Humberto Beguín) is some 15 blocks northwest of the monument. There are north- and southbound services along RN 3, but also westbound connections from Comodoro Rivadavia to Los Antiguos and Chile Chico via paved RP 43.

Typical fares include Comodoro Rivadavia (US$2.50, one hour), Puerto Deseado (US$6, 3.5 hours), Río Gallegos (US$12, eight hours), Los Antiguos (US$10, five hours), and Buenos Aires (US$35, 26 hours).

PUERTO DESEADO AND VICINITY

Bypassed by rerouted RN 3—but not by nature or history—Puerto Deseado is one of Patagonia's hidden, vastly underrated pleasures. Visited by Magellan, originally settled by Spanish whalers, explored by Darwin in 1833, and resettled half a century later, it hasn't lost its 19th-century pioneer ambiance. In recent years, it's become a homeport for the booming South Atlantic shrimp fishery—some businesses have signs in Spanish, English, and Russian. In an area that Francisco P. Moreno called "the most picturesque place on the eastern Patagonian coast," though, the star attraction is the Ría Deseado, where strong tides rush dozens of kilometers up the estuary to create a wildlife-rich zone that's the focus of a growing ecotourism sector.

Orientation

On the north shore of the Ría Deseado, Puerto Deseado (population 10,252) is 216 kilometers southeast of Caleta Olivia and 295 kilometers from Comodoro Rivadavia via RN 3 and paved RN 281. It is, however, 125 kilometers from the RN 3 junction.

Compact Deseado is a walker's town, with most sights and services on and around the waterfront and Avenida San Martín.

Sights

For a small town, Deseado has plenty to see; the big draw is the **Reserva Provincial Ría Deseado** (see the separate entry below). The town's various historical monuments, though, all have good stories behind them.

By the late 19th century, Deseado seem destined to become a railroad town, as authorities planned a northwesterly line for freight and passengers to Bariloche. Service never progressed beyond Las Heras, 283 kilometers to the northwest; it closed in 1977, leaving the stately **Estación del Ferrocarril Patagónico** (Avenida Oneto s/n) as an empty shell that's slowly undergoing restoration for municipal offices.

Several historic monuments date from this era, most notably the railroad's **Vagón Histórico** (1898), a historical railcar placed in a small plaza at San Martín and Almirante Brown. To the west, immediately across the street, **Banco de la Nación** has preserved its classic lava-block style; unfortunately, the supermarket that occupies the former **Compañía Argentina del Sud** (1919), immediately north, has concealed its vintage features with hideous painted signs on all sides of the building—for no reason whatsoever, as they have no competition in town (perhaps the people who stood up for the Vagón Histórico will make this their next cause). One block west, dating from 1915, stands the **Sociedad Española.**

Along the waterfront, the **Museo Regional Mario Brozoski** (Brown and Colón, tel. 0297/487-0673) holds artifacts from the English corvette *Swift,* sunk nearby in 1770 and only located in 1982. Hours are 8 A.M.–5 P.M. weekdays. Several kilometers northeast of town,

abandoned railroad station at Puerto Deseado

The architecture at Puerto Deseado resembles that of the Great Plains.

Balneario Las Piletas is a volcanic beach area where retreating tides leave shallow pools warm enough for swimming, at least in summer.

At the north end of Almirante Zar, after passing beneath a railroad bridge, the road leads five kilometers into the isolated **Cañadon Quitapeña,** offering excellent camping sites (no services). Ten kilometers west of town, a southbound lateral off RN 281 leads to the **Gruta de Lourdes,** a secluded pilgrimage site where the faithful have left devotional plaques (it might be sacrilegious to say this would be a good rock-climbing area, but that would be no less respectful than spray-painting the rocks themselves already is). Rare rainstorms can produce ephemeral waterfalls here.

Reserva Natural Ría Deseado

One of coastal Patagonia's primo wildlife sites, the Ría Deseado differs from a typical estuary in that it submerges a long, narrow valley that, in the past, probably carried a much greater volume of fresh water. As the fresh-water flow diminishes, seawater penetrates farther and farther inland, creating new islands and other fauna-rich habitats. Offshore islands also form part of the reserve.

Several local operators organize wildlife-watching excursions in and around the Ría, to locations including the Magellanic penguin colony at **Isla Chaffers** and cliffside colonies of rock cormorants *(Phalacrocorax magellanicus)* and grey or red-legged cormorants *(Phalacrocorax gaimardi)* at **Banca Cormorán,** where deep water permits close approaches to the nests. On any excursion, swiftly swimming *toninas overas* (*Cephalorhynchus commersonii,* Commerson's dolphin) breach and dive around and under the outboard launches; in mating season, they leap completely out of the water.

At **Isla de los Pingüinos,** 30 kilometers offshore, there are breeding elephant seals and the northernmost colonies of the tireless rockhopper penguin *(Eudyptes crestatus),* which braves crashing waves to bound up steep stone faces to get to its nesting sites. Some operators also follow Darwin's route up the *ría* where, wrote the great naturalist, "I do not think I ever saw a spot which appeared more secluded from the rest of the world, than this rocky crevice in the wild plain."

Three Deseado operators organize excursions for the increasing number of Argentine and foreign visitors. Ricardo Pérez of **Darwin Expediciones** (Avenida España s/n, tel. 0297/15-624-7554,

DEATH RODE THE RAILS

The handsome wooden railcar that now stands at the corner of San Martín and Almirante Brown is more than an object of train-spotter nostalgia. During the Santa Cruz Anarchist rebellion of 1921 (a struggle dramatized in Osvaldo Bayer's film *La Patagonia Rebelde*), it was the mobile command center for Colonel Héctor Benigno Varela, who led government forces against striking farm workers throughout the province. At Jaramillo station, near the present-day junction of RN 281 and RN 3, Varela himself executed gaucho insurgent José Font (popularly known as "Facón Grande" or "Big Knife") under false pretenses (fittingly, Varela died from a bomb and bullets by German Anarchist Kurt Gustav Wilckens in Buenos Aires in 1923).

As a symbol of military brutality in Santa Cruz—in total, some 1,500 people died at the hands of Varela's forces—the car is an enduring monument. Nearly six decades later, in a December 1980 demonstration of defiance against Argentina's fiercest dictatorship ever, Deseado residents encircled the historic railcar with 40 private automobiles to prevent its removal by a truck. Not only did they challenge armed authority—in a town with a tank regiment, yet—but the demonstrators boldly signed their names and ID-card numbers in a petition to the province's military governor. Astonishingly, under pressure, the de facto government backed down.

www.darwin-expeditions.com, info@darwin-expeditions.com) has extensive experience here, and also does sea kayaking. Half-day trips to Isla Chaffers cost only about US$20 per person; full-day trips, following Darwin's route up the Deseado estuary, costs US$80. A full-day excursion to the rockhopper colony at offshore Isla de los Pingüinos runs about US$90 per person, with a four-passenger minimum.

Turismo Aventura Los Vikingos (Estrada 1275, tel. 0297/487-0020, tel. 0297/15-624-4283) also organizes a diversity of itineraries, and goes farther afield to destinations like the petrified araucaria forest at Monumento Natural Bosque Petrificado. A new entrant is **Kren Excursiones Náuticas** (Pueyrredón 238, tel. 0297/15-621-0875, www.krenturismo.com, krenturismo@hotmail.com).

Entertainment

Deseado is no nightlife mecca, but for drinks there's the bar at **Hotel Los Acantilados** (España and Pueyrredón), which has views across the *ría*. The **Jackaroe Boliche** (Moreno 633) is a dance club.

Accommodations and Food

Open all year, but windy and exposed, **Camping Refugio de la Ría** (Avenida Marcelo Lotufo s/n, tel. 0297/15-625-2980) charges US$2.50 per site, and also has claustrophobic trailers for US$2.50 per person. At the western approach to town, **Camping Cañadón Giménez** (US$2 per tent) is more protected.

There are several shoestring options: **Hotel Colon** (Brown and Ameghino, tel. 0297/487-0522, US$8/13 s/d); **Residencial Sur** (Ameghino 1640, tel. 0297/487-0522, US$8/13 s/d); and **Hotel Oneto** (Doctor Fernández and Oneto, tel. 0297/487-0455, US$5.50 pp with shared bath, US$11/15 s/d with private bath).

Hotel Chaffers (San Martín and Moreno, tel. 0297/487-2246 or 0297/487-2168, US$17/24 s/d) is a substantial upgrade. At **Hotel los Acantilados** (España and Pueyrredón, tel. 0297/487-2167, acantour@puertodeseado.com.ar, US$13–20 s, US$18–26 d), downstairs budget rooms come with small but serviceable baths; the upstairs rooms are better furnished and have sea views, but the baths are equally small and lack tubs. Its bar/*confitería,* with high ceilings and sea vistas, is the best place in town for a drink.

Dining options are limited, but good enough at places like **Pizzería La Balsa** (12 de Octubre 641, tel. 0297/487-1275), **Kokomos Pizza** (San Martín and Sarmiento, tel. 0297/487-2134), and the *parrilla* **El Pingüino** (Piedrabuena 958, tel. 0297/487-0373). Both **Viejo Marino** (Pueyrredón

224, tel. 0297/487-0509) and **Puerto Cristal** (España 1698, tel. 0297/487-0387) have decent seafood, but the intangibles are lacking.

Information and Services

Deseado's **Dirección Municipal de Turismo** (Avenida San Martín 1525, tel. 0297/487-0220, turismo@pdeseado.com.ar) is open 8 A.M.–9 P.M. daily in summer, 9 A.M.–4 P.M. daily the rest of the year. From December through Semana Santa, there is also an information table within the Vagón Histórico (San Martín and Almirante Brown), the city's historic rail car (see above for more detail); hours are 10 A.M.–9 P.M. daily.

Banco de la Nación (San Martín 1001) and **Banco de Santa Cruz** (San Martín 1056) have ATMs.

Correo Argentino is at San Martín 1075; the postal code is 9050. **Telefonía Deseado** is at Almirante Brown 544. **TPP** (San Martín 1259) has slow Internet connections.

For medical services, try the **Hospital Distrital** (Brown and Colón, tel. 0297/487-0200).

Getting There and Around

Deseado has limited public transportation options, both by air and land. The government air service **LADE** (tel. 0297/487-1204) has its offices at the **Terminal de Ómnibus** (Sargento Cabral 1302), about 10 blocks northeast of downtown. The only flights are to and from Comodoro Rivadavia, usually Mondays and Fridays; cabs and *remises* are the only options to the airport, which is about six kilometers from town.

There are five buses daily to Caleta Olivia (US$6, 3.5 hours) and Comodoro Rivadavia (US$8, 4.5 hours), three with **Transporte La Unión** (tel. 0297/15-592-8598) and two with **Sportman** (tel. 0297/487-0013).

MONUMENTO NATURAL BOSQUES PETRIFICADOS

One of RN 3's most desolate stretches is the 350 kilometers between Caleta Olivia and Puerto San Julián, but just north of the midway point there's an incomparable detour to this 13,700-hectare desert badland, scattered with fossil tree trunks. In Jurassic times, long before the Andes rose in the west, this was a humid region of coniferous *Proaraucaria* woodlands before catastrophic volcanic eruptions flattened the forests and covered them with ash. In the 130 million years since, water and wind have eroded the ash layers and left the petrified trunks strewn on the surface.

Measuring up to three meters in diameter and 35 meters in length, *Proaraucaria* was a forerunner of the contemporary araucaria of the Andes. Until 1954, when the area became a natural monument (meriting Argentina's highest possible level of protection), the best and biggest specimens were regularly looted. Proposed additions would increase the protected area to 60,000 hectares.

Solitary Bosques Petrificados, 50 kilometers west of RN 3 via graveled RP 49, gets about 3,500 visitors per year, mostly in summer. In addition to its petrified forests, it has typical desert steppe vegetation and wildlife like guanacos and rheas. It has no water, and there is no public transportation, but tour operators in Río Deseado will organize excursions to the site. For camping, try Estancia La Paloma, midway between RN 3 and the forest; in the past, authorities have permitted camping near the ranger station.

For more information, contact the APN office in Caleta Olivia (Hipólito Irigoyen 2044, tel. 0297/485-1000, bosquespetrificados@apn.gov.ar).

PUERTO SAN JULIÁN AND VICINITY

Possibly coastal Patagonia's single most historical settlement, windswept Puerto San Julián was the place where Magellan's crew wintered in 1520, en route to the first circumnavigation of the globe. Both Magellan and Sir Francis Drake, half a century later, faced mutinies that they put down ruthlessly, while Antonio de Viedma founded a short-lived Spanish colony at nearby Floridablanca—southern Patagonia's first European settlement—in 1780. Darwin, who found the countryside here "more sterile" than Deseado, uncovered a fossil specimen of the llama-like *Macrauchenia patachonica,* with an elephantine trunk.

In the 1890s, British settlers from the Falkland

Islands and Scotland finally established a permanent presence in the area, with the powerful San Julián Sheep Farming Company. Even in the late 1930s, according to John Locke Blake, "English was spoken freely round town," and the Company's extensive holdings—175,000 hectares of pastureland—dominated economic life into the 1960s. Today the town is a minor ecotourism destination, thanks to the presence of dolphins and penguins, and a common stopover as the largest town between Caleta Olivia and Río Gallegos.

Orientation

San Julián (population 6,152) is 351 kilometers south of Caleta Olivia and 355 kilometers north of the provincial capital of Río Gallegos via RN 3. Avenida San Martín, the main thoroughfare, is an extension of the eastward lateral than connects the town with the highway.

Sights and Entertainment

In the bay just north of town, **Isla Cormorán** has a substantial Magellanic penguin colony; there's a king cormorant colony nearby at the sardonically named **Isla Justicia,** the site where Magellan suppressed a mutiny by decapitating one rebel, quartering another, and leaving two others to starve. With its office in a salvage hulk, **Pinocho Expediciones** (Avenida Costanera and Mitre, tel. 02962/452856, expino@videodata.com.ar) takes visitors on harbor tours (US$6 pp) that also include dolphin-watching, but when the winds are too strong it may not be able to sail.

Occupying an archetypal Patagonian house, San Julián's **Museo Regional y de Arte Marino** (Vieytes and Rivadavia) is so bursting with archaeological and historical artifacts that it may have to move to new quarters. Fortunately enough, it has knowledgeable staff, since the clutter means it's poorly organized; summer hours are 9 A.M.–noon and 4–9 P.M. weekdays, 10 A.M.–1 P.M. and 4–9 P.M. weekends. Even these are inconsistently kept, and winter hours are shorter.

Immediately across from the museum entrance, the memorial **Plazoleta Albino Argüelles** commemorates one of the army's victims in the Anarchist rebellion of 1921. From here, the coastal Avenida Hernán de Magallanes leads north along the coast, past the marked grave of *Beagle* crewman Robert Sholl, who died on the voyage prior to Darwin's. The road continues to the abandoned **Frigorífico Swift,** a mutton freezer that operated from 1912 to 1967; its crumbling shell and pier are suitable subjects for post-industrial photographers.

In a century-old building, atmospheric **Casa Lara** (Avenida San Martín and Ameghino) is the only bar worthy of the name.

Accommodations and Food

The waterfront **Autocamping Municipal** (Avenida Hernán de Magallanes 560, tel. 02962/452806, US$1 pp plus US$1.50 per vehicle) has well-sheltered sites with picnic tables and firepits, clean bathrooms with hot showers, laundry facilities, and even a playground.

Hotel Alamo (RN 3 s/n, tel. 02962/454092, US$9/12 s/d) is a utilitarian motel-style facility at the highway junction. **Hospedaje La Casona** (Avenida Hernando de Magallanes s/n, tel. 02962/452434, miramar@sanjulian.com.ar, US$9/13 s/d with shared bath) is a B&B occupying a recycled waterfront house—the most distinctively Patagonian lodgings in town. It has comfortable beds, spacious and attractive common areas, and a kitchen, with a basic self-serve breakfast.

Government-run hotels have a reputation for shoddy service and maintenance, but the **Hostería Municipal de Turismo** (25 de Mayo 917, tel. 02962/452300, US$13/19 s/d) is an exception. It's not luxurious, but the staff take pride in the place, and the rooms are comfortable and spotless (though the breakfast is forgettable).

Under new management, **Hotel Sada** (Avenida San Martín 1112, tel. 02962/452013, US$12/18 s/d) has 18 rooms with private bath. **Hotel Bahía** (Avenida San Martín 1075, tel. 02962/454028, hbahia@sanjulian.com, US$20–22 s, US$26–29 d) is an attractive new hotel that fills up fast.

Right on the waterfront, the popular **Cantina El Muelle Viejo** (9 de Julio 1106, tel. 02962/453009) has a quick kitchen and attentive service, with fish and seafood at the top of the menu. Try the fresh and tasty *robalo a la maitre'd* (US$4), garnished with garlic, butter, and parsley, and the diverse house salad of lettuce, tomato, green beans, palm hearts, and hard-boiled egg.

Crowded even on weekdays, **La Rural** (Ameghino 811, tel. 02962/454066) is primarily a *parrilla* serving beef and lamb, but has expanded its fish and seafood offerings; there are also fine pastas (particularly *sorrentinos*) from their own factory, outstanding salads, reasonable prices, and excellent service.

La Juliana (Zeballos 1130, tel. 02962/454149) has made good early impressions with relatively expensive home-style cooking. **Popeye** (Moreno 1170, tel. 02962/452045) is the best choice for pizza.

M&M (Avenida San Martín 387) has superb ice cream; there's another branch in El Calafate.

Information and Services

Mid-December–March, there's a municipal information office, open 10 A.M.–10 P.M. daily, in a trailer at the highway junction. On the main avenue median, the municipal **Centro de Informes** (Avenida San Martín s/n, between Moreno and Rivadavia, tel. 02962/452871, Interno 116, centur@videodata.com.ar) is open 7 A.M.–midnight in summer, 7 A.M.–2 P.M. weekdays only the rest of the year.

Banco de Santa Cruz (Avenida San Martín and Moreno) and **Banco de la Nación** (Mitre 101) have ATMs.

Correo Argentino is at Avenida San Martín 155; the postal code is 9310. For telecommunications, try **Cabinas Telefónicas Noé** (Avenida San Martín 1375). **CTK.com** (San Martín and Moreno) provides greatly improved Internet access, but it's also the rowdy home-away-from-home for San Julián's adolescent computer gamers.

Lavandería Arco Iris (Roca 1077) does the washing.

For medical services, try the **Hospital Distrital Miguel Lombardich** (9 de Julio s/n, tel. 02962/452020) or the private **Clínica Austral** (San Martín 979, tel. 02962/452044).

Getting There

LADE (tel. 02962/452137) maintains an office in the Terminal de Ómnibus (Avenida San Martín 1552), with occasional flights to Comodoro Rivadavia, Gobernador Gregores, and Río Gallegos; flights normally leave from the airfield near the highway junction.

On a highway the length of RN 3, somebody has to draw the short straw, and nearly all San Julián buses arrive and leave between midnight and 6 A.M., most of these between 1:30 and 4 A.M. There are several services to Buenos Aires and intermediates, and south to Río Gallegos.

Cerro San Lorenzo (Berutti 970, tel. 02962/452403) goes to Gobernador Gregores (US$9) at 7:30 A.M. Tuesday, Thursday, and Saturday and 11 A.M. Sunday. Return buses from Gregores leave the same days at 6 P.M.

ESTANCIA LA MARÍA

Though it's 150 kilometers northwest of San Julián via graveled RP 25 and RP 77, Estancia La María is beginning to attract visitors to pre-Columbian rock-art sites that resemble the far more famous Cueva de las Manos, in western Santa Cruz. With nearly 90 caves in a dozen valleys and canyons, it's home to an active archaeological research project operated by the Universidad Nacional de La Plata (www.arqueologialamaria.com.ar), which organizes 10-day workshops (US$640).

Open October–April, the *estancia* itself offers accommodations (US$20 pp), camping (US$5 pp), and meals (US$7 pp for lunch or dinner, US$2 pp for breakfast). For details, contact Fernando Behm through Estancia La María (Saavedra 1168, San Julián, tel./fax 02966/452328, tel. 02966/452233 or 02966/15-449827).

COMANDANTE LUIS PIEDRA BUENA

When Darwin and the *Beagle*'s crew ascended the Río Santa Cruz in 1834, the swift current beyond Isla Pavón obliged them to walk the shore and drag their boats on lines—a process that limited their progress to about 10 miles per day. Twenty-five years later, naval explorer Luis Piedra Buena first raised the Argentine flag near where the mostly forgettable town that bears his name now stands; Perito Moreno ascended it part way in 1879, and territorial governor Ramon Lista made the first arduous steamer ascent in 1890, all the way to Lago Argentino and Lago Viedma.

While Piedra Buena itself is nothing to speak of, the agreeably surprising quality of its limited services makes it worth a lunch break or even an overnight before visiting the new Parque Nacional Monte León.

On the Río Santa Cruz's north bank, Piedra Buena (population 4,175) is 127 kilometers south of Puerto San Julián and 235 kilometers north of Río Gallegos via RN 3. About 45 kilometers south of town, westbound RP 9 provides a motorist's or cyclist's shortcut along the Río Santa Cruz valley to El Calafate.

While Piedra Buena itself is nondescript, **Isla Pavón,** reached by a turnoff from the bridge over the Río Santa Cruz about three kilometers south of the highway junction, is a beautiful wooded spot that's popular for fishing; a small museum honors Comandante Piedra Buena's efforts.

Accommodations and Food

On the island, the **Camping Vial Isla Pavón** (tel. 02962/497303, US$2.50 per site) has electricity, clean toilets, and hot showers (which cost US$.50 extra).

Its name lacks attraction and imagination, but the **Hotel Sur Atlantic Oil** (RN 3 Km 2404, tel. 02962/497008, suratlantic@alantec psc.com.ar, US$15 s or d) has spacious, comfortable motel-style rooms alongside its gas station. Popular with southbound travelers, it also has a remarkable restaurant with a diverse menu, and particularly choice pastas (take lunch in the restaurant proper, rather than the utilitarian *confitería*).

On Isla Pavón itself, **Confitería y Hostería Isla Pavón** (tel. 02966/15-638380, US$14/23 s/d) offers 10 attractive rooms, a sauna, and one Jacuzzi-equipped suite. While parts of the grounds can flood at high tide, the hotel itself would be a good value even at the old 1:1 exchange rate, and the restaurant is equally inviting.

Getting There and Around

The **Terminal de Ómnibus** is at Ibáñez Norte 130, in the town proper. There are north- and southbound services along RN 3, but it's also possible to catch buses on the highway.

Itinerarios y Travesias offers a weekly service from Piedra Buena to the El Chaltén sector of Parque Nacional Los Glaciares, at 6 A.M. Thursday (US$26, seven hours). Bicycles cost an extra US$5.

PARQUE NACIONAL MONTE LEÓN

Recently donated to the APN by the Fundación Vida Silvestre and the Patagonia Land Trust—by environmental philanthropists Doug Tompkins and Kris McDivitt—62,000-hectare Monte León's 30-kilometer shoreline and headlands are an ecological wonderland of copious wildlife and uncommon landscapes. Little known and even less visited, this former *estancia* is only Argentina's second coastal national park, after Parque Nacional Tierra del Fuego (other reserves in Río Negro, Chubut, and Santa Cruz are provincial domains).

Flora and Fauna

Monte León's coastline is home to some 60,000 Magellanic penguins, as well as gray and king cormorants, snowy sheathbills, Patagonian crested and steamer ducks, Dominican gulls, and sea lions, while its interior grazes guanacos and rheas and shelters armadillos and *liebres* (Patagonian hares), among other species. The vegetation is primarily grasses and prostrate shrubs associated with the Patagonian steppe. There are also puma and red and grey foxes.

Sights and Activities

Wildlife-watching is, of course, the principal activity, but the landscape itself is something special: Where the tides meet the headlands, the sea has eroded deep caverns. One of these, **La Olla** ("the kettle"), is so called because, seen from the steppe above, it has an almost perfectly circular opening (for safety's sake, do not approach this fenced-off feature too closely).

The coastline itself differs from elsewhere in Patagonia in that it abounds with prominent offshore rocks and stacks. Guano collectors worked one of these, **Isla Monte León,** by string-

© WAYNE BERNHARDSON

In Parque Nacional Monte León, an aerial tramway once allowed workers to move guano from Isla Monte León to the mainland.

ing a still-existing cable tram from the mainland. Exploring both La Olla and the base of Isla Monte León is possible by walking along the beach at low tide, but hikers should be aware of the tide tables to avoid being stranded in a potentially dangerous situation—or worse. It's best to descend about an hour before low tide—ask for times at the visitors center on RN 3. La Olla itself fills with kelp and can be a slog to walk through—take off your shoes and roll up your trousers. Much of the route exposed at low tide is slippery rock, and the tide comes in fast.

Accommodations and Food

At Monte León proper, camping is possible, but there are better accommodations at **Hostería Monte León** (RN 3 Km 2385, tel. 011/4621-4780 in Buenos Aires, www.monteleon-patagonia.com, monteleon@infovia.com.ar, US$150/240 s/d with full board), the former *estancia*'s *casco*, which also arranges excursions to the shoreline.

While donating the *estancia* to the park service through their Patagonia Land Trust, Tompkins and McDivitt have retained about 330 hectares and left management of the *hostería* to former owner Silvia Braun and her Swiss-Argentine husband Juan Kuriger. The *casco* itself is a spacious, high-ceilinged beauty with four guest rooms and a small museum; much of the produce comes from Silvia Braun's organic garden.

At the same time, the managers have turned the former *gallinero* (henhouse) into a cheaper accommodations alternative, and are also rehabbing the *casco* at nearby **Dor Aike** (opposite the park entrance, but four kilometers east of the highway) as a second and cheaper *hostería* with coal-burning fireplaces (now decorative).

Other Practicalities

For information (especially on the state of the road, which is subject to washouts) ask at Hostería Monte León (www.monteleon-patagonia.com), where there are rangers stationed nearby (tel. 02962/498184 in Puerto Santa Cruz, monteleon@apn.gov.ar).

There is no public transportation to Monte León, which is 58 kilometers south of Piedra Buena via paved RN 3 and graveled RP 63, but heavy rains can cause washouts on this route; if so, the gate will be locked.

RÍO GALLEGOS

Travelers often dismiss windy Río Gallegos as merely a port and service center for Anglo-Argentine wool *estancias* and, more recently, the petroleum industry. Dating from 1885, near continental Argentina's southern tip, it has a handful of worthwhile museums, historical landmarks, and other distinctive Magellanic buildings; it's also the gateway to one of the continent's largest penguin colonies and several historic *estancias* that have become guest ranches. It is no longer the main gateway to El Calafate, since construction of the new international airport there, but many overland travelers to or from Punta Arenas (Chile) and Tierra del Fuego still have to spend a night here.

Orientation

Río Gallegos (population 79,072) is 696 kilometers south of Comodoro Rivadavia and 351 kilometers south of Puerto San Julián via RN 3, and 67 kilometers north of the Chilean border post of Monte Aymond; from Monte Aymond, it's another 196 kilometers to Punta Arenas or, alternatively, 571 kilometers to Ushuaia, Tierra del Fuego (including a ferry crossing at Primera Angostura. It is 305 kilometers southeast of El Calafate via paved RP 5.

Most points of interest and services are on and around Avenida Roca, which runs northwest-southeast, and the perpendicular Avenida San Martín. The redeveloped open space along the waterfront, to the northeast, has added a touch of class, but it can't stop the almost incessant winds.

Sights

Opposite Plaza San Martín, dating from 1899, the **Catedral Nuestra Señora de Luján** (Avenida San Martín 755) was the work of the Salesian priest Juan Bernabé, who was also responsible for the cathedrals of Punta Arenas and Ushuaia. Like other pioneer buildings, it reflects the typically Magellanic wood-framed, metal-clad style. Guided tours are available 10 A.M.–3 P.M. daily except Sunday, when hours are 2–6 P.M.

On the plaza's south side, named for a local sculptor, the **Museo de Arte Eduardo Minnicelli** (Maipú 13, tel. 02966/436323, museominnicelli@aike.zzn.com) showcases provincial artists. Hours are 8 A.M.–7 P.M. weekdays except Monday, 3–7 P.M. weekends and holidays. It's closed December 20–February 10.

Three blocks south, the **Museo Provincial Padre Jesús Molina** (Ramón y Cajal 51, tel. 02966/423290, cultura@spse.com.ar) is a comprehensive museum in the Complejo Cultural Santa Cruz, a larger cultural center; its holdings include material on geology, paleontology, natural history, ethnology, and local history, including a good photographic collection. Hours are 10 A.M.–6 P.M. weekdays, 11 A.M.–7 P.M. weekends and holidays.

Appropriately located in a pioneer house that was the residence of Arthur and Victor Fenton, the city's first physicians, the **Museo de los Pioneros** (Elcano and Alberdi, tel. 02966/437763, turismo@riogallegos.gov.ar) does an outstanding job of documenting southern Patagonia's early settlers. English-speaking Scottish-Argentine volunteers greet visitors and explain the details. Hours are 9 A.M.–8 P.M. daily, but in winter it may close as early as 6 P.M. Admission is free.

Entertainment and Shopping

The **Cine Carrera** (Avenida Roca 1012, tel. 02966/420204) shows recent movies.

Artesanías Santacruceñas Yatén (Sarmiento 80, tel. 02966/420026) contains handmade items from throughout the province, some of which are made on the premises. **Rincón Gaucho** (Avenida Roca 619, tel. 02966/420669) specializes in horsegear and the like.

Originally sponsored by *estancieros,* **Artesanías Keokén** (Avenida San Martín 336, tel. 02966/420335) specializes in woolens, but also sells leather goods and food items including preserves and candies.

El Carretón (Piedrabuena 129, tel. 02966/422927) offers homemade products from Estancia Rupai Pacha (see separate entry below).

Accommodations

Traditionally, accommodations prices are high and quality mediocre, but things are improving. Demand is also high, so reservations are a good idea.

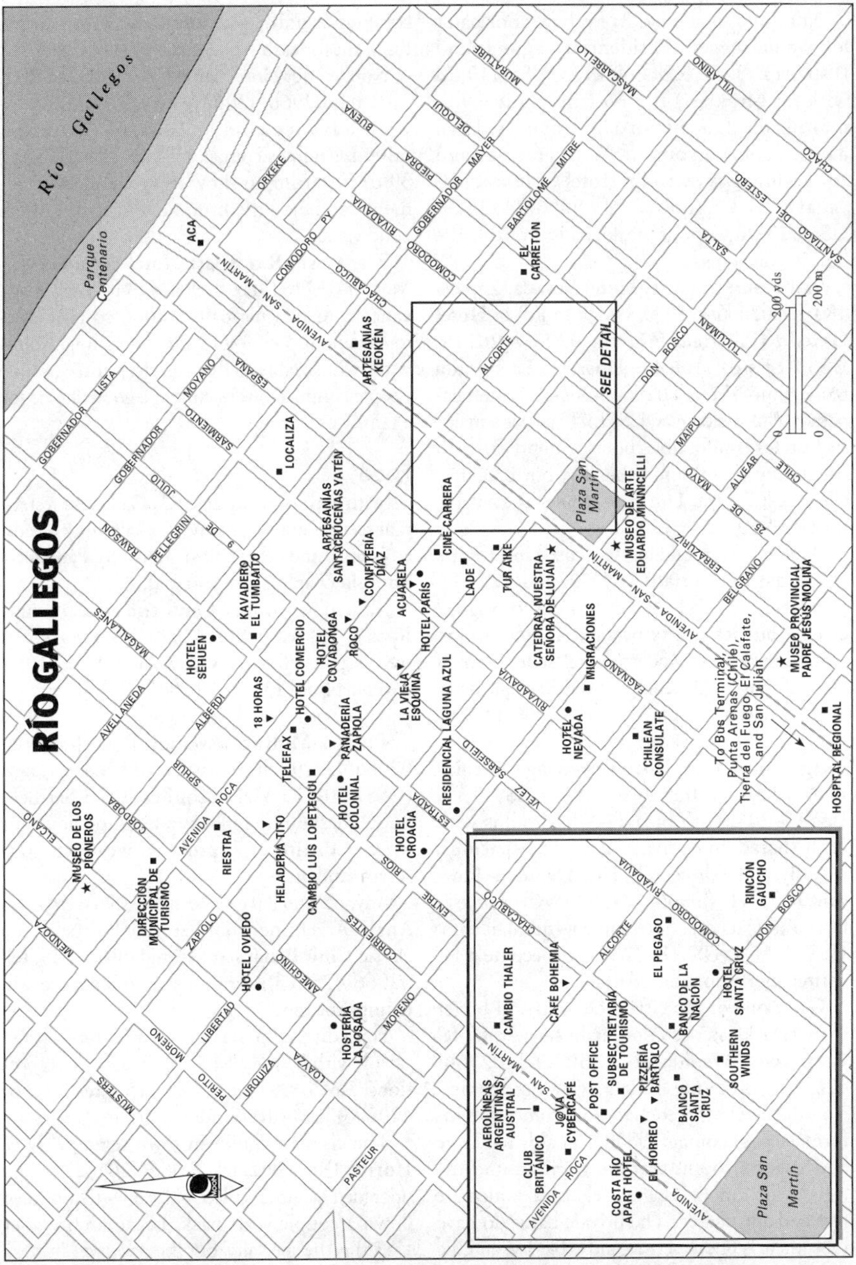
RÍO GALLEGOS
Río Gallegos
Parque Centenario
ACA
EL CARRETÓN
ARTESANÍAS KEOKEN
SEE DETAIL
LOCALIZA
ARTESANÍAS SANTACRUCEÑAS YATEN
CONFITERÍA DÍAZ
CINE CARRERA
Plaza San Martín
MUSEO DE ARTE EDUARDO MINNICELLI
TUR AIKE
CATEDRAL NUESTRA SEÑORA DE LUJÁN
LADE
ACUARELA
HOTEL PARÍS
KAVADERO EL TUMBAITO
HOTEL SEHUEN
18 HORAS
HOTEL COMERCIO
HOTEL COVADONGA
ROCO
LA VIEJA ESQUINA
RESIDENCIAL LAGUNA AZUL
MIGRACIONES
HOTEL NEVADA
CHILEAN CONSULATE
To Bus Terminal, Punta Arenas (Chile), Tierra del Fuego, El Calafate, and San Julián
MUSEO PROVINCIAL PADRE JESÚS MOLINA
HOSPITAL REGIONAL
TELEFAX
PANADERÍA ZAPIOLA
CAMBIO LUIS LOPETEGUI
HOTEL COLONIAL
HELADERÍA TITO
RIESTRA
HOTEL CROACIA
MUSEO DE LOS PIONEROS
DIRECCIÓN MUNICIPAL DE TURISMO
HOTEL OVIEDO
HOSTERÍA LA POSADA
AEROLÍNEAS ARGENTINAS/ AUSTRAL
CLUB BRITÁNICO
J@VA CYBERCAFÉ
COSTA RÍO APART HOTEL
EL HORREO
PIZZERÍA BARTOLO
POST OFFICE
SUBSECRETARÍA DE TURISMO
CAMBIO THALER
CAFÉ BOHEMIA
BANCO SANTA CRUZ
BANCO DE LA NACIÓN
EL PEGASO
HOTEL SANTA CRUZ
SOUTHERN WINDS
RINCÓN GAUCHO
AVENIDA SAN MARTÍN
AVENIDA ROCA
CHACABUCO
ALCORTE
COMODORO RIVADAVIA
DON BOSCO
ORKEKE
BUENA
DELOQUI
MURATURE
MASCARELLO
VILLARINO
CHACO
SANTIAGO DEL ESTERO
SALTA
TUCUMÁN
MAIPÚ
25 DE MAYO
ALVEAR
CHILE
ERRAZURIZ
BELGRANO
FAGNANO
RIVADAVIA
SARSFIELD
VELEZ
ESTRADA
RÍOS
ENTRE
CORRIENTES
AMEGHINO
MORENO
LOAYZA
URQUIZA
PERITO
MORENO
MUSTERS
PASTEUR
LIBERTAD
ZAPIOLA
MENDOZA
ELCANO
CÓRDOBA
SPHUR
ALBERDI
AVELLANEDA
MAGALLANES
RAWSON
PELLEGRINI
9 DE JULIO
GOBERNADOR
SARMIENTO
MOYANO
LISTA
GOBERNADOR
ESPAÑA
COMODORO PY
PIEDRA
GOBERNADOR MAYER
BARTOLOMÉ MITRE
0 200 yds
0 200 m

Not quite so good as its fresh exterior paint job would suggest, **Residencial Laguna Azul** (Estrada 298, tel. 02966/422165, US$7/10 s/d without breakfast) is a no-frills choice with multi-bedded rooms; for a little more, you can have a room to yourself. With gracious and conscientious ownership, **Hotel Colonial** (Rivadavia and Urquiza, tel. 02966/422329, US$9/13 s/d without breakfast) is probably the best in this range.

In the same range, try **Hotel Nevada** (Zapiola 480, tel. 02966/425990, US$9/13 s/d) or **Hotel Oviedo** (Libertad 746, tel. 02966/420118, US$9/13 s/d). Amiable **Hostería La Posada** (Ameghino 331, tel. 02966/436445, hosterialaposada@infovia.com.ar, US$13/17 s/d) is a major step up for comfortable rooms with private bath (including a tub) and cable TV, but breakfast costs US$1 extra. Lunch or dinner is available for US$3.50.

Ill-advised remodeling has cost **Hotel París** (Avenida Roca 1040, tel. 02966/422432, US$10–13 s, US$13–20 d) most of its original charm, but it's still respectable though rough around the edges. Modern motel-style rooms at the back have high ceilings and firm single beds. **Hotel Croacia** (Urquiza 431, tel. 02966/422997, US$15/22 s/d) is a shade better.

Aging but reliable **Hotel Covadonga** (Avenida Roca 1244, tel. 02966/420190, US$9–13 s, US$15–20 d with breakfast) has rooms with both shared and private bath. The spacious, friendly, and well-kept **Hotel Sehuen** (Rawson 160, tel. 02966/425683, www.hotelsehuen.unlugar.com, hotelsehuen@hotmail.com, US$13–16 s, US$18–22 d) has become a favorite; reservations are advisable.

Once one of the city's best, and still better than its lackluster exterior might suggest, **Hotel Comercio** (Avenida Roca 1302, tel. 02966/420209, fax 02966/422172, www.hotelcomercio.informacionrgl.com.ar, hotelcomercio@informacionrgl.com.ar, US$21/33 s/d) has large and spotless rooms that are worn around the edges, with dim lighting; the electrical outlets are few and antiquated. The private baths do have tubs, there is phone service and cable TV, and the public areas including the bar are excellent. The breakfast is only so-so, but there's a 10 percent discount for cash payments.

Nondescript **Hotel Santa Cruz** (Avenida Roca 701, tel. 02966/420601, fax 02966/420603, www.advance.com.ar/usuarios/htlscruz, htlscruz@infovia.com.ar, US$16–29 s, US$23–39 d) is starting to show its age, and management can be a little brusque, but it still offers good value.

The **Costa Río Apart Hotel** (Avenida San Martín 673, tel./fax 02966/423412, www.advance.com.ar/usuarios/fjmontes, costario@infovia.com.ar, US$37/45 s/d) offers huge suites with twin-sized beds that can sleep three or four people comfortably, making it a good choice for a family or a group.

Food

As with accommodations, Río Gallegos's restaurant scene is also improving. For takeaway breads, croissants, and other baked goods, try **Panadería Zapiola** (Zapiola and Estrada).

Misleadingly named **Confitería Díaz** (Avenida Roca 1143, tel. 02966/420203) is a *parrilla* as well as a breakfast and sandwich spot. **18 Horas** (Avenida Roca 1315, tel. 02966/434541) is comparable, with a fixed-price lunch.

Puesto Molino (Avenida Roca 854, tel. 02966/427297) has a particularly fine *fugazzeta* (US$2.50). **La Vieja Esquina** (Vélez Sarsfield 96, tel. 02966/438400) is a backup choice for pizza. **Confitería Zapiola** (Chacabuco 104) serves sandwiches.

Anyone who has ever been, or aspired to be, an Anglo-Argentine wool baron will dine at the classic **Club Británico** (Avenida Roca 935, tel. 02966/425223), though the atmosphere still trumps the food.

For a diverse menu of specialties like salmon ravioli with pesto (US$3.50), in enormous portions, **RoCo** (Avenida Roca 1157, tel. 02966/420203) is worth consideration.

The classiest choice in town remains **El Horreo** (Roca 862, tel. 02966/426462), whose upgraded facilities replace older ones that burned down a couple years back. Local lamb (about US$5) is the specialty, but the *empanada gallega* makes an ideal appetizer.

Acuarela (Avenida Roca 1084, tel. 02966/420249) produces exceptional ice cream, perhaps even better than the traditional favorite **Heladería Tito** (Zapiola and Corrientes, tel. 02966/422008).

Information

One of Argentina's most efficient tourist offices, the **Subsecretaría de Turismo de la Provincia** (Avenida Roca 863, tel. 02966/422702, 02966/438725, www.scruz.gov.ar/turismo, turismosantacruz@speedy.com.ar) is open 9 A.M.–9 P.M. weekdays, 10 A.M.–10 P.M. weekends in the peak summer season; the rest of the year, hours are 9 A.M.–8 P.M. weekdays, 9 A.M.–3 P.M. weekends. It has maps and extensive details on accommodations, excursions, and transportation.

The **Dirección Municipal de Turismo** (Avenida Roca and Córdoba, tel. 02966/436917, turismo@riogallegos.gov.ar) is open 8 A.M.–8 P.M. weekdays only. It also maintains a **Centro de Informes** (tel. 02966/442159) at the bus terminal, open 8 A.M.–9 P.M. weekdays and 10 A.M.–1 P.M. and 4-8 P.M. weekends and holidays.

For motorists, **ACA** is at Orkeke 10, tel. 02966/420477, on the riverfront end of Avenida San Martín.

Services

Cambio Luis Lopetegui (Zapiola 469) and **Cambio Thaler** (Avenida San Martín 484) exchange U.S. dollars, Chilean pesos, and traveler's checks. There are numerous ATMs, such as **Banco Santa Cruz** (Avenida Roca 809) and **Banco de la Nación** (Avenida Roca 799).

Correo Argentino occupies a historic building at Avenida Julio Roca 893; the postal code is 9400. **Telefax** (Avenida Roca 1328), one of many *locutorios,* also has Internet services. **J@va Cybercafé** (Avenida Roca 923, tel. 02966/422775) is the comfiest Internet outlet.

Tur Aike (Zapiola 63, tel. 02966/422436) is one of the city's best established travel agencies.

For visa matters, **Migraciones** (Urquiza 144, tel. 02966/420205) is open 8 A.M.–8 P.M. weekdays only. The **Chilean consulate** (Mariano Moreno 148, tel. 02966/422364) is open 9 A.M.–2 P.M. weekdays only.

Lavadero El Tumbaito (Alberdi 397) can handle the laundry.

For medical attention, try the **Hospital Regional** (José Ingenieros 98, tel. 02966/420025).

Getting There

Río Gallegos is still a hub for southern Patagonian travel, though air services are less important since the opening of El Calafate's airport. Overland, there are westbound connections to El Calafate and Parque Nacional Los Glaciares, as well as the coaltown of Río Turbio, and to Chile's Puerto Natales and Parque Nacional Torres del Paine; and southbound links to Punta Arenas, Chile, and to the Argentine Tierra del Fuego.

Aerolíneas Argentinas/Austral (Avenida San Martín 545, tel. 02966/422020) flies daily to Aeroparque and to Ushuaia.

LADE (Fagnano 53, tel. 02966/422316) flies northbound to San Julián, Comodoro Rivadavia, and Buenos Aires; westbound to Río Turbio, El Calafate, and Gobernador Gregores; and southbound to Río Grande and Ushuaia.

Once a month, Saturday **LAN** flights between Punta Arenas and the Falkland Islands pick up and drop off passengers in Río Gallegos; for details, contact travel agencies.

About two kilometers west of downtown, Río Gallegos's **Terminal de Omnibus** (Charlotte Fairchild s/n, tel. 02966/442159) fronts directly on RN 3 near Avenida Eva Perón. There are provincial, long-distance, and international services (to Chile).

One recent, welcome development is direct service to Río Grande (US$19, eight hours) and Ushuaia (US$27, 12 hours), in Argentine Tierra del Fuego, with **Tecni-Austral** (tel. 02966/442447), daily except Sunday in high season. This avoids the former necessity of traveling to Punta Arenas, Chile (which is still possible but longer and slower).

Between them, **El Pulgarcito** (Avenida Roca 1074, Local 2, tel. 02966/15-623780) and **El Pegaso** (Comodoro Rivadavia 35, Local 3, tel. 02966/426758) alternate almost-daily service to Gobernador Gregores (US$13, 6.5 hours), the quasi-gateway to Parque Nacional Perito Moreno (*not* the famous Moreno Glacier). Departures are 7–8 A.M.

Other typical destinations, fares, and times include San Julián (US$8, 4.5 hours), Río Turbio (US$10, six hours), El Calafate (US$10, four hours), Caleta Olivia (US$13, eight hours), Comodoro Rivadavia (US$15, nine hours), Trelew (US$23, 13 hours), Puerto Madryn (US$25, 14 hours), and Buenos Aires (US$40–55, 36 hours).

Several carriers go to Punta Arenas, Chile (US$9, 5.5 hours), including **El Pingüino** (tel. 02966/442169), **Buses Ghisoni** (tel. 02966/442687), **Magallanes Tour** (tel. 02966/442765), and **Pacheco** (also tel. 02966/442765). El Pingüino and **Bus Sur** (tel. 02966/442687) both go to Puerto Natales, the gateway to Torres del Paine, but it's also possible to bus to the Argentine border town of Río Turbio, where there are frequent shuttles over the line.

Getting Around

Taxis and *remises* (about US$3.50) provide the only public transport to **Aeropuerto Internacional Brigadier General D.A. Parodi,** about five kilometers west of town on RN 3.

From downtown Avenida Roca, city buses Nos. 1 and 12 ("Terminal") go directly to the Terminal de Omnibus, on the southwestern outskirts of town, but cabs are also a reasonable option.

Car-rental agencies include **Localiza** (Sarmiento 237, tel. 02966/424417) and **Riestra** (Avenida San Martín 1504, tel. 02966/421321).

VICINITY OF RÍO GALLEGOS

Thanks to its proximity to historic *estancias* and wildlife sites, most notably the Cabo Vírgenes penguin colony, Río Gallegos is earning a newfound respect even though it's not a major destination in itself. Río Gallegos travel agencies, such as **Tur Aike** (Zapiola 63, tel. 02966/422436), can arrange excursions to outlying attractions.

Returning from Cabo Vírgenes, Chile-bound travelers with their own vehicles can take the RP 51 shortcut to the Monte Aymond border post, but should ask directions before doing so, as it is not always obvious or clearly marked.

Estancia Monte Dinero

At a junction about 15 kilometers south of Río Gallegos, RP 1 turns southeast through an area of rolling pasturelands and, increasingly, gas-and-oil derricks reminding you that Santa Cruz is an energy storehouse. The gravel road is smooth as far as **Estancia Cóndor,** an immaculate settlement that belongs on picture postcards (though neighboring farmers consider that the Benetton empire, which now owns Cóndor, is an indifferent neighbor in what was once a close-knit community).

Beyond Cóndor, the road deteriorates toward **Estancia Monte Dinero,** a pioneering sheep farm that has also opened its doors to tourists. Some 120 kilometers from Río Gallegos, 26,000-hectare Monte Dinero benefits from its proximity to the Cabo Vírgenes penguin colony, but it's also interesting as a ranch that, unlike most others in the area, is subdivided into relatively small paddocks to manage its 19,500 sheep and fragile pastures more intensively. Also unlike other *estancias,* it trains its own contract shearers to use manual rather than electric shears, pays them a premium to do so, and shears the ewes before lambing to ensure a higher lambing rate.

Founded by the Fentons, another pioneer Patagonian family, the **Hostería Monte Dinero** has four downstairs bedrooms, three with private bath, and two with shared bath upstairs, while the *casco*'s former sun porch has been expanded into an attractive and spacious, but not extravagant, bar and dining room. A small museum holds family keepsakes (including a perfect puma skull), and there's also a billiard table (*not* a pool table).

Estancia Monte Dinero (tel./fax 02966/428922, tel./fax 02966/426900, ext. 23, www.montedinero.com.ar, turismo@montedinero.com.ar) is open October–April. Rates are US$45 per person with half-board, US$90 per person with full board and a variety of farm activities that include dog trials, sheep shearing, and hiking.

For nonguests, there's a *día de campo* (US$25 pp) that includes farm activities and lunch. Neither accommodations nor day trips include drinks or the 21 percent IVA. Excursions to Cabo Vírgenes cost about US$30 per person, while horseback riding is available for US$10 per hour.

© WAYNE BERNHARDSON

The coastline at Cabo Vírgenes is one of Argentina's largest penguin reserves.

Reserva Provincial Cabo Vírgenes

Beyond Monte Dinero, the road improves as it approaches Cabo Vírgenes, second only to Punta Tombo among Argentina's Magellanic penguin colonies with about 120,000 breeding pairs. It is also growing rapidly, having increased by a third since 1998.

The abundance of brush here, though, means the birds are less visible than at Dos Bahías, and there's no direct access to the beach. A 1,500-meter nature trail, though, permits close approach to the birds, and there's an interpretive brochure in good English. There's an admission fee of US$2.50 for foreigners, US$1.60 for Argentines, and US$.80 for Santa Cruz residents.

At the northeast corner of the reserve, the Universidad Nacional de la Patagonia is rehabbing the hilltop **Faro Cabo Vírgenes,** the historic Argentine lighthouse, as a museum. Outside the lighthouse, facing the ocean, there remain foxholes dug to repel British commandos who might have landed here during the 1982 Falklands war (the Brits did conduct operations in Argentine Patagonia and Tierra del Fuego, escaping into Chile with collusion from the Pinochet dictatorship, which feared an Argentine attack).

At the so-called **Cementerio Histórico,** the only truly legitimate tomb may be that of Conrado Assinbom, a hermit who lived in the shack beneath the lighthouse. One older cross is almost illegible, and there's no certainty anyone's buried there.

At the reserve's southern edge, visitors can cross the border—technically illegally—for a guided tour of **Faro Punta Dungeness** (1897), the Chilean lighthouse at the end of Chile's narrow latitudinal strip along the Strait of Magellan. When duties permit, Chilean navy personnel show visitors around the facility.

Estancia Monte Dinero has the nearest accommodations, while its sparkling *confitería* **Al Fin y al Cabo** has become the place to stop for lunch and sweets—try the rhubarb cake with *calafate* sauce. While it's fairly expensive, the quality is excellent and the building has a magnificent shoreline view south to Cabo Dungeness.

Interior Santa Cruz Province

EL CALAFATE

Spreading along the south shore of Lago Argentino, a giant glacial trough fed by meltwater from the Campo de Hielo Sur, fast-growing El Calafate is the poster child for Argentina's tourism boom. The gateway to Argentina's Parque Nacional Los Glaciares and its spectacular Moreno Glacier—tourists swamped the town in early 2004, anticipating the glacier's rupture—El Calafate has few points of interest in itself. Still, it has good and improving services, including hotels and restaurants, and it's southwestern Santa Cruz province's transport hub.

Calafate owes its three-pronged growth to 1) a sparkling new international airport that's nearly eliminated the overland route from Río Gallegos for long-distance passengers; 2) the competitive Argentine peso; 3) the fact that current president Néstor Kirchner, a Santa Cruz native, has built a (relatively modest) home here and invited high-profile international figures, such as Brazilian president Luis Inacio da Silva (Lula) and Chilean president Ricardo Lagos, to admire the Moreno Glacier with him.

The boom has had drawbacks, though. As Calafate's population has more than doubled in a decade, real-estate prices have skyrocketed, and lots that went for barely US$1,500 a couple years ago are now fetching six times that. Tourist demand trumps housing for an army of construction workers—some of whom sleep in shipping containers after building hotels and holiday houses during the daytime—and seasonal employees like guides have spent the summer living in tents in the municipal campground. Local property owners prefer to rent their houses and apartments to free-spending tourists.

Orientation

El Calafate (population 6,439) is 320 kilometers northwest of Río Gallegos and 32 kilometers west of northbound RP 40, which leads to the wilder El Chaltén sector of Parque Nacional Los Glaciares and a rugged, rarely used overland route back to Chile. While it's only about 50 or 60 kilometers from Torres del Paine as the crow flies, El Calafate is 215 kilometers from the Cerro Castillo border crossing and about 305 kilometers from Puerto Natales via RN 40, RP 5, and RP 11, including a small additional distance on the Chilean side.

A former stage stop, El Calafate has an elongated city plan that has spread only a few blocks north and south of its main east-west thoroughfare, the pompously named Avenida del Libertador General José de San Martín. Nearly all services and points of interest are close to what is colloquially known as "Avenida Libertador" or simply "San Martín."

Sights

After years of apparent abandonment, the **Museo Regional El Calafate** (Avenida Libertador 575, tel. 02902/491924) has reopened, but it's hard to say that the sparse and poorly presented exhibits on paleontology, natural history, geology, and ethnology were worth the wait. The photographic histories of pioneer families show promise, but it would be nice to have some explanation of the 1920s labor unrest that led to several shooting deaths on the *estancias.* It's open 10 A.M.–5 P.M. weekdays only.

More promising is the **Centro de Interpretación Histórica** (Almirante Brown and Bonarelli, tel. 02902/492799, calafatecentro@cotecal.com.ar), whose sophisticated timeline puts southern Patagonian natural, cultural and historical events in context; it has many photographs, good English translations, and a small but quality library. Hours are 10 A.M.–9 P.M. daily from September to Semana Santa, 10 A.M.–6 P.M. the rest of the year. Admission (US$3 pp) includes *remise* transportation from downtown Calafate.

Nearby, at the north edge of town, municipal authorities have transformed a onetime sewage pond into **Reserva Municipal Laguna Nimez,** a fresh water body now frequented by more than 100 bird species. It's open 8 A.M.–9 P.M. daily; English-speaking biologist Cecilia

Scarafoni leads two-hour bird-watching excursions (US$4 pp) here through her Ecowalks (tel. 02902/493196, ecowalks@cotecal.com.ar). Scheduled walks take place at 9 A.M. and 6 P.M. daily except Sunday, unless there is rain.

Entertainment and Shopping

El Calafate is surprisingly light on nightlife, which consists mostly of dining out and drinking at venues like the **The Grouse** (Avenida del Libertador 351, tel. 02902/491281), a Celtic-style pub that occasionally has live music. The brew pub **Whirra** (Almirante Brown 1391, tel. 02902/492515), on the Laguna Nimez road, also offers *picadas* (bar snacks). On Calafate's western outskirts, the best place for drinks is the **Shackleton Lounge** (Avenida Libertador 3287, tel. 02902/493516), which has lake views.

Downtown Avenida del Libertador is lined with souvenir shops such as **Open Calafate** (Avenida Libertador 996, tel. 02902/491254), which also sells books and maps. For premium homemade chocolates, try **Casa Guerrero** (Avenida Libertador 1246, tel. 02902/491042), or any of several similar locales.

Accommodations

El Calafate has a wide variety of accommodations at generally high standards in each category, ranging from camping to five-star comfort. Its growing number of custom-built hostels, with stylish architecture, often including high ceilings, engaging common areas with stunning views, and even restaurants and bars, are far better the dingy no-frills reputation that the word sometimes implies.

Occupancy rates are at an all-time high, and places that once stayed open January and February only now stay open all year. Unless otherwise indicated, prices below are for high season, usually October–April, but specific dates can vary and, if business is slow, rates can be negotiable. Breakfast is usually (though not always) extra.

Under US$10

At the eastern approach to town, flanking the Arroyo Calafate, the fenced and forested **Camping Municipal** (José Pantín s/n, tel. 02902/492622, campingmunicipal@cotecal.com.ar, US$2 pp) has good common toilets and hot showers, and each site has its own fire pit. Areas on the east side of the creek are for walk-in campers only.

On the grounds of its namesake *hospedaje,* **Camping Jorgito** (Moyano 943, tel. 02902/491323, US$2 pp) is decent enough. The similar **Camping Los Dos Pinos** (9 de Julio 218, tel. 02902/491271, losdospinos@cotecal.com.ar, US$2.50 pp plus US$2 per car) has basic tent sites.

US$10–25

A block south of the bus terminal, the so-so **Albergue Lago Argentino** (Campaña del Desierto 1050, tel. 02902/491423, fax 02902/491139, hostellagoargentino@cotecal.com.ar, US$6 pp) offers hostel-style accommodations. Adolescent boys—not necessarily bad kids, but still adolescents—hang around friendly **Hospedaje Jorgito** (Moyano 943, tel. 02902/491323, US$12–16 d), which has good multi-bedded rooms with shared or private bath. The Chilean-run **Hospedaje Alejandra** (Espora 60, tel. 02902/491328, US$13/17 s/d) is old and a bit dark but otherwise OK.

"Think big" seems the motto at **Calafate Hostel** (Gobernador Moyano 1296, tel. 02902/492450, www.hostelspatagonia.com, calafatehostel@cotecal.com.ar, US$8 pp), which has hostel accommodations with shared bath and balconies, in a stylish new building with vast common areas; it also has better rooms with private bath (US$20/27 s/d).

East of the arroyo, open October–mid-April, the HI affiliate **Hostal del Glaciar Pioneros** (Los Pioneros 251, tel./fax 02902/491243, www.glaciar.com, info@glaciar.com, US$7 pp, US$27/32 s/d) has extensive common spaces, including a large lounge, kitchen space, and laundry facilities. It offers its own excursions to the Moreno glacier. There is also floor space above the restaurant for US$2 per person, as well as large and comfortable but no-frills hotel-style rooms.

Under the same management, with identical prices, the new **Hostal del Glaciar Libertador** (Avenida Libertador 587, tel./fax 02902/491792, www.glaciar.com, info@glaciar.com)

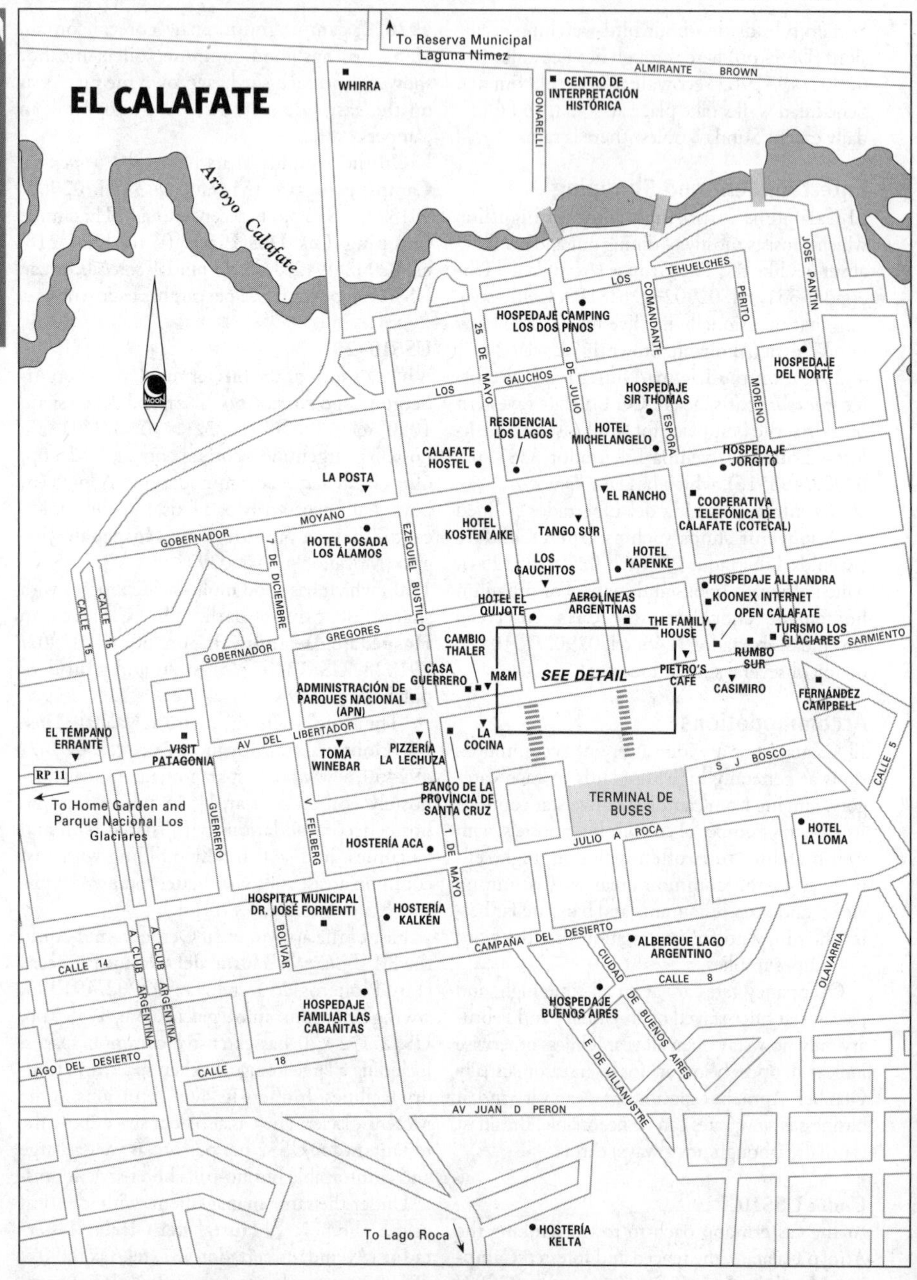
EL CALAFATE
To Reserva Municipal Laguna Nimez
WHIRRA
CENTRO DE INTERPRETACIÓN HISTÓRICA
ALMIRANTE BROWN
BONARELLI
Arroyo Calafate
LOS TEHUELCHES
JOSÉ PANTIN
COMANDANTE
PERITO
HOSPEDAJE CAMPING LOS DOS PINOS
HOSPEDAJE DEL NORTE
25 DE MAYO
9 DE JULIO
LOS GAUCHOS
MORENO
ESPORA
HOSPEDAJE SIR THOMAS
RESIDENCIAL LOS LAGOS
HOTEL MICHELANGELO
HOSPEDAJE JORGITO
CALAFATE HOSTEL
LA POSTA
EL RANCHO
COOPERATIVA TELEFÓNICA DE CALAFATE (COTECAL)
MOYANO
HOTEL KOSTEN AIKE
TANGO SUR
GOBERNADOR
7 DE DICIEMBRE
HOTEL POSADA LOS ÁLAMOS
EZEQUIEL BUSTILLO
LOS GAUCHITOS
HOTEL KAPENKE
HOSPEDAJE ALEJANDRA
KOONEX INTERNET
CALLE 15
HOTEL EL QUIJOTE
AEROLÍNEAS ARGENTINAS
OPEN CALAFATE
GREGORES
THE FAMILY HOUSE
TURISMO LOS GLACIARES
SARMIENTO
GOBERNADOR
CAMBIO THALER
RUMBO SUR
CASA GUERRERO
M&M
SEE DETAIL
PIETRO'S CAFÉ
CASIMIRO
ADMINISTRACIÓN DE PARQUES NACIONAL (APN)
FERNÁNDEZ CAMPBELL
EL TÉMPANO ERRANTE
AV DEL LIBERTADOR
LA COCINA
VISIT PATAGONIA
TOMA WINEBAR
PIZZERÍA LA LECHUZA
CALLE 5
S J BOSCO
RP 11
To Home Garden and Parque Nacional Los Glaciares
GUERRERO
V FEILBERG
BANCO DE LA PROVINCIA DE SANTA CRUZ
TERMINAL DE BUSES
HOTEL LA LOMA
JULIO A ROCA
HOSTERÍA ACA
1 DE MAYO
HOSPITAL MUNICIPAL DR. JOSÉ FORMENTI
HOSTERÍA KALKEN
A CLUB ARGENTINA
BOLÍVAR
CAMPAÑA DEL DESIERTO
ALBERGUE LAGO ARGENTINO
OLAVARRIA
CALLE 14
CIUDAD DE BUENOS AIRES
CALLE 8
HOSPEDAJE FAMILIAR LAS CABAÑITAS
HOSPEDAJE BUENOS AIRES
LAGO DEL DESIERTO
CALLE 18
E DE VILLANUSTRE
AV JUAN D PERON
HOSTERÍA KELTA
To Lago Roca

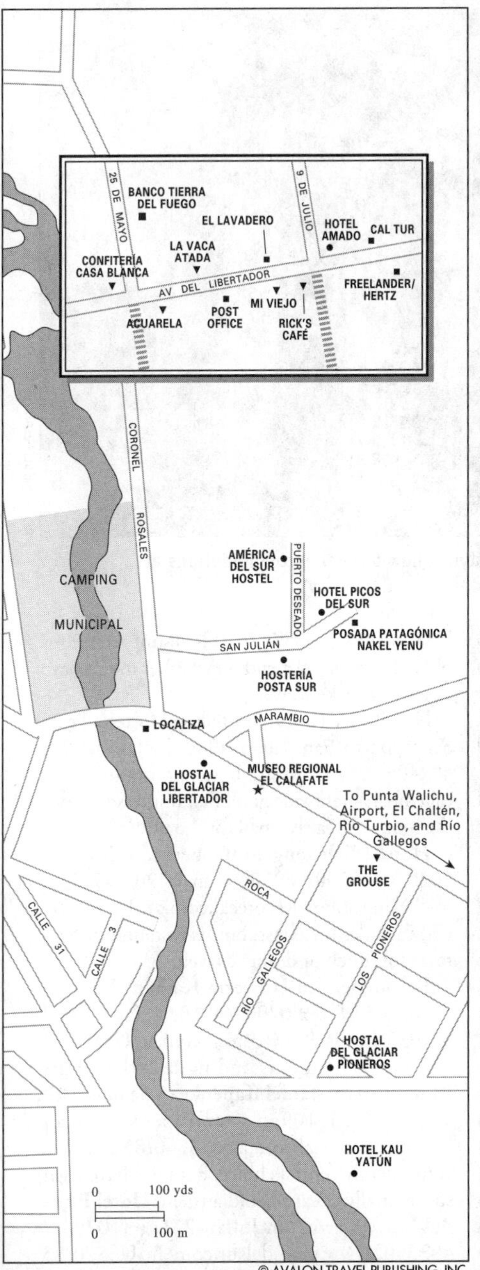

has 22 rooms with private bath; some are four-bed dorms, while others are twins or doubles. Both hostels offer roughly 15 percent discounts for HI members, and 30 percent low-season discounts in October and April (except for Semana Santa).

On the hilltop immediately east of the municipal campground, custom-built **América del Sur Hostel** (Puerto Deseado s/n, tel. 02902/493525, www.americahostel.com.ar, info@americahostel.com.ar, US$9 pp, US$36 d) has friendly management, spectacular common spaces with panoramic views, and free transfers from the bus terminal. Nearby, tidy **Posada Patagónica Nakel Yenu** (San Julián 244, tel. 02902/493711, US$9 pp) is another fine new hostel, but lacks the vibes of América del Sur.

At **Hospedaje del Norte** (Los Gauchos 813, tel. 02902/491117, caltur@cotecal.com.ar, US$13–17 s, US$17–23 d), rates vary for rooms with shared or private bath; breakfast costs US$2 extra.

Just south of the bus terminal is the basic **Hospedaje Buenos Aires** (Ciudad de Buenos Aires 296, tel. 02902/491147, buenosaires@cotecal.com.ar, US$13/23 s/d). **Hospedaje los dos Pinos** (9 de Julio 358, tel./fax 02902/491271, losdospinos@cotecal.com.ar, US$25 d) has plain but spacious and immaculate accommodations with in-room heating.

US$25–50

Toward the west end of town, just beyond the EG3 gas station on Avenida Libertador, **Home Garden** (Guillermo Eike 14, tel./fax 02902/493396, homegardencal@yahoo.com.ar, US$20/30 s/d) has smallish rooms with private bath and breakfast, and an exceptionally friendly family atmosphere.

Hospedaje Familiar Las Cabañitas (Valentín Feilberg 218, tel. 02902/491118, lascabanitas@cotecal.com.ar, US$29 d) offers chalet-style accommodations and perhaps Calafate's most *simpático* management. This is a popular choice, and reservations are advisable; despite the suggestive name, the rooms lack kitchen facilities.

Tidy, well-regarded **Residencial Los Lagos** (25 de Mayo 220, tel. 02902/491170, fax

© WAYNE BERNHARDSON

Hostal del Glaciar Libertador is one of several stylish new budget accommodations at El Calafate.

02902/491347, loslagos@cotecal.com.ar, US$33 d) charges extra for breakfast. Breakfast is also additional at the appealing **Hospedaje Sir Thomas** (Espora 257, tel. 02902/492220, fax 02902/491300, hospedajesirthomas@cotecal.com.ar, US$33/36 s/d).

Rates differ for members (including those of overseas affiliates) and nonmembers at the **Hostería ACA** (Primero de Mayo 50, tel. 02902/491004, fax 02902/491027, robertolugo@cotecal.com.ar, US$33–45 s, US$43–55 d), which has fallen behind other more contemporary places.

Hotel Amado (Avenida Libertador 1072, tel. 02902/491134, familiagomez@cotecal.com.ar, US$24/44 s/d) is central but otherwise so-so; breakfast costs extra. **Hostería Kelta** (F.M. Portoriero 109, tel. 02902/491966, www.kelta.com.ar, kelta@kelta.com.ar, US$43/50 s/d), by contrast, is a handsome, homey new B&B with 11 rooms.

US$50–100

Set back from the street, hillside **Hotel La Loma** (Avenida Roca 849, tel. 02902/491016, www.lalomahotel.com, lalomahotel@cotecal.com.ar, US$38–45 s, US$57–73 d) is an unpretentious place where rates depend on whether rooms have a garden or lake view.

Near the old airfield, the hilltop **Hostería Posta Sur** (Puerto San Julián 490, tel./fax 02902/492406, US$53/58 s/d, hosteriapostasur@cotecal.com.ar) has made good first impressions, but the rooms are fairly small for the price.

Hotel Michelangelo (Gobernador Moyano 1020, tel. 02902/491045, fax 02902/491058, michelangelohotel@cotecal.com.ar, US$46/61 s/d) includes breakfast, but its restaurant draws raves for lunch or dinner as well.

Recommended **Hostería Kalkén** (Valentín Feilberg 119, tel. 02902/491073, fax 02902/491036, hotelkalken@cotecal.com.ar, US$56/63 s/d) includes an outstanding breakfast in its rates. Attractive **Hotel Kapenke** (9 de Julio 112, tel. 02902/491093, www.kapenke.com.ar, kapenke@cotecal.com.ar, US$60/83 s/d) is a conveniently central choice, but rates have risen substantially. Near the old airfield, **Hotel Picos del Sur** (Puerto San Julián 271, tel. 02902/493650, www.picosdelsur.com.ar, US$70/83 s/d) is another recent development.

Over US$100

Its exterior handsomely rehabbed in wood and glass, the pastel rooms at **Hotel El Quijote** (Gregores 1191, tel. 02902/491017, fax 02902/491103, elquijote@cotecal.com.ar, US$85/105 s/d) make it one of El Calafate's most stylish hotels. Rates include breakfast.

When El Calafate was smaller, four-star **Hotel Kau Yatún** (tel. 02902/491259, fax 02902/491260, www.kauyatun.com, kauyatun@cotecal.com.ar, US$112/126 s/d) was part of Estancia 25 de Mayo; the older part was the *casco,* whose suites have a Jacuzzi, fireplace, and other amenities, including a full buffet breakfast. In January only, it offers a nightly string quartet. Note that its business address of Avenida Libertador 1190 is not the same as the property itself, which is east of the arroyo and up the hill from the Albergue del Glaciar.

The 60-room **Hotel Kosten Aike** (Gobernador Moyano 1243, tel. 02902/492424, fax 02902/491538, kostenaike@cotecal.com.ar, US$146 s or d) is an impressive four-star facility with every modern convenience, including gym and spa, modem access, and even handicapped facilities.

In the same range is **Hotel Posada Los Álamos** (Gobernador Moyano 1355, tel. 02902/491144, www.posadalosalamos.com.ar, posada losalamos@cotecal.com.ar, US$153/176 s/d).

Food

El Calafate has several decent *confiterías* for *minutas* (short orders), sandwiches, coffee, and the like. Among them are **Pietro's Café** (Avenida Libertador 1000, tel. 02902/492334); **Confitería Casa Blanca** (Avenida Libertador 1202, tel. 02902/491402); and **Rick's Café** (Avenida Libertador 1105, tel. 02902/492148). **Los Gauchitos** (Gregores 1170, tel. 02902/492298) has the best takeaway empanadas.

Decorated in a Buenos Aires motif, **Tango Sur** (9 de Julio 265, tel. 02902/491550) has pizzas in the US$4.50–7.50 range, with more complex entrées around US$10. Another fine choice is **El Rancho** (Gobernador Moyano and 9 de Julio, tel. 02902/491644), back in action after an unfortunate absence. A breakaway from El Rancho, **Pizzería La Lechuza** (Avenida Libertador and 1° de Mayo, tel. 02902/491610) deserves special mention for its *super cebolla y jamón crudo* (onion and raw ham).

The most imaginative Italian option, though, is **La Cocina** (Avenida Libertador 1245, tel. 02902/491758, where entrées start around US$6. Relocated **El Témpano Errante** (Avenida Libertador 1630, tel. 02902/493723) deserves a detour for its diverse menu and cheerful ambiance.

Simply decorated, appropriately named **The Family House** (Comandante Espora 18, tel. 02902/492156) is a respectable *parrilla* that also serves trout and pasta dishes in the US$4–5-and-up range, with good service as well. **La Vaca Atada** (Avenida Libertador 1176, tel. 02902/491227) is a popular *parrilla* that also has fine soups and pasta, with most entrées in the US$4–7 range. **Mi Viejo** (Avenida Libertador 1111, tel. 02902/491691) is comparable but a bit dearer.

Hotel El Quijote's **Sancho** (25 de Mayo 80, tel. 02902/492442) has become one of the top dining options, with entrées ranging from pasta to lamb in the US$5–8 range and large portions—the half *picada* of appetizers easily feeds four hungry mouths. It also has a credible nonsmoking section.

Even better is **Casimiro** (Avenida Libertador 963, tel. 02902/492590), which would be a good choice almost anywhere in the world; the plate of smoked Patagonian appetizers is exquisite. Other entrées, in the US$5–11 range, are close behind but less unique, though portions are large in pastas, trout, and lamb. It's also a by-the-glass wine bar, with an enormous list of vintages ranging up to US$100 per bottle (truly extravagant by current Argentine standards).

More than its name suggests, the inconspicuous but stylish **Toma Winebar** (Avenida Libertador 1359, tel. 02902/492993) also serves Patagonian specialties in the US$6–10 range. The smoked appetizers are only so-so, but the trout-stuffed chicken breast is exceptional.

Fine in conception but less so in execution, **La Posta** (Bustillo and Moyano, tel. 02902/491144) is the upscale restaurant at Hotel Posada Los Alamos (though it's across the street from the hotel proper); entrées are upwards of US$10 except for pastas, which start around US$5–6. It's big and spacious, but the service can be shaky.

Astonishingly, El Calafate went nearly a decade without a quality ice creamery, but now it has two outstanding ones. **Acuarela** (Avenida Libertador 1177, tel. 02902/491315) and **M&M** (Avenida Libertador 1222, tel. 02902/492422) can aspire toward Buenos Aires's best; for a local treat, try the fresh *calafate* berry flavor at M&M, which is slightly better than that at Acuarela (which nevertheless has many very fine flavors).

Information

At the bus terminal, the **Secretaría de Turismo de la Municipalidad de El Calafate** (Avenida Roca 1004, tel. 02902/491466, fax 02902/491090, www.elcalafate.gov.ar, info@elcalafate.gov.ar) maintains a database of hotels and other services, and has English-speaking personnel, maps, brochures, and a message board. Hours are 8 A.M.–10 P.M. November–March, 8 A.M.–8 P.M. the rest of the year.

The **Administración de Parques Nacionales** (APN, Avenida Libertador 1302, tel. 02902/491755 or 02902/491545, losglaciares@apn.gov.ar) is open 7 A.M.–2 P.M. weekdays only.

There is a useful private website, www.losglaciares.com, that contains considerable information on El Calafate and the surrounding area.

Services

As the gateway to the glaciers, El Calafate has a full complement of services.

Cambio Thaler (Avenida Libertador 1242, tel. 02902/493245) is the only formal exchange house. Both **Banco de la Provincia de Santa Cruz** (Avenida Libertador 1285) and **Banco de Tierra del Fuego** (25 de Mayo 40) have ATMs; the latter is more reliable.

Correo Argentino is at Avenida Libertador 1133; the postal code is 9405.

The **Cooperativa Telefónica de Calafate** (Cotecal, Espora 194) also has the best and cheapest Internet access; there are no collect phone calls, though. **Open Calafate** (Avenida Libertador 996, tel. 02902/491254) provides some competition in both telephone and Internet services, but its connections are slower than Cotecal's. **Koonex Internet** (Comandante Espora 44, tel. 02902/493750), which will let you plug your own machine in, is open 9 A.M.–3 A.M. daily.

El Lavadero (Avenida Libertador 1118, tel. 02902/492182) charges around US$3.50 per laundry load.

The **Hospital Municipal Dr. José Formenti** is at Avenida Roca 1487, tel. 02902/491001, 02902/491173.

Getting There

El Calafate is western Santa Cruz's transport hub, thanks to its sparkling new airport, road connections to Río Gallegos, and improving links north and south along RN 40. The international airport provides direct connections to Buenos Aires and even, in season, to Puerto Natales (Chile).

Aerolíneas Argentinas (9 de Julio 57, tel. 02902/492815) normally flies north to Trelew and Aeroparque, and south to Ushuaia, but sometimes has service to or from Bariloche as well. Almost next door, **Southern Winds** (9 de Julio 69, tel. 02902/491349) flies north to Bariloche and Buenos Aires.

LADE (tel. 02902/491262, ladecalafate@cotecal.com.ar) keeps an office at the bus terminal, Avenida Roca 1004. It flies northbound to Comodoro Rivadavia and Buenos Aires, and southbound to Río Gallegos, Río Grande, and Ushuaia.

November–March, Chilean carrier **Aerovías DAP** flies to Puerto Natales (US$50) twice each weekday. Its representative is **Rumbo Sur** (Avenida Libertador 960, tel. 02902/492155, 02902/491854).

El Calafate's **Terminal de Ómnibus** overlooks the town from its perch at Avenida Roca 1004; for pedestrians, the easiest approach is a staircase from the corner of Avenida Libertador and 9 de Julio. For long-distance connections to most of the rest of the country, it's necessary to backtrack to Río Gallegos.

Interlagos (tel. 02902/491179) and **Taqsa** (tel. 02902/491843) shuttle between El Calafate and the Santa Cruz provincial capital of Río Gallegos (US$10, four hours), where there are northbound connections to Buenos Aires and intermediates, and southbound connections to Punta Arenas (Chile). These buses will also drop passengers at the Río Gallegos airport.

In summer, three carriers connect El Calafate with El Chaltén (US$14, 4.5 hours) in the Fitz Roy sector of Parque Nacional Los Glaciares: **Cal Tur** (tel. 02902/491842), **Chaltén Travel** (tel. 02902/491833), and **Los Glaciares** (tel. 02902/491158). Services generally leave between 7:30–8 A.M., though there are sometimes afternoon buses around 5–6 P.M. Winter services may be only once or twice weekly. Taqsa may add a regular service from Río Gallegos to El Calafate and on to Perito Moreno.

December–April or so, Chaltén Travel provides alternate-day bus service from El Calafate to Perito Moreno and Los Antiguos (the border crossing for Chile Chico), in Chubut province, along desolate RN 40 (US$66, 12 hours); while this is more expensive than comparable distances elsewhere, it's also more direct, quicker, and cheaper than alternative routes via coastal RN 3, especially if you factor in accommodations. Passengers from El Chaltén can board the northbound bus from El Calafate at the junction of RN 40 and RP 23 without having to return to El Calafate. Buses depart Calafate on odd-numbered days and return from Los Antiguos on even-numbered days.

In summer, **Turismo Zaahj/Bus Sur** (tel. 02902/491631) and **Cootra** (tel. 02902/491444) alternate daily services to Puerto Natales, Chile (US$15, 4.5 hours); occasionally there are direct services to Parque Nacional Torres del Paine. In winter, these services may be as infrequently as once a week.

Getting Around

Aerobús (tel. 02902/492492) provides door-to-door service to the glossy new **Aeropuerto Internacional El Calafate** (tel. 02902/491220, aerocal@cotecal.com.ar), 23 kilometers east of town, just north of RP 11.

The local Hertz representative is **Freelander** (Avenida Libertador 1029, tel. 02902/491437). Try also **Localiza** (Avenida Libertador 687, tel. 02902/491398) or **Servicar** (Avenida del Libertador 695, tel. 02902/492301).

VICINITY OF EL CALAFATE

Tours and transport to the Moreno Glacier and other nearby attractions are possible with a variety of operators. Among them are **Turismo Los Glaciares** (Avenida Libertador 924, tel. 02902/491159, losglaciares@cotecal.com.ar), **Solo Patagonia** (Avenida Libertador 867, tel. 02902/491298, fax 02902/491790, www.solopatagonia.com.ar), **Cal Tur** (Avenida Libertador 1080, tel. 02902/491368, caltur@cotecal.com.ar), **Mundo Austral** (Avenida Libertador 1114, tel. 02902/492365, fax 02902/492116, mundoaustral@cotecal.com.ar), **Aventura Andina** (Avenida del Libertador 761, Local 4, tel. 02902/491726, aventuraandina@cotecal.com.ar), **Visit Patagonia** (Avenida del Libertador 1532, 02902/491119, visitpatagonia@cotecal.com.ar), and **Interlagos Turismo** (Avenida Libertador 1175, tel. 02902/491175, interlagos@cotecal.com.ar), which some locals suggest has been living on its reputation.

Punta Walichu

Seven kilometers west of El Calafate, a northbound dirt road leads three kilometers to Punta Walichu (tel. 02902/491280), a commercialized pre-Columbian rock-art grotto on the south shore of Lago Argentino. A small visitors center displays a few fossils and some stone tools, and shows a 25-minute video, not to mention spurious replicas of similar sites elsewhere in the province. On the plus side, devaluation has dropped the admission price to about US$2.50 per person.

Punta Walichu also has a small library, a souvenir stand, a *confitería,* and bathroom facilities.

Estancia Rincón

A recent entry in the rural tourism category, open for day tours only, this Italian-run *estancia* (Avenida Libertador 1130, El Calafate, tel. 02902/491965, www.estanciarincon.com.ar) occupies a blufftop site just north of the Río Santa Cruz on the east side of RN 40, barely half an hour from El Calafate. Rates are US$25 per person for excursions that include a ranch tour, viewing the gathering and shearing, and lunch or dinner with wine; other activities, like fishing or a photographic safari, are also possible.

Estancia Alice

One of El Calafate's most convenient *estancias,* west of El Calafate en route to the Moreno glacier, Estancia Alice (RP 11 Km 22) is open for day tours that may include breakfast and outdoor activities like birding and horseback riding, as well as exhibitions of sheep herding and shearing, afternoon tea, and a barbecued-lamb dinner. Morning excursions cost around US$20 per person, afternoon excursions with dinner around US$25, horseback rides around US$10 per hour.

Estancia Alice also offers accommodations for US$105/114 s/d with breakfast and limited activities included; there are also multiday packages with more comprehensive services. For details, contact Agroturismo El Galpón (Avenida Libertador 761, El Calafate, tel. 02902/491793, www.estanciaalice.com.ar, elgalpon@estanciaalice.com.ar). The *estancia*'s Buenos Aires office is at Avenida Leandro Alem 822, 3rd floor, tel./fax 011/4313-0679.

Hostería Alta Vista

Once a separate *estancia,* since absorbed by the adjacent **Estancia Anita,** Hostería Alta Vista (RP 15 Km 33, tel./fax 02902/491247, altavista@cotecal.com.ar, US$220 s or d) is an outpost of the Braun dynasty that dominated the Patagonian wool industry of Chile and Argentina. As such, its seven-room *casco,* which includes one luxury suite, is the place to be spoiled; surrounded by luxuriant gardens in a sheltered location at the foot of 1,294-meter Cerro Freile, it has a first-rate bar/restaurant open to guests only, a separate *quincho* for lamb *asados,* and flawless service from its English-speaking staff.

In addition to accommodations, Alta Vista offers excursions that include horseback riding in the hills immediately behind the *estancia,* offering a small lagoon full of wildfowl, with condors soaring above, and distant views of the Moreno glacier. Nonguests may take tours of the *estancia,* which is clearly the most upscale *estancia* near El Calafate—unlike Nibepo Aike, it has been gentrified beyond rusticism.

Near Estancia Anita's entrance stands a memorial to the "Patagonia Rebelde" strikers of 1921–1922; erected by the provincial legislature, it reads "If the winners write history, that means there's another history: the Santa Cruz strikers, their histories present in our memory."

Accommodations at Hostería Alta Vista are all-inclusive except for incidentals like telephone charges and laundry.

PARQUE NACIONAL LOS GLACIARES

On the eastern slope of the Andes, Parque Nacional Los Glaciares comprises more than 759,000 hectares of slowly flowing ice, interspersed with Magellanic forests, that give birth to clear, frigid rivers and vast lakes along the Chilean border east and north of El Calafate. A UNESCO World Heritage Site, it's most famous for the Moreno glacier, which draws thousands of relatively sedentary visitors on day trips but also pulls in international scientists absorbed in glaciology and climate studies. The northerly sector—a 4.5-hour bus trip from El Calafate—attracts those seeking to spend several days in vigorous exercise, either trekking or the far more demanding and dangerous technical climbing for which the area is well known. The park's wildlife includes the endangered Andean *huemul.*

Geography and Climate

When the Campo de Hielo Sur receded at the end of the Pleistocene, it left behind the two huge glacial troughs that are now Lago Argentino and, to the north, the roughly parallel Lago Viedma. While these lakes lie only about 250 meters above sea level, the Andean summits along the Chilean border rise to 3,375 meters on Cerro Fitz Roy and nearly as high on pinnacles like 3,102-meter Cerro Torre, which matches Chile's Torres del Paine for sheer majesty.

Most of these bodies of water lie outside the park boundaries, but the eastern Andean slopes still contain their remnants, some of the world's most impressive, and accessible, glaciers. Thirteen major glaciers flow toward the Argentine side, including the benchmark Moreno glacier; ice covers 30 percent of the park's surface.

Despite the accumulated snow and ice, the

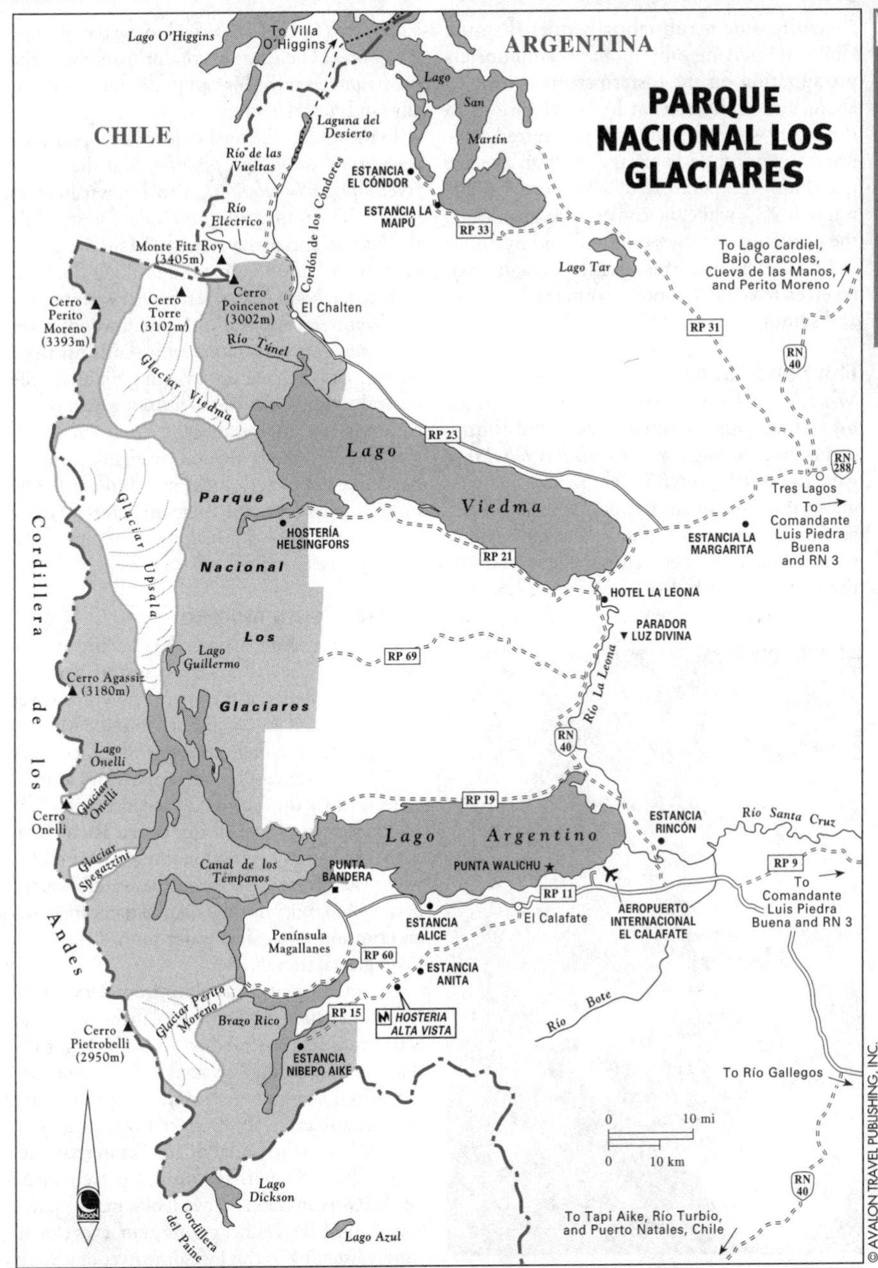
PARQUE NACIONAL LOS GLACIARES
ARGENTINA
CHILE
Lago O'Higgins
To Villa O'Higgins
Lago San Martín
Laguna del Desierto
Río de las Vueltas
Cordón de los Cóndores
ESTANCIA EL CÓNDOR
ESTANCIA LA MAIPÚ
RP 33
Río Eléctrico
Monte Fitz Roy (3405m)
Cerro Poincenot (3002m)
Cerro Torre (3102m)
Cerro Perito Moreno (3393m)
El Chalten
Lago Tar
To Lago Cardiel, Bajo Caracoles, Cueva de las Manos, and Perito Moreno
RP 31
RN 40
Río Túnel
Glaciar Viedma
RP 23
Lago Viedma
RN 288
Tres Lagos
To Comandante Luis Piedra Buena and RN 3
Parque Nacional Los Glaciares
Glaciar Upsala
HOSTERÍA HELSINGFORS
RP 21
ESTANCIA LA MARGARITA
HOTEL LA LEONA
PARADOR LUZ DIVINA
Cordillera de los Andes
Lago Guillermo
RP 69
Cerro Agassiz (3180m)
Río La Leona
RN 40
Lago Onelli
Cerro Onelli
Glaciar Onelli
RP 19
Lago Argentino
ESTANCIA RINCÓN
Río Santa Cruz
Glaciar Spegazzini
Canal de los Témpanos
PUNTA BANDERA
PUNTA WALICHU
RP 9
To Comandante Luis Piedra Buena and RN 3
RP 11
ESTANCIA ALICE
El Calafate
AEROPUERTO INTERNACIONAL EL CALAFATE
Península Magallanes
RP 60
ESTANCIA ANITA
Glaciar Perito Moreno
Brazo Rico
RP 15
HOSTERIA ALTA VISTA
Río Bote
Cerro Pietrobelli (2950m)
ESTANCIA NIBEPO AIKE
To Río Gallegos
0 10 mi
0 10 km
MOON
Lago Dickson
Cordillera del Paine
Lago Azul
RN 40
To Tapi Aike, Río Turbio, and Puerto Natales, Chile

Argentine side is substantially drier than the Chilean, receiving only about 400 millimeters precipitation on the eastern steppe, rising to about 900 millimeters at higher elevations to the west, where the terrain is forested. The warmest month is February, with an average maximum temperature of 22°C and a minimum of 9°C, while the coolest is August, when the maximum averages only 5°C and the minimum -1°C. Like the rest of Patagonia, it often receives ferocious winds, strongest in spring and summer.

Flora and Fauna

Where rainfall is insufficient to support anything other than *coirón* bunch grasses and thorny shrubs like the *calafate (Berberis buxifolia)* that gave the nearby town its name, the guanaco grazes the Patagonian steppe. Foxes and Patagonian skunks are also conspicuous, the flightless rhea or *ñandú* scampers across the open country, the *bandurria* or buff-necked ibis *(Theristicus caudatus)* hunts invertebrates, and flocks of upland geese *(Chloephaga picta)* browse the swampy lakeshores. The Andean condor soars above the plains and even the highest peaks, but occasionally lands to feast on carrion.

In the forests, the predominant tree species are the *lenga (Nothofagus pumilio)* and the *coigue (Nothofagus betuloides),* also known here as *guindo.* The puma still prowls the forest, while the *huemul* and perhaps the *pudú* survive in the vicinity of Lago Viedma. Squawking flocks of austral parakeets *(Enicognathus ferruginaeus)* flit between trees, and the Patagonian woodpecker *(Campephilus magellanicus)* pounds on their trunks. Perching calmly, awaiting nightfall, the austral pygmy owl *(Glaucidium nanum)* is a common late-afternoon sight.

Along the lakeshores and riverbanks, aquatic birds like coots and ducks are abundant. The most picturesque is the Patagonian torrent duck *(Merganetta armata),* which dives for prey in the rushing creeks.

Cerro Torre, Parque Nacional Los Glaciares

Glaciar Perito Moreno

Where a low Andean pass lets Pacific storms cross the cordillera, countless storms have deposited hundreds of meters of snow that, over the millennia, have compressed into the Moreno Glacier, the groaning, rasping river of ice that's one of the continent's greatest sights and sounds. Fifteen times during the 20th century, the advancing glacier blocked the **Brazo Rico** (Rico Arm) of Lago Argentino to form a rising body of water that eventually, when the water's weight became too much for the natural dam, triggered an eruption of ice and water toward the lake's main glacial trough.

No such event took place from 1988 until March 14, 2004, when the avalanche of ice and water could have served as a metaphor for the flood of tourists that invaded El Calafate in anticipation. On any given day, though, massive icebergs still calve off the glacier's 60-meter face and crash into the **Canal de los Témpanos** (Iceberg Channel) with astonishing frequency. Perched on catwalks and overlooks, many visitors spend entire days either gazing at or, eyes closed, simply listening to this awesome river of ice as it rumbles forward. Descending to lake level is pro-

The Moreno Glacier, west of El Calafate, is one of South America's great visitor attractions.

hibited because of the danger of backwash and flying chunks of ice; it is possible, however, to contract a full-day "minitrekking" excursion onto the ice for about US$60 per person with **Hielo y Aventura** (Avenida Libertador 935, El Calafate, tel. 02902/491053, www.hieloyaventura.com). Hielo y Aventura also does one-hour boat excursions on the lake, approaching the glacier's face, for US$9 per person.

The Moreno glacier is 80 kilometers southwest of El Calafate via RP 11. Organized tours from town leave every day, as does scheduled transportation (see below); normally transportation is extra for everything except the bus tours to the glacier.

Glaciar Upsala

Even larger than the Moreno glacier, 50 kilometers long and 10 kilometers wide at its foot, the Upsala glacier is accessible only by crowded catamaran excursions from Puerto Bandera via Lago Argentino's Brazo Norte (North Arm). Impressive for its sheer extent, the size of the bergs that have calved off it, and their shapes and colors, it's the trip's outstanding sight.

At midday, the boat anchors at Bahía Onelli, but bring a bag lunch (skipping the restaurant) to walk to ice-clogged **Lago Onelli.** The land portion of this excursion is highly regimented, and the pace the guides suggest—30 minutes from the dock to the shores of Onelli—is appropriate for those on crutches. Smoking is prohibited on the forest trail.

Travelers should realize that this is a mass-tourism excursion that may frustrate hikers accustomed to the freedom of the hills. If you take it, choose the biggest available ship, which offers the greatest deck space to see the Spegazzini and Upsala glaciers. On board, the freshest air is within the cabin of the *ALM,* whose seats are cramped but where smoking is prohibited; on deck, desperate smokers congregate even in freezing rain. Reasonably priced cakes, sandwiches, coffee, tea, and hot chocolate are available on board.

Puerto Bandera is 45 kilometers west of Calafate via RP 11 and RP 8. For information and reservations, contact concessionaire René Fernández Campbell (Avenida Libertador 867, El Calafate, tel. 02902/491155 or 02902/491428, fax 02902/491154, rfcino@cotecal.com.ar). The full-day trip costs about US$60 per person; the fare does not include transportation from El

Calafate (about US$4 pp round-trip) to Puerto Bandera or the obligatory US$7 park admission fee for nonresidents of Argentina.

Lago Roca

Less visited than other parts of the park, the southwesterly sector also known as La Jerónima, along Lago Roca's Brazo Sur (South Arm), offers camping and cross-country hiking—there are no formal trails, only routes like the one up the summit of **Cerro Cristal** from the campground, 55 kilometers from El Calafate. The landscape's most striking characteristic, though, is the conspicuously high, but now dry, shoreline from the days when the lake backed up behind the advancing Moreno glacier. Unlike other sectors, Lago Roca charges no admission fee.

Sector Fitz Roy

In the park's most northerly sector, the Fitz Roy Range has sheer vertical spires to match Torres del Paine, but even if you're not one of the world's top technical climbers, the several trails from the village of El Chaltén to the base of summits like Fitz Roy and Cerro Torre make some of the southern hemisphere's most enthralling hiking. It's even possible to traverse the southern Patagonian icefields, but visitors looking for a more sedate outdoor experience will find a handful of former sheep *estancias,* onetime Patagonian wool producers that have reinvented themselves as tourist accommodations.

From a signposted trailhead at the north end of El Chaltén, just south of the basic Camping Madsen, the **Sendero Laguna Torre** is an 11-kilometer track gaining about 200 meters in elevation as it winds through southern beech forests to the climbers' base camp for Cerro Torre; figure about three to 3.5 hours. At the lake itself, in clear weather, there are extraordinary views of 3,102-meter summit of Cerro Torre, crowned by the so-called "mushroom" of snow and ice that technical climbers must surmount. While the Italian Cesare Maestri claimed that he and the Austrian Toni Egger reached the summit in 1959 (Egger died in an avalanche, taking the expedition's camera with him), the first undisputed ascent was by the Italian Casimiro Ferrari in 1974.

From the Madsen pack station, the more demanding **Sendero Río Blanco** rises steeply at the outset before leveling out through boggy beech forest and continuing to the Cerro Fitz Roy base camp, a total climb of about 350 meters in 10 kilometers. About midway to Río Blanco, a signed lateral leads south to **Laguna Capri,** which has backcountry campsites.

From Río Blanco, the vertiginous zigzag trail ascends 400 meters in only 2.5 kilometers to **Laguna de los Tres,** a glacial tarn whose name commemorates three members of the French expedition, René Ferlet, Lionel Terray, and Guido Magnone, who reached Fitz Roy's summit in 1952. Truly a top-of-the-world experience, Laguna de los Tres offers some of Patagonia's finest Andean panoramas.

From the Río Blanco campground (reserved for climbers only), a northbound trail follows the river's west bank north to **Laguna Piedras Blancas,** whose namesake glacier continually calves small icebergs into the lake. The trail continues north to the Río Eléctrico, beyond the park boundaries, where a westbound trail climbs the river to Piedra del Fraile and a possible circuit of the Campo de Hielo Sur, suitable only for experienced snow-and-ice trekkers. At the Río Eléctrico, it's also possible to rejoin the road from El Chaltén to Lago del Desierto.

Glaciar Viedma

From Puerto Bahía Túnel on Lago Viedma's north shore but south of El Chaltén, the park's best lake excursion is the catamaran *Viedma Discovery*'s voyage to the face of the Viedma glacier, a full-day trip that includes an ice-climbing exploration of the glacier itself.

Sailing from Bahía Túnel, the ship rounds the ironically named **Cabo de Hornos** ("Cape Horn") to enter an iceberg-cluttered section of the lake (Glaciar Viedma is Argentina's largest, though its lakeside face is small) before anchoring in a rocky cove. After disembarking, visitors hike to an overlook of the glacier and 2,677-meter Cerro Huemul; those who wish can strap on crampons and continue with the guides onto the glacier for about 1.5 hours (even some pretty sedentary Porteños do so).

The bilingual guides are well-versed in glaciology and provide much more personalized service than the Fernández Campbell excursion from Puerto Bandera. While the excursion price here does not include lunch, they do provide an aperitif on the glacial rocks.

Departure time from El Chaltén is 8:30 A.M., while the boat sails from Bahía Túnel at 9 A.M.; the cost is US$50 per person plus US$6.50 for transportation from El Chaltén for those who need it. For details, contact Patagonia Aventura (Güemes s/n, tel. 02962/493110, fax 02962/493017, El Chaltén). **Restaurant at Bahía Túnel** is a good breakfast choice, with exceptional picture-window views across the lake, and also serves lunch, afternoon tea, and especially the sunset dinner.

Lago del Desierto

Elongated Lago del Desierto, 37 kilometers north of El Chaltén, is a scenic end-of-the-road destination with several worthwhile hiking trails, boat excursions, and even a challenging border crossing to the remote Chilean settlement of Villa O'Higgins.

From the south end of the lake, a short trail winds west through dense southern beech forest to a vista point and the hanging glacier at **Laguna Huemul,** while a longer route follows the eastern shore to the border, a 20-kilometer trek over relatively gentle terrain. In 2002, more than 200 people crossed the Argentine-Chilean border in a place that was once such a bone of contention between Chile and Argentina that, decades ago, a Chilean Carabinero even lost his life in a firefight with Argentine soldiers.

Despite objections by a handful of extreme Chilean nationalists, the matter is resolved, the border is peaceable, and determined hikers or mountain bikers can readily cross to Villa O'Higgins. Before attempting this route, though, verify the latest details with the Argentine Gendarmería (Border Patrol) in El Chaltén, and read the sidebar "The New Cruce de Lagos" in the Villa O'Higgins entry in the Aisén chapter.

From El Chaltén, **Mermoz** (San Martín s/n, tel. 02962/493098) minibuses go to Lago del Desierto (US$9 round-trip pp) at 9:30 A.M. daily, returning at 4:30 P.M. Hitching is feasible but vehicles are few and often full. At the lake itself, the launches *Viedma 1* and *La Mariana* take passengers to the north end for US$15 per person.

Accommodations and Food

There are limited accommodations and food in the southern sector of the park since most people stay at El Calafate, but they're increasingly abundant at El Chaltén; for details, see the separate El Chaltén entry below.

Backpackers should note that no campfires are permitted within the park—campstoves are obligatory for cooking. According to rangers, water is potable throughout the park.

Glaciar Moreno: Only seven kilometers east of the glacier, **Camping Bahía Escondida** (tel. 02902/491005, US$3 pp) has 30 sites with running water and fire pits; there are hot showers 7–10 P.M. only and electricity 8 P.M.–midnight only. Backpackers can camp free at the Seccional de Guardaparques, the ranger station at the glacier itself, two nights maximum.

The only accommodations near the glacier, the lavish **Hostería Los Notros** (tel. 02902/499510, fax 02902/499511 in El Calafate, US$670–960 s, US$880–1,080 d) rivals Torres del Paine's Hotel Explora in the "room-with-a-view" category; all 32 rooms face the ice. Reservations are essential here, and multiday package with full board and excursions included are the rule rather than the exception. For details, contact Hostería Los Notros (Arenales 1457, 7th floor, Buenos Aires, tel. 011/4814-3934, fax 011/4815-7645, www.losnotros.com, info@losnotros.com).

Also at the glacier, the **Unidad Turística Ventisquero Moreno** operates both a snack bar (sandwiches for US$2.50–4, plus coffee and desserts) and a separate restaurant with set meals for US$7–12; there's also an a la carte menu.

Lago Roca: La Jerónima's **Camping Lago Roca** (tel. 02902/499500, lagoroca@yahoo.com.ar) charges US$3 per adult, US$1 for children, and also has four-bed *cabañas* for US$20. Hot showers are available, and its restaurant/*confitería* serves decent meals.

At the terminus of RP 15, 56 kilometers southwest of El Calafate, the *casco* at Croatian-founded **Estancia Nibepo Aike** (Perito Moreno 229, Río

Gallegos, tel./fax 02966/436010, www.nibepoaike.com.ar) preserves its original rustic style but is now a five-room guesthouse with contemporary conveniences—all rooms have private bath, for instance. Rates are US$100/130 s/d with half-board, with a minimum two-night stay. Open October 1–April 30, it also has a newer **Quincho Don Juan** for day-trippers to lunch or dine, though overnight guests may eat in the restaurant rather than the main house's dining room if they wish.

Information

At the Río Mitre entrance, the main Moreno glacier approach, the Administración de Parques Nacionales (APN) collects a US$7 park-admission fee for nonresidents of Argentina. At present, no fee is collected at either the Lago Roca or El Chaltén sectors.

Hikers may want to consult Tim Burford's *Chile and Argentina: The Bradt Trekking Guide* (Bradt Travel Guides, 2001), or Clem Lindenmayer's and Nick Tapp's *Trekking in the Patagonian Andes* (Lonely Planet, 2003); the former has thorough text, but the latter has better maps. There is also the new edition of Miguel A. Alonso's locally available, bilingual *Trekking en Chaltén y Lago del Desierto* (Los Glaciares Publishers, 2003), which covers numerous hikes in the vicinity. Alonso has also written *Lago Argentino & Glaciar Perito Moreno Handbook* (Buenos Aires: Zagier & Urruty, 1997), a more general guide that's available in English, Italian, German, and French.

Getting There and Around

The Moreno glacier is about 80 kilometers west of El Calafate by RP 11, which is paved to the park entrance; the trip takes somewhat more than an hour. Both **Interlagos** and **Taqsa,** at El Calafate's bus terminal, have scheduled services at 9 A.M. daily (US$17 round-trip), returning in the afternoon.

In addition to regularly scheduled services, guided bus tours are frequent, but both are less frequent in winter; for suggested operators, see the listing under the Vicinity of El Calafate heading. El Calafate's **Albergue del Glaciar** runs its own minivan excursions, leaving about 8:30 A.M. and returning about 5 P.M., for US$25 per person, including the navigation in front of the glacier.

EL CHALTÉN

Billing itself as "Capital Nacional del Trekking," Argentina's national trekking capital, El Chaltén has become popular for its easy access to Fitz Roy–range trailheads in Parque Nacional Los Glaciares. While many of the trails are suitable for overnight backpacks, access is so good that day hikers can cover nearly as much ground.

Exposed to fierce westerly winds and to potential floods from the Río de las Vueltas, El Chaltén has still managed to achieve a sense of permanence in what, just a few years ago, seemed a bleak assortment of government offices aimed to uphold Argentina's presence in a then disputed border zone (the last of many Chilean-Argentine territorial quarrels, over Lago del Desierto to the north, was finalized only a few years ago). With the highway from the RN 40 junction recently paved, it's growing so rapidly that some fear it will become the next El Calafate, where real estate development (and speculation) are rampant. When the rest of the route is paved, travel time from El Calafate will fall from about five hours to three.

Orientation

El Chaltén is 220 kilometers northwest of El Calafate via eastbound RP 11 to the Río Bote junction, northbound RN 40, and westbound RP 23 along the north shore of Lago Viedma. It has street names and addresses, but they don't mean much in a town this size, and people pay little attention to them. While it remains small and compact enough for pedestrians, signs of sprawl are appearing.

Events

El Chaltén celebrates several events, including October 12's **Aniversario de El Chaltén,** marking the town's formal founding in 1985; November 10's **Día de la Tradición,** celebrating the gaucho heritage; and early February's **Fiesta Nacional del Trekking,** which lasts a week.

Recreation

For suggestions on hiking and climbing in the vicinity of El Chaltén, see the separate entry under Parque Nacional Los Glaciares.

From here, it's possible to arrange a one-day trek and ice climb on Glaciar Torre (US$45 pp) with **Fitz Roy Expediciones** (Lionel Terray 212, tel./fax 02962/493017, www.fitzroyexpediciones.com.ar), which also offers lengthier guided hikes—nine-day expeditions, really—on the Campo de Hielo Sur, the Southern Continental Ice Field (US$950 pp). **Camino Abierto** (San Martín s/n, tel. 02962/493043, www.caminoabierto.com), **Alta Montaña** (Lionel Terray s/n, tel. 02962/493018, altamont@infovia.com.ar), and **Viviendo Montañas** (Avenida Güemes 68, tel. 02962/493068, www.vivmont.com.ar) also conduct expeditions onto the great icefields.

NYCA Adventure (San Martín 591, tel. 02962/493093, www.nyca.com.ar) offers half-day excursions including activities like climbing, hiking, mountain biking, rafting, and rappelling. **Lago San Martín** (Riquelme and Rojo, tel. 02962/493045) arranges excursions to and from Lago San Martín, across the mountains to the northeast, with *estancia* accommodations.

Just north of Albergue Rancho Grande, **Viento Oeste** (San Martín s/n tel. 02962/493021, vientooeste@infovia.com.ar) rents and sells climbing, camping, and wet-weather gear.

Accommodations

El Chaltén has a reasonable selection of accommodations, some of them very good, but high summer demand makes reservations advisable. Many places close in winter, but there's always something available.

At the north edge of town, the APN's woodsy **Camping Madsen** has running water and is free of charge but lacks toilets—dig a latrine—and fires are prohibited. Directly across from the APN office, on the banks of the Río Fitz Roy, there's another free site, but it's more exposed.

Commercial campgrounds, with services like hot showers, generally cost around US$3 per person, plus an additional peso or two for hot showers. These include **Camping El Relincho** (San Martín s/n, tel. 02962/493010, elrelincho@cotecal.com.ar) and **Camping El Refugio** (San Martín s/n).

El Chaltén has several hostel-style accommodations, starting with the economical, four-room **Albergue Elal** (Perito Moreno 152, tel. 02962/493088, travesias_r40@hotmail.com, US$5 pp), where guests need their own sleeping bags; common areas include a kitchen and living room. Others include the smallish **Albergue Los Ñires** (Lago del Desierto s/n, tel. 02962/493009, losnires@videodata.com.ar, US$7 pp); HI-affiliated **Cóndor de los Andes** (Avenida Río de las Vueltas and Halvorsen, tel. 02962/493101, www.condordelosandes.com, US$7 pp); and **Albergue del Lago** (Lago del Desierto 135, tel. 02962/493010, US$7 pp).

Open all year, the HI affiliate **Albergue Patagonia** (San Martín 493, tel. 02962/493019, alpatagonia@infovia.com.ar, US$7–8 pp) has cozy dorm accommodations—four–six beds per room—and also provides cooking facilities, laundry service, meals, a book exchange, and bike rentals, and organizes excursions. English and Dutch are spoken; its main drawback is that the bathroom facilities, while good enough, are arguably too small.

The spacious 44-bed **Albergue Rancho Grande** (San Martín 635, tel./fax 02962/493005, rancho@cotecal.com.ar, US$8 pp) also offers B&B packages with transportation from El Calafate. For reservations in El Calafate, contact Chaltén Travel (Avenida Libertador 1177, tel. 02902/491833, chaltentravel@cotecal.com.ar).

Alongside its namesake hotel, the no-frills **Hostería Los Ñires** (Lago del Desierto s/n, tel. 02962/493009, US$17 pp) has awkwardly shaped but reasonably spacious rooms with private bath, excellent beds, and furniture, but lacking closet space. Separated from its bar/restaurant by a long corridor, the sleeping quarters are remarkably quiet; rates include a decent breakfast.

Cozy, friendly **Nothofagus Bed & Breakfast** (Hensen s/n, tel. 02962/493087, nothofagus@infovia.com.ar, US$22–28 s, US$25–33 d) is also tobacco-free; rates depend on whether the room has shared or private bath. Family-run **Hospedaje La Base** (Lago del Desierto 97, tel./fax 02962/493031, US$30/33 s/d) has two firm beds per room, which are two-bedroom *cabañas* that share a kitchen but have private bath. Like many other places, it closes June–November.

New on the scene, **Hostería Thiamalu** (Lago del Desierto 99, tel. 02962/493736, thiamalu_chalten@yahoo.com, US$34 s or d) is a four-room work in progress. Recently opened **Posada Altas Cumbres** (Lionel Terray 342, tel. 02962/493060, altas_cumbres@hotmail.com, US$40 s or d) has five spacious new rooms and a restaurant.

Hotel Lago del Desierto (Lago del Desierto 137, tel. 02962/493010, hotelldd@infovia.com.ar, US$60 s or d) closes May–October; it also rents six-bed *cabañas* with kitchen facilities for US$110, and has camping facilities for US$2.50 per person. Comparably priced **Hostería Kalenshen** (Lionel Terray 50, tel. 02962/493108, kalenshen@videodata.com.ar, US$60/70 s/d) is a promising new option.

North of El Chaltén, in an out-of-the-way location on the Lago del Desierto road, **Hostería El Pilar** (tel./fax 02962/493002, www.hosteriaelpilar.com.ar, US$91/111 s/d with breakfast and taxes; tel. 011/5031-0755 in Buenos Aires) has the classic style of a Patagonian *casco,* but it's really a recent construction (1996). Room reservations are essential for this cozy and increasingly popular place (open October–April), but it's possible to dine (US$14 pp) in the restaurant without. Shuttle transportation from El Chaltén is free for guests.

Rates at the **Fitz Roy Inn** (San Martín 520, tel. 02962/493062, US$50–65 s, US$53–68 d, caltur@cotecal.com.ar) vary from low season (September–October and April) and high season (November–March); it also has multiday packages with half-board or full board, but the full-board option would preclude eating at other good places in town.

Rates have risen substantially at **Casa de Piedra** (Lago del Desierto s/n, tel./fax 02962/493015, US$64/69 s/d), which provides large and comfy but tackily decorated rooms with private bath but without breakfast. It has well-kept grounds and is quiet, but the new power plant going up nearby could change things.

It's still a work in progress—the landscaping needs attention—but **Hostería Posada Lunajuim** (Trevisan s/n, tel. 02962/493047, posadalunajuim@yahoo.com, US$85/100 s/d) has made good first impressions with its appealing common areas (including a bar/restaurant) and with private bath, central heating, and breakfast.

The eight-room **Hostería El Puma** (Lionel Terray 212, tel. 02962/493095, hosteria-elpuma@infovia.com.ar, US$95/110 s/d) is another impressive addition to Chaltén's accommodations scene.

Food

Hikers and climbers can stock up on groceries at **El Chaltén** (Lago del Desierto s/n), **Kiosko Charito** (Güemes s/n), and **El Gringuito** (San Martín s/n). Otherwise, for its size, El Chaltén offers a good and improving selection of restaurants.

Chocolatería Josh Aike (Lago del Desierto s/n, tel. 02962/493008) is more than it sounds—while the desserts are good enough, the breakfasts and pizzas are also excellent. **Domo Blanco** (Costanera Sur 90, tel. 02962/493036) serves exceptional ice cream but closes in winter.

Open in summer only, **Ruca Mahuida** (Lionel Terray 501, tel. 02962/493018) is one of Chaltén's most imaginative eateries and also sends smokers outside to indulge their habit, but the service can be forgetful. Lamb is the specialty at **La Casita** (San Martín 535, tel. 02962/493042), which otherwise serves a standard Argentine menu—beef, pizza, pasta, and the like—its major downside is the cramped and tobacco-heavy atmosphere. In mid-summer, it can be hard to get a table at popular **Pizzería Patagonicus** (Güemes s/n, tel. 02962/493025), perhaps the only Argentine eatery to have lamb on the pizza menu; the decor, with natural wood and mountaineering photos, embodies Chaltén's style.

Reservations are advisable at **Fuegia** (San Martín s/n, tel. 02962/493019), Albergue Patagonia's cozy bistro-style restaurant, especially in summer. Likewise, call ahead for the unpretentious **Estepa** (Cerro Solo and Antonio Rojo, tel. 02962/493069), a snug, tobacco-free, nine-table place whose windows face Cerro Fitz Roy. Offering home-style cooking at a high level, its specialty is *cordero estepa,* lamb with *calafate* sauce, but there are also pizzas and empanadas, with most entrées in the US$5–7.50 range.

Information and Services

El Chaltén's **Comisión de Fomento** (Avenida Güemes 21, tel. 02962/493011, www.elchalten.com) is just north of the bridge across the Río Fitz Roy. At the southern approach to town, the **APN** (tel. 02962/493004) has turned the former *hostería* into a national-parks visitors center, which also issues climbing permits (free of charge). Hours are 8 A.M.–8 P.M. daily.

El Chaltén has limited services, including long-distance phone service and relatively slow and expensive Internet connections.

Locutorio de la Morsa (Güemes s/n) has long-distance phone and fax service. **Chaltén Travel** (Avenida Güemes and Lago del Desierto) has relatively but not outrageously expensive Internet connections.

Getting There

Several companies connect El Chaltén with El Calafate (US$14, 4.5 hours): **Cal Tur** (San Martín s/n, tel. 02962/493062); **Chaltén Travel** (San Martín s/n, tel. 02962/493005); and **Los Glaciares** (Güemes s/n, tel. 02962/493084). Departures are usually in late afternoon, between 5 and 6 P.M. There are several buses daily in summer, but only one or two weekly in winter.

With Chaltén Travel, it's possible to travel north on gravel RN 40 to the towns of Perito Moreno and Los Antiguos (the border crossing for Chile Chico), in Chubut province (US$55 pp, 13 hours). These services leave El Calafate on alternate days in summer; passengers from El Chaltén can board the bus from La Leona, on RN 40, without having to return to El Calafate. The rest of the year, there may be only one bus weekly.

An alternative is Daniel Bagnera's **Itinerarios y Travesías** (Perito Moreno 152, tel. 02962/493088, travesias_r40@hotmail.com), a minivan to Perito Moreno and Los Antiguos (US$50 pp) that sometimes makes a side excursion to the pre-Columbian rock-art site of Cueva de las Manos. Departures are almost daily in summer, but weekly at most in the winter months; schedules may vary according to the Chilean ferry from the border post of Chile Chico. I&T also offers occasional departures for Comandante Luis Piedra Buena (US$28), on coastal RN 3, with northbound connections.

RN 40 SOUTH

Southeast of El Calafate, RN 40 and RP 5 are contiguous as far as El Cerrito, where RN 40 forks southwest toward the Chilean border. At the junction of RN 40 and east-west RP 7, about halfway to Puerto Natales, Tapi Aike is a wide spot in the road where there's a gas station, a convenience store, and accommodations at nearby Estancia Tapi Aike.

From here, the road continues southwest to the border crossing at **Cancha Carrera,** the easiest access to Torres del Paine, but it is being slightly rerouted and there is no regular public transportation there. Most travelers cross into Chile at Río Turbio, a bleak coal town that features a surprisingly contemporary ski resort and a historic narrow-gauge railway.

Estancia Tapi Aike

Historically part of the Braun empire, the Tapi Aike sheep ranch sprawls over 60,000 hectares of the southern Santa Cruz steppes, but the settlement itself is a compact one near the RN 40 junction with RP 7. Open November–April, the *estancia's* comfortable *casco,* reinvented as **Posada Tapi Aike** (tel. 02966/420092 in Río Gallegos, lilianagfernandez@speedy.com.ar, US$60 pp), offers B&B accommodations between Calafate and the border; some visitors stay here and make Torres del Paine a day trip.

In addition to accommodations, Tapi Aike prepares simple but well-made lunches and dinners (US$20 pp), including a main dish, salad, soda, wine, and dessert. The Viel family, descendents of the Brauns, speak English as well as Spanish. Estancia Tapi Aike also has a Buenos Aires contact (tel./fax 011/4784-4360).

Estancia Rupai Pacha

From Tapi Aike, RN 40 leads southwest past the **Hotel Fuentes del Coyle,** a barebones country inn that's a local landmark; about 22 kilometers southwest, soon to be bypassed by the rerouted highway, the Sturtzenbaum family's Estancia Rupai Pacha (Piedra Buena 129, Río Gallegos, tel. 02966/422927, www.rupaipacha.com.ar, US$43/52 s/d) provides organic produce for El Calafate and raises sheep on 26,000 hectares of rolling steppe, 200–400 meters above sea level. With views of Torres del Paine to the southwest, it also offers congenial farmstay accommodations, with opportunities for hiking, riding, and especially birding on its marshy lowlands. Founded only in 1973, it's not a historic *estancia,* but the gardens are a treasure, with delectable raspberries and other fresh fruits in season, and there's also a handicrafts shop.

About 180 kilometers south of El Calafate and 70 kilometers north of Río Turbio, Rupai Pacha will be about nine kilometers west of the rerouted highway. Rates include breakfast, while additional meals cost US$15 per person; there is also a sheltered campground (US$5 pp). English and German are spoken.

Río Turbio

In one of Argentina's most remote corners, the gritty coal town of Río Turbio has been slowly declining as its underground seams reach exhaustion, but it got an ironic shot in the arm with the 2001 peso meltdown—as locals could no longer afford to do their shopping in Chile, supermarkets and other businesses here actually opened and expanded during the country's worst economic crisis ever.

Even the coal mines recovered as a national energy crisis made the local mineral a competitive energy source, but this had a serious downside as well. In mid-2004, an underground fire killed 14 miners, plunging the community into mourning and raising questions about cost-cutting measures by the private concessionaire.

Though it's not exactly beautiful, Río Turbio holds some interest for its aging locomotives and railcars—the narrow-gauge railway still carries coal to Punta Loyola, near Río Gallegos and its modest winter-sports center.

Visits from Chile have increased from 200 to 1,500 per weekend, as Chileans go for cheaper goods here. Industry is recovering, and there are plans for a tourist train to Gallegos, but the city suffered a serious setback due to the mining accident.

Río Turbio (population 6,652) is 270 kilo-

Trainspotters enjoy the antique railcars at Río Turbio.

meters west of Río Gallegos via RN 40, and 30 kilometers north of Puerto Natales, Chile. It's 242 kilometers south of El Calafate via RN 40 and RP 11.

Near the Villa Dorotea border post, about four kilometers south of town, the **Centro de Deportes de Invierno Valdelén** (tel. 02902/421900, angeli@oyikil.com.ar) is a modest but lighted ski area, with elevations ranging 180–690 meters; there are about 12 hectares of downhill slopes and 160 suitable for cross-country. Hours are 10 A.M.–10 P.M. daily when snow is sufficient, usually in June, July, and August.

Whatever its shortcomings as a place to live, Río Turbio has decent accommodations, starting with **Hospedaje Yenu** (2 de Abril 170, Barrio Islas Malvinas, tel. 02902/421694, US$7 pp with breakfast). Other good options include **Hotel Nazo** (Gobernador Moyano 464, tel. 02902/421800, nazo@oyikil.com.ar, US$17/27 s/d), and the Valdelén ski area's **Hostería de la Frontera** (tel. 02902/421979, US$20/33 s/d), an exceptional value.

Don Pablo I (Pellegrini and Roque Saenz Peña, tel. 02902/421220) is a pizzeria (US$3–5) that also serves *minutas* (US$2–5). With more atmosphere than other local places, **El Granero** (Teniente del Castillo and Gobernador Lista, tel. 02902/421493) is a fine breakfast choice, with good croissants and *submarinos,* and also offers *minutas.*

Río Turbio's **Centro de Información Turística** (Plazoleta Agustín del Castillo s/n, tel. 02902/421950, www.turismorioturbio.com.ar) is presumably open 8 A.M.–9 P.M. weekdays and 9 A.M.–9 P.M. weekends; in practice, it keeps irregular hours.

Banco de Santa Cruz (Gobernador Lista s/n) has an ATM. For postal services, **Correo Argentino** is at Avenida De los Mineros and Roque Saenz Peña.

Neyem Turismo (Teniente Ramón del Castillo 32, tel. 02902/421671, neyem@latinmail.com, neyem8@hotmail.com) arranges local excursions.

LADE (Avenida Mineros 375, tel. 02902/421224) flies to Río Gallegos and Río Grande (Tierra del Fuego).

Unlike other cities, Río Turbio has no central bus terminal, but all the companies are fairly close to each other. **Cootra** (Teniente del Castillo 01, tel. 02902/421448) operates five–seven buses daily to Puerto Natales (US$2–3, one hour) except on weekends, when there are only two or three. **Bus Sur** (Avenida Mineros 262) goes once or twice daily. Cootra also goes to El Calafate at 7 A.M. daily (US$10, 4.5 hours).

Taqsa (Teniente del Castillo 130, tel. 02902/421422) goes to Río Gallegos (US$10, five hours) at 2 and 11:30 A.M. daily.

RN 40 NORTH

About 30 kilometers east of El Calafate, northbound RN 40 covers 596 kilometers of rugged gravel road—scheduled to be completely paved within four years—in the arid eastern Andean foothills, before finally arriving at the cowtown of Perito Moreno near Lago Buenos Aires, the oasis of Los Antiguos, and the Chilean border town of Chile Chico. In recent years, this desolate highway has seen increasing numbers of overland travelers but mixed reviews indicate it's not for everyone: the unrelenting westerlies bowl over cyclists and bikers alike, sharp rocks blow tires and shatter windshields, and vehicles can break down in the middle of nowhere.

Still, this particular section of "La Cuarenta"—running from Río Gallegos almost to the Bolivian border, RN 40 is Argentina's longest interior highway—has a mystique all its own. Some love it, some loathe it, and others are ambivalent, but no one forgets it.

Parador Luz Divina

Ninety kilometers from El Calafate and 10 kilometers south of La Leona, buses often stop at this roadside *confitería* for snacks, cakes, and coffee. It also has camping, but it's less sheltered than La Leona.

La Leona

Little more than a wide turnout alongside the road, at the Helsingfors junction of RN 40 and westbound RP 21, **Hotel La Leona** is a longtime local landmark where travelers brake for chocolate and lemon pie, banana bread, and tea

GET YOUR FLATS ON LA CUARENTA

From the Bolivian border near La Quiaca to its terminus near Río Gallegos, RN 40 is Argentina's great unfinished interior highway. Some segments of "La Cuarenta," in the central Cuyo provinces, are smoothly paved, while others in the Andean northwest are rough and rugged. None of those, though, enjoys the notoriety of the segment between the El Calafate junction and the town of Perito Moreno, on the cusp between the Patagonian steppe and the icy southern Andes.

It may not be Argentina's loneliest road—some of the dead-end routes that spin off it seem simply *abandoned*—but for Argentines and foreigners alike it's become the standard for adventurous driving and cycling, thanks to its secluded Andean lakes, isolated *estancias,* plentiful wildlife, and rare sights like the pre-Columbian rock art of Cueva de las Manos. Even the advent of (infrequent) public transportation has not diminished its mystique.

When the author first drove the 594 kilometers in early 1991, he saw only three other vehicles in four days, and services were almost nil. Since then, traffic has not exactly burgeoned, but the peak summer season now sees a small but steady procession of motorists, motorcyclists, and bicyclists. It's as if a selective bunch have absorbed Darwin's insight that the appeal of the bleak Patagonian plains was "the free scope given to the imagination."

It's clearly not for everyone, though, and a trip up or down La Cuarenta requires planning. With accommodations and supplies few and far between, bicyclists and motorcyclists *must* carry tents and cold-weather gear, even in midsummer, and plenty of food. Detailed maps, like ACA's newest regional sheets, are essential. Preferably, automobiles should carry at least two spare tires.

© WAYNE BERNHARDSON

Settlements are few and far between on "La Cuarenta" in Santa Cruz province.

and coffee. At the same site since 1916, it has only two simple rooms with a total of four beds, but makes an excellent stop for cyclists, either north or southbound, who can't be bothered to set up the tent. Water-shortage warning in the toilet: "If it's yellow, let it mellow; if it's brown, flush it down."

Nearby, the newly discovered **Bosque Petrificado La Leona** is a badlands reserve of petrified forests and dinosaur fossils on nearby Estancia Santa Teresita, accessible by guided tour only. For details on this full-day excursion (US$45), contact any El Calafate travel agency.

Estancia La Margarita

Beyond La Leona, after passing the westbound turnoff to El Chaltén, RN 40 turns east and, after about 17 kilometers, passes the entrance to Estancia La Margarita, where a dirt road leads south from the highway. La Margarita (RN 40, Km 2544, www.lamargarita.8k.com, srr69@hotmail.com, US$9 pp) is a 20,000-hectare sheep ranch with a smattering of wildlife—foxes, guanacos, and rheas—along with simple *cabaña* accommodations and meals (US$2 for breakfast, US$5 for lunch or dinner; wine extra). It's open December–February; reservations are advisable.

Also carry extra fuel—between El Calafate and Perito Moreno, the only dependable supplies are at El Chaltén (a 90-km detour), Tres Lagos, Gobernador Gregores (a 70-km detour), and Bajo Caracoles. Some tourist *estancias* will sell gasoline to their clients or in an emergency, but don't count on it.

Road hazards are numerous. Bicyclists and motorcyclists must contend with powerful Patagonian winds that can knock them down in an instant, and deep gravel adds to the danger. Even high-clearance vehicles are vulnerable to flipping on loose gravel, especially when braking suddenly, and 50-knot gusts make things worse. Though four-wheel drive is not essential, some drivers prefer it to avoid fishtailing on gravel.

Chipped, cracked, and even shattered windshields are par for the course on RN 40 and other graveled Patagonian roads. Normally, rental-car insurance policies do *not* cover such damage, and replacements are expensive in Argentina (though fairly cheap in Punta Arenas, Chile). Approaching vehicles usually brake to minimize the possibility of such damage, but some drivers find they need to play chicken to slow down an onrushing SUV.

The big news is that by 2008, thanks to former Santa Cruz governor and current Argentine president Néstor Kirchner, this segment of RN 40 will be paved, and rerouted to pass through Gobernador Gregores (whose tourism director is delighted). Hearing that RN 40 will be paved evokes enough nostalgia for a tango, but there will remain plenty of unpaved gravel roads to last for the lifetime of most of this book's readers.

If driving or cycling doesn't appeal to you, but you still want to see the loneliest highway, summer bus and minivan services now connect El Calafate and El Chaltén, at the south end, with Perito Moreno and Los Antiguos at the north end of the province; for details, see the appropriate geographical entries.

For a more relaxing itinerary, Bariloche's **Overland Patagonia** (tel. 02944/461564, www.overlandpatagonia.com) offers a four-day excursion from Bariloche to El Calafate that overnights in Río Mayo (Chubut), Estancia Los Toldos (for Cueva de las Manos), and Estancia Menelik (for Parque Nacional Perito Moreno).

Tres Lagos and Vicinity

Beyond La Margarita, RN 40 climbs over the volcanic Meseta Escorial before dropping into the enigmatically named hamlet of Tres Lagos (the only water in the vicinity is the humble Río Shehuen). Northbound motorists *must* fill up at the YPF station, which has the only gasoline this side of Bajo Caracoles, 338 kilometers to the north.

Tres Lagos has few other services, though there is a pretty good municipal **Camping Comunal** (tel. 02962/495031, US$1 pp plus US$1 per vehicle) with hot showers (US$.65). Very good fresh-baked empanadas and other lesser snacks are available at the YPF station.

To the northwest, gravel RP 31 and RP 33 leads 100 kilometers to **Lago San Martín** and 19 kilometers farther to **Estancia La Maipú,** which has upscale facilities with breakfast (US$86/103 s/d) but also a bring-your-own-sleeping-bag backpackers' *refugio* (US$10 pp) with hot water and showers, but without indoor toilets. Lunch costs US$8 per person, dinner US$15; there are also horseback rides (US$28 pp). For details, contact Estancia La Maipú (Chaco 167 2° B, Buenos Aires, tel. 011/4901-5591, fax 011/4311-6689, www.estancialamaipu.com.ar); there is also a contact in Puerto Santa Cruz (9 de Julio 570, tel. 02962/498233), on the coast.

About nine kilometers beyond La Maipú by an increasingly rough road that requires high clearance, the 42,666-hectare, British-founded **Estancia El Cóndor** (Corrientes 531, 7th floor, Buenos Aires, tel. 011/5371-5580, fax 011/5371-5581,

HOSTERÍA HELSINGFORS

In an incomparably dramatic setting at the base of glacier-covered mountains, on Lago Viedma's secluded south shore, Helsingfors was one of southwestern Santa Cruz's earliest *estancias,* and also one of the first to open its gates to tourists. Though its services, elevated prices, and isolation imply exclusivity, it's surprisingly unpretentious—the comfortable *casco* has an inviting reception area, a cozy sitting room with beamed ceilings, a large brick fireplace, a bar, and a dining room with a young but talented chef who spends his winters at the prestigious Las Leñas ski resort.

One of Helsingfors's recreational highlights is a 2.5-hour hike through meadows and *lenga* forest to Laguna Azul, a cirque lake beneath a hanging glacier. Despite the name, it's more turquoise than blue. There is also a rigid inflatable Zodiac for excursions to Glaciar Viedma, wind and weather permitting.

Legally, Helsingfors may not even be an *estancia,* as the founders apparently never registered their title and the land on which it sits probably belongs to Parque Nacional Los Glaciares. Laguna Azul and other surrounding areas certainly are, and Helsingfors's owners are concerned that Calafate operators could bring an influx of hikers that could impact a nearly pristine part of the park and, of course, reduce its appeal to high-paying guests.

Most visitors spend two or three nights at Helsingfors, which is 179 kilometers from El Calafate via eastbound RP 11, northbound RN 40, and westbound RP 21. It has eight double rooms, some of them detached from the *casco,* and there are plans to add three more double rooms and expand the dining area. Open mid-October–mid-April, Hostería Helsingfors (San Martín 516, Río Gallegos, tel. 02966/420719; Avenida Córdoba 827, 11° A, C1054AAH Buenos Aires, tel. 011/4315-1222, www.helsingfors.com.ar, US$195/350 s/d) includes full board, transportation to and from El Calafate or its airport, and all excursions. Children under age eight pay half.

Parque Nacional Los Glaciares's Laguna Azul lies just south of Hostería Helsingfors, on Lago Viedma's south shore.

www.cielospatagonicos.com, US$60 s or d with breakfast, US$90/120 s/d with full board) has 35 kilometers of lakefront. Lunch or dinner costs US$15 per person; there are also horseback rides (US$20 pp) and other activities.

Lago Cardiel and Vicinity

North of Tres Lagos, RN 40 winds north over the Meseta Cascajosa before coming within sight of **Lago Cardiel,** a deep interior drainage lake that's a bellwether for ongoing climate-change studies. It also enjoys a certain popularity for fishing excursions, but even then it's remote enough that there's not much competition.

On the west side of the highway, 22 kilometers south of the RP 29 junction to Gobernador Gregores, English-speaking Alejandro Luiz has leased **Estancia Siberia,** the casual doppelganger of the stereotypical tourist *estancia.* With little livestock, set amongst an aging orchard of apricot, cherry, pear, and plum trees, it's been open September–March or April, but there are reports that it's been sold. For the time being, Luiz operates a one-of-a-kind *confitería*/bar with light meals and desserts, a large CD collection, and a *fogón* for *parrilladas.* He also rents rooms (US$17 pp) with shared bath and hot showers; camping is free, so it's a popular stop for cyclists.

As RN 40 is paved and rerouted over the next several years, RP 29 to Gobernador Gregores will become the principal route north, though it's longer than the existing RN 40. At the junction, westbound RP 29 leads 23 kilometers to **Estancia Las Tunas** (tel. 011/4668-1491 in Buenos Aires, las_tunas@hotmail.com, US$72/120 s/d), recently opened to tourist trade, on Cardiel's north shore. Rates include full board and excursions, including horseback rides.

Estancia La Angostura and Vicinity

About 60 kilometers northwest of La Siberia on RN 40, midway between RP 29 and RP 25, an eastbound dirt road drops into the Río Chico marshlands, dotted with birds including upland geese, coots, and lapwings. In a sheltered location among densely planted trees, La Angostura has seven comfortable guest rooms (US$30 pp with breakfast), but also has a decent campground (US$3.50 pp) on a farm that's closer to the rustic end of the tourist *estancia* continuum. The food is heavy on Argentine standards like *milanesa.* For more details, contact Estancia La Angostura (tel. 02902/491208, jck@intervia.com.ar); it's open September–May. As RN 40 is rerouted to Gobernador Gregores, this will be more an off-the-paved-track place to experience the old highway.

North of La Angostura, the 200 or so kilometers of northbound RN 40 to Bajo Caracoles is one of Patagonia's most service-free areas, especially since the owner's death forced closure of the landmark **Hotel Las Horquetas,** an out-of-the-wind dive near the junction with westbound RP 37. Some campers like the sites along the Río Chico near the junction of RN 40 and RP 25, but the best spots go early. There's a basic alternative at **Río Olnie,** about 30 kilometers south of Bajo Caracoles (see separate entry below).

Gobernador Gregores

Though it's 60–70 kilometers east of RN 40 via either RP 29 or RP 25, Gobernador Gregores (population 2,513) can be an essential detour for bikers or motorists running short of gasoline. It's also the easiest place to obtain other supplies, and to hire a car and driver to otherwise inaccessible Parque Nacional Perito Moreno, some 200-plus kilometers to the northwest. RN 40's paving and rerouting to Gregores figures to reinvigorate the town as a tourist service center over the next several years, especially as a base for improved access to the park.

The **Camping Municipal Nuestra Señora del Valle** (Roca and Chile, tel. 02962/491038, US$1 pp) has hot showers. There's a pair of decent hotels: **Hotel San Francisco** (San Martín 463, tel. 02962/491039, US$5.50 pp), and **Hotel Cañadón León** (Roca 397, tel. 02962/491082, US$7/13 s/d), which also has the best restaurant.

Other choices for dining include **Pizzería Chicho** (Barrenechea and Belgrano) and the *parrilla* **El Palenque** (San Martín s/n).

The **Dirección Municipal de Turismo** (Barrenechea 492) can help with general information. The **APN** (San Martín 882, tel./fax 02962/491477, peritomoreno@apn.gov.ar) deals with Parque Nacional Perito Moreno.

LADE (Colón 544, tel. 02962/491008) flies northbound to Comodoro Rivadavia and Buenos Aires, and southbound to San Julián and Río Gallegos.

Cerro San Lorenzo (San Martín and Alberdi, tel. 02966/15-631768) has bus service to San Julián (US$9) at 6 P.M. Wednesday, Friday, Saturday, and Sunday, returning from San Julián at 7 A.M. Tuesday and Saturday and 1 P.M. Thursday and Sunday.

El Pulgarcito (San Martín 704, tel. 02962/491102) goes to Río Gallegos (US$12, 6.5 hours) Tuesday, Thursday, and Saturday at 6 A.M., returning Wednesday, Friday, and Sunday at 7 A.M. **El Pegazo** (Mariano Peikovic 520, tel. 02962/491274) goes to Gallegos Monday, Wednesday, and Friday at 6 A.M., returning at 8 A.M. Tuesday, Thursday, and Saturday.

Parque Nacional Perito Moreno

The intensely colored sedimentary summits of the Sierra Colorada are the backdrop for the lake-laden, wind-whipped, and wildlife-rich high country of Parque Nacional Perito Francisco P. Moreno, named for the founder of Argentina's national park system. Possibly Patagonia's wildest park, where Paleo-Indians covered cave walls with images of guanacos and human hands, it's one major reason travelers are braving the rigors of La Cuarenta.

In addition to the park itself, the Patagonia Land Trust has acquired 14,000 hectares in the adjacent area of El Rincón, which may be incorporated into the park.

Comprising 115,000 hectares of Patagonian steppe, sub-Antarctic forest, glacial lakes and fjords, and high Andean pastures, Parque Nacional Perito Moreno is 220 kilometers northwest of Gobernador Gregores via RP 25, RN 40, and RP 37. It's 310 kilometers southwest of the town of Perito Moreno via RN 40 and RP 37.

At 900 meters above sea level, the park's base altitude is significantly higher than Los Glaciares, and its climate colder, wetter, and more unpredictable. Its highest summit is 2,254-meter Cerro Mié, but snow-capped 3,700-meter Cerro San Lorenzo, north of the park boundary, is the area's highest peak.

In the drier eastern steppes, the dominant vegetation consists of bunch grasses known collectively as *coirón;* to the west, there's a transitional wind-flagged, sub-Antarctic forest of *lenga* and *ñire,* the ubiquitous southern beeches (*Nothofagus* spp.) In more sheltered areas, there are dense and nearly pure *lenga* forest along the shores of Lago Azara and Lago Nansen.

Troops of guanacos patrol the steppes and even some of the high country where there's summer pasture; the *huemul* (Andean deer) also grazes the uplands in summer but winters at lower altitudes. The puma is the alpha predator, but there are also smaller killers in the persons of red and grey foxes. The *pilquín* or *chinchillón anaranjado (Lagidium wolffsohni)* is a species of vizcacha unique to Santa Cruz province and southernmost Chile.

The largest birds are the Andean condor and the flightless rhea, but other impressive species include the *águila mora* (*Geranoaetus melanoleucus,* black-chested buzzard eagle), the large owl *ñacurutú (Bubo virginianus),* Patagonian wood-

© WAYNE BERNHARDSON

Parque Nacional Perito Moreno contains some of southern Patagonia's wildest high country.

peckers, and the *carancho* (crested caracara). Perito Moreno's many lakes and streams support abundant wildfowl, including flamingos, black-necked swans, grebes, wild geese, and steamer ducks. Unlike other Patagonian lakes, those within the park have remained free of introduced fish species.

Sights and Recreation

While **Lago Burmeister** is worth a visit, the cave paintings have been closed to public access. There are large troops of guanacos on **Península Belgrano,** reached by an isthmus immediately west of Estancia Belgrano (which is not a tourist *estancia*).

One of the best day hikes is 1,434-meter **Cerro León,** a 2.5-hour climb immediately north of Estancia La Oriental, which offers the best easily accessible panoramas in the vicinity (though hikers must be prepared for the changeable weather). The nearby volcanic overhang known as the **Cerro de los Cóndores** is the flight school for condor chicks.

Accommodations and Food

There are free but barren campsites with pit toilets at the APN's Centro de Informes, at the park entrance; the more appealing campground at Lago Burmeister consists of Tehuelche-style lean-tos in dense *lenga* forest. The water here is potable, but no supplies are available within the park; campers must bring everything they need.

Open November–March, within the park boundary on the north shore of Lago Belgrano, **Estancia La Oriental** (Rivadavia 936, San Julián, tel. 02962/452196, fax 02962/452445, elada@uvc.com.ar, US$50 s/d) has both conventional accommodations (seven rooms sleeping up to 22 guests) and protected campsites (US$6, with hot showers) near the lodge. The US$5 homemade breakfasts (homemade scones, bread, and jam, plus ham and cheese) deserve a detour, but the dinners (US$14 pp) can't quite match them.

Just outside the park boundary, **Estancia Menelik** occupies a windy, oddly exposed site—most *estancieros* chose protected valley-bottom locations for their settlements—but the popular explanation is that its original German homesteader wanted to advertise his presence, and spot the approach of any strangers. Despite the barren landscape, the welcome is warm at both the comfortably furnished farmhouse, which has ample bedrooms (US$70 d with breakfast) plus a large sitting room (with library) and dining areas, and at its simpler **Refugio Río Belgrano** (a rehabbed bunkhouse, US$10 pp). Though well off the beaten path, it does get tour groups, so reservations are advisable; for details, contact Cielos Patagónicos (Corrientes 531, 7th floor, Buenos Aires, tel. 011/5371-5580, fax 011/5371-5581, www.cielospatagonicos.com). Given Menelik's isolation, the quality of the food (US$5 for breakfast, US$15 for lunch or dinner) is very good. It's open November–April.

Other Practicalities

Rangers at Perito Moreno's Centro de Informes, at the park entrance, provide maps and brochures, and offer a variety of guided hikes and visits; they can also be reached through the APN in Gobernador Gregores (tel./fax 02962/491477, peritomoreno@apn.gov.ar); the postal address is Casilla de Correo 103, (9311) Gobernador Gregores.

Rental cars offer the greatest flexibility, though it's possible to hire a car and driver in Gobernador Gregores or the town of Perito Moreno. Hitching from the highway junction is feasible but by no means certain.

In season, Overland Patagonia's four-day "safari" from Bariloche to El Calafate visits the park during the day and spends the night at Menelik; for details, see the sidebar "Get Your Flats on La Cuarenta."

Río Olnie

Thirty kilometers south of Bajo Caracoles, Río Olnie is a wide spot at a curve in the road where a recent settler who goes by the nickname "Arroz Crudo" ("Raw Rice") has reopened the country bar known as **Hotel Olnie** after a 12-year closure. He is slowly—*very slowly*—rehabbing the building with "luxuries" like indoor plumbing and showers. Cyclists, among the hotel's most reliable clientele, pay US$2 per person for bunks, while there are also a couple simple singles for US$3.50.

While likely to improve, this is a boisterous macho environment (though not threatening), and single women might feel uncomfortable here. Simple meals are also available, and any additional services on RN 40 are welcome ones.

Bajo Caracoles

Midway between Las Horquetas and the town of Perito Moreno, barren Bajo Caracoles is an oasis for automobiles and motorcycles, as it has the only gas station in nearly 500 kilometers of RN 40. Southbound travelers should fill the tank here, but northbound travelers should buy only enough to reach Perito Moreno, 128 kilometers to the north.

Bajo Caracoles is also the southern gateway to the major rock-art site of Cueva de las Manos, 41 kilometers to the northeast via RP 57, but there are alternative access points farther north. RP 39 leads east to the hamlet of Hipólito Yrigoyen and **Lago Posadas,** near the Chilean border, while RP 41, a short distance north of Bajo Caracoles, goes directly to the border crossing at **Paso Roballos.**

With recently modernized bathrooms, the legendary **Hotel Bajo Caracoles** (tel. 02963/490100, US$17 s or d) is far better than anyone might expect in this remote outpost, and it fills up early despite its cantankerous owner—after all, it's the only option. It also has groceries and surprisingly good meals.

Lago Posadas and Vicinity

Bajo Caracoles is not known for its beauty, but it's hard to improve on aquamarine Lago Posadas, 90 kilometers to the east, and nearby Lago Pueyrredón, nudging the Chilean border. While the main route from Bajo Caracoles to the border passes Lago Ghío, along RP 41 to the north, southerly RP 39 via Lago Posadas is a more scenic alternative.

It also permits a stay at **Estancia Turística Lagos del Furioso,** an unpretentious but more-than-comfortable getaway occupying a privileged site on the isthmus between Lago Pueyrredón and Lago Posadas. Porteño owners Ana Bas and Jorge Cramer oversee attentive service, a first-rate restaurant, and excursions to the wild surrounding countryside with rates starting at US$179–242 d. Lunches cost US$10, dinners US$20.

Lagos del Furioso (Paraná 1255 6° D, Buenos Aires, tel. 011/4812-0959, www.lagosdelfurioso.com, info@lagosdelfurioso.com) can also be reached via Estancias Turísticas de Santa Cruz (Suipacha 1120, Buenos Aires, tel. 011/4325-3098, www.estanciasdesantacruz.com). It's open November–April; the minimum stay is two nights.

Cueva de las Manos and Vicinity

Beyond Baja Caracoles, rugged RN 40 traverses the northern steppe until the point where, over millions of years, the Río Pinturas has cut a deep, scenic canyon. In the process, it has left countless *aleros,* stony overhangs often mistakenly called *cuevas* or caves. One of these is the famous **Cueva de las Manos,** a UNESCO World Heritage Site where stencils of hundreds of human hands, guanacos, and abstract forms cover the rock walls in orange, red, and yellow ochres.

The canyon of the Río Pinturas is the location of Cueva de las Manos, a pre-Columbian rock-art site recognized by UNESCO.

Dating from around 7370 B.C. the oldest paintings at Cueva de las Manos represent hunter-gatherers from immediate post-glacial times, but the more abstract designs, which are fewer, are far more recent. Oddly enough, nearly all the hands from which the site takes its name are left hands.

Along with Parque Nacional Perito Moreno, this is one of the finest detours off RN 40, with two main access points. From Bajo Caracoles in the south, gravel RP 41 goes directly to the site, where the municipality of Perito Moreno operates a small *confitería* and a rocky campground (US$1 per tent), and charges US$1.50 admission to the caves. Bars now block close access to the paintings, to discourage vandalism (even repeatedly touching the paintings could damage them), but do not obscure the view.

The other main access point is from the Río Pinturas drainage itself, with two separate alternatives (both of which also offer accommodations). From **Estancia Casa de Piedra** (tel. 02963/432199 in Perito Moreno), 45 kilometers north of Bajo Caracoles, there's a 12-kilometer access road, at the end of which it's a three-kilometer hike to the paintings; from **Estancia los Toldos,** another 23 kilometers north and seven kilometers east, another 15-kilometer access road permits a close approach. Note that, by either the northern or southern route, mountain bikers can avoid backtracking to RN 40 by hauling their bikes over the river (there's a pedestrian bridge) and out the other direction.

On the east side of RN 40 (ideal for cyclists), the bucolic **Estancia Casa de Piedra** (tel. 02963/432199) allows camping for $1.25 per tent, plus US$1 for showers; it also rents basic but passable rooms for US$5.50/9 s/d with shared bath. At Estancia Los Toldos, **Hostería Cueva de las Manos** (tel. 011/4901-0436, fax 011/4903-7161, cuevadelasmanos@hotmail.com, cdelasmanos@fibertel.com.ar) has four modern carpeted rooms with private bath (US$70 d) with breakfast, plus very fine hostel accommodations (US$16 pp) without breakfast. Restaurant lunches and dinners cost about US$15, afternoon tea US$5. It's open November–March, and sometimes for Semana Santa. They will also arrange transfers from the town of Perito Moreno (US$25 one way for a minimum two passengers) and offer a variety of excursions.

Estancia Telken

Only 30 kilometers south of Perito Moreno, a short drive west of the highway, Estancia Telken is a 21,000-hectare working ranch that doubles as a restful guest house and campground. Hosted by a gracious Dutch-Argentine family—who share meals and conversation with their guests—Telken also offers excursions in the vicinity, most notably to the rock-art site of Cañadón del Arroyo Feo, as well as Cueva de las Manos, Los Antiguos, Lago Posadas, and other provincial destinations.

Dating from 1915, Telken has a main house comprising two rooms with private bath and one with shared bath, while a separate guest house has a triple with private bath and an apartment that can sleep up to five persons. Guests dine with owner/proprietors Coco and Petty Nauta, who speak Spanish, English, and Dutch. The grassy campground has a covered *quincho* with a full kitchen for cooking and a full bath with hot showers.

Open October to the end of April, Estancia Telken (tel. 02963/432079, tel./fax 02963/432303, jarinauta@yahoo.com.ar, telkenpatagonia@argentina.com) charges US$44/50 s/d with shared bath, US$54/60 s/d with private bath, both with breakfast. With half-board, rates are US$59/80 s/d with shared bath, US$69/90 s/d with private bath. Camping costs US$5 per tent or vehicle, plus US$5 per person. In addition to more distant excursions, visitors can rent horses (US$10 for the first hour).

In the off-season, contact Coco and Petty Nauta (Roque Sáenz Peña 2480, (1636) Olivos, Provincia de Buenos Aires, tel. 011/4797-7216).

Perito Moreno

Where RN 40 meets the smoothly paved international highway from Comodoro Rivadavia to Chile Chico, the nondescript cowtown of Perito Moreno marks the return to civilization for northbound travelers and the start of the adventure for the Calafate-bound. Often confused with its namesake national park, as well as the eponymous glacier in Parque Nacional Los Glaciares, it has reasonably good services, but many visitors prefer the lakeside town of Los Antiguos to the west.

Perito Moreno (population 3,598) is 398 kilometers southwest of Comodoro Rivadavia via Caleta Olivia, and 58 kilometers east of Los Antiguos via smoothly paved RP 43. It is 124 kilometers south of Río Mayo, Chubut province, via one of the more rugged stretches of RN 40, which continues toward Esquel and the Andean lake district; for more details on this route, see the Northern Patagonia chapter. Note that there is no regularly scheduled public transportation between Perito Moreno and Río Mayo.

Early February's **Festival Folklórico Cueva de las Manos** is a musical event that capitalizes on the proximity of Santa Cruz's world heritage site.

Practicalities

Opposite Laguna de los Cisnes, the city park at the south end of town, the **Camping Municipal** (Roca and Moreno, US$1.30 plus US$1.30 per vehicle or tent) is small but sheltered from the wind, and has flawless bathrooms with hot showers (US$1 extra).

Otherwise, the pickings are slim. **Hotel Santa Cruz** (Belgrano 1565, tel. 02963/432133, US$9 d) is a no-frills shoestring option, while **Hotel Americano** (San Martín 1327, tel. 02963/432074, juanpablo_leiva@hotmail.com, US$9/13 s/d) is a hair better. The respectable **Hotel Belgrano** (Avenida San Martín 1001, tel. 02963/432019, US$9/15 s/d) also has a restaurant, but the best option is the homey B&B **Posada del Caminante** (Rivadavia 937, tel. 02963/432204, matejedor@interlap.com.ar, US$10/15 s/d); since it has only three rooms, call ahead.

The **Oficina Municipal de Turismo** (Avenida San Martín 1059, tel. 02963/432732, turismompm@interlap.com.ar) is open 7 A.M.–11 P.M. and 8 A.M.–10 P.M. daily the rest of the year, but closes noon–2 P.M. on weekends.

Banco de la Nación (Avenida San Martín 1385) has an ATM.

Correo Argentino is at Avenida Juan D. Perón 1331; the postal code is 9040. The **Call Center** (Rivadavia 1055) has long-distance services, while **Crazy.net** (Perito Moreno 1070) has Internet connections including perhaps Argentine Patagonia's only iMac.

Family to Estancia Telken, bilingual **Guanacondor Tours & Expeditions** (Perito Moreno 1087, tel. 02963/432303, jarinauta@yahoo.com.ar, jarinauta@santacruz.com.ar) arranges excursions including Cañadón del Arroyo Feo.

For medical services, the **Hospital Distrital** is at Colón 1237, tel. 02963/432045.

LADE (Avenida San Martín 1065, tel. 02963/432055) was flightless as of last pass. The airstrip at the north end of town, though, is undergoing a major upgrade.

The sharp new **Terminal de Ómnibus** is also at the north end of town, at the traffic circle where RN 40 (Avenida San Martín) meets RP 43. Note, however, that there are is no regular overland transport on that stretch of RN 40 between Perito Moreno and Río Mayo, 124 kilometers to the north.

La Unión (tel. 02963/432638) and **Sportman** (tel. 02963/432177) have westbound service to Los Antiguos (US$1.50, one hour) and eastbound service to Comodoro Rivadavia (US$9, five hours). Sportman also has a daily service to Río Gallegos (US$20, 12 hours).

Transporte Lago Posadas (Saavedra 1357, tel. 02963/432431) has irregular minibus service to Lago Posadas US$8, four hours).

Chaltén Travel buses from Los Antiguos to El Calafate will pick up passengers at the terminal here; for details, see the El Calafate entry. For southbound travel to El Chaltén, contact **Itinerarios y Travesías** (tel. 02963/432268, tel. 0297/15-400-0335); for more details, see the Parque Nacional Los Glaciares entry above.

Los Antiguos

Rows of upright poplars announce the approach to laid-back Los Antiguos, the garden spot of Santa Cruz province, where riotously colorful flowerbeds fill the median strip of Avenida 11 de Julio, flats of soft fruits like raspberries, cherries, and strawberries go for a song, and baskets of apples, apricots, pears, peaches, plums, and prunes adorn the storefronts.

Thanks to its mild microclimate, Los Antiguos

has been a getaway since Tehuelche times, its Spanish name ("the ancient ones") derived from an indigenous term meaning "Place of the Elders." For a few years, after the eruption of Chile's nearby Volcán Hudson in August 1991 buried the area in ash, both the fruit harvest and the tourist trade suffered, but there's been a recent recovery. Fishing and hiking are the main attractions.

On the south shore of Lago Buenos Aires, Los Antiguos (population 2,047) is 58 kilometers west of Perito Moreno via RP 43. Entering town, the highway becomes the divided Avenida 11 de Julio, which continues to the Chilean border; the Argentine border post is on the western edge of town, while the Chilean Carabineros are across the Río Jeinemeni, about five kilometers farther.

Early January's three-day **Fiesta de la Cereza** (cherry festival) can put a strain on accommodations and other facilities. February 5's **Día de los Antiguos** marks the town's anniversary, while **Día del Lago Buenos Aires** takes place October 29.

For fresh fruit, as well as preserves, try any of several farms such as **Chacra El Porvenir** (walking distance from Avenida 11 de Julio) and the lakeshore **Chacra El Paraíso.**

Practicalities

Protected by poplars and cypresses, the lakeshore **Camping Municipal** (Avenida 11 de Julio s/n, tel. 02963/491265, US$1 pp plus US$1 per tent) provides picnic tables and fire pits at every site. Hot showers are available 5:30–10 P.M. only.

Hotel Argentino (Avenida 11 de Julio 850, tel. 02963/491132, US$10/18 s/d) is a utilitarian hotel with a decent restaurant. On the eastern outskirts of town, **Hostería Antigua Patagonia** (RP 43 s/n, tel. 02963/491055, www.antiguapatagonia.com.ar, US$36/50 s/d) is a modern three-story hotel.

The **Subsecretaría de Turismo** (Avenida 11 de Julio 432, tel. 02963/491261, fax 02963/491261, www.losantiguos-sc.com.ar) is open 7 A.M.–8 P.M. daily October–March, 9 A.M.–4 P.M. weekdays only the rest of the year.

Banco de Santa Cruz (Avenida 11 de Julio 531) has an ATM.

Correo Argentino is at Gobernador Gregores 19; the postal code is 9041. **Locutorio Los Antiguos** (Alameda 436) has long-distance telephone services, but has been slow to enter the digital age.

La Unión (Alameda 428, tel. 02963/491078) and **Sportman** (Patagonia Argentina 170, tel. 02963/15-621-6082) both go to Caleta Olivia (US$8, five hours) and Comodoro Rivadavia (US$10, six hours). Sportman also has daily service to Río Gallegos.

Acotrans (Patagonia Argentina 170, tel. 02963/15-621-6082) crosses the border to Chile Chico (US$1 pp) three times every weekday and twice Saturday, but never on Sunday.

For up-to-date information on Chaltén Travel buses and Itinerarios y Travesías trips to El Chaltén (US$45, 13 hours) via southbound RN 40, contact the **Subsecretaría de Turismo** (Avenida 11 de Julio 432, tel. 02963/491261).

Magallanes

Thanks to the Torres del Paine, the magnificent granite needles that rise above the Patagonian plains, Chile's most southerly region has acquired international fame. Pacific storms drench the nearly uninhabited western Andean cordillera, feeding alpine and continental glaciers and rushing rivers, but rolling grasslands and almost unstoppable winds typify the eastern areas in the Andean rain shadow. Along the Strait of Magellan, the city of Punta Arenas is the center for excursions to a variety of attractions, including easily accessible penguin colonies and Tierra del Fuego's remote fjords. The region has no direct road connections to the rest of Chile—travelers must arrive by air, sea, and through Argentine Patagonia.

Administratively, Region XII (Magallanes) includes all Chilean territory beyond 49° S—theoretically all the way to the South Pole, as Chile claims a slice of Antarctica between 53° and 90° W longitude. It also takes in the Chilean half of the Isla Grande de Tierra del Fuego, west of about 68° 35', and most of archipelagic Tierra del Fuego.

Over the past decade, improved cross-border communications have meant that many visitors to the Argentine side also visit Chile to see Puerto Natales, Torres del Paine, and other Chilean attractions. While prices are presently higher in Chile than in Argentina, they are also stable and, after the initial surprise, most visitors adapt accordingly.

As in Argentina, January and February are the

Must-Sees

Look for [M] to find the sights and activities you can't miss and [N] for the best dining and lodging.

Casa Braun-Menéndez (Museo Regional de Magallanes): Magallanes's regional museum now occupies what was the mansion of Patagonia's wool aristocracy (page 380).

Monumento Natural Los Pingüinos: In the summer season, penguins occupy every square centimeter of Isla Magdalena, also home to a historic lighthouse (page 391).

Parque Nacional Pali Aike: Hugging the Argentine border, the caves of the northern Magallanes's volcanic steppe feature some of the continent's prime "Early Man" sites (page 395).

The Fjords of Fuegia: It may be expensive to cruise the ice-clogged inlets of the archipelago of Tierra del Fuego, from Punta Arenas to Ushuaia, Cape Horn, and back, but it's still cheaper than chartering your own yacht. Even backpackers occasionally splurge for a leg of this unforgettable itinerary (page 395).

Cuernos del Paine, Parque Nacional Torres del Paine

Torres del Paine: The granite needles that rise above the Patagonian steppe are a beacon drawing travelers from around the world to Chile's premier national park, **Parque Nacional Torres del Paine** (page 413).

Cuernos del Paine: This jagged interface between igneous and metamorphic rock, also in Parque Nacional Torres del Paine, comprises some of the world's most breathtaking alpine scenery (page 414).

Puerto Williams: On Isla Navarino, across the Beagle Channel from Ushuaia, tiny Williams retains much of the "uttermost part of the earth" ambiance that the Argentine city once offered. It also provides access to the rugged hiking trails of the Dientes de Navarino, a series of summits that rise like inverted vampire's fangs (page 423).

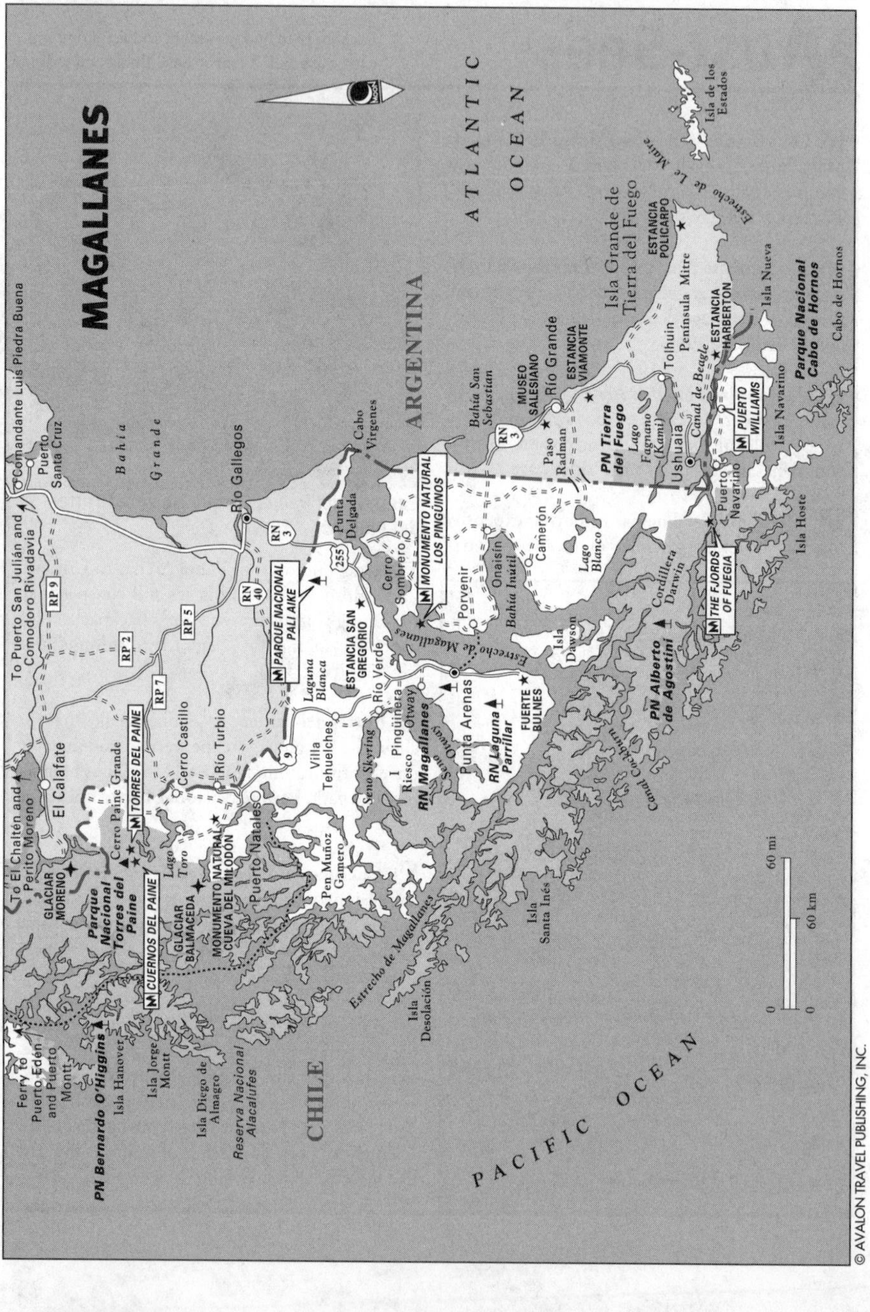

MAGALLANES

ATLANTIC OCEAN
PACIFIC OCEAN
ARGENTINA
CHILE
Bahía Grande
To Puerto San Julián and Comodoro Rivadavia
Comandante Luis Piedra Buena
Puerto Santa Cruz
To El Chaltén and Perito Moreno
El Calafate
GLACIAR MORENO
Parque Nacional Torres del Paine
CUERNOS DEL PAINE
TORRES DEL PAINE
Cerro Paine Grande
Lago Toro
Cerro Castillo
Río Turbio
GLACIAR BALMACEDA
MONUMENTO NATURAL CUEVA DEL MILODÓN
Puerto Natales
RP 9
RP 2
RP 5
RP 7
RN 40
RN 3
9
255
Río Gallegos
Cabo Vírgenes
Punta Delgada
PARQUE NACIONAL PALI AIKE
Laguna Blanca
ESTANCIA SAN GREGORIO
Villa Tehuelches
Río Verde
Pen Muñoz Gamero
I Riesco
Pingüinera Otway
Seno Skyring
Seno Otway
RN Magallanes
Punta Arenas
RN Laguna Parrillar
FUERTE BULNES
Cerro Sombrero
MONUMENTO NATURAL LOS PINGÜINOS
Porvenir
Onaisín
Bahía Inútil
Estrecho de Magallanes
Isla Dawson
Cameron
Lago Blanco
Bahía San Sebastián
MUSEO SALESIANO
Río Grande
ESTANCIA VIAMONTE
Paso Radman
PN Tierra del Fuego
Lago Fagnano (Kami)
Tolhuin
Ushuaia
Canal de Beagle
ESTANCIA HARBERTON
Península Mitre
ESTANCIA POLICARPO
Isla Grande de Tierra del Fuego
Estrecho de Le Maire
Isla de los Estados
Puerto Navarino
PUERTO WILLIAMS
Isla Navarino
Isla Nueva
Parque Nacional Cabo de Hornos
Cabo de Hornos
Isla Hoste
THE FJORDS OF FUEGIA
Cordillera Darwin
PN Alberto de Agostini
Canal Cockburn
Isla Santa Inés
Isla Desolación
Ferry to Puerto Edén and Puerto Montt
PN Bernardo O'Higgins
Isla Hanover
Isla Jorge Montt
Isla Diego de Almagro
Reserva Nacional Alacalufes
0 60 mi
0 60 km

peak months, and prices drop considerably in the off-season—though many places also close. Like Argentina's El Calafate, the area enjoys a lengthening tourist season.

PLANNING YOUR TIME

Like Ushuaia, Punta Arenas can be a base for sightseeing, but usually only for a day or two; for those who haven't seen Magellanic penguins elsewhere, it's worth scheduling or waiting for the boat to Isla Magdalena. It's also the home port for the spectacular cruise to Tierra del Fuego's remotest fjords and Cape Horn, a trip that deserves its full week but is worth doing even in a three- or four-day segment.

Exploring the thinly populated Chilean part of Tierra del Fuego requires a vehicle or even an airplane—connections to Puerto Williams, though it's not far from Ushuaia as the crow flies, are haphazard except by commercial flights from Punta Arenas. Once you're there, it takes at least a week to hike the Dientes circuit.

Puerto Natales, the urban gateway to Torres del Paine, is primarily a place to prepare for the trek, but its seaside setting, the youthful exuberance of its visitors, and nearby hiking excursions often extend the stay. The park itself deserves no less than a week, for day-hikers and backpackers alike, but even an abbreviated day trip—some people do it, despite the time and difficulty of getting here—is worth the trouble.

A new attraction is the *Skorpios III* cruise through the fjords on the west side of the Campos de Hielo Sur, across the ice from Torres del Paine. In the summer season, this pioneering five-day, four-night excursion promises to become a regional highlight.

HISTORY

Some of the oldest archaeological evidence for human habitation on the entire continent comes from Magallanes, from volcanic rock shelters in and near Parque Nacional Pali Aike on the Argentine border. Pleistocene hunter-gatherers once stalked now-extinct species like giant ground sloths and native American horses, but later adopted more broad-spectrum forms of subsistence that included marine and coastal resources. These peoples were the predecessors of today's few surviving Tehuelche and Kawasqar (Alacaluf) peoples, and the nearly extinct Selknam (Ona) and Yámana (Yahgan) who gathered shellfish on the coast and hunted guanaco and rhea with bows and arrows and *boleadoras.*

European familiarity with southernmost South America dates from 1520, when the Portuguese navigator Fernando Magalhaes, in the service of Spain, sailed through the strait that now bears his name (Magallanes in Spanish, Magellan in English). Ranging from three to 25 kilometers in width, the Strait of Magellan became a major maritime thoroughfare en route to the Pacific.

Spain's 16th-century colonization attempts failed miserably, as did the initial Chilean and Argentine efforts, but the city of Punta Arenas finally took hold after 1848—thanks largely to the fortuitous discovery of gold in California only a year later. While gold fever soon subsided, the introduction of sheep brought a wool and mutton boom that benefited from the Franco-Prussian War of the 1870s, and helped create enormous *estancias* that dominated the region's political, social, and economic life for nearly a century.

While the livestock industry hangs on, commercial fisheries, the state-run oil industry, and the tourist trade have superseded it in the regional economy. Even these industries, though, have proved vulnerable to fluctuations, declining reserves, and international developments beyond their control, so that Magallanes cannot count on the prosperity that once seemed assured. The Zona Franca free-trade zone that once fueled the regional economy, even drawing immigrants from central Chile, has largely stagnated.

Punta Arenas and Vicinity

Patagonia's largest city, Punta Arenas is also the regional capital and the traditional port of entry, whether by sea, land, or air. Stretching north-south along the Strait of Magellan, the city boasts an architectural heritage that ranges from the Magellanic vernacular of metal-clad houses with steeply pitched roofs to elaborate Francophile mansions commissioned by 19th-century wool barons. Home to several museums, it's a good base for excursions to historical sites and nearby penguin colonies.

Punta Arenas's diverse economy depends on fishing, shipping, petroleum, duty-free retail, and tourism. Historically, it's one of the main gateways to Antarctica for both research and tourism, but in recent years the Argentine port of Ushuaia has taken away much of this traffic. Ironically, in a region that grazes millions of sheep, it's hard to find woolens here because of the influx of artificial fabrics through the duty-free Zona Franca.

HISTORY

After the collapse of Chile's initial Patagonian settlement at Fuerte Bulnes, Governor José Santos Mardones relocated northward to a site on the western shore of the Strait of Magellan, long known to British seamen as "Sandy Point." Soon expanded to include a penal colony, the town adopted that name in Spanish translation.

The Chileans' timing was propitious, as the 1849 California Gold Rush spurred a surge of shipping through the Strait that helped keep the new city afloat—even if supplying sealskins, coal, firewood, and lumber did not exactly portend prosperity. A mutiny that resulted in the death of Governor Benjamín Muñoz Gamero did little to improve matters, and traffic fell off in the following years.

What did bring prosperity was Governor Diego Dublé Almeyda's introduction of breeding sheep from the Falkland Islands. Their proliferation on the Patagonian plains, along with a vigorous immigration policy that brought entrepreneurs like the Portuguese José Nogueira, the Spaniard José Menéndez, and the Irishman Thomas Fenton—not to mention the polyglot laborers who made their fortunes possible—helped transform the city from a dreary presidio to the booming port of a pastoral empire. Its mansions matched many in Buenos Aires, though the maldistribution of wealth and political power remained an intractable issue well into the 20th century.

As the wool economy declined around the end of World War II, petroleum discoveries on Tierra del Fuego and commercial fishing sustained the economy. Creation of Zona Franca duty-free zones gave commercial advantages to both Punta Arenas and the northern city of Iquique in the 1970s, and the tourist trade has flourished since the end of military dictatorship in 1989.

ORIENTATION

Punta Arenas (population 116,105) is 210 kilometers southwest of Río Gallegos via the Argentine RN 3 and the Chilean Ruta 255 and Ruta 9; it is 241 kilometers southeast of Puerto Natales via Ruta 9. A daily vehicle ferry connects Punta with Porvenir, while a gravel road, the most southerly on the South American continent, leads to Fuerte Bulnes and Cabo San Isidro.

On the western shore of the Strait of Magellan, Punta Arenas occupies a narrow north-south wave-cut terrace, but the ground rises steeply farther west. Only in recent years has the city begun to spread eastward rather than north to south.

Most landmarks and services are within a few blocks of the central Plaza Muñoz Gamero; street names change on each side of the plaza, but the numbering system is continuous.

SIGHTS

For a panoramic overview of the city's layout, the Strait of Magellan, and the island of Tierra del Fuego in the distance, climb to **Mirador La Cruz,** four blocks west of Plaza Muñoz Gamero via a staircase at the corner of the Fagnano and Señoret.

I HEARD IT THROUGH THE GRAPEVINE

When the Patagonian wool barons built their mansions and *cascos* in the 19th century, one amenity they all demanded was a glassed-in greenhouse or conservatory. In a region where high winds, hail, and snowstorms were not unusual at any season, they could enjoy balmy indoor sunshine on long summer days, and grow vegetables like eggplants and tomatoes that could never survive the weather outdoors.

Both Argentina and Chile are famous for their grapes (thanks to their wine industries), but the two countries can also boast the world's southernmost grape arbors. The most readily seen is the one at the conservatory restaurant at Punta Arenas's Hotel José Nogueira, the former Sara Braun mansion, at 53° 9' S. So far, though, even visiting experts have been unable to identify its origins.

According to Sara Braun's descendent Julia Braun, vines at the *casco* of Estancia Sara, on the Argentine side of Tierra del Fuego, push the grape line to 53° 25' S. The original *casco* at Estancia María Behety (53° 48' S), west of the city of Río Grande, may have had vines, but the house burned to the ground several years back.

One of the most luxuriant austral grapevines, though, flourishes in Government House in Stanley, in the Falkland Islands. Introduced by Governor Cosmo Haskard in the 1960s, at 51° 45' S, it's not so far south as Punta Arenas or Estancia Sara, but its Black Hamburg table grapes may provide the most abundant harvest of any of them.

In the Islands, grapes have been such a luxury that Government House dinner guests eat them dipped in chocolate during the March/April harvest. According to Stanley market gardener Tim Miller, he purchases the surplus and labels them "'by Royal Appointment,' as the Governor is the Queen's representative at the end of the day!"

© WAYNE BERNHARDSON

Some of the world's southernmost grapes grow in the conservatory restaurant of the former Sara Braun mansion in Punta Arenas.

Plaza Muñoz Gamero and Vicinity

Unlike plazas founded in colonial Chilean cities, Punta Arenas's central plaza was not initially the focus of civic life, but thanks to European immigration and wealth generated by mining, livestock, commerce, and fishing, it became so by the 1880s. Landscaped with Monterey cypress and other exotic conifers, the plaza and surrounding buildings constitute a *zona típica* national monument; the plaza proper underwent a major renovation in 2004.

The plaza takes its name from early provincial governor Benjamín Muñoz Gamero, who died in an 1851 mutiny. Among its features are the Victorian kiosk (1910) that now houses the municipal tourist office and sculptor Guillermo Córdova's elaborate monument sponsored by wool magnate José Menéndez on the 400th anniversary of Magellan's 1520 voyage. Magellan's imposing figure, embellished with a globe and a copy of his log, stand above a Selknam Indian representing Tierra del Fuego, a Tehuelche symbolizing Patagonia, and a mermaid with Chilean and regional coats-of-arms. According to local legend, anyone touching the Tehuelche's now well-worn toe—enough have done so to change its color—will return to Punta Arenas.

After about 1880, the city's burgeoning elite began to build monuments to their own good fortune, such as the ornate **Palacio Sara Braun** (1895), a national monument in its own right, at the plaza's northwest corner. Only six years after marrying the Portuguese José Nogueira, Punta's most prominent businessman, the newly widowed Sara Braun contracted French architect Numa Mayer, who applied contemporary Parisian style in designing a two-story mansard building that contrasted dramatically with the city's earlier utilitarian architecture. Now home to the Club de la Unión and Hotel José Nogueira, the building retains most of its original features, including the west-facing winter garden that now serves as the hotel's bar/restaurant.

Mid-block, immediately to the east, the **Casa José Menéndez** belonged to another of Punta's wool barons, while at the plaza's northeast corner, the Comapa travel agency now occupies the former headquarters of the influential **Sociedad Menéndez Behety** (Magallanes 990). Half a block north, dating from 1904, the **Casa Braun-Menéndez** (Magallanes 949) houses the regional museum.

At the plaza's southwest corner, Punta Arenas's **Iglesia Matriz** (1901) now enjoys cathedral status. Immediately to its north, both the **Residencia del Gobernador** (Governors' Residence) and the **Gobernación** date from the same period, filling the rest of the block with offices of the Intendencia Regional, the regional government. On the south side, directly opposite the Victorian tourist kiosk, the former **Palacio Montes** now holds municipal government offices; at the southeast corner, the **Sociedad Braun Blanchard** belonged to another powerful commercial group (as should be obvious from the names, Punta Arenas's first families were, commercially at least, an incestuous bunch).

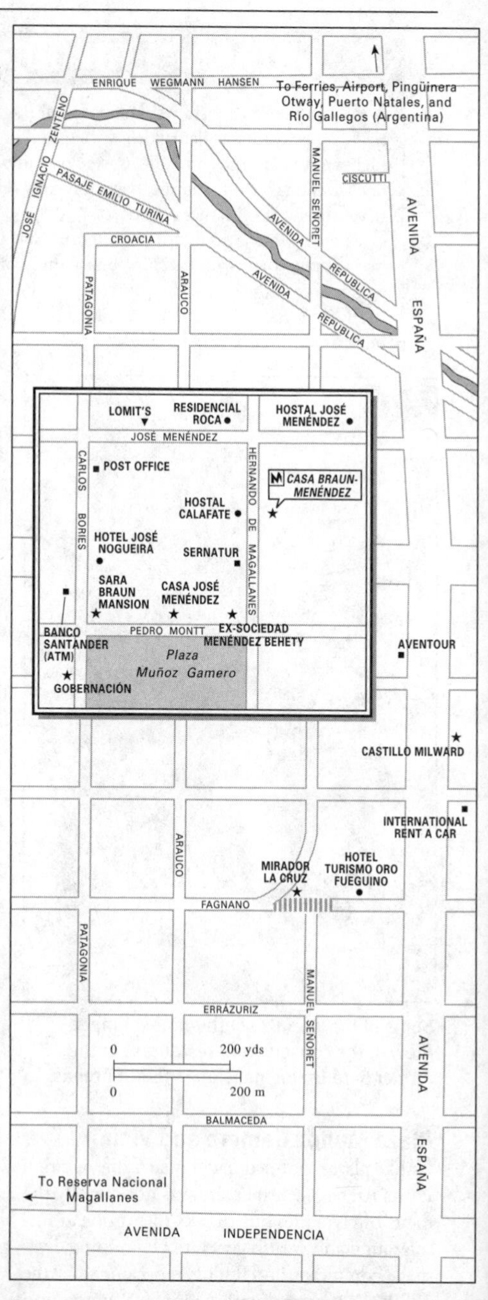

PUNTA ARENAS

To Cementerio Municipal, Museo del Recuerdo, Zona Franca, Ferries, Airport, Pingüinera Otway, Puerto Natales, and Río Gallegos (Argentina)

To Hospedaje Costanera

MUSEO REGIONAL SALESIANO MAYORINO BORGATELLO
AV BULNES
LAVASECO VICARS
HOSTAL CARPA MANZANO
CLAUDIO BOTTEN
SARMIENTO DE GAMBOA
DON BOSCO
ARMANDO
CHILOÉ
TRES ARROYOS
AUSTRO INTERNET
CARLOS BORIES
LAUTARO NAVARRO
HOSTAL LUNA
O'HIGGINS
QUILLOTA
CROACIA
SANHUEZA
DONDE MARÍN
HERNANDO DE MAGALLANES
MEJICANA
EL MERCADO
SALA ESTRELLA
TURISMO AONIKENK
Plaza Sampaio
HOSPEDAJE MANUEL
HOSPEDAJE MEJICANA
EL ESTRIBO
DAMIANA ELENA
ALBERGUE BACKPACKER'S PARADISE
IGNACIO CARRERA PINTO
ROTISERÍA LA MAMÁ
Río de las Minas
CHILE TÍPICO
HOSTAL TERRASUR
JORGE MONTT
BUSES FERNÁNDEZ
HOSTAL LA ESTANCIA
VALESSE
SCOTT CAMBIOS/ CENTRAL DE PASAJEROS
BUSES PACHECO
HOTEL TIERRA DEL FUEGO
HOTEL CÓNDOR DE PLATA
HOTEL FINIS TERRAE
AVENIDA COLÓN
MURAL GABRIELA MISTRAL
HOTEL MONTECARLO
LOS PATIPERROS
HOSTAL FITZROY
TURISMO LAGUNA AZUL
TURISMO PEHOÉ
AEROVÍAS DAP
HOSTAL DEL ESTRECHO
LA CARIOCA
JOSÉ MENÉNDEZ
HOTEL SAVOY
BUS SUR
HOTEL LOS NAVEGANTES
SEE DETAIL
ENTEL
AUTOMÓVIL CLUB DE CHILE
CONAF
PJE DUBLE ALMEYDA
BUDGET RENT A CAR
BUSES GHISONI/ TECNI-AUSTRAL
BUSES TRANSFER
LAVANDERÍA RECORD
LANEXPRESS
HERTZ
WALDO SEGUEL
PEDRO MONTT
LA LUNA
LABERINTO
HOSTAL AL FIN DEL MUNDO
MUSEO NAVAL Y MARÍTIMO
RESIDENCIA DEL GOBERNADOR
Plaza Muñoz Gamero
HOTEL CABO DE HORNOS
BROCCOLINO
PJE KORNER
IGLESIA MATRIZ
QUIJOTE
HOSTAL DEL REY
ROCA
TURISMO VIENTO SUR
HOTEL MERCURIO
TELEFÓNICA CTC
PALACIO MONTES
SOCIEDAD BRAUN BLANCHARD
TURISMO PALI AIKE
SOTITO'S BAR
PJE J. PEDRALS
HOTEL PLAZA
OLIJOE PUB
ERRÁZURIZ
Estrecho de Magallanes
HOTEL ISLA REY JORGE
TURISMO YÁMANA
HOSTAL O'HIGGINS
NOGUEIRA
21 DE MAYO
PUERTO VIEJO
To Colegio Pierre Fauré
To Reserva Nacional Laguna Parrillar and Fuerte Bulnes
AVENIDA INDEPENDENCIA
ARTESANÍAS RAMA CHILE
PUERTO DEL ESTRECHO
MUELLE FISCAL ARTURO PRAT
MOON

Casa Braun-Menéndez (Museo Regional de Magallanes)

Like European royalty, Punta's first families formed alliances sealed by matrimony, and the Casa Braun-Menéndez (1904) is a classic example: the product of a marriage between Mauricio Braun (Sara's brother) and Josefina Menéndez Behety (daughter of José Menéndez and María Behety, a major wool-growing family in Argentina—though international borders meant little to wool merchants).

Still furnished with the family's belongings, preserving Mauricio Braun's office and other rooms virtually intact, the house boasts marble fireplaces and other elaborate architectural features. The servants' quarters in the newly opened basement reveals the classic upstairs-downstairs division of early-20th-century society.

Today, the Casa Braun-Menéndez (Magallanes 949, tel. 061/244216, museomag@tie.cl) serves as the regional museum, replete with pioneer settlers' artifacts and historical photographs. There are imperfect but readable English descriptions of the exhibits. On some days, a pianist plays beneath the atrium's stained-glass skylight.

November–April, the Casa Braun-Menéndez is open 10 A.M.–5 P.M. daily except for major holidays; the rest of the year, it closes at 2 P.M. Admission costs US$1.50 for adults, US$1 for children.

Museo Regional Salesiano Mayorino Borgatello

From the 19th century, the Salesian order played a key role in evangelizing southern Patagonia and Tierra del Fuego, in both Chile and Argentina. Punta Arenas was their base and, while their rosy view of Christianity's impact on the region's native people may be debatable, figures like the Italian mountaineer priest Alberto de Agostini (1883–1960) made major contributions to both physical geography and ethnographic understanding of the region.

Agostini left a sizeable collection of photographs, both ethnographic and geographical, preserved in the museum (Avenida Bulnes 336, tel. 061/221001, musborga@tnet.cl), which also has a library and a small regionally oriented art gallery. Permanent exhibits deal with regional flora and fauna, a handful of early colonial artifacts, regional ethnography, the missionization of Isla Dawson and other nearby areas, cartogra-

The former Braun-Menéndez mansion is home to Punta Arenas's regional museum.

phy, and the petroleum industry. For Darwinists, there's a scale model of the *Beagle* and, for Chilean patriots, one of the *Ancud,* which sailed from Chiloé to claim the region in 1843.

The Museo Regional Salesiano is open daily except Monday 10 A.M.–6 P.M. Admission costs US$1.50 for adults, US$.40 for children.

Museo Naval y Marítimo

Pleasantly surprising, Punta Arenas's naval and maritime museum (Pedro Montt 981, tel. 061/205479, terzona@armada.cl) provides perspectives on topics like ethnography—in the context of the Strait of Magellan's seagoing indigenous peoples—even while stressing its military mission. It features interactive exhibits, such as a credible warship's bridge, a selection of model ships, and information on the naval history of the southern oceans.

The most riveting material, though, concerns Chilean pilot Luis Pardo Villalón's 1916 rescue of British explorer Ernest Shackleton's crew at Elephant Island, on the Antarctic peninsula. On the cutter *Yelcho,* with neither heat, electricity, nor radio in foggy and stormy winter weather, Pardo returned the entire crew to Punta Arenas in short order; he later served as Chilean consul in Liverpool.

The Museo Naval is open 9:30 A.M.–12:30 P.M. and 2–5 P.M. daily except Sunday and Monday. Admission costs US$1.10 for adults, US$.45 for children.

Museo del Recuerdo

Run by the Instituto de la Patagonia, itself part of the Universidad de Magallanes, the Museo del Recuerdo (Avenida Bulnes 01890, tel. 061/207056) is a mostly open-air facility displaying pioneer agricultural implements and industrial machinery, reconstructions of a traditional house and shearing shed, and a restored shepherd's trailer house (hauled across the Patagonian plains on wooden wheels). In addition to a modest botanical garden, the Instituto itself has a library/bookshop with impressive cartographic exhibits.

Admission to the Museo del Recuerdo costs US$1.50 for adults, free for children. Hours are 8:30 A.M.–11 P.M. and 2:30–6 P.M. weekdays. From downtown Punta Arenas, taxi *colectivos* to the Zona Franca (duty-free zone) stop directly opposite the entrance.

Other Sights

Four blocks south of Plaza Muñoz Gamero, at the foot of Avenida Independencia, naval vessels, freighters, cruise ships, Antarctic icebreakers, and yachts from many countries dock at the **Muelle Fiscal Arturo Prat,** the city's major port facility until recently. Open to the public 10 A.M.–6 P.M. only, it's also the departure point for cruises to the fjords of Tierra del Fuego and to Antarctica.

The late, gifted travel writer Bruce Chatwin found the inspiration for his legendary vignettes of *In Patagonia* through tales of his eccentric distant relative Charley Milward, who built and resided at the **Castillo Milward** (Milward's Castle, Avenida España 959). Described by Chatwin as "a Victorian parsonage translated to the Strait of

© WAYNE BERNHARDSON

A crypt at Punta Arenas's Cementerio Municipal memorializes Yugoslav immigrants, who were mostly Croatian.

Magellan," with "high-pitched gables and gothic windows," the building features a square tower street-side and an octagonal one at the back.

At the corner of Avenida Colón and O'Higgins, gracing the walls of the former **Liceo de Niñas Sara Braun** (Sara Braun Girls' School), rises a seven-meter **Mural Gabriela Mistral,** honoring the Nobel Prize poetess.

Ten blocks north of Plaza Muñoz Gamero, the **Cementerio Municipal** (Avenida Bulnes 029) is home to the extravagant crypts of José Menéndez, José Nogueira, and Sara Braun, but the multinational immigrants who worked for them—English, Scots, Welsh, Croat, German, and Scandinavian—repose in more modest circumstances. A separate monument honors the vanished Selknam (Ona) Indians who once flourished in the Strait, while another memorializes German fatalities of the Battle of the Falklands (1914).

ENTERTAINMENT

Except on Sunday, when the city seems as dead as the cemetery, there's usually something to do at night.

Punta Arenas has one surviving cinema, the **Sala Estrella** (Mejicana 777, tel. 061/241262).

Laberinto (Pedro Montt 951, tel. 061/223667) is primarily a dance club. The stylish **Olijoe Pub** (Errázuriz 970) has the feel of an upscale English pub, with paneled walls, ceiling, and bar, and reasonably priced drinks; the music, though, can get a little loud for conversation.

At the north end of town, **Makanudo** (El Ovejero 474, tel. 09/6492031) has 7–10 P.M. happy hours weekdays except Friday, and live music Friday and Saturday nights from around 1:30 A.M.

The **Club Hípico** (municipal racetrack) fronts on Avenida Bulnes between Coronel Mardones and Manantiales, north of downtown. Professional soccer matches take place at the **Estadio Fiscal** (stadium), a few blocks north at Avenida Bulnes and José González.

SHOPPING

Though it's faltered in recent years, Punta Arenas's major shopping destination is the duty-free Zona Franca, four kilometers north of downtown but easily reached by *taxi colectivo* from Calle Magallanes. Traditionally, consumer electronics were the big attraction—Santiaguinos even flew here for the bargains, but price differentials are smaller than they used to be. Motorists, though, can find replacement tires and similar items much cheaper than in Argentina or mainland Chile.

Puerto del Estrecho (O'Higgins 1401, tel. 061/241022) serves as the waiting room for *Mare Australis* cruises to the Chilean fjords, but is also a good if fairly pricey souvenir shop; in addition, it has an upstairs café, Internet access, and long-distance telephone service.

For crafts, well-stocked **Artesanías Rama Chile** (Independencia 799, tel. 061/244244) contains items like wool socks and sweaters and wood carvings of penguins. For media like metal (copper and bronze) and semi-precious stones (lapis lazuli), visit **Chile Típico** (Ignacio Carrera Pinto 1015, tel. 061/225827). **Tres Arroyos** (Bories 448, tel. 061/241522) specializes in custom chocolates.

For books (including some local guidebooks and travel literature in English), maps, and keepsakes, try **Southern Patagonia Souvenirs & Books**; since its Bories location burned down, it has outlets at the airport (tel. 061/211591) and at the Zona Franca (tel. 061/216759).

ACCOMMODATIONS

Sernatur maintains a complete list of accommodations with up-to-date prices. Note that what in many other parts of Chile would be called *residenciales* are *hostales* (B&Bs) in Punta Arenas. Some relatively expensive places have cheaper rooms with shared bath that can be excellent values.

US$10–25

Open November–March only, the **Albergue Backpacker's Paradise** (Ignacio Carrera Pinto 1022, tel. 061/240104, backpackersparadise@hotmail.com, US$4.50 pp) is a hostel facility that crowds 30 bunks into only four dorm rooms, but for the price it has its public. On the plus side, it has adequate common spaces with cable

TV, cooking privileges, and Internet access. Open January and February only, six blocks south of Plaza Muñoz Gamero, the **Colegio Pierre Fauré** (Bellavista 697, tel. 061/226256, cpfaure@hotmail.com, US$5 pp) also offers the option of camping (US$2.50 pp) in the adjacent garden (or pitching a tent indoors in the gymnasium); a simple breakfast costs US$1 more.

Israeli favorite **Hospedaje Manuel** (O'Higgins 648, tel. 061/245441, fax 061/220567, turmanmi@entelchile.net, US$5 pp for dorms) has more spacious quarters for US$7/12 s/d with shared bath.

Along the shoreline, east of the racetrack at the foot of Quillota, **Hospedaje Costanera** (Rómulo Correa 1221, tel. 061/240175, hospedajecostanera@hotmail.com, US$6.50 pp) has drawn favorable commentary.

Near the old port, improved **Hostal O'Higgins** (O'Higgins 1205, tel. 061/227999, US$10 pp, US$25 d) has rooms with shared and private bath. Plain but clean and friendly, it also has ample secure parking. **Hospedaje Mejicana** (Mejicana 1174, tel. 061/227678, yoya_h@hotmail.com, US$10/13 s/d) has made favorable early impressions.

Only a block from the plaza, the creaky **Residencial Roca** (Magallanes 888, 2nd floor, tel./fax 061/243903, US$10/17 s/d) has cable TV, laundry service, and a book exchange. **Hostal del Rey** (Fagnano 589, Departamento B, tel./fax 061/223924, delrey@chileaustral.com, US$10/17 s/d) is a friendly family place with only three doubles and two singles, so it's often full—call ahead. Rates include an ample breakfast, but the toxic tobacco-laden atmosphere may tip the balance against it.

Often full, despite mixed reviews, **Hostal Dinka's House** (Caupolicán 169, tel. 061/226056, tel./fax 061/244292, www.dinkaspatagonia.com, hostal@dinkaspatagonia.com, US$11 pp) has rooms with private and shared bath, with breakfast included; the nearby annex is definitely substandard.

About 10 blocks northwest of the Plaza, **Hostal Sonia** (Pasaje Darwin 175, tel./fax 061/248543, www.hostalsk.50megs.com, hostalsk@entelchile.net, US$13 pp) has hostel accommodations for HI members only at an otherwise midrange place.

Hostal La Estancia (O'Higgins 765, tel./fax 061/249130, carmenalecl@yahoo.com, US$9 pp for dorms, US$17/25 s/d) has spacious rooms with cable TV, telephone, and shared bath only, with breakfast included.

US$25–50

In a large old house that's been subdivided, **Hostal Al Fin del Mundo** (O'Higgins 1026, tel. 061/710185, alfindelmundo@123.cl, US$13 pp) has rooms that vary considerably in size and quality, but it has its good points. Rates include breakfast and shared bath.

Well-regarded **Hostal Sonia** (Pasaje Darwin 175, tel. 061/248543, hostalsk@entelchile.net, US$19/27 s/d) has rooms with private bath and breakfast included, in addition to its hostel accommodations.

Some rooms are a bit small at well-kept **Hostal José Menéndez** (José Menéndez 882, tel. 061/221279, josemenendez@chileaustral.com, US$21/28 s/d with shared bath, US$30/33 s/d with private bath), but it's friendly, central, arranges tours, has parking, and offers a decent breakfast.

Near the cemetery, **Hostal Parediso** (Angamos 1073, tel./fax 061/224212, US$13–25 s, US$20–33 d) compensates for kitsch decor—note the stalactite ceilings—with genuine hospitality and reasonable comfort. Despite occasional overheating, each room has comfy beds, telephone, and cable TV, though the building can squeak when someone walks to the shared baths. Rates include a simple but abundant breakfast, and kitchen privileges are available; the more expensive rooms have private bath.

Hostal FitzRoy (Lautaro Navarro 850, tel./fax 061/240430, US$17 pp) is an old-fashioned B&B offering some modern comforts—notably cable TV and phones in each room—along with peace and quiet, and a good breakfast. Returned to its original configuration thanks to enlightened new ownership, the rooms are more spacious, but buildings of this vintage still have creaky floors and staircases.

Despite its misleadingly small street-side façade, **Hostal Calafate** (Magallanes 922, www.calafate.cl, hostal@calafate.cl, tel./fax 061/241281, US$19–28 s, US$28–34 d) is a rambling building with spacious rooms that once held the former Hotel Oviedo; recently remodeled, it keeps a couple so-called *celdas de castigo* ("prison cells") for backpacker clients for US$10 per person—a pretty good deal in a well-kept, central facility. It also has the best Internet facilities, also open to nonguests, in town.

Hostal Luna (O'Higgins 424, tel. 061/221764, fax 061/224637, hostalluna@hotmail.com, US$17 pp) has plain but well-furnished and even homey rooms—every bed has a cozy duvet—with a simple breakfast included. The spacious dining room has cable TV, but the rooms do not.

Rehabbed and improved **Hotel Montecarlo** (Avenida Colón 605, tel. 061/222120, fax 061/243438, montecarlo@enelmundo.com, US$16/24 s/d with shared bath, US$25/37 with private bath) is once again worth consideration, though it lacks parking. For the price, **Hotel Cóndor de Plata** (Avenida Colón 556, tel. 061/247987, fax 061/241149, US$30/40) is an excellent choice with private bath and breakfast.

Low-key, family-run **Hostal Terrasur** (O'Higgins 723, tel. 061/225618, hostalterrasur@entelchile.net, US$33/50 s/d) is one of the more appealing B&B-style places in its range. Rates include cable TV, telephone, and continental breakfast.

Hostal Turismo Oro Fueguino (Fagnano 356, tel./fax 061/249401 or 061/246677, tel. 09/2183690, orofueguino@terra.cl, US$20–38 s, US$30–47 d) occupies a deco-style house with an outlandish interior paint job that somehow holds the place together. Rates include cable TV, telephone, central heating, breakfast, and private bath; some rooms are windowless but have skylights. A few cheaper rooms have shared bath.

The so-so **Hostal del Estrecho** (José Menéndez 1048, tel./fax 061/241011, estrecho@chileanpatagonia.com, US$20/35 s/d with shared bath, US$30/48 s/d with private bath) is suitable in a pinch. **Hostal de la Avenida** (Avenida Colón 534, tel./fax 061/247532 or 061/249486, US$42/50 s/d) is a respectable choice for the price.

US$50–100

Hotel Savoy José Menéndez 1073, tel./fax 061/247979, info@hotelsavoy.cl, US$39–48 s, US$50–60 d) lacks style—some interior walls have cheap plywood paneling—but the rooms are large and comfortable, and the staff is responsive.

Occupying a stylishly modernized building, **Hotel Mercurio** (Fagnano 595, tel./fax 061/242300, mercurio@chileaustral.com, US$49/64 s/d) offers both convenience and charm, with gracious staff to boot. Rates include private bath and breakfast.

Hostal Carpa Manzano (Lautaro Navarro 336, tel. 061/242296, fax 061/248864, carpamanzano@terra.cl, US$40/55 s/d) gets good marks in its category. Half a block south of Plaza Muñoz Gamero, **Hotel Plaza** (Nogueira 1116, tel. 061/241300, fax 061/248613, hplaza@chileaustral.com, US$72/87) is a classic of its era, but the business-oriented **Hotel Tierra del Fuego** (Avenida Colón 716, tel./fax 061/226200, tierradelfuego@entelchile.net, US$89/98 s/d) has better contemporary fixtures.

Over US$100

Punta Arenas has a good selection of upscale, mostly modern hotels, such as **Hotel Los Navegantes** (José Menéndez 647, tel. 061/244677, fax 061/247545, www.hotel-losnavegantes.com, hotelnav@chilesat.net, US$78–98 s, US$86–110 d), which has standard conveniences in midsized rooms.

Hotel Isla Rey Jorge (21 de Mayo 1243, tel. 061/222681, fax 061/248220, www.islareyjorge.com, reyjorge@ctcinternet.cl, US$119/146 s/d) is a favorite with foreign tour groups.

Hotel Finis Terrae (Avenida Colón 766, tel. 061/228200, fax 061/248124, www.hotelfinisterrae.com, finister@ctcreuna.cl, US$89–140 s, US$101–160 d) is a fine newer hotel.

Traditionally one of Punta's best, built by the Sociedad Ganadera Tierra del Fuego, the 1960s high-rise **Hotel Cabo de Hornos** (Plaza Muñoz Gamero 1025, tel./fax 061/242134, www.hotelcabodehornos.cl, rescabo@entelchile.net, US$165–184 s, US$195–217 d) is steadily recovering from years of neglect. Off-season rates are about 25 percent cheaper; there are also more expensive suites.

Punta Arenas's most distinctively historic accommodations, the **Hotel José Nogueira**

(Bories 959, tel. 061/248840, fax 061/248832, www.hotelnogueira.com, nogueira@chileaustral.com, US$95–149 s, US$115–179 d) occupies part of the Sara Braun mansion. Its greenhouse bar/restaurant merits a visit even if you can't afford to stay here.

FOOD

Punta Arenas's fast-improving gastronomic scene ranges from fast food to haute cuisine. Prices, however, are also increasing rapidly.

Los Patiperros (Avenida Colón 782, tel. 061/245298) is a modest but popular café serving full meals in the US$5 range. **Quijote** (Lautaro Navarro 1087, tel. 061/241225) also serves inexpensive lunches, as does the outstanding **Rotisería La Mamá** (Sanhueza 720, tel. 061/225812), a good place to grab a meal while waiting for the bus.

Upstairs in the Casa del Turista, at the entrance to Muelle Prat, **Café Puerto del Estrecho** (O'Higgins 1401, tel. 061/241022) has a variety of espresso-based specialty coffees, such as mocha and amaretto, plus snacks and desserts to accompany them.

Punta Arenas's best fast-food alternative is **Lomit's** (José Menéndez 722, tel. 061/243399), a dependable sandwich-and-beer chain that's almost always packed. Sandwiches fall into the US$3–5 range. **La Carioca** (José Menéndez 600, tel. 061/224809), by contrast, is a one-of-a-kind sandwich outlet that also serves passable pizza, pasta, and draft beer.

Dónde Marín (O'Higgins 504, tel. 061/245291) delivers on its modest pretensions, serving fine if simply prepared fish entrées, including a side order, in the US$6–8 range. The decor is only utilitarian, but the service is professional.

At first glance, painted in primary colors and decorated with Argentine cinema posters and maps that indicate the origins of their clientele, **La Luna** (O'Higgins 974, tel. 061/228555) looks more a scene than a restaurant. Buzzing with activity, it misses the mark with the *ostiones al pil pil* (scallops) appetizer, but the *chupe de centolla* (king crab casserole) is worth twice its US$7.50 price tag. Beef and pastas are also on the menu.

Stick with the meat at **El Estribo** (Ignacio Carrera Pinto 762, tel. 061/244714); their fish is only so-so, but the beef and lamb dishes, in the US$5–10 range, are consistently strong. The English menu translation is occasionally hilarious, but the service is attentive.

Punta's best new restaurant is **Damiana Elena** (O'Higgins 694, tel. 061/222818), where reservations are essential on weekends and advisable even on weeknights. Decorated with antiques, this restored period house serves beef and seafood specialties in the US$5–10 range—very modest prices for the quality it offers—with unobtrusive service. There is limited tobacco-free seating, for which reservations are particularly advisable.

A good seafood choice is the nautically themed **Puerto Viejo** (O'Higgins 1205, tel. 061/225103), doing bang-up business with an almost exclusively seafood menu. Open for lunch and dinner, with knowledgeable waiters and terrific service, it serves specialties like *centolla* (king crab) and *merluza* (hake); for US$12, the *centolla al Puerto* appetizer can satisfy two hungry diners. On the down side, the pisco/*calafate* sours are mixed in advance, though they're still pretty fresh.

Under the same management, a couple kilometers north of the plaza, **Los Ganaderos** (Avenida Bulnes 0977, tel. 061/214597) is a classy *parrilla* specializing in succulent Patagonian lamb grilled on a vertical spit—for US$12 *tenedor libre* (all-you-can-eat) per person. There is also a more diverse *parrillada* for two (US$25), and pasta dishes in the US$8 range. Try the regional Patagonian desserts, such as *mousse de calafate* and *mousse de ruibarbo* (rhubarb).

Four blocks south of the plaza, the creative **La Leyenda del Remezón** (21 de Mayo 1469, tel. 061/241029) serves game dishes (beaver and guanaco are now being farmed in the region) in the US$17 range—not cheap, obviously, but unique. Seafood specialties include krill, king crab, and spider crab.

Punta Arenas's classic seafood locale, open 24/7, is **El Mercado** (Mejicana 617, 2nd floor, tel. 061/247415; serving a diverse fish and shellfish menu at midrange prices, it affixes a 10 percent surcharge 1–8 A.M. Another seafood classic, the upstairs **Centro Español** (Plaza

Muñoz Gamero 771, tel. 061/242807) never seems to have many clients, but still manages to turn out good food at slightly higher prices than El Mercado.

Promising **Brocolino** (O'Higgins 1049, tel. 061/710479) serves a fine risotto with *centolla* and scallops, along with beef, lamb, and pastas in the US$10–12 range. Traditionally, **Sotito's Bar** (O'Higgins 1138, tel. 061/245365) has set the seafood standard for Punta Arenas, and it still deserves consideration.

INFORMATION

A couple doors north of Plaza Muñoz Gamero, **Sernatur** (Magallanes 960, tel. 061/225385, infomagallanes@sernatur.cl) is open 8:15 A.M.–6 P.M. weekdays only. One of Chile's better regional tourist offices, it has English-speaking personnel, up-to-date accommodations and transportation information, and a message board.

In summer, Plaza Muñoz Gamero's municipal **Kiosko de Informaciones** (tel. 061/200610, informacionturistica@puntaarenas.cl) is open 8 A.M.–8 P.M. weekdays, 9 A.M.–6 P.M. Saturday, and 9:30 A.M.–2:30 P.M. Sunday. It also has free Internet access for brief periods (longer if no one is waiting).

For motorists, the local branch of the **Automóvil Club de Chile** (Acchi, O'Higgins 931, tel. 061/243675) also rents cars.

Conaf (José Menéndez 1147, tel. 061/223841) provides information on the region's national parks.

SERVICES

Punta Arenas is one of the easier Chilean cities to change both cash and traveler's checks, especially at travel agencies along Lautaro Navarro. Most close by midday Saturday, but **Scott Cambios** (Avenida Colón and Magallanes, tel. 061/245811) will cash traveler's checks then.

Several banks in the vicinity of Plaza Muñoz Gamero have ATMs, such as **Banco Santander** (Magallanes 997).

Correos de Chile is at Bories 911, just north of Plaza Muñoz Gamero.

Long-distance call centers include **Telefónica CTC** (Nogueira 1116), at the southwest corner of Plaza Muñoz Gamero, and **Entel** (Lautaro Navarro 931). Try also **Hostal Calafate** (Magallanes 922), which has expanded its hotel business with an Internet café and phone center, now the best in town.

Austro Internet (Croacia 690, tel. 061/229297) is open 9 A.M.–8 P.M. weekdays, 10 A.M.–8 P.M. Saturday, and 4–8 P.M. Sunday, but also keeps Sunday-morning hours (9 A.M.–1 P.M.) when cruise ships are in port.

The **Argentine consulate** (21 de Mayo 1878, tel. 061/261912) is open 10 A.M.–3:30 P.M. weekdays only. Countries with honorary consulates include Brazil (Arauco 769, tel. 061/241093), Spain (José Menéndez 910, tel. 061/243566), and the United Kingdom (tel. 061/211535).

For clean clothes, try **Lavandería Record** (O'Higgins 969, tel. 061/243607) or **Lavaseco Vicars** (Sarmiento de Gamboa 726, tel. 061/241516).

Punta Arenas's **Hospital Regional** (Arauco and Angamos, tel. 061/244040) is north of downtown.

GETTING THERE

Punta Arenas has good air connections to mainland Chile, frequent air service to Chilean Tierra del Fuego, infrequent flights to Argentine Tierra del Fuego, and regular weekly service to the Falkland Islands. There are roundabout overland routes to mainland Chile via Argentina, regular bus service to Argentine Tierra del Fuego via a ferry link, direct ferry service to Chilean Tierra del Fuego, and expensive (but extraordinarily scenic) cruise-ship service to Ushuaia, in Argentine Tierra del Fuego.

Air

LAN/LanExpress (Lautaro Navarro 999, tel. 061/241232) flies four times daily to Santiago, normally via Puerto Montt, but some flights stop at Balmaceda, near Coyhaique. It also flies three times weekly to Ushuaia, Argentina, and Saturday to the Falkland Islands; one Falklands flight per month stops in the Argentine city of Río Gallegos.

AIR ANTARCTICA

For many visitors, one of the great disincentives to Antarctic travel is the fact that, even though southern South America offers the closest approach to the frozen continent, it usually involves a stomach-churning two-day crossing of the stormy Drake Passage—in each direction. If Chilean entrepreneurs have their way, though, well-heeled travelers will soon skip the seasickness.

In the summer of 2004, though, Punta Arenas–based **Antarctica XXI** organized the first commercial air-sea excursion to the Antarctic Peninsula, eliminating the Drake Passage segment. Arriving at the Base Aérea Presidente Eduardo Frei Montalva, the Chilean air force's main Antarctic base on Isla Rey Jorge, passengers almost immediately board the Russian research vessel *Grigoriy Mikheev* for a five-day cruise among the relatively sheltered waters of the peninsula.

The convenience comes at a price, though; the cheapest rate for the all-inclusive tour is US$5,900 per person, double occupancy. For more details, contact Antarctica XXI (Roca 998, Oficina 104, Punta Arenas, tel. 061/228783, fax 061/220694, www.antarcticaxxi.com). While there were only three trips in the summer of 2004–2005, because of the ship's previous commitments, the number is likely to increase in the coming years.

Check at travel agencies for Puerto Montt/Santiago flights with **Sky Airline,** which has new routes here, and the new carrier **Aerolíneas del Sur** (Pedro Montt 969, tel. 061/220700).

Aerovías DAP (O'Higgins 891, tel. 061/223340, fax 061/221693, www.aeroviasdap.cl, ventas@aeroviasdap.cl) flies seven-seat Cessnas to and from Porvenir (US$23), in Chilean Tierra del Fuego, at least daily except Sunday, more often in summer. Daily except Sunday and Monday, it flies 20-seater Twin Otters to and from Puerto Williams on Isla Navarino (US$64 one way). In summer, it also flies Twin Otters to Ushuaia Monday and Wednesday only (US$100). In addition, it has extensive charter services, and occasionally goes to Antarctica.

Bus

Punta Arenas has no central terminal, though some companies share facilities and the **Central de Pasajeros** (Avenida Colón and Magallanes, tel. 061/245811) sells tickets to all bus companies. Most terminals are within a few blocks of each other, north of Plaza Muñoz Gamero. Note that services vary seasonally, with the greatest number of buses in January and February.

Several carriers serve Puerto Natales (US$5, three hours), including **Bus Sur** (José Menéndez 565, tel. 061/227145), with four buses daily; **Buses Fernández** (Armando Sanhueza 745, tel. 061/242313, seven daily); **Buses Pacheco** (Avenida Colón 900, tel. 061/225527, three daily), and **Buses Transfer** (Pedro Montt 966, tel. 061/229613, one daily).

In addition to its Puerto Natales services, Buses Pacheco goes to the Chilean cities of Osorno, Puerto Montt, and Castro (US$60, 28–36 hours) Wednesday at 9 A.M., via Argentina. **Queilén Bus** (Armando Sanhueza 745, tel. 061/221812) and **Cruz del Sur** (Armando Sanhueza 745, tel. 061/227970) alternate services to Puerto Montt and Castro most mornings at 9:30 A.M. In addition to its Puerto Natales services, Bus Sur goes to Coyhaique (US$50, 20 hours) Monday at 10:30 A.M.

Several carriers go to Río Gallegos (US$10, four hours): **Buses Pingüino** (Armando Sanhueza 745, tel. 061/221812 or 061/242313), **Buses Ghisoni** (Lautaro Navarro 975, tel. 061/222078), and Buses Pacheco (see above for contact details).

Tecni-Austral (Lautaro Navarro 975, tel. 061/222078) goes directly to Río Grande (US$22–25, eight hours), in Argentine Tierra del Fuego, daily except Monday at 8:30 A.M.; the Tuesday, Thursday, and Saturday buses continue to Ushuaia (US$32, 12 hours). **Bus Sur** goes Monday, Wednesday, and Friday at 9 A.M. to Río Grande, with connections to Ushuaia, while Central de Pasajeros goes Monday, Wednesday, Friday, and Sunday.

Sea

Transbordadora Austral Broom (Avenida Bulnes 05075, tel. 061/218100, tabsa@entelchile.net) sails from Punta Arenas to Porvenir

(2.5 hours) at 9 A.M. daily except Sunday, when sailing time is 9:30 A.M. Adult passengers pay US$6 per person except for the drivers, whose own fare is included in the US$37 charge per vehicle (motorcycles pay US$11). Children pay US$2.50 per person. Since the ferry has limited vehicle capacity, reservations are a good idea on the *Melinka,* which leaves from Terminal Tres Puentes, at the north end of town but easily accessible by *taxi colectivo* from the Casa Braun-Menéndez, on Magallanes half a block north of Plaza Muñoz Gamero.

Broom also sails the ferry *Cruz Australis* to Puerto Williams (36 hours) every Wednesday at 6 P.M., returning Friday at 10 P.M. The fare is US$150 for a bunk, US$120 for a reclining seat.

It's neither cheap nor a conventional way of getting to Argentina, but passengers on the luxury MV *Mare Australis,* which sails from Punta Arenas every Saturday for a week-long cruise of the fjords of Chilean Tierra del Fuego, can disembark in Ushuaia (or board there for that matter). Normally the *Mare Australis* requires reservations well in advance. For more details, see the Fjords of Fuegia section.

GETTING AROUND

Punta Arenas's **Aeropuerto Presidente Carlos Ibáñez del Campo** is 20 kilometers north of town on Ruta 9, the Puerto Natales highway. **Transfer Sandy Point** (Pedro Montt 840, tel. 061/222241, toursandypoint@entelchile.net) arranges door-to-door transfers for US$4 pp.

Buses returning from Puerto Natales will normally drop their passengers at the airport to meet outgoing flights on request, but make arrangements before boarding. Natales-bound buses will also pick up arriving passengers, but again make arrangements in advance.

Punta Arenas has numerous car-rental options, including **Adel Rent a Car** (Pedro Montt 962, tel. 061/235472, gerson@adentalrentacar.cl), **Budget** (O'Higgins 964, tel./fax 061/241696, budget@ctcinternet.cl), **Emsa/Avis** (Roca 1044, tel./fax 061/241182, rentacar@viaterra.cl), **Hertz** (O'Higgins 987, tel. 061/248742, fax 061/244729), **International** (Waldo Seguel 443, tel. 061/228323, fax 061/226334, internationalrac@entelchile.net), and **Lubag** (Magallanes 970, tel./fax 061/242023, luis_barra@entelchile.net).

For rental bikes, contact **Claudio Botten** (Sarmiento de Gamboa 1132, tel. 061/242107, 09/1684118, cbotten@ze.cl).

VICINITY OF PUNTA ARENAS

Punta Arenas's many travel agencies operate a variety of excursions in the vicinity, to nearby destinations like Reserva Nacional Magallanes, Fuerte Bulnes, the Seno Otway penguin colony, Río Verde, Estancia San Gregorio, and even Parque Nacional Torres del Paine. The most popular half-day excursions, like Fuerte Bulnes and Otway, cost US$10–15 per person, while full-day trips like Pali Aike can cost up to US$70 per person.

Among the established operators are **Aventour** (Avenida España 872, tel. 061/244197, fax 061/220174, www.aventourpatagonia.com, aventour@entelchile.net), **Turismo Aónikenk** (Magallanes 619, tel. 061/228332, fax 061/221982, www.aonikenk.com, turismo@aonikenk.com), **Turismo Laguna Azul** (José Menéndez 631, tel. 061/225200, fax 061/240278, www.payne.cl, lagunaazul@chileaustral.com), **Turismo Pali Aike** (Lautaro Navarro 1125, tel. 061/229388, fax 061/223301, www.turismopaliaike.com, paliaike@entelchile.net), **Turismo Viento Sur** (Fagnano 585, tel. 061/226930, fax 061/225167, www.vientosur.com, agencia@vientosur.com), and **Turismo Yámana** (Errázuriz 932, tel. 061/710567, fax 061/240056, www.turismoyamana.cl, turismo@yamana.cl).

Reserva Nacional Magallanes

Only eight kilometers west of downtown Punta Arenas, 13,500-hectare Reserva Nacional Magallanes is a combination of Patagonian steppe and southern beech forest which, in good winters, accumulates enough snow for skiing. Despite its proximity to Punta Arenas, official statistics say it gets barely 8,000 visitors per year, and fewer than 300 of those are foreigners.

From westbound Avenida Independencia, a good gravel road that may require chains in winter climbs gradually to a fork whose southern branch

PINGÜINOS AND PINGÜINERAS

Chilean Patagonia's largest city is close to two breeding colonies of the burrowing Magellanic penguin, *Spheniscus magellanicus.* The Otway Sound colony is about a 45-minute drive from the city, and is interesting enough, but the larger colony on Isla Magdalena, an island in the Strait of Magellan, is two hours away by ferry.

Also known as the jackass penguin to English speakers, because its call resembles that of a braying burro, the Magellanic is present October–April. It is most numerous in January and February, when the chicks hatch in the sandy burrows that the birds have dug beneath the coastal turf. After the chicks have hatched, the parents alternate fishing trips in search of food that they later regurgitate to their young (combined with the scent of bird droppings, this makes any visit to a penguin colony an olfactory as well as a visual and auditory experience).

While the birds appear tame, they are wild animals and their sharp beaks can draw blood—photographers need to stay out of pecking distance. Even though both the Otway and Magdalena colonies have fenced walking routes to restrain tourists, the birds themselves frequently cross these routes.

Besides the countless seabirds and dolphins en route, the Magdalena trip has the added bonus of a historic lighthouse that now serves as a visitors center on an island that's one Swiss-cheese warren of penguin burrows. While neither trip is strenuous, any walk in the roaring Patagonian winds can be a workout.

Otway trips leave every day, but Magdalena trips are no more than two or three times a week in January and February, with fewer or no trips outside those months.

© WAYNE BERNHARDSON

Magellanic penguins

leads to the reserve's **Sector Andino,** where the local Club Andino's **Centro de Esquí Cerro Mirador** includes a *refugio* that serves meals, a ski school, and a single well-maintained chairlift. In summer, try the **Sendero Mirador,** a two-hour loop hike that winds through the forest and crosses the ski area; there's also a mountain-bike circuit.

The northwesterly **Sector Las Minas,** which includes a gated picnic area, charges US$1.50 per person for adult admission, but nothing for kids. A longer footpath links up with the trail to the El Mirador summit, which offers panoramas east toward Punta Arenas, the strait, and Tierra del Fuego, and west toward Seno Otway.

Though some Punta Arenas travel agencies offer tours to the reserve, it would also be a good mountain-bike excursion from town.

Pingüinera Seno Otway

Burrowing Magellanic penguins abound along

THE WHALES OF MAGALLANES

For decades now, the great whales have drawn travelers to Mexico's Baja California, Argentina's Península Valdés, and other breeding and feeding sites in the Americas. The latest entry in the whale-watching sweepstakes is one of Chile's first maritime reserves, Parque Marino Francisco Coloane, in the Strait of Magellan southwest of Punta Arenas.

Established in July 2003, named in honor of a Chilean author who chronicled the southern seas, the 67,000-hectare park is the result of five years' biological investigations that pinpointed the area around Isla Carlos III as a prime feeding grounds for the southern humpback whale *(Megaptera novaeangliae)* from mid-December to late April. In addition to the humpbacks, which migrate the length of the South American coast from Colombia, the park's seas and shorelines are home to breeding populations of Magellanic penguins, cormorants, many other southern seabirds, and sea lions. Orcas are also present.

Whalesound (tel./fax 061/266312 in Punta Arenas, www.whalesound.com) is a recent startup that offers three-day sailboat expeditions (US$700 pp) to the park, where guests stay in domed tents, with comfortable Japanese beds and solar-powered electricity, on Isla Carlos III. Departures take place from Fuerte Bulnes, an hour south of Punta Arenas by road, on the yacht *Esturión;* if sea conditions are too rough, they go overland to Isla Riesco and then a shorter trip to Carlos III on rigid inflatables. The cost includes daily excursions with specialized bilingual guides and gourmet meals from a French-trained Chilean chef. Sea kayaks are also available.

the Atlantic coast of Argentine Patagonia, but they are fewer in Chile. Barely an hour from Punta Arenas, though, the *Spheniscus magellanicus* colony at Seno Otway (Otway Sound) is the closest to any major city on the continent. Under the administration of the nonprofit Fundación Otway, it grew in a decade from no more than 400 penguins to about 8,000 breeding pairs at present. From October, when the first birds arrive, to April, when the last stragglers head to sea, it draws up to 40,000 visitors. The peak season, though, is December–February.

While the site is fenced to keep human visitors out of critical habitat, the birds are relatively tame and easy to photograph; on the down side, this did not prevent stray dogs from killing more than a hundred birds in 2001. The land-owning Kusanovic family has recently taken over management from the Fundación Otway.

During the season, any number of Punta Arenas operators shuttle visitors to and from the Otway site for about US$10–12 per person, not including the US$4 per person admission charge. Half-day tours take place either in morning (which photographers may prefer) or afternoon.

Otway is only about 70 kilometers northwest of Punta Arenas via Ruta 9 and a gravel road that leads west from a signed junction at the Carabineros Kon Aikén checkpoint; the gravel road passes the **Mina Pecket** coal mine before arriving at the *pingüinera.*

During the season, the **Pinguin Adventure Line** (Gabriela Mistral 679, Puerto Natales, tel. 061/411113, pinguin_adventure@yahoo.com) connects Puerto Natales with Punta Arenas (US$19 pp) via the scenic Río Verde alternative and the Otway colony, which makes it easy to combine the penguin colony with door-to-door transportation. It departs from Puerto Natales at 8 A.M., arriving at Punta Arenas at 1 P.M.; the return trip leaves Punta Arenas at 3 P.M., arriving 8 P.M. at Natales.

While the Otway colony is a worthwhile excursion, visitors with flexible schedules and a little more money should consider the larger Isla Magdalena colony in Monumento Natural Los Pingüinos, in the Strait of Magellan (see below).

Monumento Natural Los Pingüinos

From early October, more than 60,000 breeding pairs of Magellanic penguins paddle ashore and waddle to burrows that cover nearly all of 97-hectare Isla Magdalena, 20 nautical miles northeast of Punta Arenas, before returning to sea in April. Also the site of a landmark lighthouse, Isla Magdalena is the focal point of Monumento Natural Los Pingüinos, one of Conaf's smallest but most interesting reserves.

While the mainland Otway penguin colony gets upwards of 40,000 visitors per year, Isla Magdalena gets fewer than 9,000—90 percent of them foreigners—because of its limited accessibility. In summer, though, the ferry *Melinka* visits the island three times weekly from Punta Arenas. Though more expensive than Otway tours, these excursions also offer the chance to see penguins and dolphins in the water, as well as black-browed albatrosses, cormorants, kelp gulls, skuas, South American terns, and other seabirds in the surrounding skies.

From a floating dock on the east side of the island, a short trail leads along the beach and up the hill to Scottish engineer George Slight's **Faro Magdalena** (1901), a lighthouse whose iron tower rises 13.5 meters above the island's highest point; still functioning, the light has a range of 10 nautical miles. A narrow spiral staircase ascends the tower.

In the building's first five decades, a resident caretaker maintained the acetylene light, but after its automation in 1955 the building was abandoned and vandalized. In 1981, though, the Chilean navy entrusted the building to Conaf; declared a national monument, it has since become a visitors center. It boasts remarkably good exhibits on the island's history (discovery, and early navigation, cartography, and construction of the lighthouse) and natural history in both Spanish and English (though the English text is less complete). The U.S. archaeologist Junius Bird, best known for his 1930s work at the mainland site of Pali Aike, also undertook excavations here.

For excursions to Isla Magdalena, contact **Turismo Comapa** (Magallanes 990, tel. 061/200200, fax 061/225804, tcomapa@entelchile.net). In December, January, and February, after its regular Tuesday/Thursday/Saturday ferry run to Porvenir, the *Melinka* makes a passengers-only trip to Isla Magdalena (US$30) from Terminal Tres Puentes; sailing time is 3 P.M. (bring food—the *Melinka*'s snack bar is pretty dire). Visitors spend about 1.5 hours on the island, returning to Punta Arenas around 9 P.M.

Passengers on the *Mare Australis* cruise through the Tierra del Fuego fjords stop here on the return leg of the trip.

Fuerte Bulnes

In 1584, Spanish explorer Pedro Sarmiento de Gamboa organized an expedition of 15 ships and 4,000 men to control the Strait of Magellan, but after a series of disasters only three ships with 300 colonists arrived to found **Ciudad del Rey don Felipe,** at Punta Santa Ana south of present-day Punta Arenas. Even worse for the Spaniards, the inhospitable climate and unsuitable soils made agriculture impossible; when British privateer Thomas Cavendish landed three years later, in 1587, he found only a handful of survivors and gave it the name Port Famine, which has survived as the Spanish **Puerto del Hambre.**

For many years, the consensus was that starvation alone determined the fate of Puerto Hambre, but Punta Arenas historian Mateo Martinic has suggested that disease, mutual acts of violence, Tehuelche attacks, and a simple sense of anguish or abandonment contributed to its demise. Unfortunately, the Chilean military control much of the area, making archaeological excavations that might resolve the question difficult.

The area remained unsettled until 1843, when President Manuel Bulnes ordered the cutter *Ancud* south from Chiloé with tools, construction materials, food, and livestock to take possession for the expansionist Chilean state. The result was Fuerte Bulnes, a military outpost that survived only a little longer than the original Spanish settlement before being relocated to Punta Arenas in 1848.

Modern Fuerte Bulnes, on the site of the first Chilean settlement, is a national monument more for its site than for its reconstructions of 19th-century buildings and the defensive walls, of sharpened stakes, which surround them. Among

© WAYNE BERNHARDSON

Estancia Río Verde is an appealing detour on the Magellanic steppe between Punta Arenas and Puerto Natales.

the structures were residences, stables, a blockhouse, a chapel, a jail, and warehouse.

Archaeologists located nearby remnants of Ciudad del Rey don Felipe in 1955, and later excavations turned up human remains, bullets, tombs, and ruins of Puerto Hambre's church. A relatively recent plaque (1965) celebrates the 125th anniversary of the Pacific Steam Navigation Company's ships *Chile* and *Peru* and their routes around the Horn.

Puerto Hambre and Fuerte Bulnes are 58 kilometers south of Punta Arenas via Ruta 9, which is paved about halfway; the rest is bumpy but always passable. There is no regular public transportation, but most Punta Arenas tour operators offer half-day excursions. Admission is free of charge.

Reserva Nacional Laguna Parrillar

About 45 kilometers southwest of Punta Arenas via paved Ruta 9 and a gravel westbound lateral, Laguna Parrillar attracts only about 4,400 visitors per year to its 18,000 hectares of forest and wetland. While it's open to day use only, it has picnic areas and hiking trails to commend it, and makes a worthwhile excursion from the city. Admission costs US$1.50.

Río Verde

Some 43 kilometers north of Punta Arenas on Ruta 9, a gravel road loops northwest along the shore of Seno Otway to Seno Skyring and Estancia Río Verde, which has seemingly made the transition from a shipshape sheep farm to a model municipality of exquisitely maintained public buildings in the Magellanic style. Note particularly the manicured gardens surrounding the **Escuela Básica,** the local boarding school.

Off to a good start, in one wing of the boarding school, the **Museo Comunal Río Verde** has exhibits on local history, natural history (taxidermy), ethnology, and local and regional literature. Hours are 10 A.M.–5 P.M. daily; admission costs US$1.

Unfortunately, only the foundations remain of the recently created *municipalidad,* which burned to the ground a couple years back and destroyed some museum exhibits; municipal offices have since moved to the former Hostería Río Verde, 90 kilometers from Punta Arenas and six kilometers south of the *estancia.*

Across from the former *hostería,* a small on-demand ferry shuttles vehicles and passengers to **Isla Riesco.** Nearby, Paola Vizzani González's *Escultura Monumental,* a beached whale built of concrete and driftwood, honors the region's early colonists. Also nearby, the **Hito El Vapor** marks the final resting place of the steamer *Los Amigos,* which carried coal to outlying farms until it ran aground in a storm.

The loop road rejoins Ruta 9 at Villa Tehuelches, a wide spot in the road about 90 kilometers from Punta Arenas. This would make a good alternative route north or south for both motorists and mountain bikers, and is now part of an alternative tour between Puerto Natales and Punta Arenas that takes in the Otway penguin colony; for details, see the Otway entry above.

While the *hostería* at the ferry crossing no longer provides accommodations, the Chilean-Uruguayan **Estancia Río Verde** (Km 98 Norte, tel. 061/311123 or 061/311131, jmma@entelchile.net, US$50/60 s/d) offers stylish accommodations, day tours that can include horseback riding and fishing, and *asados,* lunches, and tea in its restaurant. A bargain by *estancia* standards, it also has gracious English-speaking owners.

Río Rubens

About halfway between Villa Tehuelches and Puerto Natales, Río Rubens is a prime trout stream that flows northeast into Argentina. At Km 183 on Ruta 9, the nearby **Hotel Río Rubens** (tel. 09/6401583) has resisted the temptation to upgrade itself from a modest rural inn, with a decent restaurant at modest prices, though it has added *cabañas* and camping. Hotel rates are US$12 per person with private bath and breakfast.

Estancia San Gregorio

From a highway junction about 45 kilometers north of Punta Arenas, paved Ruta 225 leads east-northeast to the Argentine border at Monte Aymond, passing the former Estancia San Gregorio, once one of Chilean Patagonia's largest landholdings. Part of the Menéndez wool empire, San Gregorio dates from the 1890s, though it reached its peak between 1910 and 1930. Besides wool, it produced frozen mutton, hides, and tallow.

The rusting hulk of the British clipper *Ambassador* rests on the shoreline at San Gregorio.

Now run as a cooperative, 120 kilometers from Punta Arenas, San Gregorio is a *zona típica* national historical monument. It exemplified the Anglo-Scottish model of the Patagonian sheep *estancia,* in which each unit was a self-sufficient hierarchy with a nearly omnipotent administrator at the top. Geographically, it consisted of discrete residential and production sectors: The former included the administrator's house, employee residences, shearers' dormitories, chapel, and the like, while the latter consisted of the shearing shed, warehouses, a smithery, company store, and similarly functional buildings. It had its own pier and railroad and a pier to move the wool clip directly to freighters.

Most of San Gregorio's construction dates from the 1890s, but French architect Antoine Beaulier's **Casa Patronal,** still occupied by a descendent of the Menéndez dynasty, dates from 1925. The farm featured an extensive system of windbreaks ranging upwards of five meters in height, later planted with Monterey cypress for beautification.

While San Gregorio is technically not open to the public, many of its buildings line both sides of the highway to Monte Aymond. Beached on shore are the corroded hulks of the British clipper *Ambassador* (a national monument) and the company steamer *Amadeo,* which gave up the ghost in the 1940s.

Kimiri Aike

About 30 kilometers east of San Gregorio, paved Ruta 257 leads southeast to **Punta Delgada,** the port for the ferry crossing to Tierra del Fuego via the Primera Angostura narrows. Depending sometimes on tidal conditions, the ferries *Bahía Azul* and *Patagonia* shuttle across the channel every 1.5 hours 8:30 A.M.–11 P.M. Fares are US$2 per person for passengers, US$1 for kids ages 10–14, US$17 for automobiles, and US$5 for motorcycles. Most buses to Argentine Tierra del Fuego use this route because the longer ferry to Porvenir goes only once daily.

At the highway junction, **Hostería Tehuelche** (tel. 061/1983002) was once the *casco* (big house) for the formerly British-run Estancia Kimiri Aike; now, November–May, it offers satisfactory accommodations for US$28/38 s/d in huge rooms with shared bath. Buses between Punta Arenas and Río Gallegos often stop here for lunch; breakfast, dinner, and snacks are also available. The Barros Luco sandwich can be good, but ask them to hold the mayonnaise.

guanacos, Parque Nacional Pali Aike

Parque Nacional Pali Aike

Hugging the Argentine border north of Kimiri Aike and west of the Monte Aymond border crossing, little-visited Pali Aike is an area of volcanic steppe and rugged lava beds that once supported megafauna like the ground sloth milodon and the native American horse, both of which disappeared soon after humans first inhabited the area some 11,000 years ago.

While Paleo-Indians hunters may have contributed to their extinction, environmental changes after the last major glaciation may also have played a role. In the 1930s, self-taught archaeologist Junius Bird, of New York's American Museum of Natural History, conducted the earliest systematic excavations of Paleo-Indian sites like Cueva Pali Aike, within the park boundaries, and Cueva Fell, a short distance to the west. These archaeologically rich volcanic shelters (not caves in the strictest sense of the word) are the prime reason Chilean authorities have nominated the area as a UNESCO World Heritage Site.

Findings at Cueva Pali Aike include human remains that have yielded insights on Paleo-Indian funerary customs, while materials from Cueva Fell have helped reveal the transition from relatively simple Paleo-Indian hunting to more complex forms of subsistence. These include sophisticated hunting tools like the bow and arrow and *boleadoras,* and a greater reliance on coastal and marine resources. There are also indicators of ceremonial artifacts.

Part of arid eastern Magallanes, 5,030-hectare Pali Aike consists of rolling steppe grasslands whose porous volcanic soils and slag absorb water quickly. Almost constant high winds and cool temperatures make it a better summer or autumn excursion.

While the milodon and native horse may have disappeared, the park's grasslands swarm with herds of wild guanaco and flocks of rheas, upland geese, *bandurria* (ibis), and other birds. Pumas and foxes are the major predators.

Accessible by road, **Cueva Pali Aike** is a volcanic tube seven meters wide and five meters high at its mouth; it is 17 meters deep but tapers as it advances. In the 1930s, Bird discovered both human and megafauna remains, at least 8,600 years old and probably much older, in the cave.

Tours from Punta Arenas visit Cueva Pali Aike and usually hike the 1.7-kilometer trail through the **Escorial del Diablo** (the appropriately named Devil's Slag Heap, which is hell on hiking boots). The trail ends at the volcanic **Crater Morada del Diablo.**

From Cueva Pali Aike, a nine-kilometer footpath leads to **Laguna Ana,** where waterfowl are abundant, and the main road, five kilometers from the park entrance. Mountain bikes should be ideal for this sort of rolling terrain, but it could be even tougher on tires than it is on boots.

A campground is under construction, but there are no tourist services as yet, so bring supplies.

At the main park entrance, Conaf has a ranger station but collects no admission fee. A great destination for solitude seekers, Pali Aike officially gets fewer than 1,200 visitors per annum, only a quarter of them foreigners.

Parque Nacional Pali Aike is 196 kilometers northeast of Punta Arenas via Ruta 9, Ruta 255, and a graveled secondary road from the hamlet of Cooperativa Villa O'Higgins, 11 kilometers beyond Kimiri Aike. Just south of the Chilean border post at Monte Aymond, a hard-to-follow dirt road also leads to the park.

There is no public transportation, but Punta Arenas travel agencies can arrange visits. Hiring a car, though, is probably the best option, especially if shared among several people.

THE FJORDS OF FUEGIA

Short of Antarctica itself, some of the Southern Hemisphere's most awesome scenery occurs in the Beagle Channel and southern Tierra del Fuego. And as usual, Charles Darwin left one of the most vivid descriptions of the channel named for the famous vessel on which he sailed:

> ***The scenery here becomes even grander than before. The lofty mountains on the north side compose the granitic axis, or backbone***

of the country, and boldly rise to a height of between three and four thousand feet, with one peak above six thousand feet. They are covered by a wide mantle of perpetual snow, and numerous cascades pour their waters, through the woods, into the narrow channel below. In many parts, magnificent glaciers extend from the mountain side to the water's edge. It is scarcely possible to imagine anything more beautiful than the beryl-like blue of these glaciers, and especially as contrasted with the dead white of the upper expanse of the snow. The fragments which had fallen from the glacier into the water, were floating away, and the channel with the icebergs presented, for the space of a mile, a miniature likeness of the Polar Sea.

Even today, fairly few visitors still see Tierra del Fuego's splendid fjords, barely changed since Darwin described them in 1833; many of those do so on board the week-long excursion from Punta Arenas to Ushuaia and back on the Chilean vessels *Mare Australis* and *Via Australis.* Unlike the Navimag ferry from Puerto Montt to Puerto Natales, these are cruises in the traditional sense—the passengers are waited on hand and foot, and they're not cheap. Yet for the foreseeable future, this remains the only way to see the area short of sailing or hiring your own private yacht, and for that reason it's worth consideration even for those with limited finances.

Routes can vary depending on weather conditions in this notoriously changeable climate. After an evening departure from Punta Arenas's Muelle Prat, the vessel crosses the Strait of Magellan to enter the **Seno del Almirantazgo** (Admiralty Sound), a westward maritime extension of the freshwater Lago Fagnano trough. Passengers usually go ashore at the sound's lesser inlet **Bahía Parry,** on the north side of the Cordillera Darwin; here, hikers can approach the groaning **Ventisquero Parry** (Parry Glacier), named by Philip Parker King, captain of HMS *Adventure* and hydrographer on the *Beagle* expedition, in honor of Sir William Edward Parry (1790–1855), who made four unsuccessful attempts at the Northwest passage to the Pacific. With its numerous icebergs and low salinity, Bahía Parry has little wildlife.

From Bahía Parry, the ship sails back west, pausing at a small elephant seal colony at **Bahía Ainsworth,** near the **Ventisquero Marinelli,** where there's a short hiking trail through what was once forest until escaped beavers dammed the area into a series of ponds. Farther west, at **Isla Tucker,** there's a small Magellanic penguin colony and it's also possible to see the rare striated caracara, *Phalcoboenus australis.*

After a night's sailing, the ship enters the **Fiordo D'Agostini,** a glacial inlet named for the Italian priest and mountaineer who explored the farthest recesses of the Cordillera Darwin in the early 20th century. When high winds make it impossible to approach the **Glaciar Serrano** (named for Chilean naval Lieutenant Ramón Serrano Montaner, who charted the Strait in 1879), an option is the more sheltered **Glaciar D'Agostini.** Even here, though, seracs crack off the glacier's face, touching off a rapid surge of water and ice that runs parallel to a broad gravel beach and, when it subsides, leaves the beach littered with boulders of ice.

Darwin, again, described the dangers of travel in a land that sea kayakers are just beginning to explore:

The boats being hauled on shore at our dinner hour, we were admiring from the distance of half a mile a perpendicular cliff of ice, and were wishing that some more fragments would fall. At last, down came a mass with a roaring noise, and immediately we saw the smooth outline of a wave traveling toward us. The men ran down as quickly as they could to the boats; for the chance of their being dashed to pieces was evident. One of the seamen just caught hold of the bows, as the curling breaker reached it: he was knocked over and over, but not hurt; and the boats, though thrice lifted on high and let fall again, received no damage. . . . I had previously noted that some large fragments of rock on the beach had been lately displaced; but until seeing this wave, I did not understand the cause.

Prior to navigating Canal Cockburn, the ship stops at **Ventisquero Cóndor** where condors glide low and cormorants nest on the bluffs. Briefly exposed to swells from the open ocean, the vessel turns into the calmer **Canal Ocasión** and eventually enters the north arm of the Beagle Channel, sailing past the so-called **Avenida de los Glaciares,** a series of glaciers named for various European countries, sometimes anchoring at Yendegaia for brief shore-based excursions; for more information, see the separate entry for Estancia Yendegaia.

Traditionally, the ship proceeds to **Puerto Williams,** where it spends a few hours before sailing for the Argentine port of Ushuaia; now, though, it takes a variant to **Cabo de Hornos** (Cape Horn). The opening, a new Chilean port of entry at Puerto Navarino, directly south of Ushuaia, may expedite immigration formalities and the itineraries, as it will allow the ships to avoid doubling back to Puerto Williams, to reenter Chile, after leaving Ushuaia; for more information on Ushuaia, see the separate geographical entry.

After reentering Chile at Puerto Williams, the ship sails south to **Cabo de Hornos** (Cape Horn) and then back north to **Bahía Wulaia** where passengers go ashore at the site of a one-time Yámana mission. Returning to the Beagle Channel, it turns westward through the Beagle Channel's North Arm, again passing the Avenida de los Glaciares and entering Fiordo Pía (Pía Fjord), where dozens of waterfalls cascade down sheer metamorphic slopes from the **Glaciar Pía.** A bit farther west, it enters **Fiordo Garibaldi,** at least to the point where pack ice prohibits any further progress—even on a comfortable cruise ship, sailing through Tierra del Fuego fuels the sensation of passing through uncharted waters. After a short backtrack, the most vigorous passengers disembark for a short but strenuous and slippery hike through sopping Magellanic rain forest.

On the last full day, the boat sails through the Angostura Gabriel, a narrows only about 250 meters wide, before entering **Bahía Brooke,** where a nameless river of ice is slowly but inexorably transporting granite boulders down to the sea, and fresh snow avalanches off hanging glaciers. On the final morning, it sails north to **Isla Magdalena** (see the separate entry for Monumento Natural Los Pingüinos) before returning to Punta Arenas.

Practicalities

Well-organized without being regimented, the cruise is informal in terms of dress and behavior. As the start, passengers sign up for meal tables; places are fixed for the duration except at the buffet breakfast, when people tend to straggle in at different times. In general, passengers are grouped according to language, though they often place together people who speak English as a second language. The staff themselves can handle Spanish, English, German, French, and occasionally other languages.

After a welcome drink, usually pisco sour or *vaina* accompanied by mini-empanadas and other finger food in the bar, there's an introduction of the captain, crew, and staff, a brief folkloric show, and an obligatory safety drill. Smoking is prohibited everywhere except on the topmost deck and outdoors; bar consumption is now included in the package.

The cabins themselves are simple but spacious, with either a double or two single beds, built-in reading lights, a writing desk, and a private bath with good hot showers (though it takes a while for the hot water to arrive if you're the first shower of the morning). Each room has a closet with hangars and a small lock box for valuables. The food is ample and occasionally excellent, though breakfasts are a little monotonous; the wine is superb, and the service exceptional. Vegetarian menus are available on request.

For those who tire of the landscape or when the weather is bad, on-board activities include line-dancing(!), PowerPoint lectures on flora and fauna, engine-room tours, and culinary demonstrations of carved cucumbers, peppers, zucchinis, and other vegetables, in the shapes of birds and flowers. The farewell dinner is a fairly gala affair, followed by champagne on the topmost deck. As on the *Puerto Edén* ferry from Puerto Montt to Puerto Natales, the crew hands out diplomas on the final night.

At several locations, there are optional shore-based activities as well. At Puerto Williams, supplementary excursions include a US$30 anthropological bus trip, led by the local museum director, and a US$180-per-person Twin Otter over-flight of Cabo de Hornos for a maximum of 20 passengers. Many passengers leave and others board at Ushuaia, where the possibilities for full-day excursions are numerous. Many, though, opt for independent sightseeing.

Punta Arenas is home port for both the *Mare Australis* and the *Via Australis,* which have staggered schedules; check-in takes place at the Casa del Turista (O'Higgins 1401), at the entrance to Muelle Prat, while late-afternoon boarding begins either Saturday *(Mare Australis)* or Wednesday *(Via Australis).* Only a handful of passengers now take the entire seven-day cruise; most take the shorter three- or four-day options, beginning or ending the trip in Ushuaia.

Usually this very popular cruise runs full October–April, except for the last trip before Christmas, which may be only half full; in this case, it may be possible to negotiate a deal in Punta Arenas, getting a private cabin without paying a single supplement, for instance. In addition, at this time of year, days are so long that it's possible to enjoy the landscape until after 11 P.M., and there's sufficient light to read by 4 A.M. Note that cabins have 110-volt outlets, with U.S.-style plugs.

Reservations are made through **Cruceros Australis** (Avenida Bosque Norte 0440, 11th floor, Las Condes, Santiago, tel. 02/4423110, fax 02/2035173, www.australis.com), which also has offices in Buenos Aires (Carlos Pellegrini 989, Retiro, tel. 011/4325-8400, fax 011/4325-6600) and in Miami (4014 Chase Ave., Suite 202, Miami Beach, FL 33140, tel. 305/695-9618 or 877/678-3772, fax 305/534-9276). Per-person rates on the Punta Arenas–Ushuaia leg start at US$785–1,393 in low season up to US$1,244–2,229 in high season. On the Ushuaia–Punta Arenas leg, the comparable rates are US$681–1,207 in low season to US$1,078–1,931 in high season.

Puerto Natales and Vicinity

In the past 20 years, Puerto Natales has changed from a sleepy wool and fishing port on what seemed the aptly named Seno Última Esperanza—"Last Hope Sound"—to a bustling tourist town whose season has lengthened well beyond the traditional summer months of January and February. Its proximity to the famous Parque Nacional Torres del Paine, coupled with its status as the southern terminus for the scenic and increasingly popular ferry route from Puerto Montt, has placed it on the international travel map, utterly transforming the local economy.

While Puerto Natales has no knockout attractions in its own right, the town enjoys a magnificent seaside setting, with the snow-capped Cordillera Sarmiento and Campo de Hielo Sur, the southern Patagonian ice cap, visible over the water to the west. For visitors to Paine and other regional sights, it has abundant services, including tour operators and rental equipment, while there are also convenient connections to the Argentine town of El Calafate and Parque Nacional Los Glaciares.

In the aftermath of the Argentine economic meltdown of 2001–2002, though, Natales took a triple hit: retired Chilean coal workers from Río Turbio saw their incomes trapped in Argentine banking restrictions and their pensions cut by two thirds because of the Argentine devaluation, even as their cost of living remained high, and active workers have seen their wages decline. At the same time, local merchants have seen their Argentine business dry up as things are no longer cheaper on the Chilean side. Only tourism remains reliable.

One possible strong point is the pending construction of a 150-meter cruise-ship pier, which would simplify transfers from both the ferry and visiting cruisers to land. Meanwhile, private initiative has built a smaller jetty for local cruises near Puerto Bories, north of town.

HISTORY

Última Esperanza acquired its name because expeditions led by the 16th-century Spaniards Juan

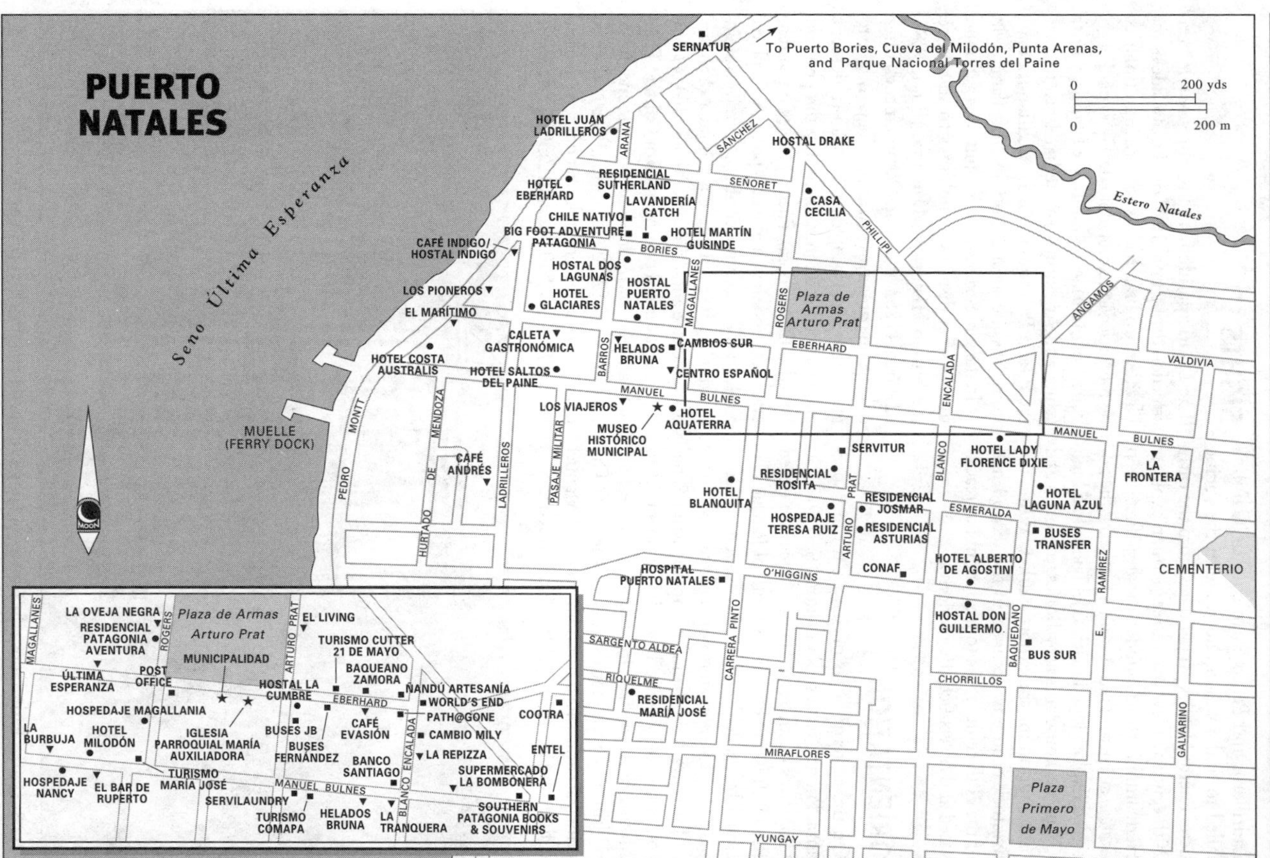
PUERTO NATALES
Seno Última Esperanza
Estero Natales
To Puerto Bories, Cueva del Milodón, Punta Arenas, and Parque Nacional Torres del Paine
0 200 yds
0 200 m
SERNATUR
HOTEL JUAN LADRILLEROS
HOSTAL DRAKE
CASA CECILIA
HOTEL EBERHARD
RESIDENCIAL SUTHERLAND
CHILE NATIVO
LAVANDERÍA CATCH
BIG FOOT ADVENTURE PATAGONIA
HOTEL MARTÍN GUSINDE
CAFÉ INDIGO/ HOSTAL INDIGO
HOSTAL DOS LAGUNAS
HOSTAL PUERTO NATALES
LOS PIONEROS
HOTEL GLACIARES
EL MARÍTIMO
Plaza de Armas Arturo Prat
CALETA GASTRONÓMICA
HELADOS BRUNA
CAMBIOS SUR
HOTEL COSTA AUSTRALIS
HOTEL SALTOS DEL PAINE
CENTRO ESPAÑOL
LOS VIAJEROS
HOTEL AQUATERRA
MUSEO HISTÓRICO MUNICIPAL
MUELLE (FERRY DOCK)
CAFÉ ANDRÉS
SERVITUR
HOTEL LADY FLORENCE DIXIE
LA FRONTERA
RESIDENCIAL ROSITA
HOTEL BLANQUITA
RESIDENCIAL JOSMAR
HOTEL LAGUNA AZUL
HOSPEDAJE TERESA RUIZ
RESIDENCIAL ASTURIAS
BUSES TRANSFER
HOTEL ALBERTO DE AGOSTINI
CONAF
CEMENTERIO
HOSPITAL PUERTO NATALES
HOSTAL DON GUILLERMO
BUS SUR
RESIDENCIAL MARÍA JOSÉ
Plaza Primero de Mayo
ARANA
SÁNCHEZ
SEÑORET
PHILLIPI
BORIES
MAGALLANES
ROGERS
EBERHARD
ANGAMOS
VALDIVIA
ENCALADA
BARROS
MANUEL BULNES
PEDRO MONTT
HURTADO DE MENDOZA
LADRILLEROS
PASAJE MILITAR
BLANCO
ARTURO PRAT
ESMERALDA
RAMIREZ
O'HIGGINS
BAQUEDANO
E.
CARRERA PINTO
SARGENTO ALDEA
RIQUELME
CHORRILLOS
GALVARINO
MIRAFLORES
YUNGAY
LA OVEJA NEGRA
Plaza de Armas Arturo Prat
EL LIVING
RESIDENCIAL PATAGONIA AVENTURA
TURISMO CUTTER 21 DE MAYO
MUNICIPALIDAD
BAQUEANO ZAMORA
ÚLTIMA ESPERANZA
POST OFFICE
HOSTAL LA CUMBRE
ÑANDÚ ARTESANÍA
WORLD'S END
HOSPEDAJE MAGALLANIA
PATH@GONE
COOTRA
LA BURBUJA
HOTEL MILODÓN
IGLESIA PARROQUIAL MARÍA AUXILIADORA
BUSES JB
CAFÉ EVASIÓN
CAMBIO MILY
BUSES FERNÁNDEZ
LA REPIZZA
ENTEL
TURISMO MARÍA JOSÉ
BANCO SANTIAGO
HOSPEDAJE NANCY
EL BAR DE RUPERTO
SUPERMERCADO LA BOMBONERA
SERVILAUNDRY
SOUTHERN PATAGONIA BOOKS & SOUVENIRS
TURISMO COMAPA
HELADOS BRUNA
LA TRANQUERA
© AVALON TRAVEL PUBLISHING, INC.
Magallanes

Ladrilleros and Pedro Sarmiento de Gamboa failed to find a westbound route to the Pacific here. Puerto Natales proper dates from the early 20th century, a few years after German explorer Hermann Eberhard founded the area's first sheep *estancia* at Puerto Prat. Within a few years, the Sociedad Explotadora de Tierra del Fuego had built a slaughterhouse at nearby Bories to process and pack mutton for the export market. While the livestock economy declined in the second half of the 20th century, the tourist boom has reactivated and diversified the economy.

ORIENTATION

On the eastern shores of Seno Último Esperanza, Puerto Natales (population 16,978) is 250 kilometers northwest of Punta Arenas via paved Ruta 9. It is 150 kilometers south of Parque Nacional Torres del Paine, also by Ruta 9, which is paved for 13 kilometers north of the city.

Entering town from the north, Ruta 9 becomes the roughly north-south Costanera Pedro Montt; most services and points of interest are within easy walking distance to the east. The principal commercial streets are east-west Manuel Bulnes and north-south Avenida Baquedano.

SIGHTS

The **Municipalidad,** a gingerbread-style construction dating from 1929 on the east side of the Plaza Arturo Prat, had its construction financed by the Sociedad Explotadora de Tierra del Fuego, which owned large amounts of land in both Chile and Argentina. Immediately to its east, the **Iglesia Parroquial María Auxiliadora** dates from the same era and shares its Magellanic style.

In the same exterior fashion but with a roomier interior that displays its holdings to advantage, the **Museo Histórico Municipal** (Bulnes 285, tel. 061/411263, muninata@ctcinternet.cl) offers displays on natural history, archaeology, and the region's aboriginal peoples, European settlement, and the rural economy (including the powerful Sociedad Explotadora), Puerto Natales' own urban evolution, and the Carabineros police, who played a role in the museum's creation. Noteworthy individual artifacts include a Yámana (Yahgan) dugout canoe and Aónikenk (Tehuelche) *boleadoras,* plus historical photographs of Captain Eberhard and the town's development. Summer hours are 8:30 A.M.–12:30 P.M. and 2:30–8 P.M. weekdays, 3–8 P.M. weekends; the rest of the year, hours are 8:30 A.M.–12:30 P.M. and 2:30–6 P.M. week-

The Sociedad Explotadora de Tierra del Fuego financed construction of Puerto Natales's Municipalidad.

days, 3–6 P.M. weekends. Admission costs US$1 for adults, US$.35 for children.

ENTERTAINMENT

Puerto Natales' nightlife is limited mostly to low-key bars like **Café Indigo** (Ladrilleros 105), a Chilean-run but gringo-oriented gathering place with nightly slide shows about Natales and Torres del Paine.

El Bar de Ruperto (Bulnes 371) takes its name from the pisco-swilling burro once popular on Chilean TV ads.

SHOPPING

For books, travel literature (some of it in English), maps, and the like, there's a branch of **Southern Patagonia Souvenirs & Books** (Bulnes 688, tel. 061/413017).

Ñandú Artesanía (Eberhard 586) sells maps and books in addition to a selection of quality crafts. **World's End** (Blanco Encalada 226, tel. 061/414725) is a Chilean map specialist.

ACCOMMODATIONS

Over the past two decades, Puerto Natales has developed one of the densest offerings of accommodations in all Chile. This is especially true in the budget category, where competition keeps prices low. There are good values in all categories, but plenty of mediocre and ordinary places as well. Off-season rates can drop dramatically.

Under US$10

Residencial Josmar (Prat and Esmeralda, tel. 061/414417, US$3 pp) has built a spacious campground with clearly delineated sites, privacy from the street, electricity, and hot showers. Among the regular accommodations, Israeli favorite **Residencial María José** (Magallanes 646, tel. 061/412218, juan_lasa@hotmail.com, US$5 pp) is one of Natales' best bargains.

US$10–25

Residencial Asturias (Prat 426, tel. 061/412105, US$5 pp) is a little cramped but otherwise fine. **Hospedaje Magallania** (Tomás Rogers 255, tel. 061/414950, magallania@yahoo.com, US$8 pp for dorms, US$20 d) is an informal hostel-style facility with spacious dorms and a few doubles, including breakfast, kitchen privileges, a TV room, and *buena onda* (good vibes).

Residencial Rosita (Prat 367, tel. 061/412259, US$6 pp) occupies the upstairs of a crowded family house; the rooms, all with shared bath, are smallish but fairly priced. **Hospedaje Teresa Ruiz** (Esmeralda 463, tel. 061/410472, freepatagonia@hotmail.com, US$6–7 pp) gets high marks for congeniality, cleanliness, and outstanding breakfasts with homemade rhubarb preserves. **Residencial Sutherland** (Barros Arana 155, tel. 061/410359, US$7 pp) is also a respectable choice.

The local HI affiliate is **Albergue Path@gone** (Eberhard 595, tel. 061/413291, pathgone@entelchile.net, US$7.50 pp), which has very good facilities. Friendly **Residencial Patagonia Aventura** (Tomás Rogers 179, tel. 061/411028, US$7 pp) provides a bit more privacy than others in its range, with knowledgeable operators who also rent equipment. Rates at friendly, responsive **Hospedaje Nancy** (Bulnes 343, tel. 061/411186, nancy@patagoniadiscovery.cl, US$8 pp) include breakfast.

In an older house with substantial character, steadily upgrading **Hostal Dos Lagunas** (Barros Arana 104, tel. 061/415733, doslagunas@hotmail.com, US$11 pp) is fast becoming a travelers' favorite; rates include an ample and varied breakfast.

US$25–50

Stuck in an off-the-beaten-sidewalk location, looking more expensive than it is, the immaculate **Hostal Don Guillermo** (O'Higgins 657, tel./fax 061/414506, US$13–21 s, US$23–27 d) is seriously underpriced compared to nearby competitors. It does lack private baths, and some rooms are small, but the breakfast is excellent; rates vary according to whether the room has cable TV.

Its decor is tacky—the interior looks more like a house trailer than a house—but cheerful **Hotel Blanquita** (Ignacio Carrera Pinto 409, tel. 061/411674, US$10 pp, US$23/33 s/d) is spotlessly maintained and often full. Rates include breakfast, but vary according to shared or private bath. **Hostal La Cumbre** (Eberhard 533, tel. 061/412422, lacumbre_hostal@yahoo.es, US$17 pp) occupies one of the town's better-preserved landmark houses.

Now a Natales institution, **Casa Cecilia** (Tomás Rogers 60, tel. 061/411797, redcecilia@entelchile.net, US$12 pp, US$30/38 s/d) deserves credit for improving accommodations standards here—it's such a legend that, on occasion, nonguests even ask for tours of the hospitable Swiss-Chilean B&B. The rooms are simple, and some are small, but all enjoy central heating, there are kitchen facilities, and the cheerful atrium is a popular gathering place. Rates, which vary according to shared or private bath, include the usual sumptuous breakfast.

Hip **Hostal Indigo** (Ladrilleros 105, tel. 061/413609, fax 061/410169, indigo@entelchile.net, US$17 pp, US$40 d with breakfast) has carved itself a niche as much for its ground-floor pub/restaurant as for its comfortable upstairs accommodations; most but not all rooms have private bath. Climbers can work out on the free-standing wall outside.

US$50–100

Rehabbed **Hostal Drake** (Philippi 383, tel./fax 061/411553, francisdrake@chileaustral.com, US$40/55 s/d) is a comfortable hostelry in a quiet location that tour operators often choose for their clients. Rates include breakfast, but you need persistence to get IVA discounts.

Other good values include **Hotel Milodón** (Bulnes 356, tel. 061/411727, fax 061/411286, US$45/62 s/d), and **Hotel Laguna Azul** (Baquedano 380, tel./fax 061/411207, laguna.azul@entelchile.net, US$55/68 s/d).

Natales's most engaging new place, though, is **Hotel Aquaterra** (Bulnes 299, tel. 061/412239, info@aquaterrapatagonia.com, US$55/65 s/d), a purpose-built hotel that combines style and substance, including an unconventional restaurant menu with items like pot stickers and fajitas.

The striking **Hotel Lady Florence Dixie** (Manuel Bulnes 659, tel. 061/411158, fax 061/411943, florence@chileanpatagonia.com, US$66/76 s/d) has expanded and upgraded what was already a good hotel without becoming a budget-breaker. Off-season rates, barely half the above, are a real bargain.

It's getting competition, though, from the **Hotel Glaciares** (Eberhard 104, tel./fax 061/411452, www.hotelglaciares.co.cl, glaciares@entelchile.net, US$74/86); again, off-season rates are a virtual gift.

Over US$100

Moribund despite its relative newness, **Hotel Internacional Alberto de Agostini** (O'Higgins 632, tel. 061/410060, fax 061/410070, hotelagostini@entelchile.net, US$68/102) does have spacious rooms with good natural light. While it's dropped its rack rates, it's still worth bargaining here—there are better values in lesser categories.

Hotel Eberhard (Costanera Pedro Montt 58, tel. 061/411208, fax 061/411209, hoteleberhard@busesfernandez.com, US$95/104 s/d) used to be one of the best in its range; it's still OK, but there are better options for fewer pesos. **Hotel Juan Ladrilleros** (Pedro Montt 161, tel. 061/411652, fax 061/412109, aventour@entelchile.net, US$93/105) is about average in this category; try instead the handsome **Hotel Saltos del Paine** (Bulnes 156, tel. 061/413607, fax 061/410261, www.saltosdelpaine.cl, informacion@saltosdelpaine.cl, US$76/106 s/d).

The best value in its range is **Hotel Martín Gusinde** (Bories 278, tel. 061/412770, fax 061/412401, www.austrohoteles.cl, hgrey@terra.cl, US$116/140 s/d); the off-season rates, dropping by more than 50 percent, are an exceptional value.

Rates at the waterfront classic **Hotel Costa Australis** (Costanera Pedro Montt 262, tel. 061/412000, fax 061/411881, costaus@ctcreuna.cl, US$130–164 s, US$147–181 d) depend on whether the room has a city or sea view. Off-season rates also fall substantially.

FOOD

To stock up on supplies for hiking at Puerto Natales, visit **Supermercado La Bombonera** (Bulnes

646). For breakfast, sandwiches, and desserts (especially the Sachertorte), try the vegetarian **El Living** (Arturo Prat 156, tel. 061/411140, US$4 for sandwiches), on the north side of the Plaza de Armas. The British owner arrived here by way of Explora's extravagant Hotel Salto Chico, in Torres del Paine, but his food is more upscale than his prices; hours are 11 A.M.–11 P.M. daily, but it closes May–mid-October.

Known for its seafood, Puerto Natales has several moderately priced eateries and a handful of upscale choices, if nothing truly exceptional. Relying on their waterfront locations to draw crowds, **El Marítimo** (Pedro Montt 214, tel. 061/410819) and **Los Pioneros** (Pedro Montt 166, tel. 061/410783) offer good value for money. For better atmosphere, try the casual **La Tranquera** (Bulnes 579, tel. 061/411039).

La Caleta Gastronómica (Eberhard 169, tel. 061/413969) is a moderately priced (US$5–8) locale that offers excellent value—try the salmon with king crab sauce. Another well-established option is **Café Andrés** (Ladrilleros 381, tel. 061/412380), for cooked-to-order seafood.

La Burbuja (Bulnes 300, tel. 061/414204) specializes in seafood and meats, but also has vegetarian offerings; try the *ostiones al pil pil* (US$5), a slightly spicy scallop appetizer, and the *congrio* (conger eel) for an entrée.

Offering exceptional views of the sound, and perhaps the most diverse food in town, **Café Indigo** (Ladrilleros 105, tel. 061/413609) is part of its namesake accommodations. Sandwiches, pastas, and a variety of vegetarian options are on the menu.

Greatly improved, opposite the plaza, **La Oveja Negra** (Tomás Rogers 169, tel. 061/415711, US$6–10) is the choice for a quiet meal in relaxed, if not quite intimate, surroundings. For either seafood or beef, its upscale aspirations make for more elaborate dining than at most of its competitors.

Part of its eponymous hotel, **Aquaterra** (Bulnes 299, tel. 061/412239, US$8–10) is an upscale restaurant with menu items like Mexican fajitas and Japanese *gyoza* (pot stickers) not often seen in this part of the world. For more conservative diners, it offers traditional beef dishes.

Underrated **Última Esperanza** (Eberhard 354, tel. 061/413626) deserves more attention than it gets for exceptional seafood at reasonable prices with outstanding service. **Los Viajeros** (Bulnes 291, tel. 061/411156) is a recent entry in the seafood category but also serves grilled Patagonian lamb. The **Centro Español** (Magallanes 247, tel. 061/411181) promises Spanish cuisine, but it remains a work in progress.

Café Evasión (Eberhard 595-B, tel. 061/414605) is a moderately priced café restaurant with daily lunch specials. **La Frontera** (Bulnes 819), open for lunch only, is comparable. Basic Chilean dishes outshine the Italian at **La Repizza** (Blanco Encalada 294, tel. 061/410361).

Natales's best ice creamery, **Helados Bruna,** has two locales: Bulnes 585 and Eberhard 217. Rhubarb is the regional specialty.

INFORMATION AND SERVICES

In a freestanding chalet-style structure on the waterfront, **Sernatur**'s local delegation (Pedro Montt 19, tel./fax 061/412125) is open 8:30 A.M.–1 P.M. and 2:30–6:30 P.M. weekdays throughout the year; December–March, it's also open 9 A.M.–1 P.M. weekends. It has helpful personnel, occasionally English-speaking, and fairly thorough information on accommodations, restaurants, and transportation.

For national-park information, contact **Conaf** (O'Higgins 584, tel. 061/411438).

Puerto Natales has several exchange houses: **Cambio Mily** (Blanco Encalada 266), **Cambios Sur** (Eberhard 285), and **Stop Cambios** (Baquedano 380), at Hotel Laguna Azul. **Banco Santiago** (Bulnes 598) has an ATM.

Correos de Chile (Eberhard 429) is at the southwest corner of Plaza Arturo Prat.

Long-distance operators include **Telefónica CTC** (Blanco Encalada and Bulnes) and **Entel** (Baquedano 270).

Internet connections are improving and cheapening. Try **World's End** (Blanco Encalada 226) for high-speed connections, but new outlets are appearing all the time.

Servilaundry (Bulnes 513, tel. 061/412869) or **Lavandería Catch** (Bories 218) can do the washing.

Hospital Puerto Natales (tel. 061/411582) is at Ignacio Carrera Pinto 537.

GETTING THERE

Air

LanChile/LanExpress no longer has a separate office here, but **Turismo Comapa** (Bulnes 533, tel. 061/414300, fax 061/414361) can handle reservations and tickets. Punta Arenas-bound buses will drop passengers at that city's Aeropuerto Presidente Carlos Ibáñez del Campo.

Path@gone (Eberhard 599, tel./fax 061/413290) represents Aerovías DAP, which flies weekdays to El Calafate (Argentina) November–March. Puerto Natales has a small but modern airfield just north of town.

Bus

There is frequent bus service to and from Punta Arenas and Torres del Paine, and regular but less frequent service to the Argentine destinations of Río Turbio, Río Gallegos, and El Calafate.

Carriers serving Punta Arenas (US$5.50, three hours) include **Bus Sur** (Baquedano 558, tel. 061/411325), **Buses Fernández** (Eberhard 555, tel. 061/411111), **Buses Pacheco** (Baquedano 500, tel. 061/414513), and **Buses Transfer** (Baquedano 414, tel. 061/412616). Round-trip tickets offer small discounts, but less flexibility.

Services to Torres del Paine (US$12, two hours) vary seasonally, and there is often frequent turnover among the agencies; again, there are small discounts for round-trip fares. Carriers include **Buses JB** (Prat 258, tel. 061/412824), **Buses Fortaleza** (Prat 234, tel. 061/410595), **Buses María José** (Bulnes 386, tel. 061/414312), and **Bus Sur.**

For the Argentine border town of Río Turbio (US$2, one hour), where there are connections to El Calafate and Río Gallegos, try **Buses Cootra** (Baquedano 244, tel. 061/412785), which has five to seven daily except on weekends, when there are only two or three. Bus Sur has fewer departures.

To the Argentine town of El Calafate (US$17, 5.5 hours), the carriers are Buses Cootra, Bus Sur, and **Turismo Zaahj** (Prat 236, tel. 061/412260). While these services are frequent in high season, in winter they may be weekly only.

At the Fernández terminal, **Buses El Pingüino** (Eberhard 555, tel. 061/411111) goes Sunday at 11 A.M. to Río Gallegos (US$10–13, 4.5 hours). Bus Sur goes Monday, Tuesday, and Friday at 6:30 A.M.

Ferry

Turismo Comapa/Navimag (Bulnes 533, tel. 061/414300, www.navimag.cl) operates the weekly car/passenger ferry MV *Magallanes* to the mainland Chilean city of Puerto Montt. Northbound sailing day is usually Friday at 4 A.M., but weather and tides can change schedules. For fares, see the Puerto Montt entry in the Sur Chico chapter.

Passengers often spend the night on board before early-morning departures, but Navimag also has a Sala de Espera (waiting room) improvised from two shipping containers at the corner of the Pedro Montt and O'Higgins.

GETTING AROUND

Emsa/Avis (Bulnes 632, tel. 061/410775) and **MotorCars** (Blanco Encalada 330, tel. 061/413593) rent cars, but there's a wider selection in Punta Arenas. **World's End** (Blanco Encalada 226, tel. 061/414725) rents bicycles and motorcycles. **Path@gone** (Eberhard 599, tel./fax 061/413290) also rents bicycles.

VICINITY OF PUERTO NATALES

A growing number of operators arrange excursions to nearby sites of interest and, of course, to Parque Nacional Torres del Paine and even Argentina's Parque Nacional Los Glaciares.

Several operators have organized complementary, one-stop arrangements for Torres del Paine under the umbrella of **Path@gone** (Eberhard 599, tel./fax 061/413290, www.pathagone.com, pathgone@chileaustral.com, pathagone@entelchile.net). These include **Andescape** (tel./fax 061/412592, www.andescape.cl, andescape@terra.cl); **Fantástico Sur** (Magallanes 960, Punta Arenas, tel. 061/710050, www.lastorres.com,

© WAYNE BERNHARDSON

roadside shrine to Argentine folk saint Difunta Correa, near Puerto Natales

info@lastorres.com); **Onas Aventura Patagonia** (tel./fax 061/412707, www.onaspatagonia.com, onas@chileaustral.com), which also does sea kayaking, trekking, and full-day excursions to Paine; and **Turismo Stipe** (tel./fax 061/411125, turismostipe@entelchile.net).

Other agencies include **Big Foot Adventure Patagonia** (Bories 206, tel. 061/414611, fax 061/414276, www.bigfootpatagonia.com, explore@bigfootpatagonia.com) for sea kayaking, trekking, ice hiking, climbing, mountaineering, and more general excursions as well; **Chile Nativo** (Barros Arana 176, tel. 061/411385, fax 061/415474, www.chilenativo.com, info@chilenativo.com) for riding, trekking, and birding; and **Servitur** (Prat 353, tel./fax 061/411858, servitur@entelchile.net). **Baqueano Zamora** (Eberhard 566, tel. 061/413953, baqueano@chileaustral.com) specializes in horseback trips in the park and is also the concessionaire for Posada Río Serrano and Hostería El Pionero.

Frigorífico Bories

Only four kilometers north of Puerto Natales, the Sociedad Explotadora de Tierra del Fuego built this state-of-the-art (for its time) meat freezer to prepare excess livestock, primarily sheep, for shipment to Europe. Built of brick masonry between 1912 and 1914, in the Magellanic style, it's the only plant of its kind in a reasonable state of preservation. After expropriation by the Allende government in 1971, the plant was partially dismantled and finally shut down a few years back.

Among the remaining structures are the rendering plant, which converted animal fat into tallow, the tannery that prepared hides for shipment, and the main offices, smithery, locomotive repair shop (Bories had its own short line), freight jetty, power plant, and boilers. The power plant still works.

Accommodations and food are available here at **Hotel Cisne Cuello Negro**; make reservations through **Turismo Pehoé** (José Menéndez 918, Punta Arenas, tel. 061/244506, fax 061/248052, ventas@pehoe.cl, US$90/100 s/d). Rates include private bath and breakfast; there is also a restaurant.

Puerto Prat

About 15 kilometers northwest of Puerto Natales via a gravel road, sheltered Puerto Prat is the nearest thing to a beach getaway that *Natalinos* have—on rare hot days, its shallow waters warm up enough to let the truly intrepid dip their toes into the sea. It is also the starting point for one-day sea kayak trips to **Fiordo Eberhard** (US$90 pp); for details, contact Big Foot Adventure Patagonia in Puerto Natales.

A short distance north, settled by Captain Hermann Eberhard, **Estancia Puerto Consuelo** was the area's first sheep farm. Now open to the public for day visits (US$10 pp), it also has a small museum. It's open 9 A.M.–7 P.M. daily; for details, contact Turismo Comapa in Natales.

Difunta Correa Shrine

About six kilometers east of Puerto Natales, on the south side of Ruta 9, the spreading mountain of water-filled plastic bottles at this spontaneous roadside shrine suggests one of two things: either many Argentines are traveling here, or Chileans are becoming devoted to the folk saint of Argentina's San Juan province. Or it may be a changing combination of the two, as the recent Argentine economic crisis has reversed the traditional flow of Argentine tourists into Chile.

Cerro Dorotea

About seven kilometers east of town on Ruta 9, nudging the Argentine border, the hike to the ridge top of the Sierra Dorotea makes an ideal half-day excursion, offering some of the Natales area's finest panoramas. Well-marked with red blazes and signs, the route to the summit of 549-meter Cerro Dorotea is, after the initial approach, unrelentingly uphill but never exhaustingly steep. This is not pristine nature—much of the lower slopes are cutover *lenga* forest, some of which has regenerated itself into an even-aged woodland. The ridge itself is barren, with a telephone relay antenna on the top.

Trailhead access is over private property, where farmer Juan de Dios Saavedra Ortiz collects US$4 per person. The fee, though, includes a simple but welcome Chilean *onces* (afternoon tea with homemade bread, butter, ham, and cheese) on your return from the hike.

Centro Turístico Llanuras de Diana

In the sheltered valley of the Río Casas Viejas, 30 kilometers east of Puerto Natales, Llanuras de Diana (Ruta 9 Km 215, tel. 061/410661, www.cajalosandes.cl, US$52 s or d) is a garden spot on the steppe that's close enough to Natales for those with their own vehicles, but almost equally convenient by public transportation. Buses between Punta Arenas and Natales pass right by the entrance. Open to the public, though employees of its savings-and-loan owners have priority, it offers 16 finely decorated rooms with private bath, as well as a restaurant, bar, and extensive gardens. Reservations are essential, as it often gets tour groups.

Monumento Natural Cueva del Milodón

Northwest of present-day Puerto Natales, on the shores of a small inlet known as Fiordo Eberhard, the giant Pleistocene ground sloth known as the mylodon *(Mylodon darwini)* took shelter in this wave-cut grotto some 30 meters high and 80 meters wide at its mouth, and 200 meters deep. While the mylodon has been extinct for nearly as long as humans have inhabited the area—some 11,000 years ago—the discovery of its remains caused a sensation in Europe, as their state of preservation induced some scientists to believe the animal might still be alive.

German pioneer sheep farmer Hermann Eberhard gets credit for discovering the cave in 1895, but Erland Nordenskjöld (1900) was the first scientist to study the cave, taking sample bones and skin back to Sweden. Its manure has been carbon-dated at roughly 10,400 years before the present, meaning the large herbivore coexisted with humans, but it was most definitely *not* a domesticate. In all probability, though, hunting pressure contributed to its demise (and that of many other Pleistocene megafauna). Oddly enough, no complete skeleton has been found.

The mylodon has gained a spot in the Western imagination, both among scientists and the lay public. U.S. archaeologist Junius Bird described the animal in his journals, published as *Travel and Archaeology in South Chile* (University of Iowa Press, 1988), edited by John Hyslop of the American Museum of Natural History. Family tales inspired Bruce Chatwin to write his masterpiece *In Patagonia,* which relates far-fetched legends that Paleo-Indians penned the mylodon in the cave and that some animals survived into the 19th century.

Conaf's **Museo de Sitio,** open 8 A.M.–8 P.M. daily, has excellent information on the 192-hectare park, which attracted nearly 46,000 visitors in 2003, more than half of them Chilean. A tacky life-size statue of the mylodon stands in the cave itself.

Admission costs US$5 for adult foreigners, US$2.50 for Chilean residents, with nominal rates for children. Many Natales-based tours take in the sight, but there is no regular public transport except for Paine-bound buses that pass on Ruta 9, five kilometers to the east. Mountain-bike rental could be a good option. In addition to the park's picnic area, there's now a good restaurant nearby.

Glaciar Balmaceda (Parque Nacional Bernardo O'Higgins)

Chile's largest national park, covering 3,525,901 hectares of islands and icecaps from near Tortel in Region XI (Aisén) to Última Esperanza in Region XII (Magallanes), has few easy access points, but the Balmaceda glacier at the outlet of the Río Serrano is one of them. From Puerto Natales, the closest approach is a four-hour sail northwest—where Juan Ladrilleros and Pedro de Sarmiento de Gamboa ended their futile quests for a sheltered route to the Pacific—past Puerto Bories, several wool *estancias* reachable only by sea, and nesting colonies of seabirds and breeding colonies of southern sea lions, among U-shaped valleys with glaciers and waterfalls. Andean condors have been sighted in the area.

At the end of the cruise, passengers disembark for an hour or so at **Puerto Toro,** where a half-hour walk through southern beech forest leads to the fast-receding **Glaciar Balmaceda.** Visitors remain about an hour before returning to Natales, unless they take advantage of the option to travel upriver to Torres del Paine, which may be visible in the distance.

A new option for visiting remote parts of the park, in comfort, is the five-day, four-night Skorpios cruise of the so-called "Ruta Kawéskar." For more information, see the sidebar "The Channels of the Kawéskar."

There are no formal accommodations in the park proper. However, across the sound from Puerto Toro, in virtually the most peaceful location imaginable—but for the wind—the nearly new **Hostería Monte Balmaceda** (c/o Aventour Patagonia, Avenida España 872, tel. 061/244197, fax 061/220174, www.aventourpatagonia.com, aventour@entelchile.net) charges US$89–99 s, US$108–131 d with breakfast. Rates, which include breakfast, depend on the view.

In addition to the hostería, Aventour now operates **Refugio Monte Balmaceda** (US$15 pp), a comfortable tent-style hostel (sleeping bags not provided) with shared baths. Guests at both the *hostería* and the *refugio* can lunch or sup at the restaurant for US$18 per person.

As it's mostly accessible by sea, a stay here is usually part of a package including a visit to the park and/or Torres del Paine. There is, however, a footpath suitable for a two-day trek to or from Torres del Paine.

Two Puerto Natales operators sail up the sound to the Balmaceda glacier, usually daily in summer, less frequently the rest of the year. Bad weather and high winds may cause cancellations at any time of year.

Turismo Cutter 21 de Mayo (Eberhard 554, tel. 061/411978, 21demayo@chileaustral.com; Ladrilleros 171, tel./fax 061/411176) operates its eponymous vessel or the yacht *Alberto de Agostini* to the park. Fares are US$60 per person; on the return the boat stops at Estancias Los Perales, where there's an optional *asado* for US$12 per person. The 18-meter yacht *Nueva Galicia* (Eberhard 169, tel. 061/412352, nuevagalicia@terra.cl) does the same circuit.

Instead of returning to Puerto Natales, it's possible to continue upriver to Torres del Paine with either 21 de Mayo or with **Onas Patagonia** (Eberhard 599, tel. 061/414349, tel./fax 061/412707, onas@chileaustral.com). In open Zodiac rafts, supplying all passengers with warm wet weather gear, Onas passes scenic areas not normally seen by visitors to Paine, makes a lunch stop along the Río Serrano, and requires a brief portage around the Serrano rapids before arriving at the Río Serrano campground. The total cost is US$90; the excursion can also be done in the opposite direction.

THE CHANNELS OF THE KAWÉSKAR

From the Golfo de Penas to Tierra del Fuego, southwestern Patagonia is one of the planet's most thinly populated and little visited areas. Its pre-Columbian inhabitants were "Canoe Indians," a general term applied to the Yámana and Kawéskar Indians who used precarious vessels to hunt seals and gather shellfish on the region's coasts and in myriad inlets. Never numerous, they prospered on local resources until catastrophic contact with Europeans—first violence and then disease—nearly obliterated them.

Today, ironically enough, it's possible to explore the dramatically scenic channels and icy fjords of the Kawéskar—also known as the Alacaluf—on board a comfortable cruise ship. Long known for its voyages from Puerto Montt to Laguna San Rafael, the Chilean Skorpios line has incorporated the glacial fjords between Puerto Natales and Puerto Edén into a five-day, four-night, 600-mile **Ruta Kawéskar** itinerary that pays symbolic homage, at least, to the last sad survivors.

The *Skorpios III* normally sails late Saturday from the company's new jetty, four kilometers north of Puerto Natales at the Puerto Bories junction. At the beginning, it follows the northbound Navimag ferry route as far as Isla Chatham, where it turns east to enter **Parque Nacional Bernardo O'Higgins** and anchor briefly at the fishing camp of **Caleta Villarrica.** It then enters **Fiordo Amalia,** where the flowing tongue of **Glaciar Amalia** protrudes from the Campo de Hielo Sur, the southern continental ice field, almost directly opposite Torres del Paine. Here passengers transfer onto double-hull, flat-bottom boats that are in fact mini-icebreakers, slicing through the pack ice to approach the glacier's face (these boats also have flat roofs, which helps keep off the rain and snow—except when the wind makes the rain horizontal).

From Amalia, the ship sails north to **Fiordo Calvo,** a site of magnificent hanging glaciers, a breeding sea-lion colony, and a rock-cormorant colony. Unfortunately, when the icebreakers' noisy diesels approach too closely, the lions and their pups scramble over the rocks and into the sea.

Retracing its route and then sailing north most of the night, again following the Navimag route, the *Skorpios III* eventually turns northeast into **Fiordo Eyre** and steams to **Glaciar Pío XI,** the South American continent's largest glacier—62 kilometers long and six kilometers wide. Since the icebreakers spend the season at Caleta Villarrica and Fiordo Amalia, passengers approach the glacier in smaller, quieter lifeboats, floating past deep blue icebergs that are constantly calving off the face. Before reversing direction south, the ship pays a brief visit to **Puerto Edén,** home of the last remaining Kawéskar.

The area's finest scenery, arguably, is the return trip's **Fiordo de la Montaña,** a sheer-sided north-south canyon between the Cordillera Sarmiento and Cordillera Riesco, only a short distance west of Puerto Natales. A candidate for future day trips from Natales, it includes the cruise's

Puerto Edén and Vicinity

Thanks to nearly incessant rains, misleadingly named Puerto Edén is as verdant as Adam and Eve's Biblical garden, but red-tide conditions have placed the shellfish livelihood of the remaining 15 or so Kawéskar Indians at risk. Their only other income sources are government handouts and some sadly crude crafts—tiny carved canoes and shells, for instance. Alcoholism is unfortunately common.

Vicinity is a relative term with respect to Puerto Edén (population about 300), the last outpost of the Kawéskar, which is about 400 kilometers northwest of Puerto Natales. It is on the weekly Navimag ferry route to and from Puerto Montt and also gets *Skorpios III* cruise-ship passengers and private yachts, which can explore the ice fields of the Campo de Hielo Sur, in Parque Nacional Bernardo O'Higgins, from the west.

Cruise passengers typically spend a couple hours on shore, where the subsidized Proyecto only other shore-based excursion—a hike to the relatively small but accessible **Glaciar Bernal.** The last night on board, which includes a gala dinner-dance, is spent in the lee of **Isla Focus,** within sight of Natales.

Accommodating only 110 passengers in 48 cabins, *Skorpios III* is a relatively small cruise ship. Decorated with handsome wood veneer, with view windows rather than portholes, the cabins are spacious and have excellent bathrooms and showers. Some beds, though, are on the soft side. The food and wine are excellent, and the service personalized.

The Kochifas family, Greek-Chilean shipbuilders based in Puerto Montt, have pioneered an appealing itinerary. What the Ruta Kawéskar trip lacks, as yet, is information: The guides' main task seems to be pointing out photo opportunities—already obvious enough in this extraordinary landscape. The *Skorpios III* would benefit from a library of books on the region, and presentations on history, environment, and ecology—at present, it's simply "eat well and enjoy the scenery."

The *Skorpios III* operates early September–mid-May, on a five-day, four-night schedule, leaving late Saturday night or Sunday morning; high-season is mid-December–mid-March. Rates start at US$2,140–2,500 s, US$1,340–$1,570 pp in Doble B, US$1,450–1,700 pp in Doble A, US$1,700–2,100 pp in Doble Matrimonial. There are also suites.

Ice is the attraction on the Ruta Kawéskar through the fjords northwest of Puerto Natales.

Yekchal has built a boardwalk over soggy terrain to an overlook where, on clear days, the view is magnificent. There's also a replica of a traditional Kawéskar house, but nobody lives in these sorts of dwellings anymore.

Puerto Edén's only accommodations and food are available at the **Hospedería Yekchal,** on the boardwalk north of the boat dock. Ships of any size cannot get very close to the shore and need to shuttle passengers on smaller boats.

Cerro Castillo and Vicinity

North of Natales, one of Chile's most thinly populated municipalities, the *comuna* of Torres del Paine has only 739 inhabitants by the 2002 census; more than half of them live in the hamlet of Cerro Castillo, 60 kilometers north of Puerto Natales on Ruta 9, alongside the Río Don Guillermo border crossing. Called Cancha Carrera on the Argentine side, this is the most direct route from Parque Nacional Torres del Paine to El Calafate

(Argentina) and Parque Nacional Los Glaciares. Formerly seasonal, it is now open all year.

Formerly an *estancia* belonging to the powerful Sociedad Explotadora de Tierra del Fuego, Cerro Castillo has an assortment of services, including a dismal museum at the municipal **Departamento de Turismo** (Avenida Bernardo O'Higgins s/n, tel. 061/691932) and the only gas station north of Puerto Natales (if continuing to Argentina, though, fuel is much cheaper on the Argentine side).

En route to and at Cerro Castillo, there are several accommodations options. The most southerly, **Hostería Patagonia Inn** (Km 26 Norte, Sector Dos Lagunas, tel. 061/228117 or 061/415153, US$20/33 s/d) is a former Braun-Menéndez property and its own small museum still holds some of the *estancia*'s record books. For the price, its 15 rooms with private bath, central heating, and TV offer good value; it also has a restaurant.

On the site of an older namesake that burned to the ground, **Hotel Tres Pasos** (Km 38 Norte, tel. 02/1969630 or 02/1969631, www.vientosur.com, hotel3pasos@terra.com, US$63/92 s/d) is a contemporary roadside inn that's well above average for the area. Lunch or dinner costs US$15 at its restaurant.

At Cerro Castillo itself, there are basic accommodations at **Residencial Loreto Belén** (tel. 061/691932, Anexo 728, US$17 pp) and more elaborate lodgings at **Hostería El Pionero** (tel. 061/413953, tel./fax 061/412911, baqueanoz@terra.cl, US$45–95 s, US$55–115 d); the cheaper rooms belong to an annex. Open September–April only, it serves meals to nonguests as well as guests, and also rents horses.

Parque Nacional Torres del Paine

Several years ago, when a major Pacific Coast shipping company placed a two-page ad in Alaska Airlines' in-flight magazine, the landscape chosen to represent Alaska's grandeur was . . . Parque Nacional Torres del Paine! While an uninformed photo editor may have been the culprit—interestingly enough for a Southern Hemisphere destination, the image was reversed—the soaring granite spires of Chile's premiere national park have become an international emblem of alpine majesty.

But there's more—unlike many of South American's national parks, Torres del Paine has an integrated network of hiking trails suitable for day-trips and backpack treks, endangered species like the wild guanaco in a UNESCO-recognized World Biosphere Reserve, and accommodations options ranging from rustic campgrounds to cozy trail huts and five-star luxury hotels. Popular enough that some visitors prefer the shoulder seasons of spring (November–December) or fall (March–April)—the park receives nearly 90,000 visitors annually, more than two-thirds of them foreigners—Torres del Paine has become a major international destination, but it's still wild country.

Nearly everybody visits the park to behold extraordinary natural features like the **Torres del Paine,** the sheer granite towers that have defied erosion even as the weaker sedimentary strata around them have weathered, and the jagged **Cuernos del Paine,** with their striking interface between igneous and metamorphic rocks. Most hike its trails uneventfully, but for all its popularity, this is still hazardous terrain. Hikers have disappeared, the rivers run fast and cold, the weather is unpredictable, and there is one documented case of a tourist attacked and killed by a puma.

ORIENTATION

Parque Nacional Torres del Paine is 112 kilometers northwest of Puerto Natales via Ruta 9 through Cerro Castillo; 38 kilometers beyond Castillo, a westbound lateral traces the southern shore of Lago Sarmiento de Gamboa to the park's isolated Laguna Verde sector. Three kilometers beyond the Laguna Verde junction, another westbound lateral leaves Ruta 9 to follow Lago Sarmiento's north shore to Portería Sarmiento, the park's main gate; it continues southwest for 37 kilometers to the Administración, the park headquarters at the west end of Lago del Toro.

Twelve kilometers east of Portería Sarmiento, another lateral branches northwest and, three kilometers farther on, splits again; the former leads to Guardería Laguna Azul, in the park's little-visited northern sector, while the latter enters the park at Guardería Laguna Amarga, the most common starting point for the popular Paine Circuit, and follows the south shore of Lago Nordenskjöld and Lago Pehoé en route to the Administración visitors center. Most public transportation takes this route.

Under construction, though, a bridge over the Río Serrano will soon permit access to the park via Cueva del Milodón and the western shore of Lago del Toro. It remains to be seen how this will affect public transportation.

GEOGRAPHY AND CLIMATE

Parque Nacional Torres del Paine comprises 181,414 hectares of Patagonian steppe, lowland and alpine glacial lakes, glacier-fed torrents and waterfalls, forested uplands, and nearly vertical granite needles. Altitudes range from only about 50 meters above sea level along the lower Río Serrano to 3,050 meters on the summit of Paine Grande, the central massif's tallest peak.

Paine has a cool temperate climate characterized by frequent high winds, especially in spring and summer. The average summer temperature is about 10.8°C, with maxima reaching around 23°C, while the average minimum in winter is around freezing. Average figures are misleading, though, as the weather is highly changeable. The park lies in the rain shadow of the Campo de Hielo Sur, where westerly storms drop most of their load as snow, so it receives only about 600 millimeters rainfall per annum. Still, snow and hail can fall even in midsummer. Spring is probably the windiest time; in autumn, March and April, winds tend to moderate, but days are shorter.

It should go without saying that at higher elevations temperatures are somewhat cooler and snow is likelier to fall. In some areas it's possible to hut-hop between *refugios,* eliminating the need for a tent and sleeping bag—but not for warm clothing and impermeable rain gear.

FLORA AND FAUNA

Less diverse than in areas farther north, Paine's vegetation still varies with altitude and distance from the Andes. Bunch grasses of the genera *Festuca* and *Stipa,* known collectively as *coirón,* cover the park's arid southeastern steppes, often interspersed with thorny shrubs like the calafate *(Berberis buxifolia),* which produces edible fruit, and *neneo (Anathrophillum desideratum).* There are also miniature ground-hugging orchids like the *zapatito (Calceolaria uniflora)* and *capachito (Calceolaria biflora).*

THE TORRES DEL FUEGO

In February 2005, in an incident that will have consequences for years to come, a careless camper overturned his campstove, starting a fire that burned for nearly a month in Parque Nacional Torres del Paine. The conflagration scorched 15,470 hectares of native vegetation, including forest, scrubland, and steppe, in the park's popular northeastern sector.

Most of the burned area consisted of steppe grasses and shrubs that should recover quickly, but the 2,400 hectares of slow-growing southern beech forest are more problematical. West of the Río Paine and the Lago Paine road, Conaf is placing priority on restoring 800 hectares of *lenga* and *ñirre.* At a cost of about US$1,700 per hectare, the government forestry agency is collecting seeds and will build several greenhouses to nurture seedlings for transplanting to the burned area in spring 2006. Some parts of the fire area will be fenced off to prevent humans trampling on, and guanacos feeding off, the newly planted trees.

Some parts of the park may be off limits to hikers for several years, though it's possible trails may be rerouted. While the fire came perilously close to the Cascada Ecocamp and the Hostería Las Torres, it damaged no major structures.

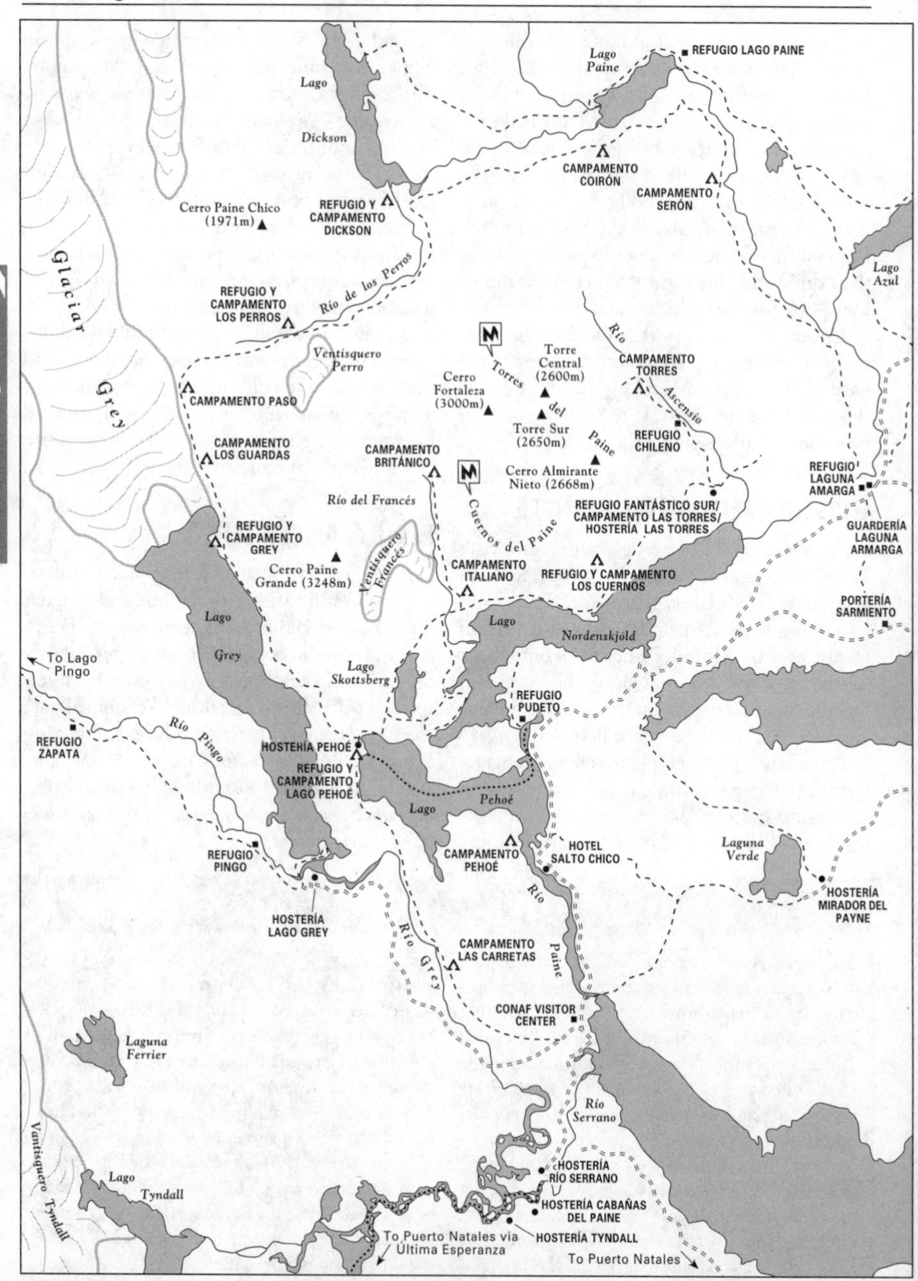

REFUGIO LAGO PAINE
Lago Paine
Lago Dickson
CAMPAMENTO COIRÓN
CAMPAMENTO SERÓN
Cerro Paine Chico (1971m)
REFUGIO Y CAMPAMENTO DICKSON
Glaciar Grey
Lago Azul
REFUGIO Y CAMPAMENTO LOS PERROS
Río de los Perros
Ventisquero Perro
Río Ascensio
CAMPAMENTO TORRES
Torre Central (2600m)
Torres del Paine
Cerro Fortaleza (3000m)
CAMPAMENTO PASO
Torre Sur (2650m)
REFUGIO CHILENO
CAMPAMENTO LOS GUARDAS
CAMPAMENTO BRITÁNICO
Cerro Almirante Nieto (2668m)
REFUGIO LAGUNA AMARGA
Río del Francés
REFUGIO FANTÁSTICO SUR/ CAMPAMENTO LAS TORRES/ HOSTERÍA LAS TORRES
Cuernos del Paine
GUARDERÍA LAGUNA ARMARGA
REFUGIO Y CAMPAMENTO GREY
Ventisquero Francés
Cerro Paine Grande (3248m)
CAMPAMENTO ITALIANO
REFUGIO Y CAMPAMENTO LOS CUERNOS
PORTERÍA SARMIENTO
Lago Grey
Lago Nordenskjöld
To Lago Pingo
Lago Skottsberg
REFUGIO PUDETO
Río Pingo
REFUGIO ZAPATA
HOSTERÍA PEHOÉ
REFUGIO Y CAMPAMENTO LAGO PEHOÉ
Lago Pehoé
Laguna Verde
REFUGIO PINGO
CAMPAMENTO PEHOÉ
HOTEL SALTO CHICO
HOSTERÍA MIRADOR DEL PAYNE
HOSTERÍA LAGO GREY
Río Grey
Río Paine
CAMPAMENTO LAS CARRETAS
CONAF VISITOR CENTER
Laguna Ferrier
Río Serrano
Ventisquero Tyndall
Lago Tyndall
HOSTERÍA RÍO SERRANO
HOSTERÍA CABAÑAS DEL PAINE
HOSTERÍA TYNDALL
To Puerto Natales via Última Esperanza
To Puerto Natales

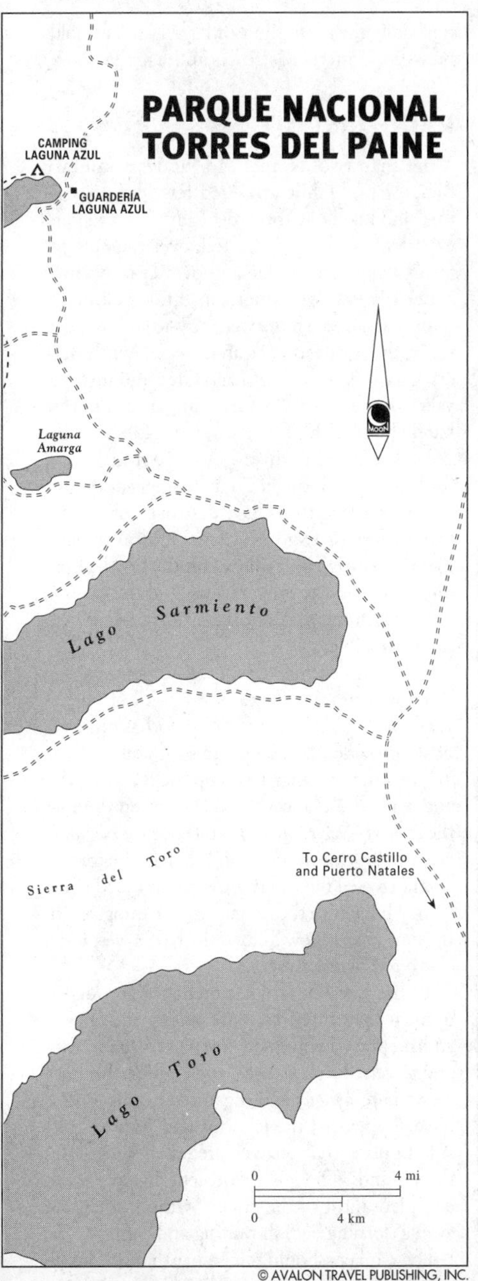

Approaching the Andes, forests of deciduous *lenga (Nothofagus pumilio)* blanket the hillsides, along with the evergreen *coigue de Magallanes (Nothofagus betuloides)* and the deciduous *ñirre (Nothofagus antarctica)*. At the highest elevations, there is little vegetation of any kind among the alpine fell fields.

Among Paine's mammals, the most conspicuous is the guanaco *(Lama guanicoe)*, whose numbers—and tameness—have increased dramatically over the past two decades. Many of its young, known as *chulengos,* fall prey to the puma *(Felis concolor)*. A more common predator, or at least a more visible one, is the gray fox *(Dusicyon griseus)*, which feeds off the introduced European hare and, beyond park boundaries, off sheep. The endangered *huemul* or Andean deer *(Hippocamelus bisulcus)* is a rare sight.

The monarch of South American birds, of course, is the Andean condor *(Vultur gryphus)*, not a rare sight here. Filtering the lake shallows for plankton, the Chilean flamingo *(Phoenicopterus chilensis)* summers here after breeding in the northern altiplano. The *caiquén* or upland goose *(Chloephaga picta)* grazes the moist grasslands around the lakes, while the black-necked swan *(Cygnus melancoryphus)* paddles peacefully on the surface. The fleet but flightless rhea or *ñandú (Pterocnemia pennata)* scampers over the steppes.

TORRES DEL PAINE

Some of the Andes' youngest peaks, the Torres del Paine are among the most emblematic in the entire range. Some 10 million years ago, a magma intrusion failed to reach the earth's surface, cooling underground into resistant granite; in the interim, water, ice, and snow have eroded softer surrounding terrain to liberate the spires of Torres del Paine into one of South America's most dramatic landscapes.

So strong a draw are the Torres that some visitors pressed for time settle for day tours that allow only a few hours in the park. Many others walk to the base of the Torres from Hostería Las Torres, a relatively simple day hike where it's hard to avoid the crowds. A longer and more tiring alternative, up the steep canyon of the Río Bader, provides a different perspective and the solitude that many hikers seek in the mountains.

CUERNOS DEL PAINE

Many visitors to the park misidentify the Cuernos del Paine (Horns of Paine) as the Torres. Located almost immediately south of the Torres proper, the saw-toothed Cuernos retain a cap of darker but softer metamorphic rock atop a broader granitic batholith that, like the Torres, never reached the surface before cooling. It's the sharp contrast between the two that gives the Cuernos their striking aspect.

As with the Torres, daytrippers can admire the Cuernos from the highway through the park. The best views, though, come from the "W" trail along the north shore of Lago Nordenskjöld, between Hostería Las Torres and Lago Pehoé.

Cuernos del Paine, Parque Nacional Torres del Paine

PAINE CIRCUIT

More than two decades ago, under a military dictatorship, Chile attracted few foreign visitors, and hiking in Torres del Paine was a solitary experience—on a 10-day trek over the now famous Paine circuit, the author met only three other hikers, two Americans and a Chilean. Some parts of the route were easy-to-follow stock trails (the park was once an *estancia*), while others, on the east shore of Lago Grey and into the valley of the Río de los Perros in particular, were barely boot-width tracks on steep slopes, or involved scrambling over granite boulders and fording waist-deep glacial meltwater. In the interim, as raging rivers have destroyed bridges at the outlets of Lago Nordenskjöld and Lago Paine, the original trailhead on the north shore on Lago Pehoé no longer exists, and the Laguna Azul exit in the park's northeastern corner is no longer feasible.

At the same time, completion of a trail along the north shore of Lago Nordenskjöld several years back created a new loop and simultaneously provided access to the south side of the Torres, offering easier access up the Río Ascencio and Valle del Francés in what is often done as the shorter "W" route to Lago Pehoé (see separate entry below for more detail). Where the former circuit crossed the Río Paine and continued along its north bank to the Laguna Azul campground, the new circuit now follows the river's west bank south to Laguna Amarga.

In the interim, trail maintenance and development have improved, rudimentary and not-so-rudimentary bridges have replaced fallen logs and traversed stream fords, and comfortable concessionaire *refugios* and organized campgrounds have supplanted the lean-tos and *puestos* (outside houses) that once sheltered shepherds on their rounds. Though it's theoretically possible to complete most of the circuit without a tent or even a sleeping bag, showering and eating at the *refugios,* hikers should remember that this is still rugged country with unpredictable weather.

Most hikers now tackle the circuit counterclockwise from Guardería Laguna Amarga, where buses from Puerto Natales stop for passengers to pay the park admission fee. An alternative is to continue to Pudeto and take a passenger launch to Refugio Pehoé, or else to the park's Administración (involving a longer and less interesting approach); both of these mean doing the trek clockwise.

At least a week is desirable for the circuit; before beginning, registration with park rangers is obligatory. Camping is permitted only at designated sites, a few of which are free. Purchase supplies in Puerto Natales, as only limited goods are available with the park, at premium prices.

Accommodations and Food

For counterclockwise hikers beginning at Laguna Amarga, there is no *refugio* until Lago Dickson (roughly 11 hours), though there is a fee campground at **Campamento Serón** (five hours) and a free one at **Campamento Coirón** (three hours farther).

Under Conaf concession to Puerto Natales's **Andescape** (Eberhard 599, tel. 061/412877, fax 061/412592, andescape@terra.cl) are **Refugio Lago Grey** and **Refugio Lago Dickson,** where there are also campgrounds, plus the **Campamento Río de los Perros.** All these *refugios* resemble each other, with 32 bunks charging US$16 per person, with kitchen privileges and hot showers, but without sheets or sleeping bags, which are available for rental but sometimes scarce. Breakfast costs US$6–7, lunch US$8, dinner US$11; a bunk with full board costs US$38 per person. Campers pay US$5 each, plus US$1.50 for showers (*refugio* guests, though, have shower priority). Rental tents, sleeping bags, mats, and campstoves are also available.

Puerto Natales's **Vértice** (tel. 061/412742) is the new concessionaire for cramped and traditionally overcrowded **Refugio Lago Pehoé** (but make reservations, which are strongly recommended, at Turismo Comapa, Bulnes 533, tel. 061/414300); a new *refugio* has been under construction here and should be operating by the time this book appears. Rates are US$20 per person without breakfast.

THE "W" VARIANT

From Guardería Laguna Amarga, a narrow undulating road crosses the Río Paine on a narrow bridge to the grounds of **Estancia Cerro Paine,** beneath the 2,640-meter summit of Monte Almirante Nieto. The *estancia* operates a hotel, *refugios,* and campgrounds, and also shuttles hikers back and forth from Laguna Amarga for US$4 per person.

From Estancia Cerro Paine, a northbound trail parallels the route from Guardería Laguna Amarga, eventually meeting it just south of Campamento Serón. The *estancia* is more notable, though, as the starting point for the "W" route to Lago Pehoé, a scenic and popular option for hikers lacking time for the full circuit. On the western edge of the *estancia* grounds, the trail crosses the Río Ascencio on a footbridge to a junction where a northbound lateral climbs the river canyon to Campamento Torres, where a short but very steep trail ascends to a nameless, glacial tarn at the foot of the Torres proper. This is an easy day hike from the *estancia,* though many people prefer to camp or spend the night at the *refugio* (see below for information on accommodations and food).

From the junction, the main trail follows Lago Nordenskjöld's north shore, past another *refugio* and campground, to the free Campamento Italiano at the base of the **Río del Francés** valley. While the main trail continues west toward Lago Pehoé, another northbound lateral climbs steeply up the valley, between the striking metamorphic Cuernos del Paine to the east and the 3,050-meter granite summit of Paine Grande to the west, to the free Campamento Británico.

Hikers in search of peace and quiet can make a strenuous detour up the **Valle Bader,** a steep rugged river valley that's home to a climber's camp at the base of the Cuernos. This involves a very stiff climb, and the route is mostly unmarked, but experienced cross-country hikers should be able to handle it.

Accommodations and Food

Technically outside the park boundaries, most of the "W" route along the north shore of Lago Nordenskjöld is under the private control of

Fantástico Sur (Magallanes 960, Punta Arenas, tel./fax 061/710050, www.lastorres.com, info@ lastorres@com), which runs the 36-bunk **Refugio Las Torres** on the *estancia's* main grounds, the 36-bunk **Refugio Chileno** in the upper Río Ascencio valley, and the 28-bunk **Refugio Los Cuernos,** all of which also have campgrounds. Fantástico Sur's *refugios* are more spacious, diverse and attractive in design than the Conaf *refugios,* and the food is better as well.

Bunks at any of the Fantástico Sur *refugios* cost US$24 per person (US$50 pp with full board), while camping costs US$6 per person with hot showers. Separately, a continental breakfast costs US$6, a U.S.-style breakfast US$8, lunch US$12, or dinner US$14; a full meal package costs US$27. Rental tents, sleeping bags, mats, and stoves are also available.

OTHER TRAILS

After heavy runoff destroyed the once-sturdy bridge at the outlet of Lago Paine in the early 1980s, the north shore of the Río Paine became, and has remained, isolated from the rest of the park. A good road, though, still goes from Guardería Laguna Amarga to the east end of Laguna Azul, where there are a campground and *cabañas,* and the **Sendero Lago Paine,** a four-hour walk to the lake and a simple *refugio.* A trekkers' alternative is the **Sendero Desembocadura,** which leads north from Guardería Laguna Amarga through open country to the west end of Laguna Azul and continues to Lago Paine, but this takes about eight hours. From the north shore of Lago Paine, the **Sendero Lago Dickson** (5.5 hours) leads to the Dickson glacier.

Several easy day hikes are possible near Guardería Lago Pehoé, directly on the road from Laguna Amarga to the Administración visitors center. The short **Sendero Salto Grande** leads to the thunderous waterfall, at the outlet of Lago Sarmiento, that was the starting point of the Paine Circuit until unprecedented runoff swept away the iron bridge that crossed to Península Pehoé. From Salto Grande, the **Sendero Mirador Nordenskjöld** is a slightly longer but still easy hike to a vista point on the

© WAYNE BERNHARDSON

Though it lies on private land, Hostería Las Torres is the starting point for many hikes into the Paine backcountry.

lakeshore, directly opposite the stunning Cuernos del Paine.

From Guardería Lago Grey, 18 kilometers northwest of the Administración by road, a short footpath leads to a sandy beach on the south shore of Lago Grey, where westerly winds often beach icebergs from Glaciar Grey. The longer and less visited **Sendero Lago Pingo** ascends the valley of the Río Pingo to its namesake lake (5.5–6 hours); there are two basic *refugios* along the route.

FURTHER RECREATION

Though popular, hiking is not the only recreational option for Paine visitors.

Despite the similarity of terrain, Paine attracts fewer climbers than Argentina's neighboring Parque Nacional Los Glaciares, perhaps because fees for climbing permits have been very high here. At present, permits are free of charge; before being granted permission, though, climbers must present Conaf with current climbing résumés, emergency contact numbers, and authorization from their consulate.

When climbing in sensitive border areas (meaning most of Andean Chile), climbers must also have permission from the Dirección de Fronteras y Límites (Difrol) in Santiago. It's possible to do this through a Chilean consulate overseas or at Difrol's Santiago offices; if you arrive in Puerto Natales without permission, it's possible to request it through the **Gobernación Provincial** (tel. 061/411423, fax 061/411992), the regional government offices on the south side of Plaza Arturo Prat. The turnaround time is 48 hours. Ask Conaf for more time than you'll need, as each separate trip could require a separate fee.

While climbing and mountaineering activities may be undertaken independently, local concessionaires can provide training and lead groups or individuals with less experience on snow and ice. Puerto Natales's Big Foot Adventure Patagonia, for instance, has a Refugio Grey base camp, where it leads full-day traverses of the west side of Glaciar Grey (US$75 pp) daily at 9 A.M. and 3 P.M., returning at 2 and 8 P.M. Except for warm, weather-proof clothing, they provide all equipment. For more detail, contact **Big Foot Adventure Patagonia** (Bories 206, tel./fax 061/413247, explore@bigfootpatagonia.com).

Big Foot also arranges guided three-day, two-night descents of the Río Serrano for US$500 per person.

The only park concessionaire offering horseback trips is Río Serrano–based **Baqueano Zamora** (Eberhard 534, Puerto Natales, tel. 061/413953, fax 061/412911, www.baqueano zamora.com). Rates are about US$75 per day (including lunch). Just outside the park boundaries, though, Hostería Las Torres has its own stables; for contact details, see the Accommodations entry below.

ACCOMMODATIONS AND FOOD

Park accommodations range from free trailside campgrounds to first-rate luxury hotels with just about everything in between; in summer, reservations are almost obligatory at hotels and advisable at campgrounds and *refugios.* For options along the Paine Circuit and other trails, see the separate entries above.

Camping

River water and pit toilets are the only amenities at Conaf's free **Refugio y Camping Laguna Amarga,** where backpackers wait for the bus to Puerto Natales. At Estancia Cerro Paine, **Camping Las Torres** (US$5 pp) draws hikers heading up the Río Ascencio valley to the Paine overlook and/or west on the "W" route to Lago Pehoé, or finishing up the circuit here. Formerly insufficient shower and toilet facilities have improved substantially.

Also at Las Torres, the **Cascada Eco-Camp** is a dome-tent facility designed for minimum-impact accommodations; on raised platforms, heated by gas stoves, each tent is five meters wide, with wooden floors and two single beds, with towels and bedding including down comforters. A larger tent contains a common living area, dining room, and kitchen; the separate bathrooms have hot showers and composting toilets (from some of them, it's a long walk for middle-of-the-night toilet visits). It's open, however, only to Cascada clients; for more detail consult their listing under Organized Tours in the Know Patagonia chapter, or see their website (www.cascada-expediciones.com).

On the small peninsula on the eastern shore of its namesake lake, just west of the road to the Administración, sites at the concessionaire-run **Camping Lago Pehoé** (tel. 061/249501 or 061/249581, campingpehoe@sodexho.cl, in Punta Arenas, US$20) hold up to six people; fees include firewood and hot showers. A few kilometers farther south, **Camping Río Serrano** has recently been closed but should reopen in the near future.

In the park's isolated northeastern sector is **Camping Laguna Azul** (tel. 061/411157 in Puerto Natales, US$17 per site).

Refugios, Hosterías, and Hotels

Near the Administración, Conaf's **Refugio Lago Toro** charges US$5 per person for bunks (bring your own sleeping bag) plus US$2 for hot showers. The extremely basic **Refugio Pudeto,** on the north shore of Lago Pehoé, has long needed a makeover to put it on a par with other *refugios,* but for the moment it remains a backpackers' crash pad.

Posada Río Serrano (tel. 061/413953, baqueanoz@terra.cl, US$95–129 d) is a former *estancia* house retrofitted as a B&B. Rates, which include breakfast, depend on whether the room has shared or private bath; there a restaurant/bar for other meals and for drinks. While it's improved under new management, and quadruples and sextuples can be cheaper per person, it's really overpriced for what it offers.

Reachable by road along Lago Sarmiento's south shore or by foot or horseback from the Río Paine, well-regarded **Hostería Mirador del Payne** (tel. 061/410498, www.miradordelpayne.com, US$123/152 s/d) lies in the park's isolated southeastern Laguna Verde sector. Its Punta Arenas representative is **Turismo Viento Sur** (Fagnano 585, tel./fax 061/226930, www.vientosur.com).

Where Lago Grey becomes the Río Grey, you'll find **Hostería Lago Grey** (US$173/199 s/d with breakfast); lunch or dinner costs US$24 per person. For reservations, contact **Austro Hoteles** (Lautaro Navarro 1061, Punta Arenas, tel./fax 061/225986, hgrey@terra.cl). Off-season rates are about half; it also arranges excursions.

On a five-hectare island linked to the mainland by a footbridge, the 25-room **Hostería Pehoé** US$145–180 s, US$160–195 d) has improved substantially since the operator won a lawsuit against Conaf and began to reinvest in what had been a rundown facility, with substandard service, in an undeniably spectacular setting. For reservations, contact **Turismo Pehoé** (José Menéndez 918, Punta Arenas, tel. 061/244506, fax 061/248052, pehoe1@ctcreuna.cl).

At Estancia Cerro Paine, seven kilometers west of Guardería Laguna Amarga, the sprawling but well-run **Hostería Las Torres** (US$131–179 s, US$149–197 d) is one of the park's gems for its setting beneath Monte Almirante Nieto, its professionalism, and the recent addition of a spa, which offers saunas and massages. While it's an upscale option, it's conscientiously eco-friendly in terms of waste disposal, and management is constantly seeking feedback from guests. Open to both guests and nonguests, the tobacco-free restaurant prepares quality food in cruise-ship quantities. For reservations, contact Hostería Las Torres (Magallanes 960, Punta Arenas, tel. 061/226054, fax 061/222641, www.lastorres.com, info@lastorres.com); off-season rates are about half.

Open for packages only, **Hotel Salto Chico** is a mega-luxury resort that, somehow, manages to blend inconspicuously into the landscape while offering some of the grandest views of any hotel on the globe. Rates start at US$1,974/2,876 s/d for three nights in the least expensive room, ranging up to US$6,808/8,544 s/d for seven nights in the costliest suite, including transfer to and from Punta Arenas and unlimited excursions within the park. Low-season rates are about 20 percent cheaper. For details and/or reservations, contact **Explora Hotels** (Américo Vespucio Sur 80, 5th floor, Las Condes, Santiago, tel. 02/3952533, fax 02/2284655, www.explora.com, reservexplora@explora.com).

Just beyond park boundaries, reached by launch over the Río Serrano, the stylish **Hostería Lago Tyndall** (Croacia 731, Punta Arenas, tel./fax 061/2354457, www.hosteriatyndall.com, hosteriatyndall@terra.cl, US$130/150 s/d) enjoys peace, quiet, and magnificent views. Nearby is the less stylish **Hostería Cabañas del Paine** (tel. 061/220174, fax 061/243354 in Punta Arenas, aventour@entelchile.net, US$110/140 s/d).

INFORMATION

Conaf's principal facility is its **Centro de Informaciones Ecológicas** (tel. 061/691931), at the Administración building on the shores of Lago del Toro, which features good natural-history exhibits. It's open 8:30 A.M.–8 P.M. daily in summer. Ranger stations at Guardería Laguna Amarga, Portería Lago Sarmiento, Guardería Laguna Azul, Guardería Lago Verde, and Guardería Lago Grey can also provide information.

Entry Fee

For foreigners, Torres del Paine is Chile's most expensive national park—US$13 per person except May 1–September 30, when it's only US$7 per person. Rangers at Portería Lago Sarmiento, Guardería Laguna Amarga (where most inbound buses now stop), Guardería Lago Verde, or Guardería Laguna Azul collect the fee and issue receipts.

Books and Maps

The text and coverage of the 5th edition of Tim Burford's *Chile & Argentina: The Bradt Trekking Guide* (Bradt Publications, 2001) are greatly improved over previous editions, though the maps are only so-so. Clem Lindenmayer and Nick Tapp's new 3rd edition of *Trekking in the Patagonian Andes* (Lonely Planet, 2003) has significantly better maps than Bradt and expanded coverage compared to its own previous editions. Only a few of those maps, though, are as large as the 1:100,000 scale that's desirable for hiking, though the rest are suitable for planning hikes.

Climbers should look for Alan Kearney's *Mountaineering in Patagonia* (Seattle: The Mountaineers, 1998), which includes both historical and practical information on climbing in Torres del Paine and Argentina's Parque Nacional Los Glaciares. Gladys Garay N. and Oscar Guineo N. have collaborated in *The Fauna of Torres del Paine* (1993), a locally produced guide to the park's animal life.

Conaf sells a very inexpensive map, at a scale of 1:160,000 with erratic contour intervals, that's suitable for orientation but not for trekking. The trekking map of choice, for about US$5.50, is Daniel Bruhin's *Torres del Paine,* at a scale of 1:100,000. At the same scale and about the same price, JLM Mapas' *Torres del Paine Trekking Map* is widely available in Punta Arenas and Puerto Natales, and less dependably available at Portería Lago Sarmiento and at the park's Centro de Informaciones Ecológicas.

GETTING THERE

Most people choose the bus as the cheapest and quickest way to and from the park, but the more expensive trip up Seno Última Esperanza and the Río Serrano by cutter and Zodiac is a viable and more interesting alternative.

Bus

For overland transportation details, see the Puerto Natales entry. All bus companies enter the park at Guardería Laguna Amarga, where many people begin the Paine circuit, before continuing to the Administración at Río Serrano. Round-trips from Natales are slightly cheaper, but companies do not accept each others' tickets.

In summer only, there may be direct bus service from Torres del Paine to El Calafate, Argentina, the closest town to that country's Parque Nacional Los Glaciares. Inquire in Puerto Natales or at the park Administración.

River

Transportation up and down the Río Serrano, between the park and Puerto Natales, has become a popular if considerably more expensive alternative than the bus; for details, see the separate entry for Parque Nacional Bernardo O'Higgins and the Balmaceda glacier. Visitors who only want to see this sector of the river, without continuing to Puerto Natales, can do so as a day trip to Puerto Toro and back.

GETTING AROUND

Buses to and from Puerto Natales will also carry passengers along the main park road, but as their schedules are very similar, there are substantial blocks of time with no public transportation. Hitching is common, but competition is heavy and most Chilean vehicles are full with families. There is a regular shuttle between Guardería Laguna Amarga and Estancia Cerro Paine (Hostería Las Torres).

October–April, reliable transportation is now available from Refugio Pudeto to Refugio Pehoé (US$17 one way, 30 minutes; US$30 round-trip) with the catamaran *Hielos Patagónicos* (tel. 061/411380 in Puerto Natales). In October and April, there is one departure daily, at noon, from Pudeto, returning at 12:30 P.M. In November and mid-March–April, there are departures at noon and 6 P.M., returning at 12:30 and 6:30 P.M.

December–mid-March, there is another departure at 9:30 A.M., returning at 10 A.M. Schedules are subject to change, may be canceled due to bad weather, and there are no services on Christmas and New Year's Day.

Also in season, the catamaran *Grey II* goes daily from Hotel Lago Grey to Glaciar Grey (US$60 pp) at 9 A.M. and 3 P.M. daily. There is a US$3.50 shuttle between the Administración and Hotel Lago Grey that connects with the cruise.

Chilean Tierra del Fuego

Across the Strait from Punta Arenas, Chilean Tierra del Fuego is a thinly populated area with only one major settlement, the town of Porvenir, on its northerly steppes. To the south, its rugged alpine terrain is a westward extension of the Argentine cordillera, with scenic fjords that few other landscapes can match. Across the Beagle Channel, Isla Navarino's Puerto Williams, the southernmost permanent settlement in the world, is part of an archipelagic maze that stretches south to the famous Cape Horn.

PORVENIR

Chilean Tierra del Fuego's main town, Porvenir sits on a sheltered harbor on the east side of the Strait of Magellan. Local settlement dates from the 1880s, when the area experienced a brief gold rush, but stabilized with the establishment of wool *estancias* around the turn of the century. After the wool boom fizzled in the 1920s, it settled into an economic torpor that, appropriately enough, has left it a remarkable assortment of corroding metal-clad Magellanic buildings.

Porvenir's inner harbor is a great place for spotting kelp geese, gulls, cormorants, steamer ducks, and other seabirds, but its main tourist role has been as a gateway to the Argentine sector of the Isla Grande. This may change as small local enterprises begin to provide access to parts of the archipelago that, up to now, have only been accessible through expensive cruises.

Orientation

Only 30 nautical miles east of Punta Arenas, Porvenir (population 4,734) occupies a protected site at the east end of Bahía Porvenir, an inlet of the Strait of Magellan. Its port, though, is three kilometers west of the town proper, whose mostly regular grid occupies a sloping south-facing site centered on the Plaza de Armas.

From Porvenir Ruta 215, a smooth gravel road, leads south and then east along the shore of Bahía Inútil to the Argentine border at San Sebastián, 150 kilometers away; an interesting alternate route leads directly east through the Cordón Baquedano before rejoining Ruta 215 about 55 kilometers to the east. If it's too late to catch the ferry back to Punta Arenas, another gravel road follows the coast to Puerto Espora, 141 kilometers to the northeast.

Sights

Directly on the water, **Parque Yugoslavo** is a memorial to the earliest gold-seeking immigrants, most of whom were Croatians; it's also one of the best birding spots in town. The tourist office provides a small map/brochure, in English, of the city's distinctive architectural heritage; many of its houses, and other buildings, were also Croatian-built.

Most public buildings surround the neatly landscaped **Plaza de Armas,** two blocks north of Parque Yugoslavo. Among them is the expanded and improved **Museo de Tierra del Fuego Fernando Rusque Cordero** (Zavattaro 402, tel. 061/580098), a regional museum that deals with the island's natural history, indigenous heritage, the early gold rush, the later but longer-lasting wool rush, and even cinematography—German-born local filmmaker José Bohr actually went to Hollywood in 1929, and enjoyed a long if inconsistent career. It has added a skillfully done replica of an early rural store, and a good photographic display on local architecture.

The museum takes its name from a Carabineros officer who helped found it—and was no doubt responsible for the permanent exhibit on police uniforms. Hours are 9 A.M.–5 P.M. weekdays; in January and February only, weekend hours are 10:30 A.M.–1:30 P.M. and 3–5 P.M. Admission costs US$.80.

Accommodations and Food

Residencial Colón (Damián Riobó 198, tel. 061/581157, US$8 pp) and **Hostal los Canelos** (Croacia 356, tel. 061/581223, US$8 pp) are comparable, though the latter occupies a more distinctive Magellanic house. Rates at **Hotel España** (Croacia 698, tel. 061/580160, US$10–13 pp) depend on whether the room has shared or private bath. It also has a restaurant, but breakfast costs extra.

Hotel Central (Philippi 295, tel. 061/580077, US$21–26 s, US$31–35 d) also varies according to shared or private bath, but rates include breakfast. All rooms at **Hotel Rosas** (Philippi 296, tel. 02901/580088, US$25/33 s/d) have private bath and include breakfast; its restaurant is one of Porvenir's best values in a town with, admittedly, only a few options.

Hostería Los Flamencos (Teniente Merino s/n, tel. 061/580049, US$35–42 s, US$44–54 d, ventas@hosterialosflamencos.com) has undergone a recent rehab, including much-needed interior and exterior paint, but kept prices reasonable for what it offers. The higher rates are from peak season, October–April.

Other than hotel restaurants, the main dining options are the basic **Puerto Montt** (Croacia 1199, tel. 061/580207), the very decent waterfront **Club Social Croata** (Señoret 542, tel. 061/580053), and the **Club Social Catef** (Zavattaro 94, tel. 061/581399). **El Chispa** (Señoret 202, tel. 061/580054) is a *picada,* a Chilean term denoting good home cooking at moderate prices.

Information and Services

Porvenir's steadily improving **Oficina Municipal de Turismo,** in the museum building at Padre Mario Zavattaro 434 (tel. 061/580098, ext. 324, muniporvenir@terra.cl) is open 8:30 A.M.–5 P.M. weekdays except Friday, when it closes at 4 P.M. Weekend hours are 11 A.M.–2 P.M. and 3–5 P.M. If e-mailing them, include *asunto turismo* in the header.

Information is also available at the kiosk on the Costanera between Mardones and Muñoz Gamero.

Banco del Estado (Philippi 263) is the only option for changing money.

Correos de Chile (Phillipi 176) is at the southwest corner of the Plaza de Armas. The **Compañía Chilena de Teléfonos** is at Philippi 277.

For medical services, try the **Hospital Porvenir** (Carlos Wood s/n, between Señoret and Guerrero, tel. 061/580034).

Getting There and Around

Porvenir has regular but infrequent connections to the mainland and to Argentina.

Aerovías DAP (Manuel Señoret s/n and Muñoz Gamero, tel. 061/580089) operates air taxi service to Punta Arenas (US$23) at least daily, often more frequently.

Unfortunately, there are no longer regular buses between Porvenir and Río Grande, on the Argentine side, so hitching is the only option.

Tuesday and Friday at 4 P.M., there's a free municipal bus from the DAP offices on Señoret to Camerón and Timaukel (2.5 hours), in the southwestern corner of the island; another goes to **Cerro Sombrero** (1.5 hours) at 5 P.M. Monday, Wednesday, and Friday from Santos Mardones 330.

There are also buses to Camerón and Timaukel (US$6, 2.5 hours) Monday, Wednesday, and Friday at 5 P.M.; these leave from Aerovías DAP offices on Señoret.

In the same office as DAP, **Transbordadora Broom** (Manuel Señoret s/n, tel. 061/580089) sails the car-passenger ferry *Melinka* to Punta Arenas (2.5 hours) Tuesday, Thursday, and Saturday at 1 P.M., Wednesday, and Friday at 2 P.M., and Sunday and holidays at 5 P.M. The ferry leaves from Bahía Chilote, about three kilometers west of town. For fares, see the Punta Arenas entry.

VICINITY OF PORVENIR

Vicinity is a relative term on Tierra del Fuego, as some fascinating locales are exceptionally difficult or expensive—or both—to reach. **Cordillera Darwin, Ltda.** (Croacia 675, tel. 061/580296, 09/6407204, www.explorepatagonia.cl, info@explorepatagonia.cl) does brief launch tours around

wool truck at Porvenir ferry dock

Bahía Chilote, three-day horseback excursions to the Río Cóndor, and a six-day trip to the Cordillera Darwin that's substantially cheaper than the only other option, the week-long luxury cruise on the *Mare Australis* (see the Fjords of Fuegia section for details).

Monumento Natural Laguna de los Cisnes

Birding groups often make a detour to this 25-hectare saline lake reserve, which desiccates during droughts, just north of Porvenir. While it takes its name from the elegant black-necked swan, it's also home to many other species.

Cordón Baquedano

After Chilean naval officer Ramón Serrano Montaner found gold in the rolling hills east of Porvenir in 1879, gold-panners from Chile and Croatia flocked to the Río del Oro valley, between the Cordón Baquedano and the Sierra Boquerón. Living in sod huts that shielded them from the wind and cold, hoping to eke out a kilogram per year—though yields were usually smaller—more than 200 worked the placers until they gave out. By the turn of the century, California miners introduced dredges and steam shovels, but decreasing yields ended the rush by 1908–1909. A few hardy individuals hang on even today.

From Porvenir, the eastbound road through the Cordón Baquedano passes several gold-rush sites, some marked with interpretive panels; the literal high point is the **Mirador de la Isla,** an overlook 500 meters above sea level. In many places guanacos, which seem to outnumber sheep, gracefully vault meter-high fences that stop the sheep cold.

Onaisín

About 100 kilometers east of Porvenir, a major north-south road crosses Ruta 215 at Onaisín, a former Sociedad Explotadora *estancia* whose **Cementerio Inglés** is a national historical monument. Northbound, the road goes to the petroleum company town of Cerro Sombrero, while southbound it goes to Camerón and Lago Blanco.

Lago Blanco

Some 50 kilometers southwest of Onaisín, the road passes through **Camerón,** an erstwhile picture-postcard *estancia* that is now a municipal-

© WAYNE BERNHARDSON

Estancia Yendegaia and Cordillera Darwin

ity, then angles southeast to Lago Blanco, an area known for its fishing and, until recently, a speculative and controversial project for native forest exploitation by the U.S.-based Trillium Corporation. In summer, there's a bumpy border crossing to Río Grande, Argentina, via a dirt road, with many livestock gates, and a ford of the Río Rasmussen. The Argentine border post is called Radman.

On Isla Victoria, in the middle of Lago Blanco, **Lodge de Pesca Isla Victoria** (tel. 061/243354) caters to fly-fishermen for US$144/174 s/d.

Estancia Yendegaia

Visited primarily by Chilean cruise ships and private yachts, Estancia Yendegaia conserves 44,000 hectares of native Fuegian forest in the Cordillera Darwin between the Argentine border and Parque Nacional Alberto de Agostini. While the owners hope to establish a private national park and create an unbroken preservation corridor along the Beagle Channel (Yendegaia borders Argentina's Parque Nacional Tierra del Fuego), there is government pressure to pave the *estancia*'s airstrip at Caleta María, at the northern end of the property, and a road south from Lago Blanco is already under construction. The owners, for their part, would rather see the border opened to foot traffic from Argentina, but they have consulted with public-works officials to minimize the road's environmental impact.

In the meantime, the *estancia* is open to visitors—though access is difficult without chartering a plane or boat, or taking an expensive tour like the *Mare Australis* cruise through the Fuegian fjords; even this stops only on occasion. While naval boats between Punta Arenas and Puerto Williams may drop passengers here, these are so infrequent that getting back could be a problem. In the near future, there should be accommodations available.

CERRO SOMBRERO

About 70 kilometers north of Onaisín and 43 kilometers south of the Puerto Espora ferry landing, Cerro Sombrero is a company town where employees of Chile's Empresa Nacional de Petróleo (ENAP, National Petroleum Company) reside in orderly surroundings with remarkable amenities for a town with only about 150 houses. Dating from the early 1960s, it boasts an astronomical observatory, a bank, a botanical garden, a cinema, a hospital, recreational facilities including a heated swimming pool, and restaurants. Buses between Río Grande and Punta Arenas take a meal break at **Restaurant El Conti,** just outside town.

Overnighters will find accommodations at **Hostería Tunkelén** (Arturo Prat 101, tel. 061/345001, US$12.50 pp, US$38 d).

PUERTO WILLIAMS

On the north shore of Isla Navarino, across the Beagle Channel from Argentine Tierra del Fuego, Puerto Williams is the so-called "Capital of Antarctica" and gateway to the rugged Los Dientes backcountry circuit, a difficult five-day slog through soggy mountainous terrain. Local residents look forward to establishment of a permanent ferry link to nearby Argentina, but there is much political opposition across the channel because myopic Ushuaia impresarios fear losing business to tiny Williams—however unlikely that possibility.

Founded in the 1950s, formerly known as Puerto Luisa, the town (population 1,952) has paved sidewalks but gravel streets. Most of its residents are Chilean naval personnel living in relatively stylish prefabs, but there are also some 60 remaining descendants of the Yámana, of whom only about five speak the language—now a hybrid including many Spanish and English words—among themselves.

Sights

Overlooking the harbor is the **Proa del Escampavía Yelcho,** the prow of the famous cutter which, at the command of Luis Pardo Villalón, rescued British Antarctic explorer Edward Shackleton's crew from Elephant Island, on the Antarctic Peninsula, in 1916. A national monument, the bow survived collisions with icebergs to get to its destination; returning to Punta Arenas, the entire ship makes a cameo appearance in original newsreel footage in British director George Butler's *Endurance,* an extraordinary documentary of the Shackleton expedition.

directional signs at Puerto Williams

Very professional for a small-town museum, Williams's **Museo Martin Gusinde** has small exhibits on geology, economic plants and taxidermy, a marker for the former post office, and a sign for the coal mine at Caleta Banner, on nearby Isla Picton, which provisioned the *Yelcho* on its mission to rescue Shackleton's crew. Admission costs US$1.75 per person; nearby is the **Parque Botánico Omora,** an organized selection of native plants.

Built in Germany for operations on the Rhine, the **MV *Micalvi*** shipped supplies between remote *estancias* and other settlements before sinking in Puerto Williams' inner harbor in 1962; the upper deck and bridge remain as the yacht club's bar/restaurant.

Practicalities

The **Pingüino Pub** is at the Centro Comercial.

Pensión Temuco (Piloto Pardo 224, tel. 061/621113) charges US$12.50 per person with shared bath, US$17 per person with private bath, and also serves meals. Try also the nearby **Residencial Pusaky** (Piloto Pardo 242, tel. 061/621116, US$14–18 pp); rates vary according to shared or private bath.

Refugio Coirón (Ricardo Maragaño 168, tel. 061/621227, fax 061/621150, coiron@simltd.com, US$13.50 pp) has very good accommodations with kitchen privileges and shared bath. It's a better choice than the friendly but basic **Hostería Onashaga** (Uspachún 290, tel. 061/621081), which costs US$16 per person for multi-bedded rooms with shared bath; those with private bath go for US$33 d. Lunch or dinner costs US$3.

South America's southernmost bar/restaurant, the **Club de Yates Micalvi,** occupies the main deck and the bridge of the historic vessel that lies grounded in Puerto Williams's inner harbor.

Nearly all of Puerto Williams's services are concentrated around the Centro Comercial, a cluster of storefronts just uphill from the Muelle Guardián Brito, the main passenger pier. These include the post office, several telephone offices, Banco de Chile, the Cema-Chile crafts shop, and Manualidades, which rents mountain bikes.

DAP (tel. 061/621051), at the Centro Comercial, flies 20-seat Twin Otters to Punta Arenas (US$64) Tuesday, Thursday, and Saturday April–October. The rest of the year, flights leave daily except Sunday. DAP flights are often heavily booked, so make reservations as far in advance as possible.

Regular connections between Puerto Williams and Ushuaia, on Argentine Tierra del Fuego, continue to be problematical, but hitching a lift across the channel with a yacht is feasible—for a price. For up-to-date information, contact the **Gobernación Marítima** (tel. 061/621090), the **Club de Yates** (tel. 061/621041, Ext. 4250), or **Turismo Sim** (tel. 061/621150). There are occasional charter flights as well.

In summer, the **ferry** *Patagonia* sails to Punta Arenas (38 hours) Friday at 7 P.M. Fares are US$150 in a bunk, US$120 for a reclining seat.

VICINITY OF PUERTO WILLIAMS

The Williams-based, German-Venezuelan **Sea & Ice & Mountains Adventures Unlimited** (Austral 74, tel./fax 061/621150, tel. 061/621227, www.simtld.com, coiron@simltd.com) organizes trekking, climbing, and riding expeditions on Isla Navarino and the Cordillera Darwin, week-long yacht excursions around the Beagle Channel and to Cape Horn, and even Antarctica. Advance booking is essential.

The Coastal Road

From Puerto Williams, a coastal road runs 54 kilometers west to the village of Puerto Navarino, now a legal port of entry, and 28 kilometers east to Caleta Eugenia; only two kilometers east of Williams, **Villa Ukika** is the last refuge of the Yámana. From Caleta Eugenia, the road is gradually advancing southeast to **Puerto Toro,** where some 60 boats employ about four persons each in search of *centolla* (king crab).

Cordón de los Dientes

Immediately south of Puerto Williams, **Cordón de los Dientes** is a range of jagged peaks rising more than 1,000 meters above sea level that offers the world's southernmost trekking opportunities. There are, however, few trails through this rugged countryside—anyone undertaking the four- to five-day "circuit" should be experienced in route finding.

Argentine Tierra del Fuego

If Patagonia is exciting, Tierra del Fuego—with its reputation as the "uttermost part of the earth"—is electrifying. In the days of sail, the reputation of its sub-Antarctic weather and ferocious westerlies obsessed navigators whether or not they had ever had experienced the thrill—or terror—of "rounding the Horn." After Richard Henry Dana survived the southern seas en route to California in November 1834, he vividly described conditions that could change from calm to chaos in an instant:

"Here comes Cape Horn!" said the chief mate; and we had hardly time to haul down and clew up, before it was upon us. In a few moments, a heavier sea was raised than I had ever seen before, and . . . the little brig . . . plunged into it, and all the forward part of her was under water; the sea pouring in through the bow ports and hawse-hole, and over the knight-heads, threatening to wash everything overboard. . . . At the same time sleet and hail were driving with all fury against us.

© WAYNE BERNHARDSON

Must-Sees

Look for [M] to find the sights and activities you can't miss and [N] for the best dining and lodging.

Museo Marítimo de Ushuaia: Much more than its name suggests, Ushuaia's best museum needs more than one visit to absorb its maritime heritage and appreciate the way in which one of the world's most remote prisons affected the city's development (page 432).

Estancia Harberton: East of Ushuaia, this historic *estancia* is, arguably, the nucleus of the "uttermost part of the earth" (page 441).

Glaciar Martial: Whether entirely by foot or partly by chairlift, the climb to Ushuaia's nearby glacier, part of **Parque Nacional Tierra del Fuego,** rewards visitors with panoramic views of the city and the storied Beagle Channel (page 443).

Misión Salesiana: North of Río Grande, the priests at this national historical monument did their best to salvage the remains of Fuegia's indigenous cultures from the European onslaught, but they themselves inadvertently contributed to the holocaust (page 447).

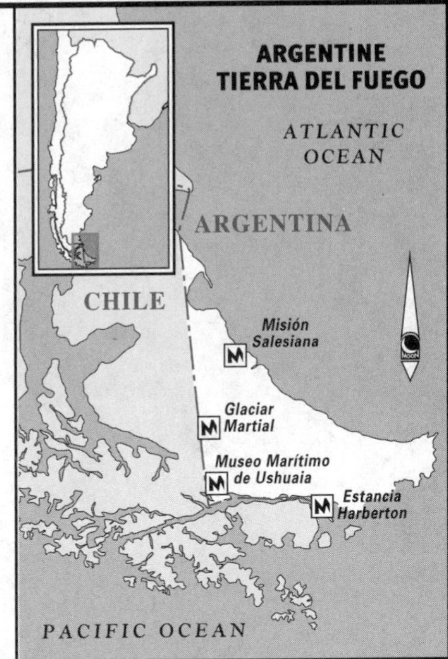

In Dana's time, such voyages were the price of admission to one of the earth's most spectacular combinations of sea, land, ice, and sky. In a landscape whose granite pinnacles rise nearly 2,000 meters straight out of the ocean, only a handful of hunter-gatherers foraging in the fjords and forests could know the area with any intimacy. Today, fortunately, there are ways to reach the archipelago of Tierra del Fuego that involve less hardship—not to mention motion sickness—than Dana and his contemporaries suffered.

In his autobiography, pioneer settler Lucas Bridges labeled Tierra del Fuego the "Uttermost Part of the Earth" for its splendid isolation at the southern tip of the southern American continent. It's still a place where fur seals, sea lions, and penguins cavort in the choppy seas of the Strait named for the celebrated navigator Ferdinand Magellan, where Darwin sailed on the *Beagle* and the first 49ers found their route to California. From the seashore, behind the city of Ushuaia, glacial horns rise like sacred steeples nearly 2,000 meters above sea level. The beaches and southern beech forests of Parque Nacional Tierra del Fuego, west of the city, are the terminus of the world's southernmost highway.

Tierra del Fuego is not just one island, but an archipelago, though the Isla Grande de Tierra del Fuego is South America's largest island. Argentina shares the territory with Chile; while parts of the Argentine side are urbanized, the Chilean side has only a few small towns and isolated *estancias.* Roads are relatively few but improving, and some of them are now paved, especially on the Argentine side; the unpaved roads, though, are hazardous to windshields, which are mostly cheaply replaced in the mainland city of Punta Arenas (Chile).

Though it has much in common with Santa Cruz, Chubut, and Argentina's other Patagonian

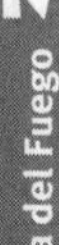

ARGENTINE TIERRA DEL FUEGO

ATLANTIC OCEAN

PACIFIC OCEAN

ARGENTINA

CHILE

Comandante Luis Piedra Buena
Puerto Santa Cruz
Bahía Grande
Río Gallegos
To Puerto San Julián and Comodoro Rivadavia
RP 9
RP 2
RP 5
RP 7
RN 40
RN 3
9
255
To El Chaltén and Perito Moreno
El Calafate
GLACIAR MORENO
Parque Nacional Torres del Paine
Cerro Paine Grande
Lago del Toro
GLACIAR BALMACEDA
MONUMENTO NATURAL CUEVA DEL MILODÓN
Villa Cerro Castillo
Río Turbio
Puerto Natales
Ferry to Puerto Montt
Isla Hanover
Isla Jorge Montt
Isla Diego de Almagro
Reserva Nacional Alacalufes
Pen Muñoz Gamero
Villa Tehuelches
Laguna Blanca
ESTANCIA SAN GREGORIO
PN Pali Aike
Punta Delgada
Cabo Vírgenes
Cerro Sombrero
Seno Skyring
Isla Riesco
RN Magallanes
Pingüinera Otway
Seno Otway
Río Verde
RN Laguna Parrillar
Punta Arenas
FUERTE BULNES
Estrecho de Magallanes
Isla Desolación
Isla Santa Inés
Porvenir
Onaisín
Bahía Inútil
Isla Dawson
Cameron
Lago Blanco
Bahía San Sebastián
ESTANCIA MARÍA BEHETY
MISIÓN SALESIANO
Río Grande
ESTANCIA VIAMONTE
ESTANCIA JOSÉ MENÉNDEZ
Paso Radman
Lago Fagnano (Kami)
Parque Nacional Tierra del Fuego
GLACIAR MARTIAL
Ushuaia
Tolhuin
Canal de Beagle
Isla Grande de Tierra del Fuego
Península Mitre
ESTANCIA HARBERTON
ESTANCIA POLICARPO
Estrecho de Le Maire
Isla de los Estados
Puerto Williams
Puerto Navarino
Isla Navarino
Isla Hoste
Isla Nueva
Parque Nacional Cabo de Hornos
Cabo de Hornos
Cordillera Darwin
PN Alberto de Agostini
Canal Cockburn
0 60 mi
0 60 km

provinces, Tierra del Fuego retains its own distinctive identity. Most major attractions and services—undoubtedly the most accessible ones—are on the Argentine side.

There are two ferry routes from the Chilean mainland to Tierra del Fuego: a shuttle from Punta Delgada, only 45 kilometers south of the Argentine border, across the Primera Angostura narrows to Puerto Espora, and a daily service from Punta Arenas to Porvenir, one of the Strait's widest parts.

PLANNING YOUR TIME

Like the rest of southern South America, Tierra del Fuego deserves all the time you can give it, but most visitors have to make choices. Ushuaia is the best base for sightseeing in Tierra del Fuego proper, given its access for excursions to the nearby national park, the Beagle Channel, and Estancia Harberton, with a minimum of three days. Hikers may wish to spend several days more and fly-fishing aficionados—who often prefer the vicinity of Río Grande—can easily stay a week or two.

HISTORY

Prior to their European "discovery" by Magellan in 1520, southern South America's insular extremes were inhabited by dispersed bands of hunter-gatherers like the Selknam (Ona), Kawasqar (Alacaluf), and Yámana (Yahgan) who lived off maritime and terrestrial resources that they considered abundant—only in the European view was this a land of privation. The archipelago acquired its name from the fires set by the region's so-called "Canoe Indians," the Kawasqar and Yámana, for heating and cooking; in this soggy region, though, it might have been more accurate to call it Tierra del Humo ("Land of Smoke").

Early navigators dreaded Cape Horn's wild seas, and their reports gave their countrymen little reason to settle in or even explore the area. In the early 1830s, Captain Robert Fitzroy of the *Beagle* abducted several Yámana, including the famous Jemmy Button, to England, and subjected them to missionary indoctrination before returning them to their home on a later voyage. On that voyage, a perplexed Charles Darwin commented on the simplicity of their society: "The perfect equality among the individuals composing the Fuegian tribes, must for a long time retard their civilization."

The first to try to bring civilization to the Yámana, rather than the opposite, were Anglican missionaries from the Falkland Islands, some of whose descendents still live in Tierra del Fuego. After abortive attempts that included both Fuegian assaults and the starvation death of British evangelist Allen Gardiner, the Anglican Thomas Bridges settled at present-day Ushuaia, on the Argentine side of the Isla Grande, where he compiled an English-Yahgan dictionary. His son Lucas, who grew up with Yámana playmates, wrote the extraordinary memoir *The Uttermost Part of the Earth,* published a few years before his death in 1950.

In the meantime, both the Chilean and Argentine governments established a presence in the region, and gigantic sheep *estancias* occupied the sprawling grasslands at the expense of native peoples who once hunted guanaco and other game on them. When, as the guanaco slowly disappeared, the desperate Fuegians began to hunt domestic sheep, they often found themselves facing the wrong end of a rifle—though introduced European diseases like typhoid and measles killed more native people than did bullets.

Borders in the archipelago were never clearly defined and the two countries nearly went to war over three small islands in the Beagle Channel in 1979. Positions were uncompromising—one Argentine poster boldly declared "We will never surrender what is ours!"—but papal mediation successfully avoided warfare and brought a settlement within a few years. There are lingering issues, though, like transportation across the Channel from Ushuaia to Puerto Williams.

Since then, travel to the uttermost part of the earth has boomed, especially on the Argentine side in the summer months. Other important economic sectors are sheep farming and petroleum, on both the Chilean and Argentine sides.

Ushuaia and Vicinity

Beneath the Martial range's serrated spires, on the Beagle Channel's north shore, the city of Ushuaia is both an end (virtually the terminus of the world's most southerly highway) and a beginning (the gateway to Antarctica). The surrounding countryside is increasingly popular with activities-oriented visitors who enjoy hiking, mountain biking, fishing, and skiing.

After two decades-plus of economic growth and physical sprawl, the provincial capital is both declining and improving. On the one hand, the duty-free manufacturing, fishing, and tourist boom that transformed a onetime penal colony and naval base into a bustling city has weakened. On the other, it's begun to clean up the waterfront and restore historic buildings that gave the town its personality. The streets are cleaner, and there are parks and plazas and green spaces, but it still has one of the worst particulate pollution problems of any Argentine city because high winds kick up dust in the unpaved streets of its newer neighborhoods.

HISTORY

Ushuaia dates from 1870, when the Anglican South American Missionary Society decided to place the archipelago's first permanent European settlement here. Pioneer missionary Thomas Bridges and his descendants have left an enduring legacy in Bridges' Yahgan (Yámana) dictionary, his son Lucas's memoir, and the family estancia at nearby Harberton (sadly, the Yahgans whom Thomas Bridges hoped to save succumbed to introduced diseases and conflict with other settlers).

Not long after Ushuaia's settlement, Argentina, alarmed by the British presence, moved to establish its own authority at Ushuaia and did so with a penal settlement for its most infamous criminals and political undesirables. It remained a penal settlement until almost 1950, when Juan Domingo Perón's government created a major naval base to support Argentina's claim to a share of Antarctica. Only since the end of the

© WAYNE BERNHARDSON

city of Ushuaia, with the Martial range in the background

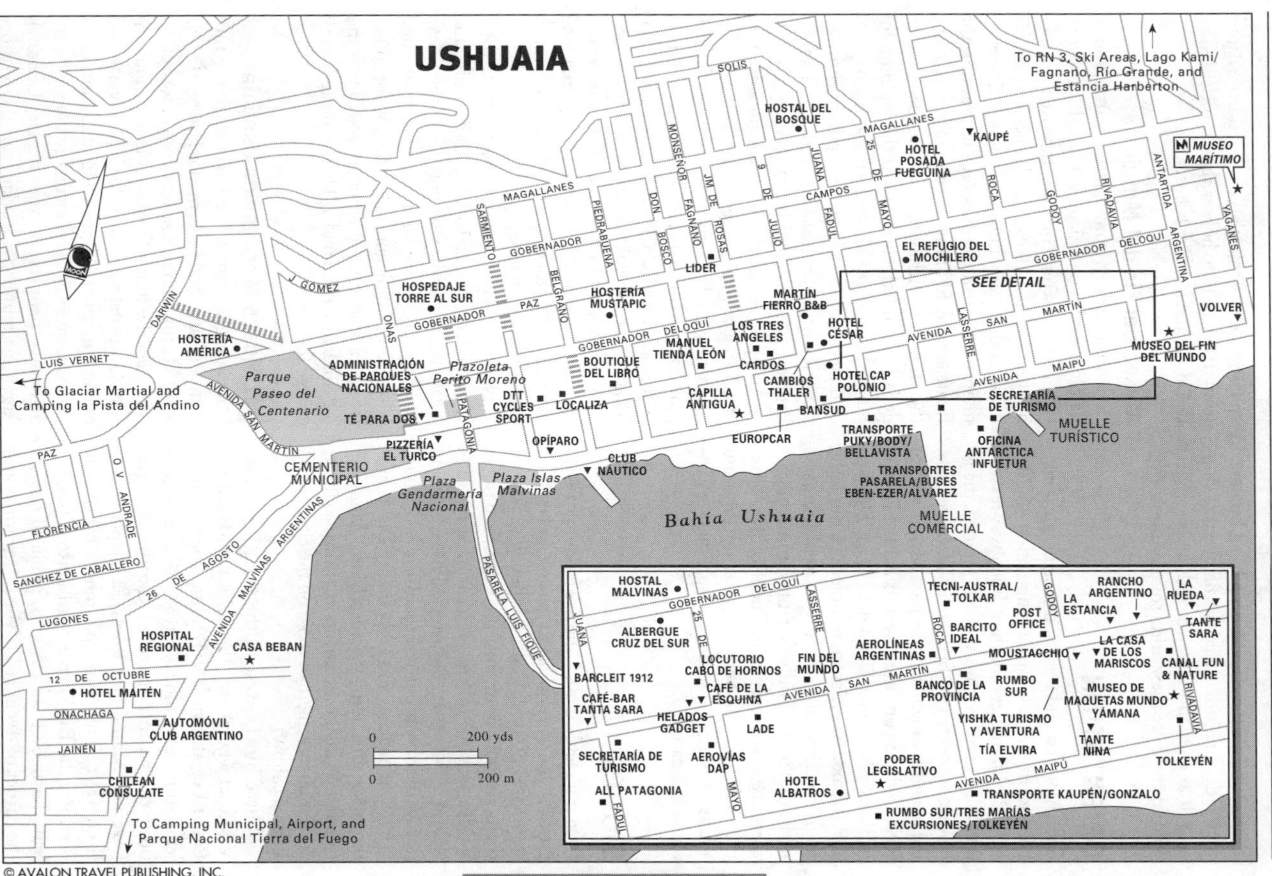
USHUAIA
To RN 3, Ski Areas, Lago Kami/Fagnano, Río Grande, and Estancia Harberton
MUSEO MARÍTIMO
MUSEO DEL FIN DEL MUNDO
VOLVER
YAGANES
ANTARTIDA ARGENTINA
RIVADAVIA
GODOY
ROCA
LASSERRE
25 DE MAYO
FADUL
JUANA
9 DE JULIO
JM DE ROSAS
MONSEÑOR FAGNANO
DON BOSCO
PIEDRABUENA
BELGRANO
SARMIENTO
ONAS
PATAGONIA
MAGALLANES
CAMPOS
SOLIS
GOBERNADOR DELOQUI
GOBERNADOR PAZ
AVENIDA SAN MARTÍN
AVENIDA MAIPÚ
KAUPÉ
HOTEL POSADA FUEGUINA
HOSTAL DEL BOSQUE
EL REFUGIO DEL MOCHILERO
SEE DETAIL
SECRETARÍA DE TURISMO
MUELLE TURÍSTICO
OFICINA ANTARCTICA INFUETUR
TRANSPORTES PASARELA/BUSES EBEN-EZER/ALVAREZ
MUELLE COMERCIAL
TRANSPORTE PUKY/BODY/BELLAVISTA
HOTEL CAP POLONIO
HOTEL CÉSAR
MARTÍN FIERRO B&B
BANSUD
CAMBIOS THALER
CARDOS
LOS TRES ANGELES
EUROPCAR
CAPILLA ANTIGUA
MANUEL TIENDA LEÓN
LÍDER
HOSTERÍA MUSTAPIC
BOUTIQUE DEL LIBRO
LOCALIZA
CLUB NÁUTICO
OPÍPARO
DTT CYCLES SPORT
Plazoleta Perito Moreno
Plaza Islas Malvinas
Plaza Gendarmería Nacional
HOSPEDAJE TORRE AL SUR
ADMINISTRACIÓN DE PARQUES NACIONALES
TÉ PARA DOS
PIZZERÍA EL TURCO
CEMENTERIO MUNICIPAL
Parque Paseo del Centenario
J. GÓMEZ
HOSTERÍA AMÉRICA
AVENIDA SAN MARTÍN
DARWIN
To Glaciar Martial and Camping la Pista del Andino
LUIS VERNET
O V ANDRADE
PAZ
FLORENCIA
SANCHEZ DE CABALLERO
LUGONES
12 DE OCTUBRE
HOTEL MAITÉN
ONACHAGA
JAINEN
HOSPITAL REGIONAL
AUTOMÓVIL CLUB ARGENTINO
CHILEAN CONSULATE
CASA BEBAN
26 DE AGOSTO
AVENIDA MALVINAS ARGENTINAS
PASARELA LUIS FIQUE
Bahía Ushuaia
To Camping Municipal, Airport, and Parque Nacional Tierra del Fuego
0 200 yds
0 200 m
LA RUEDA
TANTE SARA
CANAL FUN & NATURE
TOLKEYÉN
RANCHO ARGENTINO
LA ESTANCIA
LA CASA DE LOS MARISCOS
MUSEO DE MAQUETAS MUNDO YÁMANA
TANTE NINA
POST OFFICE
MOUSTACCHIO
RUMBO SUR
YISHKA TURISMO Y AVENTURA
TÍA ELVIRA
TRANSPORTE KAUPÉN/GONZALO
TECNI-AUSTRAL/TOLKAR
BARCITO IDEAL
BANCO DE LA PROVINCIA
RUMBO SUR/TRES MARÍAS EXCURSIONES/TOLKEYÉN
AEROLÍNEAS ARGENTINAS
PODER LEGISLATIVO
FIN DEL MUNDO
HOTEL ALBATROS
LOCUTORIO CABO DE HORNOS
CAFÉ DE LA ESQUINA
LADE
HOSTAL MALVINAS
ALBERGUE CRUZ DEL SUR
HELADOS GADGET
AEROVÍAS DAP
BARCLEIT 1912
CAFÉ-BAR TANTA SARA
SECRETARÍA DE TURISMO
ALL PATAGONIA
© AVALON TRAVEL PUBLISHING, INC.

1976–1983 military dictatorship has it become a tourist destination, visited by many cruise ships as well as overland travelers and air passengers who come to see the world's southernmost city.

ORIENTATION

Stretching east and west along the Beagle Channel's north shore, Ushuaia (population 45,205) is 3,220 kilometers south of Buenos Aires and 240 kilometers southwest of Río Grande, the island's only other city. Bedecked with flowerbeds, the main thoroughfare is Avenida Maipú, part of RN 3, which continues west to Bahía Lapataia in Parque Nacional Tierra del Fuego. The parallel Avenida San Martín, one block north, is the main commercial street; the focus of Ushuaia's night life, it gets gridlocked on summer nights as surely as any avenue in Buenos Aires. From the shoreline, the perpendicular northbound streets rise steeply—some so steeply that they become staircases.

SIGHTS

Even if it's leveled off, Ushuaia's economic boom provided the wherewithal to preserve and even restore some of the city's historic buildings. Two of them are now museums: the **Casa Fernández Valdés** (1903), on the waterfront at Avenida Maipú 175, houses the historical Museo del Fin del Mundo, while the **Presidio de Ushuaia** (1896), at Yaganes and Gobernador Paz, is now the rather misleadingly named Museo Marítimo (while not insignificant, its maritime exhibits are less interesting than those on the city's role as a penal colony).

Three blocks west of the Casa Fernández Valdés, at Maipú 465, the classically Magellanic **Poder Legislativo** (1894) houses the provincial legislature. Five blocks farther west, prisoners built the recently restored **Capilla Antigua** (Avenida Maipú and Rosas), a chapel dating from 1898. The municipal tourist office now occupies the **Biblioteca Sarmiento** (1926) at San Martín 674, the city's first public library. At the corner of Avenida Malvinas Argentinas and 12 de Octubre, the waterfront **Casa Beban** is an elaborate reassembled pioneer residence dating from 1913; it now houses the municipal Casa de la Cultura, a cultural center.

Museo del Fin del Mundo

Benefiting greatly from exterior restoration of its block-style construction, Ushuaia's evolving historical museum contains improved exhibits on the Yámana, Selknam, and other Fuegian Indians, and on early European voyages. There remain permanent exhibits on the presidio, the Fique family's El Primer Argentino general store, the original branch of the state-run bank Banco de la Nación (which occupied the building for more than 60 years), and natural history, including run-of-the-mill taxidermy. Its celebrity artifact is one of few existing copies of Thomas Bridges' Yámana-English dictionary.

An open-air sector includes representations of a Yámana encampment and dwellings, plus machinery used in early agriculture and forestry projects. The Museo del Fin del Mundo (Avenida Maipú 175, tel. 02901/421863, www.tierradelfuego.org.ar/museo) also contains a bookstore/souvenir shop and a specialized library on southernmost Argentina, the surrounding oceans, and Antarctica. The exceptional website places much of this material online.

November–April, hours are 9 A.M.–8 P.M. daily, with guided tours at 10 A.M., noon, and 2 and 5 P.M.; the rest of the year, hours are noon–7 P.M. daily except Sunday, with guided tours at 2 and 5 P.M. daily. Admission costs US$3.50 for adults, US$2 for students and retired people, and is free for children 14 and under. There is no additional charge for tours.

Museo Marítimo de Ushuaia

Misleadingly named, Ushuaia's maritime museum (Yaganes and Gobernador Paz, tel. 02901/437481, museomar@satlink.com) most effectively tells the story of Ushuaia's inauspicious origins as a penal settlement for both civilian and military prisoners. Alarmed over the South American Missionary Society's incursions among the indigenous peoples of the Beagle Channel, Argentina reinforced its claims to the territory by building, in 1884, a military prison on Isla de los Estados (Staten Island), across the Strait of Lemaire at the southeastern tip of the Isla Grande.

Barely a decade later, in 1896, it established Ushuaia's civilian Cárcel de Reincidentes for repeat offenders; after finally deciding, in 1902, that Isla de los Estados was a hardship post even for prisoners, the military moved their own facility to Ushuaia. Then, in 1911, the two institutions fused in this building that, over the first half of the 20th century, held some of the country's most famous political prisoners, celebrated rogues, and notorious psychopaths.

Divided into five two-story pavilions, with 380 cells intended for one prisoner each, the prison held as many as 600 prisoners at a time before closing in 1947. Its most famous inmates were political detainees like immigrant Russian anarchist Simón Radowitzsky, who killed Buenos Aires police chief Ramón Falcón with a bomb in 1909; Radical politicians Ricardo Rojas, Honorio Pueyrredón, and Mario Guido (the deceptively named Radicals are in fact an insipid middle-class party); and Peronist politician Héctor Cámpora, who was briefly president in the 1970s.

Many if not most of the prisoners, though, were long-termers or lifers like the diminutive strangler Cayetano Santos Godino, a serial killer dubbed "El Orejudo" for his oversized ears (interestingly enough, the nickname also describes a large-eared bat that is native to the archipelago). Julio Ordano has written a play, performed in Buenos Aires, about Santos Godino, "El Petiso Orejudo."

Life-size figures of the most infamous inmates, modified department store dummies clad in prison stripes, occupy many cells. One particularly interesting exhibit is a wide-ranging comparison with other prisons that have become museums, such as San Francisco's Alcatraz and South Africa's Robben Island.

The museum does justify its name with an exceptional exhibit of scale models of ships that have played a role in local history, such as Magellan's galleon *Trinidad,* the legendary *Beagle,* the South American Missionary Society's three successive sailboats known as the *Allen Gardiner,* and Antarctic explorer and conqueror Roald Amundsen's *Fram.* In addition, there are materials on Argentina's Antarctic presence since the early 20th century, when the corvette *Uruguay* rescued Otto Nordenskjöld's Norwegian expedition, whose crew included the Argentine José María Sobral. On the grounds is a full-size replica of the Faro San Juan de Salvamento, the Isla de los Estados (Staten Island) lighthouse that figures in Jules Verne's story "The Lighthouse at the End of the World."

In addition, this exceptional museum contains a philatelic room, natural history exhibits, and admirable accounts of the region's aboriginal peoples. In fact, it has only two drawbacks: There's too much to see in a single day, and the English translations could use some polishing—to say the least.

The Museo Marítimo is open 9 A.M.–8 P.M. daily from mid-October to the end of April; the rest of the year, it opens an hour later. Guided tours are at 11:30 A.M. and 6:15 P.M. daily, but schedules can change.

Admission costs US$5 per person but, on request, the staff will validate your ticket for another day; since there's so much here, splitting up sightseeing sessions is a good idea. There are discounts for children under age six (US$1), students and senior citizens (both US$1.75), and families (US$10 including up to four children). It has an excellent book and souvenir shop, and a fine *confitería* for snacks and coffee.

Museo de Maquetas Mundo Yámana

While both the Museo del Fin del Mundo and Museo Marítimo do a creditable job on Tierra del Fuego's indigenous heritage, this small private museum (Rivadavia 56, tel. 02901/422874, mundoyamana@infovia.com.ar) consists of skillfully assembled dioramas of life along the Beagle Channel prior to the European presence, at a scale of 1:15. It also includes cartographic representations of the Yámana and their neighbors, interpretations of the European impact, and panels of historical photographs.

Open 10 A.M.–8 P.M. daily, the Museo de Maquetas Mundo Yámana charges US$1.75 per person for adults, US$1 for students and retired people, and is free for children under 13. The staff speak fluent English.

SOUTH TO THE ICE

Since the demise of the Soviet Union, Ushuaia has become the main jumping-off point for Antarctic excursions on Russian icebreakers that, despite being chartered under American officers, sometimes still carry the shield of the hammer and sickle on their bows. For travelers with flexible schedules, it's sometimes possible to make last-minute arrangements at huge discounts—no ship wants to sail with empty berths—for as little as US$1,500. Normal rates, though, are around US$3,000 or more for 9–14 days, including several days' transit across the stormy Drake Passage—medication is advisable.

If your timing is bad and budget cruises are not available, many Ushuaia travel agencies can make alternative arrangements. The season runs mid-November–mid-March.

© WAYNE BERNHARDSON

former Soviet research icebreaker, now an Antarctic cruise ship, in Ushuaia

On the waterfront Muelle Comercial, Ushuaia's **Oficina Antártida Infuetur** (tel. 02901/424431, antartida@tierradelfuego.org.ar) has the latest information on Antarctic cruises. Guidebooks to the white continent include Jeff Rubin's *Antarctica* (Lonely Planet, 2005), Ron Naveen's *Oceanites Site Guide to the Antarctic Peninsula* (Chevy Chase, MD: Oceanites, 1997), and the third edition of Tony Soper's and Dafila Scott's *Antarctica: a Guide to the Wildlife* (Bradt Publications, 2000).

SHOPPING

Boutique del Libro (San Martín 1129, tel. 02901/424750) offers an excellent selection of Spanish-language books and a smaller choice of English-language materials. **Fin del Mundo** (San Martín 505) has a wide selection of kitschy souvenirs but also maps and books.

ACCOMMODATIONS

Ushuaia has abundant accommodations, but it's long been one of the most expensive destinations in what was, until recently, an expensive country. Demand is also high, though, in the summer months of January and February, when prices rise and reservations are advisable. One heartening development is the arrival of several bed-and-breakfasts—known by the semi-English acronym ByB—several of which are excellent alternatives.

Under US$10

Eight kilometers west of Ushuaia on the road to Parque Nacional Tierra del Fuego, the **Camping Municipal** is free of charge but has limited facilities (fire pits and pit toilets only). Four kilometers west of town, the **Camping del Rugby Club Ushuaia** (tel. 02901/435796, campingpipo@tierradelfuego.org.ar, US$2 pp) has sites with running water, bathrooms with hot showers, and fire pits with barbecue grills.

A stiff climb to the northwest of downtown

Ushuaia, **La Pista del Andino** (Alem 2873, tel. 02901/435890 or 02901/15-568626, lapistadel andino@infovia.com.ar, US$3 pp) has slightly sloping campsites at the Club Andino's ski area; the first transfer from downtown or the airport is free. It also lets guests with sleeping bags crash in the *refugio* above its bar/restaurant, but this is less than ideal for anyone who wants to get to bed early.

US$10–25

On the edge of downtown, high enough to offer spectacular views of the Beagle Channel, HI affiliate **Albergue Torre al Sur** (Gobernador Paz 1437, tel. 02901/437291, fax 02901/430745, www.torrealsur.com.ar, torrealsur@impsat1.com.ar, US$5–6 pp) has been one of Argentina's finest backpacker facilities, but it's gotten mixed reviews recently because of overcrowding and noise. Rooms have two or four beds, with lockers; there's hot water, Internet access, and free luggage storage.

HI has recently added a promising new affiliate, **Albergue Los Cormoranes** (Kamshen 788, tel. 02902/423459, www.loscormoranes.com.ar, loscormoranes@speedy.com.ar, US$5–6 pp). Most directly reached by climbing Don Bosco and taking a left, it's about eight steep blocks north of the waterfront.

Central but quiet, **Albergue Cruz del Sur** (Deloqui 636, tel. 02901/423110, www.xdelsur.com.ar, ibar72@yahoo.com, xdelsur@yahoo.com, US$6 pp) is an independent hostel whose rooms have four, six, or eight beds; there is also cable TV, Internet access, two kitchens, and a free initial pick up. Guests also get a series of discounts and specials at various services around town.

The hostel-style **El Refugio del Mochilero** (25 de Mayo 241, tel. 02901/436129, refugio delmochilero@hotmail.com, US$5–6 pp) has almost equally good facilities but a little less ambiance than it once had.

US$25–50

Hostería América (Gobernador Paz 1665, tel. 02901/423358, fax 02901/431362, hosteriaamerica@speedy.com.ar, US$20/30 s/d) is a good choice enjoying a fine location above the Parque Paseo del Centenario.

Improvements at rehabbed **Hotel César** (Avenida San Martín 753, tel. 02901/421460, fax 02901/432721, hotelcesarhostal@speedy.com.ar, US$22/30 s/d) have turned it into one of the central area's better values. **Hotel Maitén** (12 de Octubre 140, tel. 02901/422745, maiten@tierradelfuego.org.ar, US$25/33 s/d) remains a reasonable budget choice.

Management has turned grumpy at **Hostería Mustapic** (Piedrabuena 230, tel. 02901/421718, mustapic@sinectis.com.ar, US$23/35 s/d with shared bath, US$33/41 s/d with private bath), but it's still adequate and fairly central. Rates include breakfast.

Hostal Malvinas (Gobernador Deloqui 615, tel./fax 02901/422626, info@hostalmalvinas.com, US$25–37 s, US$30–43 d) provides simple but quiet and immaculate rooms with large baths and no frills—not even TV—but croissants and coffee are free all day.

Martín Fierro B&B (9 de Julio 175, tel. 02901/430525, javiersplace@hotmail.com, US$37 d) is a stylish hillside place with bunks—two people each in small but well-designed rooms with shared baths. The common areas are simultaneously spacious and cozy, and the breakfast is varied and filling; the tiny shower stalls, though, make bathing with a friend impossible without being *really* intimate. There are also two downstairs "aparthotel" rooms (US$50) sleeping up to four people.

US$50–100

Only its location on a busy street detracts from the bright and cheerful **Hotel Cap Polonio** (San Martín 746, tel. 02901/422140 or 02901/422131, www.hotelcappolonio.com.ar, US$70 s or d). All rooms are carpeted, with cable TV; the private baths have tubs as well as showers, and there's a good restaurant/*confitería* with breakfast included. Tango shows take place at 10 P.M. Saturday.

Hostal del Bosque (Magallanes 709, tel./fax 02901/430777 or 02901/421723, www.hostal delbosque.com.ar, info@hostaldelbosque.com.ar, US$90 s or d) is an "aparthotel" whose two-room suites, with kitchenette, can sleep up to four people. There are large baths, with shower and tub, and cable TV; it also has its own restaurant.

Over US$100

Hillside, four-star **Hotel Ushuaia** (Lasserre 933, tel. 02901/430671, hotelushuaia@yahoo.com.ar, US$60–80 s, US$80–110 d) is a good value in its price range.

Offering awesome views from its cul-de-sac hillside perch, **Hotel Posada Fueguina** (Lasserre 438, tel. 02901/423467, www.posadafueguina.com.ar, info@posadafueguino.com.ar, US$97/130 s/d) also provides breakfast, cable TV, and similar amenities.

The spacious, three-star **Hotel Albatros** (Avenida Maipú 505, tel. 02901/433446, www.albatroshotel.com.ar, reservas@albatroshotel.com.ar, US$95–130 s, US$115–156 d) is the pick of the waterfront accommodations.

The interior is more impressive than the surprisingly plain exterior at the luxury **Hotel del Glaciar** (Luis Martial 2355, tel. 02901/430640, fax 02901/430636, www.hoteldelglaciar.com, delglaciar@speedy.com.ar, US$143–179 s or d). At Km 3.5 on the road to the Martial glacier, each room has either a mountain or ocean view.

At Km 3 on the glacier road, the nearby **Hotel y Resort Las Hayas** (Luis Martial 1650, tel. 02901/430710, fax 02901/430719, www.lashayas.com.ar, lashayas@overnet.com.ar, US$205 s or d) enjoys nearly all conceivable luxuries, including an elaborate buffet breakfast, gym, sauna, Jacuzzi, and a heated indoor pool; it picks up guests with reservations at the airport, and offers a regular shuttle to and from downtown Ushuaia. Behind its surprisingly utilitarian exterior, some of its 102 rooms suffer from hideous decor—the wallpaper is to cringe at—but all are comfortable and its staff are highly professional.

FOOD

Ushuaia has always been one of Argentina's more expensive places to eat, but the peso collapse of 2001–2002 has reined in prices. That said, there are still some truly expensive choices; the financially challenged should look for *tenedor libre* specials, or be particularly cautious with extras like dessert and coffee.

The Hotel Cap Polonio's **Marcopolo** (San Martín 730, tel. 02901/430001) is a café-restaurant that serves excellent coffee, chocolate, and croissants for breakfast—try the *submarino* for a cold morning's pickup. **Café de la Esquina** (Avenida San Martín 602, tel. 02901/423676) is a popular meeting place with similar offerings, as well as sandwiches for late-afternoon tea.

Open for lunch only weekdays, but with Saturday evening hours, **Pizzería El Turco** (San Martín 1440, tel. 02901/424711) is good and moderately priced, but it lacks the variety found at the slightly more expensive **Opíparo** (Avenida Maipú 1255, tel. 02901/434022), which also serves pasta dishes. Well-established **Barcleit 1912** (Fadul 148, tel. 02901/433105) seems to have fallen a step behind some of the other pizzerias, but also has a variety of moderately priced short orders.

One of Ushuaia's finest, **Tante Sara** (San Martín 137, tel./fax 02901/435005) serves outstanding pasta with a broad selection of imaginative sauces, as well as pizza, with good service in pleasant surroundings. Most entrées, such as ravioli with king crab, fall into the US$5–7 range. For coffee, sandwiches, and desserts, try their **Café-Bar Tanta Sara** (San Martín 701, tel. O2901/423912).

Barcito Ideal (San Martín 393, tel. 02901/437860) seems always to draw crowds to its US$6 *tenedor libre* buffet. **La Rueda** (San Martín 193, tel. 02901/436540) charges only slightly more for its own buffet *parrillada.* Nearby **La Estancia** (San Martín 253, tel. 02901/436540) has similar fare.

For US$6, **Rancho Argentino** (San Martín 237, tel. 02901/430100) serves a fixed-price four-course meal including grilled Fuegian lamb, but it also has a more diverse a la carte menu including beef and baked empanadas. The well-established **Moustacchio** (Avenida San Martín 298, tel. 02901/423308) has similar fare but also emphasizes seafood.

Ushuaia has a wider choice of seafood restaurants than almost any other Argentine provincial city. **La Casa de los Mariscos** (San Martín 232, tel. 02901/421928) specializes in *centolla* (king crab), but also has many other fish and shellfish options in the US$4–8 range. Looking like a Porteño antique shop housed in a classic Magellanic residence, tango-themed **Volver** (Avenida Maipú 37, tel. 02901/423977) doesn't quite live up to its potential—the fish and seafood dishes, like *abadejo al ajillo* (US$5) and king crab soup (US$3) are disappointingly bland. With a 30-year history, **Tante Nina** (Gobernador Godoy 15, tel. 02901/432444) focuses on Fuegian fish and seafood, but also serves Patagonian lamb and "homely pasta."

Other possibilities include the **El Náutico** (Avenida Maipú and Belgrano, tel. 02901/430415), where entrées start around US$4.50; **Tía Elvira** (Avenida Maipú 349, tel. 02901/424725), where four-course dinners cost around US$10–12; and **Kaupé** (Roca 470, tel. 02901/422704), which serves an exclusively (and exclusive) a la carte menu. The latter has specialties like king crab (US$12), exquisite lemon ice cream, carpaccio, and wine by the glass. Even post-devaluation, a full meal here costs upwards of US$25, but it's worth the splurge.

Equally top-of-the-line—both literally and geographically—is the dining-with-a-panoramic-view at **Chez Manu** (Luis Martial 2135, tel. 02901/423253), immediately below the Hotel del Glaciar. Using local ingredients like king crab and lamb, the French-run restaurant is *the* place for a truly elaborate meal at equally elaborate prices: US$25 and up. Along with Kaupé, this is one Ushuaia restaurant with food to match its views.

Té Para Dos (San Martín 1463, tel. 02901/435535) is a promising teahouse. **Helados Gadget** (Avenida San Martín 621) has all the conventional Argentine ice-cream flavors—good enough in their own right—but also incorporates regional specialties like *calafate* and rhubarb.

INFORMATION

Ushuaia's well-organized municipal **Secretaría de Turismo** (San Martín 674, tel. 02901/424550, www.e-ushuaia.com, info@e-ushuaia.com) is open 8 A.M.–10 P.M. weekdays and 9 A.M.–8 P.M. weekends and holidays. English-speaking staff are normally present.

There's a subsidiary office at the **Muelle Turístico** (tel. 02901/437666, puertos_st@e-ushuaia.com), open 8 A.M.–6 P.M. daily, and another at the airport (tel. 02901/423970) that's open for arriving flights only.

The provincial **Instituto Fueguino de Turismo (Infuetur)** has ground-floor offices at Hotel Albatros (Avenida Maipú 505, tel. 02901/423340, info@tierradelfuego.org.ar).

For motorists, the **Automóvil Club Argentino** (ACA, tel. 02901/421121) is at Malvinas Argentinas and Onachaga.

The **Administración de Parques Nacionales** (APN, Avenida San Martín 1395, tel. 02901/421315, tierradelfuego@apn.gov.ar) is open 9 A.M.–noon weekdays.

At the waterfront Muelle Comercial, the **Oficina Antárctica Infuetur** (tel. 02901/423340 or 02901/421423, antartida@tierradelfuego.org.ar) has the latest information on Antarctic sailings and tours. Hours are 8 A.M.–5 P.M. daily in summer, 9 A.M.–4 P.M. weekdays the rest of the year.

SERVICES

Ushuaia has abundant tourist and general services.

Several banks have ATMs, including **BanSud** (Avenida Maipú 781) and **Banco de la Provincia** (San Martín 396); the latter accepts traveler's checks at a three percent commission. **Cambio Thaler** (Avenida San Martín 788, tel. 02901/421911) also takes three percent on traveler's checks but keeps longer hours: 9:30 A.M.–1:30 P.M. and 4–8 P.M. weekdays, 10 A.M.–1:30 P.M. and 5:30–8 P.M. Saturday and 5:30–8 P.M. Sunday.

Correo Argentino is at San Martín 309; Ushuaia's postal code is 9410.

Locutorio Cabo de Hornos (25 de Mayo 112) provides telephone, fax, and Internet access, but there are many others.

The **Chilean consulate** (Jainén 50, tel. 02901/430970) is open 9 A.M.–1 P.M. weekdays only.

The **Dirección Nacional de Migraciones** (Beauvoir 1536, tel. 02901/422334) is open 9 A.M.–5 P.M. weekdays only.

Los Tres Angeles (Juan Manuel de Rosas 139, tel. 02901/422687) offers quick and reliable laundry service.

The **Hospital Regional** (tel. 02901/422950, tel. 107 for emergencies) is at Maipú and 12 de Octubre.

GETTING THERE

Ushuaia has good air connections to Buenos Aires and intermediate points, and improving overland transportation from mainland Argentina and from Chile. Maritime transportation is either tenuous or expensive.

Aerolíneas Argentinas/Austral (Roca 116, tel. 02901/421218) normally flies two or three times daily to Aeroparque, sometimes via Río Gallegos, El Calafate, or Trelew. Occasional Buenos Aires-bound flights land at Ezeiza instead of Aeroparque.

In the Galería Albatros, **LADE** (Avenida San Martín 564, Local 5, tel. 02901/421123) flies irregularly to Río Gallegos, El Calafate, Comodoro Rivadavia, and Buenos Aires.

November–March, the Chilean carrier **Aerovías DAP** (25 de Mayo 64, tel. 02901/431110) flies 20-passenger Twin Otters Monday, Wednesday, and Friday to Punta Arenas, Chile (US$100), Ushuaia's only scheduled international service.

For Puerto Williams, across the Channel in Chile, it may be possible to arrange a private charter flight through the **Aeroclub Ushuaia** (tel. 02901/421717, tel. 02901/421892) for about US$100 per person.

Ushuaia lacks a central bus terminal. **Lider** (Gobernador Paz 921, tel. 02901/436421) goes to Tolhuín (US$4.50) and Río Grande (US$8, 3.5 hours) eight times daily except Sunday and holidays, when it goes only five times. **Transportes Montiel** (Marcos Zar 330, tel. 02901/421366) goes to Río Grande seven times daily except Sundays and holidays, when it goes six times only.

Tecni-Austral (Roca 157, tel. 02901/431612) goes daily at 6 A.M. to Río Grande, sometimes continuing to Río Gallegos (US$27, 12 hours) and others to Punta Arenas, Chile (US$25, 12 hours).

The Chilean MV *Mare Australis* operates luxury sightseeing cruises to Puerto Williams, Cape Horn, and through the fjords of Chilean Tierra del Fuego to Punta Arenas; while not intended as simple transportation, they can serve the same purpose for those who can afford them. It's possible to either disembark in Punta Arenas (three days) or return to Ushuaia (in a week). For more details, see the Punta Arenas entry. These cruises are usually booked far in advance, but on rare occasion—normally just before Christmas—it may be possible to board more spontaneously.

Political complications between Chile and Argentina have held up regular transportation across the Beagle Channel to Puerto Williams, but in December 2001 the two countries agreed to open Puerto Navarino, at the east end of Isla Navarino, as a port of entry to Chile.

What that means for regular public transportation remains unclear. In the meantime, ask around the Club Náutico (Avenida Maipú and Belgrano) for private yachts that may take passengers (a large enough group should be able to charter a boat for around US$70–100 pp). One possibility is Claudio Don Vito (claudio_don_vito@hotmail.com).

GETTING AROUND

A causeway links the city with **Aeropuerto Internacional Malvinas Argentinas,** which has the country's highest airport taxes: US$5 for elsewhere in Argentina, and US$20 for international flights. Taxis and *remises* cost only about US$2–3 per person with **Manuel Tienda León** (San Martín 995, tel. 02901/422222).

Several bus companies all charge around US$7.50 round-trip per person to Parque Nacional Tierra del Fuego; it's normally possible to stay in the park and return on the following day. Note that the companies below, as indicated, use several different stops along the waterfront, but do not have offices there; some have telephones and others do not. The schedules below are summer hours that may change; at other seasons, schedules are reduced.

From Avenida Maipú and 25 de Mayo, **Transporte Pasarela** (tel. 02901/433712), **Buses Eben-Ezer** (tel. 02901/431133), and **Transportes Alvarez** have 21 buses daily to the park between 7:30 A.M. and 8 P.M., returning between 9 A.M. and 8 P.M.

From Maipú and Fadul, **Transporte Puky** (tel. 02901/435418, tel. 02901/15-618547), **Body,** and **Bellavista** go a dozen times daily between 8:30 A.M. and 7:45 P.M., returning between 9:30 A.M. and 8:30 P.M.

From Maipú and Roca, **Transportes Kaupén** and **Gonzalo** operate seven buses daily between 9 A.M. and 7 P.M., returning between 10 A.M. and 8 P.M.

Most of the same companies have slightly less frequent services to the chairlift at the Glaciar Martial (US$2.50 pp), normally with a minimum of two passengers. Trips to Estancia Harberton (US$14 pp) need a minimum of three passengers.

Car rentals start around US$35 per day and range up to US$200 per day for a four-wheel-drive vehicle. Some agencies offer unlimited mileage within the province of Tierra del Fuego, but others limit this to 150 kilometers per day or even less, so verify before signing the contact.

Ushuaia rental agencies include **Cardos** (San Martín 845, tel. 02901/436388, cardosr@hotmail.com), **Europcar** (Maipú 857, tel./fax 02901/430786, europcar@carletti.com.ar), **Hertz** (at the airport, tel. 02901/432429, hertzushuaia@infovia.com.ar), and **Localiza** (San Martín 1222, tel. 02901/430739, ultimoconfin@tierradelfuego.com.ar).

DTT Cycles Sport (Avenida San Martín 903, tel. 02901/434939) rents mountain bikes.

VICINITY OF USHUAIA

Ushuaia has more than a dozen travel agencies offering excursions in and around Ushuaia, ranging from double-decker-bus city tours (US$8, 1.5 hours) to Parque Nacional Tierra del Fuego (US$14, 4–5 hours) and historic Estancia

UNLEASHING THE BEAGLE

In 1978, the military dictatorships of Chile and Argentina barely avoided war over three small islands in the Beagle Channel and, though successive civilian governments have resolved the territorial dispute, ease of movement across the channel is still not what it could be.

According to the Chilean viewpoint, the Argentines have failed to live up to their part of the 1978 agreement, which implied reciprocal border openings at Agua Negra (between the Argentine city of San Juan and the Chilean city of La Serena) for Argentina and Puerto Almanza (opposite Puerto Williams) for Chile. For the Chileans, it's also a matter of principle that, as they provide overland access to Argentine Tierra del Fuego through Chilean territory, the Argentines should supply access to Isla Navarino for the Chileans.

This sounds reasonable enough, but at the same time Argentina's federal government (unlike Chile, which is a unitary state) has to deal with elected provincial authorities still obsessed with territoriality, as well as Ushuaia business interests who fear a loss of commerce to flyspeck Puerto Williams. In practice, improved communications would probably encourage more tourists to stay longer in the area, and Puerto Williams shoppers to cross to Ushuaia, where prices are lower.

In early 2001, at the invitation of the Chilean navy, President Ricardo Lagos paid a visit to Puerto Williams in the company of Sernatur head Oscar Santelices and Argentine ambassador Daniel Olmos, but so far there have been no concrete transportation developments between Williams and Puerto Almanza. In December of that year, though, Chile declared Puerto Navarino a port of entry for Chilean-flagged vessels, permitting day excursions from Ushuaia to the southern Beagle Channel fjords.

Because excursionists would have to stay in Argentina, there were hopes that this step would begin to satisfy Ushuaia interests who, apparently, worry that Puerto Williams might undermine Ushuaia's claim to be the world's southernmost city. Reportedly, a Chilean businessman purchased a catamaran for this purpose, but no further movement has taken place. Still, the situation bears watching.

Harberton (US$50–65, eight hours). They also organize activities such as hiking, climbing, horseback riding, fishing, and mountain biking.

Local operators include **All Patagonia** (Juana Fadul 60, tel. 02901/433622, fax 02901/430707, www.allpatagonia.com), which is the AmEx representative; **Canal Fun & Nature** (Rivadavia 82, tel. 02901/437395, www.canalfun.com); **Rumbo Sur** (San Martín 342, tel. 02901/422441, fax 02901/430699, www.rumbosur.com.ar); **Tolkar** (Roca 157, Local 1, tel. 02901/431408, www.tolkarturismo.com.ar); **Tolkeyén** (Maipú 237, tel. 02901/437073); and **Yishka Turismo y Aventura** (Gobernador Godoy 62, tel./fax 02901/437606, yishka@tierradelfuego.org.ar).

Beagle Channel Boat Excursions

From the Muelle Turístico, at the foot of Lasserre, there are boat trips to Beagle Channel wildlife sites like **Isla de los Lobos,** home to the southern sea lion *(Otaria flavescens)* and the rarer southern fur seal *(Arctocephalus australis),* and **Isla de Pájaros,** a nesting site for seabirds, mostly cormorants. These excursions cost around US$20–25 per person for a 2.5-hour trip on oversized catamarans like the *Ana B, Ezequiel B,* and *Luciano Beta.* With extensions to the penguin colony at Estancia Harberton and a visit to the estancia itself, the cost is about US$50.

© WAYNE BERNHARDSON

view of the Beagle Channel from Glaciar Martial, Parque Nacional Tierra del Fuego

Rumbo Sur and Tolkeyén sell tickets for these excursions from offices at the foot of the Muelle Turístico, where Héctor Monsalve's **Tres Marías Excursiones** (tel./fax 02901/421897, marias3@satlink.com) operates four-hour trips (US$30–35 pp) on a smaller vessel (eight passengers maximum) that can approach Isla de Lobos more closely than the large catamarans. They also land on Isla Bridges, a small but diverse island with cormorant colonies, shell mounds, and even the odd penguin.

Ferrocarril Austral Fueguino

During Ushuaia's early days, prison labor built a short-line, narrow-gauge steam-driven railroad west into what is now Parque Nacional Tierra del Fuego to haul the timber that built the city. Only a few years ago, commercial interests rehabilitated part of the roadbed to create a gentrified, antiseptic tourist version of the earlier line that pretty much ignores the unsavory aspects of its history to focus on the admittedly appealing forest scenery of the Cañadon del Toro.

The train leaves from the **Estación del Fin del Mundo** (tel. 02901/431600, fax 02901/437696, www.trendelfindelmundo.com.ar), eight kilometers west of Ushuaia at the municipal campground. October–mid-April, there are three departures daily, while the rest of the year there are only one or perhaps two if demand is sufficient. The two-hour-plus excursion costs US$17 per person in tourist class, US$32 per person in first class, and US$75–100 per person with a buffet lunch or dinner.

Round-trip transportation from Ushuaia to the station costs US$5 per person with **Manuel Tienda León** (San Martín 995, tel. 02901/422222). Passengers can also use the buses from Ushuaia to Parque Nacional Tierra del Fuego.

Ski Areas

Ushuaia gets most of its visitors in summer, but it's becoming a winter sports center as well, thanks to its proximity to the mountains. Downhill skiing, snowboarding, cross-country skiing, and even dogsledding are possibilities.

The major ski event is mid-August's **Marcha Blanca,** which symbolically repeats Argentine liberator José de San Martín's heroic winter crossing of the Andes from Mendoza to assist his Chilean counterpart Bernardo O'Higgins against the Spaniards. Luring upwards of 400 skiers, it starts from the Las Cotorras cross-country area and climbs to Paso Garibaldi, the 430-meter pass between the Sierra Alvear and the Sierra Lucas Bridges. Ideally, it takes place August 17, the anniversary of San Martín's death (Argentine novelist Tomás Eloy Martínez has called his countrymen "cadaver cultists" for their apparent obsession with celebrating death rather than birth dates of their national icons).

The nearest area, only three kilometers west of downtown, is the Club Andino's modest **Pista Andina Wolfgang Wallner,** which has a single lift, capable of carrying 300 skiers, and one 859-meter run on a 30-degree slope. For more information, contact the **Club Andino Ushuaia** (Juana Fadul 48, tel. 02901/422335, www.clubandinoushuaia.com.ar).

The principal downhill area, though, is the **Centro de Deportes Invernales Luis Martial** (Luis Martial 3995, tel. 02901/15-613890, tel. 02901/15-568587, esquiush@tierradelfuego.org.ar), seven kilometers northwest of town at the end of the road. It has a single 1,130-meter run on a 23-degree slope, with a double-seat chairlift capable of carrying 224 skiers per hour.

Most areas east of Ushuaia, along RN 3, are for cross-country skiers: **Tierra Mayor** (Km 21, tel. 02901/437454, tierramayor@tierradelfuego.org.ar), **Las Cotorras** (Km 26, tel. 02901/499300), and **Haruwen** (Km 35, tel./fax 02901/424058, haruwen@tierradelfuego.org.ar). All of them rent equipment and offer transportation from Ushuaia.

The only downhill resort east of Ushuaia is the modern **Cerro Castor** (RN 3 Km 27, www.cerrocastor.com, castor@infovia.com.ar), which has up-to-the-minute facilities, including four lifts and 15 different runs. Daily lift tickets cost US$18–26, with discounts for multiday packages.

Estancia Harberton

Historic Harberton dates from 1886, when missionary pioneer Thomas Bridges resigned from the Anglican mission at Ushuaia to settle at his new estancia at Downeast, later renamed for the Devonshire home town of his wife Mary Ann Varder. Thomas Bridges, of course, was the author of the famous English-Yámana dictionary, and their son Lucas continued the family literary tradition with *The Uttermost Part of the Earth,* an extraordinary memoir of a boyhood and life among the Yámana and Ona (Selknam) Indians.

Harberton continues to be a family enterprise—its present manager and part-owner, Tommy Goodall, is Thomas Bridges' great-grandson. While the wool industry that spawned it has declined in recent years (though it has about 1,000 cattle), the estancia has opened its doors to organized English- and Spanish-language tours of its grounds and outbuildings; these include the family cemetery, flower gardens, woolshed, woodshop, boathouse, and a native botanical garden whose Yámana-style lean-tos are far more realistic than their Disneyfied counterparts along the Ferrocarril Austral Fueguino tourist train. Photographs in the woolshed illustrate the process of cutting firewood by axes and transporting it by raft and oxcart, and the tasks of gathering and shearing sheep.

In addition, American biologist Rae Natalie Prosser (Tommy Goodall's wife) has also created the **Museo Acatushún de Aves y Mamíferos Marinos Australes** (www.acatushun.com, US$2 pp), a bone museum stressing the region's marine mammals but also seabirds and a few shorebirds; it's open 10 A.M.–7 P.M. daily mid-October–mid-April. It's also possible to visit Magellanic penguin rookeries at Isla Martillo (Yecapasela) with Piratur for US$18 per person; a small colony of gentoo penguins has recently established itself on the island, making this a more intriguing trip for those who've seen Magellanic penguins elsewhere.

Estancia Harberton (tel. 02901/422742, fax 029091/422743 in Ushuaia, estanciaharberton@tierradelfuego.org.ar) is 85 kilometers east of

© WAYNE BERNHARDSON

Estancia Harberton is one of Patagonia's most historic ranches.

Ushuaia via paved RN 3 and gravel RC-j, but work has stopped on a new coastal road from Ushuaia that would shorten the distance. Mid-October–mid-April, the estancia is open for guided tours (US$4 pp) 10 A.M.–7 P.M. daily except Christmas, New Year's, and Easter. Note that because of Harberton's isolation there is no telephone and email communications can be slow, as they require a trip to Ushuaia.

With written permission, **camping** is permitted at unimproved sites; the estancia has also remodeled the former cookhouse (two rooms with 4–5 beds each and shared bath) and shepherds' house (two rooms of three beds with private bath), which are available for US$60–80 per person, depending on the room.

Harberton's **Casa de Té Mánacatush** serves a tasty afternoon tea (US$4.50 pp) and serves lunch and dinner as well (US$11, reservations advised).

In summer, Transportes Pasarela and others provides round-trip transportation from Ushuaia (US$20–30 pp), but services change frequently. Ushuaia's Piratur (tel. 02901/15-604646) offers a US$50 package with overland transportation and a visit to the penguin colony.

Catamaran tours from Ushuaia are more expensive and spend less time at Harberton, but do include the farm-tour fee.

Parque Nacional Tierra del Fuego

For pilgrims to the uttermost part of the earth, mecca is Parque Nacional Tierra del Fuego's Bahía Lapataia, where RN 3 ends on the Beagle Channel's north shore. It's a worthy goal but, sadly, most visitors see only the area in and around the highway because most of the park's mountainous interior, with its alpine lakes, limpid rivers, blue-tinged glaciers, and jagged summits, are closed to public access.

GEOGRAPHY AND CLIMATE

About 18 kilometers west of Ushuaia, Parque Nacional Tierra del Fuego hugs the Chilean border as its 63,000 hectares stretch from the Beagle Channel north across Lago Fagnano (Kami). Elevations range from sea level on the channel to 1,450 meters on the summit of Monte Vinciguerra.

Most of the park has a maritime climate, with frequent high winds. Rainfall is moderate at about 750 millimeters per annum, but humidity is fairly high, as relatively low temperatures inhibit evapotranspiration—the summer average is only about 10°C. The record maximum temperature is 31°C, while the record minimum is a fairly mild -12°C. At sea level, snow rarely sticks for long, but at higher elevations there are permanent snowfields and glaciers.

FLORA AND FAUNA

As in southernmost Chile, thick southern beech forests cover the Argentine sector of Tierra del Fuego. Along the coast, the deciduous *lenga (Nothofagus pumilio)* and the Magellanic evergreen *coigüe (Nothofagus betuloides)* are the main tree species; at higher elevations, the stunted, deciduous *ñirre (Nothofagus antarctica)* forms nearly pure stands. In some low-lying areas, where cool annual temperatures inhibit complete decomposition, dead plant material compresses into *sphagnum* peat bogs with a cover of ferns and other moisture-loving plants; the insectivorous *Drosera uniflora* swallows unsuspecting bugs.

Until recently Argentina's only protected coastal area, Parque Nacional Tierra del Fuego has a seashore protected by thick kelp beds that serve as incubators for fish fry. Especially around Bahía Ensenada and Bahía Lapataia, the shoreline and inshore waters swarm with cormorants, grebes, gulls, kelp geese, oystercatchers, flightless and flying steamer ducks, snowy sheathbills, and terns. The maritime black-browed albatross skims the Beagle's waters, while the Andean condor sometimes soars overhead. Marine mammals, mostly sea lions but also fur seals and elephant seals, cavort in the ocean. The rare southern sea otter *(Lutra felina)* may exist here.

Inland areas are fauna-poor, though foxes and guanacos are present in small numbers. The most conspicuous mammals are the European rabbit *(Oryctolagus cunniculus)* and the Canadian beaver *(Castor canadiensis)*, both of which were introduced for their pelts but have proved to be pests.

GLACIAR MARTIAL

Within the park boundaries, but also within walking distance of Ushuaia, the Glaciar Martial is the area's best single hike, offering expansive views of the Beagle Channel and across to the jagged peaks of Chile's Isla Navarino. Reached not by RN 3 but rather by the zigzag Camino al Glaciar (also known as Luis Martial) that climbs northwest out of town, the trailhead begins at the Aerosilla del Glaciar, the ski area's chairlift, which operates 10 A.M.–4:30 P.M. daily except Monday. The 1.2-kilometer chairlift (US$2 pp) reduces the two-hour climb to the foot of the glacier by half. In summer there are frequent buses to the lift (US$2.50–3 round-trip) with Pasarela, Eben Ezer, and Bellavista from the corner of Avenida Maipú and 25 de Mayo, 9 A.M.–9 P.M. Though easy to follow, the trail—especially the middle segment—is steep, and the descent requires particular caution because of loose rocks and soil. There is no admission charge to this sector of the park.

hikers at Glacier Martial, Parque Nacional Tierra del Fuego

© WAYNE BERNHARDSON

OTHER SIGHTS AND ACTIVITIES

Where freshwater Lago Roca drains into the sea at Bahía Lapataia, the park's main sector has several short nature trails and a handful of longer ones; most of the backcountry is off limits to casual hikers. Slightly less than one kilometer long, the **Senda Laguna Negra** uses a boardwalk to negotiate boggy terrain studded with ferns, wildflowers, and other water-tolerant species. The 400-meter **Senda de los Castores** (Beaver Trail) winds among southern beeches gnawed to death to form dams and ponds where the beavers themselves occasionally peek out of their dens.

The five-kilometer **Senda Hito XXIV** follows Lago Roca's northeastern shore to a small obelisk that marks the Chilean border. If, someday, Argentine and Chilean authorities can get it together, this would be an ideal entry point to the wild backcountry of Estancia Yendegaia, but at present it's illegal to continue beyond the marker. From a junction about one kilometer up the Hito XXIV trail, **Senda Cerro Guanaco** climbs four kilometers northeast up the Arroyo Guanaco to the 970-meter summit of its namesake peak.

From Bahía Ensenada, near the southeastern edge of the park, there are boat shuttles to **Isla Redonda** (US$14 pp) 10 A.M.–5:30 P.M.

PRACTICALITIES

Accommodations and Food

Camping is the only option in the park itself, where there are free sites with little or no infrastructure at **Camping Ensenada, Camping Río Pipo, Camping Las Bandurrias, Camping Laguna Verde,** and **Camping Los Cauquenes.** While these are improving, they're less tidy than the commercial **Camping Lago Roca** (tel. 02901/433313, lagoroca@speedy.com.ar, US$2–3 pp), whose more expensive "A" sector has hot showers, a grocery, and the restaurant/*confitería* **La Cabaña del Bosque.**

Information

At the park entrance on RN 3, the APN has a Centro de Información where it collects a US$4-per-person entry fee. Argentine residents pay half.

Several books have useful information on Parque Nacional Tierra del Fuego, including William Leitch's *South America's National Parks* (Seattle: The Mountaineers, 1990), which is now out of print; the fifth edition of Tim Burford's *Backpacking in Chile & Argentina* (Bradt Publications, 2001); and the third edition of Clem Lindenmayer's *Trekking in the Patagonian Andes* (Lonely Planet, 2003). The latter two are hiking guides.

Birders may want to acquire Claudio Venegas Canelo's *Aves de Patagonia y Tierra del Fuego Chileno-Argentina,* Ricardo Clark's *Aves de Tierra del Fuego y Cabo de Hornos* (Buenos Aires: Literature of Latin America, 1986), or Enrique Couve and Claudio Vidal Ojeda's bilingual *Birds of the Beagle Channel* (Punta Arenas: Fantástico Sur Birding & Nature, 2000).

Getting There and Around

For transportation details to and from the park, see the Getting Around entry for Ushuaia.

Río Grande and Vicinity

Most visitors who stay in and around Río Grande, on the Isla Grande's barren, blustery Atlantic shoreline, do so for the fishing. For the rest, the once desolate city is more a point of transit than a destination in itself, but thanks to smoothly paved streets, the huge dust clouds that once blew through this wool and oil town have subsided. There are limits to beautification, though, as all the trees planted in Plaza Almirante Brown are stiffly wind-flagged.

Bus schedules used to dictate that travelers pass the night here, but recent improvements mean quicker connections to Ushuaia for overland travelers. Still, services have improved, and there's enough to do that an afternoon spent here need not be a wasted one.

ORIENTATION

On the north bank of its namesake river, Río Grande (population 52,786) is 79 kilometers southeast of the Chilean border post at San Sebastián and 190 kilometers northeast of Ushuaia via RN 3, which is still unpaved between Tolhuin and Rancho Hambre. As of this writing, the mountainous section between Tolhuin and the Hostería Petrel turnoff was still a loose gravel surface on which cracked windshields were a daily event. The blinding dust kicked up by every vehicle makes this one of the country's most hazardous roads.

RN 3 bypasses the compact city center, which is reached by southeasterly Avenida San Martín, the main commercial street. Most services are within a few blocks of the axis formed by San Martín and the perpendicular Avenida Manuel Belgrano, which leads east toward the waterfront.

SIGHTS

Río Grande's **Museo de La Ciudad Virginia Choquintel** (Alberdi 553, tel. 02962/430647) does a lot with a little, with good materials on natural history, surprisingly sophisticated exhibits on ethnology and aboriginal subsistence, and historic displays on maps and mapmaking, the evolution of communications on the island, and astronomical science. Now occupying the former storehouses of the Asociación Rural de Tierra del Fuego, the Museo de la Ciudad is open 9 A.M.–8 P.M. weekdays and 3–7 P.M. Saturday.

Río Grande has few architectural landmarks—

North of Río Grande, the Salesian chapel was the focus of efforts to catechize Selknam Indians in the early 20th century.

or few buildings of any antiquity for that matter—but the **Obras Sanitarias** (1954) waterworks tower (Lasserre 386), at the northeast corner of the Plaza, dates from the Juan Perón era.

PRACTICALITIES

Entertainment

El Cine 1 & 2 (Perito Moreno 211, tel. 02962/433260) shows current films in modern facilities, but sometimes turns up the volume to excruciating levels—bring or improvise ear plugs, just in case.

La Guanaca (Lasserre 592) is an informal, low-key bar with live music.

Accommodations

Accommodations are fairly scarce, but there are good values, particularly at the budget end. Nearly every mid- to upscale place offers a 10 percent discount for payment in cash.

Río Grande's first backpackers' hostel, at the south end of town, is the promising **Hotel Argentino** (San Martín 64, tel. 02964/422546, hotelargentino@hotmail.com, US$7 pp). It gets especially high marks from cyclists; standards are good for B&B with shared bath, there are kitchen facilities and other usable common spaces, and they'll fetch guests from the bus terminal for free.

The simple but spotless, family-run **Hospedaje Noal,** (Obligado 557, tel. 02964/427516, US$7/12 d) has spacious rooms with shared bath but plenty of closet space and good beds. Perhaps the next best value, cozy **Hotel Rawson** (J.M. Estrada 750, tel. 02964/430352, US$8/12 s/d) has smallish rooms with private bath.

Close to the bus terminal, the seaside **Hotel Isla del Mar** (Güemes 936, tel. 02964/422883, fax 02964/427283, isladelmar@arnet.com.ar, US$23/27 s/d) is frayed, rather than just worn around the edges, with loose doorknobs, scuffed walls, and slowly eroding wooden built-ins. Still, it exudes a certain funky charm, even if "seaview" is a relative term here—with Río Grande's enormous tidal range, the Atlantic tides sometimes seem to be on the distant horizon. Rates include breakfast, and there's a cash discount.

A glass palace that looks out of place in Río Grande, **Hotel Atlántida** (Avenida Belgrano 582, tel./fax 02964/431914, atlantida@netcombbs.com.ar, US$30/36 s/d) has decent rooms, but it's also well worn. Beds are softer than some might prefer in the aging but tidy rooms at **Hotel Federico Ibarra** (Rosales 357, tel. 02964/430071, hotelibarra@netcombbs.com.ar, US$33/40 s/d), but it's worth consideration with breakfast and a 10 percent cash discount.

Río Grande's most professional operation, **Posada de los Sauces** (Elcano 839, tel. 02964/432895, info@posadadelossauces.com, US$42–54 s, US$52–67 d) is easily the top of the line. One of the suite bathrooms is large enough for a hot-tub party, and the restaurant is far and away the city's most elegant.

Food

La Nueva Piamontesa (Belgrano and Mackinlay, tel. 02964/424366) is a longstanding favorite for varied and delicate baked empanadas and the pizzas in its deli. An inexpensive sit-down restaurant as well, it's open 24/7.

Two other places specialize in pizza and pasta: **Café Sonora** (Perito Moreno 705, tel. 02964/423102) and **La Nueva Colonial** (Fagnano 669, tel. 02964/425353).

Leymi (25 de Mayo 1335, tel. 02964/421683) serves fixed-price lunches for about US$3.50, and has a broad menu of *parrillada,* pasta, and other short orders. **El Rincón de Julio** (Elcano 805, tel. 02964/15-604261) is a hole-in-the-wall *parrilla,* highly regarded by locals, with lunch-counter-style service.

Mamá Flora (Avenida Belgrano 1101, tel. 02964/424087) is a good breakfast choice that also has coffee and exquisite chocolates. There are two outstanding ice creameries on the Plaza: **Limoncello** (Rosal and Fagnano, tel. 02964/420134) and **Lusso** (Fagnano and Lasserre).

Several upscale hotels have their own restaurants, most notably the **Posada de los Sauces** (Elcano 839, tel. 02964/430868), which deserves special mention for superb service, the cooked-to-order *lomo a la pimienta* (pepper steak, US$6.50), and their complimentary glass of wine. There's also a 10 percent cash discount.

Information and Services

Río Grande's municipal **Oficina de Información Turística** (Rosales 350, tel. 02964/431324, rg-turismo@netcombbs.com.ar) is a kiosk on Plaza Almirante Brown; open 9 A.M.–9 P.M. daily in summer, 9 A.M.–8 P.M. weekdays and 10 A.M.–5 P.M. Saturday the rest of the year, it's exceptionally helpful.

The provincial **Instituto Fueguino de Turismo** (Infuetur, Belgrano 319, tel. 02962/422887) is open 10 A.M.–4 P.M. weekdays only.

Cambio Thaler (Rosales 259, tel. 02964/421154) is the only exchange house. Banks with ATMs include **Banco de Tierra del Fuego** (San Martín 193) and **Banca Nazionale del Lavoro** (San Martín 194).

Correo Argentino (Rivadavia 968) is two blocks west of San Martín; the postal code is 9420. **Locutorio Cabo Domingo** (Avenida San Martín 458) has long-distance services, while **Telefónica** (San Martín and 9 de Julio) has Internet access.

El Lavadero (Perito Moreno 221) does the washing.

For medical services, the **Hospital Regional** (tel. 02964/422088) is at Ameghino s/n.

Getting There

Aerolíneas Argentinas/Austral (San Martín 607, tel. 02964/422748) flies daily to Río Gallegos and Buenos Aires. **LADE** (Lasserre 425, tel. 02964/422968) flies with some frequency to Río Gallegos, less frequently to Comodoro Rivadavia.

Río Grande's **Terminal de Buses** (Avenida Belgrano 16, tel. 02964/421339) is near the waterfront, but some companies have offices elsewhere in town. At the main terminal, **Lider** (tel. 02964/420003), **Transportes Montiel** (tel. 02964/420997), and **Tolkeyén** (tel. 02964/427354) have multiple departures to Tolhuín (US$3.50) and Ushuaia (US$7.50). **Buses Pacheco** (tel. 02964/425611) goes to Punta Arenas, Chile (US$18, eight hours) Tuesday, Thursday, and Saturday at 10:30 A.M.

Tecni-Austral (Moyano 516, tel. 02964/430610) goes to Punta Arenas Monday, Wednesday, and Friday at 9:30 A.M., to Río Gallegos (US$20, eight hours) via Chile daily except Sunday at 9:30 A.M., and to Ushuaia (US$9, four hours) daily at 6 P.M.

Getting Around

City bus Línea C goes directly to **Aeropuerto Internacional Río Grande** (tel. 02964/420600), a short distance west of downtown on RN 3, for US$.50. It's also a reasonable cab ride.

Europcar (Avenida Belgrano 423, tel. 02964/432022) rents cars and pickup trucks.

VICINITY OF RÍO GRANDE

As the area surrounding Río Grande does not have a well-developed transport infrastructure, hiring a vehicle is worth consideration.

Reserva Provincial Costa Atlántica de Tierra del Fuego

From Cabo Nombre, at the north end of Bahía San Sebastián, to the mouth of the Río Ewan southeast of Río Grande, the Isla Grande's entire shoreline is a bird sanctuary because of the abundant plovers and sandpipers, some of which migrate yearly between the Arctic and South America. Near the San Sebastián border post is the privately owned **Refugio de Vida Silvestre Dicky,** a prime wetland habitat of 1,900 hectares.

Misión Salesiana

One exception to Río Grande's lack of historic sites is the Salesian mission (RN 3 Km 2980, tel. 02964/421642, www.misionrg.com.ar), founded by the order to catechize the Selknam; after the aboriginals died out from unintentionally introduced diseases and intentional outright slaughter, the fathers turned their attention to educating rural youth in their boarding school. The well-preserved **Capilla** (chapel), a national historical monument, and similar Magellanic buildings comprise part of the mission's **Museo de Historia, Antropología y de Ciencias Naturales,** whose recently improved facilities display their natural history and ethnography exhibits far better than in the not-too-distant past.

From Río Grande, Línea B goes hourly to the Misión Salesiana, about 11 kilometers north of Río Grande, from 7:30 A.M.–8:30 P.M. The

FISHING IN FUEGIA

Fishing for Atlantic salmon, brown trout, and rainbow trout is a popular pastime throughout Argentine Tierra del Fuego, but rules are a little intricate. In the first instance, there are separate licenses for Parque Nacional Tierra del Fuego and for the rest of the island, and fees differ for residents of the province, nonresidents of the province, and foreigners.

For fishing within the park, licenses are available only from the APN in Ushuaia; rates are US$5 per day or US$20 per season (November–mid-April) for residents. For nonresidents or foreigners, rates are US$11 per day, US$53 per week, or US$71 per season. Children under age 18 pay US$3.50 and retired Argentine citizens pay nothing.

For fishing beyond park boundaries, daily rates vary depending on the river, but range US$17–34 for foreigners; there's a 15-day license for US$34–67, and seasonal rates are US$67–133. Fuegian and Argentine residents pay a fraction of these rates.

In Ushuaia, licenses are available at the **Asociación Caza y Pesca** (Maipú 822, tel. 02901/423168, cazpescush@infoviar.com.ar) or **Óptica Eduardo's** (San Martín 830, tel. 02901/433252). In Río Grande, contact the **Club de Pesca John Goodall** (Ricardo Rojas 606, tel. 02964/424324).

museum is open 10 A.M.–12:30 P.M. and 3–7 P.M. daily except Sunday, when it keeps afternoon hours only; admission costs US$1 for adults, US$.50 for children.

Historic Estancias

Several of the region's largest and most important *estancias* are in the vicinity of Río Grande. Founded by the Menéndez dynasty's Sociedad Explotadora de Tierra del Fuego, **Estancia María Behety,** 17 kilometers west via gravel RC-c, is the site of the world's largest shearing shed.

Also Sociedad Explotadora property, **Estancia José Menéndez,** 25 kilometers southwest of town via RN 3 and RC-b, is one of the island's most historic ranches. RC-b continues west to an obscure summer border crossing at **Radman,** where few visitors of any kind cross the line to Lago Blanco on the Chilean side.

For potential overnighters, though, the Sea View Guest House at the Simon Goodall family's **Estancia Viamonte** (tel. 02964/430861, www.estanciaviamonte.com, info@estanciaviamonte.com, US$100/165 s/d for bed and breakfast, US$150 pp with full board and activities) is the only place on the island that can offer the opportunity to sleep in Lucas Bridges' bedroom. Directly on RN 3, about 42 kilometers southeast of Río Grande, it fronts on a bird-rich beach; the house itself can sleep up to six people with two shared baths, plus living and dining rooms. There are extensive gardens, and chances for fishing, riding, and farm activities.

Lago Fagnano (Kami) and Vicinity

Named for the priest who headed the Salesian evangelical effort among the Selknam, this elongated body of water fills a structural depression that stretches across the Chilean border to the west. Also known by its Selknam name Kami, its shoreline is nearly 200 kilometers long and its surface covers nearly 600 square kilometers.

The most westerly part of the lake, along the Chilean border, belongs to Parque Nacional Tierra del Fuego but is virtually inaccessible except by boat. As might be expected, the lake is popular with fishing enthusiasts.

At the moment, since the closure of Hostería Kaikén at the east end of the lake, the main accommodations this side of Ushuaia are at Lago Escondido's **Hostería Petrel** (RN 3 Km 3186, tel. 02901/433569, US$47 d), which has lake-view rooms with Jacuzzis and a restaurant that's a popular stopover for tour groups.

At the east end of the lake, about midway between Río Grande and Ushuaia, pilgrims pause at the town of **Tolhuin** to taste the goods at **Panadería la Unión,** a bakery whose celebrity visitors have ranged from ex-President Carlos Menem to folk-rocker León Gieco, hard-rockers Los Caballeros de la Quema, and actress China Zorrilla. It has the usual fine bread but also loads of *facturas* (pastries), *alfajores,* and sandwiches; what it lacks, astonishingly for Argentina, is any coffee other than machine-dispensed instant.

The Falkland Islands (Islas Malvinas)

In 1982, the isolated Falkland Islands made world news when Britain and Argentina fought a 10-week South Atlantic war that ended in a decisive British victory and, serendipitously, ended a brutal military dictatorship. The territorial dispute over the Islands, which Argentina claims as the Malvinas, has not gone away, but the islands' tourism profile has risen as a destination for cruise ships and a select group of independent travelers interested primarily in sub-Antarctic wildlife.

What the Falklands can offer, as a Patagonian outlier 500 kilometers east of the South American continent, is enormous colonies of seabirds (the six species of penguins include easy access to the uncommon king and gentoo), black-browed albatrosses and several species of cormorants in particular, and marine mammals including elephant seals, sea lions, and fur seals. Most of these are rarely seen on the continent, and many of them would require a trip to either remote South Georgia or Antarctica.

Despite their small permanent population, only about 2,500, the Islands have good tourist infrastructure in the capital city of Stanley and in main island and offshore lodges, close to wildlife sites, that are the local counterpart to Argentine

Must-Sees

Look for M to find the sights and activities you can't miss and M for the best dining and lodging.

The Falkland Islands Museum and National Trust: In only an hour or so, visitors can get a grasp of the Islands' local, maritime, military, and natural history, with a touch of Antarctica to boot, before exploring the rest of Stanley (page 458).

Johnson's Harbour and Volunteer Point: Johnson's Harbour on East Falkland is a key stop for its large and growing king-penguin colony, which spends the entire year at the scenic lagoon Volunteer Point. There's even more to see in the summer (page 468).

Bleaker Island: For visitors on a budget, Bleaker has excellent accommodations and much of the same wildlife as Sea Lion, but its penguins, cormorants, and petrels are more dispersed (page 470).

Sea Lion Island: Sea Lion may be one of the Falklands' most expensive destinations, but there's more wildlife in a smaller area than any other easily accessible part of the Islands (page 470).

Port Howard, West Falkland

Port Howard: On West Falkland, guests at Port Howard Lodge can enjoy the comforts of the former manager's house in what is now the last survivor of the large sheep farms that once monopolized the Islands' wool industry. Since construction of the West Falklands road, it's a great base for visiting other settlements and wildlife sites on the island (page 471).

Pebble Island: In addition to penguin and petrel colonies, Pebble has endless crescent beaches and lagoons full of wildfowl, all within easy reach of one of the Islands' best-run lodges (page 473).

Saunders Island: Both the hiking and the wildlife—especially the black-browed albatrosses—are extraordinary on mountainous Saunders, whose historic resources include ruins of Britain's original 18th-century outpost (page 475).

Carcass Island: The Falklands may be a more commercial destination than they were 20 years ago, but Rob and Lorraine McGill's wildlife-rich West Falkland ranch feels like a throwback to the days when it would never have occurred to any Islander to charge for bed and breakfast (page 477).

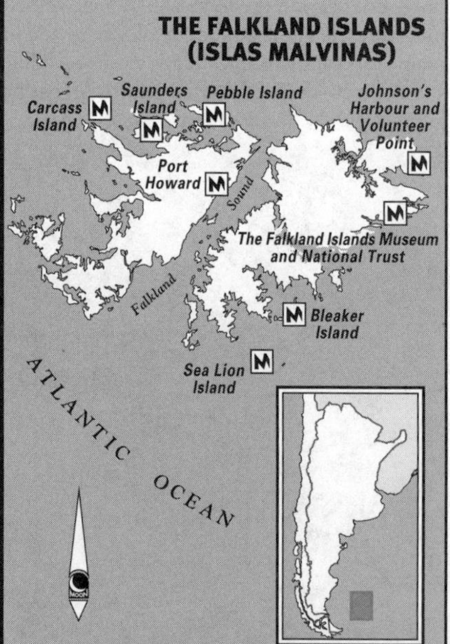

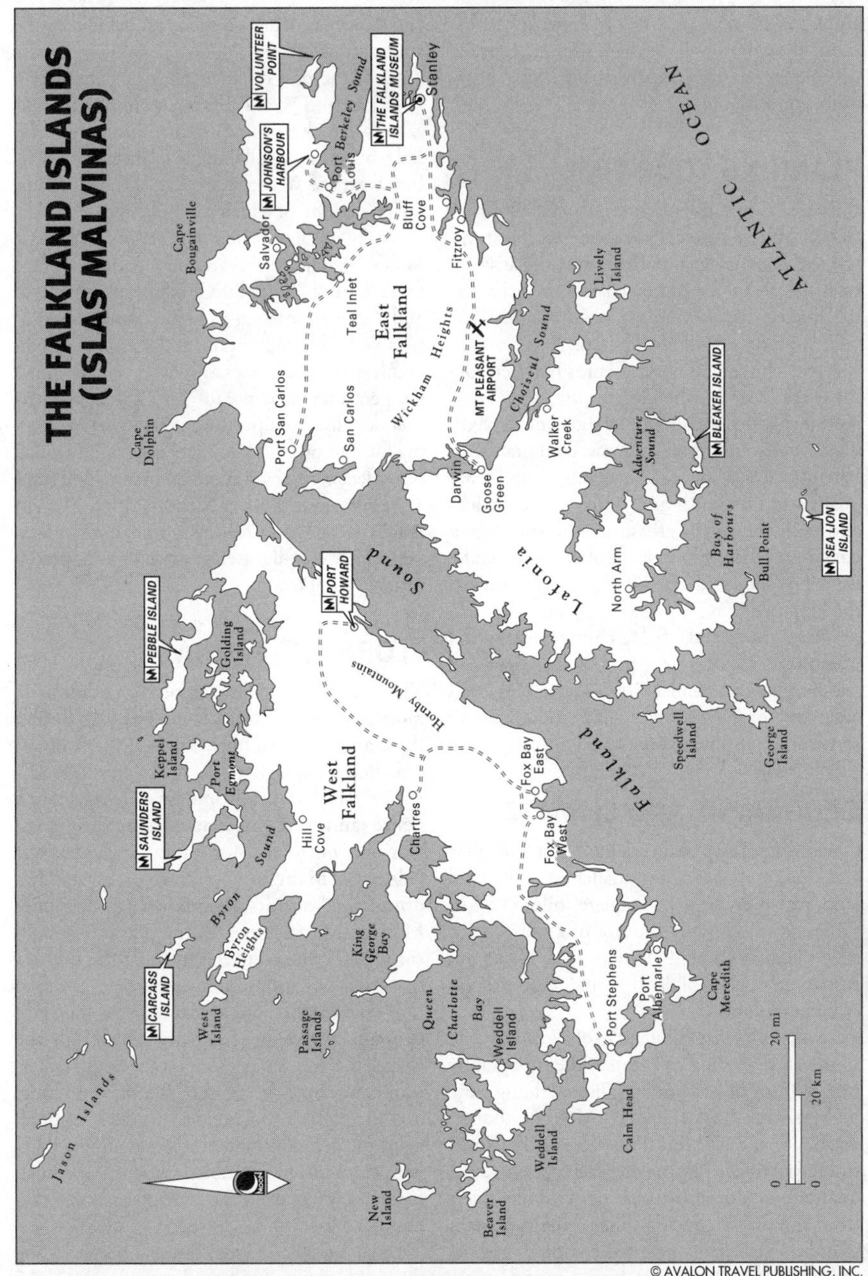
THE FALKLAND ISLANDS (ISLAS MALVINAS)
VOLUNTEER POINT
THE FALKLAND ISLANDS MUSEUM
Stanley
JOHNSON'S HARBOUR
Port Louis
Berkeley Sound
Cape Bougainville
Salvador
Bluff Cove
Fitzroy
Teal Inlet
East Falkland
Wickham Heights
MT PLEASANT AIRPORT
Choiseul Sound
Lively Island
ATLANTIC OCEAN
Cape Dolphin
Port San Carlos
San Carlos
Darwin
Goose Green
Walker Creek
Adventure Sound
BLEAKER ISLAND
Lafonia
Bay of Harbours
North Arm
Bull Point
SEA LION ISLAND
PEBBLE ISLAND
PORT HOWARD
Sound
Golding Island
Hornby Mountains
Keppel Island
Port Egmont
SAUNDERS ISLAND
West Falkland
Hill Cove
Chartres
Fox Bay East
Fox Bay West
Falkland
Speedwell Island
George Island
Byron Sound
Byron Heights
CARCASS ISLAND
King George Bay
West Island
Passage Islands
Queen Charlotte Bay
Weddell Island
Port Stephens
Port Albemarle
Cape Meredith
Calm Head
Jason Islands
New Island
Beaver Island
0
20 mi
20 km
© AVALON TRAVEL PUBLISHING, INC.

and Chilean *estancias.* The big drawback is that most, though not all, of these sites are only accessible by relatively expensive air taxis that require good timing.

PLANNING YOUR TIME

Because of infrequent international flights—weekly at best—unless your time is almost unlimited, organizing your itinerary before arrival is essential. Without your own plane or yacht, visits shorter than a week are nearly impossible, and two weeks would be desirable.

Most visitors enjoy the Islands between October and March, when migratory seabirds and marine mammals return to the shoreline to breed. The concentrations of penguins, cormorants, albatrosses, elephant seals, and other species are greatest in December and January, when chicks and pups are present; these are also the longest days of summer, with more flexibility for wildlife-watching. That said, signature bird species such as the king penguin are present all year.

Given the Islands' fickle climate, warm and waterproof clothing, such as woolen sweaters and windbreakers, is essential. Rubber boots ("wellies") are useful for slogging over peaty ground, but it's sometimes possible to borrow them.

GEOGRAPHY AND CLIMATE

Consisting of two main islands (East and West Falkland) and nearly 700 smaller ones, the total land area is about 4,700 square miles (12,173 square km). Roughly the size of Connecticut, they measure about 155 miles (250 km) from east to west; the Falkland Sound separates the two main islands.

Except for East Falkland's softly undulating southern peninsula of Lafonia, the topography ranges from hilly to mountainous, though the highest point, East Falkland's Mount Usborne, reaches only 2,312 feet (705 meters). The most striking landforms are the periglacial "stone runs," quartzite boulder fields that descend like rivers from the ridges and summits of the two main islands. The heavily indented coastline, with its sandy and gravelly beaches, bays, estuaries, inlets, and scenic headlands, is the main habitat for the abundant wildlife.

Over the past decade, the road network on both East and West Falkland has improved considerably, making some destinations more accessible, but air taxis still link the relatively populous East with the West and smaller offshore islands, only a handful of which are inhabited.

While it might be fair to describe the climate as "sub-Antarctic" because low annual average temperatures (around 6°C) inhibit plant growth and decomposition as well, the latitude is comparable to that of London, and the surrounding South Atlantic alleviates the winter cold. Summer temperatures rarely rise to 75°F (25°C), but neither do winter temperatures remain below freezing for days on end. Humidity is high but rainfall is moderate, reaching about 24 inches (600 mm) at Stanley, but West Falkland is drier. The climate's most trying feature is the almost incessant westerlies—the average annual wind speed is nearly 14 knots.

FLORA AND FAUNA

The Islands' relatively simple flora comprise mostly extensive grasslands and prostrate shrubs; there are no native trees. Fringing parts of the coastline is the high, dense tussac grass *(Parodiochloa flabellata),* a prime wildlife habitat so dense and verdant that passing European mariners mistook it for forest. Because it was vulnerable to fire and overgrazing, its range has diminished and its abundance has declined. Most native pasture is "white grass" *(Cortaderia pilosa),* which covers much of the interior but is less nutritious for livestock.

It's the fauna, though, that draw visitors. Five penguin species breed here, of which only the Magellanic is normally seen on the South American continent; the gentoo, the majestic king, and the crested rockhopper are easily sighted, while the occasional macaroni nests among rockhoppers, which it resembles. Other species, such as the chinstrap, make the odd appearance but do not breed here.

Large numbers of king cormorants nest among the rockhoppers, while predatory skuas raid the

© WAYNE BERNHARDSON

giant petrel chick, Bleaker Island

colonies to steal eggs. The most interesting bird of prey, though, is the striated caracara or Johnny Rook, so fearless that it will approach humans on foot and steal small, shiny objects. The most striking of breeding birds is the black-browed albatross, so flawlessly beautifully that photographs can make living individuals look like perfectly preserved museum specimens.

Other common birds on the Islands' shoreline include rock cormorants, giant petrels, various gulls, black and Magellanic oystercatchers, snowy sheathbills, kelp geese, and flightless steamer ducks. The grasslands and wetlands are home to crested caracaras, red-backed hawks, black-necked swans, peregrine falcons, and several species of sheldgeese. Nearly all the birds are surprisingly tame and easily photographed.

In addition, marine mammals include breeding populations of elephant seals, southern sea lions, and southern fur seals (whose inaccessible colonies are more difficult to visit), six species of dolphins, and orcas. The large South Atlantic whales are uncommon, however.

HISTORY

The Falklands' early history is murky. In pre-Columbian times, Fuegian Indians may have sailed here in bark canoes, but there is no evidence of permanent occupation; an unidentified ship from Magellan's 1520 expedition may have wintered here after being blown off course. Various Spanish, Dutch, British, and French navigators frequented the area over the next two centuries.

Nobody established a settlement, though, until the Frenchman Louis de Bougainville brought colonists to Port Louis, East Falkland, in 1764 (the Islands' Spanish name, Malvinas, is an adaptation of St. Malo, the Channel homeport for many French vessels).

In 1766, unaware of the French presence, Britain built its own garrison at Port Egmont on Saunders Island, West Falkland. In 1767, meanwhile, Spain replaced France at Port Louis after invoking the Treaty of Tordesillas (1494), under which the Pope had divided the New World between Spain and Portugal. In 1770, after happening upon the Port Egmont settlement, the Spaniards ejected the British but, under threat of war, permitted them to return.

In 1774, the British left Port Egmont without relinquishing their claims. A desolate penal settlement for nearly four decades, the Islands became a haven for whalers and sealers after Spain's departure in 1811.

A decade later, the newly independent United Provinces of the River Plate sent a governor whose tenure was short, while Buenos Aires businessman Louis Vernet asserted rights to the seal fishery and the feral livestock, cattle, and horses, that the Spaniards had abandoned. When Vernet attempted to enforce his rights against American sealers, though, a U.S. naval officer wrecked the Port Louis settlement and forced Vernet's return to Buenos Aires.

In early 1833, a British naval vessel evicted the United Provinces' remaining forces, but its Argentine successor state has steadfastly maintained its claim to the Islands, usually diplomatically—but more aggressively when a military dictatorship launched a surprise invasion in 1982.

After the British takeover, Montevideo-based

Englishman Samuel Lafone created the Falkland Islands Company to commercialize the cattle herds and then transformed the economy by introducing wool-bearing sheep. For well over a century, the FIC owned nearly half the property in the Islands and dominated shipping as well, though other immigrants created similar large sheep farms with a resident labor force.

About half the population, which grew slowly and has never exceeded about 2,500, lived on the farms; the other half resided in the port capital of Stanley, established in 1844. Starting in the 1970s, though, political uncertainty and the wool industry's decline led farm owners to sell off their properties; nearly all of them are now family farms, but the population has shifted dramatically toward the capital for reasons that have only partly to do with the wool industry.

The South Atlantic Conflict

The Falklands' peculiar political status, as an isolated British possession in the decolonization era that followed World War II, led to negotiations that might have resulted in their absorption by Argentina—despite Islanders' determination to remain British (perhaps a dozen Argentines, nearly all of them married to Islanders or other British citizens, resided on the Falklands). Granting Argentina's military airline LADE the first regular routes from the continent to the Islands, a 1971 communications agreement also gave Buenos Aires a de facto say in immigration and other matters.

Argentina's 1976–1983 military dictatorship, which increased Islanders' misgivings about Argentine instability, was collapsing beneath the weight of its own brutality, corruption, and ineptitude when it made a last-gasp grab for domestic popularity by invading the Falklands on April 2, 1982. The Argentine generals and admirals, though, underestimated British prime minister Margaret Thatcher's resolve; even worse, they misjudged her military's ability to organize the task force that retook the Islands within ten weeks (Argentine forces, for their part, had not fought a real shooting war since 19th-century conflicts with Paraguay and the Mapuche).

The Post-War Period

In the conflict's aftermath, Britain's declaration of a fisheries protection zone and licensing regime made the Islands in general, and Stanley in particular, one of the world's most prosperous places on a per-capita basis. While the Islanders themselves did not crew the ships that came from Europe and Asia, the revenue from squid licenses and joint ventures enabled local government to invest in schools, medical care, and roads, and individuals to improve their living standards. Tourism revenues also increased dramatically, as 'round-the-Horn and Antarctica-bound cruise ships called to visit the Islands' capital and enjoy the spectacular coastal wildlife.

Meanwhile, relations with the continent remained distant through the 1980s but improved in the 1990s as Argentine president Carlos Menem's administration attempted to persuade skeptical Islanders of its goodwill. The biggest step forward was a communications agreement that allowed the Chilean airline LAN to fly weekly from Santiago and Punta Arenas to the Islands' Mount Pleasant Airport, but subsequent Argentine governments have taken a harder line—in 2003, President Néstor Kirchner's administration revoked LAN's permission for Mount Pleasant–bound charter flights that simplified cruise-ship passenger exchange.

Stanley benefited most from the newfound prosperity and the population shift, as family-owned farms did not need—and could not afford—the large labor force employed by traditional sheep ranches.

RECREATION

For most visitors, **wildlife watching** is the main activity. Because of the Islands' isolation and small human population, many species show no fear of people, but the Falklands Islands Countryside Code, adapted from rules for comparable sites in Antarctica, recommends that visitors get no closer than six meters to birds and marine mammals. Be especially cautious with the southern sea lion, which can be aggressive and surprisingly quick on land.

Fishing for sea trout requires a license (£10) from the Stanley Post Office; the trout season runs September 1–April 30. Fishermen must return the license's logbook to the Fisheries Department (tel. 27260) at the floating Falkland Islands Port and Storage System (FIPASS), anchored in Stanley Harbor east of town.

Opportunities for **hiking** are almost limitless, but government and landowners discourage camping because of fire danger and livestock disturbances. Since nearly all land is privately held, hikers must inform the landowner.

Diving among the Islands' numerous shipwrecks, kelp forests, and reefs is possible with Stanley operator Dave Eynon's Falklands Underwater, which rents equipment and organizes tours; for details, see the Stanley entry.

Golfers seeking a real challenge can take on the courses at Stanley, Darwin, and Port Howard, taking a penalty if their ball lands among landmines (this is not a common occurrence, and minefields from the 1982 conflict are well-signed). In all honesty, these are improvised courses on boggy, undulating terrain, and the Islands' nearly constant winds complicate play even more.

HEALTH AND SAFETY

Probably one of the world's safest destinations—true crime is virtually nonexistent—the Falklands pose no major health problems and have good medical infrastructure in case of illness or injury. It is worth mentioning, though, the unfortunate legacy of landmines laid by the Argentine military; though dangerous, minefields are fenced and clearly marked, and no civilian has been injured since hostilities ceased in 1982. Entering minefields or tampering with signs can expose you to fines of £1,000. To report landmines or other questionable objects, contact the Joint Service Explosive Ordnance Disposal (tel. 72393).

While the weather can be changeable, the Falklands' intense sunshine and brisk winds make visitors vulnerable to sunburn even with very brief exposure.

GETTING THERE

Chile's **LAN** (www.lan.com) offers the only regular commercial flight to the Falklands' **Mount Pleasant International Airport (MPA),** 35 miles (60 km) southwest of Stanley, every Saturday from Santiago and Punta Arenas; it turns around immediately at MPA. One Saturday per month in each direction, it picks up passengers in Río Gallegos, Argentina; the following Saturday, it drops them off.

LAN fares from Santiago start at US$680 round-trip; from Punta Arenas, it's US$540 round-trip. Through fares from Europe or North America can be cheaper for those already planning to visit South America; from the UK, the economy fare is £922 (US$1,660) round-trip, with two stopovers permitted. LAN also has good connections from North America, Mexico, and Australia.

Britain's **Ministry of Defence (MOD)** operates or charters six or seven flights per month from RAF Brize Norton, near Burford, Oxfordshire, via the tiny South Atlantic island of Ascension. The flight takes 18 hours, including an hour's stopover for refueling on Ascension; fares start at £1,608 round-trip, considerably more expensive than the Santiago-Punta Arenas route, but Chile-bound travelers can purchase one-way tickets. The MOD baggage limit is normally 60 lbs (27 kg); enforcement is lax, but overweight charges run £13.40 per pound.

For reservations on MOD flights, contact the Travel Coordinator at **Falkland House** (14 Broadway, Westminster, London SW1H 0BH, tel. 020/7222-2542, fax 020/7222-2375, travel@falklands.gov.fk). In the Falklands, for both LAN and MOD flights, contact **International Tours and Travel Ltd** (Beauchene Shopping Center, John Street, tel. 22041, fax 22042; se.itt@horizon.co.fk).

GETTING AROUND

Except between Stanley and Mount Pleasant Airport, there is no regular public transportation on roads, though **taxis** and **rental cars** (with or without guides) are available on both East and West Falkland. Off-road driving is not advisable for drivers without local experience, who frequently get "bogged" in the soggy terrain and have to call or trek for help. Visitors may use their own state or national driver's licenses in the Falklands for up to 12 months.

To West Falkland and offshore islands, the only regular public transportation is the **Falkland Islands Government Air Service (FIGAS),** an air-taxi service that flies 10-passenger Norman-Britten Islander aircraft to grass airstrips throughout the Islands. At the approximate rate of £1 per minute, the fare from Stanley to Saunders Island, north of West Falkland, is about £120 round-trip. For safety reasons, pilots enforce the baggage limitation of 30 lbs (14 kg) per passenger.

On an ad hoc basis, **Island Shipping** (tel. 22345, fax 22347, www.shipping.horizon.co.fk) can take a few passengers on its freighter MV *Tamar* on its rounds to pick up wool and deliver other goods to settlements around the Islands, and even to Punta Arenas. Rates are £25 per person, per day, with meals included.

Stanley and Vicinity

Its setting often compared with the moorlands of Scotland's outer isles, fast-growing Stanley claims to be the "world's smallest capital," and it's modernizing rapidly as commercial fishing and tourism supplant wool in the Islands' economy. The sweet scent of smoldering peat no longer permeates the evening atmosphere, as heating oil now warms the houses and fuels the cookstoves of most aging stone cottages and newer kit constructions alike, and streets once lined with utilitarian Land Rovers now sport shiny new SUVs.

While few Islanders work directly in the fishery, their joint ventures with overseas fishing companies and local government's infrastructural investments have, since the 1982 South Atlantic conflict, transformed a forlorn-looking village into a much more presentable place. Many local residents have remodeled and repainted their houses, or built new ones, and continue their tradition of self-sufficiency by tending tidy kitchen gardens even though more commercial produce is now available.

HISTORY

After the Colonial Office shifted the Islands' capital from Port Louis to sheltered Port Jackson (soon renamed Stanley Harbour) in 1844, Stanley became the new seat of government but its permanent population was a ragtag assortment of roving mariners, holdover gauchos, and Chelsea military pensioners. Except in emergencies, though, 'round-the-Horn shipping avoided the Islands, because Stanley gained a reputation for cargo-shipping losses—"condemned at Stanley" became a cliché among insurers.

In the early days, feral cattle rather than sheep roamed the Islands' pastures, and low-value hides attracted little commercial interest. After mid-century, though, when the newly founded Falkland Islands Company shifted from cattle to sheep and other recently created farms followed suit, Stanley grew rapidly as the transshipment point for wool between camp and the UK.

In addition to being the Islands' largest landholder, the FIC dominated commerce as the Islands' only significant merchant house, and Stanley's biggest employer, and remained so for more than a century. Its impact on the townscape was palpable—many if not most Stanley houses belonged to the company, whose workers lived in them only so long as they remained employees.

With declining wool prices after World War II, and political uncertainties due to relations with Argentina in the 1970s, Stanley stagnated until the outbreak of hostilities in 1982. While the capital was heavily occupied by Argentine troops, their last-minute surrender to approaching British forces avoided serious damage.

Stanley still transships the Islands' wool, but fisheries income since 1986 has transformed it into one of the most prosperous communities of its size in the world. It's far from pretentious, and the boom-and-bust of squidding makes the economy vulnerable, but the changes since the conflict are the most dramatic in the capital's history. Only oil, rumored to be present offshore, could have a bigger impact.

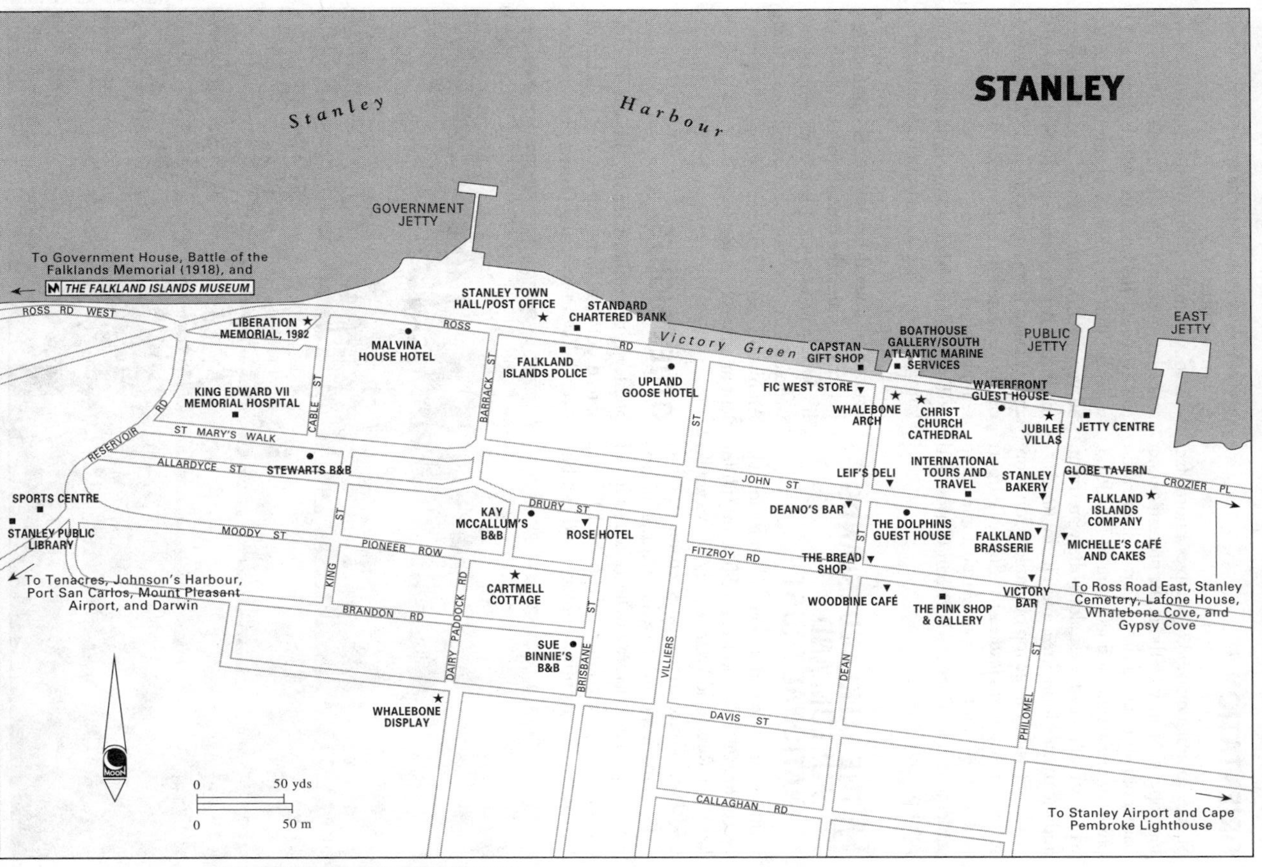
STANLEY
Stanley Harbour
GOVERNMENT JETTY
To Government House, Battle of the Falklands Memorial (1918), and
THE FALKLAND ISLANDS MUSEUM
ROSS RD WEST
LIBERATION MEMORIAL, 1982
MALVINA HOUSE HOTEL
STANLEY TOWN HALL/POST OFFICE
STANDARD CHARTERED BANK
ROSS RD
Victory Green
CAPSTAN GIFT SHOP
BOATHOUSE GALLERY/SOUTH ATLANTIC MARINE SERVICES
PUBLIC JETTY
EAST JETTY
FALKLAND ISLANDS POLICE
UPLAND GOOSE HOTEL
FIC WEST STORE
WATERFRONT GUEST HOUSE
KING EDWARD VII MEMORIAL HOSPITAL
CABLE ST
BARRACK ST
ST
WHALEBONE ARCH
CHRIST CHURCH CATHEDRAL
JUBILEE VILLAS
JETTY CENTRE
RESERVOIR RD
ST MARY'S WALK
ALLARDYCE ST
STEWARTS B&B
INTERNATIONAL TOURS AND TRAVEL
LEIF'S DELI
STANLEY BAKERY
GLOBE TAVERN
JOHN ST
CROZIER PL
SPORTS CENTRE
STANLEY PUBLIC LIBRARY
KAY MCCALLUM'S B&B
DRURY ST
ROSE HOTEL
DEANO'S BAR
THE DOLPHINS GUEST HOUSE
FALKLAND BRASSERIE
FALKLAND ISLANDS COMPANY
MICHELLE'S CAFÉ AND CAKES
MOODY ST
PIONEER ROW
FITZROY RD
THE BREAD SHOP
To Tenacres, Johnson's Harbour, Port San Carlos, Mount Pleasant Airport, and Darwin
KING ST
CARTMELL COTTAGE
WOODBINE CAFÉ
THE PINK SHOP & GALLERY
VICTORY BAR
To Ross Road East, Stanley Cemetery, Lafone House, Whalebone Cove, and Gypsy Cove
BRANDON RD
DAIRY PADDOCK RD
SUE BINNIE'S B&B
BRISBANE ST
VILLIERS
DEAN ST
PHILOMEL ST
WHALEBONE DISPLAY
DAVIS ST
MOON
0 50 yds
0 50 m
CALLAGHAN RD
To Stanley Airport and Cape Pembroke Lighthouse

ORIENTATION

Stanley (population 1,989) occupies a north-facing slope on Stanley Harbour, the protected inner harbor of East Falkland's larger Port William. Most points of interest and businesses are on Ross Road, which stretches east-west along the waterfront, and the parallel John Street and Fitzroy Road.

On the windy ridge top of Stanley Common, south of town, roads lead east to Stanley Airport and west to Mount Pleasant Airport and camp settlements like Darwin, Port San Carlos, and Johnson's Harbour.

THE FALKLAND ISLANDS MUSEUM AND NATIONAL TRUST

Comprehensive in conception and professional in execution, the Falkland Islands Museum (Holdfast Road, Ross Road West, tel. 22727, www.falklands-museum.com) dedicates separate exhibits to local, maritime, military, and natural history. Among the standouts are a well-stocked replica of an early general store, materials on the 1982 war (including an Argentine bunker), and exhibits on camp life, including changing communications transportation.

Dating from the 1950s on the Antarctic Peninsula, the museum's current prize exhibit is the reconstructed **Reclus Hut,** which sheltered researchers from the Falkland Islands Dependencies Survey (FIDS), later renamed and still active as the British Antarctic Survey (BAS). Dismantled and removed from Antarctica in 1996, it was recently reerected here alongside the main museum building.

The Falkland Islands Museum occupies Britannia House, originally built as headquarters for the Argentine airline LADE; after the 1982 conflict, it housed British forces commanders before becoming the museum a few years back. It's open 9:30 A.M.–4 P.M. weekdays and 2–4 P.M. weekends, and also when cruise ships are in town. Admission costs £2.50 per person or its equivalent in dollars or euros.

OTHER SIGHTS

Stanley is pedestrian-friendly, though it's more spread out than some expect, and walking the steep hills can be tiring (especially for elderly

© WAYNE BERNHARDSON

An exhibit at the Falklands Museum recreates an early Islands store.

EIGHT DAYS IN THE FALKLANDS

For visitors to southernmost Patagonia, the Falkland Islands make an intriguing detour, but an inflexible one. There is only one flight weekly, on Saturday, from the Chilean city of Punta Arenas to the Islands' Mount Pleasant Airport. Likewise, travel within the islands requires, for the most part, using air taxis whose itineraries depend on demand rather than fixed schedules. For a visit this short, and with limited accommodations, advance arrangements are virtually essential; depending on availability, other sites could be substituted for those mentioned below.

Day 1

Arrival at Mount Pleasant Airport, with immediate air-taxi connection to Pebble Island, West Falkland. Overnight at Pebble Island Lodge, with visit to 1982 combat sites and nearby seabird and marine-mammal colonies. Alternatively, flight to Saunders Island, with self-catering accommodations; visit to 18th-century ruins of earliest British settlement and bird-rich shoreline.

Day 2

Full-day exploration of Pebble Island wildlife sites, with gentoo and rockhopper penguins, the occasional king penguin, and sea lions. Alternatively, on Saunders, long but rewarding hike to diverse penguin and black-browed albatross colonies at "The Neck."

Days 3–4

Air taxi to Carcass Island, West Falkland, with substantial elephant-seal colonies and many other birds, including an abundance of the rare striated caracara, a remarkably tame predator. Accommodations at Carcass Island Lodge.

Day 5

Air taxi to Sea Lion Island, East Falkland, home to four species of penguins, large elephant-seal and sea-lion colonies, giant petrels, uncommon small birds, and the Falklands' largest remaining stands of native tussock grass, more than two meters high. Accommodations at Sea Lion Lodge.

Day 6

Morning sightseeing on Sea Lion Island, with afternoon air taxi to Stanley. Hotel or B&B accommodations in town.

Day 7

Full-day overland excursion to Volunteer Point to visit king-penguin colony, returning to Stanley in the afternoon. Friday-night pub crawl, if desired.

Day 8

Morning free for sightseeing in Stanley, with early-afternoon departure for Punta Arenas.

© WAYNE BERNHARDSON

Stanley's Christ Church Cathedral and Whalebone Arch are probably the capital's most photographed landmarks.

cruise-ship passengers); the perpetual wind can also be trying. Most visitors start along the waterfront Ross Road, at the Jetty Centre tourist office, and walk west.

Ross Road and Ross Road West

Dating from 1887, built to celebrate Queen Victoria's 50th year on the throne, the **Jubilee Villas** (Ross Road and Philomel Street) are private homes that, with their British brick, bay-window, terraced-row style, seem to have been plucked out of working-class London boroughs.

One block west, dating from 1892, the capital's most imposing building is the Anglican **Christ Church Cathedral** (Ross Road and Dean Street), the seat of the Church of England. Built of brick and stone, with a soaring steeple and stained-glass windows, its interior also memorializes local men who served in two world wars. The cathedral overlooks the **Whalebone Arch,** a sculpture joining the jawbones of two blue whales, erected for the colony's 1933 centennial in the center of an open green.

Stretching west along the waterfront from Dean Street, **Victory Green** commemorates the Allied triumph in World War I; several cannon from the Port Louis settlement, functional 19th-century Hotchkiss guns (fired on ceremonial occasions), and the mizzenmast of HMS *Great Britain* punctuate the neatly trimmed lawns.

One block west, the rehabbed **Stanley Town Hall** is home to the post office, public meetings, and events such as winter dances. A block farther, the **Liberation Memorial** (1982) honors the British soldiers and sailors who died in the 1982 conflict with Argentina; every June 14, Stanley residents gather for a memorial service here.

Appointed by London, the Colony's highest officials have resided in **Government House** (Ross Road West) since the mid-19th century. Bright yellow in summer, spiny gorse hedges and broad lawns separate the house from the street, but not so long ago it was customary for all Island visitors to sign the guest register. With all the economic activity and personnel movement since the 1982 war, the governor has more to do than just socialize, and this tradition has virtually disappeared.

On the shoreline side of Government House, the **Monument to the Battle of the Falklands**

(1918) is an obelisk commemorating the 1914 confrontation in which British naval forces surprised and sank several German vessels. Farther west, one of few still-identifiable Stanley Harbour shipwrecks, the Liverpool-built barque *Jhelum* tilts offshore after being scuttled here in 1870. Nearby is the excellent **Falkland Islands Museum** (Holdfast Road; see separate entry).

Central Stanley

Many of Stanley's surviving stone houses from the 19th century line John Street, one block south of Ross Road. Erected for the Chelsea pensioners, mid-19th century kit houses line **Pioneer Row,** directly uphill from Stanley Town Hall; one of these, **Cartmell Cottage** (7 Pioneer Row), is now open as a museum.

Two blocks farther uphill, local conservationist Mike Butcher displays part of his salvaged **whalebone collection,** including the skull, jaws, and teeth of a gigantic sperm whale, in his yard at Dairy Paddock Road and Davis Street.

Ross Road East and Vicinity

East of Philomel Street, the **Falkland Islands Company** headquarters occupies most of block-long Crozier Place, beyond which Ross Road resumes as Ross Road East and passes **Stanley Cemetery,** whose weathering tombstones tell a great deal about the origins of the Islands' immigrant population.

At the east end of Stanley Harbour, **Whalebone Cove** is the final resting place for several rusting hulks, most notably the handsome three-masted freighter *Lady Elizabeth,* left here after striking a reef in 1913. To the north, still a feasible walk from town, **Gypsy Cove** is home to about 320 breeding pairs of Magellanic penguins, as well as cormorants, night herons, oystercatchers, and small birds; stick to the signed nature trail, as landmines left by the Argentines in 1982 are still a potential hazard on the beach and in some other areas.

Farther east, about seven miles from town, **Cape Pembroke Lighthouse** (1854) is a bit distant for

Conservationist Mike Butcher's garden, at Dairy Paddock Road and Davis Street, expresses local sentiment for saving the great whales.

© WAYNE BERNHARDSON

East of Stanley, Gypsy Cove has a signed nature trail but the beach itself is off limits because of landmines left from the 1982 conflict with Argentina.

most hikers, but it's a common destination for tours out of Stanley. During the 1982 conflict, lighthouse keeper Reginald Silvey used an illegal radio to keep British forces informed of Argentine movements.

ENTERTAINMENT

For most Stanley residents, nightly entertainment involves watching videos at home, but there's always a pub crawl starting at the relatively low-key **Victory Bar** (1-A Philomel Street, tel. 21199, www.victorybar.com), commonly known as "the Vic." One block north, the **Globe Tavern** (Crozier Place and Philomel Street, tel. 22703) is the capital's traditional and, in some ways, more colorful watering hole. A few blocks west, the **Rose Hotel** (1 Brisbane Road, tel. 21067) is another option (it is not, note, a hotel in the accommodations sense).

Live music with local bands, and occasional visitors, takes place in the pubs and on occasion in Stanley Town Hall. Once or twice a month, when the pubs close, Stanley's Fighting Pig Band (www.fightingpigband.com) hosts a show and dance at their home sty The Trough, a remodeled assemblage of eight military Portakabins on Stanley Airport Road. Admission costs £3 and, since it has no liquor license, it's BYOB only.

EVENTS

Under the sponsorship of the Falkland Islands Horticultural Society, March's **Horticultural Show** is a competitive event which, at the end of the day, finishes with an auction of produce and baked goods from Stanley and the camp.

August's Town Hall **Crafts Fair** showcases the efforts of leatherworkers (whose bridles, stirrups, and other gear resemble those of early gauchos), weavers, artists, and photographers.

On Boxing Day, the day after Christmas, **Stanley Sports** resembles a North American rodeo, with horse racing (betting is legal), bull riding, and similar competitions.

SHOPPING

Locally produced items include knitted woolens and leatherwork, and children's toys with penguin motifs, but many souvenirs are imported from the UK.

Stanley has a growing number of outlets, starting with books and maps at the **Jetty Centre** (Ross Road and Philomel Street). Directly opposite Whalebone Arch, the **Boathouse Gallery** (Ross Road, tel. 21145, fax 22674) has a photo gallery, with landscape, wildlife, and underwater prints, and also sells local crafts and standard souvenirs. Immediately west, the FIC's **Capstan Gift Shop** (Ross Road, tel. 27654) also carries local souvenirs and photographic equipment.

Two blocks uphill from the Jetty Centre and half a block west, **The Pink Shop & Gallery** (33 Fitzroy Road, tel. 21399) has prints and crafts by local artists, as well as books and maps.

SPORTS AND RECREATION

Immediately south of Government House, Stanley's **Sports Centre** (Reservoir Road, tel. 27291) includes a public swimming pool, but hours vary—phone ahead or ask the tourist office.

For **fishing,** the nearest site is the Murrell River at the west end of Ross Road, but the improved road network has made other East Falkland sites almost equally accessible.

South Atlantic Marine Services (Ross Road and Dean Street, tel. 21145, fax 22674, www.falklands-underwater.com, dceynon@horizon.co.fk) rents diving equipment and does dive tours. In and around Stanley, shipwrecks, kelp forests, and reefs (with their sea lions and elephant seals) are great attractions for divers.

ACCOMMODATIONS

Reservations are almost essential in Stanley, since accommodations are limited even though quality is good to high.

Conspicuous for its colorful flowerbeds and even more colorful garden gnomes, **Kay McCallum's B&B** (14 Drury Street, tel. 21071, fax 21148, £18 pp) is homey and comfy, with excellent lunches and dinners at modest prices; she's particularly good at curries. Kay's smoking has bothered some guests, but apparently she's reformed. **Stewarts B&B** (12 St. Mary's Walk, tel. 21191, www.tourism.org.fk/pages/scotia.htm, £18.50 pp) is similar.

FALKLANDS PHILATELY

Until the 1982 South Atlantic conflict, the Falkland Islands had a low international profile except among one serious constituency—they made their mark in philately. Since the Islands' first postage stamps appeared in 1878, collectors have treasured Falklands issues, and for more than a century, they were one of the colony's main revenue earners. Economically, they're no longer so important, but neither are they insignificant.

Unlike many newly independent countries in post-colonial Africa and Asia, the Falklands never flooded the market with their stamps, and thus they've kept their credibility among collectors. Falklands stamps are also works of art, thanks to local talents like illustrators Ian Strange and Tony Chater, and painter James Peck.

In Stanley Town Hall, adjacent to the Post Office, the **Philatelic Bureau** (Ross Road, tel. 27159, www.falklands.gov.fk/pb/home.htm) sells Falklands stamps and first-day covers for up to a year after their initial appearance. It's open 9 A.M.–noon and 1:15–4 P.M. weekdays, with longer hours when cruise ships are in port.

Dating from 1863, a stone structure that originally housed a pub, **The Dolphin's Guest House** (46 John Street, tel. 22950, commersons@horizon.co.fk, fprintz@horizon.co.fk, £24 pp) now has 10 modernized guest rooms, a sunny north-facing conservatory for breakfast and tea, and a cozy lounge with a bar and satellite TV.

In a quiet location beyond the cemetery, **Lafone House** (Ross Road East, tel. 22891, arlette@horizon.co.fk, £25 pp with shared bath, £35 pp with private bath, both with breakfast) is a new, immaculate, and spacious private home with a couple spare rooms on a B&B basis. Owner Arlette Betts is also one of Stanley's most hospitable innkeepers.

On the edge of Stanley Common, about 15 minutes out of Stanley on the Mount Pleasant highway, Sharon Halford's **Tenacres** (tel. 21155, fax 21950, www.tenacrestours.horizon.co.fk, £25 pp) is a blend of B&B and farmstay in a comfortable, contemporary house.

MAKING THE CONTINENTAL CONNECTION

Because Buenos Aires has prohibited Chilean charters from using Argentine airspace en route to the Falklands, LAN's scheduled Saturday flights to and from Punta Arenas are increasingly full of cruise-ship passengers. This means, in turn, that independent travelers need to make travel plans carefully or they might have to remain longer than expected in the Islands.

Returning from the Islands, if disembarking in Río Gallegos, Argentina, insist that immigration officials stamp your passport; some travelers exiting Argentina at more northerly border posts have had problems with immigration officials who have accused them of entering the country illegally or overstaying their visas. Some, on the other hand, have backdated entry stamps to the date the individual arrived in the Falklands, which Argentina considers its territory.

Box lunches are available for £5 and evening meals for £10.

Sue Binnie's B&B (3 Brandon Rd, tel. 21051, £30 pp) is a comfortable traditional house with soft-spoken, Spanish-speaking ownership. The centrally located **Waterfront Guest House** (36 Ross Road, tel. 22331, fax 23234, www.thewaterfront@horizon.co.fk, £33 pp) offers B&B accommodations in a rambling house with harbor views.

Stanley's most venerable existing accommodations, the FIC's **Upland Goose Hotel** (20/22 Ross Road, tel. 21455, fax 21520, www.tourism.org.fk/pages/upland-goose.htm, £30 pp, £55/95 s/d), has 17 guest rooms with TV and private bath, a restaurant, and a bar. Rates vary according to the room.

Generally considered Stanley's best, **Malvina House Hotel** (3 Ross Road, tel. 21355, fax 21357, www.tourism.org.fk/pages/malvina.htm, £76/100 s/d with breakfast) is a contemporary hotel on attractive grounds, with a conservatory restaurant.

FOOD

For the largest selection of groceries, there's the FIC's **West Store** (Ross Road and Dean Street, tel. 27660). Open early, **The Bread Shop** (Dean Street, tel. 21273) has excellent fresh bread, pies, pizzas, sausage rolls, and sandwiches. **Stanley Bakery** (Waverley House, Philomel Street, tel. 22692) is also good.

There are several good takeaway choices, starting with **Leif's Deli** (23 John Street, tel. 22721), the **Woodbine Café** (29 Fitzroy Road, tel. 22696) for fish and chips, and **Michelle's Café and Cakes** (2 Philomel Street, tel. 21123), which also serves breakfast and lunch.

Tobacco-free **Shorty's Diner** (Snake Hill and Davis Street East, tel. 22855) has sandwiches, short orders, and desserts. **Deano's Bar** (40 John Street, tel. 21296) serves pub grub including fish and chips, burgers, and curries and fishcakes.

Malvina House Hotel (3 Ross Road, tel. 21355) is traditionally one of the best dinner choices, with full meals in the £16 range.

On the site of the classic Globe Store, which burned to the ground at the end of the 1982 war, the present star on the food scene is the Chilean-run **Falklands Brasserie** (3 Philomel Street, tel. 21159). It would be a good restaurant anywhere, with appetizers such as chicken satay (£4) and parma ham with melon (£5), entrées like garlic chicken (£12) and grilled Falklands lamb (£11), and desserts like tiramisu (£3.25). There's a strong list of mostly Chilean and Spanish wines, and a cheaper lunch menu of sandwiches, pastas, pizzas, and fish and chips.

INFORMATION

At the foot of Philomel Street, the **Jetty Visitor Centre** (Ross Road, tel. 22281, www.tourism.org.fk, jettycentre@horizon.co.fk) is open 8:30 A.M.–5 P.M. weekdays in the summer peak, but keeps weekend and longer hours when cruise

AIRBORNE WITH EDDIE

For anyone who enjoys small planes, FIGAS flights are a treat. With an excellent safety record, the government air service covers every remote settlement, though weight restrictions limit access to some airstrips, particularly on small islands like West Point and New Island. Still, there's no better overview of the Islands and, because flight schedules are demand-driven, tourists sometimes get a lengthy tour before reaching their final destination.

Though the odds are against it, one of FIGAS's outstanding experiences is sharing the cockpit headphones with head pilot Eddie Anderson, who can identify every farmstead and islet he flies over. An outspoken conservationist, he's also been buying up prime conservation sites such as the outer Passage Islands and Elephant Keys, the key breeding site for the notoriously timid giant petrel.

FIGAS comes in for a landing at Pebble Island.

ships are in port. Off-season, hours are noon–3 P.M. daily except Monday.

The local weekly publishes the annual *Penguin News Tourist Guide,* a newsprint booklet with brief description of sights and services both in Stanley and throughout the Islands. It's free of charge at the Jetty Centre.

In the Falkland Islands Community School, the **Stanley Public Library** (Reservoir Road, tel. 27290) holds a large collection of books and papers relating to the Falklands (including the author's 781-page doctoral dissertation!) and Antarctica. Hours are 9 A.M.–noon weekdays, 1:30–5:30 P.M. Monday, Tuesday, and Thursday, 2:30–5:30 P.M. Wednesday, 3–6 P.M. Friday, and 1:45–5 P.M. Saturday.

SERVICES

Standard Chartered Bank (Ross Road between Barrack and Villiers Streets) changes US dollars and euros to British and local pounds, from 8:30 A.M.–3 P.M. weekdays only. There's no ATM, but they'll issue cash advances against MasterCard and Visa.

The **Post Office** (Ross Road at Barrack Street, tel. 27180) occupies part of Town Hall. Hours are 8 A.M.–noon and 1:15 P.M.–4:30 P.M., but it keeps longer and weekend hours when cruise ships are in port.

Public phones, in the Jetty Visitor Centre, the FIC West Store, and some other locations, require prepaid Cable and Wireless phone cards. Internet service at the Jetty Centre, with modem-only connections, is fairly expensive at £1.80 per half-hour.

For efficiently arranging a visit to the Islands, especially for short-term guests, the best choice is **International Tours and Travel** (Beauchene Centre, John Street, tel. 22041, fax 22042, www.falklandstravel.com), which is also the LAN airline rep here.

The other option is **Stanley Services Ltd.** (Airport Road, tel. 22622, fax 22623, www.stanley-services.co.fk).

Alongside the Dolphins Guest House, **Falkland Printz** (John Street, tel. 32185) stocks and develops both color print and slide film.

Near the museum, the **Customs & Immigration Department** (H Jones Road 3, tel. 27340) also sells nautical charts of the Islands. For emergencies, contact the **Falkland Islands Police** (Ross Road between Barrack Street and Villiers Street, tel. 999).

King Edward VII Memorial Hospital (St. Mary's Walk, tel. 27328) has 90 staff and 32 beds; in true emergencies, British military specialists are also available. Care is on a fee-for-service basis, though, and visitors should be certain to have insurance.

The hospital **pharmacy** (tel. 27329) can fill prescriptions.

GETTING THERE

For several years after the 1982 war, the only way to reach the Islands was an expensive Royal Air Force flight from England via Ascension Island. That route still exists, with an irregular schedule, but for the last several years LAN has offered Saturday flights to and from Punta Arenas; one flight per month picks up and drops off passengers in the Argentine city of Río Gallegos. For details, see the Getting There entry at the beginning of this chapter.

GETTING AROUND

FIGAS (tel. 27219, tel. 27303 at check-in desk) flies 10-seat Norman-Britten Islanders to grass airstrips around the Islands on demand, but clients may need to be flexible; **Stanley Airport** (tel. 27309) is about four kilometers east of town.

Typical FIGAS destinations and one-way fares include Bleaker Island (£40), Port Howard (£47), Sea Lion Island (£48), Pebble Island (£54), Saunders Island (£61), and Carcass Island (£73).

For international flights, **Falkland Islands Tours & Travel** (tel. 21775, astewart@horizon.co.fk) offers door-to-door bus service (£13 pp) to Mount Pleasant International Airport.

B.K. Cabs (3 Fitzroy Road, tel. 21344) and Lowe's Taxis (tel. 21381) provide service around town; the average fare is about £2.

For rental cars, try **FIC Automotive** (Crozier Place and Hebe Street, tel. 27680).

East Falkland

East Falkland still has the Islands' best road network, though very little outside town is paved. The best is the Stanley-Mount Pleasant Highway, which links the capital with the airport, continuing to Darwin and Goose Green, but even this is almost entirely gravel and requires caution. From Pony's Pass, about eight miles west of town on this route, the North Camp Road leads to Estancia, where it forks north to Port Louis and Johnson's Harbour, and west to Teal Inlet, Douglas Station, and Port San Carlos. All other routes are four-wheel-drive tracks that are not advisable for locally inexperienced drivers (more than a few British military visitors, for instance, have had to ask farmers for tractors to pull them out of the boggy terrain).

Several Stanley-based operators offer tours in and around Stanley, and overland on East Falkland by road and off-road. In alphabetical order, they include Patrick Watts's **Adventure Falklands** (P.O. Box 223, Stanley, tel. 21383, pwatts@horizon.co.fk), which covers Stanley, wildlife sites at Volunteer Point and Cape Bougainville, and 1982 battlefields (Patrick manned the FIBS radio coverage during the 1982 Argentine invasion); Tony Smith's **Discovery Falklands** (38 Ross Road, tel. 21027, www.discoveryfalklands.com), which does natural history, historical, and battlefield excursions throughout East Falkland; Graham France's **Falklands Forays** (7 Snake Hill, tel. 21624, www.tourism.org.fk/pages/france.htm), which focuses on Stanley and vicinity, including golf and Gypsy Cove; Neil Rowlands's **Hebe Tours** (tel./fax 21561, nrowlands@horizon.co.fk), specializing in wildlife and trout fishing, with rental gear available; and Sharon Halford's **Tenacres Tours** (tel. 21155, fax 21950, www.tenacrestours.horizon.co.fk), whose offerings range from Stanley and nearby battlefields to wildlife sites at Long Island, Volunteer Point, Cape Bougainville, and Cape Dolphin.

THE CAMP

Traditionally, in the Falklands, everything outside Stanley is camp, and camp has been a synonym for hospitality. The term itself derives from the Spanish *campo* (countryside), and it's a common usage among Anglo-Argentines and Anglo-Chileans as well.

In the heyday of sheep farming, Falklands settlements were small company towns on or near sheltered harbors. Since the land reform and subdivision of the 1980s, though, this pattern has changed; many campers have moved to Stanley, the settlements have fewer residents, and many farmers now live in isolated homesteads, at what were once "outside houses." Still, on East and West Falkland, an improved road network has partly compensated for the decline of traditional settlements and their social amenities.

While many camp residents are still involved in sheep farming, an increasing number work wholly or partially in tourism and cottage industries. Some of the best wildlife sites—Sea Lion, Bleaker, Pebble, Saunders, and Carcass Islands, for instance—now boast comfortable lodges and/or self-catering accommodations.

Not so long ago, the idea of charging someone who came to spend a weekend in camp was almost unthinkable—though it was customary to present the host with rum or another small gift. Now, though, for better or worse, the custom of a free bed has nearly disappeared. According to Pebble Island Hotel's Allan White, "I preferred the old way," but the pressure for economic diversification has nearly—though not entirely—eliminated that option. Even so, the hospitality remains.

PORT LOUIS

Open to the public only occasionally, Port Louis still holds ruins of Louis de Bougainville's French settlement of 1764, of Louis Vernet's early-19th-century colony, and the tomb of Vernet's deputy Matthew Brisbane, who took charge after the British displaced Buenos Aires in 1833 (Brisbane died at the hands of renegade gauchos, and other colonists had to flee to an offshore island for their lives). Dating from 1843, the handsome ivy-covered farmhouse is the Islands' oldest habitable building; a museum may be in the works.

Several hours north of the settlement, **Seal Bay** is one of East Falkland's finest wildlife sites, with southern sea lions and many penguins, including Magellanics, rockhoppers, and the occasional macaroni. While access is restricted, some Stanley operators may get permission.

For information on Port Louis, including self-catering accommodations at the settlement's **Garden House,** contact farm owner Peter Gilding (tel. 31060, fax 31061).

JOHNSON'S HARBOUR AND VOLUNTEER POINT

Northeast of Port Louis settlement by a good road, Johnson's Harbour is an essential stop on the Islands' tourist circuit for its thousand-strong colony of king penguins, which are present all year, at its easterly Volunteer Point sector. In addition, there are gentoos, Magellanics, cormorants, and many other birds.

The colorful king, the Islands' largest penguin, has an unusual breeding cycle that can range from 10 months (in the Falklands, at the northern limit of its range) to 14 months (at sub-Antarctic South Georgia). Moreover, that cycle is much less season-specific than its migratory counterparts or even the gentoo, which is also present throughout the year. At the site itself, do not enter the stone circle intended to mark an undisturbed king penguin area.

Owned by Smith Brothers, Johnson's Harbour is a 36,000-acre (14,570-hectare) sheep farm that charges £12.50 per person, per day to visit the colony. From the settlement, the soggy four-wheel-drive track is difficult even for locally experienced drivers, so don't even think about renting a car to get here, in either summer or winter (when vehicle access is almost impossible).

Visitors to the colony can stay at **Volunteer Shanty** (£8 pp), a basic but well-kept shelter. For details, contact George Smith (tel./fax 22190) or the Johnson's Harbour Farm (tel. 31395).

SALVADOR AND CAPE BOUGAINVILLE

Northwest of Stanley via Estancia, Teal Inlet, and Douglas Station, Salvador is the gateway to Cape Bougainville, home to large colonies of rockhopper penguins and the occasional macaroni, plus other seabirds and sea lions. In the hands of the same family since its Gibraltarian founder, Andrés Pitaluga, arrived from South America in the 1830s, it also has elephant seal and sea lion colonies on Centre Island in the estuary of Port Salvador (Salvador Water), near the settlement.

From Stanley, Cape Bougainville is a feasible full-day excursion, but there are also self-catering accommodations at the settlement's **Salvador Lodge** (tel. 31194 or 31193, £10 per person per night, £5 for children under 12).

PORT SAN CARLOS AND CAPE DOLPHIN

At the end of the North Camp Road, the settlement of Port San Carlos is the gateway to Cape Dolphin, a wildlife-rich area a long day's excursion from Stanley. Its long white-sand beach and headlands are home to gentoo penguins, king and rock cormorants, and sea lions, while black-necked swans, grebes, and teals paddle its ponds.

A protected wildlife reserve, Cape Dolphin is irregularly open to the public and it's best to go with a tour from town. At the settlement itself, **Smylie's Cottage** (tel. 41013, £12 pp) is a self-catering unit with central heating and a gas cookstove.

From Stanley, Port San Carlos (commonly known as "KC" for the initials of founder Keith Cameron) is about two hours by road, but the overland track to the Cape is slower.

DARWIN AND GOOSE GREEN

Where a slender isthmus links East Falkland's mountainous north with its undulating southern peninsula of Lafonia, about 60 miles west of Stanley, Darwin once had a population of nearly 200 that has fallen to only four, as most of the farm buildings and houses shifted to nearby

© WAYNE BERNHARDSON

The only surviving ship to have served San Francisco during the California Gold Rush, the *Vicar of Bray* (1841) has formed part of the jetty at Darwin for nearly a century.

Goose Green in the 1920s. The peninsula, whose highest point is only 90 meters above sea level, takes its name from Montevideo merchant Samuel Fisher Lafone, founder of what became the Falklands Islands Company; Lafone's gauchos hunted feral cattle to be slaughtered, their hides processed, at his *saladero.*

Darwin is a historic site, starting with the circular **corral** that dates from *saladero* days before sheep replaced cattle, and it became the center of the FIC's camp operations for more than a century; the weathering headstones at **Darwin Cemetery** tell part of the story. In 1982, the South Atlantic war's deadliest combat took place at Goose Green; military landmarks include a **monument** to British Colonel H Jones, who died leading an assault on Argentine positions, and the **Argentine military cemetery.**

At Goose Green itself, part of the FIC jetty, the decaying remains of the barque ***Vicar of Bray*** (1841) belong to the only surviving ship to have served San Francisco during the California Gold Rush. After spending several decades coasting the Islands, it was blown ashore here in 1912 and incorporated into the jetty.

South of Goose Green, dating from 1927, the **Bodie Creek Bridge** is the world's southernmost suspension span. In the middle of the FIC camp, it simplified communications with the outlying Walker Creek and North Arm settlements.

Former police chief Ken Greenland and his wife Bonnie operate the tastefully modernized **Darwin House** (tel. 32255, fax 32253, darwin.h@horizon.co.fk, £27 pp for B&B accommodations, £46 with half-board, £59 with full board). A nonsmoking facility, its five comfortable guest rooms share baths, while common areas include a sunny north-facing conservatory, large sitting and dining rooms, a substantial library, and a small bar.

The Greenlands also rent the nearby self-catering **Commerson Cottage** and **Peale Cottage** (£15 pp with a £30 minimum). Cottage guests may take meals at the main lodge, where nonguests need reservations except for light snacks. Fresh oysters, farmed nearby by Gavin Hardcastle, sometimes appear on the menu, but mussels are on hold because of red tide conditions.

BLEAKER ISLAND

For wildlife-oriented visitors on a budget, Bleaker Island is an exceptional alternative to more distant and/or costly destinations like Sea Lion and Carcass Islands, which require longer flights and have more expensive accommodations and food. Bleaker can't quite match the diversity of those islands, but it has a scenic rocky shoreline with Magellanic, rockhopper, and gentoo penguins, as well as the occasional king, plus king cormorants and night herons, and a breeding colony of giant petrels.

Because Bleaker has no cats, it also has thriving populations of small birds, and owners Mike and Phyl Rendell are removing rats from offshore islands to further encourage the diminutive species like tussac birds. While there are no breeding sea lions or elephant seals, Bleaker gets occasional visitors.

Bleaker's **Cobb Cottage** (tel. 21355, fax 21357, mrendell@horizon.co.fk, £20 pp) is a comfortable and attractive self-catering kit house with three bedrooms, sleeping a maximum of five persons; if it's full, the Rendells can accommodate extra people in the main house. Rates include a leg of mutton, and there's a small store for supplementary needs.

At its closest, Bleaker is barely half a mile from East Falkland; FIC managers used to ride 20 miles southeast from North Arm and row across to Bleaker, but visitors today prefer FIGAS. Most wildlife is within easy walking distance of the settlement, but there's a Land Rover available for rent (on Bleaker's "hard camp," unlike much of East Falkland, getting bogged is not a serious hazard).

SEA LION ISLAND

For wildlife-lovers who can afford it, compact Sea Lion Island offers more in a smaller area than any other destination in the Islands. Five miles long and barely a mile wide, with landscapes ranging from broad sandy beaches to rocky tussac-topped cliffs, it can boast 47 breeding bird species (including four penguins and five predators), plus large breeding colonies and elephant seals and sea lions.

Sea Lion's single most impressive feature may be the sprawling mixed colonies of rockhopper penguins and king cormorants—for both their visual impact and their odor—but the most ex-

a king cormorant colony at Sea Lion Island

citing one may be the dense plantations of native tussac grass that sometimes conceal bull sea lions that gave the island its name. An unexpected encounter with these large, fierce beasts can be disconcerting.

In the summer breeding season, elephant seals nearly cover the sandy beaches within a few minutes' walking distance of the island's comfortable lodge. Frequenting the nearby tussac, the striated caracara or Johnny Rook *(Phalcoboenus australis)* is one of the world's rarest predatory birds, but it's remarkably tolerant of the human presence.

Owned by the Falkland Islands Development Corporation (FIDC), Sea Lion has very few sheep since its 1990s purchase from Terry and Doreen Clifton, who had restored the native tussac for both wildlife habitat and controlled grazing. In 1986, FIDC chose Sea Lion for the Islands' first dedicated wildlife lodge, where those who are staying only a day can see a bit of everything, while those spending several days can orient themselves and then choose where they wish to concentrate their efforts.

Under a 150-year lease, a British company now operates **Sea Lion Lodge** (tel. 32004, fax 32003, www.sealionisland.com, £95 pp with full board); the onsite manager is Rob McKay, an enthusiastic Scotsman who gives an informative introductory Land Rover tour (£20 pp). Purpose-built from a kit, with a Chilean cook and mostly Chilean staff, the 24-bed lodge is probably the most economically successful of the Islands' wildlife destinations.

West Falkland

Beyond the Falkland Sound, which runs northeast-southwest, the west was the site of Britain's first settlement, at Port Egmont on Saunders Island. Nobody settled West Falkland proper, though, until J.L. Waldron founded a sheep station at Port Howard in the late 1860s, and settlements like Fox Bay, Hill Cove, and Port Stephens followed in short order. Some of these farms remained in the same hands for over a century, while others became FIC property. Several offshore islands, some of them exceptional wildlife destinations, were home to small independent farmers; one of them, Keppel Island, witnessed a curious experiment in missionizing Indians from Tierra del Fuego.

While the population of West Falkland has been declining since the agrarian reform of the 1980s, there's hope that the improved road network and the establishment of Fox Bay Village, on the south coast, as a wool transshipment point, will revitalize the island. The only other surviving large settlement, still run as a traditional sheep station, Port Howard has only 21 permanent residents and has had to lay off personnel. One Falklands humorist has suggested that it would be easy to repopulate the west by enforcing prohibition in Stanley and declaring open licensing hours here.

PORT HOWARD AND VICINITY

Every house has a view at Port Howard, West Falkland's only surviving large farm and the starting point for an improving road system. Most of the island's wildlife sites are a bit distant, but a visit here offers insights into how the large sheep stations worked. Since its sale to former employees in 1987, though, hard times in the wool industry have caused unemployment, population has fallen from 40 to a little more than 20, and the school has closed because there are no children.

One of Howard's outstanding features is the former **manager's house,** now a visitors' lodge. In its present state, this is a gem, but in the past it could also be a burden. According to one experienced observer, a large house was not necessarily a luxury, especially as labor became more scarce and expensive:

> ***Managers' houses have tended to be large not for the convenience of the managers—rather the opposite. They have been used as free hotels by official visitors—OK when servants were obtainable but a burden on wives in particular since in general they were not.***

© WAYNE BERNHARDSON

Port Howard, West Falkland, is a picture-postcard settlement.

Still, as it grazes 42,000 sheep on about 200,000 acres, Port Howard offers possibilities for hiking near Mount Maria, fishing in the Warrah River, golf on a nine-hole course in the settlement, and highway and off-road tours. Occupied by a thousand Argentines in 1982, it saw no serious combat, but there's a small **war museum** here and the British military's occasional live-fire exercises are a reminder of the continuing territorial dispute.

Jim and Lesley Woodward operate the cozy, remodeled, and child-friendly **Guest House at Port Howard** (tel./fax 42175, www.guesthouseporthoward.horizon.co.fk, £16.50 pp with breakfast, £27.50 pp with half-board, £38.50 pp with full board), one of the Islands' best values.

Port Howard Lodge (tel./fax 42187, www.tourism.org.fk/pages/port-howard.htm, £60–65 pp with full board; discounts for children depending on age) provides a glimpse into the apparent comforts that came with privilege—spacious, well-furnished bedrooms with private bath, a large sitting room that now serves as a bar, a dining room that's now the restaurant, and a sunny conservatory that yields luscious grapes in summer. The operators have preserved historic features like the antique crank telephone exchange (since replaced by a digital network), and a handsome assortment of gaucho-style horse gear adorns the walls.

In addition, Howard Lodge offers farm tours (£5 pp) and eight-hour four-wheel-drive and wildlife tours (£30 pp, with a two-person minimum).

HILL COVE AND VICINITY

Almost directly west of Port Howard, now reached by a good road, Hill Cove acquired a certain fame for being the only place in the Islands where a forest plantation, primarily conifers such as pines and Sitka spruce, has been successful. Some specimens reach 50 feet in a land where most ornamentals are stunted and wind-flagged.

Since its subdivision and sale, the settlement is a lesser focus than the outside houses, some of which offer accommodations. On the site of the initial settlement, northeast of Hill Cove proper, Paul and Davina Peck's **Shallow Bay Guest House** (tel. 41007, www.shallowbayfalklands.horizon.co.fk, £20 pp self-catering, £25 pp half-board, £30 pp full board) occupies one of the Islands' oldest stone houses.

Rates at Peter and Shelley Nightingale's **West Lagoons Farm** (tel. 41194, www.westlagoons.com, £33 pp) include full board.

PORT STEPHENS AND VICINITY

Now accessible by road, from Port Howard via Fox Bay Village, the far western settlement of Port Stephens lies on the edge of one of the Islands' most scenic and wildlife-rich areas. Unfortunately, it lacks formal tourist facilities, but for visitors with time and flexibility it's worth exploring the options—perhaps by renting a vehicle at Port Howard, about three hours away.

Just southwest of the settlement, the wildlife sites include **Wood Cove** and **Stephens Peak,** home to enormous mixed colonies of cormorants and rockhopper penguins. **Calm Head,** about two hours from the settlement, provides some of the Islands' most spectacular coastal panoramas. Peter and Anne Robertson, who own this area, do not permit vehicles to enter it; visitors *must* hike from the settlement.

© WAYNE BERNHARDSON

tossing the fleece at Fox Bay West, West Falkland

Formerly part of Port Stephens, **Port Albemarle** was the site of an industrial sealing station, a Colonial Development Corporation fiasco that—fortunately—failed to commercialize sea lion oil after World War II. Most of its ruins have been dismantled, as current owners Leon and Pam Berntsen now live here, but the factory was a suitable metaphor for the misjudgments and neglect that so long characterized London's attitude toward the Islands.

Beyond the sealing station, a large gentoo colony faces the stunning **Arch Islands,** where the South Atlantic seas have eroded a passageway in the largest of the group.

Intending visitors need permission from landowners Peter and Anne Robertson (tel. 42307, par@horizon.co.fk) at the settlement, and Leon and Pam Berntsen (tel./fax 42309, l.p.berntsen@horizon.co.fk) at Albemarle Station. When it's not needed for shearers, the Robertsons rent the **Cadet's Quarters** on a self-catering basis (£30 d, £40 t).

PEBBLE ISLAND

Just off West Falkland's north coast, Pebble Island takes its name from the colorful agates, sometimes polished and turned into jewelry, that litter its westernmost beaches. Visitors come to the 24-mile-long offshore island for its diverse wildlife and landscape: east of the settlement isthmus, a pond-filled plain teems with wildfowl while sea lions breed along the shore; to the west, several penguin species have colonized the coastal greens and headlands, along with giant petrels. There are more than 40 resident bird species.

Immediately north of the settlement, ironically enough, horseshoe-shaped **Elephant Bay** has no elephant seals, but its white crescent beach is the starting point for a two-hour walk to **Little Wreck Point**; at the end, there's a shoreline graveyard of beaked whale skulls, ribs, and vertebrae. Magellanic penguins breed here and swim in the large pond.

On the night of May 14–15, 1982, Pebble was the site of a British commando raid that destroyed 11 Argentine spotter planes—an action that made their naval counter-invasion of East Falkland feasible. On the slope of **First Mount,** just west of

THE FALKLANDS BOOKSHELF

For a good general account of history and natural history, look for Ian J. Strange's *The Falkland Islands* (David & Charles, 1983), but it barely anticipates the dramatic economic and political changes since the 1982 South Atlantic war. Robert Fox's *Antarctica and the South Atlantic: Discovery, Development and Dispute* (BBC Books, 1985) places the territorial controversy in historical context. For military and political details on the war, try Max Hastings' and Simon Jenkins's *Battle for the Falklands* (London, Pan, 1983).

For detail on natural history, try Strange's *Field Guide to the Wildlife of the Falkland Islands and South Georgia* (Harper Collins, 1992), illustrated with the author's exceptional color and black-and-white drawings, and black-and-white photographs. Also well illustrated, Robin Woods' *Guide to Birds of the Falkland Islands* (Anthony Nelson, 1988) focuses exclusively on birds, while Strange covers marine mammals, introduced land mammals, and flora as well.

For a Darwinian perspective, based on archival research at Cambridge, there's Patrick Armstrong's *Darwin's Desolate Islands: A Naturalist in the Falklands, 1833 and 1834* (Picton, 1992). Based on private papers, Michael Mainwaring's *From the Falklands to Patagonia* (Allison & Busby, 1983) chronicles one 19th-century shepherd's family's departure from the Islands to pioneer an *estancia* on "The Coast" of Argentine Patagonia.

In cooperation with the Falkland Islands Trust, the small British publisher Bluntisham Books has a series of well-illustrated booklets that include T. H. Davies' and J. H. McAdam's *Wild Flowers of the Falkland Islands* (1989), John Smith's historical *Those Were the Days* (1989) on Stanley's past, and Julian Fisher's *Walks and Climbs in the Falkland Islands* (1992).

The annual *Falklands Islands Journal* covers a variety of historical and natural-history topics, including local memoirs. It's available in Stanley or in the UK from Jim McAdam (Department of Applied Plant Science, Queens University, Newforge Lane, Belfast BT9 5PX, Northern Ireland, jim.mcadam@dardmo.gov.uk).

Beautifully illustrated with color photographs, and contributions from local writers, Debbie Summers' excellent *Visitor's Guide to the Falkland Islands* (Falklands Conservation, 2001) makes an ideal souvenir; it's available in the Islands for £9.

the settlement, there's a monument to HMS *Coventry*, which sank with at least 10 British helicopters on board after being hit by a missile, about 10 miles to the north. A nearby gravesite marks the resting place of two Argentine pilots whose Learjet came down a short distance from here, but the remains went undetected until 1992.

Some distance west, on a coastal green, there's a substantial gentoo colony with the occasional king, and a mid-sized rockhopper colony with the odd macaroni. Giant petrels also nest on a nearby slope, but visitors should not approach too closely as these easily disturbed birds many abandon their nests.

The former manager's house, **Pebble Island Lodge** (tel./fax 41093, pebblelodge@horizon.co.fk, £65 pp with full board for adults, half-price for children 5–15) has six spacious doubles and one odd compact single entered through its own bathroom; all baths are private but have showers rather than tubs. The enormous sitting room, with excellent natural light, has a self-service bar on the honor system. There is 24-hour electricity from a wind turbine and storage batteries, and 24-hour hot water.

The food—particularly the hake—is well above average by camp standards, with very fine homemade bread and good desserts. There's a respectable choice of wines, mostly Chilean.

Islanders Allan White and Jacqui Jennings, who run Pebble Lodge, offer eight-hour Land Rover tours (£30 pp) that cover western Pebble thoroughly; Allan, who has substantial cruise ship experience in both the South Atlantic and South Pacific, is particularly knowledgeable on natural history but also on the 1982 conflict ("When I

An adult king penguin stands behind a gentoo chick, Pebble Island.

was in England in school, I watched the TV news every night to see what was happening...").

For hikers, the Lodge has Land Rover drop-off service that depends on the distance from the settlement: £5 per person up to four miles, £10 per person up to eight miles, and £15 per person up to 12 miles.

KEPPEL ISLAND

Immediately west of Pebble and north of Hill Cove, rarely visited Keppel has wildlife including penguins and black-browed albatrosses, no permanent inhabitants, and the most extraordinary history of any offshore island. In the early 1850s, the South American Missionary Society occupied Keppel as part of an ambitious project to make Fuegian Indians abandon their livelihood as mobile hunter-gatherers and become sedentary horticulturalists—evangelizing them, of course, in the process.

Among the inhabitants at Cranmer, as the SAMS settlement was known, was Jemmy Button, history's most famous Fuegian. Having traveled to England with Captain Fitzroy on the *Beagle,* learned English, and even met the Queen, Button returned to Tierra del Fuego and resumed his aboriginal ways, though he spent five months on Keppel shortly after it opened. In 1859, in an incident that's still subject to much speculation, he was implicated in the murder of SAMS missionaries at Tierra del Fuego, but acquitted in a Stanley trial.

At remote Keppel, the SAMS operated with little government oversight and even less transparency, leading to suspicions of forced labor and abuse. Many Fuegians died at Cranmer, their graves unmarked, but in all probability crowded living fomented diseases like tuberculosis. In their homeland, living in the open air, the Fuegians survived almost without clothing.

Despite these setbacks, Keppel remained a missionary station until 1898 and, while the number of Fuegians decreased, its produce brought substantial income on the Stanley market. Sold in 1911 to Dean Brothers, owners of nearby Pebble, it operated as a sheep farm until 1992.

Cruise ships often stop at Keppel, where a high relief SAMS emblem embellishes the arch of the mission's woolshed. Several other mission structures are fairly intact, and there remain foundations of several Yahgan houses. More recent buildings are in good condition.

While it's hard to reach Keppel other than on cruise ships, because FIGAS planes cannot land unless there is someone there in case of emergency, some locals have spoken of offering boat tours from nearby Pebble or Saunders, so it's worth asking around. In conjunction with the Falkland Islands Museum & National Trust, the Liverpool Museum has published an excellent, well-illustrated and laminated *Keppel Island Site Guide,* available in Stanley.

SAUNDERS ISLAND

Better than any other island in the archipelago, Saunders blends the attractions of natural history and history—its wildlife is abundant and accessible, but it's also a case study in the Falklands/Malvinas controversy.

© WAYNE BERNHARDSON

trumpeting chinstrap penguin, a rare Antarctic visitor to Saunders Island

The Falklands' second-largest offshore island, at 31,000 acres, Saunders is a roughly U-shaped landmass nearly cut into unequal halves by the roughly east-west Brett Harbour. The settlement, though, occupies a site at Port Egmont, on the relatively sheltered east coast, almost facing Keppel.

History

British marines first established themselves here in 1765, but after France withdrew from Port Louis, Spain discovered and expelled the Port Egmont settlement two years later—nearly sparking a shooting war in Europe. Under pressure, the Spaniards restored the Saunders settlement but, in 1774, Britain suspended its presence for, it said, budgetary reasons. After the British departure, Spanish forces leveled the settlement.

Just north of the current settlement, Port Egmont's surviving ruins include extensive foundations and even some walls, jetties, and garden terraces that, by one account, yielded plentiful produce—mostly root crops such as potatoes and carrots, but also green vegetables such as broccoli, celery, lettuce and spinach.

Ironically enough, long after Britain regained the Islands from Buenos Aires, Saunders became Argentine property. Scottish sheep farmer John Hamilton, who came to the Islands as an FIC shepherd in the late 19th century, re-emigrated to Santa Cruz territory, where he became a major *estanciero;* never losing interest in the Falklands, he purchased several island properties including Saunders. When Hamilton died, though, his Argentine children inherited the property and, until its sale to resident employees in 1987, its ownership was a sore point among Islanders.

Sights

For wildlife-oriented visitors, the big attraction is **The Neck,** a sandy isthmus about four hours' walk from the settlement on the north side of Brett Harbour. On its north side, facing the open ocean, a large gentoo colony and a smaller contingent of kings breed; for some years, a solitary chinstrap penguin has made its home among the gentoos.

The Neck's real highlight is the enormous breeding colonies of rockhopper penguins, cormorants, and especially black-browed albatrosses, who need the steep cliffs and stiff northwesterly winds beneath **Mount Richards** to launch themselves into flight. On land, these stunningly beautiful birds are a bit ungainly but, nearly fearless of humans, they will reward photographers by waddling into close-up range. For tireless hikers, this scenic northern coastline is an ideal way to return to the settlement, but its steepness, slipperiness, and high winds make it potentially hazardous.

Immediately west of The Neck, Magellanic penguins burrow in the coastal greens en route to **Elephant Point** (another four hours on foot), which has a substantial elephant-seal breeding colony, as well as kelp gulls, skuas, and other birds.

February–May, there are whales offshore.

Accommodations and Food

In the settlement proper, farm owners/managers David and Suzan Pole-Evans (tel. 41298, fax 41296, davidpe@horizon.co.fk) rent the self-catering, six-bed **Stone Cottage,** dating from 1875 but with a modernized interior, and the separate 10-bed **R&R House,** most often used by military guests from Mount Pleasant. Rates are £20 per person.

Wildlife enthusiasts, though, usually prefer the **Portakabin** (£40 pp) at The Neck, which has electricity and hot water, and can sleep six, though four would be more comfortable. It also has a gas cookstove and a chemical toilet.

In addition, **Freddie's Karavan** (£10 pp), 40 minutes' ride from the settlement near rockhopper and albatross colonies at Rookery Mountain, sleeps two and has hot and cold water, a peat stove, electric light, and a small gas cookstove; Rover transfers cost £15 per person round-trip. The farm also permits camping (£10 pp) anywhere except The Neck proper (though it's possible not too far away).

Farm schedules permitting, the Pole-Evanses can provide Land Rover transfers to The Neck (£20 pp round-trip), and day tours for visitors who stay at the settlement (£15–20 pp). The farm has a small store and may sell fresh milk and eggs, but visitors should bring supplies from Stanley.

CARCASS ISLAND

For many Islanders and visitors alike, remote and tiny Carcass is their favorite island in the Falklands. At the northwestern edge of the archipelago, it's full of wildlife but, at the same time, it's equally notable for a home-style hospitality that belies its dependence on the tourist trade.

On the island's south shore, Carcass settlement is a sheltered beauty spot whose honeysuckle aroma and 10-foot dracaenas lend it an almost tropical aura. Curious caracaras perch in the Monterey cypress windbreaks outside the lodge's dining-room windows, the younger ones playing like kittens with string that droops from the limbs.

Unlike the larger islands, Carcass has always been a family farm, though it's changed hands several times in nearly a century and a half. The present owners, Rob and Lorraine McGill, run only about 900 sheep and make much of their living from brief cruise-ship visits and overnight guests. On meeting the FIGAS flight, Rob McGill even offers chocolates and juice on the Rover ride into the settlement.

On the shoreline in front of the settlement, the birdlife is numerous and diverse, with kelp geese,

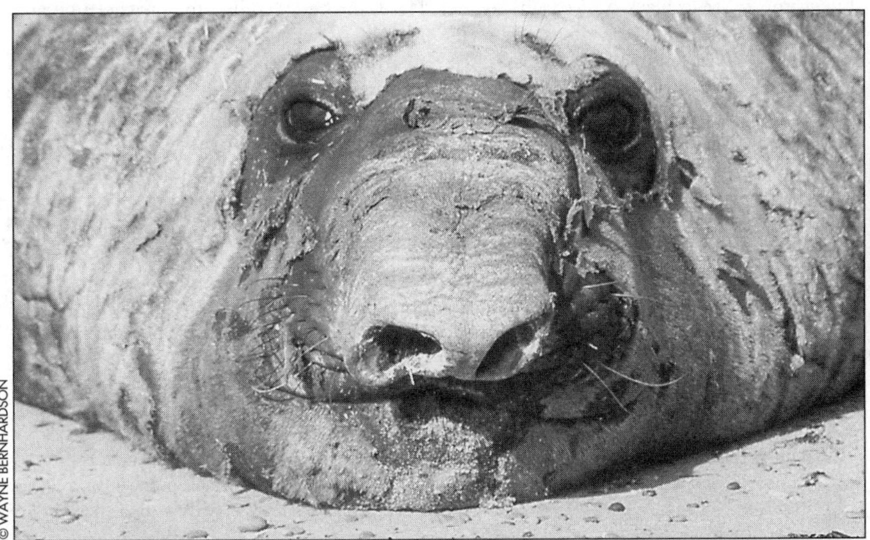

An elephant seal stares warily at Carcass Island.

steamer ducks, Magellanic oystercatchers, Patagonian crested ducks, Cobb's wren, and *tussac* birds (small birds flourish in the absence of cats, rats, and mice). South of the settlement, there's a large tussac grass plantation with gentoo and Magellanic penguins.

At Northwest Point, several miles from the settlement but not far from the airstrip, there's a colony of about 200 elephant seals. The highest point, 723-foot Mt. Bing, yields views of the remote, uninhabited Jason Islands to the northwest.

Carcass, which takes its name from the 18th-century naval vessel HMS *Carcass,* has rooms with private bath in the main house (£60 pp with full board). Thanks to a wind turbine and backup generator, it now enjoys 24-hour electricity. For reservations and/or information, contact Rob or Lorraine McGill (tel. 41106, fax 41107, lorraine@horizon.co.fk).

WEST POINT ISLAND

Southwest of Carcass, separated from West Falkland by a narrow strait called The Woolly Gut, West Point Island has been in the same family since 1879. Like Carcass, it gets plenty of cruise-ship visitors to see its black-browed albatrosses, Johnny Rooks, Magellanic penguins, and rockhoppers, and owner Roddy Napier has replanted native tussac grass on much of the shoreline. Unfortunately, because of its short and thrilling airstrip—probably too thrilling for timid fliers—FIGAS cannot land more than two passengers at a time.

WEDDELL ISLAND

On the southwestern edge of the archipelago, sprawling Weddell is the Falklands' third-largest island, with a representative sample of wildlife and an intriguing history. Like Saunders Island, Weddell belonged to Scottish *estanciero* John Hamilton, and he and his managers undertook audacious agricultural experiments here.

Some of these projects, such as replanting native tussac grass, cultivating experimental forests, and diversifying the livestock with dozens of Highland cattle and more than a hundred Shetland ponies, were commendable even if they met limited success. Others, such as introducing Patagonian foxes, were foolish; expected to provide pelts, the proliferating foxes not only caused high lamb mortality, but also preyed on bird eggs.

Like Saunders, Weddell became Argentine property but, after the war, it was sold to its resident managers, and has since changed hands again to a British owner. Visitors can go to Loop Head, the best wildlife site, for its gentoo and Magellanic penguins, giant petrels, great skuas, night herons, and striated caracaras. For self-catering accommodations, contact **Weddell House** (tel. 42398, fax 42399, www.weddellisland.com, £35 pp).

THE STAATS ISLAND GUANACOS

West of Weddell, uninhabited Staats Island is notable for supporting a population of roughly 400 guanacos, first introduced by John Hamilton in the 1930s. In such a restricted habitat, as its 500 hectares of natural vegetation declined under grazing pressure, biologists would expect large die-offs to keep the population in equilibrium. Into the 1950s, though, hunting kept the population in check—on sporadic visits, Islanders culled upwards of a hundred in a week.

The culling records are, in fact, scratched into the walls of **Waldron's Shanty,** where the hunters sought shelter from wind and rain. Since 1997, though, no culling has taken place—though 20 or so animals may have been poached in 2002. The remarkably stable numbers since then have piqued biologists' interest in the species' population dynamics in what is, for all practical purposes, an ideal natural laboratory.

NEW ISLAND

In more than one sense, New Islands has always been the Falklands' "Wild West." Its rugged, precipitous headlands bursting with wildlife, including rockhopper penguins, black-browed albatrosses, and southern fur seals, it was also a lawless refuge for British and North American sealers and whalers in the late 18th and early 19th centuries. In one celebrated case, during the War of 1812, New England whaler Charles Barnard spent 18 months marooned here after being abandoned by British marines he had rescued from a shipwreck.

Remains of **Barnard's House** still stand here, as do rusting ruins of an early-20th-century **Norwegian Whaling Factory** that folded for lack of whales. In all, New Islands has 41 breeding bird species, including crested and striated caracaras, and the rare thin-billed prion.

Most New Island visitors come from cruise ships, as the airstrip does not permit FIGAS to carry more than two passengers. Its two owners both manage their properties as nature reserves, and only about 50 sheep remain, primarily for food. No smoking is permitted anywhere on the island.

Wildlife illustrator and photographer Tony Chater is the owner of **New Island North Nature Reserve** (tel./fax 42318, tony.kim@horizon.co.fk), while Ian J. Strange established the **New Island South Conservation Trust** (tel. 42317, www.newislandtrust.com) to protect wildlife colonies and historical constructions on the south side.

For an account of Barnard's New Island stranding, look for his memoir *Marooned* (Middletown, CT: Wesleyan University Press, 1979), edited and with an illuminating introduction by Bertha S. Dodge.

Know Patagonia

The Land

Patagonia's diverse geography rises from sea level through desert steppe to Andean forests and fell fields, and continental glaciers. On the Chilean side, west of the Andes, Patagonia is a well-watered and often lushly forested region, while the sparsely vegetated eastern Argentine side lies mostly in the rain shadow of the cordillera.

GEOGRAPHY

Because there's no agreement on what precisely constitutes Patagonia, it's hard to calculate its size, but it's larger than most of the world's countries. From its northernmost point at the source of Argentina's Río Colorado, around 36° S latitude, it's about 2,200 kilometers as the crow flies to Cape Horn, at nearly 56° S. At the widest point, roughly 40° S, it measures nearly 1,000 kilometers from the Atlantic to the Pacific, but it narrows to barely 400 kilometers toward the tip of the continent.

Argentine Patagonia, comprising the provinces of Neuquén, Río Negro, Chubut, Santa Cruz, and Tierra del Fuego, has an area of 786,983 square kilometers, larger than Texas and about the same size as Turkey. This calculation excludes parts of Buenos Aires province north of the Río Negro and south of the Río Colorado, Argentine Patagonia's traditional boundary.

Chilean Patagonia's limits are even more imprecise. South of the traditional Mapuche frontier on the Río Biobío, Chile's contemporary Andean lake district of La Araucanía and Los Lagos, plus the more southerly regions of Aisén and Magallanes, add up to 339,914 square kilometers, only a little smaller than present-day Germany. Counting only the "truly" Patagonian regions of Aisén and Magallanes, though, it would be just 241,058 square kilometers—still as large as the United Kingdom.

Together, the Argentine and Chilean sectors of Patagonia would total 1,126,897 square kilometers, about the size of France, Germany, and the United Kingdom combined, or of California and Texas combined.

Mountains

Patagonia's most imposing physiographic feature is the longitudinal Andean range that extends the length of the continent to southernmost Patagonia, where it gradually disappears beneath the Pacific Ocean. The southern Patagonian Andes are not so high as the uplands of Peru, Bolivia, and northernmost Chile and Argentina, but have many heavily glaciated peaks because of their higher latitude.

One of the world's most seismically active countries, Chile lies at the juncture of the Nazca and South American plates. Positioned along the so-called Pacific "ring of fire," it also has numerous active volcanoes—some of them *very*

© WAYNE BERNHARDSON

According to local legend, anyone who touches the Tehuelche's toe on Plaza Muñoz Gamero in Punta Arenas, Chile, will return to the region.

DEFINING PATAGONIA

Most literary accounts of Patagonia, ranging from Darwin's *Voyage of the Beagle* to Bruce Chatwin's contemporary classic *In Patagonia,* deal primarily with sprawling, thinly populated Argentine Patagonia, not the lesser-known narrow strip of Pacific Chile (possibly even more thinly populated) in the same latitudes.

Part of the problem in defining Patagonia derives from the fact that, in Argentina, there's broad agreement that it's the enormous territory south of the Río Colorado, comprising the provinces of Neuquén, Río Negro, Chubut, and Santa Cruz, and the Argentine sector of the archipelago of Tierra del Fuego (though despite having much in common with those provinces, Tierra del Fuego has its own distinct identity). Neuquén province's northernmost point is only slightly southeast of the Chilean city of Talca, part of a Mediterranean vineyard zone that is clearly not Patagonia. Drawing any line, though, is sure to engender controversy, as the Río Colorado boundary would include parts of Buenos Aires province.

Chilean Patagonia's exact boundaries are imprecise because, in a sense, it's an imaginary region with no formal boundaries, though nearly everybody would agree that both Region XI (Aisén) and Region XII (Magallanes) are at least part of it. Other more northerly areas would like to be included, if only to partake of the Patagonian mystique.

One recent academic collection defines Patagonia as the territory between 39° and 55° S latitude, which would place it slightly south of the Chilean city of Temuco and almost precisely at the Argentine provincial capital of Neuquén. This, though, would still expand the traditional boundaries of Chilean Patagonia and substantially reduce Argentine Patagonia by excluding much of Neuquén province.

Another approach might be ecological. The same collection posits four broad vegetation zones: Patagonian steppe, *coigüe*-dominated southern beech forest, Magellanic moorland, and ice-fields and glaciers. This, though, would disregard Neuquén's northerly steppe and some forested Andean areas (the northernmost occurrence of *coigüe (Nothofagus betuloides)* is around 40° S). It would also omit areas of araucaria forest, a species often identified with Patagonia's northern reaches, especially on the Argentine side, and with its native peoples.

No portrayal of Patagonia can, in fact, overlook its aboriginal peoples. Many were mobile hunter-gatherers like the land-based Tehuelche (with northern and southern branches) and the coastal Kawéskar, Selk'nam, and Yámana in more southerly areas. This pre-Columbian distribution, though, was soon complicated by the trans-Andean movement of semisedentary Araucanians, for whom political borders were merely lines on paper.

It was the combative Mapuche, in fact, whose presence marked the frontier on both sides of the border—deterring colonial Spain and making Argentine and Chilean colonization precarious almost until the 20th century. Even much of present-day Buenos Aires and La Pampa provinces were dangerous for colonists, who suffered raids on their cattle, horses, properties, and persons. In the early 1880s, Chile's southward military advances and General Julio Argentino Roca's euphemistically titled *Conquista del Desierto* (Conquest of the Desert) pushed the frontier south.

In reality, Patagonia does not lend itself to any easy, precise definition. Like the people, plants, and animals that migrate with the season, the years, the decades, the centuries, and even millennia, it shifts with time and perspective. Pinning it down is less important than appreciating and enjoying what it's offered in the past, still offers today, and will offer tomorrow.

active—and many active earthquake faults. The 1960 earthquake centered near the southern city of Valdivia brought a tsunami that devastated coastal areas from Concepción to Chiloé, and left many thousands homeless. In the interim, seismic safety has improved, but earthquakes are not going to disappear.

Steppes

In Patagonia's high latitudes, in the rain shadow of the Andes, bunch grasses and shrubs punctuate the arid, mostly level *meseta* that stretches to the Atlantic. In a few areas, eastward-flowing rivers have cut deep, scenic canyons through the bedrock.

Rivers

On both sides of the Andes, rushing transverse rivers create recreational rafting runs and water to irrigate the vineyards of Neuquén. Some Argentine rivers reverse direction to flow through gaps into the Pacific on the Chilean side, while others like the Río Negro and the Río Santa Cruz traverse the Patagonian steppe to reach the Atlantic.

Chile's largest and most important rivers are the Futaleufú, still providing recreational thrills but threatened with major dam projects; and the remote Baker, which carries the largest flow of any Chilean river.

landscape of Cerro López, Parque Nacional Nahuel Huapi, Argentina

© WAYNE BERNHARDSON

Lakes

Both Argentina and Chile are famous for their Andean lake districts, where the melting ice of Pleistocene glaciers has left a legacy of indigo-filled troughs. Chile's remote Aisén region and Argentina's Chubut and Santa Cruz provinces have countless large lakes barely touched by fishermen. There are also large interior drainage lakes such as Chubut's Lago Musters and Lago Colhué Huapi, and Santa Cruz's Lago Cardiel.

CLIMATE

In the Southern Hemisphere, Patagonia's seasons are reversed from the Northern Hemisphere: the summer solstice falls on December 21, the autumn equinox on March 21, the winter solstice on June 21, and the spring equinox on September 21. For most Argentines and Chileans, the summer months are January and February, when schools are out of session and families take their holidays.

In Patagonia's far southern latitudes, blustery maritime conditions are the rule and seasonal variations can be dramatic, but it's difficult to generalize about climate. Moreover, altitude plays a major role in all areas.

Its receding glaciers particularly sensitive to warming, Patagonia is a living laboratory for climate-change studies. While it's the coolest part of the country, its inclemency is often overstated—despite its geographical position at the southern tip of the continent, it is not Antarctica. Eastern portions of Argentina's Patagonian provinces are even arid steppe, with low rainfall but frequent high winds, especially in summer. Climatically, Tierra del Fuego is an extension of mainland Patagonia.

Flora and Fauna

Much of Patagonia's flora and fauna will be novel to foreign visitors, especially those from the Northern Hemisphere.

CONSERVATION ORGANIZATIONS

Argentina, Chile, and the Falkland Islands all have their own conservation-oriented entities, both governmental and nongovernmental.

Argentina

For information on protected areas, contact the **Administración de Parques Nacionales** (Avenida Santa Fe 680, Retiro, tel. 011/4312-0820, www.parquesnacionales.gov.ar); for more details on the parks themselves, see the summary under Outdoor Recreation in this chapter.

Argentina's preeminent wildlife advocacy organization is the **Fundación Vida Silvestre Argentina** (Defensa 251, tel. 011/4331-4864, Monserrat, Buenos Aires, www.vidasilvestre.org.ar). Foreign membership rates are US$60 per annum; it publishes a monthly newsletter *Otioso* and the magazine *Revista Vida Silvestre.*

For birders, it's the **Asociación Ornitológica del Plata** (25 de Mayo 749, 2nd floor, Buenos Aires, tel. 011/4312-8958, www.avesargentinas.org.ar); hours are 3–9 P.M. weekdays.

The international conservation organization **Greenpeace** also has a Buenos Aires representative (Mansilla 3046, Barrio Norte, tel. 011/4962-0404, www.greenpeace.org.ar).

© WAYNE BERNHARDSON

flower of *Mutisia ilicifolia,* Parque Nacional Lanín, Argentina

Chile

Chile's main government environmental organization, in charge of national parks and other protected areas, is the **Corporación Nacional Forestal** (Conaf, Avenida Bulnes 291, Santiago, tel. 02/3900282 or 02/3900125, www.conaf.cl), which provides information and also sells maps, books, and pamphlets at its Santiago headquarters. It also has offices in every regional capital and some other cities, and visitors centers and/or ranger stations at nearly all its units.

In recent years, nonprofit environmental organizations have proliferated—so much so that that their abundance may have diluted their influence. Many focus on forest preservation, arguably the country's most hot-button issue.

Renace (Seminario 774768, Ñuñoa, Santiago, tel. 02/2234483, www.renace.cl) is a loose alliance of Chilean environmental organizations. The highly professional **Fundación Terram** (General Bustamante 2451, Providencia, Santiago, tel. 02/2694499, www.terram.cl) stresses sustainable-development issues.

The best known forest-preservation organization is **Defensores del Bosque Chileno** (Defenders of the Chilean Forest, Diagonal Oriente 1413, Ñuñoa, Santiago, tel. 02/2041914, www.elbosquechileno.cl). Once again headed by founder Adriana Hoffman, a botanist who served for nearly two years as the Lagos administration's major environmental official, its focus is native forest preservation and restoration.

Chile's oldest environmental organization is the **Comité de la Defensa de Flora y Fauna** (Committee for the Defense of Flora and Fauna, Codeff, Luis Uribe 2620, Ñuñoa, Santiago, tel. 02/2747461, www.codeff.cl). Since 1968, it has primarily focused on practical projects to preserve and restore native plants and animals, often in cooperation with government agencies like Conaf.

Falkland Islands

Falklands Conservation (Jetty Centre, P.O. Box 26, Stanley, tel. 500/22247, www.falklandsconservation.com) is the Islands' main conservation organization. It also has a UK office (1 Princes Avenue, Finchley, London N3 2DA, tel. 44/20/8343-0481).

VEGETATION ZONES

Floral associations are strongly, but not perfectly correlated with latitude and altitude. The environments below appear in greater detail in individual national parks and other geographical entries.

Broadleaf and Coniferous Forest

In the Patagonian lake district, various species of broadleaved southern beech (*Nothofagus* spp.), both evergreen and deciduous, are the most abundant trees. Notable conifers include the *paraguas* (umbrella) or monkey-puzzle tree *Araucaria araucaria,* so called because its crown resembles an umbrella and its limbs resemble the form of a monkey's curled tail. The long-lived *alerce* or *lawen (Fitzroya cupressoides)* is an endangered species because of its high timber value, though most stands of the tree are now protected; it is more common on the well-watered Chilean side.

Except for specialists, Argentines and Chileans refer indiscriminately to conifers as *pinos* (pines), even though the Southern Hemisphere's only true pines (of the genus *Pinus*) occur as garden ornamentals or plantation timber species.

Temperate Rain Forest

In southwestern Chilean Patagonia, heavy rainfall supports dense and verdant coastal and upland forests of mostly *Nothofagus,* though there are many other broadleaf trees and even the occasional conifer such as the *ciprés del los Guaitecas* (*Pilgerodendron*

© WAYNE BERNHARDSON

nalca (Gunnera chilensis), Parque Nacional Queulat, Chile

© WAYNE BERNHARDSON

bark of araucaria tree, Parque Nacional Conguillío, Chile

uviferum, Guaytecas cypress). In some areas, though, this forest has suffered severe depredations at the hands of corporations and colonists.

Patagonian Steppe

In the Andean rain shadow, on the eastern Patagonia plains, Chilean Magallanes, and even parts of Tierra del Fuego, decreased rainfall supports extensive grasslands where the wind blows almost ceaselessly. In some areas, thorn scrub such as the fruit-bearing barberry *calafate (Berberis buxifolia)* is abundant. From the late 19th century, sheep grazing for wool had a tremendous detrimental impact on these natural pastures, but some are recovering as some *estancias* have folded.

Magellanic Forest

From southern Patagonia to the tip of Tierra del Fuego, Argentine and Chilean woodlands consist primarily of dense *Nothofagus* forests that, because of winds and climatic extremes, are nearly prostrate except where high mountains shelter them.

FAUNA

As with the flora, Patagonian fauna are largely correlated with latitude and altitude. The following paragraphs offer only a sample; for details, see individual geographic entries, especially those for national parks and other reserves.

Marine, Coastal, and Aquatic Fauna

The temperate to sub-Antarctic southern Atlantic and Pacific, with their lengthy coastlines and many estuaries, are a storehouse of biological wealth. That wealth, though, is more abundant in numbers of individuals than in diversity of species.

Upwelling nutrients and the north-flowing Peru (Humboldt) Current makes Chile's coastline one of the world's richest fishing grounds (giving Chile's cuisine its character). In the far south, peoples like the Yámana and Kawasqar lived largely on maritime resources.

The main pelagic **fish** in the southern oceans include *congrio* (conger eel, *Genypterus* spp.), *cojinova* (*Seriolella* spp.), corvina *(Cilus gilberti),* and the overexploited *merluza* (hake, *Merluccius hubbsi*) and *merluza negra* (Chilean sea bass or Patagonian toothfish, *Dissostichus eleginoides*). Shellfish and crustaceans, all of them edible, include the relatively commonplace mussel, *centolla* (king crab, *Lithodes Antarctica*), the *ostión* (scallop, *Argopecten purpuratus* or *Chlamys patagonica*), and *calamares* (squid, both *Loligo gahi* and *Ilex argentinus*), the target of a burgeoning fishery between the Argentine mainland and the Falklands. Particularly notable in Chile are the *loco* (abalone, *Concholepas concholepas*), *erizo* (sea urchin, *Loxechinus albus*), and *picoroco* (giant barnacle, *Megabalanus psittacus).*

For more information on seafood, see the Food and Drink entry in this chapter.

Marine mammals include the *lobo marino* (southern sea lion, *Otaria flavescens*), which inhabits the coastline from the River Plate all the way south to Tierra del Fuego and well north into the Pacific. From Argentina's Chubut province south, the southern elephant seal *(Mirounga leonina)* and southern fur seal *(Arctocephalus australis)* are both on Appendix II of the Endangered Species

© WAYNE BERNHARDSON

Commerson's dolphins in the Ría Deseado, Argentina

List (CITES), classified as threatened or regionally endangered.

The most famous of Argentine whales is the southern right whale *(Eubalaena australis),* which breeds in growing numbers in the waters around Península Valdés. Other cetaceans found in southern waters include the blue whale *(Balaenoptera musculus),* the humpback whale *(Megaptera novaeangliae),* the fin whale *(Balaenoptera physalus),* sei whale *(Balaenoptera borealis),* Minke whale, *(Balaenoptera acutorostrata),* pygmy right whale *(Caperea marginata),* and beaked whales (*Berardius* or *Mesoplodon* spp.). The orca or killer whale *(Orcinus orca)* is also present, along with smaller marine mammals such as Commerson's dolphin *(Cephalorhynchus commersonii).*

Terrestrial Fauna

Patagonia's land fauna, especially large mammals, are often nocturnal or otherwise inconspicuous, but they are a diverse lot.

The largest, most widely distributed carnivore is the secretive puma or mountain lion *(Felis concolor).* The smaller Andean cat *(Felis jacobita)* is an endangered species.

The southern river otter *(Lutra provocax)* is an endangered species, while the Argentine gray fox *(Dusicyon griseus)* qualifies as threatened.

Wild grazing mammals include the widely distributed guanaco *(Lama guanicoe),* a relative of the domestic llama and alpaca, which is most abundant on the Patagonian steppe but also inhabits parts of the high Andes. Domestic livestock like cattle, horses, burros, and goats are, of course, very common.

The South Andean *huemul (Hippocamelus bisulcus),* a cervid that appears on Chile's coat-of-arms, is the subject of a joint conservation effort between the two countries. In the mid-19th century, there were some 22,000 in both countries, but at present only about 1,000 survive in each country south of Chile's Río Biobío because of habitat destruction, contagious livestock diseases, and unregulated hunting.

The *pudú (Pudu pudu)* is a miniature deer found in densely wooded areas on both sides of the Patagonian Andes; like the *huemul,* it's difficult to spot.

Chile lacks poisonous snakes, but some species of the venomous, aggressive pit vipers known

A Patagonian fox relaxes at Chile's Parque Nacional Torres del Paine.

collectively as *yarará* (*Bothrops* spp.) range into the northernmost parts of Argentine Patagonia, even south of Península Valdés. They are less common in the southern part of their range than in the subtropical north, however.

Freshwater Fish

In the Andean lake district, introduced species include brook trout *(Salvenilus fontinalis),* European brown trout *(Salmo trutta),* and rainbow trout, and landlocked Atlantic salmon *(Salmo selar Sebago).* Native species (catch-and-release only) include *perca bocona* (big-mouthed perch, *Percichtys colhuapiensis*), *perca boca chica* (small-mouthed perch, *Percichtys trucha*), *puyén* (*Galaxis* spp.), Patagonian *pejerrey (Basilichtys microlepidotus),* and *peladilla (Aplochiton taeniatus).*

Birds

Southern Patagonia's steppes, seacoasts, oceans, and forests can be a wonderland for birders; for visitors and especially dedicated birders from the Northern Hemisphere, the great majority are new additions to their life lists. For recommended birding guides, see Suggested Reading.

The Argentine Pampas' signature species may be the southern lapwing or *tero (Vanellus chilensis),* whose local name derives from its call, but it and other similar species have a wide distribution. With its curved beak, the widely distributed buff-necked ibis or *bandurria* is a striking presence.

The Andean condor soars along the length of the cordillera, while migratory birds like flamingos, along with coots, ducks, and geese, frequent shallow steppe lakes like Lago Musters and even much smaller bodies of water.

In northern Patagonia's dense forests, some birds are heard as often as seen, especially the reticent songbird *chucao.* Others, like the flocks of squawking Patagonian parakeets that flit through the woods, are more visibly conspicuous.

Some 240 bird species inhabit the south Atlantic coastline and Tierra del Fuego, including the wandering albatross *(Diomedea exulans),* with its awesome four-meter wingspan, the black-necked swan *(Cygnus melanocoryphus),* Coscoroba swan *(Coscoroba coscoroba),* flightless steamer duck *(Tachyeres pteneres),* kelp gull *(Larus dominicanus),* and several penguin species, most commonly the Magellanic or jackass penguin *(Spheniscus magellanicus).* Its close relative the Humboldt penguin *(Spheniscus humboldtii)* is an endangered species that ranges far to the north on the Chilean side.

Its numbers reduced on the Pampas, where it roamed before cattle, horses and humans turned native grasslands into ranches and granaries, the

Black-necked swans paddle near the wooden jetty at Puerto Natales, Chile.

ostrich-like *choike* or *ñandú* (greater rhea, *Rhea americana*) still strides across some less densely settled parts of Argentine and Chilean Patagonia. The smaller *ñandú petiso* (lesser rhea, *Pterocnemia pennata*) is fairly common in the provinces of Neuquén, Río Negro, Chubut, and Santa Cruz.

Invertebrates

For purely practical purposes, visitors should pay attention to pests and dangers like mosquitoes, flies, and ticks, which can be serious disease vectors, even though maladies like malaria and dengue are almost unheard of (the mosquito vector for dengue has been spreading southward from the tropics, but the disease itself has not yet been detected). In well-watered rural areas, mosquitoes can be a real plague, so a good repellent is imperative.

The Reduvid, or assassin bug, which bears trypanosomiasis (Chagas' disease) is present in Argentina, though it is hardly cause for hysteria. For detailed information, see the Health and Safety entry in this chapter.

The Cultural Landscape

While Patagonia's natural landscapes, flora, and fauna are fascinating and enchanting, the region also has a cultural landscape, one transformed by human agency over the millennia. Few parts of the region are truly pristine, but their landscapes are no less interesting for all that.

Most of pre-Columbian Patagonia was a thinly populated place of hunter-gatherers who left few conspicuous landmarks—notwithstanding globally significant aboriginal rock-art sites like Santa Cruz province's Cueva de las Manos. Some of the continent's most important early-man archaeological sites are just over the border from Santa Cruz, in the Chile's Magallanes region, and at Monte Verde near Puerto Montt.

In immediate pre-Columbian times, bands of nomadic hunter-gatherers peopled much of Patagonia. Living in smallish bands with no permanent settlements, they relied on wild game like the guanaco (a relative of the domestic llama) and the flightless ostrich-like *ñandú* or rhea, as well as fish, for subsistence. What remains of their material culture is primarily lithic (arrowheads, spear points, and the rounded stone balls known as *boleadoras*).

AGRICULTURE AND THE LANDSCAPE

From the Pampas south, the European invasion utterly transformed Argentina's landscape into first, an open range cattle zone, and then, successively, large fenced sheep and cattle ranches known as *estancias* that dominated the rural economy for over a century. In Patagonia, this took the form of the sheep *estancia,* an extensive unit producing wool for export to Europe and North America.

Across the Biobío, in the Andean lake district, southern Chile's pre-Columbian peoples were shifting cultivators and, as such, their impact on the landscape was not always obvious. Because they cut the forest and used fire to clear the fields before planting, their impact was significant, but long fallow periods allowed the woodlands to recover. Much of what seems to be virgin forest today may in fact be secondary growth.

Because Araucanian Indians on both sides of the Andes resisted the advance of the Spaniards and, then, the Argentines and Chileans, agricultural colonization of Patagonia was spotty until the late 19th century (this, though, did not prevent the Araucanians from adopting European livestock and planting orchards of European fruits such as apples). By the early 1880s, though, Argentine General Julio Roca's ruthless military campaign against them and Chile's advance south of the Biobío ended indigenous autonomy.

On the Chilean side of the border, European settlers transformed the landscape by deforesting large areas and turning them into dairy farms and croplands; in the Aisén region, government incentives encouraged settlers to slash and burn the forest even when they lacked manpower to produce crops that, in any event, had no market.

© WAYNE BERNHARDSON

sorting sheep at Estancia Monte Dinero, Argentina

On the drier Argentine side, irrigation was necessary to develop the Patagonian fruit basket in localities such as the Río Negro and Río Chubut valleys. A few remote localities achieved a certain success, such as Argentina's Los Antiguos and, just across the border, Chile Chico, but their very remoteness made it difficult to get their products to market.

The greatest factors in transforming the natural landscape of the Falkland Islands have been the introduction of domestic animals, first cattle and then sheep, and the impact of fire. Both have nearly eliminated the lush and nutritious native tussac grass, which fringed virtually the entire coastline before the Islands were settled. Other plant species, better adapted to grazing and trampling, have flourished over the landscape.

SETTLEMENT LANDSCAPES

As in the rest of their American dominions, when the Spaniards took control of present-day Argentina and Chile they tried to institute a policy of *congregación* or *reducción.* This meant concentrating native populations in villages or towns for the purpose of political control, tribute or taxation, and religious evangelization. This model had limited success in the northernmost parts of Chile's Andean lake district, and small, dispersed populations made it utterly impractical elsewhere in Patagonia.

Cities, of course, differ greatly from the countryside. By royal decree, Spanish-American cities were organized according to a rectangular grid surrounding a central plaza where all the major public institutions—*cabildo* (town council), cathedral, and market—were located. The logical outgrowth of *reducción* policies, Buenos Aires, Santiago, and other cities were no exception to the rule; the transformation from colonial city to modern metropolis obliterated some landmarks, but the essential grid pattern became an almost universal model for the former Spanish empire.

In the Mapuche countryside south of the Biobío, traditional *rucas,* plank houses with thatched roofs erected with community labor rather than by individual families, have nearly disappeared; they are more common on the Chilean side, where the indigenous population is larger and more cohesive. On the Chiloé archipelago, some neighborhoods of *palafitos* (fishermen's houses on stilts or pilings) have managed to withstand earthquakes and tsunamis.

In colonial cities and towns, houses fronted

directly on the street or sidewalk, with an interior patio or garden for family use; any setback was almost unheard of. This general pattern has persisted, though building materials have mostly changed from adobe to concrete, and high-rise apartment blocks have replaced single-family houses in many urban neighborhoods. Covered by metal cladding and topped by corrugated zinc roofs, southernmost Patagonia's wood-framed, 19th-century "Magellanic" houses affect a Victorian style.

In recent decades, wealthier Argentines and Chileans have built houses with large gardens, on the North American suburban model, in a frenzy of conspicuous consumption—but still surrounded by high fences and state-of-the-art security. Some lie within so-called "gated communities," known in Argentina as *"countries,"* but these are uncommon in Patagonia.

On the Falkland Islands, in the camp, settlement landscapes resemble those of Patagonia's sprawling *estancias,* though in fact these were the prototype for the mainland as landless shepherds emigrated to take up farming in Chile and Argentina. In the Falklands case, they were located close to the shore, to simplify the transfer of wool to Stanley.

Stanley, the Islands' only real "urban" settlement, reminds many visitors of towns and villages in Scotland or Ireland. The capital's older stone houses fit that mold, but the "Magellanic" style of brightly painted, metal-clad houses is as common here as it is on the southern Patagonia mainland and Tierra del Fuego.

Environmental Issues

Like other countries, Argentina and Chile suffer from environmental degradation, though not all indicators are negative.

AIR, WATER, AND NOISE POLLUTION

Aging diesel buses may be the primary culprit in deteriorating urban air quality, but private vehicles (some of which still run on leaded gasoline in Argentina) and taxis contribute more than their share (many taxis and private vehicles, though, run on natural gas). Superannuated factories, with subsidized smokestacks, are another source.

In Patagonia, a different sort of atmospheric problem is critical. Deterioration of the Antarctic ozone layer has exposed both humans and livestock to ultraviolet radiation in summer; though ozone depletion from aerosols is a global problem over which Argentines and Chileans have relatively little control, they suffer the consequences of the growing ozone hole.

Just as motor vehicles cause urban air pollution, so they produce most of its noise pollution, due partly to inadequate mufflers. Buses and motorcycles are the worst offenders, but jet skis on otherwise placid lakes are a source of growing concern.

Drinking water is normally potable, but a historical legacy of polluted waterways derives from, first, the proliferation of European livestock, followed by the processing of hides and livestock, and then by industry. Mining is also a factor; near the town of Esquel, Chubut, there has been concern and vociferous opposition to a Canadian project that would use cyanide, which might find its way into streams and aquifers, to extract gold from local ores.

Salmon farming, a booming and increasingly concentrated industry (10 of 40 registered companies control half the production) cause problems with runoff, from Chile's Andean lake district south into Aisén. Moreover, salmon often escape to colonize streams and seas at the expense of native fish, and some farmers have been accused of killing sea lions that prey on the caged fish.

SOLID WASTE

Like other urban and rural areas, Patagonian cities can produce prodigious amounts of garbage;

despite the presence of isolated landfills, gusting winds can carry their contents for dozens of kilometers or more.

Despite the disposal problems, city streets are relatively clean even if, in the course of the rush toward "development," there's an unfortunate reliance on disposable beverage containers and other undesirable packaging.

ENERGY

Argentina is self-sufficient in fossil fuels and has substantial hydroelectric resources in the subtropical north and along the Andean foothills, but Argentine governments have promoted nuclear power since the 1950s. Not known for its transparency, the Comisión Nacional de Energía Atómica (CNEA, National Atomic Energy Commission) is located in San Carlos de Bariloche.

Even hydroelectricity is no panacea, as it threatens key natural sites in both Argentina and Chile. The most threatened areas are Chile's Río Futaleufú, one of the world's top whitewater rivers, and the isolated Río Baker.

DEFORESTATION AND SOIL CONSERVATION

Native forest conservation is a hot-button issue for many Chilean activists, who have led determined and successful opposition to schemes like the Cascada Chile wood chip project in Region X (Los Lagos), which was canceled in early 2001. In recent years, clandestine logging of protected *alerce* trees in the Andean lake district has caused a scandal.

According to the industry-oriented Corporación de Madera (Corma), 90 percent of the wood that arrives in Chilean factories comes from forest plantations and only 10 percent from native forests. This figure is misleading, though, in the sense that plantations of eucalyptus and Monterey pine have replaced heavily logged native woodlands. Moreover, of the 10 million cubic meters of wood used annually for heating and cooking in Chilean households, 70 percent comes from native forests.

Centuries of livestock activities, both grazing and trampling, have caused serious erosion even in areas where there were never native forests, such as the Pampas and the Patagonian steppes. Even today, some forested national parks—most notably Argentina's Lanín and Los Glaciares—have been unable to eliminate grazing within their boundaries. There has been pressure to create presumably sustainable forest-exploitation projects in Tierra del Fuego's Magellanic woodlands, and road-building into these areas has caused substantial damage.

FISHING

What happens beneath the seas may be less observable than deforestation or air pollution, but there is serious concern that both small and large fisheries are overexploited on both sides of the Andes. Pelagic species like Patagonian toothfish, often known as Chilean sea bass, are clearly vulnerable to overfishing, and some shellfish such as *locos* (abalone) are traditionally vulnerable to overexploitation.

This has repercussions in the region's natural assets—overfishing for squid, for instance, *may* have contributed to Magellanic penguin deaths in the Falklands, but this is a controversial issue that's a reasonable hypothesis rather than a fact. Such issues, unfortunately, often get tied up in political disputes such as Argentina's territorial claims to the Islands, or Chilean fishermen's claims that predation by sea lions is reducing their catches.

The Falklands' big environmental issue for most of their history had been the deterioration of overgrazed pastures, due to high stocking rates and insufficient fencing. In the 1980s, though, the "Squid Rush" of Asian and European fishing fleets forced the British government to declare a conservation zone and licensing regime in offshore waters that had previously been a free-for-all.

Commercial fishing has revolutionized the economy and given the Islands some of the world's highest per-capita income and living standards. At the same time, some have worried that the fishery could collapse if, under pressure to maintain those standards, authorities grant too many licenses.

History

Patagonia has an epic and complex multinational history that started long before it lodged in the European imagination.

PREHISTORY

Human occupation of the Americas is relatively recent. The earliest immigrants reached North America from East Asia more than 12,500 years ago, when sea levels fell during the last major continental glaciation and united the two continents via a land bridge across the Bering Strait. Some researchers believe this migration, interrupted by various interglacial periods during which rising sea levels submerged the crossing, began tens of thousands of years earlier. Nevertheless, by the time the bridge last closed about 10,000 years ago, the entire Western Hemisphere was populated, at least thinly, with hunter-gatherer bands occupying environments that ranged from barren, torrid deserts to sopping rainforests to frigid uplands and everything in between.

One of the continent's oldest confirmed archaeological sites is at Monte Verde, Chile, near present-day Puerto Montt. Radiocarbon dating here has given a figure of 13,000 years at a site at which, according to University of Kentucky archaeologist Tom Dillehay, has some of the continent's earliest evidence of architecture, as well as use of wild potatoes and other native tubers. The most geographically proximate Early Man sites–later than Monte Verde—are 900 kilometers or more to the north.

At least 11,000 years ago, probably several thousand years earlier, the first inhabitants arrived as aboriginal hunter-gatherers who subsisted on guanaco, rhea, and other wild game, and may even have contributed to extinction of megafauna like the ground sloth *Mylodon* and the American horse *Onohippidium saldiasi*.

In cave sites ranging from present-day Neuquén to the tip of Tierra del Fuego, they left clues as to the peopling of Patagonia. Their successors left vivid visual evidence of their way of life in rocky overhangs like Cueva de las Manos, in Santa Cruz province. These were essentially self-sufficient bands; only much later, around A.D. 1000, does ceramic evidence suggest contact between northernmost Patagonia and the central Andean civilizations.

As important as hunting was to the first Americans, gathering wild foods probably contributed more to the diet. As population gradually reached saturation point under hunter-gatherer technology, they began to rely on so-called incipient agriculture, one of whose hearths was the Peruvian highlands, but real farming did not arrive in what is now Patagonia until much later.

In any event, from around 6000 B.C., beans (*Phaseolus* spp.), squash (*Cucurbita* spp.), and potatoes (*Solanum* spp.) became the staples of an agricultural complex that, as population grew, supported a settled village life and, eventually, great Andean civilizations. Maize was a later addition, acquired from Mexico.

When the Spaniards finally arrived, according to one scholar, they found "the richest assemblage of food plants in the western hemisphere." Domestic animals were few, though—only the dog (sometimes raised for food), the guinea pig (definitely raised for food), and the llama and alpaca (both raised for food and fiber, with the llama also serving as a pack animal).

Slower to develop than the Andean region, at least partly due to late demographic saturation, most Patagonian peoples remained nomadic or semi-sedentary until shortly before the Spanish invasion. Some of them sustained a hunter-gatherer way of life even into the 20th century.

PRE-COLUMBIAN CULTURES

In Pre-Columbian times, then, what is now Chile and Argentina comprised a diversity of native peoples who ranged from small isolated bands of hunter-gatherers to semi-urbanized outliers of Inka Cuzco (in present-day Peru). The Inkas' southernmost penetration took them beyond present-day Santiago, but they never managed to conquer the Araucanians—the semi-sedentary Mapuche and the closely related Pehuenche and Puelche withstood both the Inka expansion and, for more than three centuries, the invasion of the Spaniards and their successors. More numerous on the Chilean side of the Andes, they survived because of distance from Cuzco, their mobility as shifting cultivators, and their decentralized political structure—not easily conquered or co-opted by the bureaucratic Inka.

In Patagonia, groups like the Chonos, Tehuelche (Aónikenk), Kawasqar (Alacaluf), Yámana (Yahgan), and Selkn'am (Ona) subsisted by hunting, fishing, and gathering, but introduced European diseases and outright extermination devastated their already small numbers, and sheep displaced the guanaco and rhea on which their livelihood depended.

Toward the end of the 15th century, then, just prior to the Spanish invasion of the New World, southernmost South America was a mosaic of remote peoples who either resisted domination from "civilized" outsiders, or had little or no contact with them.

EARLY HISTORY

Early Patagonian history is complex because of multiple currents of European exploration and settlement. Ferdinand Magellan's legendary expedition of 1519 spent the winter of 1520 in San Julián, Santa Cruz province, before rounding the Horn; Magellan died before returning to Spain on the first circumnavigation of the globe, but his Italian chronicler Antonio Pigafetta aroused European imaginations with exaggerated tales of Patagonian "giants." This first meeting between Europeans and Patagonians was a cordial meeting, but many succeeding encounters were not.

Pigafetta's fanciful description of the Tehuelche was not the only one of its kind, and it took more than two and a half centuries for this sort of exaggeration to fade away. As late as the 1770s John Byron, grandfather of the celebrated poet Lord Byron, fabricated tales of Patagonians whose "middle stature seemed to be about eight feet; their extreme nine feet and upwards . . ."

The word Patagonia itself is a matter of confusion. One explanation is that it derived from the Tehuelches' supposedly oversized feet, but the Spanish word *pata* more correctly means "paw." More probably, it came from the Spanish romance *Primaleón,* in which a giant named Patagón inhabits an island of fur-wearing hunter-gatherers.

Though little explored, the Patagonian interior was also a source of tall tales like the kingdom of Trapalanda or Trapananda, a southern El Dorado (ironically enough, no European saw real geographical marvels like the Moreno Glacier until the 19th century). If Patagonia was a source of tall tales, though, it also saw scientifically serious expeditions like those of the Englishman John Narborough, the Frenchman Louis de Bougainville, the Spaniard Alejandro Malaspina, and, of course, Darwin on the *Beagle.* It was Darwin, in fact, who credibly debunked the lingering legends of "Patagonian giants":

> ***We had an interview at Cape Gregory with the famous so-called gigantic Patagonians, who gave us cordial reception. Their height appears greater than it really is, from their large guanaco mantles, their long flowing hair, and general figure; on an average their height is about six feet, with some men taller and only a few shorter; and the women are also tall; altogether they are certainly the tallest race which we anywhere saw.***

From the North

Christopher Columbus's so-called "discovery" of the "New World" was, of course, one of the signal events of human history. While he may have bungled his way into fame—according to geographer Carl Sauer, "The geography in the mind of Columbus was a mixture of fact, fancy and credulity"—the incompetently audacious Genoan sailor excited the interest and imagination of Spaniards and others who, within barely half a century, brought virtually all of what is now known as Latin America under at least nominal control.

Europeans had roamed the Caribbean for more than three decades after Columbus's initial voyage, but the impulse to conquest in South America came from Mexico and especially Panama, which Francisco Pizarro and his brothers used as a base to take Peru. From Peru, in 1535, Pizarro's partner/rival Diego de Almagro made the first attempt to take Chile by traveling south through what is now northwestern Argentina. Crossing the 4,748-meter Paso de San Francisco from the east, Almagro's poorly organized expedition ended in grisly failure—most of his personnel, retainers, and even livestock died—but this marked the start of the Spanish presence in Argentina and Chile.

Four years later, after defeating an uprising by Almagro, Pizarro designated Pedro de Valdivia to undertake Chile's conquest and, by 1541, Valdivia had founded Santiago. In short order, he founded several other cities on or south of the Biobío, including Concepción, Villarrica, and his namesake city Valdivia, before finally meeting his match, his own former Araucanian slave Lautaro, at the Battle of Tucapel. Before his death—according to some accounts, Valdivia pleaded for his life by offering his captors unimaginable wealth, before dying from a blow to the head—he had laid the groundwork for the country that was to become Chile.

Spanish institutions were most easily imposed in areas that had been under Inka influence, as a long history of hierarchical government made it possible for the Spaniards to place themselves at the top of the pyramid. In much of Spanish America, peoples accustomed to paying tribute to the Inka's delegate now paid it to the *encomendero,* the Spanish Crown's representative.

In the Andean lake district, though, the mobile Araucanians staved off the Spaniards and then the Argentines and Chileans for more than three centuries. In southernmost Patagonia, the Spaniards' situation was even more tenuous, as colonization efforts failed disastrously because of poor planning and difficult environmental conditions.

COLONIAL PATAGONIA

Not permanently settled until 1580, Buenos Aires was not Patagonia, but what happened there affected Patagonia dramatically. On the surrounding Pampas, the Querandí and other indigenous groups had subsisted on guanacos, rheas, and other game, in addition to edible fruits and plants they gathered, but these resources were inadequate, and culturally inconceivable, for the Spaniards.

The failed Pedro de Mendoza expedition of 1535, though, had left behind horses that proliferated on the lush but thinly populated pampas pastures, and the multiplication of escaped cattle from Juan de Garay's 1580 expedition rapidly transformed the Buenos Aires backcountry and northernmost Patagonia into a fenceless feral cattle ranch. The abundance of horses and cattle, nearly free for the taking, resulted in the gaucho culture for which Argentina became famous.

After 1776, when Buenos Aires became capital of the newly created Virreinato del Río de la Plata (Viceroyalty of the River Plate), the Spaniards began to establish a presence in Atlantic Patagonia, founding the cities of Carmen de Patagones and Viedma.

South of the Chilean heartland, the Araucanians quickly adopted the Spanish-introduced horse—bringing mounts across the Andes from Argentina—and staved off the Spaniards and then the Chileans for more than three centuries. In fact, the area south of the Biobío was widely known as a separate country called "Arauco." In distant Patagonia and Tierra del Fuego, the situation was even more tenuous, as tentative Spanish colonization efforts failed disastrously because of poor planning and environmental conditions for which they were unprepared.

The Demise of Colonial Spain

When Napoleon invaded Spain, in the early 19th century, the glue that held its colonial possessions together began to dissolve, leading to independence in several steps. Patagonia was marginal to this struggle, in which an evolving sense of metropolitan identity contributed to political change.

© WAYNE BERNHARDSON

The Victorian-style Kiosco del Centenario marked the centennial of Argentine independence on Plaza Independencia, Trelew.

In the early generations, people identified themselves as Spaniards, but over time criollos (American-born Spaniards) began to differentiate themselves from *peninsulares* (European-born Spaniards). It bears mention that while the mestizos and even the remaining indigenous population may have identified more closely with Argentina or Chile than Spain, it was the criollo intelligentsia to whom independence had the greatest appeal.

The South American independence movements commenced on the periphery, led by figures like Argentina's José de San Martín, Venezuela's Simón Bolívar, and Chile's Bernardo O'Higgins, but their heroism rested on a broad base of support. In Buenos Aires, this base developed as opportunistic and unauthorized British forces, taking advantage of Spain's perceived weakness, occupied the city in 1806 and 1807, but a grassroots uprising ejected the invaders and gave the Porteños confidence.

Returning from Spain, San Martín led criollo forces against royalist armies deployed from Peru, in what is now northwestern Argentina and over the Andes into Chile. As both countries soon declared independence, the polities that would rule Patagonia began to take shape; San Martín honorably refused to head the new Chilean government, leaving it to his colleague O'Higgins.

THE SETTLEMENT OF PATAGONIA

Political independence meant less in Patagonia than it did in the rest of Argentina and Chile, though the isolationist dictator Juan Manuel de Rosas of Buenos Aires dominated a loose confederation of provinces from 1829 until his overthrow in 1852. In the 1830s, he drove the Araucanians westward out of Buenos Aires province toward the Andean lake district, but the real challenge was the Patagonian frontier to the south and west.

In immediate pre-Columbian times, the semisedentary Mapuche and their other Araucanian allies crossed the northern Patagonian Andes freely, occupying Tehuelche territory and mixing with them, and they continued to do so after the Spanish invasion. Acquisition of the Old World horse, which the Mapuche soon mastered, allowed them to keep their autonomy even as the Spaniards and then the Argentines advanced southward. After Darwin met Rosas, he sorrowfully foretold the demise of the aborigines:

> ***Every one here is fully convinced that this is the justest war, because it is against barbarians. Who would believe that in this age in a Christian civilised country that such atrocities were committed?... Great as it is, in another half century I think there will not be a wild Indian in the Pampas north of Río Negro.***

The Argentines and their European immigrant allies advanced on several fronts, by differing means. In the 1860s foreign minister Guillermo Rawson struck a deal granting Welsh dissidents farms in coastal Chubut, from where they moved westward up the river to the Andes. General Julio Argentino Roca, though, wanted to complete the job begun by Rosas, while the Araucanians, for their part, continued to raid the frontier for cattle and horses.

In 1879, the politically ambitious Roca initiated his *Conquista del Desierto* (Conquest of the Desert), a euphemistically titled military campaign that rode ruthlessly across La Pampa, Neuquén, and Río Negro to displace the Mapuche and other Araucanians in favor of settlers' cattle and sheep; at the same time, it was a preemptive strike against Chilean territorial ambitions. On the strength of his military victory, Roca became president in 1880; the subsequent arrival of the railway from the coast accelerated the process and opened the fertile Río Negro valley to agricultural development.

Around the same time, the government began to encourage Scottish settlers, many of them from the Falkland Islands, into the southern territories of Chubut, Santa Cruz, and Tierra del Fuego, to conquer Patagonia with sheep. With the definitive settlement of southern Patagonia, Argentina reached its maximum territorial expansion, though precise boundaries with Chile remained to be settled.

Meanwhile, at the same time Chile warred with Bolivia and Peru for control of nitrate-rich northern deserts, it also managed to turn its attention to the troublesome Araucanian frontier and, soon thereafter, consolidate its position in Patagonia. In 1881, treaties with the Mapuche paved the way for European, largely German, immigration beyond the Biobío. The war with Bolivia and Peru probably cost Chile much of what is now far southern Argentina, but the growth of Punta Arenas, thanks to the California Gold Rush and the subsequent wool boom, contributed to the country's newfound prosperity.

Argentine Patagonia remained peripheral to, though hardly exempt from, the turmoil of 20th-century Argentine phenomena like Peronism and the countless coups that eventually culminated in 1976–1983 "Dirty War," in which a bloodthirsty military dictatorship tortured and killed thousands of mostly leftist opponents and presumed opponents, and led the country into a foolish war with Great Britain over the Falklands (known to Argentines as the Malvinas).

Only a few years earlier, in 1978, the Argentine and Chilean dictatorships had nearly gone to war over three small islands in the Beagle Channel, south of Ushuaia. Papal mediation resolved that conflict without shooting, but General Augusto Pinochet's regime clearly looked the other way when British forces used Chilean territory to conduct mainland commando operations against Argentina in the Falklands war.

Southernmost Patagonia also played a role in the campaign against "subversives" that followed Pinochet's 1973 coup against constitutional president Salvador Allende. Once a Salesian missionary outpost, remote Isla Dawson, southwest of Punta Arenas, served the regime as an inescapable prison camp.

PATAGONIA TODAY

Today, thanks to fishing, industrial preferences, and tourism, Argentine Patagonia (including Tierra del Fuego) is the country's fastest-growing region, with the most positive demographic indicators. Since 1980, Tierra del Fuego's population has nearly quadrupled, while Neuquén's has nearly doubled. Santa Cruz has grown 70 percent, Chubut 57 percent.

Patagonia now has Argentina's highest employment rates outside of Buenos Aires, the highest mean monthly income at US$245, the lowest poverty rates at 18.5 percent, lowest mortality rate at 4.7 per thousand (the nationwide figure is 7.4), the lowest rate of death by heart disease and infection, and the lowest infant mortality. It has the highest percentage rate of potable water and sewer service, and the highest literacy rates.

Ironically, the Argentine economic implosion of 2001–2002 revived the wool industry, as the new exchange rate made the Argentine clip more competitive internationally; at the former one-to-one rate with the U.S. dollar, production costs were impossibly high. At the same time, Australia's depleted wool stocks raised demand elsewhere, and oil price rises made wool more competitive with petroleum-based fibers: Prices that were US$3 per kilogram rose to US$9 per kilogram and, in peso terms, earnings quadrupled. In 2002, mutton exports from Santa Cruz doubled to about US$500 million, thanks partly to worries about mad cow disease in Europe. A delegation of rabbis even visited Río Gallegos to explore the idea of setting up a kosher slaughterhouse for exports to Israel.

Before World War II, Santa Cruz province had had 1,500 *estancias* with 7.5 million sheep, a figure which fell in the 1990s from four million on 1,200 to two million on 600. After a series of bad winters and a natural disaster in the ash-laden 1992 eruption of Chile's Volcán Hudson, some farms were abandoned. Some economically desperate *estancieros* may have even set fires to collect on insurance, and even set outbuildings afire to avoid their designation as historic structures they would have been obliged to maintain (with no economic assistance).

Some beneficiaries of boom have been foreign companies who bought the best properties at bargain prices. In Santa Cruz, sheep still outnumber humans by 10 to one, and Patagonia's largest wool producer, the Italian conglomerate Benetton, owns flagship ranches like Estancia El Cóndor near Río Gallegos. In total, Benetton runs about 280,000 sheep on about 900,000 hectares.

Devaluation also made tourism competitive. For much of the 1990s, Argentines took their vacations in Chile or other "inexpensive" countries like the United States, but the exchange rate trend has totally reversed, so that Chileans and other foreigners are flocking to Argentine Patagonia. Summers since 2003 have been a bonanza for Patagonian tourism; increased demand has brought steadily rising prices, but they're still reasonable by international standards.

Chilean Patagonia's population has also grown, but less dramatically than Argentina's. Since the 1982 census, thinly settled Aisén's population has grown by 38.5 percent, but Magallanes has barely 14 percent more. Much closer and more accessible to Santiago than comparable Argentine provinces, the Andean lake district regions of La Araucanía and Los Lagos have grown by 24.5 percent and 26.4 percent respectively.

As the Chilean peso has strengthened against the dollar and held its own with the Euro, the reversal of the exchange rate has made Chile expensive for Argentine tourists, most of whom have had to take their vacations in their own country instead of Pucón or Puerto Varas. Unlike in Argentina, the Chilean wool sector has not benefited from devaluation and falling production costs for export.

Chile's relatively high travel costs have not yet deterred overseas visitors, though—there's only one Torres del Paine, for instance, and Sernatur officials estimated that, in the 2004–2005 summer season, Patagonian tourism grew nine percent over the previous year.

Government and Politics

In both Chile and Argentina, Patagonian politics differs from the rest of the country in some important ways. Argentine federalism has encouraged a certain provincial autonomy, while Chilean unitarism has engendered skepticism and even resentment in both Aisén and Magallanes. In the case of Magallanes, it's not unusual to see references to the "República Independiente de Magallanes" (Independent Republic of Magallanes), which even has its own unofficial flag.

These are not just theoretical questions. During the Argentine financial collapse of 2001–2002, for instance, Santa Cruz's then-governor (now president) Néstor Kirchner was able to shift US$660 million in provincial oil revenues to overseas banks, thus avoiding the pesification and devaluation of the province's financial assets. Chilean citizens of Magallanes, meanwhile, argue that the decisions that affect their daily lives take place in Santiago, not Punta Arenas.

Traditionally, one of Patagonia's hot-button issues has been "territorial integrity," as the two countries have argued over accurate borders for nearly a century. In the 20th century, border guards even died in shootouts, and full-scale war nearly broke out over three small Beagle Channel islands in 1978. All these disagreements have now been settled, but a handful of extreme nationalists on both sides still grit their teeth and grimace. Some Chileans fret and the more extreme seethe over U.S. environmental philanthropist Douglas Tompkins's initiatives to create private nature reserves and national parks in continental Chiloé (Los Lagos region) and Aisén, in their belief that these compromise the country's territoriality.

The highest-profile territorial issue, though, is Argentina's claims to the Islas del Atlántico Sur (including the British-ruled Falkland/Malvinas Islands and South Georgia) and Antártida Argentina (an Antarctica wedge below 60° S latitude between 25° and 74° W longitude). Many Argentine politicians and citizens of the southern Patagonian provinces, especially Santa Cruz and Tierra del Fuego, are vociferous on the Malvinas issue.

While Argentina is persistent and vocal in its claims to the Falklands and South Georgia, it acknowledges that Antarctic claims are on hold by international treaty. Chile reserves an Antarctic area between 53° and 90° W longitude, but the oldest Antarctic claim belongs to Great Britain: British Antarctic Territory lies between 20° and 80° W latitude. Fortunately, these overlapping claims have not precluded international cooperation on the frozen continent.

In Punta Arenas, Chile, increasing regional sentiment has led to manifestations of an "Independent Republic of Magallanes," which already sports its own flag.

ORGANIZATION

Argentina

Argentina's federal system superficially resembles that of the United States, with executive, legislative, and judicial branches at the national level and parallel institutions for each of the 23 provinces and the Ciudad Autónoma de Buenos Aires (Autonomous City of Buenos Aires).

At the national level, the Congreso Nacional (legislative branch) consists of a 257-member Cámara de Diputados (Chamber of Deputies) and a 72-member Senado (Senate, with three members for each province and Buenos Aires). In reality, as head of the executive branch, the president wields great discretionary powers, often governs by decree, and frequently intervenes in provincial affairs.

Provincial governments establish their own budgets, but the federal government funds them through revenue-sharing—a formula that has led to irresponsibly large deficits in some provinces that the feds are obliged to cover. This varies from province to province—oil-rich Santa Cruz, for instance, is solvent, but Neuquén's extensive social services have put a strain on local revenues.

Chile

Chile's national government consists of separate and legally independent executive, legislative and judicial branches, but its twelve regions, plus the Metropolitan Region of Santiago, lack the autonomy of Argentina's provinces—their governors, for instance, are appointed from the president's office in Santiago. At the same time, municipalities do have considerable autonomy in local matters.

At the national level, the bicameral Congreso

Nacional (National Congress) consists of a 46-member Senado (Senate) and a 120-member Cámara de Diputados, both based in Valparaíso. Only 38 senators are elected, however, as eight are "institutional," including former heads of the armed forces and ex-presidents, a controversial legacy of the Pinochet years. There is strong public sentiment to abolish the institutional senators, but reform efforts have stalled.

Falkland Islands

As a Crown Colony of the British Empire, the Falkland Islands are a political anomaly. The governor is an appointee of the Foreign and Commonwealth Office (FCO) in London and Britain controls foreign and civil service affairs, but the local Legislative Council (Legco) is an elected eight-member body with considerable autonomy. Legco members serve four-year terms, and selected members advise the governor as part of his Executive Council (Exco), along with the chief executive (generally an expatriate Briton recruited and appointed by local government) and financial secretary.

Local political issues are mostly practical matters, including education and public works. On an international level the biggest concern is Argentina, which most Islanders instinctively distrust since the 1982 invasion and before. Related practical issues include air links with Chile, on which Islanders rely for both their own convenience and for the tourism and fisheries industries. Connections with Punta Arenas, their preferred airport, are subject to permission to overfly Argentine territory; the South Atlantic fishery, which is the Islands' main revenue source, relies on migratory stocks that move from Argentine offshore waters into local seas, and vice versa.

Islanders are virtually unanimous that they wish to remain British, but some are more disposed toward friendlier commercial and political relations than others. Those opposed argue that there needs to be greater reciprocity on the Argentine side.

BUREAUCRACY

The government institutions most travelers are likely to come into contact with are immigration, customs, and police. Most visitors have little contact with the Argentine or Chilean military, who were notorious for political repression in the 1970s and 1980s, but have kept a low profile in recent years.

Argentina

Argentine immigration and customs generally treat foreigners fairly, but the police are notoriously corrupt. The capital's Policía Federal are generally superior to provincial forces, some of whom are infamous for shaking down motorists for bribes for minor equipment violations, but this is less common in the Patagonian provinces.

Chile

Unlike most other Latin American countries, Chile has a reputation for relative cleanliness and honesty in public administration—regularly, the country receives the region's highest rating from the anti-corruption organization Transparency International.

Chile's immigration, customs, and police are trustworthy as institutions; the Carabineros (national police) might be best categorized as "firm but fair." There have been instances, though, of renegade cops who rob, steal, and intimidate, especially in lower-class neighborhoods.

Falkland Islands

The Falklands bureaucracy is exemplary in terms of honesty, but unyielding in enforcing rules "by the book." Immigration officials, for instance, invariably question arriving visitors as to their local accommodations, admit them for exactly the time their resources permit, and make it clear that nonresidents may not work. Like the Chilean Carabineros, local police are firm but fair.

Economy

ARGENTINA

To most foreign observers, Argentina's economy is an enigma. Rich in natural resources, with a well-educated populace and modern infrastructure, for most of seven decades it has lurched from crisis to crisis, with the notable exception of the stable, prosperous 1990s. In late 2001, it stunned the world and even many Argentines by defaulting on part of its US$141 billion foreign debt, triggering a political and economic meltdown comparable to the Great Depression of the 1930s.

Much of the problem was attributable to high-level corruption and a rigid exchange policy that was particularly tough on Patagonia, where production costs for wool remained high in international terms. The subsequent devaluation, though, made Patagonian wool an attractive international commodity, and competitive prices spurred a tourism boom throughout the country, but especially in Patagonia.

International tourism, which accounts for about 10 percent of Argentine exports, and domestic travel are significant economic factors. As Argentina's main gateway, the city of Buenos Aires benefits more than any other locality from the tourist trade, but Patagonia is the ultimate destination for many of the two-million plus who pass through the capital.

CHILE

While not Latin America's largest economy, Chile is one of the region's most stable and dynamic. For nearly two decades, its economic performance has been one of almost uninterrupted growth, though the dramatic 7.6 percent average for the decade that ended in 1998 has fallen into the three to four percent range. Growth in southern Patagonian Region XII (Magallanes), though, was less than two percent.

Perhaps the economy's most obvious weakness is its continuing dependence on mining in general and copper in particular. It is also vulnerable to energy shortages, which have created pressure to develop its remote Patagonian rivers for hydroelectricity the country's cheapest energy source, but at great potential environmental cost.

After mining, the single most important export contributor is forestry, constituting roughly 11 percent of exports. It's a controversial sector for environmental reasons, as overexploitation of native forests and their subsequent replacement by plantations of exotics like Monterey pine and eucalyptus have created biological deserts. It's also controversial for social and political reasons, as forestry companies have occupied ancestral lands of the Mapuche, who are increasingly vocal in seeking their return.

One interesting agricultural development is a plan to establish organic agricultural standards for all of Region XI (Aisén), which would ease the export of products like beef to the European Community. This could also apply to fruit-growing in the small but productive "banana belt" around Lago General Carrera, and even to fish farming.

Thanks to the productive north-flowing Humboldt or Peru current that parallels the coast, Chile has become one of the world's leading fisheries countries. A more recent development is salmon farming in the cool ocean inlets and glacial lakes from the Andean lake district south through Aisén and into Magallanes, but this flourishing industry has had high environmental costs.

Tourism is a key economic sector from the Andean lake district to the tip of Cape Horn. Once nearly limited to January and February, the season is lengthening and overseas visitors, in particular, have flocked to Aisén and Magallanes. Chile's Andean lake district lost much of its traditional market, at least temporarily, with the Argentine economic collapse of 2001–2002, and Chilean vacationers aggravated the situation by passing their own holidays at giveaway prices in Argentina.

According to a 2003 survey, poverty is declining throughout most of the country, but southern Patagonian rates in Magallanes and Aisén (Region XII) actually increased in the previous three years, by 2.9 and 4.5 percent, respectively. These regions, though, had relatively low rates of 12 and 14.3 percent compared with the Andean lake district regions of La Araucanía (Region IX) and Los Lagos (Region X), where the rates were 29 and 21.6 percent respectively. On the other, in those regions, poverty had declined about three percent in the period in question; the Araucanía's level, the country's highest, correlates with the impoverished Mapuche population.

FALKLAND ISLANDS

For more than a century, wool dominated the Falklands' economic life through sprawling sheep farms that closely resembled or were even the forerunners of the Patagonian sheep *estancia.* Since 1986 it's a distant second or even third to fishing and tourism. There are about 630,000 sheep on 88 farms, with an average of around 6,400 sheep on about 25,000 acres. Most of the population lives in Stanley, though, where the main employers are government, the Falkland Islands Company (FIC), and small businesses.

In 1986, establishment of an exclusive fishing zone around the Islands led to a licensing regime whose revenues transformed the economy into one that, given the small population, now enjoys one of the world's highest per-capita GDPs and standards of living.

From 1988 through 2003, fishing-license revenues averaged nearly £25 million per annum, with a range from just below £20 million to just over £29 million. For a permanent population of 2,379, yearly per-capita fishing revenue has averaged about £10,500 (more than US$18,600). Though it's the economy's most vigorous sector, it's also vulnerable to boom and bust as squid, the most valuable species, has a short life cycle. In 2004, with apparently falling stocks, local government had to reduce the numbers of licenses and make budget cuts.

Some observers worry that a collapse in squid and other fish stocks could cause revenue shortfalls that would make it impossible to support the Islands' recently improved infrastructure of ports, roads, schools, and new hospital—not to mention the 400 or so civil servants who administer and maintain them. There's hope that offshore petroleum might pick up the slack, but results so far have been mixed—petroleum is present, but it's not clear that the quantity recoverable and the cost of extraction would justify the effort.

For a relatively isolated archipelago, the tourism sector is surprisingly well developed. In the 2003–2004 season, more than 40,000 cruise-ship passengers disembarked in the wildlife-rich Islands at £12 per head in landing fees. The total revenue of some £480,000 (about US$850,000) made this the local government's second-largest revenue earner after fishing. Private sector farmers with wildlife sites also earn landing fees, a valuable supplement to wool and mutton income, and service providers like wildlife lodges, bus and taxi services, a market, and a butcher have also benefited.

Thanks to fishing revenues, Islanders themselves have received a travel allowance of £1 per day (recently reduced to 50p) and can accumulate up to £1,700 before it must be used. While the allowance may be spent locally, most Islanders use it to take trips abroad.

The People

ARGENTINA

According to the 2001 census, Argentina has 36,223,947 inhabitants, but the Patagonian provinces are thinly populated. Among them, Neuquén, Río Negro, Chubut, Santa Cruz, and Tierra del Fuego have less than five percent of the country's population in more than 28 percent of its territory.

Argentina is a country of immigrants, both recent and not-so-recent, and Patagonia's population reflects that history. Spaniards, of course, first colonized what is now Argentina, but a 19th-century tidal wave of Italians, Basques, English, Irish, Welsh, and other nationalities have spread throughout the country. In Patagonia, Anglo-Argentines and Yugoslavs have a high profile, along with working-class Chilotes from the Chilean island of Chiloé.

Argentina has the smallest indigenous population of any South American country except Uruguay, though certain provinces and regions have significant concentrations. There are no definitive statistics, but about 40,000–90,000 Mapuches reside in La Pampa, Neuquén, and Río Negro provinces, with much smaller numbers of Tehuelches and others in the southern provinces of Chubut, Santa Cruz, and Tierra del Fuego.

CHILE

According to the 2002 census, Chile's population is 15,116,435, but, as in Argentina, the distribution is skewed. More than 40 percent of Chileans live in the Santiago Metropolitan Region, and nearly a third in the capital city itself. Only about 2.2 million, less than 15 percent, live in the Andean lake district regions of La Araucanía and Los Lagos, and the Patagonian regions of Aisén and Magallanes, which together comprise about 45 percent of Chilean territory.

In the truly Patagonian jurisdictions of Aisén and Magallanes, the statistics are even more extreme; only about 200,000 people, barely one percent of the population, live on nearly a third of the country's surface. In Aisén alone, fewer than 70,000 residents, less than half a percent of all Chileans, inhabit about a third of the country's territory.

Chile's population is largely mestizo, of mixed Spanish and indigenous heritage, but roughly a million Mapuche inhabit the area south of the Biobío—not to mention Santiago boroughs such as Cerro Navia, La Pintana, El Bosque, Pudahuel, and Peñalolén (80 percent of Chile's indigenous population lives in cities and towns, only 20 percent in the countryside).

The Mapuche, whose vernacular language of Mapudungun is vigorously used, constitute about 90 percent of Chile's total indigenous population; there are remnants of the Kawasqar (Alacaluf) and Yámana (Yahgan) in the southern fjords and rainforests of Aisén and Magallanes.

The surnames of Chile's nonindigenous populations suggest a potpourri of nationalities, from Spanish to Basque, Italian, German, Anglo, and many others, but they do not form such obvious ethnic communities as, say, Italian-Americans in New York or Irish-Americans in Boston. Chilean Patagonia's population ethnically resembles that of Argentine Patagonia, with a particularly strong representation of Croats.

FALKLAND ISLANDS

On a much smaller scale, the Falklands' population distribution is even more extreme than that of either Argentine or Chilean Patagonia. By the 2002 census, the permanent population was 2,379 (excluding 534 civilian support workers at the Mount Pleasant military base). In addition to civilian support staff, Mount Pleasant is home to about 2,000 British servicemen, including officers and "squaddies" on four-month assignments.

Of the Falklands' permanent residents, 1,989 (nearly 84 percent) lived in the capital of Stanley. The other 390 were dispersed among the 12,173 square kilometers of the two main islands, East and West Falkland, and the smaller offshore is-

EL VOSEO

Along with Uruguayans, Paraguayans and some Central Americans, Argentines commonly use the distinctive second-person familiar form of address known as *el voseo* (use of the pronoun *vos*). Spaniards and most other Latin Americans, by contrast, employ the *tuteo* (use of the pronoun *tú*) in most circumstances.

Use of the *voseo*, a mostly archaic form that dates from the 16th and 17th centuries, involves different verb endings for all regular and most irregular verbs. This means adding a last-syllable accent for stress—instead of *tú hablas*, for instance, Argentines will say *vos hablás*. Likewise, with an irregular verb such as *decir* (to say), Argentines will also say *vos decís* rather than *tu dices*.

In the imperative form, there are also differences—instead of *ven* (come), Argentines say *vení*. Negative imperatives, though, are the same in both the *tuteo* and the *voseo*, e.g. *no vengas* (don't come). Some very common verbs, such *ir* (to go) and *estar* (to be) are similarly irregular in both the *voseo* and the *tuteo*, but others are not. In the *voseo*, for instance, *tu eres* . . . becomes *vos sos*. . . .

Despite differing verb forms, Argentines still use the possessive article *tu* and the reflexive or conjunctive object pronoun *te* (*¿te vas?*). Alert travelers will quickly recognize the differences, but before using the form, considered substandard in some contexts, they may wish to refrain from doing so unless absolutely certain that it's appropriate. The *tuteo* is never considered incorrect, though it may sound quaint in some contexts.

lands. Some 1,326 (about 56 percent) were Falklands-born, with as many as seven generations' history in the Islands. Most of the remainder came from the United Kingdom, but there are a Chilean contingent of about 65 and more than 40 other nationalities. Of the Mount Pleasant support workers, more than 400 came from the Atlantic island of St. Helena.

Most of the original 19th-century immigrants were English and Scottish laborers and shepherds, some of whom migrated to "The Coast" of Patagonia, as they referred to it. At the same, Britain has long remained "home" and prosperous landowners traditionally sailed there to escape the austral winter and even sent their children there for secondary and university education.

Today, Falklands schools are on a United Kingdom schedule, so that students who finish their A levels here may now continue their university education in the UK without a break. Thanks to fishing revenues, local government funds university education—"even their beer money," according to one local commentator—even for indifferent students. This, ironically, is the other extreme from the time when university education was the privilege of landowners' children.

LANGUAGE

Spanish is Argentina's official language, but English is widely spoken in the tourist and business sectors of the economy. Foreign language use is also vigorous among ethnic communities such as Italo-Argentines, Anglo-Argentines, and German-Argentines. The Anglo-Argentine and business communities even support a daily tabloid, *The Buenos Aires Herald*, while the German-Argentine community has the weekly *Argentinisches Tageblatt*. Welsh is making a comeback in Chubut province.

Spanish, likewise, is Chile's dominant language, but perhaps 400,000 speak the Mapuche vernacular of Mapudungun, with half of those active users. As in Argentina, English is a fairly common second language in the tourism sector and the business community, and the Chilean government's policy is to broaden the use of the language.

In the Falklands, English is the official language and the language of preference. Many locals handle basic Spanish or better, but some are reluctant to speak it because of their antipathy toward Argentina. At the same time, others are taking Spanish lessons to improve their business communications with the South American continent—preferably with Chile.

Outdoor Recreation

Patagonia offers exciting options for hiking, climbing, and mountain-biking in the Andes; bird-watching on the long Atlantic and Pacific shorelines, the interior drainage lakes, the southern steppes, and the fjords of the southern rainforests; and sightings of marine mammals ranging from seals, sea lions, and dolphins to orcas and the great right whales of Patagonia.

On both sides of the Andes, the runoff permits whitewater rafting and kayaking from the Andean lake districts in the north to Chubut province and Aisén in the south, and sea kayaking in the southern fjords and glacier-fed lakes.

For suggestions as to possible operators, see the Organized Tours entry below.

NATIONAL PARKS AND OTHER PROTECTED AREAS

Both Argentina and Chile have impressive rosters of national parks, reserves and monuments, and some significant provincial reserves as well. In fact, Argentina and Chile were pioneers in setting aside land for conservation purposes, even if they haven't always backed up legislation with sufficient funding, and have sometimes given way to commercial pressures.

Given a land tenure situation in which nearly all its territory is privately owned, the Falkland Islands have no formal national parks, but the northwesterly Jason Islands and some other areas are Crown Reserves. Many farms protect their wildlife zealously, and some have designated parts of their properties, particularly offshore islands, as nature reserves.

Argentina

Argentina's main conservation agency is the Administración de Parques Nacionales (APN, Avenida Santa Fe 690, Retiro, Buenos Aires, tel. 011/4311-0303, www.parquesnacionales.gov.ar). While its selection of brochures on national parks and other protected areas is improving, the staff themselves are best informed on the most high-profile destinations, such as Parque Nacional Los Glaciares. Hours are 10 A.M.–5 P.M. weekdays only. The APN also maintains branch offices in cities such as San Martín de los Andes, San Carlos de Bariloche, El Calafate, and Ushuaia, while rangers staff information offices at many of its parks and reserves.

Argentina has three categories of protected areas: *parques nacionales* (national parks), *reservas nacionales* (national reserves), and *monumentos naturales* (natural monuments), though the practical distinctions among them are not always clear. According to law, the national parks are "areas to be preserved in their natural state, which are representative of biogeographical region and have natural beauty or scientific interest." Often contiguous with national parks, national reserves may be buffers that permit "conservation of ecological systems . . . or the creation of independent conservation zones . . ."

Natural monuments are "places, things, and live animal or plant species, of aesthetic, historic or scientific interest, to which is granted absolute protection." They usually have one outstanding feature, such as the petrified forest of Santa Cruz province, but may also consist of a rare or endangered species such as the southern right whale or the *huemul* (Andean deer).

The following paragraphs summarize the APN's most important units by region but omit some of the less accessible ones; for details, see individual geographical entries. They also include provincial reserves, some of which are, again, covered in detail by individual geographical entries.

In northern Neuquén province, black-necked swans float on the waters of the 11,250-hectare **Parque Nacional Laguna Blanca,** whose namesake lake formed when lava flows dammed a desert stream. Hugging the Chilean border to the southwest, 412,000-hectare **Parque Nacional Lanín** takes its name from the slightly lopsided snow-covered cone that straddles the Chilean border above extensive "monkey puzzle" (araucaria) woodlands.

© WAYNE BERNHARDSON

ice hiking on Glaciar Viedma, Parque Nacional Los Glaciares, Argentina

Pioneer conservationist Francisco P. Moreno spurred the creation of Argentina's first national park, the contiguous 750,000-hectare **Parque Nacional Nahuel Huapi** in Río Negro province, by donating his own land at the west end of the glacial Lago Nahuel Huapi. On a peninsula jutting into the lake's north shore, in Neuquén, the 1,753-hectare **Parque Nacional Los Arrayanes** is a separate unit protecting pure forests of the cinnamon-barked *arrayán* tree, a myrtle relative.

In western Chubut province, south of El Bolsón, **Parque Nacional Lago Puelo** comprises 27,675 hectares of its namesake lake, with its transparently blue-green waters, and forested Andean slopes that give way to treeless fell fields. West of Esquel, the 263,000-hectare **Parque Nacional Los Alerces** is most notable for its humid Valdivian forest, which includes the long-lived, redwood-like *alerce* (false larch).

In eastern Chubut, the Atlantic coastal **Reserva Provincial Península Valdés** is one of the country's major attractions for its diverse wildlife, including whales, sea lions, elephant seals, Magellanic penguins, and other seabirds. Southeast of Trelew, **Reserva Provincial Punta Tombo** is the largest penguin-nesting site, but there are several other reserves along or near southbound RN 3.

Argentina honored its greatest conservationist's name with the creation of northwestern Santa Cruz province's **Parque Nacional Perito Moreno,** an isolated 115,000-hectare park with aquamarine lakes, alpine peaks, and Andean-Patagonian woodlands.

In addition to the world-famous Moreno glacier, southwestern Santa Cruz's 600,000-hectare **Parque Nacional Los Glaciares** has snow and ice-covered pinnacles to match or surpass Chile's Torres del Paine.

On northern Santa Cruz's province's Patagonian steppe, scattered specimens of fossil *Proaraucaria* trees litter the surface of the 13,700-hectare **Monumento Natural Bosques Petrificados.** Thanks to a public-private initiative, the 60,000-hectare **Parque Nacional Monte León,** near the town of Luis Piedra Buena, has become Argentina's second coastal national park. Its only predecessor was the 63,000-hectare **Parque Nacional Tierra del Fuego,** which stretches from the wildlife-rich Beagle Channel coastline through Patagonian forests to the needles of the Andean uplands.

Chile

Chile's main conservation agency is the Corporación Nacional Forestal (Conaf, National Forestry Corporation), which manages the Sistema Nacional de Áreas Silvestres Protegidas (Snaspe, National Protected Areas System). Within Snaspe, Chile has three principal categories of protected areas: *parques nacionales* (national parks), *reservas nacionales* (national reserves), and *monumentos naturales* (natural monuments). In addition, Chilean law allows the establishment of *reservas naturales privadas* or *santuarios de la naturaleza,* private nature reserves of which there are only a few as yet.

Conaf defines each of its *parques nacionales* as "a generally extensive area where there exist either unique or biologically representative environments, not significantly affected by human intervention and capable of self-sustainability, whose flora and fauna or geological formations are of special educational, scientific or recreational interest." Management objectives are to preserve samples of these environments, their cultural and scenic characteristics, the continuity of natural processes, and promote activities associated with education, research, and recreation.

Monumentos naturales are generally smaller areas "characterized by the presence of native flora and fauna, or the existence of geologically relevant sites of scenic, cultural, or scientific interest. Management objectives are similar to those of national parks.

Reservas nacionales are areas "whose natural resources require special attention because of their susceptibility to degradation or importance to the welfare of nearby communities." The primary management objectives are soil and watershed conservation, the preservation of endangered wild flora and fauna, and the application of appropriate technologies to those ends.

The following paragraphs summarize Snaspe's most important Patagonia units but omit some of the least accessible ones; for details, see individual geographical entries. They also include privately owned protected areas, some of which are, again, covered in detail by individual geographical entries.

Within the city limits of the regional capital of Temuco, the 90-hectare **Monumento Natural Cerro Ñielol** is a historic site and also home to Chile's national flower, the *copihue.* Northeast of Temuco, the 6,474-hectare **Parque Nacional Tolhuaca** is a well-kept secret along the banks of the Río Malleco. Directly east of Temuco, the 60,833-hectare **Parque Nacional Conguillío** is famous for its araucaria forests and diverse volcanic landforms, including the 3,125-meter cone of Volcán Llaima. Only a short distance northeast, there's fine hiking at 13,730-hectare **Reserva Nacional Malalcahuello** and the contiguous 13,775-hectare **Reserva Nacional Las Nalcas.**

Near Pucón, southeast of Temuco, there are two popular hikers' parks: the densely forested 12,500-hectare **Parque Nacional Huerquehue** and the 63,000-hectare **Parque Nacional Villarrica,** famed for its namesake smoldering snowcapped cone, 2,840 meters above sea level and Chile's most active volcano.

East of Osorno, the 106,772-hectare **Parque Nacional Puyehue** is locally popular for its hot springs, but the barren volcanic backcountry is truly unique. To the south, east of Puerto Varas, the 231,000-hectare **Parque Nacional Vicente Pérez Rosales** is the gateway to Argentina via Lago Todos los Santos and a bus-boat shuttle to Bariloche.

Southeast of Puerto Montt are two well-forested units, the 39,255-hectare **Parque Nacional Alerce Andino,** so called for its endangered false larch trees, and 48,232-hectare **Parque Nacional Hornopirén,** a wilderness with little access except by foot. On the western shore of the Isla Grande de Chiloé is the rainy, thickly forested 43,507-hectare **Parque Nacional Chiloé.**

At the northern gateway to the Carretera Austral, north of the town of Chaitén, the private **Parque Natural Pumalín** is a 317,000-hectare unit of wondrously verdant temperate rainforest. Southwest of Chaitén, near the Argentine border, the 12,065-hectare **Reserva Nacional Futaleufú** takes its name from the wild whitewater river that flows west.

Near the hamlet of Puerto Puyuhuapi, the 154,093-hectare **Parque Nacional Queulat** is wonderland of temperate rainforest, hanging glaciers, ribbon-like waterfalls and trout-filled streams and lakes. West of the regional capital of Coyhaique, 41,634-hectare **Reserva Nacional Río Simpson** is an equally lush but lower altitude unit that also appeals to fishermen. Just north of the city, the 2,676-hectare **Reserva Nacional Coyhaique** is wild high country only a few minutes from the plaza. Southeast of the city, toward the Argentine border, the 181-hectare **Monumento Natural Dos Lagunas** is a small protected wetland. Southwest of Coyhaique, accessible only by air taxi or by ferry from Puerto Chacabuco, the Campo de Hielo Norte (Northern Continental Ice Sheet) meets the sea at the 1,742,000-hectare **Parque Nacional Laguna San Rafael.** Immediately to its south, the even larger 3,525,901-hectare **Parque Nacional Bernardo O'Higgins** stretches well into Region XII (Magallanes).

South of Coyhaique via an excellent paved road, the towering glacial summits of 179,550-hectare **Reserva Nacional Cerro Castillo** are a popular hikers' destination. Across Lago General Carrera and south of Chile Chico, 161,100-hectare **Reserva Nacional Lago Jeinemeni** is popular with fly-fishermen, as is the 6,925-hectare **Reserva Nacional Lago Cochrane,** east of the town of Cochrane. At the southern terminus of the Carretera Austral, the municipality of Villa O'Higgins has established its own **Parque Cerro Santiago,** a counterpart to Pumalín.

Contiguous with Parque Nacional Bernardo O'Higgins, the 181,414-hectare **Parque Nacional Torres del Paine** is far more famous for its soaring granite towers. To its south, the 189-hectare **Monumento Natural Cueva del Milodón** was once inhabited by the late Pleistocene ground sloth and, later, by early humans. To the southeast, along the border, the cave dwellings at the 5,030-hectare **Parque Nacional Pali Aike** constitute a major archaeological site, and the park is home to guanacos, rheas, and other wildlife.

Several reserves are in the vicinity of the city of Punta Arenas, including two scenic forest units: the 13,500-hectare **Reserva Nacional Magallanes** in the hills only a short distance west of town, and the 18,000-hectare **Reserva Nacional Laguna Parrillar,** which also features wetlands. The 97-hectare **Monumento Natural Los Pingüinos** consists of Isla Magdalena, a huge Magellanic penguin colony in the Strait of Magellan. Across the Strait, just north of the town of Porvenir, the 25-hectare **Monumento Natural Laguna de los Cisnes** is a seasonal wetland.

Several huge units occupy nearly the entirety of archipelagic Magallanes: the 1,097,975-hectare **Reserva Nacional Las Guaitecas,** 2,313,875-hectare **Reserva Nacional Alacalufes,** the 1,460,000-hectare **Parque Nacional Alberto de Agostini,** and the 63,903-hectare **Parque Nacional Cabo de Hornos.**

Falkland Islands

The Falklands have no national parks per se, but several farms are de facto wildlife reserves and a handful have been formally designated so, most notably the 1,181-hectare **New Island North Nature Reserve** and the identically sized **New Island South Wildlife Reserve.** The remote 790-hectare **Steeple Jason Island** belongs to the Wildlife Conservation Society of New York, while the neighboring **Grand Jason Island** is government property, a Crown reserve.

HIKING

Both Argentina and Chile have plenty of ideal hiking terrain, and the number of parks and reserves with integrated and well-maintained trail systems is increasing, but there are still shortcomings. Each country has an Instituto Geográfico Militar whose maps at a scale of 1:50,000 are available for parts of the country, but many trails lack clearly signposted junctions—multiple tracks are the rule. If necessary, try to contract a local guide.

Prime hiking and backpacking areas include the lake districts on both sides of the Andes, where the season tends to be longer than in the far south; throughout the region, the Argentine side tends to be drier than the Chilean side, which receives the brunt of Pacific storms. Of the more northerly parks, the best for hiking are Nahuel Huapi and Lanín on the Argentine side, and Huerquehue, Villarrica, and Puyehue on the Chilean side.

South of the temperate lakes districts, Patagonia can be inclement at any time of year. In Argentina, the northern El Chaltén sector of Parque Nacional Los Glaciares has the best trail network, but things are improving at hard-to-reach Parque Nacional Perito Moreno, which is much less crowded.

Farther south on the Chilean side, the best hiking destinations are Parque Pumalín, whose unique trails include ladders through vertiginously steep forest terrain; Reserva Nacional Cerro Castillo, the best multi-day hiking choice in the Aisén region; and of course Parque Nacional Torres del Paine, whose season is consistently lengthening. Popular Paine, of course, is the most crowded hikers' destination in all of Patagonia, but motivated walkers can still find solitude on its lesser-known trails.

In the Falkland Islands, where wildlife-watching is the main tourist activity and the coastal sites are distant from each other, most people travel by air taxi and four-wheel-drive vehicle. That said, there's plenty of open country and hiking opportunities for those willing to confront the incessant westerlies.

CLIMBING

In both Argentine and Chilean Patagonia, the long Andean cordillera offers a climber's buffet or, for truly committed pilgrims, it can be mecca. For serious technical climbers, the biggest draws are the vertical spires of the Fitz Roy range in Parque Nacional Los Glaciares's El Chaltén sector, or even Parque Nacional Nahuel Huapi's ice-covered 3,478-meter Monte Tronador. Other options include the rest of Parque Nacional Nahuel Huapi near Bariloche, and 3,776-meter Volcán Lanín near Junín de los Andes. A warning: even experienced mountaineers in prime condition have died on these peaks.

Across the Andes, Chile's volcanoes are a particular attraction—from the northernmost lake district to remotest southern Aisén region, Chile is part of the Pacific "ring of fire"—but there is snow, ice, and rock climbing on all kinds of surfaces. Summer is the season for most climbers.

The most frequently climbed Chilean volcano, near the resort town of Pucón, is 2,847-meter Volcán Villarrica, which is also one of the most active; it's a day excursion that's sometimes canceled when Conaf determines that the crater is a little too lively. A local guide is imperative. Volcán Osorno, near the town of Puerto Varas, is also commercially climbed but is more technical.

For general information on mountaineering in Argentina, try the **Centro Andino Buenos Aires** (Avenida Rivadavia 1255, Oficinas 2/3, tel. 011/4381-1566, www.caba.org.ar). There are also local and provincial mountaineering clubs, which appear under the corresponding geographical entry.

Capable independent climbers can tackle many Chilean summits on their own, but peaks near international borders require clearance from the Foreign Ministry's **Dirección de Fronteras y Límites** (Difrol, Bandera 52, 4th floor, Santiago, tel. 02/6714110, fax 02/6971909, jadministrativo@minrel.gov.cl). For this permission, which may be done prior to arrival, each participant must present complete name, passport number, nationality, birth date, residence address, profession, arrival and departure dates in Chile, and a detailed itinerary. Issuing permission usually take two to three days; climbers must present this permission to the nearest Carabineros police station before actually undertaking the climb.

For general information on climbing in Chile, including suggestions on dealing with the bureaucracy, contact the **Federación de Andinismo** (Almirante Simpson 77, Providencia, Santiago, tel. 02/2220888, fax 02/6359089, www.feach.cl, contacto@feach.cl). See also the bilingual **Chile Climbing Page** (www.escalando.cl).

While the Falkland Islands are not a climber's destination per se, the rocky summits of both main islands, though they barely reach 700 meters, can provide challenging recreation.

CYCLING AND MOUNTAIN BIKING

Both long-distance riders and recreational mountain bikers will find Patagonia's spectacular landscapes appealing and rugged terrain challenging. Because many roads have dirt or gravel surfaces, and because paved roads are often so narrow that riding on the shoulder is essential, a mountain bike is the best option. Riders without their own bikes will find rentals readily available in tourist towns like Bariloche and Pucón, but their condition varies widely—check brakes, tires, and everything else before renting.

If touring, carry rain gear, a tent, and supplementary camping gear, and acquire a knowledge of bicycle repairs—some of the finest riding areas have almost no services. Possible routes are countless, but the most popular area is the scenic lake district on both sides of the Andes.

Increasing numbers of cyclists, some of them through riders from Alaska to Tierra del Fuego, are braving the changeable weather on Chile's Carretera Austral, a discontinuous 1,100-kilometer penetration road from Puerto Montt that's now complete to the southern outpost of Villa O'Higgins and even onto El Chaltén, on the Argentine side. Mostly gravel except for a few paved segments around the regional capital of Coyhaique, it still requires several ferry crossings as it passes through some of the continent's most spectacular wild terrain. East of the Andes, between Esquel and El Calafate, Argentina's dusty but charismatic RN 40 parallels the Carretera Austral, but riders need tremendous stamina and sense of balance, as the powerful winds can either stop progress to a crawl or bowl a rider over.

Feasible as early as October, the southernmost Patagonia routes are probably best December–April. As work progresses on the Sendero de Chile, intended to link the Andean uplands for pedestrians, bicycles, and horseback riders only, this will become an even more adventurous alternative.

HORSEBACK RIDING

Gaucho Argentina was born on horseback, and recreational riding is common even in and around Buenos Aires. It's most interesting in the provinces, though, and especially in the rugged terrain of the Andean lake district around Junín de los Andes and Bariloche. Trips range from morning or afternoon trail rides to hard-riding excursions of several days, and nearly all *estancias* offer riding as an optional activity.

saddling up at Campo Aventura, Cochamó, Chile

Likewise, Chile's strong *huaso* tradition makes riding a popular pastime in many lake district and southern Patagonian destinations. The most challenging options are around Pucón and the Cochamó area near Puerto Varas, and in Parque Nacional Torres del Paine. For details in both Argentina and Chile, see the Organized Tours listing below and/or the corresponding geographical entry.

SKIING

Since the seasons are reversed in southern South America, Patagonia's Andean slopes reach their peak in August. While Argentina's international and regional ski resorts may not have the reputation of Chile's best, the mountains near Bariloche have long drawn skiers from around the continent and the world. There are also options at San Martín de los Andes, Villa la Angostura, Esquel, and even Ushuaia.

Chile's famous international ski resorts are close to the capital city of Santiago, but Parque Nacional Villarrica (near the town of Pucón) and Antillanca in Parque Nacional Puyehue (near the city of Osorno) are respectable choices. For up-to-date snowpack statistics, check the Friday edition of the English-language Chile Information Project's travel site (www.chiptravel.cl).

For more detail, see individual geographical entries and the Organized Tours listings below.

BIRDING

Patagonia's diverse natural environments—ranging from Atlantic and Pacific shorelines to boundless steppes with surprising wetlands and Andean woodlands to the sub-Antarctic—mean an opportunity to add lots of new species to your life list. The finest birding areas are the Atlantic and Pacific coasts, the arid eastern steppes, and both sides of the temperate Andean woodlands in the lake districts.

For birding suggestions in Argentina, contact the **Sociedad Ornitológica del Plata** (25 de Mayo 749, 2nd floor, Buenos Aires, tel. 011/4312-8958, www.avesargentinas.org.ar). **Hostería Las Torres** in Chile's Parque Nacional Torres del Paine is also a birding specialist with English-speaking personnel; see also the Organized Tours entry below.

WATER SPORTS

Argentines and Chileans have traditionally flocked to their countries' beaches, riversides, and southern lakes, but have only recently begun to enjoy active water sports like surfing, sea kayaking, windsurfing, diving, and whitewater rafting and kayaking.

Whitewater Rafting and Kayaking

Descending steeply from the Andes, Chile's transverse Patagonian rivers are world-class—more than a few rafters and kayakers consider the powerful Futaleufú, in a remote area near

© WAYNE BERNHARDSON

fishing on the Río Baker, Aisén, Chile

the southern Argentine border, the world's *best* whitewater. The Trancura near Pucón, the Fuy near Panguipulli, the Petrohué near Puerto Varas, and the Baker south of Coyhaique all blend wild water with exquisite scenery, but none of them quite matches the Fu's excitement level.

On the rain-shadow side of the Andes, Argentine rivers lack the tremendous spring snowmelt that turns Chilean rivers into raging whitewater, but there are commercially viable rivers from the Aluminé in northern Neuquén to Esquel in northern Chubut, and the number is growing. The country's top river is the Class IV Río Manso, south of Bariloche.

Nearly all Patagonian rivers may be run from the first October runoff to the early days of April. For details on rafting and kayaking operators, see the Organized Tours listing below, as well as the corresponding geographical entries.

Diving

Diving is not an obvious activity in Patagonia, much of whose waters are cold and lack reefs, but in summer the Argentine city of Puerto Madryn, in Chubut province, has a cluster of diving outfitters and operators for the warm and shallow waters of the Golfo Nuevo. For details, see the Puerto Madryn entry.

Surfing and Windsurfing

The good news is that, with a long coastline and small population of surfers, Patagonia means little competition for waves; the bad news is that Argentina's Atlantic surf is generally tamer than Chile's Pacific, which is wilder but much colder (wet suits are essential here).

Shallow waters and wide tidal ranges may be further deterrents in Argentine Patagonia, but places like desolate Cabo Raso (where competition is zero) are suitable. The waters of the Golfo Nuevo, at Puerto Madryn, are too sheltered for big waves, but the blustery Patagonian winds make it a windsurfer's paradise.

Most Chilean surfers frequent areas well north of the Andean lake district, but there are possibilities near the coastal city of Valdivia. Windsurfing is best on some of the lakes themselves, rather than on the ocean.

Sea Kayaking

The Chilean village of Dalcahue, on the Isla Grande de Chiloé, is a center for commercial sea kayaking, though there are many other suitable locations, among them Puerto Natales and the spectacular Cordillera Darwin on Tierra del Fuego. The channels of Pacific Chile offer exceptional opportunities, such as the river to ocean route from the mouth of the Río Futaleufú to Chaitén via Lago Yelcho and the Río Yelcho.

While the exposed coastline of Argentine Patagonia lacks the sheltered channels and inlets of Pacific Chile, Nahuel Huapi and other large glacial lakes are a more-than-adequate equivalent for sea kayakers.

Fishing

Both Argentine and Chilean Patagonia draw fly-fishing enthusiasts eager to test their skill on lakes, rivers, and fjords from both sides of the Andean lake district to Tierra del Fuego's southernmost tip.

Along the eastern Andean slopes, the rivers of Neuquén and Río Negro provinces have the greatest concentration of fly-fishing possibilities in Argentina. Along Chile's Carretera Austral, in the Aisén region, there are numerous specialized fishing lodges and other resorts that including fly-fishing among their offerings.

For details on fish and fishing, see the Flora and Fauna entry in this chapter, and appropriate geographical entries.

Arts and Entertainment

Both Argentina and Chile have made contributions to the arts and literature well beyond the size of their relatively small populations (there are about 15 million Chileans and 37 million Argentines). Patagonia, though, is still a frontier in Southern Cone arts and entertainment.

LITERATURE

Much of Argentine literature is urban and urbane, but not all of it. In the 19th century, even as the free-roaming gaucho was becoming a wage laborer on the *estancias,* Argentine literature enshrined his most positive qualities in José Hernández's epic poem *Martín Fierro* (1872 and 1879), available in many editions and in English translation. This so-called *gauchesco* (gauchesque) tradition has never completely disappeared.

Born of U.S. immigrant parents in Buenos Aires province, William Henry Hudson (1841–1922) left Argentina for London at the age of 33, but his memoir *Long Ago and Far Away* (1922) is a staple of Argentine public education. An accomplished amateur naturalist, he also wrote *Idle Days in Patagonia* (1893) about his birding explorations. Argentines know him as Guillermo Enrique Hudson.

Chile is famous for its poets; the progenitor of them all was the conquistador Alonso de Ercilla (1533–1594), who paid his indigenous adversaries tribute in his 16th-century epic *La Araucana,* about the southern frontier that is now the lake district. The first Chilean-born poet of note was Pedro de Oña (1570–1643), whose *Arauco Domado* (Arauco Tamed) extols the Spaniards' martial achievements, particularly those of García Hurtado de Mendoza, whom Ercilla had disparaged.

VISUAL ARTS

Buenos Aires is a city of monuments. Unfortunately, many if not most of them are pretentious busts of ostensible statesmen and colossal equestrian statues of military men like Patagonian invader Julio Argentino Roca, who also makes a horseback appearance in Bariloche's landmark Centro Cívico.

Chilean public art can be comparably pompous, but there are agreeable surprises like Castro's Museo de Arte Moderno (Modern Art Museum), on the Isla Grande de Chiloé.

ARCHITECTURE

Argentine architect Alejandro Bustillo, who designed many luxurious Buenos Aires buildings, also created a magnificent northern Patagonian style with Bariloche's landmark Centro Cívico. His many imitators, though, have failed to achieve the same harmony of nature and culture, and many European-styled structures in the region are clearly derivative.

Indigenous architecture survives in thatched Mapuche *rucas,* which are far more common on the Chilean side of the Andean lake district. In Chilean towns like Puerto Varas, 19th-century German immigration has left a legacy of shingled houses that seemingly might have come straight from Bavaria. The archipelago of Chiloé has become a UNESCO World Heritage Site for its remarkable assortment of shingled churches and chapels—the diversity of shingle designs is truly extraordinary—but its remaining *palafitos* (houses on stilts or pilings) are a treasure of vernacular architecture.

Southernmost Patagonia, especially the Chilean city of Punta Arenas, is notable for the mansions erected during the wool boom of the late 19th and early 20th centuries, but also for its more modest wooden-framed, metal-clad "Magellanic" houses. Some of the best of these are in the town of Porvenir, on the Chilean side of the Isla Grande de Tierra del Fuego, but many also remain along Argentine Patagonia's Atlantic coastline and on their side of Tierra del Fuego.

MUSIC

It's hard to identify a distinctive Patagonian music, but even high culture has reached the provinces. Punta Arenas tenor Tito Beltrán (born 1965), a Swedish resident for a decade and a half, is widely considered one of the world's best opera singers in his range and has sung alongside Luciano Pavarotti.

CINEMA

Like the American West, thinly populated Patagonia has a hold on the imagination, but that hasn't quite translated into a comparable cinematic notoriety. Nevertheless, cinephiles can explore the region on video, DVD, and occasionally the big screen.

Chileans have played a greater role on global cinema than most people realize, though it's best not to exaggerate. It has its origins, surprisingly enough, in the tiny Tierra del Fuego town of Porvenir, where German-born José Bohr made an early movie before eventually finding an erratic career in Hollywood.

With state support in the late 1960s and early 1970s, talented but noncommercial Chilean filmmakers like Miguel Littín (born

© WAYNE BERNHARDSON

The famed architect Alejandro Bustillo built Hostería Futalaufquen, in Argentina's Parque Nacional Los Alerces.

1942) did some truly audacious work; he's best known for *Alsino and the Condor* (1983), filmed in exile in Nicaragua, which earned an Academy Award nomination for Best Foreign Film. His most recent effort, though, is *Tierra del Fuego* (2000), characterized by the director as an "existentialist western."

The classic Patagonian film, though, is Argentine director Héctor Olivera's *La Patagonia Rebelde* (1974), based on Osvaldo Bayer's fictional treatment of the Anarchist uprising in Santa Cruz province in the early 1900s.

Fans of the offbeat can look for director Emilio Vieyra's *Sangre de Virgenes* (Blood of the Virgins, 1967), presumably the finest vampire flick ever filmed in Bariloche and available on DVD through the British distributor MondoMacabro (www.mondomacabro.co.uk).

Starting with a bungled Buenos Aires robbery, Marcelo Piñeyro's *Wild Horses* (1995) becomes a road romance that ends with a chase in the Patagonian province of Chubut.

CRAFTS

The artisanal heritage of Argentina and Chile, especially in Patagonia, is less evident than, say, the indigenous textile traditions of the Peruvian or Guatemalan highlands. Still, both the city and the countryside have characteristic crafts.

Indigenous weaving traditions are apparent in Mapuche blankets, ponchos, sweaters, and similar garments on both sides of the Andean lake district. Mapuche silversmiths are heir to an equally impressive tradition.

Befitting their origins on the Río de la Plata (literally, "River of Silver"), Argentine silversmiths create truly intricate jewelry, as well as adornments such as the large-bladed *facón* (knife) and *espuelas* (spurs) that accompany traditional gaucho clothing.

Expert leatherworkers, in turn, produce gaucho-style clothing and horse gear such as *rastras* (belts), reins, and saddles. Both these traditions come together in the production of paraphernalia for *mate,* the herbal "Paraguayan tea," whose consumption is a cultural bellwether. Traditionally, *mate* (the herb) is sipped with a silver *bombilla* (straw) from a *mate* (gourd, in a different context), which may be mounted in a leather holder.

Throughout the Chilean heartland and well into the south, *huaso* horse gear has its own unique features—look for the elaborately carved stirrups in particular. Carvers in the Chiloé archipelago produce model *dalcas* (dugouts), *palafitos* (houses on pilings), and dolls.

ENTERTAINMENT

Even in the Patagonian provinces, Argentines are night people—discos and dance clubs, for instance, may not even *open* until 1 A.M. or so, and stay open until dawn. Chileans are less so, but by North American or Northern European standards, they often keep remarkably late hours.

Bars, Clubs, and Discos

Patagonian cities like Bariloche have the largest numbers of places to dance and drink; rock and techno, but sometimes Latin styles like salsa, are the music of choice. Cavernous dance clubs *(boliches)* can have state-of-the-art sound systems and recorded techno, but some smaller, more interesting venues have live folk, rock, and even jazz.

In Argentina, the distinction between cafés and bars is not always obvious—in fact, it's often more a continuum than a dichotomy. Some of the more stylish (or pretentious) bars often go by the English "pub," but call themselves Irish.

Cinemas

In some provincial cities, the central cinemas have closed but multiplexes have also opened in suburban areas. Cultural centers and universities in regional capitals often reprise classics or show less commercial movies.

Most imported films appear in the original language, with Spanish subtitles. The major exceptions are animated and children's films, which are invariably dubbed into Spanish.

HOLIDAYS, FESTIVALS, AND EVENTS

Government offices and most businesses close on national holidays, more than half of which are religious observations. The summer months of January and February, when most leave on vacation, are generally a quiet time; things pick up after school starts in early March.

Traditionally, many Chileans take "sandwich holidays" between official holidays and the weekend, but the government is attempting to eliminate the practice by moving some holidays to the nearest Monday.

January 1 is **Año Nuevo** (New Year's Day), an official holiday in both countries and the Falkland Islands.

Semana Santa (Holy Week) is widely observed in both Argentina and Chile, though only the days from **Viernes Santo** (Good Friday) through **Pascua** (Easter) are official holidays. Many use the long weekend for a mini-vacation.

May 1 is **Día del Trabajador** (International Labor Day), an official holiday in both countries.

October 12 is **Día de la Raza** (equivalent to Columbus Day), an official holiday in both countries.

November 2's **Día de los Muertos** (All Saints' Day or Day of the Dead) is the occasion for Argentines and Chileans to visit the graves of their loved ones, though it's not the colorful event it is in, say, Mexico or Guatemala.

December 25 is **Navidad** (Christmas Day), an official holiday in both countries and the Falkland Islands.

Argentina

On May 25, Argentines observe the **Revolución de Mayo** (May Revolution of 1810), when the Porteños of Buenos Aires made their first move toward independence by declaring the Viceroy illegitimate. This is not, however, the major independence celebration, which takes place July 9 (see below).

June 10 is **Día de las Malvinas** (Malvinas Day), an official holiday commemorating Argentina's claim to the British-governed Falkland

Islands. June 20, also an official holiday, is **Día de la Bandera** (Flag Day).

July 9, **Día de la Independencia,** celebrates the formal declaration of Argentine independence at the northwestern city of Tucumán, in 1816. Later in the month, when school lets out, many Argentines take **Vacaciones de Invierno** (Winter Holidays), when flights and even buses out of the capital fill up fast.

August 17 is **Día de San Martín,** the official observance of the death (not the birth) of Argentina's independence hero.

Chile

On May 21, **Glorias Navales** commemorates the naval Battle of Iquique, in the War of the Pacific with Peru.

Corpus Christi (May 30) is a religious holiday, as are the **Día de San Pedro y San Pablo** (Saint Peter & Saint Paul's Day) on June 29 and **Asunción de la Virgen** (Assumption) on August 15.

Taking place the first Monday in September, **Día de la Unidad Nacional** (Day of National Unity) replaced the controversial **Pronunciamiento Militar de 1973,** the military coup of 1973. The future of this holiday is in doubt because of its polemical origins.

September 18's **Día de la Independencia Nacional** (Independence Day) is immediately followed by September 19's **Día del Ejército** (Armed Forces Day); together, they constitute the **Fiestas Patrias.**

December 8 marks the **Inmaculada Concepción** (Immaculate Conception), a religious holiday.

Falkland Islands

The Falklands celebrate many of the same holidays as Argentina and Chile, but several others are either derived from the British tradition or unique to the Islands. January 10, for instance, is **Margaret Thatcher Day,** as the Islanders acknowledge the birthday of the British Prime Minister who responded to the 1982 invasion by ordering a naval task force to expel the Argentines.

June 14 is **Liberation Day,** commemorating the date on which the British forced the Argentine surrender. The first Monday of October is the **Spring Holiday.**

December 8 acknowledges the **Battle of the Falklands,** a World War I confrontation with Germany that took place within sight of Stanley. The day after Christmas is **Boxing Day,** a movable holiday that can change if Christmas falls on a Saturday or Sunday.

Accommodations

Argentine and Chilean Patagonia both have accommodations in all categories, from campgrounds to youth-hostel dormitories to extravagant luxury suites and everything in between, but in some localities peak summer season demand can tax their resources. National and municipal tourist officials offer accommodations lists and brochures, but these often exclude budget options and may even omit some midrange and high-end places.

Argentine prices, especially since the devaluation of 2001–2002, are often negotiable; do not assume the *tarifa mostrador* (rack rate) is etched in stone. Visitors also should not take hotel ratings too literally as they often represent an ideal rather than a reality, and some one- or two-star places are significantly better than others that formally rank higher.

Prices in Buenos Aires and Santiago often fall during summer months of January and February, as business travel slows to a crawl; for Patagonian destinations, though, prices usually rise. Other peak seasons, when prices may rise, are Semana Santa (Holy Week), July's winter school vacations, which coincide with Argentine patriotic holidays, and mid-September' Chilean patriotic holidays.

Note that Argentine hotels levy 21 percent in Impuesto al Valor Agregado or IVA (Value Added Tax or VAT). Unless otherwise indicated, rates in this book include IVA, but if there's any question at the front desk, ask for clarification to avoid unpleasant surprises when paying the bill.

Midrange to upscale Chilean hotels levy 18 percent IVA, but can legally discount that to tourists with the appropriate documentation—passport and tourist card—who pay in dollars or by international credit card. Foreign residents of Chile are *not* eligible for this discount. At the same time, the discount can be smaller than expected if the hotel's exchange rate is unfavorable.

CAMPING

Organized camping is common on both sides of the Andean lake district and the rest of Patag-

© WAYNE BERNHARDSON

Hotel Bajo Caracoles is one of few accommodations along isolated RN 40 in Argentina's Santa Cruz province.

onia; campgrounds are generally spacious affairs, with shade, clean toilets, and bathrooms with hot showers, and even groceries and restaurants. They are often surprisingly central, and are usually cheap, rarely more than a couple dollars per person, but some Chilean campgrounds charge for a minimum of four or five persons. In Argentina, devaluation has made modest hotels more than competitive with them.

In the peak summer season and on weekends, the best sites can be crowded and noisy, as families on a budget take advantage of bargain prices. It's usually possible to find a quiet—but less desirable—site on the periphery. But remember that Argentines stay up late, very late, for their barbecues.

In the wilder, more remote areas like Santa Cruz and Aisén, it's possible to camp just about anywhere for free, though there are restrictions in the most popular destinations like Parque Nacional Los Glaciares and Parque Nacional Torres del Paine.

The América del Sur Hostel in El Calafate, Argentina, enjoys sunny common areas with views over Lago Argentino.

HOSTELS

For youth and budget travel, Argentina and Chile have growing hostel networks, plus many independent hostels, where bunks start at around US$5 per person. In Argentina, since the 2002 devaluation, these are no longer the only budget options, but they do offer an opportunity to get together with like-minded travelers. In addition to the customary dorm accommodations, many hostels offer more expensive private rooms for individuals and couples.

Note that Argentine hostels have begun to avoid the term *albergue;* in Argentine Spanish, an *albergue transitorio* means a by-the-hour hotel. Many have adapted the English word hostel, or Hispanicized into *hostal,* a term more common in Chile, where it's a step above a *hospedaje* (see below).

For up-to-the-minute information on official Argentine hostels, contact **Hostelling Internacional Argentina** (Florida 835, 3rd floor, Oficina 319-B, tel. 011/4511-8712, fax 011/4312-0089, www.hostels.org.ar). The competing but rather torpid **Asociación Argentina de Albergues de la Juventud** (AAAJ, Talcahuano 214, tel./fax 011/4372-7094, www.hostelling-aaaj.org.ar) has a smaller network of affiliates. There is also the **Argentina Hostels Club** (www.argentinahostels.com), a growing confederation that's strong in Buenos Aires and Patagonia.

For up-to-the-minute information on official Chilean hostels, contact **Hostelling International Santiago** (Cienfuegos 151, Santiago Centro, tel. 02/6718532, fax 02/6728880, www.hostelling.cl) or the **Asociación Chilena de Albergues Turísticos Juveniles** (Hernando de Aguirre 201, Oficina 602, Providencia, Santiago, tel. 02/2333220, fax 02/2322555, hostelling@hostelling.cl).

OTHER BUDGET ACCOMMODATIONS

Budget accommodations in Argentina and Chile can cost as little as US$5 per person; they go by a variety of names that may camouflage their quality—ranging from dingy fleabags with mattresses

A DAY (OR MORE) IN THE COUNTRY

Over the past decade-plus, facing economic reality, many of Argentina's great rural estates have opened themselves to the tourist trade. From the subtropical north to the sub-Antarctic south, diversification has become the word for owners of *estancias,* some of which earn more income from hosting visitors than they do growing grain or raising livestock. For some visitors, an *estancia* stay is their entire vacation.

Figures suggest the size of the phenomenon. According to the Buenos Aires–based Red Argentina de Turismo Rural (Ratur), more than a thousand *estancias* are open to the public. For 45 percent of farms, tourism comprises 10 percent of their income; for 17 percent, it represents half of their income; and for eight percent, it represents 95 percent of their income. In Patagonia, where visits are growing at 10 percent annually, tourist revenue can be the equivalent of 10,000 kilograms of wool; in Santa Cruz province, where 40 percent of wool *estancias* have failed in recent years, it represents 15 percent of income from the wool clip.

Throughout the country, some *estancias* are reasonably priced places with limited services, but others are magnificent properties with castle-like *cascos* (big houses), elaborate service that includes gourmet meals, and recreational activities such as horseback riding, tennis, swimming, and the like.

Affiliated with the Sociedad Rural Argentina, the traditionally powerful landowners' organization, the **Red Argentina de Turismo Rural** (Ratur, Florida 460, 4th floor, Buenos Aires, tel. 011/4328-0499, fax 011/4328-0878, www.raturestancias.com.ar) represents a handful of Patagonian *estancias.*

The best-organized provincial group is **Estancias de Santa Cruz** (Suipacha 1120, Retiro, Buenos Aires, tel./fax 011/4325-3098, 011/4325-3102, www.estanciasdesantacruz.com). Most of its affiliates are in the southwestern corner of its home province, but there are also a few on the Argentine side of Tierra del Fuego.

© WAYNE BERNHARDSON

West of El Calafate, Estancia Anita's Hostería Alta Vista has been reinvented as one of the top tourist *estancias* in Argentina's Santa Cruz province.

that sag like hammocks to simple but cheerful and tidy places with firm new beds.

A *hospedaje* is generally a family-run lodging with a few spare rooms; *pensiones* and *casas de huéspedes* (guesthouses) are comparable, nearly interchangeable terms. All may have long-term residents as well as overnight guests. *Residenciales* (singular *residencial*) are generally buildings constructed with short-stay accommodations in mind, but they may also have semi-permanent inhabitants. All such places may even go by the term *hotel,* though that term usually means a more formal category.

All these categories may have some exceptionally good values. Most will have shared bath and toilet *(baño general* or *baño compartido),* but some offer a choice between shared and private bath *(baño privado);* bathtubs are unusual. In some cases, they will have ceiling fans and even cable TV, but there is often an extra charge for cable and almost always a surcharge for a/c.

Travelers intending to stay at budget accommodations should bring their own towels, though some provide towels. Many but by no means all include breakfast in their rates; ask to be certain.

Showers

Many Argentine and Chilean showers use natural gas in a *calefón,* which heats the water as it passes through the gas-run water heater. Opening the tap normally triggers the *calefón,* presuming the *piloto* (pilot) is lit, but some budget-conscious accommodations light the pilot only when someone wants to take a shower. Before getting in and turning on the tap, be sure the pilot is lit.

MIDRANGE ACCOMMODATIONS

Midrange hotels generally offer larger, more comfortable, and better-furnished rooms, almost always with private bath, than even the best budget places. Ceiling fans, cable TV, and even a/c are common, but they may not have on-site parking. Some have restaurants. Rates can range anywhere from US$25 up to US$100 d; some are better values than their high-end counterparts.

HIGH-END ACCOMMODATIONS

Luxury hotels with top-flight service, which can range upwards of US$100 per night, are few outside the capital cities of Buenos Aires and Santiago and major resort areas. In capital cities, these will usually offer amenities like restaurants, swimming pools, gym facilities, business centers, Internet connections, and conference rooms; outside capital cities, these are mostly resort hotels and will lack the business facilities. Invariably they will offer secure parking.

Some of the best options are hot-springs hotels and country-inn resorts on *estancias,* which offer traditional hospitality and ambiance with style unmatchable at other high-end places. Again, prices may be upwards of US$100, often substantially upwards.

Food and Drink

Food and drink range from the economical and ordinary to the truly elegant and everything in between. In Argentina, for most of the 1990s, eating well at restaurants was financially challenging except for cheap cafeteria lunches and *tenedor libre* (literally, "free fork") buffets, but the peso collapse of 2002 has made it possible to eat diverse and imaginative food for a fraction of its former price—at least for visitors with dollars or Euros in their bank accounts.

Stereotypically, the Argentine diet consists of beef and more beef. This common perception is not entirely mistaken, but the diet has always had a Spanish touch and, for more than a century, a marked Italian influence with pizza and pasta. Over the past decade, though, the restaurant scene has become far more cosmopolitan, adventurous, and nuanced, with Brazilian, Japanese, Thai, Vietnamese, and many other once-exotic cuisines—not to mention high-quality variations on regional dishes.

Chile's long, rich coastline and productive farmland provide seafood, meat, fresh fruit, and vegetables in abundance. While the everyday Chilean diet may have some shortcomings, in most areas visitors will have no difficulty finding appealing food and drink.

On both sides of the border, it's becoming more common to find "Patagonian" cuisine that stresses fresh regional products, including wild game, lamb, seafood, greens, and soft fruits like raspberries.

WHERE TO EAT

In Argentina, places to eat range from hole-in-the-wall *comedores* (eateries) or fast-food *bares* (unavoidably but misleadingly translated as "bars") with no formal menu, in bus and train stations, to *cafés, confiterías* (teahouses) and elegant *restaurantes* in Buenos Aires and other major tourist centers.

Likewise, in Chile, *restaurante* can cover a seemingly infinite range of possibilities. About the only hard and fast rule is to avoid places in which single men—or groups of men—sit and drink beer.

RESTAURANT TERMINOLOGY

Restaurant terminology overlaps in Argentina and Chile, but there are some differences.

Argentina

Restaurante (occasionally *restorán* or, more fashionably, *restó*) usually means places with sit-down service, but within this definition there can be great diversity. Most often, the term refers to a locale with a printed menu and table service, but even this can range from any place with a basic beef and pasta menu to truly elegant settings with celebrity chefs, complex cuisine, elaborate wine lists, and professional service.

The usual international fast-food villains have franchises in Buenos Aires, but throughout the country the best cheap food normally comes from *rotiserías* (delicatessens), which serve excellent take-away fare and may have basic seating. Likewise, supermarkets like Coto and Disco have budget *cafeterías* that are excellent budget options.

Bares and *comedores* are no-frills eateries, with indifferent service, offering *minutas* (short orders); the term *comedor* can also mean a hotel breakfast nook or dining room. A *café,* by contrast, is a place whose patrons may dawdle over coffee and croissants, but its de facto purpose is to promote social interaction in personal affairs, business deals, and other transactions—even though it also serves snacks, *minutas,* and alcoholic beverages.

Argentine *confiterías,* by contrast, serve breakfast, light meals like sandwiches, snacks like cakes and other desserts, and coffee-based drinks. Generally more formal than cafes, some of them prestigious, they are suitable for afternoon tea; some have full-scale restaurant menus, often in a separate sector.

Chile

Cocinería can be a synonym for *comedor,* but there are several other terms not used in Argentina. *Fuente de soda* (literally, "soda fountain") really signifies a place with a modest menu that lacks a liquor license. *Cafeterías* provide plain meals, usually without table service, but the misleadingly named *salón de té* (literally, "teahouse") can be more like a European-style café, sometimes with sidewalk seating. *Hosterías* are generally country-style restaurants serving large numbers of customers on weekend or holiday outings. *Hostería* can also mean a type of accommodations, though such places often have restaurants as well.

One distinctively Chilean term is the *picada,* generally a small family-run eatery that begins informally, often with just a couple tables in a spare room facing the street, but can develop into something more elaborate (in Argentina, by the way, *picada* means a trail or footpath).

Marisquerías are simple but often very good fish and seafood eateries in locations where they can buy the morning's catch straight off the boat.

WHAT TO EAT

According to historian John C. Super, whatever the negative consequences of the Spanish inva-

DINING VOCABULARY AND ETIQUETTE

In both Argentina and Chile, dining vocabulary is mostly straightforward. The usual term for menu is *la carta; el menú* is almost equally common, but can also mean a fixed-price lunch or dinner. The bill is *la cuenta. Cubiertos* are silverware, while a *plato* is a plate and *vaso* a glass. A *plato principal* is a main dish or entrée.

Note that one might ask for a *vaso de agua* (glass of water), but never for a *vaso de vino* (literally but incorrectly, a glass of wine); rather, ask for a *copa de vino.* When speaking English, native Spanish speakers frequently make a comparable error in requesting "a cup of wine."

Many but not all Argentine restaurants assess a small *cubierto* (cover charge) for dishes, silverware, and bread. This is not a *propina* (tip); generally, a 10 percent tip is the norm, but Argentines themselves often ignore this norm, especially in times of economic crisis. Women in a group will often tip little or nothing, but a good rule of thumb is that anyone able to afford a restaurant meal can afford a tip.

It's worth emphasizing that the occupation of waiter is traditionally male and professional, rather than a short-term expedient for university students or aspiring actors, but this is changing in the new, stylish restaurants, where servers are just as likely to be young and female. Note, though, that *mozo,* a common and innocuous term for an Argentine waiter, implies an insulting servility in Chile. When in doubt, use *mesero* or *jóven,* even if the individual in question is not particularly young; for a female, use *señorita* unless the individual is at least of late middle-age.

sion, it actually improved a late pre-Columbian diet that was, by some accounts, nutritionally deficient (often protein-poor). In Super's opinion,

> ***The combination of European and American foods created diversified, nutritionally rich diets. Crop yields were higher than those in Europe, and longer or staggered growing seasons made fresh food available during much of the year. The potential for one of the best diets in the history of the world was evident soon after discovery of the New World. For Europeans, the introduction of livestock and wheat was an essential step in creating that diet.***

When Europeans first set foot in South America, in the densely populated Andean region, the staples were beans, squash, and a variety of potatoes and other tubers, but the diet was low in animal protein—only the llama, alpaca, guinea pig, and wild game were readily available, and not in all areas. Spanish introductions like wheat and barley, which yielded only a four-to-one harvest ratio in Europe, reached at least two to three times that in the Americas.

The Spanish introductions blended with the indigenous base to create many of the edibles found on Argentine and Chilean tables today. The abundance of seafood, combined with European animal protein and high-productivity European fruits like apples, apricots, grapes, pears, and many others, resulted in a diverse food-production and consumption system which, however, is changing today.

Cereals

Trigo (wheat), a Spanish introduction, is most common in *pan* (bread), but also appears in the form of pasta. *Arroz* (rice) is a common *guarnición* (side dish).

Maíz (maize or corn) is a main ingredient in many dishes, including the Italian-derived polenta. Maize leaves often serve as a wrapping for traditional dishes like *humitas,* an equivalent to Mexican tamales in both northwestern Argentina and throughout Chile.

Legumes, Vegetables, and Tubers

Salads are almost invariably safe, and all but the most sensitive stomachs probably need not be concerned with bugs from greens washed in tap water. In Argentine restaurants, green salads are usually large enough for two diners.

© WAYNE BERNHARDSON

With sidewalk seating on the new pedestrian mall in Coyhaique, Chile, Café Ricer is a longtime city hangout.

Porotos (beans of all sorts except green beans) are traditional in families of Spanish descent. Other common legumes include *chauchas* (green beans), *arvejas* (peas), *lentejas* (lentils), and *habas* (fava beans).

In many varieties, *zapallo* (squash) is part of the traditional diet, as is the *tomate* (tomato). Old World vegetables include *acelga* (chard), *berenjena* (eggplant), *coliflor* (cauliflower), *lechuga* (lettuce), and *repollo* (cabbage). *Chiles* (peppers) are relatively uncommon; neither Argentine nor Chilean cuisine is really *picante* (spicy), except for dishes from Argentina's Andean Northwest, and even those rarely challenge palates accustomed to Mexican or Thai cuisine.

Native to the central Andes, *papas* (potatoes) grow in well-drained soils at higher elevations in northwestern Argentina and as far south as the Chilean archipelago of Chiloé; *papas fritas* (French fries) are almost universal, but spuds also appear as *purée* (mashed potatoes) and in Italian-derived dishes such as Argentine *ñoquis* (gnocchi). Other common tubers include *zanahorias* (carrots) and *rábanos* (radishes).

Vegetarianism

While vegetarian restaurants are fairly few except in Buenos Aires and Santiago, the ingredients for quality vegetarian meals are easy to obtain, and many eateries prepare dishes such as pasta and salads which are easily adapted to vegetarian preferences. Before ordering any pasta dish, verify whether it comes with a meat sauce—*carne* means "beef" in the Southern Cone. Waiters or waitresses may consider chicken, pork, and similar items another category—sometimes called *carne blanca* (literally, "white meat"). Faced with a reticent cook, you can always plead *alergia* (allergy).

Fruits

As its seasons are reversed from the Northern Hemisphere, the temperate Southern Cone produces many of the same fruits, often available as fresh juices. Items like *manzana* (apple), *pera* (pear), *naranja* (orange), *ciruela* (plum), *sandía* (watermelon), *membrillo* (quince), *durazno* (peach), *frambuesa* (raspberry), and *frutilla* (strawberry) will be familiar to almost everyone. When requesting *jugo de naranja* (orange juice) in Argentina, be sure it comes *exprimido* (fresh-squeezed) rather than out of a can or box. In Chile, fresh-squeezed juice is a *vitamina.*

Also widely available, mostly through import, are tropical and subtropical fruits like banana and *ananá* (pineapple). Mango, *maracuyá* (passion fruit), *cherimoya,* and similar tropical fruits are less common but not unknown.

The *palta* (avocado), a Central American domesticate known as *aguacate* in its area of origin, often appears in Argentine and Chilean salads.

Meats and Poultry

Prior to the Spaniards, South America's only domesticated animals were the *cuy* (guinea pig, rare in what is now Argentina and Chile), the llama and alpaca, and the dog, sometimes used for food. The Spaniards enriched the American diet with their domestic animals, including cattle, sheep, pigs, and poultry (chickens and ducks).

Consumption of red meat, the hallmark of the Argentine diet, may be decreasing among the more affluent but it remains the entrée of choice among lower classes. Thanks to the Italian immigrant influence, an assortment of pastas is available almost everywhere. Traditionally, Chileans consume less red meat than Argentines, but it remains the entrée of choice for many of them.

© WAYNE BERNHARDSON

Lamb on a stake is part of the traditional Patagonian *asado*.

Carne, often modified as *carne de vacuno,* or *bife* (beef), is the most common menu item in both countries. Specifically Argentine terms include *bife de chorizo* (sirloin or rump steak), *bife de lomo* (tenderloin), *asado de tira* (rib roast), and *matambre* (rolled flank steak). *Milanesa* is a breaded cutlet or chicken-fried steak that, at cheaper eateries, can be intolerably greasy.

The widest selection is usually available in the *parrillada* or *asado,* a mixed grill that includes prime cuts but also *achuras,* a broad term that encompasses offal such as *chinchulines* (small intestines, known as *chunchules* in Chile), *mollejas* (sweetbreads), *criadillas* (testicles), *morcilla* (blood sausage), and *riñones* (kidneys). *Asado* can also mean a simple roast. *Chimichurri* is a garlic-based marinade that often accompanies the Argentine *parrillada.*

Sausages such as the slightly spicy Argentine *chorizo* may also form part of the *asado;* in a hot-dog bun, it becomes *choripán. Panchos* are basic hot dogs, while *fiambres* are processed meats.

Cordero (lamb), often roasted on a spit over an open fire, is common in Patagonia. *Cerdo* (pork) appears in many forms, ranging from simple *jamón* (ham) to *chuletas* (chops) to *lomito* (loin) and *matambre de cerdo. Chivo* (goat) or *chivito* (the diminutive) is a western Argentine specialty that sometimes appears on menus in the capital and occasionally in Patagonia; note that the Uruguayan *chivito* is very different, a steak sandwich or plate slathered with eggs, fries, and other high-calorie extras.

Argentine stews and casseroles include *carbonada* (beef, rice, potatoes, sweet potatoes, corn, squash, and fruit like apples and peaches) and *puchero* (beef, chicken, bacon, sausage, *morcilla,* cabbage, corn, garbanzos, peppers, tomatoes, onions, squash, and sweet potatoes). Broth-cooked rice serves as a garnish.

Ave (poultry) most often means *pollo* (chicken),

CATTLE CULTURE ON THE PAMPAS

From his hotel room on the Avenida de Mayo, U.S. poet Robert Lowell once wrote, he could hear "the bulky, beefy breathing of the herds." Ever since feral livestock changed the face of the Pampas in the 16th century, displacing the native guanaco and rhea, cattle have been a symbol of wealth and the foundation of the Argentine diet. Riding across the Pampas, Charles Darwin found the reliance on beef remarkable:

> *I had now been several days without tasting any thing besides meat: I did not at all dislike this new regimen; but I felt as if it would only have agreed with me with hard exercise. I have heard that patients in England, when desired to confine themselves exclusively to an animal diet, even with the hope of life before their eyes, have scarce been able to endure it. Yet the Gaucho in the Pampas, for months together, touches nothing but beef. . . . It is, perhaps, from their meat regimen that the Gauchos, like other carnivorous animals, can abstain long from food. I was told that at Tandeel, some troops voluntarily pursued a party of Indians for three days, without eating or drinking.*

Recent research has suggested that this diet has not been quite so universal as once imagined—urban archaeologist Daniel Schávelzon has unearthed evidence that, for instance, fish consumption was much greater in colonial Buenos Aires than once thought—but there is no doubt that the *parrilla* is a culinary institution. Beef may not be healthy in the quantities that some Argentines enjoy, and many of them will even admit it. But few can bypass traditional restaurants, where flamboyantly clad urban gauchos stir the glowing coals beneath grilled meat on a vertical spit, without craving that savory beef.

For most Argentines, *bien cocido* (well done) is the standard for steak, but *jugoso* (rare) and *a punto* (medium) are not uncommon.

which sometimes appears on menus as *gallina* (literally, hen) in a casserole or stew; eggs are *huevos. Pavo* (turkey) is becoming more common.

In Chile, the most common poultry dish is *cazuela de ave,* a stewed piece of chicken in a thin broth with potato, corn on the cob, and other vegetables.

Fish and Seafood

Argentine fish and seafood may not have the international reputation of its beef, but the long coastline, territorial seas, and freshwater rivers and lakes provide abundant options. Buenos Aires and other coastal cities have fine seafood restaurants, but these are less common in the interior. Chilean cuisine, though, makes better use of its abundant ocean resources.

Seafood, among the most abundant animal-protein sources in pre-Columbian times, includes both *pescado* (fish) and *mariscos* (shellfish and crustaceans). The most common fish are *congrio* (conger eel, covering a variety of species), sometimes called *abadejo; lenguado* (sole or flounder), *merluza* (hake), and freshwater *trucha* (trout); *salmón* (salmon) normally comes from Patagonian fish farms.

Note that the cheapest restaurants often ruin perfectly good fish by preparing it *frito* (deep fried), but on request almost all will prepare it *a la plancha* (grilled, usually with a dab of butter) or *al vapor* (steamed). Higher-priced restaurants will add elaborate sauces, often including shellfish.

Among the shellfish, visitors will recognize the relatively commonplace *almejas* (clams), *cala-*

mares (squid), *camarones* (shrimp), *cangrejo* or *jaiva* (crab), *centolla* (king crab) and *mejillones* (mussels), *ostiones* or *callos* (scallops, but beware—the latter word can also mean tripe), *ostras* (oysters), and *pulpo* (octopus). Spanish restaurants normally serve the greatest variety of fish and shellfish.

Chilean cuisine also makes use of *cholgas* and *choritos* (different varieties of mussels) and *machas* (razor clams), as well as more unusual items like the *choro zapato* ("shoe mussel," so called because of its enormous size); *erizos* (sea urchins, definitely an acquired taste and frequently exported to Japan); the oddly named *locos* (giant abalone, literally "crazies"); *picoroco* (giant barnacle); and *piure* (resembling a dirty sponge, according to food writer Robb Walsh). Many of these have closed seasons, when they may not be taken, so be aware.

Seafood often appears on the menu in the form of *ceviche,* raw fish or shellfish heavily marinated in lime juice and spiced with cilantro. Other seafood specialties worth looking for are *chupes* (thick, buttery stews) of *congrio, jaiva* and *locos,* and *curanto,* a kitchen-sink stew that can include fish, shellfish, beef, chicken, lamb, pork, potato, and vegetables.

"Fast Food" Snacks

Ignoring the invasion of international franchises, Argentina has some of the continent's best snack food. The best of the best is the *empanada,* a flaky turnover most frequently filled with ground beef, hard-boiled egg, and olive, but it may also come with ham and cheese, chicken, onion, and (rarely) with tuna or fish. The spicier ground beef *salteña* comes from northwestern Argentina but may be available elsewhere; the tangy *empanada árabe* (lamb with a touch of lemon juice) is more difficult to find. Empanadas *al horno* (oven-baked) are lighter than *fritas* (fried, sometimes in heavy oil).

Argentine pizza is also exceptional, though less diverse in terms of toppings than in North America. For slices, try the cheeseless *fugazza* with Vidalia-sweet onions or its cousin *fugazzeta,* enhanced with ham and mozzarella. Argentines embellish their slices with *fainá,* a baked chickpea dough that fits neatly atop.

Chileans also eat pizza, but it mostly lacks the zest of its Argentine counterpart. Chilean empanadas are considerably larger, with a heavier crust; the standard is the *empanada de pino* of ground beef, hard-boiled egg, and olive, but ham and cheese is an option. Only at Easter does seafood make an appearance in Chilean empanadas.

Desserts

Many Argentines have a sweet tooth. At home, the standard *postre* is fresh fruit, ranging from grapes (most single-family homes have their own arbors) to apples, pears, and oranges. In restaurants, this becomes *ensalada de frutas* (fruit salad) or, more elaborately, *macedonia. Postre vigilante,* consisting of cheese and *membrillo* (quince) or *batata* (sweet potato) preserves, is another fruit-based dessert; it also goes by the name *queso y dulce.*

Often topped with whipped cream, *arroz con leche* (rice pudding) and *flan* (egg custard) are also good choices, as is the Spanish custard *natillas.* An acquired taste is *dulce de leche,* which one international travel magazine referred to as "its own major food group." Argentines spread prodigious quantities of this sickly sweet caramelized milk, which Chileans call *manjar,* onto just about anything and even eat it directly out of the jar.

Though it stems from the Italian tradition, Argentine ice cream lacks the high international profile of gelato—when a pair of Porteños opened an ice creamery in the author's hometown of Oakland, California, they chose the compromise name of Tango Gelato, stressing its Italian origins without suppressing its Buenos Aires detour. Argentina has a remarkable number of quality ice creameries, and a diversity of flavors, ranging from the standard vanilla and chocolate (with multiple variations on those, including white chocolate and bittersweet chocolate) to lemon mousse, *sambayón* (resembling eggnog), the Argentine staple *dulce de leche,* and countless others.

Chilean ice cream is popular almost everywhere, but the quality is usually only so-so except in the capital, where *elaboración artesanal* (small-scale production) is more common, and in Patagonia, where regional flavors like *ruibarbo* (rhubarb) appear on the menu. Chile's German immigrants have left a legacy of kuchen (pastries such as apple strudel and raspberry tarts) in the south.

International and Ethnic Food

Buenos Aires and Santiago (one of the continent's underappreciated gastronomic centers) have the greatest variety of international food, though some tourist-oriented areas also have good selections. Italian and Spanish are the most common foreign cuisines, but French and Chinese venues are also numerous. Peruvian food has become popular in Santiago, but is rare in the rest of the country and even in Buenos Aires.

Brazilian, Mexican, and Middle Eastern restaurants are less common; some popular world-food cuisines, such as Japanese, Thai, and Vietnamese, have made inroads. Given the raw material that Chile's oceans offer, sushi can be a real treat here.

MEALS AND MEALTIMES

Despite some regional differences, Argentine food is relatively uniform throughout the country, except in Buenos Aires, where diverse ethnic and international cuisine is abundant; in Patagonia, game dishes are not unusual (most of this, such as venison, is either farmed or culled on *estancias* where populations have risen too high).

By North American and European standards, both Argentines and Chileans are late eaters except for *desayuno* (breakfast); Chileans, though, are notorious late risers. *Almuerzo* (lunch, sometimes called *colación* in Chile) usually starts around 1 P.M., *cena* (dinner) around 9 P.M. or later—sometimes much later in Argentina. Argentines bide their time between lunch and dinner with a late-afternoon *té* (afternoon tea) that consists of a sandwich or some sort of pastry or dessert; the Chilean counterpart is *onces*.

Since Argentines often eat *after* the theater or a movie, around 11 P.M. or even later on weekends, anyone entering a restaurant before 9 P.M. may well dine alone. One advantage of an early lunch and dinner is that fewer customers mean fewer smokers; this is not foolproof, but statistically things are on your side.

Breakfast and Brunch

Most Argentines eat a light breakfast of coffee or tea and *pan tostado* (toast, occasionally with ham and/or cheese) or *medialunas* (croissants) or *facturas* (pastries, also eaten for afternoon tea); *medialunas* may be either *de manteca* (buttery and sweet) or *salada* (saltier, baked with oil). *Mermelada* (jam) usually accompanies plain *tostados.*

As a side dish, eggs may be either *fritos* (fried) or *revueltos* (scrambled), or sometimes *duros* (hardboiled). In some fashionable restaurant zones, a more elaborate Sunday brunch has become an option.

Chilean breakfasts are similar, but usually without the croissants or pastries; North American breakfast foods like corn flakes have also made inroads. *Avena* (oatmeal) is common in wintertime.

Lunch

Lunch is often the day's main meal, usually including an *entrada* (appetizer), followed by a *plato principal* (entrée, often *plato de fondo in Chile*), accompanied by a *guarnición* (side dish, *agregado* in Chile) and a *bebida* (soft drink) or *agua mineral* (mineral water) and followed by *postre* (dessert).

Upscale restaurants often offer fixed-priced lunches that make it possible to eat well and stylishly without busting the budget. It's also possible to find local fast-food items like *hamburguesas* (hamburgers), sandwiches, pizza, and pasta, without resorting to international franchises.

Té and Onces

Filling the time between lunch and the late-dinner hour, the Argentine *té* and the Chilean *onces* can range from a late-afternoon sandwich to the equivalent of afternoon tea, with elaborate cakes and cookies, and is often a social occasion. Presumably intended to tide people over until their relatively late dinnertime, it often becomes larger and more elaborate than that would imply.

Dinner

Dinner resembles lunch, but in formal restaurants it may be substantially more elaborate (and more expensive), and it can be a major social occasion. Argentines and Chileans dine late—9 P.M. is early, and anything before that will likely earn incredulous "What are you doing here?" stares from waiters. The exception to this rule is at tourist-oriented areas like BA's Puerto Madero complex, where restaurateurs have become accustomed to North Americans and Europeans who, lodged at nearby luxury hotels, can't wait any later than 7 P.M.

BUYING GROCERIES

In Argentina, North American-style supermarkets carry a wide selection of processed foods but often a lesser variety (and quality) of fresh greens than is available in produce markets. Many of them also have cheap cafeterias with surprisingly good food.

In areas where supermarkets are fewer, almost all neighborhoods have corner shops where basic groceries and fresh produce are available, usually within just a few minutes' walk. Butchers are numerous, fishmongers somewhat less so.

Virtually every Chilean city, town, village, and hamlet has a central market where it's possible to buy fresh produce. Even in these locales that don't have central markets, there are almost always small shops where groceries are available.

BEVERAGES

Coffee, Tea, and Chocolate

Unreconstructed caffeine addicts will feel at home in Argentina, where espresso is the norm even in small provincial towns. *Café chico* is a dark viscous brew in a miniature cup, supplemented with enough sugar packets to make it overflow onto the saucer. A *cortado* comes diluted with milk—for a larger portion request a *cortado doble*–and follows lunch or dinner. *Café con leche,* equivalent to a latte, is a breakfast drink; ordering it after lunch or dinner is a serious *faux pas.*

Chilean coffee, by contrast, is a disappointment—powdered Nescafé is the norm, and espresso is a rare commodity except in the capital. *Café negro* is Nescafé mixed with hot water; *café con leche* (coffee with milk) is usually Nescafé dissolved in warm milk.

Té negro (black tea) usually comes in bags and is insipid by most standards. Visitors wanting British-style tea with milk should ask for tea first and milk later; otherwise, they may get a tea bag immersed in lukewarm milk. Herbal teas range from the nearly universal *manzanilla* (chamomile) and *rosa mosqueta* (rose hips) to *mate de coca* (coca leaf), but *yerba mate,* the so-called "Paraguayan tea," is one of Argentina's most deeply embedded customs.

In addition to the usual, Chilean herbal teas also include specialties such as *llantén* (plantain), *cedrón* (lemon verbena), *paico* (saltwort), *boldo,* and many other often better alternatives. In Patagonia, some Chileans follow the Argentine custom of *mate.*

Chocolate lovers will enjoy the Argentine *submarino,* a bar of semi-sweet chocolate that dissolves smoothly in steamed milk from the espresso machine. Powdered chocolate is also available, but less flavorful.

It's possible to get a good cup of *chocolate* (hot chocolate) in Santiago and much of Chile's Andean lake district, where Swiss-German influence is most significant. Elsewhere, it will be powdered chocolate mixed with hot water.

Water, Juices, and Soft Drinks

Tap water is potable virtually everywhere; ask for *agua de la canilla* in Argentina or *agua de la llave* in Chile. For ice, request it *con hielo.*

Visitors with truly sensitive stomachs might consider bottled water, which is widely available. Ask for *agua pura* or *agua mineral;* some brands are spring water, while others are purified. For carbonated water, add *con gas* or, in Argentina, ask for the even cheaper *soda,* which comes in large siphon bottles.

Gaseosas (in the plural) are sweetened bottled soft drinks (including most of the major transnational brands but also local versions such as the Argentine tonic water Paso de los Toros).

Fresh-squeezed *jugos* (fruit juices) are good though limited in their diversity. *Naranja* (orange) is the standard; to ensure freshness, ask for *jugo de naranja exprimido* or, in Chile, a *vitamina.*

Chilean *licuados* are fruit-based drinks mixed with water or blended with *leche* (milk). Unless you have an insatiable sweet tooth, always ask to have them prepared without sugar *(sin azúcar, por favor);* this can be a problem even with fresh-squeezed juices other than orange.

Alcoholic Beverages

Argentina is less famous for its wines than Chile, perhaps because domestic consumption traditionally overshadows exports, but it's the world's fifth-largest wine producer and its international profile is rising fast. Most production takes place in the western and northwestern provinces of Mendoza, San Juan and Salta, but the northern Patagonian provinces of Neuquén and Río Negro are starting to make an impact.

Local microbrews attract attention at the Feria Artesanal El Bolsón in Argentina.

Chile, of course, is one of the world's major wine producers, and exports have boomed since worldwide boycotts ended along with the Pinochet dictatorship. In early 2001, though, the industry's prestige received a blow when *New York Times* wine writer Frank J. Prial trashed Chilean wines in general as "second rate," the majority of cabernets "insipid," and chardonnays as "flabby and lacking in tannin."

Tinto is red wine, while *blanco* is white. The best restaurants have a wide selection, usually in full bottles though sometimes it's possible to get a *media botella* (half bottle) or, increasingly, wine by the glass. Argentines often mix their table wines—even reds—with soda water or ice.

For more information on Southern Cone wines and wineries, look for Christopher Fielden's *The Wines of Argentina, Chile, and Latin America* (New York: Faber and Faber, 2001), though it doesn't account for some recent developments. Harm de Blij's *Wine Regions of the Southern Hemisphere* (Rowman and Littlefield, 1985) is a more intellectually sophisticated overview.

While the wines are more than worthwhile, both Argentines and Chileans are leaning more toward beer, which tastes best as *chopp,* direct from the tap, rather than from bottles or cans.

Hard liquor is less popular in Argentina, but whiskey, gin, and the like are readily available. *Ginebra bols* (differing from gin) and *caña* (cane alcohol) are local specialties.

Chile is also, along with Peru, the major producer of the potent grape brandy known as pisco, the base of the legendary pisco sour. Another popular aperitif is the *vaina,* a concoction of port, cognac, cocoa, and egg white that some Chileans consider a "woman's drink."

In both Argentina and Chile, the legal drinking age is 18.

Getting There

Most overseas visitors arrive in Patagonia by air, via Buenos Aires or Santiago, but some will arrive overland and others by ship.

BY AIR

Buenos Aires and Santiago have regular air links with North America, Europe, and Australia/New Zealand, plus less-frequent routes from southern Africa across the Atlantic (some via Brazil). Both, though, are relatively expensive destinations during peak periods such as the Christmas/New Year's and Holy Week holidays; an Advance Purchase Excursion (Apex) fare can reduce the bite considerably, but may have minimum- and maximum-stay requirements, allow no stopovers, and impose financial penalties for changes. Economy-class (Y) tickets, valid for 12 months, are more expensive but allow maximum flexibility. Travelers staying longer than a year, though, have to cough up the difference for any interim price increases.

Discount ticket agents known as consolidators in North America and "bucket shops" in Britain may offer the best deals through so-called "bulk fares," but often have other drawbacks—they may not, for instance, allow mileage credit for frequent-flyer programs. Courier flights, on which passengers surrender some or all of their baggage allowance to a company sending equipment or documents to overseas affiliates or customers may be even cheaper. Available for short periods only, though, they often leave on short notice and are less common to Latin America than to other parts of the world.

Other options include Round the World (RTW) and Circle Pacific routes that permit numerous stopovers over the course of much longer multi-continental trips, but assembling an itinerary requires effort and patience. Two useful resources for researching airfares and other aspects of international travel are the third edition of Edward Hasbrouck's *The Practical Nomad* (Emeryville, CA: Avalon Travel Publishing, 2004) and the same author's *The Practical Nomad Guide to the Online Travel Marketplace* (Emeryville, CA: Avalon Travel Publishing, 2001).

Many airlines reduced their services to Argentina after the economic collapse of 2001–2002, as debt default and a steep devaluation meant fewer Argentines could splurge on overseas travel. Some, however, are restoring and even expanding services as devaluation has made the country a travel bargain for foreigners.

Buenos Aires's international airport is **Aeropuerto Internacional Ministro Pistarini** (BUE), operated by the private concessionaire Aeropuertos Argentinos 2000 (tel. 011/5480-6111, www.aa2000.com.ar). Popularly known as "Ezeiza" for the Buenos Aires province suburb where it's located, the airport is 35 kilometers southwest of downtown BA.

Santiago's international airport is the state-of-the-art **Aeropuerto Internacional Arturo Merino Benitez** (SCL, tel. 02/6901753, www.aeropuertosantiago.cl). One of the most modern and well-monitored in the world, it's in the western suburb of Pudahuel, 26 kilometers west of downtown.

From North America

Miami, Washington, D.C. (Dulles), New York, Chicago, Atlanta, Dallas, and Los Angeles are the main U.S. gateways to Buenos Aires and Santiago; Canadian passengers may also use Toronto.

Aerolíneas Argentinas and Chile's LAN are the traditional flag carriers, but other options include American Airlines, Copa, Grupo Taca, Lloyd Aéreo Boliviano (LAB), Mexicana, Transportes Aéreos Mercosur (TAM), United Airlines, and Varig. Aerolíneas Argentinas, American, Delta, LAN, and United have the only nonstop or direct services; others require changing planes either in Central or South America.

Non-Canadians can avoid the hassle of getting a U.S. transit visa by taking Air Canada's triangle route from Toronto to Buenos Aires and Santiago and back, three or four times weekly.

INTERNATIONAL AIRLINES IN BUENOS AIRES

Unless otherwise indicated, the addresses below are in the Microcentro and vicinity.

Aerolíneas Argentinas: Perú 2, Monserrat, tel. 011/4340-7777
AeroMéxico: Esmeralda 1063, 9th floor, Retiro, tel. 011/4315-1936
AeroSur: Avenida Santa Fe 851, 1st floor, tel. 011/4516-0999
Air Canada: Avenida Córdoba 656, tel. 011/4327-3640
Air France: San Martín 344, 23rd floor, tel. 011/4317-4700
Air New Zealand: Marcelo T. de Alvear 590, 10th floor, Retiro, tel. 011/4315-5494
Alitalia: Suipacha 1111, 28th floor, Retiro, tel. 011/4310-9999
American Airlines: Avenida Santa Fe 881, Retiro, tel. 011/4318-1111
American Falcon: Avenida Santa Fe 963, 4th floor, Retiro, tel. 011/4393-5700
British Airways: Carlos Pellegrini 1163, tel. 011/4320-6600
Copa/Continental;: Carlos Pellegrini 989, 2nd floor, Retiro, tel. 011/4132-3535
Delta: Reconquista 737, 3rd floor, tel. 011/4312-1200
Iberia: Carlos Pellegrini 1163, 1st floor, Retiro, tel. 011/4131-1000
KLM: Suipacha 268, 9th floor, tel. 011/4326-8422
LanChile: Cerrito 866, Retiro, tel. 011/4378-2200
Lloyd Aéreo Boliviano (LAB): Carlos Pellegrini 141, 2nd floor, tel. 011/4323-1900
Lufthansa: Marcelo T. de Alvear 636, Retiro, tel. 011/4319-0600
Mexicana: Avenida Córdoba 755, 1st floor, Retiro, tel. 011/4000-6300
Pluna: Florida 1, tel. 011/4342-4420
Qantas: Avenida Córdoba 673, 13th floor, Retiro, tel. 011/4514-4726
South African Airways: Carlos Pellegrini 1141, 5th floor, Retiro, tel. 011/5556-6666
Southern Winds: Avenida Santa Fe 784, Retiro, tel. 011/4515-8600
Swiss International: Avenida Santa Fe 846, 1st floor, Retiro, tel. 011/4319-0000
Taca: Carlos Pellegrini 1275, Retiro, tel. 011/4325-8222
Transportes Aéreos de Mercosur (TAM): Cerrito 1026, Retiro, tel. 011/4819-4800
United Airlines: Avenida Eduardo Madero 900, 9th floor, Retiro, tel. 0810/777-8648
Varig: Avenida Córdoba 972, 3rd floor, Retiro, tel. 011/4329-9211

From Mexico, Central America, and the Caribbean

Services from Mexico to either Santiago or Buenos Aires almost always require changing planes in Central America or elsewhere in South America; the main exception is LAN, which flies nonstop from Mexico City to Santiago, with connections to Buenos Aires.

Other carriers from Mexico City include Copa, which requires changing planes in Panama; Grupo Taca, via Lima, Perú; Lloyd Aéreo Boliviano, which also flies from Cancún; and Varig, which has Buenos Aires connections via Brazil.

Cubana flies daily from Havana to Buenos Aires, while Avianca has connections to both Santiago and Buenos Aires, via Bogotá, from the Caribbean, Central America, and Mexico.

Copa flies daily from Panama, with connections throughout the region.

From Europe

From Europe, there are direct services to Buenos

INTERNATIONAL AIRLINES IN SANTIAGO

This list includes only airlines that fly to and from Santiago, though several other foreign airlines also have local representatives. Unless otherwise noted, the offices are in Santiago Centro.

Aerolíneas Argentinas: Roger de Flor 2915, Las Condes, tel. 02/6393922
Aeroméxico: Ebro 2738, Las Condes, tel. 02/2345851
Air France: Alcántara 44, 6th floor, Las Condes, tel. 02/2909330
Air New Zealand: Avenida 11 de Septiembre 1881, Oficina 713, Providencia, tel. 02/3769039
Alitalia: Avenida Bosque Norte 0107, Oficina 21, tel. 02/3788230
American Airlines: Huérfanos 1199, tel. 02/6790000
British Airways: Isidora Goyenechea 2934, Oficina 302, Las Condes, tel. 02/3308600
Copa: Fidel Oteíza 1921, Oficina 703, Providencia, tel. 02/2002100
Delta: Isidora Goyenechea 2939, Oficina 401, Las Condes, tel. 02/2801600
Grupo Taca: Barros Borgoño 105, 2nd floor, Providencia, tel. 02/2355500
Iberia: Bandera 206, 8th floor, tel. 02/8701010
LanChile: Agustinas 640, tel. 02/6323442
Lloyd Aéreo Boliviano (LAB): Moneda 1170, tel. 02/6888680
Lufthansa: Moneda 970, 16th floor, tel. 02/6301655
Mexicana: Avenida 11 de Septiembre 2329, Providencia, tel. 02/2329057
Pluna: Avenida El Bosque Norte 0177, 9th floor, Las Condes, tel. 02/7078000
Qantas: Isidora Goyenechea 2934, Oficina 301, Las Condes, tel. 02/2329562
Saeta: Santa Magdalena 75, Oficina 209, Providencia, tel. 02/3344427
SAS/Spanair: Mardoqueo Fernández 128, Oficina 502, Providencia, tel. 02/2333585
South African: Zurich 221, Oficina 11, Las Condes, tel. 02/5205880
TAME (Ecuador): Moneda 970, 16th floor, tel. 02/6301681
Transportes Aéreos Mercosur (TAM): Santa Magdalena 94, Providencia, tel. 02/3811337
United Airlines: Tenderini 171, tel. 6320279; El Bosque Norte 0177, 19th floor, Las Condes, tel. 02/3370000
Varig: Avenida El Bosque Norte 0177, Oficina 903, Las Condes, tel. 02/7078000

Aires with Aerolíneas Argentinas (from Rome and Madrid); Air Europa (from Madrid); Air France (from Paris); Alitalia (from Milan and Rome); British Airways (from London): Iberia (from Barcelona and Madrid); KLM (from Amsterdam); Lufthansa (from Frankfurt via São Paulo); Southern Winds (from Madrid); and Swiss International (from Geneva and Zurich). TAM has connections from Paris via São Paulo.

Many Buenos Aires services continue to Santiago, but there are also direct services to the Chilean capital with LAN and Iberia. There are also good connections via Brazil with Varig.

From Asia, Africa, and the Pacific

The most direct service from the Pacific has been Aerolíneas Argentinas' twice-weekly service from Sydney via Auckland, but LAN has recently added direct flights from Australia and New Zealand. From Australia, Qantas links up with LAN flights via Tahiti, Easter Island, and Santiago, or with LanChile via Los Angeles. Air New Zealand also links up with LAN. From Japan, it's easiest to make connections via Los Angeles.

From Johannesburg, South African Airways flies five times or so weekly to São Paulo, where TAM and Varig offer connections to Buenos Aires.

Within South America

Buenos Aires and Santiago have connections to neighboring republics of Uruguay, Brazil, Paraguay, Peru, and Bolivia, and elsewhere on the continent as well. There are no flights to the Guyanas, however.

For passengers on a Patagonian trip, the most important connections might be between Buenos Aires and Santiago, which are frequent on many South American and trans-Atlantic carriers.

LAN has the only flights to the Falkland Islands, also covered in this book, every Saturday from Santiago and Punta Arenas; they return the same day.

OVERLAND

Overland travel from the north can be challenging, but once you reach Argentina or Chile, it's easy enough.

From North America, Mexico, and Central America

Overland travel from North America or elsewhere is problematical because Panama's Darien Gap to Colombia is time-consuming, impassable for motor vehicles, and very difficult and potentially dangerous even for those on foot. The route passes through areas controlled by drug smugglers, guerrillas, and/or brutal Colombian paramilitaries.

Those visiting Patagonia and other parts of the continent for an extended period should consider shipping a vehicle. To locate a shipper, check the Yellow Pages of your local directory under Automobile Transporters, who are normally freight consolidators rather than the company that owns the ship, which will charge higher container rates. Since more people ship vehicles to Europe than to South America, finding the right shipper may take patience; one reliable U.S. consolidator is **McClary, Swift & Co.** (360 Swift Avenue, South San Francisco, CA 94080, tel. 650/872-2121, www.unitedshipping.com/offices/partners/mcclary.php, mcclaryswift@unitedshipping.com), which has affiliates at many U.S. ports.

Argentine bureaucracy has improved in recent years, and clearing customs with a vehicle is simpler than it once was. Vehicles arrive at the **Estación Maritima Buenos Aires** (Dársena B, Avenida Ramón Castillo y Avenida Maipú, Retiro, tel. 011/4311-0692, 011/4317-0675, or 011/4312-8677); here it is necessary to present your passport, vehicle title, and the original *conocimiento de embarque* (bill of lading), and to complete a customs application. You will then obtain an appointment with a customs inspector to retrieve the vehicle, which will cost about US$300 port charges and another US$200 for the shipper; if the vehicle has been in port longer than five days, there will be additional costs. The vehicle can remain legally in Argentina for eight months, with an eight-month extension possible; any visit to a neighboring country restarts the clock. In event of any difficulty, consult a private *despachante de aduana* (customs broker), such as **José Angel Vidal Labra** (tel. 011/4345-7887, vidla@sinectis.com.ar).

Chile's ports are less bureaucratic and even safer for the vehicle than those of Argentina. The usual ports of entry are San Antonio, southwest of Santiago, and Valparaíso, northwest of the capital. It does pay to be there within a couple days of the vehicle's arrival, or storage fees can mount up. Leave the gas tank as nearly empty as possible (for safety's sake) and leave no valuables, including tools, inside.

To arrange a shipment from San Antonio or Valparaíso, contact the Santiago consolidator **Ultramar** (Moneda 970, 18th floor, Santiago Centro, tel. 02/6301817, fax 02/6986552, italia@ultramar.cl). For a trustworthy customs broker to handle the paperwork, contact the office of **Juan Alarcón Rojas** (Fidel Oteíza 1921, 12th floor, Providencia, Santiago, tel. 02/2252780, fax 02/2045302, alrcon@entelchile.net).

Bicycles, of course, can be partially dismantled, packaged, and easily shipped aboard airplanes, sometimes for no additional charge. Except that there is rarely any additional paperwork for bringing a bike into the country, many of the same cautions apply as to any other overland travel.

From Neighboring South American Countries

Argentina has numerous border crossings with Chile, in Patagonia and elsewhere. In both countries' lake districts, trans-Andean bus service is fairly common, but many southerly crossings lack public transportation. For carrier and itinerary details, see individual geographical entries.

Both international and domestic bus services normally have comfortable reclining seats (with every passenger guaranteed a seat), clean toilets, a/c, and meals and refreshments served on board, at least on the longest trips. If not, they make regular meal stops.

In northern Patagonia, Argentina-bound buses cross from Temuco to Neuquén over the 1,884-meter Paso de Pino Hachado via Curacautín and Lonquimay; the alternative 1,298-meter Paso de Icalma is slightly to the south. There is also a regular bus service from Temuco to San Martín de los Andes via the Paso de Mamuil Malal (Paso Tromen to Argentines); a bus-boat combination from Panguipulli to San Martín de los Andes via the 659-meter Paso Huahum and Lago Pirehueico; a paved highway from Osorno to Bariloche via the Paso de Cardenal Samoré that's the second-busiest crossing between the two countries; and the classic bus-boat shuttle from Puerto Montt and Puerto Varas to Bariloche.

There are many southern Patagonian crossings, but the roads are often bad and only a few have public transportation. Those with scheduled services include the mostly gravel road from Futaleufú, Chile, to Esquel (local buses only); Coyhaique to Comodoro Rivadavia on a mostly paved road via Río Mayo on comfortable long-distance coaches; Chile Chico to Los Antiguos (shuttles with onward connections in either direction; Puerto Natales to El Calafate via Río Turbio on a steadily improving but mostly gravel route; Punta Arenas to Río Gallegos via an almost entirely paved highway; and Punta Arenas to Río Grande and Ushuaia.

In addition, many border crossings are suitable for private motor vehicles and mountain bikes, and a few by foot. For information on these, see below, as well as the appropriate geographical entries.

BY WATER

The main international crossings in Patagonia are the popular and scenic but increasingly expensive bus-boat-bus route between the Argentine resort of San Carlos de Bariloche and the Chilean city of Puerto Montt, and the relatively short cruise (three days-plus) that carries passengers between Punta Arenas (Chile) and Ushuaia (Tierra del Fuego).

Getting Around

BY AIR

Argentina

In addition to international air service, Argentina has a large network of domestic airports and a handful of airlines centered on Buenos Aires; indeed, to fly between Argentine cities, changing planes in BA is often unavoidable. Most domestic flights use Aeroparque Jorge Newbery, the city airport, but some use the international airport at Ezeiza.

Aerolíneas Argentinas has domestic as well as international flights, while its affiliate Austral (the two are almost indistinguishable) serves many Patagonian destinations from Buenos Aires south to Ushuaia, Tierra del Fuego.

Other domestic airlines come and go, with the exception of Líneas Aéreas del Estado (LADE, www.lade.com.ar), the air force's heavily subsidized commercial branch. Miraculously surviving budget crises and privatizations, it flies to southern Buenos Aires province and out-of-the-way Patagonian destinations on a wing and an overdrawn bank account.

Other private airlines have consistently failed. Recently, the most viable alternative has been Southern Winds (www.sw.com.ar), whose Patagonian destinations include Neuquén, Bariloche, and El Calafate; the airline is bankrupt but still operating. LAN's Lan Argentina, which acquired some of Southern Winds' routes, is now operating as well and plans to expand.

American Falcon (www.americanfalcon.com.ar) flies from Aeroparque to the Patagonian resorts of Puerto Madryn and Bariloche.

Air fares fell with the 2002 devaluation and have remained reasonable, though foreigners are not eligible for discounts available to Argentine citizens and residents. This means, in effect, that foreigners are paying full Y-class fares, but this also means greater flexibility in purchasing one-way *cabotaje* tickets, "open jaws" itineraries that land at one city and return from another, and to mix and match airlines. There are also "Visit Argentina" air passes.

Sample Aerolíneas Argentinas/Austral destinations, with one-way fares from Aeroparque, include Bariloche (US$137), El Calafate (US$100), Trelew (US$93), and Ushuaia (US$107). These fares do not include airport taxes (about US$5 per ticket), nor the 10.5 percent value added tax (IVA) on domestic flights.

Available only in conjunction with international travel to Buenos Aires, Aerolíneas Argentinas' "Visit Argentina" pass offers a series of discount fares to foreigners and nonresident Argentines, which requires some planning to gain maximum advantage from them. Fares are notably cheaper if the international travel takes place on Aerolíneas Argentinas.

Southern Winds has slightly lower domestic fares, with no discounts for Argentines. LADE, which flies smaller, older planes and makes many stops, is known for bargains; from Buenos Aires, for instance, Bariloche costs only US$90. It is also known, though, for unreliability in honoring reservations and keeping to its schedules.

Chile

In addition to Santiago's international airport, there are domestic airports with commercial flights at Temuco, Pucón, Osorno, Puerto Montt, Chaitén, Balmaceda (Coyhaique), and Punta Arenas; some of these have short international flights to Argentina. Coyhaique has a separate aerodrome for flights to Laguna San Rafael; for details, see the appropriate geographical entries.

LAN dominates the domestic market, but its planes are fairly spacious for a country whose longest domestic flight is only about three hours.

No competitor has had sustained success challenging LAN's supremacy, but Sky Airline now holds about 20 percent of the domestic market and serves the airports at Temuco, Puerto Montt, Balmaceda, and Punta Arenas. Aerolíneas del Sur, an affiliate of Aerolíneas Argentinas, has recently begun domestic Chilean services.

Chilean domestic airfares are generally reasonable, but purchasing tickets a few days ahead of time can result in substantial discounts. For overseas visitors LanChile also has a "Visit Chile" pass that can mean substantial savings, but it's not promoting this as much as it has in the past.

For student discounts on both international and domestic flights, try the **Student Flight Center** (Hernando de Aguirre 201, Oficina 401, Providencia, Santiago, tel. 02/3350395, fax 02/3350394, www.sertur.cl).

BY BUS

In both Argentina and Chile, buses along the principal highways, and those connecting other main cities and resorts, are frequent and almost invariably spacious and comfortable—sometimes even luxurious. A handful on back-roads routes are only marginally better than Central American "chicken buses," and they may be infrequent, but distances are relatively short.

So-called Pullman buses have reclining seats, and for short to medium runs, say up to six or seven hours, they're more than adequate. Seats are guaranteed. For the longest distances, many travelers prefer the more spacious *servicio diferencial* or the nearly horizontal *coche cama* service, which provide greater legroom in seats that recline almost horizontally. Fares are very reasonable by international standards—the 23-hour trip to Bariloche, in northern Patagonia, is less than US$50.

Most cities have a central *terminal de buses* (bus terminal), but a few have multiple terminals for long-distance, regional, and rural services, or for individual companies. Some companies also have separate ticket offices in more central locations than the terminals themselves.

Services are so frequent that reservations are

© WAYNE BERNHARDSON

southbound bus on Chile's Carretera Austral

rarely necessary except for a few infrequently traveled routes and some international services, or during holiday periods like Semana Santa (Holy Week), September's Chilean patriotic holidays, Christmas/New Year's periods, and occasionally during the January/February summer and July/August winter vacation seasons. Fares can rise and fall with demand, depending on the season.

BY RAIL

Once the primary mode of interurban transportation, Argentine domestic rail service is now limited to a handful of long-distance domestic services. In Argentine Patagonia, the only long-distance service connects the Río Negro provincial capital of Viedma and the resort city of Bariloche.

In addition to regular passenger trains, there are also tourist excursions, including the narrow-gauge La Trochita in Río Negro and Chubut provinces; the latter was immortalized in Paul Theroux's overrated bestseller *The Old Patagonian Express.*

In Chile, the only long-distance train service is the longitudinal line that runs from Santiago to Temuco, with a spur to Concepción. Many tourists, though, enjoy the wood-paneled, German-built 1920s sleepers on the Temuco line; nearly all those patronizing the dining cars are foreigners.

Trains are still cheap, though rates have risen slightly, and rehabilitated rails have made them faster. Ordinary fares to Temuco are only US$16–19, while sleepers range US$29–32 for the nine-hour journey. The state-run Empresa de Ferrocarriles del Estado (EFE, www.efe.cl) has begun a modernization program that may fund an extension to the former terminus at Puerto Montt.

BY CAR AND MOTORCYCLE

Driving conditions in Argentina and Chile have similarities but there are also dramatic differences. In the Falkland Islands, where roads are few and the most interesting destinations are inaccessible except by air or very bad tracks best left to locals, driving is inadvisable for short-term visitors.

Note that members of the American Automobile Association (AAA), Britain's Automobile

Association (AA), and other foreign automobile clubs are often eligible for limited roadside assistance and towing through the **Automóvil Club Argentina** (ACA, Avenida del Libertador 1850, Buenos Aires, tel. 011/4808-4000, www.aca.org.ar) and through the **Automóvil Club Chileno** (Acchi, Avenida Vitacura 8620, Vitacura, Santiago, tel. 02/2125702, www.acchi.cl). Both have representatives in larger cities, and many smaller towns, throughout each country.

Argentina

Driving in Argentina, especially in Buenos Aires, is not for the timid. In the words of *Buenos Aires Herald* columnist Martín Gambarotta, this is a country "where pedestrians and not cars have to stop at a zebra crossing." According to United Nations statistics, the traffic death rate of 25 per 100,000 is South America's highest, nearly twice that of Chile and the United States, and almost three times that of Germany.

Argentine highways are divided into *rutas nacionales* (abbreviated here as RN, for which the federal government is responsible), and *rutas provincials* (RP, which each province maintains). Generally, but not necessarily, federal highways are better maintained; one exception is prosperous Santa Cruz province, which has large oil royalty revenues.

Speed limits on most highways are generally around 100 km/hr, but 120 km/hr on four-lane divided roads (of which Patagonia has none). Officially, helmets are obligatory for motorcyclists, but enforcement is lax, especially in cities. The most thickheaded riders appear to believe their skulls are strong enough, but emergency-room statistics have proved them wrong.

Chile

The longitudinal Panamericana or Ruta 5, which stretches from the Peruvian border to Puerto Montt and the Isla Grande de Chiloé, is Chile's main transport artery; on the mainland, it's a smoothly paved, four-lane divided highway. Even so, despite the presence of call boxes, rest areas, and *peajes* (toll booths), there are occasionally loose livestock, pedestrians crossing at unsuitable places, and even vendors hawking items ranging from sweets and ice cream to fresh produce and cheese to dressed kid goat, ready for barbecue.

Many more roads are paved or smoothly graded, though Ruta 7, the legendary Carretera Austral (Southern Highway), is often narrow, mostly gravel, and occasionally precarious (the author has wrecked two four-wheel-drive vehicles on it, with extenuating circumstances). Heavy truck traffic can make all these routes dangerous, but most Chileans are courteous and cautious drivers despite occasional road-rage incidents in Santiago. Watch, though, for Argentine license plates, as many trans-Andean visitors drive far more aggressively.

Speed limits on most highways are generally around 100 km/hr, but authorities are considering raising the maximum to 120 km/hr on those segments of the Panamericana that are four-lane divided roads. Carabineros (the national police) with radar guns are common sights along all highways.

Vehicle Documents, Driver's License, and Equipment

Most South American countries, including Argentina and Chile, have dispensed with the cumbersome *Carnet de Passage en Douanes* that required depositing a large bond in order to import a motor vehicle. Officials at the port of arrival or border post will usually issue a 90-day permit on presentation of the vehicle title, registration, bill of lading (if the vehicle is being shipped), and your passport. For shipped vehicles, there may be substantial port charges (which rise rapidly if the vehicle has been stored more than a few days).

Before traveling, obtain an International or Interamerican Driving Permit. These permits are available through the American Automobile Association (AAA) or your home country's counterpart, and are normally valid for one calendar year from date of issue. Strictly speaking, they are not valid without a state or national driver's license, but Argentine police usually ignore the latter. Legally, another form of identification, such as national ID card or passport, is also necessary.

The police, though, pay close attention to vehicle documents—*tarjeta verde* ("green card") registration for Argentine vehicles, customs permission for foreign ones, and liability insurance (many Argentines drive without it, but it's reasonably priced from the Automóvil Club Argentino and other insurers). Vehicles without registration may be impounded on the spot. Argentine vehicles should have proof of a *verificación técnica* (safety inspection).

At roadside checkpoints, Argentine police are also rigid about obligatory equipment such as headrests for the driver and each passenger, *valizas* (triangular emergency reflectors), and *matafuegos* (one-kg fire extinguishers). In any instance of document irregularity or minor equipment violation, provincial police in particular may threaten fines while really soliciting *coimas* (bribes), though this is less common in the Patagonian provinces. A firm but calm suggestion that you intend to call your consulate may help overcome any difficulty.

Chilean police checkpoints are far less common than they were under the Pinochet dictatorship, but always stop when the Carabineros signal you to do so; this is usually a routine document check. Unlike many Argentine police, the Carabineros will refuse bribes, and offering one can get you in serious trouble; if you've committed an *infracción* (traffic violation), the best thing to do is reason with them, and you may get off unless your offense is truly flagrant or particularly dangerous. Note also that the slang term *paco* for a policeman is widely considered an insult—never use it to a cop's face.

Be sure to obtain Chilean liability insurance, which is available in major cities. *Seguro mínimo,* a cheap no-fault policy with limited personal injury coverage, is obligatory but inadequate for any serious accident.

In remote areas where gas stations are few, carry additional fuel.

Road Hazards

Argentine traffic can be fast and ruthless, many roads are narrow with little or no shoulder, and others are poorly surfaced or potholed. Heavy truck traffic can make all routes dangerous, and not just because of excess speed—impatient Argentine drivers will often try to pass in dangerous

© WAYNE BERNHARDSON

Broken axles and other misfortunes are not unusual on the Carretera Austral.

situations, and head-on crashes are disturbingly common, even between passenger buses.

Porteño drivers in the city and stray cattle in the provinces might seem to be enough to deal with, but the economic crisis since 2001–2002 has led to a major increase of *piquetes* (roadblocks) of demonstrators protesting unemployment and other issues. *Piqueteros* (pickets), while they tend to focus on stopping commercial traffic, manage to slow everything else down as well; never try to run one of these roadblocks, which can raise the pickets' wrath. Rather, try to show solidarity and, in all likelihood, you'll pass without incident. In Patagonia, the main focus of picket activity has been the western Neuquén oil town of Plaza Huincul.

Unleaded fuel is available everywhere, though some older Argentine vehicles still use leaded. In remote areas where gas stations are few, carry additional fuel.

In both the city and the countryside, watch for *lomas de burro* (speedbumps), also colloquially known as *pacos acostados* (sleeping policemen) in Chile. Night driving is inadvisable in some rural areas, as domestic livestock and inebriated campesinos may roam freely.

Expenses

Prior to devaluation, Argentina had some of the Americas' most expensive *nafta* (gasoline), but prices have fallen in dollar terms—at least temporarily—even as they've risen in peso terms. Buenos Aires prices are about US$.57 per liter for Regular, US$.63 for Super, and US$.67 for Ultra; the range translates to about US$2.17–2.55 per U.S. gallon. *Gasoil* (diesel) is typically cheaper, about US$.48 per liter (about US$1.80 per gallon), but the differential is diminishing. Because gasoline prices are unregulated, they may rise quickly.

Note, however, that so-called "Patagonian prices" south of Sierra Grande on RN 3 and El Bolsón on RN 40 are more than one-third cheaper for gasoline, which goes for about US$.37 per liter (US$1.41 per gallon) for Regular and US$.42 (US$1.60) per gallon for Super. There is no significant price differential, though, for diesel.

Operating a gasoline-powered vehicle in Chile is more expensive than in the U.S. or Argentina, but still substantially cheaper than in Europe, even though Chile now imports about 90 percent of its oil. The cost of *bencina* (gasoline) has risen to about US$1 per liter (roughly US$3.80 per U.S. gallon) in Santiago and up to 10 percent more in remote parts of Aisén. At around US$.70 per liter, diesel fuel (around US$2.65 per gallon) is about 30 percent cheaper than gasoline. These prices, though, are subject to weekly fluctuations in the exchange rate and international crude oil prices.

In both countries, repairs are cheap in terms of labor, but can be expensive in terms of parts, many of which must be imported; generally, parts are cheaper in Chile. Fortunately, skilled Argentine and Chilean mechanics can rehabilitate virtually any salvageable part.

Car Rental

Both Buenos Aires and Santiago have such good public transportation that it's hardly worthwhile risking aggressive drivers (especially in the Argentine capital), traffic congestion, and lack of parking. In Patagonia's wide-open spaces, though, a car makes it easier to explore otherwise inaccessible places, especially when time is limited. To rent a car, you must present a valid driver's license, a valid credit card, and be at least 25 years old.

Rental prices are generally lower and terms are better in Chile, where unlimited mileage deals are more common; local agencies may be cheaper than major international franchises. Rates start around US$25 per day or US$150 per week for economical vehicles like the Fiat Uno and around US$75 per day or US$450 per week or up for twin-cab pickup trucks. Even more expensive are four-wheel-drive vehicles, commonly referred to as *doble tracción* or *cuatro por cuatro* (the latter usually written "4X4"). On the other hand, if they're shared among a group, they can be fairly reasonable.

Rental insurance, which is additional, does not completely cover you against losses—there is almost always a deductible of several hundred dollars or more in case of serious damage, total destruction, or theft of the vehicle.

It's possible to rent camper vehicles and motor homes in Buenos Aires and Argentine Patagonia through **Gaibu Motorhome Time** (Florida 716, 6° A, Buenos Aires, tel. 011/4322-0075, fax 011/4393/8649, www.gaibu.com).

In Santiago, camping vehicles ranging from pickup trucks with shells to fully equipped motor homes are available through **Holiday Rent** (Suecia 734, Providencia, tel. 02/2582000, fax 02/2324975, www.chile-travel.com/holiday.htm).

Note that taking a Chilean vehicle into Argentina, or vice versa, involves additional paperwork and a surcharge, as well as supplementary insurance. Returning a vehicle to an office other than the one you rented from, which is impossible with the cheapest local companies, usually means a hefty surcharge.

Buying a Vehicle

If you're visiting Chile and Argentina for several months, buying a vehicle is worth consideration. The process is simpler in Chile, especially as Argentine regulations prohibit nonresidents from taking Argentine-registered vehicles out of the country—even if they have been legally purchased there.

Santiago has the largest selection; be circumspect about purchasing a vehicle in Region XII (Magallanes), where *zona franca* duty-free regulations limit purchases of many vehicles to permanent residents. Only a vehicle that is legally *liberado* may be sold in and taken outside the region.

To purchase a Chilean car, you need a RUT (Rol Unico Tributario) tax ID number, which takes only a few minutes at any Servicio de Impuestos Internos (SII, Internal Revenue Service) office; you need not be a legal resident of Chile. The SII issues a provisional RUT, valid for any purpose, and sends the permanent card to an address that you designate; this requires, of course, having an address in the country.

Before purchasing the vehicle, request a *Certificado de Inscripción y Anotaciones Vigentes* from any office of the Registro Civil (Civil Registry); this inexpensive document will alert you to title problems if any, as well as any legal issues (such as accident settlements) pending. To be licensed, the vehicle also needs an up-to-date *revisión técnica* (safety and emissions test).

Registering the sale itself is relatively straightforward at any Registro Civil office, involving a notarized *compraventa* (bill of sale, about US$15); an official *Giro y Pago del Impuesto a la Transferencia de Vehículos Motorizados* (Proof of Payment of Motor Vehicle Transfer Tax, made at a local bank, variable depending on the vehicle's value but modest for a used car); and a *Solicitud Registro Nacional de Vehículos Motorizados* (Application to the National Registry of Motorized Vehicles, about US$25). The Registro then issues a provisional title and mails the permanent title, usually within a month, to the address on your RUT.

Legally, the *compraventa* and other documents entitle you to take the vehicle out of the country, but since purchase of a Chilean vehicle by foreigners is still a little unusual, it may be worth making a special request to accelerate the issuance of the permanent title, which requires a brief letter to the head of the Registro. Personnel at the office can help with this.

BY BICYCLE

For the physically fit, or those intending to become physically fit, cycling can be an ideal way to see Patagonia. Because so many roads are unpaved, a *todo terreno* (mountain bike) is far superior to a touring bike. Cyclists should know basic mechanics, though the increasing availability of mountain bikes means that parts and mechanics are easier to find than they once were. In an emergency, it's easy to put a bicycle on board a bus.

Some cyclists dislike the main Argentine highways because their narrowness, coupled with fast drivers and the lack of shoulders, can make them unsafe, but there are many alternative routes with less traffic. High winds can make Argentine Patagonian roads, such as coastal RN 3 and the interior RN 40, difficult for cyclists.

Likewise, some cyclists dislike Chile's busy

Panamericana, much of which is also relatively uninteresting, but its completion as a four-lane divided highway with broad paved shoulders should make it safer, at least. There are many interesting alternatives, though—the scenic Carretera Austral, especially, is a mountain biker's delight.

BY FERRY AND CATAMARAN

From Puerto Montt south through the Aisén and Magallanes regions, lacustrine and maritime transportation fills the gaps in Chile's highway network. This is true even in parts of the Andean lake district, where passenger ferries on finger lakes like Lago Todos los Santos form part of trans-Andean routes to Argentina. In addition to ferries, there are high-speed catamarans that cover some of these routes and also serve some isolated tourist destinations.

From Puerto Montt, there are ferries and catamarans to Chaitén and Puerto Chacabuco, and to the icefields of Parque Nacional Laguna San Rafael, a route also traveled by the tourist cruise ship *Skorpios* and the luxury passenger catamaran *Patagonia Connection.* For details on the former two, see the entry for Parque Nacional Laguna San Rafael in the Patagonia chapter; for the latter two, see the Organized Tours entry below.

Navimag's *Magallanes* connects Puerto Montt with Puerto Natales, a three-day journey through the scenic fjords of Aisén and northern Magallanes; for details, see the appropriate geographical entries, the Organized Tours entry below, and the sidebar on "Chile's Inside Passage" in the Sur Chico chapter.

Transmarchilay runs a shuttle ferry across the mouth of the Reloncaví estuary, from La Arena to Puelche, about 45 kilometers southeast of Puerto Montt. The village of Hornopirén, 60 kilometers farther southeast, is the port for Transmarchilay's summer-only ferry to Caleta Gonzalo, the gateway to Parque Pumalín, Chaitén, and the Carretera Austral.

Ferries also connect Pargua, on the mainland southwest of Puerto Montt, with Chacao, on the Isla Grande de Chiloé. There are also ferries from Castro, at the south end of the Isla Grande, to Chaitén and occasionally to Puerto Cha-

In Chile, for the foreseeable future, a small car ferry will connect Puerto Yungay with the southernmost portion of the Carretera Austral, which leads to Villa O'Higgins.

cabuco. For details, see the appropriate geographical entry.

From the Aisén village of Puerto Ingeniero Ibáñez, on the north shore of Lago General Carrera, the car ferry *Pilchero* sails to the south shore border town of Chile Chico; while Chile Chico is also accessible by a road around the lake, the ferry is both faster and cheaper.

In Magallanes, there's a daily ferry from Punta Arenas across the Strait of Magellan to Porvenir, on the Chilean side of the Isla Grande de Tierra del Fuego; a more frequent shuttle ferry crosses the Strait from Primera Angostura, northwest of Punta Arenas.

LOCAL TRANSPORTATION

Though cars clog the streets of Buenos Aires and Santiago, most Argentines and Chileans still rely on public transportation to get around, even in small towns.

Underground

Buenos Aires and Santiago have the Southern Cone's only subway systems. BA's **Subte** (www.metrovias.com.ar) dates from 1913, but moves city residents efficiently and is expanding to underserved neighborhoods; Santiago's exemplary **Metro** (www.metrosantiago.cl) looks as new as the day it opened in 1975.

Colectivos and Micros (Buses)

Even small cities and towns are fairly well-served by local buses, which often run 24/7. Fares are mostly in the US$.35–.50 range, but vary according to distance. Argentines use the term *colectivo,* while Chileans normally say *micro* or, for smaller buses *liebres* (literally, hares).

One of the great conveniences in Chilean public transport is the *taxi colectivo,* which operates like a city bus on a fixed route. Only slightly more expensive than a city bus, it's usually faster and often more comfortable. *Taxi colectivos* are identifiable by the illuminated plastic signs on top of their roofs, which show major destinations along the route.

In Buenos Aires, Santiago, and some other localities, buses have fare boxes that make change, but in others they require *fichas* (tokens) or magnetic cards. In a few, drivers still handle the task.

Taxi and Remise

Buenos Aires, Santiago, and other cities have abundant fleets of taxis, mostly painted black with yellow roofs. Since a spate of robberies that began some years ago, nearly all Buenos Aires cabs are now *radio taxis*—some people prefer the security of phoning for a cab—but many Argentines still flag them down in the street. If in doubt, lock the back doors so that no one can enter by surprise.

All regular cabs have digital meters. In Buenos Aires, it costs about US$.48 to *bajar la bandera* ("drop the flag," i.e., switch on the meter) and another US$.06 per 200 meters; Santiago cabs are a little more expensive than those in Buenos Aires, while provincial cities tend to be a little cheaper in both countries. Verify that the meter is set at zero.

Drivers do not expect tips; some Argentine cabbies, to avoid having to make change, will even round the fare *down.* It's best to carry small bills rather than have to rely on the driver's making change, especially if he has just come on shift. Since there are a handful of dishonest drivers, before handing over the bill you may want to ask if he has the proper change for a large note, stating the amount that you're handing over.

Remises are Argentine radio taxis that charge an agreed-upon rate based on distance; the dispatcher will let you know the fare when you call, based on the pickup and drop-off points.

Hotels, restaurants, and other businesses will gladly ring radio taxis and *remises* for customers and clients, especially when the hour is late.

Bicycle

Cycling may not be the safest way of navigating chaotic city traffic, but the number of cyclists is growing rapidly. If riding around Buenos Aires, Santiago or other cities, side streets may be safer than fast-moving avenues, but they are also narrower, with less room for maneuver. Weekend traffic is not so wild as on weekdays, and downtown areas may be virtually deserted Sundays. There are few dedicated bike paths, most of which go through city parklands.

Walking

Most Argentine cities are compact enough that walking suffices for sightseeing and other activities, but the first rule of pedestrian safety is that that you are invisible—for an overwhelming majority of Argentine drivers, crosswalks appear to be merely decorative. While making turns, drivers weave among pedestrians rather than slowing or stopping to let them pass. Jaywalking is endemic, perhaps because it's not much more hazardous than crossing at the corner with the light.

Compared with most Argentines, Chilean motorists respect crosswalks and are courteous to pedestrians. A substantial minority, though, seem to drive distractedly at times, so it pays to be attentive.

Despite the hazards, pedestrians can often move faster than automobiles in congested areas.

Visas and Officialdom

ARGENTINA

Citizens of neighboring countries—Bolivians, Brazilians, Uruguayans, and Paraguayans—need only national ID cards, but most other nationalities needs passports. U.S. and Canadian citizens, along with those of the European Community and Scandinavian countries, Switzerland, Israel, Australia, and New Zealand, and other Latin American countries need passports but not advance visas. Citizens of nearly every African and Asian country, except for South Africa and Japan, need advance visas.

Regulations change, though, and it may be helpful to check the visa page of Argentina's **Ministerio de Relaciones Exteriores** (Foreign Relations Ministry, www.mrecic.gov.ar/consulares/pagcon.html). See also the sidebar "Argentine Embassies and Consulates Abroad" for contacts of the most important Argentine embassies and consulates overseas.

Argentina routinely grants foreign visitors 90-day entry permits in the form of a tourist card. Theoretically, this card must be surrendered on departure; in practice, it's the passport stamp that counts. For US$100, entry is renewable another 90 days at the **Dirección Nacional de Migraciones** (Avenida Argentina 1355, Retiro, Buenos Aires, tel. 011/4317-0237). Hours are 8 A.M.–1 P.M. weekdays only.

In the provinces, renewal can be done at any office of the Policía Federal (Federal Police), but in smaller towns the police may not be accustomed to doing so.

Formally, arriving visitors must have a return or onward ticket, but enforcement is inconsistent—if you have a Latin American, North American, or Western European passport, for instance, it is unlikely you will be asked to show the return ticket (in the Western Hemisphere, only Cubans need advance visas to enter Argentina). The author has entered Argentina dozens of times over many years, at Buenos Aires's international airport and some of the most remote border posts, without ever having been asked for either.

Foreign airlines, though, may not permit a passenger without a round-trip ticket to board an Argentina-bound flight. Likewise, if the arriving passenger presents an Eastern European, Asian, or African passport, he or she may well be asked for proof of return transport. Immigration officials have a great deal of discretion in these matters.

Always carry identification, since either the federal or provincial police can request it at any moment, though they rarely do so without reason. Passports are also necessary for routine transactions like checking into hotels, cashing traveler's checks, or even payment by credit card.

Dependent children under age 14 traveling without both parents presumably need notarized

ARGENTINE EMBASSIES AND CONSULATES ABROAD

Argentina has wide diplomatic representation throughout the world, even though economic difficulties have reduced this presence over the past couple decades. In capital cities, embassies and consulates are often, though not always, at the same address; intending visitors should go to consulates, rather than embassies, for visas or other inquiries.

Australia:
John McEwen House, 2nd floor, 7 National Circuit, Barton, ACT, tel. 02/6273-9111
Consulate: 44 Market St., 20th floor, Sydney, NSW, tel. 02/9262-2933

Canada:
90 Sparks St., Suite 910, Ottawa, Ontario K1P 514, tel. 613/236-2351
5001 Yonge St., 1st floor, Toronto, Ontario M2N 6P6, tel. 416/955-9075
2000 Peel St., Montréal, Québec H3A 2W5, tel. 514/842-6582

Chile:
Vicuña Mackenna 41, Santiago, tel. 02/222-8977
Pedro Montt 160, Puerto Montt, tel. 065/253966
21 de Mayo 1878, Punta Arenas, tel. 056/261532

France:
6 Rue Cimarosa, Paris, tel. 1/4434-2200

Germany:
Dorotheenstraße 89, 3rd floor, Berlin, tel. 30/226-8924
Lyonerstraße 34, Frankfurt am Main, tel. 69/972-0030

Mexico:
Blvd. Manuel Ávila Camacho 1, 7th floor, Colonia Lomas de Chapultepec, México D.F., tel. 55/5395-9251

New Zealand:
142 Lambton Quay, 14th floor, Wellington, tel. 4/472-8330

Switzerland:
Jungfraustraße 1, Bern, tel. 31/356-4350

United Kingdom:
27 Three Kings Yard, London W1Y 1FL, tel. 20/7318-1340

United States of America:
1811 Q Street NW, Washington, DC 20009, tel. 202/238-6460
5550 Wilshire Blvd., Suite 210, Los Angeles, CA 90036, tel. 323/954-9155
800 Brickell Ave., Penthouse 1, Miami, FL 33131, tel. 305/373-1889
245 Peachtree Center Ave., Suite 2101, Atlanta, GA 30303, tel. 404/880-0805
205 N. Michigan Ave., Suite 4209, Chicago, IL 60601, tel. 312/819-2610
12 W. 56th St., New York, NY 10019, tel. 212/603-0400
3050 Post Oak Blvd., Suite 1625, Houston, TX 77056, tel. 713/871-8935

FOREIGN CONSULATES IN BUENOS AIRES

As a major world capital, Buenos Aires has a full complement of embassies and consulates that provide citizen services. Where the embassy and consulate are not in the same location, the list below provides the latter's address, as they are primarily responsible for dealing with individuals traveling for either business or pleasure.

Unless otherwise indicated, addresses below are in the Microcentro and vicinity.

Australia:
Villanueva 1400, Palermo,
tel. 011/4777-6580

Belgium:
Defensa 113, 8th floor, Monserrat,
tel. 011/4331-0066

Canada:
Tagle 2828, Palermo,
tel. 011/4805-3032

Chile:
San Martín 439, 9th floor,
tel. 011/4394-6582

Denmark:
Leandro N. Alem 1074, 9th floor, Retiro,
tel. 011/4312-6901

France:
Santa Fe 846, 3rd floor, Retiro,
tel. 011/4312-2409

Germany:
Villanueva 1055, Palermo,
tel. 011/4778-2500

Ireland:
Avenida del Libertador 1068, 6th floor,
Recoleta, tel. 011/5787-0801

Israel:
10th floor, Avenida de Mayo 701,
Monserrat, tel. 011/4338-2500

Italy:
Marcelo T. de Alvear 1125, Retiro,
tel. 011/4816-6132

Japan:
Bouchard 547, 17th floor,
tel. 011/4318-8200

Mexico:
Arcos 1650, Belgrano,
tel. 011/4789-8826

Netherlands:
Olga Cossentini 831, 3rd floor, Edificio
Porteño Plaza 2, Puerto Madero,
tel. 011/4338-0050

New Zealand:
Carlos Pellegrini 1427, 5th floor,
tel. 011/4328-0747

Norway:
Esmeralda 909, 3rd floor, Retiro,
tel. 011/4312-2204

Spain:
Guido 1760, Recoleta,
tel. 011/4811-0070

Sweden:
Tacuarí 147, 6th floor, Monserrat,
tel. 011/4342-1422

Switzerland:
Santa Fe 846, 10th floor, Retiro,
tel. 011/4311-6491

United Kingdom:
Dr. Luis Agote 2412,
Recoleta, tel. 011/4803-7070

United States of America:
Colombia 4300, Palermo, tel. 011/5777-4533

Uruguay:
Avenida Las Heras 1915, Recoleta,
tel. 011/4807-3040

parental consent, but the author's now teenage daughter has visited Argentina many times with only one parent, and has never been asked for such a document.

Argentine-born individuals, even if their parents were not Argentines or if they have been naturalized elsewhere, sometimes attract unwanted attention from immigration officials. Generally, they may enter the country for no more than 60 days on a non-Argentine document. Argentine passports renewed outside the country expire on reentry, often requiring a bothersome and time-consuming renewal trip to the Policía Federal.

Lost or Stolen Passports

Visitors who suffer a lost or stolen passport must obtain a replacement at their own embassy or consulate. After obtaining a replacement passport, it's necessary to visit the Dirección Nacional de Migraciones (see above) to replace the tourist card.

Customs

Traditionally notorious for flagrant corruption, Argentina's improved customs normally presents no obstacle to tourists. Short-term visitors may import personal effects including clothing, jewelry, medicine, sporting gear, camping gear and accessories, photographic and video equipment, personal computers and the like, as well as 400 cigarettes, two liters of wine or alcoholic beverages (adults over 18 only), and up to US$300 of new merchandise.

Customs inspections are usually routine, but at Buenos Aires's international airports, river ports, and at some land borders, incoming checked baggage may pass through X-rays; do not put undeveloped photographic film in checked baggage. Fresh food will be confiscated at any port of entry.

At some remote border posts, the Gendarmería Nacional (Border Guards) handle all formalities, from immigration to customs to agricultural inspections. Visitors arriving from drug-producing countries like Colombia, Peru, and Bolivia may get special attention, as may those from Paraguay, with its thriving contraband economy.

Police and Military

Argentina is so notorious for police corruption that Porteños and other Argentines scornfully call both federal and provincial police *la cana*—an insult that should never be used to their face.

The Policía Federal (Federal Police) are more professional than provincial forces, which are often despised for harassing motorists for minor equipment violations and, even worse, for their *gatillo fácil* (hair-trigger) response to minor criminal offenses. Officers often solicit *coimas* (bribes) at routine traffic stops. To avoid paying a bribe, either state your intention to contact your consulate, or else use broken Spanish even if you understand the language well. Either one may frustrate a corrupt official sufficiently to give up the effort.

Since the end of the 1976–1983 dictatorship, the Argentine military have lost prestige and appear to have acknowledged their inability to run the country, despite occasional coup clamor by fringe figures. Still, security is heavy around military bases and photography is taboo—signs still proclaim that "the sentry will shoot."

CHILE

Argentines, Brazilians, Uruguayans, and Paraguayans need only national identity cards, but every other nationality needs a passport. U.S. and Canadian citizens, along with those of the European Community, Switzerland, Norway, Israel, Mexico, Australia, and New Zealand, need passports but not advance visas.

Nationalities which *must* obtain advance visas include Indians, Jamaicans, Koreans, Poles, Russians, and Thais. For addresses and telephones of key overseas Chilean embassies and consulates, see the sidebar "Chilean Embassies and Consulates Abroad."

Chile routinely grants 90-day entry permits to foreign visitors, in the form of a tourist card which must be surrendered on departure from the country. Formally, visitors must have a return or onward ticket, but the author has entered Chile dozens of times over many years, at the international airport and some of the most remote

CHILEAN EMBASSIES AND CONSULATES ABROAD

Chile has embassies and consulates throughout much of the world; those listed below should be most useful to intending visitors. For a complete list, check the website of the foreign-relations ministry (Ministerio de Relaciones Exteriores, www.minrel.cl).

Argentina:
San Martín 439, 9th floor, Buenos Aires, tel. 011/4327-2435

Australia:
10 Culgoa Circuit, O'Malley, ACT 2606, tel. 02/6286-2430

Consulates: 80 Collins St., Level 43, Melbourne, Victoria 3000, tel. 03/9654-4982
44 Market St., Level 18, Sydney, NSW 2000, tel. 02/9299-2533

Bolivia:
Calle 14 No. 8042, Calacoto, La Paz, tel. 2/2797331

Brazil:
Praia do Flamengo 344, 7th floor, Flamengo, Rio de Janeiro, tel. 21/2552-5349
Avenida Paulista 1009, 10th floor, São Paulo, tel. 11/3284-2148

Canada:
50 O'Connor St., Suite 1413, Ottawa, Ontario K1P 6L2, tel. 613/235-4402

Consulates: 2 Bloor St. West, Suite 1801, Toronto, Ontario M4W 3E2, tel. 416/924-0106
1010 Sherbrooke St. West, Suite 710, Montréal, Québec H3A 2R7, tel. 514/499-0405
1250-1185 West Georgia St., Vancouver, British Columbia V6E 4E6, tel. 604/681-9162

France:
64 Blvd. de la Tour Maubourg, Paris, tel. 4705-4661

Germany:
Mohrenstraße 42, Berlin, tel. 30/726-203-901

Consulate: Humboldtstraße 94, Frankfurt-am-Main, tel. 69/550194

border posts, without ever having been asked for a return or onward ticket.

A frequent unpleasant surprise, though, is the hefty *arrival* tax that Chile's Ministerio de Relaciones Exteriores (Foreign Ministry) has imposed on certain nationalities: US$34 for Australians, US$55 for Canadians, US$15 for Mexicans, and US$100 for U.S. citizens. These are one-time fees, valid for the life of the user's passport, and collected only at airports.

The rationale behind these fees, officially described as a *gasto administrativo de reciprocidad* (administrative reciprocity charge) is that the governments of those countries require Chilean citizens to pay the same amounts simply to apply for a visa (with no guarantee of being issued one). That's a reasonable argument, but the misunderstandings provoked when unsuspecting arrivals are diverted to a special line to pay those additional fees often generates ill will toward Chile.

Ninety-day extensions can take several days and cost roughly US$100, plus two color photos, at the **Departamento de Extranjería** (Moneda 1342, Santiago Centro, tel. 02/6725320) or in regional capitals. Visitors close to the Argentine, Peruvian, or Bolivian borders may find it quicker and cheaper to dash across the line and return. For lost tourist cards, it's necessary to request a

Mexico:
Ejército Nacional 423, 3rd floor, Colonia Granada, Mexico City, tel. 55/5545-1043

Netherlands:
Stadhouderskade 2,5° 1054 Es, Amsterdam, tel. 20/612-0086

New Zealand:
7th floor, Willis Corroon House, 1-3 Welleston St., Wellington, tel. 4/471-6270

Peru:
Javier Prado Oeste 790, San Isidro, Lima, tel. 1/611-2200

Switzerland:
Eigerplatz 5, 12th floor, Bern, tel. 31/370-0058

United Kingdom:
12 Devonshire St., London W1N 2DS, tel. 20/7580-1023

United States of America:
1736 Massachusetts Ave. N.W., Washington, DC 20036, tel. 202/785-3159

Consulates: 6100 Wilshire Blvd., Suite 2140, Los Angeles, CA 90048, tel. 323/933-3697
870 Market St., Suite 1062, San Francisco, CA 94105, tel. 415/982-7662
800 Brickell Ave., Suite 1230, Miami, FL 33131, tel. 305/373-8623
875 N. Michigan Ave., Suite 3352, Chicago, IL 60611, tel. 312/654-8780
79 Milk St., Suite 600, Boston, MA 02109, tel. 617/426-1678
866 United Nations Plaza, Suite 601, New York, NY 10017, tel. 212/355-0612
Public Ledger Building, Suite 1030, 6th & Chestnut Sts., Philadelphia, PA 19142, tel. 215/829-9520
Edificio American Airlines, Suite 800, 1509 López Landrón, Santurce, San Juan, PR 00911, tel. 809/725-6365
1360 Post Oak Blvd., Suite 2330, Houston, TX 77056, tel. 713/621-5853

Uruguay:
Andes 1365, 1st floor, Montevideo, tel. 2/902-6316

replacement from the **Policía Internacional** (General Borgoño 1052, Independencia, Santiago, tel. 02/7371292), or from offices in regional capitals.

Always carry identification, since the Carabineros (national police) can request it at any moment, though they rarely do so without some reason. Passports are also necessary for routine transactions like checking into hotels and cashing traveler's checks.

Lost or Stolen Passports

Visitors who suffer a lost or stolen passport must obtain a replacement at their own embassy or consulate. After obtaining a replacement, it's necessary to visit the Policía Internacional (see above) to replace the tourist card.

Customs

Visitors to Chile may import personal effects including clothing, jewelry, medicine, sporting gear, camping equipment and accessories, photographic and video equipment, personal computers and the like, and wheelchairs for disabled individuals, as well as 500 grams of tobacco, three liters of wine or alcoholic beverages (adults only), and small quantities of perfume.

Customs inspections are usually routine, but at Santiago's international airport and some land

FOREIGN EMBASSIES AND CONSULATES IN SANTIAGO

All major European and South American states, plus many others, have diplomatic representation in Santiago. The bordering countries of Argentina, Bolivia, and Peru have consulates in several other cities; their addresses appear in the appropriate geographical entry.

Argentina:
Vicuña Mackenna 41, tel. 02/2228977

Australia:
Gertrudis Echeñique 420, Las Condes, tel. 02/2285065

Canada:
Nueva Tajamar 481, 12th floor, Las Condes, tel. 02/3629660

France:
Condell 65, Providencia, tel. 02/2251030

Germany:
Agustinas 785, 7th floor, tel. 02/6335031

Israel:
San Sebastián 2812, 5th floor, Las Condes, tel. 02/7500500

Italy:
Román Díaz 1270, Providencia, tel. 02/2259212

Mexico:
Félix de Amesti 128, Las Condes, tel. 02/2066132

Netherlands:
Las Violetas 2368, Providencia, tel. 02/2236825

New Zealand:
El Golf 99, Oficina 703, Las Condes, tel. 02/2909802

Spain:
Avenida 11 de Septiembre 2353, 9th floor, Providencia, tel. 02/2334070

Sweden:
Avenida 11 de Septiembre 2353, 4th floor, Providencia, tel. 02/2312733

Switzerland:
Américo Vespucio Sur 100, 14th floor, tel. 02/2634211

United Kingdom:
Avenida El Bosque Norte 0125, 3rd floor, Las Condes, tel. 02/2313737

United States of America:
Avenida Costanera Andrés Bello 2800, Las Condes, tel. 02/2322600

Uruguay:
Pedro de Valdivia 711, Providencia, tel. 02/2238398

borders, incoming checked baggage passes through X-rays; do not put photographic film in your bag en route from Mendoza, Argentina, to Santiago, for instance. At the international airport, there are drug-sniffing beagles.

Travelers bound from Region XII (Magallanes) will undergo internal customs checks because those regions have *zona franca* duty free status. At many borders, the Servicio Agrícola Ganadero (SAG, Agriculture and Livestock Service) conducts agricultural inspections—fresh food will be confiscated—and sometimes levies a small charge for doing so.

At some remote border posts, the Carabineros (national police) handle all border formalities, from immigration to customs to agricultural inspections.

Police and Military

Chile's Carabineros are probably the continent's most professional police, with a reputation for integrity and a low tolerance for bribery and similar corruption (Argentine motorists, accustomed to bribing the cops for traffic violations in their own country, have had their vehicles confiscated for trying to do so in Chile). Known popularly but scornfully as *pacos* by some Chileans, the Carabineros are normally polite and helpful in public, but can be stern with lawbreakers—or individuals they suspect of being lawbreakers.

During the Pinochet dictatorship, the military were feared, but since the return to constitutional government and, especially, since Pinochet's detention and arrest in London, they keep a low public profile.

FALKLAND ISLANDS

All visitors, including Britons, must have passports to visit the Falklands. Visitors from Britain, the European Community, most Commonwealth countries, Chile, and the Mercosur countries do not need visas, but others should contact a British consulate. Tourists must have return tickets and sufficient funds to cover their stay, and may need to arrange accommodations in advance. Visa or MasterCard are proof of sufficient funds. Visitors should also have adequate medical coverage.

Lost or Stolen Passports

Visitors who suffer a lost passport here—theft is highly unlikely—may have problems, as there are no foreign consulates. UK and EU citizens should be able to arrange a temporary passport through Customs and Immigration, but other nationalities could need to obtain a formal Declaration of Identity through their nearest embassy and obtain permission from any other country through which they might pass, with consular assistance required at the transit airport. Consequently there could be delays in departing the Islands.

Customs

Local customs permits the importation of almost anything except illegal drugs, though there are taxes on alcoholic beverages (which are readily available locally).

Police and Military

Falklands police resemble their British counterparts; they do not carry firearms, and rarely have to deal with anything more serious than a traffic violation or a bar brawl.

The British military presence is substantial, but most of them live at Mount Pleasant Airport and visitors rarely come in contact with them. Some soldiers do take advantage of R&R to visit wildlife sites, when they may meet tourists.

Conduct and Customs

Argentines and Chileans have many things in common, but some traits differ dramatically. In both countries, politeness goes a long way with officials, shopkeepers, and others with whom you may have contact. It's always good form to offer the appropriate polite salutation *buenos días* (good morning), *buenas tardes* (good afternoon), or *buenas noches* (good evening or good night), depending on the time of day.

In terms of general conduct, both women and men should dress conservatively and inconspicuously when visiting churches, chapels, and sacred sites. This, again, is an issue of respect for local customs, even if locals themselves don't also observe it.

Argentines and especially Porteños (like New Yorkers) are known as extroverts, with a stereotyped reputation for brusqueness; some even gripe about their compatriots that "nobody respects anybody here any more." Chileans, by contrast, have a reputation as the "Victorians of South America" for their reluctance to display their emotions publicly. This is certainly a stereotype as well—many Chileans are gregarious—but on balance Argentines are probably more outgoing.

PHOTOGRAPHIC ETIQUETTE

Unlike some countries with large indigenous populations, Argentines are not exactly camera-shy, though an in-your-face approach is not necessarily appropriate either. Especially when inclusion of people is incidental to, say, a landscape, it's not a problem. However, if a person is the photograph's primary subject, try to establish a rapport before asking permission to photograph, if you can manage Spanish or have another language in common. At the same time, photographers should be particularly respectful of Patagonia's indigenous peoples.

Likewise, Chileans in general are accustomed to cameras, but photographing the Mapuche of the Andean lake district or other indigenous people without first establishing a rapport would be a serious error of judgment.

Tips for Travelers

EMPLOYMENT OPPORTUNITIES

The unemployment situation may be better in Patagonia than elsewhere in Argentina or Chile, but well-paid work is still hard to come by even for legal residents, let alone visitors on tourist or student visas. Nevertheless, foreigners have found work in the tourist industry, or casual labor in bars or restaurants. Such jobs, though, may be seasonal (in the case of tourism), or poorly paid (in the case of restaurants, except in a handful of places where tips are high).

Ideally, obtaining a work permit from an Argentine consulate is better than attempting to obtain one in country, as employment may not begin until the permit is actually granted. Nevertheless, it still requires submitting documents and takes some time.

Legal residence in Chile, which permits eligibility for a greater number of better-paying jobs, usually requires local or foreign sponsorship, a substantial investment, marriage to a Chilean spouse or other permanent resident, or a reliable retirement income. In theory, temporary working visas can lead to residence, but some workers have continued on them for several years, as the Interior Ministry bureaucracy turns slowly.

BUSINESS TRAVEL

Argentina's economy has been erratic since 2001–2002, while Chile's has been the continent's most productive. For more detailed suggestions on business travel, see the author's separate Moon Handbooks on Chile, Buenos Aires, and Argentina.

There are few legal restrictions on foreign businesses operating in Argentina, but the recent business climate, thanks largely to debt default and banking restrictions, has not been conducive to investment. Political corruption has been a further disincentive.

The best investment bets include travel and tourism services, a key Patagonian sector. Thanks to devaluation, residential real estate has been a bargain, and sellers are showing increased willingness to offer properties. In any event, before signing any business deal, consult a local lawyer recommended by your embassy, consulate, or a truly trusted friend.

Chile's institutional stability and low corruption levels have made it an investor's favorite. That, however, does not eliminate the need to understand the cultural and legal context of investing in the country.

ORGANIZED TOURS

Because of Patagonia's complex travel logistics, organized tours can be a useful option for visitors with limited time, and many reputable U.S., Argentine, and Chilean operators offer and even coordinate tours on both sides of the border. Within each category, the companies below appear in alphabetical order.

North America–Based Operators

The **American Geographical Society** (P.O. Box 938, 47 Main St., Suite One, Walpole, NH 03608-0938, tel. 888/805-0884, fax 603/756-2922, www.amergeog.org) operates a 17-day luxury cruise through southernmost Patagonia and Tierra del Fuego and on to the Falkland Islands; its only Argentine stop is at Ushuaia, but it visits several other areas covered in this book, primarily in Chile. Rates start at US$6,285 per person, double occupancy, including airfare from Miami.

Primarily but not exclusively for cyclists, **Backroads** (801 Cedar St, Berkeley, CA 94710, tel. 510/527-1555 or 800/462-2848, fax 510/527-1444, www.backroads.com) offers a nine-day "Chile & Argentina Biking" tour that takes in Chile's Lago Llanquihue area, along with Bariloche and vicinity (US$3,998 pp). Their nine-day "Patagonia Walking & Hiking" (US$5,898 pp) stays at luxury lodgings in Chile's Parque Nacional Torres del Paine and Argentina's Parque Nacional Los Glaciares.

Bio Bio Expeditions (P.O. Box 2028, Truckee, CA 96160, tel. 800/246-7238, fax 530/550-9670, www.bbxrafting.com) offers weeklong trips from Puerto Montt to its cozy base camp on Chile's Río Futaleufú for kayaking and multisport trips in the US$2,000–2,600 range.

Earth River Expeditions (180 Towpath Road, Accord, NY 12404, tel. 845/626-2665 or 800/643-2784, fax 845/626-4423, www.earthriver.com) offers 10-day rafting and multi-sport trips on and around the Río Futaleufú for US$2,800–3,000 from Puerto Montt. It has its own deluxe camp on the river.

The **Earthwatch Institute** (3 Clocktower Place, Maynard, MA 01754, tel. 800/776-0188, fax 978/461-2332, www.earthwatch.org) arranges volunteer programs in which participants pay for the privilege of assisting university faculty and independent researchers in archaeological and environmental studies. Projects in Chilean Patagonia have included river otters on the Río Toltén and owls in the Cape Horn area.

For travelers at least 55 years old, **Elderhostel** (11 Avenue de Lafayette, Boston, MA 02111, tel. 877/426-8056, www.elderhostel.org) operates a variety of two-week trips on both sides of the border in the US$3,207–4,377 range. There are options for both relatively sedentary and very active individuals, with highlights like cruising the northern Chilean fjords and hiking the El Chaltén sector of Argentina's Parque Nacional Los Glaciares.

A pioneer on the Río Futaleufú, former U.S. Olympian Chris Spelius's **Expediciones Chile** (P.O. Box 752, Sun Valley, ID 83353, tel. 888/488-9082, www.exchile.com) has its own sprawling and secluded but cozy Campo Tres Monjas on the river's south bank. While they specialize in kayaking the Fu, they also offer rafting and multi-sport holidays that include birding, hiking, and horseback riding. Weeklong stays (US$1,500) at Tres Monjas include plenty of time and instruction on the river, and transportation from Chaitén; for US$8,000 you can spend the entire summer season.

The Explorers Club (46 East 70th Street, New York, NY 10021, tel. 603/756-4004 or 800/856-8951, www.explorers.org) operates a month-long, ocean-going "South American Odyssey" that begins in the Panama Canal and ends in Ushuaia, Argentina, with plenty of other Patagonian sights and stops: Chile's Parque Pumalín, Puerto Chacabuco, and Beagle Channels fjords, as well as the Falkland Islands. Rates on the 106-passenger *Orion* range US$12,995–25,995 per person; it's possible to join mid-trip in Santiago, Chile, from US$6,495–13,995 per person.

Kayak Futaleufú (379 King Street, Almonte, Ontario K0A1A0, tel. 613/256-0783, www.kayakfu.com) offers several weeklong kayaking trips (US$1,650–1,895), utilizing the Cara del Indio and Earth River base camps outside the town of Futaleufú.

Mountain Travel Sobek (1266 66th Street, Emeryville, CA 94608, tel. 888/687-6235, fax 510/594-6001, www.mtsobek.com) does a 15-day "Trekking the Paine Circuit" (US$3,790 pp), and an 11-day "Futaleufú River Adventure" (US$2,590 pp), which can include rafting, sea kayaking, mountain biking, and hiking. Their 16-day "Hiker's Patagonia" (US$4,150 pp) begins in Santiago but flies almost immediately to Punta Arenas and Parque Nacional Torres del Paine, then crosses the border to Argentina's Parque Nacional Los Glaciares and finishes with a full day in Buenos Aires. The 17-day "Patagonia Explorer" (US$5,490 pp) follows part of the "Hiker's Patagonia" itinerary, plus four nights cruising through the Fuegian fjords of Tierra del Fuego on the *Terra Australis.* For the truly intrepid, there's the "Patagonia Ice Cap Traverse" (US$4,190 pp) on the Argentine side. Mountain Travel Sobek also has a UK contact (tel. 44/1494/448901, sales@mtsobekeu.com).

Nature Expeditions International (7860 Peters Road, Suite F-103, Plantation, FL 33324, tel. 954/693-8852 or 800/869-0639, fax 954/693-8854, www.naturexp.com) operates upscale "soft adventure" and culture-oriented tours to Argentina and Chile, among other destinations. Their 16-day "Chile: Land of Extremes" (US$4,950) takes in Puerto Varas, Chiloé, Laguna San Rafael, and Torres del Paine, while "Argentina: Journey to Patagonia" includes Buenos Aires, Península Valdés, Punta Tombo, Trelew, and Bariloche, with a brief detour to Iguazú falls. The binational "Patagonia Wilderness Adventure" (US$4,625 pp) visits Torres del Paine, El Calafate and Vicinity, and Buenos Aires.

Orvis (1711 Blue Hills Drive, Roanoke, VA 24012-8613, tel. 888/235-9783, fax 540/343-7053, www.orvis.com) arranges fishing holidays in the vicinity of the northern Patagonian towns of Junín de los Andes and Esquel, southern Argentine Patagonia's Río Gallegos, and the Argentine side of Tierra del Fuego.

Owned by native Patagonians (from Neuquén and Río Gallegos), California-based **Patagonia Travel Adventures** (P.O. Box 22, Ben Lomond, CA 95005, tel. 831/336-0167, www.patagoniaadventures.com) focuses on small group tours to Península Valdés and Punta Tombo, Parque Nacional Los Glaciares, the little-visited Patagonian steppe along RN 40, and even Chile's Parque Nacional Torres del Paine.

Powderquest Tours (7108 Pinetree Road, Richmond, VA 23229, tel. 804/285-4961 or 888/565-7158, fax 240/209-4312, www.powderquest.com) runs five or six nine- to 13-day Southern Cone ski tours annually. Argentine Patagonian resorts include Chapelco, Cerro Bayo and Cerro Catedral (Ladera Sur).

REI Adventures (P.O. Box 1938, Sumner, WA 1938, tel. 800/622-2236, www.rei.com) offers a 12-day "Northern Lake District" tour (US$2,699 pp) of Argentina and Chile; destinations include Bariloche and vicinity, Villa la Angostura, San Martín de los Andes, and Pucón. The 12-day "Patagonia Explorer" (US$2,699 pp) focuses on Chile's Torres del Paine.

Affiliated with the Smithsonian Institution, **Smithsonian Journeys** (P.O. Box 23293, Washington, DC 20026-3293, tel. 202/357-4700 or

877/338-8687, www.smithsonianjourneys.org) offers a 14-day "Patagonian: Crown Jewel of Chile" excursion (US$4,995 pp) that visits Puerto Varas and vicinity, Punta Arenas, Puerto Natales and vicinity, and Torres del Paine.

Wilderness Travel (1102 Ninth Street, Berkeley, CA 94710, tel. 510/558-2488 or 800/368-2794, fax 510/558-2849, www.wildernesstravel.com) offers a variety of trips starting with an 11-day "Chile's Land of Fire & Ice" through the Andean lake district, including Argentina's Bariloche. Other trips include the 16-day "In Patagonia" excursion (US$4,295 pp) that focuses mostly on Argentina but also visits Torres del Paine; and a 15-day "Peaks of Patagonia" (US$3,795 pp) that takes in Torres del Paine, and Argentina's Moreno Glacier and Fitz Roy areas.

Wildland Adventures (3516 NE 155th St., Seattle, WA 98155, tel. 800/345-4453, fax 206/363-6615, www.wildland.com) operates small group tours (2–8 persons) through locally based guides. In Argentina, their 10-day "Best of Patagonia" (US$2,325 pp) takes in the Moreno Glacier and other sights via Buenos Aires. The 14-day "In the Wake of Magellan" trip (from US$4,290) includes both Torres del Paine and a segment of the scenic luxury cruise between Punta Arenas and Ushuaia, as well as Argentina's Moreno glacier.

UK-Based Operators

Explore Worldwide (1 Frederick St., Aldershot, Hants. GU11 1LQ, tel. 01252/760000, www.exploreworldwide.com) organizes 14- to 20-day tours primarily to the northern Andean lake district and the more southerly Torres del Paine and Argentina's El Calafate area. Rates range from US$1,950–2,970.

Journey Latin America (12/13 Heathfield Terrace, Chiswick, London W4 2JU, tel. 020/8747-3108, fax 020/8742-1312, www.journeylatinamerica.co.uk) specializes in small group tours throughout Latin America, including Argentina, Chile, and the Falkland Islands.

Muir's Tours (97a Swansea Road, Reading RG1 8HA, tel. 0119/950-2281, www.nkf-mt.org.uk) is a fair-trade adventure and cultural-travel operator that offers Torres del Paine hiking packages of five, seven, and 10 days. Rates run about US$1,100–1,300 per person, with accommodations at the Cascada Eco-camp when not actually on the trail.

Australia-Based Operators

Peregrine Adventures (258 Lonsdale St., Melbourne, Victoria 3000, tel. 03/9662-2700, fax 03/9662-2422, www.peregrineadventures.com) organizes tours to the southernmost Patagonia, covering both sides of the border.

One of Australia's biggest operators, **World Expeditions** (71 York St., Level 5, Sydney, NSW 2000, tel. 02/8270-8400, fax 02/9279-0566, www.worldexpeditions.com.au) has a variety of Patagonian tours. It also has branches in Melbourne (393 Little Bourke St., Melbourne, Victoria 3000, tel. 03/8631-3300, fax 03/9670-7474, travel@worldexpeditions.com.au), and Brisbane (36 Agnes Street, Shop 2, Fortitude Valley, Queensland 4006, tel. 07/3216-0823, fax 07/3216-0827, adventure@worldexpeditions.com.au).

Argentina-Based Operators

The operators below invariably have English-speaking personnel and have services in many parts of the country. Many locally focused operators, though, have very good services as well; see the corresponding geographical entries for suggestions. Argentina's country code is 54.

The Buenos Aires–based **Asatej Group** (Florida 835, Oficina 205, tel. 011/4114-7600, www.asatej.com) is Argentina's youth- and budget-oriented operator, which has refocused on incoming tourism since the early 2002 peso collapse.

Based in El Chaltén, activity-oriented **FitzRoy Expediciones** (Lionel Terray 212, tel. 02293/429742, tel. 02962/493017, www.fitzroyexpediciones.com.ar) focuses on that geographical area, organizing expeditions onto the southern Patagonian ice sheets and other less-demanding day trips.

Bariloche-based **Meridies** (Avenida Benito Bock 146, No. 4, Bariloche, tel. 02944/523467, www.meridies.com.ar) is primarily an adventure-oriented climbing company that does strenuous trips like Volcán Lanín, but it also does a week-long driving and hiking trip along the southern portion of Patagonia's RN 40 ("La Cuarenta").

Buenos Aires–based **Sendero Sur** (Perú 359, Oficina 608, Monserrat, tel./fax 011/4343-1571, www.senderosur.com.ar) does a series of activity-oriented trips that include cycling in the Argentine and Chilean lake districts, visits to Patagonian *estancias,* and hiking in and around Parque Nacional Los Glaciares and Ushuaia.

Chile-Based Operators

Several Chile-based operators figure in Chilean Patagonia and Tierra del Fuego, and some also work the Argentine side of the border. Chile's country code is 56.

AlSur Expediciones (Del Salvador 100, Puerto Montt, tel./fax 065/232300, www.alsur-expeditions.com) operates tours and activities in the Andean lake district and specializes in Parque Pumalín, Douglas Tompkins' large private nature reserve.

Based in summer only at the town of Dalcahue on the Isla Grande de Chiloé, **Altué Sea Kayaking** has extensive itineraries around the eastern shore of the archipelago. For reservations, their Santiago contact is Altué Active Travel (Encomenderos 83, Las Condes, Santiago, tel. 02/2332964, fax 02/2336799, www.seakayakchile.com).

Antares Patagonia Adventure (Barros Arana 111, Puerto Natales, tel. 061/414611, fax 061/414276, www.antarespatagonia.com) operates activities-oriented trips to Patagonia, mostly but not exclusively in Parque Nacional Torres del Paine, where it has concessions for activities like ice hiking, kayaking, and mountaineering. It offers a diverse set of packages ranging from four days/three nights to 13 days/12 nights for US$690–$1,900 per person, depending on the number of passengers. Its U.S. representative is Americas Travel (348 Hayes St., San Francisco, CA 94102-4421, tel. 415/703-9955, fax 415/703-9959, mdiaz@antarespatagonia.com).

U.S./Peruvian-run **Austral Adventures** (Cochrane 432, Ancud, Chiloé, tel./fax 065/625977, www.austral-adventures.com) offers custom boat tours of the archipelago from Ancud south to Parque Pumalín, as well as land-based programs on the Isla Grande. Half-day tours in the vicinity of Ancud start around US$40, while week-long expeditions to Parque Pumalín cost around US$1,600, including gourmet meals.

French-owned **Azimut 360** (General Salvo 159, Providencia, Santiago, tel. 02/2363880, fax 02/2353085, www.azimut360.com) offers a variety of Patagonian excursions ranging from traditional southern lake-district trips to northern Patagonian ice fields and technical climbs of summits like Aisén's 4,058-meter Monte San Valentín. Its personnel can handle English, French, and Spanish.

Campo Aventura (San Bernardo 318, Puerto Varas, tel./fax 065/232910, www.campo-aventura.com) offers four-day, three-night horseback explorations of the spectacularly scenic Cochamó backcountry southeast of Puerto Varas, for US$349 per person, but both shorter and longer options are possible. English, German, French, Spanish, and Luxemburgisch are spoken.

Santiago-based **Cascada Expediciones** (Avenida Las Condes 11265, Departamento 10, tel. 02/2175061, fax 02/2151949, www.cascada-expediciones.com) offers a variety of activity-oriented excursions from the city and, during the summer season, trips farther afield to destinations like Pucón, Futaleufú, and Torres del Paine, where its domed "Ecocamp" is the most distinctive accommodations option in the park.

October–April, **Cruceros Australis** (Avenida Bosque Norte 0440, 11th floor, Las Condes, Santiago, tel. 02/4423110, fax 02/2035173, www.australis.com) offers three-, four-, and seven-day cruises from Punta Arenas through southern Tierra del Fuego's fjords to Ushuaia and Cape Horn on its luxury liner *Mare Australis.* Rates vary from low-season (October and April) to mid-season (November–mid-December and all of March) and high-season (mid-December–February). Cruceros Australis also has offices in Buenos Aires (Carlos Pellegrini 989, Retiro, tel. 011/4325-8400, fax 011/4325-6600) and in Miami (4014 Chase Ave. Suite 202, Miami Beach, FL 33140, tel. 305/695-9618 or 877/678-3772, fax 305/534-9276). For more details, see the Fjords of Fuegia section in the Magallanes chapter.

September–May, **Cruceros Marítimos Skorpios** (Augusto Leguía 118, Las Condes, Santiago, tel. 02/2311030, fax 02/2322269, www.skorpios.cl) operates a fleet of small cruise ships (around 100 passengers) from Puerto Montt and Puerto Chacabuco to Laguna San Rafael, and from Puerto Natales to the fjords of Campo de Hielo Sur, the southern continental ice field west of Torres del Paine.

Explora Hotels (Américo Vespucio Sur 80, 5th floor, Las Condes, Santiago, tel. 02/2066060, fax 02/2284655, www.explora.com) offers very expensive, all-inclusive packages, ranging from three days to a week, at its magnificently sited hotel in Parque Nacional Torres del Paine.

Cruceros Australis's affiliate **Navimag** (Avenida El Bosque Norte 0440, Las Condes, 11th floor, tel. 02/4423120, fax 02/2035025, www.navimag.com) sails between the Patagonian town of Puerto Natales and the mainland city of Puerto Montt. While these are not cruises in the traditional sense, they are more than just utilitarian transportation as they pass through Pacific Chile's spectacular fjordlands. For details and fares, see their website and the sidebar "Chile's Inside Passage" in the Sur Chico chapter.

Patagonia Connection (Fidel Oteíza 1951, Oficina 1006, Providencia, Santiago, tel. 02/2256489, fax 02/2748111, www.patagonia-connection.com) offers four-day, three-night to six-day, five-night packages based at its Termas de Puyuhuapi hot-springs resort in Aisén, including a full-day catamaran excursion to Parque Nacional Laguna San Rafael. Low-season rates, depending on the type of accommodations, start around US$700–1,270 per person for the shorter tours and US$1,000–1,600 per person for the longer tours. In high season, the shorter tours cost US$920–1,670 while the longer ones are US$1,300–2,130.

Puerto Williams–based, German-run **Sea & Ice & Mountains Adventures Unlimited** (tel./fax 061/621150, tel. 061/621227, www.simltd.com) operates yacht tours through Tierra del Fuego and Cape Horn in the summer months.

TRAVELERS WITH DISABILITIES

For people with disabilities, Patagonia can be problematical, as the infrastructure is mostly unsuitable in a region whose main attractions are outdoors. Even in cities, narrow and uneven sidewalks, not to mention the fast-moving traffic, are unkind to people with disabilities, especially those who need wheelchairs. Public transportation rarely accommodates passengers with disabilities, though Avis Argentina has recently introduced rental vehicles with hand controls.

Few older buildings are specifically equipped for handicapped people, but many of these are low and can often accommodate people with disabilities. In newer high-rise hotels, disabled access is obligatory.

TRAVELING WITH CHILDREN

Argentina and Chile are child-friendly countries. In fact, since many Argentines and Chileans enjoy large extended families, they may feel little in common with people in their late twenties and older who do *not* have children, and traveling with kids can open doors.

Many parks and plazas have playground equipment, and it's easy to mix with families there. What foreign parents may find unusual is that even toddlers may be out on the swings and slides with their families at 11 P.M. or later, even in small isolated communities. Likewise, kids are off across the street, around the neighborhood, and even on the buses at ages when North American parents are driving their kids three blocks to school and waiting nervously until the doors close safely behind them.

On public transportation, strangers may spontaneously but gently touch small children and even set them on their laps. While foreigners may find this disconcerting, it's not necessarily inappropriate in cultural context.

WOMEN TRAVELERS

Like other Latin American societies, Argentina and Chile have strong *machista* (chauvinist) elements. Argentine and Chilean women are traditionally mothers, homemakers, and children's caregivers, while men are providers and decision-makers, but there are increasing numbers of professionals and other working women.

Many Argentine and Chilean men view foreign women as sexually available, but this is not necessarily discriminatory—they view women of their own nationality the same way. In Argentina, harassment often takes the form of *piropos,* sexist comments that are often innocuous and can even be poetic, but are just as likely to be vulgar. It's best to ignore verbal comments, which are obvious by tone of voice even if you don't understand them; if they're persistent, seek refuge in a café or *confitería.*

Despite problems, Argentine and Chilean women have acquired political prominence. The most prominent and notorious, of course, was Evita Perón, but her rise to the top was an unconventional one. The highest-profile females in current politics are Argentine first lady Cristina Kirchner—a senator from Santa Cruz province in her own right—and former Chilean defense minister Michelle Bachelet, a presidential candidate for the left-of-center Concertación in 2005.

GAY AND LESBIAN TRAVELERS

Despite its conspicuous Catholicism, Argentina is a fairly tolerant country for both gay males and lesbians, and public displays of affection—men kissing on the cheek, women holding hands—are relatively common even among heterosexuals. In 2003, in fact, the city of Buenos Aires passed an ordinance permitting same-sex civil unions, though the rest of the country was not exactly fast to follow.

This does not mean that homosexuals can always behave as they wish in public—the police have beaten and jailed individuals who have offended their sense of propriety. If in doubt, be circumspect.

Certain Buenos Aires districts, most notably Recoleta, Barrio Norte, and Palermo, have a number of openly gay entertainment venues and even accommodations, but these are less conspicuous in provincial cities.

Conservative Chile may be less publicly tolerant of homosexuality, but Santiago has a lively (though far from exclusively) gay scene in Barrio Bellavista. Certainly times are better than in the 1930s, when the government of authoritarian president General Carlos Ibáñez del Campo rounded up homosexuals and threw them into the ocean with concrete footwear.

Health and Safety

Midlatitude Buenos Aires and Santiago offer no major health risks beyond those associated with any large city; public health standards are good and tap water is potable almost everywhere.

A good general source on foreign health matters is Dr. Richard Dawood's *Travelers' Health* (New York: Random House, 1994), a small encyclopedia on the topic. Dr. Stuart R. Rose's regularly updated *International Travel Health Guide* (Northampton, MA: Travel Medicine Inc., 2001) is regionally focused. Try also the fifth edition of Dirk G. Schroeder's *Staying Healthy in Asia, Africa, and Latin America* (Emeryville, CA: Avalon Travel Publishing, 2000).

For up-to-date information on health issues throughout the Southern Cone, see the U.S. Centers for Disease Control (CDC) Temperate South America regional page (www.cdc.gov/travel/temsam.htm), covering Chile, Argentina, Uruguay, and the Falkland Islands. Another good source is the United Kingdom's Department of Health (www.doh.gov.uk), which provides a chart of recommended prophylaxis by country.

BEFORE YOU GO

Theoretically, Argentina and Chile demand no proof of vaccinations, but if you are coming from a tropical country where yellow fever is endemic, authorities could ask for a vaccination certificate.

Traveling to Patagonia or elsewhere without adequate medical insurance is risky. Before leaving your home country, purchase a policy that includes evacuation in case of serious emergency. Foreign health insurance may not be accepted in either country, so you may be required to pay out of pocket for later reimbursement. Often, however, private medical providers accept international credit cards in return for services.

Numerous carriers provide medical and evacuation coverage; an extensive list, including Internet links, is available at the U.S. State Department's website (http://travel.state.gov/Publications/medical.html).

GENERAL HEALTH MAINTENANCE

Common sense precautions can reduce the possibility of illness. Washing the hands frequently with soap and water, and drinking only bottled, boiled, or carbonated water reduces the risk of contagion for short-term visitors (though Argentine and Chilean tap water is potable almost everywhere).

Where purified water is impossible to obtain, such as backcountry streams where there may be livestock or problems with human waste, pass drinking water through a one-micron filter and further purify it with iodine drops or tablets (but avoid prolonged consumption of iodine-purified water).

FOOD- AND WATER-BORNE DISEASES

While relatively few visitors to Patagonia run into problems of this sort, contaminated food and drink are not unheard of. In many cases, it's simply exposure to different sorts of bugs to which your body soon becomes accustomed, but if symptoms persist the problem may be more serious.

Traveler's Diarrhea

Colloquially known as *turista* in Latin America, the classic traveler's diarrhea (TD) usually lasts just a few days and almost always less than a week. Besides "the runs," symptoms include nausea, vomiting, bloating, and general weakness. The usual cause is the notorious *Escherichia coli* bacterium from contaminated food or water; in rare cases *E. coli* infections can be fatal.

Fluids, including fruit juices, and small amounts of bland foods such as freshly cooked rice or soda crackers, may relieve symptoms and help regain strength. Dehydration can be a serious problem, especially for children, who may need to be treated with an oral rehydration solution (ORS) of carbohydrates and salt.

Over-the-counter remedies like Pepto-Bismol, Lomotil, and Immodium may relieve symptoms but can also cause problems. Prescription drugs such as doxycyline and trimethoprim/sulfamethoxazole can also shorten the cycle. These may not, however, be suitable for children, and it's better for everyone to avoid them if at all possible.

Continuing and worsening symptoms, including bloody stools, may mean dysentery, a much more serious ailment that requires a physician's attention.

Dysentery

Bacterial dysentery, resembling a more intense form of TD, responds well to antibiotics, but the more serious amoebic dysentery can lead to intestinal perforation, peritonitis, and liver abscesses. Like diarrhea, its symptoms include soft and even bloody stools, but some people may be asymptomatic even as they pass on *Entamoeba hystolica* through unsanitary toilet and food-preparation practices. Metronidazole, known by the brand names Flagyl or Protostat, is an effective treatment, but a physician's diagnosis is advisable.

Cholera

Resulting from poor hygiene, inadequate sewage disposal, and contaminated food, contemporary cholera is less devastating than its historic antecedents, which produced rapid dehydration, watery diarrhea, and imminent death without almost equally rapid rehydration. While today's cholera strains are highly infectious, most carriers do not even suffer symptoms. Existing vaccinations are ineffective, so health authorities now recommend against them.

Treatment can only relieve symptoms. On average, about five percent of victims die, but those who recover are immune. Not a common problem in either Argentina or Chile, it's not unheard of either, but it's rare in Patagonia.

Hepatitis A

Usually passed by fecal-oral contact under conditions of poor hygiene and overcrowding, hepatitis A is a virus. The traditional gamma globulin prophylaxis has limited efficacy and wears off in just a few months. New hepatitis A vaccines, though, are more effective and last longer.

Typhoid

Typhoid is a serious disease common under unsanitary conditions, but the recommended vaccination is an effective prophylaxis.

INSECT-BORNE DISEASES

Patagonia is malaria-free but the disease may exist in northern subtropical Argentina; a few other insect-borne diseases may be present if not exactly prevalent.

Dengue Fever

Like malaria, dengue is a mosquito-borne disease of the lowland tropics, but it's less common than malaria and rarely fatal. Eradicated in Argentina in 1963, the mosquito vector *Aedes egypti* is once again present as far south as Buenos Aires and health authorities believe outbreaks are possible there. The best prophylaxis is to avoid mosquito bites by covering exposed parts of the body with insect repellent or appropriate clothing.

Chagas Disease

Also known as South American trypanosomiasis, Chagas' disease is most common in Brazil but affects about 18 million people between Mexico and Argentina; 50,000 people die from it every year. Not a tropical disease per se, it has a discontinuous distribution—Panama and Costa Rica, for instance, are Chagas-free.

Since Chagas spreads by the bite of the night-feeding conenose or assassin bug, which lives in adobe structures, avoid such structures (these still exist in the countryside); if it's impossible to do so, sleep away from the walls. DEET-based insect repellents offer some protection. Chickens, dogs, and opossums may carry the disease.

Chagas' initial form is a swollen bite often accompanied by fever, which soon subsides. In the long run, though, it may cause heart damage leading to intestinal constipation, difficulty in swallowing, and sudden death; there is no cure. Charles Darwin may have been a chronic sufferer.

HANTAVIRUS

Hantavirus is an uncommon but deadly disease contracted by breathing, touching, or ingesting feces or urine of the long-tailed rat. Primarily a rural phenomenon and most prevalent in Patagonia, the virus thrives in enclosed areas; when exposed to sunlight or fresh air, it normally loses its potency. Avoid places frequented by rodents, particularly abandoned buildings, but note that there have been cases in which hikers and farm workers have apparently contracted the disease in open spaces.

RABIES

Rabies, a virus transmitted through bites or scratches by domestic animals (like dogs and cats) and wild mammals (like bats), is a concern; many domestic animals in Argentina go unvaccinated, especially in rural areas. Human prophylactic vaccination is possible.

Untreated rabies can cause an agonizingly painful death. In case of an animal bite or scratch, clean the affected area immediately with soap and running water, and then with antiseptic substances like iodine or 40 percent-plus alcohol. If possible, try to capture the animal for diagnosis, but not at the risk of further bites; where rabies is endemic, painful post-exposure vaccination may be unavoidable.

SNAKEBITE

Poisonous snakes are rare in Patagonia (Chile has none), but the range of the aggressive and highly venomous pit viper *yarará* (*Bothrops* spp.) extends into Argentina's northern Chubut province.

The *yarará,* whose venom paralyzes the nervous system, is responsible for most of the country's snakebite incidents, but strikes are uncommon. Death is not instantaneous and antivenins are available, but the wisest tactic is to be alert and avoid confrontation. If bitten, get to medical facilities as quickly as possible, but avoid excessive movement that helps the venom circulate.

ALTITUDE SICKNESS

At the highest elevations, above about 3,000 meters, *apunamiento* or *soroche* can be an annoyance and even a danger, particularly for older people with respiratory problems. Most of the Patagonian uplands are lower than the central and northern Andes, but even among young, robust individuals, a quick rise from sea level to the sierra, in the space of a couple hours, can cause intense headaches, vertigo, drowsiness or insomnia, shortness of breath, and other symptoms. Combined with hypothermia, it can be life-threatening.

For most people, rest and relaxation help relieve symptoms as the body adapts to reduced oxygen at higher altitudes; aspirin or a comparable painkiller will combat headache. Should symptoms persist or worsen, moving to a lower elevation will usually have the desired effect. Do not overeat, avoid alcohol consumption, and drink extra fluids.

Stephen Bezruchka's *Altitude Illness, Prevention & Treatment* (Seattle: The Mountaineers, 1994) deals with the topic in detail; the fifth edition of James A. Wilkerson's edited collection *Medicine for Mountaineering & other Wilderness Activities* (Seattle: The Mountaineers, 2001) discusses other potential problems as well.

HYPOTHERMIA

Hypothermia is a dangerously quick loss of body heat, most common in cold and damp weather at high altitudes or high latitudes—be particularly careful in areas with large day-night temperature variations. Symptoms include shivering, disorientation, loss of motor functions, skin numbness, and physical exhaustion. The best remedy is warmth, shelter, and food; unlike cottons, woolen clothing retains warmth even when wet. Avoid falling asleep if at all possible; in truly hazardous conditions, you may not regain consciousness. Carry high-energy snacks and drinking water.

SUNBURN

In southernmost Patagonia and Tierra del Fuego, ozone-destroying aerosols have increased the entry of ultraviolet radiation, and caused skin problems for people and even for livestock like cattle and sheep. For all outdoor activities, use a heavy sunblock; on city streets, walk in the shade whenever possible.

SEXUALLY TRANSMITTED DISEASES

While life-threatening AIDS is the most hazardous of sexually transmitted diseases (STDs) and certainly gets the most press, other STDs are more prevalent and serious if left untreated. All are spread by unprotected sexual conduct; the use of latex condoms by males can greatly reduce the possibility of contracting STDs, but not necessarily eliminate it.

Most STDs, including gonorrhea, chlamydia, and syphilis, are treatable with antibiotics, but some strains have developed immunity to penicillin and alternative treatments. If taking antibiotics, complete the prescribed course, since an interrupted treatment may not kill the infection and could even help it develop immunity.

The most common STD is **gonorrhea,** characterized by a burning sensation during urination, and penile or vaginal discharge; it may cause infertility. **Chlamydia** has milder symptoms but similar complications. **Syphilis,** the only major disease that spread from the Americas to Europe after the Spanish invasion, begins with ulcer and rash symptoms that soon disappear; long-term complications, though, can include cardiovascular problems and even derangement.

Herpes, a virus that causes small but irritating genital ulcers, has no effective treatment. It's likely to recur, easily spread when active, and can contribute to cervical cancer. **Hepatitis B,** though not exclusively an STD, can spread through the mixing of bodily fluids such as saliva, semen, and menstrual and vaginal secretions. It can also spread through unsanitary medical procedures, inadequately sterilized or shared syringes, during body piercing, and similar circumstances. Like Hepatitis A, it can lead to liver damage but is more serious; vaccination is advisable for high-risk individuals, but is expensive.

HIV/AIDS

As in most countries, HIV/AIDS is an issue of increasing concern. It is not exclusively an STD (IV drug users can get it by sharing needles), but unprotected sexual activity is a common means of transmission; the use of latex condoms can reduce the possibility of infection.

SMOKING

Approximately 40 percent of Argentines smoke, including nearly half the male population; tobacco directly causes 40,000 deaths per annum. According to one survey, three of every 10 Argentine *cardiologists* smoke, and few of those make any recommendation to their own patients on the subject. Future fatalities start early—three of 10 students between the ages of 13 and 15 are smokers.

Still, there is widespread recognition that the habit is unhealthy, and effective smoking restrictions are in force on public transportation and a few other settings. If faced with secondhand smoke in one of the few places where it's prohibited, such as buses or taxis, it's easiest to appeal to courtesy with a white lie such as *"soy asmático"* (I'm asthmatic).

Many Argentine businesses have eliminated or reduced smoking on their premises, and there's a growing movement to educate and to limit public consumption of tobacco.

Smoking is more widespread in Chile than in the U.S., but less so than in Europe. It's effectively prohibited on public transportation and many, though not all, restaurants have tobacco-free sections. Chilean smokers generally respect limitations on their habit.

LOCAL DOCTORS

Top-quality medical services, with the latest technology, are readily available in Buenos Aires and Santiago, and even in some provincial cities. Foreign embassies sometimes maintain lists of English-speaking doctors, who often have overseas training and are numerous in the capitals and other large cities.

PHARMACIES

Pharmacies serve an important public health role in Argentina and Chile, but also carry certain risks. Pharmacists may provide drugs on the basis of symptoms that they may not completely comprehend, especially if there's a language barrier; while the cumulative societal impact may be positive, individual recommendations may be erroneous.

Many medications available by prescription only in North America or Europe may be sold over the counter in Argentine or Chilean pharmacies. Travelers should be cautious about self-medication even when such drugs are available; check expiration dates, as out-of-date drugs sometimes remain on the shelf.

In large cities and even some smaller towns, pharmacies remain open all night for emergency prescription service on a rotating basis. The *farmacia de turno* and its address will usually be posted in the window of other pharmacies, or advertised in the newspaper.

CRIME

Though many Argentines and Chileans believe assaults, rapes, homicide, and crimes against property are increasing, both countries are safe by international standards, and Patagonia particularly so. Because citizens keep late hours, there are plenty of people on the street at most times—rarely will you find yourself walking alone down a dark alleyway.

Still, certain precautions almost go without saying—most crimes are crimes of opportunity. Never leave luggage unattended, store valuables in the hotel safe, keep close watch on your belongings at sidewalk cafés, and carry a photocopy of your passport with the date of entry into the country. Do not carry large amounts of cash (money belts or leg pouches are good alternatives for hiding cash), do leave valuable jewelry at home, and do keep conspicuous items such as photo and video cameras out of sight. Do not presume that any area is totally secure.

If you should be accosted by anyone with a firearm or other potentially lethal weapon, do not resist. While guns are uncommon—knives are the weapon of choice—and truly violent crime against tourists is unusual (especially in Patagonia), consequences of a misjudgment can be lethal.

One phenomenon that has disturbed Argentines in recent years is the so-called *secuestro exprés* (express kidnapping), in which criminals hold an individual for a small ransom or, alternatively, force someone to withdraw money from an ATM. Far more common in Buenos Aires province than in the capital or elsewhere in the country, these crimes have *not* targeted tourists—rather, they appear to concentrate on individuals whose movements are familiar to the lawbreaker.

More common is the crime of distraction, in which an individual bumps into the victim and spills a substance like ice cream or mustard; while the perpetrator apologizes profusely, an accomplice surreptitiously lifts items of value. Pickpocketing is also common on public transportation; carry wallets and other items of value in a front trouser pocket or, even better, an interior jacket pocket.

Information and Services

MONEY

While traveling in Patagonia, it makes sense to have a variety of money alternatives. International credit cards are widely accepted, and foreign ATM cards work almost everywhere. Because ATMs are open 24 hours, many visitors prefer this alternative, but in remotest Patagonia there are sometimes no banks. It makes sense to have a cash reserve in U.S. dollars (rather than euros; though the European currency is gaining credibility, it's not an everyday item, especially outside Buenos Aires and Santiago). Traveler's checks may be the safest way to carry money, since they're usually refundable in case of loss or theft, but changing them outside Buenos Aires or Santiago can be a nuisance, especially in Argentina.

If carrying an emergency cash reserve, use an inconspicuous leg pouch or money belt—not the bulky sort that fits around the waist, which thieves or robbers easily recognize, but a zippered leather belt that looks like any other.

Currency

Argentine banknotes exist in denominations of 2, 5, 10, 20, 50, and 100 pesos. Coins exist in denominations of 1, 5, 10, 25, and 50 centavos, but one-centavo coins have nearly disappeared and most businesses generally round off prices to the nearest 5 or 10 centavos. There are also one- and two-peso coins.

Counterfeiting of both U.S. and foreign currency appears to be increasing in Argentina. Merchants will often refuse a U.S. banknote with the smallest tear or writing on it, at the same that they will accept any peso note that is not flagrantly *trucho* (bogus). On Argentine banknotes, look for the conspicuous watermark with the initials of the historical figure depicted—J.S.M. for José de San Martín on the five-peso note, for instance.

Chile's unit of currency is also the peso (Ch$), with coins in denominations of Ch$5, Ch$10, Ch$50, Ch$100, and Ch$500. Banknotes come in values of Ch$500 (gradually disappearing),

Ch$1,000, Ch$2,000, Ch$5,000, Ch$10,000, and Ch$20,000.

Equivalent to British Sterling, the Falkland Islands pound (£) is the official currency but U.S. dollars and euros are widely accepted, as are traveler's checks. MasterCard and Visa are also widely accepted, at least in Stanley, but other credit cards are not. Stanley's Standard Chartered Bank has no ATM, but British visitors with a guarantee card can cash personal checks up to £50.

Exchange Rates

Following Argentina's early 2002 debt default, caretaker president Eduardo Duhalde's government devalued the peso from 1 to 1.4 per dollar but, when that proved unsustainable, he floated the currency. By mid-year, the peso had fallen to 3.5 to the dollar before stabilizing, and in mid-2005, it was trading around three per dollar. The Euro's strength against the dollar has made the country cheaper for European travelers.

With Chile's more stable economy, the currency has fluctuated far less and, as of mid-2005, it was trading in the Ch$580 per dollar range. Rates tend to be highest in Santiago and lower in the regions, but this is not so meaningful as it used to be, for reasons explained in the following paragraphs.

For the most up-to-date exchange rates, consult the business section of your daily newspaper or an online currency converter such as www.oanda.com.

In the Falkland Islands, the local pound is equivalent to the British Sterling, which circulates alongside it. Falklands currency, though, is useless outside the Islands.

Changing Money

During the 1990s, when the Argentine peso was at par with the dollar, changing money was a nonissue, as the two were virtually interchangeable. The floating of the peso, though, made banks, *casas de cambio* (exchange houses), and surreptitious exchanges relevant again.

ATMs, abundant except in a few remote areas, match the best bank rates and are accessible 24/7. Most ATMs, unfortunately, dispense large banknotes, often of Ar$100 and rarely smaller than Ar$50. One way around this problem is to punch in an odd amount, such as Ar$290, in order to ensure getting some smaller notes.

Conditions are similar in Chile, but note that Banco Estado ATMs, the only option in many small towns, may be incompatible with foreign ATM cards. Many villages do not even have banks, be sure to change enough money to get you to the next major town. Likewise, in the countryside, carry plenty of smaller bills—for a small shopkeeper with limited resources, changing a Ch$5,000 note may be impossible.

In the Falkland Islands, U.S. dollars, Euros, and Sterling are widely accepted, and Stanley's Standard Chartered Bank will change traveler's checks and give advances on Visa. There are no ATMs, however.

Traveler's Checks and Refunds

Despite their safeguards, traveler's checks have many drawbacks in Patagonia, particularly the Argentine side. In addition to the time-consuming bureaucracy of changing them at banks and exchange houses, they may carry a substantial penalty in terms of commission—up to three percent or even more in some cases. Businesses other than exchange houses may not accept them and, in really out-of-the-way places, almost nobody will. Traveler's checks, unfortunately, should be a last-resort means of carrying and changing money here; cash (despite the risks) and ATM cards are better options.

Bank Transfers

Many Argentine exchange houses, post offices, and other businesses are affiliated with Western Union, making it relatively straightforward to send money from overseas. For a list of Western Union affiliates in Argentina and Chile, see their website (www.westernunion.com). The American Express Money Gram is another alternative; AmEx has headquarters in Buenos Aires and Santiago, and affiliates throughout both countries.

In an emergency, it's possible to forward money to U.S. citizens via the U.S. embassy in Buenos Aires or Santiago by establishing a Department of

State trust account through its Overseas Citizens Services, Washington, D.C. 20520 (tel. 202/647-5225; there is a US$20 service charge for setting up the account). It's possible to arrange this as a wire or overnight-mail transfer through Western Union (tel. 800/325-6000 in the U.S.); for details, see the State Department's website (www.travel.state.gov).

Credit and Debit Cards

Credit cards have been common currency for many years in both Argentina and Chile. During the 2002 peso crisis, when Argentines could not withdraw their savings from frozen bank accounts, their use became even more widespread. Visa and MasterCard are most widely accepted, but there are inconsistencies—many businesses prefer American Express, sometimes to the exclusion of others, or even Diner's Club. Debit cards are also widely accepted, at least those with Visa or MasterCard affiliation.

There are possible drawbacks to using credit cards, though. During the 1990s boom, Argentine merchants generally refrained from the *recargo,* a surcharge on credit-card purchases because of slow bank payments; many have reinstituted the *recargo,* up to 10 percent, to cut their losses due to the peso's loss of value between the customer's payment and the bank's reimbursement. Note that hotels in particular may offer equivalent cash discounts.

Fluctuating exchange rates may also affect the charge that eventually appears on your overseas account. If the rate has changed in the interim between your payment in Patagonia and its posting to the home account, it may be either greater or smaller in terms of dollars (or other foreign currency), depending on the peso's performance.

Note that, in general, *propinas* (gratuities) may *not* be added to charge restaurant meals. Keep some cash, either dollars or pesos, for tips.

Costs

For most of the 1990s, a rigid exchange policy made **Argentina** South America's most expensive country, so much so that even North Americans and Europeans found it costly. Wealthy Argentines, for their part, partied in Miami, Madrid, Rome, and other inexpensive destinations.

After the February 2002 peso float, and subsequent banking restrictions that limited the amount of money in circulation, Argentina became a bargain for visitors with dollars or other hard currency. A crippling recession, with unemployment exceeding 20 percent, kept prices from skyrocketing in spite of devaluation. Businesses such as restaurants had to keep prices relatively low, attempting to sell more at a lower margin.

Though the Argentine peso has rebounded since early 2003, travel remains inexpensive by global standards, but much depends on expectations. There are suitable services for everyone from barebones budget backpackers to pampered international business travelers. Budget travelers will still find hostel bunks or hotel rooms for less than US$10 per person and some excellent values for only a little more money. Hotels and resorts of international stature, like the Hyatt and Sheraton chains and their local equivalents, normally charge international prices, but even these have had to lower their rates during the crisis.

Likewise, meals range from a couple dollars or even less at the simplest *comedores;* restaurants with sophisticated international cuisine can charge a lot more, but even here prices are lower than in North America or Europe.

As of press time, shoestring travelers could get along on US$20 per day or conceivably even less for accommodations and food. For US$50 per day it's possible to live comfortably and eat well, and a US$100 budget can seem extravagant. It's worth adding that a combination of internal and foreign demand has driven prices relatively higher than elsewhere in Chile or Argentina.

By global standards, travel in **Chile** is moderately priced, but much depends on the traveler's expectations and where in the country he or she goes. On balance, prices are about 20 percent higher than in Argentina, but this can vary depending on locality—the Argentine resort of El Calafate, for instance, is more expensive than nearby Puerto Natales, Chile.

The **Falkland Islands,** by contrast, are substantially more expensive than either Argentine or

Chilean Patagonia, because accommodations are relatively few, local wages are high, and most local transportation consists of pricey air-taxi services. For most visitors, US$100 per day for meals and accommodations alone will be a modest budget.

Prices are comparable to the UK for hotels and wildlife lodges (the latter, with full board, cost up to £100 pp per day). On the other hand, there are self-catering cottages in camp for as little as £10–20 per day, and B&B accommodations in Stanley for about the same price. Camping is an option in a few areas, but nearly all land is private and many farmers worry about fire.

Food costs except for fresh meat (mainly mutton) are also high, as many items must be imported by air or sea, and Stanley's market garden is a capital-intensive hydroponic facility. Stanley's best couple restaurants would be good anywhere, and have prices to prove it, but there are also moderately priced fast-food snacks like burgers and pub grub like fish and chips.

Internal transportation costs are high because of high capital investments for a relatively small market. Government air-taxi service links the two main islands and many smaller ones, but visitors pay higher rates than residents.

Taxes

Argentina imposes a 21 percent *impuesto al valor agregado* (IVA, value added tax or VAT) on goods and services, though this is normally included in the advertised price; if in doubt, ask for clarification *(¿Incluye los impuestos?)*. Tax evasion is a national sport, though, and hotel owners often ignore the tax for cash payments.

Tourists may request IVA refunds for purchases of Argentine products valued more than about US$25 from shops that display a "Global Refund" decal on their windows. Always double-check, though, that the decal is not out of date.

When making any such purchase, request an invoice and other appropriate forms. Then, on leaving the country, present these forms to Argentine customs; customs will then authorize payment to be cashed at Banco de la Nación branches at the international airport.

At smaller border crossings, though, do not expect officials to be prepared to deal with tax refunds. Some crossings do not even have separate customs officials, but rather are staffed by the Gendarmería (Border Guards), a branch of the armed forces.

Chile levies an 18 percent IVA on goods and services. Most midrange to upscale hotels, however, legally discount IVA for foreign visitors who receive a *factura de exportación* (export receipt) along with their hotel bill; for details, see the Accommodations entry above.

Tipping

In formal restaurants with table service, a 10 percent gratuity is customary, but in family-run eateries the practice is rare. Taxi drivers are customarily not tipped, but rounding off the fare to the next highest convenient number is appropriate. Where there is no meter, this is not an issue.

Bargaining

Bargaining is not the way of life in Argentina and Chile that it is in some other Latin American countries, but in flea or crafts markets the vendor may start at a higher price than he or she expects to receive—avoid insultingly low offers, or such a high offer that the vendor will think you a fool. Depending on your language and bargaining skills, you should be able to achieve a compromise that satisfies everybody.

Student and Senior Discounts

Student discounts are relatively few, and prices are so low for most services that it's rarely worth arguing the point. Students, though, may be eligible for discount international airfares; see the entries on Getting There and Getting Around, and student-oriented travel agencies, for details.

Travelers above age 62 are often eligible for *tercera edad* discounts for museums, transportation, and some other services.

COMMUNICATIONS AND MEDIA

Postal Services

Since the privatization of Correo Argentino, the Argentine post office, service has been more reliable than in the past, but there's some uncertainty now that the government of newly elected President Néstor Kirchner has canceled their contracts because of reported failure to meet payments. Domestic services remain generally cheap, international services more expensive. Major international couriers provide fast, reliable services at premium prices.

General delivery at Argentine and Chilean post offices is *lista de correos,* literally a list arranged in alphabetical order. There is a small charge for each item addressed to you.

Note that, in Spanish-language street addresses, the number follows rather than precedes the name; instead of "1343 Washington Avenue," for example, a comparable Spanish-language address would read "Avenida Providencia 2134." Spanish speakers normally omit the word *calle* (street) from addresses; where an English speaker might write "499 Jones Street," for instance, a Spanish speaker would simply use "Tucumán 272." It's not unusual for street addresses to lack a number, as indicated by *s/n* (*sin número,* without a number), especially in small provincial towns.

Postal services in the Falkland Islands are dependable but infrequent, as they rely on weekly flights from Chile and less-frequent RAF flights from the UK. Large parcels go by sea, four or five times per annum. FIGAS air taxis deliver mail to outer settlements and islands, sometimes without landing.

Telephone and Fax

Argentina's country code is 54; the *característica* (area code) for the Capital Federal and Gran Buenos Aires is 011, but there is a bewildering number of area codes for individual cities, smaller cities and towns, and rural areas. All telephone numbers in the Capital Federal and Gran Buenos Aires have eight digits, while those other provincial cities and rural areas vary. When calling out of the area code, it's necessary to dial zero first.

Cellular phones in Buenos Aires all have eight digits, prefixed by 15. In addition, certain toll-free and other specialty numbers have six or seven digits with a three-digit prefix.

Public telephone are abundant; some operate with coins only, but most also accept magnetic phone cards or rechargeable account cards. The basic local phone rate is A$.25 (about US$.08) for five minutes or so; domestic long-distance is more expensive. Phone cards are convenient for in-country calls but less useful for more expensive overseas calls.

For long-distance and overseas calls, and fax services, it's simplest to use *locutorios* (call centers), which are abundant in both Buenos Aires and the provinces. Especially since devaluation, prices are increasingly competitive, and now tend to be much cheaper than placing *cobro revertido* (collect) or *tarjeta de crédito* (credit card) calls to the U.S. or any other country. Calls are more expensive during peak hours, 8 A.M.–8 P.M. weekdays and 8 A.M.–1 P.M. Saturdays.

Opening a cell-phone account without a permanent Argentine address is something of a nuisance, but rental phones are available from Nolitel (tel. 011/4311-3500, reservas@nolitelgroup.com) in Buenos Aires.

Chile's country code is 56; there are a number of area codes for individual cities and, in some cases, entire regions. All telephone numbers in Santiago have seven digits, while those in the other regions generally have six, but in some rural areas they have seven digits beginning with 1.

Cellular phones all have seven digits, prefixed by 09. In addition, certain toll-free and other specialty numbers have six-digits with a three-digit prefix.

Public telephone are abundant; some operate with coins only, but most also accept rechargeable account cards. The basic local phone rate is Ch$100 (about US$.15) for five minutes or so; domestic long distance is not that much more expensive. For long-distance and overseas calls, and fax services, it's simplest to use *centros de llamados* (call centers), which are abundant in both Santiago and the regions.

The area code of the **Falkland Islands** is 500, valid for numbers in Stanley and in camp. All telecommunications are fairly expensive here, though local technology is state-of-the-art; calls may be made from private phones or Stanley's Cable and Wireless office. Cable and Wireless

PLC operates both local and long-distance telephone services; all local numbers have five digits.

Local calls cost 6p per minute, calls to the UK 99p per minute except weekends and holidays when it's 80p per minute, and calls to other countries £1.10 per minute except weekends and holidays, when it's 99p per minute. Operator-assisted calls are more expensive, and have a three-minute minimum, so it's best to buy a phone card. There's also a surcharge for collect calls (local only).

Internet Access

In the last few years, public Internet access has become abundant and so cheap that, if price trends continue, providers will soon be paying customers to use their services. Rarely does access cost more than US$1 per hour, and it's often even cheaper. Many Argentine *locutorios* offer access, but there are many Internet cafés in both Argentina and Chile. Some overseas service providers, most notably AOL, Compuserve, and Earthlink, have local dial-up numbers, but these often collect a surcharge. High-speed and WiFi coverage are increasing rapidly in both countries.

In the Falkland Islands, Internet service (modem only) can be slow and is relatively expensive at £3.60 per hour. As with phone calls, it's more convenient to purchase a card.

Media

Buenos Aires papers are also—some to a greater degree than others—national papers sold throughout **Argentina.** The middle-of-the-road tabloid *Clarín* is the Spanish-speaking world's largest-circulation daily, while the *Buenos Aires Herald* is an English-language daily whose niche market correlates highly with hotel occupancy. It stresses commerce and finance, but also produces intelligent analyses of political and economic developments; its thicker Sunday edition includes material from the *The New York Times* and several British papers including *The Independent.*

What was once a state broadcast monopoly is now far more diverse, thanks to privatization and the advent of cable, but conglomerates like the Clarín and El Cronista groups control much of the content.

Chile may have emerged from dictatorship, but the press remains in the hands of large consortia like the pro-Pinochet El Mercurio group, which publishes its namesake daily and many other papers. Pinochet's arrest and subsequent legal troubles, however, opened up a whole new space for irreverently satirical papers such as *The Clinic,* whose bimonthly circulation of some 40,000 is a remarkable success story (the paper named itself for the London clinic at which the former dictator was detained). For an English-language summary of the Chilean daily press, plus occasional original reporting, look at the Internet-only *Santiago Times* (www.chip.cl); the weekly print tabloid *News Review* is largely business-oriented and relatively bland.

In contrast with the print media, radio and TV journalism are more pluralistic, at least in terms of ownership, as private media with foreign capital have competed with local sources since the early 1990s. That said, the state-run Television Nacional (TVN) and the Universidad Católica's Canal 13 (Channel 13) are still the most important broadcast outlets.

The only print medium in the **Falkland Islands** is the weekly *Penguin News,* which often raises the hackles of local politicians. The Falkland Islands Broadcasting System (FIBS, 96.5 FM or 550 AM) provides local radio programming, but Islanders also get radio and TV from the BBC and the British Forces Broadcasting System (BFBS). The nightly FIBS announcements, at 6:30 P.M., include the following day's FIGAS flight schedules.

MAPS AND TOURIST INFORMATION

Argentina, Chile, and the Falkland Islands all have good sources for maps and tourist information, but others are available overseas.

Maps

International Travel Maps and Books (ITMB, 530 West Broadway, Vancouver BC, V5Z 1E9, tel. 604/879-3621, fax 604/879-4521, www.itmb.com) publishes a series of maps that cover all or parts of Patagonia at a variety of scales, including *Southern South America* (1:2,800,000), Argentina (1:4,000,000), Tierra del Fuego (1:750,000), and the Falkland Islands (1:300,000).

For **Argentina,** the **Automóvil Club Argentino** (ACA, Argentine Automobile Club, Avenida del Libertador 1850, Palermo, Buenos Aires, tel. 011/4808-4000, www.aca.org.ar) publishes Argentina's most comprehensive series of highway maps, covering every province and including major city plans. Members of overseas affiliate automobile clubs, like the AAA in the United States, can buy these at discount prices. For topographic maps, the best source is Argentina's **Instituto Geográfico Militar** (Avenida Cabildo 301, Palermo, Buenos Aires, tel. 011/4576-5576, www.igm.gov.ar).

For **Chile,** the annually updated three-volume *Turistel* guidebook series (Spanish only) contains the most current road maps at the back of its *Norte* (North), *Centro* (Center), and *Sur* volumes, along with numerous useful city maps which, unfortunately, lack scales.

JLM Cartografía (General del Canto 105, Oficina 1506, tel./fax 02/2364808, Providencia, Santiago, jmatassi@interactiva.cl) publishes a series of regional and local maps at varying scale (even within the same map), in both Spanish and imperfect but generally serviceable English. Some cover parts of neighboring countries. Titles include *Sudamérica* (South America); *Araucanía, Maule a Toltén* (Araucanía, from Maule to Toltén); *Pucón/San Martín de los Andes; Lagos Andinos, Temuco a Bariloche* (Andean Lakes, from Temuco to Bariloche); *Ruta de los Jesuitas, Puerto Montt a Bariloche* (Trail of the Jesuits, from Puerto Montt to Bariloche); *Chiloé/Patagonia, Costa a Costa* (Chiloé and Patagonia, from Coast to Coast); *Camino Austral/Patagonia Chilena; Torres del Paine; Patagonia Sur/Tierra del Fuego* (Southern Patagonia and Tierra del Fuego); *Tierra del Fuego;* and *Antárctica/Polo Sur* (Antarctica and the South Pole).

Chile's own **Instituto Geográfico Militar** (IGM, Dieciocho 369, Santiago Centro, tel. 02/4606800, fax 02/4608924, www.igm.cl) publishes detailed topographic maps covering the entire country at a scale of 1:50,000; some of these, however, are "proprietary" as they adjoin what the military consider to be sensitive border areas. They are also expensive at about US$15 and up. The Instituto also sells a variety of city maps, road atlases, and books that are useful to the everyday visitor, and the staff are professional and efficient.

For the **Falkland Islands,** the locally available *Falkland Islands Explorer,* published in the UK, depicts the islands' roads and topography at a scale of 1:365,000, plus a basic city map of Stanley and text on history and natural history.

In Stanley, the **Secretariat** (Ross Road, tel. 27242) offers Directorate of Overseas Surveys (DOS) topographic maps of the entire Islands at a scale of 1;50,000, but there's also a two-sheet (1:250,000) series that's adequate for most purposes. Customs & Immigration (3 H Jones Road, tel. 27340) has maritime charts.

International Travel Maps (530 West Broadway, Vancouver BC, Canada V52 1E9, tel. 604/879-3621, fax 604/879-4521, www.itmb.com) publishes *Falkland Islands/Islas Malvinas* at a scale of 1:300,000, including detailed information on wildlife sites, but it's less complete on recent road improvements.

Tourist Offices

Argentina's **Secretaría Nacional de Turismo** (www.turismo.gov.ar), the national tourism service, has its main office in Buenos Aires, but every Argentine province also maintains a tourist-information representative in the capital; for addresses and contacts of Patagonian provinces, see the accompanying sidebar.

Each Argentine province also operates an information office in its own capital, and often in specific tourist destinations as well. Almost every other locality has its own tourist office—even in very small towns; these normally keep long summer hours but may be limited the rest of the year. For details, see the corresponding geographical entries.

Sernatur (www.sernatur.cl), Chile's national tourism service, maintains public information offices in Santiago and all regional capitals, and in

PROVINCIAL TOURIST OFFICES IN BUENOS AIRES

Every Patagonian province in Argentina maintains a tourism representative in Buenos Aires.

Chubut:
Sarmiento 1172, San Nicolás, tel. 011/4383-7458, www.chubutur.gov.ar, chubuturbue@chubutur.gov.ar

Neuquén:
Maipú 48, Microcentro, tel. 011/4343-2324, www.neuquentur.gov.ar, casanqn_turismo@neuquen.gov.ar

Río Negro:
Tucumán 1916, Balvanera, tel. 011/4371-5599, www.rionegrotur.com.ar

Santa Cruz:
Suipacha 1120, Retiro, tel. 011/4325-3098 or 011/4325-3102, www.santacruz.gov.ar, infosantacruz@infovia.com.ar

Tierra del Fuego (Instituto Fueguino de Turismo):
Marcelo T. de Alvear 790, Retiro, tel. 011/4311-0233, infuebue@arnet.com.ar

Puerto Natales. Most are normally open weekdays only, but in summer and in some localities they are open weekends. For details, see the appropriate geographical entries.

In addition to Sernatur's offices, many cities and towns have their own municipal tourist offices, especially in Andean lake district resorts like Villarrica, Pucón, and Puerto Varas, which keep long summer hours but are limited the rest of the year. Many smaller towns have summer-only (January and February) offices. Again, for details, see the appropriate geographical entries.

Falkland Islands Tourism (www.tourism.org.fk) is a public-private partnership that has offices in Stanley and representatives in the United Kingdom. For details on and suggestions for travel to, from, and in the Islands, consult the thorough, well-organized website.

In the UK, **Falkland House** (14 Broadway, Westminster, London SW1H 0BH (tel. 44/20/7222-2542, travel@falklands.gov.fk) is the Islands' official representative and de facto tourist office.

Falklands Conservation (Jetty Centre, tel. 22247, fax 22288, www.falklandsconservation.com) provides information on wildlife and conservation issues. It also has a UK representative (1 Princes Avenue, Finchley, London N3 2DA).

FILM AND PHOTOGRAPHY

Color print film is widely available, color slide film less reliably so. In any event, film tends to be cheaper in North America or Europe, so it's best to bring as much as possible. If purchasing film in Argentina, check the expiration date to make sure it's current, especially in out-of-the-way places. In the capital and larger tourist centers, print film processing is readily available and moderately priced, but it's better to hold slide film until your return to your home country if possible (but store it under cool, dark, and dry conditions).

Environmental conditions can affect the quality of your shots and the type of film you should use. Bright sun can wash out photographs; in these circumstances, use a relatively slow film, around ASA 64 or 100, and a

PHOTOGRAPHIC ETIQUETTE—AND A WARNING

Most Argentines, especially Porteños, are not exactly camera-shy, but do be cautious about photographing political protests—the police are notorious for cataloguing dissidents, so protestors may be suspicious of people with cameras. Likewise, avoid photography near military installations, although "the sentry will shoot" signs are mostly a thing of the past.

Generally, if a person's presence in a photograph is incidental, as in a townscape, it's unnecessary to ask permission, but avoid the in-your-face approach. If in doubt, ask; if rejected, don't insist. If you're purchasing something from a market vendor, he or she will almost certainly agree to be photographed.

There is one absolute no-no, however—without express permission, do not even think about photographing Israeli or Jewish community sites anywhere in Argentina. Since car-bomb attacks on Retiro's Israeli Embassy in 1992 and Once's Jewish cultural center in 1994, federal police are stationed outside all these sites. They will politely or, if necessary, not-so-politely discourage would-be clickers.

polarizing filter to reduce glare. A polarizing filter also improves contrast, dramatizing the sky and clouds, but can result in a dark foreground if you're not careful.

WEIGHTS AND MEASURES

Time

Argentina is three hours behind GMT for most of the year, and does not observe daylight savings (summer time). When the U.S. Eastern Time Zone is on daylight savings, during the Northern Hemisphere summer, and Argentina is on standard time, Buenos Aires is one hour ahead of New York; the rest of the year, there is two hours' difference.

Across the Andes, Chile is four hours behind GMT and one hour behind Argentina except in summer, when Chile goes on daylight savings time and it's two hours behind. In an energy-saving measure, some northern Argentine provinces went on daylight savings time in mid-2004, but most quickly abandoned the idea when the savings were minimal.

Like Chile, the Falkland Islands are four hours behind GMT. In summer, Stanley goes on daylight saving time, but camp remains on standard time.

Electricity

Throughout Argentina and Chile, nearly all outlets are 220 volts, 50 cycles, so converters are necessary for North American appliances like computers and electric razors. Traditional plugs have two rounded prongs, but more recent Argentine plugs have three flat blades that form, roughly, an isosceles triangle; cheap adapters are widely available.

Adequately powered converters are hard to find, so it's better to bring one from overseas.

Falkland Islands outlets also run on 220 volts, 50 cycles, but plugs are identical to those in the United Kingdom.

Measurements

The metric system is official, but this doesn't completely eliminate the variety of vernacular measures that Argentines and Chileans use in everyday life. Rural folk often use the Spanish *legua* (league) of about five kilometers as a measure of distance, and the *quintal* of 46 kilos is also widely used, especially in wholesale markets and agricultural statistics.

Likewise, the metric system is now official in the Falkland Islands, but locals still use vernacular English measures such as miles in everyday situations.

Spanish Phrasebook

Spanish is Argentina's official language, but the stereotypical Porteño intonation—equivalent to a Bronx accent in New York—is unique, for better or worse. Argentine Spanish in general is distinctive, often Italian-inflected, most notable for pronouncing both the "ll" diphthong and "y" as "zh." "Llegar" (to arrive), for example, is pronounced "zhe-gar," while "yo" (I) sounds like "zho."

Another distinguishing feature is the familiar pronoun "vos" instead of "tu." Verb forms of the *voseo* differ from those of the *tuteo,* although Argentines will always under stand speakers who use "tu."

Spanish is also Chile's official language, but the local variant, which often drops terminal consonants and glides over some internal ones, may confuse those who learned Spanish elsewhere. At tourist offices, airlines, travel agencies, and upscale hotels in both countries, English is often spoken. In the provinces and regions, it's less common, though its use is spreading, especially in the travel-and-tourism sector.

PRONUNCIATION GUIDE

Spanish may be more phonetic than English, but there are still occasional variations in pronunciation, especially in Argentina.

Consonants

c - as 'c' in "cat," before 'a,' 'o,' or 'u'; like 's' before 'e' or 'i'
d - as 'd' in "dog," except between vowels, then like 'th' in "that"
g - before 'e' or 'i,' like the 'ch' in Scottish "loch"; elsewhere like 'g' in "get"
h - always silent
j - like the English 'h' in "hotel," but stronger
ll - in Argentina, like the 'z' in "azure"; in Chile, like the English 'y'
ñ - like the 'ni' in "onion"
r - always pronounced as strong 'r'
rr - trilled 'r'
v - similar to the 'b' in "boy" (not as English 'v')
y - in Argentina, like "ll," it sounds like the 'z' in azure. When standing alone, it's pronounced like the 'e' in "me." In Chile, equivalent to its English counterpart.
z - like 's' in "same"
b, f, k, l, m, n, p, q, s, t, w, x - as in English

Vowels

a - as in "father," but shorter
e - as in "hen"
i - as in "machine"
o - as in "phone"
u - usually as in "rule"; when it follows a 'q' the 'u' is silent; when it follows an 'h' or 'g,' it's pronounced like 'w,' except when it comes between 'g' and 'e' or 'i', when it's also silent (unless it has an umlaut, when it is pronounced as English 'w', as in "Güemes")

Stress

Native English speakers frequently make pronunciation errors by ignoring stress—all Spanish vowels—a, e, i, o and u—may carry accents that determine which syllable of a word gets emphasis. Often, stress seems unnatural to nonnative speakers—the surname Chávez, for instance, is stressed on the first syllable—but failure to observe this rule may mean that native speakers may not understand you.

NUMBERS

0 — *cero*
1 — *uno (masculine)*
1 — *una (feminine)*
2 — *dos*
3 — *tres*
4 — *cuatro*
5 — *cinco*
6 — *seis*
7 — *siete*
8 — *ocho*
9 — *nueve*
10 — *diez*

11 — *once*
12 — *doce*
13 — *trece*
14 — *catorce*
15 — *quince*
16 — *diez y seis*
17 — *diez y siete*
18 — *diez y ocho*
19 — *diez y nueve*
20 — *veinte*
21 — *veinte y uno*
30 — *treinta*
40 — *cuarenta*
50 — *cincuenta*
60 — *sesenta*
70 — *setenta*
80 — *ochenta*
90 — *noventa*
100 — *cien*
101 — *ciento y uno*
200 — *doscientos*
1,000 — *mil*
10,000 — *diez mil*
1,000,000 — *un millón*

DAYS OF THE WEEK

Sunday — *domingo*
Monday — *lunes*
Tuesday — *martes*
Wednesday — *miércoles*
Thursday — *jueves*
Friday — *viernes*
Saturday — *sábado*

TIME

While Argentine and Chileans normally use the 12-hour clock (A.M. and P.M.), they sometimes use the 24-hour clock, usually associated with plane or bus schedules. Under the 24-hour clock, for example, *las diez de la noche* (10 P.M.) would be *las 22 horas* (2200 hours).

What time is it? — *¿Qué hora es?*
It's one o'clock — *Es la una.*
It's two o'clock — *Son las dos.*
It's at two o'clock — *A las dos.*
It's ten to three — *Son tres menos diez.*
It's ten past three — *Son tres y diez.*
It's three fifteen — *Son las tres y cuarto.*
It's two forty five — *Son tres menos cuarto.*
It's two thirty — *Son las dos y media.*
It's 6 A.M. — *Son las seis de la mañana.*
It's 6 P.M. — *Son las seis de la tarde.*
It's 10 P.M. — *Son las diez de la noche.*
Today — *hoy*
Tomorrow — *mañana*
Morning — *la mañana*
Tomorrow morning — *mañana por la mañana*
Yesterday — *ayer*
Week — *la semana*
Month — *mes*
Year — *año*
Last night — *anoche*
The next day — *el día siguiente*

USEFUL WORDS AND PHRASES

Argentines, Chileans, and other Spanish-speaking people consider formalities important. Whenever approaching anyone for information or some other reason, do not forget the appropriate salutation—good morning, good evening, etc. Standing alone, the greeting *hola* (hello) can sound brusque.

Note that most of the words below are fairly standard, common to all Spanish-speaking countries. Many, however, have more idiomatic equivalents; refer to the glossary for these.

Hello. — *Hola.*
Good morning. — *Buenos días.*
Good afternoon. — *Buenas tardes.*
Good evening. — *Buenas noches.*
How are you? — *¿Cómo está?*
Fine. — *Muy bien.*
And you? — *¿Y usted?*
So-so. — *Más o menos.*
Thank you. — *Gracias.*
Thank you very much. — *Muchas gracias.*
You're very kind. — *Muy amable.*
You're welcome — *De nada* (literally, "It's nothing").

Yes — *sí*
No — *no*
I don't know. — *No sé.*
It's fine; okay — *Está bien.*
Good; okay — *Bueno.*
Please — *por favor*
Pleased to meet you. — *Mucho gusto.*
Excuse me (physical) — *Perdóneme.*
Excuse me (speech) — *Discúlpeme.*
I'm sorry. — *Lo siento.*
Goodbye — *adiós*
See you later — *hasta luego* (literally, "until later")
More — *más*
Less — *menos*
Better — *mejor*
Much, a lot — *mucho*
A little — *un poco*
Large — *grande*
Small — *pequeño, chico*
Quick, fast — *rápido*
Slowly — *despacio*
Bad — *malo*
Difficult — *difícil*
Easy — *fácil*
He/She/It is gone; as in "She left," "He's gone" — *Ya se fue.*
I don't speak Spanish well. — *No hablo bien el español.*
I don't understand. — *No entiendo.*
How do you say . . . in Spanish? — *¿Cómo se dice . . . en español?*
Do you understand English? — *¿Entiende el inglés?*
Is English spoken here? (Does anyone here speak English?) — *¿Se habla inglés aquí?*

TERMS OF ADDRESS

When in doubt, use the formal *usted* (you) as a form of address. If you wish to dispense with formality and feel that the desire is mutual, you can say *Me podés tutear* (you can call me "tu") even though Argentines use the slightly different verb forms that correlate with the familiar pronoun "vos." In Chile, of course, the equivalent would be *Me puedes tutear.*

I — *yo*
You (formal) — *usted*
you (familiar) — *vos*
He/him — *él*
She/her — *ella*
We/us — *nosotros*
You (plural) — *ustedes*
They/them (all males or mixed gender) — *ellos*
They/them (all females) — *ellas*
Mr., sir — *señor*
Mrs., madam — *señora*
Miss, young lady — *señorita*
Wife — *esposa*
Husband — *marido or esposo*
Friend — *amigo* (male), *amiga* (female)
Sweetheart — *novio* (male), *novia* (female)
Son, daughter — *hijo, hija*
Brother, sister — *hermano, hermana*
Father, mother — *padre, madre*
Grandfather, grandmother — *abuelo, abuela*

GETTING AROUND

Where is . . . ? — *¿Dónde está . . . ?*
How far is it to . . . ? — *¿A cuanto está . . . ?*
from . . . to . . . — *de . . . a . . .*
Highway — *la carretera*
Road — *el camino*
Street — *la calle*
Block — *la cuadra*
Kilometer — *kilómetro*
North — *norte*
South — *sur*
West — *oeste; poniente*
East — *este; oriente*
Straight ahead — *al derecho; adelante*
To the right — *a la derecha*
To the left — *a la izquierda*

ACCOMMODATIONS

¿Hay habitación? — *Is there a room?*
May I (we) see it? — *¿Puedo (podemos) verla?*
What is the rate? — *¿Cuál es el precio?*
Is that your best rate? — *¿Es su mejor precio?*
Is there something cheaper? — *¿Hay algo más económico?*

Single room — *un single*
Double room — *un doble*
Room for a couple — *matrimonial*
Key — *llave*
With private bath — *con baño privado*
With shared bath — *con baño general; con baño compartido*
Hot water — *agua caliente*
Cold water — *agua fría*
Shower — *ducha*
Electric shower — *ducha eléctrica*
Towel — *toalla*
Soap — *jabón*
Toilet paper — *papel higiénico*
Air conditioning — *aire acondicionado*
Fan — *ventilador*
Blanket — *frazada; manta*
Sheets — *sábanas*

PUBLIC TRANSPORT

Bus stop — *la parada*
Bus terminal — *terminal de buses*
Airport — *el aeropuerto*
Launch — *lancha*
Dock — *muelle*
I want a ticket to . . . — *Quiero un pasaje a . . .*
I want to get off at . . . — *Quiero bajar en . . .*
Here, please. — *Aquí, por favor.*
Where is this bus going? — *¿Adónde va este autobús?*
Roundtrip — *ida y vuelta*
What do I owe? — *¿Cuánto le debo?*

FOOD

Menu — *la carta, el menú*
Glass — *taza*
Fork — *tenedor*
Knife — *cuchillo*
Spoon — *cuchara*
Napkin — *servilleta*
Soft drink — *agua fresca*
Coffee — *café*
Cream — *crema*
Tea — *té*
Sugar — *azúcar*
Drinking water — *agua pura, agua potable*
Bottled carbonated water — *agua mineral con gas*
Bottled uncarbonated water — *agua sin gas*
Beer — *cerveza*
Wine — *vino*
Milk — *leche*
Juice — *jugo*
Eggs — *huevos*
Bread — *pan*
Watermelon — *sandía*
Banana — *banana*
Apple — *manzana*
Orange — *naranja*
Peach — *durazno*
Pineapple — *ananá*
Meat (without) — *carne (sin)*
Beef — *carne de res*
Chicken — *pollo; gallina*
Fish — *pescado*
Shellfish — *mariscos*
Shrimp — *camarones*
Fried — *frito*
Roasted — *asado*
Barbecued — *a la parrilla*
Breakfast — *desayuno*
Lunch — *almuerzo*
Dinner, or a late-night snack — *cena*
The check, or bill — *la cuenta*

MAKING PURCHASES

I need . . . — *Necesito . . .*
I want . . . — *Deseo . . . or Quiero . . .*
I would like . . . (more polite) — *Quisiera . . .*
How much does it cost? — *¿Cuánto cuesta?*
What's the exchange rate? — *¿Cuál es el tipo de cambio?*
May I see . . . ? — *¿Puedo ver . . . ?*
This one — *ésta/ésto*
Expensive — *caro*
Cheap — *barato*
Cheaper — *más barato*
Too much — *demasiado*

HEALTH

Help me please. — *Ayúdeme, por favor.*
I am ill. — *Estoy enfermo.*
Me duele. — *It hurts.*
Pain — *dolor*
Fever — *fiebre*
Stomach ache — *dolor de estómago*
Headache — *dolor de cabeza*
Vomiting — *vomitar*
Diarrhea — *diarrhea*
Drugstore — *farmacia*
Medicine — *medicina*
Pill, tablet — *pastilla*
Birth control pills — *pastillas anticonceptivas*
Condom — *condón, preservativo*

Glossary

aduana—customs
aduana paralela—"parallel customs," corrupt Argentine customs officials
agua de la canilla—in Argentina, tap water; in Chile, this is *agua de la llave*
albergue juvenil—youth hostel
albergue transitorio—a by-the-hour-hotel, frequently used by young and not-so-young couples in search of privacy
andén—platform at train station or bus terminal
anexo—telephone extension
arbolito—Argentine street money changer, so called because they are "planted" in one spot
argentinidad—nebulous notion of Argentine nationalism, often associated with the gaucho
asado—generally, a barbecue; in context, can also mean short ribs or roast prime rib
autopista—freeway
avenida—avenue
balneario—bathing or beach resort
baño compartido—shared bath (in a hotel or other accommodations)
baño general—shared or general bath (in a hotel or other accommodations)
baño privado—private bath
barrio—borough or neighborhood
boleadoras—rounded stones, tied together with leather thong, used for hunting by Pampas and Patagonian Indians; also known as *bolas*
bono—in Argentina, a provincial letter of credit serving as a parallel currency equivalent to the peso. If at all possible, visitors should avoid accepting *bonos,* which are being phased out.
bronca—a singularly Porteño combination of aggravation and frustration; there is no precise English equivalent, the closest being "wrath" or, in Britain, "aggro"
cabildo—colonial governing council
cabotaje—full-fare domestic airline ticket
cacique—indigenous chief or headman
cajero automático—automatic teller machine (ATM)
calle—street
camarote—sleeper berth on a train
camioneta—pickup truck
campo—countryside
característica—in Argentina, telephone area code
carne—in Argentina, beef; other kinds of meat are *carne blanca* (literally, "white meat")
carretera—highway
cartelera—in Argentina, discount ticket agency
casa de cambio—official money-exchange facility, often just "cambio"
casco—"big house" of an *estancia*
casilla—post office box
caudillo—in early independence times, a provincial Argentine warlord, though the term is often used for any populist leader, such as Juan Domingo Perón
cerro—hill
chopp—draft beer
cobro revertido—collect or reverse-charge telephone call
coche cama—spacious, fully reclining long-distance bus seat
coima—bribe
colectivo—in Argentina, a city bus
comedor—simple eatery or dining room
confitería—in Argentina, a restaurant/café with a menu of *minutas* (short orders)
corralito—unpopular banking restrictions imposed by Argentine government during the debt default and devaluation of 2001–2002
costanera—any road along a seashore, lakeshore or riverside
criollo—in colonial times, an American-born Spaniard; in the present, normally a descriptive term meaning "traditionally" Argentine or Chilean
desaparecido—"disappeared one," victim of the military dictatorships of the 1970s and 1980s
día de campo—"day in the countryside" on a tourist *estancia*
dique—deep water basin dredged in the harbor of Buenos Aires
doble tracción—four-wheel drive, also known as *cuatro por cuatro* (the latter written as "4X4")
edificio—building

encomienda—in colonial times, a grant of Indian labor within a given geographical area; the *encomendero* (holder of the *encomienda*) incurred the reciprocal obligation to provide instruction in the Spanish language and Catholic religion, though such obligations were rarely honored

estancia—cattle or sheep ranch controlling large extents of land, often with an absentee owner, dominant manager, and resident employees

estanciero—owner of an *estancia*

estero—estuary

facón—gaucho knife

farmacia de turno—pharmacy remaining open all night for emergencies, on a rotating basis

feria—artisans' market, outdoor crafts or antiques fair; alternately, an outdoor bookstall

gasoil—in Argentina, diesel fuel

gauchesco—adjective describing romantic art or literature about, as opposed to by, gauchos

golfo—gulf

golpe de estado—coup d'etat

Gran Aldea—"great village," Buenos Aires prior to the influx of 20th-century immigrants

heladería—ice creamery

hipódromo—horserace track

hospedaje—family-run lodging

indígena—indigenous person

indigenista—adjective describing romantically pro-Indian literature, music and art

infracción—traffic violation

isla—island

islote—islet

istmo—isthmus

IVA—*impuesto al valor agregado,* or value added tax (VAT)

lago—lake

laguna—lagoon

latifundio—large landholding, usually an estancia

local—numbered office or locale, at a given street address

locutorio—in Argentina, a telephone call center

lunfardo—Porteño street slang that developed in working-class immigrant barrios like La Boca but is now more widely used in Argentine Spanish, though not in formal situations

machista—male chauvinist

media pensión—half-board, at a hotel or guesthouse

menú—menu; also, a fixed-price meal

meseta—Patagonian steppe

mestizo—individual of mixed indigenous and Spanish ancestry

milonga—informal neighborhood dance club, which often includes tango as a participant rather than spectator activity

minuta—in Argentina, a short order meal like pasta

mirador—overlook or viewpoint

mozo—in Argentina, a term of address for a restaurant waiter; in Chile, though, this would be extremely rude

museo—museum

oligarquía terrateniente—traditional land-owning "aristocracy" of the Pampas

onces—Chilean afternoon tea

palacete—mansion

pampa—broad, flat expanse in and around Buenos Aires province

pampero—southwesterly cold front on the Argentine pampas

parada—bus stop

parque nacional—national park

pasarela—catwalk in wet or marshy area

paseaperros—professional dog walker in Buenos Aires

payador—spontaneous gaucho singer

peaje—toll booth

peatonal—pedestrian mall

pensión—family-run accommodation

pensión completa—full board, at a hotel or guesthouse

picante—spicy hot; the Argentine and Chilean tolerance for spicy food is low, however, and most visitors may find foods labeled spicy as relatively bland

pingüinera—penguin colony

piquete—protestors' roadblock

piropo—sexist remark, ranging from humorous and innocuous to truly vulgar; also, on *filete,* an aphorism

playa—beach

Porteño—native or resident of Buenos Aires

propina—tip, as at a restaurant
puente—bridge
puerto—port
Pullman—first-class bus, with reclining seats and luggage storage underneath
pulpería—general store, often the only retail outlet in a rural area
rastra—studded gaucho belt
recargo—surcharge on credit-card purchases, common in Argentina
reducción—colonial settlement where missionaries concentrated indigenous population for catechization
remis—meterless radiotaxi charging a fixed rate within a given zone
reserva nacional—in Chile, national reserve, a category of Conaf-protected land
residencial—permanent budget accommodations, often also called hotel
restó—fashionable, even pretentious, term for a restaurant, especially in Buenos Aires
río—river
rotisería—delicatessen
ruca—Mapuche plank house, with thatched roof
ruta—route or highway
ruta nacional—federal highway
ruta provincial—provincial highway
s/n—*sin número,* a street address without a number
tango canción—"tango song," with music and lyrics expressing nostalgia
tanguero—tango dancer
tarifa mostrador—hotel "rack rate," from which there are often discounts
tenedor libre—literally "free fork," all-you-can-eat restaurant
toldo—tent of animal skins, inhabited by mobile Pampas Indians in pre-Columbian times
trucho—bogus, in Argentine slang
turco—Argentine of Middle Eastern descent
ventanilla—ticket window at bus terminal or train station
viveza criolla—in Argentina, "artful deception," ranging from small-scale cheating to audacious chutzpah
voseo—use of the second person singular pronoun *vos* and its distinct verb forms in Argentina, Uruguay, Paraguay, and some other countries; most others, though, use the *tuteo* (the pronoun *tú* and its forms)

ABBREVIATIONS AND ACRONYMS

ACA—Automóvil Club Argentino
APN—Administración de Parques Nacionales (National Parks Administration, Argentina)
Codeff—Consejo de Defensa de la Flora y Fauna (Council for the Defense of Flora and Fauna, Chile)
Conaf—Corporación Nacional Forestal (National Forestry Corporation, Chile)
Conama—Comisión Nacional del Medio Ambiente (National Environmental Commission, Chile)
IVA—Impuesto al Valor Agregado
RN—Ruta Nacional (National Highway, Argentina)
RP—Ruta Provincial (Provincial Highway, Argentina)

Suggested Reading

ARCHAEOLOGY, ETHNOGRAPHY, AND ETHNOHISTORY

McEwan, Colin, Luis A. Borrero, and Alfredo Prieto, eds. *Patagonia: Natural History, Prehistory and Ethnography at the Uttermost End of the Earth.* Princeton University Press, 1997. First published under the auspices of the British Museum, this is a collection of academic but accessible essays on topics ranging from Patagonia's natural environment to early human occupation, first encounters between Europeans and indigenes, the origins of the Patagonian "giants," and even Patagonian travel literature.

GUIDEBOOKS AND TRAVELOGUES

Crouch, Gregory. *Enduring Patagonia.* New York: Random House, 2001. Details one mountaineer's experiences on Fitz Roy and Cerro Torre in Parque Nacional Los Glaciares.

Darwin, Charles. *Voyage of the Beagle* (many editions). Perhaps the greatest travel book ever written, Darwin's narrative of his 19th-century journey bursts with insights on the people, places, and even politics he saw while collecting the plants and animals that led to his revolutionary theories. The great scientist observed the city of Buenos Aires, the surrounding pampas, and Patagonia, and met key figures in the country's history, including the dictator Rosas.

Foster, Dereck, and Richard Tripp. *Food and Drink in Argentina.* Buenos Aires, Aromas y Sabores, 2003. A fine short introduction to Argentine food, with an extensive Spanish-English glossary, by the long-time restaurant critic of the *Buenos Aires Herald* and a U.S. collaborator.

Green, Toby. *Saddled with Darwin.* London: Phoenix, 1999. Audacious if uneven account by a young, talented writer of his attempt to retrace the hoofprints—not the footsteps—of Darwin's travels through Uruguay, Argentina, and Chile. Self-effacing but still serious, the author manages to compare Darwin's experience with his own, reflect on contemporary distortions of the great scientist's theories, and stay almost completely off the gringo trail.

Guevara, Ernesto. *The Motorcycle Diaries: A Journey around South America.* New York and London: Verso, 1995. Translated by Ann Wright, this is an account of an Argentine drifter's progress from Buenos Aires across the Patagonian Andes and up the Chilean coast by motorcycle and, when the bike broke down, by any means necessary. The author is better known by his nickname "Che," a common Argentine interjection.

Keenan, Brian, and John McCarty. *Between Extremes.* London: Black Swan, 2000. During four years as hostages in Lebanon, Keenan and McCarty fantasized about riding through Patagonia on horseback. Years after their release, they did it.

Lista, Ramón. *A Journey to the Southern Andes.* Olivos, Argentina: El Calafate Editores, 2000. Originally published in 1892, this journal by the governor of Santa Cruz territory recounts an arduous steamer navigation up the Río Santa Cruz, duplicating the route of Fitzroy, to Lago Argentino and Lago Viedma. Some of the naval officer's natural-history observations are badly mistaken.

Moreno, Francisco Pascasio. *Perito Moreno's Travel Journal: a Personal Reminiscence.* Buenos Aires: Elefante Blanco, 2002. Absorbing translation of the great Patagonian explorer's northern Patagonian letters and journals, including his thrilling escape down the Río Limay from his indigenous captors.

Muir, John. *John Muir's Last Journey* (Washington, D.C.: Island Press, Shearwater Books, 2001). Edited by Michael P. Branch, this annotated collection of Muir's correspondence and notes on his eight-month odyssey through South America and Africa includes his search for native araucaria forests in Chile's northern Andean lake district.

Murphy, Dallas. *Rounding the Horn.* New York: Basic Books, 2004. A hybrid of historical and contemporary navigation in the world's wildest waters, Murphy's travelogue conveys the travails of advancing against the winds of the "Furious Fifties." But it also communicates the mystique of South America's southernmost tip.

Reding, Nick. *The Last Cowboys at the End of the World.* New York: Crown Publishing, 2001. Anthropological in its approach, this account of isolated gauchos in Chilean Patagonia's upper Río Cisnes rings true for the author's admirable refusal to romanticize people with whom he clearly sympathizes and empathizes.

Roosevelt, Theodore. *A Book Lover's Holiday in the Open.* New York: Scribner's, 1916. After retiring from politics, the still vigorous U.S. president undertook numerous overseas adventures; among other stories, this collection retells his crossing of the Andes from Chile into the lake district of northern Argentine Patagonia, and his meeting with legends like Perito Moreno.

Symmes, Patrick. *Chasing Che: A Motorcycle Journey in Search of the Guevara Legend.* New York: Vintage, 2000. Symmes follows the tiremarks of Che's legendary trip from Buenos Aires through Argentina and Chile in the early 1950s.

Wangford, Hank. *Lost Cowboys.* London: Victor Gollencz, 1995. A British country musician and experienced travel writer—whose band's name and book title are identical—follows the gauchos and other Latin American horsemen.

Willis, Bailey. *A Yanqui in Patagonia.* Stanford University Press, 1947. Out of print but well worth seeking, this U.S. geologist's memoir is a vivid account of the early 20th century's northern Patagonian frontier. It's also fascinating for his assessment of the region's potential, and for his account of intrigues within the Argentine governments of the day.

HISTORY

Crow, John A. *The Epic of Latin America,* 3rd ed. Berkeley: University of California Press, 1980. A comprehensive history of the region, told more through narrative than analysis, in an immensely readable manner. Several chapters deal with Argentina.

Nouzeilles, Gabriela, and Gabriela Montaldo, eds. *The Argentina Reader: History, Culture, Politics.* Durham, NC: Duke University Press, 2002. Too big and heavy to carry along on the road, but this diverse collection of essays and extracts is an excellent introduction to the country through the eyes of Argentines, and visitors to Argentina, since colonial times.

Parry, J. H. *The Discovery of South America.* London, Paul Elek, 1979. Well-illustrated account of early voyages and overland explorations on the continent.

Rock, David. *Argentina 1516–1987: From Spanish Colonization to the Falklands War and Alfonsín.* London: I.B. Taurus, 1987. Comprehensive narrative and analysis of Argentine history prior to Carlos Menem's presidency.

Slatta, Richard. *Cowboys of the Americas.* New Haven and London: Yale University Press, 1990. Spectacularly illustrated comparative analysis of New World horsemen, including both Argentine gauchos and Chilean *huasos.*

GOVERNMENT AND POLITICS

Caviedes, César. *The Southern Cone: Realities of the Authoritarian State.* Totowa, NJ: Rowman & Allanheld, 1984. Comparative study of the military dictatorships of Chile, Argentina, Uruguay, and Brazil of the 1970s and 1980s.

LITERATURE AND LITERARY CRITICISM

For more suggestions on Argentine literature, see the Literature entry in the Arts and Entertainment section of this chapter.

Aira, César. *The Hare.* London and New York: Serpent's Tail, 1998. Touching the dangerous territory of magical realism, Aira's novel of Rosas, the Mapuche and a wandering English naturalist on the Pampas is a complex tale that ties up neatly at the end.

Martínez, Tomás Eloy. *The Perón Novel.* New York: Pantheon Books, 1988. Based on the author's own lengthy interviews with the exiled caudillo, for which fiction seemed the appropriate outlet. According to Jorge Castañeda, "Whether Perón ever actually uttered these words is in the last analysis irrelevant: he could have, he would have, and he probably did."

Wilson, Jason. *Traveler's Literary Companion: South & Central America, Including Mexico.* Lincolnwood, Illinois: Passport Books, 1995. An edited collection of excerpts from literature, including fiction, poetry, and essays, that illuminates aspects of the countries from the Río Grande to the tip of Tierra del Fuego, including Argentina, Buenos Aires, and Chile.

ENVIRONMENT AND NATURAL HISTORY

Hudson, William Henry. *The Bird Biographies of W.H. Hudson.* Santa Barbara, California, Capra Press, 1988. A partial reprint of the romantic naturalist's detailed description of the birds he knew grewing up in Buenos Aires province, with illustrations.

Internet Resources

The following list of general interest sites does not include provincial or larger municipal tourist offices, or private tour operators, which are covered earlier in this chapter. Nor does it include museums or services like hotels and restaurants, which appear in the appropriate geographical chapter.

ARGENTINE WEBSITES

Administración de Parques Nacionales
www.parquesnacionales.gov.ar
Primary government agency in charge of national parks and other conservation areas.

Aerolíneas Argentinas
www.aerolineas.com.ar
Home page for Argentina's recovering flagship airline.

Aeropuertos Argentinos 2000
www.aa2000.com.ar
Private concessionaire operating most of Argentina's international and domestic airports, including Buenos Aires's Ezeiza and Aeroparque. In English and Spanish.

American Falcon
www.americanfalcon.com.ar
Domestic airline with small planes and limited routes.

Argentina Travel Net
www.argentinatravelnet.com
Portal for Argentine travel sites, though not nearly all of the links are closely related to travel. In Spanish and English.

Asociación Argentina de Albergues de la Juventud (AAAJ)
www.hostelling-aaaj.org.ar
Argentine hostelling organization, with limited facilities throughout the country.

Asociación Ornitológica del Plata
www.avesargentinas.org.ar
Buenos Aires-based birding and conservation organization.

Automóvil Club Argentino (ACA)
www.aca.org.ar
Argentine automobile association, useful for both information and up-to-date road maps. Offers discounts for members of affiliated clubs, such as AAA in the United States and the AA in Britain.

Buenos Aires Herald
www.buenosairesherald.com
Abbreviated online version of the capital's venerable English-language daily, worthwhile for its editorials alone.

Clarín
www.clarin.com
Outstanding online version of the capital's tabloid daily, the Spanish-speaking world's largest-circulation newspaper.

Festival de Tango
www.festivaldetango.com.ar
The capital's increasingly popular series of autumn (March–April) tango events, following Brazilian Carnaval.

Fundación Vida Silvestre Argentina
www.vidasilvestre.org.ar
Nongovernmental wildlife and habitat advocates.

Greenpeace
www.greenpeace.org.ar
Argentine affiliate of the international conservation organization.

Hostelling International Argentina
www.hostels.org.ar
Argentine Hostelling International affiliate,

with information on travel and activities throughout the country.

Instituto Geográfico Militar
www.igm.gov.ar
Military geographical institute, preparing and selling maps of Argentina.

Instituto Nacional de Estadísticas y Censos INDEC, www.indec.mecon.ar
Homepage for federal government statistical agency.

Interpatagonia
www.interpatagonia.com
Probably the most complete site for content and services on both the Argentine and Chilean sides of the Southern cone's southernmost region.

Líneas Aéreas del Estado (LADE)
www.lade.com.ar
Commercial passenger arm of the Argentine air force, which serves primarily Patagonian destinations.

Metrovías
www.metrovias.com.ar
Details on Buenos Aires subway system.

Ministerio de Relaciones Exteriores
www.mrecic.gov.ar/consulares/pagcon.html
Argentine foreign ministry, with information on visas and consulates, in English and Spanish.

Páginas Amarillas
www.paginasamarillas.com.ar
Yellow Pages for the entire country.

Secretaría Nacional de Turismo
www.turismo.gov.ar
National tourism authority, with information in Spanish and English.

Southern Winds
www.sw.com.ar
More-or-less viable domestic competitor to Aerolíneas Argentinas.

CHILEAN WEBSITES

Automóvil Club Chileno
www.acchi.cl
Motorist organization that also provides services to members of overseas affiliates.

Chile Information Project
www.chip.cl
English-language site with daily Chilean news summaries and a useful travel section.

Comité de la Defensa de Flora y Fauna
www.codeff.cl
Well-established group oriented toward wildlife and habitat conservation.

Corporación de Promoción Turística
www.visitchile.org
Public-private Chilean site in English and Spanish.

Corporación Nacional de Desarrollo Indígena
www.conadi.cl
Official government page for indigenous affairs, in Spanish only.

Corporación Nacional Forestal
www.conaf.cl
Official page of quasi-governmental agency in charge of Chile's national parks and other protected areas; in Spanish only.

Defensores del Bosque Chileno
www.elbosquechileno.cl
Nongovernmental organization devoted to native forest conservation.

El Mercurio
www.emol.com
Santiago's traditional daily newspaper, with conservative editorial line; in Spanish.

Federación de Andinismo
www.feach.cl
Site devoted to climbing, including bureaucratic obstacles in sensitive border areas.

Fundación Terram
www.terram.cl
Nonprofit promoting sustainable development in Chile.

FutaFriends
www.futafriends.org
Nonprofit organization dedicated to preserving the Río Futaleufú.

Hostelling International Santiago
www.hostelling.cl
Chilean affiliate of Hostelling International, with information on hostels and activities throughout the country.

Instituto Geográfico Militar
www.igm.cl
Chilean government agency in charge of mapping, map sales, and general geographic information.

La Tercera
www.latercera.cl
Best of the Chilean tabloid dailies, serious but with a rigidly conservative editorial policy.

Parque Natural Pumalín
www.parquepumalin.cl
Exceptional site, in Spanish and English, for what may be the most audacious (and controversial) private conservation initiative ever.

ProChile
www.chiletrip.cl
Official government site with travel and tourism information.

Publiguías
www.amarillas.cl
Chilean yellow pages.

Renace
www.renace.cl
Alliance of Chilean environmental organizations.

Sernatur
www.sernatur.cl
Chilean government tourism bureau; in Spanish and English.

Viña Cousiño Macul
www.cousinomacul.cl
Classic winery within Santiago's city limits, open for tours and tasting.

FOREIGN AND GENERAL INTEREST WEBSITES

Centers for Disease Control
www.cdc.gov
U.S. government page with travel health advisories.

CIA Factbook
www.odci.gov/cia/publications/factbook
The world's most notorious spooks perform at least one admirable public service in their annual encyclopedia of the world's countries, which appears complete online.

Currency Converter
www.oanda.com
Present and historic exchange-rate information.

Department of Health
www.doh.gov.uk
British government agency with country-by-country health advice.

Department of State
www.travel.state.gov
Travel information and advisories from U.S. government; while it has a great deal of useful material, its warnings are often exaggerated.

Latin American Network Information Center (LANIC)
http://lanic.utexas.edu
Organized by the University of Texas, this site has a huge collection of quality links to Argentina, Chile, and other Latin American countries.

Mercopress News Agency
www.falkland-malvinas.com

Montevideo-based Internet news agency covering politics and business in the Mercosur common-market countries of Argentina, Brazil, Uruguay, and Paraguay, as well as Chile and the Falkland/Malvinas Islands. In English and Spanish.

USENET DISCUSSION GROUPS

Soc.culture.argentina

No-holds-barred discussion group that touches on many other issues besides travel.

Soc.culture.chile

Similar to its Argentine counterpart.

Rec.travel.latin-america

Regional discussion group dealing with all Latin American countries, with a steady amount of postings on Argentina and Chile. Since it's unmoderated, critical reading is imperative.

Index

Estancias

Glaciers

Parks

T

Wildlife-Watching

UV

WXYZ

Acknowledgments

Like my previous efforts on Guatemala, Chile, and Buenos Aires, this book owes its existence in its present form to numerous individuals in North America, Argentina, and elsewhere. Once again, praise goes to Bill Newlin, whose prerogative helped make this title a priority, and his Emeryville staff at Avalon Travel Publishing, for continuing to offer author-friendly contracts.

In the course of nearly 30 years' experience in South America, half of that as a guidebook writer, I owe enormous debts to friends, acquaintances, and officials throughout the region. My apologies to anyone I may have overlooked or perhaps omitted through an errant keystroke. To avoid favoritism, their names appear in alphabetical order in each region, though some are grouped by workplace.

In Buenos Aires and vicinity, thanks to Diego Allolio; Joaquín Allolio; Mario Banchik of Librerías Turísticas; Mirta S. Capurro and Ricardo Sangla of the municipal Subsecretaría de Turismo; Martín Chaves, Pablo Fisch, and Silvina Garay of Asatej; Josh Goodman; Carlos Enrique Meyer of the Secretaría de Turismo de la Nación; and my nephews Juan and Manuel Massolo.

In Santiago, acknowledgements to Pablo Fernández and Rodrigo Vásquez of Hostelling International; Andrés Cinovcic A. of GTS Travel; Yerko Ivelic and Javier López of Cascada Expediciones; and Eduardo Núñez of Conaf.

In northern Argentine Patagonia, thanks to my traditional research assistant Laura Alvarez of Villa Regina, Río Negro; Rodolfo Coria of Plaza Huincul; Marcelo Ferrante of Bariloche; Asunción Gallardo of San Martín de los Andes; Charly Moreno of Trevelin; Anthony Hawes and Lucrecia Ochoa of Villa la Angostura; Martín Ortiz of the municipal Secretaría de Turismo, Bariloche; Roberto Pistarini of the Administración de Parques Nacionales, Bariloche; and Jane Williams of Estancia Huechahue.

In southern Argentine Patagonia, the list is long: Juan Carlos Lamas of Ecocentro Puerto Madryn; Herman Müller and María Alicia Sacks of Puerto Madryn; Mónica Montes Roberts and Estela Maris Williams of Entretur, Trelew; Ricardo Pérez of Puerto Deseado; Miguel Angel Alonso, Leslie Scovenna, Mariano Besio, Cecilia Scarafoni, María Elisa Rodríguez, Alexis Simunovic, Dany Feldman, and the late Mario Feldman of El Calafate; Marcelo Pagani, Alejandro Caparrós, Daniel Bagnera and Rubén Vasquez of El Chaltén; Pablo Crespo of Estancia Helsingfors; Coco and Petty Nauta of Estancia Telken; and Agustín Smart of Estancia Menelik.

In Tierra del Fuego, regards to Barrie O'Byrne, Claudio Don Vito, Javier Jury, and Julio César Lovece of Ushuaia, and to Tommy and Natalie Prosser Goodall of Estancia Harberton.

In the Chilean lakes district, special mention to Tom and Eva Buschor of Malalacahuello; Armin Dubendorfer of Puerto Octay; Beat Zbinden of Villarrica; Andrea de la Rosé and Carolina Morgado of Puerto Varas; and Britt Lewis of Ancud.

In Chilean Patagonia, including Aisén and vicinity, thanks to Nicholas La Penna of Chaitén; Chris and Rosi Spelius of Futaleufú; Gabriela Neira Morales of Sernatur, Coyhaique; Ian Farmer of Coyhaique; Miguel Angel Muñoz and Andrea Lagunas Flores of Sernatur, Punta Arenas; Helen Fell and Nelson Sánchez Oyarzo of Punta Arenas; Alfonso López Rosas of Path@gone, Puerto Natales; Alejandro Cárdenas Lobos of Puerto Natales; Werner and Cecilia Ruf-Chaura, of Casa Cecilia, Puerto Natales; Hernán Jofré of Antares Patagonia, Puerto Natales; Josian Yaksic of Hostería Las Torres; and Wolf Kloss of Puerto Williams.

In Stanley, Falkland Islands, thanks to former tourism manager John Fowler and his recent replacement Connie Stevens, Debs Ford and Russell Evans, Tim Miller, David Eynon, James Peck, Antony Smith, Patrick Watts, Sally Ellis and Jennie Forrest of International Tours & Travel, government archivist Jane Cameron, and Leona Roberts of the Falkland Islands Museum. In camp, the highest appreciation to Mike and Phyl Rendell of Bleaker Island; Ken and Bonnie Greenland of

Darwin; Rob McKay of Sea Lion Island; Allan White and Jacqui Jennings of Pebble Island; Wayne Brewer, Sue Lowe, and Ron Reeves of Port Howard; Rob McGill of Carcass Island; David and Suzan Pole-Evans of Saunders Island; and Anna Robertson of Port Stephens. A special mention to former governor David Tatham.

Stateside, thanks to Dan Buck of Washington, D.C.; Bill Franklin of the University of Iowa; Fernanda Baserga and Leandro Fernández Suárez of the Argentine consulate in Los Angeles; and Patricio Rubalcaba and Misty Pinson of Lan-Chile, Miami.

And finally, thanks to my wife María Laura Massolo, my daughter Clío Bernhardson-Massolo, and my Akita Sandro, who reminds me when I need to take a nap, and to the memory of my late Alaskan malamute Gardel.

U.S.~Metric Conversion

1 inch	=	2.54 centimeters (cm)
1 foot	=	.304 meters (m)
1 yard	=	0.914 meters
1 mile	=	1.6093 kilometers (km)
1 km	=	.6214 miles
1 fathom	=	1.8288 m
1 chain	=	20.1168 m
1 furlong	=	201.168 m
1 acre	=	.4047 hectares
1 sq km	=	100 hectares
1 sq mile	=	2.59 square km
1 ounce	=	28.35 grams
1 pound	=	.4536 kilograms
1 short ton	=	.90718 metric ton
1 short ton	=	2000 pounds
1 long ton	=	1.016 metric tons
1 long ton	=	2240 pounds
1 metric ton	=	1000 kilograms
1 quart	=	.94635 liters
1 US gallon	=	3.7854 liters
1 Imperial gallon	=	4.5459 liters
1 nautical mile	=	1.852 km

To compute Celsius temperatures, subtract 32 from Fahrenheit and divide by 1.8. To go the other way, multiply Celsius by 1.8 and add 32.

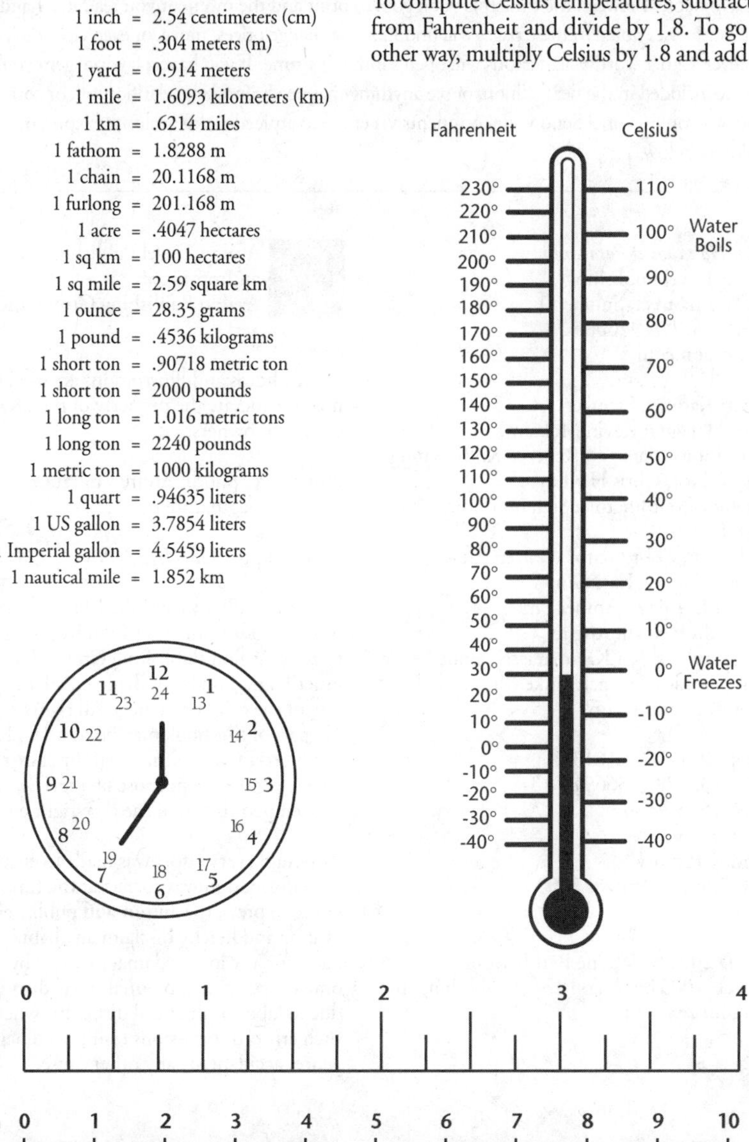

Keeping Current

Although we strive to produce the most up-to-date guidebook humanly possible, change is unavoidable. Between the time this book goes to print and the moment you read it, a handful of the businesses noted in these pages will undoubtedly change prices, move, or even close their doors forever. Other worthy attractions will open for the first time. If you have a favorite gem you'd like to see included in the next edition, or see anything that needs updating, clarification, or correction, please drop us a line. Send your comments via email to atpfeedback@avalonpub.com, or use the address below.

Moon Handbooks Patagonia
Avalon Travel Publishing
1400 65th Street, Suite 250
Emeryville, CA 94608, USA
www.moon.com

Editor: Kathryn Ettinger
Series Manager: Kevin McLain
Acquisitions Manager: Rebecca K. Browning
Copy Editor: Chris Hayhurst
Graphics Coordinators: Stefano Boni, Deb Dutcher
Production Coordinator: Darren Alessi
Cover Designer: Kari Gim
Interior Designer: Amber Pirker
Map Editor: Kevin Anglin
Cartographers: Kat Kalamaras, Suzanne Service
Cartographic Manager: Mike Morgenfeld
Indexer: Rachel Kuhn

ISBN-10: 1-56691-613-5
ISBN-13: 978-1-56691-613-4
ISSN: 1555-9386

Printing History
1st Edition—October 2005
5 4 3 2 1

Avalon Travel Publishing
an Imprint of
Avalon Publishing Group, Inc.

Front cover photo: André van Huizen/ www.imaginature.nl

Printed in the USA by Malloy